W9-CCX-904

DICTIONARY OF · THE HISTORY OF IDEAS ·

For Reference

Not to be taken from this room

# DICTIONARY OF
# THE HISTORY OF IDEAS

# DICTIONARY OF THE HISTORY OF IDEAS

## Studies of Selected Pivotal Ideas

PHILIP P. WIENER

*EDITOR IN CHIEF*

⟳⟲

VOLUME IV

*Psychological Ideas in Antiquity*

TO

Zeitgeist

CHARLES SCRIBNER'S SONS · NEW YORK

Copyright © 1973 Charles Scribner's Sons

The Publishers are grateful for permission to quote from previously published works in the following articles:

"Social Contract"

from Jean Jacques Rousseau, *The Social Contract*, trans. Maurice Cranston, © 1968, by permission of A. D. Peters & Company

"The State"

from *The Notion of the State*, by A. P. d'Entrèves, © 1967, by permission of The Clarendon Press, Oxford

"Virtuoso"

from *The Diary of John Evelyn*, ed. E. S. de Beer, © 1955, by permission of The Clarendon Press, Oxford

THIS BOOK PUBLISHED SIMULTANEOUSLY IN
THE UNITED STATES OF AMERICA AND IN CANADA—
COPYRIGHT UNDER THE BERNE CONVENTION

ALL RIGHTS RESERVED. NO PART OF THIS BOOK
MAY BE REPRODUCED IN ANY FORM WITHOUT
THE PERMISSION OF CHARLES SCRIBNER'S SONS.

5 7 9 11 13 15 17 19 M|O|C 20 18 16 14 12 10 8 6 4

PRINTED IN THE UNITED STATES OF AMERICA

*Library of Congress Catalog Card Number* 72-7943

SBN 684-13288-5   Volume I
SBN 684-13289-3   Volume II
SBN 684-13290-7   Volume III
SBN 684-13291-5   Volume IV
SBN 684-13292-3   Index
SBN 684-13293-1   Set

Memorial Library
Mars Hill College
Mars Hill, N. C.
DISCARD

# DICTIONARY OF
# THE HISTORY OF IDEAS

R
90B9
W4D3d
V. 4

750211

# PSYCHOLOGICAL IDEAS
# IN ANTIQUITY

PSYCHOLOGY is a modern term, but its components, *psyche* and *logos*, are words whose history goes back to the Indo-European parent language. For the philosophers of classical antiquity, giving an "account" (*logos*) of the *psyche* was a necessary part of intellectual inquiry. Greek philosophy was vitally concerned with many of the problems which exercise modern psychologists, but did not regard "study of the mind" as an autonomous subject with specific terms of reference. Frequently theories about the *psyche* were intimately connected with ethical, physical, and metaphysical assumptions.

In this article "antiquity" means the period of Greco-Roman civilization (ca. 750 B.C.–A.D. 450), and "psychological doctrines" means theories held about the *psyche* by philosophers. It is necessary to leave the term *psyche* untranslated initially, since it cannot be accurately rendered by a single English word such as "soul" or "mind." The meaning of *psyche* will best appear by examining its functions and what it is used to denote. Most of this survey is devoted to a chronological discussion of the major psychological doctrines, but a preliminary note on the language and popular conceptions inherited by philosophers will help to set the scene.

## THE LEGACY OF EARLY GREEK
## LANGUAGE AND THOUGHT

The Homeric poems (ca. 750–700 B.C.) are the earliest European literature. In them references to *psyche* are almost confined to descriptions of death or the dead. A man who has lost his *psyche* is either dead or unconscious (through fainting) and it is probable that the word has a primary association with breath. The precise location of *psyche* in the body is obscure, though there are good reasons for associating it with the head (R. B. Onians, *The Origins of European Thought*, Cambridge [1951], pp. 95–115). *Psyche* is sufficiently corporeal to be "breathed out" through the mouth or through a wound and to survive as a ghost when it has left the body. But though essential to the living man, *psyche* is not connected in Homer with any particular activity. *Nous* is his favorite word to describe "mental seeing" or "planning" and it can sometimes be translated "mind." To denote emotions the important word is *thumos* (physically associated with breath and blood). A man may "desire *in* his *thumos*" or his *thumos* may "urge him to do something." Though not regarded as "organs" of the body, *nous* and *thumos* are permanent possessions of the living man to which his thinking and feeling belong.

There are other words which overlap or go beyond these, but Homer does not have a single noun to denote the soul or personality. Nor does he use a single term for "body." When the Homeric hero is under emotional stress he may externalize his heart or his *thumos*, scolding it or conversing with it. The notion that emotions or intellect are in some sense independent of their possessor is illustrated by the "psychic intervention" (Dodds [1951], pp. 5–16) seen in expressions like "Zeus took away his understanding" or "A god put courage into his heart."

The survival of the *psyche* in Homer appears not to possess any important ethical or religious associations. Deprived of the body, the *psyche* lives on in Hades, a feeble transformation or residue of the living man. Essentially, the man whose *psyche* has left the body is dead. Merely to survive as a *psyche* did not make him immortal (*athanatos*). For to be *athanatos* (literally "deathless") is to possess the property of the gods, and the Homeric *psyche* is so far from being divine that it is compared to smoke. The immortality of the soul was a concept which Greeks as late as the fifth century B.C. found surprising (Herodotus IV, 93ff.).

The significance of the development between Homeric thought and early philosophy has been admirably analyzed by Snell (*Die Entdeckung des Geistes*, pp. 12ff.); but a *caveat* is perhaps needed against his claim that Homer gives a fully representative picture of Greek ways of thinking at a particular time. Homer is the culmination of a long oral tradition which has its own highly formalized expressions. In the lyric poets of the next two centuries *psyche* came to be treated as the seat of emotions, in spite of its Homeric associations with death; and it is possible that such a use of the word is not as novel as its absence from Homer might suggest. Eventually intellectual activity was also ascribed to *psyche* and by the fifth century B.C. *psyche* has changed its relation to other words and become the name for a single thing to which consciousness and vitality in general belong. How and why this happened is impossible to answer precisely, but it is certain that religious conceptions associated with the names of Orpheus and Pythagoras were highly influential.

The essence of these conceptions, which probably go back to the sixth century B.C. in northern Greece and southern Italy, is as follows: the *psyche* is an immortal (and therefore divine) being, sullied by incorporation into a mortal body but capable by initiation and ritual observances of becoming pure and eventually free of its earthly shell. Rebirth in various forms and final union with the universal divinity are essential features of this doctrine. It is clear that the Homeric concept of *psyche* has become quite transmuted here.

1

Now, far from signifying merely that which leaves a man when he dies, *psyche* must, in order to fulfill the religious belief, denote his living self or personality. The full significance of this concept was to be developed by Plato, but some earlier philosophers (whether or not they accepted the religious belief) now treated *psyche* as the center of consciousness.

### THE PSYCHOLOGICAL DOCTRINES
### OF THE PRE-SOCRATICS

*1. Thales and Anaximenes.* The first Greek thinkers who are conventionally called "philosophers" were more interested in cosmogony and cosmology than in the study of man. To Thales of Miletus *psyche* seems to have denoted both life and the source of motion. The concept of *psyche* as that which moves and animates the body is a natural development of the view that a dead (motionless) body has lost its *psyche*. In Aristotle's opinion (*De anima* 411a 7f.) Thales may have believed the world itself to possess *psyche;* and many later philosophers certainly took this view. Anaximenes, Thales' younger fellow-countryman, drew a specific analogy between the human *psyche* and the material which he supposed to surround (and control) the cosmos (frag. 2). Both were identified with breath or air, and the point of the comparison is clearly that the *psyche* in man possesses a function similar to that of air in the world. *Psyche* or air is the life-principle. Thales and Anaximenes did not apparently discuss psychology in detail, but the assumption of an affinity between the human *psyche* and the cosmic principle belongs to the same climate of ideas which gave rise to beliefs in the *psyche* as the divine element in man and the center of his consciousness.

*2. Heraclitus.* In Heraclitus of Ephesus all these concepts occur and they are also associated with an interest in sense perception and theory of knowledge. To Heraclitus the senses are the first source of information about the world, but their witness can be misleading (frag. 107). If the evidence of the senses is correctly interpreted by the soul (by which *psyche* will now be translated) it can bring about an understanding of the *logos*, the principle determining all things. This principle, which means the unity behind opposition and change, is not directly an object of perception, though Heraclitus may have supposed it to be "drawn in" physically through the senses (Guthrie [1962], p. 430). *Logos* is an object of intellectual apprehension which a soul in the right condition can grasp. The principle has as its material constituent fire, and Heraclitus probably also regarded fire as the fundamental material of soul, since "it is death to soul to become water" (frag. 36), while "a dry [i.e., hot] soul is wisest and best" (frag. 118). A number of fundamental ideas are involved here. First, the soul is now treated as the recipient of sense-impressions. Second, it is able, by interpreting these, to grasp a principle which is not strictly empirical. Third, the soul at its best is analogous to, if not identical with, the fiery cosmic principle. Aristotle, much later, was to talk of "the thought which thinks itself," and the embryo of this notion may be contained in Heraclitus' belief that the soul is both the apprehender of *logos* and in some sense identical with *logos*. These ideas were not stated in such precise terms by Heraclitus himself. Indeed he advised that the soul possesses depths which cannot be grasped (frag. 45). But they are reasonable inferences from his oracular fragments. He probably believed that the soul was immortal, and that excellence of character went along with intellectual understanding. In this he anticipated Plato, but also his near contemporary, Empedocles.

*3. Empedocles.* In Empedocles, science and mysticism are curiously blended. But though it would be improper to draw an absolute distinction between his two poems, *On Nature* and *Purifications*, the former is primarily an attempt to explain the physical world and the latter an account, in the Orphic-Pythagorean tradition, of the incarnations, rewards, and punishments of the "soul" (*daimon*). Since the work *On Nature* accounts for sense perception, emotion, and thought in purely material terms, without reference to a *psyche*, it is hard to know what role the immortal soul played in the mortal body. Empedocles' account of this is confined to the religious poem (in the evidence which survives) and it is safest to assume that he distinguished the source of physical consciousness from the moral, immortal self. If so, Empedocles has come nearer to the concept of a soul which is quite distinct from the body.

Empedocles gave detailed explanations of sense perception and thought. It is difficult to summarize these, since they are intimately connected with his basic assumptions about the world. Four elements, earth, air, fire, and water, and two polar forces, Love and Strife, constitute all that exists. To perceive is to receive in the pores of the sense organs effluences from the external elements, which are recognized by similar elements in the sense organs. Thought takes place primarily in the blood, which is composed of a nearly perfect mixture (frags. 98, 105) of the elements. It is by thought that we perceive Love and Strife, which are probably also embodied in the blood. Empedocles does not explain whether or how the evidence of the senses is organized by thought. At about this time a Pythagorean philosopher, Alcmaeon, had traced perception from the senses to the brain, but Empedocles may have regarded thought itself as a category of perception which has as its function receiving through the pores and assimilating different combinations of external elements. Even the elements are in some sense "conscious," and all processes, including emotional and mental activities, are referred to their mixture and separation. The naiveté of the theory should not obscure its achievements. Empedocles has focused attention on the mechanism of consciousness, and offered an explanation consistent with his theories about the natural world. Psychology is here related to physiology. The investigation of physical phenomena has aroused interest in the physical processes of sensation and thought.

**4. Parmenides.** Other pre-Socratic theories may be discussed more briefly. To Parmenides, whose influence on Empedocles and subsequent philosophy was profound, the physical world possessed no reality; for it contained no subject of which "exists" could always be truly asserted. Parmenides was unable to satisfy the claims of his logic by reference to changing phenomena and he rejected the senses in favor of *nous*, the mind or the application of thought: the only existent is an object of intellectual apprehension. For the history of psychology this is important. Parmenides set up the intellect as an autonomous faculty, quite independent of sense perception. Its physical basis (frag. 16) is obscure and hardly relevant to his main argument. But among philosophers like Plato and Aristotle, who were concerned with the relation between soul and body, an analogous belief in the primacy and independence of the intellectual faculty persists.

**5. Anaxagoras and Democritus.** It is improbable that any pre-Socratic philosopher regarded mind or soul as wholly immaterial. Anaxagoras made *nous* the first cause of the cosmos and the controlling principle of living things. He called it the "finest and purest of all things" (frag. 12), which suggests that he was coming close to expressing its immateriality. Unlike Empedocles, Anaxagoras regarded perception as the interaction of contraries; we recognize external heat by virtue of cold in ourselves. He was also an extreme realist, taking all qualitative differences to be fundamental differences in matter itself. This theory was opposed by his contemporary, Democritus the atomist, who referred all the qualities we perceive to changing states of the body and its interaction with atoms of different shapes. Democritus was consistent with the general pre-Socratic position in giving the soul (spherical atoms distributed over the body) the same substance as his cosmic principle.

## PLATO

Plato's psychological theory is fundamental to his whole philosophy and only its more striking aspects can be indicated here. In regarding "cultivation of the soul" as the primary duty, Plato was certainly influenced by Socrates and the Pythagoreans. Our knowledge of Socrates is largely based on the works of Plato, but it can be assumed that Socrates advocated and practiced rigorous discussion about moral concepts as the means of tending the soul and making it competent to control the body and its passions. "Soul" here means intellectual and moral self. The two attributes go hand in hand. For it is only when we know what goodness is that we can (and will) become good.

**Dualism.** Plato presents this intellectualist position most strongly in the *Phaedo*. Soul and body are alien substances. It is the aim of the soul, which is simple in essence and immortal, to rid itself of the body, for while it is embodied the soul cannot attain perfect knowledge. The only objects of knowledge are Forms—unique, incomposite, immaterial entities of which the particular objects of perception are only fleeting replicas. During embodiment the soul can apprehend the Forms only by thinking as far as possible independently of the body. Soul is the thinking, rational self in direct opposition to the passions, pleasures, and sensations associated with the body. It is still part of the soul's job to animate the body during its incarnation, but this is a regrettable incursion on its spiritual activity and Plato does not explain how the soul acts on the body.

**Differentiated Soul.** This extreme dualism was not Plato's final word. In the *Republic* (Book IV) soul loses its unity and becomes divided into *nous* ("intellect"), *thumos* ("passion"), and *epithumia* ("appetite"). To its appetitive part are ascribed bodily desires; *thumos* is the emotional element in virtue of which we feel anger, fear, etc.; *nous* is (or should be) the controlling part which subjugates the appetites with the help of *thumos*. Plato seeks justification for this theory on two counts. First, his quest for justice is based on the assumption that the state is a large-scale analogue of the individual, and therefore the components which sanction the state's division into three classes (artisans, soldiers, and guardians) are established as categories for analyzing the psychology of the individual. Second, Plato invokes the empirical fact of conflict within the individual (*Republic* IV, 436ff.). At one and the same time we may both desire to drink and be unwilling to drink. But the same thing cannot act in opposite ways with the same part of itself towards the same object at the same time. If such conflict is to be referred to the soul as a whole, then the soul must possess different parts to account for the clash. It is also the case that passion and appetite may conflict, for a man may be angry with that in himself which prompts him to do something shameful. Hence a part of the soul different from reason and appetite is required. Like the soldiers of the ideal state, passion should be the ally of the

3

governing component. The basic conflict for Plato is still between bodily desires and intellect, between sense and reason, but the dualism of the *Phaedo* has been modified by locating the division which follows from incarnation within the soul itself. At the same time Plato saw the possibility of reconciliation within the divided self, for he asserts that the two lower parts have "following reason" as their function (*Republic* IX, 586e). The true philosopher is one in whom the rule of reason is established, and in this situation all parts of the soul conspire together for a united good. Nor is the rule of reason an exercise of cold intellection. The rational part of the soul is a *lover* of wisdom, and distinguished from the appetitive part not by the absence of all desire but by having a different object of desire: the absolute, intelligible good.

This doctrine is presented mythically in the *Phaedrus* (246a ff.), where the human soul is pictured as a charioteer (reason) driving a pair of horses (passion and appetite). The passionate horse is a clean, upstanding creature which follows the guide of reason, whereas its fellow horse is a shaggy, recalcitrant beast which tries to drag the chariot down from its heavenly course. Here the soul's composite nature does not depend on incarnation; but the point of the image is the imperfect human soul's moral tension, not its multiplicity of function. Plato's division of the soul persists in later works such as the *Timaeus,* in which the rational part of the soul is stated to be divine and immortal, and is contrasted with two mortal, irrational parts: passion and appetite (69d ff.). The rational part is located in the head and is composed of immaterial ingredients blended from the basic principles of the intelligible world and the world of physical change. The irrational parts are located in the chest (passion) and the belly (appetite). Their activities are associated with the bodily organs which house them. The blood vessels seem to be the instruments by which the different parts of the soul communicate with each other.

*Knowledge and Perception.* Soul is self-moving, the principle of motion (i.e., animation) both in individual living things and in the world itself (*Phaedrus* 245c ff.). The world is an intelligent, living creature on which man himself is modelled. In its original, discarnate state the human soul has direct acquaintance with the Forms and thus acquires knowledge. This knowledge is forgotten when the soul enters a body but it can be recalled, at least in part, by "dialectic," rigorous philosophical discussion, and the judgments which we make about our perceptions presuppose it. All judgments entail the use of such terms as "exists," "is the same as," "is different from," and these are not objects of perception (*Theaetetus* 185a ff.). Learning is a process of recollecting *a priori* truths, a doctrine Plato attempts

to prove in the *Meno* (81e ff.) by an experiment in which an uneducated slave is shown how to "recall" the answer to the problem, what square has twice the area of that of a given square, by answering a series of simple questions. Since sensible objects lack the unchanging existence required by Plato of what is fully real, he took less interest in the analysis of sensation. But in later dialogues the soul is more explicitly related to the body insofar as sensations are described as movements, caused by external phenomena, which are transmitted to the soul through the body (*Timaeus* 43c); and pleasures which have their source in the body penetrate to the soul (*Republic* 457c). Plato also recognized a form of "judgment" in which the mind pronounces *rightly* or *wrongly* on what is presented to the senses (*Sophist* 263d–264b).

Plato's psychology is not a systematic doctrine, rigidly adhered to. His view of the soul developed from the uncompromising dualism of the *Phaedo* to a position in which a unitary self is attainable if harmony can be established between reason, emotion, and bodily appetite. Body and mind are related to each other through pleasure and sensation. But Plato never abandoned his belief in the priority of reason, the part of man which is akin to the fully real, unchanging world and which has as its essential function apprehending that world.

### ARISTOTLE

With Aristotle, psychology became a subject of systematic inquiry. He devoted a whole treatise (*De anima*) to defining soul and its functions, and a group of smaller works (*Parva naturalia*) covers specific topics such as memory and sleep. Aristotle regarded psychology as an aspect of physical science, and his own analysis is based on the principles which he lays down for all study of the natural world. But the *De anima* occupies a fundamental place in his entire philosophy. The biological works require constant reference to it, and it is highly relevant to the ethics, epistemology, and metaphysics. Aristotle has good claims to be the founder of "psychology," though the word itself is not used by him. All later Greek psychological theory shows his influence, in both terminology and method.

*Soul as Vital Principle.* Aristotle began his career as a student of Plato, and in his earliest works, of which only fragments survive, he argued for the preexistence and survival of the whole soul. According to that theory the relationship of body to soul is temporary and contingent. But in the *De anima,* a work of his later years, Aristotle takes body and soul to be two aspects, which are only conceptually distinguishable, of a single substance: "a body which possesses life" (II, 1). Aristotle calls these two aspects "matter" and "form." Soul is the form which *animate* matter must possess. The physical matter of an animal is not its soul, for what distinguishes animate from inanimate is not physical matter but "the possession of life." The potentiality to be alive is a natural property of certain bodies, and it is in virtue of soul that such bodies realize this potentiality.

Aristotle defines soul as "the primary actuality of a natural body which potentially has life" (*De anima* 412a 27–28). By "primary actuality" he means the actual possession of the faculties which are necessary to life, just as an eye, in order to be an eye, must possess the faculty of vision. It is clear that with this conception body and soul are necessarily related. Aristotle recognizes that emotions, desire, perception—all functions of the soul—are dependent on the body which contains them. But the influence of Plato remains strong enough to make Aristotle regard mind (*nous*) as a faculty of soul which has no physical base and which may be capable of existing apart from the body. Of this more below.

**Faculties of Soul.** In the first book of *De anima*, Aristotle surveys and criticizes earlier theories of the soul. From them he draws certain general assumptions; in particular, the soul is the principle responsible for thought, sensation and perception (Aristotle's single word *aisthesis* covers both), and movement. His detailed analysis in the next two books is concerned with these functions of soul.

Since soul is that which distinguishes animate from inanimate, Aristotle considers what characteristics are peculiar to living creatures. He nominates four: nutrition (the faculty of growth and reproduction); sensation; locomotion; and thought. The first of these is a "form of movement," and it is possessed by every living creature from plants upwards. Only man has all four faculties, which thus serve as a way of classifying all living things in ascending order of complexity.

This method of analyzing soul is an important advance on Plato's. Aristotle is not dividing the soul into parts (a procedure which he opposes) but analyzing its different functions. Possessing *aisthesis* means possessing at least one (touch) of the five senses, and it also entails imagination, pleasure and pain, and desire. The latter is not a base part of the soul, but a necessary concomitant of perception and sensation. Aristotle in some sense is a behaviorist. He wants to know how and why living creatures act, and he analyzes this in terms roughly comparable to stimulus and response. Thus an animal moves in space because its appetitive faculty is prompted by an object which presents itself as desirable (or good), and the animal is then moved to pursue it (*De anima* III, 432b 15–17; 433a 27–29). In man the psychology of action is more

complex, since mind and desire may clash; but there is no question of man's acting independently of desire since all action is prompted by the good, as the agent sees it. What man can do, if he has himself under control, is to contemplate objects of desire or aversion without acting in consequence, though physical changes, such as rapid heartbeat, may ensue (*De anima* 432b 27–32). He also has the unique capacity to deliberate and thus establish a goal of action independent of his immediate environment and physical state.

**Sensation and Perception.** Aristotle devoted considerable attention to the analysis of sensation and perception (*De anima* II, 5–12). His theories here, though hampered by inadequate physiology (the nervous system, commonly confused with the arteries, was discovered about sixty years after his death) represent a major advance on previous speculation. Aristotle takes sense perception to be an activity in which external objects so act upon each sense organ that it receives their form (perceptible properties) independently of the matter with which this form is associated in the object itself. Just as wax can be imprinted with various impressions, so the sense organ or sense can become qualified as colored, resonant, hot, etc. Neither the sense nor its (perceptible) object has any actual existence except in the act of perception, and this takes place when the appropriate medium (e.g., light in the case of vision) is acted upon by the external object and passes on its perceptible properties to the sense organ. It has been observed that an explanation of *aisthesis* as a "process of being acted on" does not square well with the active notion of "discrimination," which Aristotle also attributes to this faculty (Hamlyn, *Classical Quarterly*, 9 [1959], 12f.). Part of the difficulty arises from a lack of terms to distinguish sensation from perception. But Aristotle was not perhaps so confused as some make out. The organ is so constituted that it reacts in certain ways to the objects which fall between the ranges, light-dark, soft-hard, etc. (*De anima* 423b 30–424a 10). The sense is a "mean" between two extremes and it is in virtue of this mean that we are made aware of (or judge) the different properties of objects. Hence the reason, according to Aristotle, why we are not aware of temperature equivalent to that of our own body.

A more serious difficulty is how to explain the coordination of information received by the senses and the problem of self-consciousness. Aristotle asserts that each sense has its own object, to which it is necessarily related. (He seems to exclude the possibility of hallucination by connecting actual hearing with actual sounding, *De anima* 425b 26ff.). But there are certain properties such as motion, rest, shape, magnitude, and

5

number which are apprehended by more than one sense. Since there is no sixth sense, this "perception of common sensibles" is due to the cooperative activity of the special senses, i.e., the whole faculty, and Aristotle calls this "common sense" (*De anima* 425a 14–425b 11). Whereas we can never, in Aristotle's view, be deceived by the simple qualities (e.g., color, sound) reported by the special senses, we can make mistakes about the common sensibles; we can also relate any object of perception to the wrong external object (what Aristotle calls the "incidental" object of perception), i.e., take what we perceive to be Socrates when it is Plato. For perception does not tell us what something is (this is the job of the mind); it gives information about the qualities of an object. The precise workings of "common sense" are obscure in the *De anima*. In the *Parva naturalia* mention is made of a single, unified sense faculty, probably located in the heart, by which the data of sense are coordinated and on which self-awareness, imagination, and dreaming depend. But if Aristotle envisaged such a role for "common sense" in the *De anima* he does not say so.

*Thought.* Aristotle's account of thought is obscure and unsatisfactory. Much of the difficulty derives from the fact that he takes thought to be an activity analogous to *aisthesis*, i.e., a change brought about by an object, in this case "thinkables" or "intelligibles" (*De anima* III, 4). Now in sensation the sense organ is acted upon by external phenomena, but these are not available to actualize the mind, which "has no organ." Aristotle takes the mind to be in one respect analogous to a blank wax-tablet on which anything can be imprinted; in this sense mind is capable of receiving and becoming identical with any object of thought, but it has no actual existence until it thinks. In another respect, the mind is an ever-active power that actualizes its own capacity for thought in the manner of light which makes potential colors actual (ibid., III, 5). This doctrine of an active intellect is necessary, given Aristotle's theory of potentiality, if the capacity of the passive intellect is to result in an actual cognitive process. But the active intellect does not apparently create its own objects of thought. Where then do they come from? They cannot be independent substances, like Plato's Forms. But thought *is* concerned with "forms" or "essences"—what things really are—and it thinks them with the help of mental images (ibid., 431a 14–15). Aristotle seems to conceive of imagination as a faculty, intermediate between *aisthesis* and thought, which provides the mind with the data in which it can conceptualize the essential form of particular things, or, in the case of abstract thought, the form of, say, triangle without reference to any actual existing triangle. But the precise relationship between imagi-nation and the two aspects of mind is very uncertain.

In its active aspect mind is independent of body, eternal and immortal. It is not engendered in the physical process of conception but enters the womb "from outside." But what kind of existence the individual mind enjoys when separate from the body is not explained. God, for Aristotle, is nothing but an ever-active mind, and man has something of God present in himself through his active intellect.

This doctrine does not seriously contradict Aristotle's view of soul and body as two aspects of a single substance. Soul essentially is that which actualizes the body's vital capacities, but the active intellect has no physical correlate, though it temporarily unites with the passive intellect, which ultimately seems to depend on the body. The details of this theory are not Aristotle's main concern in the *De anima*. There he shows how the response of a living creature to its environment can be analyzed as a movement, varying in complexity from the single nutritive functions of a plant to the behavior of man, who responds by his rational and appetitive capacities to the data provided by the senses and imagination. Knowledge is the formulation of general notions by induction from the particular objects of perception. This ability to frame concepts provides man with his ethical goals and the subject matter of his scientific inquiries.

Aristotle's psychology is a general analysis of the determinate capacities of the species which fall under the genus animal. It has important metaphysical and ethical applications, but unlike Plato, Aristotle emphasized the organic unity of body and soul, and established terms of reference for investigating animal behavior.

### POST-ARISTOTELIAN PSYCHOLOGY

*1. Theophrastus and Strato.* After Aristotle's death the philosophical school (Lyceum or Peripatos) associated with his name won fame as a center of scientific research, under its successive heads, Theophrastus and Strato. Theophrastus' *De sensu*, a historical survey of theories of sensation and perception, is an invaluable source of information about the pre-Socratics, but the little that is known about his own psychological theory suggests that he followed Aristotle in most respects. He did, however, raise questions about the "external" origin of intellect and the manner of the association between the active and passive intellect (Themistius, *In De an.* 430a 25). In this context, and for what follows, Strato is a figure of major importance, a fact which has not always been fully appreciated. Evidence about him is scanty, but it reveals a thinker of the highest scientific quality. Strato departed radically from the Platonic and Aristotelian tradition in regarding sensation, perception, emotion, and thought as multiple aspects of a single, unified consciousness (Plutarch, *De libidine et aegritudine* 697b). This he located in a central organ (the front part of the brain) which communicates with the sense organs and the rest of the body via *pneuma* ("fine air or breath"). Sensations occur not in the organs themselves but in this sensorium, whence they are projected to the particular part of the body which is affected (Aëtius, IV 23, 3). Strato thus provided a firm physiological basis for consciousness lacking in Aristotle's system, and completely abandoned the distinction between rational and irrational faculties, as well as the belief in an immortal soul or a transcendent reason. Mind is not peculiar to man; rather, it is a necessary condition of sensation and perception, since the data of sense require "attention" if they are to be registered (Plutarch, *De sollertia animalium* 961a). In this theory, thought is downgraded to "consciousness," a thoroughly heretical notion in the general context of Greek philosophy. For his physiology Strato was certainly influenced by medical science which, probably shortly after his death, was revolutionized by the discovery of the nervous system. (See F. Solmsen, "Greek Philosophy and the Discovery of Nerves," *Museum Helveticum,* **18** [1961], 150–63, 169–97.) Strato's use of *pneuma* as the carrier of "messages" (Aristotle in his biological works had already assigned to *pneuma* the function of transmitting bodily movement) as well as his concept of a unified consciousness found further development in the psychology of the Stoics.

*2. Stoics and Epicureans.* In spite of their scientific achievements the Peripatetics were not the major influence on later Greek thinking in its broader sense. Epicurus and Zeno (of Citium), who founded schools in Athens at the end of the fourth century B.C., inaugurated two philosophical systems which rapidly acquired rival adherents from a wider range of society than Plato and Aristotle had affected. It is customary to invoke the conquests of Alexander the Great and the collapse of the Greek city-state in accounts of the origin of these systems. The instability of the times and the inadequacy of traditional ethics may well help to explain the success and motivation of Epicurus and Zeno, who both provided a morality which stressed the self-sufficiency of the individual. But the intellectual basis of both systems is thoroughly Greek and their psychological theories develop ideas already discussed.

These theories may conveniently be studied in concert, for Stoicism and Epicureanism possess striking similarities as well as contrasts. Both systems are a form of materialism: for Epicurus, following Democritus, all that exists is atoms, differing in size, shape, and weight (this last an innovation), which by deviating from their normal downward movement in empty space collide and form temporary compound bodies. In living things the soul itself consists of very fine atoms, resembling fiery air, which pervade the whole body. No body which lacks a soul can be alive and soul cannot be sentient or cause sensation unless it is housed in a body, a doctrine which rules out the survival of consciousness after death (*Letter to Herodotus* 63–64). The soul-atoms located in the human breast constitute "mind," which controls and issues instructions to the rest of the soul (Lucretius, III, 136–44). Mind and soul are thus in permanent contact with all parts of the body. Sensation is the result of *eidōla* (effluences exactly reproducing external objects) striking the sense organs and thus setting up a movement in the mind. And certain particularly fine "idols" (e.g., from the gods) penetrate directly to the mind. All sensations as such are true, and the only source of knowledge; but they may be misinterpreted by the mind and hence errors arise. General ideas are built up by the mind from repeated presentations of the same object, and perception occurs when individual presentations match the general idea. Scientific thought seems to operate by the juxtaposition of two sets of atoms within the mind, constituting different concepts (C. Bailey, *Epicurus* [1926], p. 269), but the evidence for this theory is notoriously obscure.

In Stoicism the soul also permeates the whole body and finds its "thinking center" in the heart. It consists not of atoms but *pneuma* ("fiery breath") in a particular state of "tension." For the Stoics, all that exists consists of bodies differentiated by *pneuma,* the active force which binds the passive material qualities, earth and water, into individual things according to its tension. (Like the pre-Socratics, Stoics and Epicureans explained soul in terms of the basic principle governing the universe.) *Pneuma* is not merely a mechanistic concept, like the Epicurean atom, but a dynamic, rational force which pervades and activates the whole world, all parts of which are thus interconnected. In perception the sense organs are acted upon by objects, either directly or through a medium, and this sets up a presentation (*phantasia*) which is reported to the central organ by currents of *pneuma.* The agent has the power to assent or not to the presentation, and his act of assent constitutes perception or "grasping" the object. The Stoics argued that presentations which completely reproduce the object are grasped as true by men of normal health, and on the basis of these, general ideas are built up by analogy, combination, etc. (Cicero, *Academica posteriora* I, 41–42; Sextus Empiricus, *Adversus mathematicos* VII, 227–60; Diogenes Laërtius, VII, 45–54). Presentations can also occur without an external cause, a theory which accounts, *inter alia,* for hallucination. Like the

7

Epicureans the Stoics based their theory of knowledge entirely on perception.

Both systems gave special attention to motivation. For the primary impulse the Stoics took "innate attraction towards those things which are peculiarly suited to preserve an animal's natural well-being and avoidance of their opposites" (Cicero, *De finibus* III, 16ff.). All living creatures are endowed with a drive, and this is naturally stimulated by awareness of the appropriate object. Without this drive no action is possible, and it follows on a mental picture stemming from something internal or external. What distinguishes man from other animals is the possession of reason. This develops through childhood, and in maturity enables a man to control his drives and so make responses to the environment which are rational and moral as well as appropriate in the instinctive sense. Assent plays its part here as a means of determining the mental attitude, which is open to the individual's control. From God's viewpoint all events are predetermined, but so far as human action is concerned the causal factor (as in Aristotle) is primarily the disposition which the agent has acquired by repeatedly acting in a certain way.

The Stoics underrated emotions, which they regarded as perverted judgments, except in the case of the sage. Like Strato they unified all functions of soul. For the Epicureans, by contrast, pleasure and avoidance of pain are the primary impulse of living creatures and the foundation of ethics. They constitute the objects of desire by which all action is prompted (Cicero, *De finibus* I, 29ff.). For any action to take place, mental images in the form of "idols" must strike the mind and obtain its attention. Then the will is activated and movement transferred from the mind to the limbs (Lucretius, II, 261–83). The freedom of the will in action is explained by reference to an indeterminate "swerve" of atoms (Lucretius, II, 250–60). This has generally been taken to imply a spontaneous movement of soul atoms for every voluntary act. But it has recently been argued that the swerve explains not particular voluntary acts but merely the fact that character is not wholly determined by antecedent causes (D. J. Furley, *Two Studies in the Greek Atomists*, Princeton [1967], pp. 169–237).

Stoicism and Epicureanism are primarily theories of ethics, and their psychology focuses attention on the motives and processes of human action. Both abandon completely any idea of an incorporeal mind; mental activity is psychosomatic activity in which the soul acts *by physical processes* upon the body. Human behavior is necessarily related to the environment, from which all the data used to form concepts are derived. Such materialism and behaviorism were completely abandoned by the last great pagan and early Christian philosophers.

## PSYCHOLOGICAL DOCTRINE IN LATE ANTIQUITY: PHILOSOPHICAL THEOLOGY

Between the foundation of Stoicism and Epicureanism and the establishment of Christianity as the official religion of the Roman empire lies a span of some six hundred years. The early part of this period produced a ferment of ideas in philosophy and science. But the first two hundred years of the Roman Empire, in spite of the achievements of the anatomist Galen and the astronomer Ptolemy, were not a time in which original thought flourished. Much was done to synthesize, modify, or reinterpret existing theories, but the dominance of Rome, so fruitful in many respects, was not conducive to philosophical speculation. Yet there were forces at work which were to produce figures of major importance in the history of ideas, in particular Plotinus and Augustine. In them classical philosophy and the eclecticism of the age combined with spiritual theology in a remarkable way.

*1. Plotinus.* As concern with moral conduct became increasingly dominant among philosophers, so interest became ever more centered on the "inner man." Already in Stoicism it was the attitude of mind, the internal disposition, which mattered in ethical judgment, but Stoicism remained earthbound by its denial of any existence to the incorporeal. In Neo-Platonism, as established by Plotinus, the highest human activity is contemplation of the transcendent Good, which is the source of various grades of being. Lowest on the scale is the material universe, including the human body with which the soul forms a mysterious and temporary union. This looks similar to Platonic dualism, but in fact it is significantly different. For Plato embodiment prevents the soul from fully grasping the Forms. But for Plotinus the body is not a necessary barrier to union with the One or ultimate Good, the goal of human endeavor. This follows because man's soul in its highest aspect is continually engaged in intellection of the Forms; it is "illumined" by Intellect, the principle second only to the One or Good. In this activity the soul is not self-conscious, since this would detract from its attention to the object of contemplation. Plotinus notes that certain activities, such as reading, go better if we are unconscious of ourselves as acting. What "comes down" to the material world and joins with body is an irradiation from the higher soul. But this lower soul is incorporeal, and Plotinus discusses the problem of its relation to the body at length (*Enneads* I, 1, 1–10; IV, 3, 9–23). He rejects all previous explanations of this relationship in favor of an analogy with light: soul is present to body as light to air. The living body is "illumined" by soul. In sensation the soul *uses* the body and reads impressions made on it. Hence there is no action of body on soul. The two remain "separate but in contact." Memory and perception both belong to soul and depend on its faculty of imaging (*Enneads* IV, 3, 27). The soul sees when it looks out at externals. In thought the faculty of imaging is acted upon by the higher soul, and this provides the principles with which reason works. Memory is a concept of great importance for Plotinus because it provides (or is) the continuity of self-consciousness. Only by memory does the embodied soul possess an image of itself. It is through desire for the lower that soul enters into body, and it is by desire for the higher that the soul can recall memory of its activity in the intellectual sphere and aspire eventually to forget all the lower (including self-awareness) in contemplation of the divine.

**2. Augustine.** Plotinus was the last great pagan philosopher of classical antiquity, but it is no coincidence that he shares much with Saint Augustine. In interpreting the scriptures Augustine was influenced by an intellectual climate common to pagan and Christian; and inner experience as revealed by introspection becomes the key to psychology. In a summary it is impossible to do more than indicate some of Augustine's major doctrines on the soul. In the *De quantitate animae* problems of the soul's relation to the body, and the nature of sensation and thought are discussed in dialogue form. The soul is incorporeal and its substance cannot be named; rather must it be inferred from the fact that God, its creator, is its proper habitation (*Patrologia Latina*, 32, 1036). The soul shares in reason and is fitted to rule the body. By its presence it vitalizes the body and forms this into a harmonious unity. In this doctrine Augustine is closer to Plotinus than to Aristotle. The soul can take note of the body's changes (and this is Augustine's definition of *sensus*) but these do not affect the soul itself. In man the soul possesses various grades of being (ibid., 1074ff.), a ranking determined by the objects of its attention. Apprehension of any kind is a result of the mind's choosing to attend to something in its field of internal vision. God is always present to the mind (whatever its activity) and by His grace the souls of the faithful at their highest possess a stable vision of the truth. It is by divine illumination that the soul has standards of judgment "impressed" on it, for the divine mind contains eternal truths (*P.L.* 42, 1052). Like Plotinus Augustine laid great weight on "memory," for this is not mere reminiscence but the storehouse of experience and the mind's knowledge of itself (ibid., 1048). In conversion the mind "remembers" God.

Augustine, for all his indebtedness to Greek thought, looks forward to the Middle Ages. But it is not the business of this article to chart the subsequent history of psychology. Needless to say, modern thinking owes more than is sometimes acknowledged to ancient psychology. Between the materialism of Democritus and the extreme spirituality of Plotinus runs a line on which intermediate positions are taken by Descartes as well as Plato, by Gilbert Ryle as well as Aristotle. In spite of inadequate technical knowledge the Greeks developed ways of analyzing mind and body and the response of an organism to its environment which continue to shape much of our thinking. They knew no "science" of psychology, and were not hampered by having to confine their attention to a neatly labeled set of "mental phenomena."

*BIBLIOGRAPHY*

For pre-philosophical psychology the best starting points are Erwin Rhode, *Psyche: Seelenkult und Unsterblichkeitsglaube der Griechen*, 4th ed. (Tübingen, 1970; Engl. trans. London, 1925); Bruno Snell, *Die Entdeckung des Geistes*, 3rd ed. (Hamburg, 1955), trans. as *The Discovery of the Mind* (Cambridge, Mass., 1953); E. R. Dodds, *The Greeks and the Irrational* (Berkeley, 1951). Texts of the pre-Socratics are collected in H. Diels and W. Kranz, *Die Fragmente der Vorsokratiker*, 6th ed. (Berlin, 1951–52). For an extended treatment see J. I. Beare, *Greek Theories of Elementary Cognition* (Oxford, 1906). W. K. C. Guthrie, *A History of Greek Philosophy*, Vols. I, II (Cambridge, 1962, 1965) has extensive notes and bibliography. For Plato the most important texts are *Phaedo, Phaedrus, Philebus, Republic* IV–VII, X; *Theaetetus, Timaeus.* For bibliography see H. Cherniss, *Lustrum* (1961), 340–82, and for recent discussion I. M. Crombie, *An Examination of Plato's Doctrines*, Vol. I (London, 1962). Aristotle's psychological theory is set out in *De anima*, ed. Hicks (Cambridge, 1907) and *Parva naturalia*, ed. W. D. Ross (Oxford, 1955); general discussion and bibliography in I. Düring, *Aristotles* (Heidelberg, 1966). See also D. W. Hamlyn, *De anima Books II and III, with Certain Passages from Book I* (Oxford and New York, 1968). Some basic texts for post-Aristotelian psychology are collected by C. J. de Vogel, *Greek Philosophy. A Collection of Texts with Notes and Explanations*, Vol. III (Leiden, 1959). Relevant works of Augustine are *De trinitate, De liberio arbitrio, De quantitate animae*, and of Plotinus, *Enneads* I, 1; IV. This period is well surveyed by E. Zeller, *Die Philosophie der Griechen*, Vol. III, 1, 5th. ed. by E. Wellmann (Leipzig, 1923), and A. H. Armstrong, ed., *Cambridge History of Later Greek and Early Medieval Philosophy* (Cambridge, 1956).

ANTHONY A. LONG

[See also Analogy in Early Greek Thought; Atomism; Behaviorism; **Biological Conceptions in Antiquity;** Cosmology; Dualism; Epicureanism; **Imprinting;** Neo-Platonism; Platonism; Pythagorean . . . ; Rationality; **Stoicism.**]

## PSYCHOLOGICAL SCHOOLS IN EUROPEAN THOUGHT

### I

THE TERM "psychology" (from *psyche,* soul; *logos,* science), invented only in the sixteenth century by an obscure Marburg professor, Goclenius, was rarely used until the eighteenth century. Furthermore, this etymological definition, "science of the soul," hardly approaches the present meaning of the term psychology, since the word "science" here meant an *a priori* theory which was indifferent to the experimentation maintained by scientific psychology around 1860; and also, the word "soul" is a term which psychology has generally rejected because of the metaphysical and religious overtones it arouses.

The idea of the soul, on the other hand, has a much longer history which undoubtedly originated in such universal phenomena as: birth and death, sleep, fainting-fits, dreams, deliriums, etc. In primitive thought, the soul appeared to have a magic correlation—which varied in different societies—with forces of life. Soul was attributed to animals as well as to man since animals also breathe and bleed. For the visible sign of death is to breathe one's last breath or to bleed to death. Also in Genesis it is said that the Eternal God, when He created man out of the dust of the Earth, "breathed the breath of life into his nostrils, and man became a living creature." What becomes of this mysterious soul which inhabits the body when the body becomes nothing more than a cadaver? The primitive mind answered this question with all sorts of imaginary pictures: a kingdom of spirits, migration of souls, ghosts of the departed, etc.

### II

In the West, Greece was the cradle of scientific knowledge insofar as certain minds, as early as the sixth century B.C., showed the necessity for a rational explanation of man and of the world, though, in the beginning aspects of both were still not clearly distinguished. The "Sophists" (Protagoras, Gorgias, et al.) were to be the first to unveil what is today called "human subjectivity," by bringing to light a problem inherent in every human being as such, that is to say, as a subject who has feelings and desires, who is capable of asking himself questions about himself and about the world, and whose very existence conditions at the same time the questions and the answers. Their great antagonist, Socrates, was to provide moral significance for this interrogation of man by himself. Socrates' dialectical irony (*maieutic*) inspired by the inscription on the Delphic Temple: "Know thyself" (*Gnothi Seauton*) brought to introspective analysis a method that lent itself to generalization. This method actually laid the foundation for introspective psychology which was to undergo, in future centuries, countless variations, all of them inscribed on the royal road opened up by the Athenian philosopher. The limits of Socratic inquiry are the very same ones of clear conscience of which Socrates was the apostle, and which prevailed in Western thought until the end of the eighteenth century.

Under Plato Socratic teaching blossomed into a grandiose metaphysics, affirming the eternity of the soul and its supermundane destiny. In Aristotle there was a more clearly manifested concern to limit the field of psychology before it was a proven science; his works, particularly *De anima,* are rich with observations which form the basis of classical psychology. Reproaching Plato for conceiving the soul in the body as a pilot in a boat, Aristotle saw in the soul the active principle of life, the organizing power already present in plants which are capable of feeding themselves and of growing; the soul guarantees the animal the power to desire and to move itself, and guarantees to man the power to think and to will. The views of the great idealistic Greek trilogy (Socrates, Plato, Aristotle) continued to feed the principal current of Western thought from the advent of Christianity until the Renaissance. When it made the shift from ancient culture, Christianity attributed in principle a greater value to the soul than to earthly matters; and inasmuch as Christianity emphasized the inner life and examination of one's conscience, it created a favorable climate for the development of introspective psychology, which Socrates had inaugurated and the Stoics had promoted further.

But the inventive mind of the Greeks opened up many other vistas. It was thus that the great physician Hippocrates, in the fifth century B.C., appeared to be the initiator of clinical observation and of characterology; and the philosopher Epicurus (341–270), who, in his quest for inward tranquility, concerned himself with interactions between the body and the soul, as in psychotherapy. These interactions led him to think that the soul and the body are of the same nature, that the soul is material like the body, but composed of more subtle atoms. Such a materialistic solution was to reappear in the modern world.

### III

With the great discoveries and the new ideals of the Renaissance there was a transformation in the relationship of man to nature. The cultural upheaval was illustrated by the persecution and burning of Giordano Bruno, apostle of the theory of the infinity and evolution of the world, as well as by the sentence to retract imposed in 1633 on Galileo Galilei, creator of mathematical physics. The great supervening transformation inspired in particular the work of René Descartes, who is a better illustration in this period of the breaking away from the ancient Greek and medieval modes of thought. A mathematician as well as a philosopher, Descartes reduced the physical universe to matter and space (Body and Extension). Convinced that the laws of Nature are, in principle, reducible to those of motion, he treated biology as though it were a branch of physics. The functions of living bodies would thus result mechanically from the arrangement of the organs. The animal to whom Descartes refused to grant any consciousness is for him nothing but a machine, an automaton. And what is man? Having discovered the basis of all knowledge in *Cogito ergo sum* and the reality of thought, whose immateriality made it impossible for thought to be reduced to matter and space, Descartes attributed a unique absolute originality to the soul. By thus affirming the coexistence of the two principles of space (*res extensa*) and thought (*res cogitans*), the Cartesian doctrine was also able to foster the revival of introspective psychology as well as mathematical physics devoted to the knowledge and mastery of the external world. This second mechanistic goal was finally to dominate European thought to the point where the *cogito*, and all that Descartes derived from it appeared as a kind of superfluous appendix.

His contemporary, Thomas Hobbes, had already counterpoised his naturalistic conception of man in which man's soul is assimilated to the physiology of the brain and nervous system (*De corpore*, 1655; *De homine*, 1656). This one-sided Cartesian development marked French materialism in the eighteenth century. A work of the physician La Mettrie (*L'homme machine*, 1748), inspired by Descartes, sanctioned the extension of automatism to include thought (*res cogitans*), the mechanism to which Descartes had reduced animal consciousness. The theory of conditioned reflexes and contemporary behaviorism fit well into this perspective. The discussions which Cartesian dualism stirred up about the relationships of the soul to the body were aimed especially at the origin of ideas. When the empiricist John Locke maintained (*Essay Concerning Human Understanding*, 1690) that all ideas come from experience, Leibniz, the rationalist, answered (*Nouveaux essais sur l'entendement humain*, 1714) that intelligence is a necessary condition for every experience. The question in point was basically one of knowing if and to what extent reason could dispense with direct observation of facts. Locke's influence, which was very great in France in the eighteenth century, had a particularly strong effect on Condillac (*Essai sur l'origine des connaissances humaines*, 1746).

In Great Britain, Locke's empiricism paved the way for David Hume's theories, which brought to light the role that repetition and habit played in knowledge; and also the theories of John Stuart Mill, author of an "associationist" system which was to have great repercussions on the Continent.

In the meantime the philosopher Immanuel Kant had cut through the Locke-Leibniz debate by revolutionizing the epistemological problem (*Kritik der reinen Vernunft*, 1781). When Kant demonstrated that knowledge is necessarily the result of a synthetic activity of the mind, his critics attacked certain illusory ideas pertaining to spiritual *substance*, such as the soul or God. Kant's *Critiques* thus undermined that ontological psychology which Christian Wolff, in keeping with the prevailing current of theological philosophical thought in Europe, still superimposed (*Psychologia rationalis*, 1734) on an empirical psychology, which he held to be valid on the level of sensory experience (*Psychologia empirica*, 1732).

Though repudiated by Kant in the domain of knowledge, the value of sensibility (*le sens intime*) was reaffirmed by Maine de Biran (1766–1824) and by the protagonists of the French "eclectic" school including Victor Cousin, Royer-Collard, and Théodore Jouffroy. Sensibility and introspection remained the surest basis for psychology, which they continued to regard as that part of philosophy whose goal was the study through direct consciousness of the soul and its aptitudes. In Germany, the Kantian condemnation of metaphysics did not prevent it from reemerging, but rather supplied metaphysics with the impetus and the motives for an unusually vigorous renewal (Fichte, Schelling, Hegel, Schopenhauer), giving new life in another form to the Leibnizian notion of the unconscious.

### IV

After this grandiose speculative flight, comparable only to that of ancient Greece, the human mind seemed to have had its wings clipped. A sluggishness was evident with regard to the great rational systems at the time when the more empirical systems continued to advance and to discredit those conceptions of nature evolved by the post-Kantians. Already J.-F. Herbart (1776–1841), a contemporary adversary of Hegel, without claiming to repudiate metaphysics, had opposed the dialectic method of Hegel with the idea of psychology as an exact science to which mathematics could be applied.

In the new cultural climate, the sciences seemed to be assured of having the last word. Under the influence of the transformist hypotheses (inheritance of acquired characteristics) of Lamarck (1744–1829) and especially of Darwin (*On the Origin of Species by means of*

*Natural Selection*, 1859), the idea that there was only a difference of degree between man and animal, which had already enticed Hobbes and continued through the eighteenth century, prevailed in France. The spiritualist demands seemed to have fallen into a state of decay and scarcely carried any weight any longer in the face of the attraction which the evolutionism of Darwin and Spencer, as well as Auguste Comte's positivism (*Cours de philosophie positive*, 1830–42), exerted on minds which had been won over to the idea of universal determinism. It was the age when Taine explained everything by the concomitant influences of race, time, and place, when Renan wrote on the future of science (*L'avenir de la science*, 1860), and when in the very country of Hegel the order was issued: *Keine Metaphysik mehr* ("No more metaphysics"). It was rather a question of substituting a metaphysical materialism for a spiritualistic metaphysics in the manner of Ludwig Büchner (1824–99) and of E. H. Haeckel (1834–1919), who glorified the ideas of matter and factual experience. In short, the times were ready to claim a scientific psychology inspired by the biology which was making constant progress and conquering many new areas of knowledge, structure, function, specific nervous energy, reflex arc, the speed of nerve stimulation, the role of certain localized cerebral responses, etc. The creation of psychology as a science posed the problem of *measurement* in a field which seemed preeminently refractory to measurement, namely, the domain of the creative spirit in philosophy and the sciences; but because scientists in astronomy and in optics were correctly preoccupied with this problem, the transition from physics to psychology was encouraged. It had been apparent for a long time that the notations which astronomers used to record the exact moment of the passage of a star to the meridian did not agree, and that the same observer always reported the same type of error. This *personal equation* brought about the passage from the external phenomena of sound and light to the implied mental processes, that is to say, to the study of hearing and sight; and especially to conceive experiments suitable for measuring *reaction time*. This is how the illustrious scientist Hermann Helmholtz undertook the explanation of certain perceptual phenomena in his physiological interpretation of Newton's optics and acoustics (*Handbuch der physiologischen Optik*, 1856–66); this led the anatomist and physiologist E. H. Weber (1795–1878) to go from physiology to psychology. Weber observed that sensation, under the influence of an increasing or decreasing continuous stimulation, varied in a discontinuous manner, and that the amount of stimulation corresponding to a *differential threshold* is in a constant and determinable relation to the initial

stimulation. To Weber's Law the philosopher G. T. Fechner (1801–87), who was determined to introduce measurement into psychology, was to give a more precise mathematical formulation: sensation increases or varies directly with the logarithm of the stimulus (*Elemente der Psychophysik*, 1860).

The conclusions of the psychophysicists were to be refuted by the French philosopher Henri Bergson who attempted to demonstrate (*Essai sur les données immédiates de la conscience*, 1889) that the stimulus could actually be measured but not the sensation itself, and that the relationship of equivalence established between the two was purely conventional.

Psychophysics having revealed its insufficiency, in the sense that Weber and Fechner had intended, because it neglected the physiological intermediaries between physical stimuli and sensations, was to be dethroned by psychophysiology, hinged exactly on the correlations between physical and physiological states (glandular, nervous, cerebral). This was the direction in which Wilhelm Wundt (1832–1920) was going to lead psychology. A physiologist of great culture, his ambition was to construct psychology as an experimental science, and its creation is rightly attributed to him. Under the influence of Cartesianism he claimed the specificity of the psychic fact against those who tended to absorb it into physiology; he invoked "parallelism" for the relationships between psychical phenomena and their organic, nervous and cerebral foundation (*Grundzüge der physiologischen Psychologie*, 1874). When his researches proved to him that the experimental method, efficacious for the study of the contents of consciousness, did not permit the application of the laws of the higher processes of the psychical life, he undertook the study of the psychology of peoples by a comparative method (*Völkerpsychologie*, 1900–20). The laboratory which he set up in Leipzig in 1879 provided with two assistants and perfectly equipped, attracted many foreign students. Such was the case also with G. Stanley Hall and J. McKeen Cattell, who in their turn set up laboratories in the United States; William James, whose work was to be a decisive contribution to the creation of American psychology, had already established a laboratory at Harvard.

In France Théodule Ribot, who held the works of Wundt in great esteem (*La psychologie allemande contemporaine*, 1879), advanced experimental psychology by theoretically endowing the new science, inspired by the biological sciences, with legal status in a complete break with tradition. In Switzerland Théodore Flournoy (1854–1920), a friend of William James, who turned his interests toward the new science, became the first one to occupy the chair in experimental psychology at Geneva with a laboratory provided for it. His young cousin Édouard Claparède (1873–1940), who studied in the department of the new science before he himself achieved fame, reported that about half a dozen neophytes, in the wake of Fechner and Wundt, had attempted to record reaction time and to determine thresholds of sensation without really understanding the significance of such experiments. Meanwhile in Germany, about 1885, a new path was opened up by certain works, especially by those of H. Ebbinghaus (1850–1909), on memory (*Ueber das Gedächtnis*, 1885), which demonstrated that it was possible to study psychical phenomena directly without having to study them from the viewpoint of their physiological concomitants. There were psychologists at that time who wanted to use the experimental method of introspection which others had wanted to banish from the laboratories. Wundt estimated that such a method was impracticable, and he was to disavow his pupil and assistant Ostwald Külpe when he adopted the introspective method to become the leader of researches which, under the name of "Thought-psychology" made the reputation of the Wurtzburg School (Külpe, Marbe, Ach, Messer, and Bühler).

Those researches implied raising questions again about the empiricist and sensualist systems inherited from the English and from Condillac, who, intending to explain the operations of mental life, including its connection with ideas and principles of reason, by the mechanical association of ideas, were able to see in thought only the end-product of the association of images. To have recourse to experimentally induced introspection was to be content no longer with recording the excitation to which a subject was exposed, and his reaction. It was asking him to take an active part in the experiments, to observe, and to give an account of what they produced in him. From their researches, conducted in this way, the Wurtzburgians had to conclude that it was necessary to admit the existence of a pure thought without pictures or words.

The reaction against the tendency to reduce mental life to a sort of mosaic was equally evident in other places. In France Alfred Binet (1857–1911), who knew intimately the methods used by the pioneers of scientific psychology in Germany, judged those researches to be excessively narrow; he was actually the first to have used controlled introspection (*L'étude expérimentale de l'intelligence*, 1903). Also, in Switzerland Édouard Claparède envisioned a much broader psychology capable of explaining mental behavior guided by intelligence (*L'association des idées*, 1903); he was to qualify his own theory as "functional," meaning by function the relationship between the psychological fact to be explained and the total behavior pattern.

His ideas were closely related to those of the Swiss psychologist Pierre Bovet (of Neuchâtel). These two men together created in 1912 the Jean-Jacques Rousseau Institute which Jean Piaget now directs under the name of Institut des Sciences de l'Éducation.

Meanwhile, in Great Britain important researches were to bring renewed vigor to the development of the new science. There were, for example, the work of Darwin's cousin, Francis Galton (1822–1911), whose researches on individual differences and heredity introduced the statistical method in psychology, and the work of the illustrious neurologist John Hughlings Jackson (1834–1911), inspired by the evolutionism of Spencer, which considered psychical functions as forming a hierarchy in which "mental illnesses" represented disintegration. The views of Jackson, which Théodule Ribot (1839–1916) had already adopted in France in his works on mental disturbances, in the sense of the inability of the functions themselves to reveal the levels of organization imperceptible in the normal state (*Maladies de la personnalité*, 1885), are the most important in psychophysiology and in psychopathology. This same kind of medico-psychological approach to problems was used again by the great psychologist Pierre Janet (1859–1947) in whose work a hierarchy of real functions is made evident and is sustained by a synthetic power requiring a psychological force and "tension." All these ideas were to play a part in the reaction which occurred in medicine and in the human sciences in general against mechanism in favor of a synthetic orientation. This orientation received a decisive thrust forward by the works of Sigmund Freud, which were at first ignored or contested. He was the discoverer of subconscious mechanisms in psychical life (*Die Traumdeutung*, 1900; *Zur Psychopathologie des Alltagsleben*, 1901), and in particular he espoused psychosomatic medicine.

Besides, the conclusions of the Wurtzburg school had posed the current psychological problem of thought and language, that could hardly be separated from the ideas which stimulated the phenomenological researches of Husserl (*Logische Untersuchungen*, 1901). He found conflicts between his researches and the current of thought which characterized scientific psychology in its early stages: the naturalism of Wundt and the introspection of Külpe. Even in the years when Wundt's researches were highly favored in Germany, some minds were repelled by the naturalistic conception of psychology. One of these was Franz Brentano, who influenced Husserl by introducing the notion of "intention" in psychical facts; also Wilhelm Dilthey strongly opposed psychology as a natural science by proposing a "psychology of understanding" (*verstehende Psychologie*) which was less preoccupied with determining laws than understanding man and his capacity to attain self-consciousness (*Ideen über eine beschreibende und zergliedernde Psychologie*, 1894). Dilthey's views fell in line with Husserl's phenomenology, thus hastening the reaction to the objectivist psychology by the philosophies based on "existence" (Heidegger, Jaspers, Sartre, and Merleau-Ponty). The theme of "understanding" as opposed to "explanation" had already appeared in the work of Karl Jaspers in 1913 in *Allgemeine Psychopathologie;* he distinguished in pathological phenomena the organic processes, which yield to causal explanation, from personality developments, which involve a living meaning which it is incumbent upon the psychiatrist to understand.

This same theme again acquired a fundamental importance in Freudian psychoanalysis, at one and the same time a therapeutic technique, an investigation of the unconscious, and a theory of man in society, whose implications have upset our cultural life. Split into rival schools, of Alfred Adler in 1910 and then of C. G. Jung in 1913, which branched out from the original trunk by challenging the Freudian conception of the "libido" and sexuality, Freudian psychoanalysis crops up in American social psychology. The views of the American "culturalists" (Karen Horney, H. S. Sullivan, Erich Fromm), who have reinterpreted psychoanalysis on the basis of more recent sociological and anthropological data, have had a considerable repercussion in continental Europe. These views have been criticized by Herbert Marcuse (*Eros and Civilization, A Philosophical Inquiry into Freud*, 1955), who reproaches them for vulgarizing Freudianism and for making it lose its corrosiveness by sacrificing it to a kind of conformism.

The current tendency, which American social psychology represents, is characteristic of a general phenomenon in our culture: an eclecticism rooted in different scientific fields and particularly in psychological schools initially opposed to one another in methodology. For example, the Russian school of Ivan Pavlov arose out of a decidedly neurophysiological orientation. His discoveries about the mechanism of conditioned reflexes, popularized to some extent by the works of W. Bechterew (1857–1927), had such a repercussion that many persons believed it would be possible henceforth to explain the human psyche itself by the role played by conditioning. It was then that John B. Watson created "behaviorism," a strongly objective psychology (*Behavior: an Introduction to Comparative Psychology*, 1914). He was convinced that the pioneers of the new science had sinned through their timidity with respect to the spiritualistic tradition. This tendency which favored the exclusion of subjectivity was shaken when the followers of the *Gestalttheorie*

(Wertheimer, Köhler, Koffka) asserted that subjectivity could not be eliminated; their argument implied at the same time the holistic idea of *Gestalt*. Beginning with the study of perception, they showed that its content is always a "Gestalt," meaning that the content is organized in such a way as to form a whole, and that the first immediately given datum furnished through experience is not the sensation but the "form," meaning an organization present in physical systems (configuration, melodies, intelligent acts, reasonings, etc.) as well as an organization in which the properties of the parts depend on the total context.

The Gestalt theory, as also phenomenology and psychoanalysis, inspired the work of the neurologist Kurt Goldstein, whose description of the organism as a unified whole (*Der Aufbau das Organismus*, 1934) also contributed to the new synthetic organization of the human sciences.

In the same way, in animal psychology, gestaltist views had had decisive repercussions. Wolfgang Köhler, one of the pioneers, had the opportunity of devoting himself during World War I, on the island of Teneriffe, to experimenting with higher apes under conditions much less artificial than he had previously had. He concluded that the apes possessed an "insight," that is to say, a total, intuitive, and concrete discernment which manifested itself in their ability to reorganize the perceived field in order to resolve certain practical problems.

Previously, aside from the Pavlov experiments and those experiments which psychology had never abandoned (destruction of organs or the removal of cerebral regions, etc.), animal psychology had studied animal behavior in a manner which intended to prove, through a kind of fear of anthropomorphism, that all forms of intelligence had to be excluded. Thus it was that the interpretations of J. Loeb (*Die Tropismen*, 1913) on the basis of experiments done with lower animals, established the neologist ideas of "phototropism" (orientation or displacement reaction in the direction of light), and of "thermotropism" (reaction directed towards a source of heat), to explain animal and perhaps also human behavior. But because it appeared to be difficult to refuse to credit the animal with at least an activity of its own, which was attested by his groupings and by his progressive adaptation in learning, the experimenters, on the basis of experiments performed with contraptions of boxes and labyrinths, chose to include "trial and error" in their theory, according to which the animal, in a difficult position in the course of random activities would, by accident, find the effective response which is established through reflex action.

After the researches of Köhler demonstrated the weakness of conclusions drawn from artificial experiments, animal psychology concerned itself particularly with the study of animal behavior in its natural habitat (ethology). The researches which they undertook revived all the traditionally debated problems concerning the innate nature and the acquired characteristics of the animal, and particularly the problems posed by Konrad Lorenz, who conducted experiments which led him to discover "imprinting" (*Einprägung*), i.e., a sort of "imprint" or "impregnation" at birth such as would cause young birds to cling, as though to their mothers, to the first of those who feed or rear them on being hatched. Also, the researches of the Dutch psychologist Buytendijk, who offered in opposition to the method of causal explanation a phenomenological interpretation of animal behavior, opened new avenues of approach which lead into the human sciences.

The role which psychoanalytical thought played in the broadening of psychological perspectives cannot be overestimated. The theme of psychoanalytic criticism with respect to the "official" psychology, which clung to the superstition of the laboratory and considered as most essential the determination of the laws which govern psychic life in general, was that it was necessary to recognize individual differences. As a result of this criticism the plan to establish "characterology" as an autonomous psychology appeared. A number of theories were born whose bases varied according to the morphological typologies they dealt with (Kretschmer, Viola, Pende, Sigaud, MacAuliffe, Louis Corman, etc.), or they were based on "properties" of fundamental "factors" (Heymans, Wiersma, Le Senne, Gaston Berger), or were opposed to *atypical* doctrines inspired by philosophical conception (Ludwig Klages).

In a general way European psychologists are more concerned with *character* than are American psychologists who are more preoccupied with *personality* and who often consider both terms synonymous (Gordon Allport). This means that alongside the tendency to discover types made up of basic traits to which any individual can be reduced, there is another tendency to consider personality in its temporal development, and which sees in personality the power of integration where the guiding elements can only be grasped in a dialectical process of interactions. In the first tendency, character is considered an invariant, a fundamental structure on which an individual's history is grafted; in the second, it is only the expression of a crystallized aspect of the personality.

The ambiguity in this area reflects that of psychology in general. Should psychical facts be "explained" by the method of the natural sciences? Or should personality rather be understood in its development? At one time the situation of their science appeared so critical

to certain German psychologists that they talked of a crisis (K. Bühler, *Die Krise der Psychologie*, 1927). Though it might have been a crisis, it did not prevent the psychological sciences from moving forward, but at the mercy of a growing complication of problems and proliferation of experiments. There still exists an official psychology, which while following in the steps of the founders has been accumulating an imposing mass of works both theoretical and experimental. However, it appears undeniable that if psychology remains confined to laboratory research by making a sort of fetish of experimentation and scientific rigor, it will lose sight of the forest for the trees; and it risks losing contact with concrete, human reality by obstinately studying only special processes and functions. The extension of methods and research is a constant reminder of the need not to lose sight of the life of the mind in its concrete manifestations.

Moreover, another important aspect of the situation is the fact that henceforth the psychological sciences are intimately connected with practical life. Psychological discoveries are utilized for all sorts of problems: educational, therapeutic, professional, commercial, advertising, military, etc. This situation tends to give research a purely "operational" direction or bent; and the danger here is to confine the mind within the existing social system, to identify the person with function by reducing the human subject to its ability to measure, to experiment, and to calculate. But from the standpoint of principles, the overlapping of data coming from rival schools, for example, in the study of the whole personality in which we find concepts of various sources, behavioristic (apprenticeship), Gestaltist (unity of self), psychoanalytical (lived situations), culturalists (socio-cultural environment), etc., a new reflection in depth has been imposed and made its appeal.

It becomes more and more clear that human behavior, taken as a whole, is so complex that any doctrinal idea claiming to be exclusive is only an illusion; in short, it is clear that psychological sciences must guard themselves above all against dehumanizing man, and must recognize that all their hypotheses are entailed by an anthropology in perpetual process, and therefore necessarily incomplete.

## BIBLIOGRAPHY

Edwin G. Boring, *A History of Experimental Psychology* (New York, 1929). George Sidney Brett, *A History of Psychology*, 3 vols. (London and New York, 1912–32), reprinted in briefer form, ed. R. S. Peters (London, 1953). Rudolf Eucken, *Die Lebensanschauungen der grossen Denker, eine des Lebensproblems der Menschheit-Entwicklungsgeschichte—von Plato bis zur Gegenwart*, 11th ed. (Leipzig, 1917). Laignel-Lavastine, ed., *Histoire générale de la médecine*, 3 vols. (Paris, 1938–49). F.-L. Mueller, *Histoire de la psychologie de l'antiquité à nos jours* (Paris, 1960); idem, *La psychologie contemporaine* (Paris, 1963). Maurice Reuclin, *Histoire de la psychologie* (Paris, 1957). M. F. Sciacca, ed., *L'Anima* (Cremona, 1954), various contributors; with ecclesiastical approval.

FERNAND-LUCIEN MUELLER

[See also **Association of Ideas; Behaviorism;** Dualism; Evolutionism; Man-Machine; Positivism; **Psychological Ideas in Antiquity; Psychological Theories in American Thought.**]

## PSYCHOLOGICAL THEORIES IN AMERICAN THOUGHT

THROUGHOUT the greater part of American intellectual history, the term "human nature" was used without explicit definition and in various ways, both descriptive and normative. It included "mental philosophy," a term gradually replaced in the later nineteenth century by "psychology," which hitherto enjoyed only infrequent use. It is possible to identify four main usages: (1) those traits that distinguish man from other creatures in "nature" and from angels and God, the traits, that is, that give him human identity; (2) man's original (genetic) equipment at birth, that is, his biological heritage and his "unlearned" impulses; (3) man's character and behavior resulting from the interaction of his heredity and his environmental experiences; and (4) the identification of human nature with the values and practical measures that different groups, classes, and factions universalize in their desire to perpetuate or to establish. Of these one or more, and sometimes several at the same time, figured in theology, political, economic, and social thought, in literature, and in proverbs and folk sayings.

Ideas in America about the nature of man were for the greater part of colonial and national experience eclectic, and in relation to the intellectual history of Europe, derivative. Nevertheless, long before Americans developed distinctive schools of psychology and the movement known as the behavioral sciences, the history of ideas about "human nature" is important because of the particular selections from and combinations of ideas accessible to the New World. That history is also important because of the bearings of these choices and combinations of ideas about human nature on political, social, and economic thought and discussion as well as on belles lettres.

A conception of human nature is implied in colonial secular writing, whether "promotional literature" to encourage migration from the Old World, personal letters and narratives, or pamphlets addressed to ad hoc political and economic issues. But for the most part an explicit discussion of human nature was closely related to three religious movements—to Puritanism, Quakerism, and Anglicanism. These discussions also reflected, to be sure, secular ideas as well as the position of the writer in the social order; but all of them, notwithstanding differences of interpretation and emphasis, shared the basic Christian idea of man's dualistic nature: an eternal soul and a corporeal body, often in conflict since each human being was subject both to divine and, because of Adam's fall, to satanic direction and influence. However limited and depraved, man's human nature still bore some residue of its original composition, that is, some power of reason and moral judgment.

Seventeenth-century Puritanism in New England, while incorporating portions of classical thought and Renaissance humanism, and while modifying both the theology and polity of Calvinism, nevertheless rested heavily on that system of thought and faith. If New England's intellectual leaders were "advanced" in accepting, in place of traditional Aristotelian logic, the system of the Huguenot reformer Petrus Ramus, dualistic and Platonic in character, their "psychology" was largely medieval and scholastic—broadly speaking, the synthesis that Thomas Aquinas made of Aristotle's *De anima*, of Plato's conception of the soul, and of Hebraic-Christian ideas and traditions. It is important to keep in mind the fact that seventeenth-century sermons varied in emphasizing in greater or lesser measure the more rationalistic concept of Aristotle and Aquinas and the emotional, intuitive, and even mystical one of the Cambridge Platonists which anticipated the image of man in such early eighteenth-century figures as the metaphysical poet Edward Taylor and in Jonathan Edwards.

It is possible to reconstruct the Puritan overall concept of the nature of man from John Winthrop's *Journal*, from sermons, and from bodies of law and court proceedings. In the main, however, the image of man presented by Charles Morton is representative of prevailing theories of human nature in seventeenth-century New England. This learned clergyman, on settling in Massachusetts Bay in 1686, brought copies of his *Compendium physicae*, which was used for a great many years in instruction at Harvard. Indebted in his discussion of "physics" to Robert Boyle and the new spirit of the Royal Academy, Morton was also familiar with Descartes and in a sense tried to reconcile much of the old with the newer learning. His "psychology," however, was for the most part traditionally scholastic.

After discussing the anatomy of the brain and the nature of "animal spirits," Morton attributes, to human beings, reason and a sentiment of the deity, faculties which "no brute has, at least to any appearance." If some men claimed there is no God, this was the result of a corrupt will and affections, rather than judgment, which comprised, with the intellect, the faculties God had implanted in man. Since Morton was primarily concerned with physics, he felt it necessary to explain the inclusion of a discussion of spirits or souls, traditionally the domain of metaphysics and, more lately, of the new "science" of pneumatics. The faculties or properties of the soul, which differentiate man from the brutes, depend somewhat, in their operation, on the body, and thus are a proper matter to be included in physics. Souls, defined as beings or forms independently created by God, are separately infused with the body at the moment of creation, so that original sin proceeds, not from body to body, nor from soul to soul, nor from the body to the soul, but from mankind to the man. The inorganic faculties, or those immediately proceeding from the nature of the soul, are intellect and will. Neither of these, in contrast with the sensory, appetitive, and locomotive powers, is affixed to any member of the body. The intellect, nevertheless, is said to reside in the head (according to Descartes, the mind acts on the body through the pineal gland), so that one speaks of "a good head." Likewise, the will, which primarily manages the appetites and affections, is said to possess the heart ("I will with all my heart").

Intellect, or the power of the reasonable (or religious) soul which enables it to understand the truth, could be improved by logic and by an understanding of how ideas are formed. The intellect receives images or "phantasms" that are then cleared by abstraction from matter and made "intelligible," as distinct from having previously been merely "potential." Morton illustrated this process by reference to the way in which the idea of a true friend is developed. When one thinks of such at first, he has a phantasm of the man's person, of the time, circumstances, and nature of his acts of kindness. Intellect transmutes this phantasm into an abstraction from the color, stature, features, and other material conditions that form and distinguish the "species" of "the real friend." Having such idea, one completes the formal execution out of the result that the intellect, acting on the object, has now "intellectuated" or made "understood." In many scholastic theories of psychology the intellect is the king of the faculties, the will the queen, but man's fall, with Adam and Eve's sin, dislocated their proper symmetry. Morton defined the will as the power of the reasonable soul, whereby, after the information

provided by the intellect, the soul "Closeth with Good, and Shuns Evill" in whatever the object or act. In contrast with these primary faculties, man also possesses the secondary faculties, properties arising from the rationality that differentiate him from brutes—that is, speech, admiration, the human passions, and laughter. Morton later supplemented this discussion of human nature. In *The Spirit of Man* (1693) he emphasized the general "grayness" of human infirmity, and individual differences in mental and moral talents. He also urged self-analysis and sustained effort for governing one's spirit, with a recognition of continual need for assistance from on High. It was not that man could "expell" his "nature," but rather that he might "order and govern" his natural dispositions and inclinations both for God's glory and service and for his own comfort and advantage.

Notwithstanding new movements of thought across the Atlantic that were greatly to alter ideas about the nature of man, traditional views persisted in America. As late as 1714 Samuel Johnson, an eighteen-year-old tutor at Yale, on the verge of discovering the new learning that was later to inform his own major philosophical treatises, made a summary abridgment of the old scholastic system. In the light of Scripture, reason, sense perception, experience, and induction, Johnson postulated the separate faculties of the "rational soul" and related these to the members of the corporeal body which are suited to the operations of the soul, which in turn is the principle of these operations. The discussion of the faculty of appetite, by which the animal spirits (which animate emotions, respiration, the beating of the pulse) are excited, added something to Morton's account. But in summing up Johnson's description of the nature of man, a historian of the early development of American psychology was not unfair in describing it as "Plato shorn of his poetry, Aristotle without his breadth and acuteness of observation and his carefully qualified conclusions, Thomas Aquinas without his logical subtlety" (Fay, p. 16).

This Ramean emphasis on the rationality of the universe and on the power of the faculty of reason at least to glimpse God's plan was supplemented by the metaphysical conception of the Covenant of Grace, the process by which God enabled His "chosen" or "elect" to become regenerate. Far from being a mere emotional cataclysm, the infusion of grace elevated reason, purifying it of its corruption and enabling the redeemed to see, with this spiritual light, further into God's plan.

The seventeenth-century Puritan conception of universal human limitations, greater in some, less in others, was reflected in social and economic pronouncements and arrangements. William Bradford justified

Plymouth's abandonment of the initial communal economy on the ground of the unequal distribution of talents and incentives for achievement. In the Puritan mind, inequality of status reflected inequality of innate endowment and thus of God's favor. In *A Brief Exposition with Practicall Observations* (1657) John Cotton declared that just as the strongest are most able to battle, just as men of knowledge are most apt to win heavenly favor, so men of understanding are most apt to attain riches. Thomas Hooker (*The Soules Vocation or Effectual Calling to Christ*, 1638) never knew a man "desperately poor, but his heart was desperately proud." While John Eliot could remind the poor that poverty must ever be an example of the price of sinful conduct (*The Harmony of the Gospels . . .*, 1678), charitable relief was, if carefully hedged, a Christian duty. "For the poor that can work and won't, the best liberality," Cotton Mather wrote, "is to *make* them." On the other hand, in view of universal human depravity, men might give way to an insatiable craving for wealth; and with this in mind John Cotton laid down the tenet that "we are never to desire more than we have good use of." Late in the century Cotton Mather emphasized anew the doctrine of the stewardship of wealth. God alone is the true owner, hence the rich man is merely His steward, to be held to account for the uses he has made of his riches, and these uses should include charity and gifts for the public weal (*Essays to Do Good*, 1710). In further recognition of human greed, and in accord with the ethical and economic teachings of Thomas Aquinas, Puritan Massachusetts tried to impose for a time "the just price" as well as "the just wage." That is, man's innately sinful tendencies were to be regulated by the state for the good of the whole.

Political theory likewise reflected the Puritan conception of human nature. In denouncing democracy, whether in church or civil government, John Cotton (*The Pouring Out of the Seven Vials*, 1642) declared that corruption always starts from the inherently corrupt, stable "people," not from the top, the superiorly endowed rulers. Similar ideas, reflecting a commitment to the inequality of human beings, found expression again and again, nowhere, perhaps, more pointedly than in the Reverend William Hubbard's Election Sermon of 1676 in which he declared that "the greatest part of mankind, are but as tools and instruments for others to work by, rather than any proper agents to effect anything for themselves. Needing a shepherd to keep them, in time of peace, from destroying themselves by sloth, they need, in war, a shepherd even more, lest they permit themselves to be destroyed by others." Yet since corruption was universal in human nature, opposition to the unlimited exercise of authority found expression in both verbal and active protests —Samuel Gorton and Roger Williams are well-known examples.

Puritan education also reflected the belief in a human nature in which intellectual gifts were unevenly distributed, despite the presence of some part of the rational faculty in everyone (the male more than the female), and in a persisting conflict between reason and the lower passions, the one pointing to truth, the other to error. Thus Harvard College was designed to provide for the cultivation of superior intellects for roles in ecclesiastical and civil leadership. The belief that metaphors and adornments in prose writing served the passions, provided a rationale for the "Plain style." The establishment of town schools testified to the belief in the possibility and importance of developing such reason as God had implanted in His human creatures, in order that they might better understand His laws as exemplified in the Bible Commonwealth, and thus keep the lower passions in check. What a few missionary-teachers did for the Indians implemented the idea that these degraded, corrupt, and vicious creatures, whom God had permitted the Devil to rule, still had capacity for Christian conversion and rational development, even if this could be effected only by exterminating the majority in a just war, that the remnant might be brought to light and civilization.

Such an oversimplified summary leaves out telling examples of ways in which the seventeenth-century Puritan image of man was reflected or applied in daily life: Winthrop's faith that notwithstanding man's total depravity, the favorable condition of the isolated environment of the New World might bring out and encourage the best human possibilities; Winthrop's further observation that a woman who had lost her "understanding and reason" because of devotion to reading and writing, should not have meddled "in such things as are proper for men, whose minds are stronger" (*Journal*, II, 225); the rejection of any non-organic or functional conception of insanity, and the consequent attribution of it either to a deformity in the brain or to the triumph of the Devil in the perpetual war he waged for the human soul; and the exemplification of almost every Puritan idea about human nature in the Salem witchcraft outbreak which, in Perry Miller's words, was "for the seventeenth century, not only plausible but scientifically rational" (Miller [1953], p. 191).

The use in Harvard classes of manuscript copies of William Brattle's *Compendium logicae secundum principia, D. Renati Cartesii* for almost half a century before its publication in 1735, was one indication of the impact of the Cartesian psychology on the teaching of logic. But the most important shifts in the Puritan concept of human nature came in the early decades of the eighteenth century and were related not only to the increasing secularization of life in New England but to the uses made of both traditional and of new movements of thought received from the Old World.

John Wise's tracts for justifying the older congregational organization of the churches and for opposing assertions of British authority in secular affairs rest in good part on a theory of human nature. This by no means broke drastically with the past. It recognized the innately good and bad in man, the existence of the elect and of superior talent, and the authority of Scripture. But it emphasized the rational component in human nature to an even greater extent than had been traditionally the case, and it invoked, in explaining the origin of civil society and in justifying the limitation of human authority and a broadly based consent if not participation in the direction of human affairs, a more secular view of natural law. In the state of nature, Wise asseverated, men possessed three "immunities" imprinted on their very nature: a sufficient reason to discover the law of nature to which man is at all times subject; a rational liberty under the law of nature; and an equality of condition, to the extent, at least, that all men are children of God and enter and leave the world in the same way. But since men possess self-love and self-interest as well as a sociable disposition or "an affection or love to mankind in general," it was expedient to move from the state of nature through contract, to the civil state, the better to control self-love and self-interest, and to make the more operationally effective the inherent associative or affectional gift. The implications of this concept of human nature, which Wise made explicit in *The Churches Quarrel Espoused* (1715) and *A Vindication of the Government of New-England Churches* (1717, 1772), pointed toward a more elevated concept of human nature, capable of coping with life's problems through reason to a greater extent than had been traditionally the case. Wise's portrait of man emphasized an innate sociability to a greater degree than had Locke's; it repudiated Hobbes's exclusion of the efficacy of an innate love for others; and it made ad hoc applications of Pufendorf's natural law philosophy.

A few decades after Wise, Jonathan Edwards, responding to some of the newer movements of thought, to the concern he felt for the attenuation of Calvinism, and to the religious revivals of the 1740's, developed a more systematic and a more original conception of man's nature. In view of its Platonic element and of the emotional intensity and anxieties of seventeenth-century Puritanism, Jonathan Edwards' emphasis on intuition and the religious affections, or on emotions, was not entirely new. Yet in accepting the rising "sensational" psychology of John Locke while he was a young student at Yale and in attaching at the same time great importance to intuitional truth, Edwards achieved an impressive synthesis of old and new in which his psychology has special importance.

In rejecting the traditional compartmentalization of body and mind of most scholastic or faculty psychologies, Edwards reduced all reality to a spiritual monism—and apparently without benefit of Berkeley. At the same time he insisted on the indispensable importance of "sensational" experience as the first step toward understanding and directing the religious emotions or affections toward the love of God—that is, toward "true virtue." The deference to Lockean "environmentalism" was evident in his explanation of why, in view of the ubiquity and identity of human nature everywhere, the Greeks developed a great philosophy of the mind in contrast with the Scythians: Edwards found the answer in the stimulating commercial exchanges of the Greeks and other peoples (*Works*, II, 477). Recognition of the Lockean psychology also explains in part why Edwards used concrete emotion-provoking rhetoric in his revivalist sermons. Since true religion involves both the understanding and the will together with the encircling emotions, Edwards felt it necessary to defend the deterministic implications of Calvinism which were being challenged by Arminianism. He developed a mediating position which held that men are free to will what their strongest inclinations (emotions) impel them toward while they are not free to "will" their inclinations—the freedom to choose without the freedom of the choices to be chosen. These were major contributions to psychological problems that helped establish Edwards' contemporary reputation at home and abroad as an original thinker—a reputation meeting with appreciation on the part of modern psychologists. Beyond this, the Great Awakening, in which he played a notable part, contributed to making the emotionally religious experience a participatory one for the newly awakened, plain people. This sense of individual self-awareness, of an immediately felt importance in the sight of God, inspired later revivalists to develop these implications in promoting both democratic action and humanitarian reform.

Though Puritanism and Anglicanism were similar in a great many ways, the only systematic colonial formulation by an Anglican brought out important differences in the concepts of man. Samuel Johnson, who was Edwards' tutor at Yale, led a small group of young men into the Church of England. Like Edwards, Johnson tried to reconcile orthodox Christian theology with the new learning of Bacon, Newton, and Locke. The Church of England offered him an opportunity

19

on the one hand to combat a trend toward "natural religion" and "deism" and, on the other hand, to find a more congenial theology than Calvinism. The philosophical idealism that Johnson found useful to this end was that of Bishop Berkeley, who lived for a time in Newport. In distinguishing between pure intellect and sensation and in his analysis of intuitive evidence, Johnson went beyond his master. His psychology, which he developed in *A System of Morality* (1746) and more comprehensively in *Elementa philosophica* . . . , which Franklin printed in 1752 as the first American textbook in philosophy, indicate familiarity with Hobbes, Hume, Leibniz, Locke, and Wolff, an important formulator of faculty psychology, as well as Berkeley. His references to man's relations with animals and his treatment of the learning process of children give him a place in the history of genetic psychology; and his discussion of cognition, judgment, affection, conation, and the sense of beauty, showed some independence of thinking. In his philosophical writings and in his sermons, Johnson stressed man's rationality and natural desire for happiness. The road to happiness, he held, lay in the glorification of God in a rational manner and in subordinating the unruly passions to reason and order. Although as an Arminian Johnson made a place for a modified "free will" and moral responsibility, he emphasized, increasingly as he grew older, the dependency of man, as a sinner, on God's grace, which perfected human nature rather than transforming it, as some evangelical revivalists held. Johnson's philosophy, which was taught at King's College (later Columbia University) during the time he presided over the institution (1754–63), made little appeal and exercised slight influence even among Anglicans. Yet a historian of American psychology finds nothing superior to it at the time on either side of the Atlantic (Fay, p. 42).

The most important exemplification of the Quaker theory of human nature is that to be found in John Woolman's *Journal and Essays* (1774; 1922). Recognizing as inborn taints and corruptions such powerful impulses as pride, vanity, greed, and self-love, Woolman nevertheless believed that God had also implanted in man the capacity for love of and compassion toward his fellow creatures. Through the power of truth and spiritual strength which is possible when the heart is opened to God, man could wean himself away from the desire for outward greatness, luxury, and greed—traits that result in such evils as slavery, war, and indifference to the impoverishment of one's fellow men. The unity of mankind would recognize no barriers of race, color, or condition—if the believer lifts himself above self-deception. Woolman had a keen sense of what modern psychology calls "ration-

alization." John Woolman's religious mysticism, a matter of the inner self, was integrally related to an outward expression of opposing social evils and the extension of Christian love to all human beings. Since Woolman perceived that customs and opinions received by youth from their parents and other superiors became like "the natural Produce of a Soil, especially when they are suited to favourite Inclinations," he attached great importance to child-rearing and education. In terms of upbringing and social environment he explained why Negroes developed sloth and other habits odious to whites. Consideration of "these and other Circumstances . . . will lessen that too great Disparity which some make between us and them."

In his emphasis on humanitarianism Woolman looked forward to one characteristic of the concept of human nature associated with the Enlightenment. At the risk of great oversimplification, it is possible to say that the similarities between what has been thought of as the Age of Reason image of man and that of Puritanism were in some ways greater than the differences. Both conceived of human nature in static rather than in evolutionary or dynamic terms; both gave an important place to reason in man's makeup; and both emphasized the limitations in man's equipment—the philosophers of the Enlightenment attaching even more importance to the lust for power than had the Puritan writers. Nevertheless the differences were also of great importance: the Age of Reason rejected the Special Providences or "interference" of God with the laws of nature and man, and emphasized the idea that the universe is a rational order capable of being understood by man's reason, if unfettered by religious dogma and if aided by the methods of natural science. Several Enlightenment thinkers attached great importance, in the molding of man, to climate and social institutions. Among these some held that man's irrational behavior resulted from the influence of outworn, irrational institutions—monarchical, feudal, priestly. Still other Enlightenment thinkers rejected the ancient dualistic conception of man, substituting for it a monistic and materialistic one.

No one American incorporated in his thinking all of these ideas. Nor did any American of the late eighteenth and early nineteenth centuries develop a systematic exposition of human nature in terms of the assumptions that Enlightenment thinkers had made. Nevertheless these ideas about human nature found expression in American thought and some of them exerted a direct and positive influence on public action.

Broadly speaking, the ideas that may be regarded as most "innovative" or "radical" played a minor role on the American scene. Such ideological orators as Tunis Wortman did, to be sure, accept the idea of human perfectibility. This concept also appealed to such writers as Joel Barlow, Philip Freneau, and Charles Brockden Brown. Another example is worth noting because it both reflected the ideas of William Godwin and his circle in Britain and anticipated the Owenite and Fourieristic communitarianism of the 1830's and 1840's. The utopian "novel," *Equality; a History of Lithconia,* first issued as a serial in 1802 in *The Temple of Reason,* a Philadelphia weekly paper, was probably written by Dr. James Reynolds, a democratic activist. The author maintained that the causes of the malevolent passions might be uprooted only in a society which repudiates private property, family pride, and jealousy, along with other prevailing institutions that thwart man's natural endowment of rational and moral gifts, the realization of which alone could result in happiness.

Nor did the monistic, "materialistic" and mechanistic conception of human nature associated with Cabanis, Tracy, d'Holbach, Helvétius, and La Mettrie become an important or widely held view of man. It is true that these writers appealed to Thomas Jefferson, who defined thinking as "a mode of action" and a "particular organization of matter." Such a position ruled out revealed religion and metaphysics as means of understanding the mind, and placed the mind squarely within nature. Religious opposition kept Jefferson from appointing Thomas Cooper to the faculty of the newly founded University of Virginia. Cooper shared the materialistic philosophy of Joseph Priestley and, like him, had fled from the reactionary England of the late eighteenth century. Cooper espoused a strict psychological materialism and translated Broussais' *On Irritation and Insanity* (1831) to support his conviction that mental processes are explicable in terms of the motions of the nervous system.

A similarly monistic materialism informed the remarkable if crude book of a Kentucky physician, inventor, champion of Pestalozzian education, and empirical investigator of vision—Joseph Buchanan. His *Philosophy of Human Nature* (1812) warranted his reputation as "the earliest native physiological psychologist" (Riley, p. 395). The much more important Benjamin Rush, who wrote *Medical Inquiries and Observations Upon the Diseases of the Mind* (1812), might be regarded as a materialist inasmuch as he attributed all operations of the mind to motions excited in the brain. But in fact he did not completely move away from dualism, since he described "the causes of insanity" as both physical (diseases, poisoning, injuries) and mental (intense concentration, worry, anxiety). It remained for his little known and eccentric son, James Rush, to present a consistently physiological and "materialistic" treatment—*A Brief Outline of an Analysis*

*of the Human Intellect* (1865). Among other things James Rush anticipated the later behavioristic concept of thought as subvocal speech.

These highly heterodox ideas associated with the Enlightenment were much less influential than "environmentalism" in both the physical and social sense. It derived in large part from Locke's and Hartley's theories that ideas are the result of sense impressions, reflections on these, and the laws of association. A well-known example of the use of the environmental theory in the discussion of race is Samuel Stanhope Smith's *An Essay on the Causes and Variety of Complexion and Figure in the Human Species* (1788). Rejecting the idea that God created diverse races, this Presbyterian divine and Princeton professor argued in favor of one original race and explained differences in color and character in terms of climate and social institutions. Jefferson, stopping short of accounting for the "inferiority" of Negroes on the basis of historical and environmental handicaps, nevertheless also set great store on the influence of environment, physical and social, in delineating man's character and conduct. Holding human nature to be the same on both sides of the Atlantic and a "constant" over time, Jefferson empirically refuted the absurd contention of Buffon and other prestigious French savants that American environment accounted for an alleged physical deterioration of animal species. On the contrary, Jefferson found that the American environment was favorable to all species, including the human. If human nature did not change, the human condition, Jefferson held, did change under favorable conditions. Thanks to America's freedom from the tyranny of kings, nobles, and priests and to its abundant free lands, Jefferson saw in the American man, particularly in the yeoman, a superior example of the human condition. Given the continuing availability of free lands and abundant resources, free schools and a free press Jefferson felt that in America the human condition, despite the menace of slavery, stood a good chance of further improvement. In emphasizing the great importance of education, the author of the Declaration of Independence expressed one of the most favored ideas associated with the belief in man's rationality and susceptibility to improvement, through the cultivation of both mind and moral sense.

In some measure Jefferson, despite the optimistic view of human nature implied in the Declaration of Independence, shared the preponderant late eighteenth-century idea that man is innately both good and bad. To be sure, his political opponents, Alexander Hamilton, John Adams, and John Marshall, emphasized to a much greater extent than he did the innate selfishness, vanity, lust for power, and corruptibility of human nature—characteristics deemed innate and ineradicable. In this regard they were influenced by the Calvinistic doctrine of depravity and even more by Machiavelli, Hobbes, and Mandeville. With such a low view of human nature it became, in their minds, imperative to devise forms of government designed to check man's baser passions: this could best be done by checks and balances and by allocating power to a "natural aristocracy" which, however susceptible to man's limitations, nevertheless, by birth, education, and wealth, could be counted on to bring rationality and morality to bear in the making of public decisions. Such a position informed discussions in the Constitutional convention (Lovejoy, Lecture 2), in *The Federalist,* and in the private correspondence of Hamilton, Jay, Madison, Adams, and, at times, Jefferson. With an ingenious system of constitutional techniques for safeguarding the interests of minorities this image of man subsequently played an important part in John C. Calhoun's political theory. In *The Disquisition on Government* (1851) the champion of southern states' rights as against federal authority argued the necessity of meeting the problem created by the fact that rulers oppress the ruled, human nature being what it is, while the ruled, when possessing the means for so doing, inevitably resist the rulers. This whole emphasis on the unequal distribution of superior faculties in a generally unfavorable portrait of human nature was also a component of the pro-slavery argument.

Benjamin Franklin shared many of his contemporaries' misgivings about human nature. Because he has been regarded as "characteristically American" his views warrant comment. Like others who subscribed to the naturalistic assumptions of the Enlightenment, Franklin rejected the idea of original sin. He did not, in consequence, assume that man might reach angelic heights. Accepting the idea of the Great Chain of Being he believed that men must operate at the particular level in the order of creation to which they are assigned. They might, however, restrain their passions and irrationality by deliberately cultivating good habits, the effect of which would be to promote both personal happiness and the well-being of mankind. Franklin's own success in overcoming hardships and in achieving fame as a self-made man, together with the cheerful "constitution" with which he appreciatively felt nature had endowed him, explained his belief that, with all man's limitations, human kind might still achieve relative virtue and happiness. Add to this a sense of human equality and the pragmatic character he ascribed to human thinking at its best, and one has what may fairly be regarded as the most widely held American view of human nature.

Franklin, like Jefferson, shared many of the concepts of the Scottish Enlightenment. The idea of an innate moral sense was especially appealing. This idea, antithetical to Locke's conception of the mind as tabula rasa at birth had, of course, a long history, reaching back at least to Stoicism. But it was the Scottish philosophers, Hutcheson, Reid, and Dugald Stewart, along with Shaftesbury, who gave it a modern idiom. The popularity in America of the Scottish common-sense philosophers can be explained by the search, during the reaction against the deism of the Enlightenment, for a philosophy that would provide support for a belief in an innate moral sense, in the unity of the soul, in freedom of the will, and for a more congenial image of man than the analytical and atomistic one of Locke's sensationalism and Hartley's associationism. The Scots taught that there is an objective reality, the proof of which was the existence of principles prior to and independent of experience (James McCosh, *The Scottish Philosophy* . . . [1874], pp. 2–10). Thus a philosophy was at hand that offered a refutation of Hume's skepticism and the materialistic implications of Lockean psychology. The Scottish philosophy was popularized by academics who prepared textbooks in mental and moral philosophy that, however simplified and eclectic, leaned heavily on it. The more widely used texts included those of Francis Bowen, Francis Wayland, Joseph Haven, Asa Mahan, and Mark Hopkins, to name only a few.

The most original of these texts were those of Thomas Upham, professor of mental and moral philosophy at Bowdoin College and a leading opponent of war and slavery. Upham borrowed not only from Reid, Stewart, and Hamilton; he was also familiar with contemporary French and German philosophy as well as with general literature and travel accounts that anticipated later ethnology. Unlike most of his colleagues in other institutions who prepared texts, he included an exposition of the nervous system, pathological behavior, and animal and child psychology. With the help of Asa Burton, an obscure but original parson in Thetford, Vermont, he conceived a way of distinguishing between the feelings and the will which put new life into the tripartite classification of the human faculties. He made the faculties of intellect, sensation, and will interdependent rather than separately operating mental functions and in so doing looked forward to what was to become a characteristically American emphasis, that is, functional psychology. What also especially distinguished Upham from the often over-intellectualist tone of his contemporaries was his emphasis on emotions—here he was looking back, perhaps, to Jonathan Edwards. "A knowledge of human nature in the common apprehension of the phrase," Upham wrote, "does not so much imply a knowledge of perception and reasoning as a knowledge of the springs of action, back of the intellect, which, in the shape of the emotions and passions, give an impulse and a character to the conduct of both individuals and communities" (*Elements of Mental Philosophy* [1831], II, 26–27). A British reviewer of Upham's *Philosophical and Practical Treatise of the Will* (1834) regarded the book as the most consistent example of the use of the Baconian method in mental science to be found in the English language, while a historian of American psychology has discovered in Upham such modern ideas as mental set, individual differences, introversion and extroversion, rationalization, the emergence of suppressed desires in perverted forms, and the James-Lange theory of emotions (Fay, pp. 106–08).

Until well after the Civil War the political economy taught in American colleges derived support both from faculty psychology, which held that mind is composed of a number of "powers" or agencies such as memory, will, and attention, and from the not incompatible image of man generally shared by the classical economists. In Benthamite terms, this ascribed to human nature a tendency to avoid pain and to realize pleasure with rational calculation of the means of advancing self-interest. In the words of Wesley C. Mitchell the common-sense philosophy saw the prevailing "economic organization as a beautiful illustration of the contrivances of the Creator for the benefit of humanity." Stress was also put on the beautiful harmony of relationships found under a competitive system which indicated precisely that "a man got what he merited and that the institution of private property contributed to general well-being by giving everybody a strong inducement to produce more than he consumed himself in order that he might add to his own ownership" (Mitchell, p. 115). As one of the best known authorities of the time, Francis Bowen of Harvard, put it, "It is true that men are usually selfish in the pursuit of wealth; but it is a wise and benevolent arrangement of Providence, that even those who are thinking only of their own credit and advantage, are led, unconsciously but surely, to benefit others. The contrivance by which this end is effected—this reconciliation of private aims with the public advantage—is often complex, far-reaching, and intricate; and thus more strongly indicates the benevolent purpose of the Designer" (*American Political Economy* . . . [1890], p. 15).

What the faculty psychology or mental and moral philosophy, with its ethical and economic implications, was to the educated classes, phrenology was to the common man. Phrenology removed psychology altogether from the realm of metaphysics. Originally, as developed by two Austrian physicians, Franz Joseph Gall and Johann Gaspar Spurzheim, phrenology was

an empirical study of the physical manifestations of temperaments (nervous, bilious, sanguine, lymphatic) and, more importantly, of the anatomy and physiology of the brain which located in its various parts the sensations and the powers of the mind—the list of "propensities" included amativeness, benevolence, combativeness, veneration, and many others. According to phrenology as it was developed, the desirable propensities might be consciously cultivated, the undesirable ones, inhibited. The visit of Spurzheim to America, where he died in 1832, and the subsequent sojourn of the Scottish phrenological leader and moral philosopher, George Combe (*Essay on the Constitution of Man*, 1828, 1833) aroused the interest of medical men and of such leading intellectuals as Benjamin Silliman, Ralph Waldo Emerson, Horace Mann, Samuel Gridley Howe, Edgar Allen Poe, Walt Whitman, and Henry Ward Beecher.

Although Calvinists and many evangelical leaders felt that phrenology contradicted Scripture, and although most physicians became critical, phrenology influenced psychiatry, criminology, and pedagogy. In contrast with its career in Europe, phrenology in America was democratized as well as commercialized through the press, the itinerant lecturer and "demonstrator," and such diagnostic and advisory centers as those of O. S. Fowler and S. R. Wells in New York City. It became a cult which for many years served the need the common man felt for a philosophy of human nature that could be readily understood, as a practical guide to the selection of proper mates and vocations and, above all, for self-improvement. The appeal of phrenology is further explained by its usefulness in the mid-nineteenth-century atmosphere of moral optimism, extreme individualism, and the widespread search for and belief in the possibility of achieving worldly success and happiness.

Competing images of man challenged the dominant mid-nineteenth-century view of human nature as it was presented by the mental and moral philosophers and, on the popular level, by the phrenologists. Unitarianism, which appealed chiefly to a small, educated and well-to-do New England elite, rejected the doctrine of original sin but retained the rational and ethical components of Calvinism. It also adopted the naturalism, environmentalism, optimism, and humanitarianism of the Age of Reason. In emphasizing the fatherhood of a loving God it endowed His sons with a larger share of divine attributes—above all with dignity—than was the case among the traditional and the more popular religious organizations. But the emphasis on reason as against emotion and on detachment led to another protest—transcendentalism. This loosely bound group of ideas attached less importance to the traditional conception of generic man than to the unique individual. The emphasis was also on each individual's capacity for imagination, sensibility, ecstasy, on an ability spontaneously and intuitively to experience the universal in the concrete, to achieve through self-culture and rapport with nature the higher self—to become one with an organic, living universe, with supreme reality, with absolute truth. This way of looking at human nature was in varying degrees influenced by Platonism and Neo-Platonism, Oriental mysticism, German idealistic philosophy, and a reaction against what appeared to be the excessive materialism of an America engaged in conquering the wilderness and in building factories, machines, and cities.

Such a "transcendentalist" image of man found expression in the educational ideas and experiments of Bronson Alcott and Elizabeth Peabody, in the communitarianism at Brook Farm and Fruitlands, in George Bancroft's historical explanation of the rise of America as the Hegelian unfolding of the world spirit, in the aesthetics and the romantic feminism of Margaret Fuller, in the nature-appreciation and social dissent of Henry David Thoreau, in the gnomic poems and evocative essays of Emerson, and in the synthesis Walt Whitman made of mystical and ego-centered views of human nature, on the one hand, and the concrete democratic realities of everyday American life, on the other. While the humanitarianism of the period owed much to evangelical Christianity, and particularly to the revivalism of Charles G. Finney, it was also indebted to the transcendentalist image of man as expressed in Emerson's remark, "Man is born to be a re-former."

Still other manifestations of the "romantic" impulse in the discussion of human nature included the Dionysian conflict in Poe's poems of mystery and beauty and in his gothic tales. The paradox in James Fenimore Cooper's novels between primitivism and civilization was another example of a "romantic" image of man.

At least two efforts to present systematically a psychology encompassing some part of this view of human nature deserve comment. Frederic Rauch, a German theologian trained at Marburg and Giessen and a member of Heidelberg's philosophical faculty until he was forced to leave, became President of Marshall College in 1836 and published, five years later, his *Psychology or a View of the Human Soul, including Anthropology* (1841). This was the first work in English both to use the term "psychology" in the title and to present in modified version the Kantian and post-Kantian, particularly the Hegelian, philosophy of human nature. Rauch expressed dissatisfaction with current views of body and mind as two substances and

suggested that they be regarded as one would regard the sunlight and raindrops in a rainbow. He denied the existence of independent faculties and regarded the growth of the mind as the growth of a plant from a seed. In his view reason and the will function interdependently—the concept of freedom of the will is rejected in view of the influence of environment on the mind as well as the influence of the mind on the body and on the environment. The treatise was somewhat exceptional in discussing individual, sexual, and racial differences and in delineating the effects of environment on temperament, sleep, and dreams.

Laurens P. Hickok's *Rational Psychology* (1849) was, like Rauch's work, inspired by German idealistic philosophy. Regarded by some as the first profound treatment of epistemology in America since Jonathan Edwards, Hickok's treatise was notable in trying to reach *a priori* principles free from the subjectivity of Kantian categories and for stressing the "constructive" powers of the mind. Hickok saw in reason, which with sensibility and understanding constitute the faculties of the mind, an intuitive insight. His ethical views were basically Kantian. Though extended through the writings and teaching of his pupil, John Bascom, Hickok's influence was relatively limited, important though his work was from a technical point of view.

The generally optimistic tone of all these images of man may in part be explained by the objective realities in American life which supported the belief in "progress" and by the fact that, save for the Civil War, the country was spared most of the great tragic experiences of many other peoples—more or less constant war, famine, pestilence, and foreign military occupation.

The faculty and rational psychology, so central in American assumptions about human nature, continued to dominate the academic scene long after a revolutionary movement known as "the new psychology" got under way in Great Britain and Germany. It began even before mid-century with Charles Bell's and Marshall Hall's investigations of the nervous systems, and made rapid strides in Germany where Ernst Weber, Gustav Fechner, Hermann von Helmholtz, and, later, Wilhelm Wundt developed laboratory methods for measuring sensation, memory, and perception. The new scientific study of mental phenomena, known as psychophysics and physiological psychology, rejected the traditional view that "mind" could be studied abstractly, by introspection alone, and without specific reference to physics and physiology. It assumed on the contrary that mental phenomena could be understood only in terms of the controlled and experimental study of the organic, unified human being. While British empiricism and associationism initially provided a philosophical context for specific laboratory investigations of mental phenomena and behavior, the publication of Darwin's three works, *Origin of Species* (1859), *Descent of Man* (1871), and *The Expression of the Emotions in Man and Animals* (1872), marked a revolutionary shift in theory. The evolutionary hypothesis substituted a dynamic view of human nature for one that had regarded man's constitution as static and unchangeable. The new view provided a new setting for the discussion of heredity and environment, and, in assuming an intimate and genetic relationship between the higher primates, human infants, and the matured individual, stimulated the development of animal and child psychology.

In the United States the first impressive discussion of the new psychology was that of Edward L. Youmans, a disciple of Herbert Spencer and an effective popularizer. In an address entitled "Observations on the Scientific Study of Human Nature" (*The Culture Demanded by Modern Life*, pp. 373–408) Youmans rejected the ancient dualism (body as the seat of a lower material nature, mind that of a higher spiritual nature). He insisted that "man, as a problem of study, is simply an organism of varied powers and activities and that the true office of scientific inquiry is to determine the mechanism, modes, and laws of its action." Citing the recent experimental literature and suggesting some of the implications of the new movement for the treatment of the mentally ill, for education, and for everyday life, Youmans concluded that the new science was only in its infancy.

Within the next two decades young Americans sought out the new psychological laboratories in Germany, especially that of Wilhelm Wundt in Leipzig, and returned to set up laboratories in the major American universities. The pioneer American contribution to the new experimental psychology, however, was that of C. S. Peirce and one of his Johns Hopkins students, Joseph Jastrow. Interested in measuring the smallest perceptible differences in sensation, Peirce and Jastrow demonstrated experimentally that when slight differences between two stimuli of weights or surfaces were reduced below the so-called physiological threshold, a subconscious registration operated. The pressure-balance devised for this investigation was the forerunner of all the improved pressure-balances later employed, the use of which confirmed the Peirce-Jastrow finding (Murchison, I, 135–36).

One young American who was to become a leader in the new psychology, James McKeen Cattell, worked not only as a student in the Leipzig laboratory, but also went to England to acquaint himself with the pioneer work of Francis Galton in devising tests and statistical measurements for intelligence. The laboratory researches of the European-trained exponents of the new psychology, and of those of their students, supplemented the work of the Europeans and in time gave new dimensions to it. By the end of the century the new psychology had largely overshadowed traditional mental philosophy except in a few centers, notably Catholic institutions. In an address at the International Congress of Arts and Sciences at St. Louis in 1904 Cattell reflected the optimism of the new psychology in declaring that he saw no reason "why the application of systematized knowledge to the control of human nature may not in the course of the present century accomplish results commensurate with the nineteenth-century applications of physical science to the natural world" (*Popular Science Monthly*, **66** [1904–05], 186).

The evolutionary theory of human nature not only affected the investigations in the laboratories. It also provided a new context for the discussion of human nature. To some intellectual leaders the evolutionary theory suggested that what was called human nature had changed but little, and that in view of this it was futile to expect melioristic changes or the elimination of institutions deeply rooted in human nature. Thus Henry Ward Beecher, the most celebrated of Protestant preachers, said, in commenting on the Franco-Prussian conflict of 1870, that war is the "remnant in man of that old fighting animal from which Mr. Darwin says we sprang." War, he went on, is a constitutional disorder belonging to human nature. A presumption in favor of Darwinian theory was the fact that war demonstrates how much of the animal there is still left in man (Sermon of July 30, 1870, in *The Plymouth Pulpit*). Similar views were later expressed by William Graham Sumner and William James. Sumner also became a leading advocate of the idea that the efforts of society to support the incompetent poor must result in still further degrading them and in discouraging those who had proved their merit by making the most of their endowments through sustained hard work (*What Social Classes Owe to Each Other*, 1883). Thus not only socialism but anything pointing to a welfare state was denounced as contrary to human nature. Such an interpretation of evolution, largely influenced by Herbert Spencer, was known as Social Darwinism.

On the other hand, the dynamic view of man which the evolutionary theory substituted for the traditional static one suggested that the evolution of human nature had not come to an end. It was to improve partly through direct adaptation, partly through the survival of the fittest, and above all through the inheritance of slowly evolving superior characteristics—characteristics that, according to the almost universally accepted theory of Lamarck, were transmitted through heredity. It was this view that John Fiske popularized. The most essential and characteristic feature of the human being, Fiske said, is his improvability. Since the first appearance of the human being enormous changes had taken place through natural selection and adaptation. Inasmuch as civilization thus far had advanced largely through fighting and the deadly struggle of competition, quick-wittedness had developed as a human trait faster than compassion and kindness. Even so, over the past thirty centuries strife had gradually lessened and cooperation, so necessary in an emerging industrial civilization, was to become a dominant trait, since, like all traits that are put to use, it would be strengthened and transmitted through heredity. "Man is slowly passing from a primitive social state in which he was little better than a brute, toward an ultimate social state in which his character shall have become so transformed that nothing of the brute can be detected in it. The ape and the tiger in human nature will become extinct" (*The Destiny of Man Viewed in the Light of His Origin* [1884], p. 103).

Lester Frank Ward, more consequential a figure than Fiske because he spoke as both a biologist and a pioneer sociologist, projected on the basis of his reading of evolutionary theory a similarly progressive improvement of human nature. This was to take place through the "telic" or purposeful guidance of man's future by the planned use of applied intelligence.

These optimistic interpretations of evolutionary theory, resting in part on the Lamarckian theory of acquired characteristics, met with a serious challenge when, in the 1880's, a new theory of heredity reached America. Although not at once or universally accepted, August Weismann's denial of the transmission of acquired characters and insistence that characteristics could be transmitted only through immutable germ plasm, raised a serious question for the reformers who rested their case in large part on evolutionary theory and the transmission of acquired characteristics. As Amos Warner, a leading figure in social welfare, wrote, "If acquired characteristics be inherited, then we have a chance permanently to improve the race independently of selection, by seeing to it that individuals acquire characteristics that it is desirable for them to transmit." But if Weismann is correct, "our only hope for the permanent improvement of the human stock would then seem to be through exercising an influence on the selective process" (Amos Warner, *American Charities* [1908], p. 22). Thus the ground was split between the hereditarians and the environmentalists for a major controversy in the changing reputation of human nature.

Even more consequential in raising doubt about the improvability of human nature through the melioristic change of the environment was Francis Galton who maintained, on the basis of genealogical data and a pioneer study of identical twins, that nature, not nurture, is the dominant force. Galton did not convince such able Americans as Chauncey Wright, Charles H. Cooley, and William James, who, in a much discussed article in *The Atlantic Monthly* for 1880, "Great Men, Great Thoughts, and Their Environment," maintained that while certain geniuses, like murder, "will out," this was by no means always the case. In another epoch Darwin and Spencer might have died "with all their music in them." The Galton study, in short, James insisted, did not take into account the limiting or encouraging factors in childhood and the excessive complexity of the conditions of effective greatness or "genius." Yet Galton and his more doctrinaire disciple, Karl Pearson, enlisted influential supporters. These included Charles W. Eliot, who in his own way reconciled Galton's elitist and hereditarian ideas with democracy, and G. Stanley Hall, whose recapitulation theory, borrowed from the hereditarian storehouse, made every individual relive the experience of the race—a position that for a time influenced the American school curriculum.

The experiments with twins and with animal and child learning that another psychologist, E. L. Thorndike, carried through, seemed to lend great weight to the dominant role of heredity. In later years this was also true of the work of other psychologists, notably Lewis Terman, a student of Hall, whose influential development of the Binet intelligence tests and whose study of a thousand California youths identified as "geniuses" seemed, to many minds, to establish the superior importance of nature over nurture. On the level of pedigree studies and field surveys Richard Dugdale (*The Jukes*, 1877), Henry Goddard, and others concluded that "poor stock" perpetuated itself in succeeding generations of criminals, insane, prostitutes, and other ne'er-do-wells. Despite the faulty records and dubious statistical procedures in these studies, they provided support for the eugenics movement initiated in Britain by Galton and his disciples. In several states the eugenicists succeeded in obtaining legislative support for the sterilization of the "unfit"—in 1927 the Virginia law was upheld by the Supreme Court, Mr. Justice Holmes speaking for the majority.

The emphasis on heredity as the major factor in human nature found additional support in the sweeping and uncritical interpretations of the inadequately devised intelligence tests administered to the rank and file of the armed forces during the First World War. Before psychologists and such critics as Walter Lippmann showed the inadequacy of the tests, the results were cited with a note of triumph by immigration restrictionists, who had long opposed the acceptance of newcomers from southern and eastern Europe on the ground of innate inferiority and unassimilability, and also by those convinced of the inherent and irremediable inferiority of American Negroes.

The contentions of the hereditarians, and the exponents of an unchangeable human nature with inherent class and race differences, met with opposition from humanitarians, including such leaders as Jane Addams, and from sociologists who insisted that unequal achievements and evidences of social ineffectiveness and dereliction were explicable in terms of the mores, and by the ways in which the environment determined the qualities and virtues that the individual in any society tries to attain or the vices that he attempts to avoid: in other words, the values in any society are the formulators of the characters of men. The most effective refutations in the nature versus nurture controversy of the extreme hereditarian position were those of a characteristically American school of psychologists—the functionalists—and of the social philosophers and social scientists who shared their basic image of man.

The dominant emphasis of Wundt and his disciples on the structure or contents of mental experience through measurement and introspective analysis met with some opposition in Europe (Oswald Külpe, Édouard Claparède, and others). But it was most tellingly challenged in America by what came to be known as functional psychology. In brief, influenced by evolutionary theory this psychology assumed that at one or another stage in the history of man the need for each mental process had become sufficiently demanding to result in the emergence of a particular process or function. Thus sense perception, emotion, and mental images developed as functions in the organism's evolution. Thinking resulted when instinct and habit failed to resolve a conflict or tension in the effort of the organism to adjust itself to an environmental situation. The functionalists attached great importance, as a result, to motor activity, to usefulness of the functional operations of the organism (i.e., mind), and to a dynamic process as opposed to a static equilibrium.

The first clear and explicit exposition of the functional view seems to have been that of John Dewey in 1884. He insisted on recognizing mental life as an organic unitary process, not as a theater for the exhibition of independent autonomous faculties or as a rendezvous in which isolated, atomic sensations and ideas gathered, held "external converse," and then parted forever. In addition, Dewey emphasized the importance of the relationships of an individual life to other lives organized in society. "The idea of environment is a necessity to the idea of organism, and with the conception of environment comes the impossibility of considering psychical life as an individual, isolated thing developing in a vacuum" ("The New Psychology"). In 1896 Dewey's famous paper on the reflex arc, which rejected the mechanistic and dualistic stimulus-response principle, noted that the organism is an active, not passive, perceiver of stimuli. Behavior, he insisted, is not disjoined into stimuli and responses but is continuous, and the sensory and motor aspects of behavior blend continuously with each other. This opened the door to technical support for a psychology of motor activity, adjustment, and functional interrelationships between organism and environment.

Meanwhile, in his vividly and racily written *Principles of Psychology* (1890) William James presented the findings of the "new psychology"—but not without critical reservations. With his imaginative, poetical zest for unresolved mysteries, exceptional personalities, peak experiences, and the reality of values no less than that of facts, James felt that "official" psychology was only a limited, however useful, means to understanding human nature. His treatment of the nervous system, the physiology of sense, the instincts, the emotions, and the will, together with the central importance he attached to habit, reflected the purposive or functional as opposed to the structural view. The associationism that characterized the structural position of Wundt and such American disciples as E. B. Titchener, was rejected for a transitory, fluctuating "stream of consciousness," unified rather than atomistic, and related to choice. In brief, James's conception of the "mind" was that of the functional and dynamic adjustment of the organism to its environment, including the unpredictable and twilight regions of experience.

The functional psychology achieved its fullest development at the University of Chicago during Dewey's affiliation with it (1894–1904) and in the years that followed. George Herbert Mead developed the idea of the inherent relatedness of self to other selves, which James had touched on, into a major concept (role theory). Of great importance also was his emphasis on the idea that thinking and social activity are aspects of the same basic process, that is, communication or symbolic behavior as mechanisms for both social control and social progress. James Rowland Angell showed, experimentally, how reaction time is a function of attention and explicated the relation of organic processes to consciousness (James Rowland Angell, *Psychology*, New York [1908], with preface to the first edition, and Murchison, III, 5–29). Others in the Chicago school applied functional psychology to ethics, law, and social institutions. Dewey himself, in his continuing work in logic, education, aesthetics, and social psychology overshadowed his sometime colleagues. Among the issues to which he addressed himself in later years were the nature-nurture controversy, which he helped resolve by showing that each is dependent on and inseparable from the other (Dewey, 1922; 1939); the contention that such social institutions as war and capitalism are the inevitable expression of human nature (or instincts), which he refuted by showing that social institutions are expressions of certain inherent human impulses or needs that might be channeled into other social expressions, as was the case in various cultures; and the question whether the very term human nature was any longer a useful concept, at least unless it was very carefully defined ("Does Human Nature Change?," *The Rotarian*, **52** [Feb. 1938], 8–11ff.).

Functionalism became absorbed into the main stream of psychology in America. Several later emphases did, however, reflect some of its special aspects. This was true, for example, of the interpersonal psychiatry of Harry Stack Sullivan, *Conceptions of Modern Psychiatry* (1956), of the opposition of the Gestalt school to a discrete, atomistic, and mechanistic conception of behavior and, in a sense, of Kurt Lewin's field theory, which held that if an individual's behavior were to be understood it must be in terms of the life space, i.e., of the relation of the individual to his environment over time and at the particular moment. Even behaviorism, despite important differences and the criticisms functionalists and behaviorists had for each other, was in some respects an outgrowth of the Chicago school.

Many insisted that behaviorism was a typically American psychology although others related it to a long line of forerunners including Democritus, La Mettrie, Condillac, and their successors. It was certainly related to the "connectionist" psychology of E. L. Thorndike who had made the stimulus-response in the context of neurons and synapses a central feature of his concept of learning. Behaviorism also derived a good deal from experimental animal psychology and from the work of the Russian "objectivists," Pavlov and Bekhterev. Though it also had immediate American forerunners other than Thorndike, behaviorism was chiefly associated with John B. Watson of Chicago and Johns Hopkins. In his expositions of behaviorism, introspection and consciousness were rejected in favor of an objective, mechanistic interpretation of behavior in terms of stimulus, response, and the conditioned reflex. Watson went further than most psychologists in making sweeping analogies between animal and human behavior and in his dogmatic and flamboyant claim that all human behavior is susceptible to prediction and control. His popular vogue rested in part on his psychology of child-rearing: parents might so con-

dition infants as to develop behavior and personalities congenial to their taste.

The critics of behaviorism included those who, like the functionalists, regarded experience as unfragmented and continuous rather than atomistic and mechanistic; those who contended that in throwing out introspection and consciousness altogether the behaviorists could not possibly explain their awareness of themselves; and those who objected that behaviorism eliminated values and ethics in any true sense. Behaviorism as modified by such criticisms and by the experimental and theoretical work of E. C. Tolman, Clark Hull, and others was fused into general psychology. What some laymen interpreted as a belated echo was B. F. Skinner's *Walden Two* (1948). This was about a model community in which elitist masters of the conditioned reflex and other behavior techniques had dehumanized (in order to make happy) the men and women who put themselves in the hands of their benevolent if dictatorial manipulators.

Some of the problems of deviant behavior were illuminated by contributions of varying importance at the hands of such nineteenth-century alienists, psychiatrists, and neurologists as Isaac Ray, William Hammond, S. Weir Mitchell, Oliver Wendell Holmes, George Beard, and Morton Prince. Of special note was the work of these and others in neurasthenia, hysteria, dreams, and other types of unconscious and nonrational behavior.

The reception of Freudianism was somewhat belated and markedly mixed. By reason of his concern with psychopathology, the theory of the unconscious, and his intellectual hospitality, William James was predisposed to give psychoanalysis an open hearing, while G. Stanley Hall's interest in sex and the psychology of deviancy led him to invite Freud and Jung to a conference at Clark University in 1909. Writing to his brother shortly after hearing and talking with the visitors, James expressed the hope that "Freud and his pupils will push their ideas to their ultimate limits; they cannot fail to throw light on human nature" (Henry James, *Letters of William James* [1920], pp. 237–38). James, however, distrusted Freud's "obsession with fixed ideas." Hall likewise distrusted Freud's way of tracing everything to one source, although he later expressed his conviction that the advent of Freudianism marked the greatest epoch in the history of psychology. Academic psychologists, in contrast with such neurologists and psychiatrists as James J. Putnam and A. A. Brill, in the main resisted the uncritical acceptance of Freud's unverified theories. These theories, nevertheless, had begun by the 1920's to exert an important influence not only in psychiatry but in such varied fields as social work, social science, labor-management problems, advertising, and public relations. In terms of the bearing of psychoanalysis on ideas about human nature the most important contributions of the American neo-Freudians involved an emphasis on the inclusion of social and cultural factors in the explanations of neuroses, psychoses, and other maladjustments.

This broadening of an imported European movement owed a good deal to several of the men and women who had come to the United States with early first-hand associations with the leaders in what was coming to be called "depth psychology." These revisionists included Karen Horney (*The Neurotic Personality of our Time,* 1937); Abram Kardiner (*The Individual and His Society,* 1939, and with others *The Psychological Frontiers of Society,* 1945); Franz Alexander (*Our Age of Unreason,* 1942); Erich Fromm (*Man for Himself . . . ,* 1947); and Erik Erikson (*Childhood and Society,* 1950; 1968). The Freudian emphasis on sex and a desire to test the incidence and character of the sexual act in wider samples than those available in clinical reports led Alfred C. Kinsey of Indiana University to interview a considerably larger population (*Sexual Behavior in the Human Male,* 1949, and *Sexual Behavior in the Human Female,* 1953).

The emphasis on quantification and on the cross-fertilization of biology, psychiatry, psychology, sociology, and anthropology led to the behavioral science movement. In 1943 Clark Hull (*Principles of Behavior*) expressed the conviction that the successful, systematic development of the behavioral sciences must await the time when students of behavior become adept at interpreting their materials in terms of mathematical equations. The proliferation of such studies, based on ideal types or models and executed with the aid of complicated computers, made contributions to the prediction and control of behavior, especially in motivation research. But the inclusion of role theory, systems theory, game theory, decision-making, and deprivation and reenforcement theory, all precisely defined in terms of the control of variables, exhibit the large scope of the behavioral sciences movement. It is true that some social scientists and virtually all humanists expressed skepticism about the more extreme claims of the movement. The concern deepened when investigations in molar biology and microgenetics suggested that the genes of inheritance might be controlled or modified, thus opening somewhat frightening possibilities for those committed to individualism and democracy.

## BIBLIOGRAPHY

The only general survey is Don H. Wolfe, *The Image of Man in America* (Dallas, 1957; New York, 1970), which, drawing on both social science material and belles lettres, focuses on ideas about "creativity" in the human person-

ality. Several articles on the idea of human nature in western thought bear on the American discussion of it. The most useful are John Dewey's article in the *Encyclopedia of the Social Sciences* (1935), VII, 531–36; James Luther Adams, "The Changing Reputation of Human Nature," *Journal of Liberal Religion,* **4** (Autumn 1942), 59–79; 4 (Winter 1943), 137–60; and Merle Curti, "Human Nature in American Thought," *Political Science Quarterly,* **68** (Sept. 1953), 354–75; (Dec. 1953), 493–510.

In terms of the discussion of the idea of human nature in formal psychology the most useful general accounts are E. G. Boring, *A History of Experimental Psychology* (New York, 1950); Carl Murchison, ed., *A History of Psychology in Autobiography,* 5 vols. (Worcester, Mass., 1930–52); and Henryk Misiak and Virginia Staudt Sexton, *History of Psychology:—An Overview* (New York, 1966). Notwithstanding the merits of this specialized account of American psychology, Jay Warton Fay, *American Psychology before William James* (New Brunswick, N.J., 1939), it is not satisfactory. Special note should be made of R. C. Davis, "American Psychology 1800–1885," *Psychological Review,* **43** (Nov. 1936), 471–93.

For the seventeenth and eighteenth centuries the most important primary sources are *The Journal of John Winthrop,* ed. James K. Hosmer, 2 vols. (New York, 1908); Charles Morton, *Compendium physicae,* Publications of the Colonial Society of Massachusetts, 33 *Collections* (1940), ed. Theodore Hornberger; Thomas Clap, *An Essay on the Nature and Foundation of Moral Virtue* (New Haven, 1765); Jonathan Edwards, *Works,* 5 vols. (London, 1840); Paul Ramsey's edition of Edwards' *Freedom of the Will* (New Haven, 1957); *Samuel Johnson, President of King's College. His Career and Writing,* ed. Herbert and Carol Schneider, 4 vols. (New York, 1929); John Woolman, *Essays and Journals* (New York, 1922); and titles of sermons and other pieces cited in the text. Benjamin Rush's *Medical Inquiries and Observations upon the Diseases of the Mind* (Philadelphia, 1812), has been reissued, with an introduction by S. Barnard Wortis, in the History of Medicine Series, No. 15 (New York, 1962). It may be supplemented by *The Autobiography of Benjamin Rush,* ed. George W. Corner, in *Memoirs of the American Philosophical Society,* **45** (Princeton, 1951).

Secondary material includes Perry Miller, *The New England Mind. The Seventeenth Century,* (New York, 1938), esp. Ch. 9; and idem, *The New England Mind, From Colony to Province* (Cambridge, Mass., 1953); Claude M. Newlin, *Philosophy and Religion in Colonial America* (New York, 1962), and the earlier work of I. Woodbridge Riley, *American Philosophy. The Early Schools* (New York, 1907). The second chapter in Arthur O. Lovejoy's *Reflections on Human Nature* (Baltimore, 1961), shows how theories of human nature entered into the making of the Constitution of the United States. Also useful is Adrienne Koch, *The Philosophy of Thomas Jefferson* (New York, 1943). An interesting example of an effort to apply modern psychological concepts to an eighteenth-century American's thought about the nature of man is Richard I. Bushman, "On the Use of Psychology: Conflict and Conciliation in Benjamin Franklin," *History and Theory,* **5** (1966), 225–40. For the use by seventeenth- and eighteenth-century historians of concepts of human nature see Merle Curti, *Human Nature in American Historical Thought* (Columbia, Mo., 1968).

The discussion of human nature in the literature of transcendentalism can best be understood through the writings of the transcendentalists themselves, although the standard biographies are also useful. Joseph Dorfman's *The Economic Mind in American Civilization*, 5 vols. (New York, 1946–59), is a good guide to the economic writings in which theories of human nature are explicitly or implicitly accessible. Also relevant is Wesley C. Mitchell's *Lecture Notes on Economic Theory* (New York, 1949). The standard authority on phrenology is John D. Davies, *Phrenology: Fad and Science; A 19th Century American Crusade* (New Haven, 1955).

Also important are Edward Youmans' essay in *The Culture Demanded by Modern Life* (New York, 1867; 1900), and John Dewey's "The New Psychology," *Andover Review*, **2** (Sept. 1884), 278–91. Much basic material is at hand in the autobiographies of pioneer psychologists, in Carl Murchison, cited above; in R. B. Perry, *Life and Letters of William James*, 2 vols. (Boston, 1935); and in G. Stanley Hall, *Life and Confessions of a Psychologist* (New York, 1923). The files of the *American Journal of Psychology* (1887—) and the *Psychological Review* (1894—) are, of course, indispensable.

The most useful brief account of the relation between Darwinism and concepts of human nature is E. G. Boring, "The Influence of Evolutionary Theory upon Psychological Thought in America," in Stow Persons, ed., *Evolutionary Thought in America* (New York, 1956), pp. 268–98. The best analysis of Chauncey Wright, William James, C. S. Peirce, and John Fiske in the context of their evolutionary, pragmatic, and idealistic philosophy in relation to the idea of human nature is that of Philip P. Wiener, *Evolution and the Founders of Pragmatism* (Cambridge, Mass., 1949), pp. 31ff. Richard Hofstadter, *Social Darwinism in American Thought 1860–1915* (New York, 1944; 1959); and Mark Haller, *Eugenics; Hereditarian Attitudes in American Thought* (New Brunswick, N.J., 1963), are standard accounts. Nicholas Pastore, *The Nature-Nurture Controversy* (New York, 1949), documents the conservative-liberal alignment of hereditarians and environmentalists.

For the functional psychology see James R. Angell, "The Province of Functional Psychology," *Psychological Review*, **14** (March 1907), 61–91. Benjamin Wolstein's "Dewey's Theory of Human Nature," *Psychiatry*, **12** (Feb. 1949), 77–85, is, of course, only one of a great many valuable commentaries on Dewey's philosophy, social ideas, and psychological contributions. Dewey's own most relevant writings are *Human Nature and Conduct* (New York, 1922), and *Freedom and Culture* (New York, 1939).

Watson's most important writings are *Psychology from the Standpoint of the Behaviorist* (Philadelphia, 1919; 2nd ed. 1929), and *Behaviorism* (New York, 1925; rev. ed., 1930). For more recent developments see the papers in "Psychology: a Behavioral Reinterpretation," *Proceedings of the American Philosophical Society*, **108** (Dec. 1964), 151–85; and C. L. Hull, *Principles of Behavior* (New York, 1943); idem, *A Behavior System* (New Haven, 1952); E. C. Tolman,

"Principles of Purposive Behavior," in S. Koch, ed., *Psychology: a Study of a Science*, 3 vols. (New York, 1959), II, 92–157; and B. F. Skinner, *Walden Two* (New York, 1948); idem, *Science and Human Behavior* (New York, 1953). See, among secondary studies, John C. Burnham, "The Origins of Behaviorism," *Journal of the History of the Behavioral Sciences*, **4** (April 1968), 143–51; and Gustav Bergmann, "The Contribution of John B. Watson," in John M. Scher, ed., *Theories of the Mind* (New York, 1962), pp. 674–87. Mention should be made of Donald H. Fleming's introduction to Jacques Loeb, *The Mechanistic Conception of Life* (Cambridge, Mass., 1964), which is a basic contribution to behaviorism.

For the reception and influence of Freud consult John C. Burnham, *Psychoanalysis and American Medicine 1894–1918*, *Psychological Issues*, Monograph 20 (Pittsburgh, 1968); and idem "The New Psychology: From Narcissism to Social Control," in Braeman, Bremner, and Brody, eds., *Change and Continuity in Twentieth-Century America: the 1920s* (Columbus, Ohio, 1968), pp. 351–98; Clarence P. Oberndorf, *A History of Psychoanalysis in America* (New York, 1953); Merle Curti, "The American Exploration of Dreams and Dreamers," *Journal of the History of Ideas*, **27** (July–Sept. 1966), 391–416. Frederick J. Hoffman, *Freudianism and the Literary Mind* (Baton Rouge, 1945); and idem, *The Twenties; American Writing in the Post-War Decade* (New York, 1955).

The literature of the behavioral sciences is too vast to do more than offer a very few samples: Leonard D. White, ed., *The State of the Social Sciences* (Chicago, 1956); idem, *The Social Studies and the Social Sciences* (New York, 1962); and Merle Curti, "The Changing Concept of "Human Nature in the Literature of American Advertising," *Business History Review*, **41** (Winter 1967), 335–57. For a criticism of the behavioral sciences from a "humanistic" point of view consult Floyd W. Watson, *The Broken Image, Man, Science and Society* (New York, 1964).

MERLE CURTI

[See also Deism; Education; Evolutionism; Genetic Continuity; Inheritance of Acquired Characteristics; Man-Machine; Organicism; Perfectibility; Philanthropy; **Pragmatism;** Progress; **Psychological Schools in European Thought;** Sin and Salvation.]

# PYTHAGOREAN DOCTRINES TO 300 B.C.

THE HISTORIAN of Pythagoreanism in the sixth and fifth centuries must make his bricks without straw. He can give us an account not of persons, events, doctrines, but only of more or less plausible reconstructions and of controversies between disparate positions. The historian of ideas is in a more fortunate position. He may accept what no one doubts, that Pythagoras lived and that he played in his time a role analogous to that of founders of religions or sects whose impact and whose message survive their persons. Nor need he question the general nature of Pythagoras' message: first, a doctrine of the soul and, second, an arithmological theory of the physical world.

These two themes, soul and number, characterized Pythagoreanism throughout antiquity. We have no reason to believe that a connection was established between them in the early period. The soul doctrine determined moral conduct. The number theory purported to explain aspects of the structure of the physical world. They were first related by Plato, when he made of soul an intermediate between intelligibles and sensibles, both of these mathematically determined. We may therefore pursue the two themes separately up to the time when they are conjoined.

Until a generation ago Erwin Rohde's account of Greek doctrines of the soul in his great study, *Psyche* (1925), found very general acceptance. It was believed that when Pythagoras migrated from Ionia to Magna Graecia he found there a flourishing sect of the worshippers of Dionysus known as Orphics (Rohde, pp. 335–61; Jaeger, pp. 55–89), and that of this Orphic sect Pythagoras and his followers formed an offshoot observance. But in 1941 Linforth reexamined critically all the evidence for this belief; and since then skepticism about it has grown, until now Dodds (p. 147) can remark: "I must confess that I know very little about early Orphism, and the more I read about it the more my knowledge diminishes." Whatever our assessment of the evidence may be, it seems clear that if Pythagoras found beliefs about the soul abroad in Magna Graecia he transformed them for his purpose. Nothing ecstatic or dionysiac remained. Even a connection with the worship of Dionysus seems improbable. Pythagoras is said to have claimed divine status (Aristotle, frag. 1) as an incarnation of Apollo, not of Dionysus, and our whole tradition connects him with Apollo. For him the soul which lodges in our bodies has come from a previous existence and is proceeding to further existences. It may pass into an animal body (Xenophanes, *Vors.* 21B 7). It may in the end achieve divinity. Its migrations are linked to rewards and punishments. It is held responsible for the deeds and the fate of the person.

We do not know what were the formal and external aspects of Pythagoreanism during the life of Pythagoras and, subsequently, through the fifth century. In the late sixth and in the first half of the fifth century Pythagoreans engaged in political activities in Magna Graecia, and apparently became a dominant faction in Croton, Metapontum, and elsewhere. But there is no evidence for the brotherhood having the quasi-monastic character of which we hear so much from Neo-Pythagorean sources (Philip [1966a], pp. 24–34). The *Symbola* or Tokens which Aristotle (frags. 5–7) has preserved for us are not any rule of a community but merely a collection of superstitious injunctions not peculiar to any one sect, nor indeed to any one country.

When at the end of the fifth century B.C. the Pythagoreans emerge in the light of history, Plato (*Republic* 600A) and Isocrates (*Busiris* 28) regard them with respect for their conduct and discipline. However, the New Comedy (*Vors.* I, 278–80) treats them as figures of fun because of their rigors in diet and clothing. We may assume that the asceticism (*askesis*) they practiced arose from beliefs about the soul: that it was entombed in the body (Plato, *Gorgias* 493A) in the sense in which Socrates says (*Phaedo* 64A) that "philosophy is a practice of dying and of the state of being dead." If the body is nothing but a temporary habitation for a soul pilgriming through earthly and other than earthly existences towards a final reward or punishment, then our concern must be to "care for the soul." A frequent corollary of care for the soul is neglect of the body. It would appear that early Pythagoreanism was not altogether exempt from this excess. Neglect of the body characterized also the Orphics of the fourth century, but what marked off Pythagoreans from Orphics was that the Pythagorean *askesis* had an intellectual character. Care for the soul implied for them a discipline not only of the body but also of the mind.

The revolutionary aspect of Pythagoras' doctrine of the soul was not transmigration, nor a system of rewards and punishments—characteristics we find in other sects—but the notion of personal and intellectual *askesis*. It may be that Pythagoras as an Ionian found the ecstatic practices of the mysteries uncongenial. He cultivated pursuits of an intellectual character (Heraclitus, *Vors.* 22B 40) and a serious demeanor (*gravitas*), and these were a part of the heritage of Pythagoreanism.

Among the thinkers of the fifth century Empedocles alone taught a similar doctrine of the soul and its migrations. Although he was only a generation older than Socrates, his thought has the characteristics of an earlier period in which each thinker faced *ex novo* the problems of the universe, making use of the ideas of his predecessors only as stimuli. Empedocles' great poem *On Nature* falls into two parts so disparate that scholars have sought to explain the yawning gap between them by the hypothesis of a conversion. One part presents a theory of the physical world, the other concerns *Purifications*. The purifications deal with the soul, its migrations through plant and animal bodies, and the means we may take to escape from this cycle

31

to divine status. So in Empedocles as in Pythagoras we have two concomitant but apparently unrelated doctrines, one of the physical world and one concerning the soul.

That Empedocles was influenced by some Pythagorean tradition we may assume if a famous fragment (*Vors.* 31B 129) alludes, as is generally thought, to Pythagoras. But the influence is remote. Empedocles is animated by a horror of the pollution incurred in eating flesh. His aim is, by avoiding such pollution, to achieve again the godhead from which he is fallen (*Vors.* 32B 115). There is no trace of the personal *askesis* that is a mark of Pythagoreanism, nor is there in the poem *On Nature* any trace of arithmological speculation except for two forces, four elements, and similar hints such as we find also in Homer. We know that in Empedocles' city, Acragas, Orphic ideas were current (Pindar, *Ol.* 2, 62–83)—ideas to which we may reasonably suppose that Empedocles subscribed. Though his notions of soul derive from the same cultural milieu as those of Pythagoras, his poems do not reveal Pythagorean influence. The peculiarly Pythagorean notion of soul, with its corollary for conduct, did not so far as we know find philosophical expression in the fifth century, and no more did the arithmological doctrines. Pythagoras' message was "Care for your soul, and endeavour to penetrate the mysteries of the universe by observing numerical correspondences." The time was not yet ripe for a philosophical development of such teachings. It was only with the emergence of mathematics as a science that number mysticism could acquire philosophical importance; and it was only when the investigation of ethical concepts began that thinkers had to concern themselves with the soul that enjoined respect of those principles.

The fifth-century vacuum in Pythagoreanism has excited the attention of scholars since antiquity. The Neo-Pythagoreans sought either by invention or adoption to people that vacuum, and Iamblichus gives us a list of their names. A century ago an attempt was made to construct for a hypothetical Pythagorean brotherhood a theory of number atomism by reaction to which the monism of Parmenides, as a dissident Pythagorean, could be explained. Tannery, the originator of this thesis, has been followed by several scholars, among them Cornford (p. 62). Von Fritz further argues that Hippasus of Metapontum, a dubious and shadowy Pythagorean, discovered incommensurability. But increasingly of late, doubt has been cast on these and similar theses on the grounds that they are built on questionable hypotheses (Philip [1966a], p. 2). They assume a formal development of the mathematical disciplines earlier than is historically possible, and they impute a mathematical character to the thought of Parmenides and Zeno for which there is

no evidence. It is much more probable that Parmenides' "One" was a revolutionary elaboration of the *nous* of Xenophanes that "sees as a whole, thinks as a whole, hears as a whole" (*Vors.* 21B 24). But we may not assume that this *nous*/mind is simply a cosmic extension of the *psyche*/soul of Pythagoras. Even when later *nous* is situated within or as a function of soul, the two concepts remain distinct. *Psyche* for Homer and Hesiod is what imparts life to bodies. Its later role as the cause of motion develops from its more primitive function, motion being the primary manifestation of life. *Nous* on the other hand is from the beginning intellective or cognitive, expressive of seeing as knowing. Plato would appear to have been the first to relate the two by locating, as he does, *nous* within soul both in the macrocosm and the microcosm.

Our tradition then suggests that the twin doctrines of Pythagoras, in spite of their potential importance, remained philosophically dormant throughout the fifth century, professed as a way of life rather than as theory by whatever persons may have espoused them. They acquired philosophical importance and the form in which they were transmitted to later antiquity only when Plato encountered them. But what of Philolaus? He is the one Pythagorean of the fifth century having a clear title to philosophical stature and of whom we have extensive fragments. It is therefore not surprising that controversies regarding early Pythagoreanism center around Philolaus. His fragments have had their defenders, but a majority of scholars has pronounced them falsifications (Burkert, p. 206, n. 17). Recently however Burkert has presented an able defense of a group of them, and the question is again open. However the question may be decided, we must observe, first, that Philolaus' main interests, astronomy and physiology, are peripheral to Pythagoreanism; second, that having apparently lived in exile from his youth until advanced years, his knowledge of Pythagoreanism must have been slight; and, third, that the fragments, if genuine, do not inspire any high opinion of Philolaus' philosophical grasp. They are no foundation for a reconstruction of fifth-century Pythagoreanism.

The Pythagoreans of the fifth century are insubstantial figures owing such character as they exhibit to Neo-Platonic fabulation (Guthrie, I, 319–33). Unlike them Archytas is an historical person, known repeatedly to have held the highest office in Tarentum. He was a contemporary of Plato's and a friend certainly from the time of Plato's second voyage to Sicily (366 B.C.) and probably from the time of his first voyage (388 B.C.). It is often suggested that the *Republic*, written between the two journeys, was influenced by Plato's encounter with Archytas and the Pythagoreans of Magna Graecia. If the encounter provoked a significant change in the complexion of Plato's thought, we must ask ourselves what new ideas he may have met with. It is unlikely that he found current in Tarentum doctrines of the soul unfamiliar to him. There were Orphic adepts in his own Attica (*Republic* 364E) and a few persons, some of them probably known to him, calling themselves Pythagoreans (*Vors.* 52, 1). He may have been impressed by the mathematical abilities of Archytas, but the fragments suggest not an adept of arithmology, of which there is no trace, but an original mind engaged in mathematical investigations. Plato had about him in Athens mathematicians of genius who were the peers of Archytas. But Archytas may have communicated to Plato arcane doctrines of the Pythagoreans. If this had been the case Aristotle, who wrote a treatise on the philosophy of Archytas in three books (Diogenes Laërtius, V. 25), could hardly have failed to have pointed out Plato's dependence on him when in the *Metaphysics* he was discussing the origins of Plato's thought. There however (987a 29–31) he tells us simply that Plato's thought was in the main a development of Pythagorean doctrines. If we can discover no individual Pythagorean whom Plato could have regarded as a master, and we have no evidence for a "brotherhood" professing a body of doctrine, what can Aristotle mean?

We can attempt to answer this question only when we have first ascertained what doctrines Aristotle imputes to the Pythagoreans. He tells us that from Limit and Unlimited as first principles there proceeds a One, and from the One somehow the numbers that are things (*Metaphysics* 986a 17–21). Further, he ascribes to the Pythagoreans doctrines, not of a philosophical nature, about the soul (*De anima* 404a 17). That there were in Plato's time Pythagoreans who professed such doctrines, and that these derived ultimately from Pythagoras himself we may easily believe. But this seems an inadequate basis for what passes as Pythagoreanism at the end of the fourth century, after Plato's death, unless we assume that Plato himself, in rethinking, transformed them. By the end of the century Pythagoreanism had acquired important tenets of which we have no trace in the early period but which continue to characterize Pythagoreanism thereafter. In particular the two principal tenets are substantially modified. Soul now no longer animates only the human person, plants, and animals. It also animates the universe. It has acquired mathematical characteristics, the souls of macrocosm and microcosm both being structured according to mathematical ratios. Further, numbers have ceased to be things. For the universe is now divided into the realm of the intelligible and the sensible, and numbers appertain primarily to the former.

We still have the two basic Pythagorean doctrines of soul and of number-things. But soul has been given a metaphysical role, and number-things have had to accommodate themselves to a *chorismos* or separation of intelligibles and sensibles. This is that mathematization of philosophy against which Aristotle protests so vigorously. It represents in its main lines the thought not only of Speusippus and Xenocrates but also, as far as we can discern, that of Plato in the *agrapha dogmata* or "unwritten doctrines" (Ross, pp. 142–53; Merlan, pp. 11–33; Krämer, pp. 1–2; Gaiser with frags.).

Can Plato himself have transformed in this manner the simpler tenets ascribed by Aristotle to "the Pythagoreans"? We observe in the dialogues how he moves from the Socratic form of refutation (*elenchus*) and a Socratic form of definition, especially of ethical ideas or concepts, towards a metaphysical structure in which these ideas can, as it were, be anchored. We observe how he differentiates between the knowledge we can have of such intelligibles and the knowledge, or better belief, we can have of sensibles. We observe his struggle to clarify the relation between intelligibles and sensibles. But can we believe that Plato was ready to adopt a whole metaphysical structure, at best implicit darkly in the dialogues, and that his dialogues serve to link and explain that structure in a way the dialogues hardly adumbrate?

We can attempt to answer that question in two ways; first, by asking whether the history of Greek thought, of which we have from Plato himself the first perceptive and imaginative accounts, would authorize any such hypothesis and, second, whether Aristotle's account of the manner in which Plato's thought evolved either confirms or at least does not contradict our hypothesis. If this proves to be the case we may then consider Speusippus and Xenocrates, as to whose speculation we are perhaps better informed, to see if their metaphysics may reasonably be supposed to have evolved from Plato's *agrapha dogmata*.

We are imputing to Plato a revolutionary rethinking of the two basic Pythagorean tenets. That someone in the early fourth century should rethink their number notions is entirely plausible. For at about that time mathematics became an organized discipline and, shortly thereafter, made tremendous strides in all its branches. In the Academy of Plato there were a number of eminent mathematicians (Proclus, in *Euclid*. 64–68, Friedlein), and our tradition tells us that Plato furthered their pursuits. His own works are a testimony to his mathematical interests. What could have been more natural than that he should modify the crude notion of number-things to adapt it to his two-realm theory? How he did so is still a matter of debate, but it would appear that he recognized a class of mathematicals intermediate between intelligibles and sensibles, and that in the *Timaeus* he regarded sensibles as somehow consisting of geometrical configurations.

How his two ultimate principles—the One or unity and the indefinite dyad or the great-and-small—generated this universe and what was the relation between them we need not attempt to determine here. Nor need we hazard a guess whether the atomism of Democritus in part suggested such a development.

The Pythagorean soul-tenet we find similarly extended and transformed. For Pythagoras the soul was what animates the body. It apparently had no cosmic function nor was it a first principle of motion. Aristotle tells us (*De anima* 405a 29) that Alcmaeon saw soul as immortal because it was in motion, like the heavenly bodies. Motion is a property of everything ensouled, but soul is not therefore a principle of motion (cf. Skemp, pp. 36–64), and Plato is the first thinker known to us who explicitly regards soul as the first principle of motion (*kinesis*). But he extends the notion of soul also in another direction. Soul animates not only all living creatures but also that living creature par excellence, the universe. How did Plato move from the individual migrating soul to the soul of the universe? He may have taken a hint from Anaxagoras. For in the account Socrates gives of his own intellectual development in the *Phaedo*, *nous* is the cause of motion. The relations between *nous* and *psyche* in Plato are a problem fraught with difficulties; but it is clear that the passage from *nous* as cosmic mover to the world soul of the *Timaeus* is an easy one and, if the theory is to leave room not only for intellection but also for perception, a necessary one.

Let us concede for the moment that, within the historical framework of preceding thought, a modification of Pythagorean tenets in the sense we have suggested is a possible one, and let us ask ourselves how Aristotle's account of the development of Plato's thought is consonant with this scheme.

In the *Metaphysics* (987a 29–988a 17) he gives us a concise account of Plato's philosophy, in the context of a survey of preceding views about first principles or causes. In the course of his survey Aristotle discusses "those who go by the name of Pythagoreans." These, he says, regard number as first principle and as material substrate (986a 16–21). Number they hold to proceed from an ultimate duality, Limited and Unlimited, from which derives the One, and thence come the numbers that constitute the physical universe. Apparently some Pythagoreans differed from this account in that they recognized not one pair of opposites but a table of opposite pairs. As their table begins with Limited and Unlimited, as its pairs are not logically or derivatively related, and as they are obviously padded to reach the number of the decad Aristotle is doubtless correct in thinking theirs only a later variant of the original doctrine. So we have for the Pythagoreans a duality

of first principles, and numbers constituting things. There is no mention of soul, probably because Pythagorean notions of soul are not at the level of theory.

Plato's philosophy, says Aristotle, in most respects followed after and conformed to Pythagorean doctrines. But it had also its own peculiar characteristic. Plato believed, with the Heracliteans, that there was no knowledge of sensibles because they exhibited no constant state, but that there was knowledge of universals and in particular of the sort of universals that Socrates sought to define. His universals Plato called "ideas." (Aristotle's polemic against the ideas arises out of this separation or *chorismos* of intelligibles and sensibles, *Metaphysics* 1040b 28 and passim.) Aristotle goes on to explain that there were differences between Plato and the Pythagoreans in matters of immanence and transcendence (how the Pythagoreans with their number-things could hold any such doctrines he does not suggest) and that though they agreed on the One as being, Plato modified the initial contrariety, substituting for the Unlimited the indefinite dyad.

Another important difference Aristotle sees is the fact that, whereas for the Pythagoreans things *are* numbers, for Platonists there exist mathematicals intermediate between ideas and sensibles and these mediate the reality we find in sensibles in respect of their idea paradigms. So Plato, according to Aristotle, has adopted the theory of dual first principles and the number-substance notion of the Pythagoreans. But as his Heraclitean views compelled Plato to recognize a gradational reality, downwards to sensibles, he modified their theories so as to achieve a procession of being from first principles and the mediation of mathematicals between ideas and particulars.

The general remarks on the origin of Platonic theories in Book A of the *Metaphysics* has as its complement in Books M and N a long and involved argument against the doctrine of idea numbers propounded by Plato, Speusippus, and Xenocrates. Though Aristotle makes little reference to persons it is possible to distinguish the aspects of the doctrine we must ascribe to the latter two (Ross, p. 152), and its substance remains imputable to Plato. Unless therefore we are willing to maintain that the whole complex structure is a fantasy of Aristotle's built on a few tentative hints in the dialogues, we must concede that Plato, at least in his later years, professed a number doctrine which was a modification of more primitive Pythagorean teaching, and that he was indeed the author of the astonishing synthesis—a unique product of historical, mathematical, and metaphysical imagination or insight.

If we find Speusippus and Xenocrates taking as their point of departure a doctrine such as we have ascribed to Plato, and if we discover that their teachings were reputed to be Pythagorean, we may regard this as substantially confirming the hypothesis of a Platonic rethinking of basic Pythagorean doctrines. Let us then turn to these two thinkers, successors to Plato in the headship of the Academy: the first a nephew who succeeded probably by Plato's nomination, the second regarded as his most faithful disciple. We find to our surprise that both of them abandon basic Platonic tenets, including belief in the ideas, and that they apparently do so under the pressure of criticism (*Metaphysics* 1086a 2). That some of this criticism came from Aristotle we cannot doubt. He was a member of the Academy until his departure for Assos on Plato's death. If he ever subscribed to the theory of ideas he had long ceased to do so, and the *Metaphysics* give us repeatedly and on many counts résumés of his objections which must have been worked out in discussion within the Academy. That Aristotle extorted concessions is however less surprising than the fact that both men appear to have retreated to Pythagorean positions. Let us consider the two thinkers separately, observing both the ground they yield and the positions they take.

To Speusippus (ca. 395–339 B.C.) and his *Encomium* of Plato (Diogenes Laërtius 3.2), we owe the curious tale that Plato's father, Ariston, attempted to force his own wife Perictione, but to no avail. When he desisted he had a vision of Apollo, and thereupon refrained from intercourse with her until Plato was born. As Wilamowitz has observed, this tale strikes us, and probably would strike an Athenian of the fourth century, as bizarre and not in the best of taste. It might even strike an Athenian as ludicrous. For Plato was the youngest child of four, and gods traditionally favored virgins. However the point of Speusippus' tale may be quite a different one. Iamblichus (*Vita Pythagorica* 4. 6) and probably also Porphyry (*Vita Pythagorae* 2) recount similar tales of Pythagoras' paternity, that he was fathered by Apollo. If this tradition goes back to the fourth century or earlier, then what Speusippus means us to infer is that Plato is a Pythagoras *redivivus*. In any event Apollinian paternity connects him with the Pythagorean tradition.

That Speusippus had for Aristotle peculiarly Pythagorean associations we see from the way in which he couples the names "Speusippus and the Pythagoreans" (*Metaphysics* 1072b 30, *Nicomachean Ethics* 1096b 5) and frequently alludes to common doctrine. We need not question Aristotle's testimony here, for our longest fragment (Lang, frag. 4) comes from Speusippus' treatise *On Pythagorean Numbers*. The first part deals with the numbers involved in the derivation of solids and with the five cosmic figures which, as Eva Sachs (pp. 42–48) has shown, are to be ascribed as mathematical constructions to Theaetetus. The second

part of the treatise is more interesting for our purposes, and Iamblichus paraphrases the words of Speusippus. Speusippus' theme is the decad. He treats it not, as we might expect, by seeking for "correspondences" after the Pythagorean manner familiar to us from Aristotle (*Metaphysics* 1092b 8–1093b 29) and by finding mystical significances. His is rather an essay in the theory of number that we later encounter in Nicomachus of Gerasa the mathematician (end of first century A.D.) and the Neo-Pythagoreans. In this he may be their precursor.

If then we have ample warrant for regarding Speusippus as a Platonist having marked and confessed Pythagorean leanings, let us now consider how he modified Plato's doctrines, and whether his modifications may be regarded as "Pythagorean." It is notorious that he abandoned the ideas (Lang, frag. 30) and together with them one of the two Platonic first principles, the indefinite dyad. In its place he recognized plurality as the companion principle of the One. From these two principles proceeded number, the whole cosmos of intelligibles and sensibles consisting of number. For Speusippus did not abandon the two-realm theory of Plato (Lang, frag. 29). But the "common ground" (Lang, frag. 4) on which he established association of intelligible universals and sensible particulars was number. Now if particulars too were essentially number it could no longer be denied that they also were knowable. So Speusippus conceded that, as a scientific rationality (*ratio*) in us enables us to know intelligibles, so a scientific perception—a judging faculty or *criterion*—enables us to know sensibles. So we have of them not belief (*doxa*) as Plato taught, but knowledge in the full sense.

Why then did Speusippus not abandon the notion of separate substance? We are told (*Metaphysics* 1090a 3–37) that he held that as objects of science they must be separate. But if he was prepared to use Ockham's razor on the ideas why should he cling to a realm of transcendent number? Much of his philosophical activity was devoted to the discovery of similarities (*homoia*), and his longest work, in ten books, bore that title. Though his classifications bore a strong resemblance to, and in some instances anticipated, Aristotle's biological classification, they were not in intent biological but were apparently meant to exhibit the structure of reality, to show how a plurality of particulars constitutes a unity and class. The numbers constituting classes and exemplified in particulars are not themselves subject to process as are the particulars, and this was the criterion on which Plato established his two realms (*Timaeus* 27D). But whereas for Plato soul mediated between these two realms, for Speusippus soul became "the form of the everywhere extended"

35

(Lang, frag. 40). This formula seems to imply a mathematical penetration of both realms, the fact of process being the only difference between them. It could be made to apply to microcosm as well as macrocosm, but it is difficult to see how such a soul could be the cause of motion; and indeed when Diogenes Laërtius attributes the definition of Speusippus to Plato he interprets this soul as *pneuma* (Diogenes Laërtius, 3. 67).

Ingenious but unsuccessful attempts have been made, in particular by Frank (pp. 130–34) to reconstruct the system of Speusippus. For this the fragments do not afford us sufficient knowledge of detail. But one aspect of this system is of special interest to us. Aristotle (*Nicomachean Ethics* 1096b 5) tells us that "the Pythagoreans seem to me to give a more convincing account (of the Good) when they situate the One on the good side of their column of opposites. Speusippus apparently conforms to this doctrine of theirs." Aristotle recognizes (*Metaphysics* 1091a 36) that Speusippus is meeting a real difficulty here, but a difficulty which, according to Aristotle, arises from making the One a first principle and principle of number, not from equating it with the Good. The Pythagoreans and Speusippus did not predicate goodness of their One, Aristotle says (*Metaphysics* 1072b 30), because they observed that in plants and animals the good was a *telos* ("goal" or "end") achieved only in the course of development. But Theophrastus' account (*Metaphysics* 11a 24) suggests that this was only an argument to buttress their case. The real reason, as Aristotle recognized (*Metaphysics* 1091b 30), was that if one of a pair of opposed first principles was said to be good or the Good, then the other must be recognized as evil. "So he [Speusippus] used to avoid predicating good of the One, on the grounds that, since process occurs from opposites, then necessarily plurality would be evil itself." (For the problems here see L. G. P., pp. 25–27.)

Speusippus (and the Pythagoreans) may have thought that this difficulty was adequately met by a pair of number first principles from which numbers proceeded, their physical manifestations achieving their good only in the course of development. But it is possible that he met it also by recognizing a One above and beyond his primary contrariety, as Plato's Good was *epekeina* ("above and beyond"). Proclus (*Comm. in Parmen.*, Klibansky 38.34) tells us that Speusippus held a doctrine he ascribed to "the ancients" (Pythagoreans?)—a doctrine differentiating between a first One not participating in being and a One in which existents participate, we assume as one of a pair of first principles. If there is a One from which the two first principles proceed, it is easier to think of them as purely mathematical and having no value

connotations. Such a theory however might lead to consequences such as those on which Aristotle remarks (*Metaphysics* 1028b 18), that differing first principles have to be recognized for numbers, magnitudes, soul, and so forth. Instead of a coherent system we have episodes, as in a bad tragedy (*Metaphysics* 1075b 37).

So we may conclude that in abandoning Platonic doctrines Speusippus reverts to simpler Pythagorean ones, especially towards the thesis that "things are number"—a position of which Aristotle says that though it is an impossible one it has the merit of being consistent. If he had abandoned it to achieve some new synthesis of his own he would no doubt have professed himself a Platonist, as Plotinus did later. But it would appear that Speusippus was driven from his Platonic positions and took refuge in a profession of Pythagoreanism, a Pythagoreanism to which he himself had contributed.

With Xenocrates (ca. 406–315 B.C.) we are on more difficult ground. He pythagorized, as Speusippus and Plato himself had pythagorized before him. But whereas Speusippus, in departing from Platonic doctrines, was an overt pythagorizer, Xenocrates professed orthodox Platonism but modified Platonic metaphysics in order to render some positions less vulnerable, and to systematize. His modifications may have been natural developments of the "unwritten doctrines." In part they may have been countenanced by Plato himself.

What positions did Xenocrates take up in respect of the twin themes of soul and number? He defined soul, in a phrase that became widely current, as "self-moving number." This definition Plutarch attributes to Xenocrates (Heinze, frag. 68), but according to Proclus (Heinze, frag. 62) Xenocrates himself attributes it to Plato. (It is attributed by the doxography, characteristically, to Pythagoras—*Dox. Gr.* 386a 13, 651.11.) If it was meant as a summary definition of the world soul of the *Timaeus*, it was an inadequate one. Its difficulties Aristotle does not fail to point out (*De anima* 408b 32), and some of the commentators, in particular Philoponus (Heinze, frag. 65), argue in Xenocrates' defense that no one who had "dipped into mathematics with the tips of a finger" could define soul so naively.

We may relate his definition of soul as self-moving number to his other famous definition of the ideas as "paradigmatic causes of physical objects as and when they occur" (Heinze, frag. 30). These ideas he identified with the idea numbers (Heinze, frag. 48). So both soul and intelligibles are number-structured. We know further that he derived physical magnitudes numerically (Heinze, frags. 37–39; cf. Philip [1966a], p. 2), indivisible lines being the atomic unit of derivation (Heinze, frags. 41–49; Pines, passim.). That he should have modified and developed Platonic doctrines seems credible. He survived Plato by thirty-three years, Aristotle by seven. So it seems clear that his modifications were in the direction of greater mathematization, and so of pythagorizing.

How his system of derivation, from first principles to physical particulars, was articulated is still a matter of controversy (Krämer, 2, 21–101). On one vital issue he seems to have been an innovator (Heinze, frags. 140–42). Plato had been singularly reticent about the relations of *nous* and *psyche*. That they were to be regarded as distinct is implied in the *Sophistes* (249a 2), and the *Philebus* (28c 7) in speaking of *nous* as "king of heaven and earth" assigns it some exalted though undefined status, as does the *Laws*. Xenocrates has a single supreme first principle, *nous,* above the One and the dyad. This *nous* is also the monad and is identified with the Zeus of popular religion. This new doctrine, which had for later Platonism consequences Xenocrates could not foresee, may derive in part from Plato's One and the Good. It had no Pythagorean origins. Nevertheless we may say of Xenocrates that, faithful Platonist though he may have held himself to be, such modifications of Plato's later metaphysics as he admitted were in the direction of pythagorizing. He commanded the respect of his contemporaries as much for his manners and morals as for his thought, thus conforming to the Pythagorean ideal of the sage.

To sum up, we have in Pythagoras a great precursor to whom is ascribed a doctrine of soul having implications for ethical conduct and a doctrine of number as the nature of the universe. It was not to these teachings however that he owed his authority. Instead, his moral dominance lent credit to his teachings. After his death his partisans formed the ruling clique of many city states of Magna Graecia and remained in power for half a century. During this period we hear little of his doctrines and know of no Pythagorean of philosophical eminence. Some time about the middle of the fifth century a wave of opposition swept the Pythagoreans out of office and into exile, if they came off with their lives. As a political party they never returned to power and it appears to have been only towards the end of the century that their return from exile was tolerated. It was under a democratic regime that Archytas, a Pythagorean, became chief magistrate of Tarentum about 375 B.C.

The fifth century was productive of great thinkers in the West—Parmenides, Zeno, Empedocles, perhaps Leucippus. But the only Pythagorean of some stature is Philolaus. He enjoys a dubious reputation as an astronomer, and for physiological speculation. His teaching was as peripheral to what we must regard as central Pythagorean doctrines as that of Archytas

was later. It is only with Plato that we find the notion of soul achieving philosophical importance and cosmic functions. It does so in a universe where things are not numbers but number-structured. We conclude that Plato seized on two basic Pythagorean notions, soul and number, and used them (together with other hints from earlier thinkers) in the construction of his own metaphysics. Plato however did not publish in detail and as a system his metaphysical doctrines. They remained largely "unwritten" partly because he believed they could not and should not be communicated by the written word.

Plato's closest disciples were less reticent. They published notes on a lecture or lectures of Plato's *On the Good,* and they developed in treatises their own metaphysical doctrines, modifying what may be inferred to have been Plato's position. They did so in the direction of a Pythagoreanism Plato himself had not merely espoused but in a measure had endowed with its characteristic tenets. When with Arcesilaus (ca. 250 B.C.) there occurred in the Academy a reaction towards a supposedly Socratic skepticism (Burkert, p. 83) pythagorizing became an embarrassment. Platonic doctrines supposed to be tinged with Pythagoreanism ceased to be imputed to Plato and were attributed holus-bolus to Pythagoras. But Plato's reorientation of thought towards mathematization and towards a doctrine of mind/soul continued to be fruitful of consequences, even when the course of its development is concealed by the endless mystifications of later pythagorizers.

### BIBLIOGRAPHY

Aristotle, *Fragmenta selecta*, ed. W. D. Ross (Oxford, 1955). W. Burkert, *Weisheit und Wissenschaft* (Nürnberg, 1962). F. M. Cornford, *Plato and Parmenides* (London, 1939). C. J. de Vogel, *Pythagoras and Early Pythagoreanism* (Utrecht, 1966); idem, *Philosophia*, Part I (Assen, 1970). H. Diels, see *Vors*. E. R. Dodds, *The Greeks and the Irrational* (Berkeley, 1951). Diogenes Laërtius, *Vita philosophorum*, ed. H. S. Long (Oxford, 1964). E. Frank, *Plato und die sogenannte Pythagoreer* (Halle, 1923). K. C. Gaiser, *Platons Ungeschriebene Lehre* (Stuttgart, 1963). W. K. C. Guthrie, *A History of Greek Philosophy* (Cambridge, Vol. 1, 1962; Vol. 2, 1965). R. Heinze, *Xenokrates* (Leipzig, 1892). Iamblichus, *Vita Pythagorica*, ed. L. Duebner (Leipzig, 1937). W. Jaeger, *The Theology of the Early Greek Philosophers* (Oxford, 1947). H. J. Krämer, *Arete bei Platon und Aristoteles* (Heidelberg, 1959); idem, *Der Ursprung der Geistesmetaphysik* (Amsterdam, 1964). P. Lang, *De Speusippi academici scriptis*, diss. (Bonn, 1911). L. G. P., *Later Greek and Early Medieval Philosophy*, ed. D. H. Armstrong (Cambridge, 1967). P. Merlan, *From Platonism to Neoplatonism*, 2nd ed. (The Hague, 1950). J. A. Philip, *Pythagoras and Early Pythagoreanism* (Toronto, 1966a);

idem, "The 'Pythagorean' Theory of the Derivation of Magnitudes," *Phoenix*, **20** (1966b), 32–50. S. Pines, *A new fragment of Xenocrates APS* (Philadelphia, 1961). Porphyrius, *Vita Pythagorae* in *Porphyrii Opuscula*, ed. O. Nauck, 2nd ed. (Leipzig, 1886). Proclus, *In primum Euclid. comm.*, ed. G. Friedlein (Leipzig, 1873). E. Rohde, *Psyche*, trans. W. B. Hillis (London, 1925). W. D. Ross, *Plato's Theory of Ideas* (Oxford, 1951). E. Sachs, *Die fünf platonische Körper* (Berlin, 1917). J. B. Skemp, *The Theory of Motion in Plato's Later Dialogues* (Cambridge, 1942). *Vors., Die Fragmente der Vorsokratiker*, ed. H. Diels and W. Kranz (Berlin, 1938; 1952)

JAMES PHILIP

[See also Analogy; **Harmony or Rapture;** Idea; Music and Science; Neo-Platonism; Number; Platonism; **Pythagorean Harmony.**]

## PYTHAGOREAN HARMONY OF THE UNIVERSE

IN THE COURSE of summarizing Pythagorean contributions to Greek thought, Aristotle, having pointed out the importance of mathematics to the Pythagoreans, adds that "since . . . they saw that the modifications and the ratios of the musical scales (ἁρμονιῶν) were expressible in numbers;—since, then, all other things seemed in their whole nature to be modelled in numbers, and numbers seemed to be the first things in the whole of nature, they supposed the elements of numbers to be the elements of all things, *and the whole heaven to be a scale and a number*" (*Metaphysica* A 5 986a, trans. W. D. Ross). Aristotle was probably describing the views of fifth- and fourth-century Pythagoreans such as Archytas of Tarentum, under whom the doctrine of a universe ordered by the same numerical proportions that govern musical harmonies was developed.

How much the semimythical Pythagoras of Samos (late sixth century B.C.) had to do with formulating the laws of cosmic harmony is not known; he is credited by Diogenes Laërtius with having discovered that the principal musical consonances result from the sounding of proportionate lengths of a stretched string, so that within the series 1–4 (the sacred Pythagorean *tetraktys*) simple ratios give forth the octave (2:1), the fifth (3:2), and the fourth (4:3). In these same proportions and their multiples, and particularly in the "means" found within multiples of the duple proportion (arithmetic = 2:3:4; geometric = 1:2:4; harmonic = 3:4:6), lay for subsequent Pythagorean thinkers the relationships between all sorts of natural phenomena. Since numbers were for them not abstractions but quantities

with real, i.e., spatial, existence, the discovery of musical laws—more tangible than vague analogies—governing the whole of creation, and especially the starry universe, was an intoxicating one, and in its precise and extended mathematical elaboration a peculiarly Greek one.

Oriental and Near-Eastern cosmologies all show some ordering principles at work, principles in many instances exerting influence on terrestrial life. The Greeks did not know where these ideas came from, but Plutarch referred to the "Chaldeans" (*De anim. procr.* 1028), and so did Philo Judaeus, who described the Chaldeans (or Babylonians) as having ". . . set up a harmony between things on earth and things on high, between heavenly things and earthly. Following as it were the laws of musical proportion (διὰ μουσικῆς λόγων), they have exhibited the universe as a perfect concord or symphony produced by a sympathetic affinity between its parts, separated indeed in space, but housemates in kinship" (*De migrat. Abrahami* XXXII, 177f., trans. F. H. Colson). It is possible that not only Greek cosmologies but also Jewish beliefs in an ordered universe hymning the praises of its Maker—expressed in the Psalms, in the visions of Isaiah and of Ezekiel, and especially in the Talmudic book of *Yoma*—may have been influenced by Babylonian lore. The same Philo who credited the Chaldeans with discovering cosmic harmony wrote a lengthy commentary on the six days of Creation (*De opificio mundi*) with constant allusions to Pythagorean theories, thus stressing what was for him the common parentage of Greek and Jewish cosmology.

Among the fragments of pre-Socratic philosophy there are a few references to symphonious order in the heavens. Anaximander (b. 610 B.C.), for whom the planets were wheels of fire visible through "breathing-holes," posited relative sizes of 27, 18, and (presumably) 9, thus 3-2-1, for the sun, moon, and "stars" (planets?) with respect to the earth. This graduated order was not accompanied by musical sound; but Anaximander did compare the "breathing-holes" in his fiery circles to the holes of musical pipes. In the Proem of the fifth-century Parmenides' "Way of Truth" the axle of a fast-moving heavenly chariot glows in its socket and sings out like a pipe; a surviving portion (frag. 12, Diels) of the second part, the "Way of Opinion," of the poem suggests further connection with Anaximander's cosmology while at the same time prefiguring one of the great statements of the music of the spheres, the Myth of Er in Plato's *Republic*. Finally, the mysterious "attunement of opposites" of Heraclitus (frag. 51, Diels) was related both to the cosmos (by Plutarch, *De anim. procr.* 1026 B) and to music (by Plato, *Symposium* 187).

To return to Pythagoras himself, it is impossible to sort out historical truth from the welter of myth surrounding this figure. But according to the doxographer Hippolytus, Pythagoras is said to have taught that the universe is put together by means of harmonic laws and so produces, through the motion of the seven planets, rhythm and melody (see Diels, *Doxographi Graeci* [1879], p. 555). The very enthusiastic Neo-Pythagorean Iamblichus went so far as to claim that Pythagoras could actually hear the cosmic music inaudible to other mortals. And since all discoveries about the Pythagorean cosmos were dependent on the numerical ratios sounded by the stretched string or monochord, it was reported by the Neo-Platonic musical theorist Aristides Quintilianus (third century A.D.) that Pythagoras' dying injunction to his students was μονοχορδίζειν ("work the monochord").

It is not from Pythagoras himself, nor yet from any of his direct followers, that we get a full and circumstantial account of the formation of the universe by the laws of harmony; the first such account—and certainly the most important—is that given in Plato's *Timaeus*. In this dialogue Timaeus the Locrian is spokesman for Plato's version of Pythagorean cosmic doctrine. (On the basis of a spurious Alexandrian dialogue paraphrasing Plato, "Timaeus of Locris" was long thought to be the source of Plato's Pythagorizing views.) The wondrous tale of the Demiurge fashioning the World-Soul is told (*Timaeus* 35–36); after this psychogony has been completed it serves as model (παράδειγμα) for the creation of the corporeal world. Out of a material blended of Sameness and Difference, ideal and bodily Existence, the Demiurge constructs a model for the universe. The psychic material is cut or marked into proportionate lengths before being split and bent into circles illustrating the makeup of the planetary system. It is these proportions, yielding the series 1-2-3-4-9-8-27, a compound of two geometric series (1-3-9-27 and 2-4-8), that outline the Pythagorean harmonic world. Plato forms a scale that "sounds" his ideal celestial distances. Within the two geometric series are placed arithmetic and harmonic means, creating proportions of 3:2, 4:3, and (their difference) 9:8. The proportion 4:3 (in musical terms an interval of a fourth) is filled in, or marked off, with intervals of the size 9:8 (in music, a whole tone), leaving in each fourth a small difference (λεῖμμα), or semitone, of 256:243. The result is a musical scale, based on a tuning of intervals that has ever since been termed Pythagorean, of nearly five octaves—truly universal, since it is by far greater in compass than any scale given by Greek musical theorists. Out of material marked with this scale, then, the Demiurge forms the World-Model, and thus it is that one could suppose

"the whole heaven to be a scale and a number," its paradigm made out of a kind of celestial monochord.

No one knows whether Plato in the *Timaeus* was himself thinking as a Pythagorean or was reporting current theories not originated, perhaps not even fully believed, by him. But the *Timaeus* is for us the main source of Pythagorean cosmology; and so it was for the later ancient world as well. A large surviving body of commentary by Neo-Platonic and Neo-Pythagorean writers (the fullest and best is that of Proclus in the fifth century A.D.) shows what fascination Plato's work had—as well as how unclear his meaning was. Through the Latin commentary of Chalcidius the *Timaeus* was known in the Middle Ages, and Renaissance Neo-Platonists, such as Marsilio Ficino, added to the body of work seeking to amplify and explicate Plato's account. The tuning system outlined in the *Timaeus* became a regular part of Greek musical theory, given full statement in the κατατομὴ κανόνος (ca. 300 B.C.) attributed to Euclid, and included in the musical treatise of the great astronomer Ptolemy (second century A.D.), whose celestial harmonies are an elaborate scientific restatement of Plato's cosmic sketch.

Plato does not describe his harmoniously conceived universe as sonorous in the *Timaeus*—the musical theory outlined there belongs to the Greek discipline of harmonics, the tuning of intervals, rather than to music itself. What is known to us as the "music of the spheres" comes from another source in Plato, the Myth of Er at the end of the *Republic*. Er the Pamphylian, a hero slain in battle, was given the privilege of seeing the next world and then returning to life to describe what he had seen. The vision of Er includes once again a model of the universe, a set of concentric rings or whorls—the planets—hung on the spindle of Necessity. The rims of these whorls are of different sizes and colors, and they revolve at different speeds—all the inner ones in opposition to the movement of the outer rim, the firmament. The Pythagorean proportions of the *Timaeus* are lacking here; but present is actual music, for as the spindle turns, "on the upper surface of each circle is a siren, who goes round with them, hymning a single tone or note. The eight together form one harmony (ἁρμονίαν)" (*Republic* X. 617, trans. B. Jowett).

Thus for Plato the universe was designed according to harmonious proportions, and this intellectual harmony could be described, in the metaphoric language of a dream-vision, as sounding music. Whether or not the cosmic myths of the *Timaeus* and the *Republic* were meant by their author to be related, most people in the ancient world took them to be so. Since the term *harmonia* could mean, among other things, the interval of the octave, some commentators made of the Sirens' music a single octave of the *Timaeus* scale—sounding simultaneously but audible successively to anyone privileged to move through the planetary realms (such a voyage is described in a long didactic poem by the encyclopedist Martianus Capella in the fifth century A.D.). Whether the scale went up or down from outer to inner planets, whether the motionless earth "sounded" in this celestial scale—these and similar questions were treated in detail by Neo-Pythagorean writers. And despite Aristotle's rejection of sounding planetary rims (in favor of his own silent, frictionless spheres; see *De caelo* II. 9. 290–91) belief continued strong in a literally musical universe, with the harmonious gradation of sound produced by the differing planetary speeds. These speeds in turn are regulated by the distances of the planets from earth, the center of the system, or from the firmament, its outer rim.

Plato's Pythagorean universe was studied, commented upon, and imitated; one of the most popular and long-lived imitations was Cicero's *Somnium Scipionis*, a dream-vision placed at the end of his *De republica* in direct imitation of Plato. For Cicero it is the motion of the spheres that produces the "great and pleasing sound" of the universe. This sound is a concord of "carefully proportioned intervals," there being seven tones in all; these seven planetary tones were equated (by Macrobius and other later commentators) with the seven numbers of Plato's geometric series in the *Timaeus*. Mortal beings, accustomed from birth to the sound of the cosmos, cannot ordinarily hear it; only in a vision, or after death, does its sublime harmony, of which terrestrial music is an imitation, reveal itself.

The core of Pythagorean belief in universal harmony is the music—heard or inaudible—of the celestial elements. But the sublunary world also partook of this harmony: the elements of fire, air, water, and earth; the seasons; the days of the week; the flow of rivers and the tides of the sea; the direction of winds; the growth of plants. These and many other earthly phenomena were viewed as directly related to the heavens, and so governed by the same principles of harmonics or musical mathematics. An elaborate set of these correspondences is given by the late Greek theorist Aristides Quintilianus (Περὶ Μουσικῆς, Book III). Man, the microcosm, shares in this harmony: everything from the gestation period of the human embryo and bodily proportions to the smallest details of human behavior is governed by analogy with, or dependence upon, celestial harmony. Even such apparently prosy dicta as ἀρχὴ δὲ τοι ἥμισμ παντός (freely rendered as "once begun is half done") could be related to the proportion 1:2, to the interval of the octave, to the midpoint of a monochord (see M. Vogler in *Festschrift J. Schmidt-Görg* [1957], pp. 377–82). Where human actions are concerned the line between cosmic harmony and astrology is a fine one; indeed there was no real distinction between the two for ancient writers, although the more vulgar aspects of astrological belief were scorned by serious thinkers.

The third book of Ptolemy's *Harmonics*, devoted to cosmic analogies of all kinds, shows a distinction between ἁρμονία κόσμου and ἁρμονία ψυχῆς; these categories, rendered in the Latin of Boethius' *De musica* (early sixth century) as *musica mundana* and *musica humana*, are joined with the music sung and played by men (*musica instrumentalis*) to form a tripartite division of the science and art of music that was to be canonical for the next thousand years in academic circles. In fact, the place of music in the curriculum, as a part of the *quadrivium* (along with geometry, astronomy, and arithmetic) is really due to the central importance of Pythagorean views of the subject in late antiquity. It should be remembered that academic study of music was primarily the study of harmonics—of tuning systems and of musical arithmetic, the properties of the *numerus sonorus*.

For the Church Fathers Pythagorean beliefs were acceptable as long as biblical parallels could be found for them; and for notions of cosmic harmony there were, as scholars like Philo discovered, plenty of parallels. The second-century Alexandrian philosopher Numenius went so far as to say "For what is Plato, but Moses speaking in Attic Greek?"—words quoted by Clement of Alexandria and other Fathers; and according to Josephus (*Contra Apionem* I, xxii), Pythagoras himself was an admirer and imitator of Jewish beliefs. Acceptance of the literal reality of the music of the spheres varied from writer to writer, but received a great boost when Saint Jerome translated from the Book of Job a passage (38:37) dealing with rainclouds as *concentum coeli quis dormire faciet*, "who can make the harmony of heaven to sleep?" (Douay trans.).

Jerome, in making this translation, drew upon the Greek version of Symmachus, a member of an early Judeo-Christian sect with strong Gnostic tendencies. Pythagorean cosmic ideas as developed by Gnostic writers took on a much more obvious astrological cast, with the planets becoming deities invoked by mystic hymns using music "proper" to each planet. This sort of thing was strongly opposed by orthodox Christian writers, but, as in the case of Jerome's translation, it may occasionally have exerted some influence. Jewish belief in the angelic habitation of the universe, colored by Gnostic angelology and given orthodox standing by the sixth century (when the nine angelic hierarchies of Dionysius the Areopagite became accepted), ultimately led to belief in a *musica coelestis*, angel-music in or above the starry heavens. This form of cosmic harmony persisted even in the later Middle Ages, when Pythagorean thinking was rather discredited because of the scholastic adherence to the anti-Pythagorean Aristotle in all things; and in Dante's *Paradiso* one finds *musica mundana* and *musica coelestis* combined in a blazing vision of light and sound.

In general, Pythagorean ideas were repeated and elaborated whenever currents of Neo-Platonism were strong: in the sixth-century commentaries of Boethius and Cassiodorus; in the ninth-century Carolingian revival (John Scotus Erigena, Regino of Prüm); in the writings of the Chartres school of the twelfth century (Guillaume de Conches, Alain de Lille). Cultivation of Neo-Platonic thought in the medieval Arab world was marked by preoccupation with *musica humana*—the harmonious makeup and workings of the human body—resulting in theories about the curative powers of music that were taken literally enough to cause music to be played as a therapeutic agent in hospitals. The great revival of Neo-Platonism among fifteenth-century humanists led to some imaginative restatements of Pythagorean cosmic belief by such men as Giorgio Anselmi of Parma (*Dialoghi*, 1434) and Marsilio Ficino (in a number of works, but most fully in a commentary on the *Timaeus*), as well as to encyclopedic compilations of everything the ancients said on the subject, the fullest being that of the theorist-composer Franchino Gafori (*Theorica musicae*, 2nd ed. [1492], I, i, "De musica mundana").

Although the literal acceptance of the Pythagorean cosmos in the early Renaissance was tempered with a certain sophisticated skepticism in the sixteenth century, enthusiastic restatements of the old beliefs continued to appear; a work like Pontus de Tyard's *Solitaire second* (1555) contained a 200-page exposition of *musique mondaine & musique humaine*. Universal harmony was described in poetry: Italian, French, and especially English. And it was depicted in fêtes and *intermedi;* Leonardo da Vinci designed the planetary sets and celestial mechanism for a *Festa del Paradiso* given at Milan in 1490. No music for this survives; but a score showing how a Renaissance musician thought of cosmic harmony does exist for a tableau staged as part of the festivities at a Medici wedding in Florence in 1589. This tableau, designed by Giovanni de' Bardi, was called "*L'Armonia delle sfere*," and contemporary accounts make it clear that Bardi was trying to depict on the stage Plato's Myth of Er.

Other aspects of Renaissance culture were touched by Pythagorean doctrine. The use of "harmonious"

proportions in architecture, perhaps practiced in antiquity, was revived in the building of the Gothic cathedrals, and became a preoccupation with architects from the time of Alberti (mid-fifteenth century). The Venetian monk Francesco di Giorgio, author of an enormous, relentlessly Pythagorean treatise called *De harmonia totius mundi* (1525), wrote a memorandum recommending the use of the *Timaeus* series in the building of a church. A generation later, when Andrea Palladio completed the facade of this church (S. Francesco della Vigna), he used a scheme of 27 *moduli*, thus Plato's outer limit, for its width.

Pythagorean ideas seem to have a less vivid appeal after the Renaissance. But before retreating, driven by seventeenth-century rationalism into poetic metaphor, the Platonic-Pythagorean cosmos received a splendid, consummatory restatement in Kepler's *Harmonices mundi* (1619), which Kepler himself describes as a work picking up where Ptolemy left off. It separates the Copernican spheres by intervals defined by the five regular solids of Greek geometry, and finds harmonic proportions expressible in musical terms—a seventeenth-century chordal complex rather than a Greek scale—in the relationships between the movements of planets and their respective medium distances from the sun. Kepler, like Ptolemy, includes a whole treatise on musical theory to lay the groundwork for his theories of cosmic harmony.

In the *Utriusque cosmi* (1617) of Robert Fludd, contemporary and archenemy of Kepler, the Ptolemaic system is still the basis for an elaboration, lengthy and formless, of Pythagorean ideas. In seventeenth-century Italy Mario Bettini (*Apiaria*, 1641–42) and Giambattista Riccioli (*Almagestum novum*, 1651) presented traditional Pythagorean cosmologies with Keplerian refinements tacked on. Polymaths such as Marin Mersenne in France (*Harmonie universelle*, 1636) and the German Jesuit Athanasius Kircher (*Musurgia universalis*, 1650) continued the process of summarizing, and in a way bringing up to date, Pythagorean lore.

Elements of Pythagorean thought have persisted among philosophers, mathematicians, and astronomers. Leibniz, for example, was fond of Pythagorean imagery (see R. Haase, "Leibniz und die pythagoreisch-harmonikale Tradition," *Antaios*, 4 [1962], 368–76), and his doctrine of "pre-established harmony" might be seen as a new version of *musica mundana/humana*. In the nineteenth century Platonic cosmology was much studied, especially by German scholars; and philosophers like Schopenhauer took up the old images of world harmony once more. One of the most interesting of nineteenth-century cosmological studies is A. von Thimus' *Die harmonikale Symbolik des Alterthums*

(1868–76), in which the presence of esoteric numerological lore is traced in the records of ancient cultures around the world.

The establishment by the German astronomer J. E. Bode (1747–1826) of a simple arithmetic series to represent planetary distances from the sun, and the later inclusion of the newly-discovered planet Neptune in the series (see Duhem, *Système*, II, 15–17) carried forward Keplerian ideas of stellar harmony; in the twentieth century a new system of harmoniously proportionate planetary distances was worked out by the cosmologist Wilhelm Kaiser (*Geometrischen Vorstellungen in der Astronomie, Kosmos und Menschenwesen*, 1930), while at the microscopic level V. Goldschmidt has found the proportions of the musical scale in the relative dimensions of crystals (*Ueber Harmonie und Complication*, 1931). The cosmos of the *Timaeus* has found twentieth-century admirers such as Sir Arthur Eddington and A. N. Whitehead; and one can call twentieth-century scholars like Hans Kayser (*Lehrbuch der Harmonik*, 1950) genuine Neo-Pythagoreans, in that their aim is to reinterpret and to reestablish, with the support of modern scientific knowledge, the basic Pythagorean concepts of world harmony.

*BIBLIOGRAPHY*

Still of fundamental importance is the first modern investigation of the subject, A. Boeckh, "Über die Bildung der Weltseele im Timaeos des Platon," *Gesammelte kleine Schriften* (Leipzig, 1866), III, 109–80. See also: R. S. Brumbaugh, *Plato's Mathematical Imagination* (Bloomington, Ind., 1954); F. M. Cornford, *Plato's Cosmology* (New York, 1937); R. Crocker, "Pythagorean Mathematics and Music," *Journal of Aesthetics and Art Criticism*, **22** (1963), 189–98, 325–35; P. Duhem, *Le système du monde. Histoire des doctrines cosmologiques de Platon à Copernic*, 10 vols. (Paris, 1913–59); E. Frank, *Plato und die sogenannten Pythagoreer* (Halle, 1923); M. Ghyka, *Le nombre d'or. Rites et rythmes pythagoriciens dans le développement de la civilisation occidentale* (Paris, 1932); R. Hammerstein, *Die Musik der Engel* (Bern, 1962); J. Handschin, *Der Toncharakter* (Zurich, 1948); J. Hutton, "Some English Poems in Praise of Music," *English Miscellany*, ed. M. Praz (Rome, 1951), II, 1–63; H. Kayser, *Lehrbuch der Harmonik* (Zurich, 1950); L. Spitzer, "Classical and Christian Ideas of World Harmony: Prolegomena to an Interpretation of the Word 'Stimmung,'" *Traditio*, **2** (1944), 409–64; **3** (1945), 307–64.

JAMES HAAR

[See also **Cosmic Images;** Cosmology; **Harmony or Rapture; Macrocosm and Microcosm;** Neo-Platonism; **Pythagorean Doctrines.**]

# RAMISM

THE TERM "Ramism" is used to designate the intellectual trends, in part philosophical and in part pedagogical, associated with the work of Pierre de la Ramée, better known as Petrus Ramus, or Peter Ramus (1515–72). Ramism was a mixture of scholasticism and humanism which spread in the sixteenth and seventeenth centuries through northern Europe and the British colonies in North America. Avowedly anti-Aristotelian, it drives toward simplification of all knowledge through a kind of noetic bookeeping, anti-iconographic and diagrammatic in form, implemented by the new art of typography. Its confident rationalism allies Ramism with the Cartesianism and *Encyclopédisme* which followed it.

*1. Ramus' Career.* Ramus was a polymath at the University of Paris, where he came as a boy from his native Picard village of Cuts (Oise), and where he received his master of arts degree, taught, became principal of the Collège de Presles, and in 1551 was named Regius Professor of Eloquence and Philosophy. Around 1562 he embraced the Protestant Reformation. Following a sojourn in Germany and Switzerland in 1568–70, he returned to the University of Paris, where he was murdered August 26, 1572, in the third day of the St. Bartholomew's Massacre.

Ramus was widely erudite, patient in working through difficult subjects, and seriously committed to the intellectual life and even more to educational reform, though his original contributions to knowledge were slight. His published works range over dialectic (logic), rhetoric, grammar (Latin, Greek, and even French), Aristotelian physics and metaphysics (both of which he ridicules), arithmetic, algebra, and geometry, and include also a few Latin translations from the Greek, classical commentaries, some of which bear on legal and military science, as well as academic orations and prefaces and remonstrances and letters, and a posthumously published systematization of Christian doctrine. His works add up to around sixty titles and those of his academic associate and lieutenant Omer Talon or Audomarus Talaeus (ca. 1510–62) to some thirteen more. Talon did the initial work on the Ramist reform of rhetoric, under Ramus' supervision. Nearly 800 extant editions of works of the two men have been identified—or, if the various works in collected editions are counted separately, over 1100, of which some 450 are editions of the works on logic and rhetoric.

*2. Ramus' Significance.* Ramus' significance and influence hinge on his reorganization of dialectic or logic, to which a reorganization of rhetoric was tied. Ramus had been educated at the University of Paris at a time when the highly formalized, scientific logic of the Middle Ages was falling into desuetude, in great part because of the attraction of the *studia humanitatis*, the studies centered on the human "lifeworld," rather than on exact science, which lie at the center of the Renaissance. Logic (or dialectic—the terms were for the most part synonymous, though careful thinkers could distinguish them, as explained below) should be something close to common sense, accessible to all, not a skill for specialists. This attitude was common throughout the humanist tradition and is found in Rudolph Agricola (Roelof Huusman, 1444–85), with whose work to a degree Ramus' work connects.

Ramus' logic rejects the works in the Aristotelian *Organon*, substituting as an approach to his subject Agricola's Ciceronian division of dialectic into invention (*inventio*) and judgment (*iudicium*), and using this division as a means of annexing some areas of instruction previously assigned to rhetoric. The classic Ciceronian rhetoric had been divided into five "parts": invention (*inventio*, discovery of "arguments"), judgment or arrangement (*iudicium* or *dispositio*, assemblage or composition of the material discovered), style (*elocutio*), memory (*memoria*), and delivery (*pronuntiatio*). Maintaining that rhetorical invention and composition were needless duplications, Ramus excised these "parts" from his (and Talon's) treatment of rhetoric, relegating them to dialectic only. He also dropped memory from rhetoric, giving as his reason that if one followed the "natural" or methodical order demanded by logic in the development of thought, memory was hardly a problem. This left rhetoric with style and delivery. Style meant the use of tropes and figures and became in effect the whole of rhetoric, for delivery was given only token treatment. Since delivery meant oral presentation, it was in fact losing relevance in a world more addicted to writing than Cicero's world had been and recently coming under the sway of print, although this quite real reason for the atrophy of delivery, and the liquidation of memory, was seldom if ever adverted to.

Some earlier thinkers had distinguished various logics in terms of degrees of logical necessity in their procedures. Scientific logic, such as that in mathematics, proceeded to necessary or inevitable conclusions. Other kinds of logic dealt rather with probabilities: dialectic was concerned with arguing for the more probable of two opposed positions, as in a formal debate; rhetoric was concerned with argumentation probable enough to conduce to action; poetry was concerned with verisimilitude. As a kind of sub-probability or reverse probability at the bottom of this scale lay sophistry, concerned with specious argumentation, falsehood proposed as truth. Ramus jettisoned all such attention to probabilities and, assigning the discovery of all arguments and their arrangement to the one sole "art" which he styled indifferently dialectic or logic, maintained adamantly that logic was logic, the same in poetry as in mathematics.

The new Ramist arrangement made up in forthrightness and simplicity for what it lacked in accuracy and suppleness, and this gave it its appeal. Once dialectic or logic was divided into invention and judgment, each of these was itself subdivided into two parts. Invention thus split into invention of "artificial" arguments (intrinsic or analytic arguments such as causes and effects, subjects, adjuncts, disparates, contraries, etc.) and invention of "inartificial" arguments (extrinsic arguments, such as testimony, less cogent than the artificial). These "parts" or headings are basically the *loci* or *topoi* (topics or "places" or commonplaces) treated by Aristotle in his *Topics* and *Rhetoric*, by Boethius, and by countless others. They constitute "seats" (*sedes*) or areas—"headings" they could be styled today—where one might find arguments to prove a point. Judgment or arrangement was likewise dichotomized into axiomatic judgment (enunciations) and dianoetic judgment (reasoning processes).

Each of these subdivisions was further divided, always into two parts, and the resulting subdivisions again dichotomized and subdichotomized until all possibility of further division was exhausted. The bipartite division employed here was itself accounted for in Ramist dialectic: it was, in fact, "method," one of the two types of reasoning processes, of which the other was syllogism. Syllogism handled shorter structures of thought, method all longer structures, whether scientific treatises (including those on dialectic itself), classroom teaching, orations (including sermons), letters, narrations, and poetry. Method in any and all subjects or genres ideally moved always from the general to the "particular." Deviations from method, proceeding from the particular to the general ("cryptic" method), were advisable or tolerable only when the audience was recalcitrant or ignorant or otherwise ill-prepared.

Although Aristotle, Galen, and others had discussed *methodos* in senses more or less related to the modern term "method," the textbook association of method and logic which Descartes learned in school and transmitted to subsequent generations of thinkers is traceable directly to Ramus and his contemporaries Johann Sturm and Philipp Melanchthon. Between the years 1543 and 1547 all three introduced sections on method into their textbooks on dialectic or logic. (Melanchthon had done a bit with method slightly earlier.)

Ramist method differed from Sturm's and Melanchthon's most effectively in its attractive diagrammatic simplicity. From classical antiquity, in academic tradition the oration or public address had served as the chief paradigm for all prose composition, often even for letter-writing. Ramist method provided as an alternative to this old oral organization of thought and expression a design more adapted to print (and to writing, too, although until print, writing had failed to modify many of the basically oral structures of primitive human culture). The typical product of Ramist method would be the modern encyclopedia article.

All the curriculum subjects, not merely dialectic or logic, could be methodized and were, if not by Ramus then by his followers. Indeed, to the Ramist mind, classroom teaching, which was both highly analytic and polemically colored, thus became somehow the paradigm for all thought and expression. By extension, the entire universe of learning and indeed the entire physical universe, which the arts mirror or picture, becomes susceptible of neat diagrammatic analysis in dichotomized outline form. In his edition of some of Ramus' works entitled *Professio regia* (1576), Ramus' disciple Johann Thomas Freige (Freigius) so analyzes Cicero's career—the first dichotomy is life/death (*vita/mors*)—and another disciple, Theodor Zwinger the Elder (1533–88), in his *Methodus apodemica* (1577) produces a dichotomized logical analysis of the Verrocchio equestrian statue of Bartolommeo Colleoni in Venice (diagrammed in terms of intrinsic causes and extrinsic causes, and so on).

The impetus to diagrammatic treatment of this sort is of course old. Diagrams such as the Tree of Porphyry can be found in the pretypographical manuscript tradition. But elaborate outlines of the sort that spread through thousands of pages of Ramist-inspired works on all subjects are extremely difficult to reproduce accurately in manuscript. On a printing press they were no more difficult to run than were pages of ordinary text. Hence it is understandable that after the development of typography they flood the world of learning. Insofar as its model of knowledge and of actuality is one which is eminently adaptable to print, Ramism is thus a post-Gutenberg phenomenon.

Ramist method is also a memory system of a special sort. Before print made massive indexing feasible by locking words into exactly the same places in thousands of copies of a given book, even in cultures with writing, knowledge had to be organized to implement mnemonic recall, and heavily symbolic or allegorical figures such as Athena and her owl, Zeus and his thunderbolts, Mercury and his wand and winged sandals, are noetically functional as well as aesthetically pleasing. From the remotest antiquity through the Renaissance, knowledge was commonly stored for recall by being associated with such mythological or otherwise iconographic figures, which, in various

memory systems, running from Cicero to Giordano Bruno, are deployed in the imagination in set spatial patterns to expedite retrieval of the knowledge associated with them. Ramism adapts this tradition. It retains the practice of deploying material in spatial patterns to expedite recall, but eliminates all iconography, substituting for statues of Athena, Zeus, and the like mere printed words connected to one another by lines in an extremely simple binary pattern forming the dichotomized Ramist charts of "methodized" noetic material. These correspond exactly to the "flow charts" with which a computer is programmed today. This Ramist substitution of lettered words for iconographic figures Frances Yates styles "inner iconoclasm" (p. 235).

From another point of view, the Ramist dichotomized charts and the mode of thought which bred them show connections with the medieval logic which Ramists and humanists generally in principle detested. It is now known that by comparison with Aristotelian logic medieval logic was highly quantified in very advanced ways. The quantifying heritage finds a new but bizarre outlet in the Ramist charting of knowledge, now under the encouragement of print, which removed words more than ever from their natural habitat in the oral world and made them maneuverable items in space.

*3. Range of Ramus' Influence.* Ramism penetrated chiefly Germany, the British Isles, Switzerland and Alsace, France, the Low Countries, and to some degree Scandinavia, as well as the British Colonies in North America, particularly New England. In all these places it tended to be most favored where Calvinism was favored, not so much because of Ramus' late-espoused Protestantism as because of the temper of his thought, which admirably suited the rising bourgeoisie from which Calvinism drew so many of its recruits. The noniconographic and neat structures which Ramism imposed on knowledge appealed to those who liked to keep account books straight and who also hated all "idols." In New England, Ramist modes of organizing and expounding knowledge are evident in Increase Mather, Cotton Mather, Samuel Johnson, John Eliot (who translated Ramus' *Dialectic* into Algonquian), and others. Significantly, Ramism exercised its greatest appeal at the pre-university level of education, although it left its often unacknowledged mark on many a university mind.

*4. Effects of Ramism.* Ramism affected virtually all knowledge with the possible exception of medicine, which vigorously resisted Ramus' anti-Aristotelianism. Making a great deal of clarity and distinctness and of analysis of all sorts—the term "logical analysis" was recognized in the sixteenth century as a characteristically Ramist term—Ramism considered branches of knowledge to be totally separated from one another in themselves, however united in use. In the lower curriculum ranges it encouraged schematization of Latin and Greek grammar—and often of vernacular grammar, even though this was not taught in school. Because it placed a high premium on logic, regardless of what kind of expression was involved, Ramism discouraged ornateness of expression and encouraged a "plain style." This was not the "low style" of classical and medieval rhetoric but rather an expository mode of expression, highly cerebral and analytic, developed out of habits of composing in or while writing (instead of using writing to "put down" what was orally composed), quite impossible in an oral culture, a style of the sort which Thomas Sprat reports the Royal Society encouraged in the immediately post-Ramist age of the late seventeenth century, as near "mathematical" expression as possible.

In philosophy Ramism encouraged a systematization which went far beyond medieval achievements or even ambitions. It encouraged a corresponding systematization in theology, where Johannes Piscator (1546–1625) undertook to do a logical analysis of every book of the Bible, clearly separating what it really "argued" from the rhetorical finery with which its logical machinery was purportedly draped.

The main thrust of Ramus' reform of learning was not toward what later became modern science. That is, it was not toward experimental observation conjoined with the application of mathematics to physics. Ramus' reform drove toward simplified analytic order in presentation of subject matter and toward an empiricism in teaching methods which skirted abstruse details. However, the practical drive which produced Ramist simplification and empiricism did also open new intellectual horizons. It encouraged giving studious attention to matters previously regarded as beneath formal academic concern. Ramus himself, although he took for granted with virtually all his contemporaries that Latin would remain the dominant language of the intellectual world, was interested also in the vernacular and published a French grammar in reformed spelling. Close, if sometimes ambiguous, connections exist between Ramism and the manual arts and crafts of the bourgeois world where Ramism had so much appeal. At a deeper level, the Ramist tendency to dissociate thought from the human context of discourse and make it into a kind of thing—a tendency derivative from but not entirely continuous with the quantification in medieval logic—favored the growing tendency to view the universe as basically an aggregate of neutral objects rather than as something vaguely animistic.

Ramus' work belongs in part to the enlarging world of humanism. Renaissance humanism extended aca-demic interest to new areas and fostered a juncture of academic learning and artisan know-how, as can be seen in the development of printing. But Ramism did not share equally all humanist enthusiasms. The imaginative interest in the human which marked much in the Renaissance and which eventually helped generate the modern fields of cultural history, sociology, anthropology, and psychology, and much else, is weak in the Ramist milieu. The resonances of human life were not congenial to this anti-iconographic, diagrammatic, encyclopedic cast of mind, which produced singularly few poets.

Ramus himself engaged in endless controversies, at least seven of which broke into printed exchanges, sometimes running over several years. His followers were equally contentious, and out of the learned world of the sixteenth and seventeenth centuries some 500 persons have been listed as Ramists, anti-Ramists, and semi-Ramists or syncretists, who undertook to harmonize Ramist and Aristotelian or other competing logics.

*BIBLIOGRAPHY*

The most extensive treatment of Ramus and Ramism is to be found in Walter J. Ong, *Ramus, Method, and the Decay of Dialogue* (Cambridge, Mass., 1958), which contains an exhaustive bibliography. The same author's *Ramus and Talon Inventory* (Cambridge, Mass., 1958) locates in quantity copies of editions of these authors' works, catalogues the Ramist controversies, and gives a list of hundreds of Ramists, anti-Ramists, and semi-Ramists or syncretists; this work is being enlarged by the author to include new discoveries. I. M. Bochenski, *A History of Formal Logic* (Notre Dame, Ind., 1961), and Wilhelm Risse, *Die Logik der Neuzeit*, Vol. I, (Stuttgart, 1964), situate Ramus' logic in the history of the science. *The Art of Memory*, by Frances A. Yates (Chicago, 1966), places Ramism in the history of mnemonics and discusses the Bruno-Dicson-Perkins dispute omitted by Ong from his catalogue of Ramist controversies. R. Hooykaas, *Humanisme, science, et réforme: Pierre de la Ramée* (Leiden, 1958), treats Ramus and the artisan-technology world. W. S. Howell's *Logic and Rhetoric in England, 1500–1700* (Princeton, 1956) situates Ramus' work in one of the major national traditions. The history of method is discussed in Neal W. Gilbert, *Renaissance Concepts of Method* (New York, 1960). *Petrus Ramus en de Wiskunde*, by J. J. Verdonk (Assen, 1966), exhaustively studies Ramus' place in the history of mathematics. See also Ong, "Peter Ramus and the Naming of Methodism," *Journal of the History of Ideas*, **14** (1953), 235–48; idem, "Ramist Classroom Procedure and the Nature of Reality," *Studies in English Literature*, **1** (1961), 31–47; and idem, "Ramist Method and the Commercial Mind," *Studies in the Renaissance*, **8** (1961), 155–72.

WALTER JACKSON ONG

[See also Iconography; Necessity; **Platonism; Renaissance Humanism; Rhetoric.**]

## RATIONALITY AMONG THE GREEKS AND ROMANS

WHEN E. R. Dodds chose to entitle his 1949 Sather Lectures "The Greeks and the Irrational," his intention was doubtless to present a paradox. For the Greeks are generally taken to be the discoverers of rationality, or at least to have made the first giant steps on the path of rational inquiry into the nature of the universe and the good life for man. Some such generalization as this is certainly acceptable. But it is not easy to pick out and describe those qualities exhibited by extant Greek writers which entitle them to be called "rational," without being vague and trivial. And there is no single equivalent in Greek for "rationality" such that one could examine its uses and leave it at that; the word *logos* comes near it, but it covers a wider range of meanings. It seems best therefore to concentrate on certain definite topics which fall within the field, in the knowledge that other quite different articles might be written under the same heading.

Section I describes some of the stages of the development from myth to rationality. The criterion that has been kept in mind to distinguish rationality is the presence of reasoned argument for preferring one alternative to others. Section II reviews the theories of Greek and Roman moralists who, in some way or other, teach that to be virtuous is to be rational. Section III discusses theories that find rationality in the cosmos and in the workings of nature.

There is little space, and the author lacks the competence, to include other topics which might well find a place under his heading, such as the origin and development of logic, the various manifestations of irrationalism in the Greco-Roman world, such as magic and astrology, and the "rationalism" of classical Greek art and architecture.

### I. FROM MYTH TO REASON

The earliest surviving Greek literature is in the realm of myth, in which rationality is not much to be expected. Even here, however, it has often and correctly been observed that Greek myth, as compared with that of other nations, contains a striking degree of rationality. For example, the powers of the gods in the Homeric poems, though supernatural, are nevertheless distributed according to a pattern in which reason can be seen. The cosmogonical myths, too, in Homer and Hesiod are not so extravagantly inconsistent and fantastic as some of the myths of the Near East. It is noteworthy that Hesiod's *Theogony* includes among the lists of gods several personifications of concepts drawn from human society—Wisdom, Right, Lawfulness, Justice, Peace.

This may help to explain why it was that the Greeks, rather than other nations, were the first to put forward theories about the natural world which could be criticized on rational criteria. The Milesians (Thales, Anaximander, and Anaximenes) in the sixth century B.C. explained the origin of the world, not by the mating of powerful divinities, but as a natural process of growth from a simple substance to a complex form. They explained the relationship of the constituent parts of the world by using analogies drawn from men's social experience (such as justice or war), or arts and crafts, in such a way that reasons could be offered for preferring one theory to another. The Milesians did not explain what the difference was between their theories and the stories about the natural world told in the myths; but it is clear that they operated with an idea of rationality which was well advanced, even if not explicitly formulated.

Towards the end of the sixth century, a significant step forward was taken by Xenophanes of Colophon, who criticized the theology of the Homeric poems and Hesiod. The surviving fragments give his criticisms and assertions without the reasoning. "Homer and Hesiod attribute all things to the gods that among men are a shame and a disgrace" (frag. 11). "God is one, greatest among gods and among men, in no way like men in form and thought" (frag. 23). "Always he remains in the same [place], moving not at all, nor is it fitting for him to move, now here, now there" (frag. 26). "If oxen and horses and lions had hands or could paint and make things with their hands like men, then they would paint the forms of gods and make their bodies each according to their own shapes, horses like horses, oxen like oxen" (frag. 15). The basis of his criticism appears to have been that he saw an inconsistency between the concept of god as something different from man, and the stories told about the gods, which made them behave as men do.

Contemporary with Xenophanes, Pythagoras moved in a new direction to explain the phenomenal world in terms of a rational structure behind appearances. "Things are numbers." It is notoriously hard to know what was the precise meaning and range of the theory propounded by the founder of the Pythagorean school; but he certainly began the way of thought later followed by Plato and all mathematical physicists in seeking for a rational system, expressible in mathematical concepts, which would unify the multifarious changing appearances presented to the senses. In the earliest form of this theory, it seems that there was a demand for extreme simplicity: the whole world was to be explained without using more than the first few integers in the number series. It was a piece of bravado typical of the pre-Socratics to claim that such a vast and complex object as the cosmos itself could be reduced to the simplest elements in this way, and so could be understood by the human mind. It was Pythagoras, according to one tradition, who used the word *cosmos* for the world for the first time, as part of his claim that there is an orderly pattern in the world which can be understood and expressed.

In this early period of Greek philosophy, the idea began to emerge that there is an order, a reasonableness, in the natural world, which somehow corresponds with the human mind. Perhaps the idea was formulated as early as Anaximenes of Miletus, who identified the stuff of which the world is made with the human *psyche*, saying that both are air. It appears unmistakably in the work of Heraclitus (ca. 500 B.C.), who professed to be the mouthpiece of the Logos according to which all things come to pass (frag. 1).

The earliest fully conscious plea for consistency in philosophical theory (or at least, the earliest that has survived) is the poem of Parmenides of Elea, "On Nature" (Περὶ Φύσεως; first half of the fifth century). One of the striking peculiarities of this work is its mixture of myth and reason. The content is presented as a revelation that was granted to Parmenides by an unnamed goddess. But at the same time it is a closely reasoned argument, and the goddess says "judge by reason (*logos*) the hard hitting criticism that I have spoken" (frag. 7.5). The criticism is aimed at earlier theories, such as those of the Milesians and Heraclitus, which asserted of things that they "are and are not." Parmenides shows clearly a characteristic that is deeply rooted in Greek thought: the desire that the words used to describe the world shall pick out with absolute and inviolable clarity the objects they are intended to identify. A statement about something in the world should state what is the case in such a way that its truth is not affected by circumstances like change of time or change of the place of observation or change in the observer. Parmenides carried this demand so far that he denied the reality of the changing world. To say that something "is not" is to say nothing about it, or rather it is to talk about nothing; and such talk is nonsensical. Hence one can only say "it is." But all descriptions of change must necessarily say that something (the state of affairs before the change) "is not," and hence they all contain this element of nonsense: "So coming to be is extinguished, and destruction is unintelligible" (frag. 8.21). He went on to make a sharp distinction between "the way of truth," which says only that "it *is*, and cannot not be . . . one, continuous," and the "way of seeming," a deceitful way, in which there is plurality and variation. It is a distinction very similar in its intention to Plato's distinction between

the Forms, perfect, unchanging, and intelligible, and the "unreal" phenomena of the sensible world.

Parmenides was thus led by the exigencies of his reasoning to reject the evidence of the senses completely. According to Plato (*Parmenides* 128d), some made fun of the argument "by showing that it led to many absurdities and contradictions"; Parmenides' pupil, Zeno, then came to the help of his master with arguments to show that the opponents' supposition that there is plurality leads to even more absurd consequences. According to this view of them (which is likely to be historically correct), Zeno's paradoxes had as their aim a *reductio ad absurdum* of the proposition that there are many things in existence. The paradoxes themselves, e.g., Achilles and the tortoise, the flight of an arrow, etc., and other *reductio ad absurdum* illustrations of change and diversity, are too well known to need description. They are typical of Eleatic philosophy as a whole, which succeeded in issuing a great intellectual challenge to all who wanted to philosophize about the nature of the world. The Eleatics showed that concepts must be examined with a new rigor, and inferences must be free from contradictions.

It has sometimes been asserted that the work of the philosophers of Elea shows the influence of mathematicians, in that the structure of their arguments is similar to that of mathematics, especially of geometry. However, the state of mathematics in the fifth century is very obscure. Some believe that by the middle of the century (approximately when Zeno was writing), there already existed a system of geometry in which theorems were deduced from a few postulates and axioms, by means of a few explicit rules of inference. Others claim that the first "Elements" must be put much nearer the date of Euclid (ca. 300 B.C.). It seems reasonable to say that to explain the characteristics of Eleatic philosophy by assuming a connection with mathematical reasoning is to explain *ignotum per ignotius*.

However this may be, the Eleatics, in the earlier half of the fifth century, adopted in its strongest form a position that was responsible for both the strengths and the weaknesses of Greek philosophy; they were confident that by reasoning or "pure thought" one might be entitled in theory to ignore and reject the evidence of sense perception.

We must now look at the growth of consciousness about method in fields of Greek thought other than philosophy.

Two of the medical writings attributed to Hippocrates, generally thought to belong to the late fifth century, are particularly interesting for their recommendations about method. *Airs, Waters, Places* begins: "Whoever wishes to pursue properly the science of medicine must proceed thus." The recommendation is to take careful note of the effects of geographical conditions and climate upon health. The statement of these effects is highly dogmatic; but the work shows clearly a remarkable interest in comparative observations of different peoples, and a desire to do better than rely on traditional lore and crude trial and error. The doctor, says the author, must have a rational theory of health, as affected by environment. *The Sacred Disease* is well known for its insistence on natural causes of the disease in question, and its rejection of superstitious ideas about its origin and attempts to cure it by "purifications and incantations."

Sometimes it has been said that there is a striking difference between the kind of reasoning employed by the Hippocratic doctors and that of the early Greek philosophers (a particularly notable expression of this view is F. M. Cornford's *Principium sapientiae*). The philosophers, it is said, demonstrated a ruthless indifference to empirical evidence, and were prepared to generalize extraordinarily widely on the basis of one or two observations or ideas. The doctors, on the other hand, resisted such all-embracing theories and recognized the need for detailed observation and even experiment. The Hippocratic treatise *On Ancient Medicine* begins with a denunciation of those who base all their work on a "hypothesis"—"heat, cold, moisture, dryness, or anything else that they may fancy"—ignoring the professional discoveries and records of earlier practitioners. However, this is a difference that should not be overstated. The medical writers denounced the "hypotheses" of the philosophers, but could not free themselves from other, equally sweeping and uncontrolled, generalizations. Scientific research into anatomy, physiology and pathology, controlled by systematic observation, began rather later, with Aristotle and his successors, and the medical writers of the Hellenistic period, e.g., Erasistratus (third century B.C.).

The second half of the fifth century saw the beginning of historiography, and the advance from straightforward storytelling to a reasoned analysis of events was dramatically swift. The beginnings of a critical approach can already be seen in Herodotus, who wrote: "I must tell what is told me, but I need not believe it entirely" (7, 152). He does indeed include some wildly improbable stories in his history, especially about the more remote regions of the earth; but he often sounds a note of rational skepticism about what he has been told. He can sometimes, although not always, make allowances for a biased source. Thucydides, by contrast, frames his story largely to bring out his own analysis of cause and effect, and of the motives—often the hidden motives—of the participants. The idea of applying reason to the explanation of the conduct of peoples and their leaders is fully developed in Thucydides.

It is clear that in the second half of the fifth century the audience for whom the Greek writers wrote became accustomed, very rapidly, to new standards of rationality in all fields of human creativity. Traditions once taken on trust were now questioned and criticized. The organization of society and even its religious institutions became subjects for debate. In Athens at least, it appears that arguing became a favorite pastime, and the subject matter might be anything under the sun.

There is no point in seeking for a simple explanation of this phenomenon; all that can be done is to mention some of its manifestations. One was the Sophistic movement. The Sophists, that is, Protagoras, Hippias, Prodicus, Antiphon, Thrasymachus, and others less famous, found that they could earn a living by teaching young men various subjects, especially the art of public speaking. There had previously been no organized higher education, and the Sophists found a ready market. The young men responded with alacrity to the invitation to join in questioning traditional beliefs and customs. The Sophists came from many parts of the Greek world and were widely travelled; their pupils learnt that the way of life in their own city-state was not the only one possible. The fact that there were wide differences in morality among different societies suggested that all moral rules might be questioned and criticized—and rejected if they could not be rationally defended. The literature of the period contains many references to the distinction between nature and custom: some Sophists claimed that the only universally applicable moral rules were those imposed by nature; all others were "merely" a matter of conventional agreement.

Naturally such a widespread questioning of tradition aroused opposition. Aristophanes' *Clouds* is a comic poet's version of the conflict. The pupil of the Sophist (Aristophanes uses Socrates as the representative of the Sophists, ignoring certain essential differences) learns that not Zeus but "Vortex" is the ruler of the world, he learns to reject the convention of filial obedience, and he learns to use argument with skillful dexterity to get what he wants. Much more seriously, there were several trials in Athens for "impiety," the most famous of course being those of Protagoras, Anaxagoras, and Socrates. The charge against Socrates, according to Plato's *Apology*, was that he was "guilty of corrupting the youth, and of believing not in the gods whom the state believes in but in other new divinities." What lay behind this charge, according to Plato, was the resentment caused by Socrates' questioning of the traditional sources of morality, and his encouragement of his young listeners to do the same.

The literature of the period in which the Sophistic movement arose (or at least, Athenian literature) shows one outstanding characteristic: an extraordinary taste for and skill in argument. The Sophists themselves taught the technique of arguing both sides of a question, as a method of imparting skill in speaking. The common occurrence of two-sided debates in Greek tragedy, especially in Euripides, shows the popularity of this kind of contest. The surviving law court speeches are of course only a small proportion of the speeches composed during this time; Athens suffered from litigation as from some endemic disease. What is to be noticed in the surviving speeches is an emphasis on rational argument, on what is "probable" or "reasonable" (*eulogon*), as opposed to irrational methods of persuasion, such as swearing oaths or offering one's slaves to be questioned on the rack.

## II. RATIONALITY AS AN ETHICAL NORM

"Socrates," Aristotle wrote, "believed all the virtues to be forms of knowledge, so that to know justice entails being just; for once we have learnt geometry and architecture we are geometers and architects" (*Eudemian Ethics*, Book 1, Ch. 5, 1216b 7). That this was truly a belief of Socrates is confirmed by the portrait of him given in Plato's earlier dialogues. It is far from clear, however, how the paradox is to be interpreted. What kind of knowledge is virtue? The analogy with the arts and crafts suggested by Aristotle and often used by the Platonic Socrates suggests some kind of skill derived from practice and instruction. But the Socratic method illustrated by Plato's dialogues was rather a search for definitions, conducted as a rule between two people, by question and answer. Socrates encouraged his listeners to ask and try to answer such questions as "What is piety?" (*Euthyphro*), "What is courage?" (*Laches*). The implication is that if one could give a satisfactory answer, then he would have the corresponding virtue. "No man willingly, does wrong." That is to say, if a man knows what is the right and virtuous thing to do in given circumstances, he will do it; failures are due to some kind of ignorance.

The most important feature, perhaps, of Socrates' belief was that it led to searching inquiries into ethical concepts and the relations between them, inquiries that had consistency as their first demand. Socrates in the Platonic dialogues is often engaged in showing one of his interlocutors that some proposition advanced by him is inconsistent with something else that he wants to assert, or with something that has already been agreed. A set of propositions about what the virtues are which was free of such inconsistencies would apparently constitute the knowledge that makes a man virtuous.

Plato's elaborate structure upon this Socratic foundation is set out in the *Republic*. The ideal state is described as wholly devoted to instilling knowledge into those who will be rulers of the state, and to making sure that they will always be in a position to bring their knowledge to bear on the life of the community. The objects of their knowledge form a far more integrated structure than Socrates envisaged, and the method of acquiring it was to be a long and single-minded educational process far different from the casual conversation of Socrates and his friends. The proposals of the *Republic* are accompanied by an analysis of the human *psyche* into three parts: the intellect, the spirited part, and the appetite. Goodness of character consists in the subordination of the two "lower" parts to the intellect, just as the virtue of the state consists in the subordination of the two lower classes of citizens, the armed forces and the producers, to the philosophic rulers. The object of the knowledge thus enthroned, both in the individual and in the state, is nothing in the sensible world: it is the eternal Forms of Plato's theory, "the Good itself," "Beauty itself," accessible only to the eye of reason after a long training in mathematics and dialectic.

Aristotle differed considerably from Plato in his view of the place of reason in ethics. He made a distinction between theoretical reason and practical reason. It was a mistake, he thought, to expect in ethics the same kind of precision that is required in the subjects studied by the theoretical sciences. Ethics deals with individual cases. Universal propositions are of course possible, and necessary, but their application to human behavior will never be direct and simple. The man of practical wisdom is one who has much experience of human affairs, and has learnt how to act both by studying the precepts and examples of others and by having acted himself.

In spite of this distinction between the theoretical intellect and practical thought, Aristotle returns in the end to an almost Platonic evaluation of the life of pure thought. It turns out that although moral goodness is not dependent on theoretical knowledge, yet the best life for man is the life of "theory" or contemplation. This is because such a life is the most godlike. The characteristic virtue of man, according to this line of thought, is the functioning of the highest part of the soul; plants have only a nutritive and reproductive soul, animals have this and a sensitive soul in addition, and only men (and gods) have souls which are also capable of reasoning. Reason is therefore the highest of men's faculties, and the exercise of reason is the best life for a man.

Rationality as a virtue was emphasized most of all by the Stoic school, beginning in the third century B.C. and adopted with much enthusiasm by many Roman thinkers. The Stoics based this emphasis, more thoroughly than Aristotle, on a view of man as part of

49

nature. The rational soul of man was declared to be part of a universal reason (*logos*), which interpenetrated the whole of the cosmos in the form of *pneuma*. The proper aim of a man's life was defined as "to live in accordance with nature"; but since the whole of nature was directed by the universal reason, this aim could also be described as living according to reason. In practice, this ideal, which could probably in theory be interpreted in an almost infinite variety of ways, turned out to have two important consequences for Stoic moral theory. First, it gave substance to the notion that those actions are morally correct for which reasons can be given; this played an important part in shaping the Stoic list of "duties" (*officia*) and in determining the Stoics' attitude to them. Secondly, the very high value placed on reason went along with a devaluation of the emotions, which were held to be merely "disturbances of the soul." The ideal Stoic, the wise man, is described by Cicero (*De finibus* 3, 75–76): once reason has taught him that moral goodness is the only thing of any real value, he is happy forever; he is more truly a king than Tarquin, who could not rule either himself or his people; more truly a leader than Sulla, who was a leader in vice; more free than anyone, because his mind is not enslaved by desires and cannot be chained.

### III. THE RATIONALITY OF THE COSMOS

It has already been mentioned that the word "cosmos" was first applied to the universe by Pythagoras, if the traditional story is correct, and that his purpose was to indicate the orderliness of the universe. From that time on, two aspects of order fascinated the philosophers: the regularity of the motions of the stars, planets, sun, and moon, with the attendant seasons and seasonal changes on earth; and the evidences of purposiveness in nature, especially in the structure of living things. The explanation of these two aspects of order was a dominating theme in the natural philosophy of the Greco-Roman world.

Anaxagoras (mid-fifth century B.C.) first named Mind as the originator of the cosmos. It appears, however, that he used this concept only to explain how the world was first set in motion, and did not go on to explain how the cosmic mind organized the cosmos into its orderly and purposive form. Plato's *Timaeus* is the first surviving account of this. He represents the world as the product of two causes: mind (or reason) and necessity. Mind is put into the world by the divine Demiurge who created it; necessity is a property of the material with which he had to work. Mind is responsible for the orderly and regular features of the cosmos, Necessity, also called "the wandering cause," for the irregularities of the cosmos.

The *Timaeus* cosmology is in the form of a myth, so that it is not easy to know how it is to be interpreted. Aristotle, however, used a similar distinction, and in a much more literal way. His model for explanation of events in the natural world is still human craftsmanship, but he is clear, as Plato is not, that this is only a model, and not to be taken at face value; there is no craftsman who made the cosmos, because the cosmos had no beginning and will have no end. Nature is like art, in that it is purposive; explanations of the phenomena of nature will therefore seek first for the "purpose" or end that they serve. Not everything is purposive; the rest must be explained as coming from the "necessity" of matter.

Aristotle's conviction that nature works "for an end" amounts to a belief in the rationality of the cosmos, since the end is always what would be chosen if the natural process were directed by a rational agent. Aristotle's idea of the activity of god was that he is perpetually engaged in thinking. Since his god's activity is the cause of the continuity of motion in the cosmos, primarily the motion of the stars and other heavenly bodies and derivatively of the continual interchange of the earthly elements, it might appear that the rationality of nature could be simply explained as the deliberate choice of a rational god. But it is clear that this connection was not made by Aristotle—or at any rate not in his most mature and serious work on cosmology. The rational working of nature is simply a fact; it has always been so, and so it does not call for any genetic explanation.

The Stoic school came closer to Plato in explaining the rationality of nature as the work of a rational god. They went, in fact, as far along this path as it is possible to go. God is identified as a rational spirit which permeates, as a physical presence, every part of the cosmos, and causes all the changes which take place in the cosmos, according to a providential plan. This faith in the rationality of everything in nature, backed up by the collection of evidences (see especially Cicero, *De natura deorum* II), was a necessary presupposition of the Stoic moral doctrine which taught that the right way to live was "in conformity with nature."

Let my first conviction be [wrote the Emperor Marcus Aurelius, *Meditations* X 6] that I am part of a Whole which is under Nature's governance; and my second, that a bond of kinship exists between myself and all other similar parts. If I bear these two thoughts in mind, then in the first place . . . I shall cheerfully accept whatever may be my lot; in the second place, I shall do nothing which might injure the common welfare of my fellow parts. . . . Thus doing, I cannot but find the current of my life flowing smoothly (trans. Maxwell Staniforth, Baltimore, 1964).

The Platonists, Aristotelians, and Stoics represent, for all the considerable differences between them, a common tradition in their assumption of rationality in the cosmos. An alternative was offered by the atomists, first Leucippus and Democritus in the late fifth century, and later Epicurus and his Roman follower Lucretius. The atomists did not deny that rational explanations could be given for natural events; indeed they insisted on it. But they denied that nature works for an end. They explained everything as the outcome of collisions of atoms, moving at random in the infinite void, with no mind of their own and no god to steer them. They did not deny the regularities and signs of purposiveness in the world. They offered the motions of atoms as an alternative explanation of the regularities; and the evidences of purpose they explained as having emerged by natural processes in the course of time, by natural selection, or trial and error. It is curious that the only words of Leucippus that survive assert that "nothing happens at random, but everything from reason (*logos*) and necessity." It can only be supposed that he meant that every event has an explanation in previous events; there are no completely spontaneous or uncaused events.

The atomists attempted to depart from the model of human reason in talking about the natural world. But the model had too strong a hold. Their mode of explanation remained less plausible in the ancient world than the teleology of Aristotle or the Stoics, and atomists were on the whole an eccentric minority. The chief reason for this (apart from the fact that the atomic theory was wedded to a peculiar moral theory by Epicurus) was that the theory could not explain the regularities of the cosmos and the artistry of nature without any knowledge of elementary laws of motion and without exact measurement.

*BIBLIOGRAPHY*

Arthur W. H. Adkins, *Merit and Responsibility: a Study in Greek Values* (Oxford, 1960). H. Boeder, "Der frühgriechische Wortgebrauch von Logos und Aletheia," *Archiv für Begriffsgeschichte*, **4** (1959), 82–209. F. M. Cornford, *Principium sapientiae* (Cambridge, 1952); see the review by G. Vlastos, *Gnomon*, **27** (1955), 65–76. E. R. Dodds, *The Greeks and the Irrational* (Berkeley, 1951). Ludwig Edelstein, *Ancient Medicine* (Baltimore, 1967). A.-J. Festugière, *La révélation d'Hermès Trismégiste*, Vol. II, *Le dieu cosmique* (Paris, 1949). W. K. C. Guthrie, *A History of Greek Philosophy*, 3 vols. (Cambridge and New York, 1962; 1965; 1970). G. S. Kirk, *Myth: Its Meaning and Function in Ancient and Other Cultures* (Cambridge and Berkeley, 1970), esp. pp. 238–51. Gilbert Murray, *Five Stages of Greek Religion*, 3rd ed. (New York, 1951). Wilhelm Nestle, *Vom Mythos zum Logos*, 2nd ed. (Stuttgart, 1942). A. S. Pease, "Caeli enarrant," *Harvard Theological Review*, **34** (1941). Max Pohlenz, *Die Stoa* (Göttingen, 1948). Karl R. Popper, "Back to the Presocratics," in his *Conjectures and Refutations* (London and New York, 1962). Gerasimos Santas, "The Socratic Paradoxes," *Philosophical Review*, **73** (1964), 147–64. Bruno Snell, *Die Entdeckung des Geistes* (Hamburg, 1948); trans. T. G. Rosenmeyer as *The Discovery of the Mind* (Oxford and Cambridge, Mass., 1953). G. Vlastos: see Cornford. James L. Walsh, *Aristotle's Conception of Moral Weakness* (New York and London, 1963).

DAVID FURLEY

[See also Historiography; Irrationalism; **Necessity; Platonism; Pre-Platonic Conceptions; Pythagorean Doctrines, Harmony; Stoicism.**]

# REALISM IN LITERATURE

THE TERM "realism" was originally used by the thirteenth-century scholastics as meaning a belief in the reality of ideas; it was contrasted with "nominalism" which supported the doctrine that ideas are only names or abstractions. In the eighteenth century its meaning was practically reversed; in Thomas Reid, in Kant, and in Schelling realism means the opposite of idealism. As a literary term, realism occurs first in a letter of Friedrich Schiller to Goethe (April 27, 1798) asserting that "realism cannot make a poet." Friedrich Schlegel, in the same year ("Ideen," No. 6) formulated the paradox that "all philosophy is idealism and there is no true realism except that of poetry." Schelling in his *Vorlesungen über die Methode des akademischen Studiums* (1802) refers to Plato's "polemic against poetic realism." The term was rather frequent in German romantic aesthetics but does not mean either specific writers or a specific period or school. It is simply used as the opposite of idealism.

The term appears next in France as early as 1826. A writer in the *Mercure français* even prophesied that "this doctrine which leads to faithful imitation not of the masterworks of art but of the originals offered by nature" will be the "literature of the nineteenth century, the literature of the true" (Borgerhoff, 1938). Gustave Planche, in his time an influential antiromantic critic, used the term "realism" from about 1833 onward almost as an equivalent of materialism, particularly for the minute description of costumes and customs in historical novels. Realism is concerned, he says, with "what escutcheon is placed over the door of a castle, what device is inscribed on a standard, and what colors are borne by a lovesick knight" ("Moralité de la poésie," in *Revue des deux mondes*, 4th ser., **1** [1835],

51

250). Clearly with Planche realism means almost the same as "local color," exactitude of description. Hippolyte Fortoul, in 1834, complains for instance of a novel by A. Thouret that it is written "with an exaggeration of realism which he borrowed from the manner of M. Hugo" ("Revue littéraire du mois," in *Revue des deux mondes*, 4th ser. [1 Nov. 1834], 339). Realism at that time is thus merely a feature observed in the method of writers whom we would today call "romantic," in Scott, in Hugo, or in Mérimée. Soon the term was transferred to the minute description of contemporary manners in Balzac and Murger, but its meaning crystallized only in the great debates which arose in the fifties around the paintings of Courbet, and through the assiduous activity of a mediocre novelist, Champfleury, who in 1857 published a volume of essays with the title *Le réalisme*, while a friend of his, Duranty, edited a short-lived review *Réalisme* between July 1856 and May 1857. (See Bernard Weinberg, 1937; H. U. Forest, "'Réalisme,' Journal de Duranty," *Modern Philology*, **24** [1926], 463–79.) In these writings a definite literary creed is formulated which centers on a very few simple ideas. Art should give a truthful representation of the real world: it should therefore study contemporary life and manners by observing meticulously and analyzing carefully. It should do so dispassionately, impersonally, objectively. What had been a widely used term for any faithful representation of nature now becomes associated with specific writers and is claimed as a slogan for a group or movement.

There was wide agreement that Mérimée, Stendhal, Balzac, Monnier, and Charles de Bernard were the precursors, while Champfleury and later Flaubert, Feydeau, the Goncourts, and the younger Dumas were the exponents of the school, though Flaubert, for instance, was annoyed at the designation and never accepted it for himself. (On Flaubert see Maxime du Camp, *Revue des deux mondes*, **51** [June 1882], 791: *Le mot [Réalisme] le blessa et, dans son for intérieur, il ne l'a jamais admis.*) There is a remarkable, tiresomely monotonous agreement in the contemporary discussion of the main features of realism. Its numerous enemies judged the same traits negatively, complaining, for instance, about the excessive use of minute external detail, of the neglect of the ideal, and seeing the vaunted impersonality and objectivity as a cloak for cynicism and immorality. With the trial of Flaubert in 1857 for *Madame Bovary* the term was completely established in France.

The French debate soon found its echoes in other countries. We must, however, distinguish between the use of the term "realism" in reporting French developments and the adoption of the term as a slogan for a local school of realistic writing. The situation in the main countries varies greatly in this respect. In England there was no realist movement of that name before George Moore and George Gissing, late in the eighties.

Still, the terms "realism" and "realist" occur in an article on Balzac as early as 1853, and Thackeray was called, rather casually, "chief of the Realist school" in 1851. George Henry Lewes was the first English critic who systematically applied standards of realism, for instance, in a severe review, "Realism in Art: Recent German Fiction" (1858). There Lewes boldly proclaims ". . . Realism the basis of all Art." In David Masson's *British Novelists and their Styles* (1859), Thackeray is contrasted as "a novelist of what is called the Real school" with Dickens, "a novelist of the Ideal or Romantic school," and the "growth among novel-writers of a wholesome spirit of Realism" is welcomed. Realistic criteria such as truth of observation and a depiction of commonplace events, characters, and settings are almost universal in Victorian novel criticism. ("Balzac and his Writings," *Westminster Review*, **60** [July and October 1853], 203, 212, 214; "William Makepeace Thackeray and Arthur Pendennis, Esquires," *Fraser's Magazine*, **43** [January 1851], 86; G. H. Lewes, *Westminster Review*, **70** [October 1858], 448–518, esp. 493; D. Masson, op. cit., Cambridge [1859], pp. 248, 257; see Richard Stang [1959].)

The situation in the United States was very similar: in 1864 Henry James recommended "the famous 'realistic system'"—obviously referring to the French—for study to a fellow novelist, Miss Harriet Prescott, who, he complained, had not "sufficiently cultivated a delicate perception of the actual" (*Notes and Reviews*, ed. Pierre de Chaignon La Rose, Cambridge, Mass. [1921], pp. 23, 32). But only W. Dean Howells, writing in 1882, speaks of Henry James as the "chief exemplar" of an American school of realism and from 1886 onwards propagated realism as a movement of which he counted himself and James as the chief proponents ("Henry James, Jr.," *Century Magazine*, **25** [1882], 26–28).

In Germany there was no self-conscious realist movement, though the term was used occasionally. In 1850 Hermann Hettner spoke of Goethe's realism, in "Die romantische Schule," *Schriften zur Literatur* (Berlin [1959], p. 66). Otto Ludwig devised the term *poetischer Realismus* in order to contrast Shakespeare with the contemporary French movement (*Gesammelte Schriften*, ed. A. Stern, Leipzig [1891], 264ff.). Julian Schmidt used the term in articles in *Die Grenzboten* from 1856, and in his history of German literature (1867) for what is usually called "Das Junge Deutschland" (*Die Grenzboten*, **14** [1856], 486ff.; "Die

Realisten 1835–1841" in Julian Schmidt, *Geschichte der deutschen Literatur seit Lessings Tod*, Vol. 3, *Die Gegenwart, 1814–1867*, 5th ed., Leipzig [1867]). Even in Marxist theory the term emerges very late. It cannot be found in early pronouncements of either Marx or Engels. It was not till 1888 that Engels, in an English letter to Miss Harkness commenting on her novel, *The City Girl*, complains that it is ". . . not quite realistic enough. Reality, to my mind, implies, besides truth to detail, the truthful reproduction of typical circumstances" (*Über Kunst und Literatur*, ed. Michail Lipschitz, Berlin [1948], pp. 103–04).

In Italy, Francesco De Sanctis defended Zola in 1878, and thought realism an "excellent antidote for a fantastic race fond of phrasemaking and display." The Italian realistic novelists invented a new term, *verismo*, though Luigi Capuana, the most prominent theorist of the group, came to reject all "isms" both for himself and his friend Giovanni Verga: *Gli 'ismi' contemporanei* (*Verismo, simbolismo, idealismo, cosmopolitismo*) *ed altri saggi* (Catania, 1898).

In Russia the situation was again different: there Vissarion Belinsky had adopted Friedrich Schlegel's term "real poetry" as early as 1836; he applied it to Shakespeare, who "reconciled poetry with real life," and Walter Scott, "the second Shakespeare, who achieved the union of poetry with life" (*Sobranie sochinenii*, ed. F. M. Golovenchenko, **1**, Moscow [1948], 103, 107–08). After 1846 Belinsky spoke of Russian writers such as Gogol as the "natural school" (ibid., **3,** 649; see note on p. 902 referring to Bulgarin's use of the term earlier in the same year). Belinsky determined the views of the radical critics of the sixties but, among them, only Dimitri Pisarev used the term as a slogan. Realism for him is, however, simply analysis, criticism. "A realist is a thinking worker" (*Sochineniya. Polnoe sobranie*, ed. F. Pavlenkov, 4th ed., St. Petersburg [1904–07], 4, 68). Dostoevsky attacked the radical critics sharply in 1863. He always disapproved of photographic naturalism and defended the interest in the fantastic and exceptional. In two well-known letters Dostoevsky asserted that he had "quite different conceptions of reality and realism than our realists and critics. My idealism is more real than their realism." His realism is pure, a realism in depth while theirs is of the surface. N. N. Strakhov, in his biography, reports Dostoevsky as saying: "they call me a psychologist: mistakenly. I am rather a realist in a higher sense, i.e. I depict all the depths of the human soul" (Letter to A. N. Maykov, 11/23 Dec. 1868, in *Pisma*, ed. A. S. Dolinin, **2**, Moscow [1928–34], 150, and letter to N. N. Strakhov, 26 Feb./10 March 1869, ibid., 169; N. N. Strakhov and O. Miller, *Biografiya, pisma . . .* , St. Petersburg [1883], p. 373). Similarly,

Tolstoy disapproved of the radical critics and showed a violent distaste for Flaubert though, surprisingly enough, he praised Maupassant and wrote an introduction to a Russian translation. Though truth and truth of emotion is mandatory for Tolstoy in *What is Art?*, the word "realism" does not occur in his writings prominently at all; e.g., Tolstoy's introduction to S. T. Semenov's *Peasant Stories* (1894) ridicules *La légende de Julien l'hospitalier* (*What is Art?* and *Essays on Art*, trans. A. Maude, Oxford [1930], pp. 17–18; the introduction to Maupassant [1894], ibid., pp. 20–45).

The term "naturalism" was in constant competition with "realism" and was often identified with it. It is an ancient philosophical term for materialism, epicureanism, or any secularism. In a literary sense it can be found again in Schiller, in the preface to *Die Braut von Messina* (1803), as something which Schiller finds worth combatting, as in "poetry everything is only a symbol of the real" (*Sämtliche Werke*, ed. Güntter-Witkowski, Leipzig [1909–11], 20, 254). Heine, in a passage of the 1831 *Salon* which profoundly impressed Baudelaire, proclaimed himself a "supernaturalist in art" in contrast to his "naturalism" in religion (*Salon* [1831], in *Werke*, ed. O. Walzel, Leipzig [1912–15], 6, 25: *In der Kunst bin ich Supernaturalist*). But again the term crystallized as a specific literary slogan only in France. It had been used before in Russia by Belinsky who usually spoke of the "natural" school in Russian literature headed by Gogol, but who in the 1847 "Survey of Russian Literature" used "naturalism" expressly as an opposite of "rhetorism" (*Sobranie sochinenii*, ed. Golovenchenko, Moscow [1948], 3, 775, 776, 789). In French, as in English, naturalist means, of course, simply student of nature, and the analogy between the writer and the naturalist, specifically the botanist and zoologist, was ready at hand. Without using the term Balzac had made the parallel between writer and zoologist the central metaphor of his preface to the *Comédie humaine* (1842). Taine, in his essay on Balzac (1858), draws the comparison explicitly when he says that "the naturalist lacks any ideal; even more so does the naturalist Balzac lack one." Hugo in the preface to *La légende des siècles* (1859) drew another parallel. "A poet or a philosopher is not forbidden to attempt with social facts what a naturalist attempts with zoological facts: the reconstruction of a monster according to the imprint of a nail or the cavity of a tooth." Cuvier's speculations on extinct antediluvian fauna had struck the imagination of his contemporaries forcibly. It is this parallel that both the early and the late Zola has in mind. "Today," Zola wrote in 1866, "in literary and artistic criticism we must imitate the naturalists: we have the duty of finding the men behind their works, to reconstruct the societies in their real

53

life, with the aid of a book or a picture" (J. W. J. Hemmings, 1964). The critic and the novelist, Zola argues, do not differ basically and both are, or should be, scientists. In the Preface to a new edition of his novel, *Thérèse Raquin* (1866), Zola proclaimed the naturalist creed most boldly. The book is "an analytical labor on two living bodies like that of a surgeon on corpses." This is substantially what Zola later expounded as the method of his "experimental novel." The preface ends with Zola claiming "the honor of belonging to the group of naturalist writers." But the distinction between "realism" and "naturalism" was not stabilized for a long time. Ferdinand Brunetière in his *Le roman naturaliste* (1883) discusses Flaubert, Daudet, Maupassant, and George Eliot as well as Zola under this title. The separation of the terms is a work of modern literary scholarship.

Thus the contemporary uses of the terms "realism" and "naturalism" should be distinguished from the process by which modern literary research has imposed the term "realism" or "realist period" on the past. The two processes are, of course, not independent of each other: the original suggestion comes from the contemporary debates. But still the two are not entirely the same. Again, the situation varies greatly in different countries.

In France the term "realism" with a distinct later stage of "naturalism" seems firmly established. In particular the books by Pierre Martino, *Le roman réaliste* (1913) and *Le naturalisme français* (1923), have confirmed the distinction: "naturalism" is the doctrine of Zola; it implies a scientific approach, it requires a philosophy of deterministic materialism while the older realists were far less clear or unified in their philosophical affiliations. In France there is one good book, Gustave Reynier's *Les origines du roman réaliste* (1912), which traces the method of realism from the *Satyricon* of Petronius to Rabelais, to the Spanish *Celestina*, and to the French literature about peasants and beggars in the sixteenth century.

In England the use of the term "realism" as a period concept is still very rare. The standard histories of English literature of the early twentieth century, the *Cambridge History of English Literature* and Garnett and Gosse, use the term only very occasionally. Gissing is called a "realist" because of Zola's influence and we hear that "Ben Jonson set out to be what we now call a 'realist' or 'naturalist.'" (On Gissing see *Cambridge History of English Literature*, 14, 458; on Ben Jonson see R. Garnett and E. Gosse, *English Literature. An Illustrated Record* [1903–04], 2, 310.) It needed an American scholar, Norman Foerster, to suggest that the term "Victorian" should be replaced by "realist," in his *The Reinterpretation of Victorian Literature* (ed. Joseph E. Baker, Princeton [1950], pp. 58–59).

In American literary scholarship the position is quite the reverse of the English position. There "realism" is firmly established, mainly since Vernon Parrington gave the title, *The Beginnings of Critical Realism* (1930), to the third volume of his *Main Currents of American Thought*. There is a collective volume, *Transitions in American Literary History* (1954), which manipulates the period concept almost with the assurance of a German literary historian. Realism, unlike naturalism, is not primarily engaged in social criticism, it is argued, but concerns itself with the conflict between the inherited American ideals of faith in man and the individual and the pessimistic, deterministic creed of modern science (Robert O. Falk, "The Rise of Realism," in *Transitions in American Literary History*, ed. H. H. Clark, Durham, N.C. [1954]). Charles Child Walcutt in *American Literary Naturalism* (Minneapolis [1956], p. 9) has well described what he called its "divided stream," "the mixture of fervid exhortation with concepts of majestic inevitableness."

In German, two recent reformulations of the concept of realism have attracted much attention. Erich Auerbach's *Mimesis: Dargestellte Wirklichkeit in der abendländischen Literatur* (1946) sketches the history of realism from Homer to Proust, always using short texts as springboards for brilliant stylistic, intellectual and sociological analyses. But it is hard to discover what he means by "realism." He tells us himself that he would like to have written his book without using any "general expressions." Auerbach tries later to combine two contradictory conceptions of realism; first something which might be called existentialism: the agonizing revelations of reality in moments of supreme decisions, in "limiting situations": Abraham about to sacrifice Isaac, Madame du Chastel deciding not to rescue her son from execution, the Duke of Saint-Simon asking the Jesuit negotiator how old he is. There is, however, a second realism in Auerbach, the French nineteenth-century realism, which he defines as depicting contemporary reality, immersed in the dynamic concreteness of the stream of history. Historicism contradicts existentialism. Existentialism sees man exposed in his nakedness and solitude, it is unhistorical, even antihistorical. These two sides of Auerbach's conception of realism differ also in their historical provenience. "Existence" descends from Kierkegaard, whose whole philosophy was a protest against Hegel, the ancestor of historicism and *Geistesgeschichte*. In Auerbach's sensitive and learned book "realism" has assumed a very special meaning: realism must not be didactic, moralistic, rhetorical, idyllic, or comic. Thus he has little to say of the bourgeois drama or the English realistic novel of the eighteenth and nineteenth century; the Russians are excluded and so are all the Germans of the nineteenth century as either

Memorial Library
Mars Hill College
Mars Hill, N. C.

didactic or idyllic. Only passages in the Bible and Dante, and among moderns, Stendhal, Balzac, Flaubert, and Zola live up to Auerbach's requirements. (See R. Wellek, "Auerbach's Special Realism," *Kenyon Review*, **16** [1954], 299–307.)

Richard Brinkmann's *Wirklichkeit und Illusion* (Tübingen, 1957) also arrives at an idiosyncratic conclusion. He ignores the historical debate and focuses on an ingenious analysis of three German stories: Grillparzer's *Arme Spielmann* (1848), Otto Ludwig's *Zwischen Himmel und Erde* (1855), and Edward von Keyserling's *Beate und Mareile* (1903). Brinkmann argues that the acme of realism is reached in Keyserling's story, as there the narrator limits himself to the representation of the feelings of a single fictional figure (a Prussian *Junker* wavering between two women). Realism or rather reality is found ultimately in the stream of consciousness technique, in the attempt to "dramatize the mind," a technique which actually achieved the most radical dissolution of ordinary reality. Brinkmann is well aware of the paradox of this "reversal," by which the attention to the factual and the individual finally led to something as "unrealistic" in the traditional sense as Joyce, Virginia Woolf, and Faulkner. The conclusion that "the subjective experience . . . is the only objective experience" (op. cit., p. 298) identifies impressionism, the exact notation of mental states of mind, with realism and proclaims it the only true realism. The accepted nineteenth-century meaning of realism is thus turned upside down. It is replaced by an individualizing, atomistic, subjective realism that refuses to recognize an objective order of things: it is even solipsism in the sense of Pater or Proust. The individual is called the "only reality" as in existential philosophy. *Lieutenant Gustl* by Arthur Schnitzler rather than *Die Buddenbrooks*, both dated 1901, is the culminating point of German realism. Bergson rather than Taine or Comte would be its philosopher.

In Germany, everybody is on his own and looks for realism wherever he wants to find it. In Italy, with the exception of Marxist critics, there is no problem of realism. Croce has taken care of that: there is no nature or reality outside the mind and the artist need not worry about the relationship. "Realism" is (like romanticism) only a pseudo-concept, a category of obsolete rhetoric. (See B. Croce, *Estetica*, Bari [1950], p. 118; "Breviario di estetica," in *Nuovi saggi di estetica*, Bari [1948], pp. 39–40; "Aestetica in nuce," in *Ultimi saggi*, Bari [1948], p. 21.)

In Russia, realism is everything. Pushkin and Gogol are considered realists, and as in Germany they argue about "critical realism," "radical democratic realism," "proletarian realism," and "socialist realism," its last stage, which according to L. I. Timofeyev's authorita-

tive *Theory of Literature* (*Teoriya literatury*, Moscow [1938]) is the "fulfilment of all art and literature."

"Socialist realism" propounds a consciously contradictory concept: the writer ought to describe society as it is but he must also describe it as it should and will be. The writer must be faithful to reality but at the same time be imbued with "party-spirit" (*partijnost*). The contradiction is solved by the demand for a "positive hero," for a prescriptive model or even ideal "type," which, e.g., Georgi Malenkov, in a speech at the nineteenth Party Congress (1952) called "the central, political problem of realism." Russian writers are literally told to find and to describe the heroes whose imitation in real life would help in transforming society toward the goal of communism.

Among the Marxists who are not mere mouthpieces of the party line, the Hungarian Georg Lukács (1885–1971) developed the most coherent theory of realism. It starts with the dogma that all literature is a "reflection of reality" (a phrase which Lukács repeats over a thousand times in the first volume of his *Aesthetik*, 1962), and that it will be the truest mirror if it fully reflects the contradictions of social development, that is, in practice, if the author shows an insight into the structure of society and the future direction of its evolution. Naturalism is rejected as concerned with the surface of everyday life and with the average, while realism creates types which are both representative and prophetic. Lukács assembles a number of criteria which allow him to judge literature in terms of its "progressiveness" (which might be unconscious, even contrary to the political opinions of the author) and in terms of the all-inclusiveness, representativeness, self-consciousness, and anticipatory power of the figures created by the great realists. Though there is much purely political polemic in Lukács and the criteria are predominantly ideological, "popular front," and later "cold war," Lukács at his best reformulates the "concrete universal" and renews the "ideal type" problem so closely in relation with the main tradition of German aesthetics that Peter Demetz could speak of him as achieving "a renaissance of originally idealistic aesthetics in the mask of Marxism" ("Zwischen Klassik und Bolschewismus. Georg Lukács als Theoretiker der Dichtung," *Merkur*, **12** [1958], 501–15).

Thus, the concept of realism vacillates today between the old meaning formulated in the nineteenth century as "an objective description of contemporary social reality" and more widely divergent recent concepts which either, as in Marxism, give realism a more specific meaning of a grasp of the social structure and its future trends or, as often in the West, show a more sophisticated awareness of the difficulties raised by the concept of reality.

Recent theorists try to redefine it either in terms of

750211

a historistic or existentialist concept of the nature of reality. While in Marxism "realism" is the only right procedure of art, most Western theorists see "realism" as only one trend of modern literature, vying but not necessarily surpassing other styles such as classicism, romanticism, or symbolism.

*BIBLIOGRAPHY*

George J. Becker, ed., *Documents of Literary Realism* (Princeton, 1963), an anthology. E. B. O. Borgerhoff, "*Réalisme* and Kindred Words: Their Use as a Term of Literary Criticism in the First Half of the Nineteenth Century," in *PMLA*, **53** (1938), 837–43. Emile Bouvier, *La bataille réaliste (1844–1857)* (Paris, 1914). F. W. J. Hemmings, "The Origin of the Terms *Naturalisme, Naturaliste*," in *French Studies*, **8** (1954), 109–21. Harry Levin, ed., "A Symposium on Realism," in *Comparative Literature*, **3** (1951), 193–285; idem, *The Gates of Horn. A Study of Five French Realists* (New York, 1963), contains much on the history of the concept. Richard Stang, *The Theory of the Novel in England, 1850–1870* (London, 1959). Bernard Weinberg, *French Realism: The Critical Reaction, 1830–1870* (New York, 1937). René Wellek, "The Concept of Realism in Literary Scholarship," in *Concepts of Criticism* (New Haven, 1963), pp. 222–55, appeared in *Neophilologus*, **44** (1960), 1–20.

RENÉ WELLEK

[See also **Existentialism;** Historicism; Impressionism; **Marxism; Naturalism in Art;** Socialism.]

# RECAPITULATION

THE THEORY of recapitulation, designated the Biogenetic Law by Ernst Heinrich Haeckel in 1872 (1872a), stated in brief that ontogeny, the development of the individual, recapitulates phylogeny, the evolutionary history of the stock to which the individual belongs. The fact that it is still appropriate to discuss it in the 1970's is a tribute to the viability of an idea that was only tenuously supported by scientific evidence when put to the test of validity.

The concept attained its greatest vigor after the publication of Darwin's *Origin of Species* (1859). When at the end of the nineteenth century a new science, experimental embryology, demonstrated that particular developmental processes might be analyzed in terms of more proximate events, embryological interest in the concept waned. When in the twentieth century the science of genetics developed and coalesced with the study of evolution, investigators in these fields also lost interest in recapitulation, yet as late as the 1950's

a prominent embryologist stated categorically in a textbook of embryology: "Today there remains no reasonable doubt about the fundamental fact that developing vertebrates pass through series of stages which in general recapitulate the evolutionary progression" (Witschi, 1956). He added some qualifications, and such a statement is rare in middle and late twentieth-century treatises, but the dogma lingers.

Before Darwin crystallized the idea that all organisms are related genealogically, the concept that organisms could be ranked from low to high on a Scale of Beings imbued the thought of philosophers and scientists. When this theory carried authority, similarities between embryos of one form and adults of another were described in generalizations that lacked evolutionary connotations. Some historians trace such concepts back to Aristotle, who believed that man during his development had first the soul of a plant, then that of an animal, before finally acquiring his rational soul. This was a metaphysical concept rather than a biological one, as perhaps also was William Harvey's expression of a parallel between embryos and animals ascending the Scale of Beings. "Nature," wrote Harvey, "ever perfect and divine, doing nothing in vain, has neither given a heart where it was not required, nor produced one before its office became necessary; but by the same stages in the development of every animal, passing through the constitutions of all, as I may say (ovum, worm, foetus) it acquires perfection in each" (Harvey, 1628).

The concept, metaphysical or otherwise, was alive apart from biological thought during the years when it began to attract scientific attention. For instance, William Blake, describing the development of Orc in the womb of Enitharmon, put it thus (Blake, 1794):

> Many sorrows and dismal throes,
> Many forms of fish, bird & beast
> Brought forth an Infant form
> Where was a worm before.

It was during Blake's time, however, that the concept began to acquire scientific status. Kohlbrugge (1911) presented a list of over seventy-two writers, beginning with Goethe and Autenrieth, who expressed ideas of parallelism or recapitulation between 1797 and 1866, the year that Haeckel formulated the recapitulation theory in a few catchwords that were to become a slogan.

Johann Friedrich Meckel was one of the most important of many who expounded laws of parallelism during the nineteenth century. He wrote in his treatise on comparative anatomy, when comparative anatomy was becoming a dominant biological discipline: "An embryo of higher animals passes through a number of stages before it attains its complete development; it is to be demonstrated here that these different stages correspond to those at which lower animals are arrested throughout their whole lives" (Meckel, 1821).

Meckel's generalization was soon to be disputed by a master as great as himself. Within five years, Karl Ernst von Baer wrote in an article that: "It has been concluded by a bold generalization from a few analogies, that the higher animals run in the course of their development through the lower animal grades, and sometimes tacitly and sometimes expressly they have been supposed to take their way through all forms. We hold this to be not only untrue, but also impossible" (von Baer, 1827). Von Baer's treatise *Ueber Entwicklungsgeschichte der Thiere* (*On the Embryology of Animals*), which established comparative embryology as a discipline that was soon to supplant comparative anatomy as the most important zoological science, devoted one of its most important sections to a refutation of the law of parallelism. In it he deduced on the basis of his own careful observations what he called "the law of individual development, 1. That the more general characters of a large group of animals appear earlier in their embryos than the more special characters. . . . 2. From the most general forms the less general are developed, and so on, until finally the most special arises. . . . 3. Every embryo of a given animal form, instead of passing through the other forms, rather becomes separated from them. . . . Fundamentally, therefore, the embryo of a higher form never resembles any other form, but only its embryo" (von Baer, 1828). As one recent authoritative critic of recapitulation theory has paraphrased it: "Instead . . . of passing through the adults of other stages of other animals during its ontogeny, a developing animal moves away from them, and the ontogenetic stages do not run parallel to the sequence of forms of the scale of beings" (de Beer, 1958).

Ironically, the law of recapitulation is often attributed to von Baer in spite of his vehement denial of the validity of the law of parallelism. This may be accounted for by the fact that Darwin, in the last four editions of the *Origin of Species* quoted a statement by von Baer to the effect that: "'Embryos of birds, lizards, and snakes, probably also of chelonia are in their earliest states exceeding like one another'" (Darwin, 1861, 1872), and Darwin himself in the final edition withdrew some earlier reservations and stated categorically that: "Several . . . highly competent judges insist that ancient animals resemble to a certain extent the embryos of recent animals belonging to the same classes; and that the geological succession of extinct forms is nearly parallel with the embryological

development of existing forms. This view accords admirably well with our theory" (Darwin, 1872).

Haeckel read the first edition of the *Origin of Species* in German translation in 1860, and, carried away by it, became Darwin's champion and popularizer in Germany. He went far beyond Darwin, and sometimes far beyond fact—he was accused of falsifying pictorial illustrations to support his theories (His, 1874)—in attempting to synthesize all that was known of nature in a single scheme based on evolutionary theory.

In his first and possibly most important general work, *Generelle Morphologie der Organismen* (1866; *General Morphology of Organisms*), Haeckel began to relate ontogeny to phylogeny (words that he invented): "Ontogenesis or the development of the organic individual, as the series of changes in form which every individual passes during the whole period of its individual existence, is immediately conditioned [*bedingt*] by the phylogenesis or the development of the organic stock (Phylon) to which it belongs. . . . Ontogenesis is the short and rapid recapitulation of phylogenesis, caused by the physiological functions of inheritance (reproduction) and adaptation (nourishment)." Already in this first of his generalizations Haeckel implied through the use of the verb *bedingen* a causal relationship between ontogenesis and phylogenesis. When in the late 1860's embryologists such as Wilhelm His (whom Haeckel singled out for particular anathema) attempted to explain the development of particular organs in terms of such mechanical factors as the folding of embryonic layers caused by unequal growth, Haeckel (1874) replied by insisting that: "Phylogenesis is the mechanical cause of ontogenesis," and would tolerate no opposition.

Haeckel was wary of claiming absolute applicability for the biogenetic law and often wrote of recapitulation as "short," "rapid," or "abbreviated." It was known by the 1860's that various nutritive, respiratory, and excretory organs (yolk-sac, allantois) characteristic of embryos are lacking in all adults. Haeckel (1875) took cognizance of such facts by classifying as *palingenetic* the embryonic processes that are transmitted by heredity from ancestral forms, in contrast to *coenogenetic* ones which appear through adaptation to the needs of embryonic or larval life.

He felt that in spite of these limitations, the clues given by embryos concerning the ancestry of their line were intelligible, and he constructed elaborate genealogies on the basis of the study of embryonic form. When there were gaps in his postulated schemes of evolutionary relationships, he was not above inventing animals to fill them. Leaning heavily on the nineteenth-century concept of fixity of origin and differentiation of the embryonic germ-layers (ectoderm,

57

mesoderm, endoderm), he postulated a two-layered organism named *Gastraea* as the ancestor of all many-celled animals (Haeckel, 1872b).

One of the most fruitful results of his forceful exposition and vehement defense of the biogenetic law was that others, like himself, studied embryos in order to ascertain the ancestry of various species, and whether or not the premises from which these studies developed were sound, a great corpus of embryological knowledge was established.

A number of factors contributed, during the late nineteenth and early twentieth centuries, toward the decline of embryologists' interest in recapitulation. As biology in general concentrated less on evolution and more on experimental physiology, embryologists became more interested in experimental than in theoretical approaches to the study of developmental mechanics. The comparability and fixity of the germ-layers in different animals were challenged by experimental evidence. As genetic data accumulated, coenogenesis became less acceptable as an explanation of deviations from strict recapitulation, since it implied the inheritance of acquired characters, the Lamarckian theory, which was unacceptable to the new genetics. In other ways also, it became clear that coenogenesis could not suffice to explain deviations from the rule. In some groups of insects, species unlike in adult form have similar larvae; in others, unlike larvae develop into similar adults (de Beer, 1958). Embryos of one order of molluscs, the cephalopods (squid, cuttlefish, octopus) have a unique type of development; they pass through no stages comparable to those of other molluscs and no other molluscs pass through stages comparable to those of cephalopods. In such organisms, genetic changes have been introduced early in the life history; Haeckel's concept called for them to occur at the end of the embryonic period.

The occurrence of mutation in genes that act early in development is a primary factor leading to the divergencies of development emphasized nearly a century and a half ago by von Baer. Since differences in development lead to differences in adults, modification of ontogeny produces new raw materials for natural selection to work upon. From this point of view (Garstang, 1922), most biologists of the late twentieth century consider ontogeny the cause of phylogeny, rather than the reverse, on the few occasions when they consider such relationships at all.

Haeckel's ideas about recapitulation appealed not only to biologists, but also to many others who became aware of them because of the popularity of the books he addressed to general readers. Like many aspects of Darwinian theory, Haeckel's concept of recapitulation had its impact on anthropology, criminology, political

theory, literature, psychology, and even history itself. An example of its influence on cultural history is provided by an organic analogy used by John W. Draper: "The march of individual existence shadows forth the march of race-existence, being, indeed, its representative on a little scale. . . . A national type pursues its way physically and intellectually through changes and developments answering to those of the individual, and being represented by Infancy, Childhood, Youth, Manhood, Old Age, and Death respectively. . . . Nations must undergo obliteration as do the transitional forms offered by the animal series. There is no more an immortality for them than there is an immobility for an embryo in any one of the manifold forms passed through in its progress of development" (Draper, 1876).

Draper's thought was of considerable significance in its influence on the development of intellectual history. At a much more popular level, the transfer of the idea of recapitulation into general thinking is exemplified in its expression in a book on child care that was a handbook in many thousands of American homes in the mid-twentieth century. "Each child," wrote Benjamin Spock, "as he develops is retracing the whole history of mankind, physically and spiritually, step by step. A baby starts off in the womb as a single tiny cell, just the way the first living thing appeared in the ocean. Weeks later, as he lies in the amniotic fluid in the womb, he has gills like a fish" (Spock, 1968).

The concept of recapitulation was especially influential in psychology, in which Haeckel himself was particularly interested. During the early part of the twentieth century it was incorporated into psychology by Carl Gustav Jung, who adopted the theory in support of his own ideas about the "race unconscious":

Experience suggests to us that we draw a parallel between the phantastical, mythological thinking of antiquity and the similar thinking of children, between the lower human races and dreams. This train of thought is . . . quite familiar through our knowledge of comparative anatomy and the history of development, which shows us how the structure and function of the human body are the results of a series of embryonic changes which correspond to similar changes in the history of the race. Therefore, the supposition is justified that ontogenesis corresponds in psychology to phylogenesis. Consequently, it would be true, as well, that the state of infantile thinking in the child's psychic life, as well as in dreams, is nothing but a re-echo of the prehistoric and ancient (Jung, 1916; trans. 1927).

Jung first developed his idea of the race or collective unconscious through the consideration of dreams, and confirmed it by his analogy to the development of the body. Analogy between the development of mind and body, on the basis of recapitulation, was made as early as 1866 by Haeckel in his *General Morphology:* "The psychic life of man obeys completely the same laws as the psychic life of other animals. . . . Like all complicated phenomena in higher organisms, so the mind, as the most complicated and highest function of all . . . can be understood only by comparing it with simpler and less complete phenomena of the same sort in lower animals and by following its gradual development step by step. We must return here not only to the biontic but also to phyletic development."

Wilhelm Preyer, Professor of Physiology at Jena during twenty-seven of Haeckel's years in the same university, extended Haeckel's ideas to child psychology. "The mind of the new-born child," he wrote in the preface to the first edition of *Die Seele des Kindes* (1882; *The Mind of the Child*), "does not resemble a *tabula rasa* upon which the senses first write their impressions, . . . but the tablet is already written upon before birth, with many illegible, even unrecognizable and invisible marks, traces of the imprint of countless sense impressions of long past generations." And Preyer went further than Haeckel to extend the concept to more specific aspects of mentality, including memory, as Jung also was to do later. "I call [personal memory]," wrote Preyer, "the memory formed by means of individual impressions, occurrences, experience, in contrast with *phyletic* memory, or instinct, the memory of the race, which results from the inheritance of the traces of individual experiences of ancestors."

Preyer may not have been the only writer in his time to believe that the life of the psyche obeys the same laws in its development as the life of the body, according to the law of recapitulation, but his *Mind of the Child* was an influential book, a pioneering analysis of child psychology. It may well have been read by Jung during his formative years, and Jung, of course, like so many of his contemporaries, may also have read books by Haeckel. Be that as it may, it was of critical importance for the subsequent history of embryology itself that *The Mind of the Child* was read by Hans Spemann, who was to perform in the first quarter of the twentieth century the experiments on embryonic induction that were so fateful for the subsequent development of experimental embryology. Spemann stated specifically in his autobiography that he was first drawn into biology as a result of reading *The Mind of the Child*. It is ironic that the same ideas that so strongly influenced psychology through Jung's acceptance of the recapitulation doctrine were also to lead up to the experimental analysis which finally destroyed the concept for biology proper.

### BIBLIOGRAPHY

K. E. von Baer, "Beiträge zur Kenntnis der niedern Thiere," *Nova Acta Physico-medica Academiae Caesareae Leopoldino-Carolinae Naturae Curiosorum*, XIII, Part 2 (1827), 525–762. Part was translated by T. H. Huxley in *Scientific Memoirs*, ed. A. Henfrey and T. H. Huxley (London, 1853); the quotation is from Huxley's translation, p. 184; idem, *Ueber Entwicklungsgeschichte der Tiere*, 2 vols. (Königsberg, 1828; 1837), I, 224; the quotation is from Huxley's translation, *Scientific Memoirs*, op. cit., p. 214. G. R. de Beer, *Embryos and Ancestors*, 3rd ed. (Oxford, 1958), is the most recent full critique of recapitulation theory. W. Blake, *The First Book of Urizen, Etched 1794*, in *Poetry and Prose of William Blake*, ed. G. Keynes (London, 1927), p. 254. C. R. Darwin, *Origin of Species* . . . , 3rd ed. (London, 1861), pp. 470–71. Darwin's quotation from von Baer is from Huxley's translation, *Scientific Memoirs*, op. cit., p. 210; *The Origin of Species* . . . , 6th ed. (London, 1872). The quotation from the 6th ed. is taken from the reprint (New York, 1902), II, 120. J. W. Draper, *History of the Intellectual Development of Europe*, rev. ed., 2 vols. (New York, 1876), I, 12, 14, 17–18. W. Garstang, "The Theory of Recapitulation. A Critical Restatement of the Biogenetic Law," *Journal of the Linnaean Society of London, Zoology*, **35** (1922), 81–101. E. H. Haeckel, "Die Gastraeatheorie, die physiologische Klassifikation des Tierreichs und die Homologie der Keimblätter," *Jenaische Zeitschrift für Naturwissenschaften*, **8** (1874), 6; idem, "Die Gastrula und die Eifurchung der Tiere," *Jenaische Zeitschrift für Naturwissenschaften*, **9** (1875), 402–19; idem, *Generelle Morphologie der Organismen*, 2 vols. (Berlin, 1866), II, 300, 344; *Die Kalkschwämme, Biologie der Kalkschwämme*, 3 vols. (Berlin, 1872b), I, 484; idem, *Natürliche Schöpfungsgeschichte*, 3rd ed. (Berlin, 1872a), p. xxxv. W. Harvey, "An Anatomical Disquisition on the Motion of the Heart and Blood in Animals," in *The Works of William Harvey, M.D.*, ed. and trans. R. Willis (London, 1847), p. 82. The original essay is in Latin. G. Heberer, ed., *Der gerechtfertigte Haeckel* (Stuttgart, 1968). This is the most comprehensive modern work available summarizing Haeckel's thought; it has extensive bibliographies. While it discusses the whole body of his work, it devotes considerable space to recapitulation. The major portion of the volume consists of long extracts from Haeckel's own writings. W. His, *Unsere Körperform und das physiologische Problem ihrer Entstehung* (Leipzig, 1874), pp. 168–71. C. J. Jung, *Psychology of the Unconscious*, trans. B. M. Hinkle (New York, 1927), pp. 27–28. J. H. F. Kohlbrugge, "Das biogenetische Grundgesetz. Eine historische Studie," *Zoologischer Anzeiger*, **37** (1911), 447–53. J. F. Meckel, *System der vergleichenden Anatomie*, 6 vols. (Halle, 1821–33), I, 396–97. W. Preyer, *Die Seele des Kindes* (Leipzig, 1884), pp. vi–vii, 260–61. H. Spemann, *Forschung und Leben* (Stuttgart, 1943). B. Spock, *Baby and Child Care*, rev. ed. (New York, 1968), p. 229. E. Witschi, *Development of Vertebrates* (Philadelphia, 1956), p. 6.

JANE OPPENHEIMER

[See also Biological Conceptions in Antiquity; Chain of Being; **Evolutionism; Inheritance of Acquired Characteristics; Macrocosm and Microcosm.**]

## REFORMATION

ALTHOUGH the concept of reformation is popularly so exclusively associated with the Protestant Reformation of the sixteenth century, "the hinge," James Froude declared, "on which all modern history turns," the religious idea of reformation is of great antiquity and of equally great complexity. It requires careful definition in order to distinguish it from other forms of renewal, renovation, revolution, rebirth, or restoration. The idea of reformation must be distinguished from deterministic, naturalistic, or supernaturalistic conceptions of renewal. Reformation is a free act or a repeated series of actions which are intended by the reformer to recover, reestablish, augment, and perfect certain essential values which at one time existed in human society but which subsequently were lost or impaired by willful neglect or due to a general decline (Ladner, 1959). To be sure, ideas of renaissance and renewal were frequently amalgamated with the idea of reformation. Nor did programs for reformation always correspond to the supposed historical original or come up to the hoped-for potential reality. Nevertheless, reformation was always characterized by man's evocative and creative effort to restore a more perfect condition which the reformer believed to have existed at some previous time. But while the reformer emphasized recovery and restoration, remaking so as to eradicate defects, he in some cases viewed reformation as an essential preliminary to further advance. Thus in Western history the idea of a return to a golden age has often been associated with a theology of hope, an eschatological expectation that the kingdom of God might be realized in whole or in part as a result of successful reformation. The words "reformation" and "reform" in certain contexts are interchangeable when used in the general sense of improvement or restoration of a better condition. But the term "reformation" has come to be preferred for a movement which has effected significant changes or improvements particularly in morals or religious tenets and practices. "Reform" is preferred for an attempt to correct corrupt practices, remove abuses, and change for the better in any way and can be applied to a specific amendment, frequently a political or legislative act, as the term "reformation" cannot.

The idea of reformation in Western intellectual history was essentially a Judeo-Christian conception associated first of all with personal regeneration and the reformed life of the individual, secondly with the restoration of the ideal community life in the monastic movement, and thirdly with a reform given institutional status within the Church as the papacy undertook to make the world safe for ecclesiastical ideals.

The advocates and carriers of individual and social reformation in the sixteenth century reached a prominence never again equalled in history, but the religious idea of reformation has remained a vital force down to the present time.

*1. Reformation and Renewal.* The idea of reformation looms largest and is most persistently recurrent in Christian thought, but it is a variant of more general renewal ideologies and has antecedents in pre-Christian literature, especially Greco-Roman, and even in pre-literate religious belief. Reformation must be distinguished from other types of renewal conceptions which were more prominent in the pre-Christian era and occurred sporadically also in later times. Gerhart Ladner, distinguished authority on the idea of reform in patristic thought, categorizes the more significant renewal ideas to be distinguished from reformation and reform as the (a) cosmological, (b) vitalistic, (c) millenarian, and (d) conversion ideologies (Ladner, 1959).

(a) Cosmological renewal ideas are very closely related to and derived from the cyclical patterns of diurnal and seasonal change and the life, death, and procreative pattern of organic beings. The myth of the eternal return reenacted in primitive religious rites and reflected in early folklore and mythology was derived from the beliefs in antiquity about the perpetual cyclical recurrence of identical or at least very similar situations, persons, and occurrences. The archaic mentality sought to negate the inexorable passage of time and the inevitable corrosion and destruction which accompanies it by positing a theory of new beginnings. All archaic and traditional societies seem to have felt the need for a periodical regeneration of the cosmos lest entropy reduce all to a state of equilibrium and usher in the stillness of death (Eliade, 1965). Examples in classical culture are plentiful, such as the Stoic doctrine of cosmic destruction and renewal, Hesiod's myth of the Golden Age at the beginning of time, or the Platonic cyclical correspondences and the Neo-Pythagorean notion of a new world year introducing cosmic renewal. This recurrence idea strikingly symbolized by New Year celebrations, which in its most radical form assumed the eternal cyclical and numerically repetitive renewal of the cosmos and with this the renewal of humanity, could not be essentially harmonized with the Christian view of history. It was cyclical rather than linear, and deterministic rather than taking into account man's freedom and the meaning of his actions in history.

(b) The vitalistic renewal ideas are related generically to the human life processes of procreation and growth. Thus the ideas of renaissance or rebirth and of upward evolutionary development in social or cultural history are by analogy based upon these processes of life. The cosmological and vitalistic renewal ideas did at times fuse with each other and combined with yet a third set of ideas.

(c) The millenarian renewal ideas were utopian and messianic, looking forward to a period of perfection. The millenarian expectations were derived from the eschatological hopes raised by the New Testament references to the thousand-year reign of Christ and the saints at the end of time and were related to certain apocalyptic notions expressed in the Old Testament prophets (especially Daniel) and developed further in the intertestamental period and expressed in the Apocrypha. The millenarian hope anticipates a perfect kingdom, in contrast to ideas of reformation which were historically relative rather than absolute, and of limited objective rather than perfectionist in goal.

(d) Within the Christian tradition the idea of spiritual renewal through baptism, which is a "washing of regeneration and renewing of the Holy Ghost," is related to personal rebirth and a beginning of the sanctified life. But while a personal reformation with implications for social improvement is associated with the regeneration in Baptism, it is a product and is not identical with the spiritual rebirth itself, given the divine initiative in the Sacrament.

Various renewal ideologies, because of their deterministic and cyclical nature, proved to be incompatible with the Judeo-Christian conception of time and history moving in a linear and irrepeatable direction and with the assumptions about man's genuine, if limited, freedom to make history. Yet, at times certain aspects of renewal ideology were adapted to and fused with reformation ideas. The idea of reformation held up a picture drawn from the past of the goal to be achieved and called for a return to a better condition once known by man. But it also presupposed that if man's intentions and will were properly applied, man could make progress in reforming himself, the Church, and society in at least a limited but real way.

*2. Medieval, Classical, and Biblical Terminology.* The terminology used for reformation was not always clearly distinguished from the language of renewal ideologies so that the substance of the conception and the program for its realization need to be examined in their historical context before a judgment is ventured as to whether a movement in question constitutes reformation, renewal, or a combination of both ideas. Medieval linguistic usage employed the words *reformare* and *reformatio* in a way parallel to such words as *regenerare* (*regeneratio*, παλιγγενεσία), *renovare, innovare* (*nova vita*), *suscitare, resuscitare, restituere, instituere, surgere, renasci, reviviscere* ("to revive"), *revirescere* ("to grow green again"). The terms

*reformare* and *reformatio* had already occurred in classical literature and were known in that context to medieval students of the classics and to Renaissance humanists. But the major sources of this terminology in the medieval and Reformation periods were unmistakably religious and specifically biblical.

In classical usage the verb *reformare* and the noun *reformatio*, which appeared a little later in the literature, did not initially suggest the active and willful reestablishing of a former state of things or the creation of a new value related to the old. In Ovid's *Metamorphoses* (an adaptation of the Greek μεταμόρφωσις) *reformare* refers to a miraculous physical restoration and to a sudden rejuvenation of an old man for one day. In Seneca and Pliny the younger *reformatio* refers to a moral, educational, and political restoration. In the Antonine and Severan periods of Roman history the great jurists applied the term *reformatio* to legal and institutional reform. Cicero, Livy, and postclassical authors used the terms *renovatio* and *renovare* to refer to renewal in various contexts (Ladner, 1959).

There were Old Testament examples of individual reform, the restoration of the law in the days of King Josiah (620 B.C., cf. II Kings 22, 23), and many prophetic admonitions to repentance and reform. The prophets were often in their own persons reformer types. They foretold the new heaven and the new earth in which even the wild beasts would honor the Lord. Isaiah 43:19 reads: "Behold, I am doing a new thing." But the terminology current throughout Western religious history was drawn predominantly from the gospels and from the epistles of Saint Paul. The New Testament tied in the idea of rebirth with an eschatological expectation of the coming of the kingdom and a new paradise. Thus Matthew 19:28 reads: "Jesus said to them, 'Truly, I say to you, in the new world, when the Son of man shall sit on his glorious throne. . . .'" The gospels also associate the spiritual regeneration of the individual through faith and in baptism with fitness for entering the kingdom of God. In John 3:3 Jesus says: "Truly, truly I say to you, unless one is born anew, he cannot see the kingdom of God" (*renatus fuerit denuo;* γεννηθῇ ἄνωθεν). Saint Paul called for the transformation of individual Christians, the improvement in morals and return to their first love of the congregation, and the preparation in the present for the perfection of the post-resurrection life. Romans 12:2 reads: "Do not be conformed to this world but be transformed by the renewal of your mind, that you may prove what is the will of God, what is good and acceptable and perfect" (Burdach, 1918). The Vulgate Latin used in the West rendered the Greek μεταμορφοῦσθαι as *reformare* or *reformari*. The two nouns most common for reformation and renewal were translated as follows: μεταμόρφωσις = *reformatio;* ἀνακαίνωσις = *renovatio.* The prefix μετά in Greek can be understood to imply a change or reversal rather than a simple direct-line transformation and thus a reformation rather than a simple renewal is suggested. In Latin patristic writings things that are *defuncta* and *deformata* need to be reformed.

*3. Reformation as Personal Reform.* During the patristic period of the Christian era reformation referred predominantly to individual reform or personal renewal. Reformation in the strictest sense of the word meant the return to a previously established norm, looking backward to something given rather than forward to a goal still awaited. The norm in a Christian context was a religious norm, the restoration in sinful man of the original image of God, and specifically the conforming to the likeness of Christ. Through spiritual regeneration and growth in sanctification and holiness of life, the individual Christian is restored in part to that original image and similitude of God which had been bestowed upon man, but which had been lost by the fall of man into sin. Genesis 1:26–27 reads: "Then God said, 'Let us make man in our image, after our likeness. . . .'" Genesis 3:1–24 records the fall of man. The restoration of the image of God in the new dispensation was given a concrete and more tangible definition as the restoration of the image of Christ. Through baptism, faith, and growth in sanctification or holiness of life man is reformed after the likeness of Christ, God-incarnate, the first-born among the sons of God. The imitation of Christ entails patterning the new man after the person of Christ, who was in every respect perfect, loving, forgiving, and gracious. The reformation of the individual in the likeness of Christ remains partial and imperfect in this present time, but will be consummated in the world to come.

Two Scripture passages from the writings of Saint Paul will serve to illustrate this conception of personal reformation and renewal patterned after Christ. I Corinthians 3:18 reads: "And we all, with unveiled face, beholding the glory of the Lord, are being changed into his likeness from one degree of glory to another; for this comes from the Lord who is the Spirit." Philippians 3:20–21 reads: "But our commonwealth is in heaven, and from it we await a Savior, the Lord Jesus Christ, who will change our lowly body to be like his glorious body, by the power which enables him even to subject all things to himself." The concept of reformation as a willed and intentional return of the individual to the perfect norm, the image of God and likeness of Christ, is amalgamated with the idea of the spiritual renewal effected by the Spirit on the divine initiative. Reformation is partial and

relative here in time and is perfected only in eternity. The Greek and Latin patristic writers derived their concept of reformation directly from the New Testament, but they developed the idea with slight variations in emphasis.

The Greek church fathers cultivated the idea of personal reformation as a restoration of the image of God and likeness of Christ. With a strong emphasis upon the centrality of the incarnation the imagery of the recovery of man's primal condition through the spiritualization of man by faith in Christ was strongly emphasized. Together with the recovery of the primal condition imagery, the Greek fathers cultivated also the notion of a return to paradise, man's first estate before the fall. Man's final return to the paradise of heaven could be anticipated by mystical participation in the here and now. They also viewed the representational embodiment of the kingdom of God on earth in the Church, the mystical body of Christ, as an ongoing reformation of the world. This conception was more meliorist than optimist, for the prayer that the Lord's kingdom should come implied an ongoing process of becoming until the Parousia at the end of time. The Christian emperor and the monastic groups were chief guardians and most dedicated promoters of the kingdom ideal.

While the creational and incarnational emphases of Eastern thought are not absent from the Latin patristic writings, a greater stress upon reformation in terms of restoration understood morally and legally is apparent. The shift in emphasis is evident in their very vocabulary. Tertullian (ca. 155–220), for example, used the word *reformare* to designate a return to a previous condition, applying the term also to the general repetitiousness of the universe. He was possibly the first to use the phrase *in melius reformare,* to reform for the better. Cyprian, Arnobius, and Lactantius, a fourth-century Christian poet who wrote on the dignity of man, conceived of personal moral meliorism as reform. Lactantius, fond of phoenix imagery, tied in the idea of reformation with his notion of a coming golden age and a glorious millennium at the end of time. Thus, just as in the early phase of the eighteenth-century romantic movement, restoration, through reform, of a golden age in the past was seen as a move toward a more perfect condition yet to be realized (Ladner, 1959).

Two heretical movements in Western Christendom made substantial contributions to the concept of reformation. The Donatists insisted that the validity of the sacrament was affected by the administrant's state of grace and opposed the readmission to the Church of the *lapsi* or fallen, those who had denied their faith in times of persecution. The Donatists were arch-

Puritans or purists who held up absolute ideals of conduct and insisted that the entire Church had to be reformed from top to bottom. The Pelagians undertook a reformation within the Church and stressed the possibility for an individual Christian to will his own moral reform and for groups of Christians to order social life according to Christian moral law. Erasmus, and before him Lorenzo Valla, learned from Jerome to pay tribute to the contribution of heretics to Christian thought. Not least of their contributions was the negative stimulation they gave to Saint Augustine. As Robert of Melun observed in the twelfth century, what the holy fathers did not find controverted they did not defend.

In Augustine the orthodox idea of reformation found an articulate spokesman. For him the reformation of man meant a great deal more than the return of an individual to the creational integrity of Adam, first man in paradise. All historical reformations are related to a creational process of formation which includes the nontemporal act of conversion to God. Augustine, of course, referred often to the restoration of the individual to the image of God or likeness of Christ. He speculated upon the nature of time and the role of numbers in leading man back to God. But above all the idea of reformation in Augustine was given a dynamic character by its association with his grand theology of history. The two kingdoms theory of his *City of God*, in which the "two churches" of Cain and Abel and their followers served as the matrix for his idea of reformation and provided the prevailing medieval context for the concept, proved to be one of the great formative forces in Western intellectual history. In the final stages of Augustine's writings, stimulated by the Pelagian controversy from A.D. 412 on, he developed a grand scheme of double succession, one line derived from Cain and another from Abel. Reformation in this scheme, whether of a single person or of the collective, meant rejecting Cain and returning to Abel. Reformation is conservative and even antirevolutionary, for Augustine saw it as a conservation and renovation, a return to that God-given and God-pleasing state of man and order of society which in history has been constantly threatened by the city of man, but never wholly lost. A subtle change in the idea of reformation is introduced by Augustine sufficiently significant for later history to merit notice. His fixation on the virtue of monastic life as a superior Christian way prompted him to speak of reform in terms not only of the indwelling Christ and of the imitation of Christ's person, but in terms of obedience to "the law of Christ."

Augustine's association of the Church with the city of God, the two never being coterminous, pointed up the Church's role as a carrier of permanent reform. The *Missale Romanum* conveyed the message of God's reforming activity not only into every cathedral but into every village chapel in Christendom. The priest at the preparation of the cup for Mass recited the words: "God who has marvelously created the dignity of human substance and has more wondrously reformed it." Not only did the idea of renewal and reform play an important part in sacramental theology, but also in restoring ecclesiastical order through periodic reforms of canon law. The revision of older conciliar canons by later councils became a regular reformatory procedure. But the predominant and most characteristic expression of the idea of reformation during the medieval period was in the constantly recurring monastic reform movements.

***4. Monastic Reform.*** In the long evolution of the monastic ideal, the theme *reformata reformanda*, things reformed must be reformed again, recurred constantly. With its hermitic and cenobitic antecedents, monasticism developed in the East, but received a unique direction in the West. The monks withdrew from society not only because it was easier to live a more perfect ascetic life, but because there they could in isolation anticipate the perfect life of devotion to God which would ultimately be consummated in heaven. In the West Saint Benedict linked monasticism with labor and made of it a most valuable instrument of social and economic progress. The glorification of work, however, had a subversive by-product, for remunerative toil produced wealth and no rules or regulations devised by the order could prevent the monks from enjoying the fruits of their labors. The passion for solitude, the desire to reform monasticism by a return to primitive poverty, drove the Benedictines into remote regions and dense forests, but a few generations later the hermitage had become a crowded monastery surrounded by serfs and tenants. For eight hundred years the monastic tide rose and fell, with reformation followed by decadence and a new effort at reconstruction (Workman, 1918).

The first of the great Benedictine reforms was inaugurated by Benedict of Aniane, the "second founder" of Western monasticism. A narrow escape from drowning while serving as a soldier in Italy under Charlemagne led him to enter the monastery of St. Seine in Burgundy. He found the monasteries in a deplorable condition, lands alienated to laymen, domination by cruel superiors, and disorder everywhere. He withdrew to an isolated gorge on the Aniane in Aquitaine and soon established a reputation as a pious reformer. In 817 he presided over the important Council of Aachen which aimed at a thorough reformation of the monastic discipline. His rule was overly rigid and a reaction toward decadence soon set in. In order to counteract this decay Duke William IX of

Aquitaine around the year 910 founded a monastery at Cluny in Burgundy. This house followed a strict interpretation of the Rule of Saint Benedict. With the Cluniac reform movement, however, a new principle entered the picture.

The reform of the eleventh century in the brief span of two generations completely altered the ecclesiastical structure and its relation to the political order. Monasticism had often been corrupted by the intrusion of worldly materialism and political domination, just as the proprietary church arrangement imposed the control of secular lords on the local churches. If the Cluniac monks could improve the secular clergy by impressing their ideals upon the entire church and if the Church could in turn exercise a real power and influence upon worldly rulers, then the Church could uplift the world rather than the world corrupt the Church. The great Pope Gregory VII plotted the strategy for the "Hildebrandine Reform." He conceived of it as "the struggle for the right order of things in the world," a moral crusade to free the Church from subservience to theocratic royal government and lay ownership of ecclesiastical institutions. The Cluniac monasteries provided the spiritual inspiration and dynamism for the movement, but the actual institutional direction came from the Gregorian reformers who aimed at a universal reform of the Church in a legal-institutional and Rome-centered plan of action. The program for the establishment of truth and justice was based upon old Church law, the *lex Christi* incorporated in the *decretum* of Gratian and other decretals of canon law. The Gregorian reformation aimed at eliminating simony, clerical concubinage and marriage, and lay investiture, and strove in a positive way to spiritualize the entire hierarchy from lowest cleric to the supreme pontiff. The Cluniac and Gregorian reform movements met with astonishing success, and yet they were not without serious defects which became evident in due course. The Cluniac movement suffered from an institutional defect, for the burden of discipline rested too exclusively upon the abbot of Cluny. The Gregorian reform suffered from an analogous flaw, but with a different effect. The assertion of Petrine or papal jurisdictional primacy paved the way for those extravagant claims to *plenitudo potestatis* asserted in behalf of the papacy by some popes, canon lawyers, and theologians in the later Middle Ages. The hierocratic conception of his office held by Innocent III, *verus imperator,* who presided over the grand Fourth Lateran Council of 1215, and the extravagant claims to preeminence asserted by Boniface VIII in the bull *Unam Sanctam* (1302), prompted fierce opposition on the part of secular rulers and precipitated the Avignonese captivity and the great schism (Ladner, 1964).

The decay of Cluny evoked yet another monastic reformation by the "white monks" or Cistercians, a nobleman Robert of Champagne initiating the reform effort. Once again as the Englishman Stephen Harding, abbot of Citeaux from 1109 to 1134, set it forth, the keynote of the Cistercian reform was a return to the literal observance of Saint Benedict's rule. The real fall of monasticism, however, as an independent force may be ascribed to its papal dependence, for when it became the auxiliary of Rome, it had clearly outlived its initial religious purpose. Bernard of Clairvaux (1091–1153) saw the dangers of ecclesiastical centralization and in a treatise *De consideratione*, addressed to Pope Eugene III, he warned against bureaucracy and fiscalism. He urged as an alternative a reformation that would be ministerial and personal rather than authoritarian and merely institutional. Because of his stress on service and spirituality he was a kind of transitional figure between Gregorian reform and the mendicant movement.

About the time of the Cluniac and Cistercian reform movements, other efforts were being made to reform by a return to more primitive eremetical life reminiscent of Eastern monasticism. Among these orders may be mentioned the Camaldulians founded by Romuald of Ravenna (d. 1027), the Vallombrosians founded by Gualbert in the Appenines, the Carthusians founded by Bruno of Cologne at Chartreuse in 1084. Ivo of Chartres (d. 1117) in the eleventh and early twelfth centuries attempted once again to bring collegiate churches and cathedrals under monastic discipline. The Canons Regular of Saint Augustine combined monastic and clerical callings in churches, schools, and hospitals. But none of the efforts at reformation within monasticism were of permanent duration. Nor were the mendicant orders able to establish a lasting reformation of the Church.

The history of monasticism was the history of constantly renewed reforms. The individual monk best incorporated the "form" of Christ and the monastic community best represented the body of Christ. Both as individuals and communities the monks were to fulfill as best they could the "law of Christ." For the mendicant friars this law was best expressed in the commission to the disciples in Matthew 10 to go into the highways and byways to serve and to save the lost. Christ gave to Francis the great commission to reform the Church in the well-known words: "Repair my house, because it is, as you can see, in the process of being completely destroyed." Saint Francis initially understood these words quite literally and with his own hands rebuilt a number of churches. Soon, however, he came to see his vocation in spiritual terms so that his conception of reformation called for personal penitence, poverty, humility, and a life of service to mankind. Unlike various heretical groups or the *pauperes Christi* in the late eleventh and twelfth centuries, who emphasized absolute poverty as the supreme good, Saint Francis stressed conversion as a change of heart, the need to emulate Christ's life of love and to lead the *vita apostolica* as a life of devotion and service. In the Rules of 1221 and 1223 as well as in his Testament Saint Francis insisted upon faithful participation in the sacraments and humble obedience to the hierarchical Church. His was to be a reformation very personal and individual within the structure of the Church.

As the conventual Franciscans in their turn grew wealthy and worldly, the spiritual Franciscans became "reformers," urging the return to apostolic poverty and the simple spirituality of Saint Francis. In the adherents to Joachim of Floris' philosophy of history an apocalyptic-utopian strain which threatened to lose all historical concreteness developed. Joachim and his commentator Gerard described the three ages of world history as the Ages of the Father, the Son, and the Holy Spirit. Gerard predicted the advent of the age of the Holy Spirit for 1260, a new age in which the Spirit, assisted by the Spiritual Franciscans, would rule. Some Joachimite tendencies were even tied in with extravagant and bizarre ideas such as Johannes von Lichtenberger's astrological calculations. If reformation in the monastic tradition had meant moral purification and a return to the norm of pristine purity, the attempts to purge and reform among the spiritualists were intended as preparation for the new and final stage of human history. All eschatological expectation concentrated on a breakthrough of an ideal time. Reformation signified the second decisive turning point in human history and would inaugurate the third and final era of world history.

**5. Late Medieval Reform.** The call for reformation at the end of the Middle Ages was very different from that sounded earlier. It was more shrill, strident, urgent. It would be difficult to overestimate the devastating impact on all areas of thought and life of the "Babylonian Captivity" of the papacy at Avignon (1309–77) and of the Great Schism, when there were two or three claimants to the papal see at once (1378–1417). Shocked reformers of various kinds responded to the confused situation. William Durand coined the phrase *reformatio in capite et in membris*, calling for reform in head and members. The conciliarists placed the blame primarily on the papacy and curia and worked for administrative and constitutional change. Typical of this criticism were the *Speculum aureum de titulis beneficiorum*, a "golden mirror" reflecting the abuses of the benefices, and the *Squalores curiae Romanae*. A popular acrostic device which appeared often in the literature was *Radix Omnium*

*Malorum Avaritia* = ROMA; love of money is the root of all evil. In 1410 Dietrich of Niem in his treatise *De modis uniendi et reformandi ecclesiam in concilio universali* argued that healing the schism had to be accompanied by the cleansing of the Church. The powers usurped by the papacy had to be taken away, the beneficiary and financial policy had to be completely reformed, and the Church restored to the *via antiqua*, its former condition.

The pre-reformers or "forerunners of the Reformation" had their individual diagnoses of ills and programs for reform. In the late Middle Ages there was still general agreement that the reform of the Church was the work of God Himself, acting through spiritual men. There was considerably less agreement as to which spiritually quickened members of the body of Christ were authorized to lead an authentic reformation or what the best method for effecting a reform might be. Marsiglio of Padua in his *Defensor pacis* (1324) not only roundly assaulted abuses in the Church, but proposed constitutional changes, on the analogy of the city-state, which would diminish the monarchical episcopate and introduce representative principles. The new constitution of the Church would not be democratic in honoring majority rule in terms of numbers, but would take into account representation by quality of office, order, and estate. William of Ockham joined the Franciscans and protested in favor of "evangelical poverty." He was a severe critic of the worldliness and wealth of Pope John XXII. Ockham saw service as a basic character of the Church which had the power of law, service to Christ first of all. The external church whose societal structure involves her in the sphere of worldly power must constantly be pressed to conform to the "true church" of service. John Wycliffe (1328–84) believed that zealous laymen, sovereign rulers who are worthy Christians, must assume the task of reforming where worldly and wicked churchmen have defaulted and should be deposed. Everyone whom the Holy Spirit moves is called to act in behalf of the Church. Every Christian who lives according to Christ's will becomes a reformer automatically in the sphere of his personal life. In this tradition the Bohemian reformer John Hus (1369–1415) exclaimed, "O Christ, it will take a long time before the proud priests will become so humble as to subject themselves to the Church for sin, as thou, being innocent, hast subjected thyself" (Schmidt, 1964). Wessel Gansfort (ca. 1420–89) conceived of reform in terms of a greater spiritualization of religious rites and dogma, exercising a considerable influence upon Luther, at least by way of confirming him in stressing the inwardness of religion.

An example of the way in which the religious idea of reformation fused in the sacramental kingship concept is provided by the fifteenth-century document known as the *Reformatio Sigismundi*. This widely circulated treatise purported to be an account of a vision of Emperor Sigismund which came to him as he lay dreaming on his bed near the dawn. In the vision Sigismund was commissioned to prepare a road for the coming of the divine order, for all written law lacks righteousness. The coming of the priest-king Frederick is foretold, who will bring into being God's own order by promoting a spiritual and secular reform program. The document was clearly intended to support the efforts of Emperor Sigismund (1410–37) to see the Council of Basel (1431–49) succeed in reform. John of Segovia, chronicler of the council, wrote: "Reform can be understood either as the extirpation of evil or as the increase of the gifts of the Holy Spirit" (Koller, 1964; Oberman, 1966).

The concept of reformation was given an immediately practical technical meaning in the Empire during the fifteenth century. Not only did poets and pamphleteers demand "reformation," but lawyers worked on the revival of Roman law (important from the twelfth century on) and the reform of the imperial order, city and territorial law. The *gravamina* or grievances of the Empire articulated regularly at the Diets throughout the fifteenth century were often coupled with appeals to the "good old law" and the superior condition of things in former times. Thus the Diet of Eger "reformed" feuding law and coinage in 1436. In the reform of city ordinances (Nuremberg, 1479; Worms, 1498; Frankfurt, 1509, etc.), the renewal and restoration of the "good old law and customs" was the program. The term "reformation" was given a legal application in the modernizing of territorial law as in the case of the 1518 "reformation of Bavarian territorial law." The lethargic Emperor Frederick III codified a "reformation of the territorial peace" in 1442 (Maurer, 1961).

**6. Reformation as a Historical Period.** The idea of reformation has come to be very closely associated with the Protestant movement as an historical epoch. In more recent ecumenical days the term "counter-reformation" has given way in historical literature to the more generous designation of "Catholic Reformation" in order to bring out the positive side of the Catholic response to Protestantism. How the concept came to be used so exclusively to designate not only a development within church history but as a term for an entire era of European history in general is an interesting question and not at all so obvious as one might suppose. For Luther himself did not use the term to describe his movement as a whole. Luther used the concept in the old legal sense and not in a utopian apocalyptic sense. He spoke of reformation as the

creation of something new only in the context of the reform of the universities and its faculties. He rarely spoke of himself as a reformer or an innovator, seeing himself rather as a mere vehicle used by Christ the Word to effect change. He wished to "let the Word rule" and not personally to lead a reform. While he drank beer with Amsdorf, he opined, the Word of God went forth into the world creating tumults. Only in his early years did Luther use the term reformation at all. The young Luther made his most comprehensive statement regarding "reformation" in his *Resolution to Thesis 89:* "The Church is in need of a reform— which is not the duty of one man, the pontiff, or of many cardinals (as the most recent council has proved both points), but of the whole world, even of God alone. But the time of this reform is known to Him alone who has founded the times" (*Weimar Ausgabe,* I, 627, 27ff.; Schmidt, 1964). Luther did not exult about effecting a reformation of the Church nor did he hope to achieve it once for all times.

The term "reformation" was applied to the new evangelical church orders which replaced the pre-Reformation territorial ecclesiastical orders. In 1526 Luther himself drew up "The German Mass and Order of Divine Service" in which he laid down the principle that every church order had to promote faith and love. When it ceased to do so, it had to be set aside quickly and decisively in favor of one more conducive to true spiritual life. An evangelical church order should never lend itself to legalism or to hierarchical tyranny as in the case of the papal order with its canon law. Uniform church orders were justified only insofar as they were necessary for right doctrinal and sacramental practice. The church orders usually contained first a section on dogma in which the agreement of the territorial church with the general Lutheran confessions was demonstrated. There followed then the rules for liturgy, holding of church offices, organization of church government, discipline, marriage laws, school ordinances, salaries, alms, and the like. The adoption of the new church orders (*Kirchenordnungen*) in territories as they turned Protestant was viewed as a formalization of ecclesiastical reformation and occasionally, as in the case of the "Cologne Reformation" of 1543, the term was specifically used.

Philipp Melanchthon (1497–1560) was reticent about using the term "reformation" even in the old legal sense. In the document of the Schmalkald Diet of 1537 the superscription *De iure reformandi* comes from a strange hand. Only when the emperor in his proposal of 1544 announced a Christian reformation did the Saxons feel justified in assembling their recommendations in the "Wittenberger Reformation" of 1545. At the Diet of Augsburg in 1548 a *Reformation guter policey* was established. In the battle against the Leipzig Interim in 1550 Pfeffinger and the conservative Lutheran Flacius Illyricus undertook "the reformation" of various rites such as confirmation. In his funeral oration for Luther and again on the second anniversary of Luther's death, Melanchthon evaluated Luther's work and the reform effort, but without using the term "reformation." He distinguished five periods of church history each of which was characterized by certain key people and outstanding accomplishments. In the final fifth period of church history Luther, Melanchthon asserted, had relit the light of the gospel, but it was really God who called the Church back to the pure sources in the apostles and prophets. He still viewed Luther as standing in a long line of teachers in the one Church extending through all the past centuries (Maurer, 1961).

The Lutheran church historians adopted this position on the place of Luther and his work in church history. Flacius Illyricus in his *Zeugen der Wahrheit* (*Catalogus testium veritatis,* 1556; "Witnesses of Truth") and the *Magdeburg Centuries* (begun in 1559) referred to reformations in the Middle Ages in the old legal sense and saw the late medieval reform ordinances as prophetic of Luther's work. The Lutheran historian Veit Ludwig von Seckendorf, author of the famous *Historia Lutheranismi,* first equated Lutheranism and Reformation. In 1688 he wrote against the Jesuit Louis Maimbourg of the Lutheran movement as the *reformatio religionis ductu Dr. Martini Lutheri.* He spoke of the Reformation as the "purification of the condition of the church." By this time general historians were operating with the concept of modern times as distinguished from the Middle Ages, with the Reformation and the Renaissance as twin sources of modernity. In 1685 the Lutheran historian Cellarius, schooled in humanist cultural values, referred to the Middle Ages as the *medium aevum.*

Like Luther and the other magisterial reformers, Calvin was concerned with the substance of Christian reform, not with personally leading a movement as such. His intention was to affirm the preeminence of Jesus Christ against all corruptions in religion which diminish the centrality and sufficiency of Christ in theology and in the life and form of the Church. His teaching was not a new legalism or a gloomy predestinarianism, but his aim was to promote the truth of the gospel and the proper form of the church, as he patiently explained in his *Reply to Sadoleto* (1539). In his preface to Olivetan's New Testament (1535) Calvin already laid down the determinative ideas of his theology which remained the leading themes to the final edition of his *Institutes:* man's blessedness is acknowledging God as the source of good; the heart of Scripture is Jesus Christ; and the Gospel is the Word of God which confers faith. Calvin answered the question of the religious meaning of "reformation" very explicitly in a treatise *On the Necessity for Reforming the Church* (1543). He described Luther as a prophet who spoke out for the Gospel against apostasy. He denied the charge that the reformers were disturbing the peace, laying the blame on those who had brought the Church to a low spiritual estate, citing the words of Elijah to Ahab: "I have not troubled Israel, but thou and thy father's house in that ye have forsaken the commandments of the Lord." The reformers, he held, were merely obedient to their vocation to preach the Gospel. For Calvin, then, "reformation" meant proclaiming the Gospel of "good news of salvation" and leaving the consequences to God. In doctrine and practice the Church had come to diminish the purity of the gospel by impairing the glory of Christ. The saints were invoked instead of Christ alone. Men were led to rely upon their own works of righteousness rather than upon Christ's all-sufficient merit and mercy. Sacramental practice was so distorted as to minimize the importance of Christ as the central reality. Reformation for Calvin, as for Luther, meant the rediscovery and renewed proclamation of the Gospel (Gerrish, 1967).

A somewhat different emphasis is evident in the case of the Zurich reformer. The Zwinglian "reformed" reading of the reformation was rooted in the Erasmian notion of a "renaissance of Christendom." Zwingli himself spoke of a "restoration of Christendom." In later years after the Zurich and Genevan Swiss Protestant movements had been amalgamated in common confessions, this way of looking at the reformation was given expression also by men in the Calvin tradition. In 1580, for example, Theodore Beza in his church history referred to the "renaissance and growth" of the reformed churches.

The radical or left-wing reformers, very commonly in that century lumped together under the term Anabaptists, had a bewildering variety of reformation conceptions. A few ideas appear, however, with considerable regularity and consistency. They expected that in their sectarian groups, having separated from official church and state, they would anticipate in the here and now the coming of the kingdom of God. They were for the most part pacifists and sought to imitate Christ and to reestablish the pristine purity of the primitive church. Whether Anabaptists, Spiritualists, or Evangelical Rationalists, the radical reformers were alike in their dissatisfaction with the Lutheran-Zwinglian-Calvinist forensic formulation of justification and original sin or predestination that seemed to them to undercut the significance of their personal religious experience. They believed that holiness or sanctification could be achieved by the saints in the here and now. They were martyr-minded like the early Christians and society obliged them by persecuting them horribly as subversives. But they persisted in exercising those personal and corporate disciplines by which they strove to imitate in their midst what they construed from the New Testament texts to have been the life of the original apostolic community (Williams, 1962).

If the Lutheran church historians contributed to the development of the idea of the Reformation as an historical epoch, the Swiss reformed church historians also contributed to this usage. In the historiography of the reformed churches the Reformation was most often dated from 1516 with Zwingli as "the first of all to reform the church." The eighteenth-century Enlightenment church historians accepted the Reformation as a period, and added new motifs of interpretation. With Johann Lorenz Mosheim, the "founder of modern church history," the view of the Reformation as a general European phenomenon gained wider currency. He introduced the conception of the church as a kind of sociological entity and stressed the importance of political factors. The Groningen professor Daniel Gerde in his *Geschichte des im 16. Jahrhundert allenthalben in Europa erneuerten Evangeliums* (1744) gave to the Reformation a trans-confessional character and treated it as a European movement. During the nineteenth century as a result of the fervor generated by the wars of liberation and the rise of nationalism, the Reformation was viewed once again as a German, French, or English phenomenon by many historians. Historicism and a stress upon the social aspects of the Reformation introduced new emphases. Thus the idea of the Reformation as an historical conception was enlarged from the narrower religious and ecclesiastical framework to include the entire social, political, and cultural development of Europe at the beginning of "modern times."

**7. Reformation in Post-Reformation Times.** The classical Reformation of the sixteenth century made such a tremendous impact upon the Western mind that the religious idea of reformation was thereafter consistently conceived in terms derived from it. Two special emphases predominated in modern times. The one was traditional in nature, namely, criticism of abuses or of indifference within the Church accompanied by a new call to revive the faith and fervor of the early Christians and of the classical reformers or founding fathers of each denomination. The second was the persistent effort to apply religion to the reformation of society.

In the second half of the seventeenth century and

into the eighteenth century, Pietism flourished as a religious movement in Germany, Switzerland, and the Netherlands. It was reformatory in the sense of making an earnest, practical application of the abstract standards of orthodoxy to private life and to Christian community. When the Enlightenment and a loss of ardor within the Church of England proved to be corrosive of personal piety and lively faith, John Wesley's Methodism served to revive religion in a way not unlike the manner in which Puritanism in its day had quickened religious fervor, largely within the structure of the official Anglican church. The Moravian Brotherhood served as a link between Pietism and Methodism. The evangelical revival in the Church of England was reminiscent of Luther's own reform efforts. Wesley was a classical reformer late in time.

The Society of Friends with its Spirit-driven movement was analogous to some of the small sects of the sixteenth century. In the nineteenth century various members of the Oxford Movement referred to the effort of the Tractarians to rekindle the flame in Anglicanism as a "reformation." In America the Great Awakening (especially in 1830–31), following the indifference to religion of the revolutionary war period, was conceived of as a reformation in the sense of an evangelical revival. It, too, was influenced by Pietism's stress on feeling. Charles Finney's *Lectures on Revivals of Religion* (1835) was the most powerful theoretical statement of the revival experience.

Within the Roman Catholic communion there have been two large-scale efforts to renew theology within this century prior to the second Vatican Council. The first was the movement known as modernism which started before the turn of the century and was cut short by Pope Pius X in 1907. The second came right after the second World War, the so-called "new theology." This theological revival now in progress may well be more lasting, for it has a broader base throughout the Church and the seriousness of the Church's situation in the world is more clearly recognized. In Catholicism as in Protestantism, the Ecumenical Movement has been hailed as an important part of the "New Reformation" of the whole Christian church on earth, the *una sancta*. The council Vatican II in its "Decree on Ecumenism" referred "to that continual reformation of which she [the Church] always has need."

The application of religion to the reformation of society was a more characteristic expression of the Anglo-Saxon world than of continental Christianity. In England one by-product of the new Methodistic piety was pressure against slavery, child labor, and other social ills. The Sunday School, Bible Society, and missionary movements were effects of religion's power to reform the world. The wedding of nondogmatic

Christianity with American pragmatism in American Christianity—e.g., in John Fiske's *Cosmic Evolution*—produced such efforts as the social gospel movement. Following the lead of such nineteenth-century theologians as Samuel Harris and Horace Bushnell, who believed that America had a special destiny and mission in realizing the kingdom of Christ on earth, the advocates of the social gospel undertook the application of the "social principles of Jesus" to American urban and industrial society, de-emphasizing personal justification and religious experience of a traditional kind. Washington Gladden (1836–1918), Josiah Strong (1847–1916), and, above all, Walter Rauschenbusch (1861–1918), author of the highly influential lecture series *A Theology of the Social Gospel* (1918), conceived of the Church's task as the reformation of society according to the will of God, whose kingdom is one of peace, justice, and love. The Christian socialist movement in Europe was a response to similar reforming impulses, although in part apologetic in aim in that it was offered as an alternative to Marxist materialism.

In the late nineteenth century American Christianity joined hands with Europe in pressing ahead with a worldwide program. John R. Mott, founder of the World's Student Christian Federation (1895), called for the "evangelization of the world in this generation" and offered to mankind Protestant Christianity and democracy as two sides of the same coin. In the twentieth century churchmen have turned to solving problems of a social nature with energy, pressing for involvement in issues of peace, civil rights, race relations, education, and income for the underprivileged, urban renewal, farm labor, and a host of similar issues. In the words of the American theologian Robert McAfee Brown, the Reformation of the sixteenth century consisted of the rediscovery of the Church, while the Reformation of the twentieth century centers in the rediscovery of the world.

While history shows that the content of the religious idea of reformation has through the ages been subjected to varying modalities, certain elements have been recurrent, if not constant. For reformation in Western thought has indeed stressed man's intentional efforts, multiple, repeated, and variegated, to reassert good old values and by personal regeneration and individual reform as well as by the restoration and improvement of community life in the Church and the world to lift man above low levels to which he has periodically fallen. If one were to take a bold look at the whole sweep of history, one might venture to conclude that in the early centuries of the Christian era renewal elements were very strong in combination with ideas of personal reformation; that in the medieval and Reformation eras reformation of the individual and of the Christian communities, regular and secular, was prominent; and that in very modern times the reform of society seems to loom large as the primary concern of religious men in the West. The religious idea of reformation has at all times been a powerful force in history. Luther, the magisterial reformer, caught the paradox implied in the religious idea of reformation. He emphasized strongly that God "works within us" but not "without us." Reformation is God's work, but at the same time it is man's work. To Luther the world was "the sphere of faith's works," one of the most powerful organizing thoughts, Wilhelm Dilthey observed, that a man has ever had (*Gesammelte Schriften*, 4th ed., Leipzig and Berlin [1940], II, 61).

*BIBLIOGRAPHY*

The principal authority on the subject is Gerhart B. Ladner, *The Idea of Reform: Its Impact on Christian Thought and Action in the Age of the Fathers* (Cambridge, Mass., 1959), pp. 35, 9–34, 39–44, 63–107, 133–42; "Reformatio," S. H. Miller and G. E. Wright, eds., *Ecumenical Dialogue at Harvard* (Cambridge, Mass., 1964), pp. 170–90, especially 172–81. Other helpful titles include: Konrad Burdach, *Reformation, Renaissance, Humanismus* (Berlin, 1918; 1926), pp. 37–42; William Clebsch, *From Sacred to Profane America* (New York, 1968); Jean Delumeau, *Naissance et affirmation de la réforme* (Paris, 1965); Mircea Eliade, *Le mythe de l'éternel retour* (Paris, 1949); idem, *The Two and the One* (London, 1965), p. 148; Wallace K. Ferguson, *The Renaissance in Historical Thought* (Boston, 1948); Brian Gerrish, "John Calvin and the Meaning of Reformation," *McCormick Quarterly*, **21** (Nov. 1967), 114–22; Heinrich Koller, ed., *Reformation Kaiser Sigismunds* (Stuttgart, 1964), pp. 4–5; Wilhelm Maurer, "Reformation," *Die Religion in Geschichte und Gegenwart*, V (Tübingen, 1961), cols. 858–73, 861–63; Heiko Oberman, *Forerunners of the Reformation* (New York, 1966); Robert D. Preus, *The Theology of Post-Reformation Lutheranism* (St. Louis, 1970); Martin Schmidt, "Who Reforms the Church?" in S. H. Miller and G. E. Wright, eds., *Ecumenical Dialogue at Harvard* (Cambridge, Mass., 1964), pp. 191–206; Lewis W. Spitz, ed., *The Reformation—Material or Spiritual?* (Boston, 1962); idem, *The Renaissance and Reformation Movements* (Chicago, 1971); Charles Trinkaus, *"In our Image and Likeness": Humanity and Divinity in Italian Humanist Thought*, 2 vols. (Chicago, 1970); George H. Williams, *The Radical Reformation* (Philadelphia, 1962), p. 865; Herbert Workman, *The Evolution of the Monastic Ideal* (London, 1918), pp. 219–24.

LEWIS W. SPITZ

[See also **Christianity in History;** Cycles; Enlightenment; **Faith;** God; **Heresy;** Hierarchy; Perfectibility; Primitivism; Prophecy; **Renaissance; Revolution.**]

## RELATIVISM IN ETHICS

THE TERM "ethical relativism" may refer to any one of a number of related views. Distinguishing these will not solve the very difficult questions involved but will at least make clearer what the problems are. Most commonly, a relativist is taken to assert that there are incompatible ultimate moral beliefs in different cultures, and that there is no sense in which one set of beliefs can be said to be correct and another mistaken. Moral beliefs, that is to say, are relative to a particular culture, much as the rules of etiquette are. We can say that it is "correct" to wear black at a funeral in some communities but not in others; there is no point in asking which is "really" correct, apart from the customs of this or that community. In the same way, it is contended, in some communities it is right to have several wives, or to kill someone who has insulted your family; in others it is wrong. Different communities have different moral codes; and there are no objective criteria by which we can judge these codes themselves as right or wrong.

It will be seen that two distinct claims are being made here: a factual claim and a philosophical claim. The factual claim is that different cultures do in fact have different ultimate moral beliefs. The philosophical claim is that, this being so, there are no criteria by which to decide between them. These need to be considered separately.

Let us take the factual claim first. Do different cultures have different ultimate moral beliefs? At first sight it might seem obvious that they do. The crimes or sins of one community (e.g., suicide, infanticide, abortion, homosexuality, wife-lending, dueling) may be blameless, or even laudable, in another. Even within a single culture moral judgments may differ radically. As Bertrand Russell has pointed out (1935), "Conscience leads some to condemn the spoliation of the rich by the poor, as advocated by communists; and others to condemn exploitation of the poor by the rich, as practised by capitalists. It tells one man that he ought to defend his country in case of invasion, while it tells another that all participation in warfare is wicked" (*Religion and Science* [1935], p. 225). One of the characters in David Hume's *Dialogue*, appended to *Enquiry concerning the Principles of Morals* (1751) gives an amusing account of an imaginary country whose most esteemed public figure kills both his infant child and his best friend, marries his own sister, who indulges him in his homosexual amours, and finally hangs himself. "So virtuous and noble a life" say his countrymen, "could not be better crowned than by so noble an end." When another character says indignantly that there could be no such country it is pointed out that all the incidents described have been taken from the lives of some of the most admired Athenians, except for the assassination, which is based on the killing of Caesar by Brutus.

Examples of this kind do not, however, settle the matter. Hume's purpose, indeed, is to defend the thesis that at bottom all men have the same moral attitudes. The most extreme differences in actual codes of conduct do not necessarily establish that ultimate moral beliefs differ; for the same general principle may dictate very different behavior in differing circumstances. "Had you asked a parent at Athens," Hume says, "why he bereaved his child of that life which he had so lately given it, it is because I love it, he would reply; and regard the poverty which it must inherit from me as a greater evil than death, which it is not capable of dreading, feeling or resenting." Again, homosexual attachments "were recommended, though absurdly, as the source of friendship, sympathy, mutual attachment, and fidelity; qualities esteemed in all nations and all ages."

A similar point was made by Francis Hutcheson, who pointed out that apparent moral diversity often sprang from difference of opinion about the facts involved. He instances differing estimates of what makes for happiness; differing opinions about the motives of other men, particularly members of other races, and so about how they deserve to be treated; and differing religious beliefs, especially about what God commands. It is not clear, however, that these are altogether disagreements about fact rather than about value: our opinions about what makes men happy, or what God commands, may well depend on—or at least be influenced by—our beliefs about what is good or right.

In the next century very much the same line was taken by W. E. H. Lecky in his *History of European Morals from Augustus to Charlemagne* (2 vols., 1869). Moral diversity, he argued, could be accounted for by differing beliefs about matters of fact (such as the existence of a life after death in which heretics are punished, or the precise stage at which an embryo becomes a separate individual) or by the misapplication of moral principles universally held. Since then, it has become possible to assess the available evidence more thoroughly, but it is not clear that the question has been settled. Some of the earlier anthropologists, like L. Lévy-Bruhl (1857–1939), were impressed by the extent of moral diversity and were inclined to conclude that "theoretical ethics" had been exploded by "science": "What scientific ethical speculation can there henceforth be except the comparative study of ethical systems that exist or have existed?" (*Ethics and Moral Science*, p. 169). Lévy-Bruhl's main point, however, is that moral beliefs are wholly the result of social conditioning, and he does not rule out the possibility that different cultures may share the same basic moral beliefs. "It may be that the characteristics of duty, and of the conscience in general, are the result of a whole mass of conditions, nearly similar, which are found in all fairly civilized human societies" (ibid., p. 121). Westermarck agrees with earlier writers that much moral disagreement depends on "knowledge or ignorance of facts, on specific religious or superstitious beliefs, on different degrees of reflection, or on different conditions of life or other external circumstances" (*Ethical Relativity*, p. 196). He thinks, however, that there is one striking difference that cannot be explained away: "Savage rules of morality" have "broadly speaking, only reference to members of the same community or tribe" (ibid., p. 197). Murder, theft, lying, and the infliction of other injuries will be disapproved of when the victim is a member of the tribe, but condoned or even applauded if he is an alien. This fact was, however, regarded by Hobhouse as evidence not of irreconcilable moral diversity, but of moral evolution: progress in morals consisted in the gradual widening of the sphere of application of moral rules. More recently, Raymond Firth has suggested that the anthropological evidence points to the existence of standards of right and wrong in all human societies. While these vary, behind the variation there is "a real measure of uniformity." No society can exist without some regulation or restraint in sexual affairs, and without some curbs on violence. There must, then, be "some general principles about the relative value of non-violence and overt harmony in social actions." He adds that the anthropologist "does not abjure moral universals. He seeks them in the very nature of his social material" (*Elements of Social Organization*, p. 214).

The factual question, then (whether cultures differ in fundamental moral beliefs) has not been decisively answered, mainly because of the difficulty of deciding which moral beliefs are fundamental. Those who argue for uniformity have usually been content to show that eccentric moral beliefs can be derived from some more normal belief. Approval of human sacrifice, for example, becomes at least understandable in a man who believes that he is at the mercy of evil spirits who will afflict the whole community unless they are appeased in some way. If this kind of explanation is accepted it will follow that moral beliefs do not differ as much as might seem at first sight: the basic moral premiss becomes, not the utterly incomprehensible one that human sacrifice is good, but the understandable (if still controversial) one that it is permissible to sacrifice one innocent person for the good of the whole community. There may still, however, be a large area of disagreement, particularly about which of two conflicting considerations should take precedence. For example,

Lecky, in commenting on the gladiatorial shows of Imperial Rome, remarks: "The Roman sought to make men brave and fearless, rather than gentle and humane, and in his eyes that spectacle was to be applauded which steeled the heart against the fear of death, even at the sacrifice of the affections" (*History of European Morals*, 1, 287). Granted that in most cultures both bravery and compassion are applauded, difference of opinion about which should take precedence may still represent a quite fundamental difference in moral attitude. It is a difference, incidentally, which may well divide men even within the same culture. And there are other differences of the same kind.

But it is clear that the philosophical question (whether moral beliefs are objective or relative in the way that rules of etiquette are relative) is an independent one. For if fundamental beliefs do vary, it is still possible that some of them are mistaken. Moreover, even if they don't vary, it might still be the case that they are not objective.

The last point comes out clearly in the eighteenth-century controversy between the moral sense school (notably Hutcheson and Hume) and their opponents. As we have seen, Hutcheson and Hume believed that all men have, at bottom, the same moral sense. An analogy may be drawn with secondary qualities like color. To say that a buttercup is yellow is to say that it will cause an impression of yellow when light-rays from it stimulate a certain kind of sense organ. An animal with different eyes might well see it as a different color. In the same way, to say that something is good is, according to the moral sense school, to say that it rouses a particular emotion (approval) in beings with certain predispositions.

On this account moral judgments are relative, but at the same time they are in a sense objective. It is objectively true that buttercups are yellow, in the sense that they appear yellow to all men with normal eyesight. This does not, however, prevent color from being relative to the sense of sight, nor does it mean that the color is a quality of the buttercup. What the buttercup has is the different quality of reflecting light-waves of a particular wavelength. It is in this way that moral judgments are, according to Hutcheson, relative to the moral sense; and it was this view that led Hume to say that moral judgments, rightly understood, do not ascribe a quality or relation to the thing judged, but express a sentiment in the breast of the person judging.

It would seem from this that to say that morality is relative is not, after all, to say that moral statements are not objective. This is the case, however, only in one sense of "objective." It is objectively true that buttercups are yellow only if we are prepared to take as our standard the judgments of men with normal sight. The buttercup is yellow, seen through human eyes; to a creature with different eyes it might not be. Similarly an action is, according to the moral sense school, wrong, seen (metaphorically speaking) through human eyes; but to a creature with a different kind of moral sense it might not be wrong. And to a neutral observer—someone who was able to transcend the limits of his own physical or mental constitution—it would be neither right nor wrong: it would simply have certain characteristics capable of arousing approval in one kind of creature and disapproval in another.

Once this is realized, the fact (if it is a fact) that men have the same basic moral beliefs becomes irrelevant. It is at least logically possible that men might (perhaps on another planet) have different basic moral beliefs. And it would seem to follow that if they did, there would be no reason for preferring one set to another. Consequently John Balguy (1686–1748), author of *The Foundation of Moral Goodness*, asks Hutcheson, very shrewdly, whether God had any reason for endowing men with the moral sense they have instead of one which, let us say, made them approve of cruelty and disapprove of kindness. If he had a reason, then there is a reason, quite apart from human dispositions, for preferring kindness to cruelty. Kindness really is better than cruelty in the eyes of God, that is, to a being who sees things as they are, and not as colored by the peculiarities of the human constitution. If God had no reason, then it would seem to follow that moral beliefs have no objective validity.

As against this, however, it may be argued that Hutcheson and Hume are in this position only because they regard morality as relative to a particular human emotion, or sentiment—the sentiment of approval. Suppose it is said instead that morality is relative to human purposes and the conditions of their realization. This would seem to give moral principles at least the objectivity of sociological laws. Hobbes, for example, regarded moral rules as stating the conditions which made harmonious cooperation in society possible. Since the conditions were the same whatever the ends cooperation was intended to achieve, this made morality "eternal and immutable" even though human desires themselves were highly mutable. This position is not, however, essentially different from that of Hutcheson and Hume. Although they said that "X is right" amounts to "I have an approving attitude to X" they did not mean that such attitudes were arbitrary, or could be adopted at will. For Hutcheson our feelings of approval are as fixed a part of human nature as our sense of smell, or of taste. This is also true of Hume, though he is more inclined than Hutcheson to concede that custom and conditioning play a part in the development of the moral sense.

Both of them would agree with Hobbes that moral beliefs are relative to human nature. If men were different, they would be different. It was just this that their opponents would not concede.

Some philosophers, however, have argued that in Hobbes or Hume relativism is attenuated to the vanishing point. Hume says, in a striking phrase, that men "invented the laws of nature" (*Treatise of Human Nature*, III, II, viii), but he also says that they could hardly have invented any other laws than those they did invent. It may be argued that this is not really a contingent matter. Any moral rule presupposes the possibility of breaking it; but it is another matter to suppose that everyone could break it all the time, and still another to suppose that the rule might not exist. It would, in a sense, be logically impossible for everyone always to tell lies. If I say "no" whenever I mean "yes" my "no" will be taken to mean "yes" and I will in effect only be using words eccentrically. If everyone said "no" when he meant "yes," the words would merely change their meaning. The rule about truthtelling, in short, is one of the conditions of communication. But the same may be said of the laws of logic; and it is not really conceivable that they could be different. To say that moral rules are the conditions of successful cooperation in society, then, may lead to the conclusion, not that they are contingent or "relative," but that they are somehow rooted in the nature of things. Something like this seems to be the position of P. Winch (1959–60).

The more usual view, however, has been that the view of Hobbes, or the moral sense view, avoids the absurdities of complete relativism only by, as it were, a lucky accident. Men happen to have the same moral sense; but they might not have had. Human nature might have been different. It is at least conceivable that we might be confronted with a tribe in which, let us say, torturing slaves for sport was approved of. It would seem to follow that we could not rationally condemn such a tribe. We would, of course, think their behavior wrong, since our own attitude to torture is one of disapproval, but we would have to admit, on reflection, that they would have the same reason for thinking our reaction wrong. We would call them cruel and they would call us squeamish. To an impartial observer it would not even make sense to ask which of us was mistaken. "We should no more call the moral sense morally good or evil," Hutcheson admitted, "than we call the sense of tasting, savoury or unsavoury, sweet or bitter" (*Essay . . .* , 3rd ed. [1742], p. 239). Moral judgments arise only within a particular moral system, in which certain moral rules or axioms are presupposed. We cannot apply moral epithets to those systems, or those axioms, themselves. The consequences are, of course, even more serious for those relativists who say that men's basic moral beliefs do actually differ. They must conclude that, objectively considered, a Hitler or a Genghis Khan is no worse than a Saint Francis or a Gandhi.

This supposed consequence has always been the chief objection to relativism. It may be argued, however, that the objection rests on a confusion. The contention is that, according to the relativist, nothing is really right or wrong. But why should the relativist say this? He is forced to say it only if he concedes an objectivist premiss which he expressly repudiates: that nothing is "really" right or wrong unless it is objectively right or wrong.

A cultural relativist, for example, believes that moral attitudes arise out of the whole complex of institutions and beliefs that constitute a culture. It is argued that, when confronted with the members of a different community whose moral attitudes differ from his own, he is logically committed to discounting his own moral revulsion from their behavior. What this implies, however, is that a moral belief or attitude that is merely a function of a culture ought to be disregarded. In other words, the relativist who draws this conclusion is not really assuming that all moral beliefs are the function of a culture, but only that mistaken ones are. A consistent relativist, on the other hand, would presumably say that "X is wrong" amounts to saying "X is not in accordance with my own fundamental moral attitudes" and that there is no other sense of "wrong" which would entitle us to add: "In that case, X cannot be 'really' wrong."

This reply may seem to commit the relativist to an even less acceptable position. For, it may be said, he is now claiming the right to condemn others simply because they happen to disagree with him, or perhaps because they happen to belong to a different culture. There are, however, two separate questions which need to be disentangled here. The principal one is what we are actually saying when we say that a given course of conduct is wrong. It would be common ground that we mean that the behavior is not in accordance with certain fundamental principles. The question at issue is how these fundamental principles are arrived at. According to the objectivist, they are statements of objective moral facts. According to the subjectivist, they express fundamental attitudes or preferences. That is to say, they are not absolute, but relative to the attitudes or preferences of the person making the judgment. If it is argued that we are not entitled to condemn a man simply for having certain fundamental attitudes, it may be asked whether we are entitled to condemn him for an intellectual error about a matter of fact. The objectivist may perhaps reply that he does not condemn a wrongdoer for believing something to be right that is in fact wrong, but for doing what he

knows to be wrong. Perhaps, however, this merely means that the wrongdoer does not realize the truth of a different proposition, namely, that it is wrong to act against one's beliefs about what is right? If so, he is still being condemned for an intellectual error. If not, it is hard to escape the conclusion that he is being condemned for being a certain kind of man: the kind of man who deliberately chooses to do what he believes to be wrong. But the subjectivist, too, would say that in the last analysis he condemns the wrongdoer for being a certain kind of man. To say that a man has certain fundamental preferences or attitudes is to say that he is a certain kind of man. If he prefers toughness to compassion (to resort to an earlier example) he will arouse disapproval, and perhaps active opposition, in someone whose fundamental preferences are different. The objectivist will say that we are only justified in disapproving if it is an objective fact that compassion is better than toughness; but (apart from the difficulty of seeing what kind of fact this could be) the relativist will ask: What added justification does this give?

The other question is whether it is fair to blame a man for having certain fundamental attitudes if those attitudes are the inevitable result of his being reared in a particular culture. But this is a separate, and not really relevant, question; for it arises equally on an objectivist theory of ethics. If "X is wrong" states a special kind of fact, it may still be the case that men will believe it or disbelieve it as a result of conditioning of one kind or another. On any ethical theory, it is necessary to distinguish the question whether a given action is wrong from the question whether a man is to be blamed for doing it.

Whether or not moral relativism is true, it is at least not as clearly false, nor as destructive of morality, as has often been maintained. In considering it, however, we have found it necessary to distinguish between the following questions: 1) Are fundamental moral beliefs sometimes different in different cultures, or between different individuals within a culture? 2) Would it follow, if they are, that morality is not objective? 3) Are moral beliefs relative to human purposes (the purposes of mankind in general) and to the conditions of their realization? 4) Are moral beliefs relative to the particular desires or attitudes of individual men? 5) Are moral beliefs arbitrary? As we have seen, there has been no quick and easy answer to any of these questions.

*BIBLIOGRAPHY*

On the nature and implications of variations in moral beliefs: E. Westermarck, *Origin and Development of the Moral Ideas*, 2 vols. (London, 1906); idem, *Ethical Relativity* (London, 1932); L. T. Hobhouse, *Morals in Evolution* (London, 1906); L. Lévy-Bruhl, *Ethics and Moral Science*

(London, 1905); W. E. H. Lecky, *History of European Morals from Augustus to Charlemagne*, 5th ed., 2 vols. (London, 1882); A. MacBeath, *Experiments in Living* (London, 1952); R. B. Brandt, *Hopi Ethics* (Chicago, 1954); J. Ladd, *The Structure of a Moral Code* (Cambridge, Mass., 1957).

The main texts for the seventeenth- and eighteenth-century controversy are: T. Hobbes, *Leviathan* (London, 1651); F. Hutcheson, *An Inquiry into the Original of our Ideas of Beauty and Virtue* (London, 1725); idem, *Essay on the Nature and Conduct of the Passions and Affections with Illustrations upon the Moral Sense* (London, 1728; 3rd. ed., London, 1745); D. Hume, *Treatise of Human Nature* (London, 1739–40); idem, *Enquiry concerning the Principles of Morals* (London, 1751); J. Balguy, *Foundation of Moral Goodness* (London, 1728–29); R. Price, *Review of the Principal Questions in Morals* (1758; 3rd ed., London, 1787).

Some recent discussions of the philosophical problems are contained in: P. Edwards, *Logic of Moral Discourse* (Glencoe, Ill., 1955); R. B. Brandt, *Ethical Theory* (Englewood Cliffs, N.J., 1959); R. M. Hare, *The Language of Morals* (Oxford and New York, 1952); D. H. Monro, *Empiricism and Ethics* (Cambridge, 1967); Charles Stevenson, *Ethics and Language* (New Haven, 1960); P. Winch, "Nature and Convention," *Aristotelian Society Proceedings, 1959–60*, **60** (London, 1961), 231–52.

D. H. MONRO

[See also **Evil;** Mathematical Rigor; **Right and Good; Utilitarianism.**]

# RELATIVITY

## I

ESSENTIALLY, Einstein's theory of relativity has its roots in the questions: Where are we? How are we moving? In connection with our present purposes, these questions posed no profound problems so long as men believed that the earth is the fixed center of the universe. With the astronomical hypothesis of a moving earth, however, the questions began to become disturbing, not only theologically but also scientifically. This article is concerned with the scientific aspects of the problem.

In the seventeenth-century concepts of Galileo, and more sharply in those of Newton, one already finds a "principle of relativity," though the phrase itself did not come into being until late in the nineteenth century. We can say that the principle has to do with the impossibility of detecting absolute motion. But to this statement we have to attach changing caveats whose nature will not become apparent until we have discussed the matter in detail.

In the nineteenth century, optical and electromagnetic theory had seemed to invalidate the principle. Reaffirming it and later generalizing it were thus revolutionary acts. Their drastic scientific consequences, affecting the basic concepts of time and space, were worked out in the twentieth century, principally by Einstein.

## II

The considerable success of the Ptolemaic system had brought high respectability to the intuitive concept of a fixed earth, a doctrine strongly reinforced by the influence of Aristotle, the dogma of the Church, and the vanity of man.

Copernicus found the idea of a moving earth in the writings of the ancients. In the dedication of his book, *De revolutionibus* to Pope Paul III, he said that at first he had thought it absurd. His greatness does not reside primarily in his daring to take it seriously but in his constructing a mathematically detailed system capable of challenging the formidable geocentric system expounded by Ptolemy. Like Ptolemy, he used epicycles (Figure 1), and his system was far from simple. And though he held that the sun was fixed at the center of the Universe, the pivotal point of the planetary motions in his system was not the center of the sun but an empty place that we may conveniently call the center of the earth's orbit. In this sense the earth, though relegated to the role of a planet, retained a certain supremacy.

Dethronement of the earth was Kepler's doing, and with it came beauty. The planets now moved in elliptical orbits about a fixed sun at a common focus, their speeds varying in orbit in such a way that the line from the sun to a planet traces out equal areas in equal times (Figure 2). No longer was there need for intricate epicycles either for shape of orbit or speed in orbit. Simplicity had taken their place.

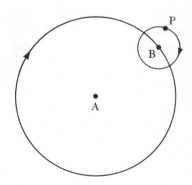

FIGURE 1. Epicycle. Planet P moves on circle (called epicycle) whose center B moves on circle (called deferent) with center A. In Ptolemaic system Earth was at A. In Copernican system A was a point near the sun.

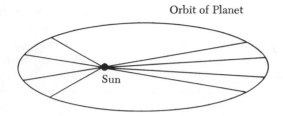

Orbit of Planet

Sun

FIGURE 2. Here the ellipticity of the orbit is highly exaggerated. In the solar system the principal planetary orbits are close to being circular.

In the drudgery of his lifelong search for laws of planetary motion Kepler was sustained by a deep, religious belief in the underlying harmony and beauty of the heavens. Let us not forget, though, that a seeking after beauty had motivated Copernicus, as it had the founders of the Ptolemaic system, who believed, with Plato, that uniform circular motion was the only one worthy of the perfection of the heavens. These aesthetic aspects of their work and the work of Kepler need to be stressed, for just such seemingly nonscientific considerations will be playing a crucial role in the developments waiting to be told, and we shall see that science in its highest manifestations is more akin to art than to the popular misconceptions concerning its nature.

### III

In the seventeenth century Galileo and Descartes adumbrated the law of inertia, which later became Newton's first law of motion: *every body continues in its state of rest, or of uniform motion in a straight line, unless it is compelled to change that state by forces impressed upon it.* That this had not been formulated millennia earlier should not surprise us, for terrestrial experience strongly suggests that bodies left to themselves come to rest, and that force is needed to maintain them in motion. True, the celestial motions seemed to continue indefinitely, but these motions were for the most part circular, and it was natural for the Greeks to believe that the heavens were subject to laws far different from those that held sway on the earth.

It is hard to overestimate the importance of the first law. Uniform motion in a straight line was now the natural motion, needing no external cause. Bodies, being possessed of an innate inertia, resisted *change* of motion; and only change of motion demanded the presence of external force. Because of this new viewpoint Newton was able to create a conceptual system that brought together the dynamics of the heavens and the earth in a mighty synthesis built seemingly on just his three laws of motion and his law of universal gravitation.

But only seemingly. By themselves, Newton's laws made no sense. Take the first law, for example. What does the phrase "uniform motion in a straight line" mean? Imagine a bead on a straight wire marked off in inches. If the bead traverses equal distances along the wire in equal times we can certainly claim that it is moving uniformly in a straight line. But our claim will be superficial and ill-founded. What, for instance, if the clock with which we timed the bead had been unreliable? Or the wire had been whirling and reeling —say with the Keplerian earth?

Newton was acutely aware of such problems. In his *Principia*, before stating his laws of motion, he carefully prepared a conceptual setting in which they could take on meaning. Saying disarmingly "I do not define time, space, place, and motion [since they are] well known to all," he nevertheless proceeded to define their absolute as distinguished from their relative aspects:

"Absolute, true, and mathematical time, of itself, and from its own nature, flows equably without relation to anything external. . . .

"Absolute space, in its own nature, without relation to anything external, remains always similar and immovable. . . ."

These are basic assertions, not operational definitions. For example, they provide no method of deciding which of our clocks comes closest to ticking uniformly.

Spurred by penetrating criticisms by Berkeley and Leibniz, Newton added a famous Scholium in a later edition of the *Principia*. Here is a short excerpt: "[God] is not eternity and infinity, but eternal and infinite; he is not duration or space, but he . . . endures forever and is everywhere present; and by existing always and everywhere he constitutes duration and space."

For Newton, absolute time and absolute space were vividly present. Without them, as we have seen, his laws would be meaningless. With them he could form cosmic concepts of absolute rest, of absolute uniform motion in a straight line, and of absolute deviations from such motion.

By noting the centrifugal effects of rotation, among them the concavity of the surface of rotating water in his famous bucket experiment, Newton had convinced himself that rotation is absolute, in powerful agreement with his concept of absolute space. However, his laws of motion did not faithfully mirror the absoluteness of their setting. To appreciate this, let us begin with everyday experience. In a vehicle, we feel no motion when the velocity is steady. We feel the *changes* in motion—the accelerations or decelerations —when the vehicle speeds up, or swerves, or jerks, or slows down. If we look out of the window we can learn of our *relative* motion, but when a sudden acceleration throws us off balance we need no view of the scenery to convince us that the ride has been unsteady.

Because of this, we sense that acceleration differs significantly from velocity and from rest. But we have been speaking in terrestrial terms. Newton's laws were set in absolute space and absolute time, which cosmically implied absolute rest, absolute velocity, and absolute acceleration. Yet the laws, while making acceleration (which term includes rotation) absolute, provided no way of detecting absolute rest or absolute velocity. According to the laws, although acceleration was absolute, both rest and velocity were, dynamically, always relative. Newton presented this as an almost immediate consequence of his laws. His *Corollary V* reads *"The motions of bodies included in a given space [i.e. reference system] are the same among themselves whether that space is at rest, or moves uniformly forward in a straight line without any circular motion."* We shall refer to this as *the Newtonian principle of relativity*, though a better phrase might well be *the Newtonian dilemma*. It troubled Newton.

Since his laws did not provide absolute location, absolute rest, or absolute velocity, he introduced an extraneous *"Hypothesis I: That the center of the system of the world is immovable."* This unmoving center could not be the center of the sun, since the sun, pulled by the planets this way and that, would be intricately accelerated. A fortiori, no point primarily related to the earth could fill the role of the fixed center of the world.

The solar system did, however, have a theoretical sort of balance point that we would now call its center of mass; and Newton argued that according to his laws the center of mass of the solar system would be unaccelerated. It would thus be either at rest or in uniform motion in a straight line—the laws could not say which. Transcending his laws, Newton now declared that this center of mass of the solar system, this abstract disembodied point never far from the sun, was the center of the world, and ipso facto immovable.

With the solar system pinned like a collector's butterfly to the immovable center of the world, absolute location, rest, and velocity acquired human vividness. Yet they did so only through Newton's ad hoc intervention. Had Newton allowed the center of mass of the solar system to move uniformly in a straight line—as it had every right to do under the laws—there would have been no dynamical effect of this motion.

A word of caution, though. In the above we have followed Newton in ignoring the possible dynamical effects of the distant stars.

## IV

Having reached this stage, we may profitably regress awhile. With a fixed earth the problem of relativity could hardly arise. But in retrospect, once we accept the idea of a moving earth, the very opposition to it argues strongly in favor of a dynamical principle of relativity. For if one could vividly feel the earth's motion or intuitively recognize dynamical effects of the motion, would men have been likely to have regarded the earth as fixed?

Evidently the earth's velocity has no noticeable dynamical effect, and this is implicit in the Newtonian principle of relativity. As for the earth's acceleration, we realize in the light of Newton's theory that it does have dynamical effects; but in everyday life these are either too small to be noticed or else do not present themselves to common sense as manifestations of the acceleration. The path to the concept of a moving earth had not been an easy one. Following Aristotle, Ptolemy had argued powerfully against it, saying, for example, that objects thrown in the air would be left behind by a moving earth. He also argued that a rotating earth would fly apart, to which argument Copernicus retorted that Ptolemy should have worried rather about the survival of the far larger sphere of the stars if that sphere and not the earth were rotating once a day.

Among the dynamical "proofs" advanced against the hypothesis of a moving earth was that heavy bodies when dropped ought to fall obliquely. By way of illustration it was said that if one dropped a stone from the top of the mast of a ship at rest it would land at the foot of the mast, but if the ship was in rapid motion the stone would "obviously" land closer to the stern. Against this Galileo argued that the stone would share the impetus of the moving ship and thus (neglecting air resistance) would land at the foot of the mast after all. In his *Dialogues on the Two World Systems* he presents the point vividly in these words of Salviati (emphasis added):

Shut yourself up with some friend in the largest room below decks of some large ship and there procure gnats, flies, and such other small winged creatures. Also get a great tub full of water and within it put certain fishes; let also a certain bottle be hung up, which drop by drop lets forth water into another narrow-necked bottle placed underneath. Then, *the ship lying still*, observe how these small winged animals fly with like velocities towards all parts of the room; how the fishes swim indifferently towards all sides; and how the distilling drops all fall into the bottle placed underneath. And casting anything towards your friend, you need not throw it with more force one way than another, provided the distances be equal . . . [Now] make the ship move with what velocity you please, *so long as the motion is uniform.* . . . You shall not be able to discern the least alteration in all the forenamed effects, *nor can you gather by any of them whether the ship moves or stands still.* . . .

Galileo then has Sagredo drive the point home by remarking:

. . . I remember that being in my cabin I have wondered a hundred times whether the ship moved or stood still; and sometimes I have imagined that it moved one way, when it moved the other way. . . .

The extent to which this is an anticipation of the Newtonian principle of relativity needs clarification. It can be interpreted in terms of the idea of inertia, but on this Galileo was somewhat confused, being unable wholly to emancipate himself from the Platonic belief in circular inertia as the basic law. Certainly the ship argument had powerful consequences. For example, the parabolic motion of projectiles, a major discovery of Galileo's, could have been deduced from it right away. For if, relative to the moving ship, the stone fell vertically with uniform acceleration, then as viewed from the shore the path would indeed be parabolic, being compounded of a vertical fall and a uniform horizontal motion.

Some twenty years before the *Principia* appeared, Huygens had used this principle of relativity brilliantly in deducing laws of perfectly elastic impact by considering simple collisions taking place on shore and asking how they would appear when viewed from a uniformly moving boat. Indeed, as Huygens realized, the first law of motion could have been deduced directly from the Newtonian principle of relativity had that principle been taken as basic. For a free body at rest in one frame of reference would be moving uniformly as viewed from a frame in uniform motion relative to the first.

But Newton relegated this principle of relativity to the minor role of a *Corollary*, and did his best to thwart it, as we have seen. His intellectual and emotional need for absolute space was overwhelming. How else could he have had absolute acceleration? Besides, the Galilean argument of the ships was not wholly satisfactory. It compared phenomena on a stationary ship with those on a ship in uniform motion, though such ships could hardly exist on a spinning earth in orbit around the sun.

As we have seen, Newton had avoided this sort of difficulty by setting his laws in absolute space and time. It is strange, therefore, that in commenting on his *Corollary V* he himself used the illustration of stationary and uniformly moving ships. And this becomes even more surprising when one notes that only a few pages earlier, in defining absolute space, he had specifically discussed how the motion of the earth is involved in the absolute motion of a ship.

The Galilean argument of the ships can be defended. Newton's laws imply that *the uniform part* of the motion in absolute space of a ship or other reference frame is not detectable within the reference frame. Therefore, whatever the effects of the *nonuniform* part

of the absolute motion of the "stationary" ship, they would be duplicated in the ship moving uniformly relative to it. Thus in retrospect we may say that Galileo, and later Huygens, did indeed have the Newtonian principle of relativity, though they could not have realized its Newtonian subtleties at the time.

## V

Though Newton regarded action at a distance as absurd, he was unable to find a satisfactory physical model that would lead to his inverse square law of gravitation. According to that law, every particle in the Universe attracts every other particle with a gravitational force that is utterly unaffected by intervening matter. Or, to put it succinctly, gravitation does not cast shadows.

Light does cast shadows, however, and this indicates that it is something propagated. That it has finite speed is by no means obvious. Important men like Kepler and Descartes believed its speed infinite. Galileo's pioneering experiment to measure its speed was inconclusive, and the first evidence that its speed was finite came in 1676, when Roemer, to account for annual variations observed in the rhythm of the eclipses of the innermost moon of Jupiter, proposed that light is propagated "gradually." Since astronomical data available at the time implied, if Roemer was correct, a speed of some 130,000 miles per second, the word "gradually" may sound like an understatement. Relativity will reveal in it an unexpected irony.

For the most part, Roemer's idea met with little favor, though Huygens and Newton were among those who took it seriously. Not till 1728 was independent corroboration found of the finite yet stupendous speed of light. In that year Bradley deduced from the *aberration* of light (tiny annual elliptic apparent motions of the stars) a speed close to the currently accepted value of some 186,300 miles per second. Since aberration has an important role to play, we briefly describe its essence. If we stand still, vertically falling rain falls on our hat. If, remaining upright, we run forward, it strikes our face. If we ran in a circle, the rain would seem to come from an ever-changing direction always somewhat ahead of us. Analogously, because of the orbital motion of the earth, light from a star seems to come to us from a position always somewhat ahead of where we would see it if we were not orbiting. The stars thus seem to move in tiny ellipses once a year, and from the size of the effect Bradley calculated the ratio of the orbital speed of the earth to the speed of light.

The discovery that light has a finite speed was to prove of world-shaking importance. It lies at the heart of the modern theory of relativity, with all its consequences. That the discovery came from astronomers,

77

as did the basis of Newton's law of gravitation, underlines the enormous practical consequences of the astronomers' seemingly ivory-tower pursuits.

Ingenious laboratory methods have been devised for measuring the speed of light with extraordinary precision, but the details need not concern us. It suffices to know that the speed is finite and can be measured in the laboratory.

### VI

In optics Newton developed a powerful particle-and-wave theory of light that, if misread, can seem an extraordinary foreshadowing of the modern quantum theory. His rejection of the pure wave theory propounded by his contemporary Huygens and others, and the superiority of his own theory in accounting for the optical phenomena known at the time were major reasons for the neglect of the wave theory during the eighteenth century.

In the early nineteenth century, however, Young and Fresnel brilliantly revived the wave theory and brought it to victory over the prevalent particle theory. The rise of the wave theory, with its ubiquitous aether as the bearer of the waves, brought a threat to the Newtonian principle of relativity, and one that Newton would probably have welcomed. For aberration implied an aether essentially undisturbed by the passage of matter through it. The aether could thus be considered stationary, so that though mechanical experiments were powerless, optical experiments had a chance to succeed in detecting absolute rest and absolute velocity —meaning now rest and velocity relative to the stationary, all-pervading aether.

The aether was not what one might reasonably consider a credible concept. Because of the phenomenon of polarization, light waves were taken to be transverse, and the aether to be an elastic solid. Yet it had to offer no perceptible impediment to the motions of the planets, for these motions were in excellent accord with Newton's system of mechanics. Nevertheless, since the wave theory of light, developed in detail by Fresnel, was as successful in encompassing the intricate phenomena of optics as Newton's laws were in encompassing the intricate phenomena of celestial and terrestrial mechanics, the aether could hardly be ignored, for all its conflicting properties.

If $v$ is the speed of the earth through the aether and $c$ the speed of light, an experiment to detect the quantity $v/c$ is said to be of the first order, as distinguished from a second-order experiment designed to detect $v^2/c^2$. A first-order experiment was soon performed, but it failed to detect $v/c$. To account for the failure, Fresnel proposed that matter carries aether wholly entrapped within it yet allows aether to pass freely through it. Moreover the amount of aether entrapped in, say, glass had to depend on the wavelength of the light passing through it, so that if various wavelengths were present, as they certainly were, the amount of entrapped aether was given by a self-contradictory formula. Fresnel's extraordinary hypothesis, which goes by the misleading name partial aether drag, proved highly successful. Without hurting the theory of aberration, it implied that every feasible first-order experiment to detect the earth's motion through the aether would fail. And since, over the years, all such experiments did fail, Fresnel's hypothesis had to be taken seriously. Indeed, it was confirmed by difficult laboratory experiments on the speed of light in streaming water.

### VII

The experimenter Faraday, being unskilled in mathematics, created simple pictorial concepts to help him interpret his pioneering researches in electromagnetism. The theorists had been content to find mathematical, action-at-a-distance formulas for the forces exerted by magnets and electric charges. But Faraday created a revolution in physics by consistently envisioning a magnet or charge as surrounded by a "field" of tentacle-like lines of force reaching through space, so that all space became the domain of the important aspects of electromagnetic phenomena.

Building on Faraday's work, Maxwell imagined an electromagnetic aether with a pseudo-mechanical structure so bizarre that he himself did not take it seriously. Nevertheless he took it just seriously enough to extract from it electromagnetic field equations that play a key role in the development of the theory of relativity. Since Maxwell required an electric current —his crucial "displacement current"—in free space, where there was no electric charge, his theory hardly seemed credible to physicists. Yet the displacement current gave an elegant mathematical symmetry to Maxwell's equations and because of it his theory predicted the existence of transverse electromagnetic waves moving with the speed of light; and when in 1888, nine years after his death, these waves were detected by Hertz, Maxwell's theory could no longer be easily resisted. It yielded a superb unification of the hitherto disparate disciplines of optics and electromagnetism, with visible light occupying a narrow band of wavelengths in a broad spectrum of electromagnetic radiation. It also dispensed with electromagnetic action at a distance by having electromagnetic effects transmitted by the aether acting as intermediary. As for the all-important aether, Maxwell's equations delineated for it an inner structure that could not be envisaged in credible Newtonian mechanical terms.

Gradually physicists, becoming accustomed to its mathematical properties, learned to live with it, and an era of mechanistic physics faded.

### VIII

By analogy with water waves and sound waves, and more specifically because of Maxwell's equations, we can expect light waves to travel through free aether with a fixed speed. If, in our laboratory, we find that light waves have different speeds in different directions, we can conclude that we are moving through the aether. Suppose, for example, that we find that their greatest speed is 186,600 miles per second in this direction → and their least speed 186,000 miles per second in this direction ←. Then we can say that our laboratory is moving through the aether in this direction → at 300 miles per second (half the difference of the speeds), and that the light waves are travelling through the aether at 186,300 miles per second (half the sum). Thus we shall have discovered our absolute velocity, and this despite Fresnel. But in speaking of Fresnel's so-called aether drag, we said it implied that *every feasible* first order experiment would fail. The above is not feasible. The direct laboratory methods of measuring the speed of light have involved not one-way but round-trip speeds.

Shortly before his death, Maxwell outlined a way to measure the earth's velocity through the aether by comparing not one-way but round-trip speeds of light in various directions in the laboratory. But since there would be only a residual effect of the second order—if $v$ is the earth's orbital speed and the sun is at rest $v^2/c^2$ is about $10^{-8}$—he dismissed the effect as "far too small to be observed."

In 1881, however, Michelson succeeded in performing the experiment with borderline accuracy for detecting the orbital speed. And in 1887, with Morley, he repeated the experiment, this time with ample accuracy. It gave a null result, and thereby precipitated a crisis. For it suggested, and this was indeed Michelson's own interpretation, that the earth carries the nearby aether along with it. But aberration implied that the earth does not.

To resolve the conflict, FitzGerald, and later Lorentz independently, proposed that objects moving through the aether contract by an amount of the second order in the direction of their motion.

Lorentz, assuming a fixed aether, untrapped and undragged, had nevertheless obtained an electromagnetic derivation of Fresnel's formula far more convincing than that given by Fresnel. Thus Lorentz could account for the null results of the feasible first-order experiments to detect absolute motion. His task was to express Maxwell's equations in a reference frame

moving uniformly through the aether with velocity $v$, and to do so in such a way that, to the first order, the $v$ did not show up. But the Maxwell equations were far from being pliable. In the moving frame they more or less forced Lorentz to replace the $t$ representing the time by a new mathematical quantity that he called "local time" because it was not the same everywhere.

By incorporating the contraction of lengths, he was able to account for the null result of the Michelson-Morley experiment without spoiling the theory of aberration. But again the Maxwell equations forced his hand, causing him to introduce with the contraction a corresponding dilatation, or slowing down, of the local time. Specifically, he found in 1904 what we now call the *Lorentz transformation*, a name given it by Poincaré in 1905. Consider two reference frames similarly oriented, one at rest in the aether and the other moving with uniform speed $v$ in the common $x$-direction. Ordinarily one would have related the coordinates $(x, y, z)$ of the former to the coordinates $(x', y', z')$ of the latter by what P. Frank named the Galilean transformation:

$$x' = x - vt, \ y' = y, \ z' = z. \tag{1}$$

But the Lorentz transformation relates $(x, y, z)$ and the true time $t$ to $(x', y', z')$ and the local time $t'$ of the moving frame as follows:

$$x' = (x - vt)/\sqrt{1 - v^2/c^2}, \ y' = y, \ z' = z \tag{2}$$
$$t' = (t - vx/c^2)/\sqrt{1 - v^2/c^2}.$$

By means of these equations, Lorentz succeeded, except for a small blemish removed by Poincaré in 1905, in transferring the Maxwell equations to the moving reference frame in such a way that they remained unchanged in form. Since no trace of the $v$ survived, neither the Michelson-Morley nor any other electromagnetic experiment could now be expected to yield a value for $v$.

It is of interest that the Lorentz transformation, (2), had already been obtained on electromagnetic grounds by Larmor in 1898, and its essentials by Voigt on the basis of wave propagation as early as 1887, the very year of the Michelson-Morley experiment.

### IX

The background has now been presented for Einstein's accomplishments of 1905, which we shall consider in conjunction with the accomplishments of Poincaré. Along with the later fame of Einstein there grew a popular mythology correctly attributing the theory of relativity to him, but seriously slighting the work of Poincaré. A considerable controversy was created when Whittaker claimed that the 1905 theory of relativity was due to Poincaré and Lorentz, with Einstein playing a negligible role. Whittaker was justified in seeking to bring the situation into better perspective, but in his zeal he went too far, forsaking his usually impeccable scholarship. This led to a counter-reaction that has also sometimes gone too far. And meanwhile the work of Larmor has received less recognition than it merits.

Maxwell led Larmor, Lorentz, and Poincaré to mathematical equations identical with equations belonging to the theory of relativity. Poincaré had so many of the crucial ideas that, in retrospect, it seems amazing that he did not put them together to create the theory of relativity. He raised aesthetic objection to the piecemeal, ad hoc patching up of theory to meet emergencies—Fresnel's entrapped aether to account for the null results of first order experiments, and the contraction to account for the second order experiment of Michelson and Morley—and as early as 1895 Poincaré adumbrated a principle of relativity that denied the possibility of detecting uniform motion through the aether. His were the aesthetic strictures that led Lorentz to seek a transformation to a moving frame that would leave Maxwell's equations invariant in form. Since, for example, the Lorentz contraction factor $\sqrt{1 - v^2/c^2}$ reduces lengths to zero when $v = c$, Lorentz had limited the application of his 1904 theory to systems moving through the aether with speeds less than $c$; it was Poincaré who suggested in 1904 the need for a new dynamics in which speeds exceeding $c$ would be impossible. And in 1905 he wrote a major article, sent in almost simultaneously with that of Einstein, in which extraordinary amounts of the *mathematics* of relativity are explicitly developed.

Einstein, in his epoch-making paper of 1905 "On the Electrodynamics of Moving Bodies," introduced a new viewpoint. He began by discussing an aesthetic blemish in electromagnetic theory as then conceived. When a magnet and a wire loop are in relative motion, there is an induced electric current in the wire. But the explanation differed according as the magnet or the wire was at rest. A moving magnet was accompanied by an electric field that was not present when the magnet was at rest and the wire moving. Thus what was essentially one phenomenon had physically different explanations within the same theory.

Because the phenomenon depended on the relative motion of magnet and wire and not on any absolute motion through the aether, and because experiments to detect motion through the aether had given null results, Einstein postulated as a basic principle that there is no way of determining absolute rest or uniform motion—he worded it more technically—and he called it *the principle of relativity*, as Poincaré had done.

The phrase was not wholly new with Poincaré. In 1877 Maxwell, in his little book *Matter and Motion*, had spoken of "the doctrine of relativity of all physical phenomena," which he proceeded to explain in these eloquent words (emphasis added): "There are no landmarks in space; one portion of space is exactly like every other portion, so that we cannot tell where we are. We are, as it were, *on an unruffled sea*, without stars, compass, soundings, wind or tide, and we cannot tell in what direction we are going. We have no log which we can cast out to take a dead reckoning by; we may compute our rate of motion with respect to the neighboring bodies but we do not know how these bodies may be moving in space."

It is surprising that these words should have come from Maxwell. Not only did he build his electromagnetic field theory on the concept of an aether but, in later propounding the idea that led to the Michelson-Morley experiment, he was envisaging the light waves that ruffle the ethereal sea as a means for determining our motion through the aether. It is not clear precisely what Maxwell had in mind when speaking of the relativity of *all* physical phenomena. There is in the phrase an echo of the views of Berkeley, of which more later. Perhaps Maxwell was not here regarding the aether as kinematically synonymous with absolute space. But later in the book, citing Newton's bucket experiment and the Foucault pendulum, he specifically contradicts the "all" by affirming the absoluteness of rotation.

Poincaré's concept of the principle of relativity, like Einstein's, went beyond what, for convenience, we have been referring to as the Newtonian principle of relativity. That principle referred to the impossibility of detecting one's absolute *uniform* motion by dynamical means. The new principle, while retaining the restriction to uniform motion, extended the impossibility to include the use of all physical means, particularly the optical. Yet it is fair to say that in Newton's time, in the absence of a generally accepted wave theory of light, the Newtonian principle of relativity could have been thought of as implying the impotence of *all* physical phenomena to detect one's absolute *uniform* motion. If so, the Newtonian principle, after a period of grave doubt as to its validity, was now being reaffirmed. But, as will appear, its reaffirmation in the Maxwellian context played havoc with fundamental tenets of Newtonian mechanics.

In speaking of the principle of relativity, Poincaré had an aether in mind. But Einstein declared that in his theory the introduction of an aether would be "superfluous" since he would not need an "absolute stationary space." Moreover, unlike Poincaré, Einstein audaciously treated the principle of relativity as a fundamental axiom suggested by the experimental hints

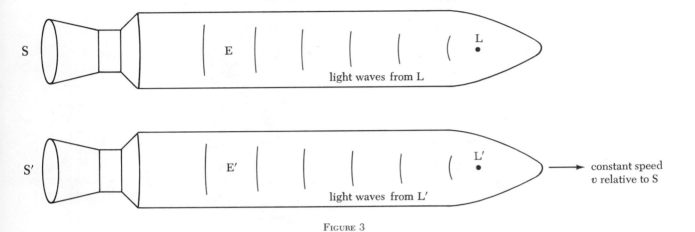

S

light waves from L

S′

light waves from L′

constant speed
$v$ relative to S

FIGURE 3

already available but not in itself subject to question.

Einstein next introduced a second postulate: that the speed of light in vacuo is constant and independent of the motion of its source—again he expressed it more technically. In terms of an aether, this postulate seems almost a truism. For a wave, once generated, is on its own. It has severed its connection with the sources that gave it birth and moves according to the dictates of the medium through which it travels.

On these two principles Einstein built his theory. Each by itself seemed reasonable and innocent. But, as Einstein well realized, they formed an explosive compound. This is easy to see, especially if, for convenience, we begin by talking in terms of an aether. Imagine two unaccelerated spaceships, S and S′, far from earth and in uniform relative motion (Figure 3). In S and S′ are lamps L, L′ and experimenters E, E′ as indicated. Assume that S happens to be at rest in the aether. E measures the speed with which the light waves from L pass him and obtains the value $c$. In S′ a similar measurement is performed by E′ using light waves from L′. What value does E′ find? Since the speed of the light waves is independent of the motion of their sources, the waves from L and L′ keep pace with one another. And since S′ is moving towards the waves with speed $v$ we expect him to find that they pass him with speed $c + v$. But the principle of relativity forbids this. For if E′ found the value $c + v$, he could place another lamp at the opposite end of S′ and measure the speed of the light waves in the opposite direction, obtaining the value $c - v$. By taking half the difference of these values he could find his speed through the aether, in violation of the principle of relativity. Therefore he must obtain not $c + v$, nor $c - v$, but simply $c$, no matter how great his speed $v$ relative to S, or indeed relative to any source of light towards which, or away from which, he is moving.

Viewing this without reference to the aether, we see from Einstein's two postulates that no matter how fast we travel towards or away from a source of light, the light waves will pass us with the same speed $c$. Clearly this is impossible within the context of Newtonian physics. Either we must give up the first postulate or else give up the second. But Einstein retained both, and found a way to keep them in harmony by giving up instead one of our most cherished beliefs about the nature of time.

## X

Einstein reexamined the concept of simultaneity. Accepting it as intuitively clear for events occurring at the same place, he asked what meaning could be given to it when the events were at different places. Realizing that this must be a matter of convention, he proposed a definition that we shall now illustrate.

Imagine the spaceships S, S′ equipped with identically constructed clocks fore and aft, as shown (Figure 4). Pretend that $c$ is small, or that the spaceships are of enormous length, so that we can use convenient numbers in what follows. When clock $C_1$ reads noon, E sends a light signal from $C_1$ to $C_2$ where it is reflected back to $C_1$. Suppose that the light reached clock $C_2$ when $C_2$ read 1 second after noon, and returned to $C_1$ when $C_1$ read 3 seconds after noon. Then Einstein would have E say that his clocks $C_1$ and $C_2$ were not synchronized. To synchronize the clocks Einstein would have E advance $C_2$ by half a second so that according to the readings of $C_1$ and $C_2$ the light would take equal times for the outward and return journeys. With $C_1$ and $C_2$ thus synchronized, if events occurred at $C_1$ and $C_2$ when these clocks read the same time, the events would be deemed simultaneous.

In 1898 Poincaré had already questioned the concept of simultaneity at different locations, and in 1900 he

81

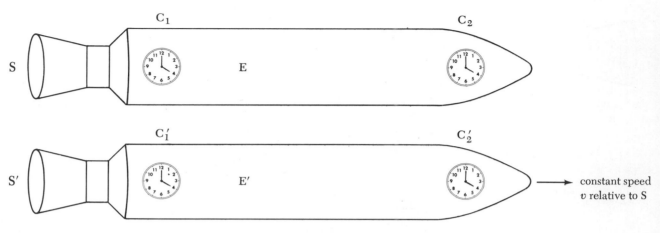

FIGURE 4

had considered the use of light signals for adjusting clocks in a manner strikingly similar to that used by Einstein in 1905. However, Poincaré was concerned with adjusting rather than synchronizing clocks. Moreover, he did not build on two kinematical postulates but worked in terms of the Maxwell equations; nor did he take the following step, and it is things such as these that set Einstein's work sharply apart.

Consider E and E' synchronizing the clocks in their respective spaceships S and S'. E arranges $C_1$ and $C_2$ so that they indicate equal durations for the forward and return light journeys, and declares them synchronized. But E', watching him from S', sees S moving backwards with speed $v$ relative to him. Therefore, according to S', the light signals sent by E did not travel equal distances there and back (Figure 5), but unequal distances (Figure 6). And so, according to E', the very fact that $C_1$ and $C_2$ indicated equal durations for the forward and backward light journeys showed that $C_1$ and $C_2$ were *not* synchronized.

However, E' has synchronized his own clocks, $C_1'$, $C_2'$, according to Einstein's recipe, and E says they are not synchronized, since relative to S the light signals used by E' travel unequal distances there and back (Figure 7).

With E and E' disagreeing about synchronization we naturally ask which of them is correct. But the principle of relativity, as Einstein rather than Poincaré viewed it, forbids our favoring one over the other. E and E' are on an equal footing, and we have to regard both as correct. Since events simultaneous according to E are not simultaneous according to E', and vice versa, Einstein concluded that *simultaneity is relative,*

being dependent on the reference frame. By so doing he gave up Newtonian universal absolute time.

Previously we spoke of measurements of the one-way speed of light as not being feasible, deliberately suggesting by the wording that this might be because of practical difficulties. The lack of feasibility can now be seen to have a deeper significance. To measure the one-way speed of light over a path AB in a given reference frame we need synchronized clocks at A and B by which to time the journey of the light. With the synchronization itself performed by means of light, the measurement of the one-way speed of light becomes, *in principle,* a tautology. The mode of synchronization is a convention permitting the convenient spreading of a time coordinate over the reference frame one uses. What can be said to transcend convention (with apologies to conventionalists) is the rejection of Newtonian absolute time, with its absolute simultaneity.

Once the concept of time is changed, havoc spreads throughout science and philosophy. Speed, for example, is altered, and acceleration too, and with it force, and work, and energy, and mass, so that we wonder if anything can remain unaffected.

Not even distance remains unscathed, as is easily seen. Imagine the spaceships S and S' marked off in yard lengths by E and E' respectively. E measures a yard length of S' by noting where the ends of the yard are at some particular time. Since E and E' disagree about simultaneity, E' accuses E of noting the positions of the yard marks *non*-simultaneously, thus obtaining an incorrect value for the length. When the roles are reversed, E similarly accuses E'. Because of the principle of relativity, both are adjudged correct. Thus once

FIGURE 5

FIGURE 6

Figure 7

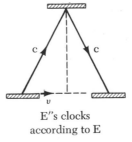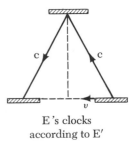

E″'s clocks
according to E

E′'s clocks
according to E′

Figure 9

simultaneity is relative, so too is length. Indeed, the disagreement as to lengths corresponds in magnitude to the FitzGerald-Lorentz contraction, but here it is a purely kinematical effect of relative motion and not an absolute effect arising from motion relative to a fixed aether. While E says that the yards of E′ are contracted, E′ says the same about those of E.

Let $x$, $y$, $z$, and $t$ denote the coordinates and synchronized clock times used by E in his spaceship reference frame S; and let $x'$, $y'$, $z'$, and $t'$ denote the corresponding quantities used by E′ in S′. Einstein derived directly from his two postulates a mathematical relation between these quantities, and it turned out to be the Lorentz transformation (2). The interpretation, though, was different, because E and E′ were now on an equal footing: $t'$, for example, was just as good a time as $t$.

Because of the principle of relativity, the relationships between E and E′ are reciprocal. We have already discussed this in connection with lengths. It is instructive to consider it in relation to time: when E and E′ compare clock rates each says the other's clocks go the more slowly. This, like the reciprocal contractions of lengths, is immediately derivable from the Lorentz transformation in its new interpretation. It can be understood more vividly by giving E and E′ "clocks," each of which consists of a framework holding facing parallel mirrors with light reflected tick-tock between them. Each experimenter regards his own clocks as using light paths as indicated (Figure 8). But because of the relative motion of E and E′, we have the situation shown (Figure 9). Since these longer light paths are also traversed with speed $c$, each experimenter finds the other's clocks ticking more slowly than his own. Indeed, a simple, yet subtle, application of Pythagoras' theorem to the above diagrams yields the mutual time dilatation factor $\sqrt{1 - v^2/c^2}$. Moreover, since E′ and E, in addition to agreeing to disagree, agree about the speed of light, each says that

the other's relative lengths are contracted in the direction of the relative motion by this same factor $\sqrt{1 - v^2/c^2}$, for otherwise the ratio distance/time for light would not be $c$ for both.

A further kinematical consequence is easily deduced directly from Einstein's postulates. We begin by noting that no matter how fast E′ moves relative to E, light waves recede from him with speed $c$: he cannot overtake them. But these light waves also move with speed $c$ relative to E. Therefore E′ cannot move relative to E with a speed greater than $c$. Nor can any material object relative to any other: *c is the speed limit*. (It has been proposed that particles exist that move faster than light. They have been named tachyons. According to the Lorentz transformation, tachyons can never move slower than light; their speed exceeds $c$ in all reference frames.)

## XI

An immediate victim of relativity was Newton's law of gravitation with its instantaneous action at a distance; for with simultaneity relative, one could no longer accept a force acting with absolute simultaneity on separated bodies. We can safely ignore the routine modifications of Newton's law that were proposed to let it fit into the relativistic framework; Einstein's by no means routine theory of gravitation will be described later.

That the startling relativistic kinematics, of which we have just seen samples, did not also play havoc with Maxwell's equations need not surprise us. Larmor, Lorentz, and Poincaré had shown the intimate relationship between Maxwell's equations and the Lorentz transformation. We can now appreciate the achievements of Fresnel and Maxwell: Fresnel's self-contradictory "aether drag" was a relativistic effect, as too was Maxwell's displacement current. Little wonder that these concepts had seemed incredible. They were valiant attempts to fit relativistic effects into the kinematics of Newtonian absolute space and absolute time. In retrospect the work of Fresnel and Maxwell takes on that aspect of inspired madness that is the highest form of the art we call science. So too does

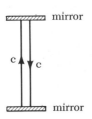

mirror

$c$ ↕ $c$

mirror

Figure 8

the work of Einstein, for his theory of 1905 was itself built on a contradiction: its basic principles assumed reference frames made out of rigid rods while denying their possibility. For a rigid rod would transmit impacts instantly and could be used to synchronize clocks in a manner conflicting with that proposed by Einstein.

### XII

Relativistic kinematics required a relativistic dynamics for which Newtonian concepts were not well suited. But the success of Newtonian dynamics for speeds small compared with $c$ had created habits of thought that could not be easily broken. Accordingly, Einstein and others sought to distort Newtonian concepts to fit relativistic kinematics. Mass became relative, increasing in value with increasing relative speed. Thus the greater the relative speed of an object, the greater its inertial resistance to change in its speed. If the object could attain speed $c$ its mass would become infinite, and no increase in speed would be possible. While this sounds like dynamics and uses Newtonian concepts, it is basically a reflection of the existence of the speed limit $c$, which, as we saw, is an immediate kinematic consequence of Einstein's two postulates. (For ordinary matter and radiation, $c$ is the upper speed limit. For tachyons, if they exist, $c$ is the lower speed limit. In either case, $c$ is a speed limit.)

In a second paper on relativity in 1905 Einstein made a daring extrapolation. He began by showing mathematically that if a body gives off an amount of energy $L$ *in the form of electromagnetic radiation*, its mass decreases by $L/c^2$. Now came these momentous words: "The fact that the energy . . . [is] energy of radiation evidently makes no difference." Therefore, Einstein concluded, all energy, of whatever sort, has mass. And herein lay the germ of the famous equation $E = mc^2$.

In 1907 Einstein completed the derivation by a further daring step. Arguing that a body of mass $m$ has the same inertia as an amount of energy $mc^2$, and that one should not make a distinction between "real" and "apparent" mass, he concluded that all mass should be regarded as a reservoir of energy. At the time, and for many years after, there was not the slightest direct experimental evidence for this, yet Einstein not only asserted the equivalence of mass and energy, but recognized it in 1907 as a result of extraordinary theoretical importance.

### XIII

In 1907 Minkowski showed in detail that the natural habitat of the equations of relativity is a four-dimensional "space-time," an idea already explicitly foreshadowed by Poincaré in 1905.

The Galilean transformation (1) exhibits the aloof absoluteness of Newtonian time. Though $t$ enters the transformation of $x$ (and, more generally, of $y$ and of $z$), it itself remains untouched: one does not even bother to write $t' = t$. In the Lorentz transformation (2), $x$ mixes with $t$ as intimately as $t$ does with $x$; and in more general Lorentz transformations $x$, $y$, $z$, and $t$ thoroughly intermingle.

In ordinary analytical geometry, if a point P has coordinates $(x, y, z)$ its distance, OP, from the origin, O, is given by

$$OP^2 = x^2 + y^2 + z^2. \tag{3}$$

If we rotate the reference frame about O to a different orientation, the coordinates of P change, say to $(x', y', z')$, but the value of the sum of their squares remains the same:

$$OP^2 = x'^2 + y'^2 + z'^2 = x^2 + y^2 + z^2. \tag{4}$$

Under the Lorentz transformation (2) there is an analogous quantity $s$ such that

$$\begin{aligned} s^2 &= x'^2 + y'^2 + z'^2 - c^2 t'^2 \\ &= x^2 + y^2 + z^2 - c^2 t^2. \end{aligned} \tag{5}$$

The analogy with (4), already close, can be made even closer by introducing $\tau = \sqrt{-1}\, ct, \tau' = \sqrt{-1}\, ct'$, for now

$$\begin{aligned} s^2 &= x'^2 + y'^2 + z'^2 + \tau'^2 \\ &= x^2 + y^2 + z^2 + \tau^2, \end{aligned} \tag{6}$$

and the Lorentz transformation (2) can be envisaged as a change to a new four-dimensional reference frame obtained by rotating the first about O to a different orientation. While (6) may give us initial confidence that relativity pertains to a four-dimensional world in which time is a fourth dimension, the nature of this four-dimensional world is more vividly seen by avoiding $\sqrt{-1}$ and returning to (5).

Let E in his spaceship S press button A on his instrument panel, and a minute later, according to his clock, press a neighboring button B; and let us refer to these pressings as events A and B. According to E, the spatial distance between events A and B is a matter of inches. According to E', because of the rapid relative motion of S and S', events A and B are separated by many miles; also, according to E', who says the clocks in S go more slowly than his own, the time interval between events A and B is very slightly longer than a minute. The importance of (5) is that, despite these disparities, it affords a basis of agreement between E and E'. If each calculates for events A and B the quantity

$$ds^2 = (\text{spatial distance})^2 - c^2(\text{time interval})^2 \tag{7}$$

he will get the same result as the other. The large

discrepancy in the spatial distances is offset by the very small discrepancy in the time intervals, this latter being greatly magnified by the factor $c^2$.

Take two other events: E switching on a lamp in S, and the light from the lamp reaching a point on the opposite wall. Here (7) gives $ds = 0$ for both E and E′, since for each of them the distance travelled by light is the travel time multiplied by $c$.

The quantity $ds$ is the relativistic analogue of distance, but the effect of the minus sign in (5) is drastic. This is easily seen if we ignore two spatial dimensions, use $x$ and $ct$ as coordinates and try to fit the resulting two-dimensional Minkowskian geometry onto the familiar Euclidean geometry of this page. We draw a unit "circle," all of whose points are such that the magnitude of $ds^2$ equals 1. Because $ds = 0$ along the lines OL, OL′ given by $x = \pm ct$, this "circle" obviously cannot cut these lines. It actually has the shape shown, consisting of two hyperbolas (Figure 10). When we add a spatial dimension the lines OL, OL′ blossom into a cone. When we add a further spatial dimension, so that we have the $x$, $y$, $z$, $ct$ of the four-dimensional Minkowski world, the cone becomes a three-dimensional conical hypersurface—do not waste time trying to visualize it. Since it represents the progress of a wavefront of light sent out from O, it is called the *light cone*; there is one at each point of Minkowski space-time.

Because a particle has duration, it is represented not by a point but a line, called its world line. If it is at rest relative to the reference frame used, its world line is parallel to the $ct$ axis. If it moves relative to the frame, its world line slants away from the $ct$ direction, the greater the speed the greater the slant. Since the speed cannot exceed $c$—we are ignoring the possibility of tachyons here—the world line must remain

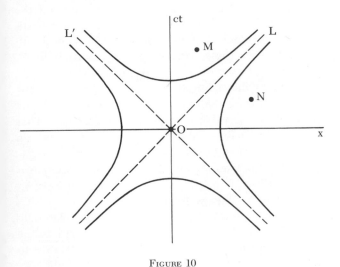

FIGURE 10

within all the light cones belonging to the points on it.

An event M within the light cone at O can be reached by an influence from event O moving with a speed less than $c$, and can thus be caused by the event O. It turns out that in all reference frames, event M is later than event O.

An event N outside the light cone at O cannot be similarly reached: the speed would have to exceed $c$. Thus O could not cause N. This is intimately related to the theorem that in some reference frames O is earlier than N and in others it is later. We have here been using the word "cause" rather loosely. The concept of causality poses enormous problems, but the situation here is superficially simple: if for some experimenters O is earlier than N while for others it is later, we are not likely to regard it as a possible cause of N.

The light cone at an event O separates space-time into three regions: the absolute future of O, the absolute past of O, and a limbo that is neither the one nor the other.

In Minkowski space-time the mutual contractions of yardsticks and the mutual slowing of clocks become mere perspective foreshortenings. Also, the hitherto unrelated laws of conservation of energy and momentum become welded together into a single space-time law. As for the hard-won Maxwell equations, they take on a special elegance. One could almost have obtained them uniquely by writing down the simplest nontrivial equations for a four-dimensional mathematical quantity (called an antisymmetric tensor of the second order) that combines electricity and magnetism into a single Minkowskian entity. These are but samples of the beauty of the theory in its Minkowskian setting. Space does not permit a discussion of the many triumphs of the theory of relativity, either by itself or when applied to the quantum theory.

No matter in what theory, the symbol $t$ is at best a pale shadow of time, lacking what, for want of better words, we may call time's nowness and flow. In treating time as a fourth dimension, Minkowski presented the bustling world as something static, laid out for all eternity in frozen immobility. This geometrization of time, however, was crucial for the development of Einstein's *general theory of relativity*, of which we must now tell.

### XIV

The absence of absolute rest and of absolute uniform motion becomes intuitively acceptable if we assume that space is featureless. In that case, though, how could there be absolute acceleration?

Berkeley, in Newton's day, had insisted that all motion must be relative and that absolute space was a fiction. As for the seemingly absolute centrifugal effects of rotation, he argued that they must indicate not absolute rotation but rotation relative to the stars. Towards the end of the nineteenth century, Mach subjected the Newtonian theory to a searching epistemological analysis that was to have a profound effect on Einstein. Amplifying Berkeley's kinematical views, Mach gave them dynamical substance by proposing that inertia—which gives rise to the seemingly absolute effects of rotation and other types of acceleration—is due to a physical interaction involving all matter in the universe. In Newton's theory, acceleration was referred to absolute space. Thus absolute space had inertial dynamical effects on bodies, yet despite Newton's third law that to every action there is an equal opposite reaction, there was no corresponding reaction by the bodies on absolute space. This anomalous, one-way dynamical influence of absolute space on matter was aesthetically and epistemologically unpleasant. Yet Einstein's theory of relativity suffered from an analogous defect. It had replaced Newton's absolute space and absolute time by a space-time in which, though the essence of the Newtonian principle of relativity was retained, acceleration was nevertheless absolute.

As early as 1907 Einstein was attacking the problem of acceleration. Aesthetically, one would like to extend the principle of relativity not just kinematically but physically to include all motion. But despite the proposals of Berkeley and Mach, experience and experiment had hitherto seemed sharply against this. Following the dictates of aesthetics, Einstein was able to show how experiment could be made to serve the ends of beauty. His weapon was the well-known observation, going back to Galileo and earlier, that all dropped bodies fall to the earth with the same acceleration $g$ (neglecting air resistance and assuming everyday heights). Newton had incorporated this by giving mass two roles to play: inertial and gravitational. The gravitational pull of the earth on a body was proportional to the mass of the body, and thus to its inertia. The larger the mass, the larger the pull but also the larger the inertia, with the result that the acceleration remained independent of the mass.

That the gravitational mass of a body should be proportional to its inertial mass was an extraneous assumption having no inherent Newtonian raison d'être. Einstein made it a cornerstone of his new theory.

Starting in purely Newtonian terms, Einstein imagined a laboratory K, far removed from external gravitational influence, moving with uniform acceleration $g$ as indicated. He compared it with a similar laboratory K' at rest in a uniform gravitational field which, for convenience, we may pretend is furnished by the earth (Figure 11).

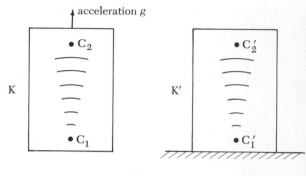

FIGURE 11

In K' all free bodies fall with acceleration $g$. Where K is, though, all free bodies are unaccelerated; but because of the "upward" acceleration of K, they "fall" *relative to K* with acceleration $g$. It is a simple exercise in Newtonian mechanics to show that, so far as *purely mechanical* experiments within K and K' are concerned, there is no way of distinguishing between K and K'.

Now came the stroke of genius: Einstein propounded a *principle of equivalence* stating that no experiment *of any sort* within the laboratories could distinguish between K and K'. At once this permitted a *general principle of relativity* embracing all motion, for if an experimenter in K, or in K', could no longer determine the extent to which physical effects were due to uniform acceleration and to what extent to uniform gravitation, acceleration need no longer be regarded as absolute. Indeed, acceleration was now seen to be intimately linked to gravitation. In addition, the equality of gravitational and inertial mass took on the aspect of a truism. For, consider equal particles suspended from equal springs in K and K'. In K, because of the acceleration, the *inertia* of the particle causes the stretching of the spring. In K', there being no acceleration, inertia does not come into play. Instead the stretching is due to the *gravitational* mass of the particle. By the principle of equivalence, one cannot distinguish between these gravitational and inertial effects.

Suppose, further, that each particle absorbs energy, thus gaining inertial mass. Since the spring in K is now extended further than before, so too, according to the principle of equivalence, must the spring in K' be. Thus the inertial mass of the energy must also have an equivalent gravitational mass.

If one looks too closely at the principle of equivalence as Einstein initially used it one finds inconsistencies. Yet its fertility was extraordinary. Consider, as a further example of this, a ray of light sent laterally across K. The acceleration of K causes the path of the light to appear to be curved "downwards" relative to K. Therefore light rays must be correspondingly bent by the gravitational field in K′. Moreover, just as the bending of a light ray passing from air to glass implies a decreased speed of propagation of the light waves, so too does the gravitational bending of light rays imply a slowing down by gravitation of the speed of light. Thus the 1905 theory, now called *the special theory of relativity,* could hold only approximately in the presence of gravitation.

Again, let $C_1$, $C_2$, $C_1'$, $C_2'$, as shown in K and K′, be "standard" clocks, by which we mean that they are *ticking at identical rates.* At each tick of $C_1$ a light signal is sent from $C_1$ towards $C_2$. Because K is moving faster and faster, each light signal has farther to travel than its predecessor to reach the receding $C_2$. So the light signals reach $C_2$ separated by greater time intervals than the time intervals separating the ticks of $C_2$. When thus compared by means of light signals, therefore, clock $C_1$, which ticks at the same rate as clock $C_2$, nevertheless seems to be going more slowly than $C_2$. The principle of equivalence now requires that the same shall hold for $C_1'$ and $C_2'$ in K′, so that standard clock $C_1'$ seems to go more slowly than standard clock $C_2'$ because of gravitation. Einstein argued that the spectral frequencies of light emitted by atoms can be regarded as standard time-keepers, and thus as substitutes for $C_1'$ and $C_2'$. Therefore spectral lines arriving at $C_2'$ from $C_1'$ would have lower frequencies than those in the spectra produced locally by $C_2'$, which would mean that they were shifted towards the red end of the spectrum. This is the famous *gravitational red shift.* But the most important lesson to be learned here is that gravitation warps time.

## XV

At this stage we must pause to consider the imposing edifice of Euclidean geometry on which Newton and Maxwell had based their theories. The Greeks had built it on idealized concepts like sizeless points and breadthless lines, and postulates concerning them. The naturalness of these postulates so deeply impressed Kant that he regarded Euclidean geometry as inescapable and existing *a priori.* Yet, from the start, Euclid's fifth postulate had caused disquiet. In context it implied that through a point P not on a line l there is one and only one line parallel to l. Because parallelism entered the dangerous realm of infinity, where intuition is particularly fallible, numerous attempts were made to avoid the fifth postulate or deduce it from the other postulates.

In 1733 Saccheri sought a *reductio ad absurdum* proof of the postulate by assuming it untrue, and managed to convince himself that the consequences were unacceptable. However, in the early nineteenth century, Gauss, Lobachevsky, and Bolyai inde-

pendently made a momentous discovery: that if one denies the fifth postulate by assuming more than one straight line through P parallel to l, a viable geometry results. Later, Riemann found a different non-Euclidean geometry in which there are no parallel lines. Thus Euclidean geometry could no longer be logically regarded as God-given or existing *a priori.*

The Cartesian coordinates indicated by the familiar uniform net of lines on ordinary graph paper have two properties of interest: first, the squares are all of unit size, so that for two neighboring points with coordinates $(x, y)$ and $(x + dx, y + dy)$ the coordinate differences $dx$ and $dy$ give direct measures of distances; and second, by Pythagoras' theorem, the distance $ds$ between the two points is given by

$$ds^2 = dx^2 + dy^2. \tag{8}$$

If we change to a coordinate mesh of wavy, irregularly-spaced lines, the new $dx$ and $dy$ will not give direct measures of distance, and (8) will take the more complicated form

$$ds^2 = g_{11}dx^2 + 2g_{12}dxdy + g_{22}dy^2, \tag{9}$$

where, in general, the values of the coefficients $g_{11}$, $g_{12}$, $g_{22}$ change from place to place. This complexity arises from our perversity in distorting the coordinate mesh. But often such distortion is unavoidable: for example, we cannot spread the familiar graph-paper mesh, without stretching, on a sphere, though we can on a cylinder. In studying the geometry of surfaces, therefore, Gauss spread on them quite general coordinate meshes having no direct metrical significance and worked with formula (9), though with different notation. Moreover, he found a mathematical quantity, now called the Gaussian curvature of a surface, that is of major importance. If this curvature is zero everywhere on the surface, as it is for a plane or a cylinder or any other shape that unstretched graph paper can take, one can spread a coordinate mesh on the surface in such a way that (8) holds everywhere, in which case the intrinsic two-dimensional geometry of the surface is essentially Euclidean. If the Gaussian curvature is not everywhere zero, one cannot find such coordinates, and the intrinsic two-dimensional geometry is not Euclidean. The crux of Gauss's discovery was that the curvature, being expressible in terms of the g's, is itself intrinsic, and can be determined at any point of the surface by measurements made solely on the surface, without appeal to an external dimension.

This powerful result led Riemann to envisage intrinsically curved three-dimensional spaces; and, thus emboldened, he considered intrinsically curved spaces of higher dimensions. In three and more dimensions the intrinsic curvature at a point, though still expressible solely in terms of the corresponding *g*'s, is no longer a single number but has many components (involving six numbers in three dimensions, and twenty in four). It is represented by what we now call the Riemann-Christoffel curvature tensor and denoted by the symbol $R^a_{bcd}$.

Gauss had already concluded that geometry is a branch of theoretical physics subject to experimental verification, and had even made an inconclusive geodetic experiment to determine whether space is indeed Euclidean or not. Riemann, and more specifically Clifford, conjectured that forces and matter might be local irregularities in the curvature of space, and in this they were strikingly prophetic, though for their pains they were dismissed at the time as visionaries.

### XVI

We now return to Einstein. It took him ten years to find the way from the special theory of relativity of 1905 to the general theory of relativity. To arrive at the general theory he had first to realize that yardsticks and standard clocks could not be used to lay out in space-time a coordinate mesh of the Cartesian sort that would directly show distances and time intervals.

This radical break with his previous habits of thought was, by his own admission, one of his most difficult steps towards the general theory of relativity. A powerful stimulus was the effect of gravitation on the comparison of clock rates as deduced from the principle of equivalence. Another was the following argument: Consider a nonrotating reference frame K and a rotating reference frame K' having the same origin and *z*-axis. On the *xy*-plane of K, draw a large circle with its center at the origin. By symmetry, it will be regarded as a circle in K'. Measure it in K' with a measuring chain, and view the process from the nonrotating frame K. Relative to K, the chain will appear contracted in length when the circumference is being measured, but not when the diameter is being measured. Therefore the circumference, as measured by the shrunken links, will have a greater value than that given by a similar measuring chain at rest in K. So the ratio of circumference to diameter as measured in K' will be greater than $\pi$, which means that the spatial geometry in K' is non-Euclidean.

That this argument can be faulted is of small consequence. It served its purpose well. Einstein seems to have known intuitively the path he had to follow and then to have found plausible, comforting arguments that would give him the courage to proceed. In the nature of things, he could not use impeccable arguments since they had to be based on theories that the general theory was destined to supersede.

What was important was Einstein's valid conclusion that space-time coordinates could not, in general, have direct metrological significance. Faced with this shattering realization, and bolstered by his conviction that all motion must be relative, Einstein decided that all coordinate systems in space-time must be on an equal footing. He therefore enunciated a *principle of general covariance* according to which the general laws of nature are to be expressed by equations that hold good for all systems of space-time coordinates. Three points need to be made concerning this principle:

(a) A general system of space-time coordinates could consist of cheap, inaccurate, unsynchronized clocks embedded in a highly flexible scaffolding in wild and writhing motion. The principle relegates the role of coordinates to that of the mere labelling of events in space-time, much as the general coordinates of Gauss label the points of a surface. To be able to accept such general four-dimensional coordinates as a basis for a physical theory, Einstein had first to arrive at a profound insight: that physical measurements are essentially the observation of *coincidences* of events, such as the arrival of a particle when the hands of the local clock point to certain marks on its dial. Such coincidences clearly remain coincidences no matter what coordinate system is used.

(b) The principle of general covariance can be said to be devoid of content. As Kretschmann pointed out in 1917, *any* physical theory capable of being expressed mathematically in terms of coordinates can be expressed in a form obeying the principle of general covariance.

(c) Nevertheless the principle was a cornerstone of the general theory of relativity.

This seeming paradox is resolved when one takes account of Einstein's powerful aesthetic sense, which made the general theory a thing of beauty. If one uses a simple reference frame in the special theory of relativity, the space-time interval *ds* between events (*x*, *y*, *z*, *t*) and (*x* + *dx*, *y* + *dy*, *z* + *dz*, *t* + *dt*) is given by

$$ds^2 = dx^2 + dy^2 + dz^2 - c^2dt^2. \qquad (10)$$

If one goes over to a more complicated reference frame writhing and accelerated relative to the former, (10) takes a more complicated form analogous to (9), namely

$$ds^2 = g_{00}dt^2 + g_{11}dx^2 + g_{22}dy^2 + g_{33}dz^2 + 2g_{01}dtdx + 2g_{02}dtdy + 2g_{03}dtdz + 2g_{12}dxdy + 2g_{13}dxdz + 2g_{23}dydz, \qquad (11)$$

where the values of the ten *g*'s change from place to place in space-time. These ten coefficients, by which one converts coordinate differences into space-time distances, are denoted collectively by the symbol $g_{ab}$

and are referred to as components of the *metrical tensor* of space-time. A convenient mathematical shorthand lets (11) be written in the compact form

$$ds^2 = g_{ab}dx^a dx^b. \tag{12}$$

With the principle of equivalence Einstein had linked gravitation with acceleration and thus with inertia. Since acceleration manifests itself in $g_{ab}$, so too should gravitation. Einstein therefore took the momentous step of regarding $g_{ab}$ as representing gravitation, and by this act he gave gravitation a geometrical significance. In assigning to the metrical tensor a dual role, he did more than achieve an aesthetically satisfying economy in the building material of his theory. For he was now able to force the seemingly empty principle of general covariance to take on powerful heuristic content and lead him directly to his goal. This he had done instinctively, since Kretschmann's argument came only after the theory was formulated. How the principle of general covariance lost its seeming impotence will be explained later.

The mathematical tool, now called the *Tensor Calculus*, for writing equations valid for all coordinate systems had already been created by Ricci (he started, interestingly enough, in the year 1887 that saw the Michelson-Morley experiment and Voigt's introduction of a transformation akin to that of Lorentz).

Einstein therefore sought tensor equations for the law of gravitation, and ultimately imposed three conditions: (a) that in free space the equations should involve only tensors formed from the metrical tensor and its first and second derivatives, (b) that the equations, ten in number, should be linear in the second derivatives of the ten *g*'s (so as to keep as close as possible to the highly successful Newtonian theory, the basic equation of which was linear in the second derivatives of a single gravitational potential), and (c) that the equations be linked by four relations corresponding to the law of conservation of energy and momentum (four relations being anyway necessary mathematically to ensure that the equations have nontrivial solutions, as was pointed out by Hilbert).

What is remarkable is that the intricate equations, which involve millions of terms, were now essentially *uniquely determined*. Naturally, they come in compact notation. From the components of the four-dimensional Riemann-Christoffel curvature tensor $R^a_{bcd}$, combinations are formed denoted by $R_{ab}$ (the Ricci tensor) and $R$ (the curvature scalar). The totality of matter, stress, radiation, etc. acting as the "sources" of the gravitational field is denoted by $T_{ab}$. Then Einstein's field equations for gravitation can be written

$$R_{ab} - \tfrac{1}{2}g_{ab}R = -T_{ab}. \tag{13}$$

## XVII

We may now consider the general theory of relativity in terms of its own concepts rather than the tentative, groping concepts on which it was built. It treats gravitation as an intrinsic curvature of space-time, the special theory of relativity becoming a limiting case valid in regions small enough for the effects of the curvature to be negligible. The special theory, like the Newtonian theory, can be expressed in terms of tensors, in conformity with the principle of general covariance. But the Kretschmann process of making equations generally covariant usually involved introducing additional physical quantities. The principle of general covariance took on importance when Einstein argued that gravitation per se must be represented solely in terms of the metrical tensor $g_{ab}$, without the introduction of additional physical quantities (other than the sources $T_{ab}$). This did more than link gravitation with geometry: it forced the seemingly impotent principle of general covariance to impose limitations so powerful that the complicated field equations of gravitation could be obtained essentially uniquely.

In linking inertia, via acceleration, to gravitation, Einstein extended the ideas of Berkeley and Mach by regarding inertia as a *gravitational* interaction. Accordingly he gave the name "Mach's Principle" to the requirement that $g_{ab}$, which defines the geometry of space-time, should be determined solely by the gravitational sources $T_{ab}$. Ironically, Einstein's theory turned out not to embrace Mach's principle unequivocally. To avoid this irony Einstein proposed a desperate remedy that did not work. Nevertheless the attempt led him to a major development that will not be considered here since it belongs to, and indeed inaugurates, the subject of relativistic cosmology.

In the special theory of relativity, as in the theory of Newton, space and time are unaffected by their contents. In the general theory space and time are no longer aloof. They mirror by their curvature the gravitational presence of matter, energy, and the like. Geometry—four-dimensional—thus becomes, more than ever before, a branch of physics; and space-time becomes a physical entity subject to field laws.

The problem of action at a distance no longer arises. Space-time itself is the mediator—the "aether"—and, in three-dimensional parlance, gravitational effects are propagated with speed $c$. Also, the self-contradiction in the special theory regarding the use of rigid rods does not apply so harshly to the general theory, since coordinate meshes are no longer constructed of rigid rods and standard clocks.

In Newton's theory the law of inertia states that a free particle moves in a straight line with constant speed. This law holds, also, in the special theory of relativity, where it is expressed by saying that a free particle has a straight world line in Minkowski space-time. Einstein essentially carried this law over into the curved space-time of the general theory by postulating that the world line of a simple free particle therein is a *geodesic*, the closest available analogue of a straight line. The law now acquired powerful new significance. Consider, for example, the curved space-time associated with the gravitational field of the sun. Calculation showed that the geodesics of particles representing planets corkscrew around the world line of the sun in such a way that, in three-dimensional language, the particles move around the sun in curves very closely approximating ellipses with the sun at a focus, their orbital speeds varying in the Keplerian manner. Remember: we are speaking of "free" particles. Thus there is no longer need to introduce a gravitational *force*. Newton's first law, the law of inertia, when adapted to Einstein's curved space-time, itself suffices to account for the gravitational influence of the sun on the motions of the planets. Indeed, all the triumphs of the Newtonian theory are inherited by the theory of Einstein.

But Einstein's theory went further than Newton's. It accounted for a previously puzzling residual advance of the perihelion of Mercury by some 43 seconds of arc per century. Moreover it implied the gravitational bending of light rays (giving twice the value that Einstein had obtained by his preliminary argument using the principle of equivalence) and also the gravitational red shift of spectral lines (giving essentially the value he had obtained from the principle of equivalence). Observations confirm the existence of these effects, but there has been a fluctuating discussion as to the extent to which the observations are in numerical agreement with the predictions. Major technological advances in the half-century since the theory was formulated have brought within range of measurement not only more precise evaluations of the above effects but also other effects hitherto beyond the reach of observation. Of particular interest is Weber's apparatus designed to detect gravitational waves.

### XVIII

An orbiting astronaut feels weightless. Does this mean that he has zero weight? Some physicists say no. They define weight as the pull of gravitation, and argue that the astronaut is not free of the gravitational pull of the earth and other bodies. The astronaut, they say, feels weightless because inertial effects balance the gravitational pull.

Actually the concept of weight is by no means easy to define satisfactorily even in Newtonian terms. In the general theory of relativity, with gravitation and inertia linked by the principle of equivalence, and with

gravitational pull replaced by space-time curvature, the concept of weight becomes quite subtle.

Perhaps one may say that the gist of the situation is this: the astronaut, being in free fall around the earth, is tracing out a geodesic world line in space-time and not only feels weightless but also has zero weight. When the rockets of his spaceship are firing, the astronaut, being no longer in free flight, departs from tracing out a geodesic. Accordingly, he acquires weight, and with it the sensation of having weight.

A man (regarded here as a point) when standing on the earth does not trace out a geodesic world line. But he does, momentarily, if he jumps. Thus we reach the somewhat startling conclusion that in the course of his jump the man has zero weight.

Since the world line of an astronaut in flight differs from that of his twin on the ground, the relativistic lengths, *s*, of the portions of their world lines between departure and return are clearly unequal. Since these lengths happen to measure the amounts of time the twins have lived between meetings, the twins will not be the same age when the astronaut returns. By imagining flights that are not yet feasible, one can infer spectacular possibilities: for example, the astronaut returning to find himself twenty years younger than his stay-at-home twin. Much fuss has been stirred up by this so-called "paradox" of the twins. But so far as the theory of relativity is concerned, it is no more paradoxical than that the total length of two sides of a triangle is not equal to the length of the third. No useful purpose will be served in discussing the matter further here, except for the following remark: The astronautical twin would seem to have a longer rather than a shorter world line than his stay-at-home brother, and thus one might expect him to be the older rather than the younger on his return. Actually his world line, as measured relativistically, is the shorter. We have to take account of the sort of distortion already encountered when we tried to draw a Minkowskian unit circle on a Euclidean page.

### XIX

By treating gravitation as space-time curvature, Einstein had geometrized a major branch of physics. In 1918 Weyl sought to carry this process of geometrization further. In curved space-time, where we have to make do with geodesics as substitutes for straight lines, directions are affected by the curvature. Weyl devised a more general space-time geometry in which not only directions but also lengths are affected; and he showed how one could thereby obtain the equations of Maxwell in a natural way alongside those of Einstein. Unfortunately, as Einstein pointed out, the idea encountered physical difficulties.

Weyl's ingenious attempt was one of the first of a

long succession of unified field theories seeking to link gravitation and electromagnetism geometrically. One trend was initiated in 1921 by Kaluza, who proposed a five-dimensional theory that was later given a four-dimensional interpretation. Another trend, growing from Weyl's work, involved introducing various geometrical features, such as torsion, directly into space-time, a notable example being the theory, based on an unsymmetric $g_{ab}$, on which Einstein was working at the time of his death.

Since electromagnetism has energy, it has a gravitational effect. In 1925 Rainich showed that electromagnetism leaves so characteristic a gravitational imprint on the curvature of space-time that the curvature itself can suffice to represent electromagnetism as well as gravitation. In this sense, the general theory of relativity could be said to be "already unified."

Because of the exuberant proliferation of unified field theories of gravitation and electromagnetism and their failure to yield new physical insights comparable to those of the special and general theories of relativity, there arose a tendency to deride attempts to reduce physics to geometry by means of unified field theories. This tendency was enhanced when atomic physicists discovered additional fundamental fields, even though, in principle, the discovery of these fields made the problem of unification, if anything, more urgent. Whether the path to unification will be via the geometrization of physics is a moot point since one cannot define the boundaries of geometry. Thus, nuclear physicists use geometrical concepts with striking success in attempting to unify the theory of fundamental particles, but these geometrical concepts are not confined to space-time.

It is worth remarking that there have been highly successful unifications lying within the special theory of relativity. For example, Dirac found relativistic equations for the electron that not only contained the spin of the electron as a kinematical consequence of Minkowskian geometry but also linked the electron to the not-then-detected positron, thus initiating the concept of antimatter. Minkowski, in his four-dimensional treatment of Maxwell's equations, had already created an elegant unified field theory of electricity and magnetism long before the term "unified field theory" was coined. And we can hardly deny that the special theory of relativity is itself a unified theory of space and time, as too is the general theory.

### XX

Transcending the triumphs of Einstein's theory is its monumental quality. This quality is manifest in the naturalness and seeming inevitability of the theory's growth, the beauty and structural simplicity of its architecture, and the interlocking economy of its basic

hypotheses. Indeed, this economy proved to be even more impressive than was originally believed: the geodesic hypothesis was found not to be needed after all, the motions of bodies being inherent in the field equations themselves. This discovery, by Einstein and collaborators among others, revealed the general theory of relativity as unique among field theories in that all others had to be supplemented by special rules linking the motions of bodies to the field.

Like every physical theory, the general theory of relativity faces great epistemological and internal difficulties. Among the latter are solutions of its equations that seem like physical nonsense, and powerful theorems discovered by Penrose, Hawkins, and others indicating that its equations carry the taint of unavoidable breakdown.

More important are the epistemological difficulties, especially in relation to the quantum theory. Bohr was of the opinion that there was no need to apply quantum concepts to the general theory of relativity; he regarded the latter as an essentially macroscopic theory linked to the macroscopic aspects of matter. Other physicists, however, have sought to quantize Einstein's gravitational theory much as Maxwell's theory of light has been quantized. In the latter the electromagnetic field is regarded as consisting of quantum-mechanical particles called photons. Accordingly one attempts to treat the gravitational field as consisting of quantum-mechanical particles to which the name *graviton* has been given. Two difficulties arise. The first has to do with the sheer complexity of Einstein's field equations (13) when written out in detail. While this inner complexity underscores Einstein's genius in obtaining the equations essentially uniquely, it also prevents a straightforward application of the familiar techniques of quantization. The second difficulty is more fundamental: if one quantizes gravitation in Einstein's theory, one automatically quantizes the metrical tensor and thus the very basis of space-time geometry. The epistemological problems posed by a quantized geometry are formidable indeed.

Even on a more superficial level the quantum theory raises deep problems concerning measurement in the general theory of relativity. The light cones, which are crucial ingredients of the geometry of space-time, are defined directly by $g_{ab}$ and represent the propagation of infinitely sharp pulses of light. But, as Einstein realized, such pulses would involve infinitely high frequencies and thus, according to the quantum relation $E = h\nu$ (energy equals Planck's constant times frequency) infinitely high energies. These in turn would imply, among other calamities, infinitely large gravitational curvatures not present in the original $g_{ab}$.

From the two basic constants, the speed of light and the Newtonian gravitational constant, that enter the general theory of relativity, we cannot form a quantity representing a length. The theory thus has no built-in scale of size. If we introduce Planck's constant, however, we can form a fundamental length. It turns out to be $10^{-33}$cm. The diameter of an atomic nucleus is enormously larger, being of the order $10^{-13}$cm. Wheeler has therefore proposed that space-time, so seemingly smooth, has a spongy structure of enormous complexity when envisaged at the $10^{-33}$cm level.

It may well be that the general theory of relativity is a macroscopic theory that breaks down at the microscopic level. Or that it survives there in an almost unrecognizable foamlike form. But all our basic physical theories suffer from a common malaise: even when they seek to avoid the idea of a space-time continuum, they use $x$, $y$, $z$, $t$ in their equations and treat them as continuous quantities. The reason is simple: no one has yet found a satisfactory way of doing without them.

Perhaps, as Einstein hoped, space and time are fundamental things out of which matter is made. Perhaps, though, matter, or something else, is the more fundamental, with space and time mere macroscopic reflections of its deeper regularities. Fundamental or not, space and time remain the very essence of our being. And Einstein's theory, for all its problems and whatever its fate, will endure as a towering masterpiece in one of the most difficult and demanding of art forms: theoretical physics.

*BIBLIOGRAPHY*

Galileo Galilei, *Dialogue on the Great World Systems*, ed. G. de Santillana (Chicago, 1953), is a classic; this edition contains illuminating editorial notes. Newton's *Principia*, trans. A. Motte, 2 vols. (Berkeley, 1962), also has editorial notes but unfortunately no index. Of other pre-relativity works, the following are particularly relevant to this article: J. C. Maxwell, *Matter and Motion* (London, 1877; reprint, New York, n.d.), see in particular pp. 80–88; also E. Mach, *The Science of Mechanics*, trans. T. J. McCormack, 6th ed. (La Salle, Ill., 1960).

The collection of essays in *Albert Einstein: Philosopher-Scientist*, ed. P. A. Schilpp (Evanston, 1949), is indispensable; the book contains Einstein's scientific autobiography and a bibliography of his writings. Key technical papers in the development of Einstein's theory are reprinted in *The Principle of Relativity* (1923); reprint, New York, n.d.). One of the most important historical surveys is E. T. Whittaker's *A History of the Theories of Aether and Electricity* (1910; New York, 1951; and later reprint), see especially Vol. II. This highly technical work is unfortunately biased in its account of the special theory of relativity, though not of the general theory. For an antidote, see the article by G. Holton "On the Origins of the Special Theory of Relativity," *American Journal of Physics*, **28** (1960), 627–36; but in this connection see the article by C. Scribner, Jr. "Henri Poincaré and the Principle of Relativity," ibid., **32** (1964), 672–78.

W. Pauli's highly mathematical *Theory of Relativity*, trans. G. Field (London, 1959), was famous in 1921 as an encyclopedia article and remains outstanding in its updated form. It contains an abundance of references.

Of the books of medium mathematical difficulty, M. Born's *Einstein's Theory of Relativity* (New York, 1962; various reprints), is of particular interest here because of its historical approach. Note that it scants the work of Poincaré, as do other books listed below. Complementing Born's book, and admirable in its own right, is W. Rindler's *Essential Relativity* (New York, 1969). Einstein's book, *The Meaning of Relativity*, 5th ed. (Princeton, 1956), is particularly recommended to those who are able to follow the mathematics.

As to nontechnical books, nobody has bettered Einstein's own popular exposition, *Relativity* (New York, 1920; later reprints). P. W. Bridgman, *A Sophisticate's Primer of Relativity* (Middletown, Conn., 1962; reprint New York), gives important insights into the special theory but unfortunately assumes without analysis the existence of rigid rods. M. Jammer, *Concepts of Space* (Cambridge, Mass., 1954; 2nd ed. 1969), contains numerous references. A. D'Abro, *The Evolution of Scientific Thought* (New York, 1927; reprint 1950), gives a detailed nonmathematical account of the whole development of the theory. Also recommended are A. Einstein and L. Infeld, *The Evolution of Physics* (New York, 1938; also reprint), and P. Bergmann, *The Riddle of Gravitation* (New York, 1968). P. Frank, *Einstein: His Life and Times* (New York, 1947; 1953), contains both biographical and philosophical material of particular interest. For J. A. Wheeler's engrossing, if speculative, ideas about foamlike space and the concept of superspace, see his book (in German) *Einsteins Vision* (Berlin, 1968). Mention may also be made of Banesh Hoffmann, with Helen Dukas, *Albert Einstein, Creator and Rebel* (New York, 1972).

BANESH HOFFMANN

[See also Causation; Cosmic Images; **Cosmology since 1850;** Mathematical Rigor; Matter; **Space;** Time and Measurement; Unity of Science.]

# ORIGINS OF RELIGION

A CRITICAL awareness of religion as a peculiar phenomenon of human behavior first appears, so far as the extant evidence shows, in the writings of the Greek philosopher Xenophanes (sixth century B.C.). As the following fragments disclose, Xenophanes had perceived the ethnic relativity of the personification of deity, as well as its innate anthropomorphism:

Mortals think that the gods are born, and wear clothes like their own, and have a voice and bodies. But if oxen and horses or lions had hands and could draw with them and make works [of art] as men do, horses would draw the shapes of gods like horses, oxen like oxen; each would make their bodies according to their own forms. The Ethiopians say that their gods are flat-nosed and black; the Thracians that theirs are grey-eyed and have red hair (Kirk and Raven, pp. 168–69).

Sometimes this critical attitude was even more radical and involved the rejection of orthodox religious concepts; thus, about 450 B.C., Anaxagoras shocked conservative opinion in Athens by declaring that the sun and moon were red-hot stones, which meant that they could not be divinities. About 300 B.C., Euhemerus of Messene explained the origin of the gods in a so-called "Sacred History" which was really a fictitious travelogue adapted for the presentation of his theory. He told how he had visited a majestic temple of Zeus, built on an island in the Indian Ocean, where he had found an inscription concerning the exploits of Zeus, and of Uranos and Kronos whom Greek tradition regarded as divine rulers of the universe before Zeus. According to his account of the inscription, it was recorded that these gods were originally great kings of remote antiquity who had subsequently been deified. Other deities were similarly accounted for, including Aphrodite, who, first of courtesans, had been deified by her lover Cinyras, king of Cyprus. This theory, though a fantastic explanation of the Greek deities with which it deals, did unwittingly touch upon a process that has operated to produce deities in various religions; for example, Imhotep, the architect of the Step Pyramid (ca. 2780 B.C.) at Saqqara in Egypt, who was venerated for his wisdom and ability, was eventually transformed into a healing-god in Greco-Roman Egypt. In more sophisticated forms, "Euhemerism" has often recurred in modern theories about the origin of religion, notably in the ancestor-worship thesis held by the sociologist Herbert Spencer (1820–1903).

The Latin poet Lucretius (first century B.C.) explained the origin of religion along other lines. A follower of the philosopher Epicurus, whom he regarded as the true savior of mankind since he had exposed the pernicious nature of religion, Lucretius in his *De rerum natura* taught that men had dreamed of gods, to whom they attributed omnipotence and immortality. Unable to account for natural phenomena, especially in its more terrifying aspects, men had gone on to ascribe all such things to the gods, whom they consequently feared and sought to propitiate. Lucretius did not deny the existence of gods, but he held that they had no contact at all with the world and mankind. Lucretius anticipated by some seventeen centuries the view of David Hume, expressed in *The Natural History*

*of Religion* (1757), that religion stemmed from human needs and fears.

The critical attitude towards religion, evident in these attempts to find rationalistic explanations of it, represented the views of an intellectual minority in Greek and Roman society. Other attempts of a theological kind were also made in the ancient world to account for the beginnings of religion. But these efforts took the form of naive cosmogonies, notably in Egypt and Mesopotamia, which severally presented some particular god as the creator of the universe, including other gods and mankind, and told how this creator-god arranged for mankind to build temples and serve the gods. There was also a movement towards syncretism, which in the Greco-Roman world found such notable expression as the attempt of Apuleius (second century A.D.) to see the Egyptian goddess Isis, who was worshipped under different names by other peoples, as the principle of all life (*The Golden Ass*, XI. 305).

The establishment of Christianity as the official religion of the Roman Empire in the fourth century resulted in the forcible suppression of paganism. Until that final victory was achieved, Christian thinkers had been obliged to find answers to pagan criticism of their faith. One of their chief points of concern was the newness of Christianity compared with the great antiquity of the pagan cults. This objection was met by the formulation in the third and fourth centuries of a philosophy of history, to which Julius Africanus, Eusebius of Caesarea, and Augustine of Hippo made the most notable contributions. By taking over the Hebrew scriptures as their own legitimate heritage, Christians were able to show to their own satisfaction that their religion could be traced back to the very Creation. This philosophy of history, together with their exclusive soteriology, provided medieval Christians with a completely adequate account of the origin of religion, since for them there was only one true religion, and that was their own. Of the other religions which they knew, they had sufficient explanations: Judaism was due to the culpable obduracy of the Jews in rejecting Jesus as the true Messiah and persisting in the now-superseded Old Covenant, which the coming of Christ had made obsolete; the broken cults of Greece and Rome had been inventions of the Devil and the sinful blindness of men; the new religion of Islam was a false heresy. Of the great religions of Asia, such as Buddhism, medieval Christians had scarcely any knowledge, and these religions had no part in their *Weltanschauung*.

The Renaissance and maritime exploration, from the fifteenth century onwards, gradually changed the parochial outlook of medieval Christendom. The new interest in ancient Greece and Rome, which characterized the Renaissance, meant that the pagan gods were no longer regarded as devils. Their antique statues were now admired, and the Renaissance artists were eager to make these deities subjects of their paintings and sculptures, while scholars familiarized themselves and others with their legends. Maritime exploration, and the trade and colonization which resulted from it, brought contact with the great civilizations of Asia and their religions, together with knowledge of the primitive peoples of Africa, Australasia, and the Americas. All this new information gradually stirred the minds of educated men in Europe, making them aware of the diversity and complexity of the cultures of mankind, many of them far older than that of Christian Europe and of equal achievement in many things. The effects of this new knowledge and interest, so far as the evaluation of religion is concerned, began to find notable literary expression during the eighteenth century.

In 1724 a Jesuit priest, Joseph François Lafitau, published a book in Paris entitled *Moeurs des sauvages amériquains comparées aux moeurs des premiers temps*. It was significant for the thesis which its author had formulated from what he knew of the religions of the American Indians, of pagan antiquity, and of his own Catholic Christianity. By comparing these faiths, he was led to conclude from certain basic similarities which he discerned, that all religions had stemmed from one original revelation. Another attempt to explain the origin of religion, or its common primitive form, was made in 1760 by Charles de Brosses in a work entitled *Du culte des dieux fétiches ou parallèle de l'ancienne religion de l'Égypte avec la religion actuelle de Nigrite*. His definition of fetishism, which he regarded as the common primitive form of religion, is imprecise; but the following statement is significant: it defined fetishism as "the cult of animals or of inanimate earthly beings" (*j'appelle en général de ce nom toute Religion qui a pour objet de culte des animaux ou des êtres terrestres inanimés*). Another notable effort at explaining the origin of religion, or at least a significant part of it, was made by Charles-François Dupuis in his *Origine de tous les cultes* (1795). He maintained that Christ, Osiris, Bacchus, and Mithra were only allegorical personifications of the sun and its annual career. Of interest, too, is the view of Giambattista Vico (1668–1744), who in his *Scienza nuova* noted that rituals concerning birth, marriage, and death constitute a common factor in all religions.

These eighteenth-century interpretations were characterized by the rationalizing spirit of the age; but as yet scholars lacked the linguistic equipment to read the religious literature of the ancient civilizations, except that of Greece and Rome and that of the Hebrew people. This equipment was, however, gradually being provided. Already, by the end of the century, knowledge of Sanskrit and Avestan Persian had been acquired by European scholars, and during the first half of the next century much progress was made in the deciphering of the lost languages of ancient Egypt and Mesopotamia. This philological interest soon found expression in the study of religious origins, most notably in the work of Friedrich Max Müller (1823–1900), who came to Oxford as a young man to translate certain ancient religious texts of India for the East India Company, and settled there as Professor of Comparative Philology. Müller greatly promoted the comparative study of religion, especially by his initiating of the celebrated series of translations entitled *The Sacred Books of the East*. The origin of religion he traced to the mind of man:

No doubt there existed in the human mind, from the very beginning, something, whether we call it a suspicion, an innate idea, an intuition, or a sense of the Divine. What distinguishes man from the rest of the animal creation is chiefly that ineradicable feeling of dependence and reliance upon some higher power, a consciousness of bondage from which the very name of "religion" was derived (*Chips from a German Workshop*, 2 vols., London [1867], I, 239).

According to Müller, the first form of religion was *henotheism* or *cathenotheism*, which signified a vague conception of deity that found expression in the attribution of divine qualities to whatever manifestation of power an individual happened to be concerned with on a particular occasion. From such a primordial conception both polytheism and monotheism later derived. Mythology also greatly occupied the attention of Max Müller, particularly that of the Indo-European peoples, which he sought to interpret by means of comparative philology. To him mythology was "a disease of language." He believed that the various names for God could be traced back to a common origin in human speech. It was from the names given to gods and goddesses, according to him, that the various conceptions stemmed; thus, if the sun was deified and the name for "sun" in a particular language was masculine, the sun-god was thought of as a male being and actions and conduct appropriate to a male being of supernatural power were ascribed to him. Hence, in process of time, there developed the complex mythologies found in most religions.

Although the influence of Max Müller was considerable, comparative philology was generally considered as having only a limited use for research into the origins of religion—it should be noted that the method has been vigorously employed in the last two decades by Georges Dumézil in investigating the religions of the ancient Indo-European peoples, but his interpretations have also encountered much opposition (see Bibliography: "Dumézil, Georges," in *Dictionary of Comparative Religion*). The development of anthropological or ethnological studies next seemed to provide the opportunity of reaching back to the beginnings of religion. This anthropological approach was also inspired, as was so much nineteenth-century scientific thinking, by the evolutionary principle which had been so impressively employed to account for the origin of the natural species. Increasing acquaintanceship with the so-called "primitive" races of the world, which resulted from exploration and colonization, seemed to provide evidence of what human culture must have been like in the remotest antiquity; there was a natural tendency to equate culture that was comparatively primitive by nineteenth-century standards with what was chronologically primitive.

A leading exponent of the anthropological approach to the origins of religion was Sir Edward B. Tylor, who published in 1871 in England a great work entitled *Primitive Culture* which was widely influential. In this work Tylor set forth, as the "minimum definition" of religion, the theory of Animism. The term was derived from the Latin words *animus* and *anima,* which denoted life, soul, spirit, concepts closely associated with the life-breath (Greek *pneuma*) that animates the body. Tylor explained how the idea of an *anima* first came to be formed:

It seems as though thinking men, as yet at a low level of culture, were deeply impressed by two groups of biological problems. In the first place, what is it that makes the difference between a living body and a dead one; what causes waking, sleep, trance, disease, death? In the second place, what are these human shapes which appear in dreams and visions? Looking at these two groups of phenomena, the ancient savage philosophers probably made their first step by the obvious inference that every man has two things belonging to him, namely, a life and a phantom. These two are evidently in close connexion with the body, the life as enabling it to feel and think and act, the phantom as being its image or second self; both, also, are perceived to be things separable from the body, the life as being able to go away and leave it insensible or dead, the phantom as appearing to people at a distance from it (*Primitive Culture,* I, 428).

From this initial concept of an animating principle within man, according to Tylor, religion derived. For primitive man was led on to conclude that all natural phenomena, endowed with apparent vitality and movement, such as trees, streams, fire, the sun, moon, and stars, also possessed souls or spirits. Hence primitive man populated the natural world with a vast host of spirits, some friendly and some inimical to himself.

Since certain forms of natural phenomena manifested great and terrifying power, these forms, thus personified, became the great gods or daemons whom he sought to appease. It was from such primitive polydaemonism or polytheism, so Tylor maintained, that subsequent rationalization produced the idea of monotheism.

Tylor was able to cite an impressive amount of anthropological material in support of his thesis, and Animism as an explanation of the origin and evolution of religion became widely influential. It inevitably encountered criticism, most notably from a later holder of Tylor's Chair of Anthropology at Oxford, namely, R. R. Marett, who argued that Tylor's theory presupposed an awareness of personality that was unlikely to have existed at the selected primordial stage of human culture. Marett sought for an even earlier and more primitive stage, such as was indicated by the idea of *mana,* i.e., an impersonal supernatural power envisaged by certain savage peoples, with which contemporary anthropologists had become much concerned. According to Marett,

The question is whether apart from ideas of spirit, ghost, soul, and the like, and before such ideas have become the dominant factors in the constituent experience, a rudimentary religion can exist. It will suffice to prove that supernaturalism, the attitude of the mind dictated by awe of the mysterious, which provides religion with its raw material, may exist apart from animism, and, further, may provide a basis on which animistic doctrine is subsequently constructed (*The Threshold of Religion,* 1914).

To define this pre-personalized stage in the evolution of religion, Marett invented the term "Animatism."

The greatest name in this early anthropological quest for the origin and essential nature of religion is that of James George Frazer (1854–1941). His output of important works was prodigious. His *magnum opus* entitled *The Golden Bough* comprises twelve volumes, an index and bibliographical volume, and a volume called *Aftermath.* The influence which he has had on modern thinking about religion has been very great; although many of his interpretations are now outmoded, his works remain a treasury of information about the religious customs and beliefs of mankind. In *The Golden Bough* (*The Magic Art,* 3rd. ed., I, 222) he set forth his definition of religion as being "a propitiation or conciliation of powers superior to man which are believed to direct and control the course of nature and of human life." He held that man's knowledge of God was inferential, being derived "either by meditating on the operations of his own mind, or by observing the processes of external nature . . . it is the imperious need of tracing the causes of events

95

which has driven man to discover or invent a deity." However, Frazer regarded religion as representing the second stage in the evolution of man's relations with the superior powers of the natural world. The first stage he designated the Age of Magic, unknowingly developing an idea of Hegel's. The transition from the Age of Magic to the Age of Religion he accounted for as follows:

It becomes probable that magic arose before religion in the evolution of our race, and that man essayed to bend nature to his wishes by the sheer force of spells and enchantments before he strove to coax and mollify a coy, capricious, or irascible deity by the soft insinuation of prayer and sacrifice (op. cit., I, 234).

Another notable contribution made by Frazer to the study of religious origins was his exposition of the economic factor in the evolution of religious ideas and practices. He showed that man, as an agriculturalist, became profoundly concerned with the annual life-cycle of vegetation upon which his food supply depended—with the drama implicit in the burying of the seed-corn in the earth, its germination, the upward surge of its new life in spring, its cutting down at harvest and transformation into food. It was from man's personification of the principle of vegetation, according to Frazer, that the idea of a god who dies and rises again originated, finding expression in such celebrated deities as Attis, Adonis, Osiris, and Christ. It may be noted that Paul Radin later (*Primitive Religion: its Nature and Origin*, 1937) also stressed the importance of lack of economic security as a factor in religious origination, and derived religion from magic.

The tendency of the early anthropologists to seek for evidence of the origin of religion in the supposed attempts of primitive man to rationalize his experience of the natural world produced yet another interpretation. Andrew Lang (1844–1912), stressing the fact that many "primitive" peoples believed in a supreme creator-deity, a "High God" or "All-Father," argued that monotheism was the earliest form of religion and that animism represented a degeneration from this original conception. This idea of a primeval monotheism found its most devoted exponent in Father Wilhelm Schmidt (1868–1954), who maintained his case in a twelve-volume work, *Der Ursprung der Gottesidee* (1926–55). He believed that this primeval monotheism also involved a primeval morality which included the practice of monogamy; he consequently saw both polytheism and polygamy as degenerate forms of the earlier faith and practice. Although this interpretation was so obviously congenial to Christian theology, Schmidt did not however posit an original divine revelation for his primeval monotheism.

The data provided by anthropological research impressed other scholars in the early years of the present century with the importance of the factor of communal or collective consciousness in primitive society. Émile Durkheim (1858–1917), preeminent among French sociologists, saw in the institution of totemism, then a popular topic of concern among anthropologists, a concept of basic significance for understanding the social origins of religion. He wrote accordingly:

The god of the clan, the totemic principle, can therefore be nothing else than the clan itself, personified and represented to the imagination under the visible form of the animal or vegetable which serves as totem (*Elementary Forms of the Religious Life* [1915], p. 206).

Jane Harrison, a classical scholar eager to use anthropological material, produced a somewhat similar theory of the emergence of the concept of a deity (Dionysus) from the communal consciousness created by ritual dancing in early Greece: "The leader of the band of *kouroi* (κοῦροι), of young men, the real actual leader, has become by remembrance and abstraction . . . a daimon, or spirit, at the head of a band of spirits, and he brings in the new year at spring" (*Ancient Art and Ritual* [1918], p. 115).

The drawing of attention to the communal factor in primitive religion was an understandable reaction to the hitherto prevailing disposition to contemplate the origin of religion in terms of individual ratiocination. Search now began to be made in other directions, most notably in human psychology or in some supposed precognitive stage in human development. Sigmund Freud (1856–1939), whose pioneering work in psychology and psychoanalysis has had such profound influence on modern thought, sought to explain the origin of religion or its primordial form in terms of deep-seated psychological impulses, particularly in the human male. To him religion was essentially "an infantile obsessional neurosis" centered mainly on the primal father-figure. In his *Totem and Taboo* (1918), Freud propounded his thesis that "the beginnings of religion, ethics, society, and art meet in the Oedipus complex." He imagined a primordial state of human society composed of a "primitive horde," dominated by a father who kept all females for himself and repelled his growing sons. The latter banded together to slay their father, whom they both hated and admired. They ate their victim, to identify themselves with him and absorb his strength. After their parricide, remorse set in and a sense of guilt formed. Rituals of expiation were devised, centered on the totem as the "father substitute." Hence, according to Freud, the institutions of primitive society, namely, totemism, incest, taboos, exogamy, the ritual totem meal, originated from the Oedipus complex. Although Freud took his ethnological examples from Australian aboriginal society, his reconstruction of this primeval drama had the sanction of no archeological or anthropological evidence; however, its novel interpretation of the sex-instinct as the source of religion caused much excitement and gave it a publicity which it did not deserve on scientific grounds. Among Freud's followers, the most distinguished was C. J. Jung (1875–1961), who developed his own distinctive interpretation of man's mental and emotional life. Jung defined religion as

a peculiar attitude of mind which could be formulated in accordance with the original use of the word "religio," which means a careful consideration and observation of certain dynamic factors, that are conceived as "powers"; spirits, demons, gods, laws, ideals, or whatever name man has given to such factors in his world as he has found powerful, dangerous, or helpful enough to be taken into careful consideration, or grand, beautiful, and meaningful enough to be devoutly worshipped and loved (Jung, p. 8).

Jung was, however, more concerned with the forms in which religion has expressed itself than with its origin. For him those forms expressed "the living process of the unconscious in the form of the drama of repentance, sacrifice, and redemption" (op. cit., p. 46). He concentrated on the interpretation of myths as expressions of the collective unconscious, discerning therein certain "archetypes" or primordial images that exercise a formative influence upon human thought and behavior. The principal archetypes he named the *persona*, the *shadow*, the *anima* and *animus*, the *old wise man*, the *earth mother*, and the *self*. For him, "The religious myth is one of man's greatest and most significant achievements, giving him the security and inner strength not to be crushed by the monstrousness of the universe" (*Symbols of Transformation* [1956], p. 231).

These psychological interpretations of the origin of religion, and its fundamental nature, placed the source of religion below the level of the conscious self and its ratiocination. Another notable endeavor of similar intent, but of a very different approach, was made by Rudolf Otto (1869–1937), a German philosopher of religion, in his widely influential book *Das Heilige* (1917), which was translated into English as *The Idea of the Holy* (1923). Otto was concerned to emphasize the nonrational nature of religious experience. To this end he postulated the existence within man of a sense of the *numinous*, i.e., the ability to become aware of the presence of an entity "wholly other" than all else in the world of his experience. Otto derived the term "numinous" from the Latin word *numen*, which denoted a supernatural nonpersonalized being. According to Otto, the numinous presence is apprehended under two different forms of manifestation, which he

distinguished as the *Mysterium tremendum* and the *Mysterium fascinans*. The former aspect, as the designation indicates, causes terror in the one who apprehends it; but it is a terror induced by its "otherness," or uncanny, eerie nature. Yet, while the numinous presence terrified, it could also fascinate, and strangely attract to closer contact with itself. It was this sense of the numinous, so Otto maintained, that constituted the essence of holiness. Its presence made a place or anything associated with it holy, and contact with it had to be controlled by taboos. Otto accounted for the various forms of primitive religion (e.g., daemonism, totemism, worship of the dead) by the rationalization of man's experience of the numinous. Otto's book clearly reveals his theological interest in devising this explanation of the origin of religion, and his work has been much appreciated by theologians.

Of considerable significance, both in view of their author's eminence as a philosopher and their intrinsic percipience, are the statements of Alfred North Whitehead (1861–1947) on the beginnings of religion and its essential nature. He saw religion as stemming fundamentally from personal experience:

Religion is what the individual does with his own solitariness. It runs through three stages, if it evolves to its final satisfaction. It is the transition from God the void to God the enemy, and from God the enemy to God the companion. . . . Collective enthusiasms, revivals, institutions, churches, rituals, bibles, codes of behavior, are the trappings of religion, its passing forms. They may be useful, or harmful; they may be authoritatively ordained, or merely temporary expedients. But the end of religion is beyond all this (Whitehead, pp. 6–7).

The emergence of religion he described as follows:

Religion, so far as it receives external expression in human history, exhibits four factors or sides of itself. These factors are ritual, emotion, belief, rationalisation. . . . But all these four factors are not of equal influence throughout all historical epochs. The religious idea emerged gradually into human life, at first barely disengaged from other human interests. The order of the emergence of these factors was in the inverse order of the depth of their religious importance: first ritual, then emotion, then belief, then rationalisation (op. cit., p. 8).

Whitehead saw the "great rational religions" as expressive of a universal religious consciousness, in contrast to religious consciousness at the tribal or social level. This universality he identified with "the note of solitariness" which he perceived as a basic factor in "rational religion" (op. cit., pp. 37ff.).

More recently it has been proposed to trace the origin of religion to a source hitherto unexplored, viz., man's consciousness of time (cf. Brandon, 1959, 1965, 1966). Human time-consciousness is seen as an essential factor of human rationality; for awareness of the temporal categories of past, present, and future is basic to the sense of self-identity. Time-consciousness, moreover, has given mankind success in the struggle for existence by enabling it to draw upon past experience in the present, to plan for future contingencies: no other animal possesses such an effective sense of time. Man's awareness of time has, however, had an ambivalent effect. By enabling him to anticipate future events, it has made him aware of his own mortality. Hence it has bred within him a sense of fundamental insecurity, which prevents him from immersing himself wholly in the enjoyment of present experience as other animals do. He knows that the passage of time inevitably brings change, decay, and death. This time-consciousness has emerged *pari passu* with the development of the human mind; evidence of its operation is to be found in the earliest remains of human culture. Man's reaction to the prospect of his own demise has taken the form of seeking security from death, or beyond death, by attachment to what is deemed eternal or unchanging. Thus in the earliest written documents, the *Pyramid Texts* of Egypt (ca. 2400 B.C.), this urge finds expression in ritual identification with the resurrected god Osiris or by joining the sun-god Rē on his everlasting journey through the heavens. On analysis, every religion is found to be primarily concerned with offering to its devotees some form of post-mortem security. This is the basic raison d'être of all religion, to which all other concerns are subsidiary.

The purpose of this article has been to trace out the history of ideas about the origin of religion where those ideas have represented significant attempts to appraise religion objectively. Some passing reference was made to early Christian thought in this context, since it was necessary to account for the apparent hiatus in curiosity about the origin of religion that occurs from the end of pagan Greco-Roman culture until the Renaissance. The theologians and scholars of most of the other great religions have also been concerned with the origins of their own respective faiths; but their thinking has generally been conditioned by the assumption that their own faith is the true religion, and that it had been divinely revealed to, or by, their founder. Thus Judaism, Buddhism, Zoroastrianism, Islam, and Manichaeism respectively trace their origins back to a unique founder, and by that very fact claim to embody an exclusive revelation concerning man and his destiny. The study of such claims, is, however, the concern of the history and comparative study of religions.

This survey may appropriately close with a brief account of what may be inferred about the earliest form of religion evidenced by archeological data. For all *a priori* theories about religious origins must ultimately be checked against the earliest evidence that archeology can provide.

It is, accordingly, significant that the so-called Neanderthal or Mousterian Man, the immediate precursor of true man (*Homo sapiens*), buried his dead, possibly providing them also with food. The burial of the dead is exclusively a human custom, implying special concern about death and the dead. Where funerary provision of food and other equipment is made, some idea of a post-mortem existence may be reasonably assumed. Concern with death and the dead, thus adumbrated by the practice of Neanderthal Man, finds more elaborate expression in the burial customs of *Homo sapiens* in the Upper Palaeolithic era (ca. 30,000–10,000 B.C.). And diversity of mortuary practice then indicates also the existence of a variety of concepts about death and post-mortem existence. Further significant evidence is to be seen in the carved representations, found on Palaeolithic sites, of women with the maternal attributes grossly emphasized but the faces left blank: such images surely indicate a concern with fertility and birth. The celebrated cave-art of the Palaeolithic era is also important in this connection; for it is generally interpreted as magical in purpose, being concerned with the promotion of successful hunting and the fertility of the animals which furnished the chief source of food for the community. Palaeolithic archaeology suggests, therefore, that men at this remote period were concerned with three issues of basic significance: birth, death, and food. In dealing with these issues, these remote ancestors had already developed practices, compounded of religio-magical elements, to assist their own practical abilities. How far these practices involved the conception of deity is necessarily unknown; but there is some possible evidence of the deification of woman as the source of life—a kind of Palaeolithic prototype of the Great Goddess so prominent in the later religions of the ancient Near East and India.

Future progress of prehistoric archaeology will doubtless throw more light on the earliest forms of religion, as it did in the 1960's at Çatal Hüyük for the early Neolithic period. But it will surely never be able to reveal the actual chronological origins of religion; indeed, it is impossible to conceive of archaeological evidence of any kind that could do so. Archaeology has done invaluable service in indicating how man endeavored to cope with the mysterious unknown that surrounded and threatened him at the earliest known stage of culture. But behind his crude religio-magical practices, such as his burial of the dead, reside mental and emotional factors which can only be surmised, not reached by archaeological research. Attempts to understand these factors are likely to continue because of the intrinsic interest and significance of the subject; but the quest, by reason of its very nature, must inevitably remain inconclusive.

*BIBLIOGRAPHY*

There is no monograph on the subject, but information will be found in the following works. E. Pinard de la Boullaye, *L'étude comparée des religions*, 2 vols. (Paris, 1948); S. G. F. Brandon, *Dictionary of Comparative Religion* (London and New York, 1970); M. Eliade, *Patterns in Comparative Religion* (New York, 1958; also reprint); E. O. James, *Comparative Religion* (London, 1938); L. H. Jordan, *Comparative Religion: Its Genesis and Growth* (London, 1908); C. G. Jung, *Psychology and Religion* (New Haven, 1958); G. S. Kirk and J. E. Raven, *The Presocratic Philosophers* (Cambridge, 1960); G. van der Leeuw, *La religion* (Paris, 1948); A. O. Lovejoy, "Religion and the Time-Process," *American Journal of Theology*, **6** (1902); A. de Waal Malefijt, *Religion and Culture* (New York, 1968); F. M. Müller, *Chips from a German Workshop*, 2 vols. (London, 1867); E. J. Sharpe, *One Hundred Years of Comparative Religion* (London, 1972); J. Wach, *The Comparative Study of Religion* (New York, 1958); A. N. Whitehead, *Religion in the Making* (Cambridge, 1927).

For the consciousness of time, see S. G. F. Brandon, *History, Time, and Deity* (Manchester and New York, 1965); idem, *Man and his Destiny in the Great Religions* (Manchester, 1963); see also "The Origin of Religion," *Hibbert Journal*, **57** (1959); "Time and the Destiny of Man," *Voices of Time*, ed. J. T. Fraser (New York, 1966).

S. G. F. BRANDON

[See also **Buddhism; Christianity in History;** Death and Immortality; Evolutionism; **God;** Islamic Conception; Myth; Primitivism; **Religion, Ritual in;** Sin and Salvation; Time.]

# RITUAL IN RELIGION

RITUAL action finds expression in a wide variety of forms in both primitive societies and sophisticated modern states. It can be either of a religious or secular character, ranging (for example and in an increasing secular sequence) from the Catholic High Mass through coronation services and university degree ceremonies to the ceremonial of the modern Olympic Games. Action so diverse in inspiration and expression, yet qualifying to be described as "ritual," suggests the existence of some common generic factor that should be identifiable. It also suggests that such a factor may stem from some deep-seated human need or represent an instinctive response to situations embodying some similarity of challenge. It is likely, however, in view of the variety of grades of significance in the typical examples cited, that some forms of ritual action may represent a tradition of conventional behavior, carefully observed and valued but not awakening any deep personal concern on the part of the participants.

In view of the variety and complexity of ritual action current in the modern world, and the obvious antiquity of its practice, an *a priori* definition of ritual is hazardous. However, the following definition might serve as a working formula, to be checked against the empirical study of notable examples of ritual practice which follows. Such a tentative definition is necessary, since the subject has been comparatively neglected and there are no clearly established conclusions to give guidance. With this qualification, ritual may, accordingly, be defined as action of an imitative or symbolical kind designed to achieve some end, often of a supernatural character, that could not be achieved through normal means by the person who performs it or on behalf of whom it is performed.

Ritual action, when encountered today or through documents of the past, is invariably regulated by traditional prescription—indeed, its efficacy is usually deemed to depend essentially upon its careful conformity to the traditional pattern.

The statement in the definition concerning the imitative or symbolical character of ritual action may justly be regarded as preempting a decision about the essential nature of ritual; but it is made designedly, in order to introduce the fundamental issue of the origin of ritual. We shall presently consider the earliest known evidence of ritual action; but the archaeological record, though it starts at the dawn of human culture, cannot reveal the actual origins of ritual which lie back in a remote undocumented past. The original nature of ritual, therefore, is inevitably a matter for speculation only; though fortunately it can be informed speculation that can be checked against the most ancient evidence. Thus it is reasonable to assume, from what seems to be common experience, that a human being, when intensely desiring that some particular thing should happen, which he cannot actually achieve by his own effort, will tend instinctively to imitate action calculated to achieve what he desires, perhaps through another agent. Such reaction will be familiar to most spectators of a drama or athletic contest with which they have become emotionally involved: the urge will often be felt to assist action by some corresponding gesture. It is a natural extension of such imitative action in primitive minds to believe that the achievement of desired results can be assisted by consciously imitative action: for example, that the sprinkling of water on the ground will help rain to fall; or the lighting of fires in mid-winter, as was done by certain primitive northern peoples, would strengthen the weakening sun during the crisis of the winter solstice. The principle involved may be described as that of imitative magic, that like will produce like.

What appears to be the earliest evidence of such ritual action dates from the Upper Palaeolithic era (30,000–10,000 B.C.). It is provided notably by a strange figure depicted on the wall of an inner cavern of the Cave of the Trois Frères, in the *département* of Ariège, France. The figure is anthropoid in form, but has the attributes of a beast: the head is surmounted by the antlers of a stag, with furry ears, owl-like eyes and a long tongue or beard; the body is covered with a hairy pelt and tail, and the genitals are those of a male animal. The posture of the figure suggests the action of dancing, and it is known as the "Dancing Sorcerer." This descriptive title indicates the interpretation that has generally been given to it. It is taken to represent a man, disguised as an animal, engaged in a ritual dance in which he imitates characteristic movements of an animal, for some specific purpose. There is other Palaeolithic evidence of men, disguised as animals and performing mimetic dances, to prove that the "Dancing Sorcerer," though the most striking, is not a unique conception. Such dances were undoubtedly connected with the chief economic activity of these peoples, namely, hunting, and constituted a form of hunting magic designed both to promote the fertility of the animals and ensure successful hunts. Evidence of ritual dances, in which men simulate animals, is found elsewhere, in primitive, though chronologically later, cultures; for example, in the plays of the ancient Greek dramatist Aristophanes, where the chorus were dressed as birds or beasts and mimed their movements, and in the ritual imitating of kangaroos which was practiced by men of the Kangaroo-tribe among Australian aborigines.

No means exist of knowing how the Palaeolithic peoples explained the purpose and mechanism of their magical dances, if indeed their minds were equipped to make such an objective assessment of what they probably did instinctively. But in view of the instinctive nature of imitative gesture, as was noted above, these Palaeolithic figures may reasonably be interpreted as showing that already, at this remote period, ritual actions were being performed, based upon the principle of imitative or sympathetic magic. Inspiring such actions was undoubtedly the belief that assimilation to an animal by wearing its skin and other items, and by the miming of its movements, would decisively affect some issue, such as a hunt, which greatly concerned the well-being of the community.

The interpretation of this Palaeolithic evidence must necessarily remain tentative; but it is consistent with other archaeological data attesting to the practice at this time of sympathetic magic in the well-known form of cave-art. Moreover, it constitutes an intelligible anticipation of a form of a ritual action which is strikingly evidenced in the earliest written texts, namely, the *Pyramid Texts* of Egypt. These *Texts*, which are inscribed on the interior walls of the pyramids of certain pharaohs of the Fifth and Sixth Dynasties (ca. 2425–2300 B.C.), were designed to secure the safe passage of these monarchs from this world to the next. To this end the *Texts* incorporate a mortuary ritual which has proved of the greatest significance for the history of religions. It constitutes both the earliest and the classic example of ritual action based on the principle of imitative magic. This mortuary ritual was patterned on the legend of Osiris, which formed the rationale of the rites. According to the legend, which was of great antiquity, Osiris, a good king of Egypt in the remote past, had been murdered by his evil brother Set, and his body left to perish. It was found by the goddesses Isis and Nephthys, who took action to save it from physical decomposition. His body being thus preserved against corruption, the dead Osiris was revivified by the sun-god Atum-Rē and other deities. The origin of this legend has been much discussed by scholars, without any agreed conclusion being established. But what is certain is that the *Pyramid Texts* show that it was believed that a dead king could be resurrected to a new life, if he were ritually assimilated to Osiris. Consequently, a mortuary ritual was developed, according to which the embalmment of the pharaoh reproduced ritually what was supposed to have been done to preserve the corpse of Osiris. This ritual of embalmment was followed by other rites calculated to revivify the deceased as Osiris had been revivified. The following passages illustrate the *modus operandi* of this ritual action, presupposing the assimilation of the dead king to Osiris. The first takes the form of an incantation addressed to the god Atum: it was recited over the embalmed body of the dead king (his name in this text was Unas), in order to revivify him; it assumes that Unas is so essentially identified with Osiris that he will participate in the resurrection of Osiris through its ritual re-presentation: "Recite: 'O Atum, it is thy son—this one here, Osiris, whom thou has caused to live (and) to remain in life. He liveth (and) this Unas (also) liveth; he (i.e. Osiris) dieth not, (and) this Unas (also) dieth not'" (*Pyramid Texts*, 167a–c). In another passage Osiris is directly reminded of the consequences of the assimilation of the dead Unas with himself: "Thy body is the body of this Unas. Thy flesh is the flesh of this Unas. Thy bones are the bones of this Unas. (If) thou walkest, this Unas walks; (if) this Unas walks, thou walkest" (*Pyramid Texts* 193a–c).

The *Pyramid Texts* do not describe the ritual acts

that accompanied these invocations, but of another related ceremony graphic illustrations do exist. This is the "Opening of the Mouth," which was intended to restore to the embalmed body its faculties of seeing, breathing, and receiving food (a similar ritual was used to animate cult-statues). The *Pyramid Texts* give the formulae of the rites, mentioning various acts and the implements used (*Pyramid Texts* 12c–14d), and in the later *Book of the Dead* (ca. 1400 B.C.), which documents the Osirian mortuary ritual when it had become democratized, the ritual is depicted in a vignette; the mummy of the deceased, held upright, is touched on the appropriate parts of its face by a priest with a curious sickle-shaped implement, while another officiant recites the corresponding formulae. This particular ceremony, also, was supposed to reproduce what had originally been done for Osiris.

An important concomitant of the ritual action, as the *Pyramid Texts* show, was the recitation of a kind of libretto that accompanied the performance of the rites. Generally this speaking-part consisted of formulae explanatory of the ritual action that was being performed, and it contains much mythological reference, e.g., to the death and resurrection of Osiris. This relation between the myth and the ritual is important, and it will be discussed below.

The extant evidence gives no indication that the Egyptians ever produced a "theology" of this mortuary ritual, i.e., sought to explain how the gods concerned in it had sanctioned such a means of enabling human beings to obtain resurrection from death. The underlying assumption of the rites seems to have been that their proper performance alone would automatically produce the desired results. And no reference was apparently made to the will of the gods concerning the applicability of the transaction to any specific individual. The invocations addressed to the gods, which accompany the ritual action, have rather the appearance of commands and thus attest to the fundamentally magical character of the rites. It is also significant that, whereas there is no mention in this mortuary ritual of the moral qualifications of the deceased, there grew up in conjunction with it a belief in a post-mortem judgment that would determine the eternal destiny of the individual. These dual themes of the Egyptian mortuary cultus, namely of salvation and judgment, resulted in the anomalous conception of Osiris as both the savior and the judge of the dead.

Towards the end of Egyptian culture, about the second century A.D., it would seem that some attempt was made to represent pictorially the effect of the mortuary ritual. It took the form of representing on certain mummy-shrouds three figures interrelated in a ritual transaction. The central figure is that of the deceased in his ordinary attire, and he is shown as being directed by the ancient mortuary god Anubis towards an Osirian figure to his right. The theme of the depiction is evidently that of the transformation of the deceased into an Osiris, a concept that had long found expression in the custom of adding the name "Osiris" to the personal name of the deceased in funerary inscriptions and papyri.

The imitative factor in ritual, which is adumbrated in Palaeolithic culture and forms the basic principle of the Egyptian mortuary cultus, finds abundant expression in other religions. The next examples are representative of the variety of purpose which such ritual action could serve. Thus the principle of magical assimilation is clearly evident in the following ancient Mesopotamian healing ritual. Its rationale was provided by the myth of the goddess Ishtar and her divine lover Tammuz, whom she rescued from the underworld. The rites concerned took place in the month of Tammuz, when the death of Tammuz was annually mourned and the goddess was believed to be especially attentive. The directions given in the text deal with the healing of a sick man, and they are based upon the supposition that Ishtar would save a man from certain specific afflictions, if he were identified with Tammuz. The following rubrics, dealing with the crucial part of the ceremony, vividly present the ritual action of assimilating the patient to Tammuz:

The sick man shall enter to the foot of the couch, his face covered (and) his gaze directed to the foot (of the couch). With a rush (?) with seven knots touch him seven times. As soon as he is touched, he has exchanged his own self (*ramân-šu-uš-pil*). Then say: 'Ishtar, thy beloved, may he go by thy side!' He should go forth from the foot of the couch . . . clothed in a *saḫḫû*-garment, beat his arms seven times to the right; seven times to the left turn himself, and at the confessional kneel down and also say: 'Ishtar, at thy confessional I kneel (before) thee: save thy man!' (Ebeling, pp. 55–56).

Afterwards the officiating priest is directed to tear off some hair from the forehead of the sick man and take his girdle, and to cast them, together with an offering of loaves and fine meal, into the river. This action had undoubtedly an apotropaic intention.

The factor of assimilation is less realistically presented here than in the Egyptian mortuary ritual, and it seems an even less convincing transaction. For the goddess Ishtar appears to be misled into accepting the sick man as Tammuz, unless, what seems to be very improbable, the ritual assimilation was regarded as effecting a mystical transformation so complete that the sick man virtually became Tammuz in his devotion to Ishtar. However that may be, it is evident the ancient Mesopotamians also believed in the efficacy of ritual assimilation.

A notable Greek instance of ritual action of an

101

imitative kind merits a brief description, particularly since it serves to introduce another aspect of ritual. The famous Eleusinian Mysteries, which promised initiates a happy post-mortem existence, had as their rationale the myth of the Rape of Persephone, the daughter of the corn-goddess Demeter, and the quest of the sorrowing mother for her lost daughter; for it was explained that Demeter had instituted the Mysteries at Eleusis as a token of her gratitude for her kind reception there. Information about the actual rites is scarce and imprecise; but there is evidence for thinking that the initiates or *mystae* ritually imitated or re-presented various traditional episodes of Demeter's search for Persephone. Thus they fasted as Demeter had done in her grief, they wandered about at night with torches as she had done in seeking for her daughter, they tasted of the *kykeon*, a mystic drink for which Demeter had asked at Eleusis. The purpose of such ritual acts can only be surmised; but it seems likely that they fostered a sense of communion between the *mystae* and Demeter. The acts, however, have a further significance, for they point to another aspect of ritual action, closely connected with that of the imitative or sympathetic magic which has been distinguished as its original and basic principle. The ritual actions of the Eleusinian Mysteries were known as *drōmena*, "things done," and they were evidently regarded as necessary and efficacious. So far as the evidence goes, it would appear that some of these *drōmena*, possibly all, were designed to re-present the original drama of Demeter and Persephone for the purpose of renewing or perpetuating what was believed to be its original soteriological efficacy. The idea that inspired such action is an intelligible one in terms of primitive logic, and it may be defined as the "ritual perpetuation of the past." It was based on the belief that some event in the career of a divine being, who lived on earth long before, had generated a beneficial efficacy of some kind, and that this efficacy could be made available in the present by ritually re-presenting the original event. The principle was clearly operative also in the Egyptian mortuary ritual, since the rites made essential reference to what had once happened to Osiris: the ritual re-presentation of the acts that had resurrected Osiris, when enacted on behalf of a dead person identified with Osiris, was believed to generate or reproduce the same effect in that person.

The two major rites of Christianity attest to the vitality of what has been distinguished here as the primordial form of ritual action, and also to the operation of the principle of the ritual perpetuation of the past. These rites have, of course, been invested with a high spiritual significance and divine authorization has been claimed for them; but their basic phenom-

enological pattern approximates to that evident in the ritual practice of other religions.

The Christian rite of initiation, namely, baptism, in its earliest presentation by the Apostle Paul, strikingly exhibits the principle of ritual imitation and assimilation. Paul's exposition is of such basic importance for the study of ritual that it must be quoted *in extenso*. It occurs in the sixth chapter of his Epistle to the Romans (verses 3–5), and was written about A.D. 54.

Do you not know that all of us who have been baptized into Christ Jesus were baptized into his death? We were buried therefore with him by baptism into death, so that as Christ was raised from the dead by the glory of the Father, we too might walk in the newness of life. For if we have been united with him in a death like his, we shall certainly be united with him in a resurrection like his (R.S.V.).

According to Paul, therefore, the Christian neophyte was assimilated by baptism to Christ in his death. In other words, baptism ritually re-presented the death of Christ, and by descending beneath the waters of baptism the neophyte was united with Christ in his death. This ritual union or assimilation, in turn, qualified the neophyte to participate with Christ in his resurrection from death. The parallel which this presentation of baptism constitutes to the Osirian mortuary ritual is obvious and very remarkable; however, there is no evidence that Paul derived his conception from the ancient Egyptian practice; the parallel is significant as witnessing to the similarity of phenomenological pattern produced by two wholly independent religious traditions.

This Pauline doctrine found dramatic expression in the baptismal ritual of the Early Church. Special baptisteries were constructed which enabled the neophytes to descend into the water. They divested themselves of their clothes, which symbolized a dying to their former selves. On emerging from the baptismal water, they were clothed in white robes, received a new name and were given mystic food of milk and honey, thus proclaiming their rebirth by baptism to a new life in Christ. This initiatory rite has been held by Christians to be absolutely essential to salvation, for the subsequent formulation of the doctrine of Original Sin implied that the unbaptized are wholly in a state of spiritual perdition. The ritual of baptism, accordingly, when properly administered (the correct "form and matter" have been both carefully defined and disputed), is believed to effect a transformation of the neophyte which cannot be achieved in any other way. Moreover, the wording of the baptismal service clearly synchronizes the moment of spiritual rebirth with the act of baptizing. Other requirements have been incorporated into the rite of baptism, such as attestation of faith in Christ and abjuration of the Devil, with confession of sins; but these are ancillary to the ritual action of baptizing in water, with the accompanying formula pronouncing that the neophyte is being baptized in the threefold name of the Trinity.

The other rite constitutes the central act of worship in Catholic Christianity, namely, the Mass, Eucharist, or Liturgy as it is variously known in the Western and Eastern Churches. Historically, the rite derives from the Last Supper or Passover that Christ partook with his disciples before his Crucifixion. The earliest account of its institution is given by Paul in his First Epistle to the Corinthians (11:23–26), and dates from about 55 A.D. According to Paul's statement,

. . . the Lord Jesus on the night when he was betrayed took bread, and when he had given thanks, he broke it, and said, "This is my body which is [broken] for you. Do this in remembrance of me." In the same way also the cup, after supper, saying, "This cup is the new covenant in my blood. Do this, as often as you drink it, in remembrance of me." For as often as you eat this bread and drink the cup, you proclaim the Lord's death until he comes (R.S.V.).

The later Gospels (except that of John) record the institution of the rite with some variations of detail.

From its primitive form the rite gradually developed an elaborate ceremonial setting such as is found today in the Latin High Mass and the Greek Liturgy. But the quintessence of the rite has continued to inhere in the ritual re-presentation of Christ's original action at the Last Supper: the blessing and breaking of the bread and the blessing of the wine, accompanied by the solemn recitation of his words of institution. The repetition of this ritual action of imitation, each time the Mass is celebrated, is held to reproduce the same change of the bread and wine into the Body and Blood of Christ as occurred at the Last Supper. Moreover, the development of the doctrine of the Sacrifice of the Mass has meant that Catholic Christians also believe that at each celebration of the Mass the sacrifice of Christ, made through his crucifixion, is re-presented to God. In other words, the Mass or Eucharist constitutes the classic example of the ritual perpetuation of the past; for it is believed that the proper performance of the ritual, by a duly authorized priest, and with the right intention, perpetuates, and makes available to those assisting, the efficacy of the original Last Supper and the sacrificial Death of Christ outside Jerusalem about A.D. 30.

In this article, so far, an attempt has been made to show that ritual originates in imitative action done in the instinctive belief that like will (re)produce like. The examples chosen by way of illustration have provided evidence of the operation of the principle from the Palaeolithic era down to modern times, though naturally with varying degrees of sophistication. This aspect of ritual, aptly denoted by the Greek word *drōmenon*, a "thing done" to achieve some specific end, may reasonably be regarded as constituting its essential raison d'être. Characteristic also of this ritual action is its reference back to some signal event of the past, deemed to have a soteriological virtue, which can be made a present reality by ritually re-presenting it according to a prescribed form. There are, however, other forms of ritual action which, though not conceived as activity that automatically achieves something, usually of a soteriological kind, have had considerable cultural importance and are still practiced today. The following are some of the more notable instances.

Commemorative ritual, which is practiced to preserve the memory of some notable event, is a well-known form in both religious and secular life. A celebrated religious example is the Jewish Passover. The origin of the rite is graphically described in the Book of Exodus (12:1ff.): the ritual killing and eating of the lamb is explained as perpetuating the memory of the apotropaic action that the Israelites were commanded to take by Yahweh on the night that he passed over Egypt, slaying the first-born of the Egyptians. The eating of unleavened bread, as part of the Passover ritual, is accounted for by the fact that the Israelites fled so hastily from Egypt that they had no time to leaven the dough for their bread. This elaborate and carefully articulated account of the origin of the Passover is particularly interesting, because it provides an historicized interpretation of two ancient rituals of which the original meaning had probably been forgotten; for the evidence indicates that the killing of the Passover lamb derived from a primitive pastoral custom of sacrificing the first-born of the herds as an apotropaic act, while the ritual eating of unleavened bread originated in another apotropaic custom of refraining from the use of leaven made from last year's corn in bread produced from the new corn of the next harvest. Examples from many other religions could be cited of historicized interpretations of primitive rituals.

Another form of ritual action found in many religions is that of the substitutionary sacrifice, in which a victim is killed, or in some other way disposed of, instead of another person or persons. Two examples may be cited for illustration. In ancient Rome, on the Ides of May, puppets representing old men bound hand and foot, which were called *Argei*, were solemnly thrown by Vestal Virgins from the Pons Sublicius into the river Tiber. The exact meaning of the rites is unknown, but it is probable that the *Argei* substituted for human victims once offered to the river-god in compensation for the building of the bridge. In ancient Hebrew religion the ceremonies of the Day of Atonement formed an elaborate ritual scheme of substitutionary sacrifice. One of its most striking rites concerned the scapegoat; the Book of Leviticus (16:20–22) gives detailed instructions for the ritual transference of the sins of Israel to this goat: "Aaron shall lay both his hands upon the head of the live goat, and confess over him all the iniquities of the people of Israel, and all their transgressions, all their sins: and he shall put them upon the head of the goat, and send him away into the wilderness by the hand of a man who is in readiness."

In ancient India, Brahmanic speculation came to evaluate the ritual action of sacrifice as providing the very basis of cosmic existence. According to the *Purusha-sūkta*, the universe had been formed from the body of a sacrificial victim Purusha, conceived of as a giant primordial Man. This primeval sacrifice was the prototype of all sacrifices which continuously renew and sustain the cosmos. In process of time, doubtless due to the sacerdotal interests of the Brahmins, the ritual of sacrifice was imagined as generating its cosmic power *ex opere operato*, being thus wholly independent of the gods.

The idea of the cosmic significance of ritual action has been much emphasized by certain scholars who believe that many primitive peoples annually performed ceremonies designed to renew or maintain the world-order for the ensuing year. In support of this view, the *akitu* or New Year Festival, celebrated in ancient Babylon, is usually cited, especially since the *enûma elish* or Babylonian Creation Epic was solemnly recited during the ceremonies. However, closer study of the festival shows that its real theme was the explanatory commemoration of the lordship of Marduk, the tutelary god of Babylon, over the other Mesopotamian gods, together with the propitiation of Marduk who was believed to determine the fate of the state at this time for another year. But, even if the idea of cosmic renewal at such festivals is thus problematic, special rites, performed at critical points in Nature's year, have had an important role in the cultural life of many peoples. A notable example is the great annual sacrifice which the emperor of China used to perform to *Shang Ti*, the supreme Deity, at the winter solstice on behalf of the people. The ceremonies, which took place at the Altar of Heaven, near the Temple of the Prosperous Year in Peking, were an elaborate complex of ritual action, including such striking acts as the placing of a sceptre of blue jade before the shrine of Shang Ti, in token of his cosmic supremacy. However, in ceremonies of this kind, in which sacrifice was offered to a deity for some specific purpose, the accompanying ritual action was ancillary to the sacrifice and was not a *drōmenon*, in the sense of effecting something by its own enactment as in the rituals previously examined.

An important attempt to discern a common "culture-pattern" in the annual agricultural festivals of the ancient Near East was put forward in 1933 in a collaborative work entitled *Myth and Ritual*, edited by S. H. Hooke. The thesis won considerable support and is still influential in some quarters; but it has also encountered much criticism. According to its exponents, the "pattern" found its expression in an annual festival, in which a sacred king represented the ritual life-cycle of a vegetation deity. Upon the solemn enactment of this ritual each year it was believed that the prosperity and well-being of the land and people depended. The ritual drama, which is supposed to have been performed at the New Year festival, had five successive episodes: the representation of the death and resurrection of the god; the recitation or symbolic representation of the myth of creation; the ritual combat, depicting the triumph of the god over his enemies; the sacred marriage; the triumphal procession of the god, followed by a train of other related deities. The ritual-pattern, assumed here, is an intelligible one; but nowhere in the extant documents is there evidence of its existence as an integrated whole in any ancient Near Eastern religion. The "pattern" has, in fact, been pieced together from ritual episodes found in various religions of this area. Certainly fertility and harvest rituals were connected with vegetation gods such as Tammuz, Attis, Adonis, Osiris (in one aspect of his being), and Baal, which were related to the annual life-cycle of vegetation, and in some places a divine or sacred king played an important part in them. But kingship seems to have varied much in the ancient Near East, and only in Egypt is there sufficient evidence for understanding what royal divinity meant; unfortunately it is in Egypt that certain crucial episodes of the supposed ritual-pattern do not appear.

There are many other areas of human life and activity which, both in the past and the present, have been controlled by ritual action primarily concerned with the safety and well-being of the community. For example, death and funeral customs among many peoples have an essentially apotropaic function. Death being instinctively feared, the dead are regarded as dangerous and their departure from among the living must be expedited; moreover, contact with them causes contagion. Consequently, much funerary ritual has been designed to protect the living, and to purify those whose contact with the dead has rendered them unclean and potentially dangerous. Birth also has generally been regarded as making those involved, namely, the mother and child, ritually unclean, probably because of their involvement with blood, the "life-substance." Hence in many religions, including Christianity, both mother and child have to be purified by a prescribed ceremony before they can be received back into the community. It may also be noted that among many peoples adolescents have to undergo a *rite de passage* before being admitted to adult membership of the community. The rituals practiced by some primitive peoples are elaborate, and often involve severe ordeals. Their performance changes the status of the individuals concerned; but the *modus operandi* seems rather to consist of tests of fitness and the imparting of knowledge of the mores of adult life than of a magical transformation into another state of being.

Ritual has often taken the form of the solemn performance of the practical activities of life in the service of deities. For example, in ancient Egypt the daily tendance of the cult-image in temples included toilet ceremonies, probably modelled on those of the pharaoh; in most religions, where the presence of deity is located in a cult-image, worship has included the daily offering of food, flowers, unguents and the burning of incense before the image—actions obviously calculated to please the god as if he were a human potentate. In China, and to a lesser degree in some other lands, a traditional system of ritual action, relating to both religious and secular life, has been regarded as constituting a pattern of correct behavior fundamental to the well-being of the individual, the family and society. Confucius laid the utmost importance on ritual (*li*). In his *Analects* (xii:1–2), he equates goodness (*jen*) with submission to ritual, defining it as "To look at nothing in defiance of ritual, to listen to nothing in defiance of ritual, to speak of nothing in defiance of ritual, never to stir hand or foot in defiance of ritual." This ritual is embodied in three books of rites, the *Li Chi*, the *I Li*, and the *Chou Li*, which attest to the Chinese conception that the harmonious balance of the universe depended upon a complex of relationships in heaven and earth which had to be maintained by the proper performance of the requisite ritual.

The antiquity and ubiquity of ritual witness to the fundamental character of the need in human nature to which it is the practical response. A. N. Whitehead placed ritual first among the four factors or aspects which he distinguished as exhibited by religion in human history: "These factors are ritual, emotion, belief, rationalization" (*Religion in the Making*, p. 8). He also sagely observed that "Mere ritual and emotion cannot maintain themselves untouched by intellectuality. . . . Men found themselves practising various rituals, and found rituals generating emotions. The myth explains the purpose both of the ritual and of the emotion" (op. cit., p. 13). The evidence, unfor-

tunately, does not exist to prove this reasonable but *a priori* assumption of the chronological priority of ritual to myth. The earliest extant evidence, which has been cited here, namely the *Pyramid Texts*, shows that ritual action was already accompanied by the recitation of explanatory formulae. How the two evolved in the undocumented period that went before is a matter for surmise only; however, as the example of the Hebrew Passover indicates, some primitive rituals have subsequently been given historicized explanations. There also exists, in this connection, a quaint but significant Mesopotamian text dealing with toothache: before the ancient dentist could begin his practical operations, he had to recite a myth in which the origin of the worm believed to cause dental decay was traced back to the creation of the world.

*BIBLIOGRAPHY*

E. Bendann, *Death Customs* (London, 1930). H. Bonnet, *Reallexikon der ägyptischen Religionsgeschichte* (Berlin, 1952). S. G. F. Brandon, *Creation Legends of the Ancient Near East* (London, 1963); idem, *History, Time and Deity* (Manchester, 1963); idem, *The Judgment of the Dead* (London and New York, 1967–68); idem, "The Ritual Perpetuation of the Past," *Numen*, 7 (Leiden, 1959); idem, "The Ritual Technique of Salvation in the Ancient Near East," *The Savior God*, ed. S. G. F. Brandon (Manchester, 1963); idem, ed., *Dictionary of Comparative Religion* (London and New York, 1970); idem, *Man and God in Art and Ritual* (New York, 1973). E. Ebeling, *Tod und Leben nach der Vorstellungen der Babylonier*, Band I (Berlin and Leipzig, 1931). M. Eliade, *Le mythe de l'éternel retour* (Paris, 1949); idem, *Traité d'histoire des religions* (Paris, 1949). J. G. Frazer, *The Magic Art* (*The Golden Bough*), 3rd ed., 2 vols. (London, 1936). G. Furlani, *Riti babilonesi e assiri* (Udine, 1940). T. H. Gaster, *Thespis* (New York, 1950). J. Harrison, *Ancient Art and Ritual*, 5th ed. (London, 1935). S. H. Hooke, *The Origins of Early Semitic Ritual* (London, 1938); idem, ed., *Myth and Ritual* (Oxford, 1933); idem, ed., *Myth, Ritual and Kingship* (Oxford, 1958). E. O. James, *Christian Myth and Ritual* (London, 1933); idem, *Myth and Ritual in the Ancient Near East* (London, 1958); idem, *Seasonal Feasts and Festivals* (London, 1961). G. E. Mylonas, *Eleusis and the Eleusinian Mysteries* (Princeton, 1961). For *Pyramid Texts*, see K. Sethe, *Die altägyptischen Pyramidentexten* (reprint Hildesheim, 1960). C. H. Ratschow, *Magie und Religion* (Gütersloh, 1955); *Sources orientales*, Vol. VII, *Le monde du sorcier* (Paris, 1966). D. H. Smith, *Chinese Religion* (London, 1968). P. J. Ucko and A. Rosenfeld, *Palaeolithic Cave Art* (London, 1967). A. van Gennep, *Les rites de passage* (Paris, 1909). A. N. Whitehead, *Religion in the Making* (Cambridge, 1927). R. C. Zaehner, *Hinduism* (London, 1962).

S. G. F. BRANDON

[See also **Christianity in History;** Creation; **Death and Immortality;** Mimesis; **Myth; Religion, Origins of;** Sin and Salvation.]

## RELIGION AND SCIENCE IN THE NINETEENTH CENTURY

IN MANY languages other than English the word "science," when used in the phrase "Science and Religion," means all rational knowledge. The English language uses the word science to mean the study of the natural or physical sciences, and it is that which concerns us in this article. The English use has caused a measure of confusion. During the nineteenth century there was a conflict between science and religion. At bottom this conflict consisted of a contrast between the philosophies dominant in that age and a religious view of the world. But in England men often talked as though the conflict between science and religion was a contrast between the conclusions of the natural sciences and the teaching of Christianity. Such a contrast existed; but it was a smaller part of a far bigger contrast between philosophy and Christianity. Nevertheless the advance of the physical sciences contributed to the sense of contrast.

*1.* Geology proved the passage of an enormous span of time before man evolved. Here was direct conflict between the evidence of scientific enquiry and that literal understanding of Genesis and the Old Testament which many Christians still held. In England this conflict was particularly important because it gave the English an impression that the natural scientists, rather than the empirical or idealistic philosophers, tended to hold views contrary to religion, and to hold those views because of their scientific enquiry. This first impinged on a wide public after the publication (1844) of *Vestiges of Creation,* by the Scottish journalist R. Chambers, which was not a scholarly book but brilliantly popularized a crude Lamarckian doctrine of evolution and a prehistory of the world as seen in the record of the rocks.

Members of the churches were therefore compelled to drop such theories as that the world was only six thousand years old, or that the story of Noah was a literal history of a universal flood. In Germany and in England this was done easily between 1820 and 1860. But in the moment that parts of Genesis were admitted to be not history, a great impetus was given to the historical investigation already started of the biblical books, their origins and dates and validity, especially the early books of the Old Testament. Thus the churches spent much time during the sixties and seventies in internal tension over the historicity of the biblical record; and conservatives were apt to blame science for these tensions when properly speaking the physical sciences gave only a subsidiary impetus to historical enquiry.

*2.* The scientific method produced results of such importance during the middle years of the century that, especially in Germany and France, it looked as though it might be the only road to truth, and therefore in both Germany and France appeared an association between the students of the natural scientists and a philosophy of materialism; as though sooner or later physical science might be able to bring the brain and then the conscience and even the aesthetic sense under its own laws of predictability. In England this was never quite so strong as in Germany and France; but in one form through Auguste Comte and in another form through Herbert Spencer, similar associations of ideas had a significant influence on English thought between 1850 and 1880. The idea that the moral or aesthetic judgments could be brought under scientific laws never commended itself to a majority of the educated in England or America. Nevertheless, it combined with the historical investigation of the Bible to cast doubt upon the miraculous element in Christianity, so far at least as that element consisted in miracles which appeared to be breaches in "the laws of nature." Christian thinkers of the mid-century, e.g., James B. Mozley and the Duke of Argyll, examined the idea of laws of nature and showed its fallaciousness if understood to mean anything but probabilities arising from what had been in many instances observed. Intelligent scientists saw that the natural sciences could never disprove a miracle or miracles. But the habit and method of scientific enquiry made them much prefer the idea of "the not-yet-explained" to the idea of the supernatural, and therefore caused many educated people to become agnostic about the miraculous. In this way the development of the sciences helped to compel the churches to consider how far the faith which they taught was dependent upon a belief in the miraculous, and whether they could admit to membership, or (where that was answered in the affirmative) to ministry, persons who claimed to be faithful Christians but who could not profess a belief in the miraculous.

*3.* The scientific method could not allow itself any limit. It could not regard any area as exempt from its enquiry. The worst of the conflict between science and religion occurred between 1859 and 1877. The conflict was then at its worst because some churches or churchmen could not accept this unlimited possibility of enquiry, and some scientists believed that their freedom to be scientists was at stake. Moderate churchmen were content to see appearance of disharmony between the word of God and the works of God, to accept gladly what the scientists discovered, and to expect that in course of time they would be able to move towards a reconciliation. Conservative churchmen were inclined to put the truths derived from dogmas as obstacles to what the scientist was doing; and some scientists (in England, above all, T. H. Huxley and John Tyndall) regarded themselves as fighting for light and reason against the armies of superstition and obscurantism. Nothing did more than this to give the conflict of these years its peculiar intensity. Such a view among scientists was encouraged in the sixties and seventies, all over Europe and America, by the attitude of the Roman Catholic Church under Pope Pius IX, which seemed determined to concede nothing to the developments of modern science and historical criticism.

In England the famous and symbolic battle along these lines was the debate between Bishop Samuel Wilberforce and T. H. Huxley at the meeting in Oxford of the British Association, July 1860; where Wilberforce debated against Darwinism partly with real arguments for the perpetuity of the species, and partly by an appeal to the moral feeling that men are not brutes; and Huxley's famous retort exposed this second appeal as a rhetorical consideration which the scientist could not (*qua* scientist) allow to influence the debate on a purely physical question. Posterity saw the debate through Huxley's eyes, as scientific enlightenment vs. ecclesiastical obscurantism.

In the sixties therefore men began to write histories of the conflict between science and religion. The first important history was that by the American J. W. Draper. In *The Intellectual Development of Europe* (1864) and *History of the Conflict between Science and Religion* (1874) he described two mysterious entities, one called Science and the other called Religion, one light and one dark, struggling for mastery throughout the history of man. Shortly afterwards a better scholar, A. D. White, president of Cornell, formed the aim of publishing a book on the same theme; its final form was published in 1896, entitled *A History of the Warfare of Science with Theology in Christendom*. The object of the book, which was pursued with a wealth of learning and fascinating illustrations, was to show that religious interference with scientific investigation harms both religion and science; and that the freedom of the scientist will in the end help religion as well as science. The books of Draper and White did not ultimately come to seem important as contributions to the history of European ideas. But they were momentous as arising from the characteristic attitudes generated by the arguments of the sixties and seventies, and as themselves contributing to harden these attitudes by seeking to give them a historical justification.

**4.** Among particular discoveries or theories nothing did more to stimulate the conflict than Charles Darwin's *The Origin of Species* (1859). This was not because Darwin was a fighter. Though his own theism slowly faded during the sixties into agnosticism, he remained a modest and reverent enquirer with no desire for conflict. But the book, by promulgating the theory of natural selection, suddenly made the theory of evolution more probable than any other theory; and though in later editions of the *Origin* he substantially modified his exclusive reliance on natural selection as the cause of evolution, the theory of evolution was found probable in most educated minds during the seventies. The theory thus came in a form likely to emphasize a large element of purposelessness or useless suffering in the process by which man had come to be. The theodicy of the churches was long familiar with the problems of pain and determinism, but the theory forced them to contemplate these problems in a new context. In this way Darwin, without intending the result, strengthened existing tendencies towards materialistic views, and in his *Descent of Man* (1871) seemed himself to take a long step in the direction of such a philosophy as that advocated by Herbert Spencer, by whom indeed the book appeared to be influenced. The doctrine of evolution in itself, however, perturbed the churches little. It quickly became acceptable among educated Christians, though for a time, especially in the Roman Catholic Church, some sought to exclude man from the process. Darwin was buried (1882) in Westminster Abbey with an excellent sermon from a bishop afterwards. The final mark of acceptability in England occurred in 1896 when Frederick Temple, well known as one who accepted the theory of evolution, was made archbishop of Canterbury.

**5.** The acceptance of evolution laid the foundation for the science of anthropology, which began to make rapid strides during the sixties. It became an axiom that the primitive peoples still existing in various parts of the world could afford evidence of earlier stages of human development. Here was an additional ground of conflict, though a minor ground. Christianity taught that man was fallen, until recently connected this fall with remote events, and believed that sin was no integral part of human nature. The anthropologists worked upon a doctrine that man had risen from the savage and the savage from the brute, and therefore the animal looked an integral element in human constitution. Therefore the churches needed to free their doctrine of original sin from any historical reference (which in any case they were already doing, because of historical enquiry into biblical texts) and see "original sin" in terms of environment and heredity.

Thus the development of the natural sciences:

(a) encouraged the historical criticism of the Bible;

(b) strengthened already existing materialistic philosophies, especially in France and Germany;

(c) insisted that no dogma could be allowed to stand

107

in its way, and therefore encouraged churches to allow reinterpretation of dogmas in the light of better information;

(d) strengthened an already existing attitude hostile to miracle, and thereby encouraged the churches to adapt or restate their ideas of revelation;

(e) laid more stress upon the brute in human nature, because the scientific method could do no other than examine man as a physical object, not excluding the brain or psyche from that definition.

The natural scientists themselves, with certain eminent exceptions (e.g., E. H. Haeckel, Karl Pearson, Huxley), were not hostile to the Christian religion, especially in England and America, where many of the leading scientists continued throughout the nineteenth century to be professing members of their churches: men like Faraday, Asa Gray, Clerk Maxwell, Lister, Kelvin, and Stokes. But because the public had a picture of "science" as antagonistic to "religion," people began to be surprised when an eminent scientist was also found to be a religious man. It was noticeable that godly men, as in America Asa Gray and in England Clerk Maxwell, were treated as exhibits, when a generation before they would have been assumed to be typical of scientists. The impact upon European religious thought was made less by the scientists themselves than by philosophers or theologians using the physical results which they proposed.

The consequences for Christian theology were of the first importance in two especial directions:

(a) the doctrine of God's immanence within the world received a greater emphasis than ever before in religious history. Since the theory of evolution worked against the notion that God created the world and each animal by a series of (miraculous) creative acts, God must be seen more as within the process than as wholly external to the process and interfering from time to time. Many writers laid more emphasis upon God as vital force, or as sustainer, and upon creation less as an act than as a continuous creativity. Some Christian thinkers (like Otto Pfleiderer in Germany or R. J. Campbell in England) carried the doctrine of immanence so far as to provoke protests that the doctrine of God as father, and therefore of his transcendence and independence of the world, was of the essence of Christianity and was being endangered by the weight placed upon divine immanence, as if an exclusive stress laid upon God within the world would lead to pantheism or some philosophy like that of Spinoza which could not be reconciled with a Christian view of the world.

(b) Under the impact of scientific development, Christianity showed a strong inclination to throw nat-

ural theology overboard; that is, to cease to claim that an argument could be made towards God from an examination of the physical world. This was not true of Roman Catholic divinity, which was then committed to some form of Thomist philosophy and claimed to use the old "proofs" of God's existence from the necessity of the idea of a creation, or the design evident in the universe. But much Protestant theology ceased to base the claim of revelation upon any argument derived from the observation of nature, and turned to lay the ultimate stress (in some form or other) on the inward properties of the human being, the nature of religious experience, the intimate connection between religious feeling and the sense of moral duty, the feeling of awe or wonder aroused by the world, or sometimes the nature of the aesthetic judgment. This tendency existed already in the thought of Schleiermacher before the conflict proper between science and religion. The development of the conflict gave great encouragement to the tendency, and in the later years of the century elevated Schleiermacher to be the seminal mind of liberal divinity.

*BIBLIOGRAPHY*

For the relation to the philosophical background in Germany: F. A. Lange, *Geschichte des Materialismus . . .* , 2 vols. (1865–66), trans. E. C. Thomas as *The History of Materialism . . .* , 3rd ed. (London, 1925). For the pre-Darwinians: Charles C. Gillispie, *Genesis and Geology* (Cambridge, Mass., 1951); R. Hooykaas, *Natural Law and Divine Miracle: The Principle of Uniformity in Geology, Biology and Theology* (Leyden, 1963); for Chambers: M. Millhauser, *Just Before Darwin* (Middletown, Conn., 1959). For Darwin and the Darwinians: *Darwin's Autobiography*, ed. N. Barlow (London, 1958); A. Ellegård, *Darwin and the General Reader* (Göteborg, 1958); G. de Beer, *Charles Darwin* (London, 1963); W. Irvine, *Apes, Angels and Victorians* (London, 1955); G. Himmelfarb, *Darwin and the Darwinian Revolution* (London, 1959); A. H. Dupree, *Asa Gray* (Cambridge, Mass., 1959); H. C. Bibby, *T. H. Huxley* (London, 1959); W. B. Turrill, *J. D. Hooker* (London, 1964); A. S. Eve and C. H. Creasey, *Life and Work of John Tyndall* (London, 1945); E. Lurie, *Louis Agassiz: A Life in Science* (Chicago, 1960). For the historical aspect: D. H. Fleming, *J. W. Draper and the Religion of Science* (Philadelphia, 1950); A. D. White, *Autobiography* (London, 1905). In general: Owen Chadwick, *The Victorian Church Part Two* (London and New York, 1970).

W. OWEN CHADWICK

[See also **Agnosticism;** Christianity in History; Creation; **Evolutionism;** Primitivism.]

# RELIGIOUS ENLIGHTENMENT IN AMERICAN THOUGHT

## I. THE ILLUMINIST TRADITION

THE AUGUSTINIAN philosophical tradition, especially after the twelfth century when contacts between monks and laymen grew more frequent and respectable, became the intellectual source of new types of devotion and religious philosophy. The career and mind of Augustine himself served as a vivid pattern. The contrast between his experience of the transformation of sexual passion into an intimate communion with Perfect Being and the Augustinian theology of Grace as a predestined election into "the City of God" was in itself a dramatization of the difference between an emotional conversion and a moral regeneration. Gradually there developed under Augustine's influence, especially among laymen, three types of "enthusiasm," that is, of having an "indwelling Holy Spirit" as a channel of Grace independent of the sacraments. This experience was interpreted as a middle way between the mystics of the Neo-Platonic type and the Aristotelian rationalizations of the scholastics and the Jesuits. One type found expression in religious love (*philia*): the Béguines (Dutch and Flemish nuns who live in convents without taking vows), Brethren of the Free Spirit, The Friends of God (*devotio moderna*), Christian Brotherhoods (*collegia pietatis*), Societies of Friends, and "theophilanthropy." Another type centered in the covenant relationship: French and Swiss Huguenots, Scottish Presbyterians, Puritans, Covenanters, Federalists, and Christian Commonwealth Men. A third type believed that an inner light (not the "light of nature," reason) kindled in them a holy love of Perfect Being. Such love is quite distinct from friendship, secular benevolence, charity, and enlightened self-love. These were called Illuminists. Among the philosophers who were directly and significantly influenced by this type of enlightenment were: Tommaso Campanella, Vico, Malebranche, Pascal, Fénelon, Francis Hutcheson, Jonathan Edwards, Pestalozzi.

This article describes the ideology of one brief, local movement within the long history of religious enlightenment. It arose among a small group of New England Puritans and among the "new light" Presbyterians in New York, New Jersey, and Pennsylvania. It served as the philosophical explanation of the Great Awakening during a few decades after 1730, and it was submerged under a deluge of evangelical piety and theological wrangling early in the nineteenth century. The philosophical leader of this movement was Jonathan Edwards (1703–58).

## II. THE ENLIGHTENMENT OF JONATHAN EDWARDS

The enthusiasm of the Great Awakening was opposed by the sober Puritans as well as by Yankee liberals. The basic charge against all such illuminism had been formulated by Bishop Bossuet in his conflict with Archbishop Fénelon: "Pure love is opposed to the essence of love which always desires the enjoyment of its object, and also to the nature of man who necessarily desires happiness." Fénelon, Pascal, and other philosophers made elaborate and critical efforts to meet this double charge radically. Among the most radical was Jonathan Edwards.

As a child, Jonathan Edwards had been accustomed to accepting the sovereignty of the Almighty as a necessary, grim truth; and he had made repeated vain efforts to love this Sovereign Lord as he was presented in Puritan pulpits and literature. His first philosophical emancipation came from reading Locke's *Essay concerning Human Understanding*. The chapter on "Power" taught him that it is not the will that does the willing, but it is the "soul" or self that does it. Will and "inclination" are the same and in a prudent person are by nature "subject to the last dictate of the understanding." This insight implied that if, as he believed, the will is depraved, unable to enjoy its true Good, the "affections" are also benighted, and therefore the rational understanding is hopelessly led astray from its normal "light of nature." Hence, the best that a prudent understanding can do is to direct the "heart" (affections, inclinations, will) toward an enlightened self-love and a social benevolence. But to achieve "true virtue" or "pure love" to Perfect Being is naturally impossible. Being a sensitive, highly emotional youth, he became desperate, for the chances of being "elected" by Grace were, on Calvinistic calculations, very slight.

He was under this tension when, after graduating from Yale in 1720, he accepted his first charge as a minister of a Presbyterian congregation in New York. The family of John Smith, with which he boarded, was influenced by "new light" pietism and he soon found himself in intimate relations with religiously enlightened laymen. His own description of what happened to him during those months in New York and immediately following is a vivid account of illumination:

My sense of divine things seemed gradually to increase, until I went to preach in Newyork [sic] . . . and while I was there I felt them, very sensibly, in a much higher degree than I had done before. My longings after God and holiness were much increased. Pure and humble, holy and heavenly Christianity, appeared exceeding amiable to me. . . . The inward ardor of my soul, seemed to be hindered and pent up, and could not freely flame out as it would. . . . Holiness . . . appeared to me to be of a sweet, pleasant, charming, serene, calm nature; which brought an inexpressible purity, brightness, peacefulness and ravishment of the soul. . . . On January 12, 1723 I made a solemn dedication of myself to God. . . . The sweetest joys and delights I have experienced, have not been those that have arisen from a hope of my own good estate, but in a direct view of the glorious things of the gospel. . . . I have many times had a sense of the glory of the third person in the Trinity, in his office of Sanctifier, in his holy operations, communicating divine light and life to the soul, . . . as an infinite fountain of divine glory . . . like the sun in its glory, sweetly and pleasantly diffusing light and life (*Narrative of his Conversion*, ca. 1740).

In 1734 Edwards outlined his doctrine of enlightenment in a philosophical sermon published under the title: *A Divine and Supernatural Light, Immediately Imparted to the Soul by the Spirit of God.* He was now ready to develop the philosophy of divine illumination, but he was distracted by the Great Awakening. For a decade, he devoted himself to the practical problems and efforts of the revival. After the enthusiasm had somewhat abated, he returned to his theoretical analysis and in 1746 published his *Treatise concerning Religious Affections.* Part I is devoted to the thesis that religion is at bottom an affair of "the heart" and that emotional forms of religious expression must be analyzed for evidences of divine Grace. Part II is a critique of those "signs" that are not evidence of enlightenment. Part III states and defends the following major conclusions:

(1) God is amiable because of his "inherent" excellence rather than on account of his "objective" attributes. Holy love is the sense of this beauty, harmony, and light.

(2) True virtue is such enjoyment; it is not the "natural" calculated judgment of conscience, nor is it a gratitude for divine benevolence. The "moral sense" as it is emphasized by the Scottish Enlightenment is only an approximation to divinely enlightened love.

(3) Holy love is a prerequisite for the "witness of the Spirit" which is central to the "covenant of Grace."

(4) This is a "rebirth in the Spirit" and not a "regeneration" of the will.

(5) This is not mysticism. "Gracious affections are attended with a reasonable and spiritual conviction of the judgment" (Part III, Sec. V).

(6) "Holy practice" must be pursued with "highest earnestness" and a convert with an enlightened heart makes "religion eminently his work and business" (Part III, Sec. XII).

Jonathan Edwards' theory of enlightenment was based not only on his own experience and on the Great Awakening but also on his wide reading in the literature of illuminism, especially Scottish and Dutch. At the time of his death in Princeton he was planning to supplement his philosophical treatises and essays by a systematic exposition of "Lovely Christianity." It is possible that his curious sketch on "The Trinity" was intended for this systematic work of Pietist philosophy. It begins:

Tis common when speaking of the Divine happiness to say that God is Infinitely Happy in the Enjoyment of himself, in Perfectly beholding and Infinitely loving, and Rejoicing in, his own Essence and Perfections, and accordingly it must be supposed that God perpetually and Eternally has a most Perfect Idea of himself, . . . and from hence arises a most pure and Perfect act or energy in the Godhead, which is the divine Love, Complacence and Joy (*Representative Selections*, eds. Faust and Johnson, p. 375).

This is obviously a portrait of Self-enlightened Perfect Being. It attempts to express in terms of the new psychology a formal definition of the Divine Essence and Glory.

### III. ECLIPSE

While Edwards during the last years of his short life was attempting a philosophical formulation of religious enlightenment, his associates in the New Light movement were dragging him back into the theological polemics of Calvinism. He was compelled by their polemics to write *The Great Christian Doctrine of Original Sin Defended* (1758—published posthumously). His closest colleague, Joseph Bellamy of Bethlehem, Conn., published in 1750 *True Religion delineated; or experimental Religion, as distinguished from Formality on the one hand, and Enthusiasm on the other, set in a scriptural and rational Light.* This was followed in 1758 by his four sermons, including *The Wisdom of God in the Permission of Sin.* Bellamy explained that God "permitted," without "causing," sin in the universe because it was to the ultimate "advantage" of mankind. Edwards had maintained that God permitted sin to enter for the sake of his own glory, and Samuel Hopkins maintained only that sin is an "advantage to the universe." Both Bellamy and Hopkins became involved in a desperate attempt to defend the "moral government" or justice of God, and this led them to assert not only God's "disinterested benevolence" but also his "disinterested malice toward sin." They were then compelled by the insistent protests of several kinds of liberals to try to defend the endless punishment of infants. Edwards had hoped to let the doctrine that "infinite sin" leads to "infinite punishment" remain an abstract conception of justice. But now the Edwardeans were pushed into defending the endless torture of innocent infants. The more they wrote on this subject the more incredible they became.

They were pushed into other absurdities on the subject of the Church Covenant. Edwards had suggested, without getting into a theological argument, that the Covenant of Grace was more essential to religion than the "external"covenant of the Church. His followers, however, insisted on enforcing the Puritan rules of strict communion, making regeneration a prerequisite. This revived the old problem of distinguishing "visible" from "invisible" saints, and the question whether men's "natural" moral strivings and "exercises" toward salvation could be interpreted as "gracious affections." Nathanael Emmons of Franklin, Mass. became hopelessly involved in the problem, so that he did not know how to distinguish between those who profess apparent holiness and those who are apparently but not professedly really holy, or those who neither appear nor profess to be holy but really are holy. The most significant predicament into which the New Light theologians drifted was their tendency to portray human nature as thoroughly damnable in order to give the whole "glory" to the Divine Light. Edwards had approved of the "moral sense" theory of the Scottish Enlightenment and agreed that self-love could generate a disinterested benevolence under the guidance of prudent judgment, but he insisted that such social benevolence is only an "image" of true virtue and pure love. But his theologically entangled and wrangling followers were forced by an increasing liberal opposition to make caricatures both of human nature and of supernatural light. By 1833, after a protracted debate between Nathaniel Taylor and Bennett Tyler, the theologies of both New Sides and Old Sides Presbyterians had become so absurd to others that the whole issue was labelled "strictly controversial" and the enlightenment went into eclipse.

### IV. AFTERGLOW

An inquisitive historian may detect scattered vestiges of philosophical pietism in America after it had lapsed into unenlightened theology and evangelical revivalism. The most direct vestige is to be found in the Rev. William Ellery Channing, leader of the New England Unitarians. He rediscovered "likeness to God" in the human soul. Two New Light influences on him were the theory of benevolence in the works of Francis Hutcheson, and the personal benevolence of Samuel Hopkins, whose character seemed to be in striking contrast to his theology. These suggested to him that there is an element of holiness in the human soul which enables man to achieve self-culture. He appealed to this aspect of the self as motivation for "social regeneration" by "diffusive charity." He used the Edwardean

terminology: perfect love, rebirth, supernatural light, mediatorial system, and Holy Spirit.

Similar vestiges appear in Channing's Boston neighbor, Theodore Parker. He preached that all theologies are transient, but that "affectional piety" and the "absolute love of God" are "permanent" in man. This doctrine he used as a basis for promoting social reforms. He conceived "transcendentalism" to mean that life, love, and piety transcend knowledge. Though he appropriated the concepts of enlightened pietism, he devoted much of his time and energy to rational criticism of scriptures and traditions.

The most influential vestige is to be found in James Marsh, a Presbyterian New Light and President of the University of Vermont. Deeply concerned over the growing gap between philosophy and theology, seeking a new ground for "experimental religion," he found in Coleridge's *Aids to Reflection* a conception of "spirit" that met his needs. In his long essay prefacing his edition of this volume, he applied Coleridge's idea of spirituality as a way of life, not of doctrine, to philosophical reflection, to theology, and to piety. This was a fresh enlightenment to him and rapidly became one of the major sources of New England transcendentalism. The blending of the religious enlightenment with the new transcendentalism is evident in typical passages like the following:

The world of spirit enters into the life of nature. . . . In its own essence, and in its proper right, it is supernatural, and paramount to all the powers of nature.

It is only by freeing the spiritual principle from the limitations of that narrow and individual end which the individual nature prescribes, and placing it under that spiritual law which is congenial to its own essence, that it can be truly free. When brought into the liberty with which the Spirit of God clothes it, it freely strives after those noble and glorious ends which reason and the Spirit of God prescribe (Marsh, *Remains* . . . , pp. 383, 389).

Such adaptation of religious enlightenment to the "newness" of romantic idealism became a common feature of transcendentalism; it is also in the immediate background of Josiah Royce's contrast between "the world of appreciation" and "the world of description."

From 1835 to 1855 Oberlin College in Ohio was a center of Christian Perfectionism or the philosophy of "sanctification," which, though critical of Edwards' identification of "will" and "inclination," was a direct descendant of the New Light theology and of its emphasis on disinterested benevolence. The combined influence of Charles Finney (New Light evangelist) and Asa Mahan (author of *Christian Perfectionism*, 1839), who were the first Presidents of Oberlin College, made this institution well-known as a center of sanctification doctrine and anti-slavery reform. Their intuitionist or illuminist theory of benevolence, in opposition to utilitarian ethics, served as a sanction for a vigorous reform movement and for civil disobedience to the fugitive slave laws.

A curious vestige of Edwards' psychology of the will is found in the development of psychology in America during the nineteenth century. The terms "will" and "inclination" were used by Edwards as technical synonyms for "heart" as over against "head." The Edwardeans in their theological polemics used the term "propensities" in place of Edwards' "inclinations," and distinguished these from both "will" and "understanding," thus creating a "three-faculty psychology." When Nathanael Emmons began to use the term "exercises" to refer to the "strivings" of seekers for Grace, others, referred back to Edwards' use of the term "taste" to describe the affectional faculty of the mind. The first psychologist to embody this "three-faculty" doctrine in his text of 1824 was the Rev. Asa Burton of Thetford, Vermont and Dartmouth College. This led to a long controversy about the relation between taste and will. Burton identified "taste" with "heart" and called it "the principle of action" as well as of "pleasure and pain." Subsequently "taste" became "consciousness" in addition to volition and cognition. Thus, at least indirectly, the theory of the affections which developed during the Great Awakening led to the preoccupation of William James with the emotions, especially in his *Varieties of Religious Experience.*

*BIBLIOGRAPHY*

J. E. Dirks, *The Critical Theology of Theodore Parker* (New York, 1948). Jonathan Edwards, *Representative Selections. With Introduction, Bibliography and Notes,* eds. C. H. Faust and T. H. Johnson (New York, 1935; rev. ed. 1962), useful for basic writings, critical introduction, references, and notes; idem, *Treatise on the Religious Affections* (Boston, 1746), also a new edition, ed. J. E. Smith (New Haven, 1959). J. Haroutunian, *Piety versus Moralism; The Passing of the New England Theology* (New York, 1932). F. Hutcheson, *An Inquiry into the Original of our Ideas of Beauty and Virtue* (Glasgow, 1723). E. H. Madden, *Civil Disobedience and Moral Law in Nineteenth Century American Philosophy* (Seattle, 1968), especially useful for the history of Oberlin College. J. Marsh, *The Remains of the Rev. James Marsh,* ed. J. Torrey (Boston, 1843). H. A. Pochmann, *German Culture in America* (Madison, 1957), best account of Marsh's philosophy. H. W. Schneider, *The Puritan Mind* (New York, 1930), does not do justice to the illuminism and pietism in Edwards, but describes his early enlightenment.

HERBERT W. SCHNEIDER

[See also **Enlightenment;** God; Holy; Love.]

## RELIGIOUS TOLERATION

LEXICOLOGY tells us that up to the beginning of the eighteenth century the word *"tolérance"* had, in French, a pejorative meaning: a lax complacency towards evil. In 1691, in his admonition to Protestants (*VIe avertissement aux protestants,* III, ix) Bossuet still proudly described Catholicism as the least tolerant of all religions and, as if to compete with this proud boast, the Walloon Synod of Leyden (an overwhelming majority of whose members were Huguenot refugees) firmly condemned religious toleration as a heresy. In the course of the crucial years of "the crisis of the European conscience," the century-old meaning of the two words was reversed: intolerance became a vice and tolerance a virtue; an opinion which had previously been held only by isolated and suspect theoreticians was suddenly widespread and became part of the common language. Thus the ideal of religious toleration had emerged through a delayed reaction to the natural propensity of groups to penalize those members who departed from the beliefs and practices of the majority, represented by those of the ruling classes, so that the majority or dominant view acquired *ipso facto* the character of an imperative rule.

The pleas for religious toleration initially appear as protests against the measures taken by the authorities against dissenters, and later, as refutations of arguments advanced to authorize or encourage the use of force against dissenters.

As regards persecution, theory follows practice as is often the case in the history of ideas; theory is advanced to explain practice, to authorize it, to defend it against its critics, and in that way the theorists of intolerance could have helped, extended, and aggravated its practice, but they were not its instigators. Likewise the partisans of religious tolerance have probably been successful at times in alleviating the severity of some punishments inflicted on minorities. They may have speeded the end of persecutions and discriminatory practices. Sometimes even, by their influence on a prince, they played a role in establishing a precarious and tiny pocket of liberalism, although in these cases we must be careful not to lend too much weight to purely theoretical considerations. The end of religious persecution depended first of all upon the evolution of Western societies; i.e., their secularization—associated with a growing realization of their temporal interests, and consisting of a steady weakening of the once intimate solidarity between Church and State—gradually relegated the question of an individual's religious affiliation to the domain of private life, that sphere of liberty which the community is able to leave to the individual without endangering itself.

Then the varieties of belief of its members no longer appeared as a menace to the loyalty required by the group's concern for security and prosperity.

This evolution has had its ups and downs in different tempos in various countries in Europe. Only recently has a Jesuit been able to enter Sweden; theoretically Switzerland is still closed to him; the few Spanish Protestants still suffer nowadays from discriminatory measures, and in countries where parties calling themselves Marxist are in power the practice of religion is seriously hindered. On the other hand, already in the sixteenth century there were some islands of significant religious pluralism in Eastern Europe (Transylvania and Poland, particularly). Each of these instances is related to local conditions and particular historical antecedents. Besides, the historian should not be content with reading the laws. In each instance he must try to determine the actual practice of carrying out laws before drawing a conclusion, because, especially under the Old Regime, it turns out that this practice deviated appreciably, in one way or another, from the letter of the law. Thus, around 1680, in the Netherlands' United Provinces, in spite of the fact that the restrictive legislation concerning Roman Catholics had not been revoked, a religious tolerance reigned, unmatched by any other country in Europe, for the restrictions were simply not enforced.

At the same time, although the Edict of Nantes was still law in France, the Protestants came under pressures, legal chicaneries, and annoyances which already bordered upon religious persecution, because the original meaning of the text of the Edict was reduced to almost nil by means of the belittling casuistic interpretation of "the letter of the law." It is enough, then, for us to recall the extreme complexity of the evolution which led Western countries from their initial practices of persecution to their current and sometimes rather limited respect for the religious freedom of their citizens. The tortuous path of this journey can be analyzed only if one pays careful attention to its close ties to different national histories. Thus, for example, the Huguenot situation improved when France was at war: for one thing, the internal problems of the realm became of secondary consideration; on the other hand, the fear of an alliance of French Protestants with the enemy—in the eighteenth century a particular nightmare to the authorities—made it a point of wisdom not to push them to despair; so that the oscillations of European foreign policy had repercussions even in the daily life of peasants in remote corners of Languedoc.

Religious intolerance can assert itself in two directions: externally, when a persecuting religion faces believers in another religion, belonging to a separate political system backed by military force, the result is a crusade or holy war; or else, internally, with respect to dissenters, schismatics and heretics (those who choose, as indicated by etymology, and whose faith, institutions, or other rites show some differences from those of the prevalent party), the result is persecution.

The first form of intolerance—that of Charlemagne against the Saxons, for example, who were given the choice between baptism and death—is easy enough to interpret. It is the ideological side of a bellicose dispute, the warfare bringing not only two tribes or two nations, but also their gods into conflict. In the case of conquest followed by colonization, the example of the Romans shows the adaptability of polytheism: it easily accommodates a multiplicity of deities, so that in the end the initial conflict gives way to a religious coalescence. On the other hand, the unique and "jealous" nature of the God of Judeo-Christian monotheism forbade his faithful ones that "sacrifice to idols" which the imperial Roman authorities regarded above all as evidence of political loyalty. (Incidentally, the conflict between the Huguenots and the power which insisted upon their recanting, under Louis XIV, produced a misunderstanding of the same type. For the Huguenot, to convert to Catholicism was to embrace "the papist idolatry" and therefore to commit a frightful sin, while from the viewpoint of authorities, the adoption of one form of Christianity rather than another was such a trivial affair that the royal power felt justified in suspecting some sort of subversion among those who refused to obey and who thus deserved the most dire punishment.)

A new element arose with monotheism: theology, with the notion of a creed, of a precise and articulated doctrinal belief corresponding to absolute Truth (since revealed). Simultaneously there appeared the possibility of orthodoxy and heterodoxy, of correct wording and erroneous wording—by accretion, suppression, or modification, even if it were of only one article of faith. As soon as rituals cease to be self-sufficient, as in ancient paganism, and are no longer akin to traditional festivities—such as we still have in Christmas trees and Easter eggs—the notion of sacrament becomes inseparably associated with acts, intentions, and speculative content.

So long as the profession of Christianity was intermittently exposed to measures of persecution by the political authorities, Christian writers defended religious liberty, and many passages from the Church Fathers eloquently justify it. However, soon after the imperial throne was won over to Christianity, the Church hastened to enlist the secular arm against heretics. Saint Augustine in particular followed that path. In spite of his original hostility towards con-

113

straint, he ended up as its theoretician, owing to the successes that penal sanctions had against the Donatists. Quickly the pagans, in their turn, became victims of persecution. It would be an anachronism to denounce outrageously the unfairness of such a double standard. Our modern relativistic attitude tends to make us reluctant to recognize the reality, both in concept and in experience, of a view of things in which absolute truth—which one felt sure one possessed—has quite a different weight and status than error. For age after age it appeared dazzlingly evident that Truth, by definition, enjoys rights of its own—and that it would be grotesque, unthinkable, criminal to even think of extending these rights to "errors." If we do not try to gain a sympathetic understanding of this ingenuous principle, a fundamental tendency in ancient cultures, we are doomed to superficiality, and by implicitly assuming the problem solved, we ignore the slow and difficult awakening of the ideal of toleration.

The most instructive type of religious intolerance, and that which is peculiar to various monotheisms (for Islam has known it also) is persecution directed against internal dissent, against heretics. According to Aquinas (it goes without saying that the facts were far from being always true to his doctrinal views), one ought not to use constraint to convert pagans and infidels, who should be brought to Christianity only by a free conversion, moved by preaching and example. Although the Jews ought technically to be considered as infidels, their dispersion within Christian countries made them liable too often to be dealt with simply as heretics of the worst kind. The religious affinities created by a common respect for the Old Testament unleashed against them a fratricidal hostility. The sources of Western anti-Semitism are far from being wholly religious, but a theological concept such as that of deicide has played a significant role in investing with respectability and legitimacy the sociological fury of conformity, that is to say, the normative value attributed to the characteristics of the statistical majority.

Nevertheless, if fact had followed theory, the condition of the Jews would have been a little less harsh than that of the heretics (which had often been the case in Rome and in the papal States). The justification of intolerance toward the dissenter rests, in fact, on the notion of the indelible stamp given by baptism: the *compelle intrare* is precisely a *compelle remanere* ("Compel them to come in" means exactly "compel them to remain"). As one is a priest eternally, one is a Christian forever. The means of constraint are destined to compel the heretic to honor his tacit covenant and to make, as it were, his concrete mode of existence coincide with that essence which he received with the seal of baptism and which he is not in any

position to modify. As bad luck would have it for so many heretics in the course of the centuries, the conditions guaranteeing the validity of the sacrament of baptism were defined very generously: even if administered according to a heretical rite, baptism is valid if only it includes a minimal trinitarian formula which, effectively, is present in almost all Christian baptismal liturgies. From this fact there readily arises the problem, not only of individuals who, born into the "true religion," depart of their own volition as adults and ought either to be punished for their defection or compelled to return to the fold, but also of those who, born in the bosom of heresy and having never known another form of Christianity, by the fact of their baptism and often unknown to themselves, fall under the power and authority of the "True Church." In our ecumenical age, this conception of baptism creates a link between all the "separated brethren" of various denominations, but until quite recently (cf. the decree on ecumenism of Vatican II) this sacrament, common to all Christians, provided the proper base for the inalienable rights that the Roman Church arrogated to itself over all the baptized, without considering the opinion of the persons involved. Still, in 1857, in the Mortara affair, Pius IX strictly applied the traditional doctrine.

In other words, membership in the Church was established by birth, because it was sealed by the earliest sacrament. "We are Christians by the same title as we are either Perigordians or Germans" observes Montaigne (*Essays*, II, xii). A man acquires his religion as he learns his language, the sphere par excellence of pure tradition. The concept of "implicit" faith allowed the authorities to consider as orthodox anyone showing obedience to the priesthood, and the unity of faith played a role somewhat akin to that played by the "one party system" in many countries of the Third World. The prevailing point of view considered the masses as a herd which their shepherds had the task of leading; the flock was regarded, if not literally, as beings of an inferior sort to that of the rulers— nobility and clergy—at least as little, or backward, children committed to the care and decisions of adults.

We, in the West, now adopt a different attitude. Citizens are reputedly mature beings, equal and responsible. But both viewpoints are equally unrealistic, even though the first appears static, the second, dynamic. The social reality does not coincide with the theory. Many citizens in our democracies behave as minors, manipulated and manipulable by publicity and propaganda, and conversely, powerful personalities flourished in the Middle Ages and under the Old Regime, even outside of the privileged classes and the very small number of educated elite. Personalities exist

114

in all centuries and all cultures, but, on the other hand, the abstract concept of an autonomous individual is scarcely meaningful in a civilization defined by a marked hierarchical stratification (family, parish, corporation, etc.) and by economical and technical structures of a pre-capitalistic nature.

In the past, the need for social conformity, gained and maintained, should the occasion demand, by force (fines, imprisonments, banishments, executions) and the spontaneous repression of deviant and disruptive tendencies, operated all the more intensely and selectively in the religious realm, because for a long time that was the only area in which centralizing tendencies operated without too much hindrance. It is not an accident that the practice of a certain religious toleration progressed—although in fits and starts—at the same time as the constitution of national states, the birth of capitalism, and the rise of modern science. The consensus, once acquired in the new areas—political loyalty, the demands of economic advance and social mobility, the mechanistic interpretation of Nature—became less necessary on the religious level, as if that which was required sociologically was a certain area of general agreement, with little concern about which particular area.

In defense of this minimal conformity, arguments multiplied—often sophistically invoked: they were scriptural arguments, drawn either from the precepts of the Old Testament against idolators and blasphemers, or from the "Compel them to come in" of the Parable of the Wedding Feast (Luke 14:23)—an exegesis advanced by Saint Augustine and revived secondarily by Calvin—or, even stranger yet, from the Parable of the Wheat and the Tares (Matthew 13:24–30, 36–43). Although the sense of this parable seems to be exactly the opposite, it was supposed that it commends long-suffering only when the distinction between the wheat and the tares is elusive (as in the case of sinners); but that the obvious characteristics which patently identify the heretic, permit without risk of error his being uprooted from the field of Christianity and command that he be committed to the flames. In other respects the revival of the study of Roman Law, encouraged by the Renaissance, furnished judicial arguments and precedents, based on a multitude of laws of the late Empire. Present-day historians surmise that these laws were a means of intimidation in their times and that they were rarely enforced. They observe that the death penalty with which those laws threatened the Manicheans had political explanations, for the seat of this heresy was in Persia, a dangerous enemy of the Eastern Empire. But in the Renaissance this legislation was taken literally, and, the dualistic character of the greater part of the medieval heresies

having rendered the term "Manichean" synonymous with "heretic," these impressive texts lent authority to the extirpation of heresy by fetter and by fire.

It is well known that the greater part of medieval heresies included economically and socially subversive elements, and that they appealed particularly to the disinherited. In the repression which heretics incurred, motives born out of social conservatism compounded the zeal to defend religious orthodoxy. The recurrence through centuries of the shock and horror felt by the privileged at a program suggesting even the faintest hint of communism is well known, as are the bright hopes that it usually awakens in the poor. Thus there are some historians who consider Marxism, in some respects, a Christian heresy because in spite of the evident paradoxical nature of that label, many of the characteristics of the communist movements allow for some curious parallels with the heresies of the past.

Let us go back to the Renaissance. Medieval law had itself also justified the most dire penalties against heretics. Likened to the poisoner of wells, the arsonist, the counterfeiter, and the murderer—the heresiarch and the votaries whom he enticed were pictured as public pests which the authorities had the solemn obligation to purge from the face of the earth. To the initial idea of extirpation and punishment—expiatory and exemplary—was joined, particularly in the case of the disciples of mischief, the desire to correct and to lead into the right path, by means of minor penalties, the lambs who had strayed.

These texts and these ideas of such diverse historical origin all concurred, at least as they were interpreted, in authorizing the idea that religious conformity, obtained, if necessary, by force, was a beneficent requirement at all levels. It was advantageous for the individual concerned that he be constrained to return to eternal salvation, (for "Outside the Church there is no salvation," as Saint Cyprian had said), and it was profitable for the collectivity, for God had not given the sword to the princes in vain, and the heretic is the most dangerous of all criminals since he is a threat to the highest good, the salvation of the soul. Finally, since his situation was reduced to that of the blasphemer and idolator, the heretic, guilty of divine lèse-majesté, was assumed to offend God himself, and the vindication of God's glory was vital, both to piety and in order to protect the group from the terrible punishments of the Lord. For a long time, in fact, the historians explained disasters—epidemics, floods, military defeats, etc.—as the results of divine wrath, which it was not wise to provoke by a careless indulgence—a "tolerance"—toward the "enemies of God."

If one reflects upon it, one is struck by the coherence and doctrinal consistency of the ideological justifications provided for the practice of religious intolerance. The system of justification stands up admirably on all levels, and the unavoidable sociological necessity for a minimum consensus gives it an imperative accent. This necessity for consensus has not disappeared from among us, but its field of application is more concerned with political or racial questions than with religious ones. We know that in most countries certain political parties are outlawed, that immigration is controlled, that certain minorities—or majorities in the case of South Africa—have to endure multiple discriminations, often very harshly applied. But the contemporary example which can help us best to penetrate the mentality of the most reflective and convinced religious persecutors is that of the laws of prophylaxis and hygiene (vaccination, quarantines, etc.) which the civil authorities impose upon the citizens. The persecutors were as convinced that they were doing their duty and acting for the common good (and, incidentally, for that of the dissidents themselves) as the governments which in our day establish decrees in order to control an epidemic; in the first case the theologians, and in the second the physicians, are the competent experts who guide the action of the "secular arm."

Considered as punishments, the penalties inflicted on heretics do not present any particular problem. They aim at checking a certain delinquency (as was the case with punishments inflicted on sorcerers). It is when constraint is supposed to call the heterodox back into the right path that an explanation becomes necessary. Indeed, to penalize an error is not to refute it, and the partisans of toleration would constantly stress this point. They would also observe that persecution creates the problems which it claims to solve: the only alternative left to the dissident group is that of armed revolt. On the *individual* level, it creates only martyrs or hypocrites. This kind of objection, consequently, makes a point of showing the complete inappropriateness of the intended goals of intolerance.

It is belatedly, toward the time of the revocation of the Edict of Nantes (1685), that the theorists of persecution presented more minutely detailed analyses which go back to Saint Augustine. They made a preliminary assumption, which is astonishingly naive, namely, that any searching comparison of their respective dogmas allows anyone to discern clearly the truth of orthodoxy and the error of heresy. The stubbornness of the dissident implies then that he "clings tenaciously to his opinions" through either conceit or indolence. The penalties which are inflicted on him are destined to counteract his obstinacy or his laziness by fostering the conditions of persuasion, but not directly to enforce conversion. (Inspired by a rudimentary pedagogy, this scheme can just as well commend the promise of re-

ward as the threat of punishment, and the former course was not neglected in France, with respect to the Protestants, until about 1679.) Only an authoritarian and paternalistic culture, prone to liken the profession of a religion to a respectful submission, was apt to encourage faith in disciplinary procedures to induce genuine conversions. Moreover, the theoretical scheme unrealistically demands a constant interplay of sanctions and preaching: but—whence the musty odor of hypocrisy which these justifications of constraint emit—no one can ignore the fact that the Huguenots saw more dragoons than missionaries worthy of that name.

All the literature of propaganda, which prepared and extolled the revocation of the Edict of Nantes, eloquently attests to a perceptible evolution of mental attitudes—contrary to what appears at first glance—for it tries hard to justify the means of constraint that previously had seemed too natural to need explanation. This so long-delayed Counter-Reformation that France experienced, had something artificial and anachronistic about it. When it happened, the ecclesiastical authorities took pains to give it an emphatic religious overtone, and to add to their credit the crushing of French Protestantism; but it seems clear that the Revocation responded mostly to certain demands—ineptly understood, but that is of little importance here—of *raison d'état*, of judicial modernism (the Edict applied to a corporate body, not to individuals), and of an increased internal security of the Realm, ensured by its religious unity.

The primary importance of that aspect of the problem is demonstrated by a counterproof. The majority of the theoreticians of religious toleration, who were all Protestants, regularly making an exception of Roman Catholics, because of their allegiance to the Pope (a foreign sovereign capable of releasing them from their requirement of fidelity to their prince), justified their subjection to certain discriminatory measures (cf. in England, the Test Act, 1673). It was not their religious convictions in themselves which were penalized, but the potential political consequences which were attributed to them—as in the case of the Huguenots, who were basically called to account for their liaisons and sympathies with England and the United Provinces. An analogous perspective explains why the majority of authors excluded atheists from the toleration which they advocated: without belief in divine sanction beyond the grave, people suspected that the individual would be a sort of outlaw with no "brake" on the road to sin. It required a whole evolution of ideas to recognize that, in fact, morality and civic-mindedness are not as necessarily integrated with religious convictions as had been traditionally assumed, or as long as ethics and political theory have remained inextricably mingled with religious dogmas.

Such a mentality was so dominant and so unquestioned that we meet it again in the schismatics and the heretics themselves; which is understandable since they claimed "to be carrying away the true Church" with them (as certain Huguenots picturesquely put it), and since their original aim had been to reform integrally the Christian Church. The events which allowed the different forms of Protestantism to dominate, at least partially, in Northern Europe frustrated the hopes of the two factions, both dedicated to the ideal of the unity of the Church. The conviction that it is the duty of the Christian magistrate to rebuke heresy had, however, consequences somewhat less sanguinary on the Protestant side than on the Catholic. It is well known that Italy, Spain, and a part of the German and Slavic countries were held or won back to obedience to Rome by methods which were too often cruel. On the other hand, while the executions of Catholics—heretics from the point of view of a Protestant—were regularly enough associated with issues of a political order, Catholics were in fact more often annoyed, persecuted, or exiled, rather than put to death.

Nevertheless, the great reformed confessions (the established churches) for a long time harshly persecuted the followers of sects, Antitrinitarians (who were subject to death in the lands of the Holy Roman Empire after 1532), and Anabaptists. In the case of the latter, once again considerations of social conservatism often played a significant role. The heretic and the revolutionary are indistinguishable in many cases, and it is difficult to know which of the two characters is responsible for the mercilessness on the part of the authorities and of public opinion. The drownings at Zurich, the decapitations at Berne, the burning at the stake of Servetus in Geneva, etc., eloquently attest that the same fundamental principles of intolerance were shared by all the authorities of Europe. That the persecutions carried out in Protestant States had been on the whole less bloody and less prolonged than those urged upon the authorities by the Society of Jesus and the Spanish Inquisition remains an ancillary statement of fact from the strict point of view of the history of ideas.

The more or less clandestine presence of sectarians in Protestant countries and the relative freedom of the press which often existed there, explain why after the Council of Trent it would only be from the reformed side of the religious frontier dividing Europe that one would meet writers arguing in favor of tolerance. Some sects, to be sure, considering that to suffer persecution is the "mark" of the true Church, responded to it simply with nonviolent fervor; however, in general, the condition of being persecuted fostered a critical approach. It was among the sectarians that we find revived a conception (held formerly by the early Church Fathers facing the Roman pagans) which, undergoing development and secularization, was to play an outstanding role in the theory of tolerance; this conception can be described in modern terms as the distinction between Church and State and between ecclesiastical and political tolerance. The small sectarian groups claimed to assemble only the elect, and consequently, contrary to the Churches with their territorial parishes, they did not aim at being coextensive with the total population. This was enough to make the sectarians distinguish expressly civil society, with its purely earthly ends, from the little band of the "Righteous," and to make them dissociate completely the second from the first (thus, originally, Anabaptists and Socinians refused to bear arms and to take cases to court). The ecclesiastical intolerance of the Anabaptists, on the other hand, was maximal. It brought about schisms, which were accompanied by reciprocal excommunications, frequently enough within the bosom of their groups.

Other sectarians, often dominated by eschatological preoccupations, deprecated the State as a sinful institution. They were then far from conceiving the idea of a legitimate but religiously neutral State. However, with time, their conceptions of millennium became more sober. Their distinction between the political and the religious realm, and their voluntaristic notion of ecclesiastical affiliation as the explicit choice of an adult individual, have been the essential ingredients of the liberal doctrine of religious toleration. Indeed, they necessarily implied that the ideas which led inevitably to persecution had to be modified. In denying to theologians the right to set in motion the secular arm, the very possibility of the constraint of conscience disappeared.

Another direction of thought tried to accomplish the same purpose by an about-face which brought about a marked subordination of the Church to the State namely, the Erastian tendency, which had meaning only in Protestant countries, and to which rallied the Arminian minority in the Netherlands. It shows a somewhat exaggerated trust (if we think of the revocation of the Edict of Nantes) in the breadth of views of civil authorities, themselves religiously involved, the magistrate being the minister of God. This trust is explained by the observation, repeated a hundred times, that the persecuting charges were always delivered by the clergy and fostered by their incurable pretentions to theocracy. We shall return below to Erastianism, with regard to the separation which it stated between the deep inner convictions of a man and their outward expression, a postulate which psychologically seemed scarcely realistic.

On the whole, the enormous conceptual structure which justified the practices of persecution as an obligation of sovereigns was a colossus with feet of clay. The argument from authority is only efficient as a sledgehammer argument, as long as it is not recognized for what it is: it is effective only when it does not have to be accompanied by *authoritarianism* to impose itself, because that which is, in fact, tradition, is perceived as an unchallenged truth, and consequently held as indisputable. An argument from authority which requires a justification, or even a simple explanation, is already virtually on the defensive and condemned in the long run. We cannot here become involved in analysis, as brief as it might be, of the many factors which have shaken the ingenious ethnocentricity of medieval culture, at the dawn of modern times, through the social upheavals which they brought about. It is sufficient to remind ourselves that the religious division of Europe, caused by the Reformation, was to deliver a mortal blow to the principle of authority which neither of the two camps had questioned. In fact, as soon as authority no longer had a monopoly, with its stranglehold broken, the initiative inevitably went to the individual, whose examination was to decide the choice to be made among the authorities competing to solicit his obedience. The Peace of Augsburg (1555) with its principle *cujus regio ejus religio* recognized the freedom of conscience of the rulers. Just as when in ancient Egypt, immortality, initially available to the Pharoah alone, was eventually offered to all the inhabitants of the Nile Valley, the principle included in the Peace of Augsburg, led, inevitably, to the subsequent opening up of the freedom of individual conscience.

The argument from authority had been contested, on the theoretical level, by all the forms of rationalism which contributed so powerfully to the emancipation—in a way, to the creation—of "the individual," if only in challenging the law of the greatest number. However, many authors deliberately excluded criticism of practical questions from the field of their investigations: they wanted to be faithful and obedient subjects to their absolute prince and fideistic in religious matters. This characteristic was common to men who were otherwise quite different. It was the case with Descartes. It was also the case with the "erudite Libertines," unbelieving, well-read persons, in whom an aristocratic egoism and a fearful scorn of bad taste resulted in an outward conformity which hid the ironic skepticism of their private thoughts. Finally, it was the case with a man as ardently religious as Pascal

(1623–62) who in a fragment of a treatise on the vacuum (*Un fragment d'un traité du vide*) advocated a break between the area in which authority rules without compromise, in which total renunciation is "sweet" (theology), and that of natural sciences in which exacting reason, powerful and critical, interpreting the testimony of experience, has the sole right to be heard. This difficult balance constituted a real issue only during a rather short cultural period. Inevitably, from the domain of science where one tended to isolate it, or from the private conviction which it was unwise to make public, rational method and bold criticisms were extended and dominated the touchy areas of scriptural exegesis and political theory, which the older generations had thought they could keep them from entering.

Many writers, however, as far back as the sixteenth century, directly challenged the practices dictated by religious intolerance. Each of them argued in his own way and used arguments differing in emphasis. But we ought to restrict ourselves here to setting out the main themes of specific indictments followed by these courageous pioneers.

A first direction, moral or irenic, distinguishes those who consider the use of violence as a monstrous inconsistency on the part of Christians, since the Gospel preaches only love and gentleness. As do all rigorists, these authors refused to allow that that which is a crime on the individual level becomes legitimate when it is done in the name of the group. It is significant that Erasmus condemned war even more decidedly than persecution. Such a perspective serves to distinguish ethics, which is the heart of the Gospel, from speculative dogmas which one can elaborate from Scripture, and gives preference to "orthopraxis" over "orthodoxy." One should be very careful to note that although such a current of thought was able, at the end of two hundred years, to influence the thought of a man like Voltaire (supremely indifferent to the content of dogmas, which he considered pure rubbish), its first representatives had theological truth much at heart. They were religious and pious men, and if obedience to the moral precepts of the Gospel seemed to them to surpass any other consideration, the dogmatic formulation retained great significance for them. But it appeared to them as the object of a humble and fervent quest rather than knowledge transmitted from the past. Unity became for them an ideal to strive for, which ought to be prefigured here and now by fraternal relations among Christians. Attentive to the frailties of the human spirit, they avoided arrogantly imposing on others personal convictions which they had been able to approach—partial, approximate truths, not absolute ones (Castellion). To their eyes the free interchange of ideas was a fruitful method of investigation, and in all areas of thought the truth could only gain by it (Milton). Heresies themselves had been useful to the early Church, in helping it to sharpen its dogmatic tenets. Religious pluralism benefited each of the competing confessions by fostering emulation in virtue and knowledge (Acontius). The indomitable freedom of spirit made appeals to physical constraint completely absurd, since force can lead to lip service but never to the forming of a conviction.

Another direction of thought brought together people perhaps less sensitive to the suffering of the victims of intolerance than concerned about peace and public order, not only on the practical level, as the Third Party of the *Politiques* who, in France, supported Henry IV and backed the Edict of Nantes, but on the theoretical level as well. These writers tried to rediscover the lost doctrinal unity by digging below differences, in order to bring to light the common root. They gave a privileged status to the dogmas on which the main churches were agreed, and proposed to hold as optional the doctrines on which they differed (somewhat in the manner followed by the Council of Trent, which had distinguished between points of dogma and scholastic opinions).

This tendency resulted quickly enough in the idea of Natural Religion—the religion which ruled from Adam to Abraham, but also the religion of which the conclusions are available to reason alone, at once extolling the principles of Natural Law and Natural Ethics; thus the passage to pure Deism was carried out imperceptibly. Other theorists challenged the necessity of a strict correlation between internal conviction and external practice. Acknowledging the individual's full liberty of conscience, they asked him to comply in the matter of the expression of his convictions in gestures and in ritual—treated consequently as *adiaphora*—with the rules promulgated by civil authorities. It was the Erastian solution, which we have already mentioned and which was defended, among others, by Hobbes and Spinoza. All believers, from this point of view, can and should to a certain extent put up with the reigning ecclesiastical organization—a stand which curiously (for the basic motives of the two breeds of writers were extremely different) meets the approval of the "spirituals," mystics who favored the inner life and to whom faith mattered infinitely more than religion. The attempts at reunion, pursued with perseverance during the seventeenth century, either among confessions drifting from the Reformation, or among all Christian churches, gathered together, momentarily, deeply religious irenics and politically minded men, primarily concerned with civil peace.

*A posteriori*, it is easy enough to see the major theoretical obstacles with which such efforts were faced.

On the one hand, the list of "fundamental articles" ought to have been all the shorter in order to get the greatest agreement, but the more traditional parties steadfastly attributed a "fundamental" character to some articles which the unifiers exerted themselves in vain to put forth as "optional." Moreover, unknown to its promoters, this kind of effort challenged the cardinal principle of intolerance less than its point of application. "None shall have wit, but we and our friends," as Molière said in another context; the circle was expanded, but not opened to all. They still remained within the confines of a Bergsonian "closed religion," of a Church outside which there is no salvation. That is to say one did not truly accept the other as different, as a being distinct from oneself, but one would strive, not without naively generous intentions, to see in one's fellow being an alter ego, a counterpart of oneself.

It is instructive to note that the two works which canonized the ideal of religious tolerance (and by which the authors who vulgarized it in the eighteenth century were inspired) had been published a few years apart, in Holland, where there was a freedom of the press unequalled at that time. They had been written (independently) by two refugees who were also laymen —the Huguenot Pierre Bayle (*Commentaire philosophique sur ces paroles de Jésus-Christ 'contrains-les d'entrer'*, 4 vols., Amsterdam, 1686–88) and the Whig John Locke (*Epistola de tolerantia*, Gouda, 1689, and soon translated into English and Dutch, and later into French). It is also noteworthy that the two books had appeared without bearing the name of their authors. Bayle's treatise, in a sense, closed a period. It exhaustively refuted all the arguments ever put forward to justify persecutions, which the new propaganda campaign, associated with the revocation of the Edict of Nantes, had provided the occasion to expound. Useless for the public good, immoral, contrary to the precepts of reason and the gospel, founded on erroneous psychological analyses, absurd and vain—such is the way religious intolerance appeared under this searching indictment. But Bayle did not stop there. He affirmed that far from being a legitimate way to serve God, persecution essentially offends Him.

Bayle in effect posed the problem no longer from the traditional point of view of "objective truth," but from that of the subjective perception made by the individual. Inverting an Augustinian phrase, he wrote: "What matters is not to which end constraint is used, but whether it is used at all" (*Commentaire philosophique*, III, xvii), which is wrong because to seek to weaken the fidelity of anyone to his inner convictions is a sacrilegious affront to the laws of God himself, who, in consideration of the intention, forgives the

119

error. Bayle's point of view is profoundly religious so the tolerance which he defines covers the heretic, the innovator, the prophet of coming revelations—and the missionary of whatever religion—an exceptionally liberal attitude. Bayle also extended tolerance to the atheist as an individual, while accepting somewhat reluctantly that the civil authorities could forbid him to proselytize. A man aware of the problems of his times, he also authorized, on the basis of purely political considerations, certain safety measures against Roman Catholics, as, for example, their ineligibility for certain civic responsibilities. Finally he decided that immoral and antisocial theories and acts should be subject to penal sanctions. In this case "fanaticism" was not prosecuted as a heresy, but simply on grounds of the danger that the conduct which it inspired in its followers might involve for the physical security of their fellow citizens.

As for the work of Locke, it is the end-product of all the intellectual ferment concerning political theory and tolerance which had seethed in England during the seventeenth century. Locke himself at the start poses the problem in terms which contain its solution, whence the brevity of the pamphlet—for he makes a formal distinction between State and Church (which is equivalent to defining the latter in sociological language, as a "sect") from which civil tolerance logically follows. Less religious than Bayle's (which demanded that we respect the image of God in all men), the doctrine of Locke had more realistic foundations inasmuch as his view appealed to a more easily understood interest: an Englishman, fervent defender of liberties which he showed to be inseparably linked together, Locke asks each man to make certain that there would be no encroachment upon his own rights, and in order to achieve that, to abandon the regimenting of the convictions of others. There we already have the individualism and utilitarianism of the eighteenth century: "enlightened self-interest." If he granted to Roman Catholicism a full liberty of conscience, Locke coupled it nevertheless with certain restrictions in civil matters, for almost the same reasons as Bayle: any religion which threatens to violate the distinction between the political and the spiritual spheres warrants a certain amount of suspicion. But quite differently from Bayle, Locke does not tolerate the atheist, who is incapable of taking an oath, and is thus an asocial being. His disciples of the Enlightenment follow him on this point and put the atheist next to the religious innovator, whom they will urge the authorities to imprison or banish before he can gather any followers. The problem here is indeed much more political than religious. Tranquility and collective prosperity are the supreme values, as is shown by the importance given to the argument from the commercial advantages which tolerance brings: money has no smell, and the contrast between the misery of Spain and the opulence of the United Provinces was to become a matter of great persuasive eloquence in the eighteenth century.

To sum up, the evolution of ideas consisted, on the level of social structures, in making religious confessions pass from the status of a "church of multitude" (with territorial pretentions and in which membership is established by birth) to that of a church of professing believers (held together, no longer automatically and passively, but by choice). On the level of values, it goes from the idea of absolute Truth as a sacred legacy received from the past, to the idea of truth as a quest and a constant reformulation in the language of cultural evolution—a reformulation which is always approximate and relative, and which implies a keen awareness of the weakness and radical inadequacies of the human mind, as well as a more and more modest agnosticism. In a more limited way this evolution occasioned a shift which brought "the heretic" close to "the infidel" (renouncing then *compelle remanere*) and dogmatic error close to ignorance (more and more liberally considered invincible, this being the only case where it is innocent, and no longer, as formerly, considered a guilt calling for punishment). This entire evolution of secularization, because of the resistance which it encountered, made way for an anticlericalism all the more powerful and diffuse as its sources and its forms multiplied. But above all the doctrine of religious tolerance appeared linked to a general splitting up, which, destroying the warm solidarities of communities and ancestral traditions, has set up the modern individual as autonomous, and, as it were, the seat of authority in the midst of social mobility. This splitting up suggested too many worldly goals for the individual's appetites and ambitions for the religious values to continue to dominate his mental world and hence express his will to power and his aggression.

## BIBLIOGRAPHY

For important statements of the theory of persecution, see Théodore de Bèze [Beza], *Traité de l'autorité du magistrat en la punition des hérétiques* (1560), the original Latin text of which had appeared in 1554, as *De haereticis a civili magistratu puniendis libellis.* . . . For the Roman Catholic side, see, for instance, *La conformité de la conduite de l'Église de France pour ramener les Protestants avec celle de l'Église d'Afrique pour ramener les Donatistes à l'Église Catholique* (Paris, 1685); and *Traité de l'Unité de l'Église et des moyens que les Princes chrétiens ont employés pour y faire rentrer ceux qui en étoient sortis*, 2 vols. (Paris, 1686–88), by the Oratorian Louis Thomassin. (A posthumous enlarged second edition appeared in 1700 under a different title: *Traité dogmatique et historique des Édits . . .*, 3 vols.) This is a serene and scholarly defense of persecution. See also, as late as the mid-eighteenth century, the different books of Abbé Caveirac.

One finds a comprehensive general bibliography in Father Joseph Lecler, S. J., *Toleration and the Reformation* (London, 1960); originally, *Histoire de la tolérance au siècle de la Réforme* (Paris, 1955). There is a useful, shorter bibliography in Henry Kamen, *The Rise of Toleration* (New York, 1967); see also idem, *The Spanish Inquisition* (London, 1965) and Léon Poliakov, *Histoire de l'antisémitisme*, 3 vols. (Paris, 1955); Volume 4 in preparation.

In *Persecution and Liberty*, essays in honor of George Lincoln Burn (New York, 1931), one finds several papers of great value, specially one by R. H. Bainton on Castellion, with respect to which, for the sake of brevity, it is enough to mention that practically all of Bainton's production is of prime importance for the present subject. In *Autour de Michel Servet et de Sébastien Castellion*, ed. B. Becker (Haarlem, 1953), appear studies in four different languages, according to the nationality of the different collaborators. W. J. Stankiewicz, *Politics and Religion in Seventeenth-Century France* (Berkeley, 1960) should be noted; and *Hérésies et sociétés dans l'Europe préindustrielle, XIe–XVIIIe siècles*, Colloque de Royaumont présenté par Jacques Le Goff (Paris and The Hague, 1968), assembles also a number of scholarly studies on its theme.

There is a recent critical reissue of the original Latin text of Locke's *Letter Concerning Toleration* in French, Italian, Polish, as well as English-German translation, all of them published under sponsorship of the Fédération Internationale des Sociétés de Philosophie and of UNESCO, in the collection "Philosophie et Communauté Mondiale." Another important edition is *Epistola de tolerantia*, trans. J. W. Gough, with an introduction by Raymond Klibansky (Oxford, 1968). The latest printing of Bayle's *Commentaire philosophique* is more than two centuries old, but it is included in the second volume of his *Oeuvres diverses*, recently photographically reissued in Germany.

Other works include: J. W. Hauer, *Toleranz und Intoleranz in der nichtchristlichen Religionen* (Stuttgart, 1961); Guido Kisch, "Toleranz und Menschenwürde," *Miscellanea Mediaevalia*, 4 (Berlin, 1966); and H. R. Schlette, "Toleranz," *Handbuch theologischer Grundbegriffe*, Vol. II, ed. Heinrich Fries (Munich, 1963).

ELISABETH LABROUSSE

[See also **Agnosticism; Church as an Institution;** Deism; Freedom; **God; Heresy;** Individualism; Law, Natural; **Reformation;** Sin and Salvation; Skepticism; Utilitarianism.]

# IDEA OF RENAISSANCE

TODAY the word "Renaissance" (rebirth) is generally applied to a series of cultural changes which began in Italy in the fourteenth century and spread to the rest of Europe in the late fifteenth century, coloring and perhaps conditioning many fundamental assumptions about art, scholarship, and morality until at least the eighteenth century. The word is also applied to the period when these innovations occurred and assumed a dominant position. The word, as commonly used in the English-speaking world, follows the French form. Some writers in English—they are a minority—prefer "Renascence." The French word is used in German and many other European languages save Italian, where *Rinascita* first emerged (see below) and where the alternative *Rinascimento* is now also used, especially for the purposes of periodization.

As a synoptic abstraction both for cultural change and for an epoch the word is unlike similar expressions in being both autonomous and contemporary with the events it describes. By "autonomous" we mean that it had no earlier employment. No classical Latin word for rebirth existed. Christian doctrine is based on the notion of rebirth and *regeneratio* is used in the New Testament, and was thence monopolized by the literature of the theologians. The metaphor was, of course, obvious enough both in the loose sense of "renewal" (e.g., the *renovatio imperii*), in the regular opposition of day and night, sleeping and reawaking, and the cycle of the seasons, as well as in scriptural exegesis and homiletics where the terms regeneration and resurrection were available. A few writers in the fourteenth and fifteenth centuries invented Latin words (*renacium, renascentia, renascitura*) which summarized the processes, but none of this would have led to the subsequent employment of "Renaissance" had there not arisen the need for a word to describe the awareness of intellectuals in the fifteenth century and later that their world was characteristically different from what had gone before, and that their times had spiritual and perhaps historical affinities with an antiquity of which they were witnessing the rebirth. "Rebirth" was to be the term which prevailed, rather than "renovation," "reflowering," "renewal," or others. "Regeneration" was presumably too closely associated with the usage of the divines, "renewal" too colorless.

Such an awareness has been traced in a number of fourteenth-century Italians and in particular it was provoked by the life and work of Petrarch (Francesco Petrarca). To the accepted educational and theological conventions of his day Petrarch deliberately opposed an urgent plea for the cultivation of Latin literature and of a moral philosophy closely based on classical models. Traditionally the Church had frowned on the study of Roman writers and thinkers save as means for teaching the clergy to be proficient in the service of a religion whose scriptures (the Vulgate) and whose service books were written in Latin. It is true that classical elements were prominent in speculation, artistic literature, and the fine arts of Europe between the fall of Rome and the fourteenth century; and it is also true that in the twelfth and thirteenth centuries the works of Aristotle had come to play a dominant role in the study and teaching of logic, metaphysics, and theology. But Greek and Roman influences were, at least in theory, subordinated to the requirements of clerical education: Ovid was "moralized," Aristotle reigned in the university schools at the price of his rationalism being lost to view.

Interest in pagan authors beyond such pedagogical and professional uses was only justified on the principle of spoiling the Egyptians and this dangerous and tempting procedure had from the start had its puritanical critics. Of course there had always been men (many of them clergy) who had enjoyed self-expression in the vernaculars and in Latin regardless of censure, just as there had always been heretics in the religious sphere. But such men had been a minority without significant public support. For Petrarch, for his growing number of disciples, and friends and for a steadily widening audience, both lay and clerical, the cultural achievements of Greece and Rome acquired fresh relevance. "Poetry" was defended as morally inspiring. "Philosophy" should be cultivated, not in the arid syllogisms of the schools, but as a devout love of wisdom. Literature thus became a vehicle for the good life, its perfection the duty and the joy of the literate Christian. While Petrarch was far from overthrowing all the conventions of his own times and although he was somewhat contemptuous of the culture of his contemporaries, his convictions did lead him to despise the barbarism of an earlier epoch and thus prepared the way for a tripartite periodization—ancient, middle, modern—which had a development concomitant with that of the idea of renewal or rebirth. This notion is explicit in Petrarch's friend Giovanni Boccaccio who referred to Dante as the man who had brought the Muses back to Italy and to Giotto as the restorer of the art of painting. Even more telling is the conviction of a renewal evident in the pages of the chronicler Filippo Villani writing towards the end of the fourteenth century an account of the great men of Florence. The idea was beginning to leave the learned coteries and establish itself as part of the mythology of a major Italian city.

Dante, Petrarch, and Boccaccio were all Florentines, though Dante lived much of his later life in exile and Petrarch was the son of another banned citizen. The association of new moral, scholarly, and artistic attitudes with Florence grew ever stronger in the decades on either side of 1400. The Republic appointed a series of humanist chancellors (the executive secretaries of the state) beginning with Coluccio Salutati in 1375; the most influential of these officials was Leonardo Bruni, chancellor in 1410–11 and from 1427 to his death in 1444. At the same time there were scores of scholars and citizens eager to participate in the debates and researches of the leading thinkers and writers. This coincided with an astonishing development in the fine arts, painting, sculpture, and architecture, which was to transform the structure and the decoration of Florentine buildings in the first half of the fifteenth century.

None of this could have happened without the active support of the leading oligarchs of the city, hardheaded businessmen intent on prosecuting their own interests and the welfare of the city whose affairs they managed. To explain this phenomenon it has been argued that the political threat to Florence of the Milanese state under the Visconti acted as a spur. Progressively isolated, the Republic and its citizens were forced to ask themselves why resistance to the Visconti was worthwhile. Humanists answered his questions with an analysis of the unique qualities of the commune: the inspiration of republican liberty as against Caesarian absolutism, the superiority of the active as against the contemplative life, an acceptance of wealth and beauty as God-given elements in the human situation in spite of the long-standing reverence for the merit of poverty and the contempt for seductive art. Stimulated in these ways the consciousness of renewal was regularly displayed by contemporaries. For example, here is Matteo Palmieri in his *Vita civile* (ca. 1436):

Where was the painter's art till Giotto tardily restored it? . . . Sculpture and architecture, for long years sunk to the merest travesty of art, are only today in process of rescue from obscurity; only now are they being brought to a new pitch of perfection by men of genius and erudition. Of Letters and liberal studies at large it were best to be silent altogether. For these, the real guides to distinction in all the arts, the solid foundation of all civilization, have been lost to mankind for 800 years or more. It is but in our own day that men dare boast that they see the dawn of better things. . . . Now indeed may every thoughtful spirit thank God that it has been permitted him to be born in this new age, so full of hope and promise, which already rejoices in a greater array of nobly-gifted souls than the world has seen in the thousand years that have preceded it (trans. W. H. Woodward).

In this passage the Florentine merchant indicated most of the elements in the Renaissance concept: the sense of belonging to a new age, the antecedent period of darkness, and behind that the ancient world of light; the assumption that Latin letters are the basis for all cultural activity, in the fine arts as well as in literature. The notion of renewal, the figure of rebirth meet one constantly in the literature of the fifteenth century, and not only in Florentine sources, but in other parts of Italy and in Northern Europe among scholars in touch with Italian developments.

It was, however, to be, if not another Florentine, at least another Tuscan, the painter and architect Giorgio Vasari (1511–74), who finally invented the word "Renaissance" (*Rinascita*) in his *Lives of the Most Excellent Italian Architects, Painters and Sculptors from Cimabue to our own Times,* which was first published at Florence in 1550. In the Preface to this influential work Vasari explains the origin of art in the divine gift of God and briefly traces its manifestations down to the perfection it reached with the ancient Greeks and the high esteem in which it was held by the Romans. Then, in the later Roman Empire, decline set in: "when human affairs begin to decline, they grow steadily worse until the time comes when they can no longer deteriorate any further." This decline was followed by the final destruction which followed the barbarian invasions. Triumphant Christianity obliterated pagan monuments and rifled old buildings for new churches. A long period of barbaric insensitivity then followed, with some better work being occasionally produced, as for example by Nicola Pisano (ca. 1220–87), but no reversal of the trend, no consistent attempt to study the "admirable sculptures and paintings buried in the ruins of Italy." He concludes by stressing that "the arts resemble nature as shown in our human bodies; and have their birth, growth, age and death." "I hope," he writes, "by this means they [the artists of his own day] will be enabled more easily to recognise the progress of the renaissance (*rinascita*) of the arts and the perfection to which they have attained in our own time."

Vasari's Renaissance was strictly applied to the fine arts but, as we have seen, the metaphor of rebirth had earlier and regularly been applied also to literature and scholarship as well; fleetingly in Petrarch and Machiavelli even to political situations. But what was to gain rapid acceptance for the term was the extension far beyond Florence and Tuscany of the phenomena epitomized in the idea. One after another the courts of Italy accepted the new learning and literature, the new painting and architecture, and the new moral value which they exemplified. First the smaller centers (Urbino, Mantua, Ferrara), then the papal court from the mid-fifteenth century and finally the capitals of the Neapolitan kingdom and the Sforza dukes. In the early sixteenth century Rome was the greatest center of scholarship and artistic patronage and Venice had begun to understand the message. By this time trans-Alpine Europe was beginning to be interested. The republicanism of Florence found little sympathy in the courts of princes, but everything else was welcome. A new generation of civil servants emerged to staff chanceries and diplomatic posts and a new kind of schoolmaster educated princes, courtiers, and their men of business in the techniques now felt to be essential for good government and the good life. The basis was Latin; the aim was the perfection of what we would nowadays call "communication"; Cicero filled the educational role which had been occupied in the schools of the Middle Ages by Aristotle. The slow and subtle adaptation of Renaissance techniques and attitudes in France and Germany, in England and Spain, produced endless variations of the basic theme; as indeed had the earlier reception in the various Italian centers. But the assumption that all culture depended on a mastery of Latin (for scholars Greek was added), and a thorough knowledge of the main classical writers was pervasive and was to color European society for centuries to come. A gentleman was by definition well educated in the "humanities." The humanities were (to quote a canonical definition) "grammar, rhetoric, history, poetry, and moral philosophy" studied in the "standard ancient writers in Latin and, to a lesser extent, in Greek." The aim was an illuminated and public-spirited elite.

Clearly the non-Italian peoples of Europe identified themselves less passionately with classical Rome than the Italians had done. Indeed the Germans, the French, and the rest looked back to an antiquity in which their ancestors had been subjugated by the legions. Nothing is more remarkable therefore than the rapid and irrevocable penetration of Italian ideas and practices among the "barbarians," as the Italian writers referred to them, some of whom were currently invading the peninsula. The concept of rebirth may sometimes (as in Germany) have provoked anti-Roman and nationalist sentiment; but the *gymnasia* of Philip Melanchthon (1497–1560) bore tribute to a new educational ideal. The "battle of the books" might lead the French to dispute the primacy in all fields of Italians or even Romans but everywhere among the literate there was an acceptance of the proposition that, so far as scholarship, literature, and the fine arts were concerned, the new age had recovered a sophistication and a mastery which had been lost for centuries. Obviously the tensions produced in the Middle Ages by an official condemnation of the world and natural beauty, of artistic achievement as an end in itself, of wealth and education as more than mere embellishments or social display (*noblesse oblige*)—obviously these tensions between how men actually lived, and how they ought to have lived, were by no means confined to Italy, and this is the ultimate explanation for the sure finality with which the Florentine discoveries moved from Tuscany to Italy and from Italy to Europe. Italy (on this sole occasion) solved the moral problems of the Continent.

It was to be in the North that the word Renaissance was regularly applied to more than the painting, sculpture, and architecture of Vasari's usage. It was, in fact, Erasmus who first stressed the rebirth of "good literature," reflecting the early interest of humanists in Paris in the literary developments in Italy, and recapturing in his affirmation of a *docta pietas* something of Petrarch's spirit. The movement was, however, more broadly based than it had been in the Italy of the mid-Trecento. A new conviction of the remarkable certainty afforded by philological scholarship enriched both patristic and classical studies; and soon the élan of the neo-Latinists was taken over into the vernaculars, producing the "golden" prose and poetry of the second half of the sixteenth century in English, French, and Spanish. From this was to come a generalized sentiment that there was a *renaissance des lettres* alongside the artistic Renaissance. Such a view was explicit by the end of the seventeenth century, in the dictionaries of Pierre Bayle (1647–1706) and of the French Academy. Such a view was generally accepted in Europe (and North America). The excitement was now dimmed. A Reformation had occurred (for some the Renaissance had been its John the Baptist). But Roman Catholics and most varieties of Protestants agreed on canons of artistic style and of literary relevance (the Bible together with the classics of Greece and Rome), scholarly precision and the morality of public service.

Such a series of related convictions dominated the eighteenth century. By then the existence of a Middle Age was an accepted part of the mental furniture of the educated. This benighted period ran from the Sack of Rome (A.D. 410) to the Fall of Constantinople (1453), when (so ran the legend) the escaping Greeks carried their manuscripts and wisdom to the West. For Voltaire there was surprise that so much illumination had come out of an Italy politically divided and sub-divided: "it may appear somewhat extraordinary that so many great geniuses should have started up of a sudden in Italy." But in reality he did not find it so extraordinary, because it was right, and because "the pest of religious controversy left Italy on one side," enabling Italians to cultivate "the never fading glory of the fine arts." These *obiter dicta* (from the *Essai sur les moeurs* of 1756) are echoed in most of the writers of the Enlightenment. One of them, Thomas Warton, described what had occurred as a "revolution." This transformation, he felt, "was the most fortunate and important" in breaking the "bonds of barbarism . . . in which the mouldering Gothic fabrics of false religion and false philosophy fell together" (*History of English Poetry,*

1774–81). Soon another revolution was to disturb these well-established platitudes.

The events in France in and after 1789, the social and emotional developments which flowed from them throughout Europe, coincided with a further and independent enrichment of the Renaissance: its association with the "Greek spirit." It was, of course, the case that the scholars of the fifteenth and sixteenth centuries had cultivated Greek scholarship, but it was never as important an inspiration as Rome had been and Greek scholarship had so far failed to attain the expertise of Latin learning. Knowledge of ancient Greek history (for example) was rudimentary compared with the scientific study of Rome.

From the mid-eighteenth century onwards this situation changed. A new and profounder attempt to understand the art and the literature of the Greek world is associated with Winckelmann, Lessing, and Friedrich August Wolf. The living embodiment of much of this was Goethe. Under the influence of these writers a fresh interpretation of aesthetics emerged (neo-classicism) and the traditional "humanities" began to assume a different aspect as "humanism" (the word *Humanismus* was apparently first used by F. J. Niethammer in 1808). A humanist in the Renaissance period itself had meant a teacher or student of the humanities (as defined above). From the start of the nineteenth century "humanist" began to acquire its alternative and vaguer meaning as a sympathizer with a human as opposed to a divine set of values. The "spirit of Greece" contributed largely to the idealization of Man. Lessing even attacked Latin: ". . . the monks let loose on us [the Germans] the barbarous deluge of *Latin* literature, *Latin* religion, and *Latin* speculation. . . . Latin, being considered as an end in itself, is ruining our education." Such opinions would have been incomprehensible to Petrarch, Bruni, or Erasmus.

The Renaissance school curriculum survived such criticism, and it survived too the forces released by the French Revolution which were to lead to the replacement of the social and political dominance of the gentleman and the courtier, trained to be citizens of the world, by that of the middle class, urban-based and marked by a bitter chauvinistic nationalism. All of this was to produce, both in sympathy and hostility, men who looked back at the now receding Renaissance with new eyes. They had, of course, all been educated traditionally enough in *lycées, gymnasia,* and grammar schools. The art they admired, however much it seemed to them daringly to break new ground, was firmly linked to the Italian masters of the Quattrocento and Cinquecento. Stendhal, Michelet, Voigt, Burckhardt were products of a Renaissance world, even if by their day it was a world of shadows from the past. The call of Italy and the attraction of the Renaissance centuries were often drenched in romanticism and associated with contemporary political and artistic aspirations. Genius was what mattered. National genius was an identifiable commodity. There was a "spirit of Germany," and of France, as well as a "Greek spirit." Such a sentiment was to further the final stage in the evolution of the notion of the Renaissance: its identification with a whole civilization. This had many antecedents. Its two brightest apostles were Frenchmen, Stendhal (Henri Beyle, 1783–1842) and Jules Michelet (1798–1874). Stendhal, novelist and art critic, found in Italy and especially in Renaissance Italy an antidote for the bourgeois philistinism and mediocrity of the France of the post-Napoleonic period. His Italy was a world of men of *virtù*: Cesare Borgia was the type who dared everything.

In Italy, a man distinguished himself by *all forms* of merit . . . and a woman of the sixteenth century loved a man learned in Greek as well as, if not more than, she would have loved a man famous for his martial valour. Then one saw passions, and not the habit of gallantry. That is the great difference between Italy and France . . . (*Abbesse de Castro*, trans. Scott-Moncrieff).

In these lines we see the identification of a Renaissance period and the assumption that the fundamental elements in it are based on national characteristics. Similarly the historian Michelet poured fire into the Renaissance in the volume so entitled of his *Histoire de France*. He came to this section of the work after completing the *Middle Ages* (1833–44) and the *Revolution* (1847–53). In this last section (*Renaissance to Revolution*, 1855–67) his prose-poetry is wilder and an attempt has been made to relate the vehemence of his approach to a crisis in his own emotional life. However that may be, the pages of glowing generalization were to be remarkably influential. The traditional achievements of the Renaissance—a new art and the renewal of classical studies—Michelet sweeps aside: such was a mere arabesque, a nothingness.

So great a power of will is said to have remained fruitless. What could be more discouraging for human thought!
 Only these over-prejudiced minds have forgotten two things, two little things, which belong to that age more than to any of its predecessors: the discovery of the world and the discovery of man. . . .
 And, definitively, the Middle Ages are at death's door in the fifteenth and sixteenth centuries, when the blazing beacons of printing, of classical antiquity, of America, the Orient and the true system of the world converge on them their withering light. . . .
 A vast event had taken place. The world was changed. Not one state in Europe, even the most immobile of them, but did not find itself, now, involved in a wholly novel movement forward. . . . The discovery of Italy had an infinitely greater effect on the sixteenth century than that of America. All the nations followed in France's footsteps, to be initiated in their turn and to see clearly by the light of this new sun (trans. A. R. Press).

One is tempted to go on quoting from the tempestuous words, not least because they are so refreshingly unlike the careful academic precisions of our own prosaic day. Yet the academic was already pressing forward with detailed studies which were to fill in the picture. In art history the most influential figures were Franz Kugler (*Handbook of the History of Painting*, 1837; 2nd ed. 1847) and John Ruskin (*Lectures on Architecture and Painting*, 1854), for both of whom in different ways the Renaissance marked a watershed. In the history of literature and scholarship the greatest work of the mid-nineteenth century was Georg Voigt's *Revival of Classical Antiquity* which was published in German in 1859. This solid and imaginative book covers the history of humanism from Petrarch down to the early fifteenth century and is still a mine of exact information. Its assumption was, however, a broad generalization. "At this moment there developed in Italy the seed of a new civilization, which was to bear its fruits first in the literary and artistic field and later to gather under the standard of literature and scholarship not merely Italy but the whole civilized world." He explained that the "heart" of this change "was the adoption of *humanitas*, all that was uniquely human in the spirit and soul of man, human in the Greek and Roman sense, and so in contradiction to the outlook of Christendom and the Church." This, he adds, could only have taken place in Italy: "In Italy such [classical] studies aroused sentiment and passion, and became matters of flesh and blood."

After all this blood and thunder, coloring even the precise erudition of Voigt, it is curious to read the *Civilization [Kultur] of the Renaissance in Italy* by Jacob Burckhardt. Published first at Basel in 1860, this was to be the most significant single treatment of its subject. It defined a period and its content. All subsequent discussion of the Renaissance turns on this remarkable work. Burckhardt was born and brought up in Basel. Thoroughly grounded in the classics at school, he read theology at the university. He later studied history with Ranke at Berlin before developing the interest in art history which was to be his main concern in later years. After a period of sporadic teaching and journalism, undertaken to finance visits to Italy, he became professor of history at Basel in 1858 and taught there almost to the end of his life. By the time of his appointment he had published a revised and extended version of Kugler's *Handbook* (1847), *The Age of*

*Constantine the Great* (1853), and the *Cicerone* (1855). Though some of his other works were to appear after his death, the *Civilization of the Renaissance in Italy* was to be the last major book published in his lifetime. Burckhardt saw his Renaissance "essay" (for this is his emphatic description of it) gradually acquire a world reputation. He never revised it, though he allowed others to annotate it—the *eruditi* for whom he felt boredom tinged with contempt. The monumental controversies the work was to produce, the mountains of commentary and analysis, were far from being to his taste.

In a profound way the sympathies of this lonely man lay with Goethe and not with the professors and their diligent seminars. It is one of the most curious of paradoxes that the scholar who, more than any other, delineated the Renaissance for the next three generations lost interest in the subject. In view of this one must ask why Burckhardt's interpretation has, on the whole, stood the test of time. The reason is partly the artistry and subtlety of his style, partly the novelty of his technique of research and exposition, partly the happy coincidence in his synthesis of many elements which had already proved enduring. What earlier writers had often enunciated as shattering truths, were filled by Burckhardt with cautious qualifications. His approach to his subject was total—all the sources readily accessible to him were ransacked for a view of society and culture in the round; no such balanced and integrated view of a whole epoch in all its aspects had been attempted. As for his indebtedness to earlier writers we cannot do better than to quote the following words of Wallace K. Ferguson:

The time was ripe for a new idealization of the Renaissance analogous to the neo-classical idealization of ancient Greece or the Romantic rehabilitation of the Middle Ages. . . . The closely associated currents of liberalism, new humanism and German idealism in nineteenth-century thought had combined to establish as essential attributes of modern progress the growth of individual freedom of thought and expression, the full development of self-conscious personality, and the evolution of moral autonomy founded upon a high conception of the dignity of man. . . . And by the middle of the nineteenth century, a long series of interpretations, approaching the problem from various angles, had taught men to see in the Renaissance, bounded on one side by the Middle Ages and on the other by the Reformation and Counter-Reformation, the age in which all these traits of the modern world had first appeared and had flourished with youthful vigor. Burckhardt's decisive contribution was to gather all these trends of interpretation together into one coherent synthesis, based upon a respectable foundation of historical scholarship (Ferguson, pp. 180, 182).

The book, encountered in our own days by most students in survey courses, is too familiar to need detailed description: it will be sufficient to indicate its contents in a few words. Part i is devoted to "the State as a work of art," and summarizes the Italian history of the thirteenth to the sixteenth centuries in terms of tyrannies and republics, with a heavy priority to the former. Part ii is devoted to "the development of the individual" and in it Burckhardt contrasts medieval anonymity with "universal men" and the idea of fame. Part iii deals with "the revival of antiquity," that is the humanists, their care for texts, their scholarship, and their literary exercises. Part iv, entitled from Michelet's phrase "the discovery of the world and of man," discusses natural science, the appreciation of natural beauty, the desire to analyze the human situation and describe the human scene. Part v, "society and festivals," deals partly with the social structure of peninsular society, partly with outward display. Finally in Part vi Burckhardt turns to "morality and religion," and assembles evidence for mounting superstition and a steady erosion of Christian morality. Throughout the work the author is dealing consciously with the spirit of Italy, the "genius of the Italian people," who are "the first born among the sons of Europe," ushering in the modern world and paying for their priority with the harsh and cynical situation of the sixteenth century, moderated by the syncretism of Ficino and Pico della Mirandola. "Echoes of medieval mysticism here flow into one current with Platonic doctrines, and with a characteristically modern spirit. One of the most precious fruits of the knowledge of the world and of man here comes to maturity, on whose account alone the Italian Renaissance must be called the leader of the modern ages." These are the final sentences in the book.

Burckhardt fairly and firmly asserted four propositions: there was indeed a Renaissance, a definable and important moment in the spiritual and material evolution of Western man; this moment was sharply opposed to the Middle Ages (which accordingly came into clearer focus from the acceptance of this view); the Renaissance inaugurated the modern world; and it was a product initially of the Italian people (though its ultimate relevance was to be worldwide). These assumptions were soon challenged, and so were many of the subsidiary arguments of the book. The studies by Wallace K. Ferguson, Franco Simone, and others referred to in the Bibliography below form a guide to the ensuing debates, which cannot be rehearsed here. Some points must, however, be briefly touched on if the reader is to be aware of the present status of the idea of the Renaissance.

One of the assumptions of Burckhardt and his contemporaries has been commonly and quietly abandoned. No one could now pretend that the Renaissance ushered in the modern world if by modern we mean the world of the twentieth century. The notion of popular sovereignty to which all governments pay at any rate lip service, the aim of universal education, the abandonment in educational practice of the teaching of the old "humanities," these are only a few of the ways in which the Renaissance world, still lingering on in nineteenth-century Europe, has now been left behind. To them we may add the art and architecture of our own times which no longer look back to Masaccio and Michelangelo, to Bramante and Palladio. Even more important, we entirely lack any one accepted style in the arts or in literature. We enjoy (or pretend to) a Greek vase alongside a medieval altarpiece, a statue by Bernini along with a jocular construction by Picasso. We admire (or pretend to) at the same instant the *Decameron* and *Finnegans Wake*. Our model is to have all models or no model. It was not thus as late as Reynolds and Dr. Johnson, even as late as Burckhardt. Yet the passing of Renaissance values as an influence has naturally lent definition to the periodic concept. We have now, at any rate in our centers of so-called higher learning, digested the European past, not into the tripartite division of the humanist, but into four divisions: ancient, medieval, Renaissance, and modern. It is true that much nice argument has revolved round the delimitation of frontiers; boundary commissioners regularly snarl at each other. And it is probably the case that the Renaissance as a period has found readier recognition in the academies of North America than in those of Europe, where university departments labelled "Renaissance" are to be found, if at all, in literature rather than in history or the fine arts. None of this has much significance, being the small change in which dons delight. The acceptance that the Renaissance is dead and gone is, however, important as it has removed at any rate some of the acerbities from the discussion of this part of the past. We may still feel inspiration or relevance in fifteenth- and sixteenth-century situations. We need no longer feel that this involves identifying ourselves with them.

Two aspects of post-Burckhardt Renaissance argument are sufficiently important to merit a further word: the emergence of other Renaissances besides that which started in Italy in the Trecento; and the problem of the Renaissance as a radical transformation of society in all its aspects.

It was natural that writers interested in medieval history and culture should react sharply to the denigration of their period by Burckhardt and scores of lesser men. This reaction has taken many forms. It has been argued that the roots of all that occurred in the time of Petrarch and later are to be found in earlier centuries. For example the love of nature has been traced to Saint Francis. Or again, the medievalist has been able to show that a high degree of representational art can be found in the thirteenth century. Gilson went further and argued that in Abelard was to be seen a "Renaissance man" and that therefore the category was meaningless. Much of this, while illuminating, even (in the case of Gilson) deeply moving, is beside the point. One swallow does not make a summer. But those scholars who have stressed the "revival of antiquity" as the essential ingredient of the Renaissance have been forced to admit that there were earlier examples of a conscious attempt to resuscitate ancient (Latin) language and ideals. Did this not happen among the scholars at the court of Charlemagne? Is there not plentiful evidence of such interests among the contemporaries of John of Salisbury (ca. 1115–80) at Chartres and Paris? So have emerged the "Carolingian Renaissance" and the "Renaissance of the Twelfth Century." From these researches much light has been shed on the rich tapestry of medieval thought and art. Yet, as with the exceptional Abelard, so with Alcuin and his friends, so with John of Salisbury's circle, one fails to find the wide support, the association with the new ideas of the men who were politically and socially of weight. These medieval Latinizers were antiquaries, they were not involving antiquity in the pursuit of solutions of current dilemmas.

The rival "Renaissances" are perhaps by now superannuated. Not so the question of the Renaissance as a fundamental reorientation of the human predicament. If it was significant (so runs the argument) then it must have been significant in the fields of politics, of science, of religion, as well as in those of literature, morality, and the arts. Yet it is not difficult to show that in these spheres the innovations of the Italians, even as developed at large through Europe, had little direct influence. The devices of governments were perhaps enriched a little by the humanities, but they were hardly transformed. Princes employed laymen educated in the new Latin instead of clerks educated in the old Latin: a significant change but hardly catastrophic. We can no longer pretend that Machiavelli's *Prince* described a situation which was new rather than one of which the earliest protagonists were Cain and Abel. That he dotted the i's and crossed the t's was important, and so was the aversion he provoked in many decent conventional men. But none of this exactly altered the structure of politics.

It is not so different with the case of religion. It would be generally conceded that the new philology contributed something towards the Reformation and so did the equation of wisdom with book-learning. But Burckhardt's assumption, shared by many of his con-

127

temporaries and followers, that the Renaissance was in some sense "pagan" does not bear examination. Atheists are *rarissimi* among the humanists, though the charge was happily bandied about (along with illegitimacy) in the acrimony of learned diatribe. In Protestant as in Catholic Europe (after the Reformation) a basic acceptance of the Christian verities prevailed and it is hard, if not impossible, to discern any important change directly due to the Renaissance.

Science is in a somewhat special category. We are, and since the nineteenth century have been, in a "modern" world largely determined by the physical scientists. If this is our modernity and the Renaissance contributed nothing to it, was there a Renaissance? Some (Lynn Thorndike was one) would say No. The humanist of the fifteenth and sixteenth centuries certainly contributed very little to the stock of ideas from which Galileo and Newton were to nourish themselves. We can no longer regard, with Bacon, the compass, gunpowder, and the printing press as occurring suddenly or as constituting the instruments of sudden change. It is fair to add, however, that there were scientists at work in the Renaissance period and their activities are in this sense "Renaissance."

Overall it seems therefore inescapable that the Renaissance can no longer arrogate to itself all the elements which were to influence subsequent history. It was a profound change, affecting public life in many of its aspects, but not in all of them. Its modes of thought, its aesthetic standards, its techniques of education, and the social and moral principles on which all these rested were to be long-lived, but they became irrelevant in the course of the nineteenth century.

At a more popular level the Renaissance idea has percolated to many areas of vulgarization, high and low. Besides the competing Renaissances of scholars mentioned above it is not uncommon for the word to be applied loosely to any revival: "the Renaissance of Scottish literature," "the Renaissance of Irish drama." As used in this way the word has often little meaning. Such a use of the word is often equivalent to "birth," rather than "rebirth," as no antecedent period or culture is in question. More important is the persistence of the Renaissance as the symbol of a spiritual state. As has been noted, this goes back to early nineteenth-century writers like Stendhal. The concepts of freedom and paganism, of men of unbridled genius and of universal men have had a secure place in literary tradition since Burckhardt and (for the English-speaking world) since John Addington Symonds' large scale *Renaissance in Italy* (7 vols., 1875–86). Such myths remain impervious to scholarly criticism and are lying about to be put to use by novelists and film producers. The continued physical attraction of Italy nourishes this general awareness of the Renaissance. Millions of Germans, Swiss, Austrians, French, British, and Americans still pour into the peninsula each year, though fewer of them live there for long periods, as they did before the First World War. And the Italy which meets the visitor's eye is overwhelmingly an Italy of the late Renaissance. The relatively tidy concept of the Renaissance currently held by academics must be placed against this larger, amorphous but influential popular feeling.

## BIBLIOGRAPHY

There is a vast literature, to which a number of specialized reviews and bibliographies are now devoted: e.g., *Bibliothèque d'Humanisme et Renaissance* (Geneva, since 1941), and earlier as *Humanisme et Renaissance* (Paris, 1934–41); *Renaissance News* (New York, since 1948), and *Studies in the Renaissance* (New York, since 1954); *Bibliographie internationale d'Humanisme et de Renaissance* (Geneva, since 1966). The indispensable guide to the history of the idea is Wallace K. Ferguson, *The Renaissance in Historical Thought* (Boston, 1948), which should be read in conjunction with Franco Simone, *La coscienza della Rinascita negli umanisti francesi* (Rome, 1949), and *Il Rinascimento francese* (Turin, 1961). For Burckhardt, see W. Kaegi, *Jacob Burckhardt, eine Biographie*, 4 vols. (Basel, 1947–67). A recent discussion of the word itself will be found in B. L. Ullman, *Studies in the Italian Renaissance* (Rome, 1955), pp. 11–25. For philosophical aspects see the many works of P. O. Kristeller and of E. Garin. Kristeller's definition of humanism is quoted above from *The Classics and Renaissance Thought* (Cambridge, Mass., 1955), reprinted as *Renaissance Thought: The Classic, Scholastic and Humanist Strains* (New York, 1961). Recent fundamental studies of the structure of Renaissance concepts are by Hans Baron, *Crisis of the Early Italian Renaissance*, 2nd rev. ed. (Princeton, 1966), together with earlier papers of which two may be instanced: "Cicero and the Roman Civic Spirit in the Middle Ages and Early Renaissance," *Bull. J. Rylands Library*, **22** (1938), and "Franciscan Poverty and Civic Wealth in Humanistic Thought," *Speculum*, **13** (1938). See Eugenio Garin, *L'umanesimo italiano* (Bari, 1952; trans. Munz, Oxford, 1965). The best single study of educational theory remains W. H. Woodward, *Studies in Education during the Age of the Renaissance* (Cambridge, 1906; reprint New York, 1967). For the revival of antiquity, besides Voigt as in the text above, see J. E. Sandys, *A History of Classical Scholarship*, 3 vols. (Cambridge, 1903–08); R. R. Bolgar, *The Classical Heritage and its Beneficiaries* (Cambridge, 1954). For the debate over the earlier "Renaissances" two brilliant books are: C. H. Haskins, *The Renaissance of the Twelfth Century* (Cambridge, Mass., 1927), and É. Gilson, *Héloïse et Abélard* (Paris, 1938; trans. L. K. Shook, Ann Arbor, 1960); see in general E. Panofsky, *Renaissance and Renascences in Western Art* (Stockholm, 1960). For discussion of the Renaissance and politics see, *inter alia*, F. Chabod's contribution to *Actes du colloque sur la Renaissance* (Paris, 1958);

the matter really needs to be studied, so to speak, on the ground: e.g., F. Gilbert, *Machiavelli and Guicciardini* (Princeton, 1965). There is nothing adequate on religion in the Renaissance, but there is an elaborate bibliography by C. Angeleri, *Il problema religioso del Rinascimento* (Florence, 1952). Lynn Thorndike's criticism from the point of view of a historian of science is briefly presented in "Renaissance or Prenaissance," in *Journal of the History of Ideas*, **4** (1943), 65–74.

DENYS HAY

[See also **Classicism in Literature;** Cycles; Enlightenment; Gothic; **Humanism in Italy;** Nationalism; **Periodization;** Reformation; **Renaissance Humanism;** Romanticism; *Virtù.*]

# RENAISSANCE HUMANISM

***Two Interpretations.*** Renaissance humanism is the name for an intellectual movement that developed in Italy from the middle of the fourteenth century to the end of the fifteenth, and which had as its aim a new evaluation of man, of his place in nature and in history, and of the disciplines which concern him. The first characteristic feature of this movement is that it originated and was carried on not by professional philosophers but by men of letters, historians, moralists, and statesmen, in dispute with the philosophers of the time, to whom they opposed the *aurea sapientia* ("golden wisdom") of the philosophers and writers of the classical period. The philosophers of that time who were teaching in the Italian universities, or in those of Paris or Oxford, were to all intents and purposes Ockhamists, followers of the *logica moderna*, that is of nominalistic or terministic logic. Very often they used this logic in treating physical and mathematical questions and especially in the solution of the difficulties inherent in the concept of *infinite* quantity; that is, of a quantity which can be made greater or smaller than any given quantity. The *De sensu composito et diviso* ("Of Compounded and Divided Meaning") of Heytesbury (fl. 1340) and above all the *Liber calculationum* ("Book of Calculation") of Swineshead (fl. 1340) (also called Suseth or Suiseth) found in the Italian schools of the second half of the fourteenth century numerous imitators and followers, and there was a proliferation of *Sophismata, Insolubilia,* and *Obligationes* which claimed to solve innumerable paradoxes; from the more ancient ones, characteristic of the Megarian-Stoic School (like that of the liar), to the later ones connected with the augmentation or diminution *ad infinitum* of size, intensity, motion, velocity, weight, etc.

When between 1351 and 1353 Petrarch collected his *Familiares* ("Familiar Letters"), he placed among the first some letters which contained a stringent criticism of this type of philosophy. It seemed to Petrarch to be a *dialectic* in the worst sense of the word; that is, not a genuine logic, but a sophistic artifice aimed at routing the adversary without respect for truth. The questions treated by this dialectic appeared futile and idle to Petrarch, unworthy of the attention of men preoccupied with attaining true wisdom. True wisdom concerns mankind and his deeds, the conduct of private life and the governance of the state, the enjoyment of beauty and the contemplation of truth. These have always been the ends which the classical philosophers pursued. Modern philosophers disregard these ends and mistakenly take dialectic, which is a simple means of inquiry, for an end in itself. But if it is useful for training youth in discussion, it becomes a futile and ridiculous game in the hands of mature men who ought to confront the real problems of life.

This polemical position was renewed by all the Italian humanists between the fourteenth and fifteenth centuries.

Coluccio Salutati, who for thirty years was chancellor of the Signoria of Florence, Leonardo Bruni, and Lorenzo Valla to name only the major figures, took over as their task Petrarch's condemnation, and insisted on the necessity of a man's education being based on the disciplines which are closely connected with the nature and conduct of man, such as poetry, eloquence, history, philosophy, ethics, politics, and economics; on those disciplines, in short, which already in Cicero's time, Aulus Gellius (*Noctes Atticae*, XIII, 17) had maintained constituted the true *paideia* and *humanitas*, that is, the education of man as man, insofar as he is distinguished from all the other animals.

This debate between humanists and Scholastics might at first sight seem like a debate between the "two cultures," that is, between a culture of a scientific tendency and one of a rhetorical or literary tendency. In fact, that is how it has been interpreted by some who have seen in humanism an "essentially medieval and essentially Christian" phenomenon; hence the continuation and elaboration of a doctrine that had already been prevalent (Bush, p. 30).

From this point of view humanism has no specific character. Already in the thirteenth century there had been a rebirth of classical culture and especially of the theological conceptions of Plato and Aristotle, to which Saint Thomas had given a new form. Werner Jaeger in particular insisted on this point in an essay *Humanism and Theology* (Milwaukee, 1943), which has thrown light upon the close connection between classical theology and the concept of *paideia*, that is, humanistic education. A corollary of this interpretation

129

is that far from aiding in the birth of modern science —which coincided with the work of Leonardo and Galileo—humanism really constituted a retarding influence; that it is thus a "counter-Renaissance," actually a counter-humanism, according to Hiram Haydn (*The Counter-Renaissance*, 1950); and that the antecedents of science should be sought (as Duhem had already done) in the development of medieval Aristotelianism. Even the latter had been retarded, and not promoted, by Renaissance humanism (M. C. Clagett, 1959; John H. Randall, Jr., 1961).

This interpretation, however, is opposed not only to the explicit assertions of the humanists, who believed they were living in a new epoch, but also to the other interpretation which takes literally the assertions of the humanists seeking to justify its validity by showing that if humanistic culture has from many points of view the same content as medieval culture, it has a different *form* which shows a new spirit, that is, a new attitude towards the world. This thesis has been sustained in classic works (Burckhardt, Dilthey, Voigt, Cassirer), and has been taken up with renewed vigor and greater balance by competent scholars, both Italian and non-Italian. In its more aware and modern form this interpretation does not take literally *all* the theses of the humanists. It does not deny the historical continuity between medieval and humanistic culture which are both fed from the same sources, those of classical antiquity. It does not deny the permanence in humanism of the theological presuppositions that classical antiquity and medieval philosophy had made their own. It does not agree with those humanists when they pretend that the whole medieval period was an epoch of barbarism, and that man's every effort must be directed towards emerging from this state of barbarism, and entering into the promised land of truth and freedom. At the same time they retain the idea that humanism constituted a force of radical innovation and that it alone had laid the foundations of what today we call "the modern world."

**The Historical Method.** The comparison and critical evaluation of these two interpretations, which in their extreme or simplified form are antithetical, can be made not by expounding merely the ideas of the humanists but also and above all by considering if and how far they form a turning point in the civilization of their time, and if they have indicated the directions along which civilization developed in the centuries that followed. The crucial problem of Italian humanism can be expressed then as follows: has this humanism made a decisive contribution to the history of the ideas that still today constitute the patrimony of western civilization, and in what does this contribution consist?

Put in this form the problem becomes susceptible of a solution which takes account of all the fundamental facts. Let us begin by considering the primary and most obvious aspect of humanism: the rebirth of classical studies. These certainly had not been neglected in the preceding centuries, which had indeed used them as the principal source of their culture. But when Lorenzo Valla, in his celebrated *De falso credita et ementita Constantini donatione Declamatio* (1440), proved the falsity of the donation that the Emperor Constantine was supposed to have made to Pope Silvester, the donation of the supreme political authority over the whole Roman Empire. In order to show the "stupidity of the concepts and words" which emerged from this document, that is, their incongruity and inexactitude, he made use of the lack of reliable testimony or other historical sources which would have validated it and of its contrast with Roman, Hebrew, and Christian law. He thus showed that he knew how to make use of all the instruments of which modern historical investigation still avails itself. The discovery and use of these instruments was the first great conquest of Italian humanism.

The humanists did not accept classical antiquity in the form which it had assumed during the preceding centuries. They wished to discover its authenticity and its original sources, both in their true perspective. The medieval writers ignored this perspective, just as medieval painting ignored optical perspective, which was developed in the great painting of the Renaissance. For them, the "ancients" were contemporaries or, better, were out of time and history, as, in fact, they felt themselves to be. The perception of historical *distance*, which is an indispensable condition of historiographical work, hence of the situation of a work, of a person, of a fact of any sort, in a determinate time and place, was lacking almost entirely. The humanists acquired this perception and made the best possible use of it. The humanists found medieval language "barbarous," because it was a deformation or corruption of classical Latin. They saw that the interpretation which medieval writers had given of ancient works was weakened by ignorance of the genuine texts, and of many works which they did not possess or of which they took no notice, by their confusion of doctrines and diverse points of view, and by their inability to recognize in their true nature the writers (or the works), of classical antiquity. They continued, it is true, like all medieval authors, to esteem such writers as the masters of all wisdom, as models of all art, of all poetry, and of all human achievement. But they were far from accepting them just as they stood, from attempting to imitate them. They wished to rediscover them as guides and masters of a kind of work which had been initiated by them, and which, interrupted by "barbarism," should be taken up again and carried forward.

There is no doubt that these demands have been answered at times adequately and at times inadequately. But there is no doubt either that these demands, just as they were formulated, still constitute the directives today of historiography.

*Freedom.* But the rebirth of classical studies was not an end in itself for the humanists. Nor was its range limited to the domain of language, of literature, of art, and of history. Its main scope was that of returning to man capacities, powers, and attitudes that medieval culture had obscured or negated. The humanists were aware that they were living in a world which was rapidly changing and in which the medieval structures (the Empire, the Church, feudalism) had lost their validity. The Italian republics and signorial states were headed by the new bourgeois class which, moreover, was beginning to acquire political importance also in the great monarchies of France, England, and Spain. It was the era in which trade, voyages, and exchanges of all sorts came to the forefront: the era which starts with Columbus' undertaking the discovery of the new world.

In these circumstances the humanists claim for man a new position in the world. The old political hierarchies, which held themselves to be representatives and guardians of a cosmic order, ordained and established directly by God, still made their force felt; fires were still kindled for witches and heretics, and life itself in the Italian cities was lacerated by internecine quarrels. The Golden Age, the peaceful and happy republic of which Plato had spoken, was very remote from the reality in which the humanists lived. But they held that man could and should work to construct it.

This is the significance of the "discovery of man" in which many historians have seen the principal accomplishment of humanism. The humanists had faith in man's power to plan his life in the world, to command his destiny and direct it towards freedom, justice, and peace. All Christian, patristic, and scholastic philosophy had defended "free will," and had made countless attempts to reconcile it with divine providence and the immutable cosmic order in which it is manifested. The humanists frequently took over these attempts and repeated more or less the same solutions. But what truly interested them was not free will as an attribute inseparable from nature and the human will, but what free will makes it possible for man to be and to do, the capacity which it gives him of transforming himself and his world. Giannozzo Manetti,

Pico della Mirandola, and Marsilio Ficino take their cue from the old discussions of free will precisely in order to show that capacity in mankind. Manetti expressed the significance of human life with the formula, *Agere et intelligere,* which he understood as meaning "to know how and to be able to govern and rule the world which was made for man." In Pico's oration, *De dignitate hominis* (1486), which has been called the "Manifesto of the Italian Renaissance," he speaks of man as a being who, unlike all others, has no fixed location nor aspect, nor determined form, nor laws which determine his nature; but is one who can choose for himself his location or nature, or whatever form he wishes, and give his own laws to himself. Man can, says Pico, either *degenerate* among inferior beings or be *regenerated* among superior and divine beings. All depends on his choice.

This confidence is shared by all the humanists and not only the Italians. As has been said, it is only partially an expression of the historical situation in which humanism flourished, a situation in which, while new forces were arising, the old forces of traditional institutions and beliefs still fought vigorously and often had the upper hand. It was rather a seed sown for the future, a new plan of life for man and human society, a new model of the relations that should be established between man and the world of nature and of history. It is an optimistic plan of which, now at a distance of centuries, we can perceive the *naïveté,* because we know that the real possibilities that are offered to man are not infinite, but subject to restrictive conditions of all kinds. In any event the humanists, making their own the maxim *Agere et intelligere,* set as their first aim a principle which we can hardly doubt today: the limits of human planning are the same as the limits of human knowledge.

*The Return to Origins.* It is a fact that the humanists maintained the theological conception substantially intact. They held that the natural world has an order which is rational and that the origin of this order is God. Their preference went nevertheless towards Plato, or better towards Neo-Platonism, although Aristotelianism also had an important role in the thought of the Renaissance (to which we shall return below). The foundation of the Platonic Academy in Florence and the work of Marsilio Ficino and his followers are the best evidence of the preference of the humanists for Platonism. What were the reasons for this preference?

Platonism was better suited than Aristotelianism to placing man in the ideal center of the world. In the *Theologia platonica* (1482) Marsilio Ficino distinguished five levels of reality: body, quality, soul, the

131

angel, and God. The soul is at the middle point and is the *third* essence or *median* essence; whether ascending from body to God or descending from God to body, it is on the third level. Thus it is the living knot of reality. God and body are at the two extremes of reality and neither the angels nor quality mediate these two extremes, because the angels are turned towards God, and quality towards body. As a creature endowed with soul, man can therefore turn either towards corporeal things or towards divine things and is thus free, because what he is or becomes depends on his choice.

These features of Ficino's Platonism, which recur also in his numerous followers, have nothing in common with classical and medieval Platonism. The conceptual structures of Platonism remain, but are utilized only in granting to man a specific capacity, a freedom of choice not even known to beings superior to man.

The second reason for the diffusion of Platonism among the humanists is that the doctrine furnished them with a theme which returns like a leitmotiv in their writings: that of the return to origins. In ancient and medieval Neo-Platonism this theme is of a strictly religious nature. The origin is God and the return to this origin consists in reversing the emanative process which goes from God to things, in remounting the pathway upward and in tending to identify oneself with God. This religious meaning remains in the works of the humanists, but to it is joined, or at times substituted, a worldly and historical meaning, according to which the origin to which one should return is not God but the earthly origin of man and the human world.

Already Dante had written in the *Convivio* (IV, 12), "The highest desire of each thing, and the first given by nature, is the return to its origin." Pico della Mirandola in *De ente et uno* defined happiness as "the return to the origin," which is also the return to the primordial knowledge of man; this knowledge is diffused and diversified through the many channels of his history, but remains one in its substance and in its unity, and ought to be reintegrated by reconciling religion and philosophy, Platonism and Aristotelianism, moral science and natural philosophy, natural philosophy and theology.

With the return to origins, according to Pico, authentic religious peace can be realized, because it can be seen that all religions, all philosophies, and the most diverse forms of wisdom which humanity possesses derive from a single source which is God Himself. Renaissance humanism means by religious tolerance not the peaceful coexistence of different religious professions, but something founded on the unity of origin which deprives religious differences of any value. Obviously in classical Platonism or Neo-Platonism

there was nothing similar. The return to origins was only the mystic *ascesis* for the reunification of the soul with God.

But outside of Platonism the return to origins assumed a definitely worldly and historical character. Machiavelli understood it as the instrument which human communities used to renew themselves and to recapture their primordial strength. In states, he says, the reduction to origins is brought about by extrinsic accident or intrinsic prudence. In ancient Rome defeats (in battle) were often the cause of men's seeking to return to the original order of their community; these were extrinsic accidents. And appropriate institutions, such as that of the tribunes of the people or of the censors, as well as the work of individuals of exceptional virtue, had the task of recalling the citizens to their original virtue; this was the intrinsic prudence of the Roman state. But also, religious communities are saved only by a return to their origins. The Christian religion would have dwindled to nought if it had not been returned to its origin by Saint Francis and Saint Dominic, who with the poverty and example of the life of Christ, restored its primitive strength (*Discorsi sopra la prima deca di Tito Livio*, III, Ch. 1). And in fact the historical research of Machiavelli was carried on precisely as a model by which the Italian community, finding new knowledge of itself in its original political orders, might renew itself and regain strength and political unity. In Renaissance humanism these innovative graftings of new interpretations on old trunks are very frequent. If one looks only at the old trunks, one does not see the originality of humanism. But if one sees what has been grafted onto the trunks, its originality and its modernity emerge as obvious.

**Naturalism.** If one considers the frequent polemics that the humanists conducted against the study of physics, and particularly that of Aristotle, humanism would appear to be an antinaturalism. In his *De nobilitate legum et medicinae* Coluccio Salutati put the study of law, which concerns men and their interrelations, above that of medicine, and in general above the sciences of nature, which are concerned with things. In the *Isagogicon moralis disciplinae* Leonardo Bruni asserted that those who passed over moral philosophy and devoted themselves, on the contrary, to physical science, seemed, so to speak, to be occupied with matters that are foreign to them while neglecting those that are close. Analogous ideas were expressed by Matteo Palmieri in his work *Della vita civile* (ca. 1440) and Bartolommeo de' Sacchi in *De optimo cive*. All these humanists contrast the "moral Aristotle" with the "physical Aristotle." The same Leonardo Bruni translated from Greek into Latin the *Nicomachean*

*Ethics*, the *Politics*, and the *Economics* of Aristotle, with the polemical purpose of calling attention to that part of Aristotle's work that deals precisely with man and his life in society and which had been neglected or even ignored by the medieval writers.

But this polemical attitude did not prevent the humanists from finding, translating, or retranslating, and circulating the basic texts of ancient science. The *De medicina* of Celsus (42 B.C.–A.D. 37), unknown in the Middle Ages, had just been discovered in 1426 by Guarino and was then widely circulated and studied (printed in 1476, English trans., 1876). It was quoted by Leonardo da Vinci. The writings of Hippocrates and Galen were, still in the fifteenth century, retranslated and provided with commentaries. The works of Archimedes already circulated in Greek in the first decades of the fifteenth century and were translated towards the middle of the century. From these works Galileo obtained decisive inspiration for his own work. Precisely through the knowledge of these texts, provided by the humanists, the renewal of science was being prepared. "Endeavoring to see in nature what Greek writers had declared to be there, European scientists slowly came to see what really was there" (Marie Boas, p. 49).

At the same time the flowering of painting with its new perspective, of architecture, and of craftsmanship in many forms and refinements, demonstrated the increasing search for new techniques and for the knowledge which was indispensable for putting them into practice. The ideal approach towards art, in that period, and towards the Renaissance itself, is characterized by a *return to nature,* in contention against the stereotyped symbolic forms of medieval art; that is, by a tendency to seek in nature and to represent in art the authentic aspects of nature herself, no longer mediated by the symbolic-linguistic forms that the Middle Ages had used.

However, the same Renaissance Aristotelianism that had flourished between 1400 and 1600, above all in the school of Padua, drew its sustenance from the texts rescued by the humanists, and from their researches and contributions to the affirmation of scientific naturalism; especially in their refusal to admit the possibility of miracles, and their insistence on the necessary order which governs all natural objects.

But notwithstanding the polemics against the study of Aristotelian physics, a study which the humanists thought of as a *piétiner sur place* ("marking time") and incapable of leading to knowledge that was really new and useful to man, Italian Renaissance humanism can be considered as a naturalism in the most exact sense of the term, i.e., the belief that man is not a casual guest of the natural world but must make of this world his home and thereby recognize that the fundamental needs of his life bind him to it. The humanists in general did not deny the transcendent end of man, his supernatural life and beatitude. But they set up a new evaluation of man's needs and of the relations that bind him to nature, and hence they tried from this point of view to modify radically the scale of moral values. The *De voluptate* (1431) of Lorenzo Valla is the basic document concerning this point. The thesis of the work is that only pleasure is the authentic good of man and that all the other goods can be reduced to pleasure. It is the end that nature herself has indicated to man, furnishing him also with the means of obtaining it. External goods, like riches, health, honor, power, are desirable only because of their being sources of pleasure. Music, song, wine are sources of pleasure that one need not depreciate; and vice is an evil because it does not leave the soul in peace but disturbs it by the memory of that which has been done. The heroic sacrifices of which both ancients and moderns speak have also been made for pleasure; because he who is placed in the impossibility of finding it seeks at least, in subordinate order, to avoid the pain of its privation. Glory and contemplative life are likewise desired for the pleasure that they confer. And Valla does not hesitate to say that "courtesans and harlots are more deserving of humankind than holy and chaste virgins" (*De voluptate*, I). On pleasure is founded human solidarity itself, because since the origins of humanity no one has desired or seen with joy another's evil, but on the contrary has desired the good of another and has rejoiced when it has befallen him. One can miscalculate all this and desire something that seems to be a pleasure both for oneself and others, and then reveals itself on the contrary to be a pain and an evil. But the error can be avoided by prudent calculation.

These ideas of Lorenzo Valla have inspired a vast humanistic literature in which the polemic against asceticism, held to be one of the basic values in medieval life, was united to a reevaluation of Epicurus, whose doctrine was believed in the Middle Ages to be synonymous with impiety and immorality, and whom on the contrary the humanists recognized as a true master of human wisdom. "Epicurus," said Cosma Raimondi, "put the highest good in pleasure because he examined more deeply the force of nature and understood that we have been formed by nature in such a way that nothing is more akin to us than having all the members of the body whole and healthy and preserving them in this condition without being affected by any spiritual or corporeal evil."

When one contrasts the literary and rhetorical character of humanism with the scientific interest which had animated certain scholastics of the fourteenth century (John Buridan, Nicolas of Oresme, Albert of Saxony), and from this comparison concludes that there was a retarding action of humanism on natural science, which would have been better promoted by these Scholastics, an important fact is neglected: the Scholasticism of the fourteenth century derives its interest from being a *critique* of traditional Aristotelianism, and from having initiated its dissolution. The theory of *impetus* which Buridan applied to the motion of the heavens and which thus rendered useless the moving intelligence assumed by Aristotle to explain this motion; the doubts of Nicolas of Oresme expressed in his *Commentario* (ca. 1377) on the *De caelo*, on the entire Aristotelian cosmology; and in general the empiricist and critical orientation which the major Scholastics of the fourteenth century showed in their Aristotelian commentaries, constituted decisive attacks on the authority of Aristotle. But it is precisely against this authority that the humanists' criticism was directed. The *Dialecticae disputationes* (1439) of Lorenzo Valla attacked the Scholastics who accepted supinely the authority of Aristotle and induced their pupils to swear not to discuss him. These, says Valla, are superstitious and nonsensical men who depreciate their own merits and deprive themselves of the faculty of seeking the truth. That which, in the Scholasticism of the fourteenth century, indicated the beginning of an independent investigation of the natural world, found a support, not an obstacle, in the humanistic *critique* of Aristotle.

We must finally recall that the first steps of modern science were taken by Copernicus, Kepler, and Galileo and were guided by the belief that nature has a mathematical order or, as Galileo says, "The book of nature is written in mathematical characters." This belief is an integral part of the Platonic tradition which the humanists brought back to life. And it was this belief which inspired the work of Leonardo da Vinci, who called himself "a man without letters," whose only intention was to read "the book of nature." He maintained that this book could be read only by consulting *experience* directly and that through experience can be discovered the *reason* which operates in nature, a reason that is made manifest in immutable laws which, however, can be interpreted and understood only in terms of number, weight, and measure (*numero, pondere, et mensura*).

On the other hand the sympathy that the humanists showed for magic was inspired especially by the active or operative character of the magical practices, i.e., of their capacity for intervening in natural events, putting them, to a certain extent, under the control of man.

Most probably without the proclamation of the

humanists that man is part of nature and that in her we must live and work; without the close connection that humanism established between man and his worldly activity, and not only with literature and art, but also with the crafts and daily labor, the empirical investigation of nature which avails itself primarily of direct observation would not have been initiated, or would have been initiated only much later. The scholastic doctors, at whom the humanists shot their arrows, made many fine speeches on cosmology and Aristotelian physics, but did not put a hand to operations of research. The polemic of Galileo against "the paper world" of the Aristotelians, which gave rise to modern science, continued and carried to its legitimate conclusion the battle of the humanists.

***Towards a New Logic.*** A methodological consideration regarding the historiographic approach to a phenomenon like Italian humanism of the Renaissance (or any other historical phenomenon) might perhaps be appropriate here. Some historians emphasize with good reasons the *continuity* of humanism with the Christian philosophy of the Middle Ages; others with equally good reasons insist on the *discontinuity* between the two phenomena, hence on the originality of humanism itself. The contrast between the two schools derives principally from the ambiguousness of the concept of "continuity." If by continuity is meant the existence of discoverable relations between the recurrent theses of humanism and those of Christian medieval philosophy, it is undeniable. But relations are not only of similarity and identity. They can be of a different nature.

They can be the result of a greater or lesser importance attributed to certain conceptions; and of the use which is made of them and of the polemical ends to which they are subordinated. The revival of Platonism, for example, is not the simple repetition of medieval Platonism; it takes issue with the Aristotelian conception of the world and tends to disseminate another conception in which the position of man and his capacity for planning have a determining part. The harmony, in which the humanists believed, between faith and reason, between the teachings of Christianity and the results of philosophic research, is another trait which binds them to the medieval world; but this harmony served Saint Thomas, for instance, to subordinate reason to faith while it served the humanists to give reason a new dimension of freedom. The substantial identity which Pico maintained existed between different faiths and different philosophies would have been a heresy in the medieval world; but this was the interpretation which he gave to the principle of harmony between reason and faith that had been predominant in that world.

When one opposes to Renaissance humanism—as, for instance, Haydn does in the book already mentioned—a "counter-Renaissance," in which, in the polemic against the humanists' enthronement of the intellect and reason as normative principles in every sector of life, an almost exclusive value is attributed to faith, to natural instinct, to "the facts," to what is empirically real; and when Machiavelli, Montaigne, Luther (and in general the whole Protestant Reformation) are designated as representatives of this counter-Renaissance, one forgets the manifold relations which bind these figures and movements to Renaissance humanism. Machiavelli shared substantially with the humanists their interest in the world of humanity and the principle of the "return to origins." Montaigne like the humanists turned back to classical wisdom and obtained from it (and especially from Stoicism and Skepticism) data for interpreting the human condition. And the entire Protestant Reformation (the real precursor of which was the humanist Erasmus) was an attempt to bring Christianity back to its sources, i.e., to reattach it directly to the Bible, setting aside the ecclesiastical tradition which had constituted the base of medieval religion. The reevaluation of social life, of work, of human activity as the only "divine service" by which the Christian bore witness to his inner faith, is another humanistic aspect of the work of Luther. On the other hand, the criticism of the intellect and of reason which is common to the cohorts of the so-called Counter-Renaissance is in reality the *critique* of the intellect and of reason in the Aristotelian sense of those terms, that is, of the intellect as the faculty of apprehending first principles as self-evident, and of reason as the faculty of deducing or drawing necessary conclusions by means of the syllogism from those principles. But the *critique* of those faculties thus understood was initiated actually by the humanists. In the *Dialecticae disputationes* of Lorenzo Valla, which is a fundamental text in this respect, logic is conceived as an art which does not have absolute principles at its disposal and does not guarantee the truth of its demonstrations. It is merely an *organon*, i.e., an instrument to give order and coherence to human language, to the discourse which men commonly use in their affairs. Aristotle, according to Valla, had been wrong in his failure to concern himself with these affairs, and thus his logic is useless for the purpose of disciplining communication among men, communication which deals with objectives such as the administration of provinces, the leading of armies, the discussion of lawsuits, the practice of medicine, legislation, the writing of history, or the composition of poems. Superior to Aristotle have been those who, like Hippocrates and Euclid, restricted themselves to a single science but at least elucidated the indubitable principles of that science. As for the syllogism, Lorenzo Valla compared it to the art of making bread: the three parts that compose it, the major premiss (*propositio*), and the minor premiss (*assumptio*) are the water and the flour from which the baker makes the dough, the conclusion (*conclusio*), which is good if its components are good.

Valla's controversy led to this new approach toward logic, which a century later was to be developed in the work of Peter Ramus; to the contrast between the logic of *invention*, which aimed at disciplining human discourse and which was directed towards the discovery of new truths, and syllogistic logic, which was capable only of giving order to truths already known.

It is certainly to the criticism of Lorenzo Valla (or of his many followers) that Galileo refers when in the First Day (*Prima Giornata*) of the Two Main Systems . . . (*Due massimi sistemi . . .*, 1632) he asserted that if logic is the instrument with which one philosophizes, one learns to play the instrument from him who knows how to play it and not from the instrument maker. And so demonstration is learned by reading books full of demonstrations, which are those of mathematicians and not of logicians.

In conclusion, if Italian Renaissance humanism was not an explosion of absolute novelty in the history of ideas (and perhaps no movement in this history is an explosion of this kind), neither was it merely the continuation of the ideas that dominated the medieval world. It was, in the first place, an attempt to regain possession of the authentic legacy of the classical world and hence of the techniques suitable to discovering this legacy. In the second place, it was an effort to rescue human knowledge from the authority which still oppressed it and to vindicate its freedom. In the third place, it was the first attempt to construct a body of knowledge which met the demands of man's daily life, private and public, and therefore could serve as an effective instrument for his plans in the future.

From the distance of centuries, we can recognize that the attempt made by the humanists to break with their recent past, and to open to man the possibility of a different kind of life, was not in vain. This attempt has not always been maintained along the lines which they indicated, and even when it has, there have been deviations and stagnations; but when all is said and done it is still the direction followed by human knowledge today.

## BIBLIOGRAPHY

For a systematic bibliography, see Hans Baron, "Renaissance in Italy," *Archiv für Kulturgeschichte*, Band XVII (1927), 266ff.; Band XXI (1931), 95f. P. O. Kristeller and J. H. Randall, Jr., "The Study of the Philosophies of the

Renaissance," *Journal of the History of Ideas,* **2** (1941), 449–96. W. K. Ferguson, *The Renaissance in Historical Thought* (Cambridge, Mass., 1948).

For references in the article see Marie Boas, *The Scientific Renaissance, 1450–1630* (London, 1962); Douglas Bush, *Renaissance and English Humanism* (London, 1939); Marshall C. Clagett, *The Science of Mechanics in the Middle Ages: 1200–1400* (Madison, 1959); Hiram Haydn, *Counter-Renaissance* (New York, 1950); John H. Randall, Jr., *The School of Padua and the Emergence of Modern Science* (Padua, 1961).

The following books by Eugenio Garin probably contain the most balanced and documented interpretation of humanism: *L'umanesimo italiano* (Bari, 1952), trans. P. Munz as *Italian Humanism* (New York, 1966); *Medioevo e Rinascimento* (Bari, 1954); *La cultura filosofica del Rinascimento italiano* (Bari, 1961); *La cultura del Rinascimento* (Bari, 1967). On the same subject see also Cesare Vasoli, *La dialettica e la retorica dell'umanesimo* (Milan, 1968).

NICOLA ABBAGNANO

[See also Ancients and Moderns; Education; **Humanism in Italy;** Machiavellism; **Platonism in the Renaissance;** Ramism; Reformation; **Renaissance.**]

# RENAISSANCE IDEA OF THE DIGNITY OF MAN

THE DIGNITY of man attained its greatest prominence and was given its characteristic meaning in the Italian Renaissance. As an idea it is usually ill-defined and tends to express a complex of notions, classical and Christian, which writers of the period desired to assert. The word *dignitas* is a Latin rhetorical and political term indicating either the possession of high political or social rank or the moral qualities associated with it. It is used with great frequency by Cicero who begins to give it some of the connotations of general worthiness it acquired during the Renaissance. It is derived from the same root as *decus* and *decorum* (Sanskrit *dac-as,* "fame"). Cicero discusses dignity as the quality of masculine beauty as a subtopic to the fourth, but most emphasized, virtue to be sought by man, *decorum,* or propriety, which he derives from Panaetius' concept, *to prepon* (*De officiis,* I. 27, 36). In the course of this discussion Cicero applies the term "dignity" to the human race, as that quality which distinguishes it from animals (ibid., I. 30):

But in every investigation into the nature of duty, it is vitally necessary for us to remember always how vastly superior is man's nature to that of cattle and other animals: their only thought is for bodily satisfactions. . . . Man's mind

on the contrary, is developed by study and reflection. . . . From this we may learn that sensual pleasure is wholly unworthy of the *dignity of the human race* (emphasis added).

Passages such as this were well known to the Italian humanists, and following Cicero's precedent, they were able to identify the dignity of man with *humanitas* itself, the quality of being most truly human which was to be acquired through the study of the liberal arts—the *studia humanitatis,* from which they derived their name. The notion of the dignity of man is thus in its origins linked with the Petrarchan ideal of the *viri illustres* stressing high civic or military achievement to be attained through emulation of Roman heroes, i.e., with the pursuit of glory or fame.

Moreover, Renaissance humanists found in Cicero another even more precise depiction of the excellence of the human species, and this one also derived from Stoic-Middle Platonist Greek sources, most likely Posidonius. After discussing the rationality, design, and providential character of the cosmos as a whole and its inanimate and animate parts, the Stoic, "Balbus," presents his arguments "that the human race has been the especial beneficiary of the immortal gods" (*De natura deorum* II, 54–66). Man excels in the intricacy and functional aptness of his organs and physiology, in his erect posture from which he contemplates the heavens, in the acuteness of his senses, in his mind and intellect, in his gift of speech, in the pliancy and ingenuity of his hands with which he creates the works of civilization, has dominion over the earth, and sets about "the fashioning of another world, as it were, within the bounds and precincts of the one we have." And all of this is the outcome of a general providence with which divinity looks after the human race and of a special concern for individuals who are even assigned particular gods as their guardians.

This analysis of the excellence of man, as presented by Cicero, may be regarded as the most fully developed classical laudation of the dignity of man that has survived, and as representative of Greek rationalism and optimism at its peak. Whether it is a direct transposition of the ideas of Posidonius or a Ciceronian synthesis of other sources, it was to have a direct and powerful influence on Renaissance humanist treatises on the dignity of man. But long before this happened, in antiquity, this cluster of ideas was blended with biblical conceptions of the nature and role of man in the universe within the history of the Judeo-Christian tradition. From the combination of these two traditions the Renaissance idea of the dignity of man specifically developed.

The critical text was Genesis 1:26, "And God said, Let us make man in our image, after our likeness . . . ," supplemented by 1:28, "And God blessed them, and God said unto them, Be fruitful, and multiply, and replenish the earth, and subdue it: and have dominion over the fish of the sea, and the fowl of the air, and over every living thing that moveth upon the earth."

The critical exegesis was that of Philo Judaeus. His first-century Hellenistic Greek synthesis of the Old Testament and the current tendencies in classical thought blending Stoicism, Platonism, and Peripateticism seems indeed to have anticipated important elements of later pagan Neo-Platonism, and even certain aspects of the Hermetic myths of man and the creation. Unquestionably, and more importantly for our subject, it had a strong influence in shaping the analogous efforts of Alexandrian Christian thinkers of the second and third century to integrate acceptable elements of classical thought with their scriptural faith.

In his commentary on Genesis, *The Mosaic Creation Story* (*De opificio mundi*), Philo stresses that the divine image in man is the mind. Molded after the archetype of the Mind of the universe, the human mind is like a god in man. Man was created by God for the double purpose of utilizing the universe and contemplating its maker; therefore, it was necessary that the rest of the universe be already created and that man be made on the sixth day. God "desired that on coming into the world man might at once find both a banquet and a most sacred display. . . ." Since man's mind was created out of divine breath and man's body from clay, "man is the borderland between mortal and immortal nature . . . ," an idea repeated both by ancient and Renaissance Neo-Platonists.

The principal contributions of the Greek Fathers to the development of this theme were made by Clement of Alexandria and Origen in proximate dependence on Philo, and by Basil and Gregory of Nyssa in less direct dependence on him. Although important variations were present among them, all four were heavily influenced by Platonism. A central emphasis was on man's "similitude" to God, which in the Greek word of the Septuagint, *homoiosis*, connoted the dynamic process of becoming like God, or Platonic "assimilation." Man's creation in the divine "image" indicated his original state of perfection, whereas, after the Fall, man was involved, through the Incarnation, in a process of movement toward a restoration of the "image" in a heavenly state, finally fulfilling man's creation in the image and likeness of God. This process was a *mimesis* of God or of Christ. Regarding the soul as a "mirror," Gregory of Nyssa teaches that by "seeing" and "knowing" God in one's self, by assimilation, man becomes like God, *theopoiesis* or *theosis*, moving from *homoiosis* or *praxis* of virtue and purification to *theoria* or *gnosis* in an infinite mystical progression.

Gregory of Nyssa's most specific treatment of the status of man was his *De opificio hominis* (*On the Creation of Man*), extending his brother Basil's uncompleted commentary on the creation, his *Hexaemeron*, to the divine work of the sixth day. Gregory's treatise was translated into Latin in the late fifth century by Dionysius Exiguus and again by Scotus Erigena in the ninth, and thus was available in the Latin West as a model for successive schools of Christian Platonism.

Somewhat out of the main line of Greek development, but also influential in the West through eleventh- and twelfth-century translations by Alfanus and by Burgundio of Pisa, was the late fourth-century treatise of Nemesius of Emesa, *De natura hominis*, ordinarily confused by Latin copyists with the treatise of Gregory just mentioned. Man, in his own person, joins mortals with immortals, rational beings with irrational; as a microcosm (*mikros kosmos*) he reflects the whole creation; by divine providence all creatures have their being for him; for man's sake God became man so that man might reign on high being made in the image and likeness of God: "how can we exaggerate the dignity of his place in the creation?" Echoing Sophocles' *Antigone*, Nemesius proclaims:

Man crosses the mighty deep, contemplates the range of the heavens, notes the motion, position, and size of the stars, and reaps a harvest from both land and sea, learns all kinds of knowledge, gains skill in arts, pursues scientific inquiry. . . . He gives order to creation. Devils are subject to him. He explores the nature of every kind of being. He busies himself with the knowing of God and is God's house and temple (*De natura hominis*, trans. W. Telfer, Library of Christian Classics, Philadelphia [1955], IV, 254–55).

Stressing man's this-worldly role and powers, as well as his eschatological ends, drawing on a wider range of classical sources than Gregory, and certainly dependent on the Stoic tradition associated with Posidonius, and on Galen and the Peripatetics, Nemesius was a rich source of both classical and Christian ideas about the nature of man. His treatise was available and used by twelfth- and thirteenth-century theologians. In its emphasis on both the sacred and secular goals of man, it clearly anticipates the Renaissance conception of the dignity of man. It enjoyed sufficient prestige to be included in the library prepared for Federigo, Duke of Urbino (Bibliotheca Vaticana, Codex Urbinatus latinus 485), and among the Greek manuscripts assembled by Giannozzo Manetti (Palatinus graecus 385), himself a principal author of the genre among the Italian humanists. An even more popular and widely diffused Greek patristic work in Latin translation in the Western Middle Ages and Renaissance contained generous excerpts from that of

Nemesius, John Damascene's *De orthodoxa fide*. Thus there was no lack of texts offering models of the Greek Fathers' synthesis of Platonic and Stoic conceptions of the key position of man in the universe with the biblical and Christian visions of man's dignity based on his Creation and on the Incarnation.

It was, however, the teachings of the Latin Fathers which, through the depth of their influence within the Western theological tradition and through the constant availability of texts, contributed in the most formative way to the development of the Renaissance idea of the dignity of man. The great and dominating figure was, of course, Augustine of Hippo. But prior to Saint Augustine significant differences from the strongly established Greek theological tradition became apparent in the works of Tertullian, Arnobius, Lactantius, and Ambrose. Greek patristic thought in its dependence on Platonism tended to regard the creation in emanationist terms, so that in a sense the presence of the divine image in man was an estrangement of the divine nature; the reformation of man toward his divine origins, after the Fall, through incarnational grace, was a return to an original perfection. Latin patristic thought placed greater stress on *creatio ex nihilo*, where even the unformed matter of corporeality and earth had a value in a divine order, and the justification of man through the atonement meant a *reformatio in meliore*. In place of a cyclical "renewal" ideology, the germs of a notion of eschatological and even historical progress were present. Perhaps these differences were due to the circumstances that Western theologians tended to be jurists and rhetoricians rather than philosophers, as such more influenced by Stoic notions of an immanent justice and order in human affairs, and more oriented toward "action" as a fulfillment of ideals rather than contemplation or mysticism as a release from and transcendence of material chaos. Even though strongly Platonist elements were present in Cicero's eclectic adaptation of Greek philosophy to rhetorical uses, it may well be argued that Western Church Fathers tended to be "Ciceronian" rather than "Platonist" in the classical influences operating upon them.

For Augustine the notion of man's creation in the "image" of God was far more crucial than his "similitude" to his Maker, which was a quality of an image. Whereas creation according to an "image" was a directly purposive act that established a specific relationship between creator and creature, "similitude" signified a formal relationship only, which of course could increase with a man's progress toward his ultimate fruition. Two works of Augustine were central in establishing the tradition of Western thought concerning the nature and dignity of man as a consequence of the character of his creation in the "image" of God.

His *De Genesi ad litteram* is a carefully analytical exegetic work that provided answers for most of the thorny questions raised by the complicated language of Genesis as well as by the twofold account of man's creation. Subsequent medieval exegetes relied heavily upon it; it was a major authority for Peter Lombard's *Sententia*, for example. In his work Augustine interprets the use of the plural in "Let *us* make man in *our* image . . ." as indicating that the entire Trinity participated in man's creation, a thought that was seized upon later as further evidence of the great honor paid man by his Maker. The Fall was interpreted as seriously and severely corrupting the "image" of God in man but not entirely obliterating it, whereas man's similitude, which lay in his capacity to perform virtues, was entirely lost until restored by the divine grace of the Atonement.

A deeper and more significant influence came from Augustine's *De Trinitate*, a work which not only sought to establish the nature of the divine Trinity but also examined all of the creaturely trinities to be found in the *vestigia* of divinity immanent in the creation. Chief among these was the trinity in man. Augustine saw a correspondence between Father, Son, and Spirit and the divine mind or memory, the divine intellect, and the divine will or love. In the most particular sense man's possession of the image of God meant that his soul also was triune in the simultaneous and inseparable possession of these three faculties.

Although man with his trinitarian soul was a spiritual being (as were also God and the angels), it is significant that Augustine gave full and equal value to the affects and passions of the will, along with memory and intellect. Intellect and will were regarded as equally imbued with goodness or subject to sin, depending on the direction of their exercise, good if directed toward divinity, the creative power of the universe, defective and thus evil if turned away. In this respect Augustine and the Western theological anthropology influenced by him were closer to the Latin rhetorical tradition than to Hellenistic intellectualism and mysticism. Moreover, though not denying the existence, need, and value of mysticism and contemplation, there is an inherent stress on dynamic action in which the human will acts co-efficiently with divine grace.

Augustine managed to avoid the opposite dangers of gnostic dualism and Pelagianism by this conception. Moreover, his view of the body and of matter accepts their full validity in their properly subordinated role within the totality of the divinely sanctified creation. Thus he regarded both an unformed spirit and body as present in the initial creation of man in God's image and likeness, which, possessing *rationes seminales*, are given their form in man's second creation out of clay and divine breath. It is in the discovery of the beauty of form and the vestiges of divinity even in corporeal things that man in his terrestrial existence is drawn toward the Creator, but for this he needs the illumination of grace. Thus while an authentic structure of Neo-Platonism is at the core of Augustine's thought, derived from the influence of Victorinus and Ambrose, and from his direct reading of the Platonists, this structure was significantly modified in a way that differed from the Christian Platonism of the Greek Fathers and which can be regarded as coming from his familiarity with the attitudes of Roman Stoicism embodied in the rhetorical tradition, above all those of Cicero.

Other classical ideas concerning the nature and cosmic role and destiny of man were transmitted to the Latin West (as well as to Byzantine East, medieval Judaism, and, soon, the Arab world). Works such as Boethius' *Consolation of Philosophy*, Macrobius' *Saturnalia*, and especially his *Commentary on the Dream of Scipio* (an excerpt from Cicero's *De republica*) were late classical compilations containing a mélange of ancient notions on creation, the eternity of the world, the place of man, his goals, and destiny that fed into and influenced medieval as well as Renaissance ideas. Strikingly important among these sources for future attempts to look at the dignity of man's creation, nature, redemption, and even deification were the legendary writings of Hermes Trismegistus, regarded as an Egyptian prophet-sage of equal sanctity with the sybils as early as Lactantius. These writings, dating from the first to the third centuries A.D., were broadly concerned with the role of man in the universe in relation to the Great God and to the lesser gods; mythological in mode of presentation, they purported to be early revelations of Hermes, a supposed contemporary of Moses.

The corpus in large extent survived in the Greek East. In the West a translation of a portion of it known as *Aesculapius* and attributed to Apuleius circulated as early as the time of Augustine who quotes it extensively in book eight of *The City of God*. A number of passages attributing divine powers and a destiny of deification to man were frequently cited by medieval discussants of the theme of the dignity of man as well as by such Renaissance luminaries as Ficino and Pico della Mirandola who begins his famous oration with the quotation "A great miracle, Aesculapius, is man."

Other later classical works and translations of a Neo-Platonic provenance also entered into the body of writings associated with discussions of our theme. A work attributed also to the same Apuleius, *On the God of Socrates* and Chalcidius' partial translation and commentary on Plato's *Timaeus* were among the few available Platonic writings in the Latin West.

The problem of the theme of the dignity of man in the Latin Middle Ages is complex and by no means adequately investigated. Certain major tendencies or occasions for discussing it may be distinguished as well as certain chronological phases which did not necessarily influence succeeding ones in a developmental way. The first of four tendencies or occasions lay in the continuing efforts at exegesis of Genesis and the compilation of works entitled *Hexaemeron* or *On the Six Days' Work*. Here Augustine's interpretations from the *De Genesi ad litteram* were formative. Medieval hexameral literature is extensive and by no means sufficiently studied, though an obvious means of tracing the history of cosmological, physical, and anthropological ideas. One may mention Bede's, Abelard's, Thierry of Chartres', and Robert Grosseteste's versions, all of which were influential. Works of this nature were not confined to a single line of interpretation but reflected the controversies and movements of their particular ages.

A second type of speculation that gave rise to discussions of man's dignity and place in the cosmos were the efforts to construct a Platonic-Christian theology utilizing essentially Greek patristic and non-Christian Neo-Platonic sources rather than Augustine's precedents and version of Neo-Platonism. Unquestionably the most important figure among those engaged in efforts of this type was the ninth-century theologian Scotus Erigena. His own work *De divisione naturae* was an original Christian Platonist theology which placed man centrally in the cosmic hierarchy as a link between the spiritual and corporeal worlds. Moreover, he added to the sources of Christian Platonism available in the West by his translation of Gregory of Nyssa's *De opificio hominis* referred to above, and, most significantly, of the writings of the fifth-century Greek theologian who is known as (Pseudo-) Dionysius the Areopagite. These, with their emphasis on a celestial and an ecclesiastical hierarchy mirroring the former, on the epistemological difficulties of passing from the uncertainties of human knowledge of visibles to a knowledge of divine invisibles, had a wide and varied influence not only on the three major phases of a revival of Christian Platonism, the Carolingian, the Chartrain, and the Florentine, but also on the Christian Aristotelianism of the scholastic period. These latter thinkers found a certain parallel between the Christian Platonist hierarchical thinking of the Pseudo-Dionysius and the concern with hierarchy among the Arabic commentators, both the Neo-Platonic and their Aristotelian opponents. But in all these instances the question of the place of man in the chain of being became crucial.

Twelfth-century Chartrain Platonism was indebted 139

to Scotus Erigena both for his own writings and his translations. More important were the number of attempted new syntheses of Platonism and Christianity, returning again, on the model of the Greek Fathers, to the problem of man as an image of the divine engaged in a process of assimilation in the recovery of the lost glory of his creation and in a progress toward a new, higher sanctification through the Incarnation and the Atonement. Among the twelfth-century Platonists who discussed man as both a microcosm and a being able to ascend to the divine or descend to the brute were Bernard Silvester in his *De universitate mundi,* Alain of Lille in his *De planctu naturae,* Thierry of Chartres in his *De sex dierum operibus,* William of Conches in his *Philosophia* and his commentaries on the *Timaeus* and on *Boethius.* Outside of the more strictly Neo-Platonic circles the theme of man's creation in the divine image and likeness, his fall and the recovery of the divine image through the incarnate Christ found expression in the writings of such diverse figures as Honorius of Autun, Peter Abelard, William of St. Thierry, Hugh of St. Victor, and most importantly Peter Lombard who attempts a systematization of earlier, chiefly Augustinian, Christian thought on the meaning and dignity of man's creation.

A third thematic direction became manifest in the late twelfth and early thirteenth centuries. As early as Lactantius' fourth-century laudation of man in his *Divine Institutes* and *God's Creation,* an opposing genre to the dignity of man, namely, the topic of "the misery of the human condition" was to be found in Arnobius' *Contra nationes,* and Lactantius' work seems to have been a direct refutation. In both Arnobius and Lactantius theme and counter-theme are arrayed against each other. When at the end of the twelfth century the deacon, Lotario de' Conti, the future Pope Innocent III, wrote his famous *De contemptu mundi, seu de miseria humanae conditionis libri tres,* he also promised, but failed, to write a companion treatise on the dignity of man. By this time these two themes had become recognized literary genres. Earlier in the century a Cistercian follower of Saint Bernard of Clairvaux, Alcherus of Clairvaux, had written a treatise, *De spiritu et anima,* and had entitled the thirty-fifth chapter, *De dignitate humanae conditionis;* the work as a whole was a miscellaneous compilation of quotations on the soul, and this chapter repeats the theme of the nobility of man's creation. The chapter in question itself closely paralleled a little work attributed to Ambrose (but more likely Alcuin's) of the same title.

A fourth aspect of the medieval consideration of the dignity of man comes with the development of scholasticism and the preponderant influence of Aristotelian and metaphysical modes of speculation in the thirteenth century. Even though there remain certain influences of the earlier Augustinian and Neo-Platonic interpretations, even though the same critical sources are known and quoted by the scholastics, a major new emphasis, even among the anti-Aristotelians, is placed on a more naturalistic treatment of the nature and powers of man, directly dependent upon Aristotle's *De anima.* Along with the formal consideration of the nature and powers of the different parts of the soul, there remains some concern with man's position in the universe, but this is regarded essentially in static, hieratic terms rather than as a dynamic, operative potential for restoration of the divine image, or for irremediable bestialization. While it would be ridiculous to argue that there was a decline in concern for the pastoral and homiletic role of theology in the cure of souls, the impetus toward discovering a philosophic, metaphysical, or scientific basis for the Christian vision of the world was so powerful as to all but overshadow the more traditional emphasis.

Typically the dignity of man was discussed in the many commentaries on the *Sentences* of Peter Lombard, not at Book I, Distinction II, Question VII, "In what way is the image of the Trinity in the soul?," the traditional Augustinian occasion for stressing man's dignity, but at Book II, Distinctions XVI and XVII, "On the creation of man," and "On the creation of the soul," where the question is typically raised of whether the dignity of man, or the image of God in man, is more excellent than in the angel. The answers vary with subtlety.

Thomas Aquinas may be cited as one out of many discussions:

. . . properly and principally the image follows the intellectual nature; . . . where the intellectual nature is more perfect, there the image is more express, and thus, since the intellectual nature is of far greater dignity in angels than in man, . . . it is necessary that the image of God is more express in angels than in the soul. . . . The image of God is also assigned to man, but not so properly, with reference to certain subsequent properties, such as that man dominates the inferior creatures . . . and according to this and other conditions of this sort, nothing prevents man from being more in the image of God than the angel. But this is relatively [*secundum quid*] and not absolutely because the judgment of similitude and diversity which is assumed from the essentials of a thing is much more firm (*Commentum in quattuor libros sententiarum,* Lib. II, D. XVI, Q. I, art. iii, Parma [1856], I, 526; passage translated by Charles Trinkaus).

Nominalist theology in the fourteenth and fifteenth centuries, in keeping with its premises, was skeptical of such discussions. Gabriel Biel, for example, in his commentary on the *Sentences*, avers: "Properly speaking no creature is a vestige of the Trinity but only improperly, metaphorically, or by assumption because it accords with a corporeal vestige in many things."

While the theme of the dignity of man had a variegated history in classical and Christian antiquity and in the Latin Middle Ages, it had not been developed into either a clearly defined literary form or an internally consistent set of ideas.

There were, on the other hand, certain elements in the history and culture of the Renaissance which favored its development into a definitive literary and philosophical genre. One such element, certainly, was the humanist movement, which in its commitment to a revival of classical motifs in literature (rhetoric and poetry) and classical attitudes in history and moral philosophy was eager to demonstrate its equally strong conviction that antique rhetoric, poetry, history, and philosophy were not in conflict with Christianity but could actually strengthen religion. The available theme of the dignity of man, a genuine blend of classical and Christian ideas and topics in its inherited forms, fitted perfectly this requirement.

In the second place the very notion of "dignity" involved the question of relative status, as its medieval comparison of man and angel had shown; it thus fitted with equal ease into the spread of a rhetorical outlook through the influence of humanism in which the function of the arts is seen to be to praise or blame, the encomium and the diatribe, and to establish the place of the individual in the eyes of contemporaries, posterity, and ultimately eternity by this means.

In a moral order guided by rhetoric there is, moreover, an emphasis on individual achievement in action as well as on inner moral worth as manifested outwardly by virtue. Whether the so-called individualism of the Renaissance was the cause or the consequence of the rhetorical outlook, there can be no doubt of its existence, and this also, with its stress on freedom of choice, was to find appropriate expression in the theme of the dignity of man.

Finally, it may be argued, there was an inherent tension between the increasing secularism manifested in the expanding economic, political, and social activities of late medieval Europe and those elements of medieval Christianity which stressed asceticism, withdrawal, contemplation, poverty, humility, the anguish, misery, and worthlessness of *homo viator*, earthly man. There was no such tension between these new manifestations of the historical dynamism of human energy and the equally Christian vision of the dignity and excellence of man. This theme must therefore be considered as a deeply formative pattern of Renaissance thought and expression through its capacity to offer a resolution of this tension.

The Trecento Italian humanist and poet, Francesco Petrarca, was the first Renaissance figure to write on this theme, and his circumstances and motivation are revealing. He was perennially concerned with the troubled consciousness and consciences of his own age, its formlessness, its lack of depth of Christian commitment, its morally and spiritually ruinous materialism, its need for a sense of historical direction, its emotional volatility, its shallow and shortsighted vanity, and its intense personal and religious despair. More significantly, he also felt that he knew where the remedy lay, or at least the direction in which it could be sought.

A work of his old age, *On His Own Ignorance and that of Many Others*, was a diatribe against the preoccupation of the established intellectuals of his day with Aristotelian natural philosophy. He was not so much opposed to Aristotle as to the unrelatedness of his study to the moral and spiritual anguish of his contemporaries. By this he aligned himself against both the physicians and other lay intellectuals of the university arts faculties and against the scholastic theologians for this remoteness from the pastoral role of the clergy. He cast himself into the new role of a lay moral counselor to his contemporaries and called on others to adopt this role as well, offering as models Seneca, Cicero, Livy, Vergil, and Horace, who as Roman moral philosophers, rhetoricians, historians, and poets had cast themselves into similar roles. He sought to emulate the work of these figures in his own writings. His numerous letters to contemporaries are full of moral counsel. His major historical work *De viris illustribus* offered the lives of great Roman statesmen as examples of men of dignity to be emulated for their moral virtues by his contemporaries. His epic poem, *Africa*, was to offer Scipio Africanus as a new Roman-Italian culture-hero.

In turning to the pagan Romans as models of the utilization of culture for moral elevation, Petrarch had no confusion (despite many scholars' perplexity over his seeming ambiguity) about the fundamentally Christian character of his enterprise. Petrarch was deeply Christian and deeply religious. He was quite clear and quite aware that these classical authors were not. An even more compelling and admired mentor was Saint Augustine who had found for himself and offered to the world a way of reconciling the Christian revelation with those values of the ancients which were culturally, morally, and politically necessary for responsible life in the chaotic historical and natural world. In his *Secret Conflict of My Cares*, Petrarch portrays himself, for the benefit of his contemporaries, as experiencing a similar conflict to that resolved by

Augustine in his *Confessions*. The resolution lay, he thought, in a religious renewal of faith and a trust in salvation by grace that could overcome the prevailing self-doubt and despair—and this should be combined with a secular renewal of self-confidence in man's ability to perform morally and socially worthy actions as exemplified by the sense of civic responsibility of the virtuous pagans. To stand firm and virtuous in the midst of the blows of Fortune was more than to achieve individual security or material success. It meant the restoration of man's inner spiritual dignity without which he would sink into and become part of the chaotic morass of sin and disorder that were the conditions of earthly existence. It meant the retention of a spiritual self-confidence that was identical with a confidence in the ever-available, divine mercy of the Creator. The great perils in the life of man, which endangered him in this world and the next, were the superficial elation of *superbia*, when by whatever accident Fortune favored him, and the ruinous desperation of *accidia* and *dolor*, when Fortune frowned. It was essential for man to know his true condition and his true worth.

Such were the motivations that led him to seize upon the fragmentary elements of the theme of the dignity of man that were present in the medieval and classical sources known to him and to give them a literary formulation that anticipated the Renaissance development of this theme in its central aspects if it did not necessarily serve as its specific model. Appropriately, his treatise on the dignity of man occurred as a chapter in his most popular work, *The Remedies of Both Kinds of Fortune* (II, 93, *De tristitia et miseria*).

Later humanist and Platonist discussions of the dignity of man were more extensive and elaborate, involving more complex theological and philosophical concepts. Through all their variations, however, the two basic arguments presented by Petrarch with rhetorical succinctness remained fundamentals. Theologically and philosophically, man's dignity derived from the character and purpose of his creation and the resulting position and role this gave man in the universe, from the freedom and the capacity to ascend toward the divine, conditions inherent in the image of God in which he was created and restored to man in the Incarnation. Historically and existentially, man's dignity derived from his individual and collective actions and creations in this world from which came his earthly fame and greatness, tokens of the individual's contributions to the high cultures and civilizations mankind invented and constructed.

The writings of two Italian humanists on the nature and powers of man and his goals and place in the universe were particularly critical in preparing the way

for the further development and a more general acceptance and explicit expression of the theme of the dignity of man when it was resumed some eight decades after Petrarch in the mid-Quattrocento. Coluccio Salutati's *De fato et fortuna* of the 1390's sought a reconciliation of the Stoic philosophy of the relationship of the individual and "providence" with the contemporary Christian discussions of the theme. It was again the ideas of Augustine that gave him his cue. As did Petrarch and many other humanists, Salutati affirmed the primacy of the will, and found the basic creative force in the universe to be divine providence as the manifestation of divine will. Within it and in fulfillment of it human will acted creatively in organizing the affairs of men in this world, and by the very definition of will had to be free. Yet it was totally in harmony with divine providence. Through being voluntarily operative in the world, man expressed his condition of having been created in the image of God.

Man would seek worthy ends both for this life and the next and would manifest his active, providential, voluntarist nature as the image of God, but he would also accept the limitation of being God-like but not God, Himself. In the ultimate deification of heavenly fruition, however, he would attain the full realization of his dignity which he could only partially attain in this life in emulation of God and fulfillment of his role as an image of God.

Although, for both Petrarch and Salutati, salvation was a matter of supernatural grace whose actuality man should fully accept to avoid the catastrophe of despair and willful defection from his nature, men were susceptible to rhetorical inducements to rational behavior and could be moved to love and dignity by the incitements of their wills. For both humanists the Roman Stoicism of Cicero and Seneca had shown the way, though ignorance of Christ had left them blind to the true faith.

Lorenzo Valla, on the other hand, found in Augustine certain eudaimonistic elements which he transformed into a Christianized Epicureanism and into a rhetorical theology that was radically voluntaristic and even erotic in its basic conception of human nature. Man, in the image and likeness of God, was a trinitarian spirit or soul, a single substance with the three qualities of energy, intellect, emotion. Energy and emotion, weak or strong, guided the intellect in its determinations, used it as an instrument of their purposes, distorted it out of extremes of cowardice or rage. Thus man acted upon the world in pursuit of his pleasures, in fulfillment of the urges of his passions and his love. If he possessed faith and the hope of heavenly fulfillment, the divine pleasures of fruition and the love of God for the sake of the loving, not for His own sake, were his goals. If, as after the Fall, and before the Advent, man had no knowledge of the Christian promises, or other more powerful allures weakened or suppressed his faith in them, he became pleasure-seeking and utilitarian in his instrumental use of the things of this world for gratification. Valla was a striking apostle and advocate of the power of man, when armed with faith, to transcend all the basically animal-like qualities of his nature and to rise to the semi-divine. He laid great stress upon action, passionate and providential, in which man not only emulated God but fulfilled his nature and dignity as the divine image and likeness.

The most precise and straightforward statement of these views of human nature is contained in the first book of Valla's *Dialectical Disputations* (in its first redaction called *Repastinatio dialecticae et philosophiae*). On the other hand, he defended Epicureanism obliquely in his *On True Good* (*De vero bono*, or *De voluptate* in its first version). In dialogue form he presents first a Stoic's complaint of the ills of life to be remedied by virtue, then an Epicurean's refutation of virtue as an end and his praise of pleasure, and finally a Christian's defense of heavenly pleasure as the true good of man. The first version was written by 1432 and the third and final one by 1442. In 1445 or 1446 Bartolomeo Facio wrote *On the Happiness of Life* (*De vitae felicitate*) as a hostile imitation of Valla, defending Stoicism and refuting Epicureanism but setting man's true good in a Christian-Stoic vision of true happiness as residing in the restoration of man's immortal soul to its heavenly place of origin after a life of virtuous restraint among the miseries of this life.

Discussions such as these of man's happiness and true good, as also those on free will and fate and fortune, were centrally concerned with the problem of the nature and status of man in the cosmos and in this life, and they led straight into the renewed treatment of the theme of the dignity of man. In 1447 the same Bartolomeo Facio was sent an outline of a treatise on the dignity of man composed by an Olivetan monk, Antonia da Barga (*Libellus de dignitate et excellentia humanae vitae*). Da Barga urged Facio to take this treatise and add the polish and elegance a humanist could give it, and thus produce the treatise on the dignity of man that Innocent III had promised and never completed. Facio did so, and his *On the Excellence of Man* (*De excellentia hominis*) appeared in 1448, dedicated to Pope Nicholas V, but making no mention of Antonio da Barga. Facio's treatise follows da Barga's quite closely, introducing, however, some amplifications and variants, some of which were borrowed from his own *De vitae felicitate*.

Facio's was promptly followed by Giannozzo Manetti's much more elaborate, erudite, and laudatory treatise, *On the Dignity and Excellence of Man* (*De dignitate et excellentia hominis libri IV*). Manetti was apparently prompted by King Alfonso of Naples to write the treatise because Facio had dedicated his to Pope Nicholas V, and it was completed by late 1452 or early the next year in the version in which we have received it in manuscript. However, the same Antonio da Barga mentions in another work of his of 1449 that Manetti had written a work *De dignitate hominis ad Anthonium Bargensem*. Thus da Barga, who was certainly a friend of Manetti, may also have urged him to write a now-lost earlier version.

Manetti retains all of the traditional religious arguments for man's dignity to which he adds any that he can draw from classical sources such as Cicero, *On the Nature of the Gods*, Aristotle's *De anima* and *Ethics*. Moreover, he makes a number of assertions that are quite clearly original. However, as in his other writings, he tries to mask his own originality behind lengthy citations. He also utilizes a far wider range of sources than he admits to or cites directly, sources which he possessed in his extensive library of Latin, Greek, and Hebrew philosophical, theological, and exegetical works which he read in all three languages. His background as a Florentine merchant, statesman, civic-humanist, pupil, and follower of Ambrogio Traversari (followed later after the composition of this work by his role as advisor to both Nicholas V and King Alfonso) undoubtedly helped to influence the much more appreciative view of man's this-worldly dignity and achievements which he incorporated into his theological conception of the dignity of man. There is no question that Manetti made explicit the new conception of man, which was already implicit in Petrarch, Salutati, and Valla and which was supportable from both Greek and Latin classical and patristic texts. Manetti, of course, sought to project a new Christian synthesis of these sources, and this determined the form of his work.

Manetti's was not a profound work, but it was an insistent and an impressive one for the completeness of its arguments on behalf of the dignity of man and for the fullness and almost lack of restraint in their assertion. It was significant also as indicating that the cultural environment, within which the Platonists' views of the dignity of man were shortly to follow, was already highly receptive to their ideas. Other important humanist defenses of human greatness and progress were also being produced, such as the Bolognese humanist Benedetto Morandi's defense of man against Giovanni Garzoni's repetition of the traditional view of human misery (in two works of 1468–70, *De humana felicitate* and *Secunda reluctatio*

143

*contra calumniatorem naturae humanae*) of especial interest because of Morandi's clear projection of the doctrine of progress under human guidance. Another important defense of man came in the 1480's by Aurelio Brandolini, an Italian humanist at the court of Matthias Corvinus of Hungary (*Dialogus de humanae vitae conditione et toleranda corporis aegritudine*).

The theme of the dignity of man, which had thus been given a definite literary form by the Italian humanists, derived from and contained within itself two divergent theological and philosophical positions. Man's dignity lay in his creation in the image and likeness of God, which could be interpreted as meaning either that it was man's destiny to transcend the limitations of his image-likeness and to ascend to eventual deification by a progress toward perfect assimilation of image and model, or that man thought, felt, and acted in a godlike manner in his domination, utilization, guidance, and reconstruction of the world of sub-human nature. The first position was both Neo-Platonist and Greek patristic in its provenance, the second was more closely related to a loose syncretism of Stoicism and Middle Platonism best expressed in Roman rhetorical philosophizing but which also could find some confirmation in a literal interpretation of certain biblical passages.

The Italian humanist movement found it natural to juxtapose the two positions contained in the traditional treatments of the theme without necessarily providing any logical or systematic reconciliation, and in fact Augustine had wrought a theologically more integrated reconciliation of the transcendental and immanent elements in the theme which was a precedent and a model for the humanists. This humanist juxtaposition or merely rhetorical reconciliation was of great historical significance for it provided a system of thinking whereby sanction and justification could be offered to a life of activism and worldly achievement which was at the same time incorporated into traditional religious values and goals. The humanists, prompted by the needs of their contemporaries, sought and devised a way to make the best of both worlds, as it were.

It was however, the revival of Platonism, which occurred in Florence in the '70's, '80's, and '90's of the Quattrocento and was widely disseminated from there, that provided a philosophical and systematic integration of these two motifs involved in the consideration of the dignity of man. The principal author of this new synthesis, which indeed pulled together disparate elements within the biblical-Christian tradition as well as within the classical tradition and then sought parallel elements in the two, was Marsilio Ficino. Ficino, who had been set to work as a young man translating the works of Plato by Cosimo de'

Medici, did not by any means produce what modern philosophers could recognize as a pure and historically accurate interpretation of Plato in his own philosophical writings. He was, on the contrary, deeply affected by a number of influences operating upon him. One was the tradition of lay piety of which the humanist writings on the dignity of man had been a notable expression and within which Ficino, ordained as a priest in 1473, had always actively participated. Another was the humanist movement, itself, with its zeal for the recovery of classical texts and monuments to which Ficino's many important translations not only of the corpus of Plato but of the principal Neo-Platonic philosophers, the Hermetic *Poimandres*, the *Orphic Hymns*, and the *Chaldaic Oracles* made a major contribution. A third was the Western Latin theological tradition within which Augustine, of course, played a leading role as a model of a Christian Platonist, but which also influenced Ficino through his early scholastic training and subsequent studies, so that he was very well versed in the varying currents of Latin theology. Moreover, though the influence of Aristotle had been dominant in thirteenth-century scholastic theology and continued to be within the Thomist tradition, this was to a high degree permeated with the hierarchical ideas of the Christian Neo-Platonist, the Pseudo-Dionysius, as well as by those of the Arabic commentators. It was not difficult to "Platonize" what was already so Neo-Platonic.

That these were the dominant movements shaping Ficino's thought is significant because from them the impulse toward a reconciliation of the transcendental and immanentist elements in the theme of the dignity of man could be found, especially in Augustine and the humanists. It is notable that, although he knew of them, Ficino seems not to have been especially influenced by the medieval Neo-Platonism of Chartres or of his near-contemporary Nicholas of Cusa, or by contemporary Byzantine Platonic doctrines such as Plethon's or Bessarion's. What he wrought was an original synthesis of Christianity and ancient Platonism and Neo-Platonism, but one that also definitely reflected the Augustinian departures from Greek patristic thought and the Renaissance humanists' stress on the validity and importance of the this-worldly dignity of man within the framework of his continuous pursuit and ultimate achievement of immortality and deification. But this was a fully articulated and unified philosophy rather than merely rhetorical juxtaposition as in the case of the humanists.

This position was manifested in two aspects of Ficino's thought. One was the stress on the role of reason in man, as a free faculty, not bound into any of the traditional Plotinian determinist systems projected by Ficino—providence to which man was tied by his highest faculty of the intelligence, fate operating through astral influences to which man was tied by his faculty of imagination, and nature which claimed man's senses and corporeality as a part. Thus while man contained within himself and was dynamically linked to all parts of the universe, was its node and coupling, through reason and the cognate will man could freely favor and resist any of these levels of being. This meant that although man was part of and had a place in the universal hierarchy, he could also transcend it and escape from it and had a more dignified role than any other created being, approaching in freedom and creativity the state of divinity, itself.

The second aspect of Ficino's thought which manifested his position on the dignity of man was his stress on man's natural appetite for immortality and deification. This could be discovered in the character of man's thought and actions which Ficino analyzed systematically into twelve characteristics of God which man was driven by his will to make actual. In delineating man's pursuit of these divine qualities, however, he becomes certainly as eloquent as the humanists, if he does not surpass them, in his depictions of the glories of man's actions and ideas in all areas of this-worldly experience. While it is true that Ficino also emphasizes many magical and supernatural powers, with which he believes man is endowed, this is not at the expense of or in diminution of his deep appreciation of man's secular this-worldly achievements as signs of man's natural appetite to become God.

The entire striving in our soul is that it become God. Such striving is no less natural to men than the effort to flight is to birds. For it is always in men everywhere. Likewise it is not a contingent quality of some men but follows the nature itself of the species (*Theologica Platonica* XIV, 1; ed. Marcel, II, 247).

It may, thus, be argued that Ficino gave philosophical and theological form and system to central attitudes of the Renaissance humanist tradition, particularly to those associated with the theme of the dignity of man. It may also be argued that this emphasis, together with his pursuit of a universal theology and anthropology to be found in all human traditions and religions, pagan and Christian alike, constitute the central themes of his philosophy. Both these themes, the dignity of man in his pursuit of deification, and the universality of all human traditions in this pursuit, were also central to the development of Renaissance culture. Ficino and the Renaissance Platonists, in other words, do not represent a divergence from the major historical impulses of the Renaissance toward a

contemplative otherworldliness, as it is frequently claimed, but complete an intellectual response to a basic need for a mode of reconciliation of the expanding secular goals and activities of the men of the period with their still fervently held religious piety and otherworldly ends, a need which found expression and partial fulfillment in the humanist treatises on the dignity of man which preceded and accompanied the Platonist movement.

The best known expression of the Renaissance theme of the dignity of man occurs in Giovanni Pico della Mirandola's *Oration* of 1486, introducing the theses he offered for debate. Although Ficino preceded him in projecting man's transcendence of the hierarchy by a multi-level freedom which determined its being by its operative choice (Ficino's *Theologia Platonica* was published 1482, probably composed by 1474), Pico gave the position a unique dramatic and rhetorical sharpness and clarity, and followed it up by an even wider-ranging pursuit of a universality of human striving for fulfillment in the historical, religious, magical, and intellectual traditions known to him. It is significant that the theme of the dignity of man had been carried since antiquity in the form of an exegesis of Genesis 1:26, for Pico's comments in his *Oration* are applied to Adam and the mode of God's creation of man, and he followed this in 1488–89 with his *Heptaplus*, which is an extension of the traditional *Hexaemeron*, or six days work, to the seventh which includes the divine and human sabbatical. Pico presents a Neo-Platonic cosmology and anthropology in this work, but one that was notably modified by his knowledge of the medieval Jewish magical tradition, itself containing Neo-Platonic elements, the Cabala. To the three worlds of nature, the planets, and the intelligences, Pico adds the Cabalistic fourth world of man, which is outside the others, yet utilizes them, is their fulfillment. The deification and the dignity of man is central to each of the six days work of creation and is related in the sixth chapter to each of the seven books, for man was created on the sixth day. Thus Pico restores the theme of the dignity of man to the hexameral tradition but renews this exegetical tradition with new Cabalistic, Hermetic, Averroist, and Neo-Platonic ideas.

A final reference may be made to the work of the Augustinian preacher and theologian, Egidio da Viterbo (Giles of Viterbo), general of his order, of great influence in propagating Ficino's Christian Neo-Platonism at the courts of Julius II and Leo X and at the Lateran Council. His commentary on the *Sentences "ad mentem Platonis"* reverts to the scholastic argument as to whether the dignity of man exceeds that of the angel. Egidio without hesitation projects man's

145

dignity as higher not only because of Christ's Incarnation as man, but because of the dynamic freedom of man's striving to become God, which contrasts with the static, hierarchical fixity of the angels' position.

The idea of the dignity of man did not cease to find exponents among both philosophers and writers in the sixteenth and seventeenth centuries in Italy and elsewhere. The influences of both Italian humanism and Florentine Platonism were too potent for these characteristic ideas and forms of discussion of man to be lost. However, its subsequent history is beyond the scope of this article. One observation only may be permitted. Histories of single ideas or clusters of ideas are difficult to delimit because they ordinarily embody entire complexes of notions that are subject to greatly varying interpretations in different philosophical and literary schools and currents. Though the dignity of man was not primarily an Aristotelian idea, it had its Aristotelian supporters, and even such an austere Stoic-Aristotelian as Pietro Pomponazzi felt compelled to polemicize against it. But ultimately more important than its involvement in the debates of Platonists and Aristotelians was to be the impact of the Protestant Reformation and Catholic Reform, on the one hand, and of the emergence of the new science, on the other. Both these sixteenth-century developments were to drastically alter the conception of man and his place in the universe and consequently the entire conception of the dignity of man, though the Renaissance concept of man itself had important implications for both these developments.

## BIBLIOGRAPHY

Charles Trinkaus, *"In Our Image and Likeness": Humanity and Divinity in Italian Humanist Thought* (London and Chicago, 1970), for principal texts discussed and bibliography. See also the following works, and especially those by: Cassirer, Garin, Gentile, Javelet, Kristeller, Ladner, Di Napoli, Paparelli, and Yates. Javelet, Ladner (*Idea of Reform*), and Landmann have important bibliographies. Herschel Baker, *The Image of Man: A Study of Human Dignity in Classical Antiquity, the Middle Ages and the Renaissance* (Cambridge, Mass., 1947; reprint New York, 1961). Ernst Cassirer, *Individuum und Kosmos in der Philosophie der Renaissance* (Leipzig and Berlin, 1927; trans. New York, 1964); idem, "Giovanni Pico della Mirandola," *Journal of the History of Ideas*, 3 (1942), 123-44, 319-54; reprinted in P. O. Kristeller and P. P. Wiener, eds., *Renaissance Essays* (New York, 1968), 11-60. Ernst Cassirer, Paul Oskar Kristeller, John Herman Randall, Jr., eds., *The Renaissance Philosophy of Man* (Chicago, 1948). Y. M. J. Congar, "Le thème de Dieu-Créateur et les explications de l'Hexaméron dans la tradition chrétienne," in *L'homme devant Dieu: Mélanges offerts au Père Henri de Lubac* (Paris, 1963), pp. 189ff. B. Domanski, *Die Psychologie des Nemesius,*

Baeumker Beiträge, III (Münster, 1900). Ludwig Edelstein, *The Idea of Progress in Classical Antiquity* (Baltimore, 1967); idem, "The Philosophical System of Posidonius," *American Journal of Philology*, 57 (1936), 286-325. A.-J. Festugière, *La révélation d'Hermès Trismégiste*, 4 vols. (Paris, 1950-54). Eugenio Garin, "La 'Dignitas Hominis' e la letteratura patristica," *La Rinascita*, I (1938), 102-46; idem, ed., *Testi umanistici sul "De anima"* (Padua, 1951); idem, *Giovanni Pico della Mirandola* (Florence, 1937). Giovanni Gentile, "Il concetto dell'uomo nel Rinascimento" (1916), reprinted in idem, *Il pensiero italiano del Rinascimento* (Florence, 1940), pp. 47-113. P. Gerlitz, "Der mystische Bildbegriff (εἰκών und imago) in der frühchristlichen Geistesgeschichte," *Zeitschrift für Religions- und Geistesgeschichte*, 15 (1963), 244ff. Karl Gronau, *Poseidonios und die judisch-christliche Genesis-exegese* (Leipzig, 1914). J. Gross, *La divinisation du chrétien d'après les pères grecs* (Paris, 1938). Klaus Heitmann, *Fortuna und Virtus, Eine Studie zu Petrarcas Lebensweisheit* (Cologne and Graz, 1958). Werner Jaeger, *Nemesius von Emesa, Quellenforschung zum Neuplatonismus und seinen Anfängen bei Poseidonios* (Berlin, 1914). Robert Javelet, *Image et ressemblance au douzième siècle de saint Anselme à Alain de Lille*, 2 vols. (Strasbourg, 1967). J. Jervell, *Imago Dei: Genesis 1:26 f. im Spätjudentum, in der Gnosis und in den Paulinischen Briefen* (Göttingen, 1960). P. O. Kristeller, "Ficino and Pomponazzi on the Place of Man in the Universe," *Journal of the History of Ideas*, 5 (1944), 220-26, reprinted in *Studies in Renaissance Thought and Letters* (Rome, 1956), pp. 279-86; idem, "The Philosophy of Man in the Italian Renaissance," *Italica*, 24 (1947), 93-112, reprinted in *Studies in Renaissance Thought and Letters*, pp. 261-78; idem, *The Philosophy of Marsilio Ficino* (New York, 1943), Italian trans., *Il pensiero filosofico di Marsilio Ficino* (Florence, 1953). Gerhart B. Ladner, "The Concept of the Image in the Greek Fathers and the Byzantine Iconoclastic Controversy," *Dumbarton Oaks Papers*, 7 (1953), 1ff.; idem, *Ad imaginem Dei: The Image of Man in Medieval Art* (Latrobe, Pa., 1965); idem, "Homo Viator: Medieval Ideas on Alienation and Order," *Speculum*, 42 (1967), 233-59; idem, *Idea of Reform* (Cambridge, Mass., 1959; rev. ed. New York, 1967), Chapters II, V; idem, "The Philosophical Anthropology of St. Gregory of Nyssa," *Dumbarton Oaks Papers*, 12 (1958). Michael Landmann, et al., *DE HOMINE, Der Mensch im Spiegel seines Gedanken* (Freiburg and Munich, 1962). R. Leys, *L'image de Dieu chez Saint Grégoire de Nysse* (Brussels and Paris, 1951). R. A. Markus, "'Imago' and 'Similitudo' in Augustine," *Revue des études augustiniennes*, 10 (1964), 125ff. F. Masai, *Pléthon et le platonisme de Mistra* (Paris, 1956). E. Massa, "L'anima e l'uomo in Egidio Viterbo e nelle fonte classiche e medievali," in *Testi umanistici sul 'De anima.'* H. Merki, ΟΜΟΙΩΣΙΣ ΘΕΩ: *Von der platonischen Angleichen an Gott zur Gottähnlichkeit bei Gregor von Nyssa*, Paradosis VII (Fribourg, Switzerland, 1952). Rodolfo Mondolfo, *La comprensione del soggetto umano nell'antichità classica* (Florence, 1958). J. T. Muckle, "The Doctrine of Gregory of Nyssa on Man as the Image of God," *Mediaeval Studies*, 7 (1945), 55-84. Giovanni di Napoli, "'Contemptus Mundi' e 'Dignitas Hominis' nel Rinascimento," *Rivista di filosofia neoscolastica*, **48** (1956), 9–41; idem, *L'immortalità dell'anima nel Rinascimento* (Turin, 1963). Gioacchino Paparelli, *Feritas, Humanitas, Divinitas: Le componenti dell'Umanesimo* (Messina and Florence, 1960). F. E. Robbins, *The Hexaemeral Literature: A Study of Greek and Latin Commentaries on Genesis* (Chicago, 1912). A. Struker, *Die Gottesebenbildlichkeit des Menschen in der altchristlichen Literatur der ersten zwei Jahrhunderte* (Münster, 1913). J. E. Sullivan, *The Image of God: The Doctrine of St. Augustine and Its Influence* (Dubuque, Iowa, 1963). R. McL. Wilson, "The Early History of the Exegesis of Genesis 1:26," *Studia Patristica*, **1** (1957), 420ff. Frances Yates, *Giordano Bruno and the Hermetic Tradition* (London and Chicago, 1964; reprint New York, 1969).

CHARLES TRINKAUS

[See also Hermeticism; Hierarchy; Macrocosm and Micrososm; **Neo-Platonism; Platonism in the Renaissance;** Progress; **Renaissance Humanism;** Stoicism.]

# RENAISSANCE LITERATURE AND HISTORIOGRAPHY

HISTORY is a mirror by means of which the present peers into the past in order to see itself as it would wish to be seen by the future. The present either abuses the past by attributing to it unworthy qualities from which it has been able triumphantly to cleanse itself and thus to create its own character, rather in the manner of the jealous son slaying his father so that he can take his place, or it uses the past as an ideal by which it whips the present and finds its own self wanting; in neither case is the present able to see the past as it was, dooming itself in effect to a like failure of comprehension when its turn inevitably comes. Thus the Church Fathers either abjured their pagan heritage altogether or, contrariwise, claimed they were its only legitimate descendants, a technique of eating the cake of the past and having it too subsequently employed by all succeeding radical movements, religious or political. The Renaissance deprecated the Middle Ages (which it had first to invent before it could destroy) in order to assert its own identity; the neo-classicists had to find their predecessors crude and unpolished; the romantics were bound to reject neo-classicism as unnatural and to shatter its cosmopolitanism into national fragments; their own needs forced the Victorians to invent rational Greeks, contented medieval peasants, and passionate Renaissance men; and T. S. Eliot had to rewrite the history of English literature so as to support the legitimacy of his style. It is worth noting in passing that the comparative method seems almost always to end up, not as a step toward international understanding, but as a weapon in the raw hands of chauvinism and xenophobia.

Seen from the scarcely serene heights of the late twentieth century, the brute energy which the Renaissance expended and the ingenious means which it employed to tear itself out of the reluctant womb of the Middle Ages have an almost mesmeric effect. The Renaissance rewrote history with a ruthless hand, but, as we see, history is now taking its ironic revenge. For if we think of the Renaissance as ultimately the revolutionary force which succeeded in destroying a static, hierarchical, and reactionary mode of thought and behavior and replaced it with one which broke open the way to the comparatively unhindered exercise of individual *virtù* in private and public life alike; that is, the freedom, if not always the possibility, of the person to move in many directions, economic, social, political, emotional, intellectual, and moral; that is, towards capitalism, a bourgeois form of society, representative government, science, freedom of conscience and belief, faith in the rational, the supremacy of the authentic and self-justifying self, and devotion to the word as the highest form of expression; then we must be prepared to admit that that world is now in process of ending, if it has not already done so, under the impact of new (or should we not say renewed?) modes of thought and behavior: the power of the collectivity over the individual, of feeling over expression, of touching over speaking, of action over persuasion, of shapelessness over structure, of things over thoughts. In short, the story of the emergence of the Renaissance tells a story which, though it comes too late to be of use (assuming the lesson could or would be used) is, nevertheless, a plot whose mythos is well worth remembering.

In the history of ideas, there will always be found a number of assumptions about the course of history, that is to say, the way men act and under what impulses, whether recognized by them or not, which help to explain the attitudes they take toward major historical problems; sometimes these assumptions are explicit, but more often they are implicit in the work itself. By this is meant that men have certain ways of looking at and judging past events which enable them to make intelligible patterns out of the flux of phenomena, for in dealing with history, the recognition and judgment of events implies some sort of preconceived way of looking at and evaluating them which is applied to the interpretation of the material. Now, in the Renaissance there were a number of methodological assumptions about the course of history which in varying degrees affected contemporary thinking about the past and about the Renaissance itself. Of these, six are especially significant; they are the idea of progress, the theory of perfectibility, the climate theory, the cyclical theory of history, the doctrine of uniformitarianism, and the idea of decline.

These six ideas are not of equal importance and the last three are in fact in ideological opposition to the first three. Nevertheless, all are fundamental to our understanding of the ways in which the Renaissance thought. Of the six, the idea of progress is of the most consequence, for it is involved in the rise of the idea of science which marks out the modern world from the preceding eras. The concept of modernity, of the modern world emerging in the Renaissance and continuing as a unity, but with variations within it, to the present day, is at bottom the consequence of the rise of the idea of science, and therefore of the Renaissance itself. But the triumph of the idea of science was not an easy one; it had to meet the opposition of a number of powerful counter-ideas before it was accepted. The conflict between the idea of progress and the theory of perfectibility on the one hand and the cyclical theory of history, the doctrine of uniformitarianism, and the idea of decline on the other is but the first stage of a controversy which reached its height and was resolved with the victory of science in the seventeenth century.

The attack on the doctrine of the superiority of the ancients, the overcoming of the attitude of skepticism toward the achievements of the moderns, the refutation of criticisms directed against the idea of progress, the opposition to the pessimism inherent in the cyclical theory of history and the idea of decline, all these measures had to be taken in the seventeenth century before the idea of science could be securely established. But the genesis of this struggle goes back to the sixteenth century when it was first given its character and direction. Nevertheless, it should be pointed out that the conflict of ideas described in this paper is of late Renaissance origin. Up to the second half of the sixteenth century, the Renaissance still believed in the authority of the ancients. But under the impact of the discoveries and inventions and of the great changes in the economic structure of society, the influence of the ancients was gradually undermined, though the contention lasted for over a century.

The humanists have usually been depicted as men who looked backward; to them the revival of learning was literally a return to the world of a way of life which had disappeared for a thousand years but which now was back. It is as though the ancient civilization had flourished, had disappeared, and had reappeared without change, except that the man of the Renaissance looked up to the ancients for the wonders they had achieved. So far as many of the writers of the Renaissance were concerned, the Middle Ages were a blank; they looked on themselves as the inheritors and continuers of a tradition which had lapsed, and it would not be putting it too strongly to say that they felt themselves the contemporaries of the ancients.

Now, there was another group of men whose faces were not turned backward but rather forward. They too thought that the ancients had accomplished great things; they too thought that the Middle Ages had been unfruitful, but what distinguishes them is the fact that they thought their own age was different both from the classical period and the Middle Ages. In other words, it was their belief that the era of the Renaissance represented a way of life which was unique and which had never before existed on the face of the earth. In their estimation, what distinguished the modern period was the rise of science, which to them meant the discoveries and the new information they uncovered, the invention of instruments the ancients had not known, the effects of these inventions, and finally the application of science toward more discoveries and inventions in increasing numbers of disciplines so that the outlook for the future was not one of sameness but of continuous change and change to the better.

Louis Le Roy sets the pattern which the moderns followed and elaborated on. If, he proposes, we take a balance, no previous age has done more in the arts and sciences than this, neither the age of Cyrus, nor of Alexander the Great, nor of the Arabs, because within the last hundred years that which had been covered by the shades of ignorance has come into the light, but also much which had never been known has emerged: new fashions of men, laws, costumes; new plants, trees, minerals; new inventions such as printing, weapons of war, instruments of navigation; lost languages restored (Le Roy, *Considérations*, pp. 7–9). According to Étienne Pasquier (II, 605–06), the foundations of a new method of inquiry superior to that of the ancients were laid down by Copernicus, Paracelsus, and Ramus, and in such fields as far apart as surgery and the investigation of magnetism, their leading exponents could each claim superiority over the ancients (Paré, A4 recto; Gilbert, pp. ii recto–ii verso). Thus the way toward a complete working out of the methods and implications of science was surveyed before Francis Bacon. Alvarez, Ramus, Surius, and Postel agree with Le Roy that their century has seen greater progress in men and learning than has been seen in the whole course of the previous fourteen centuries.

Now, on what basis did they make this astounding claim? There is no doubt that their optimism and confidence are based on their belief in progress grounded on science. In his *Of the Interchangeable*

*Course, or Variety of Things* (1594), Le Roy has worked out the philosophy of progress in relation to science which is the manifesto of the moderns. The book is in essence a complete statement of the argument of the moderns: progress, scientific method, perfectibility, the plenitude of nature, the attack on decay, even the very title itself of the most complete exposition of the aims and methods of the moderns. So hopeful is his vision of the future that it inspires Le Roy to the heights of eloquence: "The greatest things are difficult, and long in comming. . . . How many haue bin first knowen and found out in this age? I say, new lands, new seas, new formes of men, manners, lawes, and customes; new diseases, and new remedies; new waies of the Heauen, and of the Ocean, . . . and new starres seen? . . . That which is now hidden, with time will come to light; and our successours will wonder that wee were ignorant of them" (*Variety*, pp. 127 recto–127 verso).

Of the innovations made by the rise of science none received more attention than the discoveries and the invention of gunpowder, the compass, and printing. Typical is this sentence from Jerome Cardan's autobiography. "Among the extraordinary, though quite natural circumstances of my life, the first and most unusual is that I was born in this century in which the whole world became known; whereas the ancients were familiar with but little more than a third part of it" (pp. 189–90). This note of intense self-awareness is repeated in Amerigo Vespucci's letter to Lorenzo Pietro de' Medici relating his own discoveries (p. 1). In his *Histoire Generalle des Indes Occidentales & Terres Neuues* (1552), Francisco Lopez de Gomara delivers a scathing attack on the ancients' knowledge of geography. He shows that the world is round, that it is inhabited, that there are inhabitants on the other hemispheres, and that the ancients did not know how to compute correctly longitude and latitude. Le Roy lists the new things which have come into the world as a result of the discoveries: sugar, pearls, spices, herbs, trees, fruit, and gold. George Best makes a similar list and shows how the discoveries have brought about an economy of abundance (I, 14).

The importance of the invention of printing was soon recognized, especially from the point of view of its effects on the Reformation. Many writers of the Renaissance discuss the significance of printing, and the consensus is that printing has brought about a great increase in the diffusion of knowledge and has been instrumental in causing the revival itself. But it is John Foxe who brings the praise of the printing press to its highest pitch. In a section called "The Invention and Benefit of Printing," Foxe discusses the date of the invention of the press, considers the various claimants

to its invention, and describes the process. He concludes with a recital of its accomplishments: it has come from God to abolish the papal tyranny, to confute the Church of Rome, and to bring about the victory of the truth; it has diffused knowledge, reduced the price of books, made learning and reading more easily accessible, has encouraged the composition of worthwhile books, and has caused God's word to prevail (III, 718–22).

The result of this activity in the sciences was the formulation of a doctrine of progress. It was held that the modern world was different from previous worlds because it knew more, did more, and hoped to accomplish more. The future seemed to promise ever increasing inventions and discoveries of such magnitude as made the present achievements seem small by comparison, not that the present was bad, but that the future would be better. There therefore was no turning back to the past for only the future mattered. The rise of science, then, introduced a new element into the Renaissance idea of its own times. Men were aware of their era not because it was like another period which had died away and was reborn but because it was different from any other era; its uniqueness was its mark.

Those who apply the idea of progress to nature hold that, contrary to the beliefs of those who hold to the idea of retrogression, nature is not running down, that men are as good as they once were, and that it is perfectly just to expect continued improvements in the arts and sciences. This point of view is in reality an attack on the doctrine of the superiority of the ancients; at the same time, it makes possible, as we have seen in the work of Le Roy, a justification for the study of science. For if nature has run down, there is nothing new to discover, and if men's wits are becoming feebler, there is no possibility of increasing knowledge. Gabriel Harvey argues that reason still functions as well as it always did and goes so far as to assert that the first age was not the golden age; he cites Jean Bodin to declare that the golden age is now (pp. 85–86).

Richard Eden points out that the great advances made in geometry, astronomy, architecture, music, painting, arms, inventions, and the like in modern times are an indication that men can now be superior to the ancients, for they have the same abilities as the ancients; furthermore, since the number of things to be found out is infinite, so the number of inventions and discoveries is infinite (pp. xlvi–xlvii). Le Roy reports that there is a frequent complaint to the effect that manners are getting worse daily, but if this were so, he asks, then men should ". . . ere this haue come to the height of iniquitie; and there should now be no more integrities in them: which is not true." Bodin makes a strong attack on the idea of retrogression in his *Methodus* (pp. 308–407). What the theory of perfectibility contributed to the idea of the Renaissance was the belief that it was possible to equal, if not overtake, the ancients.

According to the climate theory of history, the influence of the elements may bring about changes in men's affairs. Thus Giorgio Vasari points out that the air the early painters breathed stimulated them to produce the works of art which help bring about the revival of the arts. While Bodin is most closely identified with this idea, it was not unknown to other writers, such as Thomas Proctor (p. iiir), and Fulke Greville (iv, 78–79). Bodin makes the point that a concurrence of the proper climatic conditions will bring about changes in history and that certain areas are more favorable for the cultivation of the arts and sciences than others; he does not, however, work this out in connection with his own times.

The assumption about the course of human history which is most widely held in the Renaissance is the cyclical or tide theory. According to this point of view, men and nations and the arts have their origin, rise, flourishing, and decay; when the process is once completed, it does not stop but repeats itself over and over again. Or if we take the tide image, civilizations ebb and flow, and ebb and flow, and again the process is a continuous one. Seen in the relation to the idea of the Renaissance, this theory may be a help or a hindrance to its development, depending on the point in the cycle at which an historian wishes to place it. If the Renaissance is seen as part of the ascending curve, it will be described as the apex of human history up to that point; on the other hand, if it is part of the descending arc, it will be looked on as a state of decay in comparison with the peak reached by the ancients; in point of fact, both approaches are to be found.

Niccolò Machiavelli expresses the idea of cyclical change in *The History of Florence* (1532) and Gabriel Harvey applies the cyclical theory to the course of learning and especially to its history in his own lifetime. Indeed, the imagery which both use to express the cyclical theory is strikingly similar. Machiavelli writes:

For since it is ordained by Providence that there should be a continual ebb and flow in the things of this world; as soon as they arrive at their utmost perfection and can ascend no higher, they must of necessity decline; and on the other hand, when they have fallen, through any disorder, to the lowest degree that is possible, can sink no lower, they begin to rise again (I, 213–14).

**150**  He is echoed by Harvey:

There is a variable course and revolution of all things. Summer gettith the upperhande of wynter, and wynter agayne of summer. Nature herselfe is changeable, and most of all delightid with vanitye; and arte, after a sorte her ape, conformith to the like mutabilitye.

Similar exemplifications of the cyclical theory are found in Guicciardini (I, 2) and Vasari (I, 20–21, 32–33). Le Roy attributes the greatness of the several notable eras in history, including the Renaissance, to the cyclical course of events:

. . . the excellency of armes, and learning, to haue bin first in Egypt, Assyria, Persia, and Asia the lesser: consequently in Greece, Italie, and Sarasmenia: and finallie in this age, in which we see almost all auncient, liberal, and Mechanical Arts to be restored with the tongues; after that they had bin lost almost twelue hundred yeares, and other new, inuented in their places.

As a dynamic theory of history, the idea that events have their rise, flourishing state, and fall enabled the writers of the Renaissance to account for the emergence of a new way of life when, in their estimation, there had been no changes in human affairs for a millennium.

The central doctrine of the theory of uniformitarianism holds that human nature never changes, that men at all times and places have always been the same, and that therefore there is nothing new under the sun. Thus Montaigne makes the point that the world is neither in a state of decrepitude nor in a state of progress; it is as it always has been, and nature has neither lost its power nor suddenly produced men of outstanding qualities (III, 115–16). And Pierre Charron takes the very evidence which led Le Roy to announce the doctrine of progress to arrive at the conclusion that the world has not seen nor ever will see anything new:

That this great body which we call the world, is . . . in perpetual flux and reflux; That there is nothing said, held, believed at one time, and in one place, which is not likewise said, held, believed in another year, and contradicted, reproved, condemned elsewhere; . . . That all things are setled and comprehended in their course and revolution of nature, subject to encrease, changing ending, to the mutation of times, places, climates, heavens, airs, countries (p. 231).

By denying the possibility of change or progress, the doctrine of uniformitarianism helped to put a damper on the enthusiasm for the achievements of the modern world. Its influence was more pervasive than indicated here and it continued to exercise a retarding effect on the idea of progress into the seventeenth century.

Finally, there is the idea of decay, which held that the world was on the downgrade. The best period in history had been at the beginning of the world, and history was but the record of the increasing degeneracy of man and his works. Nature itself was running down and there was no hope for the present, and certainly none at all for the future. Thus there is developed a strong strain of pessimism which, when applied to the idea of the Renaissance, denied either the uniqueness or the advances made in modern times. If we add to this the theological opposition to the things of this world and its insistence on the depravity of man, we get a steady counter-current to the idea of progress.

Basic to the idea of decay is the belief in the existence of a past golden age from which all subsequent history is judged and found wanting; Edmund Spenser writes:

So oft as I with state of present time,
  The image of the antique world compare,
  When as mans age was in his freshest prime
  And the first blossome of fair vertue bare,
  Such oddes I finde twist those, and these which are,
  As that, through long continuance of his course,
  Me seemes the world is runne quite out of square,
  From the first point of his appointed sourse,
And being once amisse growes daily wourse and wourse
    (*Faerie Queene*, V, stanza 1 of the Proem.).

And he is echoed by Fulke Greville's "A Treatise of Monarchy" (I, 5–6, 11–12).

The golden age theme brings with it a feeling of pessimism, of lack of faith in progress and in the ability of human reason to deal adequately with the problems which confront man; and this is a strain of anti-intellectualism which merges very easily into theological distrust of the reason, as in the poems of John Davies and John Norden. The Renaissance has been described as the optimistic age; it is also the pessimistic age, for on all sides one hears the cry: "We are fallen into the barren age of the worlde," and "Our age, and aged world, even doating olde," and ". . . the world declineth to an old age, and bringeth not forth his fruites with that vigor and vertue it hath done in times past; . . . the vertue and goodnesse of man seemeth to defect from that of former ages, and to wax old and decay. . . ." The idea of decay is perhaps the strongest impediment to the immediate acceptance of the idea of the Renaissance and so great was its influence that it needed the full efforts of Bacon and his followers to put an end to its vogue in the philosophical area though it kept alive by becoming a convention in poetry.

On how these six ideological preconceptions operated to affect Renaissance thinking, however, one or two conclusions suggest themselves. One is that these ideas are widespread. They are both English and Continental in scope, and range over the length of the late Renaissance as it is ordinarily conceived. A second point to be noticed is that they are not confined to any particular type of intellectual activity but are to be found in all fields of Renaissance endeavor. Another conclusion is that these are not new ideas; their origins are deep in classical culture and some of them have, for the most part, a vigorous history through the Middle Ages. This fact suggests that much of Renaissance thinking is not altogether the jumble of ideas it is usually thought to be. What is new about the Renaissance is not so much the ideas themselves, but the ways in which they were recombined into new intellectual constructions. The clue for historical research then is not so much to seek original ideas as to discover the cumulative flow of old ideas, and to analyze what new combinations have been made and under the impetus of what new needs and forces. The ideas themselves retain certain fairly constant characters; what changes as a result of new demands is the forms of recombination of old ideas.

Revived from late classical antiquity and locked together in the Renaissance mind, the idea of progress and the cyclical theory of history, reinforced when need be by the doctrine of uniformitarianism and the concept of perfectibility, were welded together to form the idea of science as the basis of a continuously expanding future; that is, of an ever-spreading modernity to which there could be no end. It is worth asking the question: Why, if the idea of progress and the cyclical theory of history were of classical origin, did they fall into disuse, and why did their potential have to wait for recognition and use until the Renaissance? The answer, it appears, lies in yet another clustering of ideas within the Renaissance mind: the fusion, this time, of the idea of science with two ideas unique to the Renaissance, the idea of nationalism and the idea of capitalism. Nationalism gave the Renaissance its force, the motivating energy which moved men to action; capitalism gave them the economic resources from which their aspirations could be put into actual effect. Thus, for the first time in the history of man, it became possible to foresee a time when man, escaped from the tyranny of an economy of scarcity, could be free to move as they willed: nationalism motivated them, capitalism gave them security, science showed them the way, and progress gave them the hope that utopia could be had here and now, on this earth and within their literal grasp.

Some centuries have passed since this vision first burst from the imagination of the Renaissance and its realization has proved to be far more difficult than the

151

optimism of the scientists of the seventeenth century foresaw, yet it remains an indispensable, indeed central, part of the modern mind: abundance equals freedom equals happiness—except for those who have already acquired them. At the very moment when the Renaissance finally achieves its ends, it comes to an end.

*BIBLIOGRAPHY*

George Best, *The Three Voyages of Martin Frobisher,* ed. V. Steffanson and E. McCaskill, 2 vols. (London, 1934). Jean Bodin, *Methodus ad facilem historiarum cognitionem* (Lyons, 1583). Jerome Cardan, *The Book of My Life,* trans. J. Stoner (London, 1931). Pierre Charron, *Of Wisdome,* trans. S. Lennard (London, 1670). Richard Eden, *The First Three English Books on America,* ed. E. Arber (Birmingham, 1885). John Foxe, *Actes and Monuments,* eds. S. R. Cattley and G. Townsend, 8 vols. (London, 1843–49). William Gilbert, *De magnete* (1600), trans. P. Fleury Mottelay as *On the Magnet* (London, 1900). Fulke Greville, *Works,* ed. A. B. Grosart (n.p., 1870). Francesco Guicciardini, *The History of Italy,* trans. A. P. Goddard, 10 vols. (London, 1753–56). Gabriel Harvey, *Letterbook,* ed. E. J. L. Scott (London, 1884). Louis Le Roy, *Considérations sur l'histoire universelle* (Paris, 1567); idem, *Of the Interchangeable Course, or Variety of Things,* trans. R. Ashley (London, 1594). N. Machiavelli, *The Works,* trans. E. Farneworth (London, 1762). M. de Montaigne, *The Essays,* trans. J. Zeitlin, 3 vols. (New York, 1936). Ambrose Paré, *Works,* trans. T. Johnson (London, 1678). Étienne Pasquier, *Oeuvres,* 2 vols. (Amsterdam, 1723). Thomas Proctor, *Of the Knowledge and Conducte of Warres* (London, 1578). Giorgio Vasari, *Lives,* trans. Mrs. J. Foster, 5 vols. (London, 1850–52). Amerigo Vespucci, *Mundus novus* (1503), trans. G. N. Northrup (Princeton, 1916).

HERBERT WEISINGER

[See also Ancients and Moderns; **Chain of Being;** Cycles; **Historiography;** Nationalism; Perfectibility; Progress; **Renaissance Humanism;** Uniformitarianism; **Wisdom of the Fool.**]

# REVOLUTION

THE WORD "revolution" implies two elements—that of change by movement, and that of a motion which returns to its starting point. In the modern concept of revolution which originated in the times of the French Revolution the element of change effecting a forward movement prevails. But even in this notion traces of the earlier concept in which the cyclical aspects of the term were predominant are still noticeable. This justifies a careful treatment of the evolution of the idea during the centuries between the Renaissance and the French Revolution.

## I. THE IDEA OF REVOLUTION IN EARLY MODERN EUROPEAN HISTORY

*Revolutio* is a late Latin word which indicates the moving of a thing from one place to another. Although it occurred in the writings of Saint Augustine and of others, it was not a widely used term.

The great political writers of the classical world lacked an expression which corresponds to our notion of "revolution"; certainly they knew of uprisings against a ruler (ἐπανάστασις: Herodotus, Thucydides), of changes of constitutions (μεταβολή πολιτείας: Plato, Aristotle), and of people who were eager for new things (*cupidus rerum novarum:* Cicero), but they regarded the world as being constantly in motion, and the length of a rulership, the functioning or nonfunctioning of constitutions depended on human qualities, not on institutional arrangements. There existed a limited number of constitutional arrangements and all of them could be perfect, but human defects made the degeneration almost unavoidable. The decline from monarchy to tyranny is the most famous example of such degeneration. Polybius made the change from one constitutional form to another into a cycle (ἀνακύκλωσις), which runs from a state of nature to monarchy, from monarchy to tyranny, from tyranny to aristocracy, from aristocracy to oligarchy, from oligarchy to democracy, and from democracy to anarchy which represented a return to a state of nature so that the cycle would begin again. This cyclical theory has played an important role in the history of political thought and particularly also in the history of the idea of revolution. Nevertheless, because in the classical view human qualities—virtues and vices—are the only moving forces in the cycle of political history and because these classical theories are not predicated on the assumption of a generally valid norm assuring a stable order of political and social life, classical political thought lacks constitutive elements of the term "revolution."

The term "revolution" begins to be used in the late Middle Ages. In its Italian form, *rivoluzione,* Renaissance historians—Guicciardini, Machiavelli, Nardi—employed it in describing political events. In their writings, *rivoluzione* indicated the occurrence of a political disorder or of a change in rulership without containing any implication about the success or value, the desirability, the character or the aim of such disorder or change. It was a neutral, purely descriptive term and was used interchangeably with *tumulto, mutazione, moto.*

In the course of the sixteenth century, however, revolution gained its own particular physiognomy which made it stand out from those concepts with which it had previously been used synonymously. The reason is the appearance of the word in the title of the work in which Copernicus presented his theory of the movements of the stars: *De revolutionibus orbium caelestium* (1543). "Revolving" and "revolutions" have remained technical terms in astronomy and cosmology indicating the orbital movements of the planets and the time relation in which they stand to each other. In the sixteenth century the application of a term explaining celestial movements to political movements on the earth was natural. The widespread, almost general belief in astrology made it inevitable to assume that movements of the stars had their counterpart in political and social events. Revolutions on earth reflected the revolutions in the heavens.

It must be added, however, that the term "revolution"—because it implied both movement and a return to the point of departure—was particularly suited for removing difficulties which medieval political thought had not been able to overcome. The basic assumption in the Middle Ages was that there was one pattern which guaranteed the stability and permanence of the social order: a monarchy based on a hierarchically organized society. Each country ought to be governed in accordance with this pattern. Unrest and disturbances were the result of violations of the law. If they were committed by the ruler he became a tyrant and resistance was permitted, even regarded as a duty.

These assumptions of a basically stable social order, however, began to look rather unrealistic in a world which, especially in the later Middle Ages, showed great changes—accumulation of wealth, concentration of political power, new forms of military organization. Christian thought—perhaps more correctly, the Jewish legacy in Christian thought—had given some recognition to the existence of change and movement in social life; it postulated a succession of empires or ages, and chiliastic hopes and expectations which, from Joachim of Floris until the Reformation, permeated European religious thought, revitalized the idea of the imminent approach of a final age. But this golden age which would restore the situation before man's fall would be preceded by a final struggle between the followers of Christ and the armies of the anti-Christ. Victory could be attained only if man immediately set himself against the evil customs and laws which had crept into social life and restored institutions to their older and better forms. It is easy to see how the idea of revolution which contained both—motion and return to the beginnings—could serve to bridge the contrast in Christian social thought between the assumption of a generally valid norm and of a development towards an age of perfection.

However, the term "revolution" gained popularity in the sixteenth century not only because it fitted a Christian mold of thought but also because it was compatible with the ideas of the humanists who had revived classical political thought. The notion of revolution could be conceived as the all-encompassing framework into which the cyclical thought of classical political writers could be fitted.

Clearly, a chief reason for the adoption of the term "revolution" in the vocabulary of political thought was the flexibility of the term; it was associated with a great variety of images which could be used by writers who might have different opinions about the explanation of change. For an understanding of the role which the idea of revolution has played in the language of politics it is important to keep in mind that the meaning of the term reaches from simply designating a change in government to the belief in a heaven-determined, cyclical, political development.

The crucial importance of the term "revolution" in the political vocabulary became generally recognized in the seventeenth century when the events in England—which we now call the English revolution—required discussion and evaluation; revolution was used both for the description and the interpretation of these events. The official proclamations in which Charles II explained to the speaker of the House of Commons, to the Lord Mayor and the Aldermen of London, his views upon his return to England in 1660 spoke of the "many and great revolutions" (see Book 16 of Clarendon's *History of the Rebellion*) through which England had passed; this was a purely factual, almost neutral allusion to the many governmental changes which had taken place in England in the preceding twenty years, but others used the term "revolution" because it appeared to them to contain an explanation of the causes of these changes; the idea served to throw light on the forces determining the course of history. To Clarendon the events demonstrated the dependence of political movements on movements in heaven: "The motions of these last twenty years . . . have proceeded from the evil influence of a malignant star" (ibid.). Hobbes saw in the events proof of the truth of the cyclical theory of classical political science: "I have seen in this revolution a circular motion of the sovereign power through two usurpers from the late King to his son. For . . . it moved from King Charles I to the Long Parliament; from thence to the Rump; from the Rump to Oliver Cromwell and then back again from Richard Cromwell to the Rump; thence to the Long Parliament; and thence to King Charles II, where long may it remain" (Hobbes, *Behemoth*, end of the Fourth Dialogue).

Application of the term "revolution" to the events of 1688 which saw another overthrow of the Stuart dynasty was justified in a similar manner. The change

# REVOLUTION

that took place in 1688 was a revolution because it represented a return to the true old constitution of England and as such closed a cycle. The fact that the events of 1688 were called a "Glorious Revolution" did not imply a better, a truer, revolution than the previous ones, nor that it ushered in a new age. The praising adjective "Glorious" was only intended to indicate that the action against James II had had a successful outcome. Also for Locke, the great defender of the revolution of 1688, the word itself had no particular meaning or weight. He seems to have been aware of its cyclical element because in the nineteenth chapter of the *Second Treatise on Civil Government* he maintained that the "slowness and aversion in the people to quit their old constitutions has in the many revolutions which have been seen in this kingdom, in this and former ages, still kept us to, or after some interval of fruitless attempts still brought us back again to, our old legislative of king, lords and commons." A later passage in the same chapter, however, shows that Locke finds no difference between revolution and rebellion. Of course, by giving the people the "right to resume their original liberty" if the purposes for which "men enter society" are subverted, Locke gave the right of resistance a firm and broadened basis which served well to justify revolutionary action in the later part of the eighteenth century.

Undoubtedly, the events in England—the execution of a monarch, the emergence of a tyrant, the overthrow of a king by his own son-in-law—deeply stirred political thought. But there were other events—the defection of the Netherlands, the Revolt of the Catalans, the Portuguese Rebellion—which directed attention to the problem of political change. All these events combined to make "revolution" a fashionable word; this can be deduced from the frequency with which it appeared in the titles of historical works. That many popular historical writers used this term chiefly because it was fashionable, can also be derived from the fact that they did not attribute to it a very distinctive meaning. One of the writers who wrote many histories of revolution was the Abbé R. A. de Vertot (1655–1733); in the Preface of his *Révolutions de Portugal* he gave an almost frivolous explanation why in the edition of 1722 the title of this work was changed from *Conjuration* to *Révolutions*. He had added earlier and later events: *C'est cette augmentation d'événemens qui a engagé à substituer le titre de Révolutions à celuy de Conjuration*. The same, somewhat thoughtless use of the word can be found in the title which Duport-Dutertre gave to the eight volumes in which he published a collection of historical anecdotes and reports. He called his work *Histoire des Conjurations, Conspirations et Révolutions célèbres, tant anciennes que*

*modernes* (1754–60). If these writers made any distinction between conspiracies, rebellions, and revolutions it is that while conspiracies and rebellions might fail, revolutions really effected changes in government.

On the other hand, the particular and distinctive character of the notion, because of its cyclical implications, was evident to serious political writers. It might be enough to refer to Walter Moyle's *Essay on the Constitution and Government of the Roman State*. Moyle speaks of the "great revolution" which took place in Rome: "the monarchy resolved into an aristocracy; and that into a democracy; and that too relapsed into a monarchy." Moyle added that these changes did not come about as Polybius had assumed "from moral reasons such as vices and corruptions" but "from the change of the only true ground and foundation of power, property." Under the impact of the events in England Moyle was interested in finding means to escape from the cycle of unending revolutions, and by focusing on the question of how to avoid them Moyle foreshadowed later intellectual concerns. But this interest made him—and some of his English contemporaries—unique in the intellectual world of the Enlightenment, for the more usual view at that time was that the cycle could not be halted.

Hume proclaimed as a law of politics "that every government must come to a period and that death is unavoidable to the political as well as to the natural body" ("Whether the British Government Inclines More to Absolute Monarchy or to a Republic," in *Philosophical Works*, Boston [1854], III, 51). Likewise, many of the *philosophes* accepted the cyclical element in the word "revolution" and did not believe in the possibility of escape. That "empires like men must grow, decay and die" is, according to D'Alembert, "a necessary revolution" in the history of states ("Éloge de M. le Président de Montesquieu"). Montesquieu saw the same impermanency in all fields of human life: *Il arrive, tous les dix ans, des révolutions qui précipitent le riche dans la misère et enlèvent le pauvre avec des ailes rapides au comble des richesses* ("Every ten years revolutions occur which hurl the rich into poverty and send the poor on a rapid flight to abundant wealth"; *Lettres persanes*). Because of its cyclical element revolution fitted the skepticism of the *philosophes* concerning the strength and power of men.

However, the word "revolution" had many applications in the language of the *philosophes;* they also used this concept without any cyclical connotation. Then, like the popular historians whom we have mentioned, they considered revolution as a neutral term descriptive of an important change in government. This is clearly expressed by Diderot in his article on "Révolution" in the *Encyclopédie;* according to him "revolution" means *en terme de politique . . . un changement considérable arrivé dans le gouvernement d'un état.* Moreover, the meaning of the word was extended to cover any great change in human institutions. It might be enough to refer to the 28th book of *De l'esprit des lois* in which Montesquieu analyzed the development of French judicial procedure; in the 36th chapter of this book "revolution" is used to indicate a fundamental change in the French political government; in the 39th chapter of the same book revolution means only a great change in administration of laws. Every development which changed the course of history was called a revolution. That, for instance, is the sense in which Gibbon used this word in his *Decline and Fall of the Roman Empire* (particularly Chapter 46). And this was the sense of the term in the Abbé Raynal's *Histoire philosophique et politique des établissements et du commerce des Européens dans les deux Indes* (1781). Raynal at the beginning of the first volume of this work spoke about the "revolution in commerce" which the discovery of the New World caused and a close reading of this and the following passages shows that—in contrast to what has been frequently asserted—he didn't allude to the American Revolution and its possible consequences but had in mind a slow and gradual long-range development extending over three centuries. In David Hume's essay on "The Rise of Arts and Sciences" (*Hume's Philosophical Works*, London [1874–75], II, 120), the phrase "the domestic and the gradual revolutions of the state" indicates a neutral and very general meaning of the word.

However, the *philosophes*—particularly their leaders like Rousseau and Voltaire—also made a particular contribution to the development of the idea of revolution, and this new aspect of the notion might have influenced Gibbon's use of the term. Despite skepticism and occasional pessimism the *philosophes* believed in progress and particularly in the decisive contribution which their own age and they themselves made to the advance of humanity. Turgot wrote that, whereas the phenomena of nature are "enclosed in a circle of revolutions that are always the same," man can break the cycle of nature and in recent times progress has become unmistakable and irresistible (*Discours sur les progrès successifs de l'esprit humain*, *Oeuvres*, Paris [1808], II, 52). The *philosophes* were firmly persuaded that the great discoveries about the laws of nature which had taken place in the preceding century would be followed by a discovery of the laws of social order and that it would soon be possible to establish a peaceful and prosperous world. It was the general conviction that an era of great change was approaching. Some looked upon the coming events with fear. Rousseau, for instance, wrote in *Émile: Nous approchons de l'état de crise et du siècle des révolutions; qui peut vous répondre de ce que vous deviendrez alors?* ("We are approaching a crisis and a century of revolutions; who can answer to you for what will become of you then?") Voltaire, in accordance with most of the *philosophes*, expressed himself more optimistically: "Everything I see scatters the seeds of a revolution which will definitely come, though I won't have the pleasure of being its witness. Frenchmen discover everything late, but in the end they do discover it. Enlightenment has gradually spread so widely that it will burst into full light at the first right opportunity, and then there'll be a fine uproar. The young people are lucky: they will see some great things" (in a letter to Bernard Louis Chauvelin of April 2, 1764). The great changes which Voltaire envisaged would be the result of new intellectual insights. He defined what was going on as *une grande révolution dans l'esprit humain* (in a letter to François Jean de Chastellux of December 7, 1772). Because this revolution presupposed a new intellectual attitude the various fields of intellectual efforts all formed part of this great revolutionary movement and writers spoke of a revolution in the arts, in the sciences, or in anatomy. Again, we have here an extension of the notion of revolution on which scholars of the nineteenth century would elaborate and to which they would give intensive study.

The changes which would result from the great revolution of the human mind and of which the *philosophes* were protagonists would finally liberate the world from superstition, from ambitious rivalry and competition, and place reason on the throne. The world would be organized according to true rational principles; the final age of history would be reached. This beginning of a new world resembled the beginning of a new revolution of the stars. There hardly can be any doubt that the astrological connotations of the word "revolution" played their part in the minds of many who were expecting from the work of the Enlightenment a revolution which would usher in a new and final age.

For later generations a new, although not a final age began with the American Revolution. However, this was not the view of the leaders of this movement when it began. They were convinced that they were defending themselves against a conspiracy of the British rulers to establish a tyrannical regime in the Colonies, and that they were acting in accordance with the right of resistance as Locke had formulated it. The American colonists were anxious to restore the old rightful basis of government. From time to time one can find the expression "revolution," for instance, in a memorandum of William Smith of June 9, 1776: he fears that "the meditated revolution tends to light up a Civil War." Actually, in the early years of the struggle the term "revolution" was rarely applied to the War of Independence; it began to occur frequently in the 1780's when Thomas Paine, on hearing that he might be appointed Historiographer to the Continent, outlined his plan for a History of the American Revolution (October 1783), when Richard Price published his *Observations on the American Revolution* (1784), and David Ramsay wrote his *History of the Revolution of South Carolina* (1785) and his *History of the American Revolution* (1789). By then independence had been achieved. It had become evident that in consequence the mercantile powers could no longer maintain their monopolistic system of trade with colonies and that a republican constitution could create a feasible system of government. A revolution in the sense of a far-reaching change had taken place. The full implications of this change and also the pioneering role of the events on the American continent were realized only when the movement continued in Europe with the French Revolution.

## II. FROM THE FRENCH REVOLUTION TO MARX'S THEORY OF REVOLUTION

With the French Revolution the idea of revolution assumes a more sharply defined form and gains a central place in political thought. Interest in the connection of the idea of revolution with a cyclical historical movement—although, as we shall see, it did not entirely disappear—diminished. The significant new development which was brought about by the French Revolution was the combining in one concept of the two notions which previously had existed side by side: that of revolutions as changes in government; and that of revolution as ushering in a new social order and a new stage in world history. Already in 1793, when the revolutionary movement was still in full swing, Condorcet stated that the extension of the political change to wider spheres was the characteristic feature of the French Revolution: "In France, the revolution was to embrace the entire economy of society, change every social relation, and find its way down to the furthest links of the political chain, even down to those individuals who, living in peace on their private fortune or on the fruits of their labor, had no reason to participate in public affairs—neither opinion nor occupation nor the pursuit of wealth, power or fame" (Condorcet, *Esquisse d'un tableau historique des progrès de l'esprit humain, Neuvième Époque*). In the notion of revolution as it developed in this period the political change—the overthrow of the existing government—remained decisive, i.e., a revolution was assumed to culminate in one dramatic, violent event: for the contemporaries the fall of the Bastille was this decisive event. When Charles James Fox heard of it

he said in a letter to Richard Fitzpatrick (30 July 1789): "How much the greatest event in the history of the world, and how much the best," and it might be added that the fall of the Bastille for the French has remained almost identical with the French Revolution itself. In the nineteenth century the crucial struggle to decide the outcome of a revolution usually took place in the capital; the fighters for the revolution were citizens armed with rifles, checkmating the military forces through quickly erected barricades and storming over these barricades towards the center of the city. Delacroix' famous painting *Liberty Leading the People* was an apotheosis of the citizens' revolutions of the first half of the nineteenth century.

But the fall of the Bastille meant more than overthrow of a government; it was taken as the beginning of a new age, and as such, forced people to take a stand. The voices which welcomed the event were numerous. We have mentioned the enthusiasm with which Fox greeted the news of the fall of the Bastille. Richard Price, the British defender of the American Revolution, proclaimed in a sermon of September 1789: "After sharing in the benefit of one revolution I have been spared to be a witness to two other revolutions, both glorious," and Hegel, hearing about the French events in his small, despotically governed South German duchy, spoke of a "magnificent sunrise." The consensus among the educated was that revolution represented a step forward in the march of humanity. Condorcet was the most articulate spokesman for the goals at which the revolution was believed to aim: "Our hopes for the future condition of the human race can be subsumed under three important heads: the abolition of inequality between nations, the progress of equality within each nation, and the true perfection of mankind" (*Esquisse. . . , Dixième Époque*). Progress, democracy, and republic became attributes of the idea of revolution; it was filled with a positive content.

Nevertheless, a problem remained connected with this highly praised event of the French Revolution, particularly the fall of the Bastille. This action involved violence, a breach of law, and ever since the French Revolution violence also became an integral element in the concept of revolution. At the outset concern about the violence which accompanied the "triumph of the people" was not great because a revolt against despotism seemed just and could be justified with the doctrine of the "right of resistance," for which Locke and his followers had provided an enlarged theoretical basis. Still in 1804, when events in France had gone far beyond a defense against arbitrary despotism, Schiller in *Wilhelm Tell* (II, ii) upheld the right of revolution with arguments which reach back to the past rather than point to the future. His defense of violence used the cyclical element of return to the beginnings, the power of the stars, natural law, and the medieval doctrine of resistance against tyranny:

> *Nein, eine Grenze hat Tyrannenmacht.*
> *Wenn der Gedrückte nirgends Recht kann finden,*
> *Wenn unerträglich wird die Last—greift er*
> *Hinauf getrosten Mutes in den Himmel*
> *Und holt herunter seine ewgen Rechte,*
> *Die droben hangen unveräusserlich*
> *Und unzerbrechlich wie die Sterne selbst.*
> *Der alte Urstand der Natur kehrt wieder,*
> *Wo Mensch dem Menschen gegenübersteht;*
> *Zum letzten Mittel, wenn kein andres mehr*
> *Verfangen will, ist ihm das Schwert gegeben.*
> (Nay, there are bounds unto oppression's power;
> For when its victim nowhere finds redress,
> And when his burden may no more be borne,
> With hopeful courage he appears to heaven,
> And grasps from thence his everlasting rights,
> Which still inalienable hang on high,
> Inviolable as the stars themselves.
> Then nature's primal state returns once more,
> When man in conflict meets his fellow man;
> And at the last, when nothing else avails,
> The sword's fierce surgery must cure his ills;
> trans. P. Maxwell).

It should be added that when in later years the existence of a right to revolution was discussed traces of survival of the medieval right of resistance or of natural law thinking are always noticeable.

If the violence connected with the first events of the French Revolution could be explained and justified, further events gave the problem of the use of violence a more serious aspect. Under the pressure of internal and external enemies the new government continued to disregard legal restrictions and to take every measure which might serve to retain power: the period of terror began. Consequently, revolution became identified with a period of extra-legality while the government ruled arbitrarily, and this lasted as long as the government which the revolution had brought into power was threatened. When on October 10, 1793 the Convention declared that "the government of France is revolutionary until the peace" the meaning was that the government could use all measures deemed fit to secure the revolution. The period lasted until the Thermidor, the fall of Robespierre. During this period France possessed not only a "revolutionary government" but also "revolutionary tribunals" and a "revolutionary army." The word "revolutionary" therefore signified not only a person who takes an active part in a revolution but is also applied to a regime which exerts arbitrary power and to the measures which this regime might take. This meaning of the word is alluded to in a phrase by Condorcet in which he stressed that "the word revolutionary can be applied only to revolutions whose aim is freedom" (*Oeuvres*, XII, 516); a similar use of the term occurs frequently in the nineteenth century and then in connection with the Communist Revolution.

If in the summer of 1789 men had rallied enthusiastically around the cause of the French Revolution the terror diminished the number of adherents. Very early the alarm had been raised by Burke in his *Reflections on the Revolution in France* (1790). In allowing violence free rein, "We have no compass to govern us nor do we know distinctly to what part we steer." Burke had many followers who spread his views on the Continent. The impact of the writings of Burke and of his disciples was so great because they played on the fear of the people. Revolution became a destructive force which threatened the security, the property, even the life of every individual. Ever since Burke and since the terror, fear of revolution has been one of the persistent elements in the Western political atmosphere. It permeates Stendhal's *Le Rouge et le noir* in which Julien Sorel reflects: *Ils ont tant peur des Jacobins! Ils voient un Robespierre et sa charrette derrière chaque haie* ("They fear the Jacobins so much! They see a Robespierre and his cart-load behind each hedge").

Fear and condemnation became connected with a reawakening of the cyclical element in the notion of revolution. The development from monarchy to anarchy, to terror, and then to military despotism, was presented as unavoidable once the orderly road of law was abandoned. Such an argument can be found not only in the political debate and in political pamphlets but its importance is evidenced by the fact that belief in such a cycle was strongly held by the two most prominent conservative statesmen of the nineteenth century: Metternich, the leader of Europe in the age of restoration, spoke of a *cycle révolutionnaire complet* (in his *Profession de foi*); and Bismarck, the architect of a conservative Europe in the second part of the nineteenth century, maintained that, after a revolution, a historical cycle occurs which leads back to dictatorship, despotism, and absolutism (*Gedanken und Erinnerungen*, Ch. 21). When he made this statement Bismarck thought not only of the Revolution of 1789 but also of the French events from the middle of the nineteenth century which had issued in the rise of Napoleon III. But the idea of a cycle through which a revolution will end in the dictatorship of a military man was not only an antirevolutionary argument of conservatives but was generally regarded as a possibility actually inherent in any revolutionary movement. The idea of a Thermidor, i.e., the possibility that when the revolution has done its work of destruction the masses will rally behind any power who will restore order and stability, still haunted the leaders of the Russian Revolution in the twentieth century; Trotsky regarded the rise of Stalin as the Soviet Thermidor, which he defined "as a triumph of the bureaucracy over the masses."

It might be remarked that the idea of a cycle through which every revolution passes has also played a role in scholarly discussions and investigations of revolution. It was hoped that analyses of the cycle might serve to establish a law of revolution; these attempts cannot be considered to have been particularly successful; Crane Brinton, whose *Anatomy of Revolution* (1938) is one of the best studies of this kind, admitted that comparison, in order to be successful, had to be limited to a few great revolutions and this could not be regarded as a sufficient basis for valid generalizations.

Nevertheless, there is general agreement on what a revolution is. Although there are many modern definitions of revolution they all contain the same elements. They maintain that revolution is a sudden, violent change in the social location of power expressing itself in the radical transformation of processes of government, of the official foundations of sovereignty or legitimacy, and of the conception of the social order; revolutions are intended to usher in a new era in history. Clearly, all the constituent features of this definition—a violent political overthrow, a transformation of social life, a development which has relevance for all humanity—were characteristic of the French Revolution; it created the modern concept of revolution.

Nevertheless, it should not be overlooked that in the decades following the era of the French Revolution and of Napoleon the two different notions of revolution which had existed in the eighteenth century and which the modern concept of revolution combined, continued to exist as distinctive facets within the unified concept. Revolution still was regarded as indicating both: political changes in different countries; and an all-embracing general movement. There were still revolutions, and there was *the* revolution.

Violent political upheavals and changes of government—revolutions—were frequent in the nineteenth century: the July revolution of 1830 in France; the Decembrist revolution of 1825 in Russia; the Neapolitan revolution of 1820; the February revolution of 1848 in Paris; the German revolution of 1848. Of all of them it can be said that they were directed towards greater freedom. But the concrete aim of these revolutionary movements in the various countries varied widely: in one country it might be a written constitution; in another it might be an enlargement of the rights of parliament or a broader franchise; or it might be equality before the law in countries in which a feudal nobility still exerted judicial and administrative functions. The pride in national distinctiveness which the struggle against Napoleon had produced implied that each nation had a different individuality and had its particular problems which it had to solve in its own peculiar way. One might even go farther: one country might need a revolution; another might be able to live without it; and in the case of a revolution, causes and aim might differ.

Nevertheless, to explain developments which had shaken the entire European social structure as locally determined and patterned was hardly fully acceptable— particularly not to those whose position was threatened by the revolution. Friedrich von Gentz, the German translator of Burke, saw the French Revolution in its early years as a "protean monster" working in different forms and at different places. The revolution became a vast force with a life of its own: "The lava of revolution flows majestically on, sparing nothing. Who can resist it?" wrote one of its adherents, Georg Forster (*Sämtliche Schriften*, VI, 84), and his view of the revolution as a spreading, powerful, dynamic force was shared by the enemies of revolution. In their view revolution had no rational, calculable, or justifiable goal. It was a dynamic force changing the civilized order into anarchy and chaos. With the fall of Napoleon the dangers seemed to be eliminated and Metternich's entire policy aimed at protecting Europe from a renewal of the revolutionary outbreak. Yet, as the events of 1830 and then of 1848 showed, the revolutionary violence had been dormant, not extinguished, and proved again its power to break the fragile crust of civilization. The view of revolution as an elemental force, harbinger of chaos and destroyer of civilization, explains the impact which the events of 1830 and 1848 made far beyond the circle of the conservative rulers on wide groups of educated men. Barthold Georg Niebuhr, the historian of Rome, and one of the great personalities of the era of Prussian reform, collapsed when he heard of the July revolution in 1830 and never recovered. The deep impression which the outbreak of the revolution of 1848 made on Alexis de Tocqueville is reflected in the classical greatness of his own description:

*La monarchie constitutionelle avait succédé à l'ancien régime; la république, à la monarchie; à la république, l'empire; à l'empire, la restauration; puis était venue la monarchie de juillet. Après chacune de ces mutations successives, on avait dit que la Révolution française, ayant achevé ce qu'on appelait présomptueusement son oeuvre, était finie: on l'avait dit et on l'avait cru. Hélas! je l'avais espéré moi-même sous la restauration, et encore depuis que le gouvernement de la restauration fut tombé; et voici la*

*Révolution française qui recommence, car c'est toujours la même. . . . Quant à moi, je ne puis le dire, j'ignore quand finira ce long voyage; je suis fatigué de prendre successivement pour le rivage des vapeurs trompeuses, et je me demands souvent si cette terre ferme que nous cherchons depuis si longtemps existe en effet, ou si notre destinée n'est pas plutôt de battre éternellement la mer!* (*Souvenirs* in *Oeuvres complètes*, Paris [1964], XII, 87).

("The constitutional monarchy had followed the old regime; after the Republic, the Empire; after the Empire, the Restoration; then the July monarchy. After each of these successive changes, one might have said that the French Revolution, having accomplished what was presumptuously called its work, was ended; so people said and thought. Alas! I had hoped so myself during the Restoration and also after the Restoration government had fallen; but there was the French Revolution beginning all over again in the same old way. . . . As for me, I cannot agree, I don't know when this long voyage will end. I am tired of being misled by fogs, time and again, into believing that the coast is near, and I often wonder whether that solid ground which we have so long sought really exists, or whether our destiny is not rather to battle the sea forever!")

The Franco-Prussian War of 1870 filled Jakob Burckhardt's mind with anxiety and fear that unrest and revolution would put an end to European civilization; he began his lectures on the age of the French Revolution with the words:

*Zum Namen dieses Kurses ist zu bemerken, dass eigentlich alles bis auf unsere Tage im Grunde lauter Revolutionszeitalter ist, und wir stehen vielleicht erst relativ an den Anfängen oder im zweiten Akt; denn jene drei scheinbar ruhigen Dezennien von 1815 bis 1848 haben sich zu erkennen gegeben als einen blossen Zwischenakt in dem grossen Drama. Dieses aber scheint Eine Bewegung werden zu wollen, die im Gegensatz zu aller bekannten Vergangenheit unseres Globus steht. . . . Jetzt dagegen wissen wir, dass ein und derselbe Sturm, welcher seit 1789 die Menschheit fasste, auch uns weiter trägt* (*Gesamtausgabe*, Berlin [1929], VII, 426–27).

("I would like to say about the title of this course that really everything that has happened until today forms part of an age of revolution and perhaps we are only at its beginning or in its second act. For those three apparently tranquil decades from 1800 to 1848 have revealed themselves to be nothing but an entr'acte in the great drama. This drama seems to develop into a movement which stands in contrast to all the known past of our globe. . . . Now we know that one and the same storm which gripped the human world since 1789 carries us further along.")

The development of the idea of revolution in the nineteenth century was also influenced by the fact that whatever people thought about it was deeply colored by emotion. The French Revolution and subsequent upheavals created a feeling of insecurity, and insecurity creates fear; this established the undertone of all future political discussions and became the dominant voice at critical moments. However, it did not determine the middle-class attitude to revolution in more tranquil times. It is difficult to present a satisfactory statement on the question whether in the nineteenth century people regarded revolution as an evil or as a beneficial event; the problem needs more intensive and more subtle investigation than scholars have given it. The difficulty is that probably the views of the great bulk of the people, of the middle classes, on the problem of revolution, were deeply ambiguous. Because of underlying fear, the issue of violence and of terror played a great role in all the discussions. This becomes very evident in the writings of historians whose favorite topic in the first half of the nineteenth century was the history of revolutions, and that meant, of the English and French Revolutions. The inclination of the nineteenth-century historians—at least outside of France—was to place the English revolution above the French Revolution because the English had tried to maintain the old rights and not to create new ones; they had taken recourse to law, not to violence. For instance, that was the thesis of Friedrich Christoph Dahlmann, the most influential German liberal, who in the 1840's wrote books on the English as well as on the French Revolution. This thesis was not welcome to French historians who were unwilling to condemn a development which had raised their country to hegemony in Europe. François Guizot wrote about the English and French Revolutions: *Ce sont deux victoires dans la même guerre et au profit de la même cause; la gloire leur est commune; elles se relèvent mutuellement au lieu de s'éclipser* (beginning of his *Histoire de la Révolution d'Angleterre*, 1826). In the same way Auguste Mignet began his *Histoire de la Révolution française* (1824) pointedly: *Je vais tracer rapidement l'histoire de la révolution française qui commence en Europe l'ère des sociétés nouvelles, comme la révolution d'Angleterre a commencé l'ère des gouvernements nouveaux*. Nevertheless, it is evident that they had difficulty in fitting violence and terror in their benign picture of the French Revolution. Both Mignet and Adolphe Thiers, whose *Histoire de la Révolution française* appeared likewise in the twenties of the nineteenth century, recognized the necessity of extreme measures in the dangerous circumstances in which France found itself without approving or admiring them: *Il est une vérité qu'il faut répéter toujours: la passion n'est jamais ni sage, ni éclairée, mais c'est la passion seule qui peut sauver les peuples dans les grandes extrémités* ("There is a truth that must always be repeated: passion is never either wise or enlightened, but only passion can save people in great extremity"; Leipzig [1846], III, 187). And Jules Michelet, in the Preface of his *History of the French Revolution* (1847) directly attacks those who regard the revolution and terror as inextricable: "The violent terrible efforts which it was obliged to make in order not to perish in a struggle with the conspiring world have been mistaken for the revolution itself by a blind, forgetful generation." Even Carlyle who in describing the history of the French Revolution was not influenced by national or patriotic considerations gave much attention to the question of terror and represented the excesses of the revolution as a natural process, an almost unavoidable reaction to the corrupt regime which had preceded it.

The French historians of this period saw in social tension and in the struggle of classes one of the causes of revolution. Indeed, fears of revolution were kept alive by the sharpening of social conflicts in consequence of the increasing role of industrial activity in economic life. In the first half of the nineteenth century we have the "Peterloo" massacres (1819) and the Workers' Rebellion in Lyons (1832). We have in Silesia the weavers destroying the newly-installed spinning machinery. We have the beginnings of trade unions and Chartism; these movements were accompanied, and perhaps nourished, by writings which attacked the existing economic system and questioned the inviolability of private property. Louis Blanc, Pierre-Joseph Proudhon, Robert Owen, Adolphe Blanqui, began to develop socialist doctrines which implied a change in the governmental system. A bourgeoisie with the memories of the terror behind it and a threat to its property before it, began to look upon the idea of revolution with detestation. They began to accept the view of the conservative statesmen that there was a wide revolutionary conspiracy comprising such associations like the *Junge Deutschland* and the *Giovane Italia*. Even if they were liberals they rejected revolution and advocated evolution and reform as the appropriate road to social betterment.

However, if the possible social consequences of revolution deterred the middle classes they remained opponents of absolutism; moreover, they were the chief protagonists of that nationalism which the French Revolution had awakened and which kept a powerful hold over the minds of men in the nineteenth century. Revolts of oppressed people against foreign despotism were regarded as natural, national revolutions deserved support, and the actions of revolutionary movements which tried to achieve national unification had to be approved. This was the time when Europeans directed increased attention to the American Revolution because, more than the English and the French Revolutions it seemed to represent the model of a revolution which achieved national liberation. Simón Bolívar, as the leader of a similar movement in South America, was highly admired by the liberal bourgeoisie. The Greek fight against the Turks, the Polish rebellion against Russian rule, aroused general sympathy and Thaddeus Kosciusko, Giuseppe Mazzini, Giuseppe Garibaldi, and Louis Kossuth were welcomed and celebrated as heroes wherever they went. Perhaps one might say that revolutions in foreign countries when they were directed against oppression and despotism were encouraged. But revolutionary movement in one's own country, especially when they had a social content, were regarded with deep suspicion. Nevertheless, as the events of 1848 showed, because the European middle class in their attitude to revolution was ambivalent, they could participate in a revolution and try to harvest advantages from it after the revolution had broken out.

It should be added that a split mind in the attitude to revolutions was not a peculiarity of the liberal middle classes; the same split can be found among conservatives. Bismarck broke with the Gerlachs, i.e., the leaders of the conservative group to which he owed his political start, when the Gerlachs opposed any cooperation with Napoleon III whom they regarded as the incarnation of *the* revolution. Bismarck had no reservations to work together with this "heir of the revolution" if such policy would be of benefit to Prussia. Bismarck, as he wrote in his memoirs, had never any hesitation in an emergency to take recourse to revolutionary weapons.

Bismarck's dispute with the Gerlachs took place after the Revolution of 1848, and a "realistic" attitude was easy for him because the revolution in Germany had failed and the position of his class was no longer threatened.

The great influence of the events of 1848 on the thinking about revolution is unquestionable. The middle classes on the European continent could not take a purely negative attitude because of the active part which they had taken in the revolution. Moreover, the ruthlessness of the reactionary regimes, which after the failure of the revolution were in power in Central Europe, aroused resentment and the rapid increase in industrialization heightened misery. It appeared impossible to separate national and social questions; a revolution would have to have a social content. The most striking and enlightening illustration of the manner in which the thinking about revolution and about the issues of revolution was shifting can be found in Theodor Mommsen's *Römische Geschichte* (1854). The third book, which deals with the Gracchi is entitled "The Revolution." Mommsen's sympathy is on the side of the Gracchi brothers, particularly of Gaius who wanted to overthrow the regime of the aristocracy. And the reason for this revolution as Mommsen described it was the contrast between an agrarian and a money economy which with the expansion of Rome had issued in a serious conflict between capital and labor and created a proletariat living in utter misery.

It is astounding how little attention has been given to this section of Mommsen's work, which strikingly reveals a shift of the contents of the revolutionary struggle from the political to the social plane. This was the time when Marx was working out his revolutionary theory. Clearly, Marx's view was nourished from the atmosphere of the fifties. But it also opened a new chapter in the history of the idea of revolution because in entrusting the task of revolution exclusively to the proletariat it again changed the attitude of the middle classes and placed the bourgeoisie definitely in opposition to revolution.

This is not the place to present a thorough analysis of Marx's theory of revolution. Such an undertaking belongs to the article on Marxism for, as it has been said, "The revolutionary idea was the keystone of a theoretical structure . . . and an exposition of the Marxian revolutionary idea in complete form would be nothing other than an exposition of Marxism itself as a theoretical system" (Tucker, pp. 2, 5). In the following, emphasis will be placed on an analysis of the connection of the earlier ideas of a revolution with that of Marx and on Marx's influence in giving the concept a new shape.

Marx's notion of revolution is closely tied to a number of related terms and concepts and should be understood in connection with them. These notions are: world revolution; distinction between social and political evolution; class struggle; bourgeois revolution and socialist revolution; final revolution.

It is symptomatic of the central importance of the idea of revolution in Marx's general system that the word appears in so many associations. Like Hegel, Marx saw world history as an interconnected process and revolution was the engine which had this process moving from one stage to the next. Of course, there are other elements in Marx's thought which shaped his concept of revolution. There were the views that each stage of history—its political forms, institutions, intellectual outlook—was determined by its forms of production and that the struggles and conflicts in history can be explained as contrasts between classes: that all social history was essentially a history of class struggles. The further implication was that this was always a struggle between two classes, between the smaller ruling group which benefited from the prevailing mode of production and the mass of the exploited.

If Marx's ideas are placed in the context of the history of the idea of revolution it becomes evident that he accepts the notion of revolution as a movement changing and transforming *all* spheres of life; but because he sees social life as dependent on the prevailing forms of production he is able to establish a clear and well-defined relation between the general *révolution des esprits* and the particular revolutions which effected the overthrow of a political regime. The political revolution is part of the wider social revolution; it is an essential precondition because the ruling group controls power by means of political institutions, but at the same time a political revolution is only a partial phenomenon. A revolution will be complete only if it brings about a change in the modes of production so that the whole of social life will become transformed. Thus, political and social revolution are interconnected but also distinguishable: "Every revolution dissolves the old society: in that respect it is a social revolution; every revolution overthrows the old government, in that respect it is a political revolution."

Marx also accepts the notion of the simultaneous existence of one great, all-embracing revolution and of many different national revolutions, and he dissolves this apparent contradiction. Although his scheme of a world-historical progressive movement punctuated by class struggles is applicable to the whole of history, actually Marx is interested only in the most recent stages of this process: the change from the feudal to the bourgeois age, and from the bourgeois age to the age of communism. He maintained that in his own time there were bourgeois revolutions, i.e., revolutions with which the bourgeoisie ends the role of feudalism, and socialist revolutions in which the workers overthrow the rule of the capitalist bourgeoisie. Some of these revolutions may be both bourgeois and socialist according to the state of economic development which has been reached in the country in which the revolution takes place. However, one essential additional point of Marx's thought is that the communist revolution is the final revolution which will establish a form of economic life eliminating the contrast between rulers and ruled, exploiters and exploited. Being the last stage in the historical process this revolution must extend over the whole world. It is to be carried out on an international level. It must be a world revolution.

Because Marx invested revolution with a chiliastic element revolution became essential in moving the world historical process forward to its final goal; it is necessary and desirable and must be judged positively.

Because revolution designates a movement which brings about a new stage in world history it is distinguished from other similar concepts. Conspiracies or *coups d'état* might change the personnel of a government, but they do not transform the political and social system. A revolutionary is a man who recognizes the need for changing the entire system and acts accordingly. There was meaning in Marx's struggle against anarchists or terrorists. Revolutionary action could be successful only if it was carried out systematically in cooperation with the class of the exploited. It was a movement which required organization. Only those who took part in organizing the proletariat, the workers, towards action could be considered to be true revolutionaries. If the modern notion of revolution had arisen in the French Revolution, Marx's theories made revolution a clearly defined historical category.

### III. THE IDEA OF REVOLUTION FROM MARX TO LENIN

With Marx and with the emergence of Marxian socialism as a significant political factor a sharp line began to separate the bourgeois capitalist world and the world of the proletariat. Likewise in the history of the idea of revolution a distinction becomes necessary between the developments in the bourgeois attitude towards revolution and the changes which the Marxian theory underwent in the hands of socialist writers and politicians.

The formation of large Marxist mass parties openly proclaiming the need for revolution inevitably increased fear of revolution and demands for countermeasures. However, the attitude of liberal and democratic circles remained somewhat ambivalent. They were wedded to the idea of progress and although they might consider the possibility of a Marxist revolution in their own country with anxiety and abhorrence, they did not withhold approval from attempts to change the government system in countries with reactionary absolutist governments: for instance, the Russian Revolution of 1905 or the Young Turkish Revolution of 1908. However, a certain hardening in the attitude to revolution and to revolutionaries took place.

It is very difficult to determine to what extent Marxian thought exerted influence on the political and historical thinking among the bourgeoisie; it is evident that the idea of revolution became a central issue of political and historical thought. Historians found revolutions everywhere in history. What had been the defection of the Netherlands became the Dutch Revolution. The revolt of the Protestants in Prague was named the Bohemian Revolution, and, as in Max Weber's *Economics and Society*, each of the changes in city rule—from that of families to that of merchant guilds, from merchant guilds to democracy—became a "revolution." There was a tendency to fall back on

the early eighteenth-century practice of calling every violent change of government a revolution although it was now always assumed that some social change was involved.

However, the term "revolution" was now also applied to events outside the strictly political sphere and it seems likely that Marxian revolutionary theory with its stress on the close connection between political, economic, and intellectual events, had a part in this. For the first great step in widening the use of the term was made by applying it to significant, far-reaching changes in economic development. The concept of an "industrial revolution" is probably the best-known application of the term to the economic sphere. Although this combination of words had been in use since the twenties of the nineteenth century, "industrial revolution" became a well-defined concept describing the economic developments which began in England in the eighteenth century through Arnold Toynbee's *Lectures on the Industrial Revolution* published in 1884. The discovery of an "industrial revolution" spurred investigation into its causes, and they indicated that an expansion of trade which had preceded the "industrial revolution" played a significant role in accumulating the capital needed for the growth of industries: the "industrial revolution" had followed a "commercial revolution." If industry and commerce had their revolutions agriculture could not be left behind: the dissolution of the manor, the creation of individually owned landed estates, and the enclosure of areas which had been common property and in common use constituted an "agrarian revolution." To the same area of a great economic change in early modern Europe belonged two further combinations in which the word "revolution" appears—"price revolution," indicating the inflationary trend in prices during the sixteenth and seventeenth centuries caused primarily by the influx of precious metals from America—and "scientific revolution" which is meant to comprise the origin of the modern scientific outlook in the period from Galileo to Newton.

In later times these notions became independent of the particular events of early modern European history they had been coined to describe. We speak of a "second industrial revolution" in the twentieth century; we assume that the heavy plough and the use of horses produced an "agricultural revolution" in the early Middle Ages, and the "scientific revolution" of the seventeenth century was preceded by the "Copernican revolution." Nevertheless, in their original meaning all these notions—"industrial revolution," "commercial revolution," "agrarian revolution," "scientific revolution," "price revolution"—refer to various aspects of the gradual rise of a capitalist society in the period between the sixteenth and the nineteenth centuries. They are various facets of the social revolution which is both precondition and consequence of the bourgeois political revolution. Whether the scholars who introduced these notions were directly or indirectly influenced by Marx, it can hardly be an accident that the extension of the notion of revolution from the political to the economic sphere was originally concerned with those innovations and developments which Marx regarded as the economic basis of the bourgeois political revolution. In a general way it was the Marxian problem of the victory of capitalism over feudalism on which these various revolutions throw light.

Because these notions owe their origin to this crucial problem of modern history it is necessary to separate this use of the word revolution from one which is not connected with any significant intellectual or historical problem and which is primarily due to the fashionable appeal which the word revolution had gained. Frequently heard statements are: Planck's quantum theory represents a "revolution" in physics, or Freud brought about a "revolution" in psychology, or Roentgen's discovery of the X-ray "revolutionized" medicine. In all these cases the revolution to which these statements refer is limited to one field—physics, psychology, or medicine—and it is not suggested that it has any direct repercussions in other fields. Application of the word revolution is intended to indicate that Planck or Freud or Roentgen accomplished a breakthrough which placed further work in the area of their specialty on a new basis. The term revolution in these cases stresses the suddenness and the radical nature of the new development; it has no further implication than to signify a change brought about by a brief or sudden action.

We have pointed to the influence which Marxian thought might have exerted in the bourgeois camp. Unquestionably bourgeois ideas played their part also in the development of Marxian revolutionary theory. The emergence of Revisionism with its implied belief in a victory of socialism by means of democratic evolution shows some echo of the bourgeois theory that the evolution of capitalism had been a long process extending over centuries and was not due to sudden violent action. Economic developments even seem to indicate that a gradual improvement of the material situation of the workers within capitalism was not impossible. The theory of the Revisionists drew strength from the fact that developments since the middle of the nineteenth century (the failure of the revolutions of 1848 and then the Paris commune in 1871) had shown that civilians armed with rifles and barricades were of no avail against a government in possession of a disciplined army equipped with heavy weapons and

with artillery. Friedrich Engels himself directed attention to the fact that the difference in strength between those who possessed a monopoly in military power and civilians had immensely widened. Clearly, under these circumstances the writings of the orthodox Marxists anxious to refute the theses of the Revisionists tried to prove that revolution was necessary and inevitable and to outline the tactics which might make a victory of revolution feasible. It is from this point of view that Lenin's *State and Revolution* (1917) is remarkable in its argument that the state is an instrument of the ruling group and that as long as a state exists a victory of the suppressed class is impossible. Lenin also maintained that one could not rely on the political maturity of the mass of the workers; a revolution required leadership by a small select group. For Trotsky the politically and economically underdeveloped situation in Russia made a revolution necessary but the weakness of the Russian bourgeoisie made it also impossible that it could maintain itself in power. Control would come into the hands of the industrial workers and revolution would then spill over Russia's frontiers into Western Europe. Briefly, once revolution has started it could no longer be stopped. It became a "permanent revolution" until the triumph of socialism over the entire world had been achieved. The discussions on the general strike and particularly Georges Sorel's *Reflections on Violence* (1908) also served the purpose of proving the necessity and feasibility of revolution. With the general strike the workers possessed a weapon which could replace the fight of civilians on barricades. For this reason the Paris Commune on which Marx had made some brief observations became a paradigm; it exemplified the manner in which during a revolutionary struggle masses of workers could exert administrative control and form an effective power center. Briefly, the issue which dominated the Marxist camp was whether revolution remained necessary and feasible; the issue was placed on another level only after the Bolshevists had seized power in Russia.

### IV. FROM THE RUSSIAN REVOLUTION TO THE PRESENT

In the history of the idea of revolution the Russian Revolution represents, at least at this writing, the final and also the most prominent landmark. It was a political revolution which involved change in all spheres of life. As such it was also a social revolution. It was meant to extend over the entire world and to usher in a new stage in world history; it was a world revolution. Political revolution, social revolution, world revolution, all combined in what its adherents call the "Great October Revolution" of 1917.

Even if the conquest of power by the Bolsheviks was not followed by a revolutionary triumph over the entire world, the fact that a large part of the globe had cut itself off from capitalist society made the Russian Revolution an epoch-making event for friends and foes. The Russian Revolution became a paradigm of a revolution. A revolution had to bring about the seizure of power by a new class. It had to destroy the existing social structure and change all the forms of social life and this would almost necessarily involve a period of terror. One might add that a revolution had to be regarded with awe all over the globe. Any political change that did not fulfill these requirements was no longer regarded as a "true revolution."

The transformation of Germany from a monarchy to a republic in 1918 was not a revolution because, despite liberalization and democratization, the change of regime did not change the German social structure. On the other hand it is interesting and significant that both fascism and Nazism were anxious to claim that they were revolutions. Although their governments were formed by bargaining and negotiations they pretended to have attained power by a violent struggle (March of Rome, Reichstag Fire). They emphasized the thoroughness of the change which they had effected and represented their movements as "the wave of the future." In the dispirited and disillusioned decade after the First World War many insisted on the need for a thorough change; the Russian Revolution influenced the minds even of those who did not agree with its doctrines, by demonstrating that only a revolution could bring about significant changes. In a somewhat paradoxical way revolution became the legitimate instrument for change and change that was not brought about by revolution was not regarded as real change. The fascist leaders were well aware of the latent sympathy of the masses for revolutionary solutions, and so were their followers and imitators in Spain, in France, and in Eastern Europe, who used the same appeal to revolution. It is characteristic of the prestige which the word "revolution" had gained in the 1930's that even historians of American democracy designated the great ages of reform of the history of their country as periods of revolution; they introduced expressions like "the Jacksonian Revolution" or "the Rooseveltian Revolution," and even a conservative president believes that his legislative proposals will have greater appeal when he says that he expects they are effecting an "American revolution."

There were more potent reasons why the fascist leaders stressed the revolutionary character of their regimes. They wanted to free themselves from the onus of being leaders of a "counterrevolution." Originally counterrevolution signified a policy which undid what the revolution had done; but with the growing threat of socialist parties, with tensions and conflicts among the various groups of the bourgeoisie, the view began to spread that recourse to revolutionary measures and the establishment of a dictatorial regime based on force was necessary to maintain the existing order. The emphasis on the revolutionary nature of their regimes served well to mask the counterrevolutionary nature of fascist or Nazi politics.

But Mussolini and Hitler had another motive to insist on the revolutionary nature of their governments. In the times of the French Revolution the French revolutionary leaders called their government a "revolutionary government" because this name suggested extraordinary times in which strict observation of laws or legal procedure was not feasible. By stressing at every opportunity the revolutionary nature of their governments the fascist and Nazi leaders justified the use they made of arbitrary emergency legislation with disregard for legal rules and traditions; the appeal to the necessities of revolution served to embellish despotic arbitrariness.

The Russian situation was different. After they had seized power the Bolsheviks remained involved in war against counterrevolutionary forces for several years. They felt encircled and threatened by a hostile world and tried to mobilize all the oppressed and suppressed peoples of the world. This work was entrusted to the Communist International whose task was "to liberate the working people of the entire world. In its ranks the white, the yellow and the black-skinned peoples —the working people of the entire world—were fraternally united" (Theses of the Communist International on the National and Colonial Question, 1920). The communist leaders survived the civil war and outside intervention but for them the end of the war did not constitute an end of the period of emergency. Their world revolutionary aims had not been realized and since they regarded a half-socialist and a half-capitalist world as an impossibility, they continued to live in what they considered a transitional period threatened by outside enemies. While they could attempt to build socialism in their country the final order of society, communism, could be constructed only after the world revolution, which now was postponed into the future. The revolutionary period was extended for an uncertain time, and the rulers of Russia have kept the door open to fall back on revolutionary measures when it seems necessary. The same holds true for almost all the governments of a communist character. All of them assume that it will take time to build the new society at which they are aiming and until the communist revolution has conquered the world world revolution has not ended. This view is clearly reflected in the name which was given to the constitution of Castro's Cuba: it is entitled *Fundamental Law of the Revolution.*

Because of the dominant influence which the Russian Revolution exerts on all investigations and debates of the idea of revolution, issues that have seemed settled have again been opened up. Problems like the connection between culture and revolution, the question of the revolutionary character of a particular class, and the relation of anarchism and revolution, are beginning to be discussed in a new manner.

Discussion on the connection between culture and revolution focuses in the notion of a "cultural revolution"—a term which is widely used and debated. Russian scholars maintain that the term was first used by Lenin but the relation of cultural attainments, particularly of art to revolution, is an old issue of great complexity. Nearly every political regime uses the symbols of art for its own legitimation; accordingly, a new regime tends to demand and to promote a new artistic style. Although this has happened at almost all times it came out into the open as a conscious policy in the period of the French Revolution, and then in the nineteenth century the relation between art and revolution took a new form because some of the artists began to reject the idealistic tradition which had nourished art in previous centuries. They stressed the need for "revolutionizing art" and considered themselves to be the natural allies of political radicalism. In the second part of the nineteenth century, in the times of naturalism and realism, writers and poets used art for the purpose of expressing sharp social criticism and participated actively in the socialist movements. In general, however, the bond between modern artists and revolution was a radical attitude rather than agreement on a definite political program. This is shown by the fact that many of the Futurists went to fascism, others went to communism.

But if the artists acted as if they had a free political choice Marxism regarded the cultural world as a superstructure bound to the economic base of social life, and a revolution which changed the modes of production would produce, therefore, a new culture as well; the political and social revolution would be supplemented by a revolution in culture.

Indeed, in the years after the First World War when a revolutionary wave passed over Europe, writers and artists, particularly in Germany and Russia, believed they had to play a decisive role in building a new society. Walter Gropius, then a leader of modern German architecture, wrote in 1919: "Not until the political revolution is perfected in the spiritual revolution can we become free." Indeed, modern architecture in Europe owed much to commissions by the governments which political changes in Germany and Russia had installed. Yet the fact soon emerged that the Marxian concept of "cultural revolution" was not really compatible with what artists then understood by "revolutionary" art. This problem was recognized by Leon Trotsky in his book on *Literature and Revolution* (Eng. trans. 1925). The writings of modern poets like Alexander Blok and V. V. Mayakovsky are for him signs of the decline of the old civilization and forerunners of a new civilization. But Trotsky believed that a true new culture could develop only slowly and gradually on the basis of a fully developed new economic and social order. "Revolutionary art which inevitably reflects all the contradictions of a revolutionary social system should not be confused with socialist art for which no basis has as yet been made." For Trotsky modern art—which for him was identical with revolutionary art—has a certain transitional value and from this point of view it was logical that in the first years after the revolution Bolshevist cultural policy should promote modern art. But that was a brief period. After some years the Bolshevik leaders rejected modern art as standing outside real life; abstract art became prohibited—the works of modern abstract artists were literally placed into the cellars of museums. The art appropriate to communist society had to be comprehensible to the people and not only to a small, sophisticated elite. Art ought to show life in forms which could immediately be understood. It had to be "social realism." The mission of the proletarian revolution is "to convert all the gains of cultural life into an all-people's possession" and socialist culture must be "a truly national culture" (M. Kim, pp. 1–2). Of course, part of the great attention which Berthold Brecht has attracted in the East and in the West is that he was able to incorporate into his plays two different levels: on one level they teach simple lessons of political morality; on the other, they ask the lasting questions of the human condition. Marxists might make use of the prestige of a great name like that of Picasso, but in East and West the organized communist movements keep distance from the artistic avant-garde. The aims of cultural revolution are placed on a lower key. Lenin said: "For us this cultural revolution presents immense difficulties of a purely cultural (for we are illiterate) and material character (for to be cultured we must achieve a certain development of the material means of production); we must have a certain material base" (*Works*, XXXIII, 475). In concrete terms cultural revolution in Soviet Russia begins with education of the masses and is envisaged as a long-time process. It should perhaps be added that it appears that in China "cultural revolution" serves the purpose to eliminate all deviations from what the ruling group regards as Marxist-Leninist orthodoxy.

In consequence of the Bolshevist conquest of power the cause of revolution became identified with Russian policy. Russia was expected to be protector of any revolutionary movement and, on the other hand, any government that allied itself with Russia considered itself to be a revolutionary government and was regarded as such. The common bond was the enmity against Western capitalism and imperialism and this made each member of this alliance automatically a partner in revolution. The notion of revolution became absorbed in the contrast between East and West. This contrast extends over the entire globe. It can express itself as a racial struggle between blacks and whites. It can be a fight of farmers and peasants against the encroachments of urban civilization. It can be a struggle of natives against foreign rule. What the Communist International set out to do after the First World War became a reality after the Second World War. The colonial empires collapsed, and in many cases where this development involved a conflict the movements for independence and the newly independent states were anxious to get Russian support. But this has introduced great diversity into the revolutionary front. If originally in the eyes of Marxism a revolution was a class struggle, with the industrial workers on one side and the capitalist exploiters of the proletariat on the other, the composition of the army of the revolution has now become multifarious: concerted action, if it is taken, arises from political cooperation rather than from occupying an identical place in the social structure.

Although Marxism has become almost identical with revolution actually the great differences in economic problems and social structure which exist in the revolutionary camp have had the result that the name Marxism covers a great variety of aims and measures. Insofar as the debate which has developed concerns the idea of revolution it appears chiefly to discuss issues of revolutionary tactics. In the writings of Che Guevara and Régis Debray (*La Révolution dans la révolution*) the need to adapt the revolutionary struggle to the circumstances in Latin America is the main theme. Unification of the military and political command, guerrilla action aiming at control of small outlying areas, and then revolutionary propaganda to win over and train the population of these localities, that is the gist of their recommendations. They feel themselves to be true revolutionaries in contrast to the "Marxist Revisionists"—as Che Guevara as well as the Chinese

call the Moscow leaders—who have transformed the revolutionary struggle into political maneuverings. But it can hardly be doubted that, behind this dispute about tactics there lies a different idea about the world which should emerge in consequence of the revolution. The idea of using the instruments of modern civilization for organizing life in such a way that everyone receives according to his needs is confronted by the view that everything that forms part of this civilization is evil and that modern civilization has to be rejected in its entirety. The ghost which Marx believed to have laid when he drove Bakunin into the wilderness has returned. Clearly, there is an anarchist element in some of the revolutionary movements of the present—of the guerrillas, of the students, of the blacks—and it is no accident that in the May days of Paris of 1968 the black flag of anarchism could be seen next to the red flag of revolution.

In the nineteenth century revolution was envisaged as a brief, violent action which overthrows the existing government and in its consequences changes the social structure and ushers in a new period of history. Since the Russian Revolution the concept of revolution has begun to disintegrate. The sudden action if it occurs is not a culminating point but rather a beginning and the completion of a revolution is a long process. Particularly the slow and gradual changes in economic structure in underdeveloped countries are regarded as revolutions, and this has validity both for the East, where this process is called "building of a socialist society" and in the West, where it is called "modernization." The term "revolution" has somewhat lost the sharp edge which it possessed in the nineteenth century and is applied to any far-reaching change.

This is also reflected in recent scholarly discussions on the theory of revolution. They are interested less in the revolutionary event itself than in the underlying long-range reasons for revolution. They are concerned with the lack of harmony between the social system on the one hand and the political system on the other. And they try to discover the various phases in which this dysfunction develops and ask at which point a revolution becomes inevitable. Some social scientists want to eliminate the term "revolution" entirely from the scholarly terminology and replace it by "internal war." This expression hardly fits the revolutions of the past but it must be admitted that it has a certain validity in the present when revolution has become a weapon in power conflicts. Whether we think of the East or the West the belief has grown that the world can be managed and can be transformed by a series of carefully planned steps. The idea of revolution has lost the spontaneity which it possessed when people believed that they were carrying out the commands of history. As executors of this higher force they trusted that they were creating an entirely new world and it was this belief in a utopia which gave to the idea of revolution its strength in the nineteenth century and made it a powerful force in political thought from 1789 to 1917.

*BIBLIOGRAPHY*

There are a number of investigations of the term "revolution," e.g., Arthur Hatto, "'Revolution': An Enquiry into the Usefulness of an Historical Term," *Mind,* **58** (1949), 495–516; and Melvin J. Lasky, "The Birth of a Metaphor; On the Origins of Utopia & Revolution," *Encounter* (Feb. 1970), 35–45; (March 1970), 30–42. An analysis of the role which the idea of revolution played in modern history is provided by Karl Griewank, *Der neuzeitliche Revolutionsbegriff* (Frankfurt-am-Main, 1969). However, this book is somewhat fragmentary, and for the idea of revolution in the nineteenth century, see the investigation by Theodor Schieder, "Das Problem der Revolution im 19. Jahrhundert," *Historische Zeitschrift,* **170** (1950), 233–71. For a somewhat more theoretical discussion of the history of this idea in recent times see R. Koselleck, "Der neuzeitliche Revolutionsbegriff als geschichtliche Kategorie," *Studium Generale,* **22** (1969), 825–38; for an analysis of the complementary concept of counterrevolution, see Arno J. Mayer, *Dynamics of Counterrevolution in Europe, 1870–1956; An Analytic Framework* (New York and London, 1971). For investigations of the Marxist concept of revolution see Robert C. Tucker, *The Marxian Revolutionary Idea* (New York and Toronto, 1969); and Reidar Larsson, *Theories of Revolution* (Stockholm, 1970). Various aspects of the problem are discussed in Vol. VIII of *Nomos* entitled *Revolution,* ed. Carl J. Friedrich (New York, 1966). For the wider philosophical and sociological aspects of the problem see Karl Mannheim, *Ideologie und Utopie* (Bonn, 1929), trans. L. Wirth and E. Shils as *Ideology and Utopia* (London, 1936); Hannah Arendt, *On Revolution* (New York, 1963); and A. T. Van Leeuwen, *Development through Revolution* (New York, 1970). Historical studies particularly focused on the problem of revolution are Eugen Rosenstock-Huessy, *Die europäischen Revolutionen und der Charakter der Nationen* (Stuttgart and Cologne, 1951); Crane Brinton, *The Anatomy of Revolution* (New York, 1938); and idem, *Preconditions of Revolution in Early Modern Europe,* eds. Robert Forster and Jack P. Greene (Baltimore and London, 1970); Franco Venturi, *Il populismo russo* (1952), trans. Francis Haskell as *Roots of Revolution* (New York, 1960; also reprint); Michael Walzer, *The Revolution of the Saints* (Cambridge, 1965). The approach of the modern social sciences to the problem of revolution is described in Lawrence Stone, "Theories of Revolution," *World Politics,* **18** (1966), 159–76; and a work of social science character on this topic is Chalmers Johnson, *Revolutionary Change* (Boston, 1966). See also Harry Eckstein, "On the Etiology of Internal War," *History and Theory,* **4** (1965), 133–63. For Marxist views of special aspects of the problem, see J. V. Polišenský, "The Social and Scientific Revolutions of the 17th Century," XIII International Congress of Historical Sciences, Moscow, August 16–23, 1970, published by Central Department of Oriental Literature (Moscow, 1970); and M. Kim, "Some Aspects of Cultural Revolution and Distinctive Features of Soviet Experience in Its Implementation," XIII International Congress of Historical Sciences, Moscow, August 16–23, 1970, published by Central Department of Oriental Literature (Moscow, 1970), pp. 1–14; the problematic character of the concept in the present-day world is reflected in Albert Camus' famous book, *L'Homme révolté* (Paris, 1951).

FELIX GILBERT

[See also **Anarchism;** Astrology; **Crisis; Cycles; Marxism;** Nationalism; Utopia.]

# RHETORIC AFTER PLATO

SINCE the time of Greek antiquity, the definition of "rhetoric" has changed from century to century as the idea of "rhetoric" has been expanded to cover the whole of the art, or contracted to include only a part. Generally, idea and definition—responding to the political or intellectual uses to which the art was put—have moved from considerations of language to the arguments or the passions expressed by language, to the effects produced by rhetorical compositions, to the relationships between such compositions and abstract concepts ("truth" or "justice"); then back to language. But whatever the particular definition, the term has been applied to the use of language (or of special kinds of language) for the moving, pleasing, or persuading of readers or auditors to specific judgments, decisions, or actions.

In the work of Plato, consistently with his general philosophical method, rhetoric is considered in the context of other problems, metaphysical or moral, and has neither the status nor the specification of a separate art. But between Plato and Isocrates, a number of technical treatises were produced which, according to report (none of them have survived), regarded rhetoric as the art of forensic or political oratory and provided precepts for the division of a speech into its parts and for the handling of language and style. Isocrates himself practiced his art as orator, writer of speeches, and teacher, at a time when speech-making was an important part of the political life of Greece. His main writings on rhetoric (*philosophia* or *logos*) are found in his early essay *Against the Sophists* and in his late speech on the *Antidosis;* there are also fragments collected from Greek and Roman authors.

Isocrates believes that the end of persuasion is achieved less through observance of a set of rules or an "art" than through the possession by the orator of a wide range of talents, qualities, and knowledge. Among these are his true moral character and his native genius for eloquence. That genius must be developed and directed, from youth, through the model provided by the tutor's life and practice, through principles of ethical and political philosophy, through *technē* and *logos* which treat of rhetorical rules proper: the choice of the proper forms of discourse, the correct ordering of the parts, the varying of the thoughts appropriately to the matter, the achievement of rhythmical and harmonious diction. But Isocrates insists that eloquence can never be reduced to rule, that it is akin to poetry in its free search for noble subjects and elegant language.

Isocrates adds to these ideas the distinction of the various kinds of oratory—the judicial, the epideictic (or the rhetoric of display), and the political; he speaks of the necessity of winning the judges' sympathy; and he names such particularly rhetorical forms of argument as probabilities and conjectures. He thereby completes a schematism for the consideration of rhetoric that will remain at the basis of the Greek and Roman tradition. It centers about the effect to be produced on a specific audience, about the moral character of the orator, and about the rules for the making of the speech. In Isocrates these are scattered and unsystematic ideas; his successors reduce them to system and art. Aristotle's *Rhetoric* (ca. 330 B.C.) is the earliest complete treatise that we have; it is also the most systematic. His "art" is not a mere reassemblage of earlier notions about rhetoric. It is a reorienting and reorganizing of those notions in a new philosophical synthesis.

Aristotle defines rhetoric as "the faculty of discovering the possible means of persuasion in reference to any subject whatever." This extension to "any subject whatever" frees rhetoric from the limitation to fixed and conventional matters, and the concept of the "possible means of persuasion" opens the way to Aristotle's idea of the three kinds of rhetorical proofs. If persuasion is to be effected, it will be persuasion of certain persons (for Aristotle, the audience is always a particularized group, never an individual) to opinion or judgment or action; the moral character, the intellectual capacities, the state of knowledge, and the emotional potential of those persons will determine the way in which the speech is made and the arguments of which it is composed. A first set of proofs (the "emotional" or "pathetic") consists of those parts of the speech that are designed to affect the specific audience. A second set (the "ethical") presents to that audience the apparent moral character of the speaker, adjusted to the audience in the particular circumstances. (This is not the "true" character of the speaker, as with Isocrates, but "rhetorical" character.) A third set (the "logical") is the argument proper, stated in the forms appropriate to the audience of rhetoric: the enthymeme (a truncated syllogism or deduction which omits a premiss) and the example (a kind of rhetorical induction, or seeing the universal in the particular case).

Aristotle devotes his treatise to an analysis of the ways in which these proofs are adapted to each of the kinds of rhetoric (deliberative, forensic, epideictic), and to a study of the passions, of political circumstances, and of logical forms. His idea of rhetoric is primarily an idea of the proofs and arguments useful in the rhetorical situation, only secondarily an idea of the style, or language, or expression in which the argument is stated. But style is important, "for it is not sufficient to know what one ought to say, but one must also know how to say it, and this largely contributes to making the speech appear of a certain character" (III, 1). Rhetoric is never, for Aristotle, an art of language in the narrow way in which it was later considered.

In the history of the idea of rhetoric after Aristotle, those constitutive elements that Aristotle had organized into a philosophical system became separated one from another and, as isolated, became the central subjects of rhetorical treatises. Language and style are probably the chief and most recurrent of these; but the order and arrangement of the parts of a speech, the character of the orator, the nature of the proofs, or the kinds or classes of speeches frequently serve as the basic matter. Such shifts are explained by general philosophical orientations and methods at a given time, by the place of rhetoric in public life or in the schools, and by the status of related arts and disciplines.

In the two centuries following the writing of Aristotle's *Rhetoric*, oratory in Greece became less a public performance and more a form of pleading in the courts; the treatment of rhetoric took the form of technical manuals and textbooks. As the notions of ethical and pathetic proofs disappeared, matters of logical argument, of arrangement of the parts, and of style came to dominate the treatises. An example of the end product of that Hellenistic development exists in the Latin *Rhetorica ad Herennium*, written around 85 B.C. and apparently derived directly from the Greek *technai*. It distinguishes again the three kinds of speeches, epideictic, deliberative, and judicial, and divides the art into five faculties: invention (the logical argument), disposition (the arrangement of the parts), style, memory, and delivery. Most important of all is the *inventio*, which enables the orator to discover the "types of issue" involved in the individual case and to develop proofs and refutations (the whole of the discussion at this point is highly legalistic, rather than merely logical). Under *dispositio*, the author lists the quantitative parts of a speech in their proper order: the exordium, the narration, the division, proof and refutation, the conclusion. The third faculty, that of *elocutio* or style, provides the framework for a treatment of the three styles—the grand, the middle, and the simple—and their cognate defective styles, and of the figures of thought and of diction, described and exemplified in great detail.

One of Cicero's earliest writings on rhetoric was the *De inventione* (ca. 85 B.C.), the first part of a full treatise, projected but never written. It is a body of precepts intended for the speaker in the law courts, analyzing in detail the various issues, proofs, and refutations that appertain to the kinds of cases. Cicero's handling of these materials is similar to that of the *Ad Herennium*, as is his division of the speech into its six consecutive parts. About forty years later (ca. 44 B.C.), Cicero wrote another "de inventione," called the *Topica* in imitation of Aristotle's *Topica* since it aims to inquire into the general sources of argument. It is hence less closely restricted to legal cases and proofs; Cicero summarizes the sources of arguments, or "topics," as "definition, partition, etymology, conjugates, genus, species, similarity, difference, contraries, adjuncts, consequents, antecedents, contradictions, causes, effects, and comparison of things greater, less and equal" (xviii. 71). At about the same date, Cicero's *De partitione oratoria* ("of the classification of rhetoric") took a broader view of the art of rhetoric, discussing in detail once again the three functions of invention, arrangement, and style, the structural divisions of a speech, and the matter at issue. The last of these sections returns to the materials of the *De inventione*, studying at length the bases of prosecution and defense, of evidence and witness, as they may be used in the law courts.

Cicero's three treatises represent a narrower view of rhetoric, one that concentrates upon technicalities of structure and argument and that sees these as related to the instruction or the practice of the courtroom orator. In other writings on rhetoric, Cicero expressed his larger vision of the art, more broadly based both philosophically and historically. Most important of these was the *De oratore* (in three books, composed in 55 B.C.), which breaks away from the tradition of the Greek manuals and seeks its orientations in Roman public life of the time. Like Isocrates, it conceives of the orator as a man of great natural gifts who is soundly educated in all areas of philosophy (especially ethics and politics) and of science. He knows at least as much of these disciplines as he must in order to sway his listeners through a combination of emotional and intellectual appeals. He must be a master of language: eloquence of diction will impose the speaker's ideas upon his audience, will move it to the kind of action or decision that he wishes. The notion of oratory as dominating its listeners is typically Ciceronian, typically Roman; and issues and arguments or topics, the kinds of speeches and the arrangements of parts, are seen as less effective instruments—therefore less important—than the genius, the knowledge, the experience of the orator and his command of language.

In his *Brutus* (46 B.C.), Cicero wrote a history of Roman oratory and a defense of the tradition that had culminated in his own performance. Like the *Brutus*, Cicero's *Orator* (late 46 B.C.) was written as a polemical document, defending his own rhetorical practice (and his own idea of rhetoric) against the new school of "Atticists" who proposed a return to the plain and clear style, to instruction rather than the arousing of the emotions, to severe logic. Cicero devotes the major part of the letter to *elocutio* or diction, and within that category, to the placing of words and the establishment of prose rhythms. In so doing, he indicates one of the main directions that rhetorical theory will take in the century following.

Between Cicero and Quintilian, the next great Roman theorist, rhetorical theory flourished in the Greek or the Greco-Roman schools whose activity was centered in Athens, in Alexandria, even in Rome. It was dominated by the "Alexandrian" mode, the tendency to apply philological techniques to detailed matters of expression. Style in all its aspects—the several "styles," the figures, rhythms, and harmonies—came to constitute the very stuff of rhetoric. An example is the *De compositione verborum* ("on the arrangement of words") of Dionysius of Halicarnassus (ca. 30 B.C.), devoted largely to matters of rhythm in verse and in prose. The *De elocutione* ("on style") of Demetrius (ca. A.D. 70), after beginning with such a discussion of rhythmic structures, pursues primarily an analysis of the "styles." Demetrius distinguished four styles: the elevated, the elegant, the plain, and the forcible; for each one, he indicates the subject matter to which it is appropriate, the kinds of words and arrangements that characterize it, the figures that are most useful, and (continuing a long tradition) the correlative vice. As examples are drawn from every kind of writing in Greece, verse and prose, the treatise is no longer classifiable as a work on oratory, but belongs to "rhetoric" viewed broadly as "effective expression."

The treatise *On the Sublime*, supposedly by an unknown "Longinus" and dating from the first century A.D., is also pseudo-rhetorical. Its main relationship to

169

rhetoric comes in the way it considers the triad of author-work-reader with respect to the effect produced by the "sublime" or the elevated style. Longinus places that effect squarely in the special talents or the genius of the writer—in whatever literary form he may choose to operate. "Character" is replaced by the real and permanent faculties of the writer, "persuasion" by an irresistible ecstasy felt by the audience at given moments in its experience of the work. Thus the principal locus of the rhetorical effect shifts from the audience (where it had been in Aristotle) and from style (where it had been in Demetrius) to the genius of the writer. Similarly, argument disappears as structure disappears; the effect of sublimity is the instantaneous product of sublimity in the soul of the writer as it selects and presents a sublime object through appropriate artistic means.

In Quintilian's *Institutio oratoria* (ca. A.D. 90) the movement of the idea of rhetoric towards the idea of the rhetorician comes to fulfillment. The real total being of the orator is here the center of attention: the treatise is an *institutio* since it aims to form and educate the orator; his education will pursue two goals, the production of the "good man" and the provision of those kinds of knowledge and those techniques that will make him "skilled in speaking." Because the good man is the virtuous man, a necessary part of his education will be an education in philosophy, ethics, politics; and these he must know fully and substantially—rather than to the limited degree required by a particular "case." "Skill in speaking" means a mastery of all the component parts of the art of rhetoric: in this connection, Quintilian reintroduces, examines, expands, and reduces to precept all the technical principles long since developed in the Greco-Roman tradition. While some heed is given to the nature of the audience and much to the construction of arguments, fundamentally it is the moral person of the orator that achieves the ends of oratory.

At the opposite pole to Quintilian's orator-centered *Institutio* is the group of style-centered works by Hermogenes (ca. A.D. 170); they represent fully the Alexandrian mode. Neither orator nor audience is of interest to Hermogenes, whose treatises are devoted either to cases and arguments (*On Legal Issues, On the Invention of Arguments*) or to style (*On the Various Kinds of Style*)—that is, to the internal construction of the speech. His long book on the "characters" or "ideas" of the various styles (he distinguishes seven, some of which are variants of the three major styles, the perspicuous, the great or sublime, the elaborate or beautiful) perhaps represents his major concern. After setting up a mechanism of eight constituent parts for each "idea"—argument, diction, method or order

of presentation, arrangement of words, figures or tropes, numbers, periods, and clauses—Hermogenes proceeds to discover what particular form each of the parts must take in each of the styles. Contrary to most earlier theorists, he considers the "ideas" as open and flexible and as capable of being combined.

In the millennium that comprises the Middle Ages, roughly the fourth to the fourteenth centuries, a significant change came about in the idea of rhetoric. Whereas in the classical period rhetoric had been variously considered in relationship to its public functions—in the forum, in the courts, in the open letter—with the end of the Roman Empire those functions either ceased to exist or were so transformed as to demand a redefining of the art. Most of the theoretical treatises were lost; they would be rediscovered only in the Renaissance. Those that remained, Cicero's *De inventione*, the *Ad Herennium*, and Quintilian (in some parts), emphasized the more mechanical aspects of the art: precepts for organization of the argument, recommendations for expression and style. But this does not mean that rhetoric as a way of thinking and of writing disappeared; rather, it came to pervade all intellectual pursuits during the Middle Ages, to give them their basic forms and orientations. In order to see it properly during this millennium, one must consider it not as a separate art or discipline, not as a distinct part of the university curriculum, but as an approach to the intellectual disciplines that was almost universal in its application.

In the domain of civil philosophy, the Ciceronian distinction of deliberative, demonstrative, and judicial oratory provided the basis for speaking on all the matters pertinent to civil affairs. Theologians discovered in rhetoric the devices for interpreting theological writings; the recognition of the four possible "senses" of a work (literal, allegorical, moral, anagogic) resulted from a transposition into the spiritual domain of interpretative techniques developed for mundane works. The Augustinians thus made of rhetoric an instrument of theology. As a part of logic, largely in the Aristotelian tradition, rhetoric took on the function of treating "probable" (as opposed to "necessary") matters, producing for those matters the kinds of proofs of which it was especially capable. It could therefore accompany logic and dialectic as instruments for the various branches of rational philosophy. In its own right, narrowly reduced to a simple art of words, rhetoric pursued its inquiry into questions of style, the figures, and the general concerns of "elocution." It became slowly assimilated to poetry, insofar as poetry was regarded as a form of discourse using a special kind of language and achieving distinct kinds of persuasion.

The achievement of rhetoric in the Middle Ages has been summarized as follows by Richard McKeon:

In application, the art of rhetoric contributed . . . not only to the methods of speaking and writing well, of composing letters and petitions, sermons and prayers, legal documents and briefs, poetry and prose, but to the canons of interpreting laws and Scripture, to the dialectical devices of discovery and proof, to the establishment of the scholastic method, which was to come into universal use in philosophy and theology, and, finally, to the formulation of scientific inquiry, which was to separate philosophy from theology. In manner of application, the art of rhetoric was the source both of doctrines which have long since become the property of other sciences . . . and of particular devices which have been applied to a variety of subjects . . . (1952, pp. 295–96).

Conceived and applied in so many different ways, rhetoric approached in the Middle Ages the status of a universal science.

In the Renaissance, the situation of rhetoric was further complicated by the rediscovery and reinterpretations of a number of ancient treatises (Greek, Hellenistic, Alexandrian, Roman). Much humanistic and scholarly effort was devoted to this enterprise. Since some of these documents treated primarily the matter of style and the figures, they reinforced recent tendencies to regard rhetoric as an art of words and expression (for example, Demetrius *On Style* and Hermogenes). In so doing, they established a link between rhetoric and poetic that was to persist through the Renaissance and beyond. Already in the twelfth and thirteenth centuries, the so-called "arts of poetry" had devoted much of their attention to the rhetorical figures; these were parts of the "art" that could be understood, reduced to rule, and taught without worrying about more philosophical aspects. At the same time, as the Ciceronian parts of "invention, disposition, and elocution" had been extended to all forms of composition, a common ground was seen for poetic and rhetoric in the matter of style. Cicero's "elocution," the figures and styles of the rhetoricians, and Aristotle's "diction" (in the *Poetics*) became the single subject of treatises devoted to expression and style.

*Elocutio* provided a basis for joining poetic and rhetoric on the level of language; the relationship was extended, through *inventio* and *dispositio*, to the whole of the two arts. Rhetoric became the art that directed the discussion and the practice of poetry. In Italy, Alessandro Vellutello, a sixteenth-century commentator on Petrarch, considered the whole of the *Canzoniere* as a single poem whose exordium was contained in the first sonnet, its narration in the sonnets and other poems following, its conclusion (in the form of a prayer) in the final *canzone*. In France, such writers of arts of poetry as Thomas Sebillet, Jacques Peletier, and Pierre de Ronsard organized their discussions around the categories of invention, disposition, and elocution, making of the first an equivalent to plot, the second a way of regarding order in the poem, and the third a synonym of style. When, about 1550, Aristotle's *Poetics* came to be generally studied, it was assimilated both to Horace's *Ars poetica* (read rhetorically in terms of its *res:verba* distinction) and to the analytical devices found in the *De inventione* and the *Ad Herennium*.

Rhetoric also flourished again as an independent art of public oratory. One of the favorite exercises of the humanists was the set speech, in Latin or Italian or French, for the great occasion; they wrote such pieces of epideictic oratory either on the models of Cicero and Demosthenes or according to the precepts found in the formal treatises. Aristotle's *Rhetoric*, rediscovered, translated, and commented by many scholars, enriched the conception of the art throughout the late Renaissance; and although it did not alter fundamentally the Ciceronian directions, it led to more philosophical considerations with respect to the nature and the functioning of rhetoric. The new arts of rhetoric written during the sixteenth century were mostly Ciceronian in inspiration; but some, using the dialogue form of Plato (or Cicero) or imitating the Aristotelian treatise, tried to achieve a broader and more inclusive vision of the art. Still others, starting from one of the ancient treatises, either expanded upon it or raised objections to its basic positions: so Peter Ramus in his *Rhetoricae distinctiones in Quintilianum* (1559), where he attacks Quintilian's theory as an overextension of the idea of rhetoric and proposes, instead, a notion of the discipline restricted to "elocution" and "action." Writers like Ramus thought of rhetoric as a living and practical art, primarily for the teaching of writing in all literary and philosophical forms, secondarily for the formation of orators.

A tendency to restrict the art of rhetoric, rather than to expand and diversify it, proved hardly acceptable to the seventeenth century; theorists and writers then wished to develop encyclopedic attitudes (inherited from the Renaissance) that would unite and unify the various arts. In France, the prevalent Ciceronian and Quintilianesque modes, restated in the new "rhetorics" (cf. René Bary and Le Sieur Le Gras), were modified to adjust them to a contemporary situation in which deliberative, judicial, and epideictic oratory had been replaced by the "eloquence of the courts" and the "eloquence of the pulpit." Later, in René Rapin for example, the notion of "eloquence" (the current equivalent of rhetoric) was extended to all forms of expression, in poetry, in history, in philosophy as well as in oratory. Rapin saw eloquence in all areas as seeking the dual ends of instruction and pleasure, with

171

the latter serving the former. But it achieved them, not by applying innumerable technical rules, but by appealing to the taste and judgment of the audience.

Taste and judgment, in this idea of rhetoric, were found in the author as well as in the public. The author applied them in every choice that he made during the process of composition; the public applied them at every moment of its exposure to the work. In all, these qualities were formed by the kind of education that Quintilian had outlined. Both the shift from rules to taste and the loss of the idea of a separate art, in the seventeenth century, were significant modifications of the idea of rhetoric; they were the beginnings of a break with the classical-Renaissance tradition. In spite of the persistence of Horace, Cicero, and Quintilian in the manuals and in the schools, the way was being prepared for essentially new conceptions.

Those new conceptions in the eighteenth century were not without earlier sources. In Diderot and D'Alembert's *Encyclopédie* (1751–80), the place of rhetoric under the faculty of reason (in the Table of Human Knowledge) and its definition as "the science of the qualities [or of the "ornaments"] of discourse" were both derived from Francis Bacon's *Advancement of Learning* (1605). Bacon, to be sure, had assigned rhetoric to the imagination; but its use, he said, was "to apply and recommend the dictates of reason to the imagination, in order to excite the affections and will" (*Advancement*, Book VI, Ch. III). The section on rhetoric in the *Discours préliminaire* of the *Encyclopédie*, however, explains the change: rhetoric serves for the communication of passions, not of ideas; it is the product of genius, not of rules or precepts; and hence any idea of a separate art or science of rhetoric should be abandoned. For the main ideas in the article "Rhétorique" in the *Encyclopédie*, the author went back to Bernard Lamy's *La Rhétorique, ou l'art de parler* (1668), a treatise which had extended the art to the whole field of belles-lettres or "philology." Largely a work on the nature and origins of language and on the character of figurative expression, Lamy's *Rhétorique* was bound to be attractive to the *philosophes* who, in all areas, including rhetoric, wished to go to the "nature," the "origins," the "causes" of human activities.

Although the French were, in theory, destroying rhetoric as an art, the English were, in their practice, demonstrating its powers and its excellence; this was the century of Burke and Pitt, whose tradition was continued by such nineteenth-century orators as Gladstone. The practice, in both periods, was a consequence of the kinds of general education offered in the schools and universities, not of any particular attention to the art. With the ancient theorists forgotten or discarded (except for a few classical scholars), rhetoric became, both in England and in America, the schoolbook study of writing and composition, indistinguishable from simple rules of grammar and syntax. In France, the deterioration reached the point where the term *rhétorique* meant an undesirable hiding of meaning, in anything written, by excessive and meretricious ornament; this sense is still current in certain French circles. Yet something like a return to an idea of rhetoric as the marshalling and presentation of persuasive arguments has flourished in the debating societies in the British universities and in American university departments of speech and public address. Especially in the latter, "rhetoric" is sometimes extended to embrace persuasive public action as well as persuasive public speaking; so that the art returns again to the realm of politics, where it had begun.

In England and America also, in a more strictly literary development, critics have applied the general tenets of rhetorical analysis to many kinds of works that are normally considered to be nonrhetorical. Their basis for so doing is the assumption that however "pure" a work may be, it contains certain features that are directed towards influencing its audience in specific ways. These may be statements meant to give a "character" to the writer or the narrator; or they may be alterations of the argument (in a philosophical work); or they may be appeals to an audience's tastes or knowledge or predilections: in a word, the whole of the traditional rhetorical trilogy. Wayne Booth's *The Rhetoric of Fiction* (1961) is typical of this approach as used for narrative writing. There have recently been discussions of the "rhetoric of philosophy" (Kenneth Burke), of rhetorical devices used by philosophers such as Descartes, Pascal, and Bayle, by poets such as Ronsard. In this contemporary movement, the idea of rhetoric has been refined and specialized as an instrument for the analysis of all literary forms; and this has led to an expansion of its usefulness and a renewed sense of its validity.

## BIBLIOGRAPHY

C. S. Baldwin, *Ancient Rhetoric and Poetic* (New York, 1924); idem, *Medieval Rhetoric and Poetic* (New York, 1928). Wayne C. Booth, *The Rhetoric of Fiction* (Chicago, 1961). D. L. Clark, *Rhetoric in Greco-Roman Education* (New York, 1957); idem, *Rhetoric and Poetry in the Renaissance* (New York, 1922). H. M. Davidson, *Audience, Words, and Art: Studies in Seventeenth-Century French Rhetoric* (Columbus, Ohio, 1965). J. H. Freese, Introduction to Aristotle's *The "Art" of Rhetoric*, Loeb Classical Library (London and Cambridge, Mass., 1926). O. B. Hardison, Jr., *The Enduring Monument: A Study of the Idea of Praise in Renaissance Literary Theory and Practice* (Chapel Hill, N.C., 1962). G.

Kennedy, *The Art of Persuasion in Greece* (Princeton, 1963). R. McKeon, "Rhetoric in the Middle Ages," *Critics and Criticism: Ancient and Modern,* ed. R. S. Crane (Chicago, 1952). E. Olson, "The Argument of Longinus' *On the Sublime," Critics and Criticism: Ancient and Modern,* ed. R. S. Crane (Chicago, 1952). B. Weinberg, *A History of Literary Criticism in the Italian Renaissance* (Chicago, 1961).

BERNARD WEINBERG

[See also Analogy; Education; **Genius; Platonism, Rhetoric and Literary Theory in; Style;** Taste.]

# RIGHT AND GOOD

THE IDEAS of the good and the right span the greater part of the field of moral philosophy. They conceptualize basic phenomena in human life: the good, that men are purposive or goal-seeking beings who have desires and aspirations; and the right, that men carry on their lives in groups that require some modes of organization and regulation involving practices, rules, and institutions. Perhaps the only other moral idea approaching them in scope is virtue as conceptualizing forms of character.

Philosophers of each generation have analyzed the concepts, bringing to them the analytic tools of successive philosophical movements, or invoking models from the particular stages in the advance of the sciences or frontiers of human knowledge. Ordinary uses, cultural molding, philosophical formulations, interact with one another. The product finds its place in the moral consciousness of men when they think and talk in terms of the good and the right.

The story of the good and the right is not, as it has so often seemed, the tale of two isolated concepts sitting for philosophical portraits in a variety of rather grand poses. Historical changes in the dominant cultural emphases—in the patterns of aspiration and modes of institutional regulation—also transform the conceptual relations. Varied historical movements and social organizations leave their mark on the very structure of the concepts. As men's understanding of their world advances, as their consciousness gains in scope and in depth, so their moral philosophy is shaped by the leading motifs of their scientific and cultural disciplines. And the resultant moral concepts are not merely products. For the concepts themselves do not function alone, but enter into conceptual frameworks in which they give organizational direction and which they shape for use.

*Two Basic Frameworks.* The two major frameworks in which the good and the right are chiefly at home may be called, respectively, the *goal-seeking framework* and the *juridical framework.* They are not complementary portions of the moral field but alternative ways of organizing the whole field to carry out the tasks of morality.

The goal-seeking framework assumes a structure of appetition or desire in human life. The good is defined either by position of the objective in this pursuit or by some basic character of the objective. Knowledge of the good helps generate a grasp of appropriate means towards its achievement. The rules of action that achieve the good determine what is right, and the character-traits that support such a moral code are regarded as virtues. The concept of the good life, either in its own name or thought of as "the ideals of life," dominates the framework and provides the end-point in justifying action or policy. The other typical ethical concepts—right and virtue—are definitely subordinated. Such a model is found in most of the ethical theories that look to human nature for an understanding of men's basic goals or directions of striving.

The juridical framework, on the other hand, sees ethics as a system of laws or rules enjoined on human beings. They constitute the "moral law." The framework usually includes some explanatory justification for the law, grounding it in divine will or some natural order or inherent rationality. Men are taken to have an intellectual capacity for recognition of the moral law and some affective capacity through which the system normally takes hold or wins their respect and obedience. The concept of right—or others of the same cluster, such as duty or obligation—dominates this conceptual framework. Virtue is tied to the disposition of conscientious obedience, and the good, usually set off as the moral good and distinguished from the merely natural goods, the desires and satisfactions of men, is identified with the goals that the moral law renders legitimate.

Each of these frameworks purports to cover the whole field, but they interpret moral processes in markedly different ways. Each focuses what is going on in human life, to which morality applies, somewhat differently. Each selects from the repertoire of human feelings which ones are to do the heavy work of morality—the goal-seeking leaning more to desire and aspiration, or else to satisfaction and pleasure, the juridical to guilt, shame, and awe. Each organizes its selected content in a different pattern, the one usually in terms of a hierarchy of means and ends, culminating in some systematic ultimate end, the other in terms of universal rules and their special applications. Such organization-modes strongly influence the methods of decision in morality: in the goal-seeking, it is the finding of appropriate strategies, in the juridical it is deduction from principles. Each appeals to different modes of justification for its morality—the one to the ultimate good which fully satisfies men's longing and aspiration, the other to the reason that grasps ultimate principles or the will that commands them. Each tends to marshall different sanctions to support the morality—the one the operative effects of pleasure and pain, of hope and accomplishment or else dread of loss, the other the fear of authoritative punishment or the pangs of conscience. Thus each framework has a definite orientational effect in the lives of men who so construe their morals.

The goals and substantial codes of a morality, its scope and its basic attitudes, vary considerably with different cultural patterns and in different historical periods. One moral code may be concerned about sex, another about property and status, all usually about aggression in interpersonal relations and about the conditions of social order. The codes of some may focus chiefly on acts, of others on inner feelings and attitudes. Some center on familial or kin group in scope, others are more broadly national or even universalistic and individualistic. Some are broad and relaxed in attitude, others narrowly intense and stringent. All such substantial features can be cast in either basic framework, although not always as easily or comfortably. For example, a nationalistic morality may be juridical or goal-seeking, and attitudes of stringency may take shape either in the sharpness of juridical command or the narrowness of a driving goal such as success and status through work and personal effort.

The history of the relation of the good and the right in ethics is thus the history of the relation of these conceptual frameworks and their transformation under the growth of human knowledge, the changes in social and cultural forms, the emergence of varying human purposes, and the refinement of philosophical theory. It is a complex history, quite revealing about the role of categories of thought in human life, and though it exhibits a definite intellectual dialectic it is scarcely a dance of bloodless categories.

*Antiquity.* In ancient times the juridical mode of thought had its marked development in Hebraic religion, with God as the lawgiver, the Decalogue and associated rules as the code of right and wrong, obligations under original compact for the Hebrew people with God, sanctions of a familial or paternal type with a fusion of awe and love, and decision-modes that grew increasingly legalistic in Talmudic jurisprudence. The appropriate character for men and women was set in this framework, and the good operated as rewards for obedience. The spread of this outlook in Christian morality, with a change to a universalistic form, the coordination of each soul directly to the divine, and

the shift to other-worldly salvation as the unifying good, paralleled by eternal damnation as a major moral sanction, set the background for most Western morality, affecting the basic framework even when the explicit religious justification receded in philosophical thought.

In pre-Platonic Greek thought, the concept of *nomos* had an incipient juridical character. This expressed a customary morality whose rules were static and conceptualized as an eternal traditional order, eternal betokening usually divine as well. When class conflicts arose in the Greek city-states and philosophical reflection grew on the cultural variety of moral codes, the notion of *nomos* became interpreted as merely customary in the sense of conventional. This was the dominant trend in the Sophists. The social impact of this view varied somewhat. For the most part, morality was regarded as rules, different in different cultures to be sure, but directed under these varying conditions, and more or less successfully, to the maintenance of stability and social order as human needs. To an extremist wing (such as Thrasymachus in Plato's *Republic*), it became construed as merely the rules of the stronger imposed for their own interests to keep the masses in check, so that the really wise individual could quietly pursue his own predatory interests. In a few radical views the conventional character of morality meant it could be altered and improved; slavery, for example, being thus a conventional institution, not a natural requirement. In all of these, though the interpretation of what was natural for man varied, the direct contrast became that between custom (*nomos*) and nature (*physis*).

Socrates and Plato refined the goal-seeking framework. In Socrates' persistent inquiry, some of the general properties of the good began to emerge. The good has a magnetic power on us, for no man willingly does what he knows to be evil. It is in some sense capable of being grasped as an object of knowledge, or perhaps capable of being sought and glimpsed, for Socrates more modestly, constantly claimed his wisdom lay in knowing his ignorance. The knowledge involved will in some sense thus be intellectual and practical and affective, either fused or at any rate undifferentiated. When we try to understand any of our particular virtues, such as courage or temperance, we find that they lose their essence if they do not involve a knowledge of the good. Virtues are thus found to be applications, through knowledge, of the good, so that no issue arises of the possible conflict of a man's moral behavior and his true well-being. Insofar as Socrates has any explicit view of the right that is not directly bound up in the quest of the individual's soul for the good, it is seen as a contractual commitment with the institutions of one's community to share in a given mode of life and take the sufferings and even injustices when they fall on one. In this way, Socrates, in the *Crito*, justifies his refusal to escape from prison.

Plato develops both the basic theory of the good as a goal-seeking ethic and the theory of right or justice as an order in the soul which enables it to move toward the good. The former is seen in Socrates' speech in the *Symposium*, which expounds the concept of love (*eros*) as a searching of the soul for the Absolute Good. Specific aims—such as to have children, to create works of art, to order the lives of men, to achieve knowledge—are simply forms of this one ultimate quest for the Absolute. In the *Republic*, the Idea of the Good is presented as the analogue, in the domain of the eternal, to the visible sun in the changing sensible world—the source of all being, of illumination and intelligibility, and of value in existence. This gathering of the real, the rational, and the valuable into a single bundle, persisted through the religious picture of the divine, and the attempts in the modern period to derive an ethics from the picture of the order of nature and human nature. The structure did not fall apart until the twentieth-century demands for the complete autonomy of ethics.

In Plato, the part of the human being engaged in this quest is identified as the rational element (the human part). But the soul is assigned two other parts, the spirited and the appetitive (compared to the lion and the dragon). The comprehensive theory of justice or the right in the *Republic* is an attempt to justify, in both social and inner individual life, a repressive order in which reason rules and with the aid of the lion keeps the dragon in his place. Selection of goals, specific virtues, aims in life, are all assessed in terms of the character of the part of the soul involved and its contribution to the harmonious order. Even Plato's theory of history as an unavoidable deterioration from an aristocratic society through oligarchic and democratic forms down to tyranny (*Republic*, Book VIII), sees this change as the descent of the soul as the dragon is progressively unleashed. Plato's theory of right thus embodies a conservative program to control the masses by a dominant elite which in its single-minded devotion to the ultimate good will overcome the war of the rich and the poor that beset the Greek cities of his epoch.

Aristotle gave the goal-seeking framework its fullest systematic development. His *Nicomachean Ethics* is the first systematic treatise of Western moral philosophy. The framework is an immanent or indwelling teleology in things. Nature works like the artist or craftsman with a plan governing its action. Every species has its own governing plan, and its good lies in the development in its individuals of the capacities with which they are endowed. Man is a rational animal, reason supervening on and imbuing his vegetative and animal capacities. Aristotle thus rejects the unified Platonic Idea of the Good. Ethics is a practical science concerned with the human good, part of the whole science of politics in which the plan of the good for man is grasped as a guide to practice. The human good, what all men aim at, is identified as happiness or well-being, though men debate the activities in which it lies and the mode of life it demands. While the *Ethics* explores the kinds of character this life points to—the varieties of virtues and the nature of virtue, and the inner nature of associational bonds—the *Politics* deals with desirable institutions.

The place of the right in Aristotle's teleological ethics is revealing. There is no central "ought" commanding in the name of the moral law. The various functions which such a concept combines in the juridical framework are here patterned in a different way. Reason is, of course, central in the philosophy, but its ethical job is less to enunciate universal laws than to work out applications of our knowledge of the good and the virtues in which that knowledge is expressed. The concept involved is rather doing what is fitting in particular situations that differ in time, place, context of persons and relations, and with a view to the special powers and limitations of the persons and groups involved. (This is the just-right, as against too much and too little, which appears in Aristotle's doctrine of virtue as the mean.) Men pray, he tells us, for the good, but they should pray that what is good generally or simply be good for them; and in the *Politics* he compromises on a balance of democracy and oligarchy as the most suitable for the Greek city-states as they exist. The element of universality appears in a concept of natural political justice, a precursor of the later conception of natural law, but without the latter's idea of divine command; in Aristotle it is the universally applicable rules of the structure of the good life. Decision, too, is not seen by Aristotle as subsumption under rule, but as means-end analysis; the man of practical wisdom, whose experience and upbringing have brought to maturity his logical power and awareness of the good, is most sensitive in relation to the particular, and can serve as a useful model for the less mature and the uncertain.

In the individualistic ethics of the Hellenistic period, when the common social good disintegrates (together with the city-state) as a governing ideal, the good becomes cast in individualistic terms. In the Epicurean philosophy, it is pleasure, peace and relief from pain, and, if possible, quiet joy rather than hectic pursuit. The metaphysical background is an atomic materialism, including rejection of teleology, acceptance of mortality and a denial of punishment in a hereafter. Since the Epicurean sociology of human development pictures the growth of human learning and the shedding of superstition, the right appears as naturalistic rules or practices or institutions, servicing the human good.

The Stoics too seek internal peace or tranquillity of spirit as the basic good, but tie it to a notion of individual virtue as its single condition and manifestation. Their outlook represents a point of transformation away from the goal-seeking framework. A juridical element enters in their concept of nature as a rational divine order in things. Their point of view is cosmic, beginning with the cosmopolitan impulse of Alexander's conquests and going on to the late Roman empire. The moral community is that of all men, each with a fragment of the divine fire. A duty-like concept makes its appearance in that one should do what the divine has ordered or arranged, but the order comes in the assignment of *role*, or what befits one's place. Particular decisions are thus expressive of the jobs or offices in which one finds oneself. This conception of an ordered system of reason for man was extremely influential in the development of the idea of natural law. Yet back of this whole juridical aspect is a view of the world in which there is no permanence and all is precarious. As Marcus Aurelius vividly depicts it, life and achievement and memory go by in a Heraclitean flux. The only real good throughout is virtue, the maintenance of integrity of the self by stern inner rational control of what alone is in our power—our response or reaction to what happens to us, and a resignation to whatever befalls us in which our tendencies to violent emotion undergo a rational dissolution.

Thus, although Stoic ethics enters the scene under the classical concept of the good, and finds a place in practice for a system of the right, its central stress on virtue and the self is working towards a newer framework, a kind of self-development model which is, in the history of ethics, a major alternative to the right and the good. It is this framework too which best fits the many ethics of salvation that characterized the decline of the Roman world, such as the Neo-Platonic vision of the path of the self in its attempt to overcome its original estrangement from divine unity and to merge eventually with the One. Christian ethics with its early inner stress has many elements of this model, but it is firmly kept within a juridical framework by its Hebraic origin and heritage.

Yet even a self-development framework will find within itself the tension of the good and the right, or of their surrogates. This is well seen in the ethics of Augustine. The good is found in the blessedness for which he longs, the right in the straining of every effort to keep on the path to its achievement. The wrong is more evident in the multitudes of temptations that lie along the way. Even the most harmless pleasures may distract one from the goal, and even in the act of prayer Augustine is suspicious of the seductive beauty of language and of music. It is this deep probing into the willfulness of the will and the ultimate character of man's responsibility (in spite of God's selection of only a chosen few for salvation) which gives force to the Augustinian concept of sin, whether he addresses himself to portraying the child in the cradle or the youth in exuberant folly, or the whole history of mankind from creation to resurrection. The analysis of sin shows the individual soul as the battleground, for moral evil lies in acquiescence or yielding in the will itself, rather than in the consequent natural action.

**The Era of Christian Dominance.** Once established, Christian thought dominated all of ethics and political philosophy in the West until the breakaway under secular and scientific influences gained strength by the seventeenth century. Yet Christian thought itself included a multitude of differing tendencies.

The Thomistic synthesis of Christian and Aristotelian elements brought the juridical and goal-seeking frameworks into an apparent unity. The central Aristotelian conceptual apparatus, with its orientation towards the good, was incorporated as a whole. But the end changed from the kind of happiness Aristotle had delineated in his natural teleology to the salvation goal of the Christian theology. The crucial confrontation of the good and the right comes, therefore, in the meeting-point where the ultimate good is steered into the channels of the juridical right. If the soul is directed to God by its original nature in God's creation, it is guided ultimately by God's law, which is juridical in form and scope. In part, but only in part, this eternal law can be apprehended by man's reason, and so is seen as the natural law, expressive of man's nature. Beyond lies what man must obey on grounds of revelation.

In essence the concepts of right and wrong dominate the system, as can be seen in the prominence of the notion of sin, already basic in Augustine's thought. Yet the good continues to operate through the weight of the sanctions of eternal salvation and eternal damnation, and also in the justification of the system as a whole. The dramatic unity of the whole is most evident in the literary presentation of Dante's *Divine Comedy*. In the first part, the *Inferno*, there is a careful grading of sins in the descent to the bottom of Hell, the distance from God and the shutting out of God's light being the measure of sin. In the third part, the *Paradiso*, there is the ascent of the virtues towards the point of ultimate union in the direct contemplation of God; but each

176

soul stays in its allotted place according to its capacity, the spirit of love holding each and stilling its desire to move further upward. In both the heavenly areas and the nether areas, the categorial tension of good and evil as against right and wrong is resolved. In the heavenly, the love of God is the basis of that aspiration which defines the good, and the right lies in the acceptance of the divine order. In the nether regions, the clarity of the wrong is seen in the punishment of sin, and the evil in the nature and intensity of the torments.

The emergence of the Protestant ethic in its different forms was not a questioning of the good so much as a vital alteration in the structure of the right. Salvation remained the goal of aspiration but the system of rules for its achievement was transformed. In Calvinism, the assurance of salvation was to be sought in success in one's calling, and a fresh cluster of virtues—the "puritan" morality of hard work, sobriety, thrift, abstinence, justice—was required as a necessary condition. Yet through this picture of the right we can discern the content of the good changing into the worldly ideal of success and the pursuit of wealth. The relation of the Protestant ethic to the economic changes and the rise of the bourgeoisie has been explored and debated in the writings of Marx, Max Weber, R. H. Tawney, and others. The language of the right still remains as the language of natural law, in the treatises on morality and politics, shifting to that of natural rights as the concept of nature itself undergoes change, as individualism gains strength, and the process of secularization gains momentum. The concept of the good is similarly individualized and secularized, especially with the growing impact of the sciences.

*An Age of Transition: From Hobbes to Kant.* The seventeenth and eighteenth centuries constitute a revolutionary period not merely on the social scene, with new classes moving into political power, but also on the intellectual scene, with the philosophies of the old order breaking up, and even the defenses of the older ways taking new and sophisticated form. The intellectual leaven is furnished by the growth of physical science, but it casts its hopes far beyond—in physiology, in psychology and economics, in political theory, and in the reinterpretation of morality.

In ethics, Hobbes expresses a shift to the extreme; he becomes the specter that haunts moral theory. Teleology is gone: the world and man are well-organized phenomena of matter-in-motion operating under causal laws. Reason is no immediate grasping of ultimate truth by the intellect but, though profoundly mathematical, a manipulator of names; yet the beginnings of an inductive theory, in the sense of the lessons of experience, are also to be found. That which men desire they call good, that from which they seek to flee they call bad. The internal detail is complex, but the overall effect is undoubted; the good is completely naturalized in terms of individual desire. The natural is the original state of man, with the unlimited egoism of desire. The system of right is reduced to the principles of human relations that will furnish the peace, law, and order needed for men to pursue their aims. These are called natural laws, in the sense that they are what a reasoning man drawing on the lessons of experience will recognize as essential for social order. In the state of nature a man has a right to anything he can take and hold.

The Continental ethical counterpart to Hobbes, in some respects, is Spinoza. Here too, good was given a naturalistic form as the object of appetite; teleology is refuted and a deterministic pattern set in which all that happens flows with mathematical necessity from the ultimate character of nature. But Spinoza's impact is considerably softened by several features. The whole of reality is also interpreted as God. The highest good is found in the exercise of reason, and the right is primarily oriented to removing obstacles for its harmonious development. Human virtue is turned from a predatory orientation to a self-conquest: as one comes to understand the necessity in one's actions, the insight transforms the turbulent emotions into clear ideas. The active mastery replacing passive reception in such transformation constitutes human freedom and the highest good is attained in the intuitive grasp of totality. Political freedom and nobler human relations flow from a Spinozistic as against a Hobbesian necessity. Thus although the immediate reception of Spinoza was hostile, as in the case of Hobbes, in the long run he stands out sharply as the propounder of an exalted ethic.

Three trends, marked in Hobbes, set the direction for much of the moral theory that followed. First, the secular character of the inquiry became dominant. In Hobbes, religion has its place mainly as a sanction. In Bentham's formulation, by the end of the eighteenth century, it is only religious belief that operates as a sanction; the truth of religion is unnecessary. Yet the absence of religious argumentation in the inner inquiries of ethics does not remove it from the outer background. Just as Newton does not look for an evolution of matter because he assumes the physical world set up by God, so the assumption that man's nature on which ethics depends will not be transformed, that a permanent moral order can be found, is either directly dependent on religious presuppositions or else the intellectual residue of the traditional outlook. Second, the natural state of man, whether seen as historically prior or as an analytic device for understanding original components in his makeup, is cast in individualistic terms. It is not a system of inherent human relations, but somehow a set of properties of the individual. Even when Locke questions the amorality of Hobbes' state of nature, the moral rights that Locke describes—the natural rights of life, liberty, and property—stand out more as individual rights than as divine prescriptions for an ordered society.

In the third place, the locus of controversy about the good and the right is displaced from the social forum to the inner psychology of the individual. To refute Hobbesian egoism is to show that the individual has authentic inner sentiments of a social or other-oriented nature. Bishop Butler's strategy of refutation is both complex and sophisticated. He first shifts the concept of the good from the object of the individual's appetites or passions to a rational self-love, quite distinct from the passions, which seeks to maximize the harmonious achievement of the desires, since obviously desires are in conflict and can lead one away from one's good. This enables him to establish a concept of right in the regulative authority of self-love over the passions. Further introspection reveals benevolence, whether as a distinct principle or as an other-regarding sentiment. Still further lies conscience, whose authority is introspectively established, as was that of self-love, over the passions.

It remains but to reconcile conscience and self-love by the claim that their voices will in fact be found in accord, and that apparent discrepancies will be found to be simply dissident passions. In Hume and in Adam Smith the operation of sympathy as a natural principle is defended as against Hobbes' attempted reduction of compassion to an imaginative feeling of one's own suffering if one were in the particular plight that has overtaken the other. In general, the good, while still conceived as what satisfies human desire, is neatly parceled into the self-regarding and the other-regarding. This reflects the dominant growth of an individualism in the social institutions and the moral acceptability of an acquisitive worldly mode of life. The self-regarding is no longer equated with the immoral; it is, if not excessive, established as a proper part of the moral. The focus for right falls increasingly on the problem of reconciling the conflict of individual goods. Hume stresses the instrumental character of conceptions of justice, and from Butler to Adam Smith there is the assurance that the unseen hand of Providence will guarantee that each man's pursuit of his own good will produce an effect of enhancement on others' good. But it takes different shades. Sometimes the individual is being reassured that an enlightened egoism will turn out for the best. Sometimes, however, he is being prompted to directly virtuous action and assured it will turn out for his own good too. Only

occasionally, as in the maverick outlook of Mandeville, do we find an array of empirical argument that if men really practiced the virtues it would yield public poverty and consequently private misfortune, and that public welfare rests on private vices!

Indeed, a considerable part of eighteenth-century ethical theorizing is cast not in terms of the right and the good, but in terms of virtue and vice, and our appreciative responses to others' character. In this whole movement, the moral good becomes primarily the good man, as contrasted with simply the natural goods of desire and satisfaction. Major epistemological controversies in morals take the form of finding the basis of moral judgment in reason or in sentiment.

The emerging utilitarianism of the latter part of the eighteenth century inherits the framework of the good defined in individual terms and the right in terms of social utility. In Bentham, the goal-seeking framework is wholly triumphant. Every man by psychological constitution seeks pleasure and the avoidance of pain. A community is simply a mass of individuals. The community problem is to achieve the greatest happiness of the greatest number. "Good" means either pleasure or the objects which are sources of pleasure. "Right" and "ought" are terms that have a meaning only with respect to courses of conduct productive of the greatest pleasure and avoidance of pain.

Both notions in utilitarianism have a more complicated character than appears at first. Pleasure as the single goal, extracted from any and every object of striving, begins to serve as a standard of measurement rather than as a goal. The orientation of the theory is to measurement; the good is the maximum pleasure attainable in a given situation. What is desired constitutes only an initial datum for the measurement; an appeal simply to the fact of desire is arbitrary, and Bentham attacks the principle of sympathy and antipathy—deciding by likes and dislikes—as capricious. The basic orientation to the good becomes intelligible in the light of the historical context. Increasingly, in Bentham's lifetime, the industrial revolution is under way, a policy of *laissez-faire* and material progress is coming to the center, an expansive this-worldly libertarian outlook is seen as the key to progress. The stress comes to be on consciousness of aims in order to reform institutions that stand in the way.

The traditional notion of the right now appears in several ways. There is first the basic social interest in institutional forms which require analysis so that they may become vehicles for the forward energies of men rather than obstacles. The right is therefore the system of institutions to serve this purpose. There is, second, the equalitarian assumption—everyone counts as one in the reckoning of the pleasures and pains. Much of the theoretical problem in the relation of the right and the good in utilitarianism comes to take the form of controversy as to whether this equalitarian principle is derivable within the theory or is an outside assumption imported into the system—for example, whether a commitment to maximizing pleasure can be shown to involve maximizing its distribution. There is, in the third place, the practical question of reconciling individual motivations to make them aim at the greatest general happiness. Bentham, like Adam Smith, relies to some extent on a natural identity of interest among men (in economics and the theory of virtue), but supplements it with an artificial identification of interests by use of sanctions (in politics and law). And finally, there is the question of justice and the human sentiments that center about it—whether these do not contain some irreducible idea of right and wrong.

This last problem, like many of the others, is most analytically considered by J. S. Mill. Although he is entirely a nineteenth-century figure, responding to fresh problems after the changes in England that follow the Reform Bill of 1832 and the emergence of the labor movement, his treatment of justice is relevant here. In Chapter 5 of his *Utilitarianism* he distinguishes sharply between the actual sentiments men have and what is moral in them, and he elaborately examines the wholly utilitarian character of justice. In brief, he traces the root ideas of ought and of merit to the convictions that punishment and censure, and reward, will be conducive to the general welfare. As for justice, it refers basically to principles of distribution in all fields, of gains and burdens. And while men have held to all sorts of such principles, the question of which to employ in what field is a matter of utilitarian reckoning. Men's moral sentiments constitute no contrary evidence, for they are built up in social life out of rudimentary reactions such as the desire for retaliation, and contain no inner justifying principle. It is the more important human institutions that build up the more peremptory sentiments. In general, Mill is more conscious than Bentham of the way in which association develops attitudes and sentiments so as even to bring changes in the nature of man. At the end he is quite far removed from psychological hedonism in his theory of virtue as becoming a part of happiness rather than simply an instrument to it.

If Mill went as far as seems possible in reducing the concept of right to utility in the framework of the good, Kant had already in the latter part of the eighteenth century posed the opposite reduction, and in a form that has come increasingly to dominate contemporary ethics. Kant is quite ready to surrender the theory of motivation to hedonism. But men's inclina-

tions, their affections, the rules for achieving happiness, are not questions of morality. They tell us what is the case, and what to do if we wish to pursue certain ends. They do not tell us what we *ought* to do. The basic moral concept is that of duty. Its commands are absolute or categorical, not hypothetical. This he takes to be clear in the ordinary moral consciousness; our respect is directed toward the man who conscientiously obeys the moral law in spite of suffering and contrary inclinations. Kant's conceptual framework is briefly this: man is a rational being, morality presupposes freedom (a postulate incapable of rational or empirical proof but required for morality), freedom is self-determination by law willed for the community of all rational beings. Hence the test for the morality of a proposed maxim is whether one would consistently will it as a law for all men. Morality thus is not determined by inclination or external command (even by divine command). As Kant says, it is autonomous, not heteronomous. A wholly moral being will follow the moral law without inner conflict; this is a holy will. But men live in two worlds, that of inclination as well as that of freedom. Hence obligation is the sense of duty curbing inclination. This is reason being practical. Virtue lies in the continuous effort to follow the ought. The good lies in happiness coming together with virtue; unmerited happiness is not a good. Thus both virtue and the good have been brought into defining relation with obligation.

Kant's moral theory, in effect, provides a method for generating or testing moral rules by universalization. It also puts the individual as a rational being in the very center, recognizing him as of infinite worth: every man is to be treated as an end, not merely as a means.

Kant is quite explicit about his aim. He is expounding a morality that is *a priori* and alleged to be free from any empirical taint. It is not the consequences of action in existence but its rational character which determines its moral worth. Man stands out from nature and its processes as utterly unique. But his uniqueness is found not in aspiration, not in apprehension of beauty, not in his use of rationality to develop the instruments of human control and the pursuit of aims. It lies in the sense of duty.

***The Growth of Historical Consciousness and the Impact of Evolutionary Theory.*** Hitherto the search had been for eternal structures, both for the good and the right, whether based on conceptions of divinity, reason, nature, or laws of the human constitution. The nineteenth century is the age in which a growing historical consciousness took philosophical shape, and the theory of evolution gave it sweeping scientific substance in the understanding of man.

179

In the first third of the century the commanding idealist synthesis in the Hegelian philosophy saw all reality as a dialectical development in which Reason or the Divine Idea achieves the self-consciousness which is its freedom. In all his specific analyses, Hegel combined a profound sense of unity, of pattern, and of process. All dualisms were seen as phases in the development of a total plan, all apparently isolated items as embodying a wider configuration in some moment of transition, and every present configuration as a stage in a historical unfolding in which apparent opposites are transcended into a higher unity. Hence Hegel's philosophy is the great solvent of traditional and opposing ethical schools: dichotomies of abstract reason and individual immediacy, duty and happiness, inner spirit and outer institutions are put into place as stages in the growth of consciousness, the unfolding of freedom, and the development of institutions. The full realization of ethics is in the objective domain of society and history in which the good is articulated in a social system of rights and duties, themselves not abstract but expressing the organization of social life unified in the state. If Hegel's own propositions often seem too schematized in terms of abstract categories, his theoretical impact was clearly to encourage the study of morality in terms of cultural pattern and historical determination.

The theory of evolution had even more far-reaching consequences on concepts of the right and the good. Few of the traditional theories were left unscathed. Most devastating was the impact on the goal-seeking framework in its teleological form; for its basic concept of a permanent natural direction of striving as ethically determinative was thoroughly undermined. Aristotle's original criteria for the natural had combined invariance or relative invariance of behavior and development in each form of life, inherent tendency in the sense of unlearned or instinctive, supplemented by what was good for the form of life. These went in separate directions once the teleological bond was broken. Invariance now meant simply scientific laws, not natural law. Inherence or instinctiveness meant that the trait got built in during past evolutionary development because of past survival value; it might, like aggressiveness, be presently disruptive and a source of anti-moral behavior in a new environment. The goodness of a type of behavior would now have to be established on its own in some fresh manner.

Utilitarianism too was affected, but in a more complex way. Its hedonistic emphasis was deepened, yet at the same time transcended. The presumed fact that men constantly pursued pleasure would now give pleasure no special ultimate status, for it had still to be asked what this signified in the evolutionary process.

But a biological evolutionary understanding of this significance was readily forthcoming. For example, pleasure could be seen, in Herbert Spencer's account, as a sign of activities having health and survival value, and rules of right, such as demands for sacrifice, could become intelligible through their long-range survival effect on the group. Utilitarianism thus found it easier to make the social transition that had been difficult in purely individualistic hedonist terms. But the forms in which pleasure was sought would now take over importance, and evolutionary mechanisms would enable us to understand them and their changes, though in social and cultural rather than biological terms. Thus Spencer also traced the changes that took place in men's conceptions of the good and the right and in their patterns of virtue as they moved from a militaristic to an industrial society. Evolutionary interest turned some ethical inquiry into the sociology of ethics and into descriptions of primitive and early moralities, in order to discover an evolution within morality itself.

This general historical emphasis, like the older use of the Newtonian model, sought to find what had emerged in order to establish at the same time a basis of critique for alternative trends and possibilities. In such endeavors, both the underlying scientific presuppositions and the underlying ethical commitments often stood out clearly. Spencer saw the evolutionary process in terms of the struggle for existence and survival of the fittest, and posited an individualistic ethics with absolute conceptions of justice whose emergence he anticipated as the outcome of social development. Anarchist ethics, by contrast, best illustrated in the work of Kropotkin, saw mutual aid as a dominant theme, frustrated by the development of power-wielding institutions, and eventually breaking through to fresh forms of human relationship. Nietzsche posited a basic psychology of a will to power whose direct and disciplined expression constituted the obvious human good. With deep insight into the natural history of morals, and into its psychological roots, Nietzsche focused on understanding the role of moral categories as well as moral content in the psychological functioning of men. He saw most of traditional religious and humanistic morality as an expression of weakness, and the concepts of evil and sin and injustice to be rooted in envy and resentment. As against this morality of good and evil, he posed the aristocratic morality of good and bad, with its direct expression of power, and he looked to the production of a higher order of man.

Marxian ethics made perhaps the most systematic attempt to combine the historical sweep of Hegelian philosophy with the scientific materialism of an evolutionary outlook, adding also elements of the growing economic science and historical analysis of social movements. The growth of freedom is seen as the basic human aim, interpreted as the increase of productive power and control of man's career and destiny. Specific stages are delineated with reference to the historical interplay of regulative forms in society, reflecting the stages of economic development and their internal conflicts. The good is defined in time and place by the dominant goals of the society, and evaluated by the advance in human freedom that is ensured; the right is defined by the system of economic and social relations, reflecting the underlying economic needs and mode of production. Thus feudal morality is a system of ordered position, with virtues of loyalty and gratitude; bourgeois morality has goods of individual success and a system of justice embodying will-assertion, property rights, and free contract; socialist and communist morality will have an ideal of human development and collective organization. Evaluation is the progressive reckoning of direction of development in the line of basic historical aims.

While all these historically-oriented theories sought to share or to develop the evolutionary framework, other moral philosophies set out to build up lines of defense against the growing naturalism. Thus the Kantian ethical theory was revived and invoked as a foundation for theories that would stem the scientific tide and set off spirit from nature. Kant himself had consciously held on to the two irreducible worlds of noumena and phenomena, the former for morality, the latter for science. And T. H. Green, witnessing the evolutionary naturalization of man, warned that unless morality somehow represented something transcendent, the moral consciousness would be reduced to simply a complex form of fear. Whether the idealist outlooks that emerged built on the Kantian contrast of nature and spirit or on the Hegelian concept of all reality as the march of Spirit, the net effect was to establish the moral consciousness as a cosmic phenomenon. Desire itself became no isolated impulse but a movement of the self, threading its way to a systematic realization in relation to the whole.

The ethics of self-realization, for example, as propounded by F. H. Bradley in his *Ethical Studies* (1876), had no need to counterpose the juridical and the goal-seeking frameworks. Like the ancient Stoic ethics of virtue, it was operating in the framework of a distinct self-development model, and Hegel had already broken down all the sharp dichotomies. It was, however, the Hegelian emphasis on the comprehensive and total system, rather than his dynamic historicism, that dominated in self-realizationist theory. Goals could appear in human consciousness, but their significance lay in the systematic unity they gave to self-development; and rules could govern human action, but their basic

meaning lay in the institutional structures of the time and place that gave content to the integration of the self. Integration in the self and organization in society were carrying on the kind of function that went with right or obligation; the growing concrete whole of self-realization would merit the appellation of the good.

The aftermath of evolution, with its recognition of variety of form and constant change and with its removal from the scene of a determinate and definitive plan for all time, made impossible thereafter the older forms of both the goal-seeking and the juridical framework. Looking back, we can detect precursor tendencies toward the new in both Bentham and Kant. Bentham's notion of pleasure as the goal had been so broad and so thin as to determine no definitive goal but to shift the emphasis to evaluation in measurement. Kant's use of rationality as self-legislation had begun to shift the emphasis from the set of rules to the way of certifying them. With the change in cognitive orientation brought by the century of evolution, the characteristic ethical element in both frameworks could only be the *critical* component which made evaluation possible or which gave a rational character to decision. In the twentieth century it took many forms, including belated Platonic reifications of value or value domains, and belated Kantian forms of extracting basic principles from the concept of rationality. It took explicit form in outlooks that made the phenomenon of criticism or of reflective decision the central focus in ethics. It took bold experimental form in the foundation of general value theory in which a unified concept of what is called *value* took over from that of the good and by developing a theory of *value judgment* comprehending the critical element, left little for an independent notion of right to do except be the application of value judgment to a particular province of value.

In turning to these predominantly twentieth-century vicissitudes of the right and the good, the experiment with value merits consideration in terms of its basic intent and procedures. The other forms can be surveyed under the rubric of analytic formulations, and naturalistic and pragmatic formulations.

***The Right and The Good in General Value Theory.*** The general theory of value appears to have arisen from different sources, at points with opposing motives. The earliest modern source was the Benthamite emphasis on measurement. For Bentham, value is, like price in economics, the measure of a consignment of pleasure or pain entering into decision. The theoretical importance of this evaluative phenomenon was noted above. It also had practical support in the existence of a money economy in which things and services of extremely diverse type and "use value" in consump-

181

tion, acquire a comparative "exchange value." Economic analysis of exchange value furnished the earliest comprehensive model for a general theory of value. It both provided concepts and inspired hopes of a systematic account of human choices and preferences in all fields.

A second source was the naturalistic continuation of Hobbes' or Spinoza's account of good as the object of endeavor, now seen in an evolutionary light. Generic value would be the earliest or most rudimentary response—the elective act of acceptance or rejection, the exhibition of an interest, a *pro-* or *con-* attitude. While some theorists reached such a broad base simply by throwing all different forms into a common hopper and postulating a value genus for the variety of value species, others had clearly in mind the evolutionary sketch of rising complexity on different integrative levels beginning with an originally simple reaction. The explanatory derivation of the complex would show how the differentiated notions such as the right or the sense of obligation arose out of the ordinary materials of human sympathy in the reactions of men in groups held together for survival. It was the functions they performed in harmonizing or marshalling or integrating interests that kept them going. Darwin had himself led the way by attacking the exaggeration of remorse into some supernatural voice. It was, he said, just different in degree from ordinary repentance, as agony differed from pain or rage from anger.

Precisely the opposite motive operated in the idealist generalization of value. For it the drawing together of different kinds of categories into a single basic notion of value was the sign of the characteristic mark of spirit. The glimmer of the ideal now operative in bare desire or selection, now in deliberate obligation, represented the same basic phenomenon.

Phenomenological approaches have sometimes gone even farther than idealist philosophy in isolating a separate domain of value. For example, Nicolai Hartmann, in his *Ethics,* contrasts sharply the sensory domain which science explores, the ontological domain which includes both the religious and the general metaphysical accounts of reality, and the axiological or value domain which is self-sufficient and independent, grasped by sensitive insight or intuition. It has its own laws and its own structure. Ethics consists in an exploration of the different values in this domain— what ought to be, whether it exists or not, in all its rich variety and often with conflicting possibilities. This is the realm of the traditional good, broadly conceived by the theory of value. Duty is the application and selection under given conditions of the structure of existence. It is, for Hartmann, a fundamental philosophical mistake to argue that the structure of reality determines value—for example, a religious teleology

in which God's will is *therefore* good. Hartmann attacks Plato too for identifying the good and the real. Value is the independent base for evaluating even the ultimately real.

The relation of the right and the good in this new framework of general value theory has shown, however, a variety comparable to that in the older tradition. At first sight, the value concept itself seems to be wholly on the side of the good. The general questions asked are all of one type: the nature of the value phenomenon, the meaning of "value," the mode of verifying value judgments, the mode of comparing values. Yet as its very breadth carries it beyond the moral domain to include aesthetic value, religious value, economic value, and so on, some distinctive mark is then required for the more limited province of the moral. Sometimes this has been taken to be the values of character, in the older tradition of virtue, but perhaps more often there has been a reference to the values that *ought* to be brought into existence under given conditions. The ought thus becomes the distinctive mark of the moral. Similarly, where value is identified in terms of interest or desire or inclination, the additional selective element, as in the contrast of the desired and the desirable, carries the connotation of what is worth desiring or ought to be desired. Sometimes the concept of the *normative* is used for the selective or critical element; sometimes, however, the term "norm" becomes rather descriptive of some pattern of interest or desire, and "value" then carries the connotation of the standard or the desirable. In Hartmann's account, the tension of the ought is carried into the heart of the good by construing value itself as an ought-to-be. Similarly, in a quite different kind of phenomenological approach—extending to value the methods that Gestalt psychology found fruitful in the study of perception—Wolfgang Köhler attempts to identify a phenomenal quality of *requiredness* as a generic element and interprets both aesthetic and moral fittingness as special cases of it.

Whatever these skirmishes in the dialectic of nomenclature, it is clear in general value theory that the concepts represent rather functional differentiation in the one material. The critical element lies in the comparative evaluation, and the question what one ought to do or what is appropriate is readily translated into what is the best thing to do. The contrast of the right and good has lost its basic importance in general value theory. Attention has shifted rather to the whole problem of the *autonomy* of the value domain, which, interestingly enough, is indifferently termed the question of the relation between the ought and the is, and that between fact and value, as if they were the same problem.

In more recent study of the language of morals, the

old sharper distinction reappears within the new framework. A contrast is made between evaluation and prescription, and the older problems of the relation between the good and the right appear in the form of the relation between value and obligation, once again as major differences in categories.

*Analytic Formulations.* Philosophical analysis, especially in its British twentieth-century forms, has been applied in various ways to problems of ethical theory. G. E. Moore's *Principia Ethica* (1903), with its common-sense analysis, reached a position in many respects analogous to the phenomenological one. The autonomy of the moral is central to his account. The basic predicate of morals is "good" in the sense of intrinsic good. This names a simple quality which cannot be identified with any descriptive predicate, whether psychological, such as pleasure or what one desires; or metaphysical, such as what God wills; or historical, such as what evolution unfolds. To identify good with any of these "natural" qualities or predicates is to commit the *naturalistic fallacy.* Moore's chief demonstration of its fallaciousness is the so-called open-question argument—that if you identify good with such a descriptive content it is always possible meaningfully to ask of this content whether it itself is good. Thus to ask if what God wills is good, or if pleasure is good, is not to ask a meaningless question or to affirm that pleasure is pleasure. Though Moore regards this as establishing the simple nonnatural character of good, and a domain of values intuitively grasped as having a worth independent of whatever the actual state of existence may be, it is more plausible to see his argument as establishing the permanent possibility of critical evaluation for any proposed content.

With respect to right and obligation, Moore's answer is utilitarian in form. To judge an act as right is to say that it will cause the world to be better than it would be on any possible alternative act.

Contrasting relations of the right and the good were proposed by Moore's contemporaries at Oxford, who also employed the method of the conceptual analysis of ordinary moral beliefs or convictions. H. A. Prichard reversed Moore's relation. The particular judgments of obligation are the primary material; we know directly in the particular case what our obligations are, and we generalize them in rough rules. The notion of good is derivative: a good man is a man who does what is right, and the good consists in those goals that a good man pursues. On the other hand, Sir David Ross took the strikingly different path of analyzing the right and the good as coordinate independent ideas. Our duty in a particular case is hard to work out, but the *prima facie* rules which tell us that lying and stealing and so on are wrong are themselves intuitively evident.

That something is good, or even yields the greatest good, does not mean that it is our duty to do it; we may be bound by a stringent duty such as a promise to a man on his death bed to carry out his wishes, but acting in accordance with his wishes may not yield the greatest good we could disinterestedly conceive. Ross's common-sense analysis reflects quite accurately the conflicts between duty and interest in ordinary life. It simply acknowledges the tension of the right and the good, or of justice and utility, or of duty and interest, by whatever names distinguished, and takes for granted that the good is what has to be sacrificed in cases of tension.

While these contrasting patterns each claimed to be the correct analysis of ordinary moral concepts and convictions, it is apparent that they also establish definite priorities in policy and conduct. To define the right in terms of the good involves a readiness to evaluate moral rules critically in terms of the welfare they bring or frustrate in practice. The separation of the right and the good or the primacy of the right has the more conservative potential in giving priority to maintaining the stability of the existing moral pattern.

Analytic formulations moved in two somewhat different directions in the mid-twentieth century. One was toward more formal logical analysis, the other to more informal contextual linguistic analysis.

The formal analysis was prompted by the rapid development of logical techniques as well as the prestige which logical positivism attached to formal construction, while disparaging ordinary language as enshrining the mistakes and myths of the past. The most prominent work relevant to ethics has stemmed from the field of *deontic* logic, in which such concepts as permissible, imperative, ought, and others of the same group of right and obligation are analyzed and systematized in logical fashion. Thus if "permissible" is taken as a primitive term, "X is obligatory" would be translated into "It is not permissible not to do X." Differences between the operations and transformations permitted in the ordinary propositional calculus and those in the deontic system are carefully explored. This is a rapidly growing field of analysis today. While the right was first dealt with, recent work has turned also to the good, and *axiological* systems have been developed using "better" as a primitive term. The question of interpretation of such systems, and of the ways of establishing or verifying statements in these systems, would raise afresh all the problems of the right and the good. At present it is the logical complexities that stimulate interest.

The positivist analysis of meaning and verification also had a different impact on ethical theory. Since the meaning of a term was taken to lie in the mode of verification implied, and truth was established either by showing a logical proposition to be analytically true or an empirical proposition to predict correctly the course of sense-experience, there seemed no place left for the ethical propositions of the intuitionist approach, any more than for propositions of religion or aesthetics. All these were accordingly denied any cognitive status; they do not assert anything, but ethical terms rather serve a noncognitive or practical function, providing vehicles for expressing or giving vent to emotions. To say "Stealing is wrong," argued A. J. Ayer in his *Language, Truth and Logic* (1936), is equivalent to saying "Stealing!!" in a tone of horror. The difference between "good" and "right" or between any ethical terms, lies in the kind and strength of the emotion conveyed. Ethical statements are therefore neither true nor false. In a development of the emotive theory, C. L. Stevenson focused on disagreement in attitude, as distinguished from disagreement in belief, as the central moral phenomenon, and analyzed ethical statements as largely persuasive in effort—practical attempts to bring about agreement in an emotive way. To resolve an ethical issue is thus causally to secure agreement in attitude, not cognitively to establish a truth.

The distinctive feature of the emotive theory was not the recognition of the role of emotion in ethics; this had been a commonplace of the eighteenth-century theorists who stressed the moral sentiments as against the Cambridge Platonists who had looked for intellectual ethical axioms. And Westermarck, in his *Ethical Relativity* (1932), had recently expounded the view that ethical beliefs were generalizations of the retributive feelings, with "wrong" and "bad" resting on the sterner retaliatory feelings, and "right" and "good" on the kindlier retributive feelings of gratitude. The distinctive element was the tie-in with the presumed correct use of language, and the claim that indicative forms in "X is good" or "X is wrong" are incorrect syntactical expressions whose proper form would be "Would that everybody desired X" as Russell at one point analyzed "good," and "Don't do X," as Carnap translated moral rules into imperatives. Some, such as Reichenbach, stressed the more voluntaristic element, the commitment component in the will-act, in ethical statements.

The contextual mode of analysis as a systematic procedure in ethics emerged from such antecedents under the impact of the revised conception of meaning that followed upon Ludwig Wittgenstein's later work. A term was to be understood not by seeking a single definition expressive of its essence, but by examining linguistic uses, by seeing carefully how one might come to learn the use of the term. No one form of unity was antecedently presupposed; there might be an ulti-

mate plurality, or a loose unity in a kind of family resemblance. In a reverse of the positivist attitude to ordinary language as a blundering to be superseded by careful formalization, the new mode of analysis showed the greatest respect for ordinary language as a repository of the wisdom and experience of the ages in communication and interpersonal relations. Accordingly, in ethics, it canvassed the field of the uses of moral terms and turned up a multitude of differences, as far apart as expressing feelings and preferences, expressing decisions, advising, persuading, evaluating and promulgating. R. M. Hare concentrated on the commending use of "good," and the use of "ought" to indicate the need for a decision. J. L. Austin explored the performatory uses of language, and in morals the actual assignment of obligation and responsibilities, J. O. Urmson the grading uses of "good." By the time that G. H. von Wright explored the variety of uses in his *Varieties of Goodness* (1963), it was a mark of lack of philosophical sophistication to ask for "the meaning of 'good.'"

Contextualism probed even more minutely into context differences. Thus the differentiation in personal pronoun with "ought" was found to make a difference in use; for example, "I ought" was sometimes declared to express a decision, "You ought" to be prescriptive as addressed to someone in particular, "He ought" to be evaluative. Thus the kind of term became less important than the kind of function being performed. But even evaluation differed (as Toulmin showed in his *The Place of Reason in Ethics*, 1950) as one was looking for the application of a rule in a particular case, questioning a rule within a moral code, and questioning a limiting principle in terms of which codes were themselves adjudged.

The relation of the right and the good underwent changes in these developments. At first the distinction was between *deontological* terms and *teleological* terms, and the question of their relation was expressed as whether deontological statements presupposed teleological statements—that is, whether ought-assertions were meaningful only if you assumed certain purposes in the background. In the language of functions, replacing that of statements, the question was the relation of prescribing to evaluating. With the multiplication of contexts and functions it became less a question of assigning a usage to one or another function than of exploring the concrete structure of each function, whatever language it employed. In effect, all the functions could be seen as contextually differentiated modes of reflective criticism.

**Naturalistic and Pragmatic Formulations.** While the analytic formulations began with language and worked out towards the contexts and functions which characterized moral phenomena and moral processes, the naturalistic formulations went as directly as possible to the latter in order to explore them in as scientific a spirit as possible. Utilitarianism had done this by identifying the good as pleasure, studying pleasure with respect to qualities, conditions of occurrence, modes of increasing, and so on, although in a limited introspective way. The good and the right were then related as pleasure and the avoidance of pain to the stable rules of their successful pursuit.

The differences among the naturalistic formulations, especially with the emergence of general value theory, tended to follow the different assumptions about the most fruitful scientific study. R. B. Perry, in his *General Theory of Value* (1926), identified value as object of interest rather than pleasure, apparently because interest has a broader biological import and can be exhibited in behavioral terms. Thus where Bentham called intensity a measure of value, Perry spoke of the degree of arousal of the organism. The function of the right was broadly carried out by measures of the maximal achievement of interest, with such criteria as intensity, preference and inclusiveness, and with specific exploration of different levels of integration of interest. In the narrow sense, judgments of right and wrong indicated the application of such criteria in rule-formation within groups for group interests. By contrast to Perry's approach, Stephen Pepper, in his *Sources of Value* (1958), focused on the phenomenon of appetition and purposive striving. Regarding it as basic, Pepper maintained that the aspects of pleasure or satisfaction generally, as well as those of interest and direction, can be set within a framework of purpose. The structure of such appetition is generalized into a theory of value as a whole, and the concepts of the good and the right find their place in the goals and the modes of organization within that structure. Pepper's formulation consciously set out from E. C. Tolman's behaviorist studies (*Purposive Behavior in Animals and Men*). In corresponding fashion, other kinds of psychological inquiry are associated with other kinds of naturalistic ethical theory. The psychoanalytic approach exerted wide influence in the mid-twentieth century. The Freudian picture of the basic instinctual tendencies operating on the pleasure principle, restrained and channeled by the ego operating on the reality principle to postpone gratification, and by the superego with its internalized parental prohibitions, furnished a model into which ethics could readily be fitted. Moral rules of right and wrong were often interpreted as superego phenomena, basically addressed to problems of acquisitiveness, aggression, and sexuality. Ideals and aspirations constituting the good rested on ego-formation or on ego-superego relations. A great part of the ethical theory that made use of psychoanalytic knowledge concerned itself with character and virtue, falling into a self-development framework rather than the goal-seeking or the juridical. But the psychoanalytic exploration of conscience and guilt and shame formations did affect deeply the theory of duty, and the probing into phenomena of pleasure and its sources, and phenomena of aspiration, contributed greater depth to the understanding of the good.

For the most part, the utilitarian and naturalistic theories have inherited the older goal-seeking framework with its picture of the unified goal broken up by evolutionary theory, by depth psychology, and by social science and its study of historical goals and their patterning. In the pragmatic formulations, akin to the naturalistic in their close relation to the sciences, but more directly incorporating the psychological study of knowledge processes, the focus is more sharply on the critical processes of evaluation and formation of rules. In William James's *Psychology* (1890) and in Dewey's reformulation of it, experience is not the passive lining-up of sensory building-blocks; it is the active attention and selection in the stream of consciousness or the flux of events, guided by the existent state and purposes of the organism, which creates signals and stimuli out of what is going on, and guides awareness and response. Categories, and ideas generally, are instruments for organizing one's activity and for resolving problems that arise. The body of ideas and habits which characterize the self at any time is therefore constantly undergoing change or is open to change in response to the growth of experience. The process is through and through an interactive one.

The psychological exploration is initially grounded in James's great work. The logical analysis of knowledge, so as to extend the analysis of action to it, is carried out with the greatest technical refinement by C. I. Lewis. The general philosophical picture in application to a whole range of fields is most evident in the instrumentalism of John Dewey. Lewis and Dewey especially stress the unified character of knowledge as against those who, like the emotivists, reject scientific method in ethics.

James's treatment of the good and the right does not go much beyond the general naturalistic concept of the integration of men's wishes and desires, or where it does it is to stress the creative frontier element in willing. Lewis analyzes good or value as one kind of empirical knowledge, where satisfactions disclosed in experience serve as the experiential base. But such judgments, though necessary, are not sufficient to determine what is right to do, since some critique or principle is needed to rank and systematize goods—one's own as well as the relation of one's own

185

good with that of others. What is distinctive about Lewis' analysis is that such a critique, imperative or prescriptive, appears not only to guide action but in the construction of all knowledge.

These rational imperatives, thus presupposed in the enterprises of science and morality, are basically four, each of which is presupposed in the succeeding ones. The first two are the rules of consistency and cogency, establishing logic and the methods of evidence as compelling. The third is the rule of prudence, according to which a man reckons his well-being in terms of his whole life rather than in momentary or fragmentary impulse. The fourth is the rule of justice, expressing the phenomena of sociality and social grouping.

Dewey goes beyond reliance on the general character of human psychology and the knowledge process to the results of the specific sciences and the history of man. The general background of his approach is the acceptance on evolutionary and historical grounds of increasingly rapid change in human life. Hence fixity in goals, in rules, in specific forms of relevant character, in specific patterns of self-social relations and in responsibility, is not to be expected. Given such change, the basic need is for direction and guidance of change. Intelligence is a general name for man's increasingly stabilized method of evaluation. Accordingly, Dewey refashions the initial picture of a moral situation and the role of concepts of good and right. A moral situation is not primarily one in which moral principles struggle with inclination; it is rather one in which there is a problem or conflict of principles so that a decision is necessary. Ethics embodies the lessons of reflective experience as an aid to such decision.

Good refers, then, not to a set of ends, although its base of phenomena is the purposive activity of men, but to a mode of evaluating ends, that is, to the development of a standard. The traditional sharp distinction of means and ends is also reassessed. In effect, Dewey is developing fresh categories for dealing with the good, in the light of the psychological processes of purposive activity. Ends are ends-in-view, targets that are set up so that aiming at them will resolve the problems in the situation. Similarly, desire is not mere liking, but arises in a matrix in which to pursue the object of desire will satisfy needs, harmonize habit conflicts, and so on. Hence ends are constantly open to evaluation in terms of consequences met in their pursuit.

Judgments of right, duty, and rights arise in the context of claims that are a constant feature of group life. Guidance by rule, or principles, is thus unavoidable. It is this distinctive context which underlies the claim that the right is separate from the good. Dewey, consciously facing the traditional issue of the relation of the right and the good, and the attempts to reduce one to the other, decides that the categorial distinction is supported by the basic difference in the phenomena of desire and aspiration on the one hand, and interpersonal claims within the group on the other. But it does not follow that there are other standards than that of the good for deciding between alternative rules or principles of right. Hence Dewey's solution, in his and James H. Tufts' major work on *Ethics* (rev. ed., 1932), is the distinction of the concepts, but insistence on evaluation of what is right by what promotes the good. In his later *Theory of Valuation* (1939), however, the concern with right and wrong recedes, and Dewey deals rather with the way criteria for evaluation in all fields rise and operate as standards and principles. The emphasis throughout remains on the theory of reflective criticism.

***Moral Autonomy and the Theory of Criticism.*** It is this emphasis on the theory of criticism in morality, most clearly presented in the pragmatist formulation, but implicit in most twentieth-century ethics, that emerges as the distinctive mark of moral autonomy. Its basis in the history of ideas was the unsettling of all fixities in the development of evolutionary conceptions. Its sociological base in the twentieth century is the complexity, rapidity of change, and conflicts, arising in all institutions and segments of human life; the collective effect is an increase in the need for decision, and the importance of comprehensive standards as contrasted with the rules of specific fields. Even in the ethical formulations that set up a separate domain of value and took autonomy to lie in independence from existence, this independence when it functions becomes in effect the right of moral criticism of anything and everything. Thus moral autonomy becomes less the traditional emphasis on Kantian formulation of laws, or the emphasis on the isolation of ethics from the sciences and human knowledge generally; rather it maintains the integrity of moral decision as a critical process. Ethical theory becomes thus the theory of the way in which human knowledge can be used by men who become conscious of their human aims—both perennial and historically local—to criticize the direction of their striving and to reorient it on the basis of the evidence. In such a conception, both the right and the good become retranslated into phases of the critical process.

*BIBLIOGRAPHY*

References to individual moral philosophers through the nineteenth century and their works may be found in Henry Sidgwick, *Outlines of the History of Ethics*, 5th ed. (London, 1902), or in a comprehensive general history of philosophy, such as *A History of Philosophy*, 3rd ed., by B. A. G. Fuller, revised by Sterling M. McMurrin (New York, 1955). See also Alasdair MacIntyre, *A Short History of Ethics* (London, 1967).

Twentieth-century conceptions of the right and the good are found in the various schools or movements. For a study of general value theory that looks back historically, see John Laird, *The Idea of Value* (Cambridge, 1929). For phenomenological approaches to value: Nicolai Hartmann, *Ethics*, trans. Stanton Coit (London, 1932), and Wolfgang Köhler, *The Place of Value in a World of Facts* (New York, 1938). For naturalistic value theory: Ralph Barton Perry, *General Theory of Value* (New York, 1926) and *Realms of Value* (Cambridge, Mass., 1958); Stephen C. Pepper, *The Sources of Value* (Berkeley and Los Angeles, 1958). For analytic formulations in the first part of the century: G. E. Moore, *Principia Ethica* (Cambridge, 1903); H. A. Prichard, *Moral Obligation* (Oxford, 1949); W. D. Ross, *The Right and The Good* (Oxford, 1930). For emotive theory: Charles L. Stevenson, *Ethics and Language* (New Haven, 1944). For ordinary language analysis: P. H. Nowell-Smith, *Ethics* (London, 1954). For formal approaches in deontic and axiological systems: G. H. von Wright, *Norm and Action* (London, 1963) and *The Logic of Preference* (London, 1963); see also his general analytic study, *The Varieties of Goodness* (London, 1963). For pragmatic approaches: C. I. Lewis, *An Analysis of Knowledge and Valuation* (LaSalle, Ill., 1946), Part III, and *The Ground and Nature of the Right* (New York, 1955); John Dewey and James H. Tufts, *Ethics*, rev. ed. (New York, 1932) and John Dewey, *Theory of Valuation* (Chicago, 1939).

ABRAHAM EDEL

[See also **Evil; Evolutionism; Happiness and Pleasure;** Hegelian . . . ; Justice; **Nature;** Platonism; Pragmatism; Socialism; **Utilitarianism.**]

# ROMANTICISM IN LITERATURE

THE TERM "romantic" emerges in the second half of the seventeenth century both in England and France. Its meaning in the phrase "as in romances" denotes, e.g., medieval romances or the epics of Ariosto and Tasso or, most frequently, the sprawling romances of intrigue and adventure composed in France by the Scudérys and La Calprenède. It was originally a pejorative term for anything "unreal," "marvelous," "extravagantly fanciful," or "sentimental." By many metaphorical shifts, largely during the eighteenth century, the term was also applied to landscapes. It became an alternative term for "picturesque," either of the idyllic kind or, in almost total contrast, to a wild and disorderly nature. This complex history with its proliferations and ramifications has been studied very fully, most recently by François Jost (1968).

The term, however, preserved throughout its early

history its clear literary reference to medieval romances and to the verse epics of Ariosto and Tasso from which their themes and "machinery" were derived. It occurs in this sense in France in 1669, in England in 1674. (Jean Chapelain speaks of *l'épique romanesque, genre de poésie sans art* in 1667. In 1669 he contrasts *poésie romanesque* and *poésie héroïque*. René Rapin refers to *poésie romanesque du Pulci, du Boiardo, et de l'Arioste* in 1673. Thomas Rymer translates this as "Romantick Poetry of Pulci, Bojardo, and Ariosto" a year later.) Thomas Warton understood it to have this meaning when he wrote his introductory dissertation to his *History of English Poetry* (1774), "The Origin of Romantic Fiction in Europe." In Warton's writings and those of several of his contemporaries a contrast is implied between this "romantic" literature, both medieval and Renaissance, and the whole tradition of literary art as it came down from classical antiquity. The composition and "machinery" of Ariosto, Tasso, and Spenser are defended against the charges of neo-classical criticism with arguments which derive from the Renaissance defenders of Ariosto and Tasso. (For the antecedents of Warton's and Hurd's arguments, see Odell Shepard's review of Clarissa Rinaker's *Thomas Warton* in *Journal of English and German Philology*, **16** [1917], 153.) An attempt is made to justify a special taste for such "romantic" fiction and its noncompliance with classical standards and rules. The dichotomy implied has obvious analogues in other contrasts common in the eighteenth century: between the ancients and moderns, between artificial and popular poetry, the "natural" poetry of Shakespeare unconfined by rules and that of French classical tragedy. A definite juxtaposition of "Gothic" and "classical" occurs in Bishop Richard Hurd and Thomas Warton. Hurd speaks of Tasso as "trimming between the Gothic and the Classic," and of the *Faerie Queene* as a "Gothic, not a classical poem." Warton calls Dante's *Divine Comedy* a "wonderful compound of classical and romantic fancy." Here the two famous words meet, possibly for the first time, but Warton probably meant little more than that Dante used both classical mythology and chivalric motifs.

This use of the term "romantic" penetrated into Germany. In 1766 Heinrich Wilhelm Gerstenberg reviewed Warton's *Observations on the Fairy Queen*, and Herder used the learning, information, and terminology of Warton and his English contemporaries. He distinguished sometimes between the "romantic" (chivalric) and the "Gothic" (Nordic) taste, but mostly the words "Gothic" and "romantic" were used by him interchangeably. This usage then penetrated into the first handbooks of general history of literature: into Eichhorn's *Literärgeschichte* (1799) and into the first volumes, devoted to Italian and Spanish literature, of Friedrich Bouterwek's monumental *Geschichte der Poesie und Beredsamkeit seit dem Ende des dreizehnten Jahrhunderts* (1801–05). There the term *romantisch* is used in all combinations: style, manners, characters, poetry are called *romantisch*. Sometimes Bouterwek uses the term *altromantisch* to refer to the Middle Ages, and *neuromantisch* to refer to what we would call the Renaissance. This usage is substantially identical with Warton's except that its scope has been expanded more and more: not only medieval literature and Ariosto and Tasso but also Shakespeare, Cervantes, and Calderón are called "romantic." It simply means all poetry written in a tradition differing from that descended from classical antiquity. This broad historical conception was later combined with a new meaning: the typological, which is based on an elaboration of the contrast between "classical" and "romantic" due to the Schlegels. Goethe, in a conversation with Eckermann in 1830 (March 21), said that Schiller invented the distinction "naive and sentimental" and that the Schlegels merely renamed it "classical and romantic." But this is not accurate history. Schiller's *Über naive und sentimentalische Dichtung* was a statement of a typology of styles which did influence Friedrich Schlegel's turn towards modernism from his earlier Hellenism. The best analysis is in A. O. Lovejoy's "Schiller and the Genesis of German Romanticism," *Modern Language Notes*, **35** (1920), 1–10, 136–46; reprinted in *Essays in the History of Ideas* (Baltimore, 1948), pp. 207–27. But Schiller's contrast is not identical with that of the Schlegels, as is obvious from the mere fact that Shakespeare is *naiv* in Schiller and *romantisch* in Schlegel.

Much attention has, comprehensibly, been paid to the exact usage of these terms by the Schlegels and their close associates (Lovejoy [1916], pp. 385–96, and [1917], pp. 65–77; reprinted, *Essays . . .* [1948], pp. 183–206). But, if we look at the history of the word "romantic" from a wide European perspective, many of these uses must be considered purely idiosyncratic, since they had no influence on the further history of the term and did not even determine the most influential statement formulated by August Wilhelm Schlegel in the *Lectures on Dramatic Art and Literature* (1809–11), which has rightly been called the "Message of German Romanticism to Europe." (Josef Körner, *Die Botschaft der deutschen Romantik an Europa*, Augsburg [1929], is a sketch of the reception of A. W. Schlegel's lectures outside Germany.)

The terms *Romantik* and *Romantiker* as nouns were apparently inventions of Novalis in 1798–99. But, with Novalis, a *Romantiker* is a writer of romances and fairy tales of his own peculiar type, *Romantik* is a synonym of *Romankunst* in this sense. (See *Schriften*, ed.

Samuel-Kluckhohn, 3, 263; "Romantik," 3, 74–75, 88. These passages date from 1798–99, but only the first was printed in the 1802 edition of Novalis' *Schriften*, ed. F. Schlegel and L. Tieck, 2, 311.) Also the famous fragment, No. 116, of the *Athenaeum* (1798) by Friedrich Schlegel, which defines "romantic poetry" as "progressive Universalpoesie" connects it with the idea of such a romantic novel. In the later "Gespräch über die Poesie" (1800), however, the term assumed again its concrete historical meaning: Shakespeare is characterized as laying the foundation of romantic drama and the romantic is found also in Cervantes, in Italian poetry, "in the age of chivalry, love, and fairy tales, whence the thing and the word are derived." Friedrich Schlegel, at this time, does not consider his own age romantic, since he singles out the novels of Jean Paul as the "only romantic product of an unromantic age." He uses the term also quite vaguely and extravagantly as an element of all poetry and claims that all poetry must be romantic. (Reprinted in Friedrich Schlegel's *Jugendschriften*, ed. J. Minor, Vienna [1882], 2, 220–21, 365, 372.)

But the descriptions and pronouncements which were influential, both in Germany and abroad, were those of the older brother, August Wilhelm Schlegel. In the lectures on aesthetics, given at Jena in 1798, the contrast of classical and romantic is not yet drawn explicitly. But it is implied in the lengthy discussion of modern genres, which include the romantic novel culminating in the "perfect masterwork of higher romantic art," *Don Quixote*, the romantic drama of Shakespeare, Calderón, and Goethe, and the romantic folk poetry of the Spanish romances and Scottish ballads (*Vorlesungen über philosophische Kunstlehre*, ed. W. A. Wünsche, Leipzig [1911], pp. 214, 217, 221).

In the Berlin lectures, given from 1801 to 1804, though not published until 1884 (*Vorlesungen über schöne Literatur und Kunst*, ed. J. Minor, 3 vols., Heilbronn [1884]; see especially 1, 22). Schlegel formulated the contrast, classical and romantic, as that between the poetry of antiquity and modern poetry, associating romantic with the progressive and Christian. He sketched a history of romantic literature which starts with a discussion of the mythology of the Middle Ages and closes with a review of the Italian poetry of what we would today call the Renaissance. Dante, Petrarch, and Boccaccio are described as the founders of modern romantic literature, though Schlegel, of course, knew that they admired antiquity. But he argued that their form and expression were totally unclassical. They did not dream of preserving the forms of antiquity in structure and composition. "Romantic" includes the German heroic poems such as the *Nibelungen*, the cycle of Arthur, the Charlemagne romances, and Spanish literature from *El Cid* to *Don Quixote.* The lectures were well attended and from them these conceptions penetrated into print in the writings of other men. They are found in the unpublished lectures of Schelling on *Philosophie der Kunst* (1802–03), printed only in *Sämtliche Werke,* 1st. sec., 5 (Suttgart, 1859). Schelling had read the MS of Schlegel's Berlin lectures. In Jean Paul's *Vorschule der Aesthetik* (1804), and in Friedrich Ast's *System der Kunstlehre* (1805) we find the contrast elaborated. Ast had attended A. W. Schlegel's lectures at Jena in 1798. His very imperfect transcript was published in 1911. But the most important formulation was in the *Lectures* of A. W. Schlegel delivered at Vienna in 1808–09 and published in 1809–11. There romantic-classical is associated with the antithesis of organic-mechanical and plastic-picturesque. There clearly the literature of antiquity and that of neo-classicism (mainly French) is contrasted with the romantic drama of Shakespeare and Calderón, the poetry of perfection with the poetry of infinite desire.

It is easy to see how this typological and historical usage could pass into the designation of the contemporary movement, since the Schlegels were obviously strongly anticlassicist at that time and were appealing to the ancestry and models of the literature they had designated as romantic. But the process was surprisingly slow and hesitant. The designation of contemporary literature as romantic was apparently due only to the enemies of the Heidelberg group which today we are accustomed to call the Second Romantic School. Johann Heinrich Voss attacked the group for their reactionary Catholic views in 1808 and published a parodistic *Klingklingelalmanach* with the subtitle: *Ein Taschenbuch für vollendete Romantiker und angehende Mystiker.* The *Zeitschrift für Einsiedler,* the organ of Arnim and Brentano, adopted the term with alacrity. In the *Zeitschrift für Wissenschaft und Kunst* (1808), the merit of *unsere Romantiker* seems to be praised for the first time. The first historical account of *die neue literarische Partei der sogenannten Romantiker* can be found only in the eleventh volume (1819) of Bouterwek's monumental *Geschichte,* where the Jena group and Brentano are discussed together (Ullmann and Gotthard [1927], pp. 70ff.). Heine's much later *Romantische Schule* (1833) included Fouqué, Uhland, Werner, and E. T. A. Hoffmann. Rudolf Haym's standard work, *Die romantische Schule* (1870) is limited to the first Jena group: the Schlegels, Novalis, and Tieck. Thus, in German literary history, the original broad historical meaning of the term has been abandoned and *Romantik* is used for a group of writers who did not call themselves *Romantiker.*

The broad meaning of the term as used by August Wilhelm Schlegel, however, spread abroad from Germany in all directions.

In the Latin world, and in England as well as in America, the intermediary role of Madame de Staël was decisive. For France it can be shown, however, that she was anticipated by others, though far less effectively. Warton's usage of the term was apparently rare in France, though it occurs in Chateaubriand's *Essai sur les révolutions* (1797), a book written in England, where the word is coupled with *Gothique* and *tudesque,* and spelled in the English way (Baldensperger [1937], p. 90). But with the exception of such small traces, the word is not used in a literary context until the German influence was felt directly. It occurs in a letter by Charles Villers, a French emigrant in Germany and one of the first expounders of Kant, published in the *Magasin encyclopédique* in 1810. Dante and Shakespeare are spoken of as "sustaining *la Romantique*" and the new spiritual sect in Germany is praised because it favors *"la Romantique."* (Reprinted in Edmond Eggli and Pierre Martino, *Le débat romantique en France,* Paris [1933], I, 26–30.) Villers' article was hardly noticed: a translation of Bouterwek's *Geschichte der spanischen Literatur* by Philippe-Albert Stapfer, in 1812, also elicited no interest, though it was reviewed by the young Guizot. The decisive year was 1813: then Sismondi's *De la littérature du midi de l'Europe* was published in May and June. In October 1813, Madame de Staël's *De l'Allemagne* was finally published in London, though it had been ready for print in 1810. In December 1813, A. W. Schlegel's *Cours de littérature dramatique* appeared in a translation by Madame Necker de Saussure, a cousin of Madame de Staël. Most importantly, *De l'Allemagne* was reprinted in Paris in May 1814. All these works radiate from one center, Coppet, Madame de Staël's château near Geneva, and Sismondi, Bouterwek, and Madame de Staël are, as far as the concept of "romantic" is concerned, definitely dependent on Schlegel.

The exposition of classical-romantic in Chapter 11 of *De l'Allemagne,* including its parallel of classical and sculpturesque, romantic and picturesque, the contrast between Greek drama of event and modern drama of character, the poetry of Fate versus the poetry of Providence, the poetry of perfection versus the poetry of progress, clearly derive from Schlegel. Sismondi disliked Schlegel personally and was shocked by many of his "reactionary" views. In details, he may have drawn much more from Bouterwek than from Schlegel, but his view that the Romance literatures are essentially romantic in spirit, and that French literature forms an exception among them, is derived from Schlegel, as are his descriptions of the contrast between Spanish and Italian drama. (Best accounts of these relationships are by Carlo Pellegrini, *Il Sismondi e la storia delle letterature dell'Europa meridionale*, Geneva [1926], Comtesse Jean de Pange, *Auguste-Guillaume Schlegel et Madame de Staël*, Paris [1938], and Jean-R. de Salis, *Sismondi, 1773–1842*, Paris [1932].)

These three books, Sismondi's, Madame de Staël's, and Schlegel's, were reviewed and discussed very heatedly in France. M. Edmond Eggli has collected a whole volume of almost five hundred pages of these polemics, covering only the years 1813–16. The reaction to the scholarly Sismondi was fairly mild, to the foreign Schlegel violent, and to Madame de Staël it was mixed and frequently baffled. In all of these polemics, the enemies are called *les romantiques*, but it is not clear what recent literature is referred to except these three books. When Benjamin Constant published his novel *Adolphe* (1816), he was attacked as strengthening *le genre romantique*. The melodrama also was called contemptuously by this name and German drama identified with it.

But up to 1816 there was no Frenchman who called himself a romantic nor was the term *romantisme* known in France. Its history is still obscure: *Romantismus* is used as a synonym of bad rhyming and empty lyricism in a letter written by Clemens Brentano to Achim von Arnim in 1803, but this form had no future in Germany (Reinhold Steig, *Achim von Arnim und die ihm nahe standen*, Stuttgart [1894], 1, 102. Letter, Oct. 12, 1803). In 1804 Sénancour refers to *romantisme des sites alpestres* (*Obermann*, letter 87, quoted by Eggli, p. 11), using it thus as a noun corresponding to the use of "romantic" as "picturesque." But, in literary contexts, it does not seem to occur before 1816 and then it is used vaguely and jocularly. There is a letter in the *Constitutionnel*, supposedly written by a man residing near the Swiss frontier, within sight of Madame de Staël's château, who complains of his wife's enthusiasm for the "romantic" and tells of a poet who cultivates *le genre tudesque* and has read to them *des morceaux pleins de* romantisme, *les purs mystères du baiser, la sympathie primitive et l'ondoyante mélancolie des cloches* (July 19, 1816, reprinted in Eggli, pp. 472–73). Shortly afterwards, Stendhal, then at Milan, who had read Schlegel's lectures immediately after the publication of the French translation, complained that, in France, they attack Schlegel and think that they have defeated *le Romantisme* (Letters to Louis Crozet, Sept. 28, Oct. 1, and Oct. 21, 1816, in *Correspondance*, ed. Divan, Paris [1934], 4, 371, 389, and 5, 14–15). Stendhal seems to have been the first Frenchman who declared himself a romantic: *Je suis un romantique furieux c'est-à-dire, je suis pour Shakespeare contre Racine et pour Lord Byron contre Boileau* (Letter to Baron de Mareste, April 14, 1818, *Correspondance*, 5, 137).

But that was in 1818 when Stendhal was voicing his adherence to the Italian romantic movement. Thus Italy enters importantly into the history of the term since it was the first Latin country to have a romantic movement which called itself romantic. There the controversy had penetrated also in the wake of Madame de Staël's *De l'Allemagne*, which was translated as early as 1814. H. Jay's violently antiromantic *Discours sur le genre romantique en littérature*, published in 1814, appeared immediately in an Italian translation. (It appeared first in *Le Spectateur*, no. 24 [1814], 3, 145; reprinted in Eggli, pp. 243–56; in Italian in *Lo Spettatore*, no. 24, 3, 145.) Madame de Staël's article on translations from German and English elicited Lodovico di Breme's defense, but he refers, however, to the whole dispute as a French affair, and obviously thinks of "romantic" in terms which would have been comprehensible to Herder or even Warton. He quotes Gravina's arguments in favor of the composition of Ariosto's *Orlando furioso* and sees that the same criteria apply to *Romantici settentrionali, Shakespeare e Schiller*, in tragedy. ("Intorno all'ingiustizia di alcuni giudizi letterari italiani" [1816], in *Polemiche*, ed. Carlo Calcaterra, Turin [1923], pp. 36–38). Giovanni Berchet's *Lettera semiseria di Grisostomo*, with its translations from Bürger's ballads, is usually considered the manifesto of the Italian romantic movement; but Berchet does not use the noun nor does he speak of an Italian romantic movement. Tasso is one of the poets called *romantici*, and Berchet also suggests the famous contrast between classical poetry and romantic poetry as that between the poetry of the dead and the living (Giovanni Berchet, *Opere*, ed. E. Bellorini, Bari [1912], 2, 19–21). He anticipates the peculiarly "contemporaneous," and political character of the Italian romantic movement. In 1817, Schlegel's *Lectures* were translated by Giovanni Gherardini, but the great outburst of pamphlets—a whole battle—did not break out till 1818, when the term *romanticismo* was used first by antiromantic pamphleteers, Francesco Pezzi, Camillo Piciarelli, and Conte Falletti di Barolo, who wrote *Della romanticomachia*, and there drew the distinction between *genere romantico* and *il romanticismo* (*Discussioni e polemiche sul romanticismo* [1816–26], ed. Egidio Bellorini, Bari [1943], 1, 252, 358–59, 363). Berchet, in his ironical comments, professes not to understand the distinction (*Il Conciliatore*, no. 17 [Oct. 29, 1818], pp. 65–66). Ermes Visconti, in his formal articles on the term, uses shortly afterwards only *romantismo* ("Idee elementari sulla poesia romantica," in *Il Conciliatore*, no. 27 [Dec. 3, 1818], p. 105). But "romanticismo" seems to have been well established by 1819, when D. M. Dalla used it in the title of his translation of the thirtieth chapter of Sismondi's *Literature of the South*, as *Vera*

*Definizione del Romanticismo,* though the French original shows no trace of the term. Stendhal, who had used the term *romantisme,* and continued to use it, was now temporarily converted to *romanticisme,* obviously suggested by the Italian term.

But, in the meantime, *romantisme* seems to have become general in France. François Mignet used it in 1822, Villemain and Lacretelle in the following years (*Courier français* [Oct. 19, 1822], quoted by P. Martino, *L'Époque romantique en France,* Paris [1944], p. 27. Lacretelle, in *Annales de la littérature et des arts,* **13** [1823], 415, calls Schlegel *le Quintilien du romantisme;* quoted in C. M. Des Granges, *Le romantisme et la critique,* Paris [1907], p. 207). The spread and acceptance of the term was assured when Louis S. Auger, director of the French Academy, launched a *Discours sur le romantisme,* condemning the new heresy in a solemn session of the Academy on April 24, 1824. In the second edition of *Racine et Shakespeare* (1825), Stendhal himself gave up his earlier form *romanticisme* in favor of the new *romantisme.* As in Italy, a broadly typological and historical term, introduced by Madame de Staël, became the battle cry of a group of writers who found it a convenient label to express their opposition to the ideals of neo-classicism. With Hugo's preface to *Cromwell* (1827) and his play *Hernani* (1830) a French romantic movement was established under that name.

In Spain the terms "classical" and "romantic" occurred in newspapers as early as 1818, once with a specific reference to Schlegel. But apparently an Italian exile, Luigi Monteggia, who came to Spain in 1821, was the first to write elaborately on *romanticismo* in *Europeo* (1823), where shortly afterward López Soler analyzed the debate between *románticos y clasicistas.* The group of Spanish writers who called themselves *románticos* was, however, victorious only around 1838 and it soon disintegrated as a coherent "school" (E. Allison Peers, "The Term Romanticism in Spain," *Revue Hispanique,* **81** [1933], 411–18. Monteggia's article is reprinted in *Bulletin of Spanish Studies,* **8** [1931], 144–49. For the later history, see E. Allison Peers, *A History of the Romantic Movement in Spain,* 2 vols., Cambridge [1940], and Guillermo Díaz-Plaja, *Introducción al estudio del romanticismo español,* Madrid [1942]).

Among Portuguese poets, Almeida Garrett seems to have been the first to refer to *nos romanticos* in his poem, *Camões,* written in 1823 in Le Havre during his French exile (see Theophilo Braga, *Historia do Romantismo em Portugal,* Lisbon [1880], p. 175).

The Slavic countries received the term at about the same time as the countries of the Romance languages. In Bohemia the adjective *romantický* in connection with a poem occurs as early as 1805, the noun *romantismus* in 1819, the noun *romantika,* a formation from the German, in 1820, the noun *romantik* (meaning romanticist) only in 1835. (These dates come from the very complete collections of the Dictionary of the Czech Academy.) But there never was a formal romantic school.

In Poland, Casimir Brodzinski wrote a dissertation concerning classicism and romanticism in 1818. Mickiewicz wrote a long preface to his *Ballady i Romanse* (1822) in which he expounded the contrast of classical and romantic, referring to Schlegel, Bouterwek, and Eberhard, the author of one of the many German works on aesthetics of the time. The collection contains a poem, "Romantyczność," a ballad on the theme of Bürger's *Lenore* (*Poezie,* ed. J. Kallenbach, Kraków [1930], pp. 45, 51).

In Russia, Pushkin spoke of his *Prisoner from the Caucasus* as a "romantic poem" in 1821, and Prince Vyazemsky, reviewing the poem during the next year, was apparently the first to discuss the contrast between the new romantic poetry and the poetry still adhering to the rules (N. V. Bogoslovsky, ed., *Pushkin o literature,* Moscow and Leningrad [1934], pp. 15, 35, 41, etc. Vyazemsky's review in *Syn otechestva* (1822) was reprinted in *Polnoe Sobranie Sochinenii,* **1,** St. Petersburg [1878], 73–78).

We have left the English story, the most unusual development, for the conclusion. After Warton there had begun in England an extensive study of medieval romances and of "romantic fiction," but there is no instance of a juxtaposition of "classical" and "romantic," nor any awareness that the new literature inaugurated by the *Lyrical Ballads* could be called romantic. Walter Scott, in his edition of *Sir Tristram,* published in Edinburgh in 1804 calls his text "the first classical English romance." An essay by John Foster, "On the Application of the Epithet Romantic" (*Essays in a Series of Letters,* London [1805]), is merely a commonplace discussion of the relation between imagination and judgment with no hint of a literary application except to chivalrous romances.

The distinction of classical-romantic occurs for the first time in Coleridge's lectures, given in 1811, and is there clearly derived from Schlegel, since the distinction is associated with that of organic and mechanical, painterly and sculpturesque, in close verbal adherence to Schlegel's phrasing. (See Coleridge's *Shakespearean Criticism,* ed. Thomas M. Raysor, Cambridge, Mass. [1930], 1, 196–98, 2, 265, and *Miscellaneous Criticism,* ed. T. M. Raysor, Cambridge, Mass. [1936], pp. 7, 148. Coleridge himself says that he received a copy of Schlegel's *Lectures* on Dec. 12, 1811; see Coleridge's *Unpublished Letters,* ed. Earl L. Griggs, London [1932], 2, 61–67.) But these lectures were not published at that time, and thus the distinction was popularized in England only through Madame de Staël, who made Schlegel and Sismondi known in England. *De l'Allemagne*, first published in French in London, appeared almost simultaneously in an English translation. Two reviews, by Sir James Mackintosh and William Taylor of Norwich, reproduce the distinction between classical and romantic, and Taylor mentions Schlegel and knows of Madame de Staël's indebtedness to him (*Edinburgh Review*, **22** [Oct. 1813], 198–238; *Monthly Review*, **72** [1813], 421–26, **73** [1814], 63–68, 352–65, especially 364). Schlegel was in the company of Madame de Staël in England in 1814. The French translation of Schlegel's *Lectures* was very favorably reviewed in the *Quarterly Review* (**20** [Jan. 1814], 355–409), and in 1815 John Black, an Edinburgh journalist, published his English translation. This was also very well received. Some reviews reproduce Schlegel's distinction quite extensively: for instance, Hazlitt's in the *Edinburgh Review* of February 1816 (reprinted in *Complete Works*, ed. Howe, 16, 57–99). Schlegel's distinction and views on many aspects of Shakespeare were used and quoted by Hazlitt, by Nathan Drake in his *Shakespeare* (1817), by Scott in his *Essay on Drama* (1819), and in *Ollier's Literary Magazine* (1820), which contains a translation of Schlegel's old essay on *Romeo and Juliet*.

The usual impression that the classical-romantic distinction was little known in England seems not quite correct. There is further evidence in Herbert Weisinger's "English Treatment of the Classical-Romantic Problem," in *Modern Language Quarterly* (**7** [1946], 477–88). It is discussed in Thomas Campbell's *Essay on Poetry* (1819), though Campbell finds Schlegel's defense of Shakespeare's irregularities on "romantic principles" "too romantic for his conception." In Sir Edgerton Brydges' *Gnomica* and *Sylvan Wanderer* there is striking praise of romantic medieval poetry and its derivations in Tasso and Ariosto in contrast to the classical abstract poetry of the eighteenth century (issues dated Apr. 20, 1819, and Oct. 23, 1818). We find only a few uses of these terms at that time: Samuel Singer, in his introduction to Marlowe's *Hero and Leander* (London, 1821), says that "Musaeus is more classical, Hunt more romantic." He defends Marlowe's extravagances which might excite the ridicule of French critics: "but here in England their reign is over and thanks to the Germans, with the Schlegels at their head, a truer philosophical method of judging is beginning to obtain amoung us" (p. lvii). De Quincey in 1835 attempted a more original elaboration of the dichotomy by stressing the role of Christianity and the difference in the attitudes toward death; but even these ideas are all derived from the Germans. But none of the English poets recognized himself

as a romanticist or recognized the relevance of the debate to his own time and country. Neither Coleridge nor Hazlitt, who used Schlegel's *Lectures*, made such an application. Byron definitely rejects it. Though he knew (and disliked) Schlegel personally, had read *De l'Allemagne*, and even tried to read Friedrich Schlegel's *Lectures*, he considered the distinction "romantic-classical" as merely a Continental debate. In a dedication of *Marino Falieri* (1820) to Goethe Byron refers to "the great struggle, in Germany, as well as in Italy, about what they call 'classical' and 'romantic'—terms which were not subjects of classification in England, at least when I left it four or five years ago." Byron contemptuously says of the enemies of Pope in the Bowles-Byron controversy, "nobody thought them worth making a sect of." "Perhaps there may be something of the kind sprung up latterly, but I have not heard of much about it, and it would be such bad taste that I shall be very sorry to believe it." Still, during the next year, Byron used the concepts in what seems to be a plea for the relativity of poetic taste. He argues that there are no invariable principles of poetry, that reputations are bound to fluctuate. "This does not depend upon the merits [of the poets] but upon the ordinary vicissitudes of human opinion. Schlegel and Mme de Staël have endeavoured also to reduce poetry to two systems, classical and romantic. The effect is only beginning."

But there is no consciousness in Byron that he belongs to the romantics. An Austrian police spy in Italy knew better. He reported that Byron belongs to the *Romantici* and "had written and continues to write poetry of this new school." (For Madame de Staël sending Schlegel's *Lectures* to Byron, see Byron's *Letters and Journals*, ed. Lord Prothero [1901], 2, 343. On Friedrich Schlegel's *Lectures*, cf. *Letters*, 5, 191–93. The dedication of *Marino Falieri*, dated Oct. 17, 1820, ibid., 5, 100–04. The letter to Murray on Bowles, Feb. 7, 1821, ibid., 5, 553–54n. The police spy story, Sept. 10, 1819, quoted ibid., 4, 462.)

The actual application of the term "romantic" to English literature of the early nineteenth century is much later. Also the terms, "a romantic," "a romanticist," "romanticism," are very late in English and occur first in reports or notes on Continental phenomena. An article in English by Stendhal in 1823 reviews his own book, *Racine et Shakespeare*, singling out the section on "Romanticism" for special praise (*New Monthly Magazine*, **3** [1823], 522–28, signed Y. I. See Doris Gunnell, *Stendhal et l'Angleterre*, Paris [1909], pp. 162–63). Carlyle entered in his notebook in 1827 that "Grossi is a Romantic and Manzoni a romanticist." In his "State of German Literature" (1827) he speaks of the German "Romanticists." "Romanticism" occurs in his article on Schiller (1831), where he says complacently that "we are troubled with no controversies on Romanticism and Classicism, the Bowles controversy on Pope having long since evaporated without result" (*Two Note Books*, ed. C. E. Norton, New York [1898], p. 111. *Miscellanies*, London [1890], 1, 45, and 3, 71. Cf. also 2, 276).

Similarly Edward Bulwer-Lytton referred to the "good people in France who divert themselves with disputing the several merits of the Classical School, and the Romantic. The English have not disputed on the matter" and "have quietly united the two schools." Byron and Shelley are at once classical and romantic (*England and the English* [1833], Book IV. Ch. iv). As late a book as Mrs. Oliphant's *Literary History of England in the End of the Eighteenth and Beginning of the Nineteenth Century* (1882) shows no trace of the term and its derivatives. She speaks merely of the Lake School, the Satanic School, and the Cockney Group. W. Bagehot used "romantic" with "classical" in a way which shows that they were not associated in his mind with a definite, established period of English literature: he speaks of Shelley's "classical imagination" (1856) and in 1864 contrasts the "classical" Wordsworth with the "romantic" Tennyson and the "grotesque" Browning (*Literary Studies*, ed. R. H. Hutton, London [1905], 1, 231 and 2, 341).

But this does not seem to be the entire story. Among the handbooks of English literature, Thomas Shaw's *Outlines of English Literature* (1849) is the earliest exception. He speaks of Scott as the "first stage in literature towards romanticism" and calls Byron the "greatest of romanticists," but separates Wordsworth for his "metaphysical quietism" (new ed., *Complete Manual*, ed. William Smith, New York [1867], pp. 290ff., 316, 341, 348, 415). It may be significant that Shaw compiled his handbook originally for his classes at the Lyceum in St. Petersburg, where by that time, as everywhere on the Continent, the terms were established and expected.

In David Macbeth Moir's *Sketches of the Poetical Literature of the Past Half Century* (1852), Matthew Gregory Lewis is set down as the leader of the "purely romantic school" of which Scott, Coleridge, Southey, and Hogg are listed as disciples, while Wordsworth is treated independently. Scott is treated under the heading "The Revival of the Romantic School," though the term is not used in the text of the chapter (2nd ed., Edinburgh [1852]; six lectures delivered in 1850–51; cf. pp. 17, 117, 213). W. Rushton's *Afternoon Lectures on English Literature* (1863) given in Dublin, discusses the "Classical and Romantic School of English Literature as represented by Spenser, Dryden, Pope, Scott and Wordsworth." The further spread and establish-ment of the term for English literature of the early nineteenth century is probably due to Alois Brandl's *Coleridge und die romantische Schule in England*, translated by Lady Eastlake (1887), and to the vogue of Pater's discussion of "Romanticism" in *Appreciations* (1889); it is finally established in books such as those of W. L. Phelps' *The Beginnings of the English Romantic Movement* (1893) and Henry A. Beers' *A History of English Romanticism in the 18th Century* (1898).

We have to conclude that the self-designation of writers and poets as "romantic" varies in the different countries considerably; many examples are late and short-lived. If we take self-designation as the basic criterion for modern use, there would be no romantic movement in Germany before 1808, none in France before 1818 or (since the 1818 example was an isolated instance, Stendhal) before 1824, and none at all in England. If we take the use of the word "romantic" for any kind of literature (at first medieval romances, Tasso, and Ariosto) as our criterion, we are thrown back to 1669 in France, 1673 in England, 1698 in Germany. If we insist on taking the contrast between the terms "classical and romantic" as decisive, we arrive at the dates 1801 for Germany, 1810 for France, 1811 for England, 1816 for Italy, etc. If we think that the noun "romanticism" is particularly important, we would find the term *Romantik* in Germany in 1802, *romantisme* in France in 1816, *romanticismo* in Italy in 1818, and romanticism in England in 1823. All these facts point to the conclusion that the history of the term and its introduction cannot regulate the usage of the modern historian, since he would be forced to recognize milestones in his history which are not justified by the actual state of the literatures in question. The great changes happened, independently of the introduction of these terms, either before or after them and only rarely approximately at the same time.

On the other hand, the conclusion drawn from examinations of the history of the words, viz., that they are used in contradictory senses, seems exaggerated. One must grant that many German aestheticians juggle the terms in extravagant and personal ways, nor can one deny that the emphasis on different aspects of their meaning shifts from writer to writer and sometimes from nation to nation, but on the whole there was no misunderstanding about the meaning of "romanticism" as a new designation for poetry, opposed to the poetry of neo-classicism, and drawing its inspiration and models from the Middle Ages and the Renaissance. The term was understood in this sense all over Europe, and everywhere we find references to August Wilhelm Schlegel or Madame de Staël and their particular formulas contrasting "classical" and "romantic."

The fact that the convenient terms were introduced

193

sometimes much later than the time when actual repudiation of the neo-classical tradition was accomplished does not, of course, prove that the changes were not noticed at that time.

The mere use of the terms "romantic" and "romanticism" must not be overrated. English writers early had a clear consciousness that there was a movement which rejected the critical concepts and poetic practice of the eighteenth century, that it formed a unity, and had its parallels on the Continent, especially in Germany. Without the term "romantic" we can trace, within a short period, the shift from the earlier conception of the history of English poetry as one of a uniform progress from Waller and Denham to Dryden and Pope, still accepted in Johnson's *Lives of the Poets*, to Southey's opposite view in 1807, that the "time which elapsed from the days of Dryden to those of Pope is the dark age of English poetry." The reformation began with Thomson and the Wartons. The real turning point was Percy's *Reliques*, "the great literary epocha of the present reign" (Introduction to *Specimens of the Later English Poets*, ed. R. Southey, London [1807], pp. xxix and xxxii). Shortly afterwards, in Leigh Hunt's *Feast of the Poets* (1814) Wordsworth is considered "capable of being at the head of a new and great age of poetry; and in point of fact, I do not deny that he is so already, as the greatest poet of the present" (p. 83). In Wordsworth's own postscript to the 1815 edition of the *Poems*, the role of Percy's *Reliques* is again emphasized: "The poetry of the age has been absolutely redeemed by it" (Wordsworth, *Prose Works*, ed. Grosart, 2, 118, 124). In 1816 Lord Jeffrey acknowledged that the "wits of Queen Anne's time have been gradually brought down from the supremacy which they had enjoyed, without competition, for the best part of a century." He recognized that the "present revolution in literature" was due to the "French revolution—the genius of Burke—the impression of the new literature of Germany, evidently the original of our Lake School of poetry" (review of Scott's edition of Swift, in *Edinburgh Review* [Sept. 1816]; reprinted in *Contributions to Edinburgh Review*, 2nd ed., London [1846], 1, 158, 167). In Hazlitt's *Lectures on the English Poets* (1818) a new age dominated by Wordsworth is described quite clearly, with its sources in the French revolution, in German literature, and its opposition to the mechanical conventions of the followers of Pope and the old French school of poetry. Scott uses Schlegel extensively and describes the general change as a "fresh turning up of the soil" due to the Germans and necessitated by the "wearing out" of the French models ("Essay on Drama," contributed to *Encyclopaedia Britannica*, Supplement, Vol. 3 [1819]; also in *Miscellaneous Prose Works*, Edinburgh [1834], 6, 380). Carlyle

in his introduction to selections from Ludwig Tieck draws the English-German parallel quite explicitly:

Neither can the change be said to have originated with Schiller and Goethe; for it is a change originating not in individuals, but in universal circumstances, and belongs, not to Germany, but to Europe. Among ourselves, for instance, within the last thirty years, who has not lifted up his voice with double vigour in praise of Shakespeare and Nature, and vituperation of French taste and French philosophy? Who has not heard of the glories of old English literature; the wealth of Queen Elizabeth's age; the penury of Queen Anne's; and the inquiry whether Pope was a poet? A similar temper is breaking out in France itself, hermetically sealed as that country seemed to be against all foreign influences; and doubts are beginning to be entertained, and even expressed, about Corneille and the Three Unities. It seems to be substantially the same thing which has occurred in Germany . . . only that the revolution, which is here proceeding, and in France commencing, appears in Germany to be completed (*Works*, Centenary ed., London [1899], *German Romance*, 1, 261).

Scott, in a retrospective "Essay on Imitations of the Ancient Ballads" (1830), also stressed the role of Percy and the Germans in the revival. "As far back as 1788 a new species of literature began to be introduced into the country. Germany . . . was then for the first time heard of as the cradle of a style of poetry and literature much more analogous to that of Britain than either the French, Spanish or Italian schools" (in a new edition of *Minstrelsy of the Scottish Border* [1830], ed. T. Henderson, New York [1931], pp. 535–62, especially pp. 549–50).

Probably the most widely read of these pronouncements was T. B. Macaulay's account in his review of Moore's *Life of Byron*. There the period of 1750–80 is called the "most deplorable part of our literary history." The revival of Shakespeare, the ballads, Chatterton's forgeries, and Cowper are mentioned as the main agents of change. Byron and Scott are singled out as great names. Most significantly, Macaulay realizes that "Byron, though always sneering at Mr. Wordsworth, was yet, though, perhaps unconsciously, the interpreter between Mr. Wordsworth and the multitude. . . . Lord Byron founded what may be called an exoteric Lake School—what Mr. Wordsworth had said like a recluse, Lord Byron said like a man of the world" (*Edinburgh Review* [June 1831]. Reprinted in *Critical and Historical Essays*, Everyman ed., 2, 634–35). Macaulay thus, long before he knew a term for it, recognized the unity of the English romantic movement.

James Montgomery, in his *Lectures on General Literature* (1833), given in 1830–31, described the age since Cowper as the third era of modern literature.

Southey, Wordsworth, and Coleridge are called the "three pioneers, if not the absolute founders, of the existing style of English literature."

The most boldly formulated definition of the new view is again in Southey, in the "Sketches of the Progress of English Poetry from Chaucer to Cowper" (1833). There the "age from Dryden to Pope" is called "the worst age of English poetry: the age of Pope was the pinchbeck age of poetry." "If Pope closed the door against poetry, Cowper opened it" (*The Works of Cowper*, ed. R. Southey, 3, 109, 142). The same view, though less sharply expressed, can be found with increasing frequency even then in textbooks, such as Robert Chambers' *History of the English Language and Literature* (1836), in De Quincey's writings, and R. H. Horne's *New Spirit of the Age* (1844).

None of these publications use the term "romantic," but in all of them we hear that there is a new age of poetry which has a new style inimical to that of Pope. The emphasis and selections of examples vary, but in combination they say that the German influence, the revival of the ballads and the Elizabethans, and the French Revolution were the decisive influences which brought about the change. Thomson, Burns, Cowper, Gray, Collins, and Chatterton are honored as precursors, Percy and the Wartons as initiators. The trio, Wordsworth, Coleridge, and Southey, are recognized as the founders and, as time progressed, Byron, Shelley, and Keats were added in spite of the fact that this new group of poets denounced the older for political reasons.

This general scheme has been then elaborated by English and American scholarship of the late nineteenth and early twentieth century. It emphasized the revolt against the principles of neo-classical criticism, the rediscovery of older English literature, the turn toward subjectivity and the worship of external nature slowly prepared during the eighteenth century and stated boldly in Wordsworth and Shelley. On the whole academic scholarship was sympathetic to the general outlook of the romantics until, first with the American neo-humanists (Irving Babbitt in particular) and with T. S. Eliot and his followers, and later with F. R. Leavis in England and the New Critics in the United States, an antiromantic reaction set in, which on various grounds, moral, political, and aesthetic, considered the romantic movement a deplorable break with the great humanist and Christian tradition. In Irving Babbitt's *Rousseau and Romanticism* (1919) the objections are largely directed against romantic morality, its conception of love and passion, its theories of genius and inspiration, its worship of nature, and its philosophical monism. With Eliot and his followers the criticism is, at least in part, aesthetic; particularly Shelley was

attacked as monotonous, imprecise and vague but also as ethically immature and politically dangerous.

Meanwhile the prevailing conception of the coherence and unity of romanticism was subjected to a critical examination by A. O. Lovejoy. In his paper "On the Discrimination of Romanticisms" (1924) Lovejoy argued that the word "romantic has come to mean so many things that by itself, it means nothing. It has ceased to perform the function of a verbal sign." Lovejoy proposed to remedy "this scandal of literary history and criticism" by showing that the "Romanticism of one country may have little in common with that of another, that there is, in fact, a plurality of Romanticisms, of possibly quite distinct thought-complexes." He asserts that even "the romantic ideas were in large part heterogeneous, logically independent, and sometimes essentially antithetic to one another in their implications." Lovejoy's examples from Joseph Warton, Friedrich Schlegel, and René de Chateaubriand demonstrate great divergences in the views of nature, politics, imagination, and intellect in the three main countries. Lovejoy's nominalistic disintegration of the concept was pushed then much further by some scholars both in England and the United States. R. S. Crane objected in particular to the simplified view of a struggle between romanticism and classicism in the English eighteenth century and went so far as to speak of "the fairytales about neoclassicism and romanticism" (*Philological Quarterly*, **22** [1943], 143). George Sherburn managed to write a history of English eighteenth-century literature (a section of *Literary History of England*, ed. A. C. Baugh, New York [1948]), without using the term and two new volumes of the *Oxford History of English Literature* (by W. L. Renwick and Ian Jack) either avoid the term altogether or discuss it as "a bed of Procrustes on which to stretch the English literature of the time" (Ian Jack, *English Literature 1818–1832*, Oxford [1963], p. 420). Mr. Jack and many others agree with the view that "the English are notoriously lazy about general ideas and problems of historiography" and are proud of it.

In recent decades, however, new attempts were made to redefine romanticism and even to reassert its unity on a European scale. René Wellek, in "The Concept of Romanticism in Literary History" (*Comparative Literature*, **1** [1949], 1–23, 147–73), tried to show that Lovejoy's disintegration of the concept has gone too far and that it is possible to describe the common elements of all European romanticisms; he tried to show that identical or very similar views of nature, of the imagination and of symbol and myth pervade all European literature (also the minor ones) of that time and that these ideas have a profound coherence and mutual implication. Wellek also tried to show that the rejection of preromanticism (while justified against simple views of a struggle between classicism and romanticism in the eighteenth century) cannot be upheld: even George Sherburn has to describe the same phenomena under the name of "accentuated tendencies" toward the end of the eighteenth century. A new age was being prepared and the preparation can be traced under whatever name. Wellek's article elicited much discussion. Morse Peckham in "Toward a Theory of Romanticism" (*PMLA*, **56** [1951], 5–23) wanted, he says, "to reconcile Lovejoy and Wellek" by singling out the criterion of organic dynamism as the definition of romanticism. He accepts the concept of nature and imagination as central but drops the concern for symbol and myth. Peckham introduced a new term "negative romanticism," that is, despairing, nihilistic romanticism. He argues that "positive romanticism" does not fit a figure such as Byron. Other books have elaborated on these themes particularly Meyer Abrams' *The Mirror and the Lamp* (New York, 1953) which emphasizes the shift from imitation theory to theory of expression, from the mirror to the lamp; or rather, from the mechanistic metaphorical analogies of neo-classical theory to the biological imagery of the romantic critics. In a great number of books and articles, often widely divergent in the evaluation of romanticism, from Frank Kermode's *Romantic Image* (1957) which considers romanticism and its descendant symbolism a "great and in some ways noxious historical myth" to Harold Bloom's exaltation of *The Visionary Company* (1961) of the English romantics, a wide agreement has been reached that romanticism centers on a concern for the reconciliation of subject and object, man and nature, consciousness and unconsciousness. E. D. Hirsch, in *Wordsworth and Schelling* (New Haven, 1960) described, e.g., the convergence of these very different figures in a whole spectrum of ideas: the way of reconciling time and eternity, the immanent theism, the dialectic which favors what Hirsch calls "both/and thinking," the fear of alienation, the concept of living nature, and the role of the imagination which makes explicit the implicit unity of all things. H. H. H. Remak in "Western European Romanticism: Definition and Scope" (*Comparative Literature: Method and Perspective,* ed. Newton P. Stallknecht and Horst Frenz, Carbondale, Ill. [1961]) reaches the conclusion that "the evidence pointing to the existence in Western Europe of a widespread, distinct, and fairly simultaneous pattern of thought, attitudes, and beliefs associated with the connotation 'Romanticism' is overwhelming."

In France the debate about romanticism was largely determined by political considerations. Romanticism was, according to a famous dictum of Victor Hugo, identified with liberalism, with the heritage of the revolution and its supposed initiator Rousseau, and thus became the target of the conservative reaction, particularly during the Dreyfus affair. The arguments, which in English are familiar mainly from Babbitt's books, were actually formulated in France by Désiré Nisard and Ferdinand Brunetière in the nineteenth century and were elaborated particularly by Pierre Lasserre, in *Le romantisme français* (1907). Romanticism, he argues, is "the total corruption of the higher parts of human nature," "the usurpation by sensibility and imagination of the right rule of intelligence and reason," "the decomposition of art because it is the decomposition of man." The romantic worship of nature and progress leads to pantheism, to a cheap optimism and belief in progress. Antiromanticism was a slogan of the *Action française* and many, early in the twentieth century, believed in a revival of classicism including André Gide and Paul Valéry. In the meantime academic research went its even way also in France; Paul Van Tieghem in a learned compendium covering all European literatures, *Le romantisme dans la littérature européenne* (1948), came to the meager conclusion that "the suppression of the mythological style is probably the most universal trait of formal romanticism." But also in France in recent decades a new synthetic view was formulated. Albert Béguin's *L'âme romantique et le rêve* (Marseilles, 1939) sees the greatness of romanticism in its "having recognized and affirmed the profound resemblance of poetic states and the revelations of a religious order." Romanticism, for Béguin centers on myth which it discovers in dreams and the unconscious. Béguin traces the role of dream in the German romantic theorists, philosophers, and doctors of the unconscious and studies it in writers such as Jean Paul, Novalis, Brentano, Arnim, and E. T. A. Hoffmann sympathetically. He sees Nerval, Baudelaire, Rimbaud, Mallarmé, and Proust as their immediate successors. Georges Poulet, the most eminent of the new French critics, has come to conclusions not far removed from those of the recent English and American defenders and definers of the concept. In a chapter of *Les métamorphoses du cercle* (Paris, 1961) he generalizes about romanticism boldly: it is a consciousness of the fundamentally subjective nature of the mind, a withdrawal from reality to the center of the self, which serves as starting point of a return to nature. Poulet draws his examples mainly from French sources but also from Coleridge and Shelley, using insistently the figure of the circle and circumference. His conclusion corroborates the view of romanticism as an effort to overcome the opposition of subject and object in a personal experience.

In Germany, Rudolf Haym's *Romantische Schule* (1870) was the standard work which defined romanticism very narrowly in terms of the first romantic school: in practice, the thought of the Schlegels and Tieck. Haym's concern was mainly historical and descriptive. Only with the dominance of "neo-romantic" tendencies in German literature around the turn of the century did a sympathetic interest in the romantic movement revive. Ricarda Huch's *Blütezeit der Romantik* (1899) was the decisive work, while the researchers of Oskar Walzel, who published many letters and set the movement into a context of intellectual history, gave the revival a scholarly basis. In the early twenties a whole series of books was devoted specifically to definitions of the nature or essence of romanticism. They operate with dichotomies, thesis and antithesis, vast contrasts such as idea and form, idea and experience, rationalism and irrationalism, etc. Max Deutschbein, in *Das Wesen des Romantischen* (Leipzig, 1921) stressed the reconciling, synthetic imagination as the common denominator of romanticism drawing quotations from English and German sources.

A scheme of contrast is the result of Fritz Strich's *Deutsche Klassik und Romantik: oder Vollendung und Unendlichkeit* (Munich, 1922). There Strich transfers Wölfflin's *Kunstgeschichtliche Grundbegriffe* (1915) to literature. Man searches for permanence or eternity; and the history of man oscillates between the two poles of perfection and infinitude. Romanticism is dynamic, has open form, is symbolic, yearns for the infinite always in opposition to classicism documented by the classical stage of Goethe and Schiller. All these writings are surveyed in Julius Petersen's *Wesensbestimmung der deutschen Romantik* (1926). German scholarship was largely *geistesgeschichtlich* but there was also a trend which before the event of Nazism tried to explain romanticism by a kind of racial history.

Josef Nadler in *Die Berliner Romantik* (1921) argued the curious thesis that romanticism is purely a matter of the Germanized Slavs in Eastern Germany who wanted to revive the Teutonic Middle Ages while German classicism is the attempt of the West Germans to revive the Roman antiquity of their distant past. The West Germans in the romantic movement (Brentano, Görres, etc.) are explained away as belonging to a separate movement, called "The Restoration." Similar nationalistic theories which look at romanticism as a purely German affair were expounded during and after the Nazi period by serious scholars such as Richard Benz (*Die deutsche Romantik*, 1937), who seek the essence of romanticism in German music and the spirit of music. Since the second World War interest in *geistesgeschichtlich* speculation declined and German literary scholarship turned toward textual inter-

pretation. There are exceptions such as Adolf Grimme's *Vom Wesen der Romantik* (1947) which has defined romanticism as a breakthrough of what he calls "the vegetative strata of the soul": the preconscious rather than the subconscious. The preconscious includes the imagination which is raised to consciousness in romanticism. Grimme argues for a phenomenological method. The aim of a verbal definition is illusory. We can only point to what is romantic as we can only point to the color red.

But we need not conclude on such an irrationalistic note. The variety of interpretations, the divergence and multiplicity of definition need not lead to despair. One can describe the rise, dominance, and decline of a system of ideas and poetic practices which will have their anticipations and survivals. Periods and movements are not general terms of which every individual work or figure would be merely an example. They are neither mere linguistic labels nor metaphysical entities but regulative ideas, historiographical tools. Agreement on the meaning of romanticism in all the main countries has, in spite of the spate of writings on the topic, grown rather than diminished in recent decades. Romanticism clearly preserves its value as a term for a period in Western literature.

*BIBLIOGRAPHY*

Carla Apollonio, *Romantico: storia e fortuna di una parola* (Florence, 1958). Fernand Baldensperger, "Romantique—ses analogues et équivalents," in *Harvard Studies and Notes in Philology and Literature*, **14** (1937), 13–105. François Jost, "Romantique: la leçon d'un mot," in *Essais de littérature comparée* (Fribourg, 1968), II, 181–258. A. O. Lovejoy, "The Meaning of 'Romantic' in Early German Romanticism," in *Modern Language Notes*, **21** (1916), 385–96, and **22** (1917), 65–77; reprinted in *Essays in the History of Ideas* (Baltimore, 1948), pp. 183–206; idem, "On the Discrimination of Romanticisms," in *PMLA*, **39** (1924), 229–53; reprinted in *Essays in the History of Ideas* (Baltimore, 1948), pp. 228–53. Morse Peckham, "Toward a Theory of Romanticism," in *PMLA*, **66** (1951), 5–23; idem, "Toward a Theory of Romanticism II. Reconsiderations," in *Studies in Romanticism*, **1** (1961), 1–6. Julius Petersen, *Die Wesensbestimmung der deutschen Romantik* (Berlin, 1926). H. H. H. Remak, "West European Romanticism: Definition and Scope," in *Comparative Literature: Method and Perspective*, ed. Newton P. Stallknecht and Horst Frenz (Carbondale, Ill., 1961), pp. 123–59. Franz Schultz, "Romantik und Romantisch als literaturgeschichtliche Terminologie und Begriffsbildung," in *Deutsche Vierteljahrsschrift für Literaturwissenschaft und Geistesgeschichte*, **2** (1924), 349–66. Logan P. Smith, *Four Words: Romantic, Originality, Creative, Genius*, Society for Pure English, Tract No. 17 (Oxford, 1924); reprinted in *Words and Idioms* (Boston, 1925). Richard Ullmann and Helene Gotthard, *Geschichte des Begriffs 'Romantisch' in*

*Deutschland* (Berlin, 1927). René Wellek, "The Concept of Romanticism in Literary Scholarship," in *Comparative Literature*, **1** (1949), 1–23, 147–72; reprinted in *Concepts of Criticism* (New Haven, 1963), pp. 128–98; idem, "Romanticism Re-examined," in *Concepts of Criticism* (New Haven, 1963), pp. 199–221.

RENÉ WELLEK

[See also **Classicism in Literature; Gothic;** Organicism; **Romanticism;** *Zeitgeist*.]

# ROMANTICISM
## (ca. 1780–ca. 1830)

COMMON prudence, if not necessity, dictates consideration of the problem of romanticism before attempting to define or describe it. For the problem, as Arthur Lovejoy pointed out years ago, is a thorny one. In view of the many and conflicting conceptions of romanticism among historians and critics, what if anything can be stated positively about it? Do the facts themselves reveal a genuine "movement," reasonably well unified and of European scope, which peaked in the late eighteenth and early nineteenth centuries and which, because it is identifiable, can then be held responsible for a variety of intellectual and even political progeny in the modern world? Lovejoy, as is well known, came down hard on the skeptical side. "The word 'romantic'," he pointed out, "has come to mean so many things that, by itself, it means nothing" (Lovejoy, 1924). He therefore recommended learning to use the word in the plural. There was a "plurality of Romanticisms" but no "one fundamental 'Romantic' idea." Somewhat ambiguously, he was willing to speak of "a Romantic period" between 1780 and 1830, but not of *a* romantic movement.

This was and still is a useful caveat. The evidence is clear that there were important differences between "the romantic School" which arose in Germany in the 1790's and English and French romanticisms of the same period. Within each century, moreover, the nature of romanticism changes subtly from one generation to the next. "Late" German romanticism, for example, was more nativist, and more fascinated by the occult and supernatural, than the earlier phase which was closer in spirit to "classical" Weimar. In France the gap was even more marked between the "conservative" generation of Chateaubriand and the *émigrés*, and that of the liberal Victor Hugo who himself underwent a considerable change of heart, both politically and religiously, after 1830. The word "ro-

mantic," though lately come into vogue, patently did not function as a rallying cry since it signified too many different things (e.g., "anticlassical" to Friedrich Schlegel, but merely "contemporary" to Stendhal), and besides, not all the persons generally designated as romantics in today's textbooks were conscious of being or called themselves romantics. Romanticism was probably at its most self-conscious in the Berlin-Jena coterie, led by Schlegel among others, which propagated the term and eventually drew fire from Goethe. But to my knowledge neither Coleridge nor Wordsworth ever adopted the label. Save for some highly informal salons as in Berlin, or later on in the *cénacles* of Paris or in esoteric groups like the "Nazarenes" in Rome, romanticism had no institutional organization, and certainly no single great publishing venture comparable to the *Encyclopédie* of the eighteenth century, even within one country. It had no central doctrine, nor even so loose an authority as the Bible during the Protestant Reformation. Indeed, how could it have had, seeing that the romantics, if such they may be called, prided themselves on their individuality.

If carried to the extreme this caveat would indeed dictate a pluralistic and even nominalistic interpretation. But we do not need go so far, for, as René Wellek and some others believe, not only was there a romantic movement of European-wide scope but failure to identify it would mean to miss some of the salient features of nineteenth- and even twentieth-century culture. Naturally, this affirmation must stand or fall on the evidence. However, one or two methodological comments should help to clarify it. First of all, it is important not to cavil at the word itself. "Romanticism" may not be just the right word to describe certain profound changes in *Weltanschauung* which did in fact take place during the period in question. But what word would serve better, especially since tradition has by now, for better or worse, sanctioned its use and furthermore associated it with at least some widely shared assumptions and ideas. Lovejoy, it seems to me, sometimes comes very close to conceding this point despite his insistence on pluralism. Second, we need to remind ourselves that the problem of romanticism is by no means unique. How does it differ, except perhaps in greater complexity, from a host of similar historiographical problems—from, for instance, the problem of the Renaissance, or the Reformation, or even the Enlightenment? The romantic movement is, frankly, an ideal type. But so are most other "movements" in history, especially when considered broadly and transcending provincial boundaries. The historian describes their "ideal" characteristics knowing perfectly well they cannot be found anywhere or all together in a perfectly pure state. But I fail to see how he could do otherwise. Without doing so he could never get much beyond talking about individuals or narrowly circumscribed schools or groups. He could never talk about *the* Renaissance, and we should be the poorer for it.

This sort of ideal type, it should be understood, has a firm basis in reality. It represents the historian's generalizations from the evidence before him: an observed consensus, the common denominator he detects in the midst of diversity. In the case of a movement in ideas this consensus is most easily discovered in what the individuals involved were all *against*. What they were all *for* is harder to get at. But it may not be so difficult if one remembers that the area of agreement is never so much in consciously formulated conceptions (where there is usually wide difference of opinion) as in certain preconceptions, i.e., deeply felt aversions and psychological needs. One of the exciting things about the romantic consensus is that it came about with a minimum of international "influence." There were influences, of course, as of Rousseau on nearly all the Germans, Kant on Coleridge as well as his own countrymen, Herder and Walter Scott on French historiography, for example. But the big story is that the various wings of the romantic movement developed largely independently of one another, out of native impulses, but also—otherwise there would be no consensus—in reaction against a body of ideas common in certain respects to them all.

John Stuart Mill, no romantic himself but a sympathetic and informed observer, put his finger unerringly on what the European romantics disliked. Romanticism, he said in an essay on Armand Carrel (1837), represented a reaction "against the narrownesses of the eighteenth century." Though he was speaking there primarily of literature, it is clear from what follows and from other essays, conspicuously the famous one on Coleridge, that he thought of it as a revolt against narrowness on many fronts, in philosophy and science, in historical and political thought, as well as in poetry and the drama. "Fractional," "partial," "insignificant," "poor," were among the adjectives Thomas Carlyle employed in his essay on Diderot (1833); he denounced "Diderot's habitual world" as "a half-world, distorted into looking like a whole." The reference in both cases was, of course, to the European Enlightenment which by then had become a stereotype, and partly also a caricature. The romantics thought that world too narrow because of its addiction to geometric thinking and the allied doctrine of neo-classicism, or else to Lockean empiricism. The geometric spirit, though metaphysically bold, tried to subject all life to reason and thus to mechanize and demean it. Neo-classicism, similarly ambitious in seeking out Nature's ideal patterns,

imposed universal and iron rules on art and the artist. Empiricism offended for the opposite reason, because it was too skeptical, because it severely limited human knowledge to the sense world of appearances. Newton became an arch-symbol of this narrowness. Opinions about Newton varied, of course, even among the romantics (one thinks of Saint-Simon who preached a Cult of Newton), but William Blake's depiction of him was quite typical. Blake did not see in Newton the great imaginative genius celebrated by Alexander Pope. On the contrary, he demoted him to the material world, making him look downward as though trying to fathom the world by means of a pair of compasses, i.e., by measurement and "reason" alone (*Newton*, Tate Gallery, London [1795]).

A word more about origins would seem advisable at this point in order to avoid misunderstanding. Mill's favorite words—"reaction" and "revolt"—are only approximately correct. Mill viewed the history of ideas as a perpetual oscillation between extremes. One mode of thought, inevitably developed to excess sooner or later, provoked its opposite. Thus, "the eighteenth century" set on foot the romantic movement. The latter, however, must also be seen as growing out of, and not merely reacting against the Enlightenment. In any case it would not have been the same without it. It owed something to British empiricism's attack on rationalism, something to certain *philosophes* like Diderot, who though devoted to the Enlightenment nevertheless developed some decidedly un-*philosophe* notions about nature and the arts. It owed something to the French Revolution which inspired a whole generation of French romantics, especially after 1830. The Enlightenment also left its mark in less obvious ways. Surely the religious heterodoxy of many of the romantics, including pastor Schleiermacher himself, traces back in part to doubts sown by the *philosophes*. And what of the idea of progress? Did it not enhance the romantic sense of the infinite?

The roots of a great movement in opinion are always multiple and complex. Romanticism was not at all, I think, the ally of any particular social class, or, except locally, a "conservative reaction" as has often been claimed. On the other hand, there is no question that political events deepened some facets of romantic sensibility, particularly in Germany during and after the War of Liberation. The romantic movement might be compared to a mighty river into which flowed scores of tributary streams, some of them commencing far back in time, others more recently. A list of these streams would include, in addition to those already mentioned, the individualism of the sixteenth and seventeenth centuries of which romantic individualism might be considered the climax; Pietism in seventeenth-century Germany and the quarrel between *Rubénistes* and *Poussinistes* in seventeenth-century France; the growth of "sentimentalism" everywhere in eighteenth-century Europe; the *Sturm und Drang* of Goethe's Weimar which in some though not all respects is hardly distinguishable from early German romanticism itself; the new German Idealism. Toward the close of the eighteenth century all these streams had contributed to form the romantic movement. If the latter had any "beginning," doubtless it should be looked for in newly discovered and perhaps still somewhat vague tastes and aspirations; only at its height did it become acutely conscious of itself in art and philosophy. Individual thinkers therefore played the role not so much of initiators as implementers of the new tastes. The search for pioneers and precursors, and for the "influence" of one writer or artist on another, seems to me fruitless and footless unless it takes into account the many, and not merely the few, the elite, who were swept up in the romantic torrent. Nevertheless, certain individuals do stand out as important catalytic agents. Such, for example, was Rousseau, the Rousseau of the *Nouvelle Héloïse* and *Émile* which nearly everybody read. Such was Goethe (for all that he called romanticism a "sickness"); Herder for his new views of history; and Immanuel Kant whom Schlegel called the new Moses and whose writings Coleridge said "invigorated" his understanding more than any other work. Kant was particularly important for showing the limits of reason (*Verstand*) yet at the same time postulating strongly the existence of "transcendental ideas." It is important, however, to distinguish the main river from the tributaries. Fundamentally, the romantic movement was just what Mill said it was, a reaction against a certain "narrow" kind of thinking epitomized by the "scientific" Enlightenment.

It is not so easy to say what it stood *for*. "Ontological," "conservative," "religious," "concrete and historical," "poetical" says Mill of its constructive "doctrine" (Mill, "Coleridge," 1840), but he was thinking of romanticism primarily in one country, and consequently not all his adjectives apply equally well to all. Considered more broadly romanticism might better be said to have centered in several quite marked predispositions: an emphasis on particularity or individuality, and a sense of the infinite and the irrational component in human life. These predispositions provide the key (Wordsworth would say "the prelude") to romantic ideas about "Man, Nature, and Society." Without the key, the ideas—i.e., romantic answers to the perennial questions of human life: the sort of questions Wordsworth set out to explore in his philosophical poem *The Excursion*—must often seem hopelessly in conflict and to lead into a maze without end.

Since the romantic mind did not quite center in "Man," it makes sense perhaps to turn first to romantic ideas about God and Nature. Here the sense of the infinite is particularly clear. "The Infinite," said Carlyle, "is more sure than any other fact." To be sure, this sense could take secular as well as religious forms, as we shall see. But it lent itself particularly well to the romantic search for a religious reality beyond reach of reason or sensible experience. "True religion," said Schleiermacher in his famous definition, "is sense and taste for the Infinite (*das Unendliche*)." He also described it as "expansive soaring in the Whole and the Inexhaustible" (*Reden über die Religion*, 1799).

It was widely believed that the world had lost its religious bearings during the Enlightenment and that men needed to recover them if there were ever again to be heroes and great works of imagination. In "the Unbelieving Century" God had become nonexistent or peripheral and bound by rational categories. Carlyle vividly describes this feeling of loss in his chapter on "The Everlasting No" in *Sartor Resartus* (1833–34), that great source book for romantic views on God and religion. His Professor Teufelsdröckh tells there of the spiritual crisis he went through (obviously owing to the corrosive effect of Enlightenment skepticism): how, as "the spirit of Inquiry" took possession of him, he had moved from doubt to disbelief, and consequently was shut out from hope. At best, he thought, there might be "an absentee God," sitting idle since the first Sabbath and looking at the Universe from outside it.

How, then, to recover a living faith? Some romantics never succeeded in doing so, and their failure was doubtless a source, in some individuals, of melancholy. Others, however, like Teufelsdröckh-Carlyle, did rediscover God, but in new and strange places. It is true, then, that the romantic movement sparked a religious revival, but false to think of it as a simple return to orthodoxy. Even those who, like the Roman Catholic refugees and converts, flocked back to their ancestral altars found new and romantic reasons for doing so. Actually, romantic religiosity luxuriated in a great many forms, including some purely private religions like the bizarre mythology invented by William Blake. If these forms had anything in common, it was in the tendency to bring God back "inside" the Universe and to find him in the human heart and nature. In other words, the romantics emphasized the immanence rather than the transcendence of God.

This was true even of an apologist for Catholicism like the Vicomte de Chateaubriand. In the *Génie du Christianisme* (1802), called the "Bible of romanticism," he avoided the traditional kinds of rational "proofs" which Voltaire had found so easy to demolish, and somewhat in the manner of Rousseau's Savoyard

Vicar rediscovered religion through his tears, through passion (Chateaubriand defined religion as "a passion"), through the beauty and sense of awe aroused in the beholder by the presence of God in nature and Gothic churches. A parallel view is observable in Schleiermacher who changed the course of Protestant theology. He too, though more especially in his early utterances when he was closely associated with the Berlin romantic group, shifted the emphasis from rational exegesis and doctrine to individual experience or feeling. It was preeminently in "feeling," he thought, that is, in a precognitive experience, that the individual encountered the Infinite, now brought within the soul itself. Schleiermacher's "Theology of Feeling" thus united the romantic sense of the infinite and romantic individuality. Each individual experienced God in his own unique way, as did every positive religion of the world though Schleiermacher still thought Christianity superior.

But the romantics also characteristically found God in nature, not all of them, of course, not Vigny or Byron, not even Blake, but certainly an impressive number. These "natural supernaturalists," revolting against the Newtonian machine, sought to make nature a home in which man could once again live and feel close to God, and thus solve the problem of dualism which had plagued thinking men since the time of Descartes. The impetus to this new way of thinking about nature came from, among others, Rousseau whom the contemplation of nature could send into mystical ecstasies (as in Les rêveries du promeneur solitaire, 1776–78); Goethe who in his morphological studies was always trying to discover the original and inner principle of things, the invisible in the visible; Spinoza, or rather Spinoza seen through Jacobi's and Herder's eyes, who seemed to teach a God immanent in nature, indeed in all existence, as a life-force. The logical extension of such thinking was a new religion of nature, appropriately called by Carlyle—who at this point again summarizes a large body of romantic opinion—"Natural Supernaturalism." Natural Supernaturalism, rather than outworn "Church-clothes," provided Teufelsdröckh with his answer to the "Everlasting No." It meant raising the natural to the supernatural rather than the reverse process which had characterized the materialism of the Enlightenment. This line of thought had previously been worked out much more subtly by the philosopher Schelling, whose Naturphilosophie was much admired by Goethe and Coleridge. It was exemplified poetically by Wordsworth, and by romantic landscape painters like Constable in England and David Caspar Friedrich in Germany.

It is worth noting parenthetically that despite this quasi-pantheism the romantic movement was not necessarily antiscientific. It was opposed to a certain kind of mechanical science and split down the middle as to whether mechanical inventions beautified or uglified life. But not a few romantics, Schelling, for example, who became secretary of the Academy of Sciences at Munich, and Maine de Biran who admired the physicist Ampère, eagerly followed the latest developments in science, while some undoubtedly contributed positively to the advancement of science by their bold speculations especially in biology and the psychology of the unconscious. One thinks again of Schelling who postulated a natura naturans, a creative, dynamic, evolutionary nature which achieved its "goal" in man himself; or of Dr. Carus or Gottfried-Heinrich von Schubert, Schelling's colleague at the University of Erlangen and translator of Erasmus Darwin, who investigated the symbolic language of dreams or, as he so graphically put it, "the night-side of science." Much as the romantics exalted art and the artist, they showed little disposition to think in terms of "two cultures," to pit art against science unless it was mechanical science. On the contrary, there was a marked tendency to romanticize science, as Balzac did in his novel The Quest of the Absolute. Novalis, himself an amateur scientist as well as a great poet, thought of science as a gateway to the Infinite. Some of Victor Hugo's poems also repay reading on this point. Hugo became a sort of poet laureate of science, glorifying it as a great adventure into the unknown and penetrating the mystery of nature.

We have said that the romantic movement did not quite center in Man, and this remark requires some comment as we turn now from romantic ideas of God and Nature to those concerning man himself. The truth of the remark can be gauged by comparing romanticism with "classical" humanism. In the latter, man, though not necessarily unaware of wider cosmic forces, was free to set purposes for himself and, to a large degree, make his own fate. The romantics, however, commonly saw man in the context of great cosmic and historical movements which enveloped him in an "infinity" greater than himself. Man is simply not the measure in romantic landscape painting, or in the new type of "English" garden (not geometrized nor ordered by human hand as in "classical" gardens), or in those gigantic philosophies of history projected by a Herder, Hegel, or even Michelet.

Nevertheless, by comparison with the Enlightenment the romantics greatly enhanced man's capabilities. Enlightenment anthropology seemed intolerably narrow to them, belittling man, accenting, as Wordsworth said, the "inferior faculties" and thus denying him access to "principles of truth." For the wider vision

201

of reality they yearned for they obviously needed far greater candle power than Locke could provide, an image of man less passive and banal than Condillac's statue man. Hence, the romantics countered with a conception of knowledge emphasizing man's activity and creativity. This theory, derived partly from the new German Idealism, posited a special "faculty" of the human mind, superior to the discursive reason, and variously labelled (depending somewhat on the reference, whether to artistic theory, philosophy, or religion) "Reason," "Imagination," "intuition," "feeling," "faith," "the illative sense," etc. The names are legion, but what the romantics were trying to say about man comes out clearly enough in the famous distinction, made early by Jacobi and Kant and developed by Coleridge, between Reason and Understanding (*Vernunft* and *Verstand*). The latter, obviously associated with Locke and Hume, could merely apprehend appearances. In Schopenhauer's metaphor it was like a man who goes round and round a castle sketching the facade and never finding an entrance. "Reason," on the other hand, was the source of transcendental ideas, "the organ of the super-sensuous" as Coleridge called it, able to discern "invisible realities or spiritual objects" (*The Friend*, 1809). As is well known, Coleridge also distinguished sharply between the use of "Imagination" and "Fancy" by the poet, the latter being able only to copy and embellish past examples, the former, however, possessing an "esemplastic power" to see things as a whole and to bring new worlds to life, by creation and invention. The imagination, as depicted by the romantics, was obviously something more than human. The same immanentism is observable in romantic man as in "nature." The human imagination was the vessel through which the Infinite or Eternal expressed and became conscious of itself. Hence, Blake, Shelley, and others could speak of man as "the Divine Image." Human creativity was patently not considered to be an entirely conscious process. Indeed, there were those who thought that man touched reality more deeply, because removed entirely from sense perceptions, in dreams and ecstasy than in the waking state. Most of these strands of thought are brought together in Schelling's doctrine of artistic genius. The creative artist was the ideal Romantic Man. According to Schelling, he presented in his work, "as if instinctively, apart from what he has put into it with obvious intent, an infinity which no finite understanding can fully unfold" (*System des transzendentalen Idealismus*, 1800). Aesthetic intuition thus involved both conscious and unconscious activity, drawing upon a power-not-itself, and combining the real and ideal.

Romantic Man thus contrasts rather sharply with the Rational Man of the Enlightenment or the "classical" tradition. He was at once more many-sided and more complicated. In him "reason" was not preeminent (though he was not necessarily antirational; cf. the Savoyard Vicar) but took orders from the deepest feelings or intuitions. Few romantics would have disagreed with Coleridge's opinion "that deep thinking is attainable only by a man of deep feeling." And because of this emphasis on "feeling" they also insisted on man's individuality and freedom of will. In his monologues Schleiermacher tells how he revolted against the notion, still strong in Kant and Fichte, of a "universal reason," the same in all men. It finally dawned upon him—he calls it his "highest intuition"—"that each man is meant to represent humanity in his own way, combining its elements uniquely." This is a typical romantic statement, and it applied equally to that individualist par excellence, the genius, who communicated the voice of the Infinite in unique and inimitable works of art. No description of Romantic Man would be complete without also taking into account the important role played by the will. As denizens of the phenomenal world men might be subject to a sort of necessity. However, there was also the noumenal world, as Kant said, in which they freely proposed and strove after their own goals, endlessly like Goethe's Faust. Faust is a very romantic figure, not in his transcendentalism which he gives up as unattainable, but in his titanism, his restless striving, his will to wring an ever wider meaning from life. This emphasis on will is reminiscent of Schopenhauer's philosophy which, however, was pessimistic and suggests still another side to romantic anthropology. The romantics were also acutely aware of a "night-side," of an anxious and troubled human nature, of forces hidden in man which could tear him and his world apart. In other words, the unconscious cut two ways. It could lead man to a higher purpose but it could also let loose the demonic in and around him, as is made clear, for example, in Schopenhauer's *The World as Will and Idea* (1818) which depicts a blind human will achieving only unhappiness, or in the frightful monsters and phantoms released in Francisco Goya's later work, notably in some of his *Caprichos* and *Proverbios* in which reason has abandoned man altogether.

Romantic ideas about Society and the State can be understood only in the light of this complex image of Man. Of course, there was no specifically romantic politics. A romantic could almost equally well be a conservative, liberal, socialist, or even anarchist. There was, however, a "social romanticism" in the sense of certain identifiable attitudes. For instance, there is no romantic who, if he thought at all about the subject, did not object to a mechanical conception of the state (as indeed he objected to a mechanical "nature"). Edmund Burke, though himself a political conservative, therefore voiced a common "romantic" attitude when in *Reflections on the Revolution in France* (1790) he attacked the revolutionaries as mere theorists who thought they could treat politics as though it were a "geometrical demonstration," without reference to human nature or history. If it was to achieve its end, it should be adjusted, he had said, "not to human reasonings, but to human nature; of which reason is but a part, and by no means the greatest part."

Against this abstract theorizing the romantics usually put up some sort of organic theory emphasizing men's emotional ties to a historically growing community and its institutions. This preference for *Gemeinschaft* was no doubt partly a reflection of revolutionary times which made only too clear the need for order and tradition. However, it also antedated the French Revolution in the cogitations of Rousseau and Burke (not so opposed to each other politically as the latter liked to think) and Herder. Emphasis on community did not constitute a negation of romantic individuality as might be supposed. In the area of social thought the latter found outlet, not so much in the doctrine of individual "rights" (by its nature abstract and general, i.e., applying equally to all mankind) as in a growing awareness of the differences between peoples and nations, and in the belief that the national community, and perhaps also the State, was necessary to the full development of each individual's personality. Significantly, the one theorist of the Enlightenment revered by Burke was Montesquieu who understood that laws could not be the same everywhere but must be adapted to the particular environment and experience of a people. At the same time Burke (to be followed in England by Coleridge and Sir Walter Scott) was writing about the uniqueness of the English constitution and the sweetness of a man's natal soil, Herder was expounding his conception of the *Volksgeist* in Germany. Each *Volk* or people, he believed, came to have its own peculiar *Geist*, exhibited preeminently in its religion, language, and literature. This nationalism, cultural only in Herder, developed strong political overtones during the War of Liberation and possibly contributed in the long run to German racist and "fascist" thought.

However that may be, it is evident that romanticism could as easily lend itself to a political messianism, not so much to planning as to dreaming of a future age of gold characterized by universal justice and freedom, and achieved by a passionate outburst of human love or pity. Burke, of course, would have deplored this sort of utopian thinking. But it broke out all over, particularly in France after 1830 when romantic literary and social revolt at last joined hands. There

Saint-Simonians and Fourierists, as well as liberals like Hugo and the historian Michelet, had visions of infinite social improvement, and pledged themselves to relieve the suffering of *les misérables* caused by the Industrial Revolution. These mixed romantic feelings about past and future often blended, as in the social thought of those two great romantic nationalists Jules Michelet and Giuseppe Mazzini. Both men owed a considerable debt to Herder. Both preached in perfervid language a "religion" of the fatherland, resurrecting its particular past and prophesying its special mission for the future: i.e., France to spread the gospel of Liberty, Italy to reincarnate the spirit of Rome, and thus make the world better.

These ideas about politics and society provide a natural bridge to their ideas about history. It is obvious from the above that most romantics, even those who like Victor Hugo looked to the future, had a strongly developed historical sense. In other words, the romantic movement contributed powerfully to, though it did not invent, what came to be known later as "historicism." Historicism, as Friedrich Meinecke defines it, rests on the twin concepts of temporal individuality (both of epochs and peoples) and development. Thus, it represented another facet of the romantic revolt against the generalizing tendencies of the Enlightenment. Certain words of David Hume provide the perfect foil for the new attitude. (Despite his empiricism Hume often lapsed into generalist language.) "It is universally acknowledged," he had said in *An Enquiry concerning Human Understanding* (1748), "that there is a great uniformity among the actions of men, in all nations and ages, and that human nature remains still the same in its principles and operations" (Sec. VIII, Part I). This was emphatically not the way Herder or Burke thought about history. Herder compared history to a tree which throws out a great variety of branches, and is forever renewing itself; also to a chain each link of which is necessary to an unbroken succession. Like Herder the romantic could not only respect but frequently empathize with past epochs which were very different yet out of which his own had grown. This empathy, notably with the Middle Ages, did not necessarily lead to better history writing. Novalis, for instance, projected his own dreams of innocence and unity into the Middle Ages, which he glorified in his *Christenheit und Europa* (1799). On the other hand, impressive studies of the Norman Conquest, the Dukes of Burgundy, the Crusades, etc. by "romantic" historians such as Augustin Thierry, Barante, and Michaud laid the ground for the revival of medieval historical scholarship. Romantic historicism, it should be noted, commonly explained history by the operation of "spiritual" as opposed to material forces. A divine purpose unfolds in history as in nature for Burke and Herder. Heroes are "called" to perform prodigies (Carlyle), nations to carry out sublime missions. In Hegel Spirit becomes increasingly conscious of itself in both nations and "World-Historical Individuals." For Michelet *Le Peuple* alone possessed the spirit of love and self-sacrifice which would enable France to achieve hers and mankind's destiny.

Most of these romantic philosophies of history were wildly optimistic. However, there was another side to the movement, already hinted at, which was the reverse of optimistic. This was the Byronic side which was expressive of melancholy, agony, disenchantment, unfulfilled longing, and even, on occasion, rebellion— rebellion, not only against society but also the universe, as in Byron's *Cain*. How important was this *Weltschmerz*? It was much more than a pose. German literature was saturated with it long before Byron. It reached philosophic expression in Schopenhauer, and in Leopardi (despite "classical" tastes, surely a romantic at least in such *Canti* as *L'Infinito* and *La Ginestra*). It dominated the thought of French romantics like Alfred de Vigny and Alfred de Musset, the latter an admirer of Byron, and was reflected in the painting of Eugène Delacroix (*Dante and Virgil in Hell*, 1822). Musset called it *la maladie du siècle* and ascribed its vogue to the times in which young Frenchmen lived following the Revolution and Empire, between two worlds, between a past forever destroyed and a future but dimly guessed (*La confession d'un enfant du siècle*, 1836). No wonder they were melancholy. "*Je suis venu trop tard*" . . . too late to believe, as in a past age of innocence and illusion.

Were there, then, after all at least two if not a plurality of romanticisms? It is preferable to think of several sides to the same movement. On the one hand, the romantics aimed to recreate wonder in a world become narrow and prosaic. At their most optimistic they thought they might restore unity, and hence meaning, to a civilization plagued by dualisms: the unity of man, God, and nature, as in Schelling's ambitious doctrine of identity. In these respects the romantic movement might be said to constitute the first great revolt against one kind of modernity—the modernity represented by the scientific Enlightenment.

Yet the romantics themselves were very "modern" in certain respects. They were aware, far more than the *philosophes*, of living in a world of endless Becoming. This was an intoxicating experience for those who could connect up the Becoming with some sort of Being even if it was not "orthodox." But for those who could find no Being either in heaven or on earth it was a cruel experience. A drama like *Cain* (1821) has a very modern ring about it. Cain speaks of an absurd universe, of man's homelessness, of knowledge turning to ashes in his mouth ("The tree was true, though deadly"). Rather than submit meekly he rebels against "the Omnipotent tyrant." Meanwhile, Schopenhauer was tearing off men's "masks" and revealing in their unconscious minds a "will to live" which inflicted suffering on itself and others. So the romantic movement also prefigured another sort of modernity which ripened fully only later in the worlds of Darwin, Freud, and Sartre. Nietzsche thought of romanticism as a shrivelled up thing, poor in vitality, retreating from life. This is the last thing one ought to say of a movement which pursued "infinity" and exalted the "esemplastic power" of man. Nevertheless, it had different sides which could give birth to very different kinds of offspring.

### BIBLIOGRAPHY

Arthur O. Lovejoy's interpretation emerges clearly from the articles reprinted in *Essays in the History of Ideas* (Baltimore, 1948), especially the one on "The Discrimination of Romanticisms" of 1924. See also for general interpretation J. Barzun, *Romanticism and the Modern Ego* (Boston, 1943); W. J. Bate, *From Classic to Romantic* (Cambridge, Mass., 1946); H. Fairchild, *The Romantic Quest* (New York, 1931); W. T. Jones, *The Romantic Syndrome* (The Hague, 1961); H. A. Korff, *Humanismus und Romantik* (Leipzig, 1924); D. Mornet, *Le romantisme en France au XVIIIe siècle* (Paris, 1912); J. H. Randall, *The Career of Philosophy*, Vol. II (New York, 1965); H. G. Schenk, *The Mind of the European Romantics* (London, 1966); F. Strich, *Deutsche Klassik und Romantik* (Munich, 1928); R. Wellek, "The Concept of Romanticism in Literary History," *Concepts of Criticism* (New Haven, 1963), pp. 128–98. For some of the special aspects of romantic thought discussed in the text, see also R. Aris, *History of Political Thought in Germany from 1789 to 1815* (London, 1936); J. W. Beach, *The Concept of Nature in Nineteenth-Century English Poetry* (New York, 1936); A. Béguin, *L'âme romantique et le rêve* (Paris, 1939); M. Bowra, *The Romantic Imagination* (Cambridge, Mass., 1949); C. Brinton, *The Political Ideas of the English Romanticists* (London, 1926); M. Brion, *Romantic Art* (New York, 1960); K. Clark, *The Gothic Revival* (London, 1928); R. T. Clark, *Herder* (Berkeley, 1955); A. Cobban, *Edmund Burke and the Revolt against the Eighteenth Century* (London, 1929); H. Kohn, *The Idea of Nationalism* (New York, 1944); R. Picard, *Le romantisme social* (New York, 1944); A. M. Osborn, *Rousseau and Burke* (London, 1940); J. L. Talmon, *Romanticism and Revolt. Europe 1815–1848* (London, 1967).

FRANKLIN L. BAUMER

[See also Classicism; Enlightenment; Genius; **Historicism;** Individualism; Infinity; **Irrationalism;** Nationalism; Nature; **Organicism;** Progress; **Romanticism in Literature; Romanticism in Post-Kantian Philosophy;** Utopia.]

## ROMANTICISM IN POLITICAL THOUGHT

IT MAY seem rather paradoxical to tie the adjective "political" to the designation of a literary school. Indeed, the label "romantic" has been known to designate in an oscillating manner the most diverse tendencies, for example, romantic traditionalism, romantic humanitarianism, and romantic nationalism. Thus in England romantic poetry, marked for a long time by the struggle of the nation against revolutionary and imperial France, tended with Coleridge to affirm national traditions and religious mysticism in protest against the rationalistic individualism of liberal thought. However, in the second romantic generation, with Byron, Keats, and Shelley, there appeared a feeling of moral rebellion against the traditional order and its conventional lies and privileges; whence the numerous declarations of generous emotion, of lofty sarcasm, or of aesthetic detachment, and whence the appeal to the ideals of liberty and justice. In France, Chateaubriand, who was not a political theoretician and whose dilettantism was often denounced, contributed nonetheless to giving French traditionalism its style by prominently parading the political virtues of loyalty and honor, and a certain form of freedom having nothing in common with any egalitarian levelling. His idea of freedom was inseparable from the institutions of the old regime to which, despite everything, he did not believe it possible to return. It was to this cult of the past, strengthened by historical studies, that Lamartine, Vigny, and Hugo—all while they were young—were attached; their cult of the past undoubtedly contrasted with the classicism which had been indulgent towards the revolutionary ideology. But, towards 1830, most of the romantic writers turned to a sort of humanitarian socialism which, along with Lamennais, lamented as pitiful the sufferings of the poor and the oppression of subject nations; later it was the nation of the "people" which was to be the basis of Michelet's political philosophy, hostile to a Church which stood in the way of social emancipation and progress. Consequently, associated with the idea of the power of the people and its justice, there developed, during the first half of the nineteenth century in France, a romanticism of the barricades. In Italy, without rejecting the religious principles to which it remained attached, romanticism aspired to utilize for its own ends the liberal principles that had come out of the French Revolution; by appealing to past traditions a political spirit was reawakened in the thought of Manzoni and Silvio Pellico, who declared themselves liberals, nationalists, and Catholics all at the same time.

It was, however, only in Germany that, despite a certain hesitancy and wavering, romanticism was defined as a body of political doctrine to which most writers of this school, from Novalis to Eichendorff, remained faithful. Romanticism in Germany, therefore, cannot be considered only from the viewpoint of literary criticism or of philosophy of science, for it was also a "politics" located at the very heart of the European counterrevolutionary movement.

For political romanticism cannot be dissociated from the group of movements created in Europe by the fear of revolutionary ideology. To explain this fact would be unthinkable without taking into account Edmund Burke's work, *Reflections on the Revolution in France* (1790), which contrasted the proud geometry of the rationalists against the background of the ancestral wisdom of the English constitution. Furthermore, we must recall that at the same time Joseph de Maistre and L. G. A. de Bonald provided the émigrés with a philosophy of Restoration which attacked the claims of universal reason by defending the original uniqueness of each notion and culture; denied the theory of the social contract by affirming the superior excellence of human ties; and opposed the idea of the unlimited progress of the human spirit by praising the superiority of historical tradition. It was, indeed, in 1816 that the Swiss Karl Ludwig von Haller began the publication of *Restauration der Staatswissenschaft . . . (Restoration of Political Philosophy)* in which, basing the State on private relations and Natural Law, he tried to preserve the patriarchal society of the old regime. However, none of these writers was connected in any way with romanticism.

German political romanticism has to be related to the philosophical environment in which it arose. As pupils of Fichte, whose *Theory of Knowledge (Wissenschaftslehre,* 1794) they had read, the romantics, immersed in his theory of the Ego as an omnipotent demiurge and boundless principle of creation, emerged with the conviction that destiny belongs to those superior individuals who have known how to impose the law of their intellect on the external world. No morality, religion, or limiting rule could be suitable for such personalities: the romantic poet treats the universe in any way he pleases; through his irony, he makes the universe an ephemeral creation of his genius. Nevertheless the romantics recognized that this personality of the genius cannot truly be formed and developed except by contact with other men; hence, they recommended association with their fellow-beings, "reciprocal meditation," and a "common philosophy" as the highest obligation of life, seeing in this "sociability" the essential element of culture. Individuals, they thought, can attain their complete fulfilment only by trying to unite. As a result, their concern with estab-

205

lishing "guilds" of superior minds, a kind of spiritual "freemasonry," emerges. And they defined these forms of sociability not only as social gatherings but also in the form of friendship and love; this love was envisaged as an effort to comprehend through the beloved intermediary the reality of the universe. It is well known how prominent a place this idealization of social relations has occupied in romantic literature, for example, in the poetry of Novalis or F. H. Jacobi's *Woldemar* (1779), or in the novel, like Friedrich Schlegel's *Lucinde* (1799).

This idealization was the principal feature in the development of the social, political, or economic thought of the romantics. They quickly broke away from the conception of human relations held by the thinkers of the Enlightenment, whom the romantics later accused of reasoning in the abstract about people assumed to be reasonable by nature and inspired with their own conventional ideals of liberty and equality. Anxious, on the one hand, to establish rules for a genuine "human symphony," the romantics, on the other hand, accentuated every possible kind of relationship which put the individual under obligation to the group.

It was the social "organism" which became the predominant element of the romantics' way of reflection. Henceforth, the State was no longer to be considered as a "machine" or artificial creation of the legislator limiting the State to police functions; instead it would be considered as a "living creature" or "organism" growing and developing like a plant according to its own laws, without enabling the statesman to amend it by means of fallaciously conceived constitutions. It would be this living collective society—a "macro-anthropos"—whose universal spirit would direct the energies of individuals and lead them to participate in a common task. Since social contracts were useless, in the eyes of the romantics, with respect to maintaining the social structure, the result was that the State would impose itself on its citizens through sentiments of devotion, faith, and love which it would instigate. Henceforth social distinctions would have to be established on the ideas of hierarchy and obedience, and thus on the privileged relationships of man to man. The romantic idea of the State was to make no appeal to fear or utility, or the sovereignty of the law, but did so for the mystic communion of subjects on a common faith with respect to the "beloved person," or loyalty to the monarch.

This conception was defined for the first time by Novalis in 1798 in the periodical *Annals of the Prussian Monarchy* on the occasion of the accession to the throne by Frederick-William III of Prussia and Queen Louise. The ideas and the vocabulary which Novalis used on this occasion were drawn, on the one hand,

from the physical philosophers' conceptions of "Nature," then being systematized by the young Schelling; and, on the other hand, from the pietists' secret assemblies. In these assemblies for several years, all over Germany, a silent war was being waged against the philosophy of the Enlightenment and against the French Revolution which was depicted in pietist circles as a "conspiracy of Enlighteners." But this interpretation of the idea of the State was soon to become the common property of all the romantics. It is found in Schleiermacher's *Monologues* (1800), in the *Philosophical Lectures* delivered in Cologne by Friedrich Schlegel (1804–06), and especially in Adam Müller's *Elements of the Art of Politics* (1808). Müller saw the State as "the totality of human affairs." He wrote that ". . . the State is not simply a factory or a farm or an insurance company or an industrial company. It is not an artificial organization; it is not a human invention meant for the utility or pleasure of citizens; outside of the state there exists nothing for the citizen."

A political philosophy was developed around this theory of the State which opposed the legacy of French revolutionary thought in all particulars. The romantics opposed the conviction that institutions are susceptible to progress on the basis of their historical view which would place the golden age of humanity in the past. According to them, the most profound wisdom flourished in the centuries of the Middle Ages; they readily opposed the modern theory of the social contract by their vindication of feudal attachments, especially of chivalry, to which August-Wilhelm Schlegel dedicated his first works; and they thought that their ideal was realized in the court of the Holy Roman Empire for whose restoration they hoped, and whose impressive organization they supported against the leveling and destructive universalism which was the outcome of the Napoleonic conquest. Their admiration of medieval institutions led them to deduce that the Estates (*Stände*), not individuals, should be represented beside the sovereign. Finally, since all forms of liberalism, as well as the industrial civilization (which was coming into existence on the continent) were hostile to them, they opposed the free play of business transactions and exchanges; they hoped for the return of the corporative regime on the economic plane, and they vindicated land ownership which they considered as "sacrosanct" because it bound the landowner irrevocably to the soil he cultivated as an inalienable possession.

As for religion, the romantics indicated their sympathies for Catholicism, because in their eyes, it constituted an ecumenical order; condemning the Reformation for having broken Christian unity, they hoped for the restoration of that unity in the form of a "visible church," as a symbol of its universal mission. "Christianity," wrote Novalis in his famous essay of 1800, *Christenheit oder Europa,* "must be revived and make itself efficacious again. Once again, without regard for national borders, it must set up a visible church which should receive any person who was in need of the supernatural, and which would strive to become the mediator between the old and the new world." It was to this Catholicism, recognized as an efficacious antidote to revolutionary ideology, that Adam Müller was converted in 1805 in Vienna, and Friedrich Schlegel in 1808 in Cologne; their conversions were followed by those of many of their friends.

What was the influence of political romanticism in Napoleonic Germany? In placing the accent on the monarchical idea as well as on the privileges of the feudal governing classes, the romantics appeared to be the best defenders of the established order. This explains why they were so favorably received at the court in Vienna, which portrayed itself as the champion of legitimacy; it also explains the utilization which was made of their doctrine in Prussian aristocratic circles against the reforms of Hardenberg. In this respect the role played by Adam Müller, whose career was favored by his friend Friedrich von Gentz, was essential. But in standing up against revolutionary and imperial France, romanticism also took on a national character; and one of Schlegel's major preoccupations was to create that patriotic poetry which could galvanize enthusiasm against the "Usurper" and his supporters.

This nationalistic aspect of the romantic movement found support in the endeavors of the Heidelberg school, gathered around the poets Arnim and Brentano, to restore the literary national past, to revive folklore, to define in the name of the people ( *Volkstum*) a certain ethnic community or relationship cemented by language, costumes, beliefs, legal traditions, and popular morality. And when the great tests of the wars of deliverance were to come, it would be the duty of one man of this group, Joseph Görres, to make his journal, *The Mercury of the Rhine,* the rostrum in which would be discussed the reorganization of Germany, conceived as embracing all the Germanic language countries. Thus the concept of the Reich as a nation was restored, and before this Görres thought that the dualism of the great German powers would bow.

Tied to the idea of nationalism, political romanticism would not be without influence on the theater of Kleist, as well as on the nationalist diatribes of Arndt and Jahn. Nevertheless, after the fall of Napoleon, it was not the intention of Metternich, who had been barely affected by the romantic movement, to allow a political situation to develop which would lead to the unification of the great states of Central Europe.

Political romanticism had then to fall back on a purely conservative attitude, whose principal goal was to combat, in the Austrian state as well as in the Catholic states of southern Germany, tendencies which were favorable to the Enlightenment, and in particular, the last vestiges of Josephist legislation. It was around the Redemptorist Hofbauer in Vienna that the romantic circle was concentrated, and there Friedrich Schlegel and Adam Müller published their last works in the review *Concordia* (1820–23). Schlegel defined what he meant by "Christian politics," in which he opposed both the practice of absolutism and modern liberalism.

The same effort was to be attempted in the court of the king of Bavaria, Louis I, at the new university of Munich. Here the most remarkable personality was the philosopher Franz von Baader, who, developing the ideas of the romantics on society and on economics, announced (precursor of Marx) that there was an accumulation of capital in a few hands; he insisted on the necessity of the representation of the proletariat, whose role in modern society he discerned and of whose rights the Catholic Church, according to him, was the natural defender. As a result of the development of an industrial civilization and the rise of liberalism, political romanticism was more and more reduced to a defensive position. It is in the writings of the poet Josef von Eichendorff, around 1830, that the swan song of romanticism was heard.

Victim of the raillery of Heine and of the writers of "Young Germany," political romanticism was soon to fall into oblivion. Somewhat later, a Viennese economist, Othmar Spann, was to attempt to redeem the writings of Adam Müller, precursor of Friedrich List. The Nazis borrowed many ideas from Müller, and they talked about his subject as "German sociology," the restorer of a sense of the "organic" community. In fact, political romanticism was out of joint with the times. This monumental effort, at times perspicacious, too often sophisticated and purely speculative, an expression of the rancors and the terrors of a society haunted by the revolutionary spectre, searched desperately in the memory of a glorious past for a way to authorize the survival of its customs and privileges.

*BIBLIOGRAPHY*

The principal texts have been reproduced in German by J. Baxa, *Gesellschaft und Staat im Spiegel deutscher Romantik* (Jena, 1924); in English by H. S. Reiss, *The Political Thought of the German Romantics 1793–1815* (Oxford, 1955); in French by J. Droz, *Le romantisme politique en Allemagne* (Paris, 1963).

About political romanticism, besides the analyses of F. Meinecke in *Weltbürgertum und Nationalstaat* (Munich, 1909), cf. P. Kluckhohn, *Persönlichkeit und Gemeinschaft:*

*Studien zur Staatsauffassung der deutschen Romantik* (Halle, 1925); Crane Brinton, *Political Ideas of the English Romanticists* (Oxford, 1926); and J. Droz, *Le Romantisme allemand et l'État: Résistance et collaboration dans l'Allemagne napoléonienne* (Paris, 1966). The best detailed study is by R. Aris, *Die Staatslehre Adam Müllers und ihr Verhältnis zur deutschen Romantik* (Tübingen, 1929).

JACQUES DROZ

[See also Enlightenment; Counter-Enlightenment; **Genius;** Hierarchy; **Nationalism; Organicism;** Pietism; **Revolution; Romanticism;** Socialism; State.]

# ROMANTICISM IN POST-KANTIAN PHILOSOPHY

POST-KANTIAN romanticism can be construed as a reaction against the neo-classicism and rationalism of the eighteenth-century Enlightenment, of the philosophers and ideologists who dominated the European "Age of Reason"; or it can be viewed as an expression of a recurring mood in Western culture from Hellenic civilization to the present. Whenever men assert their essential unity with nature, strive for an integration of their intellectual with their emotional capacities, of consciousness with the unconscious, facts with values, and seek to identify subject with object, the term "romantic" has been applied by themselves or others to those who shared this *Weltanschauung.* However, as A. O. Lovejoy wrote, the movement which began in Germany in the seventeen-nineties is "the only one which has an indisputable title to be called Romanticism, since it invented the term for its own use" (*Essays in the History of Ideas* [1948], p. 235).

This is the romantic movement, *die Romantik,* of post-Kantian cultural history. A romanticist "school," Heine's *romantische Schule,* could only be found in Jena and nearby Weimar at the end of the eighteenth and beginning of the nineteenth centuries. In 1798, in the second issue of the *Athenaeum,* Friedrich Schlegel asserted the supremacy of *die romantische Poesie.* With his brother Wilhelm, with Tieck, Novalis, Fichte, and Schelling, he established the artistic, literary, and critical positions best designated *die Romantik.* Influenced by this outlook a broader philosophical program of romantic idealism was developed at the newly established University of Berlin by Fichte, Schleiermacher, Hegel, and, very briefly, Schelling, though Hegel soon repudiated romanticism as inadequate.

Goethe, who had been linked to the groups in Weimar and Jena, also turned from the romantic *Sturm und Drang* mood of his youth. The spirit of "storm and stress" typified in Goethe's early work was a prologue to *die Romantik.* The poets and artists of Schlegel's circle responded to Goethe's challenge to find inspiration in the plenitude of life; for them, as for him, theory seemed bleak in contrast to the fertility of life's golden tree. The spiritual atmosphere of this *Romantik* corresponded to the romanticism of poets and novelists (Wordsworth, Coleridge, Shelley, Keats, Byron, Hawthorne, Poe, Whitman, Chateaubriand, de Vigny, de Musset, and Hugo), of such painters as Delacroix and Géricault, and of composers (Schubert and Schumann, Berlioz and Chopin). But *die Romantik,* and post-Kantian romanticism in general, was distinctive in its attachment to emerging German nationalism, glorification of medieval traditions of folk stories and fairy tales, its special attention to "the voice of the heart" often heard in "forest solitude." To be sure some of the elements in this combination of themes were familiar to other romanticisms such as the gothic tradition in English fiction and the worship of nature in the Lake poets.

Lovejoy's conviction that the romanticism of one country might have little in common with those of others echoed the judgment expressed in de Musset's *Lettres de Dupuis et Cotonel* in 1836. Lovejoy's thesis has been attacked by René Wellek in a symposium, *Romanticism Reconsidered,* edited by Northrop Frye in 1963. At the end of his essay, entitled "Romanticism Re-examined," Wellek writes that, though while not "minimizing or ignoring national differences or forgetting that great writers have created something unique and individual," it is noteworthy "that progress has been made not only in defining the common features of Romanticism but in bringing out what is its peculiarity or even its essence or nature: that attempt, apparently doomed to failure and abandoned by our time, to identify subject and object, to reconcile man and nature, consciousness and unconsciousness."

Without denying the validity of Lovejoy's discriminations of various romantic traditions or failing to recognize the significance of Wellek's so-called "Pan-Romanticism," one can agree with Francis B. Randall's comment in his essay, "Marx the Romantic," that "Romanticism, like other important abstract nouns in the history of culture, is not a term to be defined but a field to be explored" (Introduction to *The Communist Manifesto,* New York, 1964).

To the extent that post-Kantian romanticism was a reaction, it stood in opposition less to the skepticism and even to such occasional atheism as existed alongside the deism of the Enlightenment, as to the "scientific" modernism and rationalistic liberalism on which the Age of Reason prided itself. The sources of later romanticism were, as will be apparent, evident in the earlier eighteenth century and, indeed, before that. It is significant that three figures such as Pascal, Spinoza, and Bach, neglected or even repudiated in the religion, philosophy, and music of the Age of Reason, were rediscovered by the romanticists and became cultural heroes of romanticism.

Opposition to the Enlightenment's attempts to apply the limited outlook of scientific rationalism, first developed in religion and the arts. Art was manifestly not created by the mere application of mechanical rules, as a narrow classical formulation might suggest, nor could religious values be construed as the products of a restricted empiricism. Romanticism proclaimed the primacy of humane interests, of man's emotional and passionate nature and of the spirit of free imagination in all creative activity. Such emphases yielded great achievements in the arts. In the history of ideas the group led by Friedrich Schlegel sought to develop a philosophy of romantic idealism by using the values of human freedom as a key to unlock the innermost secrets of man's nature and to open up an understanding of all nature more adequate than the theories of eighteenth-century mechanistic science. Kant had been concerned to overcome doubts raised by Hume and Holbach, by the skepticism and atheism of the Enlightenment. The post-Kantians undertook the more arduous task of creating a new *Weltanschauung* which would offset the established world views of Newton and Locke. Claiming to build on Kant's achievements, the post-Kantian romanticists drew useful suggestions for their views and visions from traditions of Platonism and Neo-Platonism, doctrines of medieval alchemists such as Paracelsus, mystics, notably Jacob Boehme, and aspects of the philosophies of Spinoza and Leibniz largely neglected during the eighteenth century.

Johann Gottfried von Herder, whom J. H. Randall has called the "first German Romanticist" (*The Career of Philosophy* [1965], II, 103) was a friend of Goethe's who brought him to Weimar to be court preacher. In Weimar, Herder became a member of the literary circle which surrounded Goethe and which included Schiller and the latter's protégé Hölderlin. The proximity of Weimar to Jena and its group of romanticists made Herder's influence readily available in both places. Herder, writes Randall, "hated reason; . . . he loved feeling and sentiment and the primitive, folksongs and the poetry that coming from the people expresses the soul of the race." These ideas Herder had formulated in his *Ideen zur Philosophie der Geschichte der Menschheit* (1784–91), while in *Gott, einige Gespräche* (1787), he had developed his views on religion, largely derived from his reading of Spinoza, which became a major influence on romanticist philosophy, notably in the metaphysics of Schelling and in

Schleiermacher's theology. As Hölderlin's work built a bridge from classical literature to romanticist poetry, so what Herder had absorbed of philosophical traditions in Kant's Königsberg lecture hall, together with a vision of the possibility of human greatness derived from Lessing, reappeared in the speculations of Schleiermacher and Schelling as Ernst Cassirer has shown in his *Freiheit und Form* and *Idee und Gestalt.*

Another major influence in the development of romanticist ideas, particularly in the works of Schelling, was Franz Baader whose enthusiasm for the doctrines of Jacob Boehme and for those of Herder's friend Johann Georg Hamann was transmitted to Schelling and into the mainstream of German romanticism. Their preoccupation with the nature of evil became a part of romanticist *Weltschmerz*. Echoes of this melancholy may be heard in Heinrich von Kleist, Tieck, and Novalis as well as in Byron and Baudelaire, Leopardi and Lermontov, and in Schopenhauer's pessimism.

A more generally recognized influence in the development of ideas associated with romanticism came from Rousseau and affected not only those who would by any standard be recognized by romanticists but also others who repudiated such designation—Goethe, for example, Hegel and, later, Nietzsche. As Cassirer has demonstrated in *Rousseau, Kant and Goethe,* it was, in the first instance, the somewhat surprising fact, surprising in view of obvious temperamental differences, that Kant was powerfully attracted to Rousseau's writings, particularly to his psychological observations, which impressed not only Goethe but also the succession of post-Kantian romanticist philosophers.

Johann Gottlieb Fichte was, as noted, for a time a member of the group surrounding Schlegel in Jena. He formulated an ethic and social philosophy in which the idea of Freedom was central and sounded the note of "egoism" which George Santayana found characteristic of German philosophy. Fichte held the vocation of man to be the creation of a moral order in which essential human rights and duties could be fully exercised. True individuality and personality were to be attained only in a nation in which man engaged in a constant struggle towards unattainable goals. In the First Introduction to his *Wissenschaftslehre* (1797), Fichte asserts that action, not mere knowledge, is primary in the fulfillment of human destiny. However Fichte also calls upon men to turn their attention inward towards their innermost selves. This self contemplation, *intellektuelle Anschauung*, is a prime source of that romanticist irony which characterized the literature of *die Romantik*, an awareness of the inevitable disparity between aspiration and realization.

The writings of Friedrich Schleiermacher, particularly his *Reden über die Religion* (1799) and *Monologen*

209

(1800), provide a fully articulated romanticist philosophy of religion. Drawing on his own pietistic background, Schleiermacher devoted himself as scholar, preacher, and theologian to the formulation of ideas to which the poets of *die Romantik* had given artistic expression. A sense of infinity and eternality, receptivity to diversity of cultures and variety of artistic experience, free individuality in a liberated humanity providing the fullest development of the potentialities of personality, such were the recurring themes of Schleiermacher's works.

Hölderlin, Hegel, and Schelling, schoolmates at the Tübingen seminary, had joined their friends in dancing around a "freedom tree" when they received news of the fall of the Bastille. Hölderlin became the greatest poet of *die Romantik*, but his major contribution to the history of ideas is to be found in his influence on Hegel and Schelling. The centrality of Hellenic ideas in Hegel's social philosophy and the predominant aesthetic elements in Schelling's thought give evidence of Hölderlin's pervasive influence on his friends. Though the romanticist themes of freedom, self-determination, and creativity remained central in Hegel's philosophic system he, like Goethe, repudiated romantic emotionalism. He developed a logic in which freedom was subject to law, individuality was attained in relatedness, and creativity was to be understood in the context of cultural processes. In Hegel's Faustian quest for totality he sought a systematic intellectual comprehensiveness such as Hölderlin and the other poets of *die Romantik* had endeavored to realize in art. With an imagination equal in its way to that of the poets, Hegel attempted a rational formulation of all "Reality" through a "logic of passion" applied to the data of history. Many of Hegel's followers, including so-called left-wing Hegelians, were permeated by the spirit of romantic idealism; even the materialism of Karl Marx remains romanticist insofar as Marx sees man's essence in creative activity which is negated by misdirected passion linked to greed.

Hegel attempted to escape from the romanticists' problem of deriving the rich variety and multiplicity of existence from a primal unity by positing a unity which was itself a system of particulars. Though Hegel asserted that he had attained this view by transcending the philosophical romanticism which he had, in youthful collaboration, shared with Schelling, the latter claimed throughout his long career that he had anticipated Hegel's ideas without repudiating their romanticist implications. Schelling is the most explicitly romantic of the post-Kantian idealists, "the prince of the romanticists," as Josiah Royce called him. Beginning as a Kantian with marked Fichtean overtones, he drew consciously on Neo-Platonic and medieval German

traditions, on Bruno and Boehme and Hamann, Spinoza and Leibniz, as well as on his contemporaries and collaborators among the poets and artists of *die Romantik*. He used these influences with imaginative independence and developed his thought in a series of systematic doctrines variously designated *Naturphilosophie, Identitätsphilosophie*, and *Transcendentale Idealismus*, culminating in the posthumously published *Philosophie der Mythologie und Offenbarung*. Under whatever title, his views encompassed the romanticist ideas of individuality, freedom and creativity, and an intense, quasi-religious devotion to the values of personality. Schelling shared Hegel's interest in logic and history but gave particular emphasis to a view of Nature as the unity which made intelligible the diversities encountered in experience, a view which sought to take account of the evil and irrational elements in concrete existence. Drawing on Spinoza and developing an evolutionary conception which had been outlined by Herder, Schelling more than any other romanticist thus espoused positions which attracted philosophical poets and men of letters, notably Samuel Taylor Coleridge, Thomas Carlyle, Ralph Waldo Emerson, and Edgar Allan Poe (*Eureka*). Supplementing residual overtones derived from Schopenhauer's influence, Emerson evoked romanticist elements in the work of Friedrich Nietzsche. Schelling also anticipated important aspects of later evolutionary philosophers including Henri Bergson, Samuel Alexander, a suggestion of Schelling's influence in American pragmatism. Charles Sanders Peirce in a letter cited by R. B. Perry in *Thought and Character of William James* (II, 415–16) wrote: "I consider Schelling as enormous" and "If you were to call my philosophy Schellingism transformed in the light of modern physics, I should not take it hard." John Dewey recognized in Schelling anticipations of his own emphasis on the pervasive significance of artistic experience. That contemporary existentialism owes much to Schelling is especially evident in the writings of Martin Heidegger and Paul Tillich.

## BIBLIOGRAPHY

In addition to works by Cassirer, Lovejoy, and others cited above, the following books can be consulted. Jacques Barzun, *Classic, Romantic and Modern* (New York, 1961), a revised and enlarged version of the author's *Romanticism and the Modern Ego* (Boston, 1943), a comprehensive study of romanticist achievement and critical commentary. Rudolf Haym, *Die romantische Schule* (Berlin, 1870; rev. ed. Tübingen, 1960), remains valuable as a presentation of nineteenth-century views and bibliography. Nicolai Hartmann, *Die Philosophie des deutschen Idealismus*, 2nd ed. (Berlin, 1960). Part I is devoted to Fichte, Schelling, and *die Romantik*. See also Ricarda Huch, *Die Romantik*

(Leipzig, 1908); H. A. Korff, *Humanismus und Romantik* (Leipzig, 1924); H. G. Schenk, *The Mind of the European Romanticists* (London, 1966), with an introduction by Isaiah Berlin; Walter Silz, *Early German Romanticism, Its Founders and Heinrich von Kleist* (Cambridge, Mass., 1929); L. A. Willoughby, *The Romantic Movement in Germany*, 2nd ed. (New York, 1966).

For English translations of post-Kantian romanticists, see: J. G. Fichte, *The Vocation of Man*, ed. Roderick M. Chisholm (New York, 1956); F. Schleiermacher, *Soliloquies*, ed. Horace Leland Friess (Chicago, 1926); F. Schelling, *The Ages of the World*, ed. Frederick deWolfe Bolman, Jr. (New York, 1942), and idem, *Of Human Freedom*, ed. James Gutmann (Chicago, 1936).

JAMES GUTMANN

[See also Enlightenment; Existentialism; **Hegelian** . . . ; Nationalism; Nature; Platonism; Pragmatism; **Romanticism;** Skepticism.]

# SATIRE

ARISTOTLE speaks in his *Poetics* of a kind of poetry (iambics) which portrays "the actions of inferior men" (IV, 9), but the word *satura* (originally an adjective meaning "mixed" or "of various composition") and the conception of satire as a definite type of poetry with a definable style first appears in Rome in the first century B.C., most importantly in the writings of Horace. When the first-century A.D. rhetorician Quintilian writes, *Satura . . . tota nostra est* ("Rome is preeminent in satire," *Institutio oratoria*, X, 93), he means, however, to claim Roman superiority only in that kind of satiric writing now known as formal verse satire—a collection of short verse satires in which the satirist directly attacks and denounces a variety of men and practices—written first by Lucilius, refined and stabilized by Horace, and further developed by Juvenal and Persius. The word "satire" has come, however, to be the general term for any kind of writing which attacks, directly or indirectly, something which is hated or feared. In one direction the word expands into the adjective "satiric," vaguely referring to any slightly muted expression of hostility; and in the other direction it narrows to a particular literary genre or myth, like comedy, tragedy, and epic, with a characteristic subject matter, style, and structure. As a genre, it should be distinguished from the perspectives or modes—lyric, narrative, and dramatic—through which it is variously presented.

The history of satire from its primitive beginnings to its highest levels of development is a series of attempts to manage and use a fundamental attitude or human energy which is nakedly open in the crudest satire and is still expressed in some fairly direct form in even the most polished literary satires. Juvenal's *Si natura negat, facit indignatio versum* ("Though nature says no, indignation shapes my poetry"; I, 79) reveals precisely that quality of fury and outrage which drives most satire. The desire to attack and overwhelm those things which are hated and feared, for whatever reason, comes through openly in Swift's "Drown the world! I am not content with despising it, but I would anger it, if I could with safety" (Letter to Pope, Nov. 26, 1725). It is there in Pope's "strong Antipathy of Good to Bad" (*Epilogue to the Satires, Dialogue II* [1738], 198), and in John Marston's "I cannot chuse but bite" (*The Scourge of Villanie* [1598], Satire VIII). Even when the hostility is not openly expressed, it is latent in the ugly ways in which satire characteristically presents its victims, and in the imagery traditionally associated with the satiric attack: biting, flaying, throwing acid, whipping, administering purgatives, and anatomizing. In those works where the author creates a character embodying the pure satiric impulse and develops the logic of this attitude to its absurd but revealing extreme, the satiric figure ends isolated from society, hating all that man does and is. Shakespeare's Timon retires naked to the desert to curse man and nature, to intrigue against Athens, and finally to kill himself; Gulliver goes to live in the stable, preferring the company of horses to that of men; Molière's Alceste in *Le Misanthrope* leaves Paris, and the vital though morally imperfect Célimène, for that "wild, trackless, solitary place, " where he can "forget the human race"; and Tod Hackett, the satiric painter in Nathanael West's *The Day of the Locust* (1939), ends broken and insane, wailing like a siren to announce all the disasters past and to come.

Such direct and indirect revelations of motive permit us to see the relationship of sophisticated literary satires to cruder, more direct expressions of the same power in primitive satiric spells and curses used to banish and destroy the dark forces, human and natural, which threaten the well-being of the community. In pre-classical Greece, satire was used in various early fertility rituals to invoke the good and banish evil through the imperative magic of the curse. Among the Arabian tribes the satirist rode in the van of the army hurling curses like spears at the enemies before him. The ancient Irish satirists, of whom particularly full records exist, not only were capable of dealing with community problems by means of satiric spells but were credited, down to the seventeenth century, with the ability to perform such useful but humble tasks as rhyming rats to death.

This use of language like a fist and the belief in the power of the curse have never died. Anthropologists describe shame-cultures in which public ridicule will cause a man to retire to his house and die, and we hear of flyting contests in which two opponents stand and hurl insults at one another until the weaker is overwhelmed by sheer vituperation. The crude energies of satire are present even in what Benjamin DeMott ("The Age of Overkill," *New York Times Magazine*, May 19, 1968) has called "the mindless cycle of super taunts" so characteristic of our own time of "habitual irascibility" when—like the generals who build enough weapons to kill every human being three times over—men use the language of overkill: hundred-megaton dirty weapons like, "The white race is the cancer of history," "The family is the American fascism," and, repeated like a primitive chant, "The middle class are just like pigs."

Magical spells, incantations, curses, invective, lampoons, verbal overkill, and the language of hard-attack are not satire, in the sense that the word is ordinarily used, but rather the substratum of satire, the world of verbal anger and violence which always exists in a multitude of extra-literary forms just beyond the edges of art. Civilized societies, while aware of the usefulness of invective and curse, have always been nervously alert to the dangers of uncontrolled aggressiveness and unchained fury such as can still be felt in the curse of the Greek satirist Archilochus (seventh century B.C.) on one of his enemies: "Shivering with cold, covered with filth washed up by the sea, with chattering teeth like a dog, may he lie helplessly on his face at the edge of the strand amidst the breakers—this 'tis my wish to see him suffer, who has trodden his oaths underfoot, him who was once my friend" (Strassburg frag., 97A). Beyond this, there remains always the danger that the satirist instead of employing his skills for the good of the community may use them for such personal ends as Archilochus did when he cursed King Lycambes and his daughter, causing them to hang themselves, simply because he had been denied the hand of the princess. This same arbitrary use of satiric power appears in a number of Irish stories about groups of satirists who descend upon a kingdom and make outrageous demands for food, money, and women. If their requests are denied they blight the king and his land with their curses. Even when the anger is controlled and the attack directed at a socially sanctioned target, satire still continues to generate considerable uneasiness because it seems always to go too far. An attack upon a corrupt lawyer becomes inevitably an attack upon the law itself; an attack upon excessive authority grows into a questioning of the very principle of authority.

Another Irish story, *The Great Visitation to Guaire*, suggests the way in which society has curbed and channeled the power of satire. The satirist Dallan demands from King Hugh a magic shield which makes weak all those who look upon it. Hugh refuses to part with his most precious possession, and Dallan then proceeds to curse (satirize) him. But since the curse of Dallan is unjust, used only for personal profit, and without truth, it rebounds on the satirist, and Dallan dies within three days, while King Hugh continues to live and prosper. The point is clear: satire is required to be both just and true if it is to work; if untrue, it harms the man who speaks it. The same requirement is imposed in legal terms in the Roman libel laws and in the prohibition against Greek Old Comedy and its scurrilous attacks in the plays of Aristophanes on such historical figures as Socrates and Euripides.

Perhaps because our documents are from a period when the process was far advanced, it is as impossible to trace exactly the steps by which curses were transformed into literary satire as it is to trace the parallel social and psychological movement in which education, religion, law, and the other powers of society gradually exerted some degree of control and restraint on human aggression in general. Both patterns are complicated enormously, of course, by frequent regressions of such severity as to make it doubtful if there has been any change at all. But despite such slippages, satire has evolved from curse to art, and many of the devices and techniques which we take to be characteristic of the genre function not merely to hide but to justify and make socially acceptable and useful the enormous powers of militant anger.

Most obviously the authors of satire have accepted, though often with tongue in cheek, the requirement that their attacks be true. Every satirist endeavors to persuade in some manner that he has along with Pope "stoop'd to truth, and moralized his song" (*Epistle to Dr. Arbuthnot*, line 341); that he is with Byron a "Columbus of the moral seas" who will "show mankind their Soul's antipodes" (*Don Juan*, XIV, line 101); that his subject is with Juvenal *quidquid agunt homines* ("the things men do," I, 85); and that he deals like Ben Jonson only in "deeds, and language, such as men doe use" (*Every Man In*, Prologue, 21). Despite the obvious exaggeration characteristic of the genre, satire makes extensive use of an elaborate apparatus of verisimilitude—maps are drawn, street names given, genealogies drawn up, fantastic objects precisely named and described—and solemn assurance is offered that the language is plain and simple like the subject, that truth replaces style because the satirist is only a reporter of things that are. "Shocking though it may seem," the satirist is always saying, "this is the way the world truly is," and he then proves his point by shifting from denunciation to description or presentation of idiocy and vice in all their remarkable plenitude.

This shift from denunciation to presentation, the removal of the emphasis from the attacker to the thing attacked, though it has not taken place steadily and evenly, is still the most prominent line of development in Western satire, and the major way in which satirists have met the social requirement that any display of aggression be based on truth. In Roman *satura* the attack is managed by a speaker who denounces directly the foolish and vicious world; and while it is possible to argue that the speaker is not Horace or Juvenal but a *persona* designed for the satiric purpose, the effect is still to locate, despite all protestations of objectivity, the point of view in the speaker himself, and thereby to force on him sole responsibility for the attack. The charge that the fault lies not in a corrupt world but in the intemperate character of the satirist was met in part in *satura* by portraying him in as favorable a light as possible—the mild, tolerant, amused "Horace" is the best example—and was handled in Renaissance England by the construction of a standard *persona* that the satiric poet was expected to assume. Elaborating an old false etymology which derived "satire" from "satyr," the Elizabethans constructed a satyr-satirist who incorporated all the traits thought appropriate to these rough, woodland gods and all the traditionally feared psychic qualities underlying uncontrolled attack: sadism, brutality, uncontrolled anger, prurience, envy, frustration, and imbalance. Under the cover of this *persona* several generations of English satirists—chiefly Joseph Hall, *Virgidemiarum* (1597–98), and John Marston, *The Scourge of Villanie* (1598–99)—were able to attack the social ills and the follies of Renaissance Englishmen with a savagery and violence which would ordinarily be unacceptable. Isaac Casaubon gave the true etymology of "satire" in his *De satyrica Graecorum poesi et Romanorum satira* (1605), but it was not generally understood and accepted until nearly a century later.

The more usual way, however, of handling the problem of the satirist has been to portray him as a simple, ordinary, humble figure who would never dream of doing anything so unpleasant as writing satire if the wickedness and stupidity of the world were not so overwhelming as to make it inescapably necessary. The prophet come down from the hills to the wicked cities of the plains, the gawky medieval plowman stubbornly and quietly speaking truth, the simple scholar nurtured at the university experiencing the big world for the first time, the fool too innocent to know that men do not speak of what is plain for all to see: these are all

variants of the standard type of ironic satirist brought to perfection by Alexander Pope in his *Epistle to Dr. Arbuthnot, Imitations of Horace,* and the two dialogues of the *Epilogue to the Satires.* In these works he carefully constructs a charming picture of a modest and gentle "Pope" raised in innocence by kind and harmless parents, retiring from the world, mildly accepting insults, until at last he is driven, reluctantly, into replying to his enemies. "Fools rush into my Head, and so I write" (Imitation of "The First Satire of the Second Book of Horace," line 14).

The gap between author and satirist implicit in the elaboration of fictitious *personae* in formal verse satire grows wider in those narrative and dramatic works where the author disappears and the satirist becomes a character in his own right, responsible for the attack and for any unpleasantness that may be associated with it. Such a figure may be either an ironic simpleton like Folly in Erasmus' *Praise of Folly,* Voltaire's Candide, or Joseph Heller's Yossarian in *Catch-22;* or he may be a hard attacker like Shakespeare's Thersites in *Troilus and Cressida,* Ben Jonson's Macilente in *Every Man Out of His Humour,* or Alceste in Molière's *Le Misanthrope.*

The master of the fictitious satirist is, however, Jonathan Swift, who seems to have played all possible turns on the device. His regular method is to construct a satirist who attacks effectively some aspect of human folly, as Gulliver attacks human pride, as the political economist in *A Modest Proposal* attacks the wasteful economic practices of the English in Ireland, or as the amateur scientist in *The Mechanical Operation of the Spirit* attacks religious dissent and enthusiasm. But as the attack proceeds, the satirist gradually reveals himself as being at least as foolish and wicked as his victims. Usually he is guilty of the same sins in a more intense, unsuspected way: Gulliver the misanthrope living with horses is supremely proud and stupid, the "Modest Proposer" who plans to reduce the Irish population and provide needed income by selling babies for meat is more cruel and inhumane in his science than the English in their indifference, and the fellow of the Royal Society is more mechanical and lacking in true spirit than the poor fanatics he castigates.

Swift's method for handling the satirist merges with that variety of satire where the satirist disappears altogether, and the fools and dunces are simply presented in the fullness of idiocy. This type of satire—sometimes called Menippean or Varronian, but more aptly called "situational satire" by Ricardo Quintana—existed side by side with first-person satire from the beginning, and has gradually become the dominant satiric method. Its chief virtue in accommodating satire to the restrictions placed by society on the display of anger is, of course, that it permits the author to retire altogether from the combat and leave the stage to fools who convict themselves in words and actions, as do the advocates of war and sophistry in Aristophanes' plays, the vulgar merchant Trimalchio in *The Satyricon* of Petronius, the philosophers in Lucian's satires, the greedy dreamers in Jonson's *Alchemist*, the dunces of Pope's *Dunciad*, George III and Southey in Byron's *Vision of Judgment*, the pompous, muddle-headed Englishmen of Evelyn Waugh's satiric novels.

The attempt to displace the responsibility for satiric anger and attack has been paralleled by the development of other techniques for making satire socially acceptable. Society, while demanding that charges be true, has also continued to insist that the expression of anger be limited in intensity, qualified in some manner, and that it be released only for specified reasons on sanctioned occasions. Freud perceived that aggression is acceptable when expressed indirectly in the form of a joke, and wit has been the principal means by which satire has made itself respectable. The presence of wit in the midst of anger and attack perhaps signals that the violent emotions are still under control, restrained and organized by the rational faculties, tempered by some self-awareness. Wit, in Dryden's terms, is the "difference betwixt the slovenly butchering of a man, and the fineness of a stroke that separates the head from the body, and leaves it standing in its place" (*Essay on Satire*, 1693), and no literary kind shows the exercise of such persistent ingenuity in honing its cutting edge as satire. Wit, construed not just as humor, but as cleverness, ingenuity, and style, appears most obviously in the persistent efforts of satirists to find a clever strategy, an unusual and surprising angle of attack. Diatribe and denunciation are avoided in favor of such devices as beast fables, letters of obscure men, ships of fools, presentations of fantastic schemes, praise of the ridiculous, attempts to enter Heaven, trips through a looking-glass, auctions of philosophers, and anti-utopias.

When Byron admits that "One should not rail without a decent cause" (*Don Juan*, II, line 119), he speaks for all satirists who have accepted society's view that attack must be limited to those men and practices which are dangerous and evil by generally accepted standards. Satirists have thus been forced to prove that their specific targets are indeed evil. This has been done in the crudest way by delivering a sermon on wickedness, as Juvenal frequently does, or it has been managed by forcing the fools to condemn themselves from their own mouths and bring about evil results by their actions. The required moral standard has been invoked frequently as a lost age of innocence or departed grandeur mocked by the ghastly and ludicrous pretensions of the present. Mock fairy tale, pastoral, epic, and other inverted forms are common satiric strategies. In the very greatest satire the moral standard is embedded in the texture of the work itself. The meaningful and real world, which the fools are perverting, is always present in the imagery of Ben Jonson's satiric plays, in the steady, even, balanced couplets of Dryden and Pope, and in the endless onward flow of verse and events in Byron's *Don Juan*.

It has been proposed that the most inventive and effective satire is written in times when the satirist is in real danger for his attacks. While it is not at all certain that the quality of satire increases directly with the intensity of political, literary, and ethical censorship, there is no question that the history of satire and the development of some of its most prominent characteristics can be understood as an uneven but continuing process of making anger and attack morally and socially acceptable. It would be a mistake to think, however, that the many techniques used to accomplish this end are mere disguises or concealments of human aggressiveness; rather, the aggressiveness has been shaped, ordered, and transformed into more meaningful and useful forms.

But the history of satire can be viewed in another way, contradictory at first but ultimately complementary. In the great continuing line of Western literary satire extending from Aristophanes, through the Roman and the great French and English neoclassical satirists, to such moderns as Brecht, Huxley, Waugh, Orwell, and Ionesco, the attack has been directed at a great variety of men, ways of thought, and institutions. Aristophanes attacks the war party of Athens and the new sophistry; Horace slyly mocks the frenzied busyness of the Roman status seekers; Juvenal thunders at the corrupting influences of Asiatic customs and luxury on the simple virtues of old republican Rome; uncounted numbers of medieval satirists catalogue the foulness of women and the abominations of a corrupt clergy; Ben Jonson attacks Renaissance materialism and the humanistic dream of the unlimited powers of man; Swift reveals the dreadful truth beneath unrealistic beliefs in the goodness of human nature and the inevitability of scientific progress; Voltaire follows to its bitter end the remarkable belief that this is the best of all possible worlds; Byron exposes the lifelessness and stupidity which underlie the bright surface of the early nineteenth-century establishment; Gogol tracks the callous indifference to humanity and the mechanical set of mind in Russian officialdom and society; Huxley holds up to contempt the views of modern sociology and science which seek utopia but create a hell; Orwell reveals the terror implicit in totalitarian, dictatorial government; and Ionesco makes manifest the herd instinct, the savagery, and the stupidity on which middle-class life and institutions rest.

On the surface, the objects of satire's attacks have been wide and various, but beneath the variety a remarkably similar world takes shape. The old gods of light and order die, and their places are taken by idols: Horace's Priapus (I, 8), the stupid deities of Lucian's *Icaromenippus*, Golding's *Lord of the Flies*. The sacred places are defiled: Jerome's description of the use of Christ's birthplace for an assignation; the rites perverted: the ceremonies of *bona dea* transformed to an orgy in Juvenal's Satire VI; theology becomes a mockery: Swift's argument against the abolishment of Christianity; piety a pretense: Molière's *Tartuffe*. History becomes a record of futility and loss in the inverted *translatio studii* in Book III of *The Dunciad* where ignorance rather than light moves across the world from east to west; the past is lost forever in the colossal "dream dump" of Nathanael West's *Day of the Locust*, where the record of human struggle and courage is reduced to the artificiality of Hollywood sets jumbled together in meaningless chaos.

The scene of nature darkens and the peaceable kingdom gives way to the ravaged German countryside of Voltaire's *Candide*, the fetid jungle where life abounds without meaning in which Tony Last wanders at the end of Waugh's *Handful of Dust*, or the universal darkness covering all at the end of *The Dunciad*. The innocent lamb and the gentle ox are replaced by Brecht's shark with its pretty teeth, Ionesco's thundering hippopotamus, Jonson's flesh-fly buzzing around the dying fox, and, most terrible of all, the Yahoo.

The City of Man ceases to be the emblem of community and art, and becomes the polyglot confusion of Juvenal's second-century Rome; the savage, dangerous, unlighted London of John Gay's *Trivia* (1716); James Thomson's "City of Dreadful Night" (1874); the garbage-strewn, decaying, tyrannically ruled metropolis of George Orwell's *1984*. The men of this city no longer assemble for traditional purposes but gather in gangs for pillage as in Henry Fielding's *Jonathan Wild* (1743), or swirl about, violently and mindlessly, in anarchic mobs like the aimless, chattering crowd of *The Dunciad* or the excitement-seekers who coagulate before Kahn's Persian Palace in the Hollywood of West's *Day of the Locust*. In quieter moments, men move mechanically through grotesque rituals such as the Lilliputian "leaping and creeping," or they pass bored and filled with ennui through the empty requirements of society in the country seat of the Amundevilles in *Don Juan*. In this fragmented and meaningless world, every man's hand is ultimately set against his fellow, and this relentless antagonism frequently culminates in cannibalism (Juvenal's Satire

XV, Swift's *Modest Proposal*, Byron's *Don Juan*, and Waugh's *Black Mischief*).

Traditional human relationships and the forms in which they are expressed become perverse and grotesque. The family in Jonson's *Volpone* takes the grotesque form of Volpone's household in which the "children" are a dwarf, hermaphrodite, and eunuch, begotten in drunkenness on street beggars and kept only for amusement. Eating becomes gluttony, and the banquet turns into the orgy of vulgarity at Trimalchio's in Petronius' *The Satyricon*. Love becomes the cynical bargains of Lucian's *Dialogues of the Heterae*, marriage the opportunity for adultery of William Wycherly's *Plain Dealer*, and sex the ugly perversity of Juvenal's pathic angrily protesting the immorality of the rich man who has tired of him and cast him off.

Human institutions and the arts, originally designed to further life and preserve human values, turn sour and become instruments of tyranny and means to desolation. In satire, law is the stupid, self-satisfied lawyers and cruel judges of Daumier; government is the rule of Orwell's Big Brother; education is Waugh's Scone College, Oxon., and Llanabba Hall of Dr. Augustus Fagan, Ph.D.; science is the alchemy of Jonson's projectors, the schemes of Swift's pedants, and the inhumanity of Huxley's *Brave New World*. Learning becomes the organized ignorance of Swift's Laputa, the uselessness of Lucian's philosophers in *Sale of Lives*, the sophistics of Aristophanes' Socrates; language the instrument of pretense used to mask the idiocy of Pope's Dunces, the Newspeak of *1984*, the means to domination of Ionesco's *The Lesson*.

The traditional architectonics, the ways in which the images of satire are organized and their dynamics shown, underline the disorderliness, the perversity, the sterility, and the meaninglessness inherent in the components of the satiric world. In keeping with the original meaning of the word *satura*, satire usually lacks a consistent, even development and an obviously harmonic arrangement of parts. Both first-person formal and third-person narrative satire consists of flickering vignettes, a series of brief, seemingly unrelated scenes. This newsreel technique of rapid, abrupt shifts intensifies the already powerful tendencies to fragmentation and meaninglessness.

This characteristic broken scene of satire is seldom if ever dominated by a single heroic figure, or even by a limited central cast, as is the case in comedy or tragedy. Where one figure does occupy the limelight more than others, he is likely to be either the satirist himself railing on the wicked world, or, more often, a booby hero (Voltaire's Candide, Swift's Gulliver, or Waugh's Paul Pennyfeather), innocent, trusting, and utterly ignorant, to whom the most dreadful things happen during the course of his travels. Satire does not, however, ordinarily focus on the private, individual life, and so it gives us not a hero but a great variety of diverse people, very lightly sketched, who have in common only a shared kind of grotesque idiocy, which is busily at work destroying all sense and meaning. The human litter of the satiric world is paired with a litter of inanimate objects, and the satiric world is crammed to the bursting point with dense numbers of unrelated things. If in the midst of this jumble any trace of the good or the ideal remains, it stands upon the edge of obliteration, finds itself utterly helpless and frustrated, or, despairing, allows itself to dissolve into the mob or takes its place in the empty, mechanical movements of life.

Satire is usually said to lack plot, and it does not, indeed, in its abrupt, disjunct movements have the steady Aristotelian progression from a beginning, through a middle, to an end, which is usual in tragedy and comedy. But something does happen in satire: usually all the busy efforts and frantic activities of the fools eventuate in a regression, or the pure confusion implicit in their local activities. They rush madly about, scheme, plan, talk, and cover great distances, only to end in the same place they began. They make titanic efforts to raise themselves to godhead and overcome the limits inherent in nature, only to end lower than they started. They spread over all creation and master everything, only to reduce everything to nothing. The inevitability of their defeat and the scheme of the satiric plot is contained in the projects they pursue; alchemy, the invention of a perpetual motion machine, or the creation of utopia.

The diabolic logic of the satiric world, where one must always run faster to stay in the same place, is revealed in the great irony at the center of a recent American satire, Joseph Heller's *Catch-22* (1961). In this novel the bomber pilot requests the flight surgeon to ground him for psychological reasons. The doctor points out, however, that as long as he continues flying and risking his life in this insane war he is, indeed, crazy and should be grounded. However, the fact that he is now here, trying to escape and save his life, proves his sanity, and he is therefore capable of continuing to fly. Returned to duty!

All writers of satire, whatever their particular bias, ultimately fear and attack, and by attacking seek to exorcise the fragmentation, disorder, isolation, and meaninglessness which have historically been sensed by the Western mind as the great threats to the continuity of society and the welfare of the individual. The magician satirist, the author of the great literary satires, and even the verbal overkiller of our own time, all fear and attack the same things, and all use, in varying degrees, the same traditional symbols—the jungle, the wasteland, the mob, the machine, and the beast. They also use certain structural devices—the fragmented scene, the multiplicity of characters and things, the reflexive or regressive plot. At the surface of their satires, of course, they are blaming and attacking identifiable men and specific attitudes—Cardinal Wolsey, urban and court life, Colley Cibber, Victorian prudery, modern science, and Stalinism. The strategy is extremely clever and effective, for by identifying these men and attitudes with the images of fear and by making them responsible for the great archetypal situations of hopelessness and meaninglessness, the satirist condemns his victims utterly. But in the long run, the historical and realistic content of satire may tend to be forgotten, and we may continue to read the great satires not for what they tell us about the Rome of the Caesars or the England of Walpole and Castlereagh, but for what they tell us about our most fundamental fears as men; about what kind of world is ultimately unliveable for true human beings. At this level, in a way appropriate to this most ironic of literary kinds, satire the engine of anger and hatred ceases to be divisive and frightening and becomes instead a source of unification and comfort, which tells us that beneath the hatreds and antagonisms of the moment all men ultimately are afraid of the same things.

*BIBLIOGRAPHY*

Roman *satura* is discussed most recently and completely in *Satire, Critical Essays on Roman Literature*, ed. J. P. Sullivan (Bloomington, Ind., 1963). The nature of formal verse satire is detailed by M. C. Randolph, "The Structural Design of Formal Verse Satire," *Philosophical Quarterly*, **21** (1942), 368–84. See also M. C. Randolph, "Celtic Smiths and Satirists: Partners in Sorcery," *English Literary History*, **8** (1941), 127–59, for the relation of magic to the violent metaphors used by the satirist to describe his art. Primitive satire and its development into art are the subject of R. C. Elliott, *The Power of Satire: Magic, Ritual, Art* (Princeton, 1960), the single most important book on the subject of satire, and one to which this article is heavily indebted.

The gradual shift of emphasis from the satirist to the object of attack has been traced in great detail in two recent books, which provide the most useful and complete history of Western literary satire available: Ronald Paulson, *The Fictions of Satire* (Baltimore, 1967); and idem, *Satire and the Novel in Eighteenth-Century England* (New Haven, 1967). The most useful single work on the nature of third-person narrative satire is Ricardo Quintana, "Situation as Satirical Method," *University of Toronto Quarterly*, **17** (1947–48), 130–36.

The history and development of satyr-satire is followed in A. B. Kernan, *The Cankered Muse, Satire of the English*

*Renaissance* (New Haven, 1959). The Pope *persona* and the general question of satiric *personae* are treated in Maynard Mack, "The Muse of Satire," *Yale Review*, **41** (1951–52), 80–92; and Swift's mastery of this device is helpfully discussed in W. B. Ewald, Jr., *The Masks of Jonathan Swift* (Cambridge, Mass., 1954); and in Martin Price, *Swift's Rhetorical Art* (New Haven, 1953).

The typical images and symbols of satire were first worked out by Northrop Frye, *Anatomy of Criticism* (Princeton, 1957). Frye's ideas are carried forward and focused helpfully by Philip Pinkus, "St. George and the Dragon," *Queen's Quarterly*, **70** (1963–64), 30–49, where the author argues that satire is not so much an attack on evil as a sad and contemptuous portrayal of its triumph. The characteristic structure and plot of satire are discussed in A. B. Kernan, "A Theory of Satire," *The Cankered Muse* (New Haven, 1959); and idem, *The Plot of Satire* (New Haven, 1965). The latter book attempts to define the differences between satire and the genres with which it is frequently confused, tragedy and comedy.

Edward W. Rosenheim, Jr., *Swift and the Satirist's Art* (Chicago, 1963), argues the case against the possibility of any general description of a genre so varied in its instances, and insists that the best definition can be no more than, "Satire consists of an attack by means of a manifest fiction upon discernible historical particulars" (p. 31).

For a collection of modern criticism see Ronald Paulson, ed., *Modern Essays in Criticism, Satire* (Englewood Cliffs, N.J., 1971).

ALVIN B. KERNAN

[See also **Comic;** Evil; **Irony; Literature;** Motif; **Style;** Tragic.]

# VICTORIAN SENSIBILITY AND SENTIMENT

SENSIBILITY, in its broadest and most neutral sense, designates the process by means of which intellectual perceptions and sensory experience interact according to a relatively consistent pattern. The term recognizes the psychological fact that just as there can be no human feeling without a minimum of intellectual discrimination, so men are unable to reason without experiencing some feeling. Sensibility produces sentiment, which is feeling and thought in association as distinguished from pure thought and instinctual emotion. Although sensibility and sentiments vary from individual to individual, if the members of the dominant class in a particular society share the same basic values and possess sensory mechanisms conditioned by the same environment, a particular pattern of thinking and feeling may be said to characterize a whole society.

It is in this sense that one can speak of a Victorian sensibility and Victorian sentiment.

The term "Victorian" was at first applied to the period of English history that coincided with a long reign. Recent usage, however, has tended to confine the term to a more limited and more coherent phase of English culture extending approximately from 1830 to 1880.

As in other epochs, the sensibility and sentiments characteristic of Victorian culture were shaped both by external pressures and by inherited attitudes of which the Victorians themselves were not always conscious. The major external pressures were an expanding population, spreading industrialization, greater concentration of people in large urban areas, and an increase in wealth which was diffused among growing numbers of people. The conscious Victorian response to these external changes was in large measure determined by attitudes and values inherited from the past, the most important of which were Evangelicalism in religion and utilitarianism in philosophy. The coalescence of these external pressures and internal attitudes created a social structure and cultural pattern, centering in the middle class and characterized by a distinctive mode of thinking and feeling, that gave stability to English society for approximately fifty years.

The most important conscious element in Victorian culture was its Evangelical religion, a variant of English Protestantism which combined diverse elements from the older traditions of Puritanism, Methodism, and Anglicanism. The latter forms of English Protestantism have been described as religions of the State, of the heart, and of the Church, respectively. Evangelicalism's uniqueness lay in its being a religion of the home. Like the traditions from which it derived, Evangelicalism emphasized personal faith and the direct relationship between the individual soul and God, but combined this Protestant doctrine with special emphases of its own. Unlike Puritanism and Anglicanism, which offered a coherent theology and a corporate ideal of holiness in the State or in the Church, Evangelicalism stressed the nonrational, emotional element of religious experience and personal holiness within the family; unlike Methodism, it retained ecclesiastical elements such as *The Book of Common Prayer* and a sense of the value of corporate public worship. It exercised its pervasive influence mainly by creating a strong sense of family and of self-discipline. The Evangelical watchwords of "duty" and "earnestness" appeared in the writings of professed Victorian agnostics and of working-class radicals as well as in the sermons of Evangelical ministers.

Religious censuses of the period indicate that less

than half the population of Great Britain attended Sunday church services regularly, and that not more than one in ten of the metropolitan poor attended church at all, yet Victorian England can be described as deeply religious. The virtues cultivated within the Evangelical patriarchal family structure—obedience, chaste love, self-improvement, and fellow-feeling —carried over into Victorian public life in corresponding social virtues: deference to one's superiors, marital fidelity, industry, and sympathy for the deserving poor. The sense of duty was thus both familial and social, and a sober earnestness provided the moral atmosphere in which these duties were performed. From its center in the middle-class home the tenets and tone of Evangelicalism gradually infiltrated both the Victorian aristocracy and the lower classes. The latter were exposed to Evangelical teaching and philanthropies through the literature and the charitable works of numerous religious societies which served as organized social agencies for spreading the Evangelical ethos. Except for the unreachable paupers in the great urban areas and agricultural laborers scattered in remote localities, it was the rare Victorian who was not touched, directly or indirectly, by the values and attitudes of Evangelicalism.

If Evangelical Christianity might be described as the heart of the Victorian sensibility, utilitarianism was its mind. Like Victorian religion, the dominant philosophy of the period had its roots in a variety of eighteenth-century attitudes, ranging from the common-sense deistic morality of eighteenth-century Anglican divines to the radical application of the principle of utility in legal and economic reform proposed by philosophical rationalists. Unlike Evangelicalism, utilitarianism was grounded in logic and was completely secular in orientation; it was outspokenly antireligious, resting its claims on sensory and rational experience rather than on the supernatural or the feelings of the heart. The function of philosophy in the utilitarian view was, in the words of one of the most influential writers of the period, not to make men perfect, but to make imperfect men comfortable. Utilitarianism posited self-interest, explainable on the basis of an egoistic psychology of pleasure and pain, as the governing impulse in human behavior. Its exponents were committed to the possibility of improving man's estate through rational education of individual egoism and political and legal reform of existing social structures. The "pleasure" for which the individual was to be educated and social institutions were to be designed was not the transitory pleasure of the individual but a "general utility"; the maxim which served as the guiding utilitarian principle in politics, ethics, and economics alike was "the greatest happiness of the

greatest number." The chief obstacles to the achievement of this general good were the ignorance and superstition which in the past had created irrational structures such as the Church and the aristocracy. The leading utilitarians collected and published statistics in support of their specific proposals for reform: the resolution of the inherent political antagonism between rulers and ruled through universal suffrage, and free competition in an open market in the realm both of ideas and of economic activity.

Utilitarianism was thus not only different from but intellectually incompatible with the basic attitudes underlying Evangelicalism. Yet, in what might be called the orthodox Victorian sensibility, the two traditions complemented one another in important ways. Three assumptions which were basic to the Victorian response to the problems posed by industrialization and urbanization were upheld by both, though they interpreted and defended them on quite different grounds: (1) the primacy of the individual, (2) the possibility, and the duty, of improving man's estate, and (3) the need for asceticism on the part of the individual if men were to be happy. For the Evangelical the individual soul was free before God to work out its eternal salvation through faith and good works; for the utilitarian the individual man was free to attain happiness on earth, rationally, by following certain universal laws. For both, the happiness of the individual was bound up with his willingness to help his fellowman, that is, with his development of a capacity for sympathy, or fellow-feeling, or benevolence, as it was variously called. For the Evangelical the duty to practice asceticism was based on a religiously formed conscience; for the utilitarian it was based on the Malthusian sociological theory of population growth and the Ricardian economic theory, based on Malthus, of the distribution of wealth in an open-market economy. Outward expression of fellow-feeling took the form of philanthropy for Evangelicals and of social reform for the utilitarians.

In addition to these positive beliefs, Evangelicalism and utilitarianism displayed common hostilities which were equally important: toward the merely sensuous and merely speculative; and toward idleness, play, and fictions. Because the progress of the individual, and therefore of society, was for both schools a serious and pragmatic business, anything which did not contribute to the realization of the larger goal was rejected as frivolous or worse. To the earnest middle-class Victorian the "idle" rich and the "lazy" poor were equally irresponsible.

The society brought about by the interaction between these personal attitudes and the impersonal pressures of the environment was shaped by three general qualities which characterized the middle class: (1) moral idealism; (2) intellectual nonconformity; and (3) social conformity (C. Dawson, in *Ideas and Beliefs of the Victorians*, 1949). The attitudes and sentiments attaching to these qualities overlapped and interpenetrated one another in a cohesive social culture which withstood inward contradictions and external threats despite rapid changes during the period in both the human and the natural environment.

Victorian moral idealism was nurtured primarily by the Evangelical belief in the sanctity of the home and by the sentiments connected with this belief. Accounts in contemporary diaries, letters, and religious tracts convey a sense of the powerful role played by family prayer in the training of Victorian children and domestics. The regimen of the household of an early, influential, and wealthy convert to Evangelicalism conveys something of the quality of Evangelical discipline:

Abt. a quarter before 10 oClock, the family assembled to prayers, which were read by Wilberforce in the dining room. As we passed from the drawing room I saw all the servants standing in regular order, the woeman ranged in a line against the wall & the men the same. . . . —When the whole were collected in the dining room, all knelt down against a chair or Sopha. Wilberforce knelt at a table in the middle of a room, and after a little pause began to read a prayer, which He did very slowly in a low, solemnly awful voice (Davies [1961], p. 220).

Such scenes were repeated in numerous Victorian homes. In the country more conscientious members of the squirearchy set a similar example in the Hall. The practice of daily family prayer, supplemented by spiritual reading and weekly sermons in church or chapel, generated a strong bond between Victorian parents and children, and between brothers and sisters, which persisted even when, as not seldom happened in later years, serious differences of opinion developed regarding the theological superstructure of Evangelicalism.

In addition to the Bible, one of the popular family books of the period was *Pilgrim's Progress*. The Puritan stress on self-discipline, piety, and self-improvement was disseminated through Victorian society in a flood of Evangelical treatises and didactic tales prepared by the religious press. A typical tract, *The Sinner's Friend*, published in 1821, had by 1845 sold 800,000 copies and by 1867 more than a million and a half copies (Chadwick, 1966). The twin evils of sexual promiscuity and alcohol held a prominent place in this literature, a preoccupation which deeply affected the secular literature of the period as well. The emphasis upon chastity and temperance was in part a reaction to the promiscuity and drinking so conspicuously evident in

the great underworlds of poverty in Victorian cities; in this respect Victorian reticence was a phase in the "history of the battle for refinement and civilization, and above all the better protection of women, against promiscuity, animalism, brutality and grossness which had been common even in the eighteenth century" (Clark [1962], p. 126). Even apart from this reinforcement, the Evangelical emphasis upon sexual restraint and temperance would have had the effect of idealizing chaste love, woman, and the home, and of surrounding these objects with sentiments of attachment, reverence, and even worship.

Evangelical moral idealism made itself felt outside the home in negative form in the censorship which it exercised over literature and the arts. The tradition which held that the arts should teach as well as delight was interpreted in the light of a moral aesthetic which associated delight primarily with moral teaching in a way that severely limited both the areas of experience that could be treated in art and the manner in which the matters which were treated could be presented. Thackeray, the Brontë sisters, the later Dickens, George Eliot, and other leading writers were in this respect typically Victorian. This moralism had to do not simply with prudishness in matters of sex, but with a deeper and more comprehensive alteration in sensibility which might be described as a loss of the sense of play. Dress, conversation, intellectual speculation, religious liturgy, games themselves, as well as literature and the arts, were affected. One of the notable features of the age was the Sabbatarianism which forbade not only drink and games but even secular reading on Sundays.

The other important form in which Victorian moral idealism had its effect outside the home was more positive. Generally a culture that enforces its taboos has focused energies of considerable power. The sentiments of benevolence and charity which were an important part of Victorian moral idealism resulted in prodigious philanthropic efforts and political activism. The William Wilberforce whose household was described above was largely responsible for the passage of England's first antislavery legislation; a close friend, an Evangelical banker, donated six-sevenths of his annual income to charity until he married, after which he gave one-third.

The reform of political and legal administrative procedures, as well as Victorian intellectual nonconformity, stemmed primarily from utilitarianism, the basic impulse of which was rational conviction rather than emotional commitment. The essential utilitarian virtues were likewise intellectual: sincerity in thinking, strict logic, a conscientious study of facts, and the courage to follow wherever facts and logic led. For

John Stuart Mill, the best known of the utilitarians, uncensored conflict of opinion, intellectual tolerance, and philosophical and religious pluralism were the very conditions for human advancement. Though utilitarians could be doctrinaire, in principle the utilitarian philosophy was committed to disinterested examination of the facts, including facts regarding the way in which the mind itself works. Characteristically, whereas Evangelical influence originated in the family and spread from the home into Victorian society, the utilitarian influence was exercised primarily in the discussion of public affairs in public debate and spread thence into the Victorian home. The conflict of opinion produced by their widely different assumptions helped to create an atmosphere of intellectual tolerance and a less polemical tone in the press.

The combination of moral idealism and intellectual nonconformity helped to produce the third marked characteristic of the Victorian sensibility, an extraordinary impulse to conform socially. Elements in Evangelicalism and utilitarianism made compromise and conformity possible, since neither was as extreme or as belligerent as its eighteenth-century predecessor, Methodism and Philosophical Radicalism, respectively. The memory of the social upheavals caused by the French Revolution and the Napoleonic wars early in the century was still disturbing to many Englishmen in 1830 and persuaded them that men of good will, however diverse their intellectual or religious principles, should work together to pursue the immediate practical advantages made possible by an expanding technology. In addition, the spread of poverty and urban slums after 1830 tended to unite members of the ruling classes in a common fear as well as a common sense of guilt. What distinguished Victorian England from the rest of nineteenth-century Europe, one historian has noted, was that while in France, Germany, Italy, and Russia idealists were usually extremists who despised compromise, in Victorian England devotion to compromise was strongest precisely among the most sincere idealists (Dawson, op. cit.).

The pressure of social conformity expressed itself in two popular terms—carried over from at least the Renaissance—in the Victorian vocabulary, "gentleman" and "respectability." Both terms escape precise definition because of their manifold implications for their Victorian user. In a general and vulgar sense, a gentleman was an educated man with an independent income and therefore one who ranked in the middle class or higher on the social scale. But in its narrower and more essential meaning it referred to the moral training and sensitivity which wealth and education made possible. The moral dimension was described by the novelist Thackeray when, in answer to his own question "What is it to be a gentleman?" he replied that it was "to have lofty aims, to lead a pure life, to keep your honour virgin; to have the esteem of your fellow-citizens, and the love of your fireside; to bear good fortune meekly; to suffer evil with constancy; and through evil or good to maintain truth always" (Houghton [1957], p. 359). The idea of respectability was more superficial and more widely applied than the idea of the gentleman, It included the suggestion of bodily cleanliness and neatness, particularly in its application to the lower classes.

Neatness is the outward sign of a conscious respectability, and Respectability is the name of that common level of behaviour which all families ought to reach and on which they can meet without disgust. The Respectable man in every class is one whose ways bear looking into, who need not shrink or hide or keep his door barred against visitors . . . who lives in the eye of his neighbours and can count on the approval of the great and the obedience of the humble (Young [1936], p. 25).

The notion of respectability thus had covert political implications in the relationships between social classes. A leading politician of the age remarked that "The middle classes know that the safety of their lives and property depend upon their having round them a peaceful, happy, and moral population." Respectability was the standard applied to ensure such a population, denoting "at once a select status and a universal motive. Like Roman citizenship, it could be indefinitely extended, and every extension fortified the State" (Young, op. cit.). The note of deference which predominated in Victorian social relationships underlay a strong admiration for national heroes and leaders, including a deep-rooted devotion to Queen Victoria herself and a general suspicion of persons and institutions which were not English.

The basic pattern of thought and feeling which characterized the orthodox Victorian sensibility—moral sentiments centered around the family and the virtues of duty and earnestness; intellectual sentiments centered around the ideals of intellectual sincerity and tolerance; social sentiments centered around the ideals of gentlemanliness and respectability—produced what one of its critics called "an epoch of hearts uplifted with hope, and brains active with sober and manly reason for the common good. Some ages are marked as sentimental, others stand conspicuous as rational. The Victorian age was happier than most in the flow of both these currents into a common stream of vigorous and effective talent" (Buckley [1951], p. 13). The dark shadows cast by the positive qualities of the Victorian sensibility were equally real, however, the result of the fact that a sensibility harboring ideals which were not logically related and which in some important areas were in direct contradiction to one another was inevitably subject to tensions that could not always be successfully resolved. The more sensitive Victorians were aware of these contradictions. John Ruskin pointed out to his readers that while their Evangelical religion told Victorians to love their neighbor, their utilitarian economic principles told them that the deepest instinct of man was to defraud his neighbor. He could think of no precedent in history for a nation's establishing a systematic disobedience to the first principles of its professed religion. The Victorians assimilated the contradictory attitudes as best they could. The agonized personal crises and frequent painful wrenchings of family relationships recorded in the literature of the period reflected the tensions that accompanied the attempt to reconcile them. At a still deeper level a profound psychic ambivalence expressed itself in other ways.

One way was the sentimentality which marked the popular literature and art of the age, the tendency to present scenes of "pathos feasting on itself." The most famous sentimentalist of the age was the novelist Charles Dickens, whose treatment of grief and death, particularly where children were involved, was immensely popular. He was accused of handling the death of little children "as if it were some savoury dainty which could not be too fully appreciated" (Richard Stang, *The Theory of the Novel in England 1850–1870*, New York and London [1959], p. 62). Sentimentalism likewise affected Victorian painting, which exhibited two prominent features: a love of literal detail and a tendency to exaggerate sentiment. The connection between the literalism and the sentimentality was an important one: "Victorian sentimentality is largely the imposition of feeling as an afterthought upon literalness" (H. House, *Ideas and Beliefs of the Victorians* [1949], p. 223). The scientific love of fact was utilitarian in emphasis; the price it exacted, evident in the autobiographies of Mill and Charles Darwin, was a threatened loss of the capacity to feel. The sentimental love of fact was mainly Evangelical in inspiration, and the price it exacted was a weakening of the capacity to reason. Evangelical literature and practice were not above exposing to public view the agonies of a dying child or the delirium tremens of the drunkard for purposes of edification. The utilitarians, by contrast, agnostic or atheistic in matters of religion, doubted the immortality of the soul and the possibility of rewards in another life, and therefore attached all the more importance to reducing pain in the present one. The wavering between a scientific and a sentimental view of pain reflected a dangerous split in the Victorian sensibility.

The fissure beneath the surface solidity of Victorian thought and feeling was most evident in the ambiguous relation of the Victorian sensibility to nature. During the first quarter of the nineteenth century English romantic writers had hopefully envisioned the possibility of men developing an "organic sensibility" by means of which the rival claims of intellect and feeling as sources of truth could be reconciled. The reconciliation conceived by the romantics went beyond the inward psychic integration of thought and emotion and included man's relationship to the external universe as well. The latter point rested on romantic assumptions regarding the "correspondences" that obtained between the inward forms of human thought and feeling and outward natural forms, the inward and outward worlds being regarded as so adapted to one another as to make possible an integrated participation of all the human faculties in a reassuring encounter with the universe. Two circumstances contributed to the rapid decline of this romantic faith: first, the emergence of what one Victorian poet called the "terrible muses" of astronomy and geology, and secondly, an increasing sense, as the century progressed, that the powers of reason by which men were mastering nature through technology had created a new irrational power over which men might lose control: the machine.

Of these two disturbing pressures, the impact of scientific thought, notably of geology and biology, was the earlier felt and contributed most to the ambivalence in the Victorian response to nature. Geology gave rise to a time-consciousness, later reinforced by studies of biological evidence, which stemmed from the discovery that the universe had existed for millions of years and that "whilst this planet has gone cycling on according to the fixed law of gravity, . . . endless forms most beautiful and most wonderful have been, and are being evolved." Darwin himself was deeply moved by his evolutionary vision, but the ordinary Victorian felt that the human species was dwarfed in a terrifying abyss of endless time. It was as though the roof and walls of a long-inhabited room had been removed and familiar objects were seen in a new, strange, and disturbing light. The Victorian response to this new nature reflected the same ambivalence that can be detected in Victorian art. On the one hand, there was an intense fascination with natural forms and minute details evident in Victorian word-painting in prose and the naturalism of its art; on the other hand, there was a compelling need to invest natural forms and details with moral significance. As the traditional "evidences" of the handiwork of a Creator became more difficult to discern, the orthodox Victorian sensibility found it correspondingly difficult to evoke the moral reassurances it sought in nature.

The science of biology cast a shadow of another kind as well: the threat to human life posed by the instinct to procreation. T. R. Malthus' *An Essay on the Princi-*

*ple of Population as It Affects the Future Improvement of Society,* published in 1798, evoked a dire vision of the natural tendency for human population to increase faster than the means of subsistence. It was Mathus' theory which inspired David Ricardo to construct his pessimistic theory of political economy. Whereas to Adam Smith society had been one great family, to Ricardo it was the scene of a bitter contest for supremacy and survival, the view which Darwin extended to all of organic life. The utilitarians responded characteristically by arguing that if "nature" was blind and cruel, man had the power, and the moral duty, to ameliorate its effects through social reform. Yet the specter of a nature "red in tooth and claw" haunted the Victorian imagination and contributed to the sentimentality as well as to the reticence of its treatment of nature and natural instinct.

The threat posed by the increase in population and the extension of technology involved representative institutions as well as individuals. A London clergyman who found himself assigned to a city parish with 35,000 parishioners (Clark, 1962) might wonder whether the Church could keep pace with the changing environment. Similarly, agricultural depressions threatened the competitive economy built on Ricardian principles, while all through the period a steady stream of social legislation designed to meet urban and rural problems created a growing government bureaucracy in direct opposition to the consciously held political ideals of the age. Impersonal forces were silently making the representative Victorian institutions obsolete.

The result was that alongside the dominant sentiments of confidence and hope there was another, less reassuring set of pressures and feelings creating a sensibility characterized by anxiety and fear. In addition to the more remote threat of alienation in a meaningless universe, there were immediate dangers which generated deep-seated fears: in politics the fear of mobs and revolution, in economics the fear of bankruptcy, in family life the fear of orphanhood. These fears appear again and again in the literature of the age, either consciously or unconsciously, providing the plots as well as the emotional energy of much of the writing. Debt, ruin, and madness haunt Victorian fiction: characters struck down are usually shown to have deserved their fate, while "deserving" characters are conveniently rescued by a legacy, emigration, a fortunate marriage, or a change of heart (Williams, 1958). But the arbitrariness of the solutions reinforces the impression of a serious incompatibility between conscious Victorian sentiments and the realities to which these sentiments had to be related.

In protecting itself against a seemingly blind nature and the nonrational impulses of the body and the unconscious—fear of the void, sexual desire, the play instinct—the Victorians developed a powerful will to belief and action, mobilizing the virtues in support of this will at the expense both of reason and of unconscious impulses. The law of psychic life that basic impulses cannot be thwarted without paying a price seems to be borne out in reading the private journals and correspondences of the age; one is struck by the number of "headaches" and other forms of illness which plagued the Victorians.

By the latter half of the century observers were commenting on what seemed to be a notable increase in the number of suicides. The ambivalent relationship between the conscious and unconscious elements of the Victorian experience produced a consistent pattern of behavior: the search for individual autonomy, either through religious adherence to the laws of God or through rational adherence to the laws of nature; the powerful role assigned either to the superego or conscience or to reason in this search; the prevalence of guilt, connected with violation of accepted codes; and a tendency to hysteria, related to repression. As early as the 1850's Matthew Arnold identified the characteristic feeling of the age as *ennui*, and the dominant note of its intellectual life as a "dialogue of the mind with itself."

Arnold's diagnosis of the malaise of the Victorian age in the 1850's was shared by few of his contemporaries; most men were comforted by the "march of mind" and the impressive material progress evidenced by the Great Exhibition of 1851. With few qualifications English culture seemed stable and triumphant through the fifties and sixties and England itself moving in the vanguard of human advancement. But by 1880 the contradictions which were disguised or contained for half a century by the Victorian capacity for compromise had become intolerable. The sentiments and sensibility of Victorian orthodoxy lost their energy and were increasingly placed on the defensive by new conscious attitudes and sentiments.

Imperialism, the emergence of an unscrupulous class of nouveaux riches, the second-rate quality of a second Evangelical revival, a growing "yellow press,"—these and other symptoms of decline marked the imminence of a major shift in sensibility. The influence of the Evangelical conscience was undermined from within by the spread of religious skepticism, and from without by attacks on Evangelical piety as a hypocritical use of an ostensibly Christian fervor to disguise essentially worldly ambitions. The supremacy of the utilitarian principle was similarly weakened, in part by the impact of German idealism and psychology, and more seriously by charges that its economic principles simply rationalized an inhuman social structure based on the struggle for wealth. With the questioning of these central elements of the Victorian sensibility, new attitudes and values emerged which were essentially *anti*-Victorian in their bias and which signified more a rejection of Victorianism than the arrival of a new integration of thought and feeling.

The two major forms of anti-Victorianism, although united in their common revolt against Victorian principle and practice, were opposed to one another in most other matters. The earlier of the two reactions can be described under the general term of "aestheticism," the reassertion of the play instinct not only as an end in itself but as the only possible response to a hideous environment. This development was associated primarily with the arts and literature, first in the form of Pre-Raphaelitism and later, partly in response to influences from the Continent, in the form of impressionism. But there were important social implications in aestheticism as well, notably the revival of dandyism and satirical wit, a withdrawal from politics of the usual kind, a new concern with ritual and form, and a thoroughgoing intellectual skepticism. In effect, aestheticism marked a radical disengagement from Victorian moral commitments and social concerns through escape into the amoral world of art and play. In asserting that the only stay against ugliness and meaninglessness was in the formal coherence of art, aestheticism reversed the Victorian practice of literal imitation of nature: one of the most-quoted epigrams of the new movement insisted rather that nature must imitate art.

The skepticism which underlay this aestheticism appeared in its subjectivization of experience, its carrying Victorian individualism to the *ne plus ultra* of solipsism. Each man was an island unto himself; the "facts" of experience were seen as a series of impressions which the individual memory could store and the individual imagination could rearrange, but from which no rational or objective or common knowledge could be inferred. Ugly objects and immoral action were as susceptible of artistic treatment as conventionally beautiful things or noble conduct; indeed, it was no longer possible to make such distinctions since one could only try to rescue one's private impressions from the flux of experience by capturing them in a work of art.

Aestheticism represented a turning of the Victorian sensibility in upon itself and a consequent dissolution of accepted certainties under the pressure of the dialogue of the mind with itself. The other major development, which might be generally called "politicism," represented an opposite movement. In its dissatisfaction with Victorian culture, politicism turned outward and aggressively attacked existing social structures. In

the form of socialism politicism called for the creation of a new social structure through the active intervention of the state; in the guise of anarchism it called for the abolition of social structures altogether. To both political schools aestheticism seemed an immoral retreat from responsibility: not only was great art moral, as the Victorians had insisted, but it was specifically public, political, and revolutionary in its moralism. The career of William Morris was representative: influenced in his youth by the religious revival in Oxford, he moved first through a phase in which his aesthetic conscience led him away from social concerns as alien to the artistic embodiment of idle dreams, and then to a final phase of political activism on behalf of revolutionary socialism.

Aestheticism carried Victorian individualism and intellectual nonconformity to extremes unassimilable by the orthodox Victorian sensibility. Politicism, on the other hand, refocused Victorian moral idealism through its political radicalism. Both rejected Victorian social conformity, and the ideals of the gentleman and of respectability which had sustained it. Aestheticism regarded the respectable gentleman as insensitive, dull, and prudish; politicism regarded him as rich, selfish, hypocritical, and counterrevolutionary. In its initial stage the fin de siècle revolt against Victorian orthodoxy generated an excitement and hope similar to that which had accompanied the romantic movement at the beginning of the century, but the later movement lacked both the range and the depth of the earlier one, being essentially negative in character and divided against itself in its aims. Although Queen Victoria lived on until 1901, after 1880 her name was no longer an adequate symbol for the events, values, and sentiments which were shaping and expressing a new sensibility for which historians have not yet found a satisfactory name.

*BIBLIOGRAPHY*

Valuable surveys of the period are provided in W. E. Houghton, *The Victorian Frame of Mind, 1830–1870* (New Haven, 1957); G. M. Young, *Victorian England: Portrait of an Age* (London, 1936; 2nd ed. 1953); and *Ideas and Beliefs of the Victorians* (London, 1949), a collection of BBC talks by experts on various aspects of Victorian England. Relevant social histories are G. Kitson Clark, *The Making of Victorian England* (Cambridge, Mass., 1962); G. M. Trevelyan, *Illustrated English Social History*, Vol. IV: *The Nineteenth Century* (London and New York, 1952); and G. M. Young, ed., *Early Victorian England, 1830–1865*, 2 vols. (London and New York, 1934). For utilitarianism, see É. Halévy, *The Growth of Philosophic Radicalism*, trans. M. Morris (Boston, 1955). For Evangelicalism, see H. Davies, *Worship and Theology in England: From Watts and Wesley to Maurice,*

1690–1850 (Princeton, 1961); and Owen Chadwick, *The Victorian Church: Part I* (New York, 1966). R. D. Altick's *The English Common Reader* (Chicago, 1957) studies the mass reading public. J. H. Buckley, *The Victorian Temper* (Cambridge, Mass., 1951), and R. Williams, *Culture and Society, 1780–1950* (London, 1958; New York, 1960; also reprint) gives an overview of the literature of the period.

Studies of important individual Victorians appear in Asa Briggs, *Victorian People* (Chicago, 1954); *The Great Victorians*, ed. H. J. and H. Massingham (London, 1932); and Basil Willey, *Nineteenth Century Studies* (London and New York, 1949) and *More Nineteenth Century Studies* (London and New York, 1956).

WILLIAM A. MADDEN

[See also **Agnosticism;** Deism; **Evolutionism; Religion and Science;** Romanticism; Sin and Salvation; Utilitarianism.]

# SIN AND SALVATION

## INTRODUCTION

THAT THESE two subjects should be linked together for consideration here is justified both by religious tradition and a natural association of ideas. Each subject, however, connotes, on analysis, distinctive evaluations of man's situation in the universe which do not necessarily involve mutual relationship. Thus, while sin denotes human offenses against divine law and the evil consequences that stem from them, salvation may concern divine deliverance from forms of evil, such as volcanic eruption or flood, quite unconnected with man's sin. The Litany of the Anglican Church, in the *Book of Common Prayer* (1662), provides a convenient example of this difference in the following petitions:

From fornication, and all other deadly sin . . . Good Lord, deliver us: From lightning and tempest; from plague, pestilence, and famine; from battle and murder, and from sudden death, Good Lord, deliver us.

That the ideas of sin and salvation are traditionally associated derives from a very ancient and widespread belief in deities who govern the universe, and decree laws designed to maintain a proper relationship between themselves and mankind, in order to preserve both the cosmic order and the harmony of human society. The forms in which this belief has found expression in the course of history have been many and various. They will be described here in chronological order (except Islam); and with comparative reference so that their similarities and differences may be appreciated. (Islamic ideas of sin and salvation are treated after the section on Christianity, in order to complete the survey of religions of Near Eastern origin

in this connection.) For, in a very true sense, the history of man's conception of sin, and the ways in which he has sought for salvation, reflect his interpretations of the significance of human life and destiny.

## IDEAS OF SIN AND SALVATION IN THE ANCIENT NEAR EAST

*1. Egypt.* The earliest evidence for our subject is found in Egypt. There, already by about 2400 B.C. as the *Pyramid Texts* (*Pyr.*) attest, the Egyptians believed that a person's post-mortem well-being could be jeopardized by accusations of wrongdoing brought against him after death. Since these *Texts* are an amorphous collection of prayers, incantations, hymns, and myths of diverse origin, which the priests of Heliopolis put together in the belief that they would assist a dead pharaoh to secure eternal felicity, the various references in them to a post-mortem judgment are difficult to interpret. The following passage, for example, seems to be designed to refute all kinds of accusations, even those that might be brought by animals:

There is no accuser (representing) a living person against N (the deceased king); there is no accuser (representing) a dead person against N; there is no accuser (representing) a goose against N; there is no accuser (representing) a bull against N (*Pyr.* 386 a–b).

The situation implied here is significant; for a tribunal is envisaged before which the deceased may be accused, if he had in some way abused a human being or an animal. Who presided over this post-mortem tribunal, how its transactions were ordered, and what penalties might be imposed, are not indicated. The implication that there was a divine law or order, which the deceased might have transgressed, is suggested by another *Text* (*Pyr.* 319): "N comes forth to justice (*maat*); he brings it, that it may be with him."

This reference to *maat* is of basic importance, because its appearance in the *Pyramid Texts* constitutes the earliest evidence of the idea of a transcendental moral order that recurs, under various names, in many later cultural traditions, as will be noted. For the Egyptians *maat* had several facets of meaning. It could signify justice, truth, and good order in both a social and cosmic context. In mythological imagery, *maat* was portrayed as a goddess, whose distinguishing symbol was a feather; she was regarded as the daughter of the sun-god Rē, and, by a curious transformation of imagery, as the food upon which Rē lived. Thus, Rē, who was the chief god of the Egyptian state, was regarded as embodying *maat* as the principle of order in the universe and in human society.

How these intimations in the *Pyramid Texts* of belief in a moral order, of which the sun-god Rē was the guardian, affected the lives of individuals is revealed in certain tomb inscriptions of about the same period. A notable example is that on the tomb of a noble named Herkhuf. He claims that he "gave bread to the hungry, clothing to the naked, and ferried him who had no boat." He further declares that he never said anything evil "to a powerful one against any people," for he desired "that it might be well with me in the Great God's presence." Despite its rather complacent assertion of virtue, in the history of ethics and religion this inscription is the earliest evidence of belief that positive "good-neighborly" conduct would win divine approval, particularly after death. The "Great God" of the inscription was undoubtedly Rē, and Herkhuf's statement implies that the deity was concerned with a man's moral behavior, and would punish or reward accordingly after death.

The inscription on Herkhuf's tomb reveals no consciousness of sin; but the assertion of his virtues surely implies that contrary behavior would transgress the code of conduct that the Great God required of men. Greater moral sensitivity is shown in a somewhat later (ca. 2000 B.C.) writing known as the *Instruction for King Meri-ka-rē*. Here it is stated that "more acceptable is the character of one upright of heart than the ox of the evil doer," and warning is given that each man must face judgment after death, with his deeds, good or bad, set in heaps before him.

Despite this evidence of what James Breasted and others have aptly called the "dawn of conscience," it is significant that the early Egyptian documents reveal primary concern for a form of salvation that is quite unconnected with moral issues. This salvation, which was fervently sought, was from death and its consequences. The means employed was a combination of ritual magic and practical action. A technique of ritual embalmment was developed, which was patterned on that which was believed to have been employed to revivify the divine hero Osiris after his murder by his evil brother, Set. The efficacy of this mortuary ritual depended on the careful enactment, on behalf of a deceased person, of what had once been done for Osiris; but no question was asked of the moral fitness of the deceased to enjoy this resurrection. By the New Kingdom period (from 1580 B.C.), however, belief in a post-mortem judgment was incorporated into these Osirian funerary rites. The so-called *Book of the Dead*, which was composed at this time to assist the dead to attain eternal beatitude, impressively attests to this development. Two of its chapters (XXX and CXXV) are especially concerned with the judgment which the dead had to face. In many of the manuscripts, these chapters are illustrated with vignettes which graphically present the Egyptian conception of the awful ordeal. The importance of this conception for both the history of soteriology and ethics is such that it requires a measure of detailed analysis here.

The depictions of the judgment scene invariably show a large pair of balances standing in the middle of the Hall of the Two Truths (*Maati*). In one scale-pan the feather symbol of *maat* is set, and in the other the hieroglyph sign (*ib*) of the heart of the deceased. The mortuary-god Anubis supervises the weighing, and the assessment is recorded by the scribe-god Thoth. The transaction generally takes place in the presence of Osiris, the lord of the dead, and it is watched apprehensively by the deceased. Close by a fantastic monster, with a crocodile's head awaits an adverse verdict: it is Am-mut, the Eater of the Dead.

The judgment scene usually accompanies the text of Chapter XXX of the *Book of the Dead*, which is a prayer addressed by the deceased to his heart not to witness against him at this critical juncture. The hypostatization of the heart implied here is a unique feature of ancient Egyptian thought. In texts, the heart is sometimes referred to as the "God in man," and it was evidently regarded as a conscious censor of the individual's behavior throughout life and ready to testify against him in the judgment after death.

The weighing of the heart was evidently related to another transaction with which Chapter CXXV is concerned. This Chapter is prefaced by a descriptive rubric: "Words spoken when one enters the Hall of the Two Truths. To separate N (the deceased) from his sins (*ḥww*), and to see the face of all the gods." Then follow two Declarations of Innocence, sometimes misleadingly called Negative Confessions. The first Declaration is addressed to Osiris; the second to forty-two demonic beings. Each Declaration consists of a number of asseverations of innocence of certain specified crimes. The following are representative examples from both lists, and include both moral and ritual offenses:

I have not killed . . . caused pain to anyone . . . diminished the food offerings in the temples . . . had sexual relations with a boy . . . stolen the loaves of the glorified (dead) . . . diminished the corn-measure.

How these Declarations of Innocence were related to the weighing of the heart is not formally stated in the relevant texts: but a logical nexus can be reasonably made out. It would seem that the Declarations were first made by the deceased on arrival at the Hall of the Two Truths. But these solemn protestations of innocence were not deemed enough until the moral integrity of the person making them had been proved. This was done by weighing his heart against *maat*. If the assessment was favorable, he was significantly proclaimed *maa kheru* ("true of voice") and thus justified in his protestations of innocence.

225

Considerable attention has been given here to this ancient Egyptian evidence because it is not only the earliest we have of the "dawn of conscience," but it also concerns the most elaborate conception of a postmortem judgment until the evolution of Christian eschatology. The Declarations of Innocence also provide our earliest known categories of what was considered to be sin, in that the act concerned a transgressed divine law. It is significant, too, that the ancient Egyptians, while they sought salvation from death by ritual means, believed that the individual's eternal destiny was finally determined by his own character.

*2. Mesopotamia.* In the sister-civilization of Mesopotamia ideas of sin and salvation differed profoundly from the Egyptian concepts, because the Mesopotamian peoples did not believe that a happy lot after death could be achieved. For them, death irreparably shattered the psychophysical organism that constituted an individual person. What survived the awful change was terribly transformed and descended into *kur-nu-gi-a*, the Land of No-return, which was conceived as an immense pit, deep down below the foundations of the world, where the dead dwelt in dust and gloom. All went there, great and small, good and bad; for the gods had withheld the gift of immortality from man.

Salvation, consequently, could not be hoped for from death and its consequences. There was, also, no expectation of judgment after death, since a common fate awaited all. The logic of this view of man's life and destiny meant that salvation and sin were ideas that related only to this present life. Salvation, accordingly, was security from what threatened to harm or destroy the enjoyment of life in this world. For such security men turned to the gods in prayer and service, believing that they had the power to grant long life and prosperity. They believed, too, that the gods had created mankind to serve them by building temples and offering sacrifice to them. Neglect of this service constituted sin, and it had dire consequences. The gods would withdraw their protection from those who so transgressed, thus leaving them open to demonic attack. A Babylonian text known as the *Ludlul bel nemequi* significantly reveals the doubt and anxiety that might beset a man, afflicted by evil, who was not conscious of having neglected his religious duties: "I looked backwards: persecution, woe! Like one who did not offer libation to a god . . . who did not bow his face and did not know reverence, in whose mouth prayer and supplication ceased." The texts of many so-called "penitential psalms" which have been found, appear to express a sense of contrition for sin felt towards a particular patron-god; but their purpose was essentially expiatory. They were doubtless recited during rituals of atonement prompted by misfortune, or, were of an apotropaic kind. It is improbable that they constituted evidence of an established doctrine of sin.

That the gods were believed to have delivered laws for mankind to keep finds graphic expression in the famous Code of Hammurabi, king of Babylon (ca. 1792–1750 B.C.). Carved at the top of the black basalt stele on which the laws are inscribed, is a scene of Hammurabi adoring the sun-god Shamash, from whom he had received the laws. The laws that follow, and penalties for their infringement, are concerned, however, only with the well-being of the state and the maintenance of social order. In an epilogue, Hammurabi claims that Shamash had committed these laws to him, and he threatens with divine punishment any successor who might disregard them. But throughout the Code the terms of reference relate significantly, to life in this world; and transgression of its provisions is to be punished by the civil authorities. Similarly confined to this life are the forms of salvation for which much concern is shown in Mesopotamian texts. But when acts of saving intervention are ascribed to such deities as Marduk or Ishtar, it is salvation from some kind of mundane misfortune, usually sickness; for there could be no saving from the post-mortem destiny decreed for mankind.

*3. Israel.* Until the emergence of belief in a resurrection and judgment of the dead in the second century B.C., the ancient Hebrew conception of man limited personal significance to this life. Moreover, since Hebrew religion was essentially ethnic in origin and character, the individual was significant only insofar as he affected, by his behavior, the relation between Yahweh, the god of Israel, and the holy nation, Israel. A notable instance of this situation occurs in the Book of Joshua (7: 1ff.). The Israelites had suffered a severe defeat by the people of Ai. When Joshua, the Israelite leader, inquired the reason of Yahweh, he was told that Israel had sinned because some of the spoils, dedicated to Yahweh in a previous victory, had been withheld from him. Investigation revealed that an Israelite named Achan had secretly retained certain articles. After he and his family and animals had been stoned to death by the other Israelites, Yahweh was appeased and gave Israel victory over Ai. This barbaric act graphically attests to the prevalence of a primitive sense of communal guilt for the transgression of an individual, and the need to make corporate expiation to the offended deity.

The traditional Hebrew disposition to evaluate sin primarily in terms of the relation of Yahweh and Israel demands many other illustrations. Thus, the kings of Israel are each appraised in a kind of set formula relating to their attitude towards idolatry: "he clung to the sin [i.e., idolatry] of Jeroboam the son of Nebat, which he made Israel to sin; he did not depart from it" (II Kings, 3:3; cf. 10:29; 13:2; etc.). This emphasis upon the corporate aspect of sin, especially in the matter of idolatry, has its classic expression in the second of the Ten Commandments (Exodus 20:3–17). After forbidding the making and worshipping of graven images, Yahweh is represented as declaring that he is "a jealous God, visiting the iniquity of the fathers upon the children to the third and the fourth generation of those who hate me, but showing steadfast love to thousands of those who love me and keep my commandments" (R.S.V.).

The Ten Commandments, just as the Egyptian Declarations of Innocence and some expiatory Mesopotamian texts, concern both religious and ethical actions. Priority of order is given to the religious: worship no other gods; do not commit idolatry; do not take the name of Yahweh "in vain"; and, positively, observe the sabbath. The reward promised for the faithful keeping of these injunctions is confined to this life, namely, divine beneficence and a long life "in the land which the Lord your God gives you."

Apart from these basic requirements for the maintenance of a proper relationship between Yahweh and Israel, Hebrew literature reveals a variety of ideas about the cause and nature of sin. The story of the Fall of Adam, in Genesis (Chs. 2–3), is the most notable attempt to explain the origin and consequence of sin. Since it is set in the Primeval History section of the Yahwist philosophy of history, the story has a universalistic meaning, and it does not pertain specifically to the destiny of Israel. Its theme, briefly, is that the progenitors of mankind incurred the doom of mortality for themselves and their descendants by disobedience to their Maker's command. The part played by the serpent in the fateful drama is enigmatical: it is represented as the suggesting to Eve of the advantages to be gained from disobedience; but the decision to disobey is distinctly taken by Adam and Eve. However, shortly after the account of the Fall, the Yahwist writer in describing the first murder (Genesis 4:2–7), makes a curious reference to sin as a demonic being (*rōbhēs*), "crouching at the door." But the idea that sin is a demon, which seizes the unwary, is not developed, and the consequent suggestion that an evil power seeks to win man from God does not appear in Hebrew thought until the post-Exilic period (after 538 B.C.).

Psalm 51, though of unknown date, affords valuable evidence of the currency of three distinct conceptions of sin. In verses 1 and 2 the penitent beseeches God to ". . . blot out my transgressions. Wash me thoroughly from my iniquity, and cleanse me from my sin!" In Hebrew, "transgressions" (*peshaᶜ*) meant "rebellion"; "iniquity" (*ᶜāwōn*) denoted a deliberate turning aside from the right way; and "sin" (*ḥaṭṭâth*) signified missing the mark or losing one's way through ignorance or lack of skill. The Psalms, which generally show a great sensitivity about offending God, raise many unsolved questions as to whether they should be interpreted as personal confessions or as expressions of corporate contrition, with the speaker representing Israel in a ritual of atonement.

Salvation in ancient Hebrew literature could have two connotations, namely, God's deliverance of Israel from its enemies, the classic example of which was the deliverance from the pursuing Egyptians and their destruction in the Red Sea (Exodus 14:13ff.), and the deliverance of individuals by God from misfortune (e.g., Psalms 34:6). The ethnic or nationalist idea of salvation steadily became the major theme of Jewish religion as Israel's position worsened in the interplay of power politics of the ancient Near East. The desire and hope for divine deliverance found fervent expression in an apocalyptic literature that began to proliferate from the second century B.C. The emphasis, which the prophets had earlier placed on Israel's iniquity as the cause of its political disasters, was now shifted to that of the wickedness of their Gentile oppressors. Belief in ultimate divine succor became concentrated in the idea of Yahweh's Messiah, who would come with supernatural power to overthrow and judge the Gentiles and vindicate Israel as the Elect People of God. It was this hope, that Yahweh would mightily intervene in world affairs to save Israel, that inspired the Zealots, who led the Jewish resistance to the government of Rome, and that eventually caused the fatal revolt of A.D. 66, which ended in the overthrow of the nation and the destruction of Jerusalem and its great Temple four years later.

Parallel with the development of the national hope for divine salvation, went a quest for individual salvation by divine grace. The ancient Yahwist doctrine of man had limited the enjoyment of significant personal life to this world. Yahweh, it was taught, blessed the pious with long life and material prosperity, and punished the impious by misfortune and early death. But, as a sense of individuality emerged in Israel, the speciousness of this doctrine became painfully evident. It caused the questioning of Yahweh's justice that finds such poignant expression in the Book of Job. Job is the type-case of the innocent sufferer overwhelmed by unmerited misfortune. His plight is the more tragic because he accepts the traditional teaching that death was the virtual end of personal life: beyond it lay only the misery of Sheol. Job's problem was that his piety had been unrewarded in this life, and he could expect no divine salvation after death. Within the context of the then contemporary Yahwist doctrine of man, Job's

227

problem, though faced courageously, could find no satisfying answer. A viable answer did eventually become possible in the second century B.C., when the belief was established that God would finally resurrect and judge the dead. Then the just would be rewarded by a blessed post-mortem existence, while the unjust were punished in Sheol, which was reconceived as the place of eternal torment for the damned.

**4. The Greco-Roman World.** Christianity, which is the salvation-religion par excellence, stemmed from Judaism; but its soteriology was profoundly influenced by ideas current in the Greco-Roman world, in which it spread during the formative centuries of its growth. Consequently, these ideas, which are intrinsically significant, are also of basic importance for the study of Christian soteriology.

The Olympian religion of classical Greece, of which the earliest literary evidence is found in the Homeric poems, afforded no hope of a happy afterlife. A common fate awaited all. Their shades descended, at death, into the gloom and misery of Hades, and from this fate there could be no salvation (*Odyssey* Xl.204–22). This view of man's ultimate destiny formed the pattern, with certain variations, of the official religion of Greece; it finds expression in its literature and philosophy (except that of Plato), and its influence can be traced in the sad dignity of the farewell scenes sculptured on many tombs. The Olympian gods were served to maintain the prosperity of the state, and failure to serve them aright or observe the taboos of their cults constituted sin, which involved dire punishment. Thus, the *Iliad* begins by describing how the god Apollo afflicted the Greek army, which was besieging Troy, with a deadly plague because the Greek leader Agamemnon had insulted his priest. Oedipus provides the classic instance, in Greek literature, of the pitiless exactment of divine punishment for unintentional sin. The unfortunate hero commits parricide and incest unwittingly, and thus through his pollution brings disaster to Thebes, his native city, and an awful doom upon himself. It is accordingly significant that, in Greek thought, *hubris* was distinguished as the capital sin; for it meant that the gods were relentless in striking down a man who, confident in his own achievement or good fortune, tended to forget his human status.

The Olympian religion was essentially the religion of the polis, the city-state; it did not cater to personal needs. For those who sought the comforting assurance of a happy afterlife, instead of Hades' grim prospect, there were the mystery-religions of Eleusis and Orphism. The designation "mystery-religion" connotes a cult into which a person had to be specially initiated, in order to participate in its secret rites and be instructed in its esoteric doctrine. To the initiate of the Eleusinian Mysteries, the rationale of which was provided by the myth of the goddess Demeter's search for her lost daughter Persephone, a blessed afterlife was promised. This salvation from the common lot of mankind after death depended primarily upon the magical efficacy of the initiatory rites performed at Eleusis, though certain minimal ethical qualifications were required for initiation. Unfortunately, owing doubtless to the fact that the initiates (*mystae*) kept their vows of silence, we are inadequately informed about both the doctrine and ritual of the Eleusinian Mysteries. The same cause probably accounts also for our lack of detailed knowledge about Orphism. This cult, which traditionally derived from Orpheus and was essentially connected with the myth of Dionysos-Zagreus, was concerned with the emancipation of the soul from its fatal involvement with physical matter. It taught that each soul (*psyche*) was of celestial origin and immortal; but, due to some primordial fault or error, it was doomed to a process of reincarnation in bodies of various kinds, human, animal, and vegetable. Unlike the Eleusinian Mysteries, Orphism had no specific cult-center; it was organized in small local communities. Initiation involved purificatory rites and the imparting of secret knowledge; a discipline of life was required, including vegetarianism. From texts inscribed on gold leaves (*laminae*), found in tombs thought to be those of Orphic initiates, it would appear that advice was given to enable the deceased to establish their heavenly origin and so escape from the "sorrowful, weary wheel" of unceasing reincarnation.

In process of time, other mystery-religions became established in the world of Greco-Roman culture. Chief among them were the cults of Isis and Osiris from Egypt, Attis and Adonis from Asia Minor, and Mithra from Iran. The popularity of these cults attests to the widespread need then felt for the assurance of a blessed afterlife, which was not met by the official religions of Greece and Rome. The cults of Attis and Adonis derived from primitive rituals connected with the "dying-rising" god of vegetation, whose myth commemorated the annual death and resurrection of vegetation. Certain aspects of the myth were incorporated also into the mortuary cult of Osiris. Such cults were based on ancient man's hope that a similar cycle of death and resurrection might, with divine help, be reproduced in himself. In the Mithraic mysteries, elements of solar and vegetation mythologies can be discerned; but the role of Mithra seems to have been that of saving his initiates from the dominion of Ahriman, the principle of death and evil, who was identified with the destructive process of Time under the guise of Zurvān *dareghō–chvadhāta* ("Time of the Long Dominion," i.e., Finite Time).

Together with these specifically religious cults, which offered salvation of varying kinds to their initiates, there existed in the Greco-Roman world mystical philosophies that claimed to possess esoteric (*gnōsis*) knowledge about the human situation which would gain eternal beatitude for those who possessed it. These faiths may be conveniently grouped as Gnosticism, Hermeticism, and Neo-Platonism. The first two were concerned to account for the misery of human life in a way similar to that of Orphism, except that they embodied belief in the baleful dominion of the stars over mankind. The duality of human nature, namely, of an ethereal soul's incarceration in a physical body, was explained as due to the primordial fall or descent of an archetypal *Anthropos* ("Man"), from his abode with the Father of Light, through the celestial spheres, into the lower material world, where he cohabited with *Phusis* ("Nature"). From this union mankind was born, thus partaking of the nature of each of its parents, and subject to the planetary powers that ruled the world. Salvation, consequently, consisted in the freeing of the ethereal soul of man from its involvement in corruptible matter, so that it might ascend to its true home with the Father of Light. The various Gnostic sects and the Hermeticists offered to achieve such salvation for their devotees through specially revealed knowledge (*gnōsis*) of various kinds, and disciplines and mystic techniques. Neo-Platonism, on the other hand, sought spiritual salvation through an electic philosophy and mystical experience, including particularly ecstasy, a psychic state of being outside of, or transcending, one's body.

It is important to note that in these mystery-religions and mystical philosophies, although certain moral offences such as murder constituted a bar to initiation, little concern was shown about moral qualifications or sin. Instead, emphasis was laid upon the virtue of initiation as the means to salvation; it was the un-initiated who were damned to a miserable post-mortem existence. The distinction is succinctly drawn in some lines of Sophocles: "How thrice-blessed are they of mortals who, having beheld these [Eleusinian] mysteries, depart to the house of Death. For to such alone is life bestowed there: to the others fall all ills" (frag. 753, Turchi, p. 152).

**5. Christianity.** The message of Jesus of Nazareth is summarized in Mark 1:14 as: "The time is fulfilled, and the kingdom of God is at hand; repent." This summary is significant, for it shows how thoroughly the mission of Jesus was set in the context of contemporary Jewish eschatological belief. Jesus called upon his fellow Jews to prepare themselves, by repenting of their sins, for God's intervention in the existing world order, to save His people and punish their oppressors. According to the Gospels, Jesus was con-

cerned with the deeper causes of sin, and was impatient with preoccupation about ritual offences. Thus he taught that "what comes out of the mouth proceeds from the heart, and this defiles a man. For out of the heart come evil thoughts, murder, adultery, fornication, theft, false witness, slander" (Matthew 15:18–19; R.S.V.). But, by exhorting his hearers to repent, Jesus evidently believed that the individual could by his own volition, rectify his evil disposition and merit membership of God's kingdom. It would appear also that Jesus and his original Jewish disciples accepted the contemporary demonology, and believed that the Devil, as the Adversary of God, tempted men and women to commit evil (e.g., Luke 22:3, 53).

It was Saint Paul, an Hellenistic Jew, who transformed the original Jewish movement centered on Jesus as the Messiah of Israel into a universalist savior-god religion. Paul believed that God had specially commissioned him to present Jesus to the Gentiles in a manner suited to their needs (Epistle to Galatians 1:15–16, 2:7–8). Consequently, drawing unconsciously on his knowledge of Greco-Roman culture, Paul developed a soteriology of a very esoteric kind. It had two themes, each of which envisaged mankind as being in a fatal condition and needing a divine savior to deliver them. One theme is briefly outlined in the First Epistle to the Corinthians, 2:6ff., which presupposes a form of astralism similar to that in Gnosticism and Hermeticism, namely, that mankind is in a state of hopeless subjection to the daemonic powers (*archontes*) that inhabit the planets. Paul explains how God planned, before the eons, to save mankind by sending into this sublunary world a preexistent divine being, called the Lord of Glory. Incarcerated in the person of Jesus, the *archontes* did not recognize him and crucified him (verse 8). Their error cost them their control over mankind; for they could not hold in death the divine Lord of Glory who had assumed human nature (Epistle to Colossians 2:15, 20).

Paul's other soteriological theme was based on a summary philosophy of history. He views mankind as divided between Gentiles and Jews. The former, he maintains, had failed to live according to the natural law, which God had given, and so had fallen into deep moral corruption (Epistle to Romans 1:18ff.). The Jews, to whom God had given a special Law (Torah), had also failed to keep its precepts, and thus stood even more condemned (Romans 2:17ff.). And, so Paul concluded, "there is no distinction; since all have sinned and fall short of the glory of God, they are justified by his grace as a gift, through the redemption which is in Christ Jesus, whom God put forward as an expiation by his blood, to be received by faith" (Romans, 3:22–25; R.S.V.). In this context, Paul uses the imagery of the Jewish sacrificial system, regarding Christ as "our paschal lamb," that has been sacrificed (I Corinthians 5:7). Through Christ's vicarious sacrifice mankind is reconciled to God, being "saved by his life" (Romans 5:10). Paul also reinterpreted the purificatory rite of baptism as a ritual death and rebirth. The neophyte is ritually identified in baptism with Christ in his death, so that he might be raised to a new life *in Christo*, as Christ was raised by God from death (Romans 6:3ff.).

Owing to the disappearance of the original Jewish Christian community of Jerusalem in the Roman destruction of that city in A.D. 70, Paul's interpretation, which that community had rejected, survived to become the basis of Catholic Christianity. In the subsequent elaboration of his soteriology, another of Paul's ideas was effectively utilized, particularly by Saint Augustine of Hippo. In his Epistle to the Romans (5:12–13), Paul had written with reference to Adam, "sin came into the world through one man and death through sin, and so death spread to all men because all men sinned" (R.S.V.). From this idea developed the doctrine of Original Sin, according to which every child through seminal identity with Adam, inherits the guilt of Adam's original act of disobedience and also a disposition to sin. From the stain of this inherited sin the newborn infant is deemed to be purged by baptism. An essential emphasis was thus placed upon baptism, and the Church did not hesitate to declare that the unbaptized, even if they had committed no actual sin, were doomed to perdition.

The Church has never formally defined the manner in which the death of Christ operates to save mankind from the consequences of sin, both original and actual. Three main lines of interpretation have been developed by theologians: that Christ's death was the price paid to the Devil to redeem mankind; that his dying, as the sinless representative of mankind, propitiated the just anger of God the Father towards his sinful brethren; that the exemplary effect of Christ's willingness to die on behalf of mankind is calculated to move sinners to contrition, and open the way to their reconciliation with God.

Despite this lack of formal definition, the presentation of Christ as the divine savior of mankind, who saves through his sacrificial death, constitutes the basic doctrine of Christianity, in both its Catholic and Protestant forms. It led, in the Middle Ages, to the formulation of an elaborate eschatology, which envisaged two forms of post-mortem judgment. After death, the individual soul was to be judged by God; unless its character was such that it deserved either the immediate award of Heaven or immediate consignment to Hell, it was sent to Purgatory, where it expiated the guilt of its actual sin. When Christ eventually returned for the Last Judgment (an idea inherited from Judaism), all the dead would be resurrected with their physical bodies. To them, in this resurrected form of being, their eternal destinies would then be decreed. If their faith in Christ so merited, they would pass to the eternal beatitude of the Vision of God; if they were condemned, they were doomed to eternal torment in Hell. This belief in ultimate salvation or damnation was taught also by the Protestant Reformers, although they rejected the Catholic doctrine of Purgatory.

*6. Islam.* Muhammad declared himself to the Arab people as "a warner clear" (Koran 51:50ff.), claiming that Allāh had sent him to warn them of impending judgment on their sins. The most heinous sin was that of worshipping other gods besides Allāh. Condemnation at the judgment would mean consignment to Hell, the torments of which Muhammad vividly describes. Those adjudged faithful would be rewarded by the joys of Paradise (*al-janna*, "the garden"), which are presented in equally realistic terms. The logic of Muhammad's mission implied that men were able to repent of their sins and be forgiven, and thus be saved. The very word that Muhammad chose to describe his faith, namely, "Islām," denoted the idea of personal submission to a supreme will, thus signifying freedom of will on the part of the "Muslim," who has thus submitted himself to Allāh. The implication that the individual could chose salvation or damnation for himself is, however, contradicted by other passages in the Koran that represent human destiny as predetermined by Allāh. Thus, for example, it is stated: "Allāh leadeth astray whom He willeth and guideth whom He willeth" (25:9). But Muhammad's theological immaturity was doubtless responsible for his doctrine of predestination. Faced with the refusal of many of his countrymen to accept his message, and convinced of the omniscience and omnipotence of Allāh, Muhammad concluded that Allāh had predetermined who would be saved and who damned.

It is significant that the word for "salvation"(*najāh*) occurs only once in the Koran: "O my people, why is it? I call you to salvation, but you call me to the Fire" (40:44). The fact indicates that Muhammad did not regard mankind as being in a state of perdition owing to some original defect or sin, as in Christianity, from which they needed to be redeemed and regenerated. Voluntary submission to Allāh ensured the ultimate bliss of Heaven. Such submission necessarily involved the observance of prescriptions concerning faith and practice. These prescriptions constitute the five duties of the Muslim, known as the Pillars of Practical Religion (*Arkān al-Islām*). They are: profession of faith (*Shahāda*), epitomized as "There is no deity but God; Muhammad is God's messenger"; the recitation of five stated daily prayers; fasting (especially in the month of Ramadān); payment of legal alms; pilgrimage to Mecca.

Although the Koran (2:45) pronounces that at the Last Judgment the intercession of no one will avail the guilty, nor can they be redeemed in any way from their fate, Muhammad has acquired something of the role of a mediator or intercessor in the popular faith of Muslims. It is believed that God will accept his intercession on behalf of believers guilty of grave sin (except the unforgivable sin of polytheism), and allow him to deliver them from Hell. In the Shiʿa form of Islam, it is held that the *imams*, i.e., ʿAli, the son-in-law of Muhammad, and his descendants, also have this intercessory privilege which they will exercise for the benefit of their followers.

*7. Zoroastrianism.* The teaching of Zarathustra (in Greek, Zoroaster) conceives of mankind as decisively implicated in a cosmic struggle between the principles of Good and Evil. Zarathustra regarded himself as commissioned by Ahura Mazdā (the Wise Lord) to set before his contemporaries the fateful choice that confronts each: "Hear with your ears the best things; look upon them with clear-seeing thought, for decision between two beliefs, each man for himself before the Great Consummation, bethinking you that it be accomplished to our pleasure" (*Yasna* 30:2; trans. J. H. Moulton). Each individual had thus personally to decide on which side of the contending forces to align himself; and upon his choice his destiny depended. In the extant teaching of Zarathustra only cryptic references are made to the consequences of this choice. Thus there was to be an awful ordeal of crossing the Bridge of the Separator (*Činvat*); but the devotees of Ahura Mazdā are assured that they would be led safely across by Zarathustra himself (*Yasna* 46:10). Mention is also made of molten metal and fire as forms of Ahura Mazdā's retribution (*Yasna* 30:7; 51:9). The just are promised that they will abide with Ahura Mazdā in the House of Song (*Yasna* 45:8, 48:7), while the unjust are doomed to the House of the Lie (*Drūjō·nmāna* 46:11). There is reason for thinking that the Bridge of the Separator was an ancient Iranian concept, concerned with proving the ritual fitness of the dead to enter the next world, and that Zarathustra readapted it as a post-mortem test of allegiance to Ahura Mazdā.

The dualism of Zarathustra's teaching had a strong moral character. For though the cosmic struggle was basically that of Life against Death and Light against Darkness, Zarathustra designated the *Angra Mainyu*, the Enemy Spirit, as the *Drūj* or Lie. Moreover, the emphases which he laid upon the momentous character of the individual's choice assumed a decisive measure of human free will that is truly unique in the history of religions. However, Zarathustra seems to have ignored the consequent problem of accounting for the variation of human choice, particularly, why some should decide to align themselves with the *Drūj*. No notice, also, appears to be taken of the inherited disposition to sin, with which the Christian doctrine of Original Sin attempts to deal. The logic of Zarathustra's teaching implies that the individual could, and was expected to, work out his own salvation. Zarathustra's own role was primarily that of a prophet or interpreter of Ahura Mazdā's will. Although he would lead the faithful in safety across the Bridge of the Separator, he does not appear to claim that he would or could save them from the *Angra Mainyu*.

In the later eschatology of Zoroastrianism the postmortem destiny of the individual is described in great detail. According to the *Dâtistân-i Mēnōk-i-Krat*, a Pahlavi writing of about the ninth century A.D., the deeds of the deceased were weighed by Rashnu at the Bridge of the Separator. After that ordeal, the soul meets a personification of its past conduct: to the just the personification appears as a beautiful maiden, but to the unjust as an awful hag in whose baleful company it goes to hell. Zoroastrian dualism was not, however, an eternal conflict between good and evil, and it was believed that ultimately Ohrmazd (i.e., Ahura Mazdā) would overcome Ahriman (i.e., the *Angra Mainyu* of Zarathustra). An eschatology was accordingly elaborated which looked forward to the coming of the Saoshyans or Savior, who would resurrect the dead for judgment. The righteous would then pass to heaven, and the wicked to hell where they suffer physically for their sins. But their punishment is not eternal; for the victory of Ohrmazd and the destruction of Ahriman led finally to the *Fraškart*, the ultimate "making excellent" or rehabilitation of those who had allied themselves with Ahriman.

*8. Hinduism. Mokṣa* is the word most generally used in Hinduism to denote an idea equivalent to salvation. But the word literally means liberation, and the somewhat different action or process thereby implied from that of salvation reflects the distinctive Hindu view of human nature and destiny. This view first found expression in what is known as the early Upanishadic period of Indian culture (ca. eighth century B.C.), and was based upon the twin doctrines of *samsāra* and *karma*. *Samsāra* means the stream of existence in the empirical world, involving the individual in a ceaseless cycle of birth, death, and rebirth. The form of each period of incarnate life is believed to be determined by the nature of one's actions in previous lives. By this law or process (*karma*, literally "deed" or "act"), the soul of self (*ātman*) may even be reborn in nonhuman forms, if the entail of its past lives so requires.

The operation of *karma* can be regarded as the working-out of a person's sins or misdeeds; but although an ethical factor is thus involved, in Indian thought the process of *samsāra* and *karma* is primarily seen as resulting from the disposition of the *ātman* to cling to existence in the empirical world, which it identifies with reality. This disposition stems from a primordial *avidyā* or ignorance, and it prevents the *ātman* from perceiving that *Brahman* is the true Reality and the source and ground of its own being.

How this *avidyā* originated is not explained. The great Hindu teacher Śankara (ca. 788–820 A.D.) maintained that to seek for a causal explanation of it is itself an expression of *avidyā*, for the attempt assumes the reality of the empirical world. Accordingly, the unending misery of human existence is accepted as due to some primordial ignorance on the part of the *ātman*, not to some original sin which it had committed. To emphasize the infinite extent of this misery, Indian thinkers invented an elaborate chronology of world-ages of immense duration and repetitive pattern, since Time was conceived as cyclic in its process, not linear. Through these unending cycles of Time the individual *ātman* is doomed to drag out its miserable existence, suffering the pain and degradation of innumerable births and deaths, and burdened by the ever-increasing entail of its own *karma*.

It is from this fate that liberation (*mokṣa*) is sought. Hinduism teaches that such liberation is possible, and offers various ways by which it may be attained. Of these ways the three most notable are the Advaita Vedānta, the *bhaktimārga*, and Samkhya-Yoga. Advaita Vedānta, or Non-Dualistic Vedānta, is a philosophical discipline based upon the principle *tat tuam asi* ("That art thou"), enunciated in the *Chāndogya Upanishad* VI, 8.7. The aim of the discipline is to bring the individual *ātman* to an effective realization of its essential identity with *Brahman*. The achievement of such realization liberates the *ātman* from its fatal illusion about the empirical world and its own individuality, and so delivers it from involvement in *samsāra* and *karma*. *Bhaktimārga* ("the way of *bhakti*") promises release through divine help, won by an intense personal devotion to the Hindu gods Vishnu or Shiva. In the great classic of *bhaktimārga*, the *Bhagavadgītā* ("Song of the Lord"), the ultimate goal is union with God, and the promise is made to the devotee Arjuna: "Set thy mind on me, place thy intellect in me; in me verily shalt thou dwell hereafter" (XII.8). Samkhya-Yoga aims to achieve liberation by enabling the individual to make an existential distinction between himself and the empirical world. This insight is attained by the rigorous practice of yogic techniques calculated to gain a proper state of psychophysical detachment.

In these, and the many other ways by which *mokṣa* is sought in Hinduism, the underlying assumption is that the individual must achieve the goal by his own efforts, even though he may be assisted by divine grace. And the process is essentially that of his correcting, or recovering from, a primordial error or illusion, into which he inexplicably fell; it is not one of repenting and obtaining forgiveness of sins he has committed.

*9. Buddhism.* Buddhism originated in India in the sixth century B.C., i.e., during the Upanishadic period of Indian culture. The Buddha appears to have accepted without question the twin doctrines of *samsāra* and *karma;* but he made one important qualification. According to Hindu teaching, it is the *ātman*, the individual soul or self, that is subject to the process of *samsāra:* through infinite incarnations, it bears the burden of its *karma*. The Buddha maintained that the idea of permanent soul or self was a basic illusion. Instead, he taught the doctrine of *anatta* (*an* = not; *atta* = self), according to which the so-called individual self is the illusory product of the temporary collocation of five *khandhas*, which are various psychical and physical elements that make up a human being. Consequently, there is no real self that transmigrates from body to body. However, by a piece of subtle metaphysics, it is explained that, at the end of an incarnation, the disembodied *karma*-energy causes the formation of a new set of *khandhas*, thus producing a new individual form of being.

The Buddha is reported to have laid supreme emphasis upon the pain and misery of human existence, and claimed to reveal how release could be obtained. As in Hinduism, the cause of suffering is found not in moral failing but in a primordial ignorance (*avijjā*), or failure to perceive the true nature of things. According to the formula *paticca-samuppāda* ("dependent origination"), aging, and death (*jarāmarana*), which inevitably follow each occasion of rebirth, result from a chain of psychophysical causation, beginning with the primal *avijjā* that starts the karmic process of involvement in the empirical world.

The means of release from this fatal situation is summarized in the Buddhist "Eightfold Path," or *atthangika-magga*. The scheme defines eight requirements that have to be fulfilled: right understanding; right thought; right speech; right bodily-action; right livelihood; right effort; right mindfulness; right concentration. The eight "steps" or requirements of the Path are very fully elaborated in Buddhist teaching.

The goal of Buddhist endeavor is Nirvāna (Sanskrit) or Nibbāna (Pali). The concept denoted is inherently subtle, and it has been variously interpreted. It was understood by earlier Western students of Buddhism as signifying personal extinction. There was some justification for this view, since Buddhist texts often seem to give the term Nirvāna a negative connotation.

However, what is primarily certain is that the concept represented, and still represents, a profoundly hoped-for release or liberation from the suffering of recurrent rebirth in the empirical world. The Buddha is represented in a Pali writing entitled *Udāna* as saying with reference to Nirvāna: "There, monks, I say there is neither coming nor going, nor staying nor passing away, nor arising; without support or going on or basis is it. This is the end of pain" (viii, 1–3). But positive epithets can also be found for Nirvāna in other Buddhist writings. The problem here lies ultimately in the inherent obscurity that invests the Buddhist conception of human nature. The *anatta* doctrine certainly precludes the idea of an inner essential soul or self that might attain Nirvāna; on the other hand, the Buddha is represented as having rejected the *uccheda-vāda*, i.e., the doctrine of personal annihilation. It would seem likely that early Buddhist thinkers did conceive of some kind of transcendental self, as distinct from the empirical self; but they refused to define it either positively or negatively, on the principle that all definition is limitation by means of empirical categories.

In its original form, Buddhism was essentially a way, revealed by the Buddha Gotama, whereby men could work out their own salvation or liberation. In process of time other forms of the faith developed, which were adapted to meet the need of ordinary people for divine help and the expectation of reward or punishment after a period of incarnate life. Consequently, popular Buddhism knows of many divine helpers, called *bodhisattvas*, who assist men and women to enjoy heavenly bliss and avoid post-mortem torment, before they ultimately work out their *karma* and attain Nirvāna.

### CONCLUSION

Ideas of sin as transgression of divine law, incurring divine wrath and causing ritual pollution, are to be found in most religions. Similarly prevalent has been the quest for divine salvation from evils, natural and supernatural. The conceptions of sin and salvation surveyed in this article are the most significant and representative. Each has evolved in a major religion, and characterizes its faith and practice. Each, also, has had great cultural influence, affecting art and literature and the social behavior of many generations.

*BIBLIOGRAPHY*

Encyclopedic Works. *Dictionary of Comparative Religion*, ed. S. G. F. Brandon (New York, 1970), entries under all items mentioned in article. *Encyclopaedia of Religion and Ethics*, ed. J. Hastings, 12 vols. (Edinburgh and New York, 1910), Vol. XI, entries under "Sin" and "Salvation."

*Reallexikon für Antike und Christentum*, ed. Th. Klauser (Stuttgart, 1959), entries under "Erlösung." *Religion in Geschichte und Gegenwart*, ed. K. Galling, 3rd ed. (Tübingen, 1957–62), Vol. II, entries under "Erlöser" and "Erlösung," Vol. VI, entries under "Erlösung."

See also: T. G. Allen, *The Egyptian Book of the Dead* (Chicago, 1960). S. Angus, *Religious Quests of the Graeco-Roman World* (London, 1929). R. Bell, *The Qurʾān*, 2 vols. (Edinburgh, 1937–39). C. F. Bleeker, ed., *Anthropologie religieuse* (Leiden, 1955). S. G. F. Brandon, *Man and His Destiny in the Great Religions* (Manchester and Toronto, 1962); idem, *History, Time and Deity* (Manchester, 1965); idem, *The Judgment of the Dead* (New York, 1967), all with extensive documentation and bibliographies; idem, ed., *The Saviour God* (Manchester, 1963). J. H. Breasted, *The Dawn of Conscience* (New York, 1935). R. Bultmann, *Urchristentum im Rahmen der antiken Religionen* (Zurich, 1949), trans. as *Primitive Christianity in its Contemporary Setting* (1956; reprint New York). E. Conze, *Buddhism* (Oxford, 1957); idem, *Buddhist Thought in India* (London, 1962). Fr. Cumont, *After-Life in Roman Paganism* (New York, 1959). S. Dasgupta, *A History of Indian Philosophy*, 5 vols. (Cambridge, 1922–62); idem, *Yoga as Philosophy and Religion* (London, 1924). E. Dhorme, *Les religions de Babylonie et Assyrie* (Paris, 1945). J. Duchesne-Guillemin, *Zoroastre* (Paris, 1948); idem, *The Hymns of Zarathustra* (London, 1913). C. Eliot, *Hinduism and Buddhism*, 3 vols. (London, 1954). R. O. Faulkner, *The Ancient Egyptian Pyramid Texts* (Oxford, 1969). A.-J. Festugière, *La révélation d'Hermès Trismégiste*, 4 vols. (Paris, 1950–54). M. Gaudefroy-Demonbynes, *Mahomet* (Paris, 1957). L. W. Grensted, *A Short History of the Atonement* (Manchester, 1920). H. Günther, *Das Seelenproblem in älteren Buddhismus* (Konstanz, 1949). W. K. C. Guthrie, *The Greeks and their Gods* (London, 1950); idem, *Orpheus and Greek Religion* (London, 1952). A. Harnack, *History of Doctrine*, 7 vols. (New York, 1961; also reprint). K. Kirk, *The Vision of God* (London, 1931). W. G. Lambert, *Babylonian Wisdom Literature* (Oxford, 1960). M. Molé, "Daenā, le pont Činvant et l'initiation dans le Mazdéisme," *Revue de l'histoire des religions*, **157** (1960). S. Mowinckel, *He That Cometh* (London, 1931). T. R. V. Murti, *The Central Philosophy of Buddhism* (London, 1955). G. E. Mylonas, *Eleusis and the Eleusinian Mysteries* (Princeton, 1961). M. P. Nilsson, *Geschichte der griechischen Religion*, 2 vols., Vol. I, 2nd ed. (Munich, 1955), Vol. II (Munich, 1950). W. O. E. Oesterley and T. H. Robinson, *Hebrew Religion* (London, 1930). J. D. C. Pavry, *The Zoroastrian Doctrine of a Future Life* (New York, 1929). J. Pedersen, *Israel: Its Life and Culture*, 4 vols., Vols. I and II (London and Copenhagen, 1926), Vols. III and IV (London and Copenhagen, 1940). S. Radhakrishnan, *The Principal Upanisads* (London, 1953). E. Rohde, *Psyche: Seelencult und Unsterblichkeitsglaube der Griechen*, 2 vols. (Freiburg, 1898). J. Spiegel, *Die Idee vom Totengericht in der aegyptischen Religion* (Glückstadt, 1935). E. J. Thomas, *The History of Buddhist Thought* (London, 1951); idem, *Early Buddhist Scriptures* (London, 1935). N. Turchi, *Fontes Historiae Mysteriorum Aevi Hellenistici* (Rome, 1923). W. M. Watt, *Free Will and Predestination in*

*Early Islam* (London, 1948). M. Wensinck, *The Muslim Creed* (Cambridge, 1932). N. P. Williams, *Ideas of the Fall and of Original Sin* (London, 1927). R. C. Zaehner, *The Dawn and Twilight of Zoroastrianism* (London, 1961); idem, *Hinduism* (Oxford, 1962).

S. G. F. BRANDON

[See also Buddhism; **Christianity in History;** Dualism; Gnosticism; Hermeticism; Islamic Conception; Prophecy in Hebrew Scripture; **Religion, Ritual in.**]

# SKEPTICISM IN ANTIQUITY

## I

THE HISTORIANS of ancient skepticism agree on the broad outline of its development. It began with Pyrrho of Elis (ca. 365–275 B.C.), a pupil of the Democritean Anaxarchus and of Bryson, a member of the Megaric School. Pyrrho's followers included Nausiphanes of Teos, a teacher of Epicurus, and Timon of Phlius, who defended his master by attacking rival philosophers in his *Silloi* ("Satires") and other writings. After Timon the Pyrrhonic School went into eclipse; but meanwhile the Platonic Academy, under Arcesilaus of Pitane, turned to skepticism. The greatest of the Academic Skeptics was Carneades of Cyrene, whose discourses were recorded by his pupil, Clitomachus of Carthage (his name was originally Hasdrubal). In the first century B.C. under Philo of Larissa and Antiochus of Ascalon, the Academy first compromised, then abandoned the skeptical tradition. Cicero belongs to this transitional period; he studied under both Philo and Antiochus.

With the demise of Academic Skepticism, Pyrrhonism revived. The man chiefly responsible was Aenesidemus of Crete, probably of the first century B.C., who systematized skeptical arguments under ten tropes on the problem of knowledge and eight tropes on causes. Sometime later Agrippa (otherwise unknown) reduced the tropes to five, and someone else reduced them to two.

In its final phase Pyrrhonic Skepticism became closely allied with empirical medicine, a connection that may well have begun as early as the third century B.C. Menodotus of Nicomedia, an empirical physician of the early second century A.D., wrote a number of works that restored to skepticism a certain standing. Later in the century Sextus Empiricus wrote comprehensive accounts of skeptical arguments. His surviving works are a major source for both Academic and Pyrrhonic Skepticism. Sextus' student, Saturninus, is the last known skeptic of antiquity.

## II

There is less agreement about the antecedents of ancient skepticism. Skeptical tendencies, real or alleged, in pre-Socratics, Sophists, and Socrates were traced by Victor Brochard in his Introduction. They include the many comments of the early philosophers on the unreliability of sense perception and the limitations of human knowledge. Prominent in this review are Gorgias, *On Nature, or the Non-Existent,* and the famous dictum of the Democritean Metrodorus of Chios (fourth century B.C.), "We know nothing, not even whether we know or do not know, or what it is to know or not to know, or in general whether anything exists or not" (Diels and Kranz, frag. B1). Metrodorus' name is often linked with that of Anaxarchus, the teacher of Pyrrho.

Among the ancients themselves, Plutarch (*Moralia* 1121F–1122A) says that Arcesilaus was accused of having invoked the names of Socrates, Plato, Parmenides, and Heraclitus as authorities for his skeptical views about the suspension of judgment and the fallibility of apprehension; and Cicero, in speaking for the Academy, includes Anaxagoras, Democritus, Metrodorus, Empedocles, Parmenides, Xenophanes, Socrates, and Plato in similar contexts (*Ac.* II.72–74; *Ac.* I.44). Even more extravagant boasts, including not only philosophers but in addition Homer, Archilochus, Euripides, and Hippocrates are reported by Diogenes Laërtius (IX.71–74). These exaggerated claims appear to be a feature of Academic rather than Pyrrhonic Skepticism; and indeed three of the ancient names for skeptics, *skeptikoi* ("examiners"), *zetetikoi* ("searchers"), and *aporetikoi* ("doubters") were probably meant to suggest a tie with the Platonic Socrates and perhaps even with Aristotle. (On the names see *NA* XI.5; *PH* I.7; DL IX.69–70. Aristotle appears as a skeptic in the Epicurean Diogenes of Oenoanda, ed. Chilton, frag. 4.) Arcesilaus was called *skeptikos* by Timon and others, according to Eusebius (*PE* XIV.6.5). He may have had a polemical aim in thus placing himself in the mainstream of Greek thought, in opposition to his chief antagonist, the Stoic Zeno, a non-Greek from Cyprus. No doubt Arcesilaus also found much useful material in the arguments of his predecessors, especially the Platonic Socrates (cf. *Or.* III.67).

The attitude of the Pyrrhonists toward the earlier philosophers is less clear. Timon is reported to have dedicated his *Silloi* to Xenophanes (cf. *PH* I.223–4; DL IX.18, 111), and he seems to have spared the Eleatics from his general abuse of the dogmatists (cf. DL IX.23, 25). Perhaps he did so out of regard for Pyrrho's teacher Bryson; the Megaric School, to which Bryson belonged, was influenced by the Eleatics. Timon also spoke favorably of the atomist Democritus and the

Sophist Protagoras (DL IX.40, 52). His generally mocking tone, however, makes even his praise ambiguous.

Aenesidemus had a physical theory based on Heraclitus. He held, according to Sextus (*PH* I.210), that skepticism is the path to the Heraclitean philosophy. Sextus, however, rejected this view and carefully distinguished between Heraclitean dogmatism and true skepticism. He also rejected the claims that Democritus, the Cyrenaics, Protagoras, Socrates, Plato, Xenophanes were skeptics. Even Carneades, in his view, does not entirely escape the charge of dogmatism (*PH* I.210–31).

### III

The content of skeptical teaching may be discussed under three heads: (1) the arguments used by the skeptics to refute the dogmatists; (2) the formulation of the skeptical position in terms of phrases and tropes; and (3) the defense of skepticism.

*1.* One of Pyrrho's achievements, according to Timon (cf. DL IX.65) was to break the chains of false opinion; what opinions he attacked, and by what means, we do not know. Timon himself denounces rather than refutes his adversaries; but the fragments of his works indicate that he discussed appearance as the limit of certainty (DL IX.105), the method of hypothesis (*AM* III.2), and the divisibility of time (*AM* VI.66, X.197). He also held, apparently, that nothing is by nature good (*AM* XI.140). Our information, however, is too slight to permit the identification of his opponents or the reconstruction of his arguments.

With Arcesilaus the picture is clearer but still far from complete. He undertook to argue on either side of any question (DL IV.28; cf. IX.51, where Protagoras is said to have held that for every argument there is a counterargument) and to refute whatever opinion anyone expressed (*Ac.* I.45; *ND* I.11; *Fin.* II.2; *Or.* III.67; *PE* XIV.7.15). The opinion that chiefly interested him was the Stoic view that some appearances can of themselves be apprehended as certainly true. In rebuttal he defended the thesis that no appearances can be so apprehended. This thesis was known as *akatalepsia* ("nonapprehension") (cf. *AM* VII.153–55; *PE* XIV.7.4). It was sometimes taken to be a statement of the skeptical position, along with *epochē*, "suspension of judgment" (*Ac.* II.59; Plutarch, *Moralia* 1121F–1122A). A more cautious interpretation would be that the polemical postures assumed by Arcesilaus in order to refute the Stoics are not necessarily positions to which he himself subscribed; otherwise he becomes liable to the charge of holding "dogmatically" that nothing can be known. Such an accusation was in fact made against the Academy (cf. *Ac.* II.28–29; *NA* XI.5.8; *PH* I.226);

but Cicero says quite explicitly that the Academic Skeptics suspended judgment on every question, as the arguments on both sides were of equal weight (*Ac.* I.45), and Sextus absolves Arcesilaus, at least, from the charge of dogmatism (*PH* I.232).

A second view that Arcesilaus is said to have attacked is the doctrine that pleasure is the highest good (cf. *Fin.* II.2). This was the view of two contemporary schools, the Cyrenaic and the Epicurean. Here Arcesilaus might well have drawn on Plato; but the evidence is lacking.

With Carneades our knowledge of the nature and range of skeptical polemic is greatly increased. Carneades' discussion of the problem of knowledge was broadened to refute not only the Stoics (who were still the primary target) but all others who claimed to have found an infallible test of truth. Some idea of his arguments can be got from Cicero, *Ac.* II.79–98 and from Sextus, *AM* VII.159–65. Similarly in his discussion of ethical theory he gave an exhaustive enumeration of possible views of the *summum bonum*, or "highest good" (*Fin.* V.16–20). His practice of arguing both sides of a question is illustrated by his two speeches on justice delivered at Rome on the occasion of the embassy from Athens in 155 B.C. His arguments against natural justice can be recovered in part from the fragmentary remains of Cicero, *De republica* III, where Philus is his spokesman.

Carneades also developed arguments against philosophical theology. The best-known are (1) that the powers and activities assigned to divine beings are not consistent with their being changeless and eternal (*AM* IX.137–81; *ND* III.29–34); (2) that the evils in the universe are not consistent with divine providence (Plutarch, *Moralia*, frag. 193 ed. Sandbach, from Porphyrius, *De abstinentia* III.20; *Ac.* II.120); (3) that the occurrence of accidental designs, for example, a rock that has the form of a head, invalidates the argument that a design implies a designer (*Div.* I.23); and (4) that no clear boundary can be drawn between what is divine and not divine (*ND* III.43–50; *AM* VII.182–90). This last argument is an example of the *sorites*, or "heap," a device for obscuring boundaries by pointing to continuous gradations. It was also used, presumably by Carneades (cf. *Ac.* II.49 and 92–95), to obscure the distinction between illusions and veridical sense perceptions.

Carneades' methods exhibit certain tendencies that became increasingly strong in later skepticism. One such tendency is toward the schematic formulation of alternatives, as exhibited in the discussion of the *summum bonum*. Compare also his attack on divination (*Div.* II.9–12), where the possible objects of divination are systematically enumerated and rejected.

It is tempting to assign also to Carneades the series of propositions (*PH* III.10–11) on the power and providence of god, a scheme which Lactantius assigns to Epicurus—rather improbably, inasmuch as it entails the rejection of Epicurean theology; see Lactantius, *De ira Dei*, 13.20–21 and De Lacy, *Transactions of the American Philological Association*, **79** (1948), 18–19. The tendency toward schematic analysis is seen also in the argument on fate reported by Cicero, *De fato* 31; and it is commonly supposed that Carneades formulated the "four heads" (*Ac.* II.83) from which it follows that nothing can be apprehended through sense perception. Carneades anticipates a later trend also in his examination of the notion of the divine. Comparable examinations were subsequently made of cause (*AM* IX.195–266), body (ibid. 359–440), time (*AM* X.169–247), and the like, the aim being in each case to show that no consistent account of these concepts can be given.

The development of characteristically skeptical analyses and arguments led to two levels of refutation, one level employing arguments that dogmatists use against each other, the other the distinctively skeptical arguments. There is a hint of this already in Carneades, who opposes to the Stoic doctrine of fate not only his own dialectical refutation but also the Epicurean rejection of fatalism (Cicero, *De fato* 21–23). The mutual support of Epicureans and skeptics against Stoics or Platonists appears again in *Div.* II.51 and in Sextus' attacks on the teachers of the arts and sciences (*AM* I.1–7).

A fairly good example of skeptical polemics in the Carneadean tradition is the speech of Cicero in *Ac.* II.64–146. It includes a historical sketch, arguments to discredit both sense perception and reasoning as sources of certain knowledge, a defense of Carneades' doctrine of probability (see below, III, 3), and an account of the disagreements of the dogmatists in physics, ethics, and logic.

At some time the scope of skeptical attack was broadened to include among its targets the theoretical arts and sciences. Medicine was among the first to be involved in this controversy. The split between the theoretical and empirical approaches to medicine is evident already in the Hippocratic corpus (fifth century B.C.); and an Empirical School of medicine, with strong tendencies toward skepticism, was founded by Philinus in the third century B.C. Members of this school in later times praised Pyrrho for having followed appearances in everyday activities and having suspended judgment about all else (cf. Galen, *Subfiguratio empirica*, in Deichgräber, p. 82). The statement that "Appearance prevails wherever it goes" is indeed found in the fragments of Timon (cf. *AM* VII.30), and it provides a basis for the view that the arts and sciences which limit themselves to the use of appearances are legitimate, whereas those that claim to say something about the real nature of things are not. This is the view that Sextus adopts in *AM* I–VI. There are a few indications that the Academic Skeptics also discussed the arts and sciences. In *Ac.* II.122 Cicero mentions the empirical physicians' conviction that the nature of the body cannot be discovered by dissection, as the concealed organs may be altered by the mere act of laying them bare. Cicero also rejects the argument that the skeptic's attack on knowledge is an attack also on the arts; some arts, he says, admit that they use conjecture more than knowledge, and others such as painting and sculpture are guided by what appears rather than by what is (*Ac.* II.22, 107, 146). There is no evidence, however, that the Academic Skeptics attacked mathematics.

Aenesidemus is best known for the ten tropes (see below, III, 2). Underlying the tropes is a formulation of the epistemological problem in terms of signs: if from the apparent we obtain knowledge of the nonapparent, then the apparent serves as a sign, the nonapparent as a thing signified (see Photius, III, 121). But, Aenesidemus argues (cf. *AM* VIII.215–35), if signs were apparent they would appear the same to all who are in a similar state, that is, there would be no disagreement about what they signify. But there is disagreement; therefore signs are not apparent. Sextus gives a much fuller account of this doctrine of signs. He divides the nonapparent into three kinds: (1) the absolutely nonapparent, e.g., the number of grains of sand in Libya; (2) the nonapparent by nature, e.g., the invisible pores in the skin, or the void outside the universe; and (3) the nonapparent at the moment, e.g., the city of Athens. Things absolutely nonapparent may be left out of consideration. Things by nature nonapparent can be known only if there are appearances which point to them unambiguously (indicative signs), as the movements of the body are said to be signs of the soul or motion a sign of void. Things nonapparent at the moment can be signified by present appearances that remind us of them (admonitive signs), as smoke is the sign of fire, a scab is the sign of a wound (*AM* VIII.141–55). Sextus does not challenge the possibility of admonitive signs; they presuppose no necessary connection between sign and thing signified, and they are adequate to account for the connections that we establish between things in everyday activities (*AM* VIII.155–58). Reminding is, in fact, the skeptics' substitute for proof; see for example, *PH* III.20; De Lacy, *Phronesis*, **3** (1958), 71. But about the indicative sign, which is the invention of dogmatic philosophers and theorizing physicians, the skeptic withholds judgment, as he finds the arguments against it as strong as those for it (*AM* VIII.159–298). Sextus includes the argument of Aenesidemus mentioned above as a part of his attack on the indicative sign.

The very length of Sextus' discussion of signs testifies to their importance in skeptical polemic (cf. also DL IX.96–97). His reference to theoretical medicine and his use of medical examples suggest that the terms in which he presents the problem may have been current in medical controversy. A more widespread practice was to distinguish between common signs, which are ambiguous in their reference, and particular signs, which signify one thing only. This distinction is found in medical writers, who use it in the identification of symptoms; see for example Galen, *Commentary on Hippocrates' De Officina Medici,* I.1 (ed. Kühn, XVIII, 2, 643–45). It appears also in rhetorical theory (cf. Cicero, *Partitiones oratoriae,* 34) and in philosophical controversy of the Hellenistic period (see Philodemus, *De signis,* cols. 1 and 14). There is reason to suppose that Carneades' attack on Stoic epistemology was at some time stated in terms of this distinction: the Stoics regarded some sense perceptions as particular signs, others as common signs. Carneades challenged them to show that any appearance is ever a particular sign (*Ac.* II.33–34, 84, 103).

Another matter of major concern to Aenesidemus was the notion of cause. Sextus reports an argument that he used to show that one thing cannot cause, i.e., generate, another (*AM* IX.218–26). In addition, he formulated eight ways of attacking dogmatic theories of causation (the eight tropes; cf. *PH* I.180–84; Photius, III, 122). Photius reports that Aenesidemus also discussed truth (cf. *AM* VIII.40–47), motion, the universe and the gods, the objects of choice and avoidance, the virtues and the *summum bonum* (cf. *AM* XI.42).

Sextus' treatises are by far the most extensive of the ancient skeptical writings that have survived; and although Sextus incorporates many items derived from earlier skeptics, his presentation and elaboration seem to be his own. For example, no model has been found for his six books on the special disciplines (*AM* I–VI) or for his discussion of ethics (*AM* XI, *PH* III.168–279). He also gives a long and detailed treatment of cause (*AM* IX.195–266; cf. DL IX.97–99). Of the many other matters that he takes up, perhaps the most important is his attack on Stoic and Peripatetic logic (*PH* II.134–203; *AM* VIII.300–481). Sextus had a commendable familiarity with early Greek philosophy, and he ranks as an important source of information about the pre-Socratics and others whose works have been lost. He has, besides, an obvious enthusiasm for his subject, which sometimes turns to playfulness (e.g., *PH* I.62–63). It is perhaps because his writings were more than mere compilations that they survived.

**2.** A feature of ancient skepticism throughout its history was a fondness for catchwords. The most widely current was *epochē,* "suspension of judgment," used by both Pyrrhonists and Academics (see *Ac.* II.59; Plutarch, *Moralia* 1122A; *PH* I.8, 10, 196; DL IX.61, 62). There is some question, however, whether it goes back to Pyrrho himself, and it does not appear in the fragments of Timon. Often coupled with *epochē* is *akatalepsia,* i.e., "nonapprehension," which probably derives from the Academic attack on the Stoic theory of apprehension (*katalepsis;* cf. *Ac.* II.17–18, 31). Sextus (*PH* I.1–3) assigns it to the Academy rather than to his own school (see also Photius, III, 119–20). Diogenes Laërtius, however (IX.61), uses it along with *epochē* to characterize Pyrrho's teaching. More certainly Pyrrhonic is the phrase *ou mallon* ("no more this than that"), which appears in the fragments of Timon (cf. DL IX.76; *PE* XIV.18.3), in Aenesidemus (Photius, III, 119), and in Sextus (cf. *PH* I.187–91). It also had a place in pre-Pyrrhonic philosophy; see De Lacy, *Phronesis,* **3** (1958), 59–71. The refusal to incline this way or that was expressed by *arrhepsia* (*PH* I.190; DL IX.74), the refusal to make assertions by *aphasia* (Timon in *PE* XIV.18.4, 19; *PH* I.192–93; cf. Plutarch, *Moralia* 1123C), the avoidance of distinctions by *ouden horizein* (Timon in DL IX.76; cf. 71 and 74; *PH* I.197), the avoidance of rashness in assent by *aproptosia* (DL IX.74; cf. *PH* I.20, 177, 186; II.21; *Ac.* I.45), the equal balance of arguments for and against any thesis by *isostheneia* (DL IX.73, 76, 101; *PH* I.8; *AM* IX.207; cf. *Ac.* I.45: *paria momenta*).

Such terms as these gave the skeptics a kind of identity and served as substitutes for positive doctrine. The same may be said of their many schematisms, some of which have already been mentioned. Among the most important in later skepticism were Aenesidemus' ten tropes in support of the view that although it is possible for me to describe each thing as it appears to me, I must suspend judgment as to what sort of thing it is in itself.

The tropes are listed, with minor differences, by both Sextus (*PH* I.36–163) and Diogenes (IX.79–88). As Sextus presents them, the same thing appears different (1) to different species of animals; (2) to different individuals, by virtue of their differences in mind and body; (3) to different senses, as a painting appears flat to the touch but to the eyes seems to have depth; (4) to the same sense in different states, e.g., in sickness or health, in youth or old age; (5) because of differences in position, distance, or place, as the square tower appears round at a distance, and the oar appears bent where it enters the water; (6) by virtue of differences in the things in whose company it appears, as an object heavy in air appears light in water; (7) because of differences in quantity and situation, as grains of sand when scattered appear rough but in a heap appear soft; (8) in different relations, everything being in some sense relative; (9) insofar as it is encountered continuously or rarely, as an earthquake is more frightening to those who experience it for the first time than to persons accustomed to earthquakes; (10) according to different ways of life, customs, and beliefs, as the Taurians sacrifice strangers to Artemis, but the Greeks forbid human sacrifice. Diogenes gives to the list a less arbitrary sequence; his order is 1–4, 10, 6, 5, 7, 9, 8. Aristocles (*PE* XIV.18.11) gives the number of tropes as nine; no satisfactory explanation of the discrepancy has yet been found.

The five tropes of Agrippa are broader in scope, dealing not only with appearances but also with proof. They are given at some length by Sextus (*PH* I.164–77) and summarized by Diogenes (IX.88–89). The first is that as we are not able to resolve the disagreements and conflicts in life and in philosophy, we end up by suspending judgment. The second is that as anything submitted in support of a proposition must itself be supported, an infinite regress results. The third is that a perceived object appears to be of such and such a description relative to that which makes the judgment and to the things perceived along with it, but we suspend judgment about its true nature. The fourth is that dogmatists, in order to escape infinite regress, take unproved assumptions as their starting point. The fifth is that when that which ought to establish some conclusion can only be proved from the conclusion, since we can use neither for the proof of the other, we suspend judgment.

Finally Sextus (*PH* I.178–79) assigns to certain unnamed skeptics two tropes that aim at a formula of universal application. Certainty about a thing is got either (1) from the thing itself, or (2) from some other thing. The first alternative is refuted by the unresolved disputes of the natural philosophers; the second leads to infinite regress.

*3.* There were two main attacks on skepticism in antiquity: (1) it makes action impossible; and (2) it is self-contradictory. The first rests on the observation that action presupposes decision, and decision involves a choice between alternatives. Anyone who says of things that they are "no more this than that" thereby destroys the ground for practical decisions and so makes action impossible. As Aristotle said (*Metaphysics* 1008b 26–27), "All men make unqualified judgments, if not about all things, still about what is better and worse" (trans. Ross). To this charge the skeptics gave a number of answers. First of all, they pointed out that practical decisions are made in terms of appearances. Men naturally seek what appears good and avoid what

appears bad; in this sense they follow nature as their guide. Skepticism does not challenge appearances, but only the dogmatists' claim to have certain knowledge about the nonapparent (cf. *Ac.* II.103; *PH* I.19–20). There is therefore no conflict between skepticism and practical decisions. The view that we live by appearances is attributed by Aenesidemus to Pyrrho himself (cf. DL IX.106), and it is implied by the fragment of Timon already quoted, "Appearance prevails wherever it goes." It receives explicit statement also in the Academic tradition (cf. Plutarch, *Moralia* 1122) and is accepted by Sextus (*AM* VII.30; *PH* I.21–24). Indeed, Sextus regards the observation of appearances as the basis of the practical arts (*AM* V.1–2) and of the admonitive sign (*PH* II.100; *AM* VIII.152, 156–57). One is reminded of Plato's description of the skill in observing, remembering, and predicting that was held in honor by the inhabitants of the cave (*Republic* 516C–D).

The skeptics also accepted tradition and custom as a guide to action (*PH* I.17, 231; DL IX.61, 108; *PE* XIV.18.20). Custom may be observed on the level of appearance and followed without intellectual commitment. It is on this basis, for instance, that the skeptic performs acts of piety and avoids impiety (cf. *PH* I.23–24, III.2; *AM* IX.49). Thus Cotta, the Academic spokesman in Cicero's *De natura deorum*, insists that he may be a philosophical skeptic and still participate in the traditional Roman religion (*ND* III.5, 9). It is not unlikely that skepticism helped to strengthen the trend toward traditionalism in the Greco-Roman world.

Arcesilaus advanced still another guide to practical action. According to Sextus (*AM* VII.158), he held that happiness is secured through practical wisdom, practical wisdom consists in right action, and right action is action for which a reasonable defense can be given. The reasonable (*eulogon*) is thus the guide. There is no mention of this view in the extant portions of Cicero's *Academica*, but perhaps it is not mere coincidence that several letters which Cicero wrote during the period when he was working on the *Academica* (June–July, 45 B.C.) contain the Greek word *eulogon* or *eulogia* (*Letters to Atticus*, XIII.5, 6, 7, 22). In the last of these (22) the reference is to a decision that Cicero must himself make. Another letter to Atticus (XIV.22), written a year later, uses *eulogon* in the context of making conjectures about the future. Atticus would surely have seen in these letters an allusion to the skeptical criterion.

Carneades formulated a three-step procedure for determining the probability of an appearance. The first step is to limit oneself to persuasive appearances, that is, to those which appear to be in accord with the objects from which they come, and from among these appearances to select the ones that are not dim or distant or in any way indistinct. The second step is to inspect the persuasive appearance in the context of the chain of appearances that accompany it. For example, the appearance of a man brings with it appearances of his color, size, form, movement, speech, clothing, and also of the air, light, day, sky, earth, friends, and so forth. If none of these concomitant appearances exerts a contrary pull by appearing false, our confidence is increased. Sextus compares this inspection to that of physicians who do not judge that a man has a fever from one symptom alone but from a concurrence (syndrome) of symptoms, pulse, temperature, color, and so forth. So the Academic looks for a concurrence of appearances, none of which exerts a contrary pull. When this condition is met, the initial appearance may be said to be persuasive, with no pull to the contrary. The third step is to examine closely all of the concomitant appearances in order to assure ourselves in each case that our vision is not dulled, the distance is not too great or the object too small, the duration of the appearance is not too short, etc.

When all these conditions are satisfied by all the appearances, then the appearance with which we began may be described as persuasive (pithane), having no pull to the contrary (aperispastos), and examined from all sides (periodeumene). The fullest account of the Carneadean criterion is in Sextus (AM VII.166–84); there is a shorter account in PH I.227–29. Cicero alludes to the three stages but does not explain them in Ac. II.33, 36; further, in II.105–10 he defends Carneadean probability as an adequate guide in practical matters and in the arts. The later Pyrrhonists rejected Carneadean probability as a departure from true skepticism (cf. Photius, III, 119–20; PH I.229–30); and indeed in this they had the support of Galen, who took Carneadean probability to be equivalent to Stoic apprehension (katalepsis) and to the formula, which Galen himself preferred, that whatever appears clearly to mind or senses is true (ed. Kühn, V, 778).

The charge that skepticism is self-contradictory appears most often in the following form: a person who says that nothing can be known must admit that he cannot know whether nothing can be known and therefore must admit that perhaps something can be known. Alternatively, if he claims to know that nothing can be known he thereby admits that at least one thing can be known and so contradicts his principle. Metrodorus of Chios (quoted above, II) was no doubt attempting to escape the second alternative when he said, "We know nothing, not even whether we know or do not know." Similarly, according to Cicero (Ac. I.45), Arcesilaus denied that anything could be known, not even what Socrates left for himself (he knew that

he knew nothing; cf. Ac. II.74). Cicero also reports (Ac. II.28) an exchange between Carneades and the Stoic Antipater on this point. Antipater suggested that the skeptic might make his position consistent by saying that nothing can be comprehended except this one thing, that nothing can be comprehended. Carneades, however, insisted that there be no exceptions; the person who states that nothing can be comprehended must include this statement among the things that cannot be comprehended. Lucretius probably echoes the Carneadean view when he says, "If anyone thinks that nothing is known, he also does not know whether this can be known, since he confesses that he knows nothing" (RN IV.469–70). The Academic Skeptics did not escape the ambiguity of their presentation; they were sometimes accused of affirming that nothing can be comprehended (see above, III, 1). Sextus was more cautious; he carefully avoided saying anything that might seem to commit him to such an affirmation.

It was possible to state the charge of inconsistency in terms of the ou mallon formula. Aristotle anticipated the skeptics' dilemma when he said, in discussing Heraclitus' supposed denial of the law of contradiction (Metaphysics 1062b 2–9), that from Heraclitus' position it would follow that just as when contradictory statements are taken separately the affirmation is no more true than the negation, so when the two together are taken as a single affirmation, the entire affirmation will be no more true than its negation. The answer of the earlier skeptics to this criticism is not known; but Sextus at least recognized its force. He saw that ou mallon as a principle includes itself: it is no more true than false and is therefore not a tenable position (PH I.14). It was probably in response to this difficulty that some skeptics compared ou mallon and other such formulas to a purgative that eliminates itself along with the arguments of the dogmatists (cf. DL IX.76; PE XIV.18.21). Sextus offers another way out. The skeptical ou mallon, he says, is not to be taken as an affirmation or a negation but rather as a report of the skeptic's inability to decide between conflicting statements. It is a description of his state of mind and is as much a question as a statement (PH I.15, 191–93, 200).

### IV

The ancient skeptics evoked a variety of reactions. Of the Hellenistic schools, the Stoics were the most hostile (see, for example, Epictetus' Discourses, I.5, 27; II.20). The Epicureans were less extreme. They rejected skepticism, of course (see, for example, the Epicurean Colotes' attack on Arcesilaus, reported and answered by Plutarch in his Reply to Colotes, Moralia 1121–24). But the Epicureans shared with Pyrrho a common Democritean background, and in fact Pyrrho's pupil

239

Nausiphanes was one of Epicurus' teachers. Both Epicurus and Pyrrho regarded *ataraxia,* "peace of mind," as the end of human action (DL X.128; *PE* XIV.18.4; cf. *PH* I.8). Later Epicureans and skeptics were brought together to some extent by their common enemies. Another point of contact may have been medical empiricism. For example, a characteristic term for empirical reasoning, *epilogismos,* was used by empirical physicians, Epicureans, and Sextus; see De Lacy, *American Journal of Philology,* **79** (1958), 179–83. Within the Academy, even after its return to dogmatism, some sympathy remained for the skeptical position. Plutarch is perhaps the best example. He defended Arcesilaus against Colotes, and he even wrote a work (now lost), "On the Unity of the Academy since Plato" (No. 63 in the Catalogue of Lamprias; see further De Lacy, "Plutarch and the Academic Sceptics," *Classical Journal,* **49** [1953–54], 79–85). A more enigmatic figure is Favorinus of Arles, a contemporary of Plutarch, whom Lucian and Galen considered an Academic. His writings included a work on the ten Pyrrhonic tropes and an attack on Stoic epistemology. The evidence may be found in A. Barigazzi, *Favorino di Arelate* (Florence [1966], pp. 91, 172–74, 179, 190). Another popular figure of the second century who came under the influence of skepticism was the satirist Lucian (see B. Schwarz, *Lukians Verhältnis zum Skeptizismus,* Tilsit [1914]).

There were two schools of medicine that exhibited skeptical tendencies. According to L. Edelstein, the Empirics came under the influence of Academic Skepticism, the Methodists under the influence of the skepticism of Aenesidemus (see Temkin, pp. 187, 197–98). Sextus Empiricus, in spite of his name, argued that the Methodist School was closer than the Empirical to genuine skepticism (*PH* I.236–41). The prominence of the skeptical tendency in medicine is evident from the works of Galen, who wrote extensively about the Empirics (see Deichgräber's *Stellenregister* and R. Walzer, *Galen on Medical Experience,* London, 1944). Galen found occasion also to denounce Pyrrhonism (e.g., IV, 727; XIV, 628) and to warn against the dangers of the sorites (VII, 372, 680, ed. Kühn).

Finally, skeptical material sometimes found its way even into the writings of theologians. A prominent example is Philo Judaeus' use of Aenesidemus' ten tropes in his *De ebrietate,* 171–205.

*BIBLIOGRAPHY*

The following abbreviations have been used in the citation of ancient sources:

*Ac.* I: Cicero, *Academica posteriora,* I
*Ac.* II: Cicero, *Academica priora,* II
*AM:* Sextus, *Adversus mathematicos*

*Div.:* Cicero, *De divinatione*
DL: Diogenes Laërtius, *Vitae philosophorum*
*Fin.:* Cicero, *De finibus bonorum et malorum*
*NA:* Aulus Gellius, *Noctes Atticae*
*ND:* Cicero, *De natura deorum*
*Or.:* Cicero, *De oratore*
*PE:* Eusebius, *Praeparatio evangelica*
*PH:* Sextus, *Pyrrhoniae hypotyposes*
*RN:* Lucretius, *De rerum natura*
*RP:* Cicero, *De republica.*

Diels and Kranz references are to H. Diels and W. Kranz, eds., *Die Fragmente der Vorsokratiker,* 6th ed. (Berlin, 1951–52). Texts bearing on the Empirical School of medicine are cited from K. Deichgräber, *Die Griechische Empirikerschule* (Berlin, 1930), and Owsei and C. Lillian Temkin, eds., *Ancient Medicine: Selected Papers of Ludwig Edelstein* (Baltimore, 1967). Galen, unless otherwise noted, is cited by volume and page of *Opera omnia,* ed. C. G. Kühn (Leipzig, 1821–33; reprint Hildesheim, 1964–65). Photius, the Byzantine patriarch (ninth century A.D.), is cited from Photius, *Bibliothèque,* ed. and trans. into French by R. Henry (Paris, 1959–67).

Of the histories of ancient skepticism the most highly acclaimed is V. Brochard, *Les sceptiques grecs* (Paris, 1887; reissued 1923 and 1959). Also useful are A. Goedeckemeyer, *Die Geschichte des Griechischen Skeptizismus* (Leipzig, 1905); L. Robin, *Pyrrhon et le scepticisme grec* (Paris, 1944); and M. Dal Pra, *Lo scetticismo greco* (Milan, 1950). Three histories are in English: N. Maccoll, *The Greek Sceptics from Pyrrho to Sextus* (London and Cambridge, 1869); M. Patrick, *The Greek Sceptics* (New York and London, 1929); and C. L. Stough, *Greek Skepticism: A Study in Epistemology* (Berkeley and Los Angeles, 1969). For further items consult the bibliographies in Robin and Dal Pra.

PHILLIP DE LACY

[See also **Certainty;** Epicureanism; Happiness; **Necessity;** Platonism; **Skepticism in Modern Thought;** Stoicism.]

# SKEPTICISM IN MODERN THOUGHT

THIS ARTICLE will deal with skepticism as a philosophical view, as a set of arguments directed against traditional philosophies, theologies, and beliefs, and as a critical view countering various positive intellectual positions. In these senses, skepticism encompasses both the small persistent group of thinkers who declared themselves philosophical skeptics, as well as a much larger group who made use of skeptical materials and attitudes to develop their own positions, and often, in so doing incorporated a portion of the skeptical viewpoint in their work. The latter group are skeptics in varying degrees depending upon how extensive their incorporation of skeptical views in their own positions may be, and how they try to construct another position to overcome the skeptical difficulties they raise against their opponents. As we shall see, even among the declared skeptics there are major variations in positions, and among those who are partially skeptics, or skeptics with regard to certain areas of intellectual endeavor (which almost anyone is to some extent), the variations are still more pronounced. This article will deal then with avowed skeptics, such as Montaigne, Bayle, and Hume, with those who utilize skeptical materials to reach new viewpoints, such as Descartes and Hegel, and with those who are skeptics with regard to certain kinds of knowledge claims, such as Spinoza and Kant.

Modern skepticism, which played a great role in the development of modern thought, entered the intellectual arena in the sixteenth century. Earlier forms of philosophical skepticism had appeared in ancient Greece, and had been systematized during the Hellenistic period into a series of argumentative positions attacking various forms of dogmatic philosophy. The Academic skeptics of the later Platonic Academy, Arcesilaus and Carneades, criticized the views of the Stoic and Epicurean philosophers, seeking to show that nothing could be known, in the sense of gaining unquestionable knowledge about the real nature of things. Their arguments appear in Cicero's *De academica* and *De natura deorum* (first century B.C.). The Academics instead advocated a kind of probabilism or denial of certainty.

In contrast to the strong negative position of the Academic skeptics, another skeptical school developed from the noncommittal position of Pyrrho of Elis. Aenesidemus, an Alexandrian of the first century B.C., presented a series of attacks on the dogmatists and the Academics, leading to a suspension of judgment about whether anything can or cannot be known in metaphysics or ethics. The Pyrrhonians developed a series of "tropes" that is, skeptical reasonings, leading to a mental state of neutrality and suspension of judgment (*epochē*) about all matters that are not immediately evident. In this state of imperturbability, they said, one would finally find the goal of all Hellenistic philosophy: a life of intellectual quietude and peace of mind. The arguments of the Pyrrhonians were collected by one of their last leaders, Sextus Empiricus (second or third century A.D.) in his Pyrrhonian *Hypotyposes* and *Adversus mathematicos*.

The two skeptical positions played an important role in Hellenistic thought, but gradually died out as religious movements began to dominate the late Roman world. The last major sign of skeptical concern appears in Saint Augustine's early philosophical dialogues, es-pecially his *Contra academicos* (fifth century A.D.). After Augustine there seems to have been little further interest in the skeptical attacks.

In the Middle Ages, though there were at least two Latin translations of the writings of Sextus Empiricus, there does not seem to have been any serious consideration of skeptical themes. In the Muslim world, however, where more direct contact with classical sources existed, some of the antirational theologians made use of skeptical materials in order to challenge the metaphysical views of the Jewish and Islamic philosophers. Both Judah Ha-Levi and Al-Ghazali attacked the claims of their contemporaries to knowledge of the necessary conditions of the universe, offering arguments, much like those later used by Malebranche and Hume. Judah Ha-Levi and Al-Ghazali employed skepticism to lead people to their religious mystical views.

Modern skepticism does not derive from these medieval views, but from the combined effect of several monumental cultural changes in the sixteenth century, and the rediscovery by the West of the ancient skeptical texts.

At the beginning of the sixteenth century, man's picture of the earth was being shaken and transformed by the results of the voyages of exploration. Columbus did not merely discover a new fact, that there was an inhabited land mass between Europe and Asia, but, as Vespucci realized, that there was a New World which challenged many of the assumptions and beliefs about the old one. Almost all previous views about the world had become untrue, and the science and philosophy that had led to such views could no longer be relied upon. The new worlds discovered by the early explorers appeared to function very well without the social, political, or religious institutions of Christianity, and posed a basic skeptical challenge to the European and Judeo-Christian claims about the nature and destiny of man. The influence of the idea of the "Noble Savage," presented from Columbus to Montaigne and to Rousseau, Voltaire, and others, made intellectuals increasingly critical if not skeptical of their own or accepted valuations of civilizations.

A different kind of skeptical attack came from the humanists who had rediscovered Greece and Rome, as well as the riches of early Judaism and Christianity. Led by Erasmus and Vives they cast doubt upon the whole intellectual edifice that had been constructed in the high Middle Ages. They questioned the methods, purposes, and achievements of the scholastic universities, and portrayed the entire intellectual endeavor of the universities as sterile, futile, and bankrupt. And after Erasmus' *In Praise of Folly* (*Moriae encomium*, 1509), it was hard to take the institutional intellectual world seriously. Erasmus had not refuted scholasticism in any philosophical way, but had so ridiculed it that it could no longer be considered a way to knowledge. Only a totally different approach, that of humanistic scholarship, could help.

One form of these researches further intensified the skeptical atmosphere. Jewish scholars fleeing from Spain, brought the Cabbala into Europe, with its secret way of discovering the truth. This, coupled with the rediscovery of the Greek magical writings of Hermes Trismegistus, the researches of the alchemists, the astrologers, and the numerologists, convinced many humanists that the normal ways of gaining knowledge had to be rejected in favor of esoteric ones. Thinkers during the Renaissance era, like Pico della Mirandola, Ficino, Reuchlin, and Agrippa von Nettesheim (especially the latter), cast doubt upon previous claims to knowledge.

The "new scientists," in combining some of the humanistic learning about ancient views and esoteric theories with empirical research, raised further skeptical questions about the accepted views of man and his universe. Copernicus, Tycho Brahe, Kepler, Paracelsus, Servetus, Vesalius, and others, all contributed to undermining confidence in previous theories and methods.

In addition to these factors, the religious developments of the times helped lead the European intellectual world into a general "skeptical crisis." The questions raised by the religious struggles of the sixteenth century struck at the very heart of human certainty. First, non-Christian religions challenged the assurance people had in the Christian revelation. The revival of, and admiration for, classical paganism, the impact of Judaism, thrust into Europe by the expulsion of the Jews from Spain and Portugal, and the new threat of Islam in the form of the Turkish invasions of central Europe, all caused a crisis of confidence in Christianity, which is reflected, for example, in Jean Bodin's dialogue, *Colloquium heptalomeres.* . . . In this secret work (not published until the nineteenth century, though circulated widely from the late sixteenth century) Bodin had adherents of various religions engage in debate; the Jew and the believer in natural religion won the debate, as basic criticisms were leveled against Christianity.

As Europe was being shaken by these non-Christian challenges, a more shattering development occurred—the Reformation—which tore the Christian world asunder. Starting with complaints about Catholic practices and beliefs, the reformers were quickly forced to a theoretical level to defend their criticisms. Beginning with Luther's views at the Leipzig Disputation (1519), a central issue became that of ascertaining how one gained true religious knowledge. Luther, Calvin,

and Zwingli challenged the traditional church view, as well as the criteria on which it was based, namely tradition and papal pronouncements. Instead they appealed to conscience and personal religious experience as the bases of religious knowledge.

Catholic spokesmen then pointed out that once the reformers gave up the traditional criterion of religious knowledge of the Church, they would end up in a total skepticism, "a sink of uncertainty and error." Using the recently rediscovered texts of Sextus Empiricus (published in 1562 and 1569), the Catholics contended that the Protestants would be forced into the old skeptical problem of the criterion, that of trying to establish an unquestionable standard of true knowledge. All the reformers could offer were their personal religious opinions, and any attempt to justify these would lead either to an infinite regress or to circular reasoning. The reformers, in turn, saw that the same difficulty could be raised for the Catholics, in that they could not justify their criterion of authority and also of the oral and written tradition. The problem of authenticating a criterion applied as well to an old one as to a new one.

Each side's probing the foundations of its opponent's position revealed how uncertain each side's views really were. The debate continued well into the eighteenth century and made skepticism a living issue for those enmeshed in the religious struggles. As the fight continued, the issues became more generalized, questioning whether any knowledge at all was possible, and whether there were any criteria that could be relied upon. Gentian Hervet, the editor of the first printing of Sextus' *Adversus mathematicos* (1569), proclaimed that Pyrrhonism was the answer to Calvinism, because if nothing could be known, then Calvin's doctrines could not be known either. Skepticism would make men humble and obedient, and keep them from newfangled false doctrines. The Jesuit, Juan Maldonado, and his disciples, Cardinal Bellarmine, Cardinal Du Perron, and the Jesuits, Jean Gontery and François Veron, developed "a machine of war" to devastate the Protestants by engulfing them in a series of skeptical problems. Questions were raised as to what book is the Bible, how one ascertains what it says or means. The Protestants were forced by the use of skeptical arguments to rely solely on their private experience, which they could never prove was not delusory. The Protestants made the same sort of skeptical attacks on the Catholics, e.g., Jean La Placette, *The Incurable Scepticism of the Church of Rome* (1688), and *The Pope is a Pyrrhonist* (1692), by J. A. Turretin. Each side exposed the raw nerve of the intellectual world, the bases of human certainty, and provided reasons for doubting them.

These various factors, the voyages of exploration, the humanistic revolt, the impact of cabbalistic and magical doctrines, the rise of the "new science," the religious crises, all contributed to creating a general skeptical crisis in the sixteenth century, by undermining confidence in the fabric of the intellectual world, and by raising fundamental questions about the possibility of human knowledge in any area whatsoever. As this was happening, several thinkers began to present a new version of classical skepticism as a way of living in a radically changing world. Starting with Agrippa von Nettesheim's popular diatribe, *The Vanity of the Sciences* (1526), and Gianfrancesco Pico's *Examen vanitatis doctrinae gentium* (1520), materials from Cicero, Diogenes Laërtius, and Sextus were employed against the prevailing theories of the time. The aim of this new skeptical attack, however, was not to make men suspend judgment, but rather to make them abandon the quest for knowledge by rational means, and accept the truth (that is, the true religion) on faith. Skepticism became the road to faith.

This Christian skepticism, or new Pyrrhonism, developed primarily as a Catholic position. The classical statement of this view appeared in Montaigne's *Apology for Raimond Sebond*, written mostly in 1575–76, after Montaigne read Sextus, and was undergoing his own personal skeptical crisis. His *Apology* purports to "defend" Sebond's rationalist theology by showing the inadequacy of reason to support any conclusions about man and the world, and the need to rely on faith rather than on human capacities for any intellectual guidance. Modernizing the ancient skeptical arguments, Montaigne proceeded to undermine confidence in the reliability of sense information and human rational judgments. All of the old routines about the variability of sense experience, its dependence on various conditions, the inability to find a satisfactory criterion for judging when it is veridical, etc., were woven together into a symphony of doubt. The crescendo was reached when Montaigne pointed out that

To judge the appearances that we receive of objects, we would need a judicatory instrument; to verify this instrument, we need a demonstration; to verify the demonstration, an instrument: there we are in a circle.

Since the senses cannot decide our dispute, being themselves full of uncertainty, it must be reason that does so. No reason can be established without another reason: there we go retreating back to infinity (Montaigne, *Apology for Raimond Sebond*, in *Complete Works . . .* , trans. D. Frame, Stanford [1967], p. 454).

Our judgments, Montaigne insisted, are influenced by psychological and cultural factors, and every attempt to know reality turns out to be like trying to clutch water.

All that we can do, according to Montaigne, is accept the Pyrrhonian suspension of judgment, and following the ancient Pyrrhonian advice, live according to nature and custom, and receive and accept whatever it pleases God to reveal to us. This fideistic appeal, a logical non sequitur from Montaigne's skepticism, is set forth as the only way out of the skeptical crisis. Montaigne insisted that the skeptic would not become a Protestant. His mind would remain blank, purged of false or dubious beliefs, until God revealed the true religious principles to him. Prior to that moment, custom would keep him in the old religion.

Though Montaigne professed to be a Catholic, his skepticism led him to a generally tolerant view towards all beliefs. He influenced his friend, Henri IV, to adopt the tolerant policies enunciated in the Edict of Nantes (1598). Montaigne's personal religious background (his own family was partly Jewish, partly Catholic, and partly Protestant), his skeptical criticisms of actual religious practices and beliefs and of theology, have led many, especially from the Enlightenment onward, to see his skepticism not just as an epistemological one, challenging human knowledge claims, but also as an irreligious one, challenging belief in Judeo-Christianity. Whether Montaigne was a genuine Christian, or whether he was a covert nonbeliever, is still extremely difficult to determine. He and his followers set forth a view called "Christian skepticism," which they insisted was the same as that presented by Saint Paul at the beginning of I Corinthians. By and large, Montaigne's generalized skepticism and his fideism were accepted by the counter-reformers in France as a basis for rebutting the new dogmas of Protestantism, and for accepting the traditional religion on faith.

Montaigne's presentation of Pyrrhonism became the most popular expression of the intellectual malaise of the time. This skeptical atmosphere was further reinforced by the writings of Montaigne's distant cousin, Francisco Sanchez, and by those of Montaigne's disciples, Father Pierre Charron and Bishop Jean-Pierre Camus.

Sanchez, a Portuguese forced convert from Judaism, professor of philosophy and medicine at Toulouse, wrote some skeptical works at the same time as Montaigne's *Apology*. Using brilliant dialectical skill, Sanchez attacked the Platonic and Aristotelian theories of scientific knowledge and concluded that, in a basic and serious sense, nothing can be known. Then, in contrast to the destructive conclusion of Montaigne that one should suspend judgment about the possibility of gaining knowledge by scientific means, Sanchez offered a constructive suggestion: all that can be done

243

# SKEPTICISM IN MODERN THOUGHT

is cautious, limited empirical research. This tentative approach contains the rudiments of a hypothetical pragmatic science. Sanchez added the fideistic note of the Christian skeptics as a postscript, faith as the final answer. Sanchez' version of skepticism had some influence on seventeenth-century thinkers, and his "constructive" skepticism seems to have supplied the substructure of the *via media* between skepticism and dogmatism later offered by Pierre Gassendi.

Montaigne's disciple and heir, Father Pierre Charron, further popularized skepticism. He first wrote an enormous Counter-Reformation tract, *Les trois vérités* (1595), arguing against atheists, non-Christian religions, and Calvinism, on skeptical grounds. Next he wrote as a didactic version of Montaigne's *Apology*, *La sagesse* (1601), one of the most widely read books of the seventeenth century. He advocated rejecting all opinions and beliefs that are dubious or false, in order to render the mind blank, ready to receive whatever God wishes to write upon it. The skeptic, Charron insisted, cannot be a heretic since, in having no opinions, he cannot have the wrong ones. Until one receives the Revelation, one should live according to nature while being skeptical.

A somewhat similar Christian skepticism was set forth by Jean-Pierre Camus, who later became the secretary of Saint François de Sales and then Bishop of Bellay.

In the early seventeenth century, Christian skepticism became an acceptable position amongst Catholic theologians in France, and the avant-garde view of many intellectuals in Paris. The so-called *libertins érudits*, Gabriel Naudé, secretary to cardinals Mazarin and Bagno and royal librarian, Guy Patin, rector of the medical school of the Sorbonne, and François de La Mothe Le Vayer, teacher of the Dauphin and member of the French Academy, popularized and promulgated the *nouveau pyrrhonisme* (sometimes joining it to a Machiavellism in politics). The brilliant young scientist and philosopher, Pierre Gassendi, in his first book, *Exercitationes paradoxicae adversus Aristoteleos* (1624), leveled a thoroughgoing skeptical attack on Aristotelianism and other dogmatic philosophies, ending with the news that "no science is possible, least of all Aristotle's."

In the 1620's, especially in France, the new skeptics had succeeded in undermining confidence in all previous theories, and in creating a genuine skeptical crisis in the minds of many intellectuals. The situation became so serious that attacks against the new skepticism began to appear. Some, like that of Father François Garasse, S.J., claimed that the new skepticism was undermining religious belief and practice (and he was rebuked by the Jansenist leader, l'abbé de Saint-Cyran,

who insisted that Charron's view was the same orthodoxy that Saint Augustine had set forth). Others offered answers based on Aristotle's theories. Francis Bacon hoped to overcome skepticism by the use of new instruments. Marin Mersenne and his friend, Gassendi, offered a constructive resolution to the skeptical crisis, insisting that while skepticism could not be overcome on the epistemological level, it could be ignored on the practical and scientific level. Proposing a pragmatic and positivistic interpretation of the new science, they set forth a way of living with complete skepticism on a theoretical plane, while proceeding to gain hypothetical and useful information about the world through empirical research and the employment of the hypotheses of the new physics. Herbert of Cherbury developed a most elaborate scheme for overcoming skepticism and arriving at true knowledge. Descartes' friend, Jean de Silhon, offered a combination of Aristotelian, Stoic, and pre-Cartesian "Cartesian" rebuttals to skepticism.

René Descartes was most keenly aware of the problem and also of the inadequacy of the answers being proposed by his contemporaries. Either their solutions failed to come to grips with the problem, or they failed to yield indubitable and certain knowledge. By the tactic of pushing skeptical doubts more radically than his predecessors, Descartes sought to show that skepticism could be overcome, a basis for true knowledge found, and philosophy and science secured. Employing the skeptical method of Montaigne and Charron, Descartes sought to find some truth that could not be doubted. He rejected all beliefs that might possibly be false or dubious. He intensified the skeptics' doubt by raising the possibility that there might be an evil demon who distorts all human judgments. But in refutation of all of these doubts, Descartes insisted the proposition, "I think, therefore I am," cannot be questioned. No matter how unreliable our senses and our judgment are, no matter what the demon is up to, the *cogito* must be true, and any attempt to cast doubt on it reveals its truth. When this truth is examined to find out why it is indubitable, one discovers the criterion of true knowledge, namely that whatever is clearly and distinctly perceived is true. Using the criterion, one can then establish that God exists, that He is no deceiver, and that He guarantees that the criterion really is true. With skepticism overcome, one can then prove that an external world exists and that through our clear and distinct ideas we can gain knowledge about it. The Cartesian "way of clear and distinct ideas" then becomes a means of moving from doubt to certain knowledge about the world.

Descartes attempted to establish a new philosophy on the ruins of the skepticism that had engulfed

European thought. His radical innovation in the battle against skepticism shaped the structure and the problems of subsequent philosophy. The skeptics of the period were undaunted by Descartes' alleged conquest of skepticism, and they set to work to redirect their argumentation against this new dogmatic theory to show that Descartes had failed. On the other hand, Descartes' dogmatic opponents (e.g., Gisbert Voetius, Martin Schoock, Pierre Bourdin) sought to show that, his protestations notwithstanding, he still remained a skeptic, and a most dangerous one.

As soon as Descartes' theory appeared, Father Bourdin argued that if one could actually entertain the original doubts of Descartes, one would have undermined the possibility of finding an indubitable truth, since one could not trust one's faculties or one's understanding. Mersenne and Gassendi contended that the truths claimed by Descartes to be certain and indubitable, were still in fact open to question, and might possibly, in some sense, be false. Gassendi and the later skeptic, Bishop Pierre-Daniel Huet, analyzed and reanalyzed the *cogito* to show that it really established nothing. Gassendi insisted that the whole Cartesian system might just be a subjective vision of the author's. Huet claimed that the Cartesian system was just a collection of ideas and, as ideas, could not represent reality. Both challenged the criterion of knowledge, saying that we could only tell what we thought was clear and distinct, but not what was really in fact, clear and distinct. The criterion, they insisted, could never be applied with certainty unless we possessed another criterion, and so forth. Huet joined forces with Leibniz and with the Jesuit opponents of Cartesianism, and leveled all sorts of charges against "the Father of Modern Philosophy," seeking to reduce his vaunted achievement to rubble.

The later Cartesians tried to modify the theory to meet the critic's objections, and each new modification was met with a new dogmatic bombardment hammering away at the uncertainty of the Cartesian system, and at its inability to build a secure bridge from the world of ideas to reality. When Malebranche appeared with his radically revised Cartesianism, designed in part to meet the skeptical difficulties, the skeptic, Simon Foucher, and the orthodox Cartesian, Antoine Arnauld, sought to show that Malebranchism led to a "most dangerous Pyrrhonism." Foucher, who tried in his many writings to revive Academic skepticism, offered a new skeptical objection that was to play an important role in the subsequent history of ideas. The Cartesians, he pointed out, were willing to accept the skeptical reasonings that showed that the secondary qualities (color, sound, heat, taste, and smell) were subjective and not features of reality. The same rea-

sonings, Foucher insisted, should lead one to deny that the primary qualities (extension and motion, the ingredients of the Cartesian *real* world) were objective, and hence that none of the qualities we are aware of are constituents of reality. This argument was used by Bayle, Berkeley, and Hume as a decisive challenge to the basic assumptions of the "new philosophy."

In contrast to the anti-Cartesian skepticism in France, another kind was developing in England out of the theological controversies there. In the quest for the "true" religion, some theologians starting with William Chillingworth, tried to distinguish between the kinds of doubts raised by Sextus and Descartes, which they felt were unanswerable, and reasonable doubts that common sense and probable information could deal with. These theologians conceded that we could not gain absolutely certain knowledge, but, they insisted, there is some knowledge which cannot be reasonably doubted. Bishop John Wilkins and the Reverend Joseph Glanvill, both members of the Royal Society, presented a distinction between infallibly and indubitably certain knowledge. The former, because of skeptical difficulties, cannot be attained by human beings, but the latter, in terms of the indubitable beliefs, is accepted by all reasonable men. Using these, they constructed a theory of empirical science and of law as a means for finding useful knowledge, and for deciding human problems within the limits of a "reasonable doubt." The limited skepticism of Glanvill and Wilkins developed into the theory of science of the early Royal Society and the theory of legal evidence in Anglo-American law. It also provided a basis for a tolerant latitudinarian Christianity.

John Locke's compromise with skepticism and his appeal to an intuitive and common sense rejection of complete doubt derives, in part, from these views. However, his compromise was immediately attacked by Bishop Stillingfleet as resulting in another form of extreme skepticism in his rejection of "substance." Stillingfleet saw this as denying that there was any genuine certainty about the world, and even raising the possibility of metaphysical skepticism, a doubt whether there is any reality at all.

Throughout the seventeenth century, the new theorists felt confronted by skepticism, and in their attempts to offer new answers tried to overcome the challenge. Thomas Hobbes, a personal friend of many of the French skeptics, proposed as the solution to their problem of finding a criterion for true knowledge, that it be a political rather than an epistemological matter. The ruler would decide, and thus settle the skeptical controversies, taking on himself the risk of being wrong.

Pascal, who probably felt the force of the new skep-

245

ticism more than anyone else of the time, presented a "constructive" skepticism in his scientific writings, advocating a hypothetical probabilistic science and mathematics. In the *Pensées* (1670), he first forcibly developed the skeptical case, and then insisted that nature just would not permit one to be in complete doubt: *Le coeur a ses raisons que la raison ne connaît point* ("The heart has its reasons that reason does not know," *Pensées*, #434). We are torn between dogmatism and skepticism, belief and doubt. Only by listening to God, by having mystical experience, can one get beyond the skeptical crisis. The solution for Pascal is not philosophical, but religious.

Spinoza, on the other hand, tried to offer the most rationalistic resolution. Doubt only occurred because one lacked knowledge. By attaining clear and adequate conceptions one overcame all skeptical difficulties. The clear and adequate conceptions were their own criterion and provided their own guarantee of their certainty and truth. The proper pursuit of philosophy in the geometrical manner was the answer to skepticism.

Leibniz, a close friend of the "Academic" skeptics, Huet, Foucher, and Bayle, wrote many of the basic statements of his views as answers to them. He believed that the skeptics had raised important problems, and that his system of logic, epistemology, and metaphysics had solved them. For about thirty years he argued with his skeptical friends. Bayle's article "Rorarius" was the first extended criticism of Leibniz' theory, and Leibniz' *Theodicy* was intended to answer Bayle's skepticism.

Bishop Berkeley also saw his theory as the answer to the skeptics. By accepting the skeptics' claim that all that we know are ideas, and then insisting that ideas are reality, Berkeley believed he had solved the problem. As he saw it, the seventeenth-century metaphysicians had created a gulf between appearance and reality with their insistence that there was a material reality. This allowed the skeptics to argue that only appearances were actually known. By amalgamating things and ideas, and making the world basically spiritual, Berkeley believed he had saved the world from skepticism and irreligion, and had established "the reality of human knowledge." And much to the Bishop's chagrin, for all of his valiant efforts, he was treated as the wildest of skeptics by his contemporaries.

The new skepticism of the Montaignians created a continuing skeptical crisis on the epistemological level which the theories of the great century of metaphysics tried to overcome. The debate between the new skeptics and the new dogmatists shaped the form of the new theories, and revealed their weaknesses and defects. While these theories of knowledge and metaphysical systems were being fought over, another form of skepticism was developing—irreligious skepti-

cism—which was also to have a monumental impact on modern thought. The new skepticism, from Montaigne to Bishop Huet, professed to being religious, since it was always coupled with an advocacy of fideism. All its advocates except the Huguenot Pierre Bayle were Catholics, using skepticism to attack reformers and metaphysicians in the name of true religion. Whether they were sincere or not, they did not apply their doubts to their religious tradition or to the supposed content of revelation.

The raising of skeptical doubts about the truth of Judeo-Christianity seems to have started in the sixteenth century as indicated by Bodin's dialogue. The tragic Portuguese Jewish refugee (in the Netherlands), Uriel Da Costa, started out questioning the truth of orthodox Judaism, and the immortality of the soul, and then went on to questioning all religions. He came to the conclusion that all extant religions were man-made. He finally proclaimed that one should not be a Jew or a Christian; one should just be a man. Da Costa had reached the point of rejecting Judeo-Christianity, and is probably the first European man to try to live outside of it. However, his major ideas were unknown until published posthumously in 1687.

The French courtier, Isaac La Peyrère, a friend of the leading skeptics of the time, raised a basic skepticism about the Bible in his shocking work, *Prae-Adamitae* (1655; trans. as *Men Before Adam*, 1656). La Peyrère had become convinced from his reading of the Bible, and from geographical and anthropological evidence about China, the New World, Greenland, etc.) that there must have been people before Adam, and that the Bible cannot be an accurate account of all of human history. He questioned the accuracy of the biblical texts that we have. Finally he developed a strange mystical theory that the Bible describes only Jewish history, that the rest of mankind developed separately, and that the messianic culmination of Jewish history was at hand. Needless to say, his book was immediately suppressed and the author jailed. He converted from Calvinism to Catholicism, personally apologized to the Pope, retired to the pious Oratory, and went on developing his heretical theories.

La Peyrère's bombshell led two scholars of the Bible, Baruch de Spinoza and Father Richard Simon, to develop far-reaching skepticisms with regard to religious knowledge. Spinoza carried on La Peyrère's doubts, in his *Tractatus-theologico-politicus* (1670), and questioned the Mosaic authorship of the *Pentateuch*, as well as other biblical claims. Spinoza suggested that the Bible was not Divine Revelation, but just an early record of Jewish superstitions and activities. Finally Spinoza insisted that religion was to be interpreted naturalistically in psychological and sociological terms.

He had provided a metaphysics for seeing the world apart from all revelation, and had cast doubt on the authenticity and seriousness of the purported revealed texts of Judeo-Christianity.

Father Richard Simon, an associate of La Peyrère's at the Oratory and a reader of Spinoza, was the greatest Bible scholar of his age, and, along with Spinoza, the founder of modern biblical criticism. He set out to prove that the Protestants could never find an accurate text of the Bible or discover what it meant. Building on La Peyrère's and Spinoza's points, he used his wealth of erudition to create a skepticism with regard to the message of the Bible. Simon pointed to the epistemological difficulties in ascertaining any historical fact, and insisted that all that we knew about the message were dubious historical claims of human beings, who in their fallible way had tried to record the message. Unlike Spinoza, Simon seems to have been convinced that there is a message, and tried in his own way to give the best statement of it in his time.

However, when La Peyrère, Spinoza, and Simon were done with examining the revealed religions, it was difficult for intellectuals to accept the Bible with the previous innocence. The possibility had been raised that the Bible was not true, or only partially true. The difficulties in assessing the actual text of the Bible had become insuperable. These new skeptical doubts would not be resolved by religion, but religion itself had become a proper subject of skeptical doubting.

The culmination of the many strands of seventeenth-century skepticism appears in the writings of the greatest of the seventeenth-century French skeptics, Pierre Bayle. Bayle, a Protestant, who became a Catholic and then reverted to Protestantism, fled to Rotterdam where he wrote against all sorts of religious and philosophical theories. In his masterpiece *Dictionnaire historique et critique* (1697–1702), Bayle surveyed and skeptically criticized the various facets of the seventeenth-century intellectual world. With his brilliant dialectical skill, Bayle undermined the metaphysical theories of Descartes, Spinoza, Locke, Malebranche, and Leibniz, attacked the theologies of his time, ridiculed the biblical heroes of the *Old Testament,* challenged the criterion of rational knowledge, and tried to show that the worst heresies like Manichaeism, were more plausible rationally than Christianity. Every theory, in Bayle's hands, led to perplexity and absurdity, and constituted "the high road to Pyrrhonism." And, he insisted, over and over again, all one could do after seeing the debacle of the rational world was to abandon reason and turn to faith, pure blind faith. But Bayle had so ridiculed the usual content of faith that little seemed left except complete doubt about the possibility of understanding anything, except

by historically describing it. What Bayle himself believed, if anything, is almost impossible to discern in his sea of doubts.

Bayle's *Dictionary* launched the Age of Reason, by providing what Voltaire called "The Arsenal of the Enlightenment." Bayle had pulled together all the strains of skepticism and had laid bare all the defects of the theories of the time, undermining the quest for any metaphysical or theological certainty.

The eighteenth century began bathed in Baylean doubts. However, instead of being dismayed by his shattering skeptical conclusions, eighteenth-century thinkers were willing to apply Bayle's criticisms to religion, theology, and metaphysics, but saw a new way of understanding the universe—Newtonian science. Bayle was seen as the summit of wisdom before Newton, but now there was no longer any reason to be so dubious, except about religion and metaphysics.

One of the very few who was still concerned with skepticism was the Scot, David Hume, an avid reader of Bayle. Hume apparently went through his own personal skeptical crisis as he wrote his *Treatise of Human Nature* (1739). He started off as a Newtonian, hoping to apply "the experimental method of reasoning" to moral subjects. However, as he "scientifically" examined how people think, he began to develop a skepticism about man's ability to know anything beyond the immediately felt "impressions" or beyond what was demonstrable from "relations of ideas." However, almost all our information about the world depends on causal reasoning which cannot be justified logically because we cannot discover any demonstrable necessary connection between any pair of events called "cause and effect." When we examine how we do reach conclusions about matters of fact beyond immediate experience, we find such beliefs are based on psychological habit or custom, rather than on rational evidence. We can describe how we "reason," but we cannot justify it by reason. As Hume inquired why people believe that reason can establish matters of fact or necessary causes in the external world, in the unity of the self, and in demonstrations of the existence of God, he became all the more skeptical. He found that the empirical evidence should lead to disbelief, the psychological explanations were inadequate, and his own explanations were inconsistent, but nonetheless he, like everyone else, believed what could not be proved by reasoning. "Philosophy would render us entirely Pyrrhonian, were not nature too strong for it" (Hume, *Abstract of a Treatise of Human Nature*, ed. L. A. Selby-Bigge, Oxford [1888], p. 24). "Nature, by an absolute and uncontrollable necessity has determin'd us to judge as well as to breathe and feel" (Hume, *Treatise*, p. 183). Nature did not refute skepticism, but

247

made it unbelievable enough of the time so that life could go on. By the time Hume reached the end of the first book of the *Treatise* he seemed to see a skepticism as complete as Bayle's. "We have, therefore, no choice left but betwixt a false reason and none at all." "I am ready to reject all belief and reasoning, and can look upon opinion even as more probable or likely than another" (Hume, *Treatise*, pp. 268–69). In this skeptical despair, reminiscent of Pascal's picture of man without God, Hume saw salvation only in the beneficent actions of nature that stop all doubting in time. By living according to nature, sometimes he was forced to doubt and sometimes to believe. The beliefs are not based on evidence, but only on feelings and habits. Any examination of the beliefs just reveals the skeptical difficulties, but these difficulties notwithstanding, everyone including the Humean skeptic, has to believe all sorts of things.

Hume apparently saw, as no one else in the eighteenth century did, the plight of modern man if Bayle's doubts could not be answered, and if no fideistic or supernatural solution was acceptable. The new science of Newton only described what "reasonable" men believed, operating on normal natural psychological habits and customs. It did not really tell anybody what was necessarily true, and its conclusions could never be satisfactorily justified. No religious faith could any longer be taken seriously, once the arguments of the irreligious skeptics were applied to it. Hume could not calmly survey in Bayle's manner the wreckage wrought by skepticism. He had to believe, like everyone else, but he could only see his beliefs based on an unjustified and unjustifiable animal faith, rather than on a religious one. The world and life might have no discoverable meaning, but nature benevolently made us persevere. And Hume persevered by trying to describe human nature, man and his foibles, in historical terms. History became the constructive issue of Hume's skepticism as it was for Bayle. Historical description would replace philosophy as the way of studying man, and would still further undermine man's pretensions.

Hume's skepticism had little effect on his immediate contemporaries. They found his historical and political writings exciting, his irreligious ones immoral or intriguing, but his skepticism a bore in a Newtonian age. It was admired by the reactionaries and religious fanatics in France, but not by the *philosophes*. After the Revolution, Joseph de Maistre and Félicité de Lamennais could appreciate Hume, because his skepticism undermined the new dogmatism of the revolutionaries and the atheists, and they could advocate a fideism again on the basis of it.

One who saw what Hume had accomplished was his fellow Scotsman, Thomas Reid. Reid perceived that

Hume, and Berkeley before him, had shown that the fundamental assumptions of modern philosophy following from the intellectualism of Descartes led to a total skepticism and distrust of the senses. Reid felt that a reconsideration of the rationalistic assumptions which led to so disastrous a result was required. When philosophy reached conclusions contrary to common sense, then philosophy must be wrong. Nobody can be a complete skeptic in belief or action. Therefore one should start with the beliefs people are unable psychologically to doubt, such as that there is an external world. Common-sense realism, Reid claimed, could avoid the skeptical pitfalls in the Cartesian and Lockean theories. Hume replied that Reid had seen the problem, but his solution was really the same as Hume's, skepticism cannot be answered on a theoretical level, and nature makes us live and believe.

The Scottish School following Reid was the first to see that Hume's skepticism was *the* view to oppose if philosophy was to continue to make sense of the world. However, the way developed in Germany of dealing with Hume's skepticism had the greatest effect on subsequent philosophy. The leaders of the Prussian Academy had been concerned with Pyrrhonism, had translated Hume, and had tried to refute him. Others had presented modern skeptical views, and had translated Hume's Scottish critics.

Immanuel Kant read this literature and wrote that Hume had awakened him from his dogmatic slumbers. He saw that Hume had challenged the Enlightenment view that skepticism could be ignored and replaced by science. The fundamental question, "How is knowledge possible?" now required reexamination.

Kant's answer was to admit a complete skepticism regarding the possibility of gaining metaphysical knowledge by pure reason, while insisting that universal and necessary knowledge about the conditions of all possible experience could be attained. Starting from the conviction that some knowledge is possible, Kant then tried to show how such universal and necessary information occurs. Kant's revolutionary solution to the skeptical crisis was that necessary and universal conditions are involved in having any experience and making any judgments. Through these we can gain some certain knowledge. Mathematics is the knowledge of the *a priori* conditions of experience. And we can also know certain conditions about how our judgments about experience are organized.

These conditions apply to the forms of possible experience and to judgments about them, but do not tell us about their contents, or about the realities behind them—the real world, the self, or God. For Kant the content of experience can only be learned empirically, and such information could be no more than probable. We cannot gain any metaphysical knowledge by pure reason, since there is no way of telling if our categories apply beyond all possible experience, or what they then might apply to. However, by practical reason we act as if certain conditions prevailed beyond experience.

Kant thought he had ended the age-old struggle with skepticism. However, some of Kant's contemporaries saw his accomplishment as just opening the way for a new skeptical age, rather than resolving the skeptical crisis. Some saw that the application of his theory to religion (religion within the limits of bare reason alone) provided the theoretical grounds for a thoroughgoing skepticism of all revealed religion.

Kant's critic, G. E. Schulze (also known as Schulze-Aenesidemus), contended that Kant's philosophy provided no way for attaining truths about objective reality, or things-in-themselves. All that we could know was the subjective necessity of some of our views, which Hume had already pointed out. Hence Kant's theory was really only a vindication of Hume's kind of subjective skepticism.

Another thinker, Solomon Maimon (recognized by Kant as his most astute critic), developed a "rational skepticism" from within Kant's theory. Maimon accepted the view that there are *a priori* concepts, but held that the application of these categories to experience was only known inductively and could only yield probability. Hence no universal and necessary knowledge about experience could be gained. The question of whether there was such knowledge was, for Maimon, always an experiential matter, and as Hume had shown, no final certainty could be gained on this score.

For Maimon there are *a priori* forms of thought, but the relation of these to matters of fact remains problematic. Propositions about these *a priori* concepts were true because they were about human creations, and not because they necessarily had any objective relevance. Maimon's view that human creativity was the basis of truth was developed by Fichte as a new means of overcoming skepticism and reaching knowledge of reality.

Kant's friend, the religious fanatic, J. G. Hamann, took the arguments of Hume and Kant as establishing that knowledge of reality could not be reached by rational means. Therefore he advocated an acceptance of irrational faith as the result of complete skepticism. Hamann's irrational fideism was later adopted by Lamennais as an answer to Enlightenment views in France and a new defense of conservatism and orthodoxy, and by Kierkegaard as an answer to Hegelianism and religious liberalism. Both reacted with extreme skepticism to the "progressive" intellectual and religious trends during the early nineteenth century.

Kierkegaard brilliantly exploited the skeptical possibilities against the views of his contemporaries and insisted on the need for faith, on the unjustified and unjustifiable "leap into faith," as the only way to find subjective rather than objective certainty. The anti-rational fideism of Hamann, Lamennais, and Kierkegaard has been revived by neo-orthodox and existentialist theologians in the twentieth century, arguing that skepticism reveals our inability to find ultimate truth by rational means, hence the need for faith and commitment.

After Kant, although few philosophers call themselves skeptics, skepticism has permeated many of the major movements of thought. The struggles with the new forms of skepticism from Descartes to Kant had indicated that normal rational and scientific procedures were inadequate to gain knowledge about reality, or to support claims to religious knowledge. For most subsequent thinkers a kind of partial skepticism was accepted either as a means of transcending it, or as a means of living with it. These thinkers can only be considered as partial skeptics, or users of skepticism to develop new theories.

The German metaphysicians, starting with Fichte and Hegel, tried to overcome skepticism by examining the creative and historically developing intellectual processes with skepticism as a stage in this. For Fichte skepticism makes one realize that a fundamental unjustifiable metaphysical commitment has to be made. This commitment allows one to see things in terms of creative thought processes, and to uncover a structure of the world in which everything is seen as related to the Absolute Ego.

For the Hegelians, skeptical arguments show how unintelligible is each limited picture of the world. Since the universe and our understanding of it is historically developing, there is a legitimate skepticism at each stage, in that the world and our understanding of it are incomplete and contradictory. Until the self-realization of the Absolute, and our attainment of knowledge of it, all of our knowledge is only partly true and partly false. At the final stage, skepticism will have been overcome and genuine knowledge will be possible.

The empirical, positivistic, and pragmatic movements of the nineteenth and twentieth centuries that have combatted German idealistic metaphysics have by and large adopted a thoroughgoing skepticism about the possibility of gaining any metaphysical knowledge. The empiricists and positivists have argued that there is no means of gaining knowledge beyond empirical data, except in terms of logical and mathematical tautologies. Many pragmatists have found the traditional metaphysical quest meaningless, and metaphysical assertions unverifiable and useless. The empiricists, positivists, and pragmatists have tried to absorb or obviate the skeptical challenge by restricting the quest for knowledge to the empirical world, or to mathematics, and accepting explicitly or tacitly a skepticism about metaphysics. Some, by redefining knowledge, have in effect adopted a kind of skepticism.

Another type of modern skepticism has developed from the social sciences. The work of Marx, Nietzsche, James, Freud, and others, has produced a new form of relativistic skepticism. If the views people hold are the products of human culture and behavior, and vary with social economic and psychological conditions, can any of these views be considered as true? Nietzsche and Freud have raised the possibility of value skepticism, that all value beliefs may be man-made, and that there really are no objective values. Marx indicated that all views may just be reflections of other developing factors.

In the twentieth century, when so many of the strands of modern skepticism have been absorbed into the main intellectual currents, very few thinkers have proclaimed themselves skeptics. Many have accepted a skepticism or semi-skepticism, and then ignored it and have gone on about their intellectual business. Some have developed views indicating what remains after a fundamental skepticism has been adopted, what sort of sense may still be made of man and his world.

The forms of overt skepticism in this century have varied greatly, from the naturalistic animal faith variety of George Santayana, the linguistic positivistic mystical kind of Fritz Mauthner, the skeptical solipsism and practical altruism of Adolfo Levi, the extreme anti-rational skeptical fideism of Lev Shestov (the Russian Orthodox theologian), the existentialist skepticism, if one can call it that, of Jean Grenier and his student, the novelist Albert Camus to the semi-skepticism of Vaihinger, Alain, and Popper. Each of these thinkers has pointed to the modern malaise, either in despair or with equanimity, that because of the reasons raised by the skeptics over the past four centuries, the modern intellectual era has failed to achieve the level of intellectual security and certainty of past ages.

Mauthner's analysis of language indicated the complete relativism and subjectivism of any way of describing the world, without any means being known of independently evaluating which, if any of these, corresponded to reality. Mauthner finally concluded that all that was possible was a kind of godless mystical contemplation of the world.

Santayana contended in his brilliant *Scepticism and Animal Faith* (1923) that any interpretation of immediate or intuited experience was questionable: "Nothing given exists." However, we do interpret the given in order to make life meaningful, and interpret it in terms of an "animal faith." This is consistent with a thoroughgoing skepticism, and is pursued by following natural and social tendencies and inclinations. The beliefs that result from animal faith enable us to preserve and to appreciate the richness of life.

In contrast, Shestov not only applied a complete skepticism to rational beliefs, but insisted on a radical rejection of all rational standards in order to reach faith. Shestov insisted on the need to reject even mathematical truths in order to achieve or make room for the religious life. For Shestov rationality is contradictory and cosmically dangerous.

Camus, building on Grenier's skepticism, saw man as trying to decipher the nature and meaning of a universe that is basically absurd, employing dubious rational and scientific means. Camus used the skeptical-fideistic arguments but rejected the religious solution. Accepting Nietzsche's claim that God is dead, and that the universe is ultimately meaningless, Camus painted his protagonists as having to struggle with a world that is unintelligible and senseless. They have to recognize and accept the human situation, and find whatever personal meaning is possible through struggle though it has no objective or ultimate or rational significance.

Sir Karl Popper's quasi-skepticism, much like that of the constructive skepticism of Gassendi and of the scientific Pascal, has sought to dispose of the illusions that immutably demonstrable truths could be found in logic, mathematics, and science. He has sought to show that adequate verification of truths is not possible, and has tried to offer ways of proceeding in science and mathematics that can be of value without having to resolve the basic skeptical difficulties.

All of these who have presented forms of skepticism in the twentieth century have indicated that the fundamental skeptical problems raised in ancient times and revived in the Renaissance have not been resolved by modern philosophy, theology, or science. Over the last four centuries, the skeptics have refurbished the ancient arguments, and redirected them against the new dogmatists who have arisen. Renaissance skepticism helped erode confidence in scholastic and Platonic ways of understanding the universe. The irreligious skepticism of the seventeenth and eighteenth centuries made it difficult to accept the Judeo-Christian world view in an objective and literal sense. The critical analyses of Bayle, Hume, Kant, and the post-Kantian critics undermined the new metaphysical ventures of the seventeenth century. The anti-metaphysical positivism and the social scientific relativism of the last two centuries have indicated that it is unlikely that any final truth will be discovered by human rational or scientific means.

The struggle against skepticism has been one of the dynamic factors in the development of modern thought, urging thinkers to probe for new means of answering the attacks. The erosion, through the various forms of modern skepticism, of the structure of Western European thought has left most contemporary thinkers unable or unwilling to seek any longer certain and unshakeable foundations of a system of thought for understanding man and the universe. Most have accepted some or many elements of the skeptics' challenge, and, as a result many philosophers have turned away from the quest for any ultimate truth or meaning. Instead they have sought ways of living with the unresolved skeptical crisis through humanistic, scientific, animal, or religious faiths.

*BIBLIOGRAPHY*

Don Cameron Allen, *Doubt's Boundless Sea: Skepticism and Faith in the Renaissance* (Baltimore, 1964). Samuel Atlas, *From Critical to Speculative Idealism: The Philosophy of Salomon Maimon* (The Hague, 1964). Christian Bartholmèse, *Huet, évêque d'Avranches, ou le scepticisme théologique* (Paris, 1850). George Boas, *Dominant Themes of Modern Philosophy* (New York, 1957). Tullio Gregory, *Scetticismo ed empirismo: Studio su Gassendi* (Bari, 1961). Marcellino Menendez Pelayo, *Obras completas*, Vol. XLIII, *Ensayos de crítica filosofica* (Santander, 1948), Ch. 2, "De los orígenes del criticismo y del escepticismo y especialmente de los precursores españoles de Kant," pp. 117–216. Arne Naess, *Skepticism* (New York, 1969), contains an extensive bibliography. Charles G. Nauert, *Agrippa and the Crisis of Renaissance Thought* (Urbana, 1955). John Owen, *Evening With the Skeptics* (London, 1881); idem, *The Skeptics of the French Renaissance* (London and New York, 1893). Richard H. Popkin, "David Hume: His Pyrrhonism and His Critique of Pyrrhonism," *Philosophical Quarterly*, 1 (1950–51), 385–407; idem, *The History of Scepticism From Erasmus to Descartes* (Assen, Netherlands, 1960; New York, 1964, 1968). Contains lengthy bibliography on skepticism from 1500 to 1650; idem, "Scepticism in the Enlightenment," in T. Bestermann, ed., *Studies on Voltaire and the 18th Century*, Vol. XXVI (Geneva, 1963), pp. 1321–45; idem, "The High Road to Pyrrhonism," *American Philosophical Quarterly*, 2 (1965), 1–15; idem, "Scepticism, Theology and the Scientific Revolution in the Seventeenth Century," *Problems in the Philosophy of Science*, ed. Lakatos and Musgrave, Vol. III (Amsterdam 1968), 1–39. Karl Popper, *Conjectures and Refutations*, 2nd ed. (New York, 1968). George Santayana, *Scepticism and Animal Faith* (New York, 1923; reprint 1955). Charles B. Schmitt, *Gianfrancesco Pico della Mirandola* (The Hague, 1967). Henry G. Van Leeuwen, *The Problem of Certainty in English Thought 1630–1690* (The Hague, 1963). Richard A. Watson, *The Downfall of Cartesianism* (The Hague, 1966).

RICHARD H. POPKIN

[See also **Agnosticism;** Authority; **Certainty;** Faith; Irrationalism; Machiavellism; **Positivism; Probability;** Reformation; **Relativism;** Renaissance Humanism.]

# SOCIAL CONTRACT

THE NOTION of Social Contract, although particularly influential in the seventeenth and eighteenth centuries, has a history which reaches back to the time of the ancient Greeks. The term refers to the act by which men are assumed to establish a communally agreed form of social organization. This act has been given varying characteristics by the numerous theorists who have described it. They may refer to the establishment of society as prior to the inauguration of government, or alternatively to the state and society having arisen concurrently. In the first case the Social Contract is often thought of as a pact that all men make with each other as equals, whilst in the latter case it may be a less egalitarian agreement by which the rulers and the ruled are differentiated, and their various rights and obligations made explicit.

In order to express certain variations in the assumed agreement, some writers chose to use the closely related notions of "compact" or "covenant," rather than that of "contract." A further difference is that the contract is sometimes regarded as an act that has been made and ought to be adhered to, and at other times as one that ought to be made. Amongst all these variations, however, some points of agreement do emerge. First, there is the view that human society and government are the work of man, constructed according to human will, even if sometimes operating under divine guidance. Such a notion implies a conception of man as a free agent, rather than a being totally determined by external forces. Second, the emphasis on contract implies that the nature both of society and of government ought to be based on mutual agreement rather than on force. We shall later see how these beliefs played an important role in justifying the acceptance of liberal democratic views.

The belief that men once came together to form a contract implies the prior existence of a pregovernmental condition. It is this which is usually referred to as the State of Nature. This image, by portraying what man was like without government, serves to demonstrate exactly what it is man owes to government. The idea of a State of Nature became acceptable in that it had formed part of popular mythology from the times of antiquity, being portrayed as a former Golden Age of complete equality in both Greek and Latin literature. This assumption, found in the *Metamorphoses* of Ovid and in the writings of the Stoics, gained further expression amongst the Scholastics of the later Middle Ages, and much later still was more than echoed in Rousseau's *Discours sur l'inégalité* (1754). Most later Social Contract theorists, from the time of Hobbes onwards, have taken this accepted notion of a pre-political condition, but by altering its character have inverted its function. The State of Nature, rather than being an ideal, is now provided with deficiencies. It is in order to remedy these deficiencies that the contract has to be made. The method, then, has many uses. Sometimes the State of Nature has been portrayed as a Golden Age of peace and equality, obviously superior to anything that has replaced it. Alternatively, in order to demonstrate the extreme necessity of strong government, the nongovernmental situation can be described as a terrible and wretched condition in which

there is no place for industry, because the fruit thereof is uncertain; and consequently no culture of the Earth, no Navigation . . . no commodious building . . . no account of time; no arts; no letters; no Society; and which is worst of all, continual feare, and danger of violent death; and the life of man, solitary, poore, nasty, brutish and short (Hobbes, *Leviathan* [1651], Part I, Ch. XIII).

Or again, if one's argument is that man requires government, whilst not owing all advantages to it, the State of Nature can be portrayed as reasonably adequate, but still containing deficiencies which only a state structure can remedy (Locke, *Second Treatise of Government*, 1690).

Thus the Social Contract serves the intermediary function of explaining how man transforms his condition from the State of Nature to a proposed form of civil society. The particular form of contract used will bear the marks of this relationship, of its connection both with the condition it supposedly replaces and with that which it is intended to inaugurate.

If such an account of social and governmental origins sounds both involved and implausible, we might mention that there were influential factors promoting belief not only in a State of Nature, but also in the usual narrative accounts of its replacement by society and government. Thus, the notion of contract was made familiar by Old Testament accounts of covenant, such as those that God made with Noah, and with Abraham, and that at Hebron between King David and the elders

of Israel. Once the Christian faith gained predominance in Europe, belief in the absolute historical accuracy of the Old Testament was, for many centuries, largely taken for granted. The one society of which men had early records appeared to be founded on covenant or compact, so what could be more plausible than to assume a somewhat similar origin for other societies?

That the notion of contract is also, and more usually, associated with legal and commercial terminology is a further important factor explaining its acceptance. For what metaphor could be more apt in aiding the understanding of a certain conception of government, than one derived from an activity with which men were familiar in their daily life?

**Greece and Rome.** The use of contract by the Greeks, whilst not having the significance it was later to acquire, does at least indicate the comparatively secular nature of their political thought. Being notable constitution framers, idolizing the great lawmakers, they were easily convinced that laws were the work of man rather than of the gods. Contractual views were certainly not widely held, but they were prevalent. Among the better known accounts of contract is the version in Plato's *Republic* (359a); Glaucon suggests that "men decide they would be better off if they made a compact neither to do wrong nor to suffer it. Hence they began to make laws and covenants with one another." In Plato's *Crito*, Socrates informs us of a practice that was later to become closely connected with contract theory: he presents the device whereby contract theorists allow for the consent of those citizens dwelling in the state in the period after its inception. This consists of the notion of tacit consent, in which all people dwelling within the state are assumed, merely by their continued residence within its boundaries, to consent to the laws that have been made.

Further hints of contract can be found in the writings of the Sophists, the school of Diogenes (the Cynics), Epicurus, Xenophon, and occasionally in Roman writings of the fourth century, but on the whole such sporadic use of the term is of interest mainly on account of later developments. Thus far the contract was used as a means of reinforcing obedience to law. That it might also provide the basis for resistance against the state was not yet apparent.

It is worth pointing out that those occasional writers who maintained a belief in contract were referring to a contract of government, rather than one of society. The latter only emerged from the later postulate of natural individualism, which neither the Greeks nor the Romans held. With Aristotle, they regarded man as naturally social, as the conscious instigator of government, but not as the creator of society.

***The Middle Ages.*** Following the decline of the Roman Empire, Roman law lived on into the Middle Ages, and became integrated into the philosophy of practically all writers. Hints of governmental contract do exist, but more generally the state was regarded as a consequence of sin, a divine punishment, in which the king was sent by God to execute His wrath on evildoers. However, monarchical power was not granted arbitrary usage, either from above or below. Exhortations to the king to rule in the common good were made in thousands. This already implied monarchical obligation to the ruled, the idea of which was familiarized through the Roman law concept of *Lex Regia,* and had been given early practical expression in the German successor-kingdoms of the Western Roman Empire. Such belief in the reciprocal obligations between monarch and people was made more explicit in the coronation oath. This in itself was a form of governmental contract, in the sense that the authority of the king was not accepted unless he had bound himself by oath to provide just and good government.

The use of contract as a basis for conditional popular resistance to government, most frequently associated with the name of Locke, was already apparent in the eleventh-century writings of Manegold of Lautenbach. In his view a monarch who oppresses his people breaks the contract, and thereby absolves the ruled from any further obligations of obedience. Not only was obedience no longer obligatory, but actual rebellion was justifiable, for a king who degenerates into a tyrant should be expelled like an unfaithful shepherd. This precursor of later theories, it is only fair to mention, had little influence among his contemporaries. It was only two centuries later that Saint Thomas Aquinas presented somewhat similar ideas to a wider audience. However, his radicalism was reserved for the exceptional occasion, his main theme being one of obedience to the accepted traditional order of church and king. More clearly radical were the political ideas Marsiglio of Padua and Bartolus of Sassoferrato derived from the north Italian city-states of the fourteenth century. They both regarded authority as stemming from the people, and provided for the removal of governments infringing the constitutional laws by which they were bound. Bartolus comes close to contract theory in stressing the obligations of a *pactum* which a Prince makes with his city, but the notion is not given a central place in his thought.

With the rise of "divine right" theory, belief in contract was adapted to a changed ideological environment, thereby losing its primary character as a curb on monarchical power. Now it was not so much the king who was bound to rule for the good of the people,

as the people who henceforth became bound to obey their king. Thus, by the fourteenth and fifteenth centuries the origin of the state was seen to derive from a contract of *subjection,* an act in which obligations rather than rights received the main emphasis; a conception of contract forwarded primarily by Engelbert of Volkersdorf (1250–1311) and Nicholas of Cusa (1401–64).

The relevance of the Middle Ages to the contract theory is not that this period was one in which contract was as explicitly formulated, or as fully developed as it was later to become. Rather it is that it thoroughly prepared the ground for later theories of Social Contract. The metaphor is not inapt, for it was the dominant system of land tenure, that of feudalism, which familiarized all classes of society with the contractual idea. Thus these contract theorists stressing reciprocal rights did more than just imitate the spirit of the early coronation oath, for, in some respects, they reflected the pattern of obligation that was typical of feudal society. The whole feudal system was cemented by relationships of mutual rights and duties between lord and vassal, a system which recognized individual rights even to the extent of allowing the vassal to reject the contract if the lord had not abided by its terms. That these reciprocal obligations extended up the social scale even as far as the monarch was, perhaps, particularly evident in England, for Magna Carta (1215), although no more than an agreement between king and barons, was at least an indication that the king was to be regarded as an integral part of society, rather than as an unlimited, all-powerful ruler controlling from the "outside." Thus throughout the Middle Ages in England the conception remained of the king as having been drawn into the web of political obligation. This was much less the case in France, where successive monarchs continued to stress their theocratic function of obligation to God, and God alone. In general, however, the embodiment in law and in the social consciousness of the contractual relationships of feudalism predisposed men to regard the contract as a guarantor of rights, and a basis of legitimate government—attitudes which eventually replaced the view of the contract as an act of total subjection.

The medieval conception of contract, formed in a period when the church had intellectual predominance, was later used by minority Protestant groups of the Reformation era. It was thus that the notion of a proper Social Contract came to be formulated, and the use of contract as a democratic device more fully developed. It will be clear that belief in the "divine right of kings" is profoundly undemocratic, presenting the idea that power and authority derive from God, and descend by delegation to the monarch, and so on, in ever smaller quantities, down the social scale. This "descending thesis" of authority provided no moral basis for dissent, as disobedience to the king implied disobedience to God.

Groups striving for religious freedom, however, needed a rationale for their rejection of the orthodox religious views. The Huguenot author (either Languet or Duplessis-Mornay) of the *Vindiciae contra tyrannos* (1579) justified the French wars of religion by stating the right of the people to oppose a king who persecutes religious truth, because such a king has broken the contract between God and the people. This was the Huguenot position so long as a Catholic monarch sat on the throne. With the accession of the Protestant Henry IV (1589), the Huguenots reverted to belief in the divine right of kings, whilst certain Catholics, most notably the Jesuits Juan Mariana, Luis Molina, and Francisco Suárez, became converted to the idea of Social Contract and to the right of resistance against tyrannical kings.

By this time men had learned to present rejection of divine right and disobedience to monarchy in a manner which did not involve rejection of religion as such. This theoretical feat was accomplished by the combination of Natural Law and Social Contract. The former notion provided a means by which the word of God could be received by the mind of man without the monarch acting as an intermediary. The moral need to heed the monarch's command was further eased by the belief associated with contract, that law derives from consent and that obedience to arbitrary rule is not obligatory.

The alignment of natural rights and contract is instructive, for the attempt to derive rights from a pre-social, natural condition led to the formulation of the initial contract as an act forming society, rather than an agreement between ruler and ruled in an already established state. In this manner arose the idea of a truly *social* contract. Rights deriving from God via nature, rather than from God via the king, thus provided a religious basis for opposition to tyranny. It is no coincidence, then, that Juan Mariana, writing in 1605, combines within the same work a compact of society and a justification of tyrannicide.

With his popularization of Social Contract theory in England, Richard Hooker (1552–1600) simultaneously provided an early example of a criticism that was eventually to hasten the theory's downfall. If some men found it useful to affirm the idea of a Social Contract, others found it equally useful to deny it. This they did by posing such questions as: "If the contract is the basis of society, what exactly are its terms? What evidence have we that a contract has actually been made?" Hooker does at least realize the importance of these difficulties. The terms, he tells us, "for the most part are either clean worn out of knowledge, or else known unto very few." It required the arrival of a more historically critical age before such unverified knowledge came to be considered an inadequate basis for an important social theory.

By the seventeenth century, with the writings of Althusius, and Grotius, the major period of Social Contract theory really begins. Emphasis comes to be placed on both the individual and society as being historically and logically prior to the monarchy and state. In this manner the "descending thesis" of government sank ever more into the background. Emphasis on Social Contract and government by consent led to the reformulation of what is called the "ascending thesis" of government. This is the belief that authority is delegated to government by society—from the ruled to the rulers—up, rather than down, the social scale.

The wide application of contract theory to seventeenth-century politics stems most immediately from its religious usage by Puritan groups in both England and America. A church was regarded as a voluntary association joined together in the pursuit of communally agreed religious aims. On fleeing to America, the persecuted religious minorities of western Europe thereby each became not merely a religious community, but also a political organization. In withdrawing from the allegiance of an oppressive state power, they became their own state in the same manner as they were already their own church. In this situation, allegiance to the state could only be based on the same principle that already governed allegiance to the church, that is, by voluntary agreement. In this way the notion of religious contract provided an immediate stimulus to the development of the idea of a Social Contract, a variation of which is found in the covenant made by the Pilgrim Fathers upon their arrival in New England in November 1620.

This same alignment of religious and political attitudes occurred in England without the stimulus of resettlement. We see this quite explicitly in the writings of the Leveller John Lilburne (ca. 1614–57). He had initially concentrated on the problems of religion, accepting the commonplace view that to reject the king's authority is equivalent to disobeying God. This approach did not survive his intermittent periods of imprisonment, during which time he submitted the question of the legitimacy of state power to deeper examination. About 1636 he had written of the church as a voluntary community of believers, bound together in order to pursue common religious aims. Once the English Civil War broke out, Lilburne aligned himself with the Parliamentary side, and began applying a similar approach to the composition of civil society. The consequence of this was the use of contract theory to justify disobedience against the monarchy. As Lilburne now saw it, the king had broken his contract with the people, thereby transforming their condition into a State of Nature. Men were in no way obliged to obey monarchical tyranny, and so the basic problem remaining was to remake the social-political contract, which the Levellers actually attempted to do by means of their first "Agreement of the People" (1647).

Following the execution of Charles I "contract theory became what may almost be called the official theory of the Commonwealth party" (Gough, p. 99). Cromwell declared "the king is king by contract"; the poet John Milton went further still, declaring that society is based on contract, but monarchy rests only on trust. In his view

The power of kings and magistrates is nothing else, but what is only derivative, transferred and committed to them in trust from the people to the common good of them all, in whom the power yet remains fundamentally, and cannot be taken from them, without a violation of their natural birthright (*The Tenure of Kings and Magistrates*, 1649).

***The Age of Social Contract.*** With the English Civil War begins the century and a half in which Social Contract theory was most predominant. The reasons for this are not hard to find when one considers the problems which men sought to solve by this method. These were usually concerned with the origins and legitimacy of government, and the vital question of when governments might rightfully be disobeyed. It was such issues which were directly relevant in a period encompassing the English Civil War, the establishment of new communities in North America, the English "Glorious Revolution" of 1688, the American Revolution of 1776, and the French Revolution of 1789. The major long-term consequence of these various upheavals was the practical inauguration of the liberal democracy which still predominates in Western society today. Though our modern state system may have arrived by force of arms, the values associated with it were only considered secure once it had won the philosophical battle against its predecessors. It was here that the idea of Social Contract played a crucial role.

Perhaps we should consider whether the framework in which obligation to obey government is presented may not logically impel the theorist towards a certain limited range of conclusions. At first sight such a suggestion seems implausible, as the various values held by Social Contract theorists cover such a large area of the political spectrum. However, we must note that, whatever their differences, Social Contract theorists

did hold some assumptions in common. One of the major presuppositions implicit in this particular approach concerns the degree of man's possible control over his environment. It seems that users of the Social Contract method are disposed towards viewing society as artificial rather than natural, primarily as being the work of man rather than of God or of Nature. In consequence, we often find those who accept this method having an attitude towards religion somewhat at variance with that of their opponents. They see the world of man as deriving from man's own will, rather than being merely the expression of external forces. This is certainly not to say that people holding such views were atheists, even if their opponents occasionally regarded them as such, for belief in God does not necessarily imply His being given a continuous central role in the human drama.

Coupled with belief in the human creation of society is the strong emphasis placed on the idea of consent. Contract is presented as a voluntary agreement of those who will be bound by the rules of the system they establish. In this we see the emergence of our contemporary notions of individual freedom and the self-determination of peoples, for the implication is that the authority of the system derives from the free consent of those who compose it, rather than from the commands of God or king. In this sense the contract's radical function was as a justification of the breakdown of the "descending thesis" of government. Although Richard Hooker accepted the view that some kings might possibly rule by divine right, his view was the exception rather than the rule among Social Contract theorists. More typical was the attack on divine right made by Locke in the first of his *Two Treatises of Government.*

Connected with belief in the importance of consent, we tend to find the notion of the individual as the possessor of certain inalienable rights, which the contract is intended to secure, and which the state should not infringe. This is the manner in which contract reinforced arguments for limiting government and exalting the individual, and was the basis on which resistance was considered justified against those governments not abiding by the terms of the supposed contract.

In postulating natural freedom and natural equality, in providing a basis for the notion of merely conditional obedience to government, the Social Contract was used as a framework for a theory that had potentially disruptive implications for any society with a predominantly aristocratic power structure. The emphasis on government by consent made Social Contract a weapon against not only the divine right of kings, but against any form of absolute government. As good a

255

justification of government by consent as we are likely to find was provided by the Leveller Col. Rainborough:

Really, I think that the poorest he that is in England hath a life to live as the greatest he: and therefore truly, Sir, I think it's clear that every man that is to live under a government ought first by his own consent to put himself under that government: and I do think that the poorest man in England is not at all bound in a strict sense to that government that he hath not had a voice to put himself under (Clarke, p. 301).

To base obligation on consent may not have been original, but it was still a highly radical proposal in the hierarchical societies of seventeenth-century Europe.

However, the full scope of the theoretical potentialities of Social Contract was rarely apparent to those who used the method. What to us may sound like the thin edge of a democratic wedge did not always contain such implications for the men of the seventeenth century. Government might be said to rest on consent, power might be thought of as deriving from the people, but in such instances all that was meant was that the wealthy and influential classes might provide a curb against the possible excesses of the monarchy. Rarely was it suggested that the laboring masses of the population also possessed full natural rights. "The people" connoted those who were habitually regarded as entitled to take part in the political process, and no others. This political assumption again is correlated with contemporary religious views. Thus, the New England Puritans clearly distinguished between their own congregation and the unregenerate remainder of mankind. The right to liberty was thought of in terms of rights for their own religious liberty, rather than as rights for all men irrespective of their religious beliefs. Yet, if these various groups had no intention of formulating a theory of popular sovereignty, that was just the way that others were eventually led by the logic of their anti-absolutist argument. Not for the first time in the history of thought did works of philosophy become associated with movements which their authors would have rejected.

So we see that consent need not imply democracy unless consent refers to the consent of all concerned. In the same manner Social Contract need not necessarily imply liberal democracy unless the contract is given liberal democratic terms. It has been argued that this was the general tendency during the seventeenth and eighteenth centuries. This, however, should not blind us to an important counter-current, the most notable example of which consists of Hobbes' revival of the contract of subjection. In his *Leviathan* (1651) Hobbes contended that men should regard government as if they had made a contract with it, of such a kind as to

confer all their power and strength upon one man, or upon one assembly of men that may reduce all their wills, by plurality of voices, unto one will: which is as much as to say, to appoint one man, or assembly of men, to bear their person; and every one to own, and acknowledge himself to be author of whatsoever he that so beareth their person, shall act, or cause to be acted, in those things which concern the common peace and safety; and therein to submit their wills, everyone to his will, and their judgements, to his judgement (p. 89).

This surrender of rights, this establishment of almost uncontrolled sovereignty, is not advocated as a unilateral individual act. It is a contract only to be made by "every man with every man." Behind the much criticized absolutism of Hobbes is the basic belief that peace and security are the initial prerequisites of human society, and are to be pursued even at the cost of certain individual freedoms. The State of Nature is so disadvantageous that extreme measures are justified in saving mankind from relapsing into it. Whereas contract had usually been regarded as a means of limiting sovereign power, with Hobbes such power is placed outside the restraints of contract. The people make an agreement with each other, but not with the sovereign. This is a logical derivation from Hobbes' belief that "Covenants, without the Sword, are but Words, and of no strength to secure a man at all." Agreements are only valid when there is a superior power to enforce them. In the State of Nature covenants are void, for there is no power to enforce compliance. In civil society, there can be no agreements with the sovereign, because there can, by definition, be no superior power to enforce obedience. Thus the sovereign is still in the State of Nature in respect of his relations with the society he rules. He is not bound by any obligations to the people. Thus

there can happen no breach of Covenant on the part of the Soveraigne; and consequently none of his Subjects, by any pretence of forfeiture, can be freed from his Subjection.

That Hobbes' views clashed violently with the more general "spirit of the age" is evident from even the most cursory acquaintance with late seventeenth-century opinion. Conservatives were offended by Hobbes' neglect of divine right, whilst radicals rejected his absolutism. Somewhat similar hostility greeted Spinoza's *Tractatus theologico-politicus* (1670), a work strongly influenced by the writings of Hobbes, and in which Spinoza held that "the sovereign is bound by no law, and that all citizens must obey it in all things." Such a contract of submission was again based on the need for defense against insecurity, and was presented as a necessity "advised by reason itself."

In spite of these pronouncements, the individualist and democratic kernel of contract theory could not be entirely ignored. Hobbes may have written of the individual surrendering all rights of governing himself, and of his authorizing all the actions of the sovereign, even to the extent that "every Subject is Author of every act the Soveraign doth," yet he only applied this within the limits imposed by Natural Law. Thus certain rights were maintained by the individual, and situations were envisaged in which disobedience to the sovereign was justified. First, man was at liberty to disobey if the sovereign command him to kill himself, as this was contrary to the Law of Nature "by which we are forbidden to do anything destructive of our own life." Second, he need not allow other men to kill him, even though the sovereign demand it, for the Right of Nature stipulates "the liberty each man hath, to use his own power, as he will himselfe, for the preservation of his own Nature." Likewise, a man interrogated by the sovereign concerning a crime he has committed, is not bound to confess, for there is a Law of Nature that "no man . . . can be obliged by Covenant to accuse himselfe." Finally, the obligation to obey the sovereign is conditional upon the provision of security, for which purpose government is established. Thus, the apparent total absolutism of Hobbes is limited within the individualist demands of Natural Law. This is not to say that the individual is granted explicit rights of resistance against the sovereign, but merely that circumstances are envisaged in which obedience is neither obligatory nor rational.

In spite of these individualist concessions, is the Hobbes-Spinoza position one which enables us to deny any logical connection between contract and democracy? I would argue not, and would assert the contrary proposition that their position actually highlights an important paradox in democratic theory. In spite of the apparent surrender of numerous rights to a nearly unlimited sovereign, we must bear in mind that the resulting condition is still one of voluntary contract, representing a definite choice by the members of society. That this choice is a strange one, that submission may not seem a particularly worthwhile action, is not denied. Choice is still choice, whether other people find it rational or not. Social Contract theory, being based on consent, may support all manner of values that the people might hold. In exactly the same way democratic elections may be the means by which the widest conceivable range of governments come to power. This wide range of conceivable contracts, however, does not mean that Social Contract theory has no specific values attached to it. The right to choose

is a value, even though shared basic premises may lead to widely divergent conclusions. Belief in the right of choice does not logically provide a limitation of the range of choice. The difficulty occurs if we envisage a situation in which the people may choose not to choose. The contract of submission can be a self-annihilating contract, in the same way that freedom to commit suicide can be a self-annihilating freedom, or the choice of Bonapartist or totalitarian governments can be a choice annihilating use of democratic rights. The contract of submission, then, is an extreme; it is an act of voluntary surrender on a par with the democratic choice of governments which destroy democracy. Freedom, at its full extent, includes the freedom to extinguish freedom. This paradox is shared by both Social Contract theory and democratic theory, and as such serves to demonstrate their similarities rather than their differences.

In spite of Hobbes and Spinoza, it is generally true to say that by the end of the seventeenth century those writers who were most virulent in their attacks on Social Contract were also those who held basically antiradical views. They rejected the presumptuous notion that man could have been the creator of the imposing hierarchical edifice of society. The views previously forwarded by James I of England, that the people could not limit monarchy, that rule was by hereditary right according to the will of God, and that God was the only judge of whether the coronation oath had been infringed, were all sympathetically revived in the writings of Sir Robert Filmer. In his *Patriarcha; or the Natural Power of Kings* (1680), Filmer argued that monarchy was natural rather than conventional. Royal power derived from paternal power, as granted at the creation by God to Adam. Since that time this power had been transferred by hereditary right to the various sovereigns, who are regarded as Adam's heirs. The power of the sovereign, then, derives from God, and can in no way be limited by the king's subjects. Natural equality and freedom were condemned as contrary to biblical evidence, as were "such imaginery pactions between Kings and their people as many dream of." Leaving aside the weighty question of historical evidence, Filmer asks whether the contractual act could be considered plausible. Was it likely that men in a State of Nature could ever agree on the form a contract was to take? Were they to do so, why should their terms be binding on subsequent generations? All in all Filmer regarded the idea of contract as practically implausible, socially pernicious, and theologically heretical, views which were readily received by the more conservative sections of English society, and which John Locke attempted to refute in his famous *Two Treatises of Government*.

In 1688 the Convention parliament had passed a resolution declaring that King James II of England had "endeavoured to subvert the constitution of the kingdom by breaking the original contract between king and people." It was Locke's intention to justify the so-called "Glorious Revolution" which deposed King James, thereby to "establish the Throne of Our present King William; to make good his Title, in the Consent of the People." This required the justification of conditional rights against the monarchy, and the rejection of Filmer's belief in the divine right of kings. To do this Locke meets Filmer on his own ground, the writings of the Old Testament. Both men fully accepted the Bible as historically accurate, Locke merely claiming that Filmer had misinterpreted the texts. In Locke's view

Adam . . . being neither Monarch, nor his imaginary Monarchy hereditable, the Power which is now in the World, is not that which was Adam's since all that Adam could have . . . either of Property or Fatherhood, necessarily Died with him, and could not be convey'd to Posterity by Inheritance.

In addition, there is no divine law of primogeniture, nor is there any evidence that the monarchs of the world were actually descended from Adam. In reply to Filmer's rejection of contract, Locke manages to disprove Filmer's argument on divine right.

As a replacement for it, Locke takes a position characteristic of Social Contract theory, that civil society has been consciously constructed by men. This presupposition is fully accepted as a fact of history, no less true for being unrecorded, and no less important for being of long vintage. In reply to the appeal for evidence of an original State of Nature, Locke provides an explanation, ingenious rather than convincing, which amply demonstrates his faith in reason as the key to historical knowledge. Thus

it is not at all to be wonder'd, that History gives us but very little account of Men, that lived together in the State of Nature . . . if we may not suppose Men ever to have been in the State of Nature, because we hear not much of them in such a state, we may as well suppose the armies of Salmanasser, or Xerxes, were never Children, because we hear little of them, till they were Men, and imbodied in Armies. Government is everywhere antecedent to Records . . . For 'tis with Commonwealths as with particular Persons, they are commonly ignorant of their own Births and Infancies.

With regard to the consequences Locke draws from contract, they certainly would have appeared pernicious to those sharing Filmer's approach. With Locke the act by which individuals mutually agree to leave the State of Nature is referred to as a "compact." It is only consent "which did, or could give beginning to any lawful Government in the World." Meaningful consent, however, is confined to history, for after the creation of society consent becomes tacit rather than explicit, and is signified by mere residence within the territory of a government.

Locke clearly differentiated the origins of society from the establishment of government, a point he might have learned from Pufendorf's *De jure naturae et gentium* (1672). Pufendorf saw society as resting on two covenants and a decree. The first covenant forms society, the decree settles the particular form of government, whilst by the second covenant sovereign power is constituted. Locke accepted the importance of differentiating between society and government, but explained it in rather a different way. The agreements embodied in compact are of a character in which all sides are equally bound. Locke found this type of agreement eminently suitable to describe his notion of the social relationships of mankind, but quite unsuitable as a description of the strictly political relationship that he wished to advocate. For Locke the people and their rulers were not on a par, not equally bound by arrangements made between them. Rather, he believed that the government was the servant of society, bound by the provisions for which it had been constituted by the people. To express this relationship Locke made use of the common seventeenth-century notion of "trust." The main obligation this entails is that the government should serve to implement the will of the people. Its role is, therefore, passive; it forfeits its legitimate authority when it formulates a will of its own, and seeks to distort, alter, or silence the voice of the people.

This explains why the notion of contract was only of limited use to Locke, why he sought to differentiate the inauguration of society from the establishment of government, and why he has come to be regarded as a radical. If security is to be maintained in the general interest, then the people must be dominant. If the people are to be dominant, the government must be subservient. A contractual relationship would have put the rights of the government on a par with those of the ruled, whereas one of trust stipulates their subservience. Thus rule is exercised on the people's terms, the way apparently being left open for the creation of the conditions they desire. When a breach of this trust occurs, power quite simply "devolves to the People," for "Governments are dissolved . . . when the legislative, or the Prince . . . act contrary to their trust." This conditional right of resistance is Locke's justification of the events of 1688.

If "trust" is used to limit arbitrary power, "compact" is used to delineate the proper scope of government. This is done by means of his description of the State of Nature. We have already mentioned that the State of Nature, in describing man prior to government, serves to demonstrate what man owes to government. With Hobbes man owes virtually everything to government, his security, trade, culture, and knowledge. With Locke this is not so. Locke's vision of the State of Nature includes a market economy, wage labor, large landed estates, and the use of money. The only thing men lack is a "common Judge to Appeal to on Earth for the determination of Controversies of Right betwixt them." The function of proposing such an implausible situation is to stress that economic activity and the basic rules of personal relationships do not derive their impetus from the state. His positing a tolerable pre-political condition derives from an attitude in which government is seen as of merely supplementary importance. The function of the state is not to control the economy, but rather to ensure conditions of safety in which a presumably self-regulating economy can operate. Similarly, the function of Locke's placing freedom in the natural pre-social stage is to demonstrate that this freedom does not derive from government, which merely guarantees it. Thus, Locke's positing of natural rights, of property accumulation prior to the social compact, and of the limitation on state power imposed by the notion of trust, are all intended to protect the individual from the encroachments of governmental power.

The complete rejection of the contract of government is also found in Rousseau's *Du contrat social* (1762). Here it is made clear that only the establishment of society can be based on a contract, for the role of government is one that precludes them from a position of being able to bargain with the people. Sovereign power belongs to the people, the government merely being their servants, and having no right to complain about their conditions of service.

Thus, those theorists who deny that the act by which a people submits itself to leaders is a contract are wholly correct. For that act is nothing other than a commission, a form of employment in which the governors, as simple officers of the sovereign, exercise in its name the power it has placed in their hands . . . (*The Social Contract*, trans. M. Cranston, p. 102).

We noted with Locke how the solely social contract was a means of alleviating fears of governmental tyranny. A similar purpose was obviously shared by Rousseau, who took numerous opportunities of ridiculing the contract of subjection, which he associated with Hobbes and Grotius. Such an act he saw as sheer madness.

. . . and right cannot rest on madness. . . . Whether as between one man and another, or between one man and a whole people, it would always be absurd to say: "I hereby make a covenant with you which is wholly at your expense and wholly to my advantage; I will respect it so long as I please and you shall respect it so long as I wish" (ibid., pp. 54, 58).

Thus far it might appear as if Rousseau and Locke had both used Social Contract for the same purpose of securing individual rights. This, apparently, was Rousseau's purpose. The object of the Social Contract, he told us, is to

find a form of association which will defend the person and goods of each member with the collective force of all, and under which each individual, while uniting himself with the others, obeys no one but himself, and remains as free as before (ibid., p. 60).

Rousseau differs from Locke in that he does not allow the people a right to decide the terms of the contract, for these are invariable, being logically determined by the problem they are designed to solve. Thus the contract can be revoked, but not amended. Its institution requires unanimity, and its terms allow the body politic absolute power over all its members. It also involves the total alienation of the individual and his property to the community.

However, the contract itself is not dominant in Rousseau's overall plan. Once it has been concluded, it sinks into a place of secondary importance. Its major function is then seen as the means by which the people consent to the condition, not of liberal individualism, but of extreme social cohesion guaranteed by adherence to the General Will.

The General Will expresses the common interest of all the citizens. It is what each individual would will if he saw what his real interests were. It can be arrived at when the correct attitude of mind is displayed, when men manage to subordinate their personal and sectional interests. Such an achievement is not a mark of high intellectual endeavor, but merely of simplicity and honesty, such as Rousseau assumed to exist among the Swiss peasantry. It was rather in the inane sophistication of urban society that men made government more complex than need be, by giving their own selfish aims priority over the good of the whole community. If such people can learn to will the General Will, so much the better. If not, Rousseau suggested, they "will be forced to be free." This apparent contradiction is explained by pointing out that all people really want to follow their best interests, without always knowing what they are. To allow them to follow a false path would be to deny them their aim, and so decrease, rather than increase their freedom. The assumption behind this is that the good of each individual is to be found within the General Will. Society as a whole is given overwhelming predominance over its parts. All is merged within the General Will.

Such a theory has led to the plausible suggestion that in guarding against the dangers of the governmental contract of subjection, Rousseau had unwittingly replaced it with a Social Contract of subjection. Rousseau would argue that man, being a member of such a society, could not be in a state of subjection to it, for the body cannot wish to hurt its parts. The Social Contract, by placing sovereignty in society, ensures rule in the interests of society. This is in contrast to a governmental contract, which, in granting sovereignty to the government, thereby ensures rule solely in the interests of the government.

At this point we must note that, unlike Locke, Rousseau did not regard the contract as a historical reality. Rather it was an "ideal," an arrangement that would have to be made were political right to be instituted. Hobbes had likewise suggested his system as an "ideal," but was far more optimistic regarding its practical inauguration. "I recover some hope," he wrote, "that one time or other, this writing of mine, may fall into the hands of a Soveraign, who will . . . convert this Truth of Speculation, into the Utility of Practice." Rousseau had no such hopes. Men might strive after his ideal, but were destined never to reach it, for individual wills are always threatening to undermine the dominance of the General Will. "The body politic, no less than the body of a man, begins to die as soon as it is born, and bears within itself the causes of its own destruction" (ibid., p. 134). *Du contrat social*, then, is not a call to arms. It is a criticism of existing states, the portrayal of an ideal, carrying little hope that the ideal will be put into practice. Rousseau's influence, however, was considerable, his theories having been frequently invoked by Robespierre and Saint-Just during the French Revolution. However, it might be thought that their attempts to establish an ideal political order merely served to confirm Rousseau's warning, found in *The Origin of Inequality:*

People once accustomed to masters are not in a condition to do without them. They nearly always manage, by their revolutions, to hand themselves over to seducers, who only make their chains heavier than before.

With Rousseau the line of major Social Contract theorists came to an end. Belief in contract continued into the nineteenth century, but its significance was greatly decreased—alternative grounds for political obligation being considered preferable. However, the notion, increasingly discarded by the political philosophers, was still found useful by practicing politicians, and nowhere more so than in North America. It was here that belief in the historical validity of contract was most firmly and plausibly rooted, and here also that, in the second half of the eighteenth century, the problem of obligation to government was most clearly at the forefront of political concern. The writings of this period abound with accounts of contract or compact. We find it, for example, in the *Boston Gazette* of 1766, in the 1772 "Rights of the Colonists," the latter largely written by Samuel Adams, and in the views proclaimed by the General Court of Massachusetts on January 23, 1776.

Usually it is a contract of government, rather than of society, to which reference is made. A common theme was that George III had broken the contract by which the American colonists gave allegiance to the British crown. The action of the colonists was viewed not as rebellion, but as resistance to the illegal use of authority. Their original right was to institute government on the basis of the consent of the ruled. Were these conditions no longer fulfilled, the people could reallocate political power in the manner they found most suitable. Perhaps it was this preoccupation with the exact terms of the origins of government that led a newly independent United States of America to make its distinctive contribution to modern political practice in the formulation of a written constitution. Certainly there was a widespread view that the constitution was a governmental contract instituted for the purpose of limiting state power and guaranteeing individual rights.

It is probably no mere coincidence that by the closing years of the eighteenth century the only notable English advocate of Social Contract was Tom Paine, a man who had fought in the American army during the War of Independence.

In *The Rights of Man* (1791) Paine uses the explanatory form we have already found in Locke's writings— that is, to speak of society as based on "compact," and government on "trust." Paine's usage of these terms, however, is more satisfactory than Locke's attempt to prove that the compact was a historical reality. Thus, like Rousseau, he stated not that all government and society had been formed in this way, but that they ought to be. A compact between the people "to produce a government . . . is the only mode in which Governments have a right to exist." The government is neither a superior body nor an equal partner with the people. It is a trustee, with duties rather than rights, obliged to serve rather than command. In practice Paine saw "compact" and "trust" as reaching a mutual alignment through a constitution. The constitution is a compact; it contains the terms according to which the people agree to form their society. It is the arrangement they make with each other; it is also the limitation within which government is contained. Without a constitution a government has full legislative freedom, for good or ill, during its period of office. Where there is a constitution, this freedom is curtailed; the people maintain their basic rights. "Government without a constitution is power without a right." The examples of this ideal, and mankind's hope for the future, Paine saw in the recently inaugurated governments of the United States of America and France. This he hailed as the end of violence and superstition. The Age of Reason was coming into being. The social compacts of America and France had been its inauguration; and in their constitutional form, its guarantee.

By this time use of the contract was in decline even among those consciously adhering to the views of Locke. Thus we find in his *Observations on the Nature of Civil Liberty* (London and Boston, 1776), that Richard Price had shown himself not particularly concerned with the origins of the state. What now seemed of far more value was the Lockean notion of a trust between rulers and ruled. It was in Germany, rather than England, that, particularly under the influence of Rousseau, the notion of contract continued to find favor. Not least among the reasons for this is the fact that the German philosophical tradition has always been more juristically inclined than its English counterpart, and so was better able to absorb a term with strong legal connotations. Thus in Fichte's *Grundlage des Naturrechts* (1796), we are granted the luxury of three contracts as an explanation of the state. The first is the property contract, which leads on to the second, the protection contract, and finally the union contract (*Vereinigungsvertrag*). Kant's *Philosophy of Right* (*Rechtlehre*), appearing in the same year, contained no pretense that the contract was a historical reality. It was merely to be regarded as an "idea of reason," by means of which the relationship between the individual and the state might be better understood.

***The Decline.*** It is clear that by the end of the eighteenth century acceptance of the idea of Social Contract was in rapid decline. It may seem strange that the explanatory method of Locke and Rousseau came under most serious attack just at the time when the views they held were at their most influential. Such, however, was the case. The hundred years separating the English from the French Revolution contain the most explicit arguments both for and against Social Contract.

Not that rejection of Social Contract was anything new. An important body of opinion had never accepted it. The publication of Hobbes' *Leviathan* had previously stimulated numerous hostile replies based on the implausibility of supposing that men in a State of Nature could ever have made a Social Contract. The celebrated Sacheverell trial of 1710 was faced with the tricky historical question of whether the original contract was made before Magna Carta, and if so why no mention of the contract was to be found within it. Answers to questions such as these were increasingly demanded, and decreasingly supplied, thereby gradually reducing the value that could be derived from the use of Social Contract theory.

The major eighteenth-century attack on Social Contract appeared in David Hume's essay "Of the Original Contract" (1748). Here it is suggested that we have no evidence of a Social Contract ever having taken place, and, in any case, the very idea is "far beyond the comprehension of savages" in the State of Nature. It was clear to Hume that the idea was spread by philosophers, for the ordinary person does not usually act as if his allegiance to government stems from contract. In fact, "were you to ask the far greatest part of the nation, whether they had ever consented to the authority of their rulers, or promis'd to obey them, they would be inclined to think very strangely of you." Government, Hume concludes, "was formed by violence, and submitted to from necessity." Any legitimacy that may attach to it derives from gradual acceptance, rather than from original explicit consent. This criticism, of course, only applied to thinkers such as Locke, who regarded the contract as a historical event, and not to those who considered the contract as an act that ought to take place. It was as a philosophical inquiry of the way in which society should be understood, or the structure it ought to have, that the Social Contract method was best suited. Nevertheless an increasingly historical attitude towards society was one of the main factors leading to the rejection of Social Contract, even though not all of its proponents had regarded the contract as a historical reality.

We might note that rejection of contract on grounds of its historical implausibility did not immediately result in a major attempt to find a historically accurate account of the state's origins. Rather the question of historical origins was deemed irrelevant to the problem of political legitimacy and obligation. Philosophical criteria, which had always been taken into account, became, with the rise of utilitarianism, the sole standard. Such an approach had actually been near the surface even with the most important Social Contract theorists. Thus Hobbes passed lightly over the question of the state's actual origins, merely pointing out that men should behave "as if" a contract had been made. Also his "commonwealth by acquisition" had exactly

261

similar claims to obedience as the "commonwealth by institution"; a foreign conqueror was to be obeyed for the same reasons as an indigenous monarch. In the last resort the criterion of obligation was not so much that of origins, as that of performance. If protection is secured, then obedience is the only rational reaction.

Signs of emergent utilitarianism also occur in Locke's justification of both property and political power according to the criterion of beneficial use. Property can be owned to the extent that it can be used—none must go to waste. Political power can be rightfully exercised only in accordance with the aims for which it was supposedly instituted. Locke, therefore, is torn between alternative modes of political legitimacy—the one based on origins, stressing the importance of the correct method of institution, and the other based on practice, stressing that the rulers should govern in accord with the purposes for which government was supposedly first instituted.

We have already mentioned the way in which contract was given a radical function by being used as a means whereby conditional resistance to state power could be justified. By the end of the eighteenth century this usage was all but discarded, in response to the gradual realization that the method's apparent radicalism had inherent limitations. The belief in contract began to appear double-edged; radical when presented in terms of an improvement, either as an old standard to which society ought to return (Locke), or as a new agreement that ought to be made in order to remedy current deficiencies (Rousseau); but static when presented as an agreement that has been made, is in force, and ought to be adhered to. Insofar as he used the notion of contract, Burke employed it in this latter sense. In his *Reflections on the Revolution in France* (1790), we learn of a contract that is in no way a Social Contract made by men. It has nothing to do with historical origins, free choice, or individual consent to government. Rather it is a kind of implicit understanding whereby the hierarchy of God, man, and nature is perpetually maintained.

Society is indeed a contract . . . but between those who are living, those who are dead, and those who are to be born. Each contract of each particular state is but a clause in the great primaeval contract of eternal society, linking the lower with the higher natures, connecting the visible and invisible world, according to a fixed compact sanctioned by the inviolable oath which holds all physical and all moral natures, each in their appointed place.

In the panic engendered by the French Revolution, Burke wished to stress obedience rather than resistance, duties rather than rights. Being a Whig, Burke might have found it useful to use Whig terminology, but he did so without impairing his aim, for he turned the notion of contract in a thoroughly conservative direction.

Burke's contemporary, William Godwin, was also aware of the conservative twist that could be applied to contract. The fact that it could be given this twist was one of Burke's reasons for accepting it in highly amended form, and Godwin's for rejecting it in any form. What troubled Godwin was the notion that a present generation could be shackled by decisions taken long before their time. This would be to deny the benefits of later knowledge. As such, a contract is an absurdity, for it can only have been made with the object of improving the human lot rather than impairing it. Thus the contract method was considered incompatible with the increasingly dominant Idea of Progress. Most sixteenth- and seventeenth-century opponents of contract had been believers in divine right, and had rejected the attempt to provide guarantees against misuse of state power. By the late eighteenth century it appeared that the form of these attempted guarantees also acted against hopes of continual improvement. Godwin criticized the contractualist assumption that improvement could be brought about by the immediate transformation of the unjust present into the just future. To be successful, such an act would have to be a miracle. Godwin saw as more likely a steady and continual process, in which knowledge always precedes novelty. This was the characteristic basis on which radicals came to reject the Social Contract. Improvement was desirable, but could only be achieved gradually. Progress came to be based on pseudo-scientific foundations, on apparent laws of historical development, rather than on the sudden decision of men totally to transform their society. An additional factor is that the contract was further discredited, at least in England, by its association with Rousseau and the French Revolution. The panic aroused served to create an atmosphere in which the least spark of discontent was rigorously suppressed, lest it flare into a conflagration beyond all human control. Those who had the courage to advocate reform had to do so without recourse to Social Contract or the "Rights of Man," for both were considered pernicious notions which, having reaped such havoc just across the English Channel, threatened to do likewise somewhere else.

By the nineteenth century the age of Social Contract theory was virtually at an end. The one country in which the idea remained current was that in which it had the most recent historical roots, the United States of America. Here we find it referred to in various debates on the nature of the Constitution, and of the relationship of the separate states to the central government. In 1831 John Quincy Adams suggested that the Massachusetts Constitution was a social compact and likewise the "Declaration of Independence was a social compact, by which the whole people covenanted with each citizen of the united colonies, and each citizen with the whole people, that the united colonies were, and of right ought to be, free and independent states." Final survivals of contract could be found in various state constitutions, as in those of Arkansas, until 1868, and Texas, where it reappeared in 1876, but as elsewhere, did not long survive the realization of its historical implausibility.

In Europe there was no longer any pretense that Social Contract had any historical reality, and yet there was a reluctance to discard an idea that had served the valuable purpose of emphasizing government by consent. The best that could be done was to accept contract merely as an idea expressing the moral relationship between ruler and ruled. Society could not be held together entirely by force; it still needed a kind of tacit contract, a feeling of moral obligation. It is in this sense that we find the idea employed by such diverse figures as Kant, the poet Samuel Taylor Coleridge, and later by T. H. Huxley. T. H. Green also ably defended this usage of contract by pointing out that "The supposition that some events took place that as a matter of history did not take place may be a way of conveying an essentially true conception of some moral relation of man." It was for this nonhistorical and nonlegal notion of contract that in 1896 the French politician Léon Bourgeois resurrected the term "quasi-contract," which had already been employed over a century earlier by Josiah Tucker, Dean of Gloucester. Yet even this extreme modification of contract theory was not enough to ensure its survival, for the contractualist position had been eroded on both flanks. First, there was the movement of thought which saw man no longer as the creator of his own environment, but rather as a being determined by wider forces operating according to inexorable historical laws. We have already seen how the idea of progress undermined Social Contract theory by its insistence that change could only be gradual rather than cataclysmic. This at least did not deny the role of human will in forming society. Once the idea of human progress was regarded as scientifically inevitable, laws of historical change, whether based on natural selection, or economic determinism, made the conscious role of human beings less significant. Secondly, Social Contract theory became redundant when its postulates of popular consent to government became more of a reality. The assumed consent of ancestors, or the assumed implicit consent of contemporaries gave way, at least in western Europe and North America, to the relatively frequent explicit choice of governments by increasingly large sections of the adult population. The general election thus rendered contract theory unnecessary by explicitly fulfilling its major demand.

The Social Contract, then, is no longer in favor. Its relevance for us, however, stems from its historical connection with the ideas of individual rights and government by consent. Social Contract thus remains of interest as the procedural mode which helped introduce the set of ideas which form the basis of contemporary liberal democratic thought.

*BIBLIOGRAPHY*

The major classical texts are: T. Hobbes, *Leviathan* (London, 1962); B. Spinoza, *Tractatus theologico-politicus* (1670); S. Pufendorf, *De jus naturae et gentium* (*Of the Law of Nature and of Nations*), trans. Basil Kennett (London, 1729); J. Locke, *Two Treatises of Government* (Cambridge, 1962); D. Hume, *Theory of Politics*, ed. F. Watkins (London, 1951); T. Paine, *The Rights of Man* (London, 1958). J. J. Rousseau, *The Social Contract*, trans. and Introduction Maurice Cranston (Harmondsworth, 1968).

The secondary material includes: F. Atger, *Essai sur l'histoire des doctrines du Contrat Social* (Nîmes, 1906); C. E. Vaughan, *Studies in the History of Political Philosophy before and after Rousseau*, 2 vols. (Manchester, 1925); idem, *The Political Writings of Jean Jacques Rousseau*, 2 vols. (Cambridge, 1915; Oxford, 1962); O. Gierke, *The Development of Political Theory* (London, 1939); E. Barker, *Social Contract* (London and New York, 1948); J. W. Gough, *The Social Contract* (Oxford, 1963); M. Levin, "Uses of the Social Contract Method: Vaughan's Interpretation of Rousseau," *Journal of the History of Ideas*, **28,** 4 (October–December, 1967). For Clarke, see his *Papers*, ed. C. H. Firth, Vol. I, Camden Society, N.S. **19** (1891), 301.

MICHAEL LEVIN

[See also **Balance of Power;** Conservatism; Democracy; Equality; **General Will;** Law, Ancient Greek, Ancient Roman; Liberalism; Nature; Primitivism; Progress; **Revolution; State;** Stoicism; Totalitarianism; Utopia.]

# SOCIAL DEMOCRACY IN GERMANY AND REVISIONISM

THE WORD "revisionism" carries approximately the same universal recognition and indefinite meaning as heresy did in the late Middle Ages. It needs both a heretic, an excommunicator, a body of ideas whose interpretation is at issue, and a community of believers exclusion from which is the penultimate, if not final, sanction. It is therefore a sociological or political as much as an intellectual or doctrinal phenomenon.

Hence no final objective definition of revisionism is really possible; it depends on historical circumstances as well as the body of ideas or beliefs at issue. In the present context the meaning of revisionism is best illustrated by examining the problem separately in its historical context, its intellectual structure, and finally in its current form of universalization. The origin of the particular word revisionism is historically linked with German Social Democracy before 1914 and this is where any discussion must start.

## I. THE HISTORICAL CONTEXT OF REVISIONISM

The growth of Social Democracy in Europe during the last quarter of the nineteenth century was primarily the result of the varying but generally intense rates of industrialization, and the growth and crystallization of an urban working class. In most countries of Western and Central Europe Social Democratic parties grew rapidly during this period. Their membership and electoral base were the least privileged strata of society, those who felt they had too little share in the social assets and economic benefits of existing society and were determined to obtain them. The ends were thus always social and economic, the means political; this alone already distinguished Social Democratic parties from all others. Secondly Socialist parties were the first mass political organizations in the history of Europe; their chief resource was numbers, their ideology almost invariably collectivist. While the working class constituted the major mass of organized participants and supporters, the direction, control, and programmatic articulation was, in most cases, in the hands of middle-class intellectuals, with occasionally a self-taught working man among them. But if the working man was not only the numerical raison d'être of Social Democratic politics, but also the idealized image of its beneficiary, there was little attempt at exclusivity; all supporters were welcome, and Social Democracy, as the representative of the future good society for all, regarded itself as much the bearer of a universal future as the here-and-now representative of a deprived working class. Partly because of the strong social and intellectual polarization in German society, partly because of the failure of German liberalism as a revolutionary or even reformist force, and most directly as the result of nearly twelve years of repression through special antisocialist laws, the German Social Democratic Party (SPD) from 1890 onwards was regarded as the most powerful and revolutionary party in the Second International—a model for all the others.

The SPD came into existence in 1875, the product of fusion between a primarily political organization founded in the 1860's by Ferdinand Lassalle and the more fundamentalist movement headed by Wilhelm Liebknecht and August Bebel, known as the *Eisenacher*. The party program adopted at the congress at Gotha incorporated many of the demands for political democracy of the Lassallean leaders, who hoped to use the existing Prussian-dominated imperial state for the benefits of the labor movement against the interests of the bourgeoisie. Marx strongly criticized the tenor of the party program; too many concessions to the Lassalleans for the sake of unity, too many fundamental departures from basic Marxism, especially in the reiteration of the so-called "iron law of wages," and neglect of the Marxist concepts of class struggle and social revolution. But though the Lassallean influence in the early years of the SPD provides one of the retrospective roots of revisionism, it should be born in mind that before 1890 there was no orthodoxy to "revise," but rather a strong pragmatic current for unity and an attempt to find an acceptable mean between different traditions and emphases in what was basically a movement of the socially dispossessed.

The differences between Marxists and Lassalleans, and the subsequent revisionist debate, were overtly about socialism—the means of reaching it, the way it would differ from capitalism, the antagonistic analysis of capitalism itself which in its own way helped to define its antipode, socialism. But in Germany particularly any argument over socialism had a core directly concerned with democracy. Socialists of whatever shades necessarily inherited the burden of the failure of the liberal-democratic revolution of 1848. Marx himself had realized this clearly when he edited the *Neue Rheinische Zeitung*. And Wilhelm Liebknecht, who founded in the 1860's what was later to become the SPD, always stressed liberal democratization as a here-and-now priority against the longer-term socialist and revolutionary perspectives of Marx in his London emigration. Marx opposed the Prusso-German state consistently; the Lassalleans regarded it as a means of crushing the real enemy, bourgeois capitalism. In this respect the Lassalleans represented an emphasis on socialism to which democracy was only a secondary factor—an authoritarian form of socialism, while the *Eisenachers* were democrats with a socialist tinge. The emerging supremacy of the Eisenacher leaders in the SPD during the fifteen years from 1875 to 1890 was partly due to the growing recognition that the German state was the main enemy of democracy; that democratization was impossible within its existing framework. The achievement of democracy thus remained the vital hidden issue beneath much of the socialist rhetoric of the SPD (Marx, *Critique of the Gotha Programme*, May 1875).

During the period of illegality and repression from

1878 to 1890 the SPD thus became much more radical and inclined to pin its hopes on revolution. As a party of anti-Prussian revolutionary democrats it turned away from Lassalle and to that extent towards Marx and his opposition of the German state. For twelve years the party's only permitted form of activity was participation in elections to the central German legislature (Reichstag); its votes rose from 311,961 in 1881 to 1,427,298 in 1890. A new program was adopted at the Erfurt congress of 1891, a year after the fall of Bismarck and the end of the antisocialist legislation. This new program was much more Marxist in content. It accepted specifically the main Marxist prediction of class struggle and social revolution and looked forward to a total transformation of society. The first part specifically articulated long-run predictions of social development—the first signs of ideological orthodoxy. The program also enumerated a set of short-run aims which the party would attempt to realize within the existing framework of capitalist society but whose effect was regarded as contributing materially to the ideological strengthening of the movement for the final assault on society as a whole. The maximum and the minimum program, as they came to be called, thus dealt with separate aspects of Social Democratic aims but were politically as well as ideologically linked to each other; not "either-or" but both. Marx himself had died in 1883, but Engels, who was now the official custodian of his ideas, approved substantially of the new program and only suggested a limited number of changes in phrasing. He also took this opportunity of publishing Marx's critique of the 1875 Gotha program for the first time in *Neue Zeit*, the theoretical organ of the SPD, as a commentary on the progress made, and to strengthen the hands of the stricter "Marxists" in the party. Particularly the leaders of the SPD had become more self-consciously Marxist as the party became more radical, and the impact of Marx's old critique and Engels' accompanying letters made a significant contribution in their struggle against the opponents of the new program before and at the 1891 Erfurt party congress.

The final version of what became known as the Erfurt program was one of several drafts. The party executive's own draft had been criticized earlier by Engels (Marx/Engels, *Werke*, Berlin, XXII, 225–40). Significantly it was the version prepared by Karl Kautsky, editor of *Neue Zeit* and chief theoretician of the SPD in Germany, which met Engels' approval and was adopted. The fact that this important document of principles and strategy was the work of the chief theoretician rather than of August Bebel, the political organizer and leader, provided the grounds for the problems of orthodoxy and heresy to which its inter-

pretation was to give rise during the revisionist controversy eight years later. For, it created an article of faith to which all subscribed, but at the same time this formal ritual of sanctification hid a good deal of practical flexibility for the political leadership who treated it as a symbol rather than a detailed program for action.

The Erfurt program committed the party to a fairly rigorous and self-consciously Marxist ideology. Both Marx and Engels had regarded the now dominant wing in the SPD as their own followers, though Marx had specifically refused to be associated with the party directly as an exiled leader or even as its mentor (Letter to Bracke, 5 May 1875, *Selected Works*, Moscow [1962], II, 15). After Marx's death Engels became less reticent; he helped all he could to combat the efforts of various prominent Social Democrats, among them the influential South German George von Vollmar, to opt for a more flexible and theoretically less rigorous program. From 1891 to 1898 various attempts were made to induce the party to accept specific departures from its program in order to exploit possibilities of obtaining electoral support, especially among the peasantry in South Germany. In addition the SPD leaders in South Germany, where official policies were less polarized and in some cases had a more democratic tradition, wanted to use their electoral strength for bargaining purposes in the state legislatures on a quid pro quo basis with bourgeois parties. The last decade of the nineteenth century was still a period of ideological crystallization in the SPD; it was felt that quite apart from political *practice*, the party program ought to permit such tactics. For some of the South German party leaders the Erfurt program, if strictly interpreted, actually involved a change in their traditional tactics; its implementation might endanger their success. A difference in interpretation thus began to emerge, between those of whom the Erfurt program was fast becoming traditional party policy and those who regarded it as a departure from traditional tactics. This conflict, not between innovators and traditionalists but between representatives of different traditions, came to play a significant part in the revisionist debate. But up to 1898 the great majority of party leaders and activists treated these specific attempts at tactical adjustment as part of the democratic process of open debate, and a solid Northern majority at party congresses defeated all attempts to tinker with the party program.

As the party grew in strength (measured both by membership and by voting support at elections) and as its organizational efficiency increased, it tended to become more inward looking and self-sufficient, both in its ideas and its organizational structure. Its enemies regarded the party's very existence as a threat to society, and this feeling began to be mirrored within the party itself. The last two decades of the century were a period of stability and economic growth; the party's militancy thus found expression in contemplating its own expansion and organizational consolidation rather than in industrial or political action. An important feature of this institutionalization of radicalism was the shift from ideological problems and debates to matters of internal and external tactics; the existence and progress of the party not only symbolized the correctness of the ideology expressed by the program, the party *was* the concrete expression of the ideology. The present proved that the past had correctly predicted the future, it therefore subsumed the future now. The old conflict between the application of correct Marxist theory and the political immediacy of a mass party in Germany seemed to have disappeared. When Engels just before his death protested vigorously against the heavily edited publication of his preface (1895) to a new edition of Marx's *Class Struggles in France*, after having previously agreed to certain cuts, the German leaders ignored his letters of protest, and the version which appeared in the party's daily *Vorwärts* seemed to give Engels' blessing to a policy of legal action only—the days of the barricades were, in the changed circumstances of the day, simply not considered relevant any longer. The onward march of organized mass Social Democracy irresistibily rolled forward even over its own prophets. But though the German party leaders went much further towards the pure "democratization" of Social Democracy than Engels ever did, they all agreed on the primary aim of a democratic revolution, in which the army would come to the side of the SPD and the latter would achieve power as a Jacobin mass party but without armed struggle.

By 1898 the early days of *Sturm und Drang*, of heroic struggle and theoretical precision, had given way to a time of consolidation and growth, when problems of tactics, internal well-being, and above all organization and growth reigned supreme. The responsibilities of leading a mass party were regarded as substantially different from those appropriate to Marx's own day, when socialist praxis found expression in factional struggles between small groups of intellectuals. The very existence of the SPD justified Marx's historical predictions and overall theoretical perspectives. The SPD was in this sense the institutionalization of Marxist reality. The gap between society and the SPD was large enough for all to see; the latter's pariah position alone prevented a watering down of organizational autonomy and socialist ideology. The best proof of the success of the party's policy of making no concessions to society was the fact that a growing number of distinguished academic nonsocialist intellectuals now began to support the justice of the

workers' demands and demanded that the government should accommodate them. In time society would fall into the party's lap—always providing that the party did not fall into society's lap in the meantime.

The protracted political ideological debate that came to be called the revisionist controversy was both unexpected and, as far as the leadership of the SPD was concerned, thoroughly unwelcome. It opened up problems that were thought to have been solved and once more shifted emphasis back to ideology at the expense of political structure. In 1896 Eduard Bernstein, Engels' former secretary and esteemed senior colleague of all the SPD leaders, began to publish a series of articles in *Neue Zeit* in which he submitted the current social and economic situation of party and society to detailed analysis. He was not primarily activated by any desire to prove Marx wrong, as his opponents alleged, but the course of his investigation led him more and more firmly to the conclusion that many of the Marxist predictions of crisis in the capitalist system were being contradicted by the facts of the contemporary situation. For one thing, there had been no major economic crisis for twenty years; quite the contrary, the bourgeoisie was growing in numbers and strength, while the peasantry was prosperous and contented. Moreover, the atmosphere of relationship between classes was, if anything, milder and more benevolent than it had been in the past. Could capitalism survive by evolution and reform, and change its self-contradictory nature? Could it after all provide a harmonious integration of the means of production with the relations of production, so that revolution was no longer necessary? Could a gradual process of reform enable the working classes to obtain most of their demands without the revolutionary overthrow of the existing system?

Important as these epistemological questions were, Bernstein made it clear that they were not his main concern. They merely imposed themselves because of the evidence he marshalled; better to question the theory than to explain away the facts. His main concern was with the socialist tactics that would follow if his conclusions were correct. Thus he was soon led to a reexamination of the party's strategy and tactics. Bernstein regarded the rapidly growing forces of Social Democracy as a vital factor in transforming or reforming capitalism from an oppressive system of injustice to a socialized democracy. Not that he was an apologist for capitalism; his concern was with the means of change to socialism, a change he regarded as a potential continuum of reforms based on a moral imperative (hence the insistence of his "Marxist" opponents that he was a neo-Kantian not a dialectical materialist).

Bernstein's main concern was to maintain and increase socialist strength which would result in yet further concessions and changes in society. By extrapolating recent trends into the future the SPD was bound to become a majority sooner or later and as such its pressure to transform capitalism would become irresistible. Perhaps the most important single notion put forward by Bernstein was that no real change in policy on the part of the SPD was called for in this respect; behind the rhetoric of revolutionary ideology embodied in the party program all that he proposed was already happening. The party should recognize and accept openly that it was reformist rather than revolutionary, democratic in intention now rather than socialist in its ultimate expectations; otherwise it would come to grief. "The final goal, whatever it may be, means nothing to me, the movement everything." Once again the conflict between political democracy and revolutionary socialism, which had seemingly been overcome by the Marxist anti-Prussian radicalism of the SPD after 1878, came to the fore in a new form; according to Bernstein democracy could transform and improve the existing state without a prior social and political revolution. It was the voice of 1848, not of Lassalle, but support came nonetheless from Lassalle's heirs within the party.

Culminating with this highly practical purpose of confronting Social Democratic theory and practice, and paring the former down to fit the latter, it is clear that Bernstein did not intend to revise Marx as such—though he did admit to going further in this direction than he had ever intended. (It will be shown later, however, that the subordination of theory to praxis is necessarily an irreparable revision of Marx.) If the SPD was the institutionalization of Marxism in the current epoch, then whatever it did was justified; the main point was to be clear about, and admit to itself, what it was doing. The particularities of Marx's sayings and writings were not so much wrong as dated, hence irrelevant to the immediate present. Bernstein was sufficiently a Marxist to assume that the transformation of society was still the party's main concern; the alternatives were revolution or reform. For him the concern with self-sufficiency and self-regard, the emphasis on organizational strength and electoral growth, clearly demonstrated the path of reform—also encouraged by the economic and social circumstances of the time; the revolutionary ideology was therefore claptrap and a hindrance. In fact, there was, at least for the time being, a third alternative which combined and stabilized the apparent contradiction between reformist practice and revolutionary ideology—that of abstentionism. But this was a position to which no one admitted openly, of which no one was aware for another decade.

The leaders of the SPD initially found little to which they could take exception in Bernstein's articles, mainly because theoretical discussion just was not very important. Even Kautsky found the articles published in his journal "at first sight very attractive." The reaction against Bernstein came from a quite unexpected quarter: two East European immigrants, as yet hardly known in Germany, opened a major campaign of polemics against him. Parvus (Alexander Helphand), then editor of a party paper in Saxony, unleashed a highly abusive series of articles in reply (significantly headed "Bernstein's Revolution in Marxism" after Engels' *Anti-Dühring*); Rosa Luxemburg, recently arrived from her graduate studies in Switzerland, also published a series in which the revisionist character of Bernstein's argument was analyzed and attacked in detail. Briefly these two set out to show not only that Bernstein was wrong but also his position was impossible for a socialist and intolerable for his party, since it conflicted completely with the basic ideology and program of the SPD.

The intellectual arguments will be examined separately below. Politically, it was the programmatic acceptance of Bernstein's views by a number of party members who used his arguments to justify, and above all, to provide a broad ideological foundation for their own wishes—and what was worse, their past and present actions—which brought the SPD leadership increasingly into the fray against the revisionists. The reason why a primarily intellectual debate took on highly political and even organizational overtones was that the cohesiveness and unity of the party were now suddenly threatened. The isolated activities of trade union leaders and South German socialists had always been slapped down whenever they had been put forward as a programmatic alternative or amendment to the party's policy as embodied in its program; with Bernstein's extended critique of the official ideology and his downgrading of ideology below the rationality of praxis, all these deviant activities at once acquired theoretical justification, programmatic content, and even organizational cohesion. An alternative system of unified thought and action was challenging the existing one, forcing a choice. The activities of SPD members of provincial parliaments who supported bourgeois governments with their votes for tactical reasons, the "indiscipline" of trade union leaders who put the benefit of their members before party unity, all appeared retrospectively in a much more dangerous light than hitherto. As Auer, the party secretary, wrote pityingly to Bernstein: "My dear Ede, one does not say these things, one simply *does* them."

From a political point of view therefore the revisionist controversy brought into the open a number of factors which had previously been tolerated as mere "acts," and gave them a status which could no longer be ignored. From 1898 onwards the SPD leadership became much more sensitive to breaches of party rules and political offences against the party program. It attempted to impose discipline. In 1898, 1901, and 1903 the annual party congress voted sharply-worded condemnations of the revisionists by a large majority. Eventually, even Bernstein himself, who had hitherto escaped formal censure, was condemned. But the practical problems of revisionism could not be solved by resolutions of a congress or by the disciplinary enforcements of the executive. In a mass party which prided itself on its democratic procedures and for which unity in the face of an unremittingly hostile society was the primary consideration, expulsions were reluctant and rare. Ideologically revisionism stood time and time again condemned, in practice it continued unabated except during radical periods like 1905 and 1910. The South Germans continued their "flexible" politicking, claiming special circumstances in the South, the trade unions in practice quietly obtained almost complete autonomy from the SPD, and the tacit recognition that their members were not to be treated as the party's political cannon fodder. The problem of revisionism and reformism remained with the German party until the First World War made it irrelevant by tacitly making it official policy.

It became clear to a number of intelligent outsiders, most prominent among them Max Weber and Robert Michels, that the real sociological issues of revisionism were not so much theoretical as practical. The party regarded itself as isolated, and recreated for itself a self-sufficient world whose existence depended on a sharp gulf between it and the rest of society. It was the negation of society, and of all attempts to build bridges from either side, that kept the party in being and gave it the unity and strength of which it was so proud. By the first decade of the twentieth century, not only an established leadership but a party bureaucracy quite different from any other party in Germany had grown up. The leaders, the activists, the local bureaucracy all had a position to defend which was threatened as much by closer integration of the organized workers into society ( except for the trade unions, this would make many of the party's "compensatory" activities redundant), as by revolutionary activism which would land them in jail or worse. The maintenance of the status quo was vital, and they regarded the programmatic revisionists as its disturbers. They were thus conservatives in the real sense of the word, determined to maintain a revolutionary tradition which structured their self-sufficient world and justified the party's social isolation within which it flourished. The theoretical perspectives of the future, the argument between reform or revolution, were of secondary interest to them. Since the death of Engels there was no longer anyone in authority able or willing to point out the contradiction inherent in their position. Kautsky was to prove their particular theorist. The only critics were either outside the socialist camp or on its radical margin and could safely be ignored.

The main effect of the revisionist controversy on the future communist parties was its theoretical content. Nonetheless, political and organizational conclusions were drawn, and left their mark. The sensitivity of the Bolsheviks to all forms of opposition platforms within the party, the crucial distinction Lenin made between the expression of individual opinions and the organization of collective disagreements with party policy, all date back to the experience of the SPD. There was to be much tension and conflict between the commitment of intra-party democracy and the need to control revisionist, hence inimical and bourgeois, manifestations of opinion. The German socialist failure to eradicate revisionism eventually tilted the Russian communist scales in favor of control and against democracy. The SPD was often to be accused by Bolshevik writers of failing to maintain discipline; having condemned the revisionist position, its advocates should have been expelled from the party. It was the organizational failure of the SPD to cope with revisionism that in part led to the later communist sensitivity to organizational purity, to the frequent waves of expulsions and purges. Marx's own philosophical emphasis on the unity of theory and practice came to be interpreted not only in favor of theory's primacy, but in terms of a need to reinforce theoretical differentiation with organizational absolutes; *neither* purely theoretical argument without organizational compactness *nor* organizational purity without theoretical clarification were sufficient. The whole concept of praxis got a strong organizational twist, which may or may not have been good Marxism, but won through in the Russian party mainly because it was a direct inference from German "mistakes" in dealing with revisionism.

## II. THE INTELLECTUAL STRUCTURE OF REVISIONISM

Precisely because revisionism was an onslaught of praxis against a theoretical self-image, the ideological foundation of revisionism was not articulated in any great detail at the time. There is only Bernstein's writing and subsequent discussions by his supporters; and these took on a fundamental character mainly because they were challenged as such. Almost unintentionally Bernstein found himself elaborating a whole philosophy in order to defend his original, rather eclectic comments; the series of articles in *Neue Zeit* between 1896 and 1898 were reinforced by the much more "thorough" *Voraussetzungen des Sozialismus* (1899) which became revisionism's chief theoretical text. Too much should accordingly not be read into his writing in terms of a consistent set of ideas with which to challenge another equally consistent set of ideas. The revisionist controversy differs from both the types of arguments that Marx and Engels sometimes unleashed on their opponents, and also from the later exegeses of revisionism produced by the Bolsheviks and their German supporters in order to specify their own diametrically opposed position. The fact that revisionism has come to be regarded as a consistent attack on Marxism may be partially inherent in its original formulations, but is primarily due to later efforts to characterize it as such. Revisionism has no meaning except in the context of a fundamental departure from accepted or "correct" orthodoxy.

Hence, if anything, the articulation of a consistent position was not the work of Bernstein and his supporters but of his opponents, who provided the very consistency and internal logic that his own work lacked. In the work of Parvus and particularly Rosa Luxemburg, we find an ideological systematization of Bernstein's arguments which never ceased to surprise the latter, and whose main purpose in turn was to give a grounding to the orthodox interpretation of the party's ideology. Once he had been stimulated into awareness of the intellectual dangers of revisionism, Kautsky too defended the orthodox position against the revisionist "system" of ideas.

Bernstein challenged the accepted orthodoxy on two fronts: the accuracy and relevance of the social philosophy implicit in the party program—which in turn was based largely on Marx's own philosophy—and the political implications which resulted from this challenge.

*1. The Challenge to Marxism.* We have already noted the empirical nature of this challenge; certain social and economic developments should by now have been taking place but were not. It is naturally questionable whether the social philosophy of Marxism had ever stipulated any rigid time scale for processes of crisis; much of the argument hinged on the extent to which contemporary prosperity and social peace were temporary, or structural and permanent. There was a substantial discussion about the accuracy of Bernstein's statistics, the relative status of monopolistic concentration through the development of finance capital in the hands of banks as against Bernstein's observation that small-scale capitalism was growing in numbers and prosperity. If, on economic and social grounds, capitalism was indeed capable of internal reform and hence of survival, then a substantial part of the teleological basis which made its collapse and the proletarian revolution historically necessary under certain circum-

stances simply disappeared. Bernstein opposed the potential violence of revolution, emphasizing instead the need for legal transformation (even "expropriation of the exploiters" was to take place through agreed compensation); he also argued strongly against determinist notions of historical necessity which deprived human beings of the capacity to shape their own destiny. Hence he attacked what he conceived to be the tyranny of the dominant economic base—the relations of production—over social, political, cultural, and ideological phenomena; in this he affected to see a completion of the gradual relaxation already begun by Engels in the dominance of economic factors allegedly preached by Marx ("it is not man's consciousness that determines his existence, but on the contrary his social existence that determines his consciousness"). Nothing shows more clearly the confusion of Bernstein and almost all his contemporaries on both sides of the revisionist controversy about the real nature of Marx's thoughts and the respective attitudes of Marx and Engels than this ascription of a philosophically activist role to Engels in his post-Marx years; in fact it was Engels who was primarily responsible for the mechanization of the Marxist theory of consciousness into a "mere" reflection of nature—the mechanistic materialism Marx had attacked in *The German Ideology* (cf. Avineri [1968], pp. 66–67).

Somewhat reluctantly, Bernstein attempted to found his dissent ultimately on philosophical grounds. "My natural intellectual inclination would have rather led me to a positivist philosophy and sociology," he later avowed (*Entwicklungsgang* [1924], p. 40); as it was, his very empiricism and unconscious eclecticism (formally he opposed eclecticism in the name of Marxist consistency) led him to opt for a version of neo-Kantian evolutionary idealism that had been advocated by a number of philosophers on the fringe of the SPD (Conrad Schmidt, Ludwig Woltmann, above all, Bernstein's most immediate philosophical inspirer, Friedrich Albert Lange). This was especially marked with regard to the important role Bernstein assigned to morality "as a power capable of creative action" (*Geschichte und Theorie* [1901], p. 285). With the insistence on absolutes necessarily went a commitment to a linear evolution in the direction of human perfectibility, which was very typical of nineteenth-century philosophical optimism, and was specifically taken over by Bernstein from the English Fabians. Socialism, from this point of view, became primarily a moral movement based on ethical premises. Bernstein criticized dialectical materialism—from which he believed Engels to have been departing anyhow at the end of his life. The notion of dialectical change, with its brusque cataclysms, was for Bernstein "the worst ele-

269

ment of Marxist doctrine, the snare, the obstacle blocking access to any logical perception of things" (*Voraussetzungen*, p. 46). Instead, "Social Democracy needs a Kant who will at last confront traditional ideology . . . with a critical spirit and the necessary curiosity and . . . who will show . . . that the contempt for the ideal, the raising of material factors to the level of omnipotent forces in the process of evolution, are merely an illusion" (ibid., pp. 177–78).

This brief survey of Bernstein's economic, social, and philosophical position shows the scrappy basis of the revisionist position; how feeble the attempt was to translate what one of its opponents called "the theory of a praxis" into a consistent position vis-à-vis Marxism, or at any rate what passed as Marxism at the time. Bernstein was in his way as guilty of "flattening out" Marx into an almost mechanical materialist and determinist as were the Stalinists of a much later epoch. A great deal of what was criticized in Marx was in fact Engels' interpretation, and even this was over-simplified. The contradictions of a hybrid philosophy between positivism as a commitment to action, and idealism as a source of moral objectives, were glossed over; Bernstein was simply unaware of such problems, and also seemed to have hoped that Marx and Kant could somehow be combined. The tendency to equate the Hegelian dialectic (which, Bernstein said, Marx had not really demystified at all) with violent political revolution was quite unjustified on any grounds but a highly arbitrary linkage between Kautsky's incessant advocacy of revolution (in his capacity as Marxist "pope") and its alleged Hegelian roots—when in fact the Marxism of the Second International did everything to loosen the connection with the Hegelian method, and the rediscovery of Hegel was a feature of the early Bolshevik period (Lenin during the war, G. Lukacs in the early 1920's). Marx himself had realized clearly that in grafting Feuerbach's materialism or naturalism onto the Hegelian dialectic, there was a danger that the active component in idealism might be swamped by the contemplative nature of Feuerbach's analysis; his theses on Feuerbach specifically stress the need to preserve the element of activism in the new Marxist materialism. The activist component in revisionism thus flogged the wrong philosophical horse—even though its immediately practical concerns with political action were relevant enough in the context of the "orthodox" abstentionism which underlay the radical rhetoric of the SPD's program and leadership.

The revisionist debate between Bernstein and supporters, against the orthodox on one side and the radicals (as yet undifferentiated) on the other, was only in part concerned with the interpretation of reality and the prediction of the future. These problems were rapidly subsumed by more fundamental and immediate ones of self-definition. Could a nineteenth-century evolutionary view based on strong reliance on the perfectibility of human nature and its social system, be compatible with a socialist philosophy—and, more important, a socialist party program? What was the true meaning of socialism? Regarding society as irrevocably divided into two camps, Bernstein's opponents tried to demonstrate that his views were not socialist at all. They had therefore to be considered anti-socialist, i.e., bourgeois. A significant analogy was drawn between the "bridge building" on the part of the *Kathedersozialisten*, academic sympathizers with labor (like Sombart, Schmoller, Roscher, and others) who advocated a policy of working-class integration into society through substantial concessions to the workers, and the revisionist who proposed a very similar policy from within the socialist camp. With a span being constructed from both sides across the Marxist gulf between antagonistic classes, these would disappear and society become a continuum. For Bernstein this would represent a positive achievement for Social Democracy; to his opponents it spelled the acceptance of permanent class domination.

One of the major issues in the debate was concerned with intellectual method. Bernstein had started with an empirical and eclectic analysis of the present and from this analysis had attempted to construct a philosophy and a policy based on reality as he perceived it. This form of inductive theory was characterized by Marxists as a form of opportunism, in which policy and philosophical system were tailored to meet immediate and ever changing needs (the analogy with tailoring was in fact made by Rosa Luxemburg, *Sozialreform oder Revolution?*, 1899). Since there could be no ideological vacuum, no empty spaces in the sociology of knowledge, the surface systematization of discrete phenomena must necessarily be a reflection of bourgeois ideology and help to support it. It was but a short step from such intellectual empiricism to practical opportunism—and this label was henceforth increasingly used to characterize all socialist attempts to validate epiphenomena into a justification for praxis.

Hence one of the most important elements of controversy concerned the status of theory vis-à-vis praxis. Rosa Luxemburg underlined the way in which Bernstein's revisionism provided a cover for established but hitherto "silent" practices; indeed Bernstein had specifically extrapolated from the acceptance of these practices into a theoretical justification of them. Most of his supporters were antitheorists, and much emphasis was placed on the fact that revisionism took the form of a denial of theory in favor of praxis. Bernstein's orthodox opponents defended the party program as a correct formulation of the necessary relationship between theory and praxis; the maximum program provided the theory, the minimum program the praxis. In attempting to undermine the maximum program Bernstein was in fact undermining theory altogether and replacing it with a theoretical justification of praxis *tout court*.

In raising this aspect a confrontation between party theorists and the party "practitioners" became inevitable, though this had not been Bernstein's intention; already revisionism was as much the creature of its opponents as of its supporters. Throughout the revisionist debate from 1898 until the First World War—and like an echo ever since—those who advocated the need for correct theory found themselves differentiated from, and often opposed by, those whose task it was to manage the day-to-day political affairs of the party. Again and again a sharp distinction was drawn between theorists and activists—a distinction that was reinforced by the fact that some of the most articulate theorists were immigrant Easterners who, particularly after 1905, infuriatingly taunted the passive SPD with the example of Russian activism—or anarchy—as the German leadership would have it.

This division into theorists and practitioners was one of the main consequences of the revisionist controversy. Once the party leadership had come down against the revisionists, a tacit agreement to split theoretical from practical politics provided an escape route for all concerned; the leadership had articulated the party's self-sufficiency, the revisionists could continue their practices provided they did not raise them in ideological form. Theoretical debates were discouraged as much as possible after 1903. All the theorists suffered as a result. Bernstein never ventured again into any major theoretical statement; his later pacifism and his strong democratic and anti-imperialist attitudes before and during the First World War made him respected but relatively isolated. Kautsky increasingly became the spokesman of the party's self-sufficient isolationism; provided he did not advocate revolutionary action, his analyses and interpretations of events and his historical studies provided a theoretical gloss of intellectual respectability for the SPD, which by now had become the most important party in the Second International and an example for all. The radicals were increasingly pushed to the margin of relevance in the SPD; the party leadership accused them of losing touch with political reality. In the end therefore the revisionist controversy resulted curiously enough in a virtual embargo on all fundamental controversies; the real beneficiaries were the party leadership and the practitioners.

Also inherent in the revisionist controversy was the eventual intellectual split between the party center, with its increasingly deterministic philosophy, and the radical Left, which opened out politically in 1910. Kautsky was later accused by the communists of changing from orthodox or revolutionary Marxism to a determinist (and therefore in the end revisionist) position just before or at the beginning of the First World War (Lenin, *The Proletarian Revolution and the Renegade Kautsky*, 1918; Regionieri, 1965). As against this it has been argued that his views were consistent throughout; that the strongly deterministic element in his social philosophy was there from the start (Matthias, 1957). As the SPD became more concerned with its internal affairs, and regarded its success more openly in terms of size and organizational strength rather than revolutionary action, Kautsky increasingly focussed on the inevitability of the collapse of capitalist society before a confident, ever-growing, majoritarian socialist party, winning victory after victory at the polls and gaining the support of disaffected lower middle-class elements. The middle course which he advocated against revolutionary adventurism on the Left and overt revisionism on the Right made him the official spokesman par excellence of the party leadership. After 1910, a small, though vocal group of Left Wing radicals began to crystallize. Many of them had been in the forefront of the polemics against Bernstein during the revisionist controversy, but had now become disillusioned with the inactive component of the official condemnation of revisionism and the immobile self-sufficiency of the SPD leadership and Kautsky himself. In a sense, the revisionist controversy had obscured the problem of activism versus determinism. It was this issue which later divided Center and Left, with the revisionists amused spectators on the sidelines as their enemies fell out among themselves.

*2. Political Implications of Revisionism: Activism vs. Determinism.* In one sense, Bernstein's critique of party policy was thus a positivist commitment to action. The SPD's isolationism justified itself by a determinist social philosophy; maintenance of the "correct" status quo in ideology and program would bring about the eventual collapse of self-contradictory capitalism and the victorious inheritance of socialism. As against this, Bernstein stressed the need for involvement by socialists in order to bring about further transformation in capitalist society towards the desired end—a better life for all in a better society. His theoretical justification of greater involvement with existing society legitimated precisely those elements in the party already most concerned with political action; the South German SPD, who participated directly in local government, and the Trade Unions facing the employers and the state in the economic interests of their members all the way from individual shop floor to national industrial sector. His appeal for greater realism was thus implicitly and at the same time a call for greater activation of political possibilities. Bernstein had lived in England for some years and had absorbed not only some of the underlying attitudes of Fabianism towards human nature and society but had witnessed the success of British trade unionism in its pragmatic struggle to obtain economic benefits and political representation for labor. Marx himself had already stressed the importance of working-class practicality: "not only in *thinking*, in *consciousness*, but in massively *being*, in life . . . in forming associations . . . in which social criticism becomes the living real criticism of existing society . . ."; England and France were outstanding examples, to be copied by the excessively speculative, purely philosophical Germans (*The Holy Family*, 1845; 1956 Moscow edition, pp. 73, 205). Though Bernstein did not cite Marx against current orthodox Marxism, his own prescriptions for practical activity were intended to align theory to praxis in a harmonious relationship which, he felt, had been sundered by too much veneration for an increasingly irrelevant theory no longer able to accommodate existing praxis.

But while Marx had criticized the "pure" philosophy of knowledge-seeking by the Hegelians of the Left, Bernstein was dealing with a powerful mass movement organized in a Social Democratic party. The problem of activism became one of doing, not merely being; not activism per se but its direction. Anything conducive to the internal strengthening of the party was considered legitimate by everyone, but what about those activities which related to and took place in the context of society at large? The problem had existed throughout the history of the SPD before the First World War; the revisionist controversy made it into a critical test of orthodoxy. One issue was the right of party intellectuals and journalists to write for the nonparty, i.e., bourgeois press. The revisionists encouraged such cross-fertilization, the radicals condemned it; the party executive failed to establish any clear policy. Another, more crucial matter came to the surface during the crisis of the French Socialist Party in 1898, when the first ministerial participation of a socialist, A. Millerand, in a nonsocialist government caused much controversy in Germany. The problem of "ministerialism" was closely related to the issues raised in the revisionist controversy; both the orthodox leadership of the German party and the radicals condemned it as a serious manifestation of revisionism. Though there was at the time little likelihood of the same possibility arising in Germany, the relationship of the French case with the German revisionist crisis was stressed.

But the most important German problems of participatory activism were elections and the role of socialist deputies in the Reichstag and the provincial legislatures. The 1891 party program had stressed the lowly expectations of immediate benefits from such activities, and had regarded them, together with trade union action, mainly as a means of spreading socialist propaganda and reinforcing the party's ideology. Instrumentally they were thus mere "labors of Sisyphus," in Rosa Luxemburg's telling phrase. The revisionists, however, regarded them as fruitful in themselves. Bernstein stressed that favorable election results and the activities of SPD deputies were not only an index of the party's strength but the most immediate and powerful means for the party to make itself effective in society here and now. When the SPD suffered a major setback in the 1907 elections at the hands of a Liberal-National and Conservative coalition, aimed specifically at reducing socialist representation, Kautsky and the Party leadership felt their teleological optimism about the linear growth of Social Democracy to be seriously threatened; in order to restore it they began to pay much greater attention to the instrumental aspects of elections, and thus unconsciously adopted an important aspect of revisionist activism. The problem of democracy now came openly to the fore. In electoral matters revisionists and Center henceforward collaborated against the Radicals, who continued to stress the purely ideological function of elections and protested against the party's growing preoccupation with elections, which they called "parliamentary cretinism."

In one very crucial area of activity the revisionist superordination of praxis to theory had triumphed officially. Important secondary consequences followed. As elections came to preoccupy the SPD increasingly after 1907, the status and influence of Social Democratic deputies within the party grew apace. The party caucus in the Reichstag became the most powerful organized group within the party leadership; when World War I broke out, this group swiftly and effectively took control of the party. Significantly this shift in ideology was given extended theoretical justification by Kautsky, and signifies and first major convergence between the orthodox Center and the revisionists.

Revisionist activism thus triumphed over orthodox abstentionism. In a mass party a social philosophy of criticism could only be institutionalized meaningfully in conjunction with a highly determinist theory of inevitable social collapse. Even so the pressures of practical activism were proving too strong; ideology began painfully and slowly to adjust itself to praxis. Under the traumatic shock of the First World War the remaining theoretical barriers were irretrievably breached; henceforth the SPD was to become an openly reformist party which regarded itself as integrated into society and spent most of its time and energy trying to persuade society of this. After the war Kautsky became an irrelevance. For, in becoming a reformist party, the SPD ceased to be revisionist; there was no longer any Marxist orthodoxy to defend or to "revise." Philosophically and ideologically Bernstein's revisionism foreshadowed future orthodoxy with all its eclecticism, its difficulties of identity, its negation of the party's revolutionary past, above all its commitment to all the instrumental criteria of unbridled praxis. Yet Bernstein was no prophet. His social optimism proved unjustified, his idealism and ethical emphasis irrelevant. Only the implicit critique of abstentionism and the underlying stress on the pressures of activism proved to be accurate, though these were not his main or manifest concern. Revisionism in the last resort was a struggle for orthodoxy not for tolerance; it was the challenge of an alternative ideology articulated in opposition to the existing one that set the tone of the revisionist controversy. Whatever Bernstein's intention, the official reaction turned it into a fundamental debate about the one correct ideology. The postwar SPD certainly did not regard Bernstein as its ideological prophet; as the spokesman of revisionism he too had become an irrelevance though he lived and wrote till 1932.

In any case there developed an alternative activist challenge to the party's determinist abstentionism. The Left radicals also advocated confrontation with society but of a revolutionary kind. For some the Russian revolution of 1905 came to serve as a model; others regarded the determinism elaborated by Kautsky as conflicting with the party's activist tradition and liable to put off the effective transformation of society to the Greek Calends. These radicals therefore went back on their initial wholehearted support for the party's official antirevisionist stance which they now regarded as conservative rather than revolutionary.

Kautsky characterized the official position and his own as opposed to two forms of impatience: reformist impatience which was determined here and now to act *within* society, revolutionary impatience which wanted here and now to act against society. His breakdown theory, preoccupied with the analysis of the "readiness" of objective conditions (which was the basis of his determinism), was later used to criticize the Bolshevik revolution as premature. But he did recognize clearly that in one sense revisionists and radicals shared a commitment to activism which stood in common opposition to the waiting policy of the party. And when this policy seemed in danger of leading to regression as a result of electoral defeat, the commit-

ment to electoral (hence revisionist) activism was characterized as a buttress to the established theory of societal breakdown rather than as a major concession to revisionist ideology. The dangers inherent in this commitment were later clearly understood by communists, who though always advocating electoral participation, were careful to circumscribe its ideological importance and limit the status and power of its elected deputies through strict control by the party leadership.

### III. THE UNIVERSALIZATION OF REVISIONISM

The history of revisionism since the original controversy is no less than the history of the communist movement. Yet to ignore subsequent developments is to treat the original controversy in an abstract and isolated historical manner. The very meaning of revisionism is much more the product of later emphasis than of contemporary relevance. A brief reference must therefore be made to the subsequent history of the concept.

Already at that time German emphasis on the importance of the revisionist problem was making socialists everywhere more conscious of similar problems at home. The most important consequence was that revisionism became the basic countersystem of ideas to the official ideology in the Second International. Moreover, almost every effort at accommodation with existing society was called, and treated, as a form of revisionism. This linked one party more closely to others, and greatly helped the process of ideological simplification.

The few committed theorists of Marxism in the Second International emphasized the need for philosophical clarity and defended the status of theory against mindless but still ideological praxis. Plekhanov exhorted the Germans to take philosophy seriously and to condemn revisionism with the philosophical rigor it deserved. He berated Kautsky and the German leadership for underestimating the importance of the issue. In a more directly political context, the French socialist parties used the German revisionist controversy as an important weapon against the strong radical Republican or democratic element characterized by the leadership of Jaurès. Antirevisionism was identified with correct Marxism, and between the "Right" and the traditional "Left" represented by the old communards, there emerged a rigid, largely abstentionist echo of the German Center position under the leadership of Jules Guesde. By 1904 German pressure succeeded in inducing the International Congress at Amsterdam to condemn the revisionist tendencies in the French movement; a resolution was carried which duplicated the German condemnation of their own

273

revisionists and forced the French party to adopt, at least in theory, a more rigorous socialist line. This transfer onto French soil of a German solution to a basically German problem naturally failed to deal with the issue. In France, unlike Germany, the struggle for democracy had been largely won; the problem here was to defend democracy against reaction on the one hand, and to envisage its transformation into socialism on the other by peaceful or by revolutionary means. The options were therefore more advanced and sophisticated, while the German solution merely helped to obscure them by postulating an arbitrary predemocratic situation in which, as in Germany, democracy could only be attained *through* socialism.

In some other cases where the leadership was itself inclined to reformism—as in Belgium and Austria—the German experience helped to categorize these parties among socialists and enabled their internal oppositions to express their dissent against the leadership on the grounds of its alleged revisionism. Though it would be an exaggeration to suggest that the international socialist movement was simply split into revisionists and orthodox Marxists, the German revisionist controversy nonetheless forced into the open a more consequent self-appraisal along German lines. In the parties of Eastern Europe, like the Russians and the Poles, whose leadership was largely in exile, the German example certainly helped to create a quite fundamental division between revisionists and self-styled revolutionaries. Conditions differed substantially from those in Germany, however, and the word "revisionist" provided a label of abuse and an ideological weapon against party opponents rather than reflecting any genuine replication of the German situation. In Russia and Poland the problem of integration into society hardly arose; many of those labelled revisionist were just as committed to revolution as their detractors. Revisionism thus became merely synonymous with deviance from some postulated orthodoxy anchored in Marx.

This foreshadowed later communist use of the concept. The definition of orthodoxy after 1917 became far tighter and narrower than it had ever been in the Second International—which, apart from fundamental issues, was a permissive and loosely structured association of ideas and policies. Hence revisionism became one of the major means of identifying and condemning opponents—those who questioned the current form of orthodoxy. Since this often changed sharply and frequently, revisionism came to include not only Right Wing supporters of policies of conciliation, but also extreme Left Wing positions; under Stalin Right and Left were lumped together as revisionist because Stalinist orthodoxy, whatever its current position in the

spectrum of possible policies, always identified itself as being on the Left. Revisionism, of course, lost all precise meaning in this process; any attempt to identify a continuity of ideas among those labelled as revisionist became a barren exercise in classification. In the broadest sense, however, the incompatibility between revisionism and Marxism was always emphasized. "Either we destroy revisionism or revisionism will destroy us; there is no third way" (*Moskva*, 1 [1958]). In terms of philosophical explanation of revisionism various contradictory and often irrelevant classifications were adduced by Soviet commentators, ranging from treacherous infusion of liberal ideology to subjective idealism and excessive activism based on theories of spontaneity. The current definition, resulting from the reopening of basic philosophical questions in Eastern Europe and the application of Marxist *Problematik* of postrevolutionary socialist societies, stresses the overemphasis on the early Marx—precisely those texts selected by Marxist critics of the mechanical and dogmatic Marxism of Stalinism. "The revisionists turned to the early writings of Marx, selecting from them isolated pre-Marxist statements borrowed from the German philosophical schools which were one of the sources of Marxism" (*Soviet Philosophical Encyclopaedia*, I, 415). The direct descent of contemporary revisionism from its historical ancestor in Germany is established by suggesting that contemporary revisionists, "using the 'theoretical baggage' of their predecessors, changed only some of their dogmas and supplied them with a new phraseology" (Polyanski, in *Kritika ekonomicheskikh teorii* [1960], p. 61).

Hence, revisionism today covers both the simple case of deviation from orthodoxy within the revolutionary Marxist movement as well as the actual reflection of the original revisionist position. Since almost all social democratic parties have long since abandoned any claim to Marxist revolutionary orthodoxy, the label revisionist hardly applies to them any longer; the continuity in regarding revisionism as a form of bourgeois ideology *within* the socialist camp has been maintained. Phenomena of revisionism in communist movements today are of course legion. They include not only the application of Marxist critique to current socialist societies by Marxist intellectuals in both East and West, but also whole regimes and national movements like the Yugoslav communist league since 1948, and the 1968 Czech leadership under Dubcek. The transposition of revolutionary Marxism into an armed struggle by small groups of all-purpose revolutionaries in Latin America is also qualified periodically as a form of revisionism. As the tightly defined orthodoxy centered on Moscow gave way to pluralist approaches to socialism and greater independence was attained by the communist leadership of different parties in East and West, so the definition of orthodoxy necessary loosened somewhat. Nonetheless the borderline drawn round acceptable versions of Marxist praxis does, if crossed, still lead to the universal accusation of revisionism.

Most important in this context has been the use of the concept in the struggle between the Soviet Union and China for possession of the authoritative definition of Marxism. Though the origins of this struggle have little to do with the problems of revisionism in either its historical or its contemporary definition, the very fact that fundamental issues of Marxist epistemology have been raised made the application of the dichotomy Marxism-revisionism almost inevitable. In characterizing the Soviet Union and its policy of peaceful coexistence as modern revisionism, as an application in the international sphere of Bernstein's policies of societal integration, the Chinese have linked the present to the past with more than usual attention to the details of historical analogy. In this regard the Soviet counter-accusation of Chinese dogmatism, with its emphasis on the need to apply Marxist analysis and praxis to the particular circumstances of the present time instead of a blind acceptance of old revolutionary attitudes for all time, does carry an echo of the revisionist response to their orthodox critics at the end of the nineteenth century.

There is therefore a fundamental continuity in the history of Marxism which suggests that as long as there is orthodoxy, there will be revisionism, and as long as there is revolutionary isolationism there will be pressures for integration and for an effective praxis measurable in terms of immediate payoffs. The revisionist controversy does therefore provide an objective historical example of an endemic, continuing problem for institutionalized revolutionary movements. This continuity goes well beyond the particular issues raised by Bernstein. It is based on being rooted in problems of praxis and not merely in debate about theory.

## BIBLIOGRAPHY

The literature which deals with, or touches on, revisionism in one form or another is immense, and this bibliography is therefore highly selective.

Bernstein's most important contribution to revisionism is contained in *Die Voraussetzungen des Sozialismus und die Aufgaben der Sozialdemokratie* (Stuttgart, 1899; republished in a much enlarged edition, 1920), and in the version in book form of his *Neue Zeit* articles published between 1896 and 1898: *Zur Geschichte und Theorie der Sozialismus* (Berlin, 1901). A brief and more popular version of his views is given in *Wie ist wissenschaftlicher Sozialismus moglich?* (Berlin, 1901). For his retrospective apologia and self-presentation see *Entwicklungsgang eines Sozialisten* in F.

Meiner, *Die Volkswirtschaftslehre der Gegenwart in Selbstdarstellungen*, Vol. I (Leipzig, 1924). Discussions of the intellectual and political development of Bernstein, and his impact on the history of socialism are Peter Gay, *The Dilemma of Democratic Socialism* (New York, 1952), which includes extracts in English from Bernstein's own writing, and, more recently and comprehensively, Pierre Angel, *Eduard Bernstein et l'évolution du socialisme allemand* (Paris, 1961). This book, originally a thesis, contains a very useful bibliography of Bernstein's work, as well as of important revisionist, centrist, and radical tests. For revisionism generally see "The Roots of Revisionism," *Journal of Modern History*, **11** (1939). A discussion of the structural relationship between revisionist ideas and party praxis is J. P. Nettl, "The German Social-Democratic Party 1890–1914 as a Political Model," *Past and Present*, **30** (April 1965), 65–95.

Extended historical treatment of the political problem during and after the revisionist controversy can be found in Carl E. Schorske's *German Social Democracy 1905–1917* (Cambridge, Mass., 1955); more recently in Gerhard A. Ritter, *Die Arbeiterbewegung im Wilhelminischen Reich* (Berlin, 1959). The earlier, introductory period is well treated in two recent books: Roger Morgan, *The German Social Democrats and the First International 1864–1872* (Cambridge, 1965) for the first years, and Vernon L. Lidtke, *The Outlawed Party: Social Democracy in Germany 1878–1890* (Princeton, 1967) for the second, more radical phase. Both these monographs are primarily political histories.

For a more sociological approach, see Gunther Roth, *The Social Democrats in Imperial Germany* (Totowa, N.J., 1965). The intellectual problems of revisionism in the context of Marxism and the German philosophical tradition are discussed by George Lichtheim, *Marxism: An Historical and Critical Study* (London, 1961). A recent Soviet analysis emphasizing the philosophical aspects of revisionism is B. A. Chagin, *Iz istorii bor'by protiv filosofskogo revisionisma v germanskoi sotsialdemokratii* (Moscow and Leningrad, 1961). This is of course a modern version of the basic Bolshevik text on revisionism: Lenin's "Imperialism, the Highest Stage of Capitalism" (1917), in *Collected Works* (Moscow, 1960–), Vol. XXII.

As far as the other theoretical protagonists in the revisionist debate are concerned, see, for Kautsky, Erich Matthias, "Kautsky und der Kautskyanismus," *Marxismusstudien*, Second Series (Tübingen, 1957), 151–97; Ernesto Regioneri, "All'origine del marxismo nella II internazionale," *Critica Marxista*, **5/6** (1965), 1–127. Kautsky's own major statement on Bernstein is Karl Kautsky, *Bernstein und das sozialdemokratische Programm* (Stuttgart, 1899). For Rosa Luxemburg see J. P. Nettl, *Rosa Luxemburg* (London, 1966); her major polemic with Bernstein, and the most thorough critique of revisionism is *Sozialreform oder Revolution?* in Ossip K. Flechtheim, ed., *Politische Schriften* (Frankfurt, 1966). For Parvus see Z. A. B. Zeman and W. B. Scharlau, *The Merchant of Revolution* (London and New York, 1965).

An attempt to capture the contemporary universality of revisionism, and to relate it to its origins, is made in a collection of rather summary pieces edited by Leopold

Labedz, *Revisionism: Essays on the History of Marxist Ideas* (London, 1962). This can be compared to a collective Soviet compendium on the same theme: *Kritika ekonomicheskikh teorii predshestvennikov sovremennogo revizionizma* (Moscow, 1960).

Finally, anyone interested in contrasting the subtleties of Marx's own system of ideas with both the intellectual and applied vulgarizations which resulted in the "orthodox" Marxism of the turn of the century, should refer to Shlomo Avineri, *The Social and Political Thought of Karl Marx* (Cambridge and New York, 1968).

J. P. NETTL

[See also Historical and Dialectical Materialism; Ideology; Ideology of Soviet Communism; **Marxism;** Necessity; **Revolution; Socialism.**]

# FORMAL THEORIES OF SOCIAL WELFARE

THE PURPOSE of a theory of social welfare, or social choice as it is sometimes revealingly termed, is to provide a normative rationale for making social decisions when the individual members of the society have varying opinions about or interests in the alternatives available. Any kind of decision, social or individual, can be regarded as the interaction of the preferences or desires of the decision-maker with the range of alternative decisions actually available to him, to be termed the *opportunity set*. The latter may vary from time to time because of changes in the wealth or technology of the community. The usual formalism of social welfare theory, derived from economic theory, is that preferences (or tastes or values) are first expressed for all logically possible alternatives. Then the most preferred is chosen from any given opportunity set.

As will be seen, there is serious and unresolved dispute about the strength of the statements which it is appropriate to make about preferences. One common demand is that preferences form an *ordering* of the alternatives. In terms of formal logic, a preference relation between pairs of alternatives is said to be *transitive* if whenever alternative A is preferred to alternative B and alternative B to alternative C, then A is preferred to B; and it is said to be *connected* if, for any two distinct alternatives, either A is preferred to B or B to A. An ordering of the alternatives is a preference relation which is both transitive and connected; and it will be seen that this definition corresponds to an everyday use of the term, "ordering."

(In the economic literature, it has proved essential to consider the possibility of indifference as well as preference, between pairs of alternative social decisions. For the purposes of this article, however, we assume the absence of indifference, to simplify the exposition.)

Still a stronger demand is that preferences be measurable, that there exist a numerical representation which correctly reflects preference (the more preferred of two alternatives always has a higher number associated with it). Such a numerical representation is usually termed a *utility function*. In the terminology used by mathematical psychologists, a utility function may constitute an *interval scale*, that is, statements of the form, "the preference for A over B is so many times the preference for C over D," are regarded as meaningful. In that case, the utility function is arbitrary as to the location of its zero point and its unit of measurement, but otherwise uniquely defined. A still stronger requirement is that the utility function constitute a *ratio scale*, that is, statements of the form, "the utility (or value) of A is so many times as great as that of B." Such statements imply a natural zero; the utility function is unique up to a unit of measurement. If it is assumed that no meaning can be given to quantitative comparisons of preference but only to the ordering of alternatives, it is customary to speak of *ordinal* utility or preferences; if, on the contrary, utility is considered to constitute an interval or ratio scale, the term, *cardinal* utility or preferences, is used.

The need for a theory of social welfare arises from the need in the real world for social decisions. It is simply a fact, as Hobbes pointed out, that there are a great many decisions which by their nature must be made collectively and without which all members of the society would be much worse off—decisions on legal systems, police, or *certain* economic activities best conducted collectively, such as highways, education, and the kind of insurance represented by public assistance to disadvantaged groups.

A formal theory of social welfare then has the following form: given a representation of the preferences of the individual members of the society in ordinal or cardinal form, to aggregate them in some reasonable manner to form a preference system for society as a whole. Given the social preference system, and given a particular opportunity set of alternatives, the choice which society should make is that alternative highest on the social preference system.

## I. INDIVIDUAL CHOICE AND VALUES

The historical development of the notion of social welfare cannot be easily understood without reference to the gradual evolution of a formal analysis of individual choice, which we briefly summarize. Three characteristics of this history, which are shared with the history of the concept of social welfare, are striking: (1) the form of the basic problems were established during the eighteenth century and display the characteristic rationalism and optimism of the Enlightenment; (2) the analysis retained its general form but underwent systematic transformation under the impact of twentieth-century epistemological currents; and (3) there are strong historical links with the development of the theory of probability and its applications, links which are not easy to explain on purely logical grounds.

The first work to discuss individual choice systematically is that of Daniel Bernoulli in 1738. He was concerned to explain phenomena of which insurance was typical—that individuals would engage in bets whose actuarial value was negative. Bernoulli's solution was that what guided the individual's decisions to accept or reject bets was not the money outcomes themselves but their "moral values" as he judged them. In later terminology, the individual attached utilities to different amounts of money and accepted an uncertainty if and only if it increased the expected value of the utility. He also postulated that in general utility increased by lesser and lesser amounts as the quantity of money increased, an assumption now known as *diminishing marginal utility.* Then the individual would shy away from bets which were actuarially favorable if they increased uncertainty in money terms (in particular, if they involved a very small probability of very high returns) and would accept insurance policies if they reduced monetary uncertainty, for the high returns offered in the one case had relatively little additional utility, while the low returns avoided in the second case imply large losses of utility. Bernoulli thus required a cardinal utility (in this case, an interval scale) for his explanation of human behavior under uncertainty.

The idea that the drive of an individual to increase some measure of satisfaction explained his behavior was widespread, though rather vague, in the eighteenth century; Galiani, Condillac, and Turgot argued that in some measure the prices of commodities reflected the utilities they presented to individuals, for individuals were willing to pay more for those objects which provided them more satisfaction. This particular doctrine, indeed ran into a difficulty that Adam Smith noted, that water was surely more useful than diamonds but commanded a much lower price. But the doctrine that the increase of utility or happiness is the complete explanation of individual behavior is most emphasized by Jeremy Bentham in writings extending from 1776 to his death in 1832. Further, and even more importantly, Bentham introduced the doctrine of the parallelism between the descriptive and the normative in-

terpretations of utility; not only does an individual seek happiness but he ought to do so, and society ought to help him to this end. "Nature has placed mankind under the governance of two sovereign masters, *pain* and *pleasure.* It is for them alone to point out what we ought to do, as well as to determine what we shall do. . . . By the principle of utility is meant that principle which approves or disapproves of every action whatsoever, according to the tendency which it appears to have to augment or diminish the happiness of the party whose interest is in question" (Bentham, 1780; 1961). Bentham took it for granted that utility was a measurable magnitude; he further elaborated in various ways the factors which determine utility, such as nearness in time and certainty, but at no point is there a clearly defined procedure for measuring utility, such as would be demanded by modern scientific philosophy. The one suggestion he made was that sufficiently small increments in wealth were not perceptible; therefore, a natural unit for measuring utility is the *minimum sensibile,* or just noticeable difference, as psychophysicists were later to term it.

Although Bentham's notions were widely influential, especially among English economists (as well as being violently repudiated by the romantic thinkers of the early nineteenth century), a further elaboration was not achieved until about 1870 when Bentham's simple hedonistic psychology proved to be of surprising use in economic analysis. Smith's water-diamond paradox was at last resolved; while water as a whole was more valuable than diamonds, the relevant comparison was between an additional increment of water and an additional increment of diamonds, and since water was so much more abundant, it was not surprising that the incremental or *marginal* utility of water was much lower. (Actually, Bentham had already shown Smith's error but did not directly relate utilities to prices in any form; in any case, Bentham's contribution was not recognized.) This basic point was grasped simultaneously by Stanley Jevons in England, Léon Walras in France, and Carl Menger in Austria, between 1871 and 1874; they had in fact been anticipated by Gossen in Germany in 1854.

The further technical developments of the theory of individual choice in economic contexts are not of interest here, but the power of the utility concept led among other things to an analysis of its meaning. Already in his doctoral dissertation in 1892, *Mathematical Investigations in the Theory of Value and Prices,* the American economist Irving Fisher observed that the assumption of the measurability of utility in fact was inessential to economic theory. This point was developed independently and taken up much further by Vilfredo Pareto, from 1896 on. At any moment,

277

given the prices of various goods and his income, an individual has available to him all bundles of goods whose cost does not exceed his income. The "marginal utility" theory stated that he chose among those bundles the one with the highest utility. But all that was necessary for the theoretical explanation was that the individual have an ordering of different bundles; then the individual is presumed to select that bundle among those available which is highest on his ordering. Thus only ordinal preferences matter; two utility functions which implied the same ordinal preference comparisons would predict the same choice of commodity bundles at given prices and income. But this meant in turn that no set of observations on the individual's purchasing behavior could distinguish one of these utility functions from another. In fact, more generally, no observation of the individual's choices from any set of bundles could make this distinction. But then the neo-positivist and operational epistemology, so characteristic of this century, would insist that there was no meaning to distinguishing one utility function from another. It was the ordering itself that was meaningful, and all utility functions which implied it were equally valid or invalid.

The ordinalist position, defined above, only began to spread widely in the 1930's and became orthodox, ironically enough at a moment when the foundations for a more sophisticated theory of cardinal utility had already been laid. The general approach is to make some additional hypotheses about the kind of choices which an individual will or ought to make. Then it is demonstrated that there is a way of assigning numerical utilities to different possible bundles of goods or other alternative decisions such that the utilities assigned reflect the ordering (higher utility to preferred alternatives) and that the function assigning utilities to alternatives has some especially simple form. More particularly, it is assumed that the different commodities can be divided into classes in such a way that the preferences for commodities in one class are independent of the amounts of the commodities in the other classes. Then there is a way of assigning utilities to bundles of commodities within each class and defining the utility of the entire bundle as the sum of the utilities over classes. Such a definition of utility can easily be shown to be an interval scale. This process by which utilities are simultaneously assigned within classes and in total so as to satisfy an additivity property has become known as *conjoint measurement.*

A particular case of conjoint measurement is of special significance. An ordinalist position undermined Bernoulli's theory of choice (described above) in risky situations; if cardinal utility had no meaning, there was no way of taking its mathematical expectation. But in the case of risk-bearing, it is very natural to make an appropriate independence assumption, and it is possible so to choose a utility function that an individual's behavior in accepting or rejecting risks can be described by saying that he is choosing the higher expected utility. The philosopher Frank Ramsey made this observation in a paper published posthumously in 1931, in the collection called *The Foundations of Mathematics and Other Essays* (p. 156), but it made no impact; the point was rediscovered by John von Neumann and Oskar Morgenstern, as part of their great work on the theory of games, in 1944. The cardinalist position in this case is rehabilitated, but it has changed its meaning. It is no longer a measure inherently associated with an outcome; instead, the utility function is precisely that which measures the individual's willingness to take risks.

### II. THE SOCIAL WELFARE FUNCTION

*1. Bentham's Utilitarianism.* To Bentham, the utility of each individual was an objectively meaningful magnitude; from the point of view of the community, one man's utility is the same as another's, and therefore it is the sum of the utilities of all individuals which ought to determine social policy. Bentham is indeed concerned strongly to argue that the actual measurement of another's utility is apt to be very difficult, and therefore it is best to let each individual decide as much as possible for himself. In symbols, if $U_1, \ldots, U_n$ are the utilities of the $n$ individuals in the society, each being affected by a social decision, the decision should be made so as to make the sum, $U_1 + U_2 + \cdots + U_n$, as large as possible. An expression of this form, which defines a utility for social choices as a function of the utilities of individuals, is usually termed a *social welfare function.* Bentham's conclusion is really clearly enough stated, but there are considerable gaps in the underlying argument. The addition of utilities assumes an objective or at least interpersonally valid common unit; but no argument is given for the existence of one and no procedure for determining it, except possibly the view that the just noticeable difference is such a unit. Even if the existence and meaningfulness of such a unit is established, it is logically arbitrary to add the utilities instead of combining them in some other way. The argument that all individuals should appear alike in a social judgment leads only to the conclusion that the social welfare function should be a symmetric function of individual utilities, not that it should be a sum.

The Bentham criterion was defended later by John Stuart Mill, but his arguments bear mostly on the propriety and meaning of basing social welfare judgments on individual preferences and not at all on the commensurability of different individuals' utilities or on the form of social welfare function. Mill, like Henry Sidgwick and others, considered the primary use of Bentham's doctrines to be applicability to the legal system of criminal justice; since the conclusions arrived at were qualitative, not quantitative, in nature, vagueness on questions of measurability was not noticed. After the spread of marginal utility theory, the economist F. Y. Edgeworth expounded the notion of utility much more systematically than Bentham had done, with little originality in the foundations, though with a great deal of depth in applications. In particular, he applied the sum-of-utilities criterion to the choice of taxation schemes. The implication is one of radical egalitarianism, as indeed Bentham had already perceived. If, as is usually assumed, the marginal utility of money is decreasing, if all individuals have the same utility function for money, and if a fixed sum of money is to be distributed, then the sum of utilities is maximized when money income is distributed equally. (Here, "money" may be thought of as standing for all types of desired goods.) Then the only argument against complete equality of income is that any procedure to accomplish it would also reduce total income, which is the amount to be divided. The argument can be also put this way; resources should be taken from the rich and given to the poor, not because they are poorer per se but because they place a higher value on a given quantity of goods. If it were possible to differentiate between equally wealthy individuals on the basis of their sensitivities to income increments, it would be proper to give more to the more sensitive.

Apart from Edgeworth, there was little interest in applying the sum-of-utilities criterion to economic or any other policy. Very possibly, the radically egalitarian implications were too unpalatable, as they clearly were to Edgeworth. Subsequent work on "welfare economics," as the theory of economic policy is usually known, tended to be very obscure on fundamentals (although very clarifying in other ways).

## 2. Ordinalist Views of the Social Welfare Function.

Pareto's rejection of cardinal utility rendered meaningless a sum-of-utilities criterion. If utility for an individual was not even measurable, one could hardly proceed to adding utilities for different individuals. Pareto recognized this problem.

First of all, he introduced a necessary condition for social optimality, which has come to be known as *Pareto-optimality:* a social decision is Pareto-optimal if there is no alternative decision which could have made everybody at least as well off and at least one person better off. In this definition, each individual is expressing a preference for one social alternative against another, but no measurement of preference intensity is required. Pareto-optimality is thus a purely ordinal concept.

It is, however, a weak condition. It is possible to compare two alternative social decisions only if there is essential unanimity. To put the matter another way, among any given set of alternatives there will usually be many which would satisfy the definition. A manifestly unjust allocation, with vast wealth for a few and poverty for many, will nevertheless be Pareto-optimal if there is no way of improving the lot of the many without injuring the few in some measure. Pareto himself was very clear on this point.

Pareto-optimality is nevertheless a very useful concept in clearing away a whole realm of possible decisions which are not compatible with any reasonable definition of social welfare. It might be argued that every application of utilitarianism in practice, as to law, has in fact used only the concept of Pareto-optimality. In welfare economics, similarly, it has turned also to be useful in characterizing sharply the types of institutional arrangements which lead to efficient solutions, making it possible to isolate the debate on distributive problems which it cannot solve.

Pareto later (1913) went further. He suggested that each individual in his judgments about social decisions considers the effects on others as well as on himself. The exposition is a bit obscure, but it appears to coincide with that developed later and independently by the economist, Abram Bergson (1938). Each individual has his own evaluation of a social state, which is a function of the utilities of all individuals: $W_i(U_1, \ldots, U_n)$. Since the evaluation is done by a single individual, this function has only ordinal significance. The $U_i$'s themselves may be thought of as an arbitrary numerical scaling of the individuals' preferences; they also have only ordinal significance, but this creates no conceptual problem, since the choice of the social welfare function, $W_i$, for the $i^{\text{th}}$ individual, already takes account of the particular numerical representation of individuals' ordinal utilities.

Interpersonal comparisons of utility are indeed made, but they are ethical judgments by an observer, not factual judgments.

Pareto (but not Bergson) went one step further. The "government" will form the social welfare function which will guide it in its choices by a parallel amalgamation of the social welfare functions of the individuals, i.e., a function, $V(W_1, \ldots, W_n)$. Pareto's concept of a social welfare function remained unknown, though the concept of Pareto-optimality became widely known and influential beginning with the 1930's, as is clear in Bergson's work. The latter became very influential and is accepted as a major landmark; but in fact it has had little application.

279

Bergson accepted fully the ordinalist viewpoint, so that the ethical judgments are always those of a single individual. This approach loses, however, an important feature of most thinking about social welfare, namely, its impartiality among individuals, as stressed by Bentham and given classic, if insufficiently precise, expression in the categorical imperative of Kant. In Bergson's theory, any individual's social welfare function may be what he wishes, and it is in no way excluded that his own utility plays a disproportionate role. Pareto, by his second-level social welfare function for the government implicitly recognized the need for social welfare judgments not tied to particular individuals. But the ordinalist position seems to imply that all preferences are acts of individuals, so that in fact Pareto had no basis for the second level of judgment.

3. *Conjoint Measurement and Additive Social Welfare Functions.* In the field of social choice, as in that of individual choice, the methods of conjoint measurement have led to cardinal utilities which are consistent with the general operational spirit of ordinalism.

William S. Vickrey, in 1945, suggested that the von Neumann-Morgenstern theory of utility for risk-bearing was applicable to the Bergson social welfare function. The criterion of impartiality was interpreted to mean that the ethical judge should consider himself equally likely to have any position in society. He then would prefer one decision to another if the expected utility of the first is higher. The utility function used is his von Neumann-Morgenstern utility function, i.e., that utility function which explains his behavior in risk-bearing. Since all positions are assumed to be equally likely, the expected utility is the same as the average utility of all individuals. In turn, making the average utility as large as possible is equivalent to maximizing the sum of utilities, so that Vickrey's very ingenious argument is a resuscitation, in a way, of Benthamite utilitarianism.

Though Vickrey's criterion is impartial with respect to individual's positions, it is not impartial with respect to their tastes; the maker of the social welfare judgment is implicitly ascribing his own tastes to others. Further it has the somewhat peculiar property that social choices among decisions where there may be no uncertainty are governed by attitudes towards risk-bearing.

Fleming, in 1952, took another direction, which has not been followed up but which is worthy of note. Suppose that an ethical judge is capable of making social welfare judgments for part of the society independently of the remainder. More precisely, suppose that for any social decision which changes the utilities of some individuals but not of others, the judge can specify his preferences without knowing the utility level of those unaffected by the decision. Then it can be shown that there are cardinal utility functions for the individuals and a cardinal social welfare function, such that, $W = U_1 + \cdots + U_n$. $W$ and $U_1, \ldots, U_n$ are interval scales, but the units of measurement must be common. Again there is additivity of utility, but note now that the measurements for individual utility and for social welfare are implied by the social welfare preferences and do not serve as independent bases for them.

Harsanyi in 1955 in effect synthesized the points of view of Vickrey and of Fleming. His argument was that each individual has a von Neumann-Morgenstern utility function, expressing his attitude toward risk, and society, if it were rational, must also have a von Neumann-Morgenstern utility function. It is then easy to demonstrate that society's utility function must be a weighted sum of the individuals' utilities, i.e., $W = a_1 U_1 + \cdots + a_n U_n$. Since each individual utility is an interval scale, we can choose the units so that all the coefficients $a_i$, are 1. This result differs from Vickrey's in that the utility function of the $i^{th}$ individual is used to evaluate his position, rather than the utility function of the judge.

Distantly related to these analyses is the revival, by W. E. Armstrong, and by Leo Goodman and Harry Markowitz, of Bentham's use of the just noticeable difference as an interpersonally valid unit of utility. It has proved remarkably difficult to formulate theories of this type without logical contradiction or at least paradoxical implications.

So far all these results have led to a sum-of-utilities form, though with varying interpretations. As remarked earlier, the notion of impartiality requires symmetry but not necessarily additivity. John Rawls in 1958 proposed an alternative form for the social welfare criterion, to maximize the *minimum* utility in the society. This formulation presupposes an ordinal interpersonal comparison of utilities. He shares with Vickrey and Harsanyi a hypothetical concept of an original position in which no individual knows who he is going to be in the society whose principles are being formulated. However, he does not regard this ignorance as being adequately formulated by equal probabilities of different positions; in view of the permanence of the (hypothetical) choice being made, he argues that a more conservative criterion, such as maximizing the minimum, is more appropriate than maximizing the expected value.

## III. SOCIAL WELFARE AND VOTING

1. *The Theory of Elections in the Eighteenth and Nineteenth Centuries.* In a collective context, voting provides the most obvious way by which individual

preferences are aggregated into a social choice. In a voting context, the ordinalist-cardinalist controversy becomes irrelevant, for voting is intrinsically an ordinal comparison and no more. (Indeed, the failure of voting to represent intensities of preference is frequently held to be a major charge against it.) The theory of elections thus forcibly faced the problems raised by ordinalism long before it had been formulated in economic thought.

The theoretical analysis of social welfare judgments based on voting first appeared in the form of an examination of the merits of alternative election systems in a paper of Jean-Charles de Borda, first read to the French Academy of Sciences in 1770 and published in 1784 (a translation by Alfred de Grazia is in *Isis,* 44 [1953], 42–51). Borda first demonstrated by example that, when there are more than two candidates the method of plurality voting can easily lead to choice of a candidate who is opposed by a large majority. He then proposed another method of voting, one which has been subsequently named the rank-order method (or, sometimes, the method of marks). Let each voter rank all the candidates, giving rank one to the most preferred, rank two to the second, and so forth. Then assign to each candidate a score equal to the sum of the ranks assigned to him by all the voters, and choose the candidate for which the sum of ranks is lowest.

Borda's procedure is ordinal, but the arguments advanced for it were in effect cardinal. He held that, for example, the candidate placed second by an individual was known to be located in preference between the first- and third-place candidates; in the absence of any further information, it was reasonable to argue that the preference for the second-place candidate was located half-way between those of the other two. This established an interval scale for each individual. He then further asserted that the principle of equality of the voters implied that the assignments of ranks by different individuals should count equally.

Borda thus raised most of the issues which have occupied subsequent analysis: (1) the basing of social choice on the entire orderings of all individuals of the available candidates, not merely the first choices; (2) the measurability of individual utilities; and (3) the interpersonal comparability of preference (Borda made interpersonal comparability an ethical judgment of equality, not an empirical judgment).

In 1785, Condorcet published a book on the theory of elections, which raised important new issues. Condorcet seems to have been somewhat aware of Borda's work but had not seen any written version of it when he wrote. Condorcet's aim was to use the theory of probability to provide a basis for social

choice, and this program takes up most of the work, though this aspect has had little subsequent influence. Although he purports to apply the theory of probability to the theory of elections, in fact the latter is developed in a different way.

The most important criterion which Condorcet laid down is that, if there were one candidate who would get a majority against any other in a two-candidate race, he should be elected. The argument for this criterion might be put this way. Let us agree that in a two-candidate race majority voting is the correct method. Now suppose, in an election with three candidates, A, B, and C, that C, for example, is not chosen. Then, so it is argued, it is reasonable to ask that the result of the three-candidate race be the same as if C never were a candidate. To put it another way, it is regarded as undesirable that if A is chosen as against B and C, and the voters are then told that in fact C was not even eligible, that the election should then fall on B. The Condorcet criterion is in the fullest ordinalist spirit; it is consistent with the view that the choice from any set of alternatives should use no information about voters' preferences for candidates not available. Condorcet himself noticed an objection; if an individual judges A preferred to B and B to C, there is some vague sense in which his preference for A against C is stronger than his preference for A against B. Indeed, as we have seen, this was the starting point for Borda's defense of the rank-order method.

In fact, Condorcet used his criterion to examine Borda's rank-order method. He showed that it did not necessarily lead to choosing the pairwise majority candidate. Moreover, no modification of the rank-order method which allowed for nonuniform ranks would satisfy the Condorcet criterion.

Condorcet's second major achievement was to show that his criterion had the possibility of paradoxical consequences. It was perfectly possible that, with three candidates, A be preferred to B by a majority, B to C by a majority, and C to A by a majority. For example, suppose that one-third of the voters preferred A to B and B to C, one-third preferred B to C and C to A, and one-third preferred C to A and A to B. This possibility has become known in the literature as the "paradox of voting," or the Condorcet effect. The paradox of voting, in generalized form, and the possibility of its elimination have become the main themes of recent literature.

In the terminology introduced at the beginning of this article, (pairwise) majority voting defines a relation which is connected (there must be a majority for one or the other of two alternatives, if the number of voters is odd) but need not be transitive.

Condorcet has a proposal for dealing with a case    281

of intransitivity, at least when there are three candidates. Of the three statements of majority preference, disregard the one with the smallest majority; if this is the statement, C preferred to A by a majority, then the choice is A, being preferred to B and "almost preferred" to C. He extends this proposal to cases with more than three candidates, but no one has been able to understand the extension.

Like Bernoulli's work (1738; trans. 1954) on the expected-utility criterion for choice under uncertainty, the papers of Borda and Condorcet had few significant direct successors, (Laplace however gave a more rigorous version of Borda's probabilistic argument for the rank-order method). Indeed the value of their work only came to be appreciated when others came to the problem independently, 160 years later. Since Condorcet's work made use of the theory of probability, it, like Bernoulli's, was recorded in various histories of the theory of probability during the nineteenth century; in the thorough and widely read history of Todhunter (1865), Borda's and Condorcet's theories of elections were included with the probabilistic theory.

The only significant published nineteenth-century work on the theory of election that is known today is that of the English mathematician E. J. Nanson, published in 1882 in Australia, in *Transactions and Proceedings of the Royal Society of Victoria*, **19** (1882), 197–240. Nanson makes no reference to Condorect, but it is hard to believe that his work is independent. He notes the paradox of voting, in a manner which suggests that he regarded it as well known, and accepts fully the Condorcet criterion. His work consists primarily in showing that each of several voting methods that have been proposed fail to satisfy the Condorcet criterion, in that one could find a system of preference orderings for individuals such that there exists a candidate who would get a majority against any other but would not be chosen. He then proposes a method which will satisfy the criterion: rank all candidates according to the rank-order method. Then eliminate all candidates for which the sum of ranks is above the average. With the remaining candidates form the rank-orders again, considering only those candidates, and repeat the process until one candidate is selected.

Among the methods considered and found wanting by Nanson was preferential voting, an adaptation of the Hare system of proportional representation to the election of a single candidate. In 1926 George Hallett, a leading American advocate of proportional representation, suggested a modification which met the Condorcet criterion. He developed a procedure, the details of which need not be repeated here, which, starting with the orderings of all the candidates by all the voters, picked out a candidate, A, and a set of

candidates, $B_1, \ldots, B_r$, such that A is preferred by a majority to each of $B_1, \ldots, B_r$. Then the $B_i$'s are eliminated from further consideration; the orderings of only the remaining candidates are now used, and the process is repeated. It may be added that Hallett is fully aware of the work of both Condorcet and Nanson and refers to both of them.

Duncan Black has called attention to some contributions of C. L. Dodgson (Lewis Carroll), printed but not published, particularly one of 1876. Dodgson accepted the Condorcet criterion and observed the possibility of paradox of voting; he used the criterion, as Nanson did a few years later, to criticize certain voting methods. By implication rather than directly, he suggested an ingenious solution for the cases of paradox; choose that candidate who would have a majority over all others if the original preference scales of the voters were altered in a way which involved the least possible number of interchanges of preferences. (When there are three candidates, this proposal coincides with Nanson's.)

Dodgson raised one more conceptually interesting point, that of the possibility of "no election." His discussion is inconsistent. At one point, he contends that if the paradox occurs, there should be "no election"; however, a little further on, he argues that if "no election" is a possibility, then it should be entered among the list of candidates and treated symmetrically with them. In the context of elections themselves, the possibility is uninteresting; but if we think of legislative proposals, "no election" means the preservation of the status quo. Dodgson is noting that legislative choice processes do not take all the alternatives on a par but give a special privileged status to one.

Dodgson made no reference to predecessors; however, his pamphlets were designed to influence the conduct of Oxford elections, and scholarly footnoting would have been inappropriate. Whether or not he read Todhunter's passages on Borda and Condorcet cannot now be determined. Of course, no subsequent work was influenced by him.

*2. Current Analysis of Social Welfare Based on Rankings.* After a long but exiguous history, the general theory of elections suddenly became a lively subject of research beginning with the papers of Black published in 1948 and 1949 and Arrow's 1951 monograph. Since then there has been an uninterrupted spate of discussion, which is still continuing. It is perhaps not easy to see exactly why the interest has changed so markedly. Neither Black nor Arrow were aware at the time they first wrote of any of the preceding literature, though it is hard to exclude the possibility that some of this knowledge was in a vague sense common property. Arrow has noted (*Social Choice and*

*Individual Values,* p. 93) that when he first hit upon the paradox of voting, he felt sure that it was known, though he was unable to recall any source.

Both Black and Arrow are economists, and some historical tendencies in economics, in addition to the general theory of marginal utility, played their role. (1) A number of marginal utility theorists, such as Marshall and Wicksteed, had tried to demonstrate that their theories were, as Bentham had originally held, applicable in fields wider than the purely economic. (2) In particular, economists in the field of public finance were forced to recognize that public expenditures, which are plainly a form of economic activity, were in principle regulated by voters. A voter who was also a taxpayer could usefully be thought of as making a choice between public and private goods; the actual outcome would depend upon the voting process. Problems of this type were studied by Knut Wicksell in 1896, Erik Lindahl in 1919, and Howard Bowen in 1943. These works tend in a general way to a combined theory of political-economic choice. (3) Other economists, particularly Harold Hotelling in 1929, and Joseph Schumpeter in his 1942 book *Socialism, Capitalism, and Democracy,* suggested models of the political process analogous to that of the economic system, with voters taking the place of consumers and politicians that of entrepreneurs. (4) Marginal utility theorists, e.g., Edgeworth in 1881, and the Austrians, Carl Menger and Eugen von Böhm-Bawerk, about the same time, had been concerned with problems of bargaining, where one buyer meets one seller, rather than the more usual competitive assumptions of many buyers and sellers. The development of game theory by von Neumann and Morgenstern was intended to meet this problem, but the formulation took on such general proportions that it suggested the possibility of a very general theory of social behavior based on the foundation of individual behavior as governed by utility functions. (5) The ideas of Pareto and Bergson were now widespread and raised demands for clarification.

Most of these topics could be interpreted both descriptively and normatively, and some of this duality has persisted in the current literature. There are two main themes in the literature, associated with the names of Black and Arrow, respectively: (1) demonstration that if the preference scales of individuals are not arbitrary but satisfy certain hypotheses, then majority voting is transitive; (2) formulation of sets of reasonable conditions for aggregating individual preferences through a kind of generalized voting and examining the consequences; if the set of conditions is strong enough, there can be no system of voting consistent with all of them.

Suppose that all the alternative decisions can be imagined arrayed in a certain order in such a way that each individual's preferences are single-peaked, i.e., of any two alternatives to the left of the most preferred (by an individual), he prefers the one nearest to it, and similarly with two alternatives to the right. This would be the case if the "Left-Right" ordering of political parties were a valid empirical description. Black demonstrated that if preferences are single-peaked then no paradox of voting can arise. Put another way, the relation, "alternative preferred by a majority to alternative B," is an ordering and in particular is transitive.

Current work, particularly that of Amartya Sen and Gordon Tullock, has developed generalizations of the single-peaked preference condition in different directions. The conditions are too technical for brief presentation, but, like single-peakedness, they imply certain types of similarity among the preference scales of all individuals.

Arrow stated formally a set of apparently reasonable criteria for social choice and demonstrated that they were mutually inconsistent. The study arose as an attempt to give operational content to Bergson's concept of a social welfare function. The conditions on the social decision procedure follow: (1) for any possible set of individual preference orderings, there should be defined a social preference ordering (connected and transitive) which governs social choices; (2) if everybody prefers alternative A to alternative B, then society must have the same preference (Parento-optimality); (3) the social choice made from any set of available alternatives should depend only on the orderings of individuals with respect to those alternatives; (4) the social decision procedure should not be dictatorial, in the sense that there is one whose preferences prevail regardless of the preferences of all others.

Condition (3) in effect restricts social decision procedures (or social welfare criteria) to generalized forms of voting; only preferences among the available candidates are used in deciding an election. The inconsistency of these conditions is in fact a generalized form of the paradox of voting; no system of voting, no matter how complicated, can avoid a form of the paradox. As in the original Condorcet case of simple majority voting, all that is meant by the paradox is that it could arise for certain sets of individual preference orderings. If individual preference orderings were restricted to a set for which the conditions of Black, Sen, or Tullock hold, then majority voting and many other methods would satisfy conditions (2–4).

The evaluation of the Arrow paradox has led to considerable controversy, still persisting.

In one version of Arrow's system, condition (2) was replaced by another which, loosely speaking, stated that a change of individuals' preferences in favor of a particular alternative A would raise its social preference, if possible. The existence of the paradox is not altered by this substitution. Recent work by Kenneth May and later Yasusuke Murakami showed that this condition, together with condition (3), had powerful implications for the nature of the social decision process. Specifically, it followed that the choice from any pair of alternatives is made by a sequence of majority votes, where outcomes of the vote at one step can enter as a vote at a later step. In general, some individuals may vote more than once, and some votes may be prescribed in advance. If however it is assumed in addition that all individuals should enter symmetrically into the procedure and also that the voting rule should be the same for all pairs of alternatives, then the only possible voting rule is pairwise majority decision, i.e., the Condorcet criterion.

*BIBLIOGRAPHY*

For histories of the theory of individual choice in economics, see E. Kauder, *A History of Marginal Utility Theory* (Princeton, 1965), and G. J. Stigler, "The Development of Utility Theory," *Journal of Political Economy,* **58** (1950), 307–27, 373–96. Bernoulli's paper originally appeared in *Comentarii Academiae Scientiarum Imperiales Petropolitanae,* **5** (1738), 175–92. It has been translated into English in *Econometrica,* **12** (1954), 23–36. The quotation from J. Bentham appears in his *An Introduction to the Principles of Morals and Legislation,* reprinted in *The Utilitarians* (Garden City, N.Y., 1961), p. 17. For a survey of the theory of conjoint measurement, see P. C. Fishburn, "A Note on Recent Developments in Additive Utility Theories for Multiple-Factor Situations," *Operations Research,* **14** (1966), 1143–48.

No adequate secondary sources exist for most of Part II. See Bentham's work just cited; W. Stark, ed. *Jeremy Bentham's Economic Writings* (London, 1954); M. P. Mack, *Jeremy Bentham: An Odyssey of Ideas, 1748-1792* (New York, 1963); F. Y. Edgeworth, *Mathematical Psychics* (London, 1881), and idem, "The Pure Theory of Taxation," in *Papers Relating to Political Economy* (London, 1925), II, 102; V. Pareto, *The Mind and Society* (New York, 1935), **4,** 1459–74; A. Bergson, *Essays in Normative Economics* (Cambridge, Mass., 1966), Part I; W. S. Vickrey, "Measuring Marginal Utility by Reaction to Risk," *Econometrica,* **13** (1945), 319–33, and idem, "Utility, Strategy, and Decision Rules," *Quarterly Journal of Economics,* **74** (1960), 507–35; J. M. Fleming, "A Cardinal Concept of Welfare," *Quarterly Journal of Economics,* **64** (1952), 366–84; J. Harsanyi, "Cardinal Welfare, Individualistic Ethics, and Interpersonal Comparisons of Utility," *Journal of Political Economy,* **56** (1953), 309–21; W. E. Armstrong, "Utility and the Theory of Welfare," *Oxford Economic Papers, New Series,* **3** (1951), 259–71; L. Goodman and H. Markowitz, "Social Welfare Functions Based on Individual Rankings," *American Journal of Sociology,* **58** (1952), 257–62; J. Rothenberg, *The Measurement of Social Welfare* (Englewood Cliffs, N.J., 1961); and J. Rawls, "Distributive Justice," in P. Laslett and W. G. Runciman, eds. *Philosophy, Politics, and Society, Third Series* (Oxford, 1967), pp. 58–82.

For the work discussed in Part III, see C. G. Hoag and G. Hallett, *Proportional Representation* (New York, 1926), for the work of Hallett, Hare, and others on proportional representation and preferential voting. See also: J. Rothenberg, op. cit.; K. J. Arrow, *Social Choice and Individual Values,* 2nd ed. (New York, 1963); D. Black, *The Theory of Committees and Elections* (Cambridge, 1958); I. Todhunter, *A History of the Mathematical Theory of Probability from the Time of Pascal to that of Laplace* (Cambridge and London, 1865); A. K. Sen, "A Possibility Theorem on Majority Decisions," *Econometrica,* **34** (1966), 491–99; G. Tullock, *Toward a Mathematics of Politics* (Ann Arbor, 1967), Ch. III; and Y. Murakami, *Logic and Social Choice* (London and New York, 1968). The work of Condorcet is discussed by Black, pp. 159–80; see also G. G. Granger, *La mathématique sociale du Marquis de Condorcet* (Paris, 1956), esp. pp. 94–129. Condorcet's study was entitled *Essai sur l'application de l'analyse à la probabilité des décisions rendues à la pluralité des voix* (Paris, 1785). For Laplace's work on elections, see Black, pp. 180–83.

KENNETH J. ARROW

[See also Democracy; **Economic History; Economic Theory of Natural Liberty;** Equality; **Game Theory;** Probability; Rationality; Utilitarianism; **Utility.**]

# SOCIALISM FROM ANTIQUITY TO MARX

AS A MODERN political movement, socialism arose in the early and middle decades of the nineteenth century. As an idea, it can be discerned much earlier in mythic, philosophic, and theological thought. In the simplest sense, socialism amounts to a belief that all producers ought to share equally in the fruits of combined labor. On a deeper level, socialism is more than an economic formula, and even more than a prescription for justice. It is an expression of faith in the capacity of the mass of mankind to overcome what is thought of as an alienation or estrangement from its own essential nature, which socialists contend is far more creative, pacific, and altruistic than actual experience might indicate.

Until comparatively recently, this faith was usually circumscribed by an oppressive awareness of the constraints, both natural and artificial, preventing or distorting the expression of true humanity. Material scarcity and moral weakness were held to require and even to justify social systems in which inequality and hierarchy were assumed to be synonyms of order. All egalitarian alternatives were likely to be dismissed as impractical. Equality was thought of as a standard that may once have had bearing in the remote past, or that might apply in the distant future, but that could have no great relevance to present conditions, except as an invitation to chaos. Because it was treated as an impractical ideal, the idea of equality remained vague and undifferentiated, a catch-all for panaceas of every description, and an easy target for skeptics.

Socialism was for a long time one facet of this relatively amorphous ideal, evident in romantic evocations of primitive innocence, in millenarian prophecies of future perfection, in the more radical theologies of the Protestant Reformation, in secular utopias, and in some of the social criticism of the French Enlightenment. In the nineteenth century these intimations were transformed into elaborate arguments for social change taking essentially two forms. One view held that cooperative communities are within the realm of possibility, provided they are constructed with careful attention to individual and social needs. The other, put forward by Karl Marx, conceived of socialism as a stage of historical development, destined to be achieved after a worldwide revolution by the working class against private property and those who benefit from it. In this view, the ideal community cannot be planned in advance and put into operation regardless of historical conditions; it must arise out of revolutionary activity and will be successful only when historically appropriate. This distinction between socialism as a theory of the planned community and socialism as the outcome of an historically determined revolution, starkly clear in the nineteenth century, was adumbrated even earlier, but overshadowed by the tendency to think of socialism in all its forms as an impossible phantasy.

The first traces of socialism appear in the lament for a lost "Golden Age," a common theme in antiquity. Greek myths, recorded as early as the eighth century B.C. and derived from an even older oral tradition, recall an original state—the Age of Cronus—when all shared equally in the common lot, private property was unknown, and peace and harmony reigned undisturbed. These myths, as Lovejoy and Boas point out, describe either a "soft" or a "hard" primitivism: some depict a time of abundance and luxury in which human labor is unnecessary because the earth produces its bounty spontaneously; others depict a time of simple needs and satisfactions. Poetic renderings contrast the innocence of the original conditions with the degeneracy of actual society. The Golden Age, so the accepted interpretation ran, "was enjoyed by a different breed of mortals, in a different condition of the world and (in one version) under different gods, and no practical

moral could therefore consistently be drawn from it for the guidance of the present race. It was by implication irrecoverable, at least by men's own efforts" (Lovejoy and Boas, *Primitivism*, p. 16).

The same melancholy reflection takes philosophic form in the Platonic dialogues. In the *Laws* the "Athenian Stranger," who seems to express Plato's own view, pays tribute to the ancient ideal: "The first and highest form of the state [*polis*] and of the government and of the law is that in which there prevails most widely the ancient saying, that 'Friends have all things in common'" (*Laws* 739, trans. B. Jowett). Although such perfection is beyond revival, he adds, no better system could be conceived. In the *Republic*, however, Socrates is represented as believing that even in an ideal society communism could be a way of life only for a moral and intellectual elite. The superior philosophic capacity of the guardians or rulers would enable them to ignore the demands of appetite; their role would require that they be disinterested in all but the dispensing of justice. Otherwise, equality for unequals is criticized as a self-contradictory proposition which can only result in danger for society, as the chaotic experience of democracy proves all too well.

In his *Politics* Aristotle is skeptical of all proposals for communism, including the limited version advanced in Plato's *Republic*. Collective ownership flouts the most fundamental axioms of human nature; property held in common is likely to remain untended and uncultivated. Far better, in Aristotle's view, is the practice followed in Sparta, where goods were privately owned but made available by their owners for public use. The rightly ordered polis will apply the principle of distributive justice, or proportional equality. Absolute or numerical equality reflects only one of the claims that may legitimately be made by citizens—the claim that as members of society they deserve identical treatment. If equity and stability are to be served, however, other claims must also be recognized, such as those based upon superiority of intellect, contribution to the welfare of society, and birth or status.

The notion that differences in intellect justify social inequality was challenged by the Stoic school which arose in the third century B.C. in the waning years of the Greek polis and achieved a considerable influence during the expansion of Rome. This influence was more ethical than political, however. Although the Stoics taught that the universality of reason rendered men equals by nature, they did not go on to argue that natural standards could be applied in conventional societies. Like the Cynics, they lamented the departure from the equality decreed by nature and criticized especially inhumane attitudes and practices, but could

285

see no way to return corrupt society to its natural innocence. The best that might be hoped for, according to such spokesmen for a mature Stoic view as Cicero and Seneca, was that less fortunate classes, including slaves, would be treated charitably, in recognition of the essential unity of all mankind.

In Rome the attitude shared by citizens and philosophers alike found expression in the festival of the Saturnalia. Once each year the Age of Saturn (the Roman form of Cronus) was memorialized: slaves dined with masters and distinctions were temporarily forgotten. In at least one non-Roman version of this ceremony, the moral behind the festival is said to have been made explicit beyond any doubt: a criminal was elevated to the ruler's throne during the celebration and executed as soon as it was over, as a warning to subject classes of what they might expect from attempts at revolution.

To these classes, Christian teachings may have seemed more radical than Stoicism, especially since the spiritual egalitarianism of the Gospels appeared to make the argument over degrees of rationality irrelevant. Of what consequence were differences of intellect if, in the eyes of God, every man had a soul and all souls were alike worthy? The "poor in spirit" (Luke 6:20, King James ver.) could well have read social significance into Saint Paul's announcement that with the advent of the Redeemer "there is no such thing as Jew and Greek, slave and freeman, male and female; for you are all one person in Christ Jesus" (Galatians 3:28, *The New English Bible,* London, 1961). According to Saint Luke, the apostles could be said to have practiced communism: "Not a man of them claimed any of his possessions as his own, but everything was held in common. . . . They had never a needy person among them, because all who had property in land or houses sold it, brought the proceeds of the sale, and laid the money at the feet of the apostles; it was then distributed to any who stood in need" (Acts 4:32–35, *The New English Bible*).

As the expectation of an imminent apocalypse receded, millenarian enthusiasm became an embarrassment and a threat to the order of society and the unity of the Church. Authoritative interpreters of the Gospels insisted that they must not be read as a call to social revolution. An apostle had also declared that "the authorities are in God's service" (Romans 13:6, *The New English Bible*). Although God had intended men to live together as brothers in an earthly paradise, Saint Cyprian, Saint Zeno of Verona, and Saint Ambrose, the Bishop of Milan, all observed that human wickedness had frustrated this intention. Until the Parousia or Second Coming of Christ, the Christian was obliged to endure worldly corruption with pa-

tience and obedience. The most influential of the Church Fathers, Saint Augustine, asserted in *The City of God* (A.D. 413) that the injustices of the earthly city were God's judgment upon human sinfulness. While the pious Christian lived "like a captive and a stranger" (Book 19, Ch. xvii) in the unredeemed world, he was to cling to his faith but accept his station in life, whatever it might be.

The medieval canonists, who were the principal apologists for papal supremacy, added more positive justifications of inequality. Unity required subordination and discipline. Hierarchy in the Church and society reflected the superiority of the soul to the body, as well as the order of the cosmos, the very architecture of God. Communism was appropriate only for those exceptional ascetic virtuosos in holy orders seeking to escape attachments to the flesh and the world. Movements outside the Church, however, such as those of the Cathars, Waldenses, and Free Spirits, even though they aimed at a similar perfection, if not always through asceticism, were condemned as dangerous heresies.

Both the example and the teachings of monastic and sectarian movements nevertheless stood in pointed contrast to official dogma. As feudal society disintegrated under a complex network of strains, including princely ambition, conflicts over clerical appointments, splits within the Church, the expansion of commerce, and the rise of independent cities, the hold of the orthodox view weakened and the appeal of alternatives rose. One distinctly unorthodox alternative was posed by a twelfth-century Calabrian monk, Joachim of Floris, who preached an historicized doctrine of the Trinity resembling that earlier condemned in Montanism. According to Joachim, the incarnation was to be understood as an evolutionary succession of three ages or dispensations: of the Father or law, of the Son or Gospel, and of the Holy Spirit. The process was to be completed between 1200 and 1260 under the aegis of a new order of monks which would direct the overthrow of Antichrist. Through their triumph, the Holy Spirit would permeate all mankind and servitude and obedience would be replaced by universal love. The Joachimite prophecy inspired a wing of the Franciscan order, the Franciscan Spirituals, to imagine themselves successors of the Church appointed to lead Christendom toward the millennium.

Variations of the same prophecy assigned a messianic role to the Emperor Frederick II. Even after the death of Frederick, it was widely hoped that he would somehow reappear and usher in the last days by striking down the corrupt clergy. In the fourteenth and fifteenth centuries, peasant rebellions erupted in many parts of Europe, in response to changing economic conditions as well as visionary preaching. Religious protests, such as those led by John Ball and John Wycliffe in England and by the Hussites and Taborites in Bohemia, weakened adherence to the Church and eventually brought on the full-scale reformations of the sixteenth and seventeenth centuries. In the Protestant Reformation, the eschatological underground came to the surface in the general upheaval and made a noteworthy impact. Thomas Müntzer and Gerrard Winstanley, the leaders of two distinct movements on the "left-wing of the Reformation" (Bainton) can fairly be regarded as among the most direct theoretical precursors of modern socialism.

Müntzer was a fiery zealot who broke with Martin Luther and raised a more radical and mystical standard than Luther and the other moderate reformers were willing to accept. In 1525 he led an army of peasants in an abortive revolt which ended with his capture and execution. Although there is little in Müntzer's sermons and letters explicitly advocating communism, he was regarded by his contemporaries as a revolutionary in every respect—an "uproarious spirit" (*aufrührischen Geist*) in Luther's words. Müntzer earned this reputation by demanding total reform, temporal as well as ecclesiastical. Warmly acknowledging his debt to the "weighty testimony" of Joachim, Müntzer saw himself and his Allstedt *Bund* performing the role the Franciscan Spirituals had earlier sought to assume. Unlike the monks, Müntzer saw no reason to refrain from violence against "godless" opponents. The "fifth monarchy" foretold by the prophet Daniel, he believed, could only follow the physical destruction of the first four, the last of which remained to be toppled.

Müntzer's "Revolutionary, or charismatic, Spiritualism" (Williams and Mergall, p. 32) rejects the view of more moderate reformers that the Bible and sacraments, but not a clerical hierarchy, should mediate between God and man. In order to become one with Christ (*Christformig*), he claimed, the believer had to experience an identification with God directly and without mediation. This theological radicalism enabled Müntzer to regard himself and his followers as "an élite of amoral supermen" (Cohn, Ch. vii) released from ordinary ethical injunctions in their role as a vanguard of the millennium. Sectarian quietism and withdrawal were also rejected in favor of the revolutionary activism of a mass movement. In contrast to Müntzer, the militant Anabaptists who took control of Münster and whose communism and polygamy seemed scandalous to all of Europe, were far more conventional in their views, since they continued to believe in the need to isolate themselves from worldly corruption in order to live a perfect life above the law.

Winstanley experienced a revelation in which he and his followers were instructed to seize certain lands and cultivate them in common so as to restore the "holy community," an ideal they shared with other Puritans. No one, he declared, ought to be "Lord or landlord over another, but whole mankind was made equall, and knit into one body by one spirit of love, which is Christ in you, the hope of glory" (*Works* [1649], p. 323). The creation and redemption express a dialectic of separation and reunion: spirit and man are separate at first but in the end "man is drawne up into himselfe again, or new *Jerusalem* . . . comes down to Earth, to fetch Earth up to live in that life, that is a life above objects" (*Works* [1650], p. 453). It is only a "strange conceit" to imagine a new Jerusalem "above the skies" (*Works* [1649], p. 226).

Winstanley and Müntzer share a mystical and socially activistic theological perspective. In Winstanley's case, this perspective issues in a pacifistic orientation toward labor in common; in Müntzer's, it serves to promote violent revolution. Had the left wing succeeded in impressing itself more fully upon the main carriers of reform, the distinction that was to arise in the nineteenth century between voluntaristic and revolutionary socialists might have been felt earlier. In fact, however, the impact of the left wing was ephemeral. The most significant social residue of the Reformation was the attitude Max Weber described as the "Protestant ethic," or the exhortation to economic individualism as proof of piety and predestination. Protestantism lent legitimacy to a limited egalitarianism by sanctioning economic competition and moral autonomy, but it offered no warrant for socialism, which continued to be regarded as "utopian."

The term "utopia" came into use after 1516, when Thomas More published his work of that name boldly denouncing the vicious effects of private property and commerce, especially as they were evident in the enclosure movement in England. The sheep, he wrote, had begun to devour men and to consume whole fields, houses, and cities; a true commonwealth, as distinct from those which go by the name but are merely conspiracies of rich men, would be possible only if property were held in common. More's hostility toward private property and his advocacy of communism joined a traditional Christian disapproval of worldly avarice and corruption with an attack upon contemporary economic inequities. Many later and more secular writers, including Francis Bacon and Thomas Campanella in the seventeenth century, followed More's example by inventing other utopias, both in order to give freer reign to the imagination and to publish more radical social criticism than might have been safe to broach in an essay or treatise. As a device and a literary genre, the utopia came to replace the prophecy of religious apocalypse as a vehicle for the expression of radically egalitarian sentiments.

The dominant tendency of social theorizing, in the period following the Reformation and culminating in the French Revolution, is more accurately reflected in the work of the natural rights-social contract school. These theorists secularized and transformed traditional natural law doctrines into justifications for limited government and civil liberty. In the process, the right of private property was established as one of the most fundamental of all natural rights. John Locke argued that while God had originally given the earth to men in common, He meant it for "the use of the Industrious and the Rational" (*Second Treatise of Government* [1690], Ch. V, para. 34). The right to appropriate was subject to the limits of the law of nature, but the introduction of money by tacit consent made evasion of these limits legitimate. The main objective of the social contract was therefore the protection of the right of property, broadly understood as life, liberty, and estate and more narrowly as material possessions. James Harrington argued in *Oceana* (1656) that agrarian republics could survive only if effective limits were put upon acquisition, especially of land, but neither Harrington nor any other English theorist of this century was in any sense an advocate of socialism.

The French Physiocrats, who coined the term *laissez-faire*, agreed with Locke in regarding the right to private property as the foundation of law and economic progress. Otherwise, the leading writers of the French Enlightenment were rather less enthusiastic in their support for economic individualism. Generally, the attitude of the *philosophes* resembled that of the Stoics. Equality, Voltaire wrote, "is at once the most natural and at the same time the most chimerical of things." Although nature makes men equal, "on our miserable globe it is impossible for men living in society not to be divided into two classes, one the rich who command, the other the poor who serve" (*Philosophic Dictionary* [1769], trans. P. Gay, New York [1962], I, 245). Similarly, although Rousseau issued a stinging indictment of the evils of property, he did not propose that the right of property be abolished. The most that could be hoped for, according to Rousseau, Voltaire, Montesquieu, and Louis de Jaucourt in the *Encyclopédie*, was that enlightened rulers would eliminate extreme inequalities and alleviate the plight of the poor.

In the latter half of the eighteenth century, some theorists contended that the natural condition of society must have been one of collective rather than private ownership. Among them were Thomas Raynal, Jean Meslier, Gabriel de Bonnot de Mably, Simon Linguet, and the all but anonymous Morelly. But except for Morelly's *Code de la nature* (1755), which advocates a return to communism, the others agreed with Mably that although the communism of Sparta and the religious orders was closer to nature than the modern worship of wealth and luxury, "where property has once been established it is necessary to regard it as the foundation of order, peace, and public safety" (*Oeuvres*, IX, 13).

The detached skepticism and critical resignation which characterized the Enlightenment were swept aside by the enthusiasm for total renovation accompanying the French Revolution. Even so, all but a handful of the leading figures in the Revolution, including the Jacobins, were committed to the retention of private property. The demand for a more radical reform emerged among a minority of disaffected revolutionaries. Their major spokesman was François-Noël (Caius Gracchus) Babeuf, the leader of a small "Conspiracy of the Equals" to which a larger number of Jacobins had attached themselves. Along with other conspirators, including Sylvain Maréchal, the author of the provocative *Manifesto of the Equals* (1796), Babeuf was arrested and tried for plotting to overthrow the Directory. In his defense, Babeuf insisted that he was acting in the service of the Revolution, which would remain incomplete while there was still inequality. Borrowing a distinction drawn by the moderate Girondin, the Marquis de Condorcet, Babeuf argued that the Revolution had so far established only legal equality, but not "real" equality. Since even superior intelligence and exertion do not "extend the capacity of the stomach," it was "absurd and unjust" to distribute rewards on any basis other than need (Advielle, *Babeuf*, II, 38). The revolution of 1789 was therefore merely the forerunner of "another revolution, greater and even more solemn, which will be the last" (ibid., I, 197). It would be accomplished, however, not by legislative assemblies, but by the broad masses of the people.

Although Babeuf's conspiracy was finally crushed, *babouvisme*, with its emphasis on the revolutionary role of the working class, had a lingering influence upon socialist theory. It was only after the Napoleonic Wars, however, that modern socialism took definitive form. In the usage it now has, the word "socialist" appeared in print for the first time in 1827 in the *Co-operative Magazine* published by the followers of the industrial reformer, Robert Owen. In 1832, as *le socialisme*, it made its debut across the Channel in *Le Globe*, the journal of a band of practical and visionary reformers inspired by the theories of Henri de Saint-Simon. In this germinal period, socialism had its greatest vogue in France, where the hold of more conventional ideas had been rudely shaken by waves of revolution. The aims and outcome of this series of upheavals were subjects of intense controversy and socialism appeared to its adherents and even to some of its detractors as the logical fulfillment of the process of change which had begun in 1789. By about 1840 the term was commonly applied to a fairly wide array of doctrines, all sharing an intensely critical attitude toward existing social systems and a firm conviction that radical transformation was both possible and imperative.

Socialism probably seemed an apt name for this potpourri of dissenting views because in ways both critical and constructive all these doctrines were focused on "social" rather than individual well-being. The "social question" was a subject of wide interest, but the prevailing view was that the wretched conditions endured by the poor were as inevitable as they were unfortunate. Those who challenged this complacency by subjecting social conditions to harsh criticism and by demanding that they be changed fundamentally were likely to be called socialists. All the doctrines, despite variations, stressed the need for greater collective responsibility and a "strengthening of 'socialising' influences," as Cole observed (*Socialist Thought*, I, 4). The term "communism" was sometimes used as a synonym for socialism and sometimes to denote doctrines stressing the need for revolution and community of goods.

The socialist view was advanced in direct opposition to the more widely accepted belief that the rights of the individual against society and the state were inviolable. The most popular writers on political economy in the first half of the nineteenth century generally claimed that since individual liberty was the source of all progress, its enhancement must be the paramount aim of public policy. To interfere with the freedom of exchange was to infringe upon the rights of man and to place dangerous obstacles in the way of industry and prosperity. Against this belief, the socialists argued that the legal protection of unlimited acquisition sanctioned the exploitation of wage-laborers by the owners of capital. Any prosperity that resulted from industry could therefore benefit only the privileged few—the new aristocracy of wealth—at the expense of the many, who would remain at least as impoverished as ever.

On the most universal level—and perhaps the most fundamental—this objection to the gross inequalities flowing from the protection of private property expressed a profound and bitter moral indignation. Labor was said to have become a commodity, the laborer himself to have been robbed of his humanity

and degraded into a brute instrument of production. "For the enormous majority," Karl Marx protested, the vaunted culture of European civilization amounted to no more than "a mere training to act as a machine" (*Communist Manifesto* [1848], trans. S. Moore, pp. 146f.). Charles Fourier, in effect elaborating Rousseau's earlier indictment, drew up a meticulous catalogue of the vices due to selfish absorption with the accumulation of wealth. These vices included not only the misery of the poor but also the unhappiness and boredom of the rich. A phrase coined a generation earlier by the Girondin Jean-Pierre Brissot de Warville and popularized by Pierre-Joseph Proudhon summed up the socialist critique of conventional morality in an incendiary catechism: "What is property? It is theft."

The critics differed among themselves in the explanations offered of the sources of corruption and in proposals for reform. Some believed that moral regeneration could come only in new, planned communities. To Owen, the bedrock of social reconstruction was the principle that character is shaped by environment. Moral vices, he thought, could be reformed only by changing the conditions that produced them. Étienne Cabet imagined such a new community in his *Voyage in Icaria* (1840) in terms derived from earlier utopian speculation. Fourier sought to show that it was possible to diminish frustration and increase satisfaction without changing human nature, simply by establishing planned, but voluntary communities in which the diversity of human dispositions would be matched with the requirements of the division of labor. These ideas inspired the creation of model communities in Britain and America and generated great interest among social reformers in many countries.

Others who could see little or no hope in small-scale projects argued instead for grander efforts to reorganize society. The economist Jean-Charles Simonde de Sismondi pointed out, as early as 1819, that unless gains from increased productivity were more widely distributed, national economies would suffer not only from inequity but from periodic crises of overproduction. Saint-Simon declared that the enormous potentialities of the industrial system and of scientific research should be organized to serve the needs of society. The domination of society and government by aristocratic idlers (*les oisifs*) must be replaced by a combination of the producers (*les industriels*). Louis Blanc was convinced that the evils of the property system could be eradicated without revolution or expropriation if the state would extend public credit to "social workshops" (*ateliers*) in which artisans in the various branches of industry could form cooperative associations for production and distribution. By eliminating the need for private sources of capital, the state would make exploitation impossible. Proudhon, by vocation a tradesman, by temperament an anarchist, was suspicious of all central authority and all collectivist schemes. He preferred what he called "mutualism"—a series of decentralized exchanges in which producers would enter into contracts with each other to trade goods and services. The object would be to prevent exploitation but to retain the autonomy of the producers and avoid imposing an oppressive central authority in place of the market system.

Still others thought that changes of policy or institutions could be expected only after a change of heart. Constantin Pecqueur in France, Karl Grün, Moses Hess, and Wilhelm Weitling in Germany, believed that an ethical religion of humanity was needed either to fill the void left by the decline of Christian faith or to express common humanistic values to which all could subscribe, regardless of their attitude toward religion. The disciples of Saint-Simon, led by Barthélemy-Prosper Enfantin, Olinde Rodrigues, Saint-Armand Bazard, and Pierre Leroux, organized and directed a sect to propagate the master's call for a "New Christianity." The cult was outfitted with all the appropriate trappings, including clergy, ritual, and devotional services, and took as its cardinal dogma the "principle of association," the Saint-Simonian equivalent of Fourier's "law of attraction." It served the same purpose for the Saint-Simonians that Fourier's principle did for his followers, which was to provide a social and moral analogue of Newton's law of gravitation. Philippe Buchez and Proudhon, as well as Cabet—who preached a "true Christianity"—felt that Christianity itself, properly understood, was simply socialism by another, older name. In Britain John M. F. Ludlow, with the help of Frederick D. Maurice and Charles Kingsley, both clergymen, founded a Christian Socialist movement.

None of these spokesmen for socialism had an impact comparable to that exerted by Karl Marx, whose writings became the touchstone of socialist thinking and action. Marx differed most strikingly from earlier socialists as well as from contemporaries in believing that socialism could not be established by an act of will, either through voluntary adoption or forced imposition, but would inevitably arise at an appropriate stage of history. He couched his views in a doctrine that was at once a philosophy of history, a science of society, and a handbook of revolution. As a thinker, his greatest talents were not so much those of an originator as of a trenchant critic, a skillful borrower, and a brilliant synthesizer. In the early stages of his thought, when he developed his philosophy of history, he was indebted most to Hegel. In the later period, he owed many of his sociological and economic ideas and more

than a few of his revolutionary slogans to a host of other writers.

The influence of Hegelianism upon Marx is well recognized. It is not too much to say that all of Marx's work bears the impress of his early encounter with Hegel and the Left Hegelians. What is less well appreciated is the degree to which the apocalyptic, quasi-religious character of Marxian socialism was shaped by Hegel's philosophical restatement of radical Christian theology. Hegel's first writings grew out of his study of theology at Tübingen. In them he struggled to come to terms with traditional Christianity and the new Kantian ethics. The resolution he came to is best expounded in his essay on "The Spirit of Christianity and Its Fate" (1799) where he offers an interpretation strikingly similar to the historical trinitarianism of Joachim. Kantian ethics is explained as a reversion to Judaism, or the religion of abstract law, a "juridical order" in which man is a dependent of a remote law-giving deity. Christianity, as the incarnation of God in a single man, opens a second chapter in the unfolding of morality: Jesus, as "the beautiful soul," renounces property and all other ties to the juridical order and thereby transcends it. But Christianity, as a religion of faith in God rather than of universal participation in the divine, must be superseded by a final stage of development. In this age of fulfillment, contradictions of finite and infinite, subject and object, spirit and matter, are transcended by a total identification of the divine and the human.

These early speculations were the groundwork for *The Phenomenology of the Spirit* (1807), in which the whole of intellectual history is explained as the externalization, in the "phenomena" of human thought, of the mind of God. In two sections of the *Phenomenology*, Hegel hinted at the social implications of his philosophic history by describing self-consciousness in terms of the relations between lord and servant and by suggesting that the absolute freedom advocated in the Enlightenment generated, as its dialectical opposite, the reign of terror in the Revolution. In two other works, *The Philosophy of History* (1822) and *The Philosophy of Right* (1821), the externalization of the mind of God previously depicted in the development of theology and philosophy is described in terms of social history. Philosophically understood, history is the process in which the "Idea" expresses itself concretely and comprehensively through the medium of "world historical" nations and individuals. It assumes a final form in the constitutional state, which unites universal and particular will. The state was to be distinguished, however, from "civil society" in that the state expressed the union of public and private, while civil society was the sphere of the private alone.

Hegel's teachings had their most immediate result

in the formation of two camps of disciples, the right and left Hegelians. While the right Hegelians saw in these teachings a powerful justification of existing institutions, the left Hegelians saw as Hegel's major achievement the undermining of traditional Christianity, in particular of its dualistic separation of God and man, spirit and matter. Bruno Bauer and Marx, who joined the group while a student, circulated what purported to be an attack upon Hegel's atheism, intending to demonstrate Hegel's true views. David Friedrich Strauss argued in his *Life of Jesus* (1835) that the biblical account of Christ was not to be taken as literal fact but as a mythological reflection of an incomplete stage in human consciousness, as Hegel had suggested. Ludwig Feuerbach put the left Hegelian case more radically by contending that religion was simply a product of the mind of man. In *The Essence of Christianity* (1841) he described the idea of God as a projection of what was essential in human nature "purified, freed from the limits of the individual man, made objective" (trans. G. Eliot, New York [1957], Ch. i, Sec. 2, 14). The idea of heaven was simply the opposite of all that was disagreeable in actual existence: "The future life is nothing else than the present life freed from that which appears as a limitation or an evil" (ibid., Ch. xviii, 181).

Marx broke with the Young Hegelians because he found their preoccupation with consciousness and the individual both narrow and reactionary. In *The Holy Family* (1845) and *The German Ideology* (1845–46) he satirized "Saint Bruno" Bauer and "Saint Max" Stirner for continuing to think only in terms of ideal or spiritual freedom despite their rejection of traditional Christianity. Feuerbach had at least pointed in the right direction by making it clear that man was the source and not the product of consciousness, that "*man makes religion; religion does not make man*" ("Critique of Hegel's Philosophy of Right" [1844], trans. Bottomore, p. 44). Feuerbach showed how Hegelianism must be transformed, or redirected: "The criticism of heaven is transformed into the criticism of earth, the *criticism of religion* into the *criticism of law*, and the *criticism of theology* into the *criticism of politics*" (ibid.).

To make this transformation was to criticize the social conditions which Hegel and the Hegelians had, in Marx's view, only rationalized. Whereas Hegel had defined alienation as God's estrangement from Himself, Marx redefined it as the estrangement of man from his true or essential self and located the source of this estrangement in the relation of the laborer to the process of production. "The alienation of the worker in his product," Marx wrote in an early fragment, "means not only that his labor becomes an object, assumes an external existence, but that it exists inde-

pendently, outside himself, and alien to him, and that it stands opposed to him as an autonomous power. The life which he has given to the object sets itself against him as an alien and hostile force" ("Alienated Labor" [1844], trans. Bottomore, p. 122). Because he is compelled to work at the command of others and in occupations that exhaust and debase him, the laborer can scarcely scale the Promethean heights of creativity and self-determination Marx saw as within his capacity.

It followed that Hegel's attempt to distinguish between the state and civil society and to argue that universal and particular wills could be reconciled in the state while civil society was left inviolate was only an attempt to evade the inescapable logic of the dialectic. The political economy of civil society—precisely the subject Hegel had sought to exempt from philosophic scrutiny—must be studied critically and the contradiction between the general good and the particular interest of the propertied exposed for what it was.

Marx saw clearly where this criticism would lead. Moses Hess had no trouble persuading him of the ethical validity of communism. In 1842 Lorenz von Stein explained French socialism as an ideological outgrowth of the struggle for power within the "third estate" between the middle class and the proletariat. At stake, von Stein pointed out, was the control of the democratic system that had arisen out of the revolt against absolutism. Marx himself observed, in a commentary on Hegel, that because the proletariat was effectively excluded from civil society, it was the class with the most compelling interest in the overthrow of that society. He took as his personal objective the task of providing the proletariat not simply with an ideology but with a doctrine that would have the rigor and status of science. Only if it had such a doctrine, he believed, could the proletariat develop confidence in the success of revolution and an adequate resistance both to the seductions of bourgeois propaganda and the temptation to engage in premature revolts.

Consciousness, alone, however, would not assure the triumph of the proletariat or the achievement of socialism as a result of its triumph. Proletarian consciousness must be enhanced by revolutionary activity, or *praxis*. In such activity the proletariat would train itself to perform its historical role until eventually it would accomplish the real "negation of the negation." Alienated labor, itself a negation of human potentiality, would be negated by the proletarian revolution. In the fellowship of the revolutionary cause, the proletariat would experience the beginning of a return of its lost humanity. The establishment of communism would make possible "the return of man to himself as a *social*, i.e., really human being, a complete and conscious return which assimilates all the wealth of previous

291

development" ("Private Property and Communism" [1844], trans. Bottomore, p. 155). Communism could not represent the final form of emancipation because it would still reflect a preoccupation, however negative, with production and possession. Genuine freedom or humanism, as Marx also described it, would become possible only when life activity was no longer constrained by the requirements of production or the limitations of material scarcity.

Marx came to a clear understanding of his own alternative to Hegelianism only gradually. At first he collaborated with the Young Hegelians in editing liberal political journals in Germany. In 1843, compelled to leave the country for his own safety, he went first to Paris, where he met Friedrich Engels, his lifelong collaborator, and profited from an exposure to French socialist thinking. Expelled from France in 1845, he went to Brussels, and from there to London, where, after 1849, he made his permanent home. In 1847, at the request of the Communist League, which he and Engels were instrumental in forming, he outlined his views in the single most inflammatory document of nineteenth-century socialism, the *Manifesto of the Communist Party* (1848).

In the *Manifesto* Marx summarized in bold and eloquent strokes the principal tenets of "scientific" socialism. The ponderous Hegelian and Germanic tone of the earlier writings is pushed into the background and replaced by a deceptively simple economic determinism. Material or economic conditions are said to be the main determinants of behavior and thought. Changes in economic conditions lead to changes in the relations among the producers, who invariably form antagonistic social classes. The ruling class's refusal to yield power compels its challengers to resort to violent revolution. Continuous change is inexorable because history is governed by laws of movement arising out of economic necessity. Under capitalist organization, the productive process reaches levels of size and integration at which capitalism itself, as a system of private ownership, becomes obsolete and a "fetter" upon further growth. Small-scale enterprise yields to large monopolies; society becomes increasingly divided into only two classes—the bourgeoisie, in whose hands all capital comes to be concentrated, and the proletariat, the wage earners who have only their labor power to sell. The contradictions between capitalism and the forces of production—the ensemble of technique and capacity—generate ever-deepening crises. The class consciousness of the proletariat is strengthened as workers are concentrated in large factories and as their conditions of life grow worse with every advance of capitalist production. Finally, under the leadership of

the Communists, as the most advanced element of the proletariat, the working class must rise up in response to the ringing call with which the *Manifesto* closes: "The proletarians have nothing to lose but their chains. They have a world to win. Working men of all countries, unite!" (p. 168).

In much of his later work, notably in *Capital* (1867), which remained incomplete at his death, Marx labored to explain in detail how capitalism had arisen and why it must fail, paradoxically—and dialectically—as a result of its very success. He drew upon the work of orthodox economists, including François Quesnay, Adam Smith, David Ricardo, and Jean-Baptiste Say, as well as upon such critics of capitalism as Sismondi and the British economists John Francis Bray, John Gray, Thomas Hodgskin, and William Thompson. The labor theory of value, which many other writers, from Aristotle to Locke and Smith, had also used in one form or another, became a cornerstone of Marxian theory.

Labor, according to Marx, was the sole source of value. Capital, however, did not represent an accumulation of individual labor. The "primary accumulation" of capital was a result of forceful usurpation. Although capital produced no value, to possess it in the form of means of production was to be able to draw profit from the labor of others. Profit represented the "surplus value" extracted from wage earners by capitalist exploiters, who paid the workers only enough to provide them with subsistence and appropriated for themselves that portion of the workers' product above what was required to maintain their subsistence. The wage rate was kept at this low level because the continuous introduction of machinery resulted in an "industrial reserve army" of the unemployed. In order to survive competition, however, each capitalist would be compelled to invest a part of his profits in machinery, or constant capital. Since machines could only repay their cost but could add no value independent of what was produced by labor, the increasing proportion of constant capital relative to variable capital, or wages, would inevitably lower the average rate of profit. Furthermore, as mechanization resulted in increased technological unemployment, the workers would be unable to purchase what was produced. The result would be crises of overproduction (or underconsumption), continually increasing in intensity, in which smaller capitalists would be wiped out and the proletariat would suffer "immiseration." Final disaster might be postponed by imperialistic investments in underdeveloped areas, where subsistence costs, and therefore wage rates, would still be low enough to provide a sufficient rate of profit. In time, nothing would avail: "The knell of capitalist private property sounds. The expropriators are expropriated" (*Capital*, trans. E. and C. Paul, Vol. II, Part 7, Ch. xxiv, No. 7).

The suppression of the revolutions of 1848 and 1849 was a disappointment to Marx and Engels but not a disillusionment. Much of their prodigious intellectual energy in the years that followed was devoted to explaining the failure of these revolutions and to considering the tactics and strategy of insurrection. They generally believed that revolutionary acts would not succeed until the conditions were ripe and the class consciousness of the workers fully developed. They opposed sporadic and untimely acts of terrorism or *coups d'état*, such as had been organized by Auguste Blanqui in 1848. They conceded, however, that both tactics and strategy must be a function of national conditions. In England it was reasonable to work for the advance of socialism through parliamentary politics. In backward Russia, on the other hand, it might be possible to leap directly from agrarian populism to industrial socialism, without waiting for the development of a mature capitalism.

Marx and Engels also participated in the formation of the International Working Men's Association in 1863, hoping to establish their doctrine as the theoretical basis of the socialist movement, and vied for control of the International with Ferdinand Lasalle, the German trade-union leader, and Michael Bakunin, a Russian anarchist. Marx defended the revolt of the Paris Commune in 1871 in the name of the International, even though he thought it premature, and used the occasion to expound the need for a replacement of bourgeois parliamentarianism by a "dictatorship of the proletariat" to direct the transition to socialism. This argument, in particular, was to have great force with Lenin and other practical revolutionaries who declared themselves pupils of Marx and resorted to his works for guidance and vindication.

At Marx's death in 1883, socialism was still a marginal, heterogeneous, and highly fractious political movement. As a theoretical cause, it was firmly established throughout Europe and beginning to win adherents elsewhere. The broad appeal of the doctrine was no doubt due in part to the restatement of traditional socialist objectives in modern terms, not only by Marx but also by Owen, Fourier, Saint-Simon, and Proudhon. These restatements were made possible and given special resonance by historical circumstances. Great advances in productivity due to increasing industrialization made it obvious that for the first time in history there was no need to accept material scarcity as an inevitable condition of social life. If scarcity was unnecessary, so were grinding poverty and long hours of labor for subsistence wages. For just this reason, the harsh conditions endured by factory workers, even though in some respects they may have been an improvement over rural poverty, were felt to be intolerable. Similarly, the democratic revolutions had challenged the traditional belief that inequality and hierarchy were also necessary, whether because they were divinely ordained or essential to order. Socialism could be advocated as "the industrial doctrine," as Saint-Simon described his system, and as the ultimate form of democracy, the most perfectly egalitarian, the most truly libertarian.

If conservatives saw in the new creed only the ultimate form of mediocrity and mob rule and liberals only a revived and more bureaucratic state-worship, the socialists could respond that the society of the future would resemble nothing in actual experience and therefore could not be judged by existing standards or by the failure of previous experiments. To votaries of science, socialism made a special appeal. Saint-Simon saw in "positive" science nothing less than the salvation of the modern world. Fourier compared his own discoveries in psychology with those of Copernicus, Linnaeus, Harvey, and Newton in the physical sciences. Marx was encouraged by the similarity between his view of history as a progressive outcome of dialectical conflict and the Darwinian hypothesis of biological evolution by natural selection. In an age when science was becoming an object of worship for the emancipated, socialism could claim to be the application of science to the problems of society, with its own theories of motion, its own laws of inevitability, its own calculus of motives, its own explanations of deviations and anomalies.

To the young, to the workers, to the socially rejected of all ages, all classes, all countries, socialism was also the revolutionary doctrine par excellence, far more enticing than natural-rights liberalism which, despite efforts to extend its viability as a doctrine of social reform, was badly tarnished because of its association with such causes as laissez-faire, the inviolability of property rights, and the limitation of the suffrage to those meeting a property qualification. The internationalism of the doctrine appealed to some more than to others, but it was not impossible to be both an ardent nationalist and a socialist. The red banner borne by the socialists had first been raised in the French Revolution and it continued to exert a powerful attraction upon the romantic imagination, rekindling the age-old longing for primal innocence and paradise lost with a symbolism evoking images of fire and blood.

The revolutionary socialists were convinced, like the prophets of millennium before them, that the apocalyptic finale of history required a last cataclysmic conflict between the forces of light and darkness. But all socialists could believe that regardless of how it was to come about, the new society would make it possible for alienated man to recover his lost humanity. Neither the failure of premature and small-scale communitarian experiments nor initial departures from the ideal by revolutionary regimes are considered grounds for despair. "Socialist man," it is argued, can only be expected to make his appearance and keep himself from becoming corrupted when socialist institutions are firmly and widely established. Like earlier millenarians, modern socialists cling to the faith that once the soil is prepared, a genuine and lasting egalitarianism will become a practical possibility. Actual experience, like pre-redemptive history in religious doctrines, is thought of as a time of trial and testing when the work of preparation is to be accomplished.

In this faith lies the essence of the socialist idea. The forms of thought in which it has found expression, whether mythological, prophetic, utopian, or scientific, the disagreements over strategy between advocates of evolution and revolution, the policies that have in more recent times been taken to separate orthodoxy from heresy, such as nationalization and collectivization, are all adventitious to the idea itself. The most essential element of socialism—an element shared with democracy, liberalism, and other humanistic creeds—is the moral conviction that universal autonomy is the highest object of civilization. This conviction acquires a specifically socialist connotation when it is associated with the view that genuine autonomy depends upon an equal distribution of the proceeds of industry. The ultimate aim of socialism—and the standard by which systems claiming the name may properly be tested—is, in the words of Marx in the *Manifesto*, to create "an association, in which the free development of each is the condition for the free development of all" (p. 153).

## BIBLIOGRAPHY

The relation of socialism to the development of the idea of equality is treated in S. A. Lakoff, *Equality in Political Philosophy* (Cambridge, Mass., 1964). For comprehensive accounts of the development of socialist thought see A. Gray, *The Socialist Tradition* (London, 1946); O. Jaszi, "Socialism," *Encyclopedia of the Social Sciences* (New York, 1930), XIV, 188–212, which includes a bibliography. See also, from the second edition (New York, 1968) articles by Maurice Dobb, "Socialist Thought," under "Economic Thought," IV, 446–54; Alfred G. Meyer, "Marxism," X, 40–46; Daniel Bell, "Socialism," XIV, 506–34.

The history of the concept of the "Golden Age" is treated in A. O. Lovejoy and G. Boas, *Primitivism and Related Ideas in Antiquity* (Baltimore, 1935) and G. Boas, *Essays on Primitivism and Related Ideas in Antiquity* (Baltimore,

1948). Apocalyptic ideas and movements are examined in N. Cohn, *The Pursuit of the Millennium* (London, 1957) and J. Taubes, *Abendländische Eschatologie* (Bern, 1947). G. H. Williams, *The Radical Reformation* (Philadelphia, 1962) provides the most complete classification and history of the left wing of continental Protestantism. For the Puritan left see D. W. Petegorsky, *Left-Wing Democracy in the English Civil War* (London, 1940). See also G. H. Williams and A. Mergall, eds., *Spiritual and Anabaptist Writers* (Philadelphia, 1957) and G. H. Sabine, ed., *The Works of Gerrard Winstanley* (Ithaca, N.Y., 1941). For utopian thought see J. H. Hexter, *More's Utopia: The Biography of an Idea* (Princeton, 1952) and F. E. and F. P. Manuel, eds., *French Utopias* (New York, 1966). For Babeuf see V. Advielle, *Histoire de Gracchus Babeuf et du babouvisme*, 2 vols. (Paris, 1884) and J. L. Talmon, *The Origins of Totalitarian Democracy* (London, 1952).

The best survey in English of the rise of modern socialism is G. D. H. Cole, *A History of Socialist Thought*, Vol. I, *Socialist Thought: The Forerunners, 1789–1850* (London, 1953), which contains useful bibliographic references in the notes. See also G. Lichtheim, *The Origins of Socialism* (New York, 1969), which includes a critical bibliography. See also A. E. Bestor, "The Evolution of the Socialist Vocabulary," *Journal of the History of Ideas*, **9** (June, 1948), 259–302.

For non-Marxian socialism in the nineteenth century see Charles Fourier, *Oeuvres complètes*, 6 vols. (Paris, 1841–45); E. Poulat, *Les Cahiers manuscrits de Fourier* (Paris, 1957), which includes a guide to studies of Fourierism; *Oeuvres choisies de C. H. Saint-Simon*, 3 vols. (Brussels, 1859); *Oeuvres de Saint-Simon et d'Enfantin*, 47 vols. (Paris, 1865–78); for Proudhon see C. Bouglé and H. Moysset, eds., *Oeuvres complètes*, 21 vols. (Paris, 1923–61); and R. Owen, *A New View of Society* (London, 1927). For biography and commentary see, for Fourier, F. E. Manuel, *The Prophets of Paris* (Cambridge, Mass., 1962); Ch. V, and the notes contain a valuable critical bibliography.

The complete works of Marx and Engels are available in German as *Werke*, 39 vols. (East Berlin, 1961–68). Most of these works, with the notable exception of the *Grundrisse der Kritik der Politischen Oekonomie* and private papers, are available in English. The editions cited in the text are *Communist Manifesto*, introd. H. J. Laski, trans. S. Moore (London, 1948); *Capital*, introd. G. D. H. Cole, trans. E. and C. Paul, 2 vols. (London, 1930); T. B. Bottomore, ed., *Marx's Early Writings* (New York, 1964). See also *Capital*, Vol. III, rev. ed. by E. Untermann (London, 1960). *Capital* is also available in a three-volume edition, translated by Engels and Unterman (New York, 1967). The early writings are also available in English in L. D. Easton and K. H. Giddat, eds., *Writings of the Young Marx on Philosophy and Society* (Garden City, N.Y., 1967).

SANFORD A. LAKOFF

[See also **Alienation**; Christianity in History; Democracy; Enlightenment; **Equality**; Historical and Dialectical Materialism; Law, Natural; **Liberalism**; **Marxism**; Marxist Revisionism; Millenarianism; Perfectibility; Primitivism; Revolution; Social Contract; **State**; **Utopia**.]

# SPACE

***Introduction.*** Space is a conception of many aspects, and it has arisen—under various names, appellations, and descriptions—in different areas of cognition and knowledge: in cosmology, physics, mathematics, philosophy, psychology, and theology.

There are stirring philosophemes about space in the *Timaeus* of Plato and the *Physica* of Aristotle, and they foreshadow our present-day space, or spaces, of laboratory and cosmos, of mechanics and physics, of worlds that are everlasting and stationary, and of universes that are born and grow, and perhaps even age and collapse. But, as a rule, Greek thoughts about space were only about space in cosmology and physics, and perhaps also theology; and seldom, if ever, did Greeks compose a statement, or even an aphorism, about space in any other area of insight.

Thus, the Greeks did not create a space of logical, ontological, or psychological perception. There is almost nothing about space in Plato's *Meno,* *Theaetetus, Sophistes,* or *Parmenides,* or in Aristotle's *De anima,* or *Metaphysica.* In Aristotle's collection of several treatises in logic, the so-called *Organon,* there is mention of space only once, in Chapter 6 of *Categoriae.* It is not a "research" conception of space, but an indifferent schoolbook description of it, and Aristotle had no occasion ever to recall it.

In modern philosophy, that is since 1600, any doctrine of perception since John Locke has dealt with space as a matter of course; and, within this general approach, a monumental construction, which kept the nineteenth century enthralled, was the famed *a priori* space of Immanuel Kant. In contrast, Greek philosophy knew absolutely nothing about an *a priori* space (and time) of pure intuition as expounded by Kant in the "Transcendental Aesthetics" of his *Critique of Pure Reason* (1781). It is true (see sec. 13, below) that in psychology of the twentieth century the role of space, as a primary datum, has greatly shrunk. But this shrinkage affected space in experimental psychology rather than in metaphysical perception, and a marked difference between ancient and modern attitudes remains.

More conspicuous, and almost fate-sealing, was the absence from Greek thought of a general conception of space for geometry and geometrically oriented analysis. Greek mathematics did not conceive an overall space to serve as a "background space" for geometrical figures and loci. There is no such background space for the configurations and constructs in the mathematical works of Euclid, Archimedes, or Apollonius, or even in the astronomical work *Almagest* of Ptolemy. When Ptolemy designs a path of a celestial body, it lies in the astronomical universe of Ptolemy; but as a geometrical object of mathematical design and purpose, it does not lie anywhere. In Archimedes, who, in some respects was second only to Isaac Newton, the mathematical constructs were placed in some kind of metaphysical "Nowhere" from which there was "No Exit" into a mathematical "Future."

Such a background space was rather slow in coming. Thus, Nicholas Copernicus did not have it yet. He was an innovator in astronomical interpretation, and not in mathematical operation. His mathematics was still largely Ptolemaic, and only a bare outline of a *mathematical* background space is discernible in his *De revolutionibus orbium coelestium.* Nevertheless, already a century before Copernicus, Nicholas of Cusa, churchman, theologian, mystic, and gifted mathematician, in Book II of his leading work *Of Learned Ignorance (De docta ignorantia),* adumbrated an overall space of mathematics by way of an overall mathematical framework for the space of the universe. But the leading statements of the metaphysics of Cusa were enveloped in theology and mysticism and not very comprehensible to his contemporaries and to others after him.

On the other hand, soon after the death of Copernicus, in the second half of the sixteenth century, some mathematicians began to grope for projective and descriptive geometry, and this was bound to lead to a background space. It did, but only after two hundred years. In the meantime, in the first half of the seventeenth century a background space for geometry was created, for all to see, in *La Géométrie* (1637) of René Descartes. Half a century later, Isaac Newton in his *Principia* (1687), created an ambitiously conceived *absolute space* which was intended to be a background space for mathematics, for terrestial and celestial mechanics, and for any space-seeking metaphysics. Newton even made it into a "Sensorium of God," whatever that might be, and this aroused philosophical passions which are still smoldering. A resulting correspondence between Gottfried Wilhelm Leibniz and Dr. Samuel Clarke (for a spirited account see Koyré, [1957], Ch. XI) is much prized for what it reveals about the philosophy of Leibniz. But it is less significant for what it reveals about the role of space in science.

Beginning in the late eighteenth century, and through the length of the nineteenth century, mathematics developed a duality or polarity between space and (geometrical) structure, by which, at long last—two and a half millennia after Thales of Miletus—mathematics became an artificer of space and spaces. In the twentieth century this dualism of space and structure greatly affected all of theoretical physics. For instance, there would be no General Theory of Relativity without it. In this theory, space is gravitational space; it is "curved," and thus endowed with "form." This form is affected by the presence of gravitational matter, which is the only kind of matter known to this theory. In this way, the theory establishes a novel intimacy between matter and space and between matter and form. An enthusiast might even declare that, in this theory, matter is space (or form) and space is matter.

In quantum theory, the de Broglie dualism of particles and waves offers a different version of the dualism of matter and space, since matter is built of elementary particles and waves are space-filling. Also, in quantum "field" theory, the field is highly mathematical through its conceptual provenance; and if mathematics is equated with form, then a new version of the dualism of matter and form emerges.

In the sections to follow we will have many other assertions and details. Each section will be headed either by a name for space, or by a formulaic description of space or of something resembling space. These appellations will be introduced roughly in the chronological order in which they have arisen, and each appellation will be then followed up in its development. Our first appellation will be a Hebrew term from the Old Testament, which seems to be the earliest on record; and there is hardly another case from natural philosophy in which the Old Testament fashioned a "technical" term ahead of the Greeks.

*1. Makom.* Our term "space" derives from the Latin, and is thus relatively late. The nearest to it among earlier terms in the West are the Hebrew *makom* and the Greek *topos* (τόπος). The literal meaning of these two terms is the same, namely "place," and even the scope of connotations is virtually the same (*Theol. Wörterbuch . . .* , 1966). Either term denotes: area, region, province; the room occupied by a person or an object, or by a community of persons or arrangements of objects. But by first occurrences in extant sources, *makom* seems to be the earlier term and concept. Apparently, *topos* is attested for the first time in the early fifth century B.C., in plays of Aeschylus and fragments of Parmenides, and its meaning there is a rather literal one, even in Parmenides. Now, the Hebrew book Job is more or less contemporary with these Greek sources, but in chapter 16:18 *makom* occurs in a rather figurative sense:

O earth, cover not thou my blood, and let my cry have no place (*makom*).

Late antiquity was already debating whether this *makom* is meant to be a "hiding place" or a "resting place" (Dhorme, p. 217), and there have even been suggestions that it might have the logical meaning of "occasion," "opportunity."

Long before it appears in Job, *makom* occurs in the very first chapter of Genesis, in:

And God said, Let the waters under the heaven be gathered together unto one place (*makom*) and the dry land appear, and it was so (Genesis 1:9).

This biblical account is more or less contemporary with Hesiod's *Theogony*, but the *makom* of the biblical account has a cosmological nuance as no corresponding term in Hesiod.

Elsewhere in Genesis (for instance, 22:3; 28:11; 28:19), *makom* usually refers to a place of cultic significance, where God might be worshipped, eventually if not immediately. Similarly, in the Arabic language, which however has been a written one only since the seventh century A.D., the term *makām* designates the place of a saint or of a holy tomb (Jammer, p. 27).

In post-biblical Hebrew and Aramaic, in the first centuries A.D., *makom* became a theological synonym for God, as expressed in the Talmudic sayings: "He is the place of His world," and "His world is His place" (Jammer, p. 26). Pagan Hellenism of the same era did not identify God with place, not noticeably so; except that the One (τὸ ἕν) of Plotinus (third century A.D.) was conceived as something very comprehensive (see for instance J. M. Rist, pp. 21–27) and thus may have been intended to subsume God and place, among other concepts. In the much older One of Parmenides (early fifth century B.C.), from which the Plotinian One ultimately descended, the theological aspect was only faintly discernible. But the spatial aspect was clearly visible, even emphasized (Diels, frag. 8, lines 42–49).

*2. Chaos.* In a connected essay on space (*Physica*, Book 4, Chs. 1–5) Aristotle suggests (208b 29), rather lightly, that Hesiod's "Chaos" (χάος) was one of the earliest (Greek) designations for space, or perhaps universe, and he also quotes line 116 of Hesiod's *Theogony*: "First of all things was *Chaos*, and next broad-bosomed Earth." It is true that by etymology of the word *Chaos*, and in Hesiod's own vision, *Chaos* does not actually represent space as we know it today (Kirk and Raven, pp. 27ff.), that is, space in a cosmologically articulated universe. But chaos was destined, by future developments, to have a certain relation to space, and it is this that Aristotle's suggestion is hinting at. In fact, in many "creation myths," beginning with Plato's *Timaeus*, there is an initial phase of a "primordial chaos," in which there is no ready-made space as yet, but only a space in the making, and the structure of this space unfolds not by itself but conjointly with the structure of matter, energy, and other physical attributes. Greek natural philosophy in general knew about this initial phase, and, when in a mood of historical retrospection, viewed Hesiod's *Chaos* as an aspect of it. Aristotle's suggestion expresses such a view, in such a mood.

In present-day cosmology there is an obvious need for such an initial phase whenever a model of the universe, be it expanding or pulsating, has a so-called "point origin," that is, a time point at which the radius $R$ of the universe has the value $O$ or nearly so (H. Bondi, pp. 82ff.). Or the point origin may be the time point of a "big squeeze" for all matter and energy, in consequence of a "collapse" of a universe just preceding (Gamow, p. 29). In either case, the resulting situation has been described by Arthur Eddington (1882–1944) thus:

If the world began with a single quantum, the notions of space and time would altogether fail to have a sensible meaning before the original quantum had been divided into a sufficient number of quanta. If this suggestion is correct, the beginning of the world happened a little before the beginning of space and time (Lemaître, p. 17).

It must be stated though that there is a contemporary version of evolutionary theory in which there is no "point" origin, and a space is preexistent. It assumes that evolution began with a primordial plasma, or rather "ambiplasma" (H. Alfvén, pp. 66ff.), that is with a huge mass of gas composed of various particles of energy, matter, and antimatter, and filling a spherical volume of cosmic dimensions. Such a plasma is unstable. At some stage in the past a breakup set in which led to the formation of galaxies, and this was the true beginning of creation (ibid.).

In the *Timaeus* Plato imagined that Space, or rather, Place, was preexistent, together with Being and Becoming (52D), but that Time began when creation began (38B). With this fancy Plato outdid himself.

Whatever the mode of creation, cosmologists agree that there was an initial phase of "disorder," that is, mathematically, of so-called turbulence. Greek natural philosophers knew this, in thought patterns of theirs, fairly early, certainly since Anaxagoras of Clazomenae (500–428 B.C.), and possibly since Anaximander of Miletus (610–545 B.C.). As scientists sometimes do even today, the Greek philosophers projected back this primordial disorder as far as they could. This led them to attribute it to Hesiod's *Chaos*, and hence the famed "definition":

> chaos: rudis indigestaque moles
> (chaos: a "rude" and "undigested" heap),

in *Metamorphoses* 1, 7 of Ovid.

It has been noted long ago that Hesiod's *Chaos*, in the light of later interpretations, brings to mind the *tohu wa bohu* ("without form, and void") of *Genesis* 1:2 and related biblical terms (see "Chaos" in *Der Kleine Pauly*, Vol. I, column 1129). This is of impor-

tance, because, more than any other general conception from general philosophy, our conception of space is just as much a biblical heritage as it is a Greek one (Jammer, Ch. 2; here the emphasis is on space in theology).

**3. Cosmos.** The term *cosmos* (κόσμος) is Homeric, and classicists are studying it increasingly (even the numerous bibliographical notices in Miss Jula Kerschensteiner are not exhaustive). The basic meaning in Homer is "order," and throughout the length of antiquity this original meaning remained active amidst many figurative ones.

This "order" began to be "universe," by way of "world-order," in the following saying of Heraclitus of Ephesus (Diels, frag. 30):

This cosmos [κόσμον τόνδε] did none of the gods or men make, but it always was and is and shall be; an everliving fire, kindling in measures and going out in measures (Kirk and Raven, p. 199).

The association of this *cosmos* with "everliving fire," whatever that be, need not disqualify it from representing cosmological space. In Albert Einstein's General Theory of Relativity cosmological space is most intimately associated with gravitation (Whittaker, Vol. 2, Ch. 5). Yet the nuclear structure of gravitation is so little known that a Heraclitus of today could not be silenced, or even gainsaid, if he chose to declare that gravitation is "everliving" and that "gravitational waves" are alternately kindling and going out.

In this saying of Heraclitus, order is a principle of the universe as a whole, but long afterwards, in the logico-metaphysical outlook of Leibniz it is a schema of the space around us. We quote.

*Space is the order of coexisting things*, or the order of existence for all things which are contemporaneous. In each of both orders—in that of time as that of space—we can speak of a *propinquity* or remoteness of the elements *according to whether fewer or more connecting links are required to discern their mutual order* (*Leibniz Selections*, p. 202).

. . . When it happens that one of these coexistent things changes its *relation* to a multitude of others, which do not change their relation among themselves; and that another thing, newly come, acquire the same relation to the others, as the former had; we then say it is come into the *place* of the former; and this change we call a *motion* in that body, wherein is the immediate cause of the change (ibid., 251–52).

In these reflections of Leibniz there is even a confluence of two properties of space, of *ordering* and of *relation;* and the nearest to all this from classical antiquity is in the following passage from Aristotle:

This is made plain also by the objects studied in mathematics. Though they have no real place they nevertheless, in respect of their position relative to us, have a right and

297

left, as ascribed to them only in consequence of their position relative to us, not having by nature these various characteristics (*Physica* 208b 23–24; Oxford translation).

Among forerunners of Leibniz' ideas after Aristotle, if any, one might perhaps name the late Hellenistic (or early medieval) Aristotle commentator Joannes Philoponus (ca. 575). "For Philoponus conceives space as pure dimensionality, lacking all qualitative differentiation" (M. Jammer, p. 55), and to him "space and void are identical," with "void being a logical necessity" (ibid., p. 54); and this creates a foretaste of Leibniz, perhaps.

**4. Apeiron.** The generic meaning of *apeiron* (ἄπειρον) is Infinity without a direct suggestion of space. But the term has many connotations, and late tradition makes it likely that Anaximander, the younger compatriot of Thales, denoted by it a generative substance of the universe (Kirk and Raven, Ch. 3). If this was so, then, in Anaximander's imagery, *apeiron* may have also been a part-synonym for space, since matter and space were probably proximate notions to him.

A token of this proximity is woven into the fabric of Aristotle's *Physica*. Book 4 of this treatise is made up of three essays, on place (Chs. 1–5), on void (Chs. 6–9), and on time (Chs. 10–14). Now, immediately preceding these essays (Book 3, Chs. 4–8) is an essay on *apeiron*, as if to indicate that there is a close link between infinity and space (and void).

In the seventeenth century, Baruch Spinoza went philosophically much farther, when, in his *Ethics* he imparted infinity to Extension, that is, to space and to other attributes of his God (Wolfson, 1, 154).

Before that, in the sixteenth century, Giordano Bruno ecstatically fused space and infinity in an unbridled vision of infinitely many worlds regularly distributed over a wide-open all-infinite Euclidean space (D. W. Singer, pp. 50–61). The cosmological facts were not entirely new (ibid.), nor were they presented in adequate detail to become meaningful as such, nor were Bruno's insights greatly welcomed by his contemporaries. But somehow Bruno's outpourings made an impression, and they created and fashioned, or only activated, a philosopher's yearning for the infinitude of space, which played a leading part on the stage of philosophy until well into the twentieth century. In a broad sense, the English philosophers Henry More (1614–1687) and Richard Bentley (1662–1742) were followers of Bruno (Koyré, Chs. 6–10), and so were virtually all representatives of German idealism beginning with Immanuel Kant, or even earlier.

Oswald Spengler advanced the thesis (*Decline of the West*, Vol. 1, Ch. 5 and elsewhere), which probably was not quite new either, that this hankering after the infinitude of space, especially in its extra-rational aspects, was a characteristic trait and a propellant of Western European civilization since the early Middle Ages, and he somehow also interpreted the emergence of Gothic art and architecture as a response to this hankering. This thesis, whatever its overall validity, does not properly apply to leading scientists (Bochner, *Eclosion and Synthesis*, Ch. 14). Most scientists, even when adopting some features of Bruno's cosmology, were circumspect and restrained. In scientific cosmology today, the Kinematic Relativity (J. D. North, Ch. 8) of Edward Arthur Milne (1896–1950) seems more compatible with Bruno's suggestions than other viable theories; but even in Milne the physical presence of infinity is considerably more restrained than in Bruno's paradigm.

**5. Kenon ("Void").** Early Pythagorean philosophy, when still ingenuous, apparently identified space with *kenon* (κενόν), which literally means "void." In fact, within his essay on the void in the *Physica*, Aristotle has a passage about Pythagoreans which links *kenon* with *apeiron* ("infinity"), *pneuma* ("breath"), *ouranos* ("heaven"), and *arithmos* ("number"):

The Pythagoreans, too, held that the void exists and that breath and void enter from the infinite into the heaven itself, which as it were inhales; the void distinguishes the nature of things, being a kind of separating and distinguishing factor between terms in series. This happens primarily in the case of numbers; for the void distinguishes their nature (*Physica* 4, 6; 213b 22–28; Kirk and Raven, p. 252).

This fascinating report must be allowed to speak for itself. Unlike some modern commentators, Aristotle, very prudently, does not attempt to interpret it.

Otherwise, Aristotle's essay on the void in the *Physica* suffers from an incurable weakness. As always and everywhere, Aristotle maintains in this essay that a void cannot exist, and in the present context Aristotle would really like to give a general demonstration for this thesis. But this he cannot do. Such a demonstration would require that Aristotle first define his void logically, and then argue metaphysically that it cannot exist. However Aristotle finds it impossible to give a logical definition of void that would not turn it into a kind of space, or pseudo-space, or nonspace; and the intended demonstration of his thesis dissolves into an accumulation of remarks not easy to remember.

It is true that present-day physics is also unable to define a void other than as a space devoid of matter and energy, say. But this is of no harmful consequence as long as nobody asserts, and wants to demonstrate, that "a void cannot exist"; and nobody does.

**6. Non-Being.** The concept of Non-Being (τὸ μὴ ὄν) occurs freely in Parmenides, and is probably due to him. By an unimpeachable report in Aristotle's *Meta-physica* (985 b4)—which is reinforced by a historical analysis in *De generatione et corruptione* (325 a2; Guthrie, 2, 392–94)—the Atomists Leucippus and Democritus (fifth century B.C.), from their approach, made Non-Being into an appellation for space, to alternate with, or be a replacement for *kenon*. They viewed the relation between material atoms and their spatial setting as a contrast between the full and the *void* (τὸ πλῆρες καὶ τὸ κενόν), and expressed it as a duality between Being (τὸ ὄν) and Non-Being.

This duality, in a different outlook, had been created by Parmenides. His Being, in fusion with Oneness and Thought, constituted a universe of ontology. This universe, however ontological, was somehow also endowed with physical attributes of a uniform finite sphere (σφαῖρα), and as such it was continuous, indivisible, unchangeable, and ungenerated and imperishable; whereas the Non-Being of Parmenides was only an obverse of Being, vacuous of determination, a sham polarity as it were. Now, the atomists heavily emphasized the physical aspect of this Being. In their atomistic conception, the evenly distributed Being was shrunk from continuity to discreteness and had become concentrated in discretely distributed atoms; and, by the same token, Non-Being was metaphysically elevated to the all-important role of a spatial setting for the atoms, without which the activities of the atoms cannot be imagined.

The splendidly unchangeable ontological universe of Parmenides the philosopher had of course nothing whatsoever to do with the very changeable common universe of Parmenides the citizen, which constantly exhibited changes of day-and-night, light-and-dark, hot-and-cold, dry-and-moist, etc. Parmenides the philosopher knew this. But what he did not know was that philosophically he need not, and must not concern himself with the vulgar universe of Parmenides the citizen, but that he ought to leave it in care of more practical (scientific) experts who knew something about such "vulgarities." Instead, Parmenides the philosopher considered himself "duty bound" to construct a "model" of the other universe too, calling it, quite unrealistically, the universe of mere "appearance" (*doxa*, δόξα); which of course was the opposite of what it really was. As could be foretold, the construction turned out to be quite banal (Kirk and Raven, pp. 284–85), and late tradition has, mercifully, transmitted but few original fragments of its description.

Even Leucippus and Democritus, great scientists though they were, could not quite resist the temptations of having opinions on matters which others understood better. After having described, magnificently, the workings of the "laboratory space" of their "atomic

physics," and also the creation of the corresponding "galactic space" of cosmogony (Diogenes Laërtius, Book IX, Chs. 30–33; Loeb edition, 2, 438ff.), they felt "duty bound" to discourse also on the astronomy of the planetary system. About this they had nothing to say that was in the least interesting (Kirk and Raven, p. 412); and modern commentators since around 1900 have not ceased to point this out, gratuitously.

**7. *Chora* and *Topos*.** In Plato's creation myth in the *Timaeus* space-in-the-making, that is, space in its cosmogonic nascency and formation, is called *chora* (χώρα), but after its creation has been completed it is called *topos*. In general usage, *chora* and *topos* have approximately the same range of meanings, but *chora* is used more loosely and informally, and it is less specific than *topos*. "A locus in mathematics, that is, a figure which is determined by, or results from, specific requirements, became *topos*, not *chora*. In the *Meteorologica*, when Aristotle wishes to single out a geographic district in a country, *chora* usually stands for country and *topos* for district" (Bochner [1966], p. 152).

In *De caelo* Aristotle adheres to Plato's distinction, but since his account is less cosmogonic than Plato's the occurrence of *topos* prevails. However, going beyond Plato, markedly so, Aristotle also uses the name of *topos* for an entirely different space, namely for the space of physics proper, that is, for the operational space of "laboratory physics" of today. Nowadays it is imperative that this space be kept distinct from the space of cosmology, and Aristotle confused the two but little (Bochner [1966], pp. 154–55).

Aristotle presents his "laboratory space" in the special essay on *topos* in *Physica* 4, 1–5. His leading assertion is that in a scientific study of a physical system, space is not given as the spread across the system, as the naive view has it, but is given by the total structural behavior as determined by the boundary configuration of the system; and Aristotle's first succinct definition is: "*topos* is the inner boundary of what contains" (ibid.). When attempting to elaborate this first definition into a detailed description, Aristotle encounters complications which are intrinsic to the subject matter, and he arrives at alternate descriptions which are seemingly not quite consistent with each other. However, on closer analysis these inconsistencies can be reconciled (Bochner [1966], pp. 172–75).

Furthermore, it is important to realize that in present-day physics the conception of space is pragmatically used in alternate versions which are not identical and that no serious harm arises. Thus, (i) in engineering mechanics as taught in engineering schools all over the world, and in large parts of so-called "classical" mechanics and physics, space continues to be Newtonian, that is Euclidean, as in Newton's **299**

*Principia* (i.e., *Philosophiae naturalis principia mathematica*, London, 1687). But, (ii) the theory of single electrons or other elementary particles—that is, the so-called quantum field theory—operates in the space-time of the *special* theory of relativity which is different from the space-time of Newton's mechanics. However, (iii) in the physics of our galaxy at large (the so-called Milky Way) and beyond, space is subject to the *general* theory of relativity; and most "models" of the universe presently under examination are different from the two preceding ones. Finally, (iv) the "statistical" space of quantum mechanics may be viewed as being different from, and thus inconsistent with any "non-statistical" space, Newtonian or relativistic (Bochner [1966], p. 155).

Of course, in physics of today there is, as has always been, a great quest for consistency, unity, and harmony. But, in any one science, the volume of knowledge is growing so fast and in so many subdivisions of the science, and explanation is so far behind experimentation that a detailed internal harmonization is not attainable. In particular, the concept of space is so ubiquitous, and is reached by so many avenues and channels, that it would be stifling and sterile to force upon it metaphysically a single logical schema, which, even if acceptable today, might become unsuitable tomorrow.

**8. To pan (*"The all"*).** The Homeric term *to pan* (τὸ πᾶν) occurs several times in Aristotle's *De caelo*, sometimes reinforced by *to holon* (τὸ ὅλον; the Whole), and its meaning is a near-synonym for the leading term *ouranos* ("Heaven," "World"). However, in *Physica*, Book 4, Ch. 5, at the end of the essay on *topos*, *to pan* has a somewhat special connotation. There, Aristotle raises the following question in a rumination of his: if one views the whole universe, *to pan*, not as a *cosmic* datum but as a *physical* system however vast, does it then have a physical *topos*, and how? (Bochner [1966], p. 178). This is an intriguing question, and various aspects of the question have been raised more than once since.

Thus, Nicholas of Cusa, who had a mathematical turn of thought, equated the would-be *topos* of the universe with a mathematical substratum of it, and he asked, implicitly but recognizably, whether the universe, in a suitable substratum, might escape the dichotomy of having to be finite or infinite. He divined that there are mathematical universes to which the dichotomy does not apply (Bochner [1968], p. 325), and he even knew that the space of the universe may be endowed with a mathematical homogeneity by which every point can be viewed as a center of it (Koyré, Ch. 1). Or, if we envisage not the underlying space of the universe but the matter in it, then in the words of a present-day cosmologist: "It is theoretically possible . . . for an unbounded distribution of matter to have its circumference nowhere, and center everywhere" (G. J. Whitrow, p. 43).

After Cusa, Copernicus and Newton entertained thoughts that were consonant with his. Newton may have even been perturbed by the question (even if he would not admit to it) of how to extend the mathematical substratum of our solar system beyond itself, in case some of the comets should move on hyperbolic orbits, which are mathematically possible, but mathematically are not contained within the substratum of the planetary system proper (Bochner [1969], Ch. 14).

A version of Aristotle's problem arises in present-day cosmology. In the general theory of relativity space is gravitational space and is thus largely determined by a distribution of gravitational masses. Now, if this distribution is known and if the shape of the resulting space is to be determined, then, for operational purposes, a background space, that is a kind of *topos* in the sense of Aristotle, must be chosen *a priori*; and it would be desirable to have a procedure for making this *a priori* choice in any one given case.

**9. Ouranos.** The word *ouranos* (οὐρανός) means heavens, and it is a keyword in *De caelo*. In the assertion that the world is finite, or rather in the arguments that the "body" (*soma*) of the world is finite, Aristotle uses either *ouranos* or *to pan*. But he uses mainly *ouranos* in the speculation, which in the Renaissance brought down upon him much condemnatory criticism, that the heavens rotate around the earth in concentric spheres. He also uses *ouranos* in his beautifully reasoned assertion that there is only one world (*De caelo*, Book I, Chs. 8 and 9).

*Ouranos* is a word of uncertain etymology. It occurs in Homer and other ancient poetry and has there always one complex meaning of "the region which contains the stars and in which the phenomena of weather take place, a region which was personified and considered to be divine or to be the dwelling place of the gods" (L. Elders, pp. 140–41). It thus had a well-established standing even before Aristotle put his imprint on it. Yet, Aristotle made it the center of a system "which, although Aristotle was a naturalist rather than a physicist, held the stage of physics for almost two thousand years, and which, by its flashes of insight and uncanny anticipations, evokes fascination even today" (Bochner [1966], p. 178).

**10. Spatium.** This is the main term for space in classical Latin, and it has given rise to *space* (English), *espace* (French), *spazio* (Italian), *espacio* (Spanish), etc. The common Teutonic stem *ruum*, which gave rise to English *room* and German *Raum*, had no lexical spread of comparable compass.

Within Western civilization, with *spatium*, began a widespread imposition of the vocabulary of space on the parallel conception of time. Thus Cicero uses the expression *spatium praeteriti temporis*, in the meaning of: "the space (i.e., interval) of time gone by," and his usage has the ease of a colloquialism. Furthermore, according to the *Oxford English Dictionary*, the term *space* in English had from the first, that is since around 1300, two meanings, a temporal and a spatial, and the *Dictionary* lists the temporal meaning first. A corresponding French Dictionary (Paul Robert, 3, 1703) also lists both meanings for *espace*, and it observes that from the twelfth to the sixteenth centuries the temporal meaning was the leading one. Spanish and Italian dictionaries also have both meanings, and, according to one of them, *spazio* occurs in a temporal meaning in the *Purgatory* of Dante and in a story of Boccaccio. (Niccolò Tommaseo, *Dizionario della lingua italiana*, Turin [1915], 6, 135).

Yet, two thousand years after Cicero, the *fin-de-siècle* philosopher Henri Bergson was able to build a career and reputation on an intellectual opposition to the quantitative subordination of time to space (J. A. Gunn, Ch. 6). He was pressing his conceptions of *durée*, *élan vital*, *évolution créatrice*, etc. into a lifelong campaign for reconstituting the data of human consciousness in their original intuition that was free from the idea of space and from the scientific notion of time; and he was apparently greatly admired for this by many.

Bergson's finding, which so alarmed him, that time is dominated by space is not even correct. The true fact is that both space and time are dominated by one common paradigm, namely the mathematical linear continuum, which in the early part of Bergson's career had just been perfected by Richard Dedekind and Georg Cantor; and the seemingly spatial vocabulary is in fact a joint mathematical one. Aristotle in his *Physica*, in the context of Zeno's paradoxes, had stated over and over again, in words of his own, that there must be a common paradigm for space and time if there is to be any conception of movement at all. Also, for Aristotle, movement in a broad sense, which he termed *kinesis*, separated the animate from the inanimate, and without *kinesis* there would be no soul, and thus no kind of consciousness or intuition. For Aristotle, space (and time) were features of what he viewed as "nature." He did not have a space (or time) of perception, but he also could not imagine any kind of perception without a suitable *kinesis*, and for the latter (his) space and time, in coordination, were undoubtedly prerequisite. Whatever will endure of Bergson's philosophy, his opposition to a coordination of space and time will not.

*11. Extensio.* Our term extension comes from the late Latin term *extensio*—itself derived from the classical verb *extendere*—and it became a philosophical term in the Middle Ages. The exact philosophical status in the Middle Ages is not easy to determine, and this is due to a general difficulty which is tellingly presented in the following passage from a book on Duns Scotus:

Thus the nature of Space is discussed with reference to transubstantiation and the nature of angelic operation, while that of Time, though treated more thoroughly and at greater length in the *De rerum principio*, is once more mooted in the commentaries on the Sentences in connection with the angelic experience. Nor is this all. Our difficulties are increased by the fact that the scholastic terminology is almost impossible to translate exactly. For spatial relations are expressed in terms of *accidens*, *respectus* and *fundamentum*, all logical rather than mathematical symbols. In fact, the entire physics of the medieval world reflects this logical view of things so strange to our modern scientific modes of thinking (C. R. S. Harris, 2, 173).

In philosophy after 1600, *extension* leapt into prominence when Descartes used it, together with the equivalent *étendue*, in his *Philosophical Principles*. Occasionally, Descartes writes *espace* for it, but only informally, because formally *espace* is something else for him. In fact, in *La Géométrie* Descartes introduces an *espace* (*qui a trois dimensions*) as an operational background space for coordinate geometry in mathematics, and this is the true role of *espace* in the thinking of Descartes. *Extension* however is for him something conceptually different, namely the space of physics and of the universe. In this role, *extension* is coextensive with matter, certainly with *matière subtile*, and it is the carrier of Cartesian vortices (Hesse, pp. 102–08).

After Descartes, extension gradually diminished in importance, or at least in prominence. In Spinoza's *Ethics* it is "identified" with Spinoza's God (Wolfson, Ch. VII), and it then occurs in Leibniz' reaction to Spinoza (*Leibniz Selections*, pp. 485ff.). It still has a standing in the theory of perception of George Berkeley, Bishop of Cloyne (Jammer, p. 133) but after that it began to be a philosophical term of second rank.

But the "subtle matter" of Descartes, which filled his *extension*, maintained itself longer, although it had already had a long career, starting out with the role of Aristotle's body (*soma*) which filled his *topos*. Philosophers of the eighteenth century showed signs of tiring of this "subtle matter," but, unperturbed by this, it somehow managed to become the front-page aether of James Clerk Maxwell in the nineteenth century (Whittaker, Vol. 1, Ch. IX). Only the early twentieth century finally sent it into retirement, but it took an Albert Einstein to bring this about.

Instead of aether there are nowadays various "fields;" gravitational field, electromagnetic field, fields of vari-

301

ous de Broglie waves. The fields are dual to particles of matter or energy, and energy is equivalent with mass, so that a return to a "subtle matter" has been effected. Physics has but a limited budget of ideas of cognition with which to operate, and the same ideas are likely to return every so often for reassignment.

*12. Space of Perspective.* The sixteenth century created the space of standard (rectilinear) perspective for use in representational arts. This perspective was intended to secure a two-dimensional mimetic illusion of three dimensional actuality, and the central structural device for achieving this was the introduction of a "vanishing point" at infinity. Also, this theory of perspective advanced the presumption that it created the one and only space of "true" optical vision.

It belongs to the history of art to determine the extent to which this presumption was or was not heeded in the seventeenth and eighteenth centuries, but it is a matter of public record that in the nineteenth century a school of French painting openly revolted against it. The leading revolutionary in the nineteenth century was Paul Cézanne, and he replaced the space of classical perspective by a space of illusion of his own, which although not objectively fixed, was nevertheless subjectively controlled. The twentieth century went much further. Beginning with cubism, the visual arts began to take much greater liberties with space than Cézanne had ever done or envisaged, but this again is a topic for the history of art only.

*13. Absolute Space.* The sixteenth century also initiated descriptive and projective geometry (J. L. Coolidge, Chs. 5 and 6), and when, much later, in the nineteenth century, projective geometry was fully developing, its unfolding was part of the creation of many novel structures, Euclidean and other (see sec. 16, below). In the seventeenth century there were remarkable achievements by Gérard Desargues, Blaise Pascal, and others. But after that there was a long period of very slow advance, and non-Euclidean geometry, for instance, presented itself only in the nineteenth century, although, by content and method, the eighteenth century was just as ready for it.

This retardation may have been caused in part by Isaac Newton's insistence on the Euclidean character of his absolute Space (for other such retardations caused by Newton see Bochner [1966], pp. 346f.). In Newton's *Principia*, the program was to erect a mathematical theory of mechanics, based on the inverse square law of gravitation, from which to deduce the three planetary laws of Kepler and Galileo's parabolic trajectory of a cannon ball, all in one. Newton succeeded in this endeavor, but virtually every step of his reasoning required and presupposed that his underlying space be Euclidean. Newton was keenly aware

of this prerequisite, and following a general philosophical trend of his age, he endowed his Euclidean background space with extra-formal features of physical and metaphysical uniqueness and theological excellence, by which it became "absolute." These extra-formal features are not needed for the deductions of the main results, and Newton discourses on these features in supplementary scholia only (Bochner [1969], Ch. 12).

In support of his contention that there is an absolute space, Newton adduces two arguments (experiment with two globes, and, more importantly, with the rotating bucket) which physicists find arresting even today, although the arguments do not demonstrate that there is space which is absolute in Newton's own sense. In the Victorian era, the physicist-philosopher Ernst Mach in his *The Science of Mechanics . . . (Die Mechanik in ihrer Entwicklung;* many editions and translations), which was composed from a post-Comtean positivist stance of his age, was quite critical of Newton's arguments and conclusions (Jammer, Ch. 5, esp. pp. 140–42); but a recent reassessment by Max Born leads to a balanced appraisal of importance (Born, pp. 78–85).

The opposition to absolute space by philosophers began immediately with the Leibniz-Clarke correspondence (see Introduction, above), and has not quite abated since. Yet the *Encyclopédie* of Diderot and d'Alembert, under the heading *Espace* (1755), pronounced the debate sterile: "cette question obscure est inutile à la Géométrie & à la Physique" (Jammer, pp. 137f.).

As a background for mechanics, Newton's Euclidean space eventually evolved a variant of non-Euclidean structure out of itself (Bochner [1966], pp. 192–201, 338). In fact, one hundred years after the *Principia*, Louis de Lagrange in his *Mécanique analytique* (1786), when analyzing a mechanical system of finitely many mass points with so-called "constraints," introduced de facto a multidimensional space of so-called "generalized coordinates" (or "free parameters") as a subspace of a higher-dimensional space. Implicitly, though not at all by express assertion or even awareness, Lagrange endowed this space with the non-Euclidean Riemannian metric which the imbedding in the higher dimensional Euclidean space is bound to induce.

Analysts in the nineteenth century knew this part of the Lagrangian mechanics extremely well. This may help to explain why, for instance, Carl Jacobi showed no reaction of surprise at the news of the Bolyai-Lobachevsky non-Euclidean hyperbolic geometry around 1830; nor, apparently, did William Rowan Hamilton ever mention it, or even Bernhard Riemann, who should have felt "urged" to speak about it in his great memoir on general "Riemannian" geometry, in which non-Euclidean spherical geometry is adduced as a particular case.

*14. Space of Perception.* As already stated in the Introduction, the space of John Locke led to the *a priori* space of Immanuel Kant, which is a durable creation indeed. But Kant unnecessarily (Spengler, I, 170–71) and imprudently fused it with Euclidean space; and partisans of Kant do not quite know how to disembarrass themselves of the fact that mathematics of the nineteenth century constructed other spaces, and physics of the twentieth century adopted some of these.

In the first half of the nineteenth century, psychology became experimental psychology and broke away from philosophy. This brought into being a space of psychology and physiology to which the Victorian era was very attentive (H. Weyl, secs. 14 and 18). Thus, H. L. F. Helmholtz investigated the mathematical structure of the space of experience under certain assumptions of "free mobility," in his dual capacity of physicist and physiologist.

An active preoccupation with the space of psychology continued into the beginnings of the twentieth century. Thus, a two-volume treatise of the psychologist William James had a chapter (20) of 150 pages on "the perception of space." But, not long afterwards, psychology began to lose interest in space as the Victorian age had known it, and all that it still wanted to know about space were such un-Kantian topics as: Visual angle, Monocular Movement, Parallax, Stereoscopic vision, etc. A very voluminous *Handbook* from around mid-twentieth century (S. S. Stevens) devotes only 30 pages out of 1435 to the topic of space.

*15. The Night-Sky.* At night, only our own sun is turned away from us, but all the other suns (that is fixed stars) of the universe shine upon us as by daytime. Yet, the night-sky is dark, meaning that only very little radiation energy from all the other stars reaches us and falls on our retinas. It is a leading problem about the structure of the universe to explain why this is so, that is, why and how so much radiative energy is "lost" in space, as it appears to be.

The problem was posed in the first half of the eighteenth century; first, somewhat casually, in 1720 by Edmund Halley, eminent British astronomer, translator of difficult works from antiquity, and personal friend to Isaac Newton; and then, quite formally, in 1743, by the youthful Swiss gentlemen astronomer Jean Philippe Loys de Chéseaux, owner of an observatory on his estate (North, p. 18). After that, most unbelievably, for eighty years nothing happened. Then, in 1823, the problem was stated anew, quite emphatically, by the German astronomer H. W. M. Olbers. This stirred up some notice, but not much, and, unbelievably, the problem did not move into an area of active attention for another hundred years. But after Hermann Bondi had dubbed the problem the "Olbers Paradox" it became generally known, among professionals at any rate (North, p. 18; Bondi, Ch. 3).

Specifically the problem is as follows. If, *à la* Giordano Bruno we make the assumption that the universe is Euclidean and unchanging; that it houses infinitely many stars which, on a suitable average, are uniformly distributed; and that the universe does not change in time, so that in particular it has "always" existed in the past; then, by a simple calculation, the total radiation energy reaching, at any time, a general point of the universe is not only not small, but is in fact "infinitely large." Which means that under these assumptions the sky would be just as bright by night as by day. However it is not so, and we thus have the Olbers paradox.

In the calculation which leads to the paradox most of the energy comes from distant stars, and the paradox will be overcome if a suitable change in the above assumptions will imply that distant stars contribute little or no radiation (Bondi, Ch. 3). For instance, it suffices to assume that the universe has not existed "always," but, on the contrary, has been created "relatively recently."

Another change of assumptions, a highly favored one, is the hypothesis that the universe is expanding. The expansion produces the *red-shift* in the traveling energy waves, that is a decrease of their energy. Very informally it can be said that a fraction of the radiative energy is absorbed by the space as "nutriment" for its growth, and that the fraction is the larger the more distant the source from which the radiation is emitted.

Finally, the paradox can be overcome by the assumption that the stars, or rather the galaxies, are not distributed homogeneously, but, on the contrary, are concentrated in clusters, "hierarachically" so. Thus, between 1908 and 1922, C. V. I. Charlier advanced the hypothesis that there are clusters of galaxies (clusters of the first order), clusters of clusters (clusters of the second order), clusters of clusters of clusters, etc. (North, pp. 20–22). This hypothesis is of interest in our context because it revived a suggestion made in the eighteenth century by the imaginative mathematician and natural philosopher Johann Heinrich Lambert in his *Kosmologische Briefe* . . . (1761).

This "hierarchic hypothesis" does not have many adherents, probably because it cannot be easily reconciled with the so-called "Cosmological Principle" which is in great demand for applications. This principle was expressly enunciated, and so named, by Edward Arthur Milne in the 1930's (North, pp. 156–58), and it maintains rather broadly, and not too specifically, that the total cosmological picture of the universe, in its meaningful features, is independent of the vantage point of the observer composing the picture. The principle is flexible in its specific formulations, and is in this way a great aid in speculative deductions (Bondi, Ch. 3).

It also ought to be realized that if no radiation from the stars were lost in space, ". . . no planet anywhere in the universe would be cool enough to permit biological life of any kind" (Coleman, p. 67), as we know it today.

**16. Space of Geometry.** The nineteenth century finally and fully created Euclidean space; and the venerable geometry of Euclid finally acquired a space in which to house its figures and constructs. As a mathematical object, Euclidean space had already been clearly present in Descartes and very actively so in Lagrange. But only the nineteenth century created a duality between Euclidean space and Euclidean structure, as a particular case of a general duality of "space and structure." In the twentieth century this general mathematical duality conquered and captured basic physics from within.

Metaphysically this duality revealed itself with the advent of the Bolyai-Lobachevsky non-Euclidean geometry in 1829–30; but mathematically it had manifested itself before (Bochner [1969], Ch. 13), in the differential and descriptive geometries of Gaspar Monge and the projective geometry of Jean-Victor Poncelet; and it had been foreshadowed in the work of Lagrange.

A memorable event occurred in 1854 when Riemann farsightedly set forth this duality in his renowned "Habilitationsschrift" (1868); and as an immediate application of it he outlined the so-called Riemannian Geometry, defining it as a duality between a general manifold and a so-called Riemannian metric. Leaping into the twentieth century, Riemann stated, in expressions of his, that a manifold is a space which is locally Cartesian, so that in local neighborhoods it is determined by a system of ordinary real numbers as known from ordinary mensuration.

Riemann's paper was published only in 1868, and one of the first to plumb its depth was the philosopher and mathematician William Kingdon Clifford. But the philosophers J. B. Stallo and Bertrand Russell (see Bibliography) did not appreciate Riemann's visionary thrust, and Stallo was almost abusively critical. Contemporary mathematicians were telling these philosophers that what distinguished nineteenth-century mathematics was the creation of projective geometry in which the numerical and metrical aspects are somehow derived from the descriptive and qualitative ones. Riemann, however, anticipating twentieth-century valuations, did in no wise attempt to hide the numerical behind a facade of the descriptive, and some philosophers were puzzled and even dismayed.

In the twentieth century Riemann became philosophically unassailable; and his status became enhanced when his geometry was elected to be the setting for the General Theory of Relativity, which filled philosophers with awe. As if to make it quite clear who in the past had been right and who not, the physicist and philosopher Percy Williams Bridgman, in an introduction to a 1960-reissue of the book by Stallo says that "the discussion of transcendental geometry is definitely the weakest part of the book" (p. xxiii).

In a sense, the most abstractly conceived general space in the nineteenth century was the phase space of statistical mechanics, especially in the general version of Josiah Willard Gibbs. In the twentieth century this space developed into the infinitely dimensional space of quantum mechanics, as a setting for its physical states and statistical interpretations. This space is an outright intentional mathematical construction, pure and simple. Yet by physicists' constant preoccupation with it, this space is gradually being transformed from a tool in mathematics to a "reality" in nature, if by "reality" we understand anything that evokes a sense of being immediate, familiar, inevitable, and inalienable.

**17. Logical Space and World of Analytical Philosophy.** Georg Cantor, the creator of set theory, fruitfully applied his theory to what he termed "point sets," that is general aggregates of points in general spaces, and he somehow began to view such an aggregate of points, as a "subspace" of the general space and then as a space in its own right. In consequence of this, in working mathematics of the twentieth century, the concepts of "general set," "general point set," and "general space" have gradually become nearly synonymous.

Thus, in the theory of probability and statistics, a "probability space" is a general set in which, subject to appropriate rules, certain subsets have been marked off as "events." With each event there is associated a probability value which is a non-negative real number between 0 and 1, and the total set has probability value 1. If, in Aristotelian terminology, a general set is a probability space not *actually* but only *potentially*, that is, if the set is not given as a probability space but is only supposed and expected to be one and is analyzed accordingly, then, relative to such an analysis, the general set is called a "sample space."

Such developments were not limited to mathematics and science. Thus the *Tractatus logico-philosophicus* (German edition 1918, first English translation 1922) of the linguo-philosopher Ludwig Wittgenstein makes statements about a "logical space" (*logischer Raum*), and, by the text of the *Tractatus*, this space is some kind of aggregate or congeries of logical entities like "facts," "atomic facts," "states of affairs," "propositions," etc. Some commentators of the *Tractatus* ascribe to this space some specific structural features, but even these features are not very geometrical in a traditional sense. The *Tractatus* also refers to a "world" or "universe" (*Welt*). This universe has some ontological traits, and in a sense the logical space is but a background space to it. Nevertheless, the logical space seems to be more primary than the world, inasmuch as the constituents of the world are only some kind of "pictorial" representation of the constituents of the logical space.

The air of indeterminacy and vagueness which adheres to the notions of space and world in the *Tractatus* is indicative of the fact that Wittgenstein was never greatly interested in these notions as such; in his later work, the linguo-analytical *Philosophical Investigations* (1953), these notions hardly occur at all. Also, in the *Tractatus* Wittgenstein asserted, quite unnecessarily, that his logical space is "infinite"; this was simply a standard philosophers' assertion since Giordano Bruno, and nothing more. This reduced interest in space was not an innovation of linguo-philosophers but was a neo-Hegelian trend in which even "phenomenologists" like Edmund Husserl shared.

The ontological traits of the world of the *Tractatus* could be taken straight out of the universe of Parmenides, which fused Being with Thought, and added some dosage of Truth (*Aletheia*); except that the Truth in Parmenides, although already "two-valued," was still ontological rather than logical. But with regard to the question of the size of the universe, Parmenides made the splendid assertion, which beautifully conforms with twentieth-century cosmology, that his "sphere" is both "finite" and "complete" (Bochner, *The Size of the Universe*). This assertion of Parmenides was so subtle that even his leading disciple Melissus of Samos did not comprehend it at all, and—to Aristotle's uncontrollable chagrin—made the universe infinite instead. The great handicap of Parmenides was, that, as a Greek, he did not have the concept, or even percept, of a background space in his thinking. Therefore he could not separate his universe into a "space" and a "world," and it is this which makes his fusion of ontology with physics so puzzlingly "antiquarian."

In developments since the Renaissance, the first aspects of a "logical" world are discernible in pronouncements of Leibniz, even in his pronouncements about a world which purports to be a best possible one. The innovation of Leibniz was not at all that he fused physics with metaphysics—this was done by everybody, even including Kant, his hottest protestations notwithstanding—but that he added logic as well, and that this logic, as a partner of physics and metaphysics, had an equal standing with them. It is a fusion of logical ordering with metaphysical being, and not some specific achievements in logical theory, which makes Leibniz a precursor of analytical philosophy of the twentieth century, and which makes his universe of "monads," however permeated with metaphysics, congenial and even challenging to many an analytic "skeptic" of today.

*18. The Expanding Universe.* This thrilling epithet, originally *l'expansion de l'univers*, was created in 1927 by Abbé Georges Édouard Lemaître, and cosmology has not been the same since. There had been models of an expanding universe earlier, namely since 1922 (North, pp. 113ff.), but they were described in words which had no appeal. However, an "expanding universe" caught everybody's attention, and Arthur Stanley Eddington soon began to write a book to fit this title.

Most cosmologists of today aver that the universe is expanding, meaning that the nebulae (that is, galaxies) of the universe are receding from our galaxy, that is, are moving away from our telescopes in their lines of sight. By the Cosmological Principle (sec. 15 above), if applicable, it then follows that any nebula is receding from the others.

The evidence adduced is the so-called red-shift in the (visible) spectrum of a nebula, that is the displacement of the total set of spectral "lines of absorption" towards the "red" end of the spectrum and thus away from its violet end. Also, the redistribution of the spectral lines is such that it is possible to associate a well-defined positive real number with each nebula. On the assumption that the red-shift is caused by the so-called "Doppler effect"—which asserts that a wave emanating from a receding source gains in wavelength in transit—this real number is proportional to the velocity of the recession.

Working entirely within our galaxy, and using the Doppler effect in this way, Sir William Huggins had asserted already in 1868 that the star Sirius is moving away from the Sun, and he calculated a velocity. The assertion was later confirmed and the velocity found tolerably good (Coleman, p. 48). But only the twentieth century was equipped to apply this spectroscopic procedure to nebulae as a whole.

The red-shift appears to be the greater the fainter the nebula, and in 1929 this led the American astronomer Edwin P. Hubble to suggest that *the velocity of recession of a nebula is proportional to the nebula's distance from our galaxy* (North, p. 145). This is a renowned law, called "Hubble's Law." It also permits a rough estimate of the limit of the *observable* universe, and in 1963 the universe was thus estimated to be about 13 billion light years (Coleman, p. 65).

In 1935 the British astronomer E. A. Milne gave an extremely simple derivation of Hubble's Law, within a purely kinematic study of the motion of nebulae. He treated the assemblage of nebulae of the universe almost as if it were a large assemblage of particles composing an expanding gas (North, p. 160).

It was this approach which suggested to Milne, justifiably, to expressly introduce his Cosmological Principle (sec. 15). Before Milne, the principle used to be introduced, somewhat haphazardly, as the occasion would arise; but in one form or another it had appeared in virtually every cosmological theory since the beginning of the century (North, p. 156).

Milne credited the Cosmological Principle to a remark of Albert Einstein in 1931 that *Alle Stellen des Universums sind gleichwertig* (ibid; "all the stars of the universe are equivalent"), but philosophically the principle had a long past. A certain version of it can be identified in utterances of Nicholas of Cusa (Jammer, p. 54), and a rather explicit passage is the following:

The fabric of the world (*machina mundi*) will *quasi* have its center everywhere and its circumference nowhere, because the circumference and the center are God who is everywhere and nowhere (Koyré, p. 17).

This statement refers both to the universe and to God. But long before Cusa there was a statement about God only, namely that he is "a sphere of which the center is everywhere, and the circumference nowhere" (*sphaera infinita cuius centrum est ubique, circumferencia nusquam*). The saying occurs in the *Book of XXIV Philosophers*, which appears to be a pseudo-Hermetic compilation of the twelfth century; but the Renaissance philosopher Marsilio Ficino attributes it to Hermes Trismegistus, which would make the saying even older, however shadowy the figure of this Hermes may be (Yates, p. 247).

On the other hand, long after Cusa, Johannes Kepler was opposed to a Cosmological Principle; or so it would appear from the following utterances of his:

It will never be the case that the [starry heavens] would appear to those whom we may imagine observing them from these stars as they appear to us. From which it follows that this place, in which we are, will always have a certain peculiarity that cannot be attributed to any other place in all this infinity (Koyré, p. 67).

First impressions notwithstanding, it is possible that this argument is only a special pleading for something like the uniqueness of life on earth, which in itself is not a contravention of the Cosmological Principle. Even cosmologists today sometimes contemplate that "our corner of the universe" may have some peculiarities by which to explain certain occurrences that cannot be explained otherwise. Altogether it appears that the meaning, history, origin, and past interpretations of the Cosmological Principle are still to be investigated.

*BIBLIOGRAPHY*

Hannes Alfvén, *Worlds-Antiworlds: Antimatter in Cosmology* (San Francisco and London, 1966). Salomon Bochner, *The Role of Mathematics in the Rise of Science* (Princeton, 1966); idem, "The Size of the Universe in Greek Thought," *Scientia*, **103** (1968), 511–31; idem, *Eclosion and Synthesis* (New York, 1969). H. Bondi, *Cosmology*, 2nd ed. (Cambridge and New York, 1960). Max Born, *Einstein's Theory of Relativity* [1905], revised ed. prepared with the collaboration of Günther Leibfried and Walter Biem (New York, 1962). James A. Coleman, *Modern Theories of the Universe* (New York, 1963). Julian Lowell Coolidge, *A History of Geometrical Methods* (Oxford, 1940). *Der Kleine Pauly*, ed. Konrat Ziegler and Walther Sontheimer, 2 vols. (Stuttgart, 1964; 1967; in progress). Paul Dhorme, *Le livre de Job* (Paris, 1926). H. Diels and W. Kranz, *Die Fragmente der Vorsokratiker*, 6th ed. (Berlin, 1938). Diogenes Laërtius, *The Lives of Eminent Philosophers*, 2 vols. (London and Cambridge, Mass., 1925). Leo Elders, *Aristotle's Cosmology: A Commentary on the De Caelo* (Assen [Netherlands], 1965; New York, 1966). George Gamow, *The Creation of the Universe*, revised ed. (New York, 1961). J. Alexander Gunn, *Bergson and his Philosophy* (London, 1920). W. K. C. Guthrie, *A History of Greek Philosophy*, 3 vols. (Cambridge and New York, Vol. 1, 1962; Vol. 2, 1965; Vol. 3, 1969). C. R. S. Harris, *Duns Scotus*, 2 vols. (Oxford, 1927). Mary B. Hesse, *Forces and Fields* (London, 1961). William James, *The Principles of Psychology*, 2 vols. (New York, 1890). Max Jammer, *Concepts of Space . . .* (Cambridge, Mass., 1954). Jula Kerschensteiner, *Kosmos, Quellenkritische Untersuchungen zu den Vorsokratikern* (Munich, 1962). G. S. Kirk and J. E. Raven, *The Presocratic Philosophers* (Cambridge and New York, 1957). Alexandre Koyré, *From the Closed World to the Infinite Universe* (Baltimore, 1957). P. O. Kristeller, *Eight Philosophers of the Italian Renaissance* (Stanford, 1964). Johann Heinrich Lambert, *Kosmologische Briefe über die Einrichtung des Weltbaues* (Augsburg, 1761). *Leibniz Selections*, ed. Philip P. Wiener, revised ed. (New York, 1959). Georges Édouard Lemaître, *The Primeval Atom* (New York, 1950). *Sir Isaac Newton's Mathematical Principles of Natural Philosophy and his System of the World*, trans. from the Latin (1687), by Andrew Motte (1729), revised by F. Cajori (Berkeley, 1934); the Latin title *Philosophiae naturalis principia mathematica* (London, 1687) is frequently referred to as *Principia*. Nicolas Cusanus [of Cusa], *Of Learned Ignorance*, trans. Fr. Germain Heron (London, 1954). J. D. North, *The Measure of the Universe, A History of Modern Cosmology* (Oxford, 1965). Georg Friedrich Bernhard Riemann, *Ueber die Hypothesen, welche der Geometrie zu Grunde liegen* ("Habilitationsschrift"),

*Werke,* 2nd ed. (Leipzig, 1892), pp. 272–87; trans. as "On the hypotheses which lie at the bases of geometry," in William Kingdon Clifford, *Mathematical Papers* (London, 1882), pp. 55–71; trans. also Henry S. White, in David Eugene Smith, *A Source Book in Mathematics* (New York, 1929), pp. 411–25. J. M. Rist, *Plotinus: The Road to Reality* (Cambridge, 1967). Paul Robert, *Dictionnaire alphabétique et analogique de la langue française* (Paris, 1956), 3, 1703, "espace". Bertrand Russell, *An Essay on the Foundations of Geometry* (Cambridge, 1897). His (rather mild) criticism of Riemann is on pp. 32 and 67ff. D. W. Singer, *Giordano Bruno: His Life and Thought* (New York, 1950). Oswald Spengler, *The Decline of the West,* 2 vols. (New York, 1926, 1928). J. B. Stallo, *The Concepts and Theories of Modern Physics* (New York, 1881 and 1884); a reissue, ed. Percy W. Bridgman (Cambridge, Mass., 1960), Ch. XIV. S. S. Stevens *Handbook of Experimental Psychology* (New York, 1951). *Theologisches Wörterbuch zum Neuen Testament* (1966), 8, 187–208, esp. 199ff. Hermann Weyl, *Philosophy of Mathematics and Natural Science* (Princeton, 1949). G. J. Whitrow, *The Structure and Evolution of the Universe* (London, 1959). Edmund Whittaker, *A History of the Theories of Aether and Electricity . . . ,* 2 vols. (London, 1951–54). Harry Austryn Wolfson, *The Philosophy of Spinoza,* 2 vols. (Cambridge, Mass., 1934). Frances A. Yates, *Giordano Bruno and the Hermetic Tradition* (Chicago, 1964).

SALOMON BOCHNER

[See also Astronomy; Cosmic Images; **Cosmology;** Creation; Pre-Platonic Conceptions; Pythagorean . . . ; **Relativity;** Time.]

# SPONTANEOUS GENERATION

SPONTANEOUS GENERATION is the idea that life is derived from any source other than an already existing, genetically related parent organism. Its two main versions will be further defined as *abiogenesis,* or the production of living things from nonorganic matter, and *heterogenesis,* or the rise of living things from organic matter, both animate and inanimate, without genetic resemblance or continuity.

The idea of spontaneous generation was no doubt first suggested by universally inaccurate observation of how certain "lower" types of life appeared in such environments as soil, water, and especially in decaying organic substances. From a popular opinion seemingly confirmed by daily experience, it passed into ancient Greek science with only a modicum of examination. As a rule, classical thinkers tended to attribute to spontaneous causes of one kind or another the propagation of all those vegetal and animal species about whose sexual history the difficulties of investigation left

them in the dark. Aristotle's *De generatione animalium* reflected the state of science in the fourth century, B.C., when it asserted that oysters, mussels, sponges, lice, mosquitoes, flies, and some plants spring up directly from various organic or inorganic elements. Although spontaneous generation did not square well with his doctrine of causality, Aristotle preferred not to question its factualness, but rather to view it as an "equivocal" event which, lying outside the orderly processes of nature, understandably produced "imperfect" creatures. Pliny's *Natural History* indicates that knowledge about the subject had not improved noticeably by the first century, A.D. It informs us that worms and caterpillars are begotten from dew on cabbage-leaves, house-flies from wet wood, maggots from rotting flesh, moths from woolens, anchovies from sea-foam, mice from river-mud, etc. General—as distinct from scientific—literature, expressing more faithfully popular beliefs, offered a greater number of species imagined to be born spontaneously, and the cases that it described were often more fantastic. Among the favorite substances held capable of engendering life were wood, animal-hairs, filth, excrement, stagnant water, dried sweat, paper, and the carcasses of large beasts. This last category in particular inspired some curious and stubborn illusions during antiquity, for example, that putrefaction generates hornets in dead horses, wasps and scarabs in asses, scorpions in crocodiles, locusts in mules, and bees in oxen. On occasion, vertebrates were more implausibly included among such productions, as seen in the notion that frogs came from rainwater, or serpents from the marrow of the human spine! The available evidence shows that, while spontaneous generation was unanimously accepted as a natural principle in Greco-Roman times and was invoked regarding many species, there was little agreement concerning the specific cases, or the actual manner, in which it was assumed to take place. By its very character, such an idea was bound to undergo arbitrary metamorphoses and applications.

A special version of spontaneous generation, of far greater interest in the long run, is found in the speculative tradition, launched by the Ionian cosmogonists, that dealt with the original formation on earth of all living things. Anaximander and Anaximenes supposed that, in the beginning, every species had sprung into existence from the slime of primordial seas under the vivifying action of heat and air. This doctrine of an initial abiogenesis was modified by Empedocles, who taught that all creatures had evolved gradually from chance combinations of the four elements constituting the whole of nature. Similar opinions concerning the emergence of men and animals from the "womb of earth," or from a primeval slime warmed by the sun,

307

found a logical place within Epicurean philosophy. Lucretius no doubt summed up accurately this important aspect of atomism, when in *De rerum natura* he sang of how "Mother Earth" had long ago, while in her prime, created all plant and animal species, including man himself, immediately out of her own substance—a creative power of which, in her tired old age, some traces still remained in the similar generation of certain low forms of life. Even though the thesis of a materialistic origin for all beings drew "empirical" support from the opinions then prevalent about the spontaneous generation of many extant species, this widespread and naive belief in biological spontaneity was itself less the result of naturalistic than of animistic habits of thought. It remained, at any rate, consonant with the relative unawareness in antiquity that all processes in nature obey strict and uniform laws of physical change. The idea of spontaneous generation will therefore go logically unchallenged until the time when, by virtue of the seventeenth-century revolution in science, nature will finally be stripped of its animistic qualities and mysterious powers, and will be envisaged as a system of exactly determined relations between cause and effect.

Despite its antireligious uses in Epicureanism, spontaneous generation incurred no special disfavor with the establishment of Christian theology. Because it was commonly regarded as a natural fact, the Church Fathers, far from condemning it as impious, were inclined instead to adapt it to their own ends. Lactantius, for example, adduced it as a proof of nonsexual procreation in nature against those pagans who doubted the physical possibility of the virgin birth. Saint Augustine, in whose *City of God* spontaneous generation was turned to exegetical account, played a major role in its "christianizing." He sought to render more credible the story of Noah's ark by pointing out that it had been unnecessary to include among the species assembled therein "very minute creatures, not only such as mice and lizards, but also locusts, beetles, flies, fleas, and so forth" because, in order to perpetuate all forms of life after the Flood, "there was no need for those creatures being in the ark which are born without the union of the sexes from inanimate things, or from their corruption." The broadening of this notion permitted Augustine to answer another objection regarding the historical truth of the Deluge, voiced by those who did not quite see how the account of the animals preserved on Noah's ark could explain their subsequent distribution in remote islands. He suggested, among other ways in which they might have gotten there, that "they were produced out of the earth as at their first creation, when God said, *Producat terra animam vivam.*" In the Augustinian synthesis, there was thus

no essential conflict between an original spontaneous generation of all species and the biblical teaching of their creation by God; on the contrary, the divine fiat, in the absence of pre-existing parents, was the equivalent of a spontaneous origin. Centuries later, Thomas Aquinas was also able to find a place for spontaneous generation in the all-embracing architecture of his Scholastic theology. It was not, in fact, until the Enlightenment that, in very different intellectual circumstances, the contradiction latent in the naturalistic as opposed to the Scriptural meanings of creative spontaneity came finally to the fore with far-reaching consequences.

Unhindered by Christian dogma and enjoying the endorsement of the greatest scientific and philosophical minds of antiquity, the doctrine of spontaneous generation lost none of its appeal and credibility during the Middle Ages, and indeed not until the seventeenth century. During the Renaissance, aided by the resurgence of animistic theories of nature, it reached, if anything, a high point in its fortunes. Among those at the time whose writings lent positive support to the doctrine were Paracelsus, Ambroise Paré, G. Cardano, A. Cesalpino, and Francis Bacon. Attesting to its prevalence toward the end of the sixteenth century, G. della Porta's *Magia naturalis*, a widely read compendium of scientific knowledge, viewed spontaneous generation as an unquestionable reality, and based the discussion of it on a long list of authorities—even the most improbable—extending far back into antiquity. Van Helmont was perhaps its most extraordinary exponent well into the seventeenth century: a scientist otherwise deserving of posterity's respect, he was convinced that vermin were engendered by their hosts, and that frogs, snails, shellfish, and the like, were produced by the stagnant odors of marshes. One of his recipes for the fabrication of living creatures is well known: putrid rags stuffed in a container together with wheat-grains will, after twenty days, give birth to mice! It is noteworthy that until that late period those treating the subject did not, as a rule, trouble to make any theoretical distinction between abiogenesis and heterogenesis, it being apparently just as easy for them to imagine the sudden emergence of life from such inorganic substances as mud or water, as its nonreproductive derivation from organic matter, whether living or dead.

But along with the persistence of age-old errors, the early seventeenth century witnessed new developments in science—particularly a growing resolve to observe directly and experimentally the world of nature—which were to lead to the eventual rejection of spontaneous generation, at least in its traditionally gross sense. Sir William Harvey's *Exercitationes de generatione animalium* (1651) may be said to have represented the modern outlook. From numerous experiments on the mechanics of reproduction in various animal species, he drew conclusions epitomized by the celebrated dictum: *Omne vivum ex ovo.* Despite this reassuring formula, however, Harvey did not categorically abandon spontaneous generation, for his rather vague understanding of both "ovum" and "omne vivum" prevented him from breaking with the still current belief in the rise of certain lower forms of life from putrefaction. Yet Harvey's ovist theory, together with the exact—and exacting—method in physiology that he himself did so much to accredit, posed the problem of generation in a new light by making paramount the discovery of the "eggs" belonging to each animal species. His dictum thus inspired the researches of Francesco Redi, who confirmed its truth on a radically wider scale.

Redi's *Esperienze intorno alla generazione degl'insetti* (1668) is the earliest known attempt to subject the idea of spontaneous generation to an empirical critique. His experiments, of a lucid simplicity, were concentrated on the case of the fly—an insect almost unanimously held to spring from corruption. He showed that whenever a sample of organic matter, such as meat, was protected from its surroundings by a gauze cloth, it failed to produce the familiar maggots, regardless how rotten it became. Redi perceived that, under those circumstances, flies left their eggs on the gauze covering, and he inferred correctly that the maggots which ordinarily appear in putrescent substances are nothing but the larvae of flies hatched from eggs deposited by their parents. Redi did not repeat his experiments with every other insect believed to originate as spontaneously as the fly, for he apparently did not consider it necessary to do so. On the force of the Harveyan axiom, *omnia ex ovo*, he assumed analogically that what was true of flies must hold true for other insects, all of which, in his opinion, reproduced their kind regularly by means of eggs, laid often in places likely to mislead people into thinking that putrescence as such has generative powers. Nevertheless, Redi did not apply the analogy in a wholly consistent manner. The doctrine of spontaneous generation exercising a vestigial influence over his mind, he hesitated to conclude from his discoveries that it must represent in fact something biologically impossible. Instead, he continued to accept a limited type of heterogenesis pertaining to the presumed production of gall-insects from living plant tissues and of parasitic worms by the host organism. Notwithstanding such exceptions to the rule, Redi's rejection of spontaneous generation won rapid approval and brought about a general reversal of scientific opinion on the subject—an outcome that

was owing not only to the value of his experimental proofs, but also to the fact that, at the time he adduced them, the traditional belief had already become, under the impact of revolutionary advances in natural science, an obvious anachronism.

Among those who, subsequently, contributed to the further discrediting of spontaneous generation was the great entomologist, Jan Swammerdam (1637–80). His investigations of gall-insects, completed by Malpighi and Vallisnieri, resulted before long in ruling out any heterogenetical explanation of such plant parasites. His minute anatomical descriptions made it clear, moreover, that even the "vilest" insects exhibit marvelously intricate structures which render the chance of their spontaneous origin almost as nonexistent as that of the most highly organized animals. Impressed to the point of awe by the precise structural determinateness of all living things, Swammerdam went in fact to the opposite extreme of doubting the possibility even of epigenesis. His theory of preformation, which postulated that all reproduced life must already have "preexisted" morphologically in the parental seed, then succeeded so well that it dominated, in one version or another, biological thinking for a century to come. Under the impact of preformationism, and of the rigid criteria of mechanical regularity and fixity that it introduced into the entire theory of generation, the outmoded belief in the spontaneous emergence of life now seemed, for most biologists, to contradict the universal laws of nature.

But concurrently with these developments, which promised to consign spontaneous generation to the limbo of pseudoscientific fables, the discovery by Anthony van Leeuwenhoek (1632–1723) of the world of microscopic organisms initiated, eventually if not immediately, an altogether new phase in the survival of the doctrine. The founder of protozoology was himself firmly opposed to the notion that his "animalcules" could have arisen from the putrefying matter that made up their usual environment. Having noticed the conjugation and fission of protozoa—without, however, interpreting the phenomena properly—Leeuwenhoek imagined that their offspring must result, as in the case of more visible species, from copulation. Nevertheless, the multitudes of micro-organisms appearing, after only short intervals, in originally lifeless organic infusions gave the impression of having sprung into being literally from nowhere. Because the rate of their multiplication was so different from the normal rhythm of reproduction, it seemed plausible to suppose that some extraordinary cause might be at work, such as a transmutation process in organic matter itself. But if the early progress of microbiology served thus to reshape the idea of spontaneous generation into that

309

of microcosmic heterogenesis, it should be stressed that the technical inability, in the seventeenth and eighteenth centuries, to ascertain the modes of protozoic reproduction did not lead to the revival of the idea on the same uncritical footing that it had known in the pre-Redi past. Under the new scientific goal of extending to biology the same uniformity of principles and operations that already typified physics, it was more commonly assumed that micro-organisms must reproduce their own kind by processes similar to those of the larger species. It seemed on the whole doubtful that a mere difference in size could alter the mechanics of generation. Furthermore, the determinism that mechanistic science introduced into the conception of nature made the notion of "spontaneity" itself seem specious. To this should be added the popularity enjoyed, in the first half of the eighteenth century, by various "theologies of nature," whose authors, seeking to identify the mechanically ordered cosmos with the providential designs of God, came to believe that nothing expressed so well such a harmony in creation as the preformationist view of the origin of all life. In the perspective of this natural theologizing about the basic problems of biology, the ancient idea of spontaneous generation took on, for the first time, unorthodox implications and became charged with a naturalistic and impious potential—a fact that will explain its special role in the Enlightenment. But while the great majority of scientists, until around 1750, were cautious enough—in both science and religion—to disavow heterogenesis, the question as to how the "animalcules" actually came into existence remained, in an empirical sense, quite undecided.

Such was the context of the problem when John Needham's *New Microscopical Discoveries* (1745) announced that tiny eel-like creatures could be engendered from blighted wheat-germs placed in water. Although what he had noticed on this occasion was only the vivifying of a type of nematode worm deposited originally in a dry and motionless state within the "flower" of certain grains, Needham's later memoir ("Observations upon the Generation, Composition, and Decomposition of Animal and Vegetable Substances," 1749) defended heterogenesis on clearly different and more far-reaching grounds. It was claimed that microscopic organisms can be obtained spontaneously from various infusions prepared with mutton-gravy, macerated seeds, etc. Needham believed that he had taken every measure necessary for sterilizing and isolating his culture-media. In reality, his methods of boiling and sealing the contents of his vials left much to be desired. But erroneous as they were, his observations had a considerable—and in some respects positive—impact on biological science in his day. Not only did Buffon, who had collaborated on the same experiments, champion the new version of spontaneous generation, but he made it the theoretical cornerstone of his own doctrine of "organic molecules," by means of which he hoped to replace with an epigenetical account of reproduction the misguided preformationism still very much in vogue. Needham's opinions promoted, moreover, a trend toward naturalism in biology, which, like other facets of eighteenth-century philosophy, set itself in sharp opposition to modes of thought linked with traditional metaphysics and theology. The most striking example of this was given perhaps by Diderot, whose *Rêve de d'Alembert* (1769) used the idea of spontaneous generation as a logically indispensable ingredient in its atheistic speculations about the evolutionary origins of living forms. The theme of spontaneous generation became in the French Enlightenment an ideological bone of contention between materialists and antimaterialists, with a deist such as Voltaire heaping ridicule on Needham's "eels manufactured from paste," and "orthodox" biologists such as Réaumur, Haller, and Bonnet forcefully resisting the naturalistic tendency of Buffon and certain of his followers.

In 1765, Lazzaro Spallanzani denied the heterogenesis of infusoria in his *Osservazioni microscopiche concernenti il sistema della generazione di Needham e Buffon.* By subjecting his predecessors' experiments to stricter control, he perceived that whenever a flask containing an organic infusion and some air was hermetically sealed and thoroughly heated, it produced no organisms. He reasoned that Needham's infusoria were the result less of spontaneous generation than of imperfect sterilization. But while Spallanzani's inference was altogether valid, it proved impossible, given the limitations of experimental technique at the time, to satisfy his critics. The latter objected that his experiments were inconclusive because excessive heating of the infusion-vial had vitiated chemically its contents of air and organic matter, rendering them unfit to engender or sustain life.

Owing to this impasse, biologists remained at odds concerning the spontaneous generation of microzoa until around 1860, when Pasteur came to the problem from his interest in the biochemistry of fermentation, which could not be properly investigated without first understanding the origin and role of the varieties of micro-organism present in fermenting liquids. Pasteur perfected the type of experiment already performed, though indecisively, by Schroeder and Dutsch, and thereby ascertained that sterile culture-media remained indefinitely free of microscopic life provided that the "chemically unaltered" air with which they were brought into contact had all foreign particles carefully filtered out. From these facts he concluded that the micro-organisms appearing after a time in sterile infusions, and which by their multiplication cause the latter to ferment or putrefy, come not from any vital force in deteriorating matter, but from contamination by "germs" floating generally in the atmosphere. The *panspermist* theory was further confirmed by the ingenious experiments devised by John Tyndall to prove that exposed infusions of sterile organic matter fail to produce bacteria when surrounded by optically pure air. Nevertheless, in the famous debate between Pasteur and F. A. Pouchet, the latter rested his case on two lengthy books, *Hétérogénie, ou Traité de la génération spontanée* (1859) and *Nouvelles expériences sur la génération spontanée et la résistance vitale* (1863), that described in detail numerous experiments having results opposite to those obtained by Pasteur. The fact that Pouchet and his co-workers, in performing essentially the same experiments as Pasteur's, consistently observed bacterial growth under conditions where their great critic could discover none, was probably owing less to their lack of laboratory skill than to their preference for cultures (such as hay-infusions, where the spore of the hay-bacillus can withstand the prolonged action of boiling water) which could not be completely sterilized by the methods then in use. The Pasteur-Pouchet controversy of the 1860's also had some ideological echoes reminiscent of the eighteenth century. But if materialists and anticlericals tended, once again, to approve—whilst the religious party (which included Pasteur himself) continued to oppose—spontaneous generation, this remained a quite secondary aspect of an issue that was eventually settled according to strictly scientific considerations. The banishing of heterogenesis from microbiology and the resultant recognition that micro-organisms, like all the more visible forms of life, are reproduced only by their own kind, made possible the establishment of bacteriology as a precise science and its revolutionary applications in immunology and in the treatment of infectious diseases. Since then, whenever new experimental claims have been made contrary to the law of biogenesis, such as those of H. C. Bastian in the 1870's, it has always been possible to show, simply by improving upon Pasteur's classic methods, that spontaneous generation does not in fact occur.

But if Pasteur and his followers disposed finally of heterogenesis, this did not really check the career in the modern age of another version of spontaneous generation—that connected with the problem of *archebiosis,* or the first origins of life on our planet. In the *Temple of Nature* (1802), Erasmus Darwin had set to verse his ideas on the subject: ". . . without parents, by spontaneous birth,/ Rise the first specks of animated earth./ From Nature's womb the plant or insect swims,/ And buds or breathes, with microscopic limbs." Following Erasmus Darwin, Lamarck's *Philosophie zoologique* (1809) had forged the link between a specific theory of evolution and the notion that physicochemical forces continue even now to produce spontaneously such rudimentary organisms as infusoria and algae. Lamarck contended that, whereas at present those forms of life classed above the most elementary level reproduce themselves sexually, they had all in effect evolved long ago from undifferentiated prototypes which Nature, as always, is able to bring forth "directly." In a similar vein, but reminiscent also of the early Greek cosmogonies, Lorenz Oken (1779–1851) proposed the hypothesis of an *Urschleim,* or primary organic substance, from which the evolution of all species had begun presumably in the seas, and which even now, according to him, gave rise to such simple creatures as protozoa. Thus, during the first half of the nineteenth century, the belief in spontaneous generation served to promote, as it had in the previous century, an evolutionary conception of nature.

On this aspect of the question, Pasteur's disproof of heterogenesis was not altogether decisive and was, in part, to be counterbalanced on a more theoretical plane by the success of Darwinism after 1859. The general acceptance of organic evolution on firmly scientific grounds strengthened the assumption that the first step in the ascent of life must have been, once geological conditions permitted it, the formation of some sort of primordial protoplasm from essentially physicochemical causes—causes which, moreover, might conceivably still be active, although much attenuated, in the current state of the globe. Such speculations received sensational support when, in 1867, investigation of the Atlantic floor brought to light the mysterious *Bathybius,* an amorphous gelatinous substance thought to be a sample of free-living, basic protoplasm. Although this and subsequent claims of a similar kind all turned out, of course, to be erroneous, and despite the fact that before long protoplasm was recognized to be, not a stable homogeneous mass at all, but a highly organized dynamic system in even the simplest cells, evolutionists could not but continue to suppose that some type of original living entity, even if no longer extant, had been constituted chemically in the remote past before evolving into the complex structures now found everywhere on earth. Among those who, in one way or another, affirmed such a view of archebiosis were Huxley, Pflüger, Le Dantec, Verworn, Leduc, etc. In this form, moreover, the idea of spontaneous generation was assimilated logically to monistic or materialistic tendencies of thought. For example, the later editions of Ludwig Büchner's *Kraft*   311 *und Stoff* (1855) cited the autogenesis of life as evidence that the inherent energies of matter had alone brought all things into existence. Ernst Haeckel, in particular, gave crucial importance to the concept of an initial abiogenesis in the synthesis he effected between Darwinism and naturalism. Positing a fundamental unity between the realms of animate and inanimate matter, he attributed to certain protoplasmic compounds, believed by him still to occur in nature from spontaneous chemical reactions, the formation of *monera,* that is, of what he considered to be theoretically the most primitive individual organisms.

The status of the idea of spontaneous generation has not changed radically in the present century. It is true that the idea came into discussion again during the 1920's and 1930's as a result of some puzzling aspects of virus behavior; but subsequent study of the subject made it plain that, while viruses increase by a uniquely parasitical process in host-cells, a pre-existing virus is necessary to the production of new ones. Our period has also seen various explanations proposed regarding the manner in which life first appeared on earth, among others that of its chance occurrence from the polymerization of amino acids into biogenic protein compounds. But, for obvious reasons, such conjectures have not been verifiable. Life has not yet been chemically synthesized in the laboratory, despite theories about how it might have been synthesized in the beginning by natural agents. Biogenesis—or the rule that new life is reproduced by a pre-existing parent—remains valid without exception, at least on our planet. Yet it is difficult to imagine how that could always have been the case. The idea of spontaneous generation thus persists, as an inescapable adjunct of organic evolution, in the postulate that transitional prototypic modes of life once arose abiogenetically, perhaps in different geological epochs and in more than one place, and flourished over the long spans of time required for the development of self-reproducing genetic mechanisms. Beyond such a hypothesis, spontaneous generation remains a purely speculative possibility. There is, for example, no categorical proof that it is not still going on, either in its primordial or in a modified phase, somewhere on earth. That such a process has not yet been observed anywhere might be attributed to its extreme infrequency, or to the immediate destruction of its products by other living things. Nor can either abiogenesis or heterogenesis be excluded *a priori* with respect to some ultra-virus-like, or as yet totally unknown, entities occupying a subvisible or molecular level of life between the inorganic and organic worlds. In this special sense, the idea of spontaneous generation survives today mainly as a temptation to expand or transcend the limits of biology.

*BIBLIOGRAPHY*

Horacio Damianovich, *La Doctrina de la generación espontánea; su evolución y estado actual* (Buenos Aires, 1918). José Godoy Ramírez, "El origen de la vida. Evolución de las doctrinas abiogenéticas," *Estudio,* **31** (Barcelona, 1920), 355–93. Edmund von Lippmann, *Urzeugung und Lebenskraft; zur Geschichte dieser Probleme von den ältesten Zeiten an bis zu den Anfängen des 20. Jahrhunderts* (Berlin, 1933). Jean Rostand, *La Genèse de la vie. Histoire des idées sur la génération spontanée* (Paris, 1943).

In English: Eldon J. Gardner, *History of Biology,* 2nd ed. (Minneapolis, 1965); Charles Singer, *A History of Biology,* rev. ed. (New York, 1950).

ARAM VARTANIAN

[See also **Biological Conceptions in Antiquity;** Evolutionism; **Inheritance through Pangenesis.**]

# THE STATE

*1.* The idea of the State has been under heavy criticism during the last decades. Historians tend to consider the State a comparatively modern phenomenon, while some political scientists, for different reasons, reject the notion altogether as useless and out of date. Now, if it is certainly true that "States" have not always existed, it is equally true that they have existed long before being called by that name. We may hesitate to attribute State character to the tribal organizations of primitive peoples. But who could honestly deny that the Greek *polis* was, in more than one sense, a State? What then is needed, in order to write the history of the concept, is to consider the reasons which prompted its appearance, i.e., both the peculiar experience and the particular ideal which it was devised to express.

According to a widely held opinion the merit—if it be one—of first having brought into the limelight the idea of the State belongs to the ancient Greeks. It is difficult to see how this opinion can be seriously challenged; indeed, many reasons can be given for the special relevance given to the idea of the State in classical Greek thought. The first and foremost may well be a psychological reason, linked to a typical bent of the Greek mind. The same desire for knowledge which inspired the Greeks in submitting to rational enquiry the nature of the world that surrounded them was reflected in their attitude towards social and political problems: they were a source of endless discussion, indeed of passionate controversy at times. But alongside this almost natural predisposition, there are other reasons which account for the keen interest of the Greeks in the problems of the State. They are to be found in the particular character of Greek political experience, with its complex variety, its very instability, and its constant flux. Here was something entirely different from the closed and static social systems of the East. Here too was a mine of information to exploit, of data to compare, in order to elicit the basic laws of political development, centering around the most efficient, the most elaborate, and the most "perfect" type of human organization: the organization of the *polis* or city-state.

Most efficient, elaborate, and perfect: thus did political organization appear to the Greeks; different not only quantitatively, but qualitatively, from all other types of organized social life. Thus when Aristotle says, at the beginning of his *Politics*, that the *polis* or political association is "the most sovereign and inclusive association," he immediately adds that it is not size nor numbers alone that distinguish political power from all other powers that men exercise over men, but a peculiar quality which that power possesses, a particular aim which it pursues: the attainment of justice, that is, of a system of relations between men ensuring certain standards and determined by law.

The idea of the State thus appears to be inspired from the start by the awareness that, among all human associations, there is one that stands out for combining, however differently in proportions, might, power, and authority: might, in order to be able to defend itself from outside dangers and to impose upon its members, if necessary, conformity by force; power, insofar as that force is exercised in the name of and in accordance with certain rules; authority, inasmuch as that power should be considered legitimate and entail an obligation on those who are called to obey its commands. These three properties have been stressed differently over the centuries. The types of organizations which possessed them have varied, and have been called by different names. But such diversity is no excuse for overlooking what they had in common, for it is precisely these common elements which have gone into forging the idea of the State.

**2.** To the Greeks, the benefits to be obtained by means of the State were of paramount importance and such as fully to justify its power. Greek political experience, at least in the classic age, was summed up, as we said, in the *polis*, the city-state: a small territorial unit leading a precarious existence among a number of rival cities and increasingly threatened by the appearance of new and larger types of States. Yet, in the Greek view of life, this small and exclusive concern was the very embodiment of perfection. Aristotle sums up that view when he says that in it, and in it alone, can man realize the "good life" and achieve the fulfillment of his nature. More pessimistic views about poli-

tics were certainly not lacking among Greek writers. The importance of force was not overlooked: might indeed seems at times to be conceived as equivalent to right, especially in what we now call "international relations." Thus doubt could arise about the origin of political power: however great the benefits which the existence of the State entailed, how could this existence be explained? Was it grounded on reason or force, on nature or convention? The question, which the Sophists asked, simply could not be raised so long as the State was conceived (as it was by Plato and Aristotle) as the necessary complement of man. As the bearer of the highest values, the State stood in no need of any further legitimation.

Turning from the Greeks to the Romans, we find the restricted vision of the city-state gradually broadening out into that of a universal empire. We also find a new and quite different emphasis on law as the constituent element of the State. Last, we find that the State itself is no longer a bearer of ultimate values. It is, rather, nothing but a means for obtaining certain ends. Cicero's treatment of the problem in his *De re publica* is particularly significant in this respect. The accent is here shifted from the goal to the structure of the State: it is partnership in law (*consensus iuris*) and not common interest alone (*utilitatis communio*) that makes a people into a State (*res publica*). There exists, in any political community, a supreme power (*summa potestas*) from which law emanates. In turn, this "positive" law is subordinate to, and conditioned by, the respect for a higher or "natural" law which expresses the supreme values of justice and does not vary from city to city, but remains "eternal and unchangeable . . . valid for all nations and for all times."

The idea of law was thus definitely inserted in the idea of the State—from which it was not to be dissociated again for many centuries. Indeed, the Roman lawyers of the Imperial Age developed still further the legal theory of the State by singling out, among the innumerable rules that determine human conduct, those particular rules which define the use and the distribution of power in the community. They gave these rules a name, public law (*ius publicum*). These rules expressed, in their view, the very essence of the State—the *status rei publicae*. Yet on the other hand, while contributing so decisively to the analysis of power, the Roman lawyers bear witness to the radical change that had occurred in the general view of life and of the role which political institutions play in it. The contrast between nature and convention has now become the basic assumption of political theory. And the State, like law itself and all other institutions that contradict or limit the "natural" equality and liberty of men, had to be justified either by explaining its origin or by making it an instrument for the attainment of particular values. Both philosophy and religion were at hand to provide the necessary ingredients. The State would appear for many long centuries during the Middle Ages as a consequence of and a remedy for sin.

3. But was there a State, and if so, where was it in the Middle Ages? J. N. Figgis's famous dicta are still repeated after more than half a century: the State in the Middle Ages might have been "a dream, or even a prophecy, it was nowhere a fact. . . . The real State of the Middle Ages in the modern sense—if the word is not a paradox—is the Church. . . . The State or rather the civil authority was merely the police department of the Church." Such sweeping judgments are alluring and stimulating; but they rest on a gross oversimplification of facts. If we do not let ourselves be hampered by the confusing terminology, we can find in medieval sources, at any rate since the turn of the millennium, a clear awareness of the distinctive features of political experience and a growing effort to find appropriate names for the particular associations in which these features appear. Thus, in medieval political language *civitas* usually referred to the city-state which flourished in various parts of Europe, and more particularly in Italy. *Regnum* was used to describe the territorial monarchies in process of formation from the close of the high Middle Ages onwards. *Respublica* was reserved in most cases for describing a wider community, the *respublica christiana*, which united all believers in one sheepfold. The angle of vision determined whether that community was the Empire or the Church.

There is no denying that, among these different types of social organization, the medieval Church was the one which preserved and presented most clearly two of the features which we have listed as distinctive of the State. With its claim to supreme jurisdiction—a jurisdiction universally accepted throughout Christendom—the Church could undoubtedly appear as the highest earthly power, the moderator and source of all law; while authority, almost by definition, was the essential attribute of its spiritual rule. But the medieval Church avoided in most cases the direct use of might—effective enforcement and sanctions in temporal matters—and would in fact have been unable to exercise it except in its own small territorial domains. When, at a certain comparatively late date in history, the ambitious Pope Boniface VIII (1294–1303) proclaimed and even tried, as other popes before him, to establish the universal lordship of the Church over the whole world, the attempt ended in lamentable failure. Had the attempt succeeded, then, and only then, would the Church have become a State.

Medieval political writers were much nearer the mark in tracing elsewhere the substance of the "State," even though they did not yet dispose of the proper name for indicating it. Nothing is more interesting than to watch the efforts they made to grasp the essence of the new political reality which was beginning to take shape during the last centuries of the Middle Ages. They were helped in doing so both by the inheritance of Roman legal concepts and by the rediscovery of Aristotelian political thought which took place towards the middle of the thirteenth century; indeed, it is difficult to say which of these two influences was more decisive. From their study of Roman law, medieval writers derived the idea that what distinguished the State from all other associations was the existence of a supreme, "sovereign" power, of a "will that legally commands and is not commanded by others." They further derived the distinction between public and private law, which enabled them to overcome the personal concept of power that was inherent in feudalism, and to understand adequately the legal structure of the State. To Aristotle, on the other hand, medieval political theory was indebted for an entirely new vision of the value and dignity of political life. No longer would the State be conceived merely as *poena et remedium peccati* ("the penalty and remedy for sin"). Henceforward its authority would rest on rational, positive grounds. Such views worked havoc with the old idea of the unity of the *respublica christiana*. A plurality of separate communities—of *civitates et regna*—had already in fact taken its place. The character of perfection, self-sufficiency, and sovereignty could be ascribed to each of them individually. But for the name, the modern idea of the State was at hand.

4. There is a widely held opinion that the chief merit for having definitely fixed and popularized the modern meaning of the term "State" belongs to Niccolò Machiavelli. This opinion is certainly in great measure justified, but it should not be accepted without some reservations. In fact, the word *Stato* had certainly entered the Italian vocabulary of politics before Machiavelli's times. And even by Machiavelli the word was still used in different meanings which can be traced to preceding linguistic usage. The word itself, philologists tell us, was derived from the Latin term *status*, a neutral expression meaning the condition or way of existence of a thing. As such, it could be used also to describe the condition of a person (it still survives in that sense in English: e.g., *status, estate*) and that of a class (as in the phrases the "Estates of the Realm," *États généraux, Tiers État*). A more strictly political use of the word was the one we have already encountered in the Roman sources, where *status rei publicae* is used to indicate the legal structure of the community: it

is from here, very probably, that the Italian word *Stato* is derived. Even so, however, the word was not entirely devoid of ambiguity, since we find it used indiscriminately to indicate both the actual exercise of power—the government—and the people or the territory over which that power was exercised.

If we keep all these different usages in mind, we are not surprised that Machiavelli should not always be coherent in his use of the word "State." All the meanings we have listed so far can be traced in his works, sometimes even within the same context. In *The Prince*, however, where Machiavelli's language and style are more plain and direct, and less hampered by literary tradition than in most of his other writings, we find the clearest evidence of the final adoption of the term "State" to indicate an independent organization endowed with the capacity for exerting and controlling the use of force over certain people and within a given territory. It is in this sense that the word came to be inserted in the political vocabulary of all modern nations, although in some European countries it had to compete with other terms derived from earlier usage, or transferred from Latin to the vernacular. Thus for example, *commonwealth* in English and *république* in French continued to be favored for a while, and were no doubt much closer to the Latin *respublica* than "State." It is only with Hobbes, always very careful and precise in his use of words, that we find the three terms, *civitas*, *commonwealth*, and *State*, definitely equated. No doubt, in the course of the centuries that followed Machiavelli and Hobbes, the notion of the State was going to be enlarged and enriched with many new elements. The most important of all was perhaps the idea of nationality, which provided an emotional basis for the new Nation-state. In view of the passionate appeal to Italian patriotism which closes Machiavelli's short political treatise, many authors are inclined to consider him also on this count one of the forerunners of the modern idea of the State.

In Machiavelli's thought, however, the idea of the State was bound to be deeply influenced by his sharply pessimistic and realistic view of human nature in politics. Force, and force alone, was to him the constituent element of the State. Indeed, force seems to be not only the condition of existence, but also the ultimate justification of the State, since it is force that in the long run creates authority. Machiavelli had primarily before his eyes the petty Italian tyrannies of his day, which had no solid foundation in old loyalties, and where the only element of cohesion was the *virtù* of the leader, the Prince, and his ability in wielding effective control of both internal and external matters. Hardly any mention is made of law in Machiavelli's short political treatise; it is only in the much lengthier

*Discourses on Livy* that the importance of sound legal institutions (*buoni ordini*) is adequately stressed, and characteristically enough, the reference is to the Roman republic of old and only cursorily to contemporary Europe.

**5.** It is to a French writer, Jean Bodin, that we must turn for an analysis in terms of law of the political experience which Machiavelli had considered in terms of force alone. It was a matter of making good that claim to independence of individual States which, as we saw, marked the end of the medieval idea of the *respublica christiana*. It was a matter also of defining exactly the nature of the power which, within its territorial boundaries, represented the cohesive element of the State. Bodin's chief merit was to coin an appropriate name for that particular element which, from the legal angle, was the distinctive attribute of the modern State. Others before him—the Roman lawyers particularly—had already noticed that what gives political power its special characteristic is the use of force in the name, or on the basis, of law, i.e., of a binding standard of regular procedure; and hence they had proceeded to identify the ultimate location of that power from which the law emanates, the *summa potestas* "which legally commands and is not commanded by others." Bodin called this power sovereignty, and with the help of this concept he set out to unravel the nature of the State with a precision and clarity that have left a lasting mark on subsequent political theory.

Sovereignty is, according to Bodin, what distinguishes the State from any other kind of human association. This means that it is neither size nor might that counts on the international plane: a State remains a State as long as it is sovereign. It also means, on the internal plane, that social standing is irrelevant to the impersonal bond of subjection that ties the citizen to the sovereign. Sovereignty determines the structure of the State: it may be exercised in different ways according to the variety of governments, but it is basically unitary and indivisible. Whether in the hands of one, of a few, or of many, sovereignty remains qualitatively the same, for it entails the monopoly of power—power in the sense of control and creation of law—and not only of factual supremacy and independence.

Thus was Bodin paving the way to the modern conception of the State as the supreme arbiter of human life—the conception which finds in Hobbes's *Leviathan* (1651) its completest expression. *Non est potestas super terram quae comparetur ei* ("There is no power on earth that compares with him"): the words from the Bible (Job 41:33, Vulgate version) with which Hobbes inscribes his great work sum up most concisely what was henceforth to be the claim of the State over both individual and society. No doubt the model which Hobbes provided was bound to be corrected and modified in many ways, and even in part discarded, in the course of the centuries. Hobbes taught, with Bodin, that sovereignty could not be divided. But he overlooked Bodin's important distinction between the location and the exercise of power. Later political theory, without abandoning the idea that sovereignty is the exclusive possession of the State, emphasized the different ways in which the power of the State can manifest itself and be brought to bear upon its subjects, and thus developed the doctrine of the division of power which has become the mainstay of the modern notion of the constitutional State. Hobbes further conceived State-law as the only possible type of law, and he was certainly right in maintaining that the jurisdiction of the State is supreme within its own boundaries. But his notion of law, framed after an authoritative, voluntarist pattern, was unable to explain the existence of other laws, not "positive" in the sense in which the law of the State is positive, and yet, in their own way, "valid." Last, Hobbes believed that a unified society—one where no groupings should be allowed that might foster divided allegiances—was necessary to the well-being of the State. Here too, his prophecy has been belied by later events: the modern State has successfully adapted itself to the existence of a pluralistic society. And yet the fact remains that sovereignty in Hobbesian terms is still the basic attribute of the State to the present day: of the State that combines supreme power at home with independence abroad—the "national State," under whose banner the world has moved, for good or for evil, during the last three centuries.

7. Let us then examine briefly the different arguments that have been employed in turn, during these three centuries, in order to "legitimize" or justify the power of the State, in order to endow its commands with the chrism of authority. Some of these arguments were very old, some new and original: but what links modern political theory to the past, what indeed gives political philosophy a peculiar degree of continuity and makes it into a *philosophia perennis*, is the quest for an answer to the query: Why should one obey the laws of the State?—the problem we shall henceforth call that of "political obligation."

It is obvious enough that the problem of political obligation is a meaningless question to those who conceive the State as a pure expression of force. Should Machiavelli be put among them? It would certainly seem to be the case if we consider Machiavelli's endless repetition of the need for ruthless discipline, and his apparently unshakable conviction that consent always follows constraint. But on closer examination it is not altogether too difficult to find in Machiavelli a clear awareness of bonds which prove even stronger than the iron hand of the ruler, and make for the willing subservience of the citizens to the State. Such are traditional loyalties, sound institutions, love of liberty, patriotism; and even where, as in the Italy of Machiavelli's days, such precious goods were irretrievably lost or conspicuously absent, there still remained (according to Machiavelli)—as a possible justification of the rule of even a Caesar Borgia—the benefits which stable power entailed: union, allegiance, and peace. Machiavelli, the theorist of force, certainly deserves to be remembered among the earliest "political scientists" for his detached and objective analysis of political phenomena. But he should also be given a place among political philosophers, were it only because he was keenly aware that force is not enough, and that however great the power of the State, it must, in order to last, be endowed with authority (i.e., be recognized as legitimate).

This does not seem to be the case, however, with more recent theorists who refuse to see in the State anything else than "the organized use of force by one class in order to bring another into subjection." This well-known definition is from the *Communist Manifesto*. Indeed, Marx and Engels proclaimed that the modern State was nothing more than the form of organization set up by the bourgeoisie for the defense and the guarantee of their property and interests. But the idea that the State is merely a monopoly of force is not restricted exclusively to the Marxists. It is, in fact, shared by many contemporary political theorists, and has gained wide support in connection with another theory (also of remote Marxist origin) that provides an explanation of the fact that obedience is in most cases the result not of force alone, but of acceptance. This theory stresses the importance of "ideologies" in politics; and political ideologies are described as the means by which the use of force is disguised and made acceptable in the name of beliefs and emotions widely shared in a given society. Political ideologies, so the theory goes, respond to a social need, and they are, in a way, indispensable. But at bottom and in their essence they are deceits, and the task of the political theorist is to "unmask" them and show them for what they are: skillful instruments for the domination of a particular class or a particular man; at best merely rationalization of an existing state of affairs, where force still remains the decisive argument. If coherently applied, there is not one single political ideal of the last three hundred years that would escape the strictures of this theory. Individualism as well as socialism, egalitarian as well as liberal democracy—all can be shown to be transient ideologies, destined to be discarded or rejected once they have played their part.

8. A very different interpretation of such ideals can be given, however, if we look at them not as devices to cloak the brutal facts of political life, but as attempts to interpret and give meaning to those facts, and to pass judgment upon them on the basis of a precise standard of value. From this point of view, what strikes the observer is the predominance, in what we currently call the "modern" as well as the "western" world, of one particular standard, which from the turn of the seventeenth century onwards is resorted to more and more exclusively in order to account for political obligation, and to justify the existence of the State. This standard is drawn from considering the nature of man himself. Indeed, it seems almost a paradox that at the very moment in which the modern State, as the sole holder of both force and power, emerges as the supreme arbiter and controller of man's life in society, there should have taken place the unprecedented assertion of the paramount importance of the "rights of man." Classical thought had conceived the State as logically prior to the individual, as the condition for the fulfillment of his nature and destiny. Christian and medieval thought had turned to the will of God or to the consequences of sin in order to prove the necessity of political institutions. But now, and henceforth, political theory would have to start, so to speak, from the bottom: it was going to be progressively and systematically humanized and secularized. What took place was a revolution in political philosophy; it might be called a "Copernican revolution," to paraphrase a famous simile of Kant's.

Actually, this process of secularization and humanization of politics can be traced along two separate lines, depending on whether the interest of political theorists was focused on the ground or on the purpose of the State. To provide a ground for the State, now that natural growth or providential design were no longer considered sufficient to legitimize power, political theorists turned to the notion of the "social contract"—an abstract notion for which some confirmation could be found in historical facts, but whose rational value was entirely independent of that confirmation. The notion of the social contract underwent several versions. It could be used to set up a framework for constitutional government (as with Locke) as well as one for absolute monarchy (as with Grotius and Hobbes). It could provide an argument for resistance and revolution, and at the same time one in favor of the complete surrender of the individual to the State (as is the case with Rousseau). But, however different its uses, its basic elements remained unvaried, and these in turn have become part and parcel of modern man's attitude toward the State, long after the social contract

model had been discarded. These elements consist of two propositions which are best stated in the very words with which Jefferson gave them immortal formulation, viz., "that all men are created equal," and that "governments derive their powers from the consent of the governed." Neither of these propositions was entirely new or unheard of. The equality of men had been proclaimed in the past by religious as well as by philosophical currents of thought. Consent (or acceptance) had been stressed throughout the Middle Ages as the ultimate ground of the validity of law. But if the bottle was old, the wine was an entirely new one. What was new was the vindication of an equal "right" in each individual to be respected both as a person and as a citizen. What was new was the close association of the respect for that right on the part of the State and the duty of obedience on the part of the individual.

But before we assess the final impact of such notions on the idea of the State, one word must be said of the theories concerning the purpose of State action. Here, to put it briefly and in what may well seem at first sight a paradoxical vein, the suggestion could be made that the task assigned to the modern State was, from its very inception, one of emancipation. To prove the case one example should suffice, that of an author who is usually considered a theorist of obedience and certainly not one of liberty. One has only to consider the contrast which is drawn in a famous passage of *Leviathan* between the "state of nature" and the "civil State," in order to realize what benefits, what "values," according to Hobbes, are attained in the State. These values are both material and spiritual; they concern the comforts of life as well as the improvement of the mind. They are what in modern terms we would call "cultural" values; but cultural values are always, in some way or other, associated with liberty, with the free display of human initiative and energy.

It was left to later political theory to define and to assess the means of securing that liberty, so as to make it not a concession but the very aim of the State. Liberty soon appeared as a complex and multi-faceted concept, depending on whether greater importance was given to the citizen's freedom from outside interference, or to his participation in basic decisions, or to the removal of the obstacles which made of that freedom and participation a sham. "Negative" liberty, "positive" liberty, "social" liberty: such are the names by which these different facets have come to be currently described; and to each one of them there does correspond in fact a different type of political structure—the "liberal," the "democratic," and the "socialist" State. But on closer inspection it is not all too difficult to discover the common root of what at first sight appear as widely contrasting theories, notwithstanding the fact that in actual experience they tend to be more and more intertwined and combined. That common root is, once again, the paramount importance given to the individual, the respect of whose personality and rights has become part of the modern idea of the State.

**9.** One last point must be stressed before terminating this article: the view of the State which we described in the last paragraph is a view of the State as endowed with authority, not as the holder of power nor as a pure phenomenon of force. It is the view which nowadays prevails in the West with regard to the legitimacy of power and the grounds of political obligation; but it is by no means the only "ideology" that has gained currency in the modern world to ensure discipline and obedience. Some of these ideologies are in fact new religions (for example, Hegel's theory of the State as the visible revelation of God in history), and hardly deserve to be considered by the political theorist except for the tragic consequences they have wrought. Others, to be sure, are squarely and precisely what, as we have seen, ideologies purport to be—mere disguises of a cruel reality, of the fact that always and everywhere there have been, and there are, some who command and others who obey. This is certainly the case with a theory which encounters much favor at the present day, the theory which explains and justifies political dependence on the ground of the basic inequality of men. Once again, there is nothing new in a theory of this kind. One can find it in the *Politics* of Aristotle. The superiority of race or intelligence has always been invoked as an argument by those who happened to have the upper hand. In a more sophisticated vein, the doctrine of inequality has been recast of late as the doctrine of the elites, which, in some of its versions, teaches not only that all governments have always been of the few, but that the few who govern deserve to do so because of their special gifts and mettle.

The trouble with the "elitist" doctrine is that it is inadequate by itself to provide a ground for political obligation, and hence to confer "authority" upon the "governing class" of relatively few individuals who are, according to that doctrine, the State. In fact, there are two alternatives: either the elite is "imposed" or else it is "proposed." In the first case, clearly it is not the merits or the intrinsic superiority of the elite that matter, but its capacity to seize power, if necessary by force. In the second, which is obviously the case in modern societies, since those merits and that superiority call for recognition and acceptance on the part of those on whom the elite is to exert its power, there must be one point at least where rulers and ruled are on a footing of equality. In neither case does the

"elitist" doctrine offer a third solution, in addition to the old alternative of force or consent—of might or of right.

If a conclusion may be drawn at the end of this brief enquiry, this can only be that the idea of the State does not allow a single, precise definition, but varies according to the different levels on which political phenomena can be approached. We must be aware of how greatly the idea of the State has varied in time, and of the likelihood that it will vary considerably again, even in the near future. In fact, the "national State," with its jealous assertion of sovereignty, its rigid boundaries, and also its emotional patriotism, is fast appearing to modern eyes—at any rate in Europe—as becoming a thing of the past. A new, a supra-national State, is invoked and longed for by many, one which will be the signal of the disappearance of those nationalisms which have brought Europe to the brink of ruin. But will this mean the disappearance of the State, its "withering away"—to use the familiar Marxist phrase? So long as there will be an organization capable of controlling force, regulating power, and securing allegiance, one thing seems certain: whatever its size and its shape, whatever the name by which the men of the future will choose to call it, that organization will still be a State.

*BIBLIOGRAPHY*

A. P. d'Entrèves, *The Notion of the State*, 2nd ed. (Oxford, 1969), includes an extensive bibliography, and is a source used with the permission of the publisher, The Clarendon Press.

For the history of the word "State," an article by H. C. Dowdal, "The Word 'State,'" in the *Law Quarterly Review*, **39**, No. 153 (January, 1923), is still extremely useful. In general, besides the "classics" referred to in the context, any good history of political thought, like G. H. Sabine, *A History of Political Theory*, 3rd ed. (New York, 1961), does throw light on the idea of the State, its content, and its historical development. One very stimulating book on the subject deserves special mention: E. Cassirer, *The Myth of the State* (London, 1946). J. N. Figgis' much quoted description of the State in the Middle Ages appears in the introductory lecture of his *Political Thought from Gerson to Grotius* (London, 1907). For a destructive criticism of the idea of the State from the point of view of modern political science, perhaps the most significant texts are to be found in D. Easton, *The Political System* (New York, 1953), Ch. 4, Sec. 4, and Ch. 5.

ALEXANDER PASSERIN D'ENTRÈVES

[See also **Authority;** Church as Institution; Constitutionalism; Democracy; Equality; Freedom; Ideology; Law, Concept of; Liberalism; **Machiavellism; Nation;** Nationalism; **Social Contract; Socialism.**]

# ETHICS OF STOICISM

STOICISM is the name of a comprehensive philosophical system inaugurated at Athens by Zeno of Citium in the last years of the fourth century B.C. The system was divided for the purposes of exposition into three subjects: physics, logic, and ethics; but between these there is a fundamental connection which makes Stoicism an organic unity, a philosophy of rational coherence. The ethical goal is life in accordance with nature, *physis*, and this is achieved by consistently rational or "logical" action (*kata logon zēn*). Physics, or the understanding of nature, provides the field of morality with its values; logic grasps the relationship between statements and events, which enables man to articulate nature for himself and plan his life accordingly. The significance of such familiar Stoic attitudes as uncomplaining endurance of hardship and inflexible will cannot be adequately grasped without reference to their physical and logical basis.

*1. The Physical Basis of Stoic Ethics.* In Stoic theory the world is an organic whole, a rational being, conceptually divisible into two principles, active and passive: the active principle is *pneuma* ("fiery breath"), a vital, all-pervasive power which gives quality and coherence to the passive principle, "matter" (earth and water). *Pneuma* and matter together constitute "body," and body is all that exists. Particular material objects, whether animate or inanimate, are differentiations of *pneuma* in matter, marked off from one another by their internal structure, but interconnected externally, since matter is continuous, in contradistinction to the Democritean, Epicurean Atomism, and its empty spaces. The external contact between all bodies gives rise to an eternal sequence of cause and effect, since movement is a defining characteristic of the *pneuma* which organizes all things. This organizing principle is also called reason (*logos*), providence (*pronoia*), and destiny (*moira*); all of these are predicates of Nature or God, who is conceived as the world-soul, a perfect being, which is immanent in everything and which directs events to achieve worthy ends.

Man, like all things, is pervaded by God, but he possesses a special status. The *pneuma* which gives coherence to a stone and life to a plant manifests itself as reason (*logos*) in mature men. The natural life for man is "rational" life and this makes him a partner of God, or universal Nature. As Epictetus, the Stoic slave, puts it (*Discourses* I. i, 12): "We [i.e., the gods] have given you a certain portion of ourselves, the faculty of choice and refusal, of desire and aversion; that is, the faculty to make use of the impressions presented to your mind." Natural events are outside human control, but man has the power to evaluate

them and adapt his life accordingly. The world as a whole develops in an ordered pattern, determined by immanent providence. But this does not, in the Stoic view, remove human responsibility for good and evil. It is the proper function of man's nature to grasp the cosmic order by his own *logos*. He achieves happiness and goodness when he does nothing which is inconsistent with or alien to the will of God or Nature.

How does the Stoic set about this task? He has no innate ideas, no Platonic Forms, the recollection of which can provide criteria for moral action. His knowledge is entirely empirical, and the truth of what he apprehends depends upon external impressions of a sufficiently clear and accurate kind. But there are certain guidelines laid down for human nature which can serve, at least initially, as standards for action, and which enable the developing *logos* to grasp the principles on which morality itself is based. The human being, like all creatures, has an instinctive attraction towards those things which promote its own well-being and a complementary aversion towards their opposites. Self-love, family feeling, desire for health—these are basic drives, and their specific objects are "primarily in accordance with nature." The human infant will *naturally* take something appropriate to its constitution rather than the reverse, and the same applies to the mature man. But man differs from the child in his possession of *logos*. Moral choice, unlike infantile and animal behavior, is not a simple response of the organism to the environment. It is explained by Cicero as follows (*De finibus* III, 20–21): from the system of values acquired by his instinctive responses a mature man of sound reason intuits a higher-order system, a principle of moral action, which grasps the relationship between all events and provides the ultimate category of value.

*2. The Logical Basis of Stoic Ethics.* *Logos*, hitherto translated "reason," also means "speech," and the Stoics devoted much attention to the analysis of language and logic in its formal sense. They recognized as a fundamental distinction between men and animals the fact that man alone possesses the power of "internal speech" and an idea of consequence or succession (*ennoia akolouthias*). In the content of his significant discourse man grasps connections in nature, and true statements are the expression in language of such connections. The sequence of events is ordered and a necessary consequence of the universal causal nexus. Only God, who oversees and determines all things, possesses complete foreknowledge of events. But to the human reason the world presents itself as a set of events about which some valid inferences are possible and indeed necessary if life in accordance with nature is to be realized by an act of will, rather than external necessity. In its cruder form this concern for the future stimulated beliefs in the efficacy of divination, but the basis of these was the thoroughly scientific principle that no event occurs without a cause and that signs of what will happen are available in nature. It is likely enough that the Stoics' concern for valid inference and the logical rules which they formulated concerning hypotheticals were partly prompted by the practical desire to make prediction as reliable as possible. The sage is a logician not from academic inclination but because life in accordance with nature and reason requires understanding events and the consequences which follow from them.

*Logos* is the characteristic of mature human nature; only its "seeds" are available to the child. Provided that it is not corrupted by external influences, the developed *logos* will enable man to grasp the true nature of reality, and it will stand as the moral principle which directs him to a correspondence between himself and the world. But this natural condition of the *logos* is generally not realized owing to "perversions" brought about in childhood by the environment and bad upbringing. Events themselves and human influence give rise to beliefs that pain is an evil, pleasure a good, and success or failure in the world the states to be sought or avoided. This system of values produces as its consequence actions which are *alogos*, not irrational as such, but contrary to reason in its natural or healthy condition. Actions which are properly rational or "logical" are actions prompted by a *logos* whose soundness is guaranteed by the fact that it accords with Nature or God.

The Stoics' stress on logic led them to see the moral agent as one who possesses "a body of true propositions" (Sextus Empiricus, *Adversus mathematicos* VII, 39–41) which he incorporates in his actions. The bad man is false to facts. Stoic physics, which denied existence to the incorporeal, also influenced the treatment of moral character. The *logos* itself is "*pneuma* in a certain state," and any state other than that enjoyed by the good man is *eo ipso* a bad or unhealthy *physical* condition. The fact that the good are differentiated from the bad by criteria such as true/false, or healthy/sick, helps to explain the hardness and rigidity of Stoic ethical theory.

**3. The Historical and Cultural Background of Stoic Ethics.** In looking to Nature as the source of moral principles which would be binding on any man of sound reason, Zeno was strongly influenced by historical and social considerations. The Greek city-state, which Plato and Aristotle had envisaged as the context of moral action, was destroyed as an independent political entity by the conquests of Alexander the Great. The old civic and national boundaries, though pre-

served in theory, were of little consequence in the enlarged world divided among Alexander's successors, and the new capitals of Pergamum in Asia and Alexandria in Africa came to rival Athens as centers of culture. In a period of such social and political upheaval, neither the traditional ethics, already found wanting by Socrates and Plato, nor their immediate philosophical alternatives provided adequate guides for conduct. In Alexander's own lifetime the Cynic Diogenes had challenged contemporary values by rejecting civic life as an inadequate context for the proper development of human nature. Zeno, while avoiding some of the more scandalous aspects of Cynic asceticism, was equally cosmopolitan in taking the world itself for the context of moral action, and in making virtue a disposition of the reason which it is in the power of any man to realize. But, unlike Diogenes, Zeno grounded moral theory in physics and logic, and he also incorporated features of pre-Socratic, Platonic, and Aristotelian thought. Like Heraclitus he made *logos* something common to man and the universe; like Socrates and Plato he defined virtue in terms of knowledge. And he seems to reflect Aristotle both in his treatment of the relation between moral character, action, and emotion, and in terminology and method of analysis.

Zeno was a Phoenician by birth, but he settled in Athens at an early age and established his school there. It was fashionable until recently to invoke his Semitic origin, and that of other early Stoics, as a key to understanding the particular character of Stoic ethics, but this explanation is neither useful nor necessary. Stoicism is thoroughly Greek, and its ethics derives its distinctive quality more from a synthesis of existing concepts than from the introduction of entirely new ones. Zeno's ethical aim was to provide a basis for moral action and a means to personal well-being in the natural endowments of any man, irrespective of his social status or personal circumstances.

**4. The Stoic Concept of Value and Moral Action.** The universality of Stoic ethics is attained by making goodness and happiness (the terms are interchangeable) an internal state, a disposition of the *logos*. The four cardinal virtues—practical wisdom, justice, courage, and self-control—are all aspects of the one rational disposition and none of them is possible without the other. The sage or ideal good man is one whose actions are consistently determined by a reasoning faculty which accords with the will of Nature or God. This makes him the only free man. Reason does not give the sage free will, in the sense that his actions are undetermined by character and environment. But it enables him to make what will happen part of his own will and plan. He is completely unaffected by external circumstances, since the understanding of nature has taught him that the only good is virtue, and vice is the only evil; all else is morally indifferent. Pain and misfortune in general, like pleasure and external success, fall within the category of "indifferents." The incidence of such things is not entirely within a man's control, so that his happiness cannot be assured if it depends on the gifts of fortune and pleasure. But he *has* the power to determine his own attitude to events. Hence the paradox that the sage is happy even on the rack and all other men are unhappy no matter what their situation. Strictly, pleasure and pain are irrelevant to moral action, since they have nothing to do with *logos*. The sage acts from principle or "logic"; pity and "irrational feelings" are extirpated from his disposition, though he does experience "rational" emotions such as joy, and his conduct is invariably beneficial to other good men. An action performed by the sage, such as caring for parents, may look the same as the actions of other men. But the sage's action will be good and the actions of others bad, since the moral status of any action is determined by the agent's disposition. The dispositions of all who are not consistently good are bad. Hence the further paradox that all men are either wholly good or wholly bad; there is no midway condition and there are no degrees of virtue or vice.

This is a hard doctrine, which pays scant regard to ordinary language or experience, but the reasoning behind it is clear enough. Aristotle argued that happiness requires a lifetime for its realization and that the good man will never do anything wrong. Earlier still, Plato had regarded wrongdoing as a product of ignorance, claiming that knowledge of the good will result in virtuous action. If virtue and happiness are equated it is extremely difficult to account for vicious action without reference to mistaken judgment, and this in fact is the Stoic explanation. Bad men commit errors of the kind mentioned above (Sec. 2) and though these may differ in degree they do not differ in kind: they are all equally faults. Virtuous behavior on six days of the week is not enough. It is all or nothing— either consistency with reason or inconsistency and vacillation.

Although Stoic theory divided mankind into sages and fools, it also recognized the common needs and desires of all men. Man as a species is so constituted that he naturally prefers health to sickness, wealth to poverty, etc. Such conditions of prosperity and adversity the Stoics termed "natural advantages and disadvantages," but they regarded the possession of them as something morally neutral and irrelevant to happiness. Virtue and vice are displayed in the *manner* in which a man selects "natural advantages" and rejects their opposites, and how he reacts to their attainment

and loss. The good man will be indifferent to the latter, but he deliberately selects health and wealth rather than their opposites, provided that in so doing he does nothing inconsistent with reason. There are times, as Cato showed by his suicide, when the Stoic acts contrary to his instinctive impulses.

Critics have complained of a double standard here. If health is preferable to sickness, why should it not be called "good" or "better"? The Stoic answer is uncompromising. Health in the abstract is preferable to sickness, but to call the one "good" and the other "bad" would confuse them with the category of morality. The attainment of happiness and virtue can only be offered to all men, whatever their circumstances, if its value is shown to be categorically different from that of "natural advantages." It is "appropriate" to prefer health to sickness, to care for one's parents, to take part in politics, etc., and the consistent performance of such actions is a prerequisite for the would-be good man. But though certain acts of this kind are "unconditionally appropriate," they are only morally good when performed by the sage. He, and he alone, acts always and only from right intentions.

**5. Stoic Ethics in Practice.** The Stoics themselves did not claim to be sages, and it was a matter of debate in the school whether a man of such inflexible moral will had ever lived in fact. For the majority, "progress" (προκοπή) towards this standard was the goal, and Stoic writers such as Epictetus and Marcus Aurelius are constantly urging themselves and, by implication, their readers to maintain indifference to circumstances and to value moral choice as the only property of worth. Confidence in the benevolence of divine purpose, no matter what happens, and an immense stress on the dignity of man provide the Stoic with his strength. And the reward, in Epictetus' words, is "tranquillity, fearlessness and freedom" (*Discourses* II, 1, 21). Suicide, rationally chosen, is the way out, the "open door," if circumstances make a good life impossible.

The basis of Stoic ethics remained constant throughout the five hundred and more years (ca. 301 B.C.–A.D. 270) of the school's existence. But unlike the followers of Epicurus, who handed down their founder's teaching unchanged, later Stoics modified and developed various aspects of Zeno's doctrines. Chrysippus, the third head of the Stoa, following Zeno and Cleanthes, was a scholar of immense versatility, and much of the evidence for Stoicism is derived from summaries and criticisms of his works preserved in writers like Plutarch and Galen. Panaetius and Posidonius in the second and first centuries B.C. won fame throughout the Roman world, and Cicero's influential *De officiis* is based upon a work by Panaetius. This Stoic was an intimate associate of Scipio Africanus, and the propagation of general Stoic teaching among Romans owed much to his *humanitas*. The traditional Roman attitudes of *officium* and *virtus* found further justification in Stoic ethics, which thus claimed the allegiance of many Roman statesmen. The *De officiis,* which Cicero addressed to his son, stresses practice over theory, providing a second-best morality of appropriate actions for the Roman gentleman. It lacks the moral toughness and personal commitment of Epictetus, the slave of the imperial period, so admired by the emperor Marcus.

By cutting through the barriers of birth and wealth, and by emphasizing the autonomy of the individual, Stoic ethics did much to liberalize and humanize the social practice of the Roman empire. In the second and third centuries A.D. writers as different as the Christian, Clement of Alexandria, the Aristotelian scholar, Alexander of Aphrodisias, and Plotinus attest to its influence. The rules for conduct, intended by early Stoics as preparatory to the attainment of virtue, survived to challenge the strong and support the weak in times which neither knew, nor cared to know, the physics and logic on which Zeno and Chrysippus had rigorously built their ethics. In its theory, Stoic ethics looks forward to Kant's categorical imperative. Some essential aspects of its practice are preserved in the behavior commended by our words "stoic" and "stoical."

### BIBLIOGRAPHY

Evidence for early Stoicism is collected in J. von Arnim, *Stoicorum Veterum Fragmenta,* 4 vols. (Stuttgart, repr. 1964). For the Roman period the principal sources are Cicero, *De finibus* iii, iv, and *De officiis;* Seneca, *Epistulae morales;* and the works of Epictetus (*Discourses*) and Marcus Aurelius (*Meditations*), thoroughly discussed by A. Bonhoeffer, *Epictet und die Stoa* (Stuttgart, 1894) and A. S. L. Farquharson, *The Meditations of Marcus Antoninus,* 2 vols. (Oxford, 1944). The most authoritative modern work is M. Pohlenz, *Die Stoa,* 2nd ed., 2 vols. (Göttingen, 1959), which traces the history of Stoicism down to Saint Augustine and beyond. Two French works which deserve particular mention are E. Bréhier, *Chrysippe et l'ancien stoicisme,* 2nd ed. (Paris, 1951) and V. Goldschmidt, *Le système stoicien et l'idée de temps* (Paris, 1953).

The last few years have seen a revival of interest in all aspects of Stoicism among scholars writing in English. In *The Meaning of Stoicism* (Cambridge, Mass., 1966), L. Edelstein gives a stimulating, if at times misleading, introduction. For more detailed study see J. M. Rist, *Stoic Philosophy* (Cambridge, 1969) and A. A. Long, ed., *Problems in Stoicism* (London, 1971) with contributions by F. H. Sandbach, A. C. Lloyd, S. G. Pembroke, I. G. Kidd, G. Watson, and the editor. W. W. Tarn, *Hellenistic Civilisation,* 3rd ed.

revised by G. T. Griffith (London, 1952) surveys the culture during Stoicism's formative period.

ANTHONY A. LONG

[See also Causation; **Free Will;** God; **Happiness; Nature; Necessity;** Organicism; Platonism; **Rationality;** *Virtù.*]

# STRUCTURALISM

STRUCTURALISM, as a recognizable movement in the history of ideas, was born between the two world wars and is still developing at the present time. No account of it, therefore, can pretend to be complete or final. The idea of *structure* is much older, the term having entered the vocabulary of biology in the seventeenth century and of language, literature, and philosophy in the nineteenth. The closely associated notion of "system" is of course older still. It is important at the outset to get clear the relations between these two concepts, and this can best be done be relating them both to a third, namely that of "function." According to the standard structuralist account, structures are structures *of* systems; systems function, structures in themselves do not function—but systems function because they have the structures they do. The system of traffic signals, for example, has the function of controlling traffic; its structure is a binary opposition of red and green lights in alternating sequence. The system may share its form with other systems having different functions, but structure is not merely form; form is something that can be abstracted from matter or content and considered separately, whereas structure, in the structuralist sense, is precisely the significative (as opposed to the material) content of the system.

As a first, although necessarily misleading, definition it might then be said that structuralism is the view that structure in this sense is a more fundamental characteristic of the objects it studies (all, it must be noted, products of the human mind or of human culture), than are their physical components, their genetic origins, their historical development, their function or purpose, and so on.

This article is intended, however, as an account not of the idea of structure itself but of a set of perspectives to which the recent prominence of this idea in a number of disciplines has given rise. The occurrence of the term in the writings of a historically important figure is not enough to make him a structuralist, while its absence may not prevent him from being recognized as such by other structuralists. Ferdinand de Saussure, *le structuraliste sans le savoir*, as one commentator has called him (Georges Mounin, *Saussure, ou le structuraliste sans le savoir*, Paris [1968]), hardly used the word "structure" at all, and yet if a single point of origin had to be found for the movement it could only be the posthumous publication in 1916 of his *Cours de linguistique générale*, compiled from the notes of his students, Bally, Sechehaye, and Reidlinger. The picture is complicated by the fact that there is disagreement among the leading structuralists as to the scope of the movement—whether it is to be limited to the methodology of the social sciences (or even of linguistics only) or whether its extension to literary criticism and philosophy is legitimate. Some of the most obvious structuralists in the latter categories (e.g., Michel Foucault) have disclaimed the designation.

For present purposes we may agree that a movement exists if, at a more or less precise historical juncture, some conceptual development attracts the interest of a number of thinkers, who interact (even if sometimes negatively) in virtue of this common interest, claim common intellectual ancestors, etc. It is not a question of their *belonging* to the movement, of adhering to it in any formal sense (as e.g., in the case of surrealism); intellectual relations need not be accompanied by social or professional ones. Also the title given to the movement may not be the clearest possible indication of its intellectual content. All these remarks apply to structuralism, and this may account in part for the extraordinary range of opinion about it among critics and practitioners alike: it has been dismissed as a mere fashion, and hailed as a fundamental and irreversible change in the pattern of human thought. Whatever the merits of these extreme positions, recognizably structuralist trends are now to be found in half a dozen disciplines in the social sciences and humanities, collectively the *sciences humaines* for the French, among whom the movement has chiefly taken hold.

### I. LINGUISTICS AND ANTHROPOLOGY

The master discipline of structuralism, to which all its practitioners constantly revert, is linguistics. Scientific linguistics has a long history, but two distinct stages—the comparative and the structural—can be recognized in its modern development. The first begins with J. J. Rousseau's *Essai sur l'origine des langues* (published posthumously, 1817) and was given its greatest impetus by the rediscovery in the West of Sanskrit in the early nineteenth century. The importance of the latter was to suggest a common origin and an earlier common structure at least for Indo-European languages, and also to draw attention to the details of the evolution of these languages from earlier forms. But comparative and evolutionary (*diachronic*) studies remained fragmentary in the absence of a systematic theory of language as a *synchronic* entity.

Ferdinand de Saussure, in his courses in Paris and Geneva, put forward and developed the view that a language, as actually spoken by a linguistic community at a given time (i.e., viewed synchronically), forms a self-contained system, each element of which has its place and its own relations (grammatical, etymological, etc.) to the other elements. His work was devoted to describing the structure of this system, although as remarked earlier he did not make use of the term in this sense. In the English version of the *Cours de linguistique générale* (Saussure, 1959—referred to from now on as *CGL*) the word "arrangement" comes closest to it in meaning. Saussure distinguishes between "external" and "internal" linguistics with the famous example of the game of chess:

In chess, what is external can be separated relatively easily from what is internal. The fact that the game passed from Persia to Europe is external; against that, everything having to do with its system and rules is internal. If I use ivory chessmen instead of wooden ones, the change has no effect on the system; but if I decrease or increase the number of chessmen, this change has a profound effect on the "grammar" of the game. One must always distinguish between what is internal and what is external . . . everything that changes the system in any way is internal (*CGL*, pp. 22–23).

We might now read "structure" for "system" in this last sentence. The novelty of Saussure's method was its resolute adherence to internal questions (in contrast to comparative and other earlier methods).

Some of the chief concepts of contemporary structuralism are borrowed directly from Saussure, and it will be well to introduce them in the context of his work. "Synchrony" and "diachrony" have already been referred to; the opposition between them is reflected in the opposition *langue/parole* (rendered in *CGL* as "language" and "speaking"). Both are special cases of *langage*, the general human faculty of language, of which speech is the primary manifestation, writing being an anomalous and, from the point of view of the linguist, unhelpful addition. *Langue* is the synchronic, social reality apart from its individual manifestations, which constitute *parole*. *Langue* therefore is the system whose structure at a given time and in a given community is the object of linguistic investigation; *parole* is constituted of the particular verbal acts (controlled by the conventions of *langue*) which are performed daily and forgotten, which give language its empirical and historical reality and are its diachronic medium of evolution. Without *langue*, *pa-*

*role* would be a series of isolated and meaningless utterances; without *parole*, *langue* would be an abstract and empty system.

The function of the system of language is *signification*, and its elements are *signs*. The sign, however, is a complex entity, whose two aspects—the *signans* and *signatum* of the Stoics—are called by Saussure *signifiant* and *signifié* ("the signifier" and "the signified"). Both are psychological: the signifier is a "sound-image," the signified is the concept associated with this sound-image. The sign, for Saussure, is arbitrary—that is to say, there is no internal connection between its aspects which would make a given signifier the natural or necessary vehicle for a given signified. What gives the sign its linguistic value is the system of *differences*, on the one hand between signifiers, on the other between signifieds (or significata, some writers in English preferring "significatum" to "signified" as a noun). "In language there are only differences. . . . A difference generally implies positive terms between which the difference is set up; but in language there are only differences *without positive terms*" (*CGL*, p. 120). This quotation may be taken as a key to structuralism in general. Thought on the one hand, language on the other, are not antecedently segmented, they do not exist as separable atomic units; the structuring activity *creates* the units, bringing definiteness to both sides simultaneously. The same would apply to other significative systems; Saussure himself envisaged a new science of "semiology" that would study all systems of signs and of which linguistics would be only a part.

At the end of *CGL* Saussure raises the question of a possible link between linguistics and anthropology, but concludes that the former can be of little help to the latter. He was thinking of course of the content of linguistics as a datum for anthropology, rather than of its method as a model; at the time, as Claude Lévi-Strauss remarks (*Anthropologie structurale*, hereafter *AS*, p. 39, n.); "the founders of modern linguistics placed themselves resolutely under the patronage of the social scientists. It was only after 1920 that Marcel Mauss began . . . to reverse the trend" (trans. P. C.). In fact a good deal had to happen in linguistics before its position as an exemplar for the social sciences became clear. Not the least of these developments in historical importance was the explicit emergence of the term "structure" in the sense in which it is now understood, which occurred in a programmatic document prepared for an international congress of linguists at the Hague in 1928, by Roman Jakobson, S. Karcewski, and Prince Nicolas Troubetzkoy.

Troubetzkoy was a pioneer of the science of phonology, and his *Grundzüge der Phonologie* (1939) contains a detailed treatment of the concept of *opposition* which, while worked out in terms of phonological systems, forms an essential basis for technical analysis in other domains. In an earlier article (Troubetzkoy, 1933) he suggested a distinction which was to be crucial for later structuralism between *conscious* and *unconscious* levels of structure in language. What is *actually pronounced* (which is studied by phonetics) does not necessarily exhibit directly the *system of spoken language* (which is studied by phonology); the laws of the latter have to be established by induction and hypothesis on the evidence provided by the former. Troubetzkoy himself, in his later work, placed less weight on the opposition conscious/unconscious than some of his readers (notably Lévi-Strauss, as noted below), but he would have been prepared to admit the general point that the true structure does not always appear on the surface. The notion of structure here is extended to the domain of *parole*, and, with an explicit reference to "teleological elements," to the diachronic. The article referred to ends with a general remark: "The epoch in which we live is characterized by the tendency of all scientific disciplines to replace atomism by structuralism . . ." (Troubetzkoy [1933], p. 246; trans. P. C.).

What might be called a structuralist explosion was touched off in France by the anthropological works of Lévi-Strauss (see below) and has since been the most visible manifestation of the movement. But linguistic structuralism was to take on a new direction and a new importance with the work of Noam Chomsky. Chomsky was one of the first to draw serious attention to a comparatively neglected aspect of linguistic behavior, namely its *creative* character (although he recognizes a precursor in Wilhelm von Humboldt). The structures dealt with by most grammarians are *surface structures*; generative grammar, Chomsky's main contribution to technical linguistics, takes its theoretical point of departure from *deep structures*, basic grammatical forms from which the whole variety of surface structures can be generated. The existence of deep structures explains the ability of all speakers of a language to utter sentences that may never before have been uttered, and to be understood at once by other speakers of the same language. A language then is not an actual but a potential (and potentially infinite) set of utterances, governed by the laws of its deep structure.

The interest of this work for the structuralist movement is the suggestion that languages whose surface structures are widely different may share the same deep structure, and that this may reflect in some fundamental way the structure of mind. Chomsky speculates that

. . . the linguistics of the next generation will reveal that each natural language is a specific realization of a highly restrictive schema that permits grammatical processes and structures of a very limited variety, and that there are innumerable "imaginable" languages that violate these restrictions and that are, therefore, not possible human languages in a psychologically important sense, even though they are quite able, in principle, to express the entire content of any possible human language (Chomsky [1967], p. 8).

It should be remarked that what gives Chomsky grounds at this time for this expectation is "the new understanding of recursive mechanisms and the nature of algorithms that has developed in the last thirty years" (i.e., up to 1967); the structuralist hypothesis, at least in the hands of its more responsible proponents, is no mere speculation but rests on painstaking observation and vigorous analysis. It must be said further that Chomsky himself has serious reservations about the extension of linguistic structuralism to other domains, even by comparatively careful thinkers like Lévi-Strauss (Chomsky [1968], p. 65). While we may admit with Lévi-Strauss that the success of linguistics in structural analysis is encouraging, it seems best to confront anthropological and other data on their own terms and not to assume that every significative system is in fact a kind of language.

The development of linguistics has nevertheless been intimately connected with that of anthropology. Some non-Indo-European linguistics indeed seemed for a long time to be a part of anthropology, since the data for it came from exotic societies like that of Java, whose language was studied by Wilhelm von Humboldt in the early nineteenth century, and above all those of the Indians of North America, whose extraordinarily diverse and complex languages provided the initial stimulus for American linguistics in the late nineteenth and early twentieth centuries. But just as comparative linguistics remained fragmentary until the notion of language as system came to the fore, so comparative ethnology remained fragmentary (devoted as it was to the study of tools, pottery, the practice of hunting and agriculture, etc.) until the parallel notion of society as system was worked out. This notion had been put forward earlier on the level of civilized society by Montesquieu, but the elements of his system were themselves highly developed institutions requiring analysis in their turn. The study of kinship provided for anthropology the paradigm of structure that phonology has provided for linguistics, and with the nineteenth-century American ethnographer Lewis H. Morgan, the idea of *kinship systems* became firmly established. Morgan, however, like Saussure, used other terms than "structure."

Structuralism as an explicit movement in anthropology probably begins with A. R. Radcliffe-Brown, who added to the concept of function as it is found in Émile Durkheim and B. K. Malinowski the concept of the *structure of a functioning system*, roughly in the form in which it is outlined in the opening paragraphs of this essay (Radcliffe-Brown [1952], pp. 179–80). Later structuralists tend to think of Radcliffe-Brown as a functionalist (Lévi-Strauss speaks of "that primary form of structuralism which is called functionalism"; *AS*, p. 357), and to attribute to him two errors of judgment: first the belief that every feature of every society has an explicit function, second the belief that the structure of society is to be observed directly, as a surface phenomenon. Lévi-Strauss says, with respect to the first of these points, "To say that a society functions is a truism; but to say that everything in a society functions is an absurdity" (*AS*, p. 357; trans. P. C.). But Radcliffe-Brown, speaking of the hypothesis that social systems have a functional unity, remarks that "the hypothesis does not require the dogmatic assertion that everything in the life of every community has a function. It only requires the assumption that it *may* have one, and that we are justified in seeking to discover it" (op.cit., p. 184). On the second point he says: "In the study of social structure the concrete reality with which we are concerned is the set of actually existing relations, at a given moment of time, which link together certain human beings. It is on this that we can make direct observations. But it is not this that we attempt to describe in its particularity . . . what we need for scientific purposes is an account of the form of the structure" (idem, p. 192).

Radcliffe-Brown thus prepares the way for a structuralism which will go beyond the merely descriptive. It remained for Lévi-Strauss to bring anthropological structuralism (and with it the movement as a whole) to the position it now occupies. Lévi-Strauss's early work was a sequel to that of Marcel Mauss, whose "Essai sur le don, forme archaïque de l'échange" (*Année Sociologique*, N.S. **1**, Paris [1932–34]) had provided a dynamics for social systems in terms of exchanges. There is an obvious analogy here to systems of language; languages signify, but they do so, at least in part, in order to communicate, and communication proceeds by the exchange of words. In *Les structures élémentaires de la parenté* (1949, hereafter *SEP*) Lévi-Strauss, taking as his starting point the universal prohibition (under some form or other) of incest, interprets exogamous marriage as a system of the exchange of women, and adumbrates a general theory in which gifts, women, and other media of exchange between groups would behave like signs: "the relations between the sexes might be regarded as one of the modalities of a great 'function of communication' which includes language as well" (*SEP*, p. 613; trans. P. C.). It is hardly necessary to point out that Lévi-Strauss does not regard women *merely* as signs; on the other hand, the fact that they are never consciously viewed as such (in our own or any other society) is not incompatible, for the structuralist, with their really fulfilling this role.

This *unconscious* character of the most fundamental social and psychological structures is (as was remarked above in connection with Troubetzkoy's work on linguistic structures) an important component of Lévi-Strauss's teaching. "It is necessary and sufficient to arrive at the unconscious structure underlying an institution or a custom to acquire a principle of interpretation valid for other institutions and other customs, provided of course the analysis is carried far enough" (*AS*, p. 28; trans. P. C.).

The difference between linguistics and anthropology, so far as the contribution of structuralism is concerned, lies in the fact that they start from different conditions of knowledge. In the case of language the function of the system, or at least a function of it (namely communication), has been known for a long time; structural linguistics tells us what structural elements and relations enable it to fulfill this function. In the case of kinship the elements and relations have been known for a long time; what structural anthropology tells us is how they constitute the structure of a system and what the function of that system might be (*AS*, p. 40). Just as in the case of language, however, structural characteristics reveal themselves only in a study of *differences* among customs, myths, kinship patterns, and the like: what is constant is not a particular rule of marriage but a pattern of such rules, any variant of which will lend stability to a society with limited numbers by ensuring a cyclic order of exchanges among its parts.

One of the reasons for the enormous popularity of the structuralist movement (and hence at least in part for its extension to other fields) is to be found in two books by Lévi-Strauss which depart from the purely scientific concerns of his earlier and later works. These are *Tristes tropiques* (1955) and *La pensée sauvage* (1962). The former is part autobiography, part travelogue, part philosophical reflection; it is not explicitly structuralist at all, but some of its themes nevertheless throw significant light on what might be called the moral component of structuralism. It makes clear the influence of Marxism and psychoanalysis on Lévi-Strauss's intellectual development (in another place he speaks of having "borrowed the notion of structure from Marx and Engels"; *AS*, p. 364), provides a vivid background for his later work on mythology, and reveals his preoccupation with three basic

sociologico-philosophical problems: the place of the individual in the collective, the relation between the collective and the natural world, and the role of the ethnographer with respect both to the culture he studies and to his own culture. As for Chomsky, so for Lévi-Strauss the structures he studies are rewarding insofar as they reflect the structure of mind.

In *La pensée sauvage* he takes up this theme explicitly, examining as he puts it "mind in its natural state." One of the things that stand in the way of our grasping it in this state is of course the conditioning to which our own minds have been subject, so that we superimpose on the products of other minds a grid of logical or utilitarian expectations. Hence we are inclined to think that the primitive has an inadequate science and an unformed sense of logical propriety. Lévi-Strauss argues, however, that what he calls the "science of the concrete"—the complex systems of nomenclature and association that are to be found in virtually all primitive cultures—is just as theoretical, in its way, as our own science, that the heterogeneous structures of myth and totemism follow rules just as intelligible and rigorous as those of our more neatly engineered systems.

Engineering may be taken as a paradigm of our aspirations: everything new, shiny, detachable, precise. The primitive is a *bricoleur* rather than an engineer, and *bricolage* has become one of the basic ideas of structuralism. It means, in essence, the use for purposes of construction of anything that comes to hand, particularly of elements or remnants of former constructions. So the myth will be built up from fragments of earlier myths, as language is built up from fragments of earlier languages. This heterogeneity of content is perfectly compatible with rigor of structure, and that rather than content is the important thing. But it is much less readily seen in a product of *bricolage* than in a piece of engineering, and therefore has to be sought for by a process of analysis. The structure that emerges from this process, however, being in some sense indifferent to the materials in which it is realized, is likely to reflect more accurately than a piece of engineering the natural contours of the mind that gave rise to it.

The process of analysis in the case of myth, to take the best-known example, consists in showing how one myth can be seen as a transformation of another, or both as transformations of a third that may not even occur in the corpus of myths; it is a search for the deep structure which explains and generates, in the epistemological and ontological orders respectively, the surface structure exhibited by actual myths. The deep structure is never *extracted* in order to be shown by itself, it emerges from the repeated contrasts and oppositions of variants, complementary versions and so on. The works in which Lévi-Strauss has carried on this enterprise are the various volumes of his collection *Mythologiques*, and the scale of the project can be gauged from the fact that in the first volume alone, *Le cru et le cuit* (1964, hereafter *CC*) no fewer than 187 separate myths are analyzed. Structuralist analysis does not proceed in a straight line, from a clear-cut problem to a definitive solution, but works over its data until they yield up their own intelligibility. No myth is more basic than another—"the world of mythology is round," as Lévi-Strauss remarks in *Du miel aux cendres* (p. 7)—although one or another myth may be chosen as a key myth or myth of reference for purposes of organization. The aim of the work is consistent with that of the earlier scientific researchers, namely to "draw up an inventory of mental patterns, to reduce apparently arbitrary data to some kind of order, and to attain a level at which a kind of necessity becomes apparent, underlying the illusions of liberty" (*CC*, p. 10).

## II. LITERARY CRITICISM AND PSYCHOANALYSIS

The basic tenet of structuralism at the substantive rather than the methodological level might be rendered as follows: what makes anything intelligible to man is a coincidence of structure between it and him. Nature is not intelligible except insofar as we are able to formulate its workings in theories of our own construction (that we are able to do this so readily may be, as C. S. Peirce suggested, due to the fact that we ourselves are products of the same laws as nature is). Structuralism applies chiefly to cultural domains, in which everything is directly or indirectly a product of mind, so that a coincidence of structure is not to be wondered at. (Lévi-Strauss's observations on the prohibition of incest—an apparently cultural rule which seems to have the universality of a natural law—gave one of the first impulses to his development as a structuralist.) But the coincidence may not be evident at first, or not fully so; work may be required to bring it to light. It can become intelligible in its turn only through a second-order coincidence of structure, and it is obvious that there can be no last step in this process, which explains why in the end intelligibility must be shown rather than argued.

Clearly language is the most fundamental and most universal cultural product. Its own proper structure is the concern of linguistics, but linguistics, even the linguistics of *parole*, deals with language on a universal level. Language in actual use gives rise to a number of kinds of artifact that escape merely linguistic analysis, among which are two of particular interest for structuralism: what *is made* with language, i.e., litera-

ture, which is the concern of criticism, and what *makes itself* with language, i.e., the subject, which is the concern of psychoanalysis.

One of the most striking examples of structuralist criticism—an analysis of Charles Baudelaire's sonnet "Les Chats," which appeared originally in *L'Homme*, an anthropological journal—is again due to Lévi-Strauss, in collaboration not with a literary critic but with a linguist, Roman Jakobson (Jakobson and Lévi-Strauss, 1962). Literature seems to Lévi-Strauss to occupy an area of intersection between linguistics and ethnology: "The linguist discerns in poetic works structures that bear a striking analogy to those found in myths by ethnologists. In their turn ethnologists cannot help recognizing that myths are not merely carriers of concepts: they are also works of art" (idem, p. 5). Art is a cultural product; literature is art in the medium of language. The analysis of Baudelaire's sonnet consists simply in laying out the oppositions that occur in it, on the various levels of phonology, phonetics, syntax, prosody, semantics, and so on; there is nothing critical about this process if by criticism is meant bringing to bear *external* canons of form or style. But the outcome of it is precisely a "making intelligible" of the work on levels that are not accessible to the casual reader, or even to the informed reader who lacks the technical resources of the linguist.

This is a far cry from criticism as it is practiced by professional critics, but is does not exhaust the potential contribution of structuralism to their discipline. Works of literature are linguistic constructions, but like myths they too have conceptual content, as well as thematic, social, psychological, and aesthetic aspects. Structuralism recognizes intelligibility wherever it is to be found, and its task with respect to literature is to explore the significance of these aspects also. Structuralist criticism in France has come to be classed with psychoanalytic, Marxist, and existentialist approaches as "New Criticism" or "ideological criticism" because of its refusal to observe the customs and pieties of the literary establishment, and because of its insistence on taking the work as an object in the world—a text, the product of *écriture* or "writing," a human or social *trace* comparable to a myth, or on another level to a temple or a city, open to archeological reconstruction or deciphering—rather than as the masterpiece of a particular author or an element of a chauvinistic literary heritage. Lévi-Strauss's remark that "myths have no authors," if extended to the classics, is certainly calculated to enrage traditional critics who are as conscious of their classical antecedents as the French, and the polemic over structuralist criticism has been especially bitter where it has concerned Racine, as seen in Roland Barthes, *Sur Racine* (1963), Raymond Picard,

*Nouvelle critique ou nouvelle imposture?* (1965), and Barthes' reply to this, *Critique et vérité* (1966).

Barthes is the leader of the structuralist movement in criticism; he has also attempted (in his *Éléments de sémiologie,* 1964) to summarize what can reasonably be said at this point about the system of signs in general, as a first step towards the science envisaged by Saussure as well as by Lévi-Strauss which would deal with language but go beyond it, treating it as only one among the many significative systems available to us. Not surprisingly, the only developed technical apparatus he is able to present comes precisely from linguistics, and while it is certainly correct to treat language as the principal and most obvious structured system, there may be some danger in assuming that it is paradigmatic of all of them. Other examples of Barthes' diverse and resourceful brand of structural analysis are to be found in his *Système de la mode* (1967)—which is not, as many people have supposed, a book about fashion, but rather about the language to which it gives rise—and in his commentaries on various aspects of French culture, such as the plates of Diderot's *Encyclopédie,* the Eiffel Tower, etc., and an earlier series of short essays on everyday phenomena collected in *Mythologies* (1957).

In any discussion of significance, from C. S. Peirce to the present, the question: To whom do the signs signify what they do? is bound to arise. To this we might answer, man, the conscious subject, etc., thus giving a name to the problem but not doing anything to solve it. Now it is remarkable that the subject does not in general simply *take in* significance, but characteristically *responds* to it, and this most often not by action (which might be an appropriate response to stimuli received from the natural world) but by *discourse.* Significance evokes significance in its turn (in *Sur Racine* Barthes alludes to "the silence of the work which speaks, and the speech of man who listens"). This leads naturally enough, but by a new route, to the hypothesis that mind itself is a system with the structure of discourse. Instead of inferring the structure of mind in general from the structure of its large-scale causal consequences (language, cultural artifacts, and so on), what it suggests is that we might infer the structure of particular minds, i.e., personalities, from their immediate causal consequences, the syntagmatic spoken chain that makes up the speech of each individual person. Structuralism thus has an intimate bearing on psychoanalysis, and this connection has been worked out in the writings of Jacques Lacan, a Freudian, who in spite of early disagreements with the official organization of psychoanalysts in France has continued through his own group (*l'École freudienne de Paris*) to exert a great influence on their practice.

As in the case of kinship practices, myths, and works of art, the speech of the individual man (for the psychoanalyst, the patient) is to be seen as moving on two levels simultaneously. He uses language consciously to say what he wishes to say, and at the same time unconsciously says something quite different, which it is the analyst's task to interpret. According to the Cartesian view, in which the subject (the "I") is constituted by the *cogito,* these two differing and even conflicting messages would have to be provided by two different subjects. Given that the conscious, reflective subject is the "I" of Descartes, who, Lacan asks, is the other one? His answer is that the Unconscious, which has the structure of language, is the language of the Other, who inhabits the "other place" of which Freud speaks. This Other is genetically speaking prior to the I, which constructs itself by entering into relations with the world and with itself, through language and by means of the body; the unreflective and unconscious becomes conscious and reflective in a series of quite definite stages, of which the most important in Lacan's work has been the *stade du miroir,* or "mirror stage," which in young children represents the first apprehension of their physical unity and autonomy (in its pathological form it appears as the neurosis of the "fragmented body").

The apparent personification of the Other obscures the importance of this discovery, which is double: first, the structure of the unconscious is presumably common to all men, idiosyncrasies of the conscious subject arising from differences in ontogenetic development; second, this structure is presumably the same as the structure found underlying language, kinship systems, mythology, and literature—*it* writes, ordains, and so on, in spite of the fact that men have always believed that *they* did.

### III. PHILOSOPHY

The discomfort at this anthropomorphizing of the unconscious can be resolved in one of two ways: either by accepting it and having recourse to the transcendent (i.e., theologizing) or by challenging the concept of man that leads to it in the first place. The latter approach has been taken by Michel Foucault, whose doctrine of the "end of man," worked out in *Les mots et les choses* (1966), has awakened the defenders of humanism just as the defenders of classical drama were awakened by Barthes. Foucault, whose earlier works (*Histoire de la folie,* 1961, and *Naissance de la clinique,* 1963) had dealt with the abnormal as a negative touchstone for the human, shows in this book that the concept of "man" as it has come to be understood in contemporary humanism is a comparatively recent invention, called into being as the subject matter of the *sciences humaines* and destined to disappear with the growing realization that these sciences are dealing only with surface phenomena whose explanation is to be found elsewhere.

Once again the theme of a deep unconscious structure emerges: the search for Man as a possible object of knowledge has in fact produced linguistic structures, the unconscious, etc., but never a concept of man capable of bearing the weight that humanism would place upon it. For humanism requires a concept that will give meaning to the totality of things not only now but for the future, while the condition of man is such that his meanings always come from outside himself—from elsewhere, from the Other, from the system of discourse within which he becomes aware of the possibility of meaning. No totality can be meaningful in any case, except a finished one (a *historical* humanism, an intellectual *object*, a book, some other product of *écriture*), which can only be a part of our present totality and which necessarily has a closed structure, whereas the "structurality" of our situation (to borrow a phrase from Jacques Derrida) is open.

Derrida, in a series of very difficult essays, has begun the task of bringing structuralist philosophy into relation with the recent history of Western thought, notably that of Nietzsche and Edmund Husserl. The Apollo/Dionysius opposition in Nietzsche becomes paradigmatic of the opposition between retrospective analysis in terms of *différence*, on the one hand, and, on the other, a current and dynamic presence to the world, involving the notion of *différance* (sic), which by an etymological allusion brings in the notion of temporality (one of the meanings of *différer* being "to defer or postpone") as well as the activity of making a difference, engaging in *praxis* rather than *theoria*. The philosophical analysis of this immediacy is phenomenology, itself based on a double binary structure of noesis/noema and formal/material. Derrida sees that there can be no question of *replacing* the *cogito*, either Cartesian or Husserlian, with structure, but that the more difficult task of *reconciling* them has to be undertaken. The central problem is one of self-reference, structure being what emerges when language is employed to raise the question of language, when the subject raises the question of subjectivity, when man seeks the essence of man.

Another link with philosophical antecedents, already claimed at least on a terminological level by Lévi-Strauss, is provided by Louis Althusser's work on Marx. For Althusser the concept of *ideology* plays the key role; it is the structured, unconscious system through which men relate to their world and within which they come to awareness of it. Althusser also makes use of an essentially structuralist method in his treatment of

the relation between Marxist and Hegelian dialectics, the former being in his view a structural transformation of the latter rather than the simple inversion found in the textbooks. But Althusser himself (like Foucault, Lacan, and others) strenuously denies that he is a structuralist, and in conclusion it may be worth coming back to the problem of whether it is defensible to include these diverse points of view under a common heading at all.

The objection that is so strongly felt to the title "structuralist" by so many of those who have been identified as leaders of the movement has many components, but three stand out. First is the belief, already alluded to, that structuralism is a school or an ideology, committing anybody who subscribes to it to a package of ideas and concepts that must be accepted integrally or not at all, and excluding other possible points of view or departure (historical, positivist, existentialist, etc.). Second, and especially understandable in view of the national origins of the movement, is the fact that structuralism has become fashionable; everything not obviously in open contradiction with it, everything not fully understood, is likely to be called "structuralist" in the French press, and it is natural to resist the undiscriminating epithets of the crowd. Third is the further fact that the notion of structure has a technical use, especially in mathematics and derivatively in linguistics and anthropology, so that purists may object to its loose extension into fields like literature and philosophy. Lévi-Strauss, for instance, has very little patience with critics who go beyond linguistic structuralism.

The first two of these objections can be answered reasonably. To the extent that *other* movements are ideological or scholastic, structuralism may be incompatible with them, but since there is as yet no coherent and worked-out set of propositions to constitute structuralism "officially," but only a series of suggestive and mutually reinforcing conjectures whose empirical justifications are drawn from a number of different disciplines, many other positions (although not all) may prove to be compatible with it. Fashions change, and the value of the structuralist perspective will survive these changes.

The last objection is harder to deal with, but it may be pointed out that linguistics and anthropology, the most technical of the disciplines involved, have themselves borrowed only rather simple forms of combinatory mathematics, and that while the question why there should be intelligible structures in logic and mathematics may eventually permit a structuralist answer, for the time being it is simply inappropriate to invoke the mathematical notion of structure in connection with structuralism in the human sciences.

Structuralism so far is at the descriptive level for the most part, and this provides ample opportunity for fruitful and enlightening work in a variety of disciplines. In philosophy its theories of the mind and of meaning are beginning to become clear; its logic and metaphysics remain to be developed.

*BIBLIOGRAPHY*

L. Althusser, *Pour Marx* (Paris, 1966). R. Barthes, *Sur Racine* (Paris, 1936); idem, *Le degré zéro de l'écriture,* suivi de *Éléments de sémiologie* (Paris, 1965); idem, *Critique et vérité* (Paris, 1966). N. Chomsky, "Introduction," in M. Gross and A. Lentin, *Notions sur les grammaires formelles* (Paris, 1967); idem, *Language and Mind* (New York, 1968). J. Derrida, *De la grammatologie* (Paris, 1967); idem, *L'écriture et la différence* (Paris, 1967). O. Ducrot, et al., *Qu'est-ce que le structuralisme?* (Paris, 1968). M. Foucault, *Les mots et les choses* (Pairs, 1966). R. Jakobson and C. Lévi-Strauss, "'Les Chats' de Charles Baudelaire," *L'Homme,* **2,** 1 (Jan.–Apr. 1962). J. Lacan, *Écrits* (Paris, 1966). C. Lévi-Strauss, *Les structures élémentaires de la parenté* (Paris, 1949); idem, *Tristes tropiques* (Paris, 1955); idem, *Anthropologie structurale* (Paris, 1958); idem, *La pensée sauvage* (Paris, 1962); idem, *Mythologiques:* Vol. I, *Le cru et le cuit* (Paris, 1964), trans. John and Doreen Weightman as *The Raw and the Cooked* (New York, 1969); Vol. II, *Du miel aux cendres* (Paris, 1966); Vol. III, *L'origine des manières de table* (Paris, 1968). A. R. Radcliffe-Brown, *Structure and Function in Primitive Society* (London, 1952). F. de Saussure, *Cours de linguistique générale* (Geneva, 1915); trans. Wade Baskin as *Course in General Linguistics* (New York, 1959; reprint 1966). N. Troubetzkoy. "La phonologie actuelle," in H. Delacroix, *Psychologie du langage* (Paris, 1933); idem, *Grundzüge der Phonologie* (Prague, 1939).

Translations by the author are designated by P. C.

PETER CAWS

[See also Criticism, Literary; **Language; Linguistics;** Myth.]

# STYLE IN LITERATURE

OF THE MANY senses of "style" two are particularly relevant here: (a) the use of language in a work of literature; (b) the sum of formal characteristics common to a period, school, or genre (the latter applies to all the arts, including literature). The word "style" derives from Latin *stilus,* an instrument for writing on wax tablets, hence, by metonymy, a way of writing (already classical in this sense, found in Cicero). However, other words (such as *oratio, elocutio*) were more often used, and the concept of style naturally goes back to the earliest Greek writings on rhetoric.

Most of the major problems which have since arisen in the theory of style are already present in antiquity, at least by implication: until the end of the eighteenth century, and sometimes even later, the framework of reference is nearly always that established by ancient rhetoric and there is constant harking back to the old ideas. Though important modifications occur, this makes a strict chronological sequence difficult to trace. Thus in the *Phaedrus,* Plato (or Socrates) presents an almost romantic view of style. Rhetorical devices, ornaments, image-making, are subordinate to general truth, goodness of character, and psychological insight, in some ways an anticipation of Buffon's famous eighteenth-century dictum: "Style is the man himself" (*Le style est l'homme même*), found in *Discours sur le style* (ed. Nollet [1905], p. 22). Content and form cannot really be separated. It follows too that only the rudiments of style can be taught, its essence not at all (one of the favorite ideas of the nineteenth and twentieth centuries). Aristotle, on the other hand, in the *Poetics* and *Rhetoric,* tends towards the view of style as ornament, and engages in a precise investigation of figures of speech and other devices of style, and of their aesthetic and psychological effect. Among these figures, metaphor is the hallmark of genius, a view later echoed by Longinus and by Proust. Almost from the beginning, then, though the difference between Plato and Aristotle must not be overstressed, we find clearly stated the two opposing views of style as an inevitable product of content, and as a technique which can be acquired.

Later Greek writers develop these ideas. The *De compositione* of Dionysius of Halicarnassus (ca. 20 B.C.) is concerned with word order and rhythm but this turns into a highly interesting study of style in general. He insists on beauty and the magical effect of word order, which can be ruined by transposition. The *De elocutione* of Demetrius (first century A.D.) continues and extends the Aristotelian tradition of analysis of figures and tropes but again, in an unmechanical way, conveying the spirit as well as the technique. He shows himself keenly aware of the deeper differences between prose and poetry, going beyond meter. Roughly contemporary is *On the Sublime* (not by Longinus but the name is too familiar to be dropped), which from the end of the seventeenth century (Boileau's translation, 1674) exercised immense influence on the development of European preromanticism. Loftiness of language is the keynote; a little stream is less admirable than the ocean; and in the Platonic way expression is subordinate to thought and passion (though there is also an Aristotelian mastery in the analysis of figures).

Generally speaking the Greeks are marked by freshness and strong aesthetic sense (this applies to the Aristotelian as well as to the Platonic tradition). The Romans (Cicero, Horace, and Quintilian outstanding) are much more practical. Quintilian's *Institutio oratoria* (ca. A.D. 95), in particular, is perhaps still the best repertory of the expressive resources of a language, though with few general ideas.

Of the principles which emerge from classical theorists, the most important for later developments are the definition of the qualities of style and the theory of levels. According to Quintilian style (*oratio*) has three kinds of excellence: correctness, clarity, and adornment. Elsewhere he adds propriety (fitness to context). But for him, as for Aristotle, clarity seems the most important. Although Oriental developments lie beyond the scope of this article, it is interesting to see a similar emphasis on clarity in the Sanskrit treatise *Nātyaçāstra* (ca. first century A.D.). The three levels of style are, with variations, the simple, the intermediate, and the grand (a distinction usually ascribed to the lost *Of Style* of Theophrastus, continued by most later writers including Dionysius, Cicero, and Quintilian). Demetrius adds a fourth level, the forcible.

Medieval stylistic theory (Matthieu de Vendôme, Geoffroi de Vinsauf, John Garland) is closely imitated from Latin models (Cicero and Horace especially), but with an even stronger practical bent than that of the Romans. The doctrine of the three styles is extended from style to subject and leads to Vergil's Wheel, in which the three divisions are adapted to epic, didactic, and pastoral (*Aeneid, Georgics,* and *Eclogues*). The word *stilus* itself is much more frequently used. But one great original mind naturally towers above the rest. Dante is perhaps the first to use the term in a vernacular language exactly in its modern sense:

> tu se' solo colui da cu' io tolsi
> lo bello stilo che m'ha fatto onore.

("It is you alone from whom I took the beautiful style which has brought me honor"; *Inferno*, i, 86–87).

In *De vulgari eloquentia* he offers a new interpretation of levels of style, extending the notion beyond genres to constructions and vocabulary.

During the Renaissance, understandably, dependence on classical models is still greater, especially in the series of commentaries on Aristotle by Italians, beginning with Robortello (1548). In general, Italian and French preoccupation with the problems of a national literary language tended to distract attention from style in itself. On the other hand, there is more stress on poetics and less on rhetoric than in the work of the ancients, and this helps to detach the concept of style from a narrowly practical purpose. And in the discussion of the qualities of style, though clarity still appears, beauty and splendor of language come to overshadow it, e.g., in Trissino's *La poetica* (1529) or Ronsard's *Abrégé de l'art poétique* (1565); elocution,

Ronsard says, is a splendor of words which makes verses glitter like precious stones on the fingers of a great lord—but here we are perhaps moving towards mannerism. At the same time, Scaliger (*Poetices libri septem*, 1561) multiplies the qualities of style till he has about twenty, among which beauty (*venustas*) occupies an important place. The three levels of style of course continue to appear (Scaliger and Ronsard again). Ronsard above all returns to the Platonic view that details of style are subject to the Muses and the divine fury of the poet. On the whole, Renaissance theory shows a powerful resurgence of the aesthetic emphasis we have found in the Greeks.

When we come to the end of the sixteenth century, to late mannerism or early baroque, we encounter the difficulty that the common run of critics follows classical precepts and reflects only tangentially the sometimes startling innovations in style itself. However, both Montaigne and Ben Jonson (*Timber*, 1640; posthumous) praise the concise and abrupt style of Sallust and Seneca, the "Senecan amble." And both regard style as the expression of the man himself, Montaigne by implication, Jonson (following Juan Luis Vives) fairly explicitly ("No glasse renders a mans forme, or likenesse, so true as his speech"). They are joined by Robert Burton (*Anatomy of Melancholy*, 1621): "*stylus virum arguit*, our style bewrays us," almost Buffon. A more fully baroque conception appears in Martin Opitz (*Buch von der deutschen Poeterei*, 1624), with his exaltation of decoration as a principal quality of style and his admiration for magnificent periphrases. However, for the extreme presentation of baroque theory we must turn to Tesauro's *Il cannocchiale Aristotelico* (1654), an amazing compendium of rhetorical figures, conceits, and verbal tricks (and their equivalents in painting and sculpture), with a remarkable classification of sources of metaphors by place, time, dress, and so on, which anticipates many modern studies of imagery. Everything becomes a conceit and creates astonishment. That this extravaganza claims to be (and to some extent is) based on Aristotle is a good example of the way classical models are completely transformed and distorted by baroque writers or artists.

Comparison with Tesauro demonstrates the prudent moderation of the French classical school. Boileau returns to the notion of clarity as the supreme quality, the three styles receive much attention (Boileau and Rapin both warn against the dangers of the grand style), La Bruyère insists on propriety (in Quintilian's sense of the *mot juste*). However, we must not overlook Boileau's part in popularizing the bold ideas of Longinus, and Bernard Lamy (*La rhétorique, ou l'art de parler*, 1675) moves a step further towards Buffon.

Every man has his own way of gesticulating or walking, and so it is with writing (cf. Jonson): there are as many styles as there are persons writing. But Lamy goes further: personal differences of style are the direct product of physical differences in the brain and nervous system. This materialist and scientific approach, not far removed from Locke, anticipates not only the eighteenth century but also the nineteenth (Gourmont) and the twentieth (I. A. Richards). Lamy also examines the influence of climate on national styles and distinguishes genre styles and period styles (he is perhaps one of the first to view style historically).

The eighteenth century is still dominated by classical rhetoric, but as we should expect there is a serious attempt to put it on a rational philosophical foundation. Thus when Lord Kames (*Elements of Criticism*, 1762) discusses beauty of language at great length, he in fact talks mainly about the logic of syntax. Swift and Buffon maintain that passion in style should never prevail over reason, Laharpe that style is the just and proportionate expression of feelings; Buffon and Johnson agree that things should only be named in general terms. Clarity is still put first among qualities by Kames (who goes so far as to say that it "ought not to be sacrificed to any other beauty whatever") and by Crevier (*Rhétorique françoise*, 1765). The three levels of style continue to flourish (Rollin, Voltaire, Marmontel); Crevier makes them the basis of a systematic classification of noble and low words, the latter of course to be excluded. A favorite idea of the period, which goes back at least to Quintilian, is that style is the dress of thought (Kames, Johnson, Crevier).

The works of the professional rhetoricians, like du Marsais (*Des tropes*, 1730) and Crevier, can be regarded as the ultimate point of the classical system. Their methodical treatment of figures, sensible and intelligent, is a monument of eighteenth-century rationalism. However, the most famous and influential study, Buffon's *Discours sur le style* (1753), is not the work of a rhetorician but of a scientist. As we should expect, we find the rational emphasis of the period, with traces of a more markedly scientific attitude: thoughts and ideas are what style expresses (*les idées seules forment le fond du style*); movement is given importance, appropriately to the age of Newtonian physics (*Le style n'est que l'ordre et le mouvement qu'on met dans ses pensées*); the qualities of good style are luminosity, precision, simplicity, clarity. On the other hand, Buffon anticipates the future with his insistence on color and energy, and on the organic unity of style, its resemblance to works of nature. And of course there is *Le style est l'homme même*, foreshadowed, we have seen, by earlier writers but never so clearly stated. In spite of the scientific context in which it appears, it may be considered the foundation of romantic views of style.

In some ways the study of style becomes less important during the romantic period and after, for several reasons: the literary reaction against classical rhetoric (*Guerre à la rhétorique* . . . , Hugo); the growth of historical linguistics, with consequent rejection of the static and synchronic approach of rhetoric; above all, the biographical conception of criticism which concentrates on the personality, not the text. Still, although it is in some ways a return to Plato and Longinus, romanticism is perhaps the first great revolution in the theory of style, founded on the development of two central and closely related ideas: the style is the man; content and style are inseparable. The first is vividly put by Newman: "we might as well say that one man's shadow is another's as that the style of a really gifted mind can belong to any but himself. . . . Literature is the personal use or exercise of language" (*The Idea of a University*). On the second, De Quincey records a remark of Wordsworth's: "It is in the highest degree unphilosophic to call language or diction 'the *dress* of thoughts' . . . he would call it 'the *incarnation* of thoughts.'" This demolishes not only a favorite image of the old rhetoric but also the view of style as superimposed ornament on which that rhetoric was based. Similar views are expressed in the nineteenth century by, for example, Wackernagel, Schopenhauer, G. H. Lewes, Flaubert, and Henry James. It is clear that style in this sense, since it is the inevitable expression of mind and personality, cannot be taught (again the annihilation of the old rhetoric), a view put by Chateaubriand, Brunetière, and Walter Raleigh (*Style*, 1897), but carried to extreme lengths by Remy de Gourmont (*Le Problème du style*, 1902) in his attack on the manuals of Antoine Albalat. Wackernagel (*Poetik Rhetorik und Stilistik*, 1836–37) significantly transforms the classical three levels into the style of intellect, the style of imagination, and the style of feeling.

To this mainstream of romantic thought (even today far from exhausted) we must add the scientific and perhaps the aesthetic movements of the nineteenth century. Aestheticism is an offshoot of romanticism, but its preoccupation with form tends towards a new separation of style and content, as when Walter Pater compares the writer's language to the sculptor's marble or Robert Louis Stevenson attempts to analyze verbal music. The application of science is seen incidentally in Lewes's comparison of style to an efficient machine, and systematically in Herbert Spencer's naïvely ingenious reduction of style to the law of minimum effort. More significantly, Gourmont (an interesting amalgam of scientific and aesthetic approaches) makes style a product of physiology, an idea we have already noticed in Lamy but here developed under the influence of Taine and the French Naturalist school.

The last fifty years have seen a great revival of interest, theoretical and technical, in the phenomena of style. This movement has been both literary (the reaction against biographical criticism and the realization of the supreme importance of the work itself) and linguistic (the reaction against historical linguistics; Saussure's distinction between *langue* and *parole;* the growth of structuralism). There has been a return to some of the objects of classical rhetoric, though with methods based on advances in linguistics and an attempt to go beyond mere classification. The results are too varied and too controversial to permit easy summarizing: the most striking features are perhaps, on the literary side, the new importance attached to figures, especially imagery, and, on the linguistic side, the notion of style as an individual system within a general code. The use of computers has been valuable not so much in solving particular problems of attribution as in drawing attention to style as a set of detectable patterns.

*BIBLIOGRAPHY*

There is surprisingly little on the historical development of theories of style, and the subject is best studied in general histories of criticism: J. W. H. Atkins, *Literary Criticism in Antiquity* (Cambridge, 1934); E. Faral, *Les arts poétiques du XIIe et du XIIIe siècles* (Paris, 1924), includes the key texts in full; G. Saintsbury, *A History of Criticism* (Edinburgh and London, 1900–04); B. Weinberg, *A History of Literary Criticism in the Italian Renaissance* (Chicago, 1961); R. Wellek, *A History of Literary Criticism 1750–1950* (New Haven, 1955–). A most useful work, though elementary in intention, is L. Cooper's *Theories of Style* (New York, 1907), which includes representative essays from Plato to the end of the nineteenth century, in English or translated into English. For post-1900, see, for example, J. Cohen, *Structure du langage poétique* (Paris, 1966); R. Fowler, ed., *Essays on Style and Language* (London, 1966); H. A. Hatzfeld, *A Critical Bibliography of the New Stylistics* (Chapel Hill, 1953); J. Leed, ed., *The Computer and Literary Style* (Kent, Ohio, 1966).

R. A. SAYCE

[See also Ambiguity; **Beauty;** Criticism; Form; Metaphor; Poetry and Poetics; Rationality; **Rhetoric;** Romanticism; Structuralism.]

# SUBLIME IN EXTERNAL NATURE

RADICAL though England was in the "new science," it remained conservative in literary criticism, drawing primarily from French rhetoricians. In France the

"Sublime" was for many years a rhetorical concept. Yet even though Boileau's *Traité de l'art poétique* was known in England from the time of its publication in 1674, it is many years before we find the kind of estimate of Longinus implied by Alexander Pope in *An Essay on Criticism,* first published in 1711 (lines 675–80):

> Thee, bold Longinus! all the Nine inspire,
> And bless their Critick with a Poet's Fire,
> An ardent Judge, who Zealous in his Trust,
> With warmth gives Sentence, yet is always Just;
> Whose own Example strengthens all his Laws,
> and Is himself the great Sublime he draws.

But in the meantime, during the late seventeenth century, a "natural Sublime" was developing in England with the result that travellers to the Alps were both appalled and enthralled by the vast and grand in external Nature [see Mountains, . . .]. A climax emerges in the extraordinary ambivalence of Thomas Burnet, in *A Sacred Theory of the Earth* (Latin, 1681; English, 1684), who on the one hand condemned mountains as monstrosities, the "ruines of a broken World," and on the other responded to their majesty emotionally as had no English writer before that time. In England a "natural Sublime" preceded the "rhetorical Sublime."

In 1688 John Dennis, an English dramatist and critic, crossed the Alps and left an account of the experience in a journal-letter, later published in his *Miscellanies* (1693). Like many before him, he pondered the problem whether mountains had been original with the creation of the world, or whether they were ruins, a result of destruction by the Flood. Mountain travel was still very dangerous, and some part of the "horror" and "terror" expressed by Dennis was the result of natural and instinctive fear. "We walk'd upon the very brink, in a literal sense, of Destruction," he wrote. "One Stumble and both Life and Carcass had been at once destroy'd." Everywhere about him, Dennis saw the ruins of a broken world: "Ruins upon Ruins in monstrous Heaps, and Heaven and Earth confounded." The frightful view of precipices and foaming waters that fell headlong from them "made all such a Consort up for the Eye, as that sort of Musick does for the Ear, in which Horrour can be joyn'd with Harmony." The Alps are works which "Nature seems to have design'd, and execut'd too in Fury. Yet she moves us less when she studies to please us more." Before his Alpine journey Dennis had been "delighted" at the beauty of hills and valleys, meadows and streams, but that had been "a delight that is consistent with reason. . . . But transporting Pleasures followed the sight of the Alpes, and what unusual Transports think you were those, that were mingled with Horrours, and sometimes almost with despair." In a sentence Dennis expressed the idea of the Sublime that was to become a new aesthetic experience: "The sense of all this produc'd different emotions in me, viz., a delightful Horrour, a terrible Joy, and at the same time, that I was infinitely pleas'd, I trembled." Dennis returned to England to write various works in which he developed an aesthetic only dawning when he went abroad, to attempt to establish new literary criteria, and to make the first important distinction in English literary criticism between the Beautiful and the Sublime, categories which remained sharply opposed in his mind.

Anthony Ashley Cooper, third Earl of Shaftesbury, made the Grand Tour in 1686, two years earlier than Dennis, but did not publish his memoirs of it until *The Moralists* appeared in 1709. Perhaps like Dennis he had written a journal-letter. His account of the mountain-experience is an episode in a grand tour of the universe, on which a master conducted a pupil. It begins with sight of a vast tract of sky above the mighty Atlas, rearing his snow-covered head, where "huge embodied rocks lie piled one on another." "See with what trembling steps poor mankind tread the narrow brink of the deep precipices, mistrusting even the ground which bears them." They ponder the evidences of ruin they see on all sides, "whilst the apparent spoil and irreparable breaches of the wasted mountain show them the world itself only as a noble ruin." "Midway the mountain," the travellers felt that "space astonishes"; but space did not appall Shaftesbury as it had Blaise Pascal who wrote in his *Pensées* (1670, posthumous): "The eternal silence of these infinite spaces terrifies me." To Shaftesbury the apparent infinity of space led men to thoughts of God, in whose "immensity all thought is lost, fancy gives over its flight, and wearied imagination spends itself in vain, finding no coast nor limit of this ocean." Shaftesbury made no such sharp distinction as Dennis between beauty and sublimity: to him the Sublime was a higher and a grander Beauty.

So far as England was concerned, the most important early treatment of the Sublime was that of Joseph Addison in his *Pleasures of the Imagination.* Drafts of some of the papers had been written well before the full text was published in the *Spectator* in 1712. Even in his earliest printed work, his *Oration in Praise of the New Philosophy*, delivered when he was still a student at Oxford, Addison had shown the impact upon his imagination of a greatly expanded telescopic and microscopic "Nature" in the new universe. When he set out on the Grand Tour in 1699, he was better prepared than some of his predecessors for experience with the "grand" in Nature. "The Alps," he wrote, "fill the mind with an agreeable kind of horror, and form one of the most irregular, mis-shapen scenes in the world."

*The Pleasures of the Imagination,* as published, deal with two groups of "pleasures": a "secondary" (*Spectator* 416–20), in which Addison studies the effect upon imagination of various arts, architecture and landscape-gardening in particular. These essays, like a group of papers on Milton, may be said to treat the "rhetorical Sublime." They are less original than the first group of essays (*Spectator* 411–15), in which he discussed the effect of the primary pleasures of imagination. While he was dealing with what is there called "the Sublime in external Nature," it is significant that he carefully avoided in this group of essays the word "Sublime," using such adjectives as *great, stupendous, unlimited, spacious, unbounded,* and—though on only two occasions—*vast,* which he probably considered, as did the French, an adjective of excess. The primary pleasures of the imagination are such as man receives, not through books but directly from Nature. They come to him through his senses, most of all through sight. "By pleasures of imagination," Addison said (*Spectator* 411), "I here mean such as arise from visible objects. . . . We cannot, indeed, have a single image in the fancy that did not make its first appearance through the sight." In the essays Addison discussed three categories, "the great, the uncommon and the beautiful." His treatment of "beauty" remained conventional, that of the "new or uncommon" somewhat vague. His originality lay in his stress upon the effect on imagination of greatness, particularly as it was perceived through the eyes. Classical, medieval, and Arabic philosophers had stressed the importance of sight, but in the period of the telescope and the microscope it took on new significance. To Locke, sight was "the most comprehensive of all the senses," to Berkeley "the most noble, pleasant and comprehensive of all the senses." More than one philosopher of the period paused to consider the problems of a man born blind. But although Addison shared with predecessors and contemporaries his interest in the effect of sight, he was original in his emphasis on the influence of sight less on the mind, than on the *imagination.*

In *Spectator* 414 Addison particularly developed the idea of the great as a primary stimulus to the imagination. Works of art may be beautiful, but they cannot rise to "greatness." "There is something more bold and masterly in the rough careless strokes of nature, than in the nice touches and embellishments of art." "By greatness," he wrote in *Spectator* 412, "I do not mean only the bulk of any single object, but the largeness of a whole view." His memory went back to his Continental travels:

Such are the prospects of an open champaign country, a vast uncultivated desert, of huge heaps of mountains, high rocks and precipices, or a wide expanse of waters where we are not struck with the novelty or beauty of the sight, but with that rude kind of magnificence which appears in many of these stupendous works of nature.

A reader becomes aware that Addison is greatly interested in what we now think of as psychological effects of vastness and greatness upon the imagination. In this particular essay he continued:

Our imagination loves to be filled with an object, or to grasp at anything that is too big for its capacity. We are flung into a pleasing astonishment at such unbounded views, and feel a delightful stillness and amazement in the soul at the apprehension of them. The mind of man naturally hates every thing that looks like a restraint upon it, and is apt to fancy itself under a sort of confinement when the sight is pent up in a narrow compass, and shortened on every side by the neighborhood of walls or mountains. On the contrary, a spacious horizon is an image of liberty, where the eye has room to range abroad, to expatiate at large on the immensity of its views, and to lose itself amidst the variety of objects that offer themselves to its observation. Such wide and undetermined prospects are as pleasing to the fancy, as the speculations of eternity or infinitude are to the understanding.

Here is Addison's attempt at explicating what in modern times is "agoraphobia" and "claustrophobia."

In the last analysis, Addison declares (*Spectator* 413) that such appreciation of and aspiration toward the great is man's gift from God, who has "so formed the soul of man, that nothing but himself can be its last, adequate, and proper happiness." God has made man "naturally delighted in the apprehension of what is great or unlimited." From Infinite God through the vastness of Nature to the soul of man; from the soul of man through vast Nature to God—such was the process of what can be called "The Aesthetics of the Infinite."

There was nothing particularly original in Addison's development of the categories of beauty or novelty, but his analysis of *greatness* was of the first importance. As we shall see, his ideas were versified by Mark Akenside and made into an elaborate system by Edmund Burke. His analysis of beauty and sublimity also lay behind various of Immanuel Kant's conceptions in his *Kritik der Urteilskraft* (1790). To some extent his distinction between the Beautiful and the Sublime lay behind a new descriptive poetry in eighteenth-century England (discussed in *Mountain Gloom and Mountain Glory*, 1959). The sense of a new "vast Sublime" is to be seen particularly in the "excursion" poets who sent their imaginations on grand tours of the universe to marvel at all that was vast or grand—mighty continents with mountains and oceans, majestic rivers, subterraneous regions with caverns measureless to man. "Sublimity," James Thomson wrote to David Mallett who was planning *The Excursion* (1728), "must

be the characteristic of your piece." Mallett willingly responded with "great scenes": the violence of storm, eruptions, earthquakes, volcanoes, the Deluge. This, Thomson replied, "is arousing fancy—enthusiasm—rapturous terror."

In 1744–46 appeared editions of three long poems, all concerned in part with the Sublime: James Thomson's complete *Seasons*, Mark Akenside's *The Pleasures of Imagination*, Edward Young's *Night Thoughts*. Having wisely left to Mallett the most violent manifestations of natural forces, Thomson sent his imagination over the British Isles, Europe, and upon occasion South America, which he had not seen, finding both the Beautiful and the Sublime. "Spring" alone, in which he emphasized Beauty, is limited in its canvas. In the other seasons, rivers and mountains became more and more majestic as the various books grew under the poet's hand. "Air, earth and ocean smile immense"; "Earth's universal face is one wild dazzling waste." When shadows fall, the far horizon becomes a "boundless deep immensity of shade." "Solemn and slow the shadows blacker fall/ And all is awful listening gloom around." Nature grows increasingly richer, more diversified, more boundless, more sublime:

> Nature! great parent! whose unceasing hand
> Rolls round the Seasons of the changeful year.
> How mighty, how majestic are thy works!
> With what a pleasing dread they swell the soul,
> That sees astonish'd, and astonish'd sings!
> ("Winter," lines 106–10).

In his earlier version of *The Pleasures of Imagination* (1744), Mark Akenside, like Addison before him, treated the three categories of the sublime, the wonderful, and the fair, the second of which he omitted in a later edition. Unlike Thomson, Akenside was not a descriptive but a philosophical poet, less interested in scenery than in its effect upon the imagination. There was a significant difference, he felt, between responses to the Beautiful and the Sublime:

> Diff'rent minds
> Incline to different objects: one pursues
> The vast alone, the wonderful, the wild;
> Another sighs for harmony and grace,
> And gentlest beauty (III, 546–50).

The Beautiful and the Sublime were not antithetical to Akenside as they were to Dennis. Rather—as with Shaftesbury—the Sublime was the highest Beauty:

> . . . celestial truth
> Her awful light discloses, to bestow
> A more majestic pomp on beauty's frame.
> (II, 97–99)

To Akenside as to Thomson color was equated with beauty, light with sublimity. His "high-born soul,"

335

refusing to be satisfied with "earth and this diurnal scene," spreads its wings and takes off on a cosmic voyage through streams of light, past the planets and the "devious comets" until she "looks back on all the starrs whose blended light, as with a milky zone invests the orient."

> . . . she springs aloft
> Through fields of air; pursues the flying storm;
> Rides on the volley'd lightnings thro' the heav'ns,
> Or, yok'd with whirlwinds and the northern blast
> Sweeps the long tract of day (I, 186–91).

A climax in the poetic treatment of sublimity came in the "Ninth Night" of Thomas Young's *Night Thoughts* (1745–46). Young paid no attention to Beauty, none to landscape. As the title implies, the scene is laid at night. Young's external Nature is dark and void of color. His character, Lorenzo, had remained unconvinced throughout eight long and tedious books of the *Night Thoughts,* to be converted finally as the result of a series of cosmic voyages on which his mentor conducted his imagination. Young used the technique of cosmic voyagers of the seventeenth century. "The soul of man was made to walk the skies."

In the remote past, men had found "the great" in the Seven Wonders of the World—works of Art, not Nature. More recently they had sought it in the landscape of Nature, in the

> Seas, rivers, mountains, forests, deserts, rocks,
> The promontory's height, the depth profound
> Of subterranean, excavated grots,
> Black-brow'd, and vaulted high, and yawning wide
> From Nature's structure, or the scoop of Time.
> (IX, 905–09)

But great though these may seem to man, they were not enough for Young's imagination. "But what of vast in these?" he asked, and replied, "Nothing—or we must own the skies forgot." Greatness is found not in the landscape of earth but in the space of the heavens, that "noble pasture of the mind," where the soul "expatiates, strengthens, and exults." There she

> . . . can rove at large;
> There, freely can respire, dilate, extend,
> In full proportion let loose all her powers;
> And, undeluded, grasp at something great.
> (IX, 1016–19)

In his series of cosmic voyages Young's Lorenzo found his mind and soul expanding with the enlargement of space:

> . . . How great,
> How glorious, then, appears the mind of man
> When in it all the stars, and planets, roll!
> And what it seems, it is; Great objects make

> Great minds, enlarging as their views enlarge;
> Those still more godlike, as these more divine.
> (IX, 1059–64)

Young added to the concept of infinite space an idea that had been dawning in his century—infinite time. "Eternity," he said, "is written in the stars." As Lorenzo journeyed in the heavens among stars and planets, he learned

> The boundless space through which these rovers take
> Their restless roam, suggests the sister thought
> Of boundless time (IX, 1172–74).

Lorenzo returned from his cosmic voyaging with a new feeling for grandeur, a new awareness of the range of imagination, a new sense of God:

> True, all things speak a God; but in the small,
> Men trace out him; in great, he seizes Man;
> Seizes, and elevates, and raps, and fills (IX, 772–74).

From Art through grand Nature in the landscape of an enlarged and enlarging world, then through cosmic Nature, the imagination of the eighteenth century rose to the source of eternity and infinity. From the Infinite, through the new space discovered by astronomy, vastness descended to carry a new sense of the Sublime to exalt "the wide Sea and Mountains of the Earth." Such is the process of "The Aesthetics of the Infinite."

Not long after Thomson, Akenside, and Young had published their poems, Edmund Burke, then a student of nineteen, read before a club at Trinity College, Dublin, the draft of an essay published in 1756 or 1757 as *A Philosophical Enquiry into the Origin of our Ideas of the Sublime and Beautiful.* Addison's *Pleasures of the Imagination* was clearly one of his points of departure, but similarities with the three poets may also be seen. Particularly in his penetrating analysis of color and light, his debt to Thomson, Akenside, and Young is greater than to Addison. Burke's treatment of Beauty is more conventional than that of the Sublime, which recalls the pleasure-pain theory frequently discussed by Locke, Shaftesbury, and Hume. The qualities of Beauty are pleasant ones, such as smallness, smoothness, delicacy, variation, color. Those of the Sublime are terror, obscurity, difficulty, power, vastness, leading to magnificence and infinity.

The passion caused by the great and sublime in *nature,* when their causes operate most powerfully is Astonishment; and astonishment is that state of the soul, in which all its motions are suspended, with some degree of horror. In this case the mind is so entirely filled with its objects, that it cannot entertain any other. . . . Hence arises the great power of the sublime, that far from being produced by them, it anticipates our reasonings, it hurries us on by an irresistible force.

336

"Whatever is fitted in any soul," Burke went on, "to excite the ideas of pain and danger, that is to say, whatever is in any sort terrible, or is conversant about terrible objects, or operates in a manner analogous to terror, is a source of the *sublime*, that is, it is productive of the strongest emotions which the mind is capable of feeling." "All *general* privations," he wrote, "are great, because they are all terrible; *Vacuity, Darkness, Solitude,* and *Silence.*"

Naturally Burke had much to say of color and light. Ordinarily color belongs to Beauty, but it may mount to the Sublime if it is strong and violent. But light—when it is more than "mere light"—approaches the Sublime: the light of the sun which blinds, lightning involving grandeur or terror, rapid transition from light to darkness or from darkness to light. "Extreme light, by overcoming the organs of sight, obliterates all objects, so as in its effect exactly to resemble darkness." Light may be Sublime because of either magnificence or horror. The sublimity of light partakes to some degree of all the qualities of the Sublime that have been listed: it may astonish by its suddenness, overwhelm by vastness or power, evoke an aesthetic response by its magnificence, or rouse the passions by terror in excess or by privation.

Burke rises to one of his few emotional heights in his analysis of the power of darkness. Darkness, he tells us, is more productive of sublime ideas than light. "Night increases our terror more perhaps than any thing else." If light may be Sublime, darkness is more so. Burke's usual objectivity and dispassionateness depart when he ponders the effect of darkness on human imagination. Light may be sublime in its magnificence, pain, or danger. Darkness, the greatest of the "privations," is still more sublime because more terrible. In a section on the sublimity of darkness, Burke remembered the poet who, "blinded by excess of light," closed his eyes in endless night, recollecting that although Milton's Heaven was a place of sublime light, God himself could not be seen even by Cherubim and Seraphim. God circled his throne with the majesty of darkness:

> Fountain of light, thyself invisible
> Amidst the glorious darkness where thou sitt'st
> Throned inaccessible, but when thou shadest
> The full blaze of thy beams, and through a cloud
> Drawn round about thee like a radiant shrine,
> Dark with excessive bright thy skirts appear.
> (*Paradise Lost,* III, 375–80)

It was not Burke or Young, Thomson or Akenside who best expressed the eighteenth-century response to the great "privation" of light. It was Alexander Pope who in the ending of *The Dunciad* (1728; 1741–42)

described both the majesty and terror of universal darkness:

> She comes! she comes! the stable Throne behold
> Of Night primaeval and of Chaos old. . . .
> There at her felt approach and secret might,
> Art after Art goes out and all is Night. . . .
> Lo! thy dread Empire, CHAOS! is restpr'd;
> Light dies before thy uncreating word;
> Thy hand, great Anarck! lets the curtain fall,
> And universal Darkness buries All.

*BIBLIOGRAPHY*

Joseph Addison, *The Spectator,* ed. Donald E. Bond (Oxford, 1965). Mark Akenside, *The Pleasures of Imagination* (London, 1744). B. Sprague Allen, *Tides in English Taste* (Cambridge, Mass., 1937). Edmund Burke, *A Philosophical Enquiry into the Origin of our Ideas of the Sublime and Beautiful* (London, 1958). R. G. Collingwood, *The Idea of Nature* (Oxford, 1945). Anthony Ashley Cooper, third Earl of Shaftesbury, *The Moralists: A Philosophical Rhapsody,* in *Characteristics,* ed. John M. Robertson (London, 1900), II, 122ff. John Dennis, *Miscellanies in Verse and Prose* (London, 1693), in *Critical Works,* ed. Edward Niles Hooker (Baltimore, 1939–43), II, 350ff. Christopher Hussey, *The Picturesque: Studies in a Point of View* (London, 1927). Elizabeth Manwaring, *Italian Landscape in Eighteenth Century England* (New York, 1925). Marjorie Hope Nicolson, *Mountain Gloom and Mountain Glory* (Ithaca, 1959); idem, *Newton Demands the Muse* (Princeton, 1946). James Thomson, *Complete Poetical Works,* ed. J. L. Robertson (London, 1908). Walter J. Whipple, *The Beautiful, the Sublime and the Picturesque in Eighteenth-Century British Aesthetic Theory* (Carbondale, Ill., 1957). Edward Young, *Night Thoughts* (London, 1793).

MARJORIE HOPE NICOLSON

[See also **Beauty; Cosmic Voyages;** Cosmology; Infinity; **Mountain Attitudes; Nature;** Space; Taste.]

# SYMBOL AND SYMBOLISM IN LITERATURE

THE WORD "symbol" has had a long and complex history since antiquity. Today it may designate very different sorts of concepts in the most varied contexts. The use in mathematics or symbolic logic is almost diametrically opposed to its use in literary criticism, ar.d even there it vacillates, for "symbol" often cannot be distinguished from "sign," "synecdoche" and "allegory." In Northrop Frye's influential *Anatomy of Criticism* (Princeton, 1957) it is defined "as any unit of any work of literature which can be isolated for critical attention" (p. 367).

# SYMBOL AND SYMBOLISM IN LITERATURE

The word comes from the Greek verb *symballein*, "to put together," and the noun *symbolon*, "sign," "token" which originally referred to a half-coin which the two parties to an agreement carried away as a pledge for its fulfillment. Late in the seventeenth century its use, e.g., in Leibniz, seems to have served often as a designation for a mathematical sign. Its application to literature with a clearly defined meaning, contrasting it with allegory, occurred first in Germany late in the eighteenth century. Symbol, *Sinnbild*, emblem, hieroglyph, allegory were used almost interchangeably by Winckelmann, Lessing, and Herder. Only Kant in *Die Kritik der Urteilskraft* (*Critique of Judgment;* 1790) gave symbol a more precise meaning in the context of aesthetics. He expressly rejects "the modern logicians" (i.e., Leibniz and Wolff) who use it in opposition to "intuitive representation." "Symbolic representation is only a kind of intuitive representation," and symbols are "indirect representations of the concept through the medium of analogy." "Beauty is a symbol of morality" (paragraph 59). Goethe, who began to use the term after 1797, drew then the distinction between symbol and allegory most clearly, particularly in *Maximen und Reflexionen:* "True symbolism is where the particular represents the more general, not as a dream or a shadow, but as a living momentary revelation of the Inscrutable." And perhaps most sharply: "Allegory changes a phenomenon into a concept, a concept into an image," while symbolism "changes the phenomenon into the idea, the idea into the image, in such a way that the idea remains always infinitely active and unapproachable in the image, and will remain inexpressible even though expressed in all languages" (Nos. 314, 1112, 1113). Schiller, a close student of Kant, had used the term as early as 1794 in a review of Matthisson's poems, suggesting that the poet needs a "symbolic operation" to change inanimate nature into human nature. Nature should become a "symbol of the internal harmony of the mind with itself" by a "symbolism (*Symbolik*) of the imagination." In a letter to Goethe Schiller praises Shakespeare's *Richard III* for using "symbols where nature cannot be depicted" (Nov. 28, 1797) and recommends the introduction of "symbolic devices" (*Behelfe*) to take the place of an object (Dec. 29, 1797). In the Preface to *Die Braut von Messina* (1803) Schiller asserts boldly that "everything in poetry is only a symbol of the real."

The proliferation of the term and concept is, however, due to the German romantics, to the brothers Schlegel (though in August Wilhelm's writings which stress the imagery of literature the term *Sinnbild* predominates), to F. W. Schelling, Novalis (Friedrich von Hardenburg), K. W. F. Solger and many others. In Schelling's *Philosophie der Kunst* (1802, published in 1859) a distinction between schematism (the general signifying the particular, as in abstract thought), allegory (the particular signifying the general), and symbolism (the union of the general and the particular) which alone is art, is drawn. Similarly Solger considers all art symbolic. Solger defines the beautiful in his *Vorlesungen über Ästhetik* (1829), as the union of the general and the particular, of concept and appearance, of essence (*Wesen*) and reality. "The symbol is the existence of the Idea itself. It is really what it signifies. It is the Idea in its immediate reality. The symbol is thus always true in itself: not a mere copy of something true" (p. 129). Hegel, in his *Vorlesungen über Ästhetik* (1835; the lectures were delivered in the 1820's) differs from the majority of his contemporaries by confining "symbolic" to an early stage of art, to what in their terminology would be allegorical art. Symbolic art, for Hegel, is art where there is no concrete togetherness of meaning and form: it is the first stage exemplified by the art of ancient India and Egypt. In general, German authors clung to the romantic formulas. Heinrich Heine in a passage later to be quoted by Baudelaire, proclaims himself a "supernaturalist in art." "I believe that the artist cannot find all his types in nature, but that the most significant types, as inborn symbolism of native ideas, are revealed, as it were, in the soul." "Colors, and forms, tones and words, appearance in general, are only symbols of the Idea" (*Sämtliche Werke*, ed. O. Walzel, Leipzig [1912–15], 6, 25, 23). Also Friedrich Hebbel, though highly Hegelian in his speculations on tragedy, sees "every genuine work of art as a mysterious, ambiguous, unfathomable symbol" (*Tagebücher*, 2, 96; February 2, 1841).

The German discussion continued throughout the century, and becomes increasingly suspicious of the idealist interpretation of symbol. Friedrich Theodor Vischer's last paper, "Das Symbol" (1887) (in *Altes und Neues*, N. F., 1889) marks a temporary end as Vischer moves toward a psychological and empirical aesthetic while still clinging to the essence of the idealist interpretation. He analyzes the different meanings of the term sharply distinguishing it from myth. Symbolism in poetry is animism, anthropomorphism, inspired by the truth that the universe, nature and spirit must be one at their roots. It is an act of empathy which Vischer analyzes in purely psychological terms. A third use of symbol, as consciously contrived symbolism, as the poetic representation of what is universally significant and typical seems to Vischer dangerously near to allegory which with him and all the Germans is simply non-art.

Goethe's and Schelling's concept won out abroad. It penetrated to England mainly through S. T. Coleridge and Thomas Carlyle. Coleridge in *The States-man's Manual* (1816) defines symbol "by a translucence of the special (= generic) in the individual, or of the general in the special, or of the universal in the general; above all by the translucence of the eternal through and in the temporal. It always partakes of the reality which it renders intelligible; and while it enunciates the whole, abides itself as a living part in that unity of which it is the representative." While Coleridge often wavered in his use and sometimes thought of symbol only as synecdoche ("Here comes a sail" instead of "a ship"), symbol became the central concept of the young Thomas Carlyle in life and literature. Carlyle interpreted Goethe as a symbolist. Goethe has "an emblematic intellect," "the figurativeness is in the very centre of his being" (*Essays*, Centenary edition, 1, 244; 2, 449). In *Sartor Resartus* (1831) a whole chapter called "Symbolism" develops a total view of art and life as symbolism. Carlyle influenced two great writers profoundly: Ruskin also developed a theory of symbolism in art, but tried to combine symbolism with naturalism. "Symbolic" beauty for him surpasses but must not suppress "vital" beauty (*Modern Painters*, in *Works*, Library edition, 4, 144). Carlyle's friend and correspondent Ralph Waldo Emerson was then expounding a most extreme symbolist theory of poetry. "The whole of nature is a metaphor of the human mind." Analogy is the key to the universe. Still, Emerson, differing from the tradition of Swedenborgian "correspondences" on which he drew, insists on the "accidency and fugacity" of the symbol. All symbols are "fluxional." "In the transmission of the heavenly waters, every hose fits every hydrant," says Emerson strikingly advocating the pervasiveness and shifting convertibility of symbolism, an "incessant metamorphosis" (*Complete Works*, Centenary edition, 1, 32; 3, 20, 34–35).

The symbolist conception also penetrated to France: there are echoes, in Madame de Staël who knew the Schlegels, in Alexandre Vinet, in Charles Magnin, and particularly in Pierre Leroux, an early utopian socialist. In a series of remarkable articles in the *Revue encyclo-pédique*, Vol. 52 (1831), Leroux exalted poetry as the language of symbols, as a system of correspondences, a network of "vibrations." Elsewhere Leroux recognizes that in his sense "metaphor, symbol, myth are but different degrees of allegory" and sees in symbol "an intermediary form between comparison and allegory properly speaking. It is truly an emblem, the metaphor of an idea" (in *Oeuvres* 1, 330–31). Thus the term shifts from a rhetorical category to an element in a mystical view of nature. Oddly enough another critic, Paulin Limayrac, concludes that "Symbolic poetry has no future in France, and socialism, by

monopolizing the term, has dealt symbolism a hard blow." (See "La poésie symboliste et socialiste" in *Revue des deux mondes*, N.S. **5** [1844], 669–82, trans. M. Gilman, in *The Idea of Poetry in France* [1954], p. 225.) But Limayrac's prophecy proved to be quite wrong. Baudelaire, in the fifties, espoused a theory of universal analogy and correspondences best known through his sonnet "Correspondances." But this represented only an early occult stage of his thinking. His later aesthetics centers rather on creative imagination than on symbol. Symbol occurs interchangeably with allegory, cipher, hieroglyphic, and even emblem. Baudelaire, whatever his practice, thus cannot be called a symbolist. He died in 1867 almost twenty years before the movement which appealed to him as a forerunner. Also Stéphane Mallarmé's aesthetic does not center on the symbol. He aims rather at the creation of a special poetic language which would evoke and suggest as if by magic, the central mystery, the Idea, Silence, Nothingness. Art is both abstract and obscure. Art must "evoke, in a deliberate shadow, the object which is silenced, be allusive, never direct." The "symbol," which Mallarmé uses sparingly, would be only one device to achieve this effect. Still, one sees how the whole tendency of aesthetic thinking in France was preparing for the acceptance of the term as a slogan.

The term *symbolisme* as a designation of a group of poets was first proposed by Jean Moréas (pseudonym for Jean Diamantopoulos, 1856–1910). In 1885 he was disturbed by a journalistic attack on the decadents in which he was named together with Mallarmé. He protested: "The so-called decadents seek the pure Concept and the eternal Symbol in their art, before anything else." With some contempt for the mania of critics for labels, he suggested the term *Symbolistes* to replace the inappropriate *décadents* (Michaud [1947], 2, 331). In 1886 Moréas started a review *Le Symboliste* which perished after four issues. On September 18, 1886, he published a manifesto of *Symbolisme* in *Figaro*. Moréas, however, soon deserted his own brain-child and founded another school he called *école romane*. On September 14, 1891, in another number of *Figaro* Moréas blandly announced that *symbolisme* was dead. Thus *symbolisme* was only an ephemeral name for a very small clique of French poets. The only person still remembered aside from Moréas is Gustave Kahn. It is easy to collect pronouncements by the main contemporary poets repudiating the term for themselves. Verlaine, in particular, was vehemently resentful of this *Allemandisme* and wrote even a little poem beginning *A bas le symbolisme mythe/ et termite* (*Invectives*, 1896).

In a way which would need detailed tracing, the **339**

term, however, caught on in the later 1880's and early 1890's as a blanket name for recent developments in French poetry and its anticipations. Before Moréas' manifesto, Anatole Baju, in *Décadent* (April 10, 1886), spoke of Mallarmé as "the master who was the first to formulate the symbolic doctrine." Two critics, Charles Morice, with *La littérature de tout à l'heure* (1889) and Téodor de Wyzéwa, born in Poland, first in the essay "Le Symbolisme de M. Mallarmé" (1887), seemed to have been the main agents, though Morice spoke rather of *synthèse* than of symbol, and Wyzéwa thought that "symbol" was only a pretext and explained Mallarmé's poetry purely by its analogy to music. As early as 1894 Saint Antoine (pseudonym for Henri Mazel) prophesied that "undoubtedly, symbolism will be the label under which our period will be classed in the history of French literature" (*L'Ermitage*, June 1894).

It is still a matter of debate in French literary history when this movement came to an end. It was revived several times expressly, e.g., in 1905 around a review *Vers et prose*. Its main critic, Robert de Souza, in a series of articles "Où nous en sommes" (also published separately, 1906) ridiculed the many attempts to bury symbolism as premature and proudly claimed that Gustave Kahn, Paul Verhaeren, Francis Viélé-Griffin, Maurice Maeterlinck, and Henri Régnier were then as active as ever. Valéry professed so complete an allegiance to the ideals of Mallarmé that it is difficult not to think of him as a continuer of symbolism, though in 1938, on the occasion of the fiftieth anniversary of the symbolist manifesto, Valéry doubted the existence of symbolism and denied that there is a symbolist aesthetic ("Existence du symbolisme," in Pléiade ed., [1957], I, 686–706). Marcel Proust in the posthumously published last volume of his great series, *Le temps retrouvé* (1926), formulated an explicitly symbolist aesthetic. But his own attitude to symbolist contemporaries was often ambiguous or negative. In 1896 Proust had written an essay condemning obscurity in poetry (in *Chroniques*). Proust admired Maeterlinck but disliked Charles Péguy and Paul Claudel. He even wrote a pastiche of Régnier, a mock-solemn description of a head cold. When *Le temps retrouvé* (1926) was published and when a few years later (1933) Valery Larbaud proclaimed Proust a symbolist (Preface to Eméric Figer, *L'esthétique de Marcel Proust*), symbolism had, at least in French poetry, definitely been replaced by surrealism.

André Barre's *Le symbolisme* (1911) and particularly Guy Michaud's *Message poétique du symbolisme* (1947) as well as many other books of French literary scholarship have with the hindsight of literary historians, traced the different phases of a vast French symbolist movement: the precursorship of Baudelaire who died in 1867, the second phase when Verlaine and Mallarmé were at the height of their power before the 1886 group, the third phase when the name became established, and then in the twentieth century what Michaud calls *Néo-symbolisme* represented by "La Jeune Parque" of Valéry and *L'annonce faite à la Marie* of Claudel, both dating from 1915. It is a coherent and convincing conception which needs to be extended to prose writers and dramatists: to Huysmans after *Au rebours* (1884), to the early Gide, to Proust in part and among dramatists at least to Maeterlinck who with his plays *L'intruse* and *Les aveugles* (1890) and *Pelléas et Mélisande* (1892) assured a limited penetration of symbolism on the stage.

Knowledge of the French movement and admiration for it soon spread to the other European countries. We must, however, distinguish between reporting on French events (and even the enthusiasm reflected by translations) and a genuine assimilation of the French movement by another literature. This process varies considerably from country to country; and the variation needs to be explained by the different traditions which the French importation confronted.

In English, George Moore's *Confessions of a Young Man* (1888) and his *Impressions and Opinions* (1891) gave sketchy and often poorly informed accounts of Verlaine, Mallarmé, Rimbaud, and Jules Laforgue. Mallarmé's poetry is dismissed as "aberrations of a refined mind" and symbolism is oddly defined as "saying the opposite of what you mean." The three essays on Mallarmé by Edmund Gosse, all dating from 1893, are hardly more perceptive. After the poet's death, Gosse turned sharply against him. "Now that he is no longer here the truth must be said about Mallarmé. He was hardly a poet." Even Arthur Symons, whose book, *The Symbolist Movement in Literature* (1899), made the decisive breakthrough for England and Ireland, was very lukewarm at first. While praising Verlaine (in *Academy*, 1891) he referred to the "brainsick little school of *Symbolistes*" and "the noisy little school of *Décadents*" and in later articles on Mallarmé he complained of "jargon and meaningless riddles." But then he turned around, and produced the entirely favorable *Symbolist Movement*. It should not, however, be overrated as literary criticism or history. It is a rather lame impressionistic account of Nerval, Villiers de l'Isle-Adam, Rimbaud, Verlaine, Laforgue, Mallarmé, Huysmans, and Maeterlinck with emphasis on Verlaine. There is no chapter on Baudelaire. But most importantly the book was dedicated to W. B. Yeats proclaiming him "the chief representative of that movement in our country." The edition of Blake, which Yeats had prepared with Edwin Ellis in 1893, was introduced by an essay on "The Necessity of Symbolism," and the essay "The Symbolism of Poetry" (1900) was Yeats's full statement of his symbolist creed. Symons' dedication to Yeats shows an awareness of symbolism as a truly international movement: "In Germany," Symons says, exaggerating greatly, "it seems to be permeating the whole of literature, its spirit is that which is deepest in Ibsen, it has absorbed the one new force in Italy, Gabriele D'Annunzio. I am told of a group of symbolists in Russian literature, there is another in Dutch literature, in Portugal it has a little school of its own under Eugenio de Castro. I even saw some faint stirrings that way in Spain."

Symons should have added the United States. Or could he in 1899? There were intelligent and sympathetic reports of the French movement very early. T. S. Perry wrote on "The Latest Literary Fashion in France" in *The Cosmopolitan* (1892), T. Child on "Literary Paris—The New Poetry" in *Harper's* (1896), and Aline Gorren on "The French Symbolists" in *Scribner's* (**13** [1893], 337–52). The almost forgotten Vance Thompson, who fresh from Paris, edited the oddly named review *M'lle New York*, wrote several perceptive essays, mainly on Mallarmé in 1895 (reprinted in *French Portraits* in 1900) which convey some accurate information on his theories and even attempt with some success some explication of his poetry. But only James Huneker became the main importer of recent French literature into the United States. In 1896 he defended the French symbolists against the slurs in Max Nordau's *Entartung* and began to write a long series of articles on Maeterlinck, Laforgue, and many others not bothering to conceal his dependence on his French master, Remy de Gourmont to whom he dedicated his book of essays, *Visionaries* (1905). But the actual impact of French symbolist poetry on American writing was greatly delayed. René Taupin in his *L'influence du symbolisme français sur la poésie américaine* (1929) traced some echoes in forgotten American versifiers of the turn of the century but only two Americans living then in England, Ezra Pound around 1908 and T. S. Eliot around 1914, reflect the French influence in significant poetry.

More recently and in retrospect one hears of a symbolist period in American literature: Hart Crane and Wallace Stevens are its main poets; Henry James, Faulkner, and O'Neill, in very different ways and in different stages of their career, show marked affinities with its techniques and outlook. Edmund Wilson's *Axel's Castle* (1931) was apparently the very first book which definitely conceived of symbolism as an international movement and singled out Yeats, Joyce, Eliot, Gertrude Stein, Valéry, and Proust as outstanding examples of a movement which, he believed, had come

to an end at the time of his writing. Wilson's sources were the writings of Huneker, whom he admired greatly, and the instruction in French literature he received at Princeton from Christian Gauss. But the insight into the unity and continuity of the international movement and the selection of the great names was his own. We might only wonder about the inclusion of Gertrude Stein.

In the United States, Wilson's reasonable and moderate plea for an international movement was soon displaced by attempts to make the whole of the American literary tradition symbolist. F. O. Matthiessen's *The American Renaissance* (1941) is based on the distinction introduced by Goethe. Allegory appears as inferior to symbol: Hawthorne inferior to Melville. But in Charles Feidelson's *Symbolism and American Literature* (1956) the distinction between modern symbolism and the use of symbols by romantic authors is completely obliterated. Emerson, Hawthorne, Poe, Melville, and Whitman appear as pure symbolists *avant la lettre*, and their ancestry is traced back to the Puritans who, paradoxically, appear as incomplete, frustrated symbolists. It can be objected that the old Puritans were sharply inimical to images and symbols and that there is a gulf between the religious conception of signs of God's Providence and the aesthetic use of symbols in the novels of Hawthorne and Melville and even in the Platonizing aesthetics of Emerson.

The symbolist conception of American literature is still prevalent today. It owes its dominance to the attempt to exalt the great American writers to mythmakers and providers of a substitute religion. James Baird in *Ishmael* (1956) puts it strikingly: Melville is "the supreme example of the artistic creator engaged in the act of making new symbols to replace the 'lost' symbols of Protestant Christianity." A very active trend in American criticism expanded symbolist interpretation to all types and periods of literature. The impact of ideas from the Cambridge anthropologists and from Carl Jung is obvious. In the study of medieval texts, a renewed interest in the fourfold levels of meaning in Dante's "Letter to Can Grande" has persuaded a whole group of American scholars led by D. W. Robertson, to interpret Chaucer, the *Pearl* poet, and Langland in these terms. The symbolist interpretation reaches heights of ingenuity in the writing of Northrop Frye who began with a book on Blake and, in *The Anatomy of Criticism* (1957), conceived of the whole of literature as a self-enclosed system of symbols and myths, "existing in its own universe, no longer a commentary on life or reality, but containing life and reality in a system of verbal relationships." In this grandiose conception all distinctions between periods and styles are abolished: "the literary universe is a universe in which everything is potentially identical with everything else." The old distinctions between myth, symbol, and allegory disappear. One of Frye's followers, Angus Fletcher, in his book on *Allegory* (1964), exalts allegory as the central procedure of art, absorbing symbolism.

The story of the spread of symbolism is very different in other countries. The effect in Italy was ostensibly rather small. Soffici's pamphlet on Rimbaud, in 1911, is usually considered the beginning of the French symbolist influence, but there was an early propagandist for Mallarmé, Vittorio Pica, who was heavily dependent on French sources, particularly Téodor de Wyzéwa. His articles, in the *Gazetta letteraria* (1885–86), on the French poets do not use the term; but in 1896 he replaced "decadent" and "Byzantine" by "symbolist." The poets around Ungaretti and Montale spoke rather of *ermetismo*. In a book by Mario Luzi, *L'idea simbolista* (1959), Pascoli, Dino Campana, and Arturo Onofri are called symbolist poets.

While symbolism, at least as a definite school or movement, was absent in Italy, it is central in the history of Spanish poetry. The Nicaraguan poet Rubén Darío initiated it after his short stay in Paris in 1892. He wrote poems under the symbolist influence and addressed, for instance, a fervent hymn to Verlaine. The influence of French symbolist poetry changed completely the oratorical or popular style of Spanish lyrical poetry. The closeness of Guillén to Mallarmé and Valéry seems too obvious to deny and the Uruguayan poet Julio Herrera y Reissig (1873–1909) is clearly in the symbolist tradition, often in the most obscure manner. Still, the Spanish critics favor the term *modernismo* which is used sometimes so inclusively that it covers all modern Spanish poetry and even the so-called "generation of 1898," the prose writers Azorín, Baroja, and Unamuno, whose associations with symbolism were quite tenuous. "Symbolism" can apply only to one trend in modern Spanish literature as the romantic popular tradition was stronger there than elsewhere. García Lorca's poetry can serve as the best known example of the peculiar Spanish synthesis of the folksy and the symbolical, the gypsy song and myth. Still, the continuity from Darío to Jiménez, Antonio Machado, Alberti, and then to Guillén seems evident. Jorge Guillén in his Harvard lectures, *Language and Poetry* (1961), finds "no label convincing." "A period look," he argues, does not signify a "group style." In Spain there were, he thinks, fewer "isms" than elsewhere and the break with the past was far less abrupt. He reflects that "any name seeking to give unity to a historical period is the invention of posterity" (p. 214). But while eschewing the term "symbolism" he characterizes himself and his contemporaries well

enough by expounding their common creed: their belief in the marriage of Idea and music, in short, their belief in the ideal of Mallarmé. Following a vague suggestion made by Remy de Gourmont the rediscovery of Góngora by Ortega y Gasset, Gerardo Diego, Dámaso Alonso, and Alfonso Reyes around 1927 fits into the picture: they couple Góngora and Mallarmé as the two poets who in the history of all poetry have gone furthest in the search for absolute poetry, for the quintessence of the poetic.

In Germany, the spread of symbolism was far less complete than Symons assumed in 1899. Stefan George had come to Paris in 1889, had visited Mallarmé and met many poets, but after his return to Germany he deliberately avoided the term "symbolism" for himself and his circle. He translated a selection from Baudelaire (1891) and smaller samples from Mallarmé, Verlaine, and Régnier in *Zeitgenössische Dichter* (1905), but his own poetry does not show very close parallels to the French masters. Oddly enough, the poems of Vielé-Griffin seem to have left the most clearly discernible traces on George's own writings—see B. Böschenstein in *Euphorion*, **58** (1964). As early as 1892 one of George's adherents, Carl August Klein, protested in George's periodical, *Blätter für die Kunst*, against the view of George's dependence on the French. Wagner, Nietzsche, Böcklin, and Klinger, he says, show that there is an indigenous opposition to naturalism in Germany as everywhere in the West. George himself spoke later of the French poets as his "former allies" and in Gundolf's authoritative book on George (1920), the French influence is minimized if not completely denied. Among the theorists of the George circle Friedrich Gundolf had the strongest symbolist leanings: *Shakespeare und der deutsche Geist* (1911) and *Goethe* (1916) are based on the distinction of symbol-allegory with symbol always the higher term. Still, the term symbolism did not catch on in Germany as a name for any specific poetic group, though Hofmannsthal, e.g., in "Das Gespräch über Gedichte" (1903), proclaimed the symbol the one element necessary in poetry. Later, the influence of Rimbaud—apparently largely in German translation—on Georg Trakl has been demonstrated with certainty by H. Lindenberger in *Comparative Literature*, **10** (1953), 21–35.

But if we examine German books on twentieth-century literature "symbolism" seems rarely used. A section so called in Willi Duwe's *Die Dichtung des 20. Jahrhunderts*, published in 1936, lists Hofmannsthal, Dauthendey, Calé, Rilke, and George, while E. H. Lüth's *Literatur als Geschichte (Deutsche Dichtung von 1885 bis 1947)*, published in 1947, treats the same poets under the label "Neuromantik und Impressionismus." A later section "Parasymbolismus" deals with Musil and Broch. German literary scholarship has not been converted to the term, though Wolfgang Kayser's article "Der europäische Symbolismus" (1953; included in *Die Vortragsreise*, Bern, 1958), had pleaded for a wide concept in which he included D'Annunzio, Yeats, Valéry, Proust, Virginia Woolf, and Faulkner besides the French poets.

In Russia we find the strongest self-styled "symbolist" group of poets. The close links with Paris at that time may help to explain their appearance, or possibly also the strong consciousness of a tradition of symbolism in the Russian Church and in some of the orthodox thinkers of the immediate past. Vladimir Solovëv was regarded as a precursor. In 1892 Zinaida Vengerova wrote a sympathetic account of the French symbolists for *Vestnik Evropy* while in the following year Max Nordau's *Entartung* caused a sensation for its satirical account of recent French poetry which had repercussions on Tolstoy's *What is Art?* (1898). Valery Bryusov emerged as the leading symbolist poet: he translated Maeterlinck's *L'intruse* and wrote a poem "Iz Rimbaud" as early as 1892. In 1894 he published two little volumes entitled *Russkie simvolisty*. That year Bryusov wrote poems with titles such as "In the manner of Stéphane Mallarmé" (though these were not published till 1935) and brought out a translation of Verlaine's *Romances sans paroles*. Bryusov had later contacts with René Ghil, Mallarmé's pupil, and derived from him the idea of "instrumentation" or "orchestration" in poetry which was to play a great role in the theories of the Russian formalists (*Lettres de René Ghil*, Paris, 1935). In the meantime Dimitri Merezhkovsky had, in 1893, published a manifesto: "On the causes of the decline and the new trends of contemporary Russian literature," which recommended symbolism, though Merezhkovsky appealed to the Germans as models, to Goethe and the romantics rather than to the French. Merezhkovsky's pamphlet foreshadows the split in the Russian symbolist movement. The younger men, Alexander Blok and Vyacheslav Ivanov as well as Bely, drew apart from Bryusov and Balmont. Blok in an early diary (1901–02) condemned Bryusov as decadent and opposed his Parisian symbolism with his own Russian variety, rooted in the poetry of Tyutchev, Fet, Polonsky, and Solovëv (*Literaturnoe Nasledstvo*, **27–28** [1937], 302). Vyacheslav Ivanov in 1910, shared Blok's view. The French influence seemed to him "unreasonable in an adolescent way and, in fact, not very fertile," while his own symbolism appealed to Russian nationalism and to the general mystical tradition (*Apollon*, **8** [1910], 13). Later Bely was to add occultism, Rudolf Steiner and his "anthroposophy." The group of poets who called themselves "Acmeists" (Gumilëv, Anna Akhmatova, Osip Mandelstam) was a direct outgrowth of symbolism. The mere fact that they appealed to the early symbolist Innokenty Annensky shows the continuity with symbolism in spite of their distaste for the occult and their emphasis on what they thought of as classical clarity. Symbolism dominates Russian poetry between about 1892 and 1914. Then futurism emerged as a slogan and the Russian formalists attacked the whole concept of poetry as imagery.

If we glance at the other Slavic countries we are struck by the diversity of their reactions. Poland was early informed about the French movement, and Polish poetry was influenced by the French symbolist movement but the term *Mlada Polska* ("Young Poland") was preferred. In Wilhelm Feldmann's *Współczesna literatura polska* ("Contemporary Polish Literature," 1905) contemporary poetry is discussed as "decadentism" but Wyspiański (a symbolist if ever there was one) appears under the chapter heading: "On the heights of romanticism." All the histories of Polish literature speak of "Modernism," "Decadentism," "Idealism," and "Neoromanticism" and occasionally call a poet such as Miriam (Zenon Przesmycki) a symbolist but they never seem to use the term as a general name for a period in Polish literature.

In Czech literature the situation was more like that in Russia: Březina. Sova, and Hlaváček were called symbolists and the idea of a school or at least a group of Czech symbolist poets is firmly established. The term *Moderna* (possibly because of the periodical, *Moderní Revue* founded in 1894) is definitely associated with decadentism, *fin de siècle*, a group represented by Arnošt Procházka. A hymnical, optimistic, and even chiliastic poet such as Otokar Březina cannot and could not be classed with them. The great critic F. X. Šalda wrote of the "school of symbolists" as early as 1891, calling Verlaine, Villiers, and Mallarmé its masters, but denied that there is a school of symbolists with dogmas, codices, and manifestoes. His very first important article "Synthetism in the new art" (*Literární Listy*, 1892) expounded the aesthetics of Morice and Hennequin for the benefit of the Czechs, then still mainly dependent on German models.

The unevenness of the penetration of both the influence of the French movement and notably of the acceptance of the term raises the question whether we can account for these differences in causal terms. It sounds heretical or obscurantist in this age of scientific explanation to ascribe much to chance, to chance contacts, and personal predilections. Why was the term so immensely successful in France, in the United States and in Russia, less so in England and Spain and hardly at all in Italy and Germany? In Germany there was even the tradition from Goethe and Schelling to F. T. Vischer of the continuous debate about symbol. One can think of all kinds of explanations: a deliberate decision by the poets to move away from the French developments, or the success of the terms *Die Moderne* and *Neuromantik*. Still, the very number of such explanations suggests that the variables are so great in number that we cannot account for these divergencies in any systematic manner.

Finally, if we discuss the exact contents of the term "symbolism" in literary history, we must distinguish among four concentric circles defining its scope. At its narrowest "symbolism" refers to the French group which called itself so in 1886. Its theory was rather rudimentary. These poets mainly wanted poetry to be nonrhetorical, i.e., they asked for a break with the tradition of Hugo and the Parnassiens. They wanted words not merely to state but to suggest; they wanted to use metaphors, allegories, and symbols not only as decorations but as organizing principles of their poems; they wanted their verse to be "musical," in practice to stop using the oratorical cadences of the French alexandrine and, in some cases, to break completely with rhyme. Free verse—whose invention is usually ascribed to Gustave Kahn—was possibly the most enduring achievement which has survived all vicissitudes of style. Kahn himself summed up the doctrine simply as "antinaturalism, antiprosaism in poetry, a search for freedom in the efforts in art, in reaction against the regimentation of the *Parnasse* and the naturalists" (*La société nouvelle*, April 1894).

"Symbolism" in a wider sense refers to the broad movement in France from Nerval and Baudelaire to Claudel and Valéry. We can characterize it by saying that in symbolist poetry the image becomes "thing." The relation of tenor and vehicle in the metaphor is reversed. The utterance is divorced from the situation: time and place, history and society are played down. The inner world, *la durée*, in the Bergsonian sense, is represented or often merely hinted at as "it," the thing or the person hidden. The grammatical predicate has become the subject. Clearly such poetry can easily be justified by an occult view of the world. But this is not necessary: it might simply imply a feeling for analogy, for a web of correspondences, a rhetoric of metamorphoses in which everything reflects everything else. Hence the great role of synaesthesia, which, though rooted in physiological facts, and found all over the history of poetry, became at that time merely a stylistic device, a mannerism to be easily imitated and transmitted.

On the third wider circle of abstraction the term can be applied to the whole period roughly between 1885 and 1914. "Symbolism" can be seen as an international movement which radiated originally from France but produced great writers and great poetry

also elsewhere. In English, Yeats and Eliot; in the United States, Wallace Stevens and Hart Crane; in Germany, George, Rilke, and Hofmannsthal; in Russia, Blok, Ivanov, and Bely; in Spain and South America, Darío, Machado, and Guillén. If we, as we should, extend the meaning of symbolism to prose, we can see it clearly in the late Henry James, in Joyce, the later Thomas Mann, in Proust, in the early Gide, in Faulkner and D. H. Lawrence, and if we add the drama we recognize it in the later stages of Ibsen, and in Strindberg, Hauptmann, and O'Neill. There is symbolist criticism of distinction: an aesthetics in Mallarmé and Valéry, a looser creed in Remy de Gourmont, in Eliot, and in Yeats and there is a flourishing school of symbolist interpretation particularly in the United States.

Much of the French "new criticism" is frankly symbolist. Roland Barthes' pamphlet, *Critique et vérité* (1966), pleads for a complete liberty of symbolist interpretation. Symbolism in this sense can be defended as rooted in the concepts of the period, as distinct in meaning and as clearly setting off the period from that preceding it, realism or naturalism. The difference between symbolism and romanticism is less certainly implied. Obviously there is a continuity with romanticism, and particularly German romanticism; also in France, as has been recently argued again by Werner Vordtriede in his *Novalis und die französischen Symbolisten* (1963). The direct contact of the French with the German romantics, however, came late and should not be overrated. Jean Thorel's "Les romantiques allemandes et les symbolistes français" seems to have been the first to point out the relation (in *Entretiens politiques et littéraires*, 1891). Maeterlinck's article on Novalis (1894) and his little anthology (1896) came late in the movement. But Wagner of course mediated between the symbolists and German mythology though Mallarmé's attitude, while admiring the music, was tinged with irony for Wagner's subjectmatter (*Oeuvres*, Pléiade ed., pp. 541–45). Early in the century, Heine, a *romantique défroqué* as he called himself, played the role of an intermediary (cf. Kurt Weinberg's *Henri Heine: héraut du symbolisme français*, 1954). E. T. A. Hoffmann was widely translated into French and could supply occult motifs, a transcendental view of music, and the theory and practice of synaesthesia.

Possibly even more important were the indirect contacts through the English writers discussed: through Carlyle's chapter on symbolism in *Sartor Resartus*, and his essay on Novalis; through Coleridge from whom, through another intermediary, Mrs. Crowe, Baudelaire drew his definition of "constructive imagination"; and through Emerson, who was translated by Edgar Quinet.

There was also Edgar Allan Poe who drew on Coleridge and A. W. Schlegel, and seemed so closely to anticipate Baudelaire's views that Baudelaire quoted him as if he were Poe himself, sometimes dropping all quotation marks.

The enormous influence of Poe on the French demonstrates, however, most clearly the difference between romanticism and symbolism. Poe is far from being a representative of the romantic world view or of its romantic aesthetics in which imagination is conceived as transforming nature. Poe has been aptly described as an "angel in a machine": he combines a faith in technique and even technology, a distrust of inspiration, a rationalistic eighteenth-century mind with a vague occult belief in "supernal" beauty. The distrust of inspiration, an enmity to nature, is the crucial point which sets off symbolism from romanticism. Baudelaire, Mallarmé, and Valéry all share it; while Rilke, a symbolist in many of his procedures and views, appears as highly romantic in his reliance on moments of inspiration. For this reason the attempt to make Mallarmé a spiritual descendant of Novalis, as Vordtriede tried to do, must fail. Mallarmé, one might grant, aims at transcendence but it is an empty transcendence, whereas Novalis rapturously adores the unity of the mysterious universe. In short, the romantics were Rousseauists; the symbolists, beginning with Baudelaire, believe in the fall of man or, if they do not use the religious phraseology, know that man is limited and is not, as Novalis believed, the Messiah of nature. The end of the romantic period is clearly marked by the victory of positivism and scientism, which soon led to disillusionment and pessimism. Most symbolists were non-Christians, even atheists, although they tried to find a new religion in occultism or flirted with Oriental religions. They were pessimists who need not have read Schopenhauer and Eduard von Hartmann, as Laforgue did, to succumb to the mood of decadence, *fin de siècle*, *Götterdämmerung*, or the death of God prophesied by Nietzsche.

Symbolism is also clearly set off from the new avant-garde movements after 1914, i.e., futurism, cubism, surrealism, expressionism, etc. There the faith in language has crumbled completely, while in Mallarmé and Valéry language preserves its cognitive and even magic power; Valéry's collection of poems is rightly called *Charmes*. Orpheus is the mythological hero of the poet: charming the animals, trees, and even stones. With more recent art the view of analogy disappears: Kafka has nothing of it. Post-symbolist art is abstract and allegorical rather than symbolic. The image, in surrealism, has no beyond: it wells, at most, from the subconscious of the individual.

Finally, there is the highest abstraction, the largest circle, the use of "symbolism" in all literature, of all ages. Here the term, broken loose from its historical moorings, lacks concrete content and remains merely the name for a phenomenon which is almost universal in all art.

*BIBLIOGRAPHY*

Max Schlesinger, *Geschichte des Symbols* (Berlin, 1912); still useful.

On early history much in R. Wellek, *History of Modern Criticism, 1750–1950*, 4 vols. (New Haven, 1955–65). On Goethe's predecessors: Curt Müller, *Die geschichtlichen Voraussetzungen des Symbolbegriffes in Goethes Kunstanschauung* (Berlin, 1937). On Goethe see Maurice Marache, *Le symbole dans la pensée et l'œuvre de Goethe* (Paris, 1960).

On French developments before 1886: Margaret Gilman, *The Idea of Poetry in France* (Cambridge, Mass., 1958). Angelo P. Bertocci, *From Symbolism to Baudelaire* (Carbondale, Ill., 1964).

On the French movement: André Barre, *Le symbolisme: essai historique* (Paris, 1911). E. Raynaud, *La mêlée poétique du symbolisme*, 3 vols. (Paris, 1920–23). G. Michaud, *Message poétique du symbolisme*, 3 vols. (Paris, 1947). A. G. Lehmann, *The Symbolist Aesthetic in France, 1885–1895* (Oxford, 1950). K. Cornell, *The Symbolist Movement* (New Haven, 1952). M. Décaudin, *La crise des valeurs symbolistes* (Toulouse, 1960).

On the international movement: Edmund Wilson, *Axel's Castle* (New York, 1931). Maurice Bowra, *The Heritage of Symbolism* (London, 1943). Anna Balakian, *The Symbolist Movement: A Critical Appraisal* (New York, 1967); a good sketch. Georgette Donchin, *The Influence of French Symbolism on Russian Poetry* (The Hague, 1958). René Taupin, *L'influence du symbolisme français sur la poésie américaine de 1910 à 1920* (Paris, 1929). Enid L. Duthie, *L'influence du symbolisme français dans le renouveau poétique de l'Allemagne* (Paris, 1933). Ruth Z. Temple, *The Critic's Alchemy: A Study of the Introduction of French Symbolism into England* (New York, 1953).

RENÉ WELLEK

[See also **Allegory;** Expressionism; Impressionism; Naturalism in Art; **Romanticism;** Style.]

# SYMMETRY AND ASYMMETRY

NON HABET LATINUM NOMEN SYMMETRIA ("Latin does not have a word for 'symmetry'"). This eye-opening remark occurs in the midst of Pliny's *Natural History* (Book 34, Ch. 65; Loeb edition, Vol. 9, 174/76). Having made this remark Pliny uses the word several times as if it were a well-established loan-word (from the Greek). There is corroborating evidence that indeed it was. Vitruvius, a near contemporary of Pliny, also uses the word several times in his *De architectura*, and its connotations indicate more or less the meaning which it may have in a textbook on architecture of today.

***Antiquity and After.*** "Symmetry" is a Greek term and a Greek conception, and, as Pliny already sensed, there is perhaps no *proper* verbal equivalent for it in any European idiom. However, the term does not occur in Homer, and it may have indeed been post-Homeric by formation. Homeric terms have a peculiar verbal strength, and they also have a central meaning which they usually retain even if their later connotations are spread over variant possibilities. But the term symmetry was not of this kind. Rather, in the classical Hellenic era, the term belonged to a group of terms and locutions that designated harmony, rhythm, balance, equipoise, stability, good proportions, and evenness of structure.

When translating from the Greek for the general reader it is best to follow Pliny's (and Vitruvius') example and let the term symmetry stand as it does, rather than render it by a locution that, for a scholar, might perhaps better fit the context. It is true that the dictionary meaning of the term symmetry has shifted since antiquity, but none of the original connotations has become obsolete, certainly not entirely so. What has seriously changed is this, that one of the connotations that originally was barely there—in a dictionary sense, that is—has gradually grown to prominence, and even paramountcy. It is the connotation of "bilateral" symmetry, or, what is the same, of mirror symmetry.

This symmetry allows a strictly geometric definition, which can be applied to a visual tableau of any dimension. If the tableau is spatial, that is, three-dimensional, a "mirror" is any (two-dimensional) plane in its entire extension, and it decomposes the tableau into two half-spaces, such that a design in one of the half-spaces has, by reflection, a mirror image in the other. A design and its image are geometrically congruent, except that they differ in a sense of orientation, as a right-hand glove differs from its left-hand mate.

In a two-dimensional tableau a "mirror" is a straight line, any straight line, and on a one-dimensional axis it is a point. Right and left, above and below, front and back, when paired in a three-dimensional tableau refer to mirror reflections with respect to three mutually perpendicular planes. "Before" and "after" correspond to a bilateral symmetry on the time axis, if, as usual, this axis is represented by a (Euclidean) straight line.

***Greek Dualities.*** From our retrospect, Greek philosophy was little affected by symmetries and asymmetries, but, from the first, had dualities in its thought

patterns, perhaps even to a fault. Book 13 of Euclid's *Elements* is a splendid essay on the existence, construction, and uniqueness of regular solids in space, and as such it is a triumphant exercise in mathematical symmetry in our present-day sense. It is even a hallmark and acme of Greek originality. And yet it is an isolated achievement of Greek rationality, exclusive, and compartmentalized.

However, almost every great Greek philosopher had a thematic duality in his thinking. In Anaximander it was injustice and retribution; in Heraclitus it was change and constancy in the cosmos; in Parmenides it was the ontological contrast between Being and Appearance; in Empedocles it was, quite primitively, and insensitively, Love and Strife; in Anaxagoras it was mind versus the senses; in Democritus it was the working physicist's contrast between the material and the void, or between the full and the empty, or between the particle and the field; in Plato it was the epistemologist's difference between opinion and knowledge and the idealist's dualism between body and soul, either or both of which Plato may have inherited from Socrates; and in Aristotle it was the hardiest duality of all, the gigantic contrariety between the Potential and the Actual.

Lesser Greek philosophers dwelt on lesser dualisms, unimaginative ones. Aristotle reports (*Metaphysica* 986a 23–986b 4) that a school of Pythagoreans drew up a list of ten opposites, viz., Limit-Unlimited, Odd-Even, Unity-Plurality, Right-Left, Male-Female, Rest-Motion, Straight-Crooked, Light-Darkness, Good-Evil, Square-Oblong. Aristotle is apparently not impressed with the particular selection of pairs in this list, because he adds that Alcmaeon of Croton (of whom Aristotle does not know whether he inspired the Pythagoreans or they him) held similar views, but stated that there is nothing fixed about pairs of contraries and that they can be made up as the context demands it. And Aristotle firmly adds that the real outcome of such reflections is only this that "contraries are first principles of things." If "contraries" are meant to be polarities and dualities then this finding of Aristotle is just as much a leitmotif in the natural philosophy of our century as it was in classical Greece.

In addition to dualities from nature and knowledge as listed above, there was also an all-Greek antithesis of *nomos* ("human law," or "norm") and *physis* ("natural law"), and it was a dominant trait in statements of Sophists on moral, social, and political issues (Guthrie, III, 55–134). As a curiosity we note that an anonymous Sophist (cf. Iamblichus, *Protrepticus*, Ch. 20) dwells on the contrast between lawlessness (*anomia*) and order (*eunomia*) in such a manner as to make him very like a champion of "law (*nomos*) and order (*eunomia*)" in our sense today (Guthrie, III, 71).

***Plotinus versus Romantics.*** The Greeks have somehow created the impression on romantics of all ages—perhaps beginning in antiquity with early Hellenophile Stoics, and certainly in modern times with the very early romantic Johann Joachim Winckelmann—that dualities were the embodiment of an indissoluble union of beauty, harmony, symmetry, etc., and that prominent Greeks were likely to have statues of Pindaresque symmetry, even if a Herodotus, Socrates, Aristotle, and even Plato would hardly conform to this physical ideal *au naturel.*

The first to dissent was, most unbelievably, Plotinus, one of the most nonrealistic of philosophers, and he turned his dissent into a major philosopheme about symmetry, which he presented in his renowned essay "On Beauty" (*Enneads* I, 6) and in some other passages. Plotinus asserts and reasons that symmetry (ἡ συμμετρία, τὸ σύμμετρον) is neither a necessary nor a sufficient prerequisite for beauty (τὸ καλόν), even if, admittedly, "beauty is in the eye of the beholder" (this cliché is Plotinus').

The context suggests that it is the purpose of Plotinus to refute a widely held tenet. Being a good philosopher, he first gives a clearly formulated version of what it is that he is going to refute. He announces that he is going to refute the thesis

that the symmetry of parts towards each other and towards a whole, with, besides, a certain charm of color, constitutes the beauty recognized by the eye, that in visible things, as indeed in all else, universally, the beautiful thing is essentially symmetrical, patterned (cf. Beardsley, p. 80; trans. Stephen McKenna).

Plotinus' refutation of this thesis goes as follows. A thing cannot be endowed with symmetry unless it can be decomposed into parts which are symmetrically paired. Therefore, if symmetry were a *necessary* condition of beauty, a beautiful thing would have to be decomposable, and a simple, that is, indecomposable thing could not be beautiful. This would, according to Plotinus, exclude from the contest for beauty such things as monochromatic colors, single tones, the light of the sun, gold, night lighting, and so on (ibid.), which Plotinus finds absurd. On the other hand,

Symmetry cannot be a *sufficient* condition of beauty, because an object that remains symmetrical can lose its beauty: "one face constant in symmetry, appears sometimes fair, sometimes not"—and when a body becomes lifeless, it loses most of its beauty, though not its symmetry (ibid; also, *Enneads* VI, 7, 22).

Plotinus of course, did not convert a single romantic. In the nineteenth century, the ultra-romantic historian (a very good one) Johann Gustav Droysen impressed

an Apollo-like "symmetry" on a monumentally designed figure of Alexander the Great, which the twentieth century is taking pains to redress (cf. G. T. Griffith).

Still, there have been indomitable romantics even in the twentieth century, as there always will be. Hermann Weyl, after quoting a brief poem in adoration of symmetry—the poem was published in 1921 by the poetess Anna Wickham—also transcribes it into purple prose thus:

Symmetry, as wide or as narrow as you may define its meaning, is one idea by which man through the ages has tried to comprehend the created order, beauty, and perfection (Weyl, p. 5).

To which a Plotinus could retort that it might also be the beauty of a corpse, or the order and perfection of a row of tombstones.

***The Twentieth Century.*** There are two great works about symmetry in the twentieth century, and, by content though not by exposition, the present article is intended to be, without hyperbole, only a supplement to these. One of the works is the large post-Victorian treatise *On Growth and Form* by D'Arcy Wentworth Thompson, classicist, naturalist, biologist, and a translator of Aristotle's *Historia animalium.* The other is the small mid-century volume *Symmetry* by Hermann Weyl, leading mathematician and connoisseur of physics, with an acute sense of philosophy and poetry. There are books from this century by other authors, some quite learned, but they in no wise compare with these.

Nowadays symmetry may be conceived narrowly or broadly, specifically or comprehensively. Our conception of it will be a fully comprehensive one, and it is only from an approach as broad as ours that the above-mentioned treatise of Thompson appears to be a work on symmetry, perhaps even the leading one. Still, the chapter on Bilateral Symmetry in Weyl's book (pp. 3–38) is, on the whole, unsurpassable.

Also, nowadays, symmetries, if broadly conceived, seem to occur everywhere and anywhere; in nature, in cognition, even in perception; in moral and religious tenets; in aesthetic expressions and aspirations; and, generally, in mimetic experiences of any kind. The mimesis involved may be rigorous or proximate, faithful or distorted, inward or outward, sensuous or rational, realistic or idealistic.

Any meditation on symmetry must also account for various modes or distortions of symmetry. It also becomes necessary to distinguish between mere distortions of symmetry and direct violations of symmetry, and between outright contrapuntal asymmetry and more complementary nonsymmetry.

In nature, a deviation from symmetry may be quite small, or quite large. For instance, a honeycomb is renowned for its hexagonal and dodecahedral symmetries. Its construction is a testimonial to the intelligence, industry, and social instincts of the bee. In actual physical detail, the symmetries are not quite as regular as proverbially assumed (Weyl, p. 91), but the approximation to symmetries is a really good one.

A tree in nature is another matter. In its Platonic idea, as it were, the tree is nature's most imposing model for cylindrical symmetry, and there are specimens that are impressively regular. However, a tree may also be gnarled, very much so, and this need not impair its health, and may even enhance its beauty. Ordinarily a painter would not take out the gnarls merely for the sake of restoring the "ideal" symmetry that was "ideally" intended. A "modern" painter, of whatever persuasion of modernity, is even likely to distort the distortion over-realistically, if he is interested in the tree at all.

This is perhaps the place at which to cite a pronouncement of Dagobert Frey, which, however "contemporary," is only a pale replica of the shining original of Plotinus: "Symmetry signifies rest and binding, asymmetry motion and loosening, the one order and law, the other arbitrariness and accident, the one formal rigidity and constraint, the other life, play, and freedom" (cf. Weyl, p. 16).

It is noteworthy that a very special instance of this pronouncement had been uttered by Democritus, many centuries before Plotinus: "according to Theophrastus, Democritus says that plants with straight stems have shorter lives than those with crooked stems because it is harder for the sap to mount straight up than sideways" (Regnéll, p. 51).

**Good and Evil.** The contrast between Good and Evil in *Paradise Lost*, or between Light and Darkness in, say, Zoroastrianism is, from our broad approach, a symmetry by polarity. As a religious tenet in advanced theological stages, this symmetry is rational and idealistic, in earlier creedal stages it is sensuous and realistic.

It is remarkable that in the Old Testament there is very little of this polarity in the advanced theocratic message of the leading prophets, much less than in the fully religious or only semi-secular thinking of an Anaximander, Xenophanes, Aeschylus, Empedocles, and Plato, in classical Greece. However, by religious intensity, Greece was probably less theocratic than Old Israel.

**The Human Body.** The role of symmetry in animate life is both crude and subtle, disquieting and incomprehensible.

The human body is outwardly endowed with a bilateral symmetry which seems to be a near-prerequisite for most physical activities, such as walking, seeing, hearing, using one's hands, etc. In the internal anatomy, some organs, like lungs and kidneys conform to this symmetry, but others, very basic ones, the heart and the alimentary canal do not. Why this should be so is most baffling, to the general reader at any rate. Even the outward symmetry is not very rigorous, especially in the adult. In fact, the outward deviation from symmetry, especially in facial contours frequently bespeak character and personality, even superiority.

For the comprehension of those things it is not at all helpful to read in a very scholarly (and equally dull) book that "all asymmetries occurring [in the human body] are of secondary character" (cf. Weyl, p. 26). More helpful is the suggestion, which, in depth, may have been articulated by Weyl himself, that "the deeper chemical constitution of our human body shows a screw, a screw that is turning the same way in every one of us." But some of the explanatory details bearing on this vitalistic "turning of the screw" are very disquieting, inasmuch as a "wrong" turn of the screw may be vindictively lethal (Weyl, pp. 30–38).

**Circularity.** A circle is rich in symmetries. It admits mirror symmetry with respect to everyone of its infinitely many diameters. As a mathematical consequence of this the circle can also be rotated into itself around the center by an arbitrary angle; in fact, if two diameters form an angle $\alpha$, then mirror reflection with respect to one diameter followed by a reflection with respect to the second diameter will rotate the circle by the double angle $2\alpha$.

Apparently because of this wealth of symmetry, for 2000 years, from Plato to Tycho Brahe, and including Copernicus, scientific astronomers somehow took it for granted that a celestial orbit of the kind that came under their observation is, or ought to be, a circle, or a circle rolling off on a circle (epicycle), or a figure mathematically equivalent to such a one. They undoubtedly had it in their thinking that what is aesthetically (and ontologically) appealing is also kinematically distinguished and dynamically preferable. But a mechanical preference from outward mathematical symmetry, while frequently profitable, can also be misleading, and in the present case it certainly was the latter. It was miraculously divined by Kepler, and then mathematically rationalized by Newton that, under gravitation, the closed orbit of one celestial body around another—in an "ideal" two-body setting—is not just a circle, but an ellipse, any ellipse. The ellipse can have any eccentricity, that is any measure of deviation from a circle. A circle can also occur; but it occurs then only as a case of an ellipse whose eccentricity happens to be zero. But since the eccentricity can be any real number between 0 and 1, this is a most unlikely value to occur. Even if, by an unlikely chance, a pure circle does eventuate, that form undoubtedly is very unstable; the smallest perturbation would quickly make it into an ellipse of a small but non-zero eccentricity. Thus, in this case, the figure with a wealth of symmetries is exceptional within a large family of figures each having only a few symmetries; and the wealth of symmetries makes the exceptional figure very unstable and most unlikely to occur.

Still, circular motion does play a role, in all parts of physics, as a constituent of any wave-like event; of an ordinary wave on the water or in the air; of an electromagnetic wave in the propagation of light, as a dual to the photon; and of a de Broglie wave, as a dual to the corpuscular aspect of any elementary particle of matter. A wave, wherever and however occurring, is a composite bundle of "simple" waves, so called "monochromatic" ones, and the mathematical structure of a simple wave is always the same. The pulse of a monochromatic ray of energy is rigorously invariant in time and thus constitutes a most "dependable" clock (atomic clock). The Greeks were already groping for such a clock. Aristotle reports that some philosopher(s) before him not only *measured* time by the daily rotation of the celestrial sphere but even *defined* it quantitatively in this way. Surprisingly, Aristotle frowns on this definition (*Physica* Book 4, Ch. X, 218b 1–5).

Returning to gravitation we note that physicists nowadays, out of their fertile imaginations, have imputed a nuclear structure to gravitation too, complete with corpuscles, hopefully named gravitons, and with dual de Broglie waves, hopefully spoken of as gravitational waves. Whenever these will be conclusively verified to "exist," circularity will have finally come to gravitation too; and how a Eudoxus and a Ptolemy would welcome such a newcomer would be worth knowing.

**Time's Arrow.** For whatever reasons, perhaps for "magical" ones, an asymmetry, when pronounced, can be perturbing, both to our reason and to our psyche; and nothing can be more, or more universally perturbing than the asymmetry of time, which cosmology and evolution like to call the arrow of time, and physics its irreversibility.

When Saint Augustine asked, as others had already asked before him, what God had been doing before creating the world, his query was a challenge to creed and theology. But when Schoolmen, believers in Creation, asked the parallel question how and why God had chosen to create the world at the instant of time at which he had done so, then this question was not addressed to theology only, but, in a sense, to scientific

reasoning too. In the twentieth century updated versions of this question arise in any evolutionary theory of cosmology as well, especially when there is seemingly conflicting evidence that the evolutionary process might have started ten, or thirteen, or fifteen billion years ago. Most importantly, however, while in our stream of consciousness and variety of experience, especially experience of and in the mind, there is a qualitative difference between "past" and "future," "before" and "after," yet there is also great need—in any kind of organized knowledge, scientific or historical, legal or medical, ethical or religious—for the representation of time on a geometrically interpreted time axis, on which the present is a point, and past and future are half lines that are bilaterally symmetric with regard to this point. And bilateral symmetry, in its mathematical conception, does not provide for a distinction of the two halves that are symmetrically opposed to each other or paired with each other.

The philosopher Henri Bergson was very insistent that, because of this trait and of related ones, geometrically controlled time be banished from the precincts of his *élan vital* and *évolution créatrice* and the related vitalistic manifestations. Bergson never seriously proposed to show how to keep this geometrically controlled time from intruding into the precincts of his vital processes. But even if he had done so successfully, the problem of the symmetry and asymmetry of time within the general intellectual climate of our time would not have been thereby resolved by half, because the problem is fully encountered in exact science, even in the case of physics itself. In fact, nineteenth-century physics arrived at conclusions which as a package were ill-assorted, and physicists around 1900 were discomfited by them. The following were several of the items of the odd assortment.

(1) Some physical processes are reversible, meaning that it is theoretically possible—though perhaps none too probable—that they be run totally in reverse, as when a movie is shown backwards. Of such kind are all purely mechanical processes that, schematically, do not involve the macroscopic production and propagation of heat.

(2) However, the creation and propagation of heat is irreversible, meaning that a physical process in a closed system involving them cannot be *totally* reversed so as to restore the initial situation in its entirety. Rudolf J. E. Clausius also introduced (1850) a quantitative measure of irreversibility which he termed entropy, and he posited the so-called second law of thermodynamics by which for a closed physical system the total entropy of the system cannot decrease in time but only increase or at most remain constant.

(3) And yet, the nineteenth century also erected the 349

"kinetic theory of matter" which, qualitatively and quantitatively, interpreted thermal energy in terms of mechanical motions and collision of molecules. Now, mechanical processes of this kind are totally reversible, and

It was recognized as paradoxical that the completely reversible gas model of the kinetic theory was apparently able to explain irreversible processes, i.e., phenomena whose development shows a definite direction in time (Ehrenfest, p. 13).

This paradox was somehow overcome (Ehrenfest, p. 3) by an argument from probability. There is in the argument a step that is intuitive, but, in full, the argument is "technical," and a faint residue of discomfort seems to linger on. Also, a parallel difficulty, if not a paradox, from the organic world picture remains, and it is the following.

(4) If the second law of thermodynamics is presumed to apply to the entire universe as one physical system, as physics around 1900 was bound to presume, then the total entropy of the system must be constantly on the increase. However, "entropy also measures the randomness or lack of orderliness of the system, the greater the randomness the greater the entropy" (Blum, p. 15). On the other hand,

Living organisms represent systems that are highly "organized", that is, they display less randomness than the materials from which they are "built"; and it is therefore justifiable to say that a decrease in entropy is involved in their building (Blum, p. 99).

Thus, whenever a form or unit of life comes into being on any spot of the universe then any such occurrence, taken by itself, runs counter to the general trend towards an increase of the entropy, and, in fact,

. . . the small local decrease in entropy represented in the building of the organism is coupled with a much larger increase in the entropy of the universe (ibid.).

In sum, since any organization of parts and phenomena of the universe represents, in some appropriate sense, the creation of design and symmetry in the order of the universe, and randomness represents the opposite of design and symmetry, therefore, by the second law of thermodynamics, that is, by the arrow of time, the order of the universe cannot but gradually disintegrate and dissolve. It is true that in the immediate vicinity of a rise of life there is a preservation and even a small strengthening of the symmetry. But these features are confined by location, and fleeting by duration, and they are compensated for by an acceleration of the process of decline in the remainder of the universe.

In the twentieth century it has been difficult to reconcile this bleak vista with the outlook of most cosmological theories emerging, even when no technical inconsistencies could be argued. An even greater difficulty, from entropy, is posed by any theory of a cosmogonic creation of the universe, assuming as most theories do, that there really was a Creation. In theories of today—as in fact, much more naively, in the theories of the pre-Socratics—almost any cosmogonic theory of creation starts out with a physical state in which there is some kind of turbulence, or less systematically, turbulent disorder, or at least formlessness. Out of this initial state develops some kind of gaseous or galactic organization on a comprehensive universal scale, and together with this various standard physical processes begin to take place, some reversible and some irreversible. How all this could accord with the second law of thermodynamics nobody dares to suggest, but there seems to be an understanding among cosmologists in the second half of the twentieth century not to allow this difficulty to prevent speculation.

*Present-day Dualities.* In bilateral symmetry, however much it might deviate towards asymmetry, the parts that are "symmetrically" opposed are expected to be, at least in a recognizable approximation, equal and conformable, by congruence or other modes of equality. In a duality however—or in a polarity, which is an intensified duality—the entities that are opposed are expected to be different, and even contrary, by contrast, or otherwise. Usually, a duality contraposes two contrasting aspects of the same whole, and an asymmetry contraposes two complementary parts of a whole larger than either part. But this criterion is sometimes not easy to apply, and, altogether, symmetries, asymmetries, and dualities overlap in important ways.

Thus, Plato's dichotomy, which is meant to be a logical procedure for arriving at a definition of anything definable (*Sophist* 218D–231B) proceeds by exhibiting a succession of dyads; and it cannot be readily made out whether in Plato's construction the two elements in a dyad are symmetric, asymmetric, or dual. Leaping ahead from Plato's procedure by an ingenuous dichotomy to a present-day procedure by an intricate computer, in which so-called "information" is coded, produced, and transmitted by a succession of dyadic yes-or-no signals, it is again not easy to decide whether the two possibilities "yes" and "no" are symmetric, asymmetric, or dual.

But there are significant contemporary cases in which there are no such doubts. For instance, the opposition between corpuscles and de Broglie waves in particle physics is a pronounced duality, because the selfsame particle is sometimes a corpuscle and sometimes a wave, depending on the context. That is, an elementary particle exhibits properties that can be best explained by endowing the particle with features of both a corpuscle and a wave. In an ontological interpretation of the entire theory, corpuscle and wave may perhaps be viewed as complementary parts of a unit larger than either, but in the prevalent interpretation in working physics they are different but coextensive aspects of the same whole. Furthermore, in its purely mathematical apparatus, this duality is but an instance of an extremely comprehensive duality, the only one of its kind, which is spread through all parts of mathematical analysis, and in which the two magnitudes which are contraposed are distinctly heterogeneous.

Yet, there is another case from particle physics, a baffling one, which again belongs to the doubtful category, namely the opposition between matter and antimatter. The transformation which creates the opposition is "charge conjugation" that is the replacement of electrons by positrons (=anti-electrons) and of positrons by electrons throughout a physical system in its entirety. It would be a case of symmetry rather than of asymmetry, except for the fact that in our part of the universe, at any rate, the anti-particles are much less stable than the particles. Furthermore, the unstable "free" positron becomes very stable when bound with a neutron to form a proton. And the resulting pair composed of electron and proton is in a sense only a duality, because by its mass the proton is quite unequal to the electron, being about 1835 times larger.

*General Symmetries.* Let us suppose that a three-dimensional tableau consists of a mirror, a design in front of the mirror, and its reflection in the back of the mirror. If we "erase" the physical trace of the mirror, making it thus "invisible" and "two-sided," then there is no front and back of it, and the design and its reflection have become indistinguishable and interchangeable. That is, mathematically, a mirror reflection does not actually break up the space into two halves, one in front and one in back, and transform the front half into the back half, but it transforms the *entire* space into itself. And this transformation happens to be such that any of the two halves goes into the other and that the points on the mirror itself remain each where it is. Now, a tableau in the space is (bilaterally) symmetric with respect to a mirror, if the transformation we have just described leaves the tableau unchanged, that is, leaves it looking after the transformation as it looked before the transformation.

Inasmuch as a mirror reflection of the space is a transformation of the *entire* space into itself it is called an *automorphism*. In general, an automorphism of a space, any space, is an invertible transformation of the entire space into itself, and such a transformation is nothing other than a rearrangement of the totality of the points of the space from their given ordering into any other. In order to arrive at a general mathematically oriented notion of symmetry, it is also necessary to consider not only single automorphisms but certain assemblages of automorphisms called *groups* (for the definition of a "group" see Weyl, pp. 47, 144, and passages on other pages listed in the index to the book under "group"). Now, the mathematical notion of symmetry demands that there shall be given some group of automorphisms. If such a group is given and held fast, then a figure in space is called symmetric if each automorphism of the group leaves it unchanged. Thus, symmetry is a relative concept. A figure is not just symmetric *tout court*, but it is symmetric relative to a given group of automorphisms, which, in a logical sense, has to be given first.

The symmetry of a figure is "interesting," or "meaningful," or "relevant," mathematically or aesthetically, if the automorphisms of the underlying group are "interesting," or "meaningful," or "relevant"; in short, if the underlying automorphisms are "good" automorphisms.

In our Euclidean space, by "normal" standards of taste, mathematical or aesthetic, the "best" automorphisms are those that transform figures into "congruent" ones, thus leaving (Euclidean) distances and angles unchanged. These are the so-called orthogonal transformations. They consist of translations, rotations, mirror reflections, and combinations of such. Different from these, yet still very "normal" are so-called dilations (Weyl, pp. 65, 68). A dilation is merely a change of scale; all distances are changed in the same ratio, and angles remain the same. Weyl lists large numbers of finite groups of orthogonal transformations for plane and space, and notable physical and ornamental designs which are symmetric relative to these; he also asserts (pp. 66, 99), that in the case of the plane these groups were already determined in substance by Leonardo da Vinci, but he does not give a reference showing where to find them in Leonardo's works.

From this approach, an "obvious" asymmetry is frequently a regular symmetry with respect to a group of automorphisms that are not strict orthogonal transformations but obvious distortions of such. The leading case is a reflection in a curved, or rather corrugated mirror in an amusement park. A reflection in a corrugated mirror is still a reflection, and it still produces a "bilateral symmetry," even if distorted. In our "neutral" physical perception there is no difference between the distortion in the corrugated mirror of an amusement park for vulgar purposes, and the distortion in the nonrealistic painting of an artist from an exalted inspiration.

351

As an aside we note that in the physical theory of elementary particles certain approximate symmetries have been called *broken* symmetries.

*Homogeneity.* The orthogonal transformations in Euclidean space are not only arbiters of symmetry for designs that are outwardly imposed on the space as their background and framework, but their presence also creates a certain internal evenness of the structure of the space as such, taken by itself. For space as substratum of the universe, and within a theologico-metaphysical imagery, internal evenness of structure of a space was already adumbrated by Nicholas of Cusa in the first half of the fifteenth century, but professional mathematics began to be properly aware of it only in the course of the nineteenth century. In mathematics, the feature of "evenness of structure" that we have in mind, is nowadays termed homogeneity, and is defined below. It is again a relative concept and, again, a group of automorphisms of the space is involved. The demand is that the group be transitive. By this is meant that any point $P$ of the space can be carried into any other point $Q$ by at least one of the automorphisms. If this is so, then the space is homogeneous (with respect to the given group).

Obviously the homogeneity of a space is the more interesting if the underlying group of automorphism is more important. If the space is a so-called metric space, it is usually expected that the underlying automorphism shall at least be isometric, meaning that the transformations preserve the distance between any pair of points.

Our common Euclidean space is certainly homogeneous with regard to orthogonal transformations; in fact, the mere translations suffice for homogeneity, so that rotations and reflections ought to secure some further properties of Euclidean space, which might perhaps be even characteristic of it. Such at any rate was the expectation of the physicist and physiologist Hermann von Helmholtz; he took a physiologist's interest in the nature of Euclidean space, which, to him, was the space of physiological perception. Helmholtz emphasized the fact that any two planes which go through a point can be transformed into each other by a rotation around the point ("local mobility"), and he apparently was under the impression that this, together with homogeneity, holds for Euclidean space only. But Friedrich Heinrich Schur (1852–1932) demonstrated that all this also holds for any non-Euclidean space of *constant* curvature, whether the curvature is negative *à la* Bolyai-Lobatchevsky, or positive *à la* Riemann (and Beltrami). Schur even demonstrated this for spaces of any number of dimensions, no matter how large.

It is also a curious fact of present-day mathematics that it is not at all easy to draw up criteria of "internal symmetry" which fit Euclidean space and no other.

In cosmology there is a quest for homogeneity of another, though related kind. It does not refer to the structure of the spatial substratum of the universe but to the mode of distribution of matter in it. This homogeneity, when assumed present, falls under the so-called Cosmological Principle, and a report on it is given in the article on Space.

*Symmetry in Physics.* The terms "symmetry" and "symmetry law" occur frequently in present-day physics, and we now comment on this occurrence.

We have stated above that, in a spatial setting, an impression of symmetry arises if a design is not changed by a group of automorphisms of the space, and we add to this that, as far as design is concerned, the underlying space is a setting for it, and any automorphism of the space is a certain change of this setting. Quite generally, in mathematics and mathematically controlled science, the imperviousness to changes within a setting is technically called "invariance" (relative to these changes). In this sense a law of symmetry is a particular case of a law of invariance, and, to begin with, the two are not coextensive because symmetry involves a connotation of space, whereas invariance is more comprehensive. However, in physics many invariances involve space variables, or at least space data, and in this way the terms symmetry and invariance have drawn ever closer together and have become almost synonymous.

Thus, a present-day physicist may view even the nineteenth-century law of conservation of energy as a symmetry law. The nineteenth century envisaged various forms of energy, mechanical, thermal, electrical, etc., and admitted that they may be transformed into each other, that is, change over into each other. But the law maintained (and continues to maintain) that throughout such changes of form, the total amount of energy in a closed physical system remains constant, that is *invariant*. To this and the following see the first half of Eugene P. Wigner, *Symmetry and Reflection.*

It is not always easy to decide how two physical laws of symmetry relate to each other. It can be stated, for instance, that Newton's force of gravitational attraction (inverse square of the distance) obeys two laws of symmetry, a spatial and a temporal. According to the spatial law, the force of attraction is invariant for all orthogonal transformations of space, not distinguishing between points of origin or directions in space. According to the temporal law, it is invariant in time.

As just stated, these two laws of symmetry are separate, and have equal standing. However, the theory of relativity erases the separateness, and geology casts doubt upon their equal standing. In fact, the general theory of relativity, by the very formulation of the phenomenon of gravitation, fuses the two laws of symmetry into one, so that they cannot be separated. On the other hand, in geology, the temporal invariance is part of the general law of uniformitarianism which seems to assert that, say, in the rise of the solar system, or at least in the evolution of the earth, the familiar laws of "classical" physics are "eternal," that is temporally invariant, and thus have always been before what they are presently. This seems to make the temporal symmetry of the gravitational force hierarchically prior, and thus superior to the spatial one.

In basic physics of the twentieth century, as the century progressed, the number of invariance properties has shown a tendency to increase (Wigner, p. 60). There has been many a period of anguish when two leading symmetry laws were seemingly in an irreconcilable clash with each other. Occasionally such a period of anguish was followed by a period of relief when, to the soothing accompaniment of a Nobel prize, the clash was somehow composed.

On the other hand, the twentieth century also undid at least one law of the preceding century. It was the law of similitude. Although not very important, it was treated with respect. It asserted

. . . that physical experiments can be scaled; that the absolute magnitude of objects be irrelevant from the point of view of their behavior on the proper scale. The existence of atoms, of an elementary charge, and of a limiting velocity spelled the doom of this principle (Wigner, p. 5).

We might add that the elementary charge, that is the magnitude of the electron, seems to be the most implacable of the instruments of doom.

This doom reached beyond the law of similitude, which is a not-too-important law of physics. It also enveloped the serene vision of Leibniz that space is nothing but order and relations, and perhaps also with predestined harmony ensuing; it somehow also enveloped the creeds of the eighteenth and nineteenth centuries—"naive" creeds in the eighteenth century and less naive ones in the nineteenth—that, in spite of all vehemence and violence in man, everything will in the end turn out to be continuous, controllable, and adjustable to scale.

But these creeds overlooked the electron. James Clerk Maxwell, at the height of Victorianism, tried to forget about the electron, by creating a magnificent field theory in which everything can be adjusted to scale, but it was not enough for physics; the electron simply had to be considered and taken very seriously indeed. Magnetism is a close kin to electricity. When Thales of Miletus, almost twenty-six centuries ago, saw

a magnet in action, he exclaimed that the world is full of Gods. And so it is even today.

*BIBLIOGRAPHY*

Monroe C. Beardsley, *Aesthetics from Classical Greece to the Present* (New York and London, 1966). Harold F. Blum, *Time's Arrow and Evolution* (Princeton, 1951). Paul and Tatiana Ehrenfest, *The Conceptual Foundations of the Statistical Approach in Mechanics* (Ithaca, 1959). G. T. Griffith, *Alexander the Great, The Main Problems* (Cambridge and New York, 1966). W. K. C. Guthrie, *A History of Greek Philosophy*, 3 vols. (Cambridge and New York, 1962; 1965; 1969), Vol. III. Iamblichus, *Protrepticus*, ed. H. Pistelli (Stuttgart, 1888). Pliny, *Natural History*, The Loeb Classical Library, 10 vols. (Cambridge, Mass. and London, 1938–63). H. Regnéll, *Ancient Views on the Nature of Life* (Lund, 1962). D'Arcy Wentworth Thompson, *On Growth and Form* (Cambridge, 1917; 1942). Hermann Weyl, *Symmetry* (Princeton, 1952). Eugene P. Wigner, *Symmetries and Reflections* (Bloomington and London, 1967).

SALOMON BOCHNER

[See also Beauty; Cosmology; Nature; **Optics and Vision; Space.**]

# TASTE IN THE HISTORY OF AESTHETICS FROM THE RENAISSANCE TO 1770

*I*

"TASTE" is relevant to the history of ideas as the power of liking or disliking something, and of ruling one's judgment or conduct according to this power. Still, in this broader meaning, "taste" is used very widely but rather atypically; it is of major importance only as applied to aesthetics, where it becomes, during the seventeenth century, one of the central and most controversial notions. As such, it is the subject of many discussions and of extremely wide implications—the basic dimensions of which follow below.

The main feature of aesthetic taste is that it is conceived as an instinctive feeling, independent of reasoning; but, for many authors, reflection may at least partially modify its responses. An inferior kind of taste is considered to cherish some aspects of beauty which do not, or do not necessarily, correspond to absolute aesthetic value as established by the rules of art; a superior kind of taste, increasing its importance with the crisis of "classical" aesthetics, is itself the standard of aesthetic value and the foundation of the rules. As such, taste is first considered as the power of evaluating beauty insofar as it is inherent in objects; afterwards, it is rather seen as the power of evaluating the response of the mind to objects, with beauty no longer being a characteristic of things in themselves, but consisting in a relationship between the mind and its objects.

The increased importance of taste as a standard of beauty raises the problem of its being universal or merely relative, a problem particularly felt by "neo-classical" aesthetics, once more in quest of established values; but as tastes are manifestly different in mankind, a universality of taste may be asserted only with respect to "good" taste, in contrast to a "bad" taste which is relative. But who is endowed with "good" taste? A minority of people, of course; for some authors, only a few connoisseurs living in nonbarbaric ages. The basic condition for belonging to this minority may be that of having a good education and polished manners; here it is assumed, as most authors do, that taste may be educated by exercise or by study. On the other hand, the factual disparity of tastes in different nations and eras raises the problem of elaborating a typology, and of justifying historically and psychologically this diversity, which, though generally considered as not consistent with perfect "good" taste, is not always referred to as altogether "bad" or "perverted" taste, but as an intermediate condition.

Another question is that of the foundation of taste. Is taste a simple, unique faculty or an assemblage of different faculties? How is it connected with other faculties, especially with reason and with other feelings? Its relationship to reason does not only concern the possibility of arguing about taste, but, more basically, the problem as to whether taste should be considered as a power related to that of immediate assent to basic truths, i.e., to right reason (common sense, natural light of reason). If so, in taste, is the judgment about beauty founded on the pleasurable feeling raised by beauty, or vice versa? An identification of "taste" and "judgment" (of beauty) is frequent, but neither universal nor univocal. A further basic problem is that of the relationship of taste to the judgment of truth, and to the judgment (or feeling) of utility, of bodily pleasure, and of goodness. In the course of the eighteenth century taste grows more and more independent of other factors: at that time aesthetics is being recognized as a particular science, and it tries to assert its individuality by claiming to rest on an original principle, not subordinated to those of other branches of knowledge.

## II

Taste (Italian, *gusto*) seems to have been connected for the first time with beauty in Renaissance Italy. Filarete wrote in 1464: *Ancora a me solevano piacere*

*questi moderni; ma poi, ch'io comenciai a gustare questi antichi, mi sono venuti in odio quelli moderni. . . .* ("I also used to like the Moderns; but, as soon as I began tasting the Ancients, I came to hate the Moderns. . . ."; *Quellenschriften*, 1890). Other Renaissance views include F. Rinuccini, who used *gusto* as a synonym of "right judgment" (Rinuccini, 1840). *Gusto* is used in connection with beauty by Michelangelo (Buonarroti, 1863), by Ariosto in 1532 (Ariosto, 1532), by Leone Ebreo in 1535 (Leone Ebreo, 1929), by Cellini and Varchi (Cellini, 1857; Varchi, 1857–58), by Dolce in 1557 (Dolce, 1557), by Zuccolo in 1623 (Croce, 1946b), by Graziani in 1671 (Graziani, 1671), but only occasionally; it does not become an important notion in Italian aesthetics until C. Ettorri's *Il buon gusto ne' componimenti rettorici* (1696), and then probably under Spanish or French influence. Afterwards, its fortune was assured, as shown in 1708 by a work of L. A. Muratori, *Delle riflessioni sopra il buon gusto . . .* (1708), and by the foundation in Palermo in 1718 of an "Accademia del buon gusto" (Mazzucchelli, 1753–63). For Muratori, taste (also called *giudizio* and *dritta ragione*) is a power of judging individual cases which cannot be decided according to universal rules (Baeumler, 1923). In fact, the first extensive use of "taste" as a mysterious, instinctive power enabling man to make the right choice in the different circumstances of life, as the foundation for a civilized behavior, occurs in the works of the Spaniard Gracián, in 1647 (Borinski, 1894); but he also uses it in a specifically aesthetic sense (Gracián, ed. del Hoyo, 1960). Nevertheless, taste had (in Gracián's day) not yet become a central notion in Spanish aesthetics: Feijóo, in his *Razón del gusto* (1727–30), still applies this term indiscriminately to food, drink, music, etc., identifying it with the feeling for the pleasurable.

## III

In France, taste is applied to beauty at least as early as 1645 by Guez de Balzac (Borgerhoff, 1950), and used with this meaning by Molière in 1659 (Molière, 1659; 1663; 1669), and by La Fontaine in 1668. La Rochefoucauld, in a posthumous essay, *Du goût*, is probably the first theorist of taste in France. Taste is variable, depending on personal inclinations and circumstances, but good taste (*bon goût*) is an instinctive power of correct evaluation based on judgment (*juger sainement, discernement, lumière naturelle*) rather than on feeling; it concerns all kinds of intellectual, moral, and aesthetic objects (La Rochefoucauld, 1949). Méré's *bon goust* (1677) is very similar; it is thought to be *un sens intérieur peu connu*, independent of learning, but founded *sur des raisons très-solides; mais le plus souvent sans raisonner* (Méré, 1930). For Saint-

Evremond, on the contrary, taste may, as *bon goût, bon sens,* be close to reason, but more generally it is relative and whimsical (von Stein, 1886). Malebranche in *La Recherche de la vérité* (1674) regards taste as pertaining to sensory things (*beautez sensibles*), an inferior, sensitive kind of beauty, and holds it as relative (Malebranche, 1958f.). But, if for Rapin and Bouhours taste is relative to centuries and to nations (von Stein, 1886), for Bouhours *good* taste, especially connected with aesthetics, is a sort of instinctive good judgment, *une espèce d'instinct de la droite raison.* And La Bruyère writes that good taste is the effect of sound judgment: *Entre le bon sens et le bon goût il y a la différence de la cause à son effet* (*Les Caractères,* "Des Jugements," 1694). This rationalist conception of good taste, shared by Mme Dacier (Dacier, 1684), reaches a climax in aesthetics with Crousaz (1715), who considers taste a sentimental substitute for reason, which can be improved by education (Baeumler, 1923).

This attitude is opposed, under English influence, by the Abbé Dubos (1719); taste as a sensitivity to beauty is for him basically a matter of feeling; this feeling is not a substitute for reason, or the expression of an unconscious rational judgment: it is the basis of the judgment of beauty, as a special faculty, defined as a "sixth sense" (Baeumler, 1923). A lively discussion with Charles Rollin ensued (Rollin, 1725). Cartaud de la Vilate was also inclined to irrationalism; and he was especially interested in the study of the evolution of taste through the ages (Cartaud, 1736).

But the rationalist trend still dominated in French aesthetics. For the Abbé Batteux (1747), taste is knowledge of rules through a feeling which can be educated (Baeumler, 1923, von Stein, 1886). Diderot conceives taste as a faculty of immediate judgment; a faculty acquired through recurrent experiences, of grasping the true and the good, with whatever renders it beautiful, and of being instantly and vividly affected (*faculté acquise par des expériences réitérées, à saisir le vrai et le bon, avec la circonstance qui le rend beau, et d'en être promptement et vivement touché;* Belaval, 1950). Vauvenargues (1746) and D'Alembert (*Encyclopédie,* 1757) seem to subordinate taste to reasoning (Vauvenargues, 1746; Baeumler, 1923; *Encyclopédie,* 1757; von Stein, 1886). For Voltaire too taste comes close to reasoning, and may be corrected by reasoning; really good taste is universal, in spite of national and other differences of taste in general (*Encyclopédie,* 1757; Wellek, 1955). One of Voltaire's most famous critical works is entitled *Le Temple du goût* (1733). A later supporter of rationalism in taste is Pierre Mingard (Felice, 1773; see also: Duclos, 1805). But Montesquieu revives, at least partially, the irrationalism of Dubos, for whom taste is independent of

reasoning; it is the faculty enabling one to apply to individual cases the rules of art, and to establish exceptions to them (*Encyclopédie,* 1757; von Stein, 1886).

## IV

In Britain, taste as "inclination" is used by Caxton in 1477 (Caxton, 1893); it appears later (1502) with the meaning of "intuitive judgment" (Atkynson, 1893), and in the seventeenth century this is connected with beauty, e.g., by Milton and Congreve (Milton, 1671; Congreve, 1694). Norris, in 1691, mentions a "moral tast" [*sic*]. But a theory is not developed until the eighteenth century, when it centers on aesthetics much more in Britain than in France. The irrationalist view appears with Shaftesbury. Taste as a sense for beauty is closely connected with common sense and with moral sense, which reveal themselves through internal sensations. Taste is the internal sense of a harmonic order perceived in certain objects and belonging to them and to the perceiving mind as well; it is inborn, but it needs refining; it depends on the character of a nation, but, stripped of accidental influences, it is universal (Formigari, 1962; Morpurgo, 1962b). For Addison, ". . . the Taste is not to conform to the [rules of] Art, but the Art to the Taste"; taste is universal if it is duly educated (admiration for the classics), but in some degree it is innate if present at all (Addison, *The Spectator,* No. 29, 1711; No. 409, 1712). Hutcheson (1725) proceeds on the same line as Shaftesbury, stressing the universality of taste, and the fact that the taste for beauty is independent of considerations of utility (von Stein, 1886; Tonelli, 1955a); and Webb insists on the universality of taste (Tonelli, 1955a). The connections between beauty and utility, and even that between beauty and morality, taken for granted in French aesthetics, are no longer taken for granted in Britain after Hutcheson questions the first, and Gerard (see below) the second.

Hume declares in his essay "On the Standard of Taste" (1757) that beauty does not belong to things in themselves: taste expresses the reaction of the mind to things. Nevertheless taste, judging about beauty and about virtue as well, is universal, due to the uniformity of human nature, in spite of accidental differences (Wellek, 1955; Tonelli, 1955a). Hume's aesthetic subjectivism marks a turning point in British aesthetics. For Burke (1759), taste is a composite of different powers; it is universal, and independent of utility (Tonelli, 1955a; Formigari, 1962; Morpurgo, 1962c). Gerard (1759) carefully distinguishes taste from moral sense, but if beauty is independent of virtue, it is not independent of utility. Taste seems to be universal (Tonelli, 1955a). For him, as well as for other authors, taste is not a simple power: judgment is one of its components (Green, 1934). Hume (1762) considers taste universal, although this universality is restricted to a few connoisseurs; taste is not independent of considerations of utility (Tonelli, 1955a; Wellek, 1955). Although Dr. Johnson makes concessions to relativism in taste, he asserts after all the presence of universal common sense (Wellek, 1955). The only significant supporter of absolute relativism in taste is Joseph Priestley (1777), who applies to this subject the aesthetic principles elaborated by Mandeville and Hartley (Tonelli, 1955b). During the late eighteenth century, interest in the problem of taste is less intense in Britain: much attention is given to the theory of sublimity, and usually theories of the sublime are not referred to taste.

V

In the seventeenth century in Germany *Geschmack* ("taste") is used occasionally in the modern sense (Harsdörffer, 1651), but as late as 1687 Christian Thomasius prefers the term *bon goût* for a quality he requires of gentlemen. Aesthetic interest in the subject is not yet aroused: Leibniz, in 1712, is satisfied with a short personal interpretation of Shaftesbury's doctrine (Leibniz, 1887). Only with Bodmer (1727) taste becomes a basic subject in aesthetics, but it is conceived as a purely intellectual judgment which generates a subsequent feeling (von Stein, 1886). Gottsched (1730), referring to Leibniz, defines good taste as a correct judgment of the senses on beauty (i.e., sensitive perfection) which is known clearly but not distinctly; this judgment is confirmed by reason, applying the rational rules of perfection (Gottsched, 1751; Tonelli, 1955a). Similar ideas are expounded in 1734 by J. U. König (Tonelli, 1955a; Baeumler, 1923), by A. G. Baumgarten in *Metaphysica* (Baumgarten, 1739) and by G. F. Meier (Tonelli, 1955a; Baeumler, 1923). Lessing about 1758 still sponsors a rationalist view (Tonelli, 1955a); the same is true for what R. Mengs calls "the best taste" (Mengs, 1762). Th. Abbt in 1762 considers taste as required not only for appreciating art but also for science (Abbt, 1780). But Crusius' "moral taste" is conceived as an individually variable capacity to enjoy goodness and beauty (Crusius, 1744)—and even philosophy, according to G. H. Schramm, a pupil of Crusius (Schramm, 1772). With Moses Mendelssohn, the rationalist view is questioned: taste is independent of intellect, and it is considered as relative; it is related also to the sublime, and in this respect it seems to be universal (Braitmaier, 1888; Tonelli, 1855a).

For Kant in 1764, taste is independent of intellect and of considerations of utility, and it is different from the moral sense; it is related to the sublime also. Kant develops an extensive national typology of taste (Tonelli, 1955a). For Riedel (1767) taste is irrational and almost completely relative (Tonelli, 1955a). After 1768, Kant develops in a very original way his notion of taste in the framework of his new philosophy. Taste is considered as universal, but *a posteriori* and subjective, as a sensible judgment on the form of intuition (Tonelli, 1955a). Sulzer's position is eclectic (1771): taste is a special power, distinct from reason and moral feeling, and nevertheless it is the internal feeling for truth and goodness; beauty, perceived by taste, is neither perfection nor goodness, but the highest beauty is connected with both. Taste is universal, and its judgment can be rationally tested (Sulzer, 1792). In 1755, Herder was awarded a prize in a competition announced by the Berlin Academy on the "causes of the corruption of taste." For Herder, on Hamann's suggestion (Grappin, 1952), taste is a product of genius, as it corresponds to the orderly use of the genius's powers; it acts through reason and judgment, but it is not the same as virtue (*Ursachen des gesunknen Geschmacks . . .* [1775], sec. 1).

## BIBLIOGRAPHY

Th. Abbt, *Vermischte Werke* (Berlin and Stettin, 1780), IV, 46. J. Addison, *The Spectator*, No. 29 (1711); No. 409 (1712). L. Ariosto, *Orlando Furioso* (1532), Canto XXXV, 26. W. Atkynson, *Th. à Kempis: a full devout and gostely treatyse*, Early English Text Society (1893), Book I, Ch. XXII, 171. A. Baeumler, *Kants Kritik der Urteilskraft. Ihre Geschichte und Systematik* (Halle, 1923); reprinted as *Das Irrationalitätsproblem in der Aesthetik und Logik des 18. Jahrhunderts bis zur Kritik der Urteilskraft* (Darmstadt, 1967): Crousaz, pp. 43–49; Dubos, pp. 49–51; Muratori, pp. 51–53; Batteux, Voltaire, d'Alembert, pp. 74–75; König, p. 82; Meier, pp. 90f. A. G. Baumgarten, *Metaphysica* (Halle, 1739), sections 607–08. Y. Belaval, *L'esthétique sans paradoxe de Diderot* (Paris, 1950), pp. 75–80. E. B. O. Borgerhoff, *The Freedom of French Classicism* (Princeton, 1950), p. 14. K. Borinski, *Baltasar Gracián und die Hofliteratur in Deutschland* (Halle, 1894), pp. 40–43. F. Braitmaier, *Geschichte der poetischen Theorie und Kritik von den Diskursen der Maler bis auf Lessing* (Frauenfeld, 1888), II, 192f. D. Bouhours, *La manière de bien penser dans les ouvrages de l'esprit* (Paris, 1687), p. 382. M. Buonarroti, *Le rime* (Florence, 1863), pp. 27, 253. F. Cartaud de la Vilate, *Essay critique et philosophique sur le goust* (Paris, 1736). [W.] Caxton's *Historie of Jason*, Early English Text Society (1912), p. 72. B. Cellini, *I trattati dell'oreficeria e della scultura* (Florence, 1857), p. 41. W. Congreve, *The Double Dealer* (1694), I, 2. B. Croce, *Estètica come scienza dell'espressione e linguistica generale* (Bari, 1946a), "Storia," Ch. III; idem, *Storia della età barocca in Italia* (Bari, 1946b), Ch. V: Zuccolo, p. 167. C. A. Crusius, *Anweisung, vernünftig zu leben* (Leipzig, 1744), sec. 108f. Mme Anne Lefèvre Dacier, *Préface* to her translation of Aristophanes' *Plutus* and *Les Nuées* (Paris, 1684). L. Dolce, *Diàlogo della pittura* (Venice,

1557). C. Pinot-Duclos, *Oeuvres complètes* (Paris, 1806), Vol. X, *Considérations sur le goût. Encyclopédie, ou dictionnaire raisonné des arts, des sciences et des métiers*, Vol. VII (Paris, 1757), art. "Goût" by Voltaire, Montesquieu, d'Alembert. C. Ettorri, *Il buon gusto ne' componimenti rettorici* (Bologna, 1696). B. J. Feijóo y Montenegro, *Teatro crítico universal* (Madrid, 1727–30), Vol. VI, Disc. XI. F. B. de Felice, *L'Encyclopédie, ou dictionnaire universel raisonné des connaissances humaines*, Vol. XXII (Yverdon, 1773), art. "Goût" by Mingard and d'Alembert. L. Formigari, *L'estètica del gusto nel Settecento inglese* (Florence, 1962): Shaftesbury, pp. 28, 31f., 33f., 53f., 62f.; Burke, p. 81. F. Gallaway, *Reason, Rule and Revolt in English Classicism* (New York, 1940). B. Gracián, *El Criticon*, Part I, Crisis III, in *Obras completas*, ed. del Hoyo (Madrid, 1960), p. 533a. J. C. Gottsched, *Versuch einer critischen Dichtkunst . . .* (1730; Leipzig, 1751; reprint Darmstadt, 1962), pp. 123f. P. Grappin, *La théorie du génie dans le préclassicisme allemand* (Paris, 1952), p. 217. G. Graziani, *Cromuele* (Bologna, 1671), Preface. C. C. Green, *The Neo-Classic Theory of Tragedy in England during the XVIII Century* (Cambridge, Mass., 1934), pp. 738, 760f. G. P. Harsdörffer, *Die Fortpflanzung der Hochlöblich Fruchtbringenden Gesellschaft, mit einer Rede von dem Geschmack vermehret* (Nürnberg, 1651). J. G. Herder, *Ursachen des gesunknen Geschmacks bei den verschiednen Völkern, da er geblüht* (Berlin, 1775), Sec. I. E. N. Hooker, "The Discussion of Taste, from 1750 to 1770, and the New Trends in Literary Criticism," *PMLA*, **49** (1934). H. Klein, *There is no Disputing about Taste. Unters. zum englischen Geschmacksbegreiff im 18. Jhdt.* (Münster, 1967). J. de La Bruyère, *Les Caractères . . .* , eds. Servois and Rébelliaux (Paris, 1923), "Des jugements." J. de La Fontaine, *Fables* (1668), Book V, 1. F. de Marcillac de La Rochefoucauld, *Maximes et autres oeuvres morales* (1655), ed. Borrot (Paris, 1949), p. 131: *Réflexions diverses*, X, "Du goût." G. W. Leibniz, *Die philosophischen Schriften*, ed. C. I. Gerhardt (Berlin, 1887), III, 430f. Leone Ebreo, *Dialoghi d'Amore*, ed. Gebhardt (Heidelberg, London, 1929), p. 133. N. Malebranche, *Recherche de la vérité* (1674), in *Oeuvres complètes* (Paris, 1958f.), I, 149; idem, *Méditations chrétiennes* (1683), ibid., X, 43. G. M. Mazzucchelli, *Gli scrittori d'Italia* (Brescia, 1753–63), Vol. II, Part IV, p. 2389. G. McKenzie, *Critical Responsiveness. A Study of the Psychological Current in Later XVIII Century Criticism* (Berkeley and Los Angeles, 1949), Ch. IV. R. Mengs, *Gedanken über die Schönheit und den Geschmak in der Mahlerei* (Zurich, 1762), Ch. II. A. Gombaud de Méré, *Oeuvres complètes*, ed. Boudhors (Paris, 1930), II, 127–29; see also pp. 38f. J. Milton, *Paradise Regained* (1671), Book IV, line 347. Molière, *Les précieuses ridicules* (1659), Scene X; idem, *La critique de l'école des femmes* (1663), Scene VII; idem, *La Gloire du Dôme du Val-de-Grâce* (1669), line 360. G. Morpurgo Tagliabue, *Il concetto di gusto nell'Italia del Settecento* (Florence, 1962a); idem, "La nozione di gusto nel secolo XVIII: Shaftesbury e Addison," *Rivista di Estetica*, **8** (1962b); idem, *La nozione di gusto nel XVIII secolo: E. Burke* (Milan, 1962c). L. A. Muratori, *Delle riflessioni sopra il buon gusto nelle scienze e nell'arti* (Venice, 1708). J. Norris, *Practical Discourses upon several Divine Subjects*, 3 vols.

(London, 1691–93), I, 186. *Quellenschriften für Kunstgeschichte*, New Series III (Vienna, 1890), IX, 291. F. Rinuccini, *Ricordi storici dal 1282 al 1460* (Florence, 1840), "Documenti," p. 148. C. Rollin, *Traité de la manière d'étudier et d'enseigner les belles-lettres* (Paris, 1726), Vol. I, *Réflexions générales sur le goût*. R. G. Saisselin, *Taste in Eighteenth Century France* (Syracuse, N.Y., 1965). G. H. Schramm, *Versuch über den philosophischen Geschmack* (Jena, 1772), pp. 12, 49. H. von Stein, *Die Entstehung der neueren Ästhetik* (Stuttgart, 1886): Saint-Evremond, p. 93; Rapin, Bouhours, p. 93; Batteux, p. 94; Montesquieu, p. 95; Hutcheson, pp. 188–90; d'Alembert, p. 287; Bodmer, pp. 286–89. J. G. Sulzer, *Allgemeine Theorie der schönen Künste* (Leipzig, 1792), Vol. II, art. "Geschmack," with important bibliography. C. Thomasius, *Kleine deutsche Schriften* (Halle, 1701), p. 48; idem, *Discurs, welchergestalt man denen Frantzosen im gemeinen Leben nachahmen solle* (1687). G. Tonelli, *Kant, dall'estetica metafisica all'estetica psicoempirica, Memorie della Accademia delle Scienze di Torino*, Series 3, Vol. 3, Part II (Turin, 1955a): Hutcheson, pp. 111f.; Hume, pp. 100f., 212; Burke, pp. 111f.; Gerard, pp. 102, 112f.; Gottsched, p. 24; König, p. 31; Meier, p. 32; Lessing, Mendelssohn, Riedel, p. 212; Kant, pp. 59–63, 111, 113f., 174–77; idem, "Estetici minori britannici del Settecento," in *Giornale critico della filosofia italiana*, **9** (1955b): Mandeville, p. 31; Hartley, pp. 37f.; Priestley, pp. 204f. B. Varchi, *Storie Fiorentine* (Florence, 1857–58), Book VIII, p. 191. L. de Clapier de Vauvenargues, *Introduction à la connaissance de l'esprit humain* (Paris, 1746), Book I., n. 12, "Du goût." R. Wellek, *A History of Modern Criticism: 1750–1950*, Vol. I (New Haven, 1955): Voltaire, I, 38–42; Hume, I, 107; Home, I, 109; Johnson, I, 95.

GIORGIO TONELLI

[See also **Beauty;** Neo-Classicism; Relativism in Ethics; **Sublime.**]

# TECHNOLOGY

CIVILIZATION, even in a most elementary form, implies a degree of command over nature. Indeed, in its early stages, a civilized community, so far as it can be studied, may be said to be coextensive with its technics. It seems likely however that once a society reaches a certain stage in the development of technics and of social organization it faces, in effect, a wide choice of options. Thus it may seek wealth and power by enslaving its neighbors or by compelling them to pay tribute; it may evolve a bureaucratic form of government, or become a theocracy or a military tyranny. In any of these cases it is unlikely that there will be much further progress in technics; for they provide alternative and rival solutions to the problems which would otherwise be solved by technics, or else they induce a static society in which inventive impulses are stifled.

The civilization of China, ancient, extensive, and resilient, gave the world a number of great inventions of which the most prominent were probably paper and gunpowder. Yet, in spite of the evident genius of the individual Chinese inventor, the total achievement was disappointing. Chinese technics could not overcome the obstacles which, one infers, a static society put in the way. Inventiveness in China seems to have been diverted from its basic purpose of satisfying wants and needs; instead a great deal of effort was apparently put into what may be called "frivolous invention"; that is, into creating amusing toys such as kites, puzzles, games, automata, and firecrackers. It is only fair to add, however, that "frivolous invention" was well known in medieval and Renaissance Europe and is not uncommon in the modern world! In the case of China we may tentatively assume that the diversion and ultimate frustration of the inventive impulse was due to the values inculcated by the powerful bureaucracy, the low esteem in which utilitarian motives were held, and the real lack of incentives to economic activity.

The experiences of classical antiquity tend to confirm that the progress of technics can be arrested at any stage by unfavorable social influence. In particular it has frequently, and plausibly, been suggested that the institution of slavery accounts for the ultimate failure of Greek and Roman science and technics. On the other hand it must be admitted that the ancient civilizations of the Middle East had many technical achievements to their credit, especially in such fields as metallurgy and civil engineering. The Greeks, who were seafarers and traders, were little concerned with technics and made few significant inventions. Yet one may hazard the guess that, after the foundation of Alexandria, when Greek genius fused with the more pedestrian but complementary abilities of the Egyptians, there was at last the real possibility of a progressive science and technology. Egyptians seem to have been in some respects curiously free from that deep-seated fear of nature which troubled all other men, including Greeks and Romans. The Egyptians practiced human dissection; they were also skilled metallurgists. By repute experimental chemistry, in the form of alchemy, began in Egypt. Egyptians were of necessity expert irrigation engineers and hydrologists and they introduced such useful inventions as the water clock, or clepsydra, and the Archimedean screw. Was it perhaps symbolic that the only one of the Seven Wonders of the ancient world which served a useful purpose and was not an instance of conspicuous consumption was the Pharos at Alexandria?

The science of Alexandrians like Eratosthenes, Hero,

and Ptolemy had the professional touch which was lacking in Hellenic speculative thought. But unfortunately Alexandria, with its famous Museum and Library, had no rival, no stimulating partner, anywhere in the ancient world. Experience suggests that if science and technics are to flourish several competing centers of excellence are required: if there is only one the opportunities for profitable debates are so restricted that intellectual stagnation is sooner or later inevitable. As for the rest of the then civilized world, the major cities exemplified not so much technical abilities as the administrative gifts of the Roman rulers.

With the slow rise of Christian Europe from the ruins of the Roman Empire, a new form of society emerged that was to prove favorable for the renewed advance of technics. The reasons for this are probably many and certainly complex. Nevertheless specific and readily identifiable features of this society must have been important. For one thing the universal acceptance of a dogmatic monotheistic religion was associated with the establishment of a common educational or cultural system of which a characteristic feature was the medieval university. Again, the nature of Christian teaching meant, or at least could mean, the dismissal from nature of all arbitrary wills—the whole pantheon of gods, goddesses, and minor spirits—and the substitution of one rational, omnipotent, and benevolent God as Architect of the Universe and ruler of all things. The consequence of such a belief for the advance of technics as well as of science need hardly be emphasized. But perhaps most important of all, the Europeans revealed an admirable willingness to learn from outsiders.

At the dawn of the Middle Ages, which we assume began with the reign of Charlemagne, the Europeans were undoubtedly inferior to the contemporary Arabs and Chinese in both technics and the arts of living. They had, however, sufficient humility to admit this, tacitly at least, and in the following centuries they freely copied the inventions and the arts of the civilizations of Asia and Africa. In fact, a readiness to imitate appears to be essential for the spread of invention and for the furtherance of technics in general: this seems to be as much a characteristic of progressive industrial enterprises in the modern world as of progressive nations and civilizations in the past. It is only by imitating, by copying and adapting, that a class of technicians can be built up; and it is mainly from such a class that one may expect original inventors to emerge in due course. It follows that historians who extol the Arab and Chinese civilizations at the expense of medieval Europe miss an essential point. After all, the first question to ask about any invention is not who made it, but how widespread was its use.

If we assume that the Middle Ages ended with the fifteenth century then a simple count of inventions made or adopted by Europeans during the period confirms that it was, as regards technics, more creative than any previous epoch in recorded history. Among the more important medieval inventions were the stirrup, paper, gunpowder, firearms, the weight-driven clock, the mariner's compass, the spinning wheel, the Saxon plough, the windmill, the crank, the horse collar, the steering rudder, the printing press, and the three-masted ship. Most of the earlier inventions were copied from the Arabs and the Chinese; most of the later ones were made by Europeans themselves. Many were most likely made simultaneously but independently by different men in Europe and elsewhere; scholars have long recognized that simultaneous invention is a very common occurrence.

The weight-driven clock, perhaps the most remarkable of all medieval inventions, appeared, it is believed, towards the end of the thirteenth century having in all probability evolved from a long line of astronomical models. The mechanical clock does not measure the duration between two events, as an hour glass or a calibrated candle does; as its circular dial and moving hand indicate, it is really a device for indicating the position of the sun with respect to a meridian of the (supposedly) fixed earth.

The apparent diurnal motion of the sun is for all practical purposes uniform. But it is impossible to obtain continuous uniform motion from any motive agent without some form of self-controlling or feedback mechanism.

In the medieval weight-driven clock this problem is solved by combining a basic principle with a brilliantly ingenious kinematic invention. The uniform and constant force of gravity, acting on a suspended weight, is transformed by means of an escapement wheel into an alternating horizontal force which is then applied to an inertial system consisting of two equal masses at the opposite ends of a horizontal, centrally pivotted rod. The inertial system, driven by the cyclic force, oscillates to and fro with a uniform beat whose period, or duration, is determined by the geometry of the machine and the magnitudes of the weights and masses. The invention of the escapement wheel could, in principle at any rate, have been made at any time; but the basic physics of the weight-driven clock was not formulated until the seventeenth century: as the foregoing words "force," "inertial," and "masses" imply. One may, therefore, properly designate this invention as precocious, for it was based on principles which could not be scientifically explained at the time.

Crude as the first weight-driven clocks were, the process of "evolutionary" improvement assured rapidly rising standards of precision, reliability, and lightness: a process punctuated and expedited by such "revolutionary" improvements as the inventions of the fusee, the stackfreed, the spring or "clockwork" drive, the pendulum clock, and the anchor escapement. Before very long a class of skilled clockmakers, the first of the precision engineers, was established. This had obvious economic and technical importance. On another plane, however, the mechanization of time measurement had very far-reaching consequences. Throughout antiquity and up to the middle of the fourteenth century it had been customary to divide the period between sunrise and sunset into an equal number of hours with the consequence that the length of the hour varied with the length of the day; with, that is, the time of the year. This was a reasonable procedure in days when there were no powerful sources of artificial light so that most communal activities ceased with nightfall. Accordingly it was the practice to calibrate sundials with hour marks to suit the time of year. But with the advent of the mechanical clock the practice of astronomers, who had long taken the length of the hour to be uniform by day and by night, now became the common practice of all men. The public clock, on church or castle, proclaimed the time to all men. With the improvement in clocks went the further subdivision of the uniform hour into uniform minutes and seconds. This meant that all men could now regard time as an infinitely extended dimension against which all events and affairs were ordered. It was not so much the interval between specific events as an eternal process underlying them. Ever since the Middle Ages the steady, uniform tick of the clock has marked the passage of time in this cosmic sense. It is hardly surprising therefore that the mechanical clock inspired the familiar and persuasive seventeenth-century image of a "clockwork" universe and no doubt it contributed to Newton's formulation of absolute, true, and mathematical time which, he asserted, flows equably without relation to anything external.

No doubt, the geometrization of time also owed something to the revival of interest in Euclid in the Middle Ages and to mathematically inclined philosophies such as the various forms of Platonism. So, too, did the geometrization of space which helped artists to invent new techniques of painting pictures as "true to nature" and not as symbolic representations. At a more humdrum level the development of cartography marked the same sort of change when symbolic diagrams, such as the T-O maps, gave place to realistic representations of land forms.

Accompanying and reinforcing the emergent technics of the Middle Ages was a new attitude to nature which was, in part, a product of Christian teaching.

But it had other roots too, for an important component of the new attitude was the rise of what have been called the heretical sciences—alchemy, astrology, and magic. These represented a bold attempt to appropriate the secret and innermost processes of nature; in Robert Lenoble's expressive phrase, to break the "tabu on the natural." However we apportion the credit for the new attitude, there can be no doubt that men became more courageous and enterprising in the face of nature. One aspect of this was the relaxation in the medical schools of the medieval universities of the ancient prohibition of human dissection.

At the same time the mining industries of Europe were being developed, differing from the practice of the ancient world in that the miners were now free men and not condemned slaves. Mining was, from the early days, big business. It needed not only large-scale social and financial organization but also the services of a wide range of technics. It posed problems in civil engineering, in ventilating and pumping and hence in the generation of power, in underground and surface transport, and in the treatment of metals. Accordingly mining expedited the growth of applied sciences such as metallurgy and "pure" sciences such as chemistry and geology. Indeed, the acknowledged excellence of German chemistry was said to have been due to the extensive mining industries of that country. In short, mining has been one of the seedbeds of Western science and technology.

The last aspect of medieval and Renaissance technics that we shall mention was the proliferation of attempts to devise a perpetual motion machine. This utilitarian aspiration was based on the consideration that perpetual motion was not an absurdity: the motion of the heavens, the tides, streams and rivers, and the winds are all apparently "perpetual." And it was not until after the "Scientific Revolution" of the seventeenth century and the demonstration that the atmosphere acts as a heat engine powered by solar energy that the rational basis for the attempt to make such machines was finally destroyed.

Medieval and Renaissance perpetual motion machines, indeed machines in general, were characterized by an exuberant delight in elaboration: gear trains were added merely for the sake of complexity as well as in the hope of hitting on a more subtle science of mechanics that would transcend mere earthbound mechanics. The latter endeavor failed, but not before men had taught themselves a great deal about the principles of machines. The period was intensely machine-conscious, as the famous notebooks of Leonardo testify.

When we consider medieval technics in retrospect we can see that they affected intellectual life in several different ways. In the first place certain inventions may of themselves cause fundamental changes in thought. Thus the widespread application of the mechanical or weight-driven clock necessarily changed, or helped to change, men's ideas about time, compelling everyone to accept the notion of the uniform hour, minute, and second and furthermore to consider time as a process which transcends all particular events. In addition the machine itself suggested a model for the universe which many found particularly satisfying. Again, technics provides men with new and improved tools which, in enabling him to extend his mastery over nature, also serve to extend his knowledge. The invention of the mariner's compass coupled with improvements in ship building and design enabled Portuguese and Spanish navigators to extend knowledge of the world from the margins of Europe to the vast globe itself—now actually confirmed to be a globe—over which the observed laws of nature were found everywhere to be uniform and constant. Finally, we recognize that the development of technics may change the course of thought by ameliorating the conditions of life, by providing cumulative evidence that men may hope increasingly to determine their own destinies—that is, by giving sanction to the idea of progress—and by assisting in the spread of secular learning. The last is exemplified by the great medieval invention of the printing press.

The achievements of the period which ended in 1500 A.D. provided a good deal of the knowledge, in terms of hard-won experience, and much of the morale and inspiration for that remarkable movement which swept Western Europe in the seventeenth century and which is known as the "Scientific Revolution." The distinctive creed of the new movement was the "mechanical philosophy," an expression which neatly summed up its adherents' indebtedness to medieval and Renaissance mechanical inventors: those whom Leonardo Olschki has called the "artist-engineers" who flourished notably in northern Italy. Only a mature civilization, urban and technical rather than rural, could have given rise to the mechanical philosophy. In fact the greater part of medieval technics had been forged in the cities of northern Italy and of southern Germany. The Italian cities tended to excel in the mechanical arts, architecture, and civil engineering; the German cities in the metallurgical and chemical arts (Gutenberg, the inventor of the printing press was, significantly, a goldsmith by trade).

Peripheral Europe—i.e., Britain, Scandinavia, the Iberian Peninsula, North Germany, and Poland had, in comparison, done very little. Yet with the scientific revolution the center of gravity of technics—and of science—began to move towards the north and the west, just as, five hundred years earlier, it had moved in the same direction when the Italians and South Germans took up the technics of Africa and Asia.

The century of revolution and of change was notable for many men of genius. We shall consider, briefly, two such men whose works proved to be complementary. One, Galileo, was a genius who built on the achievements of his predecessors. The other, Francis Bacon, contemplating the triumphs of the past and considering the negligible contributions that his fellow countrymen had made, drew up a program or plan for the conscious advancement of technics which, in detail, in insight, and in eloquence of exposition, had not been rivalled up to his day; nor, one may guess, has it been rivalled since.

Galileo's method of science need not be discussed in detail. It was based on a Platonic faith in a mathematical order in nature, on the practice of abstraction and intuition of the form of individual mathematical laws of nature, and also on the use of experimental test, under conditions as close to the ideal as possible. The rise of such a philosophy in a machine-conscious community is hardly surprising. But if it owed something to practical mechanics—as the opening words of Galileo's *Two New Sciences* indicate—it was in return able to make a fundamental contribution to the advancement of practical mechanics. For, following Galileo's work, an ancient but fundamental fallacy founded in common sense and experience was removed from mechanics. Experience shows that it always requires more effort to work a machine than merely to hold it in equilibrium. This had been generalized into a plausible law; that the force required for motion is always greater than the force required for equilibrium. But the application of Galileo's principles of abstraction and idealization shows that this is not so: the inequality arises not from some basic principle but from the fact that all machines are imperfect: they distort under load and they suffer from friction. A friction-free and otherwise perfect machine would ultimately be as easy to move as to hold in equilibrium.

This insight opened up a new vista for technics. A numerical measure of the efficiency of machines now became possible. The efficiency of a machine need not be expressed in normative terms—this machine is "better" than that one—but as a simple fraction. In the case of a machine which is perfect in both design and construction the fraction, which is the ratio of the output of work to the input of power—or "effect" to "effort"—is necessarily equal to unity. In any practicable and therefore imperfect machine the fraction must be less than one. But Galileo's work also leads us to express the effort of any motive agent in terms of a measurable unit of power since, if the agent is applied to the simple and perfect machines (levers,

pulleys, gears, etc.), its effect, or the work done, must always be numerically the same, for nothing is lost in the working of a perfect machine.

Entailed therefore by the axioms of the seventeenth-century science of mechanics were two basic and related concepts: that of the quantifiable efficiency of machines and that of power. The quest for perpetual motion was abandoned, for the logical implication of the concept of efficiency is that restoration, or recovery, of the initial situation is the utmost that can be expected even of an ideal engine. In 1704 Antoine Parent initiated a fruitful debate when he computed, using the newly invented calculus, the maximum efficiency of an "undershot" waterwheel of perfect construction but inherently incapable, he believed wrongly, of perfect operation. (The fact that the wheel rotates diminishes the impact of the water on its blades, while the water leaving the machine—the tailrace—must have some residual velocity. These, apparently unavoidable, defects must reduce the efficiency of the machine. Eighteenth-century engineers were to demonstrate how they could be eliminated.)

Francis Bacon's ideas were interesting mainly from the social and political points of view. He commended technical innovation in preference to military conquest as the humane way of augmenting national wealth; he identified the obstacles to the progress of science and he pointed out that the supremacy of Europe was due not so much to military or civic superiority, as to the possession of certain key inventions such as firearms, the printing press, and the mariner's compass.

Inventions, according to Bacon, fall into two more or less distinct categories; those which can be made only if the appropriate knowledge is available—we call these science-based inventions—and those which are substantially independent of scientific knowledge and which could, therefore, have been made at any time in the history of civilization; we may call the latter "empirical" inventions. The obvious importance of the former provides, in Bacon's view, strong additional grounds for encouraging the progress of science, of the acquisition of knowledge.

Bacon wrote before the "mechanical philosophy" (e.g., of Boyle and Newton) appeared in England. He was no mechanic and his advice, that if one wants to command nature one must first learn to obey her, suggests an attitude favorable for biological sciences and technics. Generally, however, since his day the mechanistic approach, exemplified by mechanical engineering, physics, and chemistry, has triumphed. Bacon serves to remind us that an alternative form of technics might, conceivably, have developed since the seventeenth century. But this is merely conjectural. What is undeniable is that if we combine Bacon's broad vision with the practical aspects of the new science of mechanics we see how the practice of technics was becoming self-conscious and at the same time increasingly science-based. In short, "technology"—the word was a neologism in the seventeenth century—was beginning to replace the more elementary "technics."

Up to the seventeenth century the English had been mere imitators of German, French, Italian, and Dutch inventions; they had been, indeed almost notoriously, incapable of making inventions of their own. Nevertheless a considerable body of native craftsmen had been built up and they began to show their quality when, in 1712, Thomas Newcomen invented the first successful "fire" engine. This was, in Bacon's sense, a science-based invention for its operation depended on harnessing the pressure of the atmosphere; a phenomenon which had been discovered by seventeenth-century scientists. Huygens and Papin, among others, had envisaged such a machine. Newcomen's achievement lay in devising it in thoroughly practicable form— steam in a cylinder, fitted with a piston, is condensed, leaving a void, so that the external atmospheric pressure can act on the piston—and in making the engine automatic or self-acting. His was not only a major invention in its own right but one of the greatest achievements in the history of technology, comparable with the weight-driven clock and the printing press.

The main use for Newcomen's engine was as a mine pumping engine and as such its progress in the first half of the eighteenth century was slow but assured. But in the second half it was associated with two remarkable events. The first was when the engineer John Smeaton (1724–92) applied to the design and operation of the engine a new technique which can be described as systematic evolutionary improvement. One component of the engine is systematically varied, all the rest being kept constant. The change in performance of the engine is then noted with each variation of the component. The variation which gives the best result is selected and the procedure is repeated for each component in turn. In this way Smeaton could obtain the best design and the conditions for the best performance of a machine of given size.

This systematic technique had obvious affinities with the experimental procedures of the time and, quite possibly, with those of Newton in particular. Equally, it was obviously a corollary of the Galilean theory of machines, for the possibility of optimizing the performance of an engine in such a way depends on prior recognition of the concept of quantifiable efficiency. Smeaton had, as it happened, already applied his technique to the improvement of the performance of waterwheels. But while this technique is important, indeed essential, in any society with an advanced technology, it cannot of itself lead to radical new departures; it can lead only to the progressive improvement of the machine as specified and that within the limits of the materials and auxiliary devices available.

The second notable event was the *revolutionary* invention by James Watt of a practicable form of steam engine. This followed painstaking fundamental research in the new science of heat; a science to which Watt's friend Joseph Black had contributed. Watt's engine worked, as did Newcomen's, by condensing steam to form a vacuum but condensation was now carried out in a separate cylinder, or "condenser," which could be kept cold all the time and did not have to be heated up once a cycle. This gave a great economy of heat and therefore of fuel; it also clarified the idea that a heat engine works by virtue of a flow of heat from a hot to a cold body, the cold body being no less essential than the hot body, or furnace. Further to reduce waste of heat, Watt used steam at atmospheric pressure rather than cold air to drive the piston in the hot or working cylinder. Finally, to obtain the best possible economy he proposed to operate the engine "expansively" allowing the pressure of driving steam to fall steadily as the piston travelled down the cylinder. In this way he sought to extract the last ounce of "duty," or as we should now say energy, from the hot steam.

If the industrial revolution may be said to have begun in one particular industry it was in that of textiles rather than in power or mining. In 1769 Richard Arkwright was awarded a patent for the roller spinning of cotton. Roller spinning was not a novel idea, but Arkwright was the first to achieve it in practice. To do this the design of his machine had to satisfy four critical requirements. It had to have more than one set of rollers, their relative speeds of rotation had to be correct, their distance apart had to be about the same as the average length of the fibers (much less and the fibers are broken, much more and the thread comes apart), and, lastly, the pressures between each pair of rollers had to be correct. There was wide scope for error and therefore failure. It is to the credit of Arkwright that he eventually succeeded and made the mechanical spinning of cotton, the key to the mechanization of the textile industries, possible.

Arkwright's spinning machine, or "water frame" stimulated the mechanization of the other textile processes. By the beginning of the nineteenth century every such process from the preliminary treatment of the raw fibers to the final weaving of the threads had been successfully mechanized and could be driven either by water or by steam power. And all the essential inventions, from the early fly shuttle to Richard Roberts' self-acting mule, were, in Bacon's sense, "empirical." Science was not involved at any stage: the details and operations of the machines could have been easily understood by a contemporary of Leonardo. There is no evidence that the pioneers of textile technology made scientific studies of fibers by using microscopes or any other scientific devices available at that time. Furthermore, few of them bothered to become Fellows of the Royal Society. The textile revolution was, in short, initially based on empirical inventions. So, too, was the new technology of industrial machine tools which developed in America and England in the first half of the nineteenth century, and which certainly owed something in its early days to the rapid progress of textile machinery.

The mechanization of the textile industries, and the successful harnessing of waterwheels and early steam engines to power such delicate processes as spinning and weaving, constituted one of the great triumphs of technology. It was the first instance of what is now exemplified in the wide range of mass production industries. As early as 1835 Andrew Ure, in the course of a paean of praise for the new textile factories, asserted that the essence of the system lay in dividing the production process into stages, each of which could then be dealt with by self-regulating automatic machinery. He underestimated the difficulties of taking this one stage further, but his insight was nonetheless remarkable for the time.

Science may not have been involved in the invention of textile machinery; but it played a vital role in the solution of the related problems of power. In England and in France throughout the eighteenth century increasing attention had been paid to the efficient generation and transformation of power. In England industrial revolution made this particularly urgent for the best river sites for water power were quickly taken; and, as mills prospered and expanded, even these were found to be inadequate. The demand for power was insatiable; the need for efficient generation was paramount.

Inevitably, the two major power technologies tended to converge. Techniques and devices used in steam engines were applied to water power and vice versa: designers of industrial waterwheels were often designers of steam engines also. For a long period the advantages of steam and water power were fairly evenly balanced. But the efficiency of the steam engine was steadily being increased and the appearance of the high pressure steam engine after 1800 widened the field of application to include land and sea transport and a great range of industrial purposes. Further, it became apparent in the first two decades of the century that the economy of high pressure steam engines could be increased considerably above that of low pressure en-

gines. What, indeed, were the limits of efficiency of the steam engine?

In 1824 a French engineer of genius, Sadi Carnot, propounded a remarkable synthesis of knowledge. It was known by then that radiant heat from the sun was responsible for the movements of the atmosphere and, ultimately, for the hydrologic cycle: it was also known that heat, or rather the flow of heat, caused many other natural phenomena. The steam, or heat engine works by virtue of the flow of heat from a hot body, or furnace, to a cold body, or condenser. By considering the principles of Watt's expansive engine and by treating the flow of heat as strictly analogous to the flow of water, Carnot was able to envisage an ideal heat engine: one which could, from a given flow of heat, yield enough power to restore, or recover the initial (thermal) situation. Carnot did not consider the actual conversion of heat into mechanical energy: he believed, with the majority of engineers and scientists of the time, that heat is always conserved. Although some of his assumptions were incorrect, the basis of his argument was sound and his realization—derived from an obvious hydraulic analogy—that the greater the "fall" of heat, or the temperature difference over which an engine works, the greater its efficiency, was correct. This was consistent with, if it did not explain, the superior efficiency of high pressure (or high temperature) steam engines and it led him to recognize the theoretical (and the ultimately practical) superiority of the hot air engine, a judgment which was vindicated by the invention of the Diesel engine at the end of the century. In fact the history of the steam engine and of heat engines generally, must be divided into two distinct periods, before and after Carnot.

The ideal Carnot engine may be considered, in abstract terms, as marking the end of the spectrum of all thermo-mechanical transformations in nature and in art. In this Galilean sense, it provided the basis for a new science—thermodynamics—which when it was reconciled with the correct, dynamical theory of heat proved to be as fundamental as Newtonian mechanics. Thermodynamics is concerned with the transformations of energy and the conditions under which they take place. After Carnot, notable contributions were made by Joule, Helmholtz, Thomson, Clausius, and Gibbs. But besides its applications to sciences such as physics, chemistry, and meteorology, thermodynamics has influenced the development of cosmological thought. Its implications in this respect were understood from the beginning, but the idea of a thermodynamically doomed universe is still plausible.

The intellectual and psychological origins of thermodynamics are to be found partly in the science of heat, but mainly in Carnot's deep understanding of 363 the mode of operation of the Watt-type expansive condensing engine, in the increasingly wide range of application of steam power in the early nineteenth century, and in the impressive amount of mechanical work that steam engines could perform. In fact the establishment of thermodynamics was the second occasion on which a major technological advance led to new departures in science and to a change in general thought. As the mechanical clock contributed to the formulation in the seventeenth century of the idea of a "clockwork" universe, so the refinement of the heat engine left its mark on the cosmology of the nineteenth century.

The middle of the nineteenth century was a period of intellectual synthesis, when electromagnetic field-theory, the principle of natural selection, the conservation of energy, and the laws of thermodynamics were all established. Since then social changes have hastened the proliferation of science if not necessarily its rate of progress. The recent increase in the numbers of scientists has been accompanied by the greatly increased application of science to the processes of innovation. It may even be said that a new mode of technological innovation has emerged. Applied science laboratories, copied originally from nineteenth-century German university laboratories, now study materials and processes relevant to the needs of industry and also serve as sources of scientific invention. The discovery of the technique of directed scientific research has brought developments in social organization whereby scientific manpower can be deployed to solve such massive problems as those of nuclear power and space travel. The Baconian dream has, in the course of eighty years or so, become reality. With all this there has occurred a subtle shift in conventional ideas: the notion of "open-ended" technology is now widely accepted. It would be considered foolish, today, to try to specify the limits, other than those imposed by logic, of the possible achievements of technology.

There is evidence to suggest that during the nineteenth century the absolute laws of Newtonian physics, the indestructible atoms of Daltonian chemistry, and the "iron" laws of classical economics together with a reasonably complete knowledge of the size, nature, and resources of the planet constituted, between them, barriers beyond which technological development could not proceed. The limits were known and any suggestion that technology might be capable of indefinite extension would have been rejected. This has now changed, due largely to the recent achievements of technology and, no less, to the dissolution of the old nineteenth-century certainties, social and economic as well as scientific.

The impressive innovations of the twentieth century —automobiles, air travel, communications technology, computers, control systems, and a multitude of consumer goods—have enormously improved the material conditions of life. In other respects their direct effects have not yet become clear although there is no doubt that they have had a cumulative if ambiguous influence on the commonly accepted idea of progress. Historians have usually related the rise of this idea to the substitution of social theories for religious beliefs and to the advance of pure science. Although it is clear that technology, too, has been concerned, this aspect has not been studied in any detail. The time is certainly ripe for such a study for in some quarters technology has, today, become suspect. It is said to have put immense destructive powers in the hands of irresponsible politicians; reckless technological developments often cause pollution of the environment; technology generally is accused of debasing the quality of life by imposing excessive specialization and an undue mechanization of the conditions of work. But the first two are as much the outcome of common human failings as a consequence of our inability to develop a system of technology more in accord with Bacon's organic precepts. The last is a product of social organization and not, directly, of technology. Indeed, there are grounds for believing that the inventive faculty and invention generally might be harmed by excessive specialization.

There are, as we have seen, a number of different modes of technological innovation. Before the seventeenth century inventions (empirical or scientific) were diffused by imitation and adaptation while improvement was established by the survival of the fittest. Now, technology has become a complex but consciously directed group of social activities involving a wide range of skills, exemplified by scientific research, managerial expertise, and practical and inventive abilities. The powers of technology appear to be unlimited. If some of the dangers may be great, the potential rewards are greater still. This is not simply a matter of material benefits for, as we have seen, major changes in thought have, in the past, occurred as consequences of technological advances.

*BIBLIOGRAPHY*

General Works. Eugene S. Ferguson, *Bibliography of the History of Technology* (Cambridge, Mass., 1968). Friedrich Klemm, *Technik: eine Geschichte ihrer Probleme* (Munich, 1954), trans. Mrs. D. W. Singer as *A History of Western Technology* (London and New York, 1959). Joseph Needham, *Science and Civilisation in China* (Cambridge, 1954– ). Charles Singer, E. J. Holmyard, A. R. Hall, and T. I.

Williams, *A History of Technology,* 5 vols. (Oxford and New York, 1954–58). A. P. Usher, *A History of Mechanical Inventions,* 2nd ed. (Cambridge, Mass., 1954; reprint 1959).

Works Relating Technology to Science and Other Social Activities. A. C. Crombie, *Augustine to Galileo: the History of Science.* A.D. *400–1650* (London, 1952); reprinted as *Medieval and Early Modern Science,* 2 vols. (London and New York, 1959). R. J. Forbes and E. J. Dijksterhuis, *A History of Science and Technology,* 2 vols. (London, 1963). Lewis Mumford, *Technics and Civilization* (New York, 1934; reprint 1963). Lynn White, Jr., *Medieval Technology and Social Change* (Oxford and New York, 1962).

Works Having Relevance for the History of Technology. J. B. Bury, *The Idea of Progress. An Inquiry into its Origin and Growth* (London, 1920; various reprints). A. R. Hall, *The Scientific Revolution,* 2nd ed. (London, 1962; reprint 1957). Robert Lenoble, "La pensée scientifique," in Maurice Daumas, ed., *Histoire de la science* (Paris, 1963). W. Warren Wagar, "Modern Views of the Origins of the Idea of Progress," *Journal of the History of Ideas,* **28** (1967), 55–70. A. N. Whitehead, *Science and the Modern World* (London and New York, 1925; reprint 1957).

Works Dealing with Individuals, Topics, or Periods. D. S. L. Cardwell, *Watt to Kelvin and Clausius. The Rise of Thermodynamics and the Early Industrial Age* (London, 1970). Sadi Carnot, *Réflexions sur la puissance motrice du feu* (Paris, 1824; facsimile ed. 1953), trans. R. H. Thurston, republished with introduction by E. Mendoza as *Reflections on the Motive Power of Fire* (reprint, 1960). Carlo Cipolla, *Clocks and Culture, 1300–1700* (London, 1967). See also the various papers by Derek J. de Solla Price and by Silvio A. Bedini in *Technology and Culture,* and elsewhere. John Diebold, *Automation: the Advent of the Automatic Factory* (New York, 1952). Galileo Galilei, *De motu* and *Le meccaniche,* trans. I. E. Drabkin and Stillman Drake as *On Motion and On Mechanics* (Madison, 1960), with useful introductions and notes by the translators; idem, *Discorsi . . . intorno a due Nuove Scienze* (1638), trans. H. Crew and A. de Salvio as *Dialogues . . . Concerning Two New Sciences* (New York, 1914; also reprint). Norman T. Gridgeman, article on Charles Babbage, *Dictionary of Scientific Biography* (New York, 1970–), I, 354–56. H. J. Habbakuk, *American and British Technology in the Nineteenth Century* (Cambridge, 1962). R. L. Hills, *Power in the Industrial Revolution* (Manchester, 1970). Thomas P. Hughes, ed., *Selections from the Lives of the Engineers . . . by Samuel Smiles* (Cambridge, Mass., 1966). John Jewkes, David Sawers, and Richard Stillerman, *The Sources of Invention* (London, 1958). A. G. Keller, *A Theatre of Machines* (London, 1964). Leonardo Olschki, *Geschichte der neusprechlichen wissenschaftlichen Literatur,* 3 vols. (Leipzig and Halle, 1919–27). L. T. C. Rolt, *A Short History of Machine Tools* (Cambridge, Mass., 1965). Andrew Ure, *The Philosophy of Manufactures* (London, 1835; reprint 1967). Edgar Zilzel, "Concept of Scientific Progress," *Journal of the History of Ideas,* **6** (1946), 325–49.

The main journals for the history of technology are: *Technology and Culture,* and *Transactions of the Newcomen Society.* Articles dealing with the impact of technology on culture frequently appear in such journals as *Archives Internationales d'Histoire des Sciences, Isis, Annals of Science,* and *Journal of the History of Ideas.*

D. S. L. CARDWELL

[See also Alchemy; **Baconianism; Newton on Method;** Progress; Work.]

# TEMPERANCE (*SŌPHROSYNĒ*) AND THE CANON OF THE CARDINAL VIRTUES

THE HISTORY of temperance is the history of sōphrosynē (σωφροσύνη). The cardinal virtue of moderation, self-knowledge, and self-restraint—*sōphrosynē* in Greek—took the Latin name *temperantia* in Cicero's rhetorical and philosophical works, which set the style for later usage in the West. Sōphrosynē derives from the adjective *sōphrōn* (*saophrōn* in Homer): "of sound mind"—used at first to describe a person (either human or divine) who behaves in a way consistent with his nature or station (like Apollo in *Iliad* 21. 462–64, when he refuses to fight with another god on behalf of "wretched mortals") or who shows good sense, as opposed to frivolity or even witlessness (*Odyssey* 23. 11–13, 30). The words *saophrosynē* and *saophrōn* are rare in Homer, but later Greeks read the concept back into many situations in epic poetry that seemed to typify the classical idea of the virtue. Hence certain Homeric characters became exemplars of sōphrosynē in its several aspects, masculine and feminine: Odysseus for his endurance and especially for his triumph over Circe, Nestor for having the wisdom of old age, Penelope and Andromache for being good wives.

It was in the archaic age that sōphrosynē first became a "cardinal" virtue in the true sense, a quality on which hinged personal or political well-being and success. It had not been essential to the *aretē* ("excellence") of the hero in the age idealized by Homer, whose primary needs were for courage and skill in battle, but in the seventh and sixth centuries B.C. changed conditions in the Greek world led to the rise of the *polis* ("city-state") and with the polis came new values essential for its welfare. To adapt the words of M. I. Finley, Jr. (p. 129), it was necessary to tame the hero in order that the community might grow, and one of the forces that tamed the hero—and made him a citizen—was sōphrosynē.

The Delphic code with its cautionary maxims, "Know thyself," "Nothing in excess," "Think mortal thoughts," expressed the chief implications of sōphros-

# TEMPERANCE (SŌPHROSYNĒ)

yně in the archaic age. Apollo, the "far-darter," the god of remoteness and limitation, who punished hybris and defended the frontier that separates man from the gods, was the divine teacher of archaic sōphrosynē, and the Seven Wise Men—including Pittacus, Solon, Chilon, Thales, and the rest—applied Apolline morality to the problems of the polis. Elegiac and lyric poetry in the sixth and fifth centuries reveal what sōphrosynē now meant for the individual and society. Theognis of Megara, writing in the middle of the sixth century, is the first to oppose sōphrosynē to hybris in political life. His view is that of the conservative oligarchy; the sōphrosynē he admires is essentially the kind of repressive discipline later identified with Sparta. He also accepts the older, Homeric sōphrosynē—soundness of mind, good sense—and like contemporary poets extends still further the meaning of the word, which now begins to imply sobriety, both actual and metaphorical, sanity, the conduct proper to a good wife, and in general the avoidance of immoderate or irrational behavior.

Theognis (sixth century B.C.) is an innovator in two ways especially important for the later treatment of sōphrosynē in literature and art: he is the first to personify the virtue and the first to cite an exemplar. The exemplar is the mythical Cretan king, Rhadamanthys, mentioned in a context that suggests intellectual, rather than moral, implications for sōphrosynē (*Theognidea*, lines 699–718). The personification occurs in a passage modelled on Hesiod's famous description of how the Iron Age will come to an end, with the departure from the earth of *Aidōs* (Modesty) and *Nemesis* (*Works and Days*, lines 190–200). Theognis substitutes Sōphrosynē for Aidōs and lists her companions as *Pistis* (Good Faith) and the Graces (lines 1135–42). Sōphrosynē is here considered a social virtue, and it is notable both that she is the archaic successor to the epic Aidōs and that she is linked with other values that elsewhere form part of the aristocratic, Dorian ethos.

The archaic age made a further contribution to the history of sōphrosynē by popularizing themes, myths, and gnomic sayings related to hybris and its consequences, a subject destined in tragedy to provide the principal context for the development of the classical concept of sōphrosynē. Lyric poetry, especially the choral odes of Pindar, abounds in reflections on man's fatal tendency to indulge in excessive hopes and ambitions, to refuse to limit his thoughts to what befits his mortal nature, to aspire, in the clichés of archaic lyric, to "marry the daughter of Zeus" or "climb the brazen heavens." Ixion and Bellerophon become types of this kind of hybris; their fall is interpreted as a lesson to "think mortal thoughts"—the primary text of archaic sōphrosynē. It was a lyric poet, Pindar, who made the

first recorded reference to what later came to be called the "cardinal" virtues. In his eighth Isthmian Ode, Peleus and the other Aeacids are cited as models of justice, courage, sōphrosynē, wisdom, and piety (a fifth virtue often included in the canon). The implications here are primarily political, since the Aeacids stand for the people of Aegina, who, only two years before the composition of the Ode in 478 B.C., had shared with Athens the glory of defeating the Persians at Salamis.

The choral odes of Attic tragedy employ both the mythical and the gnomic themes of earlier lyric poetry to comment on the situation of the tragic hero, who is often conspicuously deficient in sōphrosynē (self-knowledge, self-restraint, moderation). Attic tragedy, in fact, reflects the first great flowering of sōphrosynē. There is clearly an intimate connection between the conditions in Athens that gave rise to tragedy in the late sixth century B.C. and those that caused sōphrosynē to be recognized at just this time as one of the essential values for the polis. Attic epitaphs now begin to describe the excellence of the dead in terms of aretē and sōphrosynē, testifying to the emergence of a new civic ideal which combines the heroism of the soldier in time of war with the sobriety and moderation of the patriotic citizen in time of peace. It has often been observed that tragedy owes much to the historical conflict resulting from the encounter of the heroic individual with the restrictions necessary for the survival and prosperity of the polis. The expression of these restrictions, both social and religious, was sōphrosynē, which inhibited its possessor from overstepping boundaries set by the gods or his fellow citizens.

A principal theme of Greek tragedy is the catastrophe that befalls the hero whose self-assertion leads him to ignore such limits. The situation is clearest in Aeschylean tragedy, which consistently links sōphrosynē with a set of desirable qualities (justice, piety, freedom, masculinity) and opposes it to arrogance, unrestrained emotionalism, immoderate behavior, and other forms of hybris. It is in Aeschylus, moreover, that we first begin to see sōphrosynē as an Athenian *aretē politikē*, different in important ways from the Dorian brand. From the final scene of the trilogy of the *Oresteia* we learn that sōphrosynē constitutes a mean between tyranny and anarchy, and that it is to be for the Athenians one of the cornerstones of their democratic constitution. The timing of the *Oresteia* in the year 458 B.C., so soon after the great extension of Attic democracy by Ephialtes, makes this trilogy a significant comment on political affairs in a period when other sources are rare. Athenian political history in the next hundred years reflects the ebb and flow of her citizens' fidelity to the gift bestowed on them at the end of the trial scene in the *Eumenides,* when the Furies, transformed into goddesses of bliss and blessing, utter their majestic benediction and visualize the Athenians "seated beside Zeus, beloved by Athena, *sōphronountes en chronōi*—learning temperance as time goes on" (line 1000).

If the Aeschylean conception of sōphrosynē can be glossed by the Apolline "Nothing in excess" and "Think mortal thoughts," the Sophoclean virtue is closer to "Know thyself." The failure in sōphrosynē that marks such heroes as Ajax, Antigone, Oedipus, Electra, and Deianeira is a failure in self-knowledge, amounting sometimes to delusion, sometimes almost to madness. The hero is blind to something essential in himself or his situation, and tragedy arises from the interplay between his circumstances and his admirable but imperfect nature. Secondary characters and Choruses typically urge a kind of sōphrosynē already recommended by Oceanus in *Prometheus Bound*—a cautionary, self-protective quality, equivalent in conduct to obedience. Rightly regarding such sōphrosynē as incompatible with the heroic ideal for which he will sacrifice everything, including life itself, the Sophoclean hero rejects it as ignoble, and it remains for the poet to show, through a variety of dramatic devices, what sōphrosynē really is: the self-knowledge that enables man to face reality, renounce delusion, and understand his part in the cosmic pattern. The speech in which Ajax interprets the procession of the seasons and the alternation of night and day as examples of the limits imposed on all elements in the universe (*Ajax,* lines 646–77) is a striking forerunner of the "cosmic justification" for the practice of sōphrosynē that Plato was to express a century later in the *Gorgias* (506D–508C). It is also typical of the Sophoclean irony by which the poet reveals to us a fundamental aspect of his tragic view through the words of a hero who is tragic precisely because he is unable to accept that view. Ajax's hostility to sōphrosynē represents an extreme version of the polarity (seen throughout Greek history) between sōphrosynē and the heroic principle. But it also reflects the sharp and specific questioning of traditional values that marked the sophistic revolution in education and permeated Greek thought during the last third of the fifth century.

The plays of Euripides reflect still more directly this crisis in Athenian culture. They reveal far less of a conscious hostility to sōphrosynē on the part of the tragic hero, but a much greater sense of helplessness to achieve so rational an excellence. They incidentally display a tremendous increase in the scope of the word sōphrosynē as it was popularly understood, and a keen interest in the contrast between various implications of the word. Euripides consistently relates it to the conflict between the rational and the irrational that forms the core of his tragedy. For him its basic meaning is "self-restraint," and only now does it regularly have such connotations as chastity, sobriety, continence, in preference to the older implications—good sense, soundness of mind, sanity—although these are by no means forgotten. It is characteristic of Euripides to play off one meaning against another—chastity against moderation, sobriety against wisdom—and thus to show the danger of a one-sided virtue. The *Hippolytus* and the *Bacchae,* each of which presents a hero who is at once sōphrōn and hybristic, fanatically virtuous and yet blind to the wholeness of life, reflect an advanced stage of the criticism of conventional values that had been initiated by the pre-Socratic philosophers, carried further by the Sophists, and intensified by the abnormal conditions resulting from the war with Sparta.

Other themes to which Euripides frequently recurs are the question of how sōphrosynē and other virtues originate, whether in nature or training—an important aspect of the current debate over the priority of *physis* ("nature") or *nomos* ("convention"); the possibility of a *sōphrōn erōs,* love guided by reason and thus less destructive than the immoderate passions of Medea and Phaedra (a topic taken up in the next generation by Plato); the claim of Athens to a mythical past in which her kings and people had excelled in sōphrosynē (manifested in the compassionate treatment of enemies and suppliants); and the efficacy of sōphrosynē as a curb on anger and cruelty, always, in Greek tragedy, more dangerous passions than sexual excess.

In his manipulation of the last two of these themes Euripides has much in common with Thucydides, whose *History of the Peloponnesian War* depicts the disastrous victory of the irrational over the rational in public life and often shows the tragic consequences of savagery and hatred. The most significant contribution of Thucydides to the history of sōphrosynē lies in his analysis of its political implications. In the contrast between Athens and Sparta that is the primary theme of the *History* he consistently treats sōphrosynē as a Spartan quality, emphasizing its relation to the Spartan characteristics of conservatism, discipline, slowness to act, and isolationism in foreign policy. It commonly denotes moderation or stability in government. In spite of his admiration for Pericles' own moderation and astute balance of political values, Thucydides rarely describes Athenian policy as sōphrōn; he reserves the word for the Dorian ethos to such an extent that sōphrosynē sometimes amounts to a slogan for the oligarchic factions and the Spartan sympathizers in the Greek cities. This situation is accepted by other writers of the late fifth century, especially

# TEMPERANCE (SŌPHROSYNĒ)

the poets of Old Comedy and the Attic orators, for whom the closest equivalents to sōphrosynē are terms like *apragmosynē* ("minding one's own business") and *hēsychia* ("quietness"), both of which had been part of the aristocratic and Dorian set of values from the age of lyric and elegiac poetry.

In the fourth century the situation abruptly changes. Now the Attic orators regularly claim sōphrosynē as a specifically Athenian virtue and a democratic one at that. The disillusionment with pro-Spartan and oligarchic politics that resulted from the Tyranny of the Thirty in 404 B.C. was the immediate cause of the change, and the *sōphrōn politēs* ("citizen") depicted by the fourth-century orators, is invariably a fervent democrat, a foe of both oligarchy and Sparta, a citizen who benefits the state by his inoffensive, law-abiding conduct and his generosity in the performance of "liturgies"—outfitting warships, subsidizing religious processions, and the like. There is even a commonplace, used by both Lysias and Isaeus, according to which the most valuable liturgy is to be a *kosmios* ("orderly") and sōphrōn citizen.

The political aspects of sōphrosynē are much discussed by the fourth-century philosophers also. Plato, in fact, makes sōphrosynē so central to his conception of the ideal state and the soul in optimum condition that at times—especially in his late dialogues—it becomes for him the most important of the cardinal virtues.

Socrates dominates the first stage in the development of Plato's concept of sōphrosynē. To judge by the picture that emerges from the dialogues of his admirers (not only Plato, but Xenophon, Antisthenes, and Aeschines of Sphettus), his own sōphrosynē was marked by a rigorous self-knowledge and a kind of asceticism often described in such terms as *enkrateia* ("self-control"), *autarkeia* ("independence"), and *euteleia* ("frugality")—all words that are linked with sōphrosynē in later Cynic writings. Plato's early dialogues are permeated by the Socratic conception of virtue as knowledge, and by Socrates himself as the exemplar of sōphrosynē (dramatized in the *Charmides*). A somewhat later stage finds Plato refining and deepening the popular definition of sōphrosynē as the restraint of appetite. His own distinctive contribution is the theory that all virtue depends on the orderly arrangement of faculties within the soul, a condition achieved by the practice of sōphrosynē. This view is first advanced in the *Gorgias* and is developed in great detail in the *Republic*.

Few of Plato's achievements in the *Republic* have more enduring significance for the history of ideas than his establishment, in Book IV, of the four cardinal virtues as an exclusive canon, consisting of wisdom (*phronēsis* or *sophia*), justice (*dikaiosynē*), courage (*andreia*), and temperance (*sōphrosynē*). Hitherto a shifting group, unstable in number and content, they owed their origin as a vaguely defined canon to the needs of the developing polis; hence they first appear in literature in the time of Pindar and Aeschylus, both of whom recognize piety (*eusebeia*) as a member of the group. What Plato did in *Republic* IV was to exclude piety and establish the other four as the excellences proper to the soul and the state, when each is in its ideal condition. Sōphrosynē is at first (389D–E) defined as obedience, and control of the appetites for food, drink, and sexual indulgence, a definition explicitly described as a popular one. Hence it is the aretē proper to the third class in society (the farmers, craftsmen, and tradesmen) and to the corresponding part of the soul, the appetitive faculty. But sōphrosynē as Plato further defines it is also a kind of harmony in the soul and the state, "sounding the same note in perfect unison throughout the whole" (432A), and as such it is necessary to each class and each faculty. It is the virtue that enables all classes and all parts to agree on the rule of the naturally superior—the philosophers in the state, the rational faculty in the soul (442C–D). Sōphrosynē produces a polis that is just and peaceful and a soul that is balanced and harmonious.

So great is Plato's temperamental affinity for sōphrosynē that he tends to expand its functions and make it virtually synonymous with justice in some contexts, with wisdom in others. He is concerned always to reconcile it with courage, and in the *Statesman* and the *Laws*, as well as the *Republic*, he devises modes of education that will prevent the soul and the state from being damaged by the conflicting demands of the two polar tendencies.

The importance of sōphrosynē increases in Plato's later dialogues, keeping pace with his increasing interest in movement and change, of which the irrational—the appetites and passions—forms one aspect. The study of physics and cosmology gave new support to the view expressed as early as the *Gorgias* (503–08) that identical principles produce excellence in every context, so that *cosmos* in the universe, justice in the state, health in the body, and sōphrosynē in the soul are completely analogous, all of them manifestations of order and harmony. No passage concerned with sōphrosynē in the *Laws* proved more influential than the statement that "likeness to God" (*homoiōsis theōi*) depends on this virtue (716C–D). Later philosophers and Church Fathers, who were keenly interested both in the imitation of God and the question whether moral virtue is proper to the Divine nature, quoted and commented on this passage more than on any other dealing with sōphrosynē, except for the great myth of

368

the *Phaedrus*. The image of the charioteer controlling the two horses and using their motive power to rise through the heavens to the realm of the Forms became a symbol of sōphrosynē for patristic writers, who sometimes conflated the Platonic myth with biblical allusions, often to Ezekiel (Ambrose, *De Virginitate* I. 17–18).

In contrast to the expansive tendencies of Plato, who makes all the virtues ultimately identical with one another, Aristotle tends to define each one as precisely as possible, severely limiting their scope and also distinguishing moral from intellectual aretē. He finds the Platonic tetrad, newly defined according to his own standards, insufficient to do justice to the entire range of human conduct, and in both the *Nicomachean Ethics* and the *Rhetoric* adds several other moral virtues to the canon of the *Republic*. His most enduring contribution to ethical doctrine is the theory of the Mean, according to which each moral virtue is a *mesotēs*, a mean state (relative to the person concerned), located between the two extremes of excess and defect. This theory is an outgrowth of the traditional Greek feeling for moderation which had already given rise to the Delphic maxims, the pre-Socratic search for balance and proportion in the physical universe, the myths of hybris in lyric and tragic poetry, and Plato's efforts in the *Philebus* to apply an absolute *metron* ("measure") to moral decisions. It is, in fact, a manifestation of sōphrosynē, which thus becomes the true basis of Aristotle's moral doctrine. When used to arrive at a definition of sōphrosynē itself, however, the theory of the Mean produces a virtue much more limited than that which in Plato's later dialogues had sometimes threatened to swallow the entire canon. It is very close to Plato's first definition of sōphrosynē in the *Republic*: for Aristotle sōphrosynē is a mesotēs concerned with three kinds of bodily pleasure: eating, drinking, and sexual intercourse (1118a 23–26). The vice of excess is undue indulgence in these appetites (*akolasia*, "wantonness"), while the vice of defect is insufficient enjoyment (*anaisthēsia*, "lack of feeling"), a vice that Aristotle admits is rarely encountered. Such a sōphrosynē is stripped of the intellectual, political, and aesthetic nuances that had clustered around it in earlier Greek thought.

In the *Rhetoric* and *Politics*, however, Aristotle admits more traditional definitions (modesty, obedience, opposition to hybris). His discussion of sōphrosynē in the *Rhetoric* is of special interest because it was through Peripatetic and Stoic rhetoric that knowledge of the cardinal virtues was transmitted to most educated Romans, and thence to the Middle Ages and the Renaissance. Aristotle's is the first extant consideration of the role of sōphrosynē in rhetoric; he studies it in connection with epideictic oratory and ethical persuasion, defining it, with an eye to its social significance, as the virtue that disposes men in regard to the pleasures of the body as the law commands (1366b 13–15). In his celebrated discussion of age-groups and character-types he assigns sōphrosynē to men in their prime, who alone combine courage with temperance (1390b 3–4).

The Hellenistic philosophical schools afford several different views of sōphrosynē. The Epicureans accept the popular definition (restraint of appetite), and concede that sōphrosynē is necessary for a life of tranquillity, but virtue is to them only the means; pleasure is the goal. The Cynics fear pleasure and exalt a kind of sōphrosynē verging on asceticism. They relate it to frugality (euteleia), and independence (autarkeia), and divorce it entirely from the theoretical life. The antithesis to sōphrosynē in Cynic thought is neither hybris nor *akolasia*, but extravagance (*tryphē*). The Cynic diatribe, often called a *sōphronizōn logos* ("a sobering discourse"), influenced a wide variety of literary types, the Stoic moral treatise, Roman satire, the oratory of the Second Sophistic, and the homilies of certain Church Fathers, to all of which it imparted a strong flavor of Cynic sōphrosynē. Hence the wide diffusion in Greco-Roman literature of the ascetic concept of the virtue, which Antipater summed up in his epitaph for Diogenes, when he described the famous wallet, cloak, and staff of the Cynic prototype as the weapons of *autarkēs sōphrosynē* (*Palatine Anthology*, Book 7.65).

For sōphrosynē, however, by far the most important of the Hellenistic schools was the Stoic, which revived the Platonic canon (henceforth more often called Stoic) and made it the center of its moral teaching. Rejecting Aristotle's distinction between moral and intellectual virtue, the Old Stoa regarded all virtues as manifestations of phronēsis in different situations. Thus sōphrosynē was defined as phronēsis in matters of choice and avoidance (*Stoicorum veterum fragmenta*, 1. 201); the opposing vice, however, was still the Aristotelian akolasia. The traditional connection of sōphrosynē with self-restraint was not forgotten; Ariston of Chios assigned to it the power to regulate the appetites (ibid., 1. 375), and Chrysippus, with his doctrine that sōphrosynē renders the impulses steady (ibid., 3. 280), provided a bridge to the great innovator of the Middle Stoa, Panaetius, who emphasized the role of the impulses in moral conduct. Panaetius, conflating some doctrines of Plato and Aristotle with those of Zeno, moderated the rigors of the Old Stoa and made it more acceptable to the Roman ruling class. He considered sōphrosynē a practical, not a theoretical, virtue, and he taught that all forms of virtue have their origin in the appetites and impulses natural to man. Sōphrosynē arises from the human instinct for order, propriety, and moderation (Cicero, *De officiis* 1. 4. 11–14); since this (unlike the impulses which give rise to courage and justice) is an impulse peculiar to man, not shared by animals, Panaetius sets it high on the scale of virtue, and he associates with it the principle of *decorum* (*to prepon*), which is essential for every form of excellence. There is a strong aesthetic element in Panaetius' view of sōphrosynē, related to his belief that this virtue assures the development of a harmonious and attractive personality. Cicero's tendency to link sōphrosynē with *humanitas* owes much to Panaetius.

Rome's earliest contacts with Greek literature probably occurred in the theater, where before the end of the second century B.C. translations and adaptations of tragedy and comedy must have introduced many Romans to the concept of sōphrosynē. A little later came the systematic study of rhetoric and philosophy, in both of which the canon of Platonic-Stoic virtues held a prominent place. Sōphrosynē, the most Hellenic of these virtues, was the hardest to transplant, but in some of its nuances it bore a sufficient resemblance to certain traditional Roman values—*pudicitia* ("chastity"), *modestia* ("moderation"), *frugalitas*, and *verecundia* ("modesty")—to encourage the Romans to naturalize it and even claim it as their own, by ascribing it to some of the heroes and heroines of the early Republic—the Elder Cato, Piso Frugi, Scipio Africanus Major, Lucretia, and Verginia in particular. Cicero, as part of his attempt to give Rome a philosophical vocabulary, suggested several Latin renderings for sōphrosynē—*temperantia*, *moderatio*, *modestia*, and *frugalitas* (*Tusculan Disputations* 3.8)—of which *temperantia* became the most popular, although by no means the only accepted equivalent.

It was Cicero who made the first systematic efforts to naturalize sōphrosynē. His contribution took two forms: the translation or adaptation of rhetorical and philosophical treatises in which sōphrosynē was defined and discussed with reference to various modes of persuasion or the ethics of the individual and the state, and the use in his own oratory of the topic of the virtues and vices. His succinct exposition of the rhetorical function of the Stoic virtues in *De inventione* constituted a principal source for medieval definitions of the canon; adaptations and commentaries on this brief text (and on the corresponding passage in the nearly contemporaneous *Rhetorica ad Herennium*) had enormous impact on the Latin West. The most influential of his philosophical expositions of the virtues was *De officiis* (based on Panaetius' interpretation of the canon), which became, in the Renaissance particularly, a favorite source of advice, the model for vernacular handbooks on morality and conduct. Almost all

Cicero's speeches employ *laudatio* and *vituperatio*, in which, among the four virtues, temperantia (with its antitheses) receives by far the greatest attention, not only because accusations of *luxuria* and *avaritia* had long proved most effective in arousing *indignatio* and *odium*, but also because Cicero sincerely believed that these were the vices most typical of Rome and most dangerous to the welfare of the Republic. In his highly successful manipulation of the topic of the virtues and vices Cicero goes far beyond his own technical precepts in *De inventione* and *De oratore* and even outstrips Aeschines, the Attic orator most adroit in the use of this *topos*. His praise of Pompey's temperantia, of the pudicitia of Caelius, and the *clementia* of Caesar was imitated by generations of orators and historians, while his great sequences of denunciatory speeches, the *Verrines*, the *Catilinarians*, and the *Philippics*, all of which relate temperance to the problems of the Republic, provided a model for Sallust, Livy, and Tacitus. In spite of enormous differences in style and historical method—in spite, even, of Sallust's and Tacitus' reaction against Ciceronian precedents, all three of the great Roman historians focus attention on the *vitia principum* as the source of decay in the state and recommend temperantia, moderatio, or some other aspect of sōphrosynē as a cure for the nation's ills.

Under the Empire, the virtues of the *Princeps* are naturally the subject of anxious concern, beginning with the presentation to Augustus of the shield in honor of his *virtus*, *clementia*, *iustitia*, and *pietas*. From this time on, clementia, a virtue subordinate to sōphrosynē in the Stoic system, becomes one of its two most significant aspects in Roman political life; the other is pudicitia, which is ascribed to a number of Emperors both in literary eulogies and on the imperial coinage.

The ethical commonplaces of late antiquity, transmitted with little variation in all the philosophical schools, gain fresh vitality with the coming of Christianity. At first a well-founded distrust of anything closely identified with paganism caused Christian apologists to ignore the Stoic canon, although each of the virtues separately found support in the early Church and all were transformed by the concept of Divine Grace as the source of virtue. Sōphrosynē won an especially enthusiastic welcome, being identified with those qualities of purity, chastity, sobriety, and self-denial that the Christians regarded as peculiarly their own. There was even a danger that an exaggerated regard for chastity as the essence of sōphrosynē might distort the classical virtue beyond recognition. With the triumph of Christianity, Clement, Origen, and the Cappadocians among the Greek Fathers, Lactantius, Ambrose, and Augustine among the Latin, began freely to adapt the doctrines of pagan philosophy to Christian theology and morals. Not only did they use the topic of the virtues, borrowed from pagan rhetoric, to embellish their own homilies and funeral orations, adding to the classical sōphrosynē a new emphasis on *hagneia* ("holiness") and *katharotēs* ("purity"), but they developed and refined such Platonic and Neo-Platonic teachings as the need to practice sōphrosynē in order to achieve likeness to God, and they emphasized the fundamental importance of this virtue for the ascetic life (now seen as the Christian continuation of the theoretical life extolled in Greek philosophy), and its crucial role in the conversion from evil to good. Patristic innovations included the identification of biblical figures (Joseph, Susanna, Judith) as types of sōphrosynē; the interpretation of many scriptural texts (Matthew 5:28 and 19:12, Luke 12:35–38, the Sixth and Tenth Commandments, several of the Beatitudes) as injunctions to the practice of this virtue; the derivation of all virtues from love (rather than wisdom); and the recognition of the example of Christ and His Blessed Mother as the supreme justification for the practice of temperance.

In late antiquity and the Middle Ages the most interesting additions to the classical doctrine of temperance were those that related it to the monastic life (where, because of its identification with chastity, one of the three great monastic vows, it enjoyed great prestige) and those that integrated it into the complex systems of virtues and vices that proliferated from the time of Evagrius Ponticus in the East and John Cassian in the West. The writings of Cicero, especially his rhetorical works and the commentaries they inspired, the encyclopedic works of Martianus Capella and Isidore of Seville, the *Moralia* of Gregory the Great, Macrobius' commentary on Cicero's *Somnium Scipionis*, and Martin of Braga's *Formula vitae honestae*, derived from Seneca's lost *De officiis*, were the chief transmitters of classical doctrine about the virtues. In the Carolingian Age Alcuin's *On Rhetoric and the Virtues* and similar works of the "advice to princes" type revived the political significance of the cardinal virtues. At this point they sprang to life in art.

### THE ICONOGRAPHY OF THE CARDINAL VIRTUES

Each of the cardinal virtues had an independent life in art, separate from the other three. In antiquity, justice and wisdom were most often represented, especially in Greco-Roman coinage. In the early Middle Ages and at the beginning of the Renaissance certain aspects of temperance were prominent in popular iconographic cycles: *Pudicitia* and *Sobrietas* among the victorious virtues in the *Psychomachia* of Prudentius (A.D. 410), and Chastity (*Pudicizia*) among the Trionfi

of Petrarch, which began to adorn Italian coffers (*cassoni*) around the middle of the fifteenth century. Temperance, chastity, and sobriety were among the so-called "Gift-virtues," derived from the Gifts of the Holy Spirit in Isaiah 11:2; these have a long history in art. The following discussion, however, will confine itself for the most part to instances in which the cardinal virtues appear as a group, with only occasional references to separate representations of temperance.

Late antiquity may now and then have seen the Stoic tetrad portrayed together, but no example has survived, and properly speaking the iconography of the cardinal virtues begins in the Carolingian period. A poem by Theodulf of Orleans purports to describe a plaque in the Palace at Aachen, which showed a tree rooted in a globe and bearing on its branches personifications of the cardinal virtues and the liberal arts. The virtues are identified by an elaborate set of attributes, *Prudentia* by a book, *Vis (Fortitudo)* by a dagger, a shield, and a helmet, *Iustitia* by a sword, a palm-branch, a set of balances, and a crown, and *Moderatio (Temperantia)* by a bridle and a scourge (Dümmler I, 46). The virtues as they actually appear in miniatures of the ninth century are more modestly equipped. They usually adorn the title pages of Gospel-books or other liturgical texts, and they are normally placed in the four corners of the page, enclosed in medallions, while the center is occupied by the Frankish king or the biblical David, the model for Carolingian rulers. In the earliest extant example, the Vivian Bible (843–51), all four virtues are half-figures (two male, two female), holding palm branches and stretching out their hands towards the central figure, King David. In other manuscripts of the ninth century Prudentia invariably holds a book, Fortitudo arms and armor, Iustitia a set of scales, and Temperantia a torch and jug (Figure 1). They are never accompanied by accessory virtues or opposing vices. Their portrayal is static, entirely lacking in the drama of the *psychomachia*, the combat between virtues and vices popularized since the fifth century by the manuscripts of Prudentius.

In the eleventh and twelfth centuries several innovations occur. The virtues are illustrated in important devotional treatises and theological tracts, as well as deluxe Gospel-books, sacramentaries, lectionaries, and the like. They also appear on an infinite variety of small objects, usually religious in nature: portable altars, shrines, reliquaries, tabernacles, book-covers, candlesticks, and fonts (Katzenellenbogen, 1964). New symbolic objects and animals are now added to the repertory of the artist in France, Germany, and the Low Countries. Prudence may have a serpent or a dove; Fortitude may tear apart the jaws of a lion; Justice may hold a sword, a plumbline, or a set square; and

371

# TEMPERANCE (SŌPHROSYNĒ)

FIGURE 1. Cardinal virtue page from Marmoutier Sacramentary, S19, folio 173v, executed at Tours, ca. 850. AUTUN, BIBLIOTHÈQUE MUNICIPALE

Temperance may have a spray of flowers, a sheathed sword, or (most often) two vessels, with which she mixes water and wine, a visual reminder of the root-meaning of *temperare*. In Mosan art she is sometimes identified by a bridle (Tervarent, 1964), but in spite of Theodulf's poem, this is the rarest of her attributes, until it is revived by Giotto early in the fourteenth century and popularized by Raphael in the sixteenth.

Literary sources are responsible for much of the interest in the virtues and many of the ways in which they are depicted. The theory of the macrocosm and the microcosm, set forth in Radulphus Glaber's *Historia sui temporis* (1059) inspired the equation of many tetrads—the cardinal virtues, the Rivers of Paradise, the Evangelists, the Latin Fathers, the Seasons. Mystical interpretations of the number four go back at least

to the Neo-Pythagoreans, and Philo Judaeus, imitated by Ambrose and Augustine, had long ago identified the Rivers of Paradise with the Stoic virtues. In the twelfth century and thereafter parallel groups of seven attracted attention, under the influence of such works as Hugh of St. Victor's *De quinque septenis*, Pseudo-Vincent of Beauvais's *Speculum morale*, and the *Summa* of Saint Thomas. Now the three Pauline virtues (faith, hope, and charity) are added to the Platonic quartet, and the resulting seven virtues are linked with other sevens: vices or deadly sins, Sacraments, Gifts of the Holy Spirit, the derived "Gift-virtues," and the seven petitions of the Lord's Prayer. The most effective way of illustrating the relation among the virtues was the Tree, the *arbor bona* rooted in humility and bearing among its branches the seven virtues. This device, which goes back at least to Saint Augustine, was popularized by the treatise *De fructu spiritus et carnis* ascribed to Hugh of Saint Victor and by illustrations to such widely-read works as the *Speculum virginum* usually attributed to Conrad of Hirzau, Lambert's *Liber floridus*, and Herrad of Landsberg's *Hortus deliciarum*. Miniatures in French manuscripts of the thirteenth and fourteenth centuries, especially Books of Hours, develop the iconography of the cardinal virtues, sometimes alone, sometimes in relation to the other sevens.

The most influential such book was *Somme le Roi*, compiled in 1279 for King Philip of France, and illustrated by a comprehensive set of pictures reproduced in many manuscripts. One page, in a manuscript of 1295, devoted to the cardinal virtues, shows two of them in action: Prudentia teaching three pupils, Temperantia advising a woman at table to refuse a proffered goblet, and two in heraldic fashion: Fortitudo holding a disk with a symbolic bird, and Iustitia with a sword and scales (Figure 2). A century later the derivative Belleville Breviary combines seven virtues, seven Sacraments, and seven vices in an intricate iconographical scheme which sets side by side the cardinal virtues as portrayed in the *Somme le Roi* manuscripts and the "Gift-virtues" in the same source. Thus the illustration devoted to the Sacrament of Marriage includes the scene of Temperance at table from the cardinal virtue page, and also a picture of Judith decapitating Holofernes, which in *Somme le Roi* had exemplified the vice of lechery and drunkenness, opposed to the "Gift-virtue" of Chastity (Godwin, 1951). Chastity herself was portrayed in *Somme le Roi* as a woman standing on a pig and holding a disk inscribed with a dove.

The tradition of the *Psychomachia* had little effect on the iconography of the cardinal virtues until the thirteenth century, when they began to be portrayed, not in combat with the vices, but in triumph over them.

The vices may be represented by personifications trodden underfoot, symbolic animals ridden by the virtues, historical exemplars seated at the feet of the virtues, or genre-scenes suggesting the vices in action. A series of thirteenth-century reliefs on the portals of Gothic cathedrals (Paris, Chartres, Amiens, Reims) shows twelve virtues as seated, feminine figures, each identified by the symbolic animal, bird, or plant on the disk she holds; underneath, a genre-scene suggests the opposing vice (Katzenellenbogen, 1964). The twelve virtues include two of the cardinal tetrad (Prudence and Fortitude) and subdivisions of the other two, according to the well-known Ciceronian and Macrobian lists (Chastity for Temperance, Obedience for Justice; see Tuve, 1963). The North Porch at Chartres, however, presents a different series of triumphant virtues, this time the group of eight comprising humility plus the theological and cardinal virtues. Although their triumph is portrayed in the older, Romanesque style (standing figures holding symbolic objects and trampling underfoot personified vices) the number eight and some of the attributes point towards the future, especially the Italian virtue-cycles of the fourteenth century. Thus the vice opposed to Temperance in this series is Wrath tearing her garments, just as in Giotto's fresco in the Scrovegni Chapel in Padua, possibly inspired by the North Porch at Chartres.

Previous to Giotto, the cardinal virtues had been depicted only rarely in Italian art, although Romanesque mosaic pavements in Pavia and Cremona show scenes of the psychomachia involving other sets of virtues. Very nearly unique is a portrayal of the cardinal virtues through genre-scenes, in the choir mosaics of San Savino in Piacenza (1107), where a duel suggests Fortitude; a king pronouncing judgment, Justice; a game of chess, Prudence; and a scene of revelry, Temperance. The mosaic in the Cupola of the Ascension in St. Mark's, Venice, dating from ca. 1200, includes the cardinal virtues in a group of sixteen, which reflect the influence of Byzantine processional scenes by way of Ravenna. The cardinal virtues display attributes popular in twelfth-century French manuscripts: Prudence. two serpents; Justice, scales; Fortitude, a lion whose jaws she tears apart; and Temperance, a pitcher from which she pours water into a bowl (Figure 3).

Giotto's sequence of eight virtues and eight vices (ranged along opposite walls in the Scrovegni Chapel, 1306) popularized one hitherto rare attribute of Temperance, the sheathed sword, which thereafter appeared in several Florentine and Neapolitan reliefs and statues. In the fourteenth century Italy takes the lead from France, not so much in devising new ways to represent the virtues as in finding new contexts in which to display them. The religious ambience is still important; the tetrad (with or without the Pauline virtues) adorns chapels (such as the Spanish Chapel in Santa Maria Novella, Florence), pulpits (those of the Pisani in Pisa and Siena, some of which antedate the fourteenth century), baptisteries (Florence, Bergamo), campaniles (Florence), tabernacles (Or San Michele, Florence), and tombs (Saint Peter Martyr in Milan, Saint Augustine in Pavia), but now they also appear in places of civic and secular importance, a return to the political significance that the virtues had enjoyed from the time of their origin in the fifth-century Greek city-states. In the fourteenth and fifteenth centuries conditions in the Italian cities were ripe for the revival of the virtues as *aretai politikai*, and we find, especially in Florence, the most Athenian of the communes, many examples of their display in public places.

They adorn the Loggia dei Lanzi and the seven panels painted by the Pollaiuoli and Botticelli for the Mercanzia, and they accompanied the personified Commune in Giotto's lost fresco for the Palace of the Podestà. In Venice the capitals of the columns of the Doges' Palace were adorned with the seven virtues,

FIGURE 2. *Somme le Roi*: cardinal virtues, Paris, Arsenal, MS. 6329, folio 96v, 1295. PHOTO BIBLIOTHÈQUE NATIONALE, PARIS

FIGURE 3. Mosaics from Cupola of the Ascension, St. Mark's, Venice, showing two cardinal virtues, Temperance and Prudence, ca. 1200. PHOTO ANDERSON–ART REFERENCE BUREAU

and the Porta della Carta was flanked by statues of Fortitude, Temperance, Justice, and Charity. In Perugia the Collegio del Cambio set the cardinal virtues in a wholly secular environment. In Siena the frescoes of Good and Bad Government by Ambrogio Lorenzetti in the Palazzo Pubblico constitute the most complex and original of the political cycles involving the virtues and vices. In the Fresco of Good Government the personified Commune sits in the midst of six virtues, the cardinal four augmented by *Pax* and *Magnanimitas*, while the theological virtues hover overhead. Temperance holds an hourglass (one of the earliest examples of this attribute); Justice holds an upright sword, a crown, and a severed head; Fortitude has a sword; Prudence points to an inscription.

In addition to this rebirth of their civic importance, the following are the most significant tendencies in the iconography of the cardinal virtues in fourteenth- and fifteenth-century Italy:

1. The integration of these virtues into great *summae* of human life, like that on the campanile in Florence, with its reliefs of seven virtues, seven planets, liberal arts, mechanical arts, and Sacraments, or Andrea da Firenze's Triumph of Saint Thomas in the Spanish Chapel of Santa Maria Novella, where the saint sits enthroned between saints and doctors of the church, with winged figures of the cardinal and theological virtues hovering above his head and defeated heretics crouched at his feet; in the lower register are personifications of the liberal arts and sciences, at whose feet in turn sit their historical exemplars.

2. The use of the virtues in funerary sculpture, at first for saints, popes, and bishops, then (in Naples) for royalty, and finally for laymen of less exalted rank (Figure 4).

3. The appearance of typical figures, biblical or historical, to represent virtues as well as vices.

Among the symbols and attributes popularized at this stage, and carried from Italy north into France, England (where the virtues are always rare), and the Low Countries, those of Prudence and Temperance are the more diverse. Justice and Fortitude show fewer innovations, although it is at this time that the column (recalling Samson and representing strength) becomes a popular attribute of Fortitude. Prudence now often carries a mirror, sometimes entwined by a serpent, and she usually has at least two faces, sometimes three, representing her attention to the past and the future, as well as the present. Temperance may now have a bridle (she wears the bit in her mouth in the Scrovegni Chapel) or a sheathed sword (also Giottesque), or an hourglass (a pun on *tempus*). She may even take the form of an ancient Venus Pudica, entirely nude, as on Giovanni Pisano's pulpit in the Duomo in Pisa (ca. 1310), or of a very lightly clad, classical Diana, as on the tomb of Pius II, now in Sant' Andrea della Valle in Rome (ca. 1473).

In France the virtues are not associated with sepulchral ornament in the fourteenth and fifteenth centuries, but early in the sixteenth are introduced into this context by Italian sculptors, who usually employ the attributes conventional in Italy. Suddenly, however, French sculptors, such as Michel Colombe, adorn with highly original types and emblems of the virtues the tombs of the Duke of Brittany in Nantes (1507) and the Cardinals d'Amboise in Rouen (1515). Prudence now holds a compass, as well as a mirror; Fortitude holds a tower from which emerges a dragon, whose neck she grasps; Temperance has a clock as well as a bridle, and only Justice, with scales and sword, is identical with her Italian counterpart. These attributes (the "new" or "Rouen" iconography) are simplified versions of an even more bizarre set that (see Tuve, 1963) probably originated among manuscript illuminators patronized by the Dukes of Burgundy, as early as 1410. They appear in the famous Rouen manuscript of a French translation of Aristotle's *Ethics* (Bibl. munic. MS 927), about 1454, and in various treatises of the "advice to princes" type, usually involving adaptations of the Ciceronian doctrine of the cardinal virtues. In such illustrations Temperance has not only the bridle and the clock (the bit worn in her mouth and the clock on her head), but also a pair of spectacles in one hand, spurs on her shoes, and a windmill on which she rests her feet. The other virtues have correspondingly elaborate attributes (Figure 5), explained in a set of verses that accompany the pictures in a manuscript (ca. 1470) of a French translation of Martin of Braga's *Formula vitae honestae* (Tuve, 1966).

Although in pagan antiquity certain mythical and historical figures were customarily linked with particular virtues, and Philo and the Church Fathers regarded various persons from the Old Testament or the New as types of virtue or vice, systematic correlations in early medieval art were limited to a small group (Samson as a type of fortitude, Judith, Susanna, or Joseph in Egypt as types of chastity and temperance). Typical figures were assigned to the liberal arts much earlier than to the virtues (Chartres in the thirteenth century, the Spanish Chapel in the fourteenth), and, by the fourteenth century, the personified vices trampled underfoot in Romanesque versions of the psychomachia had given way to historical exemplars, sometimes trampled, sometimes merely sitting in defeat before the personified virtue. In a series of miniatures from the early and middle years of the fourteenth

century, linked in some way to Giusto Menabuoi's lost frescoes in the Church of the Eremitani in Padua, the typical figure defeated by Temperance is likely to be Epicurus, but may be Tarquin. Prudence usually triumphs over Sardanapalus, Justice over Nero, and Fortitude over Holofernes. The subject provided a popular theme for pageants and tapestries in the sixteenth century.

Not until the fifteenth century are typical figures, whether historical or biblical, associated with the cardinal virtues, sometimes in conjunction with a similar treatment of the liberal arts. Thus Pesellino's two panels (ca. 1460) now in Birmingham, Alabama, show the liberal arts with their champions seated at their feet and the seven virtues in the same position with theirs: Faith, Charity, and Hope (with Saint Peter, Saint John the Evangelist, and Saint James Major) are

FIGURE 4. Tomb of Pope Pius II, Sant' Andrea della Valle, Rome, with four cardinal virtues, two theological virtues, ca. 1473. PHOTO ALINARI–ART REFERENCE BUREAU

FIGURE 5. Cardinal virtues with the "new iconography" from B.N. MS. fr. 9186, folio 304r, French translation of Martin of Braga's *Formula vitae honestae*, ca. 1470. PHOTO BIBLIOTHÈQUE NATIONALE, PARIS

FIGURE 6. Cardinal and theological virtues with historical representatives, Pesellino, ca. 1460. SAMUEL H. KRESS COLLECTION, BIRMINGHAM MUSEUM OF ART, BIRMINGHAM, ALABAMA

flanked by Prudence and Justice on one side, Fortitude and Temperance on the other. At the feet of the cardinal virtues sit Solon, Solomon, Samson, and Scipio Africanus (Figure 6). A more elaborate iconography dominates Perugino's series in the Collegio del Cambio in Perugia towards the end of the fifteenth century: each of the (seated) personified virtues is identified by familiar attributes and an explanatory inscription, while below her stand three historical representatives, two Roman, one Greek. With Justice are associated Camillus, Pittacus, and Trajan, with Prudence, Quintus Fabius Maximus, Socrates, and Numa Pompilius, with Fortitude, Lucius Sicinnius, Leonidas, and Horatius Cocles, and with Temperance, Scipio Africanus, Pericles, and Cincinnatus.

Symbolic animals, birds, and even fish were linked with virtues and vices in ancient literature (Aristotle, the Neo-Platonists, Plutarch, Pliny the Elder in particular), and this tradition, augmented by the writings of the Fathers (especially commentaries on the *Hexaemeron*) and popularized by the *Physiologus* and the *Bestiary*, flourished in the Middle Ages. At first, in both literature and art, animals more often represented vices than virtues, and it was natural for a virtue to be shown riding or standing on a beast symbolic of the vice she overcame, as Chastity in the 1295 manuscript of *Somme le Roi* stood on a pig, symbol of lechery. It will be recalled that she held a disk or shield with a picture of a dove (the turtledove symbolizes chastity in Aristotle's *History of Animals*); this emblematic or heraldic association of animals with virtues is familiar from the early thirteenth century on the Gothic cathedrals. In the revival of the motif of the psychomachia that occurs in the fifteenth century personified virtues sometimes ride on animals that symbolize their own characteristics, rather than the opposed vices.

In the sixteenth century the emblem books introduced a host of new symbolic animals into the company of the virtues. Thus Chastity riding an elephant fights with Lechery on the familiar pig in an engraving cited by Tervarent. The popularity of the emblem books, from the middle of the sixteenth century until the eighteenth, gave to the iconography of the cardinal virtues a last injection of new life. The earliest emblem book, that of Alciati (1531), drew upon the *Hieroglyphica* of Horapollo, dating perhaps from the fifth century in Alexandria and published by the Aldine Press in 1505; it was followed by the *Hieroglyphica* of Valeriani in 1556 and, most influential of all, the *Iconologia* of Cesare Ripa, first published in 1593 without illustrations, then in illustrated editions from 1603 to the final, five-volume production in Perugia, 1764–67. Ripa's *Iconologia* was the great source book for baroque artists, some of whose works—like the stuccoes of Serpotta in Palermo—would be impossible to interpret without the help of the emblem books.

An early reflection of Ripa's advice on how to depict the cardinal virtues is the Sala Clementina in the Vatican, painted by the Alberti brothers. An elaborate example is Gaulli's set of virtues on the cupola of Sant' Agnese in the Piazza Navona, 1667–71 (Figure 7).

Among the more abstruse emblems connected with the cardinal virtues by Ripa and his followers are the ostrich, which symbolizes Justice because its feathers are all of equal length, the deer, linked with Prudence because it ruminates like a sage, and the diamond, symbol of Fortitude because of its adamantine hardness. Temperance received a great variety of new emblems, including a pair of red-hot tongs and a bowl of water in which to temper them. Giuseppe Raffaelli depicted her with precisely these attributes in his statue for the ambulacrum of Saint Peter's Basilica in Rome.

Drawing upon many ancient and medieval sources, including the epigrams in the *Greek Anthology* and the *Bestiary*, the emblem books ascribe to each of the virtues both animal and vegetable symbols.

After the close of the eighteenth century the vogue for personified abstractions perished, along with the

FIGURE 7. Temperance and related figures, pendentive of cupola, Sant' Agnese in Agone, Piazza Navona, Rome, G. B. Gaulli (Baciccio), 1667–71. PHOTO ALINARI–ART REFERENCE BUREAU

taste for allegory and the wit that delights in learned and allusive jests, such as inspired the ceiling of the Camera di San Paolo in Parma (Panofsky, 1951). Even in Rome the nineteenth and twentieth centuries produced few additions to the historic iconography of the cardinal virtues, if we except the Torlonia Chapel in the Lateran Basilica and the four busts over the main portal of the Ministry of Grace and Justice on the Via Arenula. Yet for a thousand years the iconography of the cardinal virtues has provided an accurate indication of the ebb and flow of interest in Platonic-Stoic ethics, and of the impact made at various times, in various places, by new interpretations of the virtues, their relation to one another and to other "value-systems," and their importance for the religious, social, political, and personal life of Western man. It is undoubtedly significant that in our own time the cycle of Seven Deadly Sins executed by Sidney Waugh for Steuben Glass has never been balanced by a series of cardinal and theological virtues, as it surely would have been in thirteenth-century France or fourteenth-century Florence.

### BIBLIOGRAPHY

H. F. A. von Arnim, ed., *Stoicorum veterum fragmenta,* 4 vols. (Stuttgart, 1964). Morton W. Bloomfield, *The Seven Deadly Sins: An Introduction to the History of a Religious Concept, with Special Reference to Medieval English Literature* (East Lansing, 1952). Samuel C. Chew, *The Pilgrimage of Life* (New Haven, 1962). E. Dümmler, ed., *Poetae latini aevi Carolini,* in *Monumenta Germaniae Historica.* M. I. Finley, Jr., *The World of Odysseus* (New York, 1954), p. 129. Frances G. Godwin, "An Illustration to the *De Sacramentis* of St. Thomas Aquinas," *Speculum,* **26** (1951), 609–14. Werner Jaeger, *Early Christianity and Greek Paideia* (Cambridge, Mass., 1961). Adolf Katzenellenbogen, *Allegories of the Virtues and Vices in Mediaeval Art from Early Christian Times to the Thirteenth Century,* trans. Alan J. P. Crick (New York, 1964). Karl Künstle, *Ikonographie der christlichen Kunst,* Vol. I (Freiburg, 1928). Émile Mâle, *The Gothic Image: Religious Art in France of the Thirteenth Century,* trans. Dora Nussey (New York, 1958). Herbert Musurillo, S. J., "The Problem of Ascetical Fasting in the Greek Patristic Writers," *Traditio,* **12** (1956), 1–64. Helen North, *Sophrosyne: Self-Knowledge and Self-Restraint in Greek Literature* (Ithaca, 1966). Erwin Panofsky, *The Iconography of Coreggio's Camera di San Paolo* (London, 1951); idem, *Tomb Sculpture: Four Lectures on Its Changing Aspects from Ancient Egypt to Bernini* (New York, n.d.). Theognis, *Theognis, poèmes élégiaques,* ed. Jean Carrière (Paris, 1948). Rosamond Tuve, "Some Notes on the Virtues and Vices," *Journal of the Warburg and Courtauld Institutes,* **26** (1963), 264–303; **27** (1964), 42–72; idem, *Allegorical Imagery: Some Mediaeval Books and Their Posterity* (Princeton, 1966). Guy de Tervarent, *Attributs et symboles dans l'art profane 1450–1600: Dictionnaire d'un langage perdu* (Geneva, 1959); *Supplément et index* (Geneva, 1964), p. 437. Raimond Van Marle, *Iconographie de l'art profane au moyen âge et à la renaissance* (The Hague, 1931).

HELEN F. NORTH

[See also Cosmology; Happiness; Historiography, Influence of Ideas on; Holy; **Iconography;** Myth in Antiquity; **Platonism;** Pre-Platonic Conceptions; Rationality; Stoicism.]

# THEODICY

### I. DEFINITION OF THEODICY

IT IS GENERALLY agreed that the term "theodicy" (in French *théodicée*), formed from two Greek words, θεός ("God") and δίκη ("justice"), was devised by Leibniz late in the seventeenth century. From his youth Leibniz had habitually used the phrase "the justice of God" in discussing the problem of evil, but the term "theodicy" appears late in the 1690's. Having been trained in the law, Leibniz regarded theology itself as the highest form of jurisprudence, and consequently treated the problem of God's relation to the evils of the world after the analogy of a case at court. It was the widespread popularity of his *Essais de théodicée . . .* (1710, hereafter referred to as *Theodicy*) which brought the term into general use.

Theodicy in its narrow sense is thus the defense of God, the supreme creator, ruler, and judge of the universe, against charges brought about by a consideration of both moral and natural evil. Leibniz himself exemplified this meaning in a short treatise written as a quasi-legal brief, and published independently in the same year as the *Theodicy: The Cause of God argued in Terms of His Justice (Causa Dei asserta per justitiam eius)*.

Linked to this meaning, however, is a second one— the philosophical study of the compatibility of evil with the idea of God. Thus Leibniz, writing to Des Bosses (Feb. 5, 1712; trans. Loemker, p. 601), defined theodicy as "a kind of science, as it were, namely the doctrine of the justice of God—that is, of his wisdom together with his goodness." A theodicy in this sense should examine the interrelationships of three concepts: the nature of God and his providence, the nature of evil, and the meaning of justice.

Since these concepts require further presuppositions as broad as the field of natural theology itself, a third, broader meaning of theodicy has arisen; it has become a synonym for philosophical theology. Grounds for this use of the term may also be found in Leibniz himself, since his *Theodicy*, the only inclusive philosophical work which he published during his lifetime (1646–1716), contained wide perspectives on his whole system of thought. Christian Wolff established this wider use of the term, and the Scholastic tradition has generally followed it. In the reform of the French educational system carried through in the early nineteenth century, the year course in philosophy of the Lycée was divided into four sections: psychology, logic, morals, and theodicy (or natural theology). This usage is retained in P. Janet and G. Seailles, *L'Histoire de la philosophie: les problèmes et les écoles* (Paris, 1887; II, Part iv).

## II. THEODICY IN HISTORICAL RELIGIONS

In the narrow and proper sense of the term, theodicies can arise only in traditions of ethical theism. The problem presupposes the existence of one God with a moral character engaged in the order of the world, although a polytheism in which the gods are themselves bound by a superior moral fate, or one in which the religious loyalty of the individual or the group is restricted to one god (henotheism) also may raise the question of justice in the face of persistent evil. However, polytheism, the pantheism of a monistic absolute, and the dualism which assigns the evil to a god or demon apart from the good provide ways of avoiding the problem of theodicy altogether.

Nevertheless, complaints about the actions of the religious being or beings upon whom the values of life depend but who have permitted evil occur wherever man has faced his life with self-consciousness. In the first chapter of his book on prayer (1932) Friedrich Heiler has pointed out complaints, protests, and attempts to coerce, in the face of undeserved sufferings, in the traditions of many ancient or tribal cultures. In ancient China the question of the cause of suffering was addressed to Shang Ti, the Highest Lord. The mystical pantheism of the Vedanta in India evaded the problem through identity with the One, but in the more personalistic mysticism of the Bhagavad-Gita the dialogue between Krishna and Arguna includes a reproach for the evil in the world which is answered by the god. Although the Buddha was skeptical about the gods, the content of his enlightenment concerned the fact of evil, its subjective cause, and its resolution. Though polytheistic, the religions of the Mesopotamian river civilizations anticipate a doctrine that is firmly entrenched in the history of the Hebrews, and still prevails in the orthodox theistic faiths historically derivative from this—the conviction that there is a divinely appointed equation of suffering with sin and of reward with loyalty. As Saint Augustine expressed it, "There are two kinds of evil—sin and the penalty for sin" (*Against Fortunatus*, 15; in *Earlier Writings*). It deserves notice, however, that the Hebrew scriptures also contain the great poetic refutation of this theory of evil as retribution—the book of Job, which also makes the point that the only resolution of the problem is in the realm of personal commitment or faith. Also reflected in later books of the Hebrew canon, as well as in early Christian heresies, is the dualism of gods— good and evil—adhered to in the religion of Iran.

In Greece the highly individualized natures of the gods render the problem of theodicy meaningless, for the society of gods is almost at one with the society of men, and human responses must be adjusted to them very much as they must be adjusted to other, admittedly more powerful, humans. But in the great myths, particularly as they are treated in Greek tragedy, the gods fade into insignificance in the face of the awesome powers and harsh sufferings common to the human situation, and the treatment of themes such as pride and retribution achieves a universal human significance.

Thus there have arisen in all religious considerations of evil, both moral and natural, certain lines of thought demanding a theodicy or suggesting ways of avoiding one: by rendering evil subjective, to be overcome by the discipline of thought and will; by a dualism or pluralism of good and evil forces; by making suffering a retribution for sin; by overcoming the distinction between good and evil through mystical identification with God, so that what is, is good; or by a nonunderstanding commitment of faith to the goodness of God and to justification in a life after death. The ground is thus prepared for a philosophical theodicy.

### III. PHILOSOPHICAL THEODICIES

**1. Greek Theodicy.** The first philosophical resolution of the problem of evil is found in the dualism of the early cosmologists, which separated the good from the bad—a separation which was retained by Plato and Aristotle, however much these may have shifted the reference of the two poles. In each case, whether in Anaximander's separation of bounded order from unbounded matter (*apeiron*), or the Pythagoreans' dualism of even and odd, or Plato's and Aristotle's distinction between form and matter, the two are assigned distinct metaphysical statuses, even though the latter, the evil, is in some way subordinate or subject to the former, the good. In Heraclitus, on the other hand, and the Stoics, who appropriated his theory of the eternal *logos-fire*, the two poles are absorbed into a unity which transcends both but is in some higher way good, requiring submission by the individual to this ultimate order which determines his destiny. To oversimplify somewhat, the philosophic tendency is to resolve the problem of evil, either through a dualism in which the good is free of evil yet controls it, or through a pantheism in which evil is somehow less real and existent than the "truly" good, though inseparable from the apparent good. The two movements are fully synthesized by Plotinus and those who follow him; following both the Stoic doctrine of the One and the logic of a hierarchical scale of being, Plotinus makes matter the source of evil, but places it also at the outer extreme of nonbeing, removed from the One, the ineffable source of all goodness and harmony. In every case, evil is either reducible to some source other than the good (dualism), or it is merely a limitation of the good (negation), and the problem of a theodicy (which involves culpability of the good) is avoided.

In the Hellenistic period, however, there were two distinct approaches to a theodicy, which established precedents for later discussions. One was the challenge which Epicurus directed at God's power or goodness. According to Lactantius (*A Treatise on the Anger of God*, Ch. 13) he reasoned as follows:

God either wishes to take away evils and is unable; or he is able and is unwilling; or he is neither willing nor able; or he is both willing and able. If he is willing but unable he is feeble, which is not in accordance with the character of God. If he is able and unwilling, he is envious, which is equally at variance with God. If he is neither willing nor able, he is both envious and feeble, and therefore not God. If he is both willing and able, which alone is suitable for God, from what source then are evils? Or why does he not remove them?

The argument has been repeated by skeptics until today and various consequences drawn from it; one possibility, of course, is Epicurean deism or atheism.

The second contribution to a theodicy in late classicism is Plutarch's criticism of the Stoic ethics of obedience to the universal reason governing the world, on the charge that Stoicism makes God the source of all evils (*De Stoicarum repugnantiis*, Secs. 32–37; the criticism is levelled against Chrysippus, *Treatise on the Gods*). Plutarch's own solution is Plato's; God cannot be identified with nature as the Stoics hold; God can only be good, and evil must have some other source, whether in lesser powers or in matter.

**2. Christianity and Saint Augustine.** It is only when the Western theistic religions, all of them influenced by the Hebrew scriptures and by Greek thought, seek a clarification and defense of faith in the face of paganism and heresy that the problem of theodicy becomes vital. The retributive theory of suffering remains strong in these faiths, although protests were as old as the Book of Job and the teachings of Jesus and Paul. The eschatological hope of a final judgment and promise of eternal life with rewards for the faithful and good, and punishment for sinners, was the ultimate justification of a moral world order. But the questions of why a creator of perfect power, wisdom, and goodness can create a world containing evil, and how his foreknowledge is compatible with human freedom, developed as foci for discussion. A tough-minded orthodoxy (Tertullian, for example) turned to the paradoxes of the gospel as justification for theoretical skepticism and an affirmation of faith in the impossible. But, for most thinkers, Platonism provided an antidote for doubt and for the dualistic heresies of Gnostic and Manichee. A universe which is the creation of a perfect being must, to adequately reflect his greatness, be as full as possible of all degrees of finite goodness and thus also contain levels of evil as their negation; in such a world, Greek thought supports revelation in holding man to be free and therefore capable of evil, yet destined also to find his way from the lower level of sense and matter to the higher level of grace.

It was Saint Augustine who, after passing through Manichaean and Neo-Platonic phases of thought, provided that complex synthesis of doctrines about evil and the justification of God which came to prevail in Western Christian orthodoxy; it was adapted by Thomas Aquinas to the Scholastic tradition and by Leibniz to the context of the modern scientific and rationalistic moods.

Augustine's theodicy is eclectic and resists systematization. He modified Plotinus' theory of evil as negation by making it a matter rather of privation—in each created being that is evil which deprives it of the particular form or purpose which is natural to it. To this must be added Augustine's concern about the inwardness of experience, the motive rather than the external consequence of action. Evil is deficiency, therefore no cause can be found for it (*City of God* XII, 7). Hence evil has no independent status; it is always parasitic on the good (*Enchiridion*, Chs. 13, 14). But since being and goodness must be defined in terms of the particular final cause inherent in each created being, only free creatures can experience evil.

When the will abandons what is above itself and turns to what is lower, it becomes evil, not because that to which it turns is evil, but because the turning itself is wicked (*City of God* XII, 6).

So man's fall brought evil into the world, and it is relative to man and to other free creatures.

To this theory of evil as privation, Augustine adds analogical arguments of an aesthetic and part-whole nature. What appears to be evil seen in isolation or in too narrow context could be seen as a necessary component in a larger context. Thus evil can be understood in relation to good as ugliness stands to beauty; it provides the contrast (darkness, disharmony) which lets the good (light, harmony) stand out more brightly and perfectly. Thus death, to which everything transitory is subject, itself enhances the degrees of perfection in creation. Likewise the atonement provides a completely just balance for sin, preserving the harmony and goodness of the whole.

The wide range of arguments by which Augustine sought to exonerate God from any charge of moral or metaphysical imperfection and to derive all evil from man's sin were the foundation for theological optimism in the first centuries of the modern world. Thomas Aquinas used both his theory of privation and the so-called aesthetic argument, and although there were departures from it in such Scholastics as Ockham, it established the tradition of philosophical theology. (*Summa Theologica* I, 4–49; *On Free Will* III, 9, 26.)

The theory that evil is necessary to the total good because it serves as discipline to the moral and spiritual life is neglected in Augustine, but has been traced to another church father, Irenaeus, by John Hick in *Evil and the God of Love* (1966). The "Irenaean type of theodicy," also indebted to aspects of Platonism, holds that the evils of the world are required by a God of love who seeks the development of his free creatures from their original innocence into full spiritual beings. Hence, as in Augustine, there is no intrinsic or surd evil; evil is justified as the means of developing man from bondage to self-conscious participation in the Kingdom of God. This disciplinary view, which Hicks argues was eclipsed by the Augustinian arguments, was revived after Kant by Schleiermacher and others, and found support in theistic interpretations of evolution in the nineteenth century.

**3. *Theodicy in the Reformation and Leibniz.*** In the theological conflicts of the Reformation another critical reaction to the Augustinian theodicy developed. Both Luther and Calvin followed Augustine's doctrine that all evils follow from the sin and fall of man. But Luther in particular, in the tradition of voluntarism, stressing faith as independent of reason, repudiated the entire conception of a philosophical theodicy on fideistic grounds. Not God is to be justified, but man. To raise the speculative question of a theodicy merely reveals the entire sinful condition of man. Only faith has the assurance that God will use the evil of the world for his own ends. Faith exceeds our present understanding as does the justice of God in accepting sinners.

This skepticism of the intellect, which shifts the problem of theodicy from philosophy to revelation and faith, is, of course, as old as Job, and has continued until now, in the Neo-Orthodoxy of our times (Karl Barth, *Die kirchliche Dogmatik*, Munich [1932], Vol. 3, Parts 1–3). But theological controversy made inevitable a revival of metaphysics and natural theology, particularly the Neo-Platonic view that evil becomes meaningful in the larger and higher context of the purpose of creation. Nicholas of Cusa argued that since all creation is an image of the divine, the world is as good as it possibly could be, given its status as contingent and finite (*De ludo globi*, I). In the argument for the goodness of the world, teleological or "physico-theological" arguments eventually assume a priority over the other traditional forms, so that by the seventeenth century nature has been freed from the curse of Adam, and its newly discovered mathematical and organic harmonies appear as empirical evidence for the justice of God. The preoccupation of the early Boyle Lectures with teleological considerations marks a high point of this development.

The defense of God against the attacks of atheists and "libertines" was a prominent concern of thinkers of the seventeenth century, and the problem of man's freedom in its relation to God's omniscience and power became an important issue in the theodicic argument. In his apologetic work, left incomplete as the *Pensées*, Pascal attributed evil to man's sin, to be overcome by the redeemed in mystical revelation through faith. Spinoza, by contrast, had exonerated God from both good and evil, these being relative to what is useful or harmful to man, and capable of being understood through an adequate grasp of God and the active emotions which arise from this.

Like Spinoza, Leibniz had a sharp sense of the reality of the problem of evil, particularly the historical evils which beset Europe. The task of theodicy was therefore to show that the reality of evil is compatible with, indeed, follows from, the creation and providence of a God whose attributes are perfections. In addition to the great *Theodicy* of 1710, he wrote many briefer ones, including "Von der Allmacht und Allwissenheit Gottes und der Freiheit des Menschen" ("Of the Omnipotence and Omniscience of God and the Freedom of Man"); from the early Paris years the *Confessio philosophi* ("Confession of a Philosopher," edited by I. Jagodinski, Kazan [1915]); the *Discours de la métaphysique* ("Discourse on Metaphysics," 1686), especially section 30 (Wiener, pp. 331–34); and the *Causa Dei*, already mentioned. To the *Theodicy*, written discursively for a wide circle of readers, he added as an appendix, an "Abridgment of the Argument Reduced to Syllogistic Form" (the *Abrégé*, Gerhardt VI, 376–87; trans. Wiener, pp. 509–22), which set the arguments against God in twelve syllogisms, and refuted them in counter-syllogisms—a logical process which Hume and Kant adopted in their refutations.

Leibniz repeated, in general, the Augustinian-Thomistic arguments, with some adaptations to fit his analytic logic of propositions, his monadic theory of substance, and a quasi-mathematical conception of the principle that of all possible events, the best possible always occurs. His analysis is aided by clear definitions of justice (as the love of the wise man), of freedom as self-determination, and of will, anticipatory and consequent. As Thomas had done before him, he discusses three kinds of evil: metaphysical, moral, and natural. Metaphysical evil is essentially finiteness or privation in the law of individual natures. Moral evil or sin is real; it is based on unclear and inadequate knowledge; and God, who determined the law of each individual nature as the best possible in itself and in the harmony of the whole universe, is not responsible for it. Natural evil is determined by laws which also define the best possible consequences. Thus in every case evil must be judged teleologically in terms of the best possible whole. God is justified because evils are used to achieve greater goods than would otherwise be possible; evil historical events are processes of retrenchment and of the clearing of obstacles for a better future (*reculer pour mieux sauter*); on the same grounds suffering is justified as retribution for evil actions. The indestructibility of the monads is the assurance of an immortality in which the greatest harmony and justice will continue to be achieved. Since truths of fact lie beyond the range of any finite analysis, we cannot now completely comprehend the place of any event in the total harmony.

**4. Criticisms of Theodicy in the Enlightenment and in Kant.** The wide influence of the *Theodicy* is shown not only in the spirit of intellectual optimism of the Enlightenment, but also in the clarity and depth of the criticisms which it evoked. In spite of the harsh conflicts between Newtonians and Leibnizians, Samuel Clarke's Boyle Lectures show a great agreement on teleological and theological principles. Pope's *Essay on Man* is widely regarded as having been influenced by the *Theodicy*, perhaps through conversations with Bolingbroke. Appearing in many editions in France, Leibniz' work supported a popular optimism which Voltaire, stirred by the destructive fury of the Lisbon earthquake, satirized in *Candide* and helped to dispel. It was this theological current whose logic Hume exposed with relentless analysis in the *Dialogues concerning Natural Religion* (1779); in it Philo states Epicurus' old dilemma in the simplified form (it cannot be true, both that evil exists, and that God is both omnipotent and perfectly good) in which the problem of theodicy has recently been revived.

Immanuel Kant criticized all previous attempts at a theodicy in his short essay "Ueber das Misslingen aller philosophischen Versuche in der Theodicee" ("On the Failure of All Philosophical Attempts at a Theodicy"). It was written in 1791, after the three Critiques but before his work on "Religion within the Limits of mere Reason." In his precritical period he had still been intent upon settling the "distinctness of the fundamental principles of natural theology and morals" by placing teleology at the center of his argument. Now, having placed the problems of theology beyond the range of theoretical reason, establishing the primacy of the practical reason and the moral law, defining its postulates, and, finally, reconciling the two through teleological judgments involving feelings of perfection, he applies these insights in a revision of the problem of theodicy in a style reminiscent of Leibniz' *Causa Dei* . . . , not only in its syllogistic structure of defense and rebuttal, but in its tripartite ordering of the divine attributes: goodness, omniscience and omnipotence, and holiness. These, he holds, must be challenged by the empirical fact of disteleology or anti-purpose (*Zweckwidrigkeit*). Moral anti-purpose (*das Böse*) refutes will as means; physical anti-purpose (Evil) refutes will as end; and a third anti-purpose, the disproportion of physical suffering to moral evil, refutes the holiness of God's justice. Hence all previous theodicies, resting upon the intellect, have failed.

Yet there is the demand for cosmic justice, with inadequate support from experience, and Kant proposes that "more effective grounds may be found, which will absolve the wisdom which has faced accusation, not *ab instantia* since we can never be certain that our reason can arrive at the insight through experience alone of the relationship in which the world stands to the highest wisdom" (Academy ed., VIII, 263). Following the insight of Job's triumph over his friends, he finds these grounds not through speculative wisdom nor through moral wisdom alone, though both assure us of the possibility of a teleology, but through "truthfulness" (*Wahrhaftigkeit*)—not truth, which is unavailable—and a sense of moral uprightness and formal conscientiousness. This is not a simple justification through faith, but through the cosmic demands implicit in the moral uprightness of the individual, which are possible but not justifiable theoretically.

**5. *Theodicies after Kant.*** Kant's emphasis upon the inward, moral basis of theodicy had lasting consequences upon followers and opponents alike. The intense moralism of Fichte is shown in his view that nature is the battle-ground on which man achieves freedom. Condemning Leibniz for undertaking a theodicy with "indeterminate abstract categories," Hegel finds one in history. At the conclusion of his *Philosophy of History* he wrote, "That the history of the world is this process of development and the actual coming-into-being of spirit, underneath the variable dramas of its histories—this is the true theodicy, the justification of God in history" (Glockner ed., 11, 569; see also 11, 42). The attainment of freedom in the state, and the process of self-conscious assimilation by men of the absolute justify the sufferings of history. Leaning upon Hegel's dialectical logic, later Hegelians showed that this was a return to the Neo-Platonic theory that evil is a more complete good seen partially. (See also Josiah Royce, for instance, in *Studies in Good and Evil* [1898], passim.)

Another type of post-Kantian inversion of the problem of theodicy is found in the work of the French personalist, Henry Duméry, author of *The Problem of God in Philosophy of Religion* (Evanston, 1964), who reflects also the influence of such Kant-inspired thinkers as Henri Bergson and Nicholas Berdyaev. God cannot be objectified; to find the answer to the place of evil we must discover the immanence of God as the transcendent unity, the radical spontaneity, the power to change, within man. The internal dialogue of the person with the absolute within him is the path to the resolution of evil and the vindication of God. This is Kant with some Bergsonian support.

In the nineteenth century there were other attempts to overcome the problem of theodicy by reinterpreting the nature of God. Scientism absolved nature from all good or bad, and the growth of social injustices and concern for their reform emphasized moral evil and human responsibility rather than the justice of God. The conception of a God perfectly good but without absolute power was revived with effectiveness by John Stuart Mill, William James, E. S. Brightman, and

others, who thus vacated the theodicy problem rather than solved it. Darwin's theory of evolution intensified the meaning of evil in nature by stressing the role of struggle, but also invited a positive but hardly justified argument by the Social Darwinists that nature supports progress and the improvement of forms of life. Thinkers like R. A. Tsanoff have found natural evil to arise from the disharmonies and disturbed relations which take place between old and new orders of life, while Henderson and others offered statistical evidence of a teleological principle in nature. Thus encouraged, theistic and idealistic thinkers revived the Irenaeian theodicy, holding that evil and freedom are the divinely chosen conditions by which men are disciplined to become members of the Kingdom of God.

In the face of the great moral and historical catastrophes of this century, and the decline of philosophical theology which accompanied them, the problem of theodicy has been largely absorbed through the rise of religious humanism, or a fideism which distrusts intellect, or a secular skepticism. Yet there is renewed evidence that the problem is still alive, in recent discussions by thinkers of an analytic type who have restored and given rigorous formulation to the objections of Hume and Kant, with what must be admitted to be still inconclusive results. Since these discussions move from the question of theodicy to the question of evidence for the existence of God, they need not be discussed here. The works by Hick, Flew and MacIntyre, and Pike listed in the Bibliography will introduce the reader to these recent studies.

*BIBLIOGRAPHY*

Saint Augustine, *Earlier Writings*, trans. J. H. S. Burleigh (London and Philadelphia, 1953); idem, *The City of God*, trans. Marcus Dods (New York, 1948; also reprint), esp. Book 12. E. S. Brightman, *A Philosophy of Religion* (New York, 1940). Karl Barth, *Die kirchliche Dogmatik* (Munich, 1932), English trans. G. T. Thomson (Edinburgh, 1958), Vol. III. Henry Duméry, *The Problem of God in Philosophy of Religion*, trans. C. Courtney (Evanston, 1964). A. Flew and A. MacIntyre, eds., *New Essays in Philosophical Theology* (London, 1955). G. W. F. Hegel, *Werke*, ed. Hermann Glockner, 26 vols. (Stuttgart, 1927–40). Friedrich Heiler, *Prayer: A Study in the History and Psychology of Religion*, ed. S. McComb and J. E. Park (London and New York, 1932). L. J. Henderson, *The Fitness of the Environment* (Boston, 1958). John Hick, *Evil and the God of Love* (London, 1966); see also an abridged summary, "Evil," *Encyclopedia of Philosophy* (New York, 1967), III, 136–41. David Hume, *Dialogues concerning Natural Religion* (Edinburgh, 1779). R. Jolivet, "Evil," *New Catholic Encyclopedia* (New York, 1967), V, 665–67. Karl Jung, *Antwort auf Hiob* (Zurich, 1952); trans. K. F. C. Hull as *Answer to Job* (London, 1954). I. Kant, *Ueber das Misslingen aller philosophischen Versuche in der Theodizee,* in *Gesammelte Schriften,* 23 vols. (Berlin, 1902–55), VIII, 253–72. Lactantius, *A Treatise on the Anger of God,* trans. William Fletcher (Edinburgh, 1871). G. W. Leibniz, *Philosophische Schriften,* ed. C. I. Gerhardt, 7 vols. (Berlin, 1875–90); idem, *Sämtliche Schriften und Briefe,* published by the German Academy, formerly the Prussian Academy (Darmstadt and Berlin, 1923—; still incomplete), these are the most useful editions; idem, *Essais de théodicée sur la bonté de dieu, la liberté de l'homme, et l'origine du mal* (1710); trans. E. M. Haggard as *Essays on the Goodness of God, the Freedom of Man, and the Origin of Evil* (London, 1951). Unfortunately Haggard omitted from his translation the important appendices: Leibniz' reduction of his argument to syllogistic form is translated in the *Leibniz Selections,* ed. Philip P. Wiener (New York, 1951; 1959), pp. 509–22; *The Philosophical Papers* and *Letters of Leibniz,* ed. L. E. Loemker, rev. ed. (Dordrecht, 1969) contains early attempts at the problem (pp. 146–47, 216–27, 321–23). J. S. Mill, *Three Essays on Religion* (London, 1874); idem, *An Examination of Sir William Hamilton's Philosophy* (London, 1865), Ch. VII. Nelson Pike, ed., *God and Evil: Readings in the Theological Problem of Evil* (Englewood Cliffs, 1964). Josiah Royce, *Studies in Good and Evil* (New York, 1898). F. R. Tennant, *Philosophical Theology* (Cambridge, 1930), Vol. II, Ch. viii. R. A. Tsanoff, *The Nature of Evil* (New York, 1931).

LEROY E. LOEMKER

[See also **Evil;** Existentialism; Free Will in Theology; **God;** Hegelian . . . ; Perennial Philosophy.]

# THERIOPHILY

THERIOPHILY is a word coined in 1933 by the author of this article to name a complex of ideas which express an admiration for the ways and character of the animals. Theriophilists have asserted with various emphases that the beasts are (1) as rational as men, or less rational than men but better off without reason, or more rational than men; (2) that they are happier than men, in that Nature is a mother to them but a cruel stepmother to us; (3) that they are more moral than men.

The whole idea or movement, insofar as it is a fairly widespread set of attitudes, is a reaction against the dogma of the superiority of mankind to all other forms of life. The dogma, as it influenced Western Europe, had two sources: one in pagan antiquity, one in the Bible. The former maintained that man's uniqueness lay in his rational animality. He shared his senses and appetites, as Aristotle puts it in his *De anima* (413b) and elsewhere, with the beasts and the plants; but his reason was his possession alone and it elevated him above all creation. It is clear that anti-intellectualists would not agree with the second clause in this sentence and would put a higher value on instinct than on rationality. The biblical source of man's superiority is Genesis 1:28, where God gives man dominion "over every living thing that moveth upon the earth." In the later history of theriophily the biblical verse, as revealed evidence of human uniqueness and nobility, is used to refute the idea of animal nobility. The matter, however, was complicated since the pagans did not deny that the beasts had souls, whereas the Christians either denied it outright or granted them an inferior kind of soul which could not be said to survive death—a soul which in the words of Deuteronomy 12:23 was in their blood or was identical with it.

*The Background in Folklore.* The cleverness, the stupidity, the faithfulness, the prudence, the temperance, as well as their antitheses, of certain beasts is witnessed in fables and legends which go back to early Indian civilization. The Sanskrit book of parables *Pañchatantra,* like the Pali Buddhistic *Jātaka,* is full of such tales, and they reappear in Aesop, Babrius, and Phaedrus. They are retold, as in *Reynard the Fox* (*Le Roman de Reynard,* ca. 1170–1250), and with elegance by Jean de La Fontaine in the seventeenth century. But alongside such legends and fantasies we find Aristotle listing animal characteristics in the opening of Book VIII of his *Historia animalium.* There he points out that human psychological traits are shared by the beasts—traits such as gentleness or fierceness, mildness or cross temper, courage or timidity, fear or confidence, high spirit or low cunning, and "something akin to sagacity."

Sometimes, as in Pliny and Aelian, science and folklore were blended and stories of the most improbable kind were preserved for future generations to use as scientific fact. Such stories include that of Chrysippus' dog which, looking for its master in a wood, comes to a triple fork. He sniffs down two of the branches and finds no scent of his master. He then without sniffing darts down the third branch, thus proving his reasoning powers. It was, as appears, customary to explain the behavior of the beast in human terms, projecting into them the same psychological motives that might be found in human beings on analogous occasions.

*Diogenes of Sinope.* The first theriophilist of importance is Diogenes of Sinope (ca. 412–323 B.C.), the famous Cynic (from κύων, κυνός, "dog"). Diogenes was looking for an exemplar of the life according to nature, something that his contemporaries had often found in savages. But animals seemed even more natural than Scythians or Ethiopians; for human beings, in whatever state they might be found, were after all living in a society controlled by law and law was a human, not a natural, invention. "Natural" to the Cynic meant that which was untouched or, as he would say, uncorrupted by art. But almost every act of a man was changed by invention, technique, artificiality. Diogenes seeing a dog drinking by lapping up water from a puddle, saw that cups were a superfluity. He threw away his cup. He saw that the beasts wore no clothing except their fur or feathers; why then should a man need more than a rag or two to shield him from the rain and cold? Diogenes wrapped a coarse cloth round his body; it became known as the *tribon* or philosopher's cloak. Again, the beasts had no houses and were satisfied with dens in the ground or a cave; Diogenes crept into a wine jar. The beasts had no regulations for eating or copulation; they simply satisfied their innate appetites. Why should a man do differently? The beasts ate their food raw; why then cook? Polygamy, incest, cannibalism are wrongly censured; they all follow from natural habits and should be adopted rather than rejected.

None of this tended to show that the animals were rational, and indeed, as far as the Cynics were concerned, reason was of doubtful value. Instinct was more natural than reason and if one were seeking the life according to nature, then one would follow instinct and "divorce old barren reason from his bed." Following the animals, moreover, increased one's autonomy, one's *autarky*, that goal which the Greek ethicists strove to reach: to be free of all claims made by anything external to one's self. One became self-dependent and never dependent on externals. By abandoning family ties, social relations, political duties, and all the delights that come from one form or another of artistry, one became completely free and at the same time close to the animal.

*Plutarch.* The Cynic's point of view, since it deprecated the use of reason, did not include any theory of animal rationality. But at the beginning of the Christian period Plutarch wrote a dialogue (usually called *Gryllus,* from the name of the protagonist) in which Odysseus, cast up on the witch Circe's island, is allowed to speak with some of the Greeks whom Circe has turned into animals; if any wish to regain their human shapes, they may do so. Gryllus is a pig. He is far from wishing to become a man again. To begin with, the life of the beasts is more natural than that of human beings, for the souls of the beasts are able to produce that virtue which is peculiar to each species without any instruction. Animals moreover have more wisdom and prudence than men, for these virtues are implanted in animals by Nature, not by art. If you do not want to call this reason, says Gryllus, "it is time for you to find out a finer and more honorable name

for it as, it cannot be denied, it exhibits a power greater in its effects and more wonderful than either." Animals all reason, but some are more rational than others. "I do not believe," says Gryllus (in a sentence that was to be reproduced by Montaigne and to echo through the seventeenth and eighteenth centuries), "there is such difference between beast and beast in reason and understanding and memory, as between man and man."

***The General Superiority of the Beasts.*** Some admirers of the animals cared nothing for reason and were especially interested only in man's inferiority to the beasts in some detail or other. The question of whether or not man was favored by Nature had apparently been discussed as early as the fifth century B.C. by Xenophon; he depicts a conversation between Socrates and Aristodemus who discuss the question (*Memorabilia* I, iv, 2 and IV, iii, 9–12). Anaxagoras, another fifth-century philosopher, is also reported to have recognized degrees of intelligence in the beasts, though he admitted that mankind stood at the head of the animate hierarchy. Our real difference from the animals, he thought, is not our intelligence—for they too possess that faculty—but the fact that we have leaders, laws, arts, and cities (something that was to be said of the animals too later on).

That some people anticipated the Cynics in using the animals as exemplars is seen in a passage of the *Clouds* of Aristophanes (lines 1427–29), where Pheidippides justifies beating his father by the example of "cocks and other beasts." The joke would have meant little if some debaters had not used similar arguments. By Aristotle's time the question must have been commonly discussed, since in the *De partibus animalium* (687a), he refers to the argument that the beasts are better off than we because of their corporeal endowment—horns, claws, hooves—whereas man is born naked and defenseless. Aristotle's reply to this, a reply which hardly meets the point, is that the human hand is a better weapon than anything given to the beasts for it can vary the weapons as the need arises. Though Aristotle himself believed in the superiority of man, he was used by others to demonstrate the antithetical idea. For in his *Historia animalium* here and there he speaks of the cleverness of the swallows in building their nests, the medical knowledge of the Cretan goats, the singing lessons given by the mother nightingale to her young, and so on.

As early as Democritus (fifth century B.C.) we find the animals praised for their sobriety, for knowing the extent of their needs and never seeking to go beyond them. Diogenes again is cited as witness to the animals' health and longevity as well as to their lack of superfluities. The New Comedy also played on this theme of man's misery as compared with the animals: men use their reason for endless arguments; the beasts are free from contention. We are slaves to opinion; they simply follow the commands of Nature. In a fragment of Philemon (ca. 361–263 B.C.) we find the beasts praised for their "single nature": all lions are brave, all hares timid, all foxes live in the same way. But every man lives according to his own individual nature. In Menander (342–291 B.C.) man is the one "unnatural animal." Whatever evils happen to an animal come from Nature. But besides those which are natural, men invent evils. "We are pained if someone sneezes; if someone speaks ill, we are angry; if someone has a dream, we are frightened; if an owl hoots, we are terrified. Struggles, opinions, contests, laws, all these evils are added to those in nature." And like Gryllus, one of Menander's characters declares that if he were to be born again, he would choose any animal rather than the human. The beasts have no flatterers, no sycophants, no criminals.

One of the major sources of later theriophily is Pliny (ca. A.D. 23–79), for Pliny was read by everyone and his *Natural History* was a sort of encyclopedia. In the proemium to this work (VII, 1) he wrote the famous words, "it is hard to tell whether Nature has been a kindly parent to man or a cruel stepmother." To the other animals she has given a natural covering—shells, hulls, spines, shaggy hair, fur, feathers, scales, fleeces— but man "she casts forth on his natal day, naked upon a naked soil, casts him forth to weep and beg; and no other animal weeps from the moment of its birth." What folly, he continues, to think that such a creature is born to a high estate! Other animals know from birth whether they are to walk, swim, or fly. But man lies helpless and can neither talk, walk, nor eat without instruction. Man alone knows grief, the desire for excess or luxury, ambition, avarice, superstition. He alone worries about his sepulture and an afterlife. Man alone makes war on his kind. In short, man is the most unhappy of all animals and most of man's evils come from man.

*Montaigne.* Whether the ancients were serious in their praise of animals cannot be answered simply. Sometimes, as would seem to be true of Plutarch, they used the theme for purposes of satire. But it is likely that the Cynics at any rate were serious since they seem to have carried over their theriophily into action. The theme could not very well be continued into Christianity because of the biblical passage cited above and of the dogma of man's superiority. One could hardly rank an animal above the image of God endowed with soul. Yet the Christian belief in man's superiority was sometimes shaken by the awareness of evil, and there were plenty of writings on the problem of evil during the Middle Ages to show how worried men were by it. From Saint Augustine to Saint Thomas Aquinas and beyond runs a thread of explanation of something which is and ought not to be. Yet for all their preoccupation with human misery and sin, for all their contempt for the world and their yearning to escape into a happier realm, the men of the Middle Ages seem never to have maintained that human beings were inferior to the beasts, though some might be beastly.

In the sixteenth century, when skepticism and the depreciation of learning went hand in hand, when faith arose once more to preeminence as against reason, and when the classical writers became better known, there also began a wave of theriophily which is hard to distinguish from satire. It may be said to begin with G.-B. Gelli's *Circe* (1549). This work takes up the theme of Plutarch's *Gryllus* but extends it from the pig to all the animals, beginning with the oyster and ending with the elephant. *Circe* seems to the writer of this article to be one of those books of paradoxes which were current at the time and which go back at least to Maximus of Tyre (second century A.D.). One of the best known of such writings is Ortensio Landi's *Paradossi* (1543). The whole purpose of the paradoxes is to startle public opinion by proposing, in apparent seriousness, ideas generally supposed to be false, such as, that it is better to live as a peasant than as a courtier, better to be poor than rich. Others have maintained that *Circe* is a serious book and that its major theses are to be taken as the genuine opinion of its author. Such problems are difficult, if possible, to solve and we shall simply describe the contents of the little book.

In *Circe* Ulysses interviews a large range of animals and finds that all but one have no wish to return to humanity. Each points out some advantage that animals have over men. The oyster, relying on Pliny, says that Nature has given oysters an instinctive dread of their enemies—something which she has not given men—a shell for clothing, and a habitation. The mole, who was a farmer in his previous existence, laments man's need to work, famine, drought, and that steady war against hostile forces which is man's lot. Animals have none of this to endure. The snake, who was a physician before his enchantment, knows more than the average man about human disabilities, speaks of human intemperance which leads to so many ills. When Ulysses points out that medicine can cure these, the snake launches into one of those diatribes against medicine which were common at the time and furthermore points out that the beasts have no need of that empirical art, a fact which shows their superiority to man. And when Ulysses mentions human longevity as contrasted with the brevity of animal life, the snake replies that the beasts at any rate don't worry themselves about death. The hare, who comes next, delivers a sermon on all the forms of human misery. A man is miserable if rich, for he is surrounded by envious enemies; if poor, well, says the hare, there is no need to say why he is miserable. There are no rich nor poor among the beasts. No beast has to sell himself because of poverty. The roebuck prefers animal life for four reasons: the animal has no economic worries, no fear of the future, no suspicions of his fellows, no fear of the law. The doe, who had been a woman, gives Ulysses a feminist sermon. Female animals are not slaves to their mates; they do not bring forth their young in pain; they have no trouble rearing them; they are the equals of the males in every way. The lion objects to human psychological evils—ambition, envy, anger—none of which exists among the beasts. So it goes until Ulysses comes to the elephant. The elephant had been a philosopher and can see the superiority of human knowledge. Animals cannot know universals; their knowledge is confined to particulars. Moreover human knowledge is more certain than that of the beasts. Therefore he alone of Circe's animals will return to human form, bewailing the shortsightedness of his fellows, who prefer a momentary sensory pleasure to the lasting delights of reason.

*Circe* had a great vogue, and imitations of it and of the Gryllus theme continued down into the eighteenth century. It appeared in the theater and Merritt Hughes has shown how it was used even in Spenser's *Faerie Queene* (Hughes, 1943). To see society from the point of view of a foreigner—a Persian or Chinese or American Indian—was a favorite device for gaining distance and an apparent objectivity; to see it from the point of view of an animal was even better. The idea gained such popularity that it can be found in popular imagery in the caricatures of *Le monde renversé*, where beasts play the roles of men and men those of beasts. The device reappeared in our own time in Edmond Rostand's *Chantecler* (1910).

If one man is to be selected as the main vehicle of theriophily in the seventeenth century, it is Michel de Montaigne. In his essays *On Pedantry* (I, 25) and *On the Cannibals* (I, 31) he expresses his primitivistic sympathies, whether in earnest or not, and in the *Apology for Raimond Sebond* (II, 12) he engages in a eulogy of the animals which maintained that their brutal stupidity surpasses all that our divine intelligence can do. With that equilibrium of temper that characterizes Montaigne, he ends his essay not by concluding that the beasts are our superiors but simply by saying that Nature, "our great and puissant mother," gives to each that which is suitable to its kind. His adversaries in the seventeenth century, and they were

many, either failed to read his essay through or failed to understand it. They read into its author a theriophilic prejudice that was not there.

Montaigne did pick up from the ancients all the stories of animal intelligence and morality which had been passed on by Plutarch and Pliny. He speaks of the government of the bees; the architectural skill of the swallow; the deliberation and foresight of the spider in spinning her web; the medical knowledge, the temperance, the chastity of various animals. He argues that if it would require reason in men to produce works of art such as the beasts produce, it must require reason in the beasts as well. He substantiates his argument by resorting again to Plutarch, this time to the piece "On the Cleverness of the Beasts" (*De sollertia animalium*, in *Moralia* XII, 959A). In Thrace, for instance, the foxes when they come to a frozen river, put their ears close to the ice to test its thickness. If they hear the water running beneath, they conclude that the ice is too thin to support their weight. This is a case of syllogistic reasoning on their part. Not only can the animals reason, regardless of what tradition has said, but they are morally better than men. They do not war on others of their kind nor are they subservient, like human beings, to one another. They have their own medical lore: the goats of Candia cure their wounds by eating dittany, the tortoise purges itself by taking origanum. Many of them show that they are capable of learning things that are not relevant to their natural way of life—e.g., dancing to music, guiding the blind, working a treadmill. Finally, since it takes greater intelligence to teach than to learn, they have been our teachers; for we have learned weaving from the spider, building from the swallow, music from the swan and nightingale, medicine from various animals. Montaigne gives examples of animal piety, fidelity, gratitude, magnanimity, and thus proves an "equality and correspondence" between them and us.

Probably the most shocking thing about these thoughts was that they lowered man from his pinnacle and to all intents and purposes reduced him to the level of the animals. Man had always had a special position between the angels and the beasts and now it began to look as if he was losing that position. Montaigne, moreover, had support for his ideas; not only his main disciple, Pierre Charron, but also from the early zoologists, Rorario, Gilles the piscatologist, Franzius, Wilde, and Goedaert the entomologist, none of whom rank with the great names in their fields but all of whom were respected in their day. These men, either because they were credulous or because they had an unshakable confidence in ancient authority, repeated many of the old yarns and lent the prestige of their scientific position to the spread of such ideas.

It was Descartes who made the most effective attack on theriophily with his doctrine that animals were simply complicated machines; their soul, as the Bible seemed to say, was their blood. Descartes did not say, as has been asserted, that they had no feelings, but merely that their feelings were material effects of what were known as animal spirits, a gaseous substance which moved the muscles. But the most important point for Descartes was that if the beasts could reason, then they would have to have immaterial souls, for reason depends on the apprehension of immaterial ideas, universals. Since the immaterial is unchanging and hence indestructible, an immaterial soul would be immortal; but that would be unthinkable if their soul is their blood. Hence theriophily is contrary to Scripture. With the Cartesian thesis propounded, the seventeenth century split on the issue; and various books were written pro and con. The clash in opinion was not so much over the question of whether the animals were happier, more moral, more rational than man, but whether they had souls or were machines. The only relevance of the issue to our topic is whether the possession of a soul is in itself a mark of superiority. Some seventeenth-century writers, La Rochefoucauld for instance, saw little to praise in the mere possession of that instrument, but he may not have been typical.

***Eighteenth Century and Later.*** The eighteenth century was on the whole anti-Cartesian. Hester Hastings (1936) has shown how the scientific approach to animal life took precedence over the philosophic; and while men did not weary of the theoretical refinements of their predecessors' doctrines, theriophily became more of a feeling for the sufferings of animals than an appraisal of human life. The feeling as it grew in intensity started the Humane Societies. Because of the efforts of Richard Martin, an Irish M.P., the Royal Society for the Prevention of Cruelty to Animals was founded in 1824. In the United States the American Society for the Prevention of Cruelty to Animals (A. S. P. C. A.) was founded in 1866 by Henry Bergh. It came to be believed that whether beasts had a material or immaterial soul, whether they could reason or not, they were capable of suffering, and that sufficed to create a bond between them and us. As for the question of their rationality, instinct and its supposed wonders supplanted it; a scientific zoology took the place of natural history, the questions that had stirred the theriophilists were settled in the laboratory and field rather than in the study.

At the same time new philosophic tenets developed in the eighteenth century brought the animals and man closer together. The gap between animal and human psychology created by Cartesianism was bridged by the epistemology of John Locke as modified by E. B. de Condillac in France. Condillac's *Essai sur l'origine des connaissances humaines* (1746) puts the source of all ideas in sensation. In his *Traité des animaux* (1755) he argues that animals have the same sort of feelings that men have, on the ground that they have sense organs just like ours. They are not capable of the subtle reasoning of men but as far as their needs demand intelligence, they possess it. They are therefore not superior to men, in the opinion of Condillac, for after all we are not automata. Once it was granted that they could have ideas and feelings of the same general type as human ideas and feelings, the kinship of all animate life was established. The eighteenth century saw the quickened development of entomology and zoology; and as men investigated the behavior of the beasts and insects, they found grounds for greater admiration for these creatures. This admiration has continued into our own times and there are few men who are not awestruck by such things as the migration of birds, the dance of the bees, the provisions made by wasps of food for their larvae which they will never see. A philosopher like Henri Bergson, though hardly a theriophilist, nevertheless utilized the work of the zoologists to demonstrate his theories of intuition. The work of J. H. Fabre in entomology supplemented that of R. A. F. de Réaumur, just as the work of Konrad Lorenz supplemented that of G. J. Romanes.

If one wishes then to depreciate intelligence, one has as much material in the writings of the scientists as our forefathers had in those of Aristotle, Aelian, Pliny, and Plutarch. Moreover it is based on better evidence. Inane as some of the traditional stories are, they lie behind the long history of man's admiration for the beasts, which in modern times has been expressed in stories of animal courage, fidelity, kindness. An outstanding expression of modern theriophily is contained in the famous lines of Walt Whitman from *Song of Myself:*

I think I could turn and live with the animals, they are
   so placid and self-contain'd,
I stand and look at them long and long,
They do not sweat and whine about their condition,
They do not lie awake in the dark and weep for their sins,
They do not make me sick discussing their duty to God,
Not one is dissatisfied, not one is demented with the mania
   of owning things,
Not one kneels to another, nor to his kind that lived thousands of years ago,
Not one is respectable or unhappy over the whole earth.

The one outstanding item that is missing from Whitman's lines is mention of the rationality of the beasts. But its absence would not have been lamentable to a mystic like Whitman.

*BIBLIOGRAPHY*

For the documents illustrating ancient theriophily, see A. O. Lovejoy and G. Boas, *Primitivism and Related Ideas in Antiquity* (Baltimore, 1935), Chs. 4 and 13; for Montaigne, his predecessors, and disciples, see G. Boas, *The Happy Beast* (Baltimore, 1933); for the eighteenth century, see Hester Hastings, *Man and Beast in French Thought of the Eighteenth Century* (Baltimore, London, and Paris, 1936), which contains a detailed bibliography. For a criticism of the writer's views on the *Gryllus* and on Gelli's *Circe*, see Merritt Hughes, "Spenser's Acrasia and the Circe of the Renaissance," *Journal of the History of Ideas*, **4** (Oct. 1943). For one of the most fertile sources of theriophilist ideas in the eighteenth century, see Pierre Bayle, *Dictionnaire historique* (1697), the article on *Rorarius*, especially remarks C, E, F, G, H; see also the article on *Barbe*, remark C. A modern edition of *Circe* is Giovanni B. Gelli, *Circe*, ed. Robert M. Adams, trans. Thomas Brown (Ithaca, 1963).

GEORGE BOAS

[See also **Chain of Being**; Hierarchy; Longevity; **Man-Machine**; **Nature**; **Primitivism**; Rationality; Skepticism.]

# TIME

THE CONSCIOUSNESS of time is inseparable from that of change. But while the awareness of change as one of the most pervasive and omnipresent features of human experience is present on the lowest level of human and also probably subhuman intelligence, the consciousness of time, especially in its conceptual form, appeared much later. Just as it was difficult to separate space conceptually from its concrete content, it required a considerable effort of abstraction to differentiate time from changes and events "taking place" in it. The mythological image of time as a person which drags all things into a ceaseless flux was the first crude step in this direction.

*Greek and Medieval Thought.* A definite separation of time from its content was suggested by the early Pythagoreans: "Time is said to come from the Unlimited, that is from infinite space" (E. Zeller, *A History of Greek Philosophy*, trans. S. F. Alleyne, London [1881], I, 468–69). While time was no longer personified, it was still *reified*, and this reification was another step toward the separation of time from its concrete sensory content. The fact that time itself was regarded— rather illogically—as being subject to time (as "*coming from infinite space*") clearly showed the difficulties to which this early reification of time led. On the other hand, the fact that some early Pythagoreans identified time with the celestial sphere, or, more likely, with

its rotating motion, indicated their incapacity to separate time from its content. The reference to the celestial sphere and its revolving motion had far-reaching effects on the subsequent development of the concept of time: it focussed the attention of philosophers on the regular periodicity of the celestial motions by which time can be measured, and thus it deepened the distinction between the qualitative content of time and its metrical aspects.

The correlation of time with spatial motion became the source of *the relational theory of time* according to which "time is nothing by itself" (Lucretius, *De rerum natura*, I, 459f.) and cannot be separated from concrete changes occurring in it. Finally the alleged inseparability of time from spatial displacements created the tendency to exaggerate the analogy between space and time and, eventually, to spatialize time altogether and thus virtually to eliminate it; this extreme tendency is very conspicuous in the Eleatic school: the sphere of Parmenides is timeless because of its exclusively spatial and, consequently, immutable character. Similarly, Zeno's four arguments against the reality of motion (and, implicitly, against the reality of time) were based on the assimilation of time to a geometrical line. According to Zeno, temporal intervals are adequately symbolized by spatial segments; both are divisible ad infinitum, and to the point-like extremities of linear segments correspond the durationless extremities of temporal intervals—instants. The impossibility of building motion from motionless positions, and durations from the durationless instants, follows naturally.

Eleatism was the metaphysics of timeless Being in its most radical form; it exerted a powerful influence on the subsequent history of Western thought, even though it has never reappeared in such extreme form. In other words, time and becoming, instead of being completely eliminated in the Eleatic fashion, retained their existence, even though it was of an inferior and less dignified kind than that of immutable Being. This can be seen clearly in the atomists; although they did not deny the reality of time and motion, they did not include them among their first principles which, according to them, were matter and space only. Lucretius' view that "time is nothing in itself," quoted above, was an echo of Epicurus' view that time was no more than an "accident of accidents" ($\sigma\acute{\upsilon}\mu\pi\tau\omega\mu\alpha$ $\sigma\upsilon\pi\tau\omega\mu\acute{\alpha}\tau\omega\nu$) since its existence was merely a function of the changing configurations of atoms. This was probably the view of the early atomists as well; according to Sextus Empiricus, Democritus regarded time as "an appearance presenting itself under the aspect of day and night"; if he called time "uncreated," he meant by it that motion (on which, in his view, time

389

depended) is without beginning. With such a view of time and with their anticipation of the law of constancy of matter, the atomists greatly strengthened the static and substantialist modes of thought.

The antisubstantialist trend in Greek philosophy was represented by Heraclitus of Ephesus, a philosopher of "becoming" par excellence. In his opposition to the Eleatics, he went much farther than the atomists who, while admitting the reality of motion, still retained *its immutable vehicle*, i.e., substantial matter; for their atoms remain eternally the same in the successive positions of their trajectories. Heraclitus' denial of the immutable vehicle of motion followed from his insistence on the radical fluidity of everything and on the irreversibility of becoming: "You cannot step twice into the same river." For the motion of immutable particles Heraclitus substituted the dynamic unity of process in which each momentary phase was continuously transformed into its "opposite," that is, into a subsequent, qualitatively different phase. Heraclitus was apparently aware that the continuity of change (his dynamic "unity of opposites") resists the usual conceptual treatment and even a strict application of the law of contradiction: "We step and we do not step into the same river; we are and we are not" (frag. 81). This clearly anticipated the future Hegelian view of becoming as a synthesis of being and nonbeing.

Yet, Heraclitus' view was not free of spatial imagery, which was hardly compatible with his insistence on the qualitative aspect of time and its irreversibility. This was shown by his belief in the Great Year, i.e., the periodic recurrence of all events in the same order. This year, for Heraclitus, was equal to 10,800 years (according to another source 18,000 years). According to the testimony of the Stoics and of Simplicius (whose reliability on this point has been questioned by Friedrich Schleiermacher, Ferdinand Lasalle, John Burnet, Geoffrey S. Kirk), it measured the period separating two successive conflagrations in which the old world perishes and a new one is reborn. Heraclitus' idea of cyclical becoming was a culmination of the early pre-Socratic views about the periodicity of the worlds. The view of Anaximander, Anaxagoras, and Empedocles was that the existing universe is the result of the differentiation of the original chaos—watery, fiery, or qualitatively undetermined—into which it would eventually return and from which a similar universe will emerge. In such view the successive cosmic cycles were similar in their general features only, not in all their specific details; but the latter view, upholding a complete *identity* of the successive cycles, emerged soon. This was the idea of *eternal recurrence of everything* which some Pythagoreans accepted, influenced probably by their identification of time with

the circular motion of the heaven: "Everything will eventually return in the self-same numerical order, and I shall converse with you staff in hand, and you will sit as you are sitting now, and so it will be in everything else, and it is reasonable to assume that time too will be the same" (The testimony of Eudemus of Rhodes; cf. H. Diels and W. Kranz, *Die Fragmente der Vorsokratiker*, 6th ed., Berlin [1951], 58B34). This was also the view of Archytas of Tarentum who defined time as "the interval of the universe."

The subsequent development of Greek, medieval, and modern philosophy was largely dominated by the contrast between the timeless realm of Being and the temporal realm of change; in this sense it was a continuation of the dialogue between Parmenides and Heraclitus. In most philosophical systems Being was endowed with a more dignified status of the true reality of which the temporal realm is merely a pale, shadowy replica. For Plato, in the *Timaeus*, the basic reality belongs to the timeless essences (Ideas) while the temporal realm is that of ceaseless change, generation, and decay; time itself is of derivative nature, being merely a "moving image of eternity." To this metaphysical dichotomy of Being and Becoming, of perfection and imperfection, corresponds the epistemological dichotomy of two kinds of knowledge—true knowledge whose object is the immutable realm of Ideas, and mere opinion, concerning the temporal realm. In the philosophy of Aristotle the timeless Ideas of Plato were, so to speak, compressed into one single entity—God, the immovable source of every motion. Like Plato, Aristotle held *the relational view of time;* time is inseparable from motion for without motion (in the broader Aristotelian sense of *change*) there would be no time. But while Aristotle's Prime Mover has all the attributes of the Eleatic One, his view of the physical world—or at least of its sublunar part—was similar to the view of Heraclitus. Aristotle rejected the atomistic explanation of qualitative change and diversity by the displacement of homogeneous and unchangeable elements; he denied the existence of atoms and of the void, and reaffirmed the reality of qualitative change. He viewed the four sublunar elements as mutually transformable in a way analogous to the Heraclitean transformation of opposites. Every such transformation, including even change of position, implies a transition from potentiality to actuality; only the Unmoved Mover is exempt from this passage. In introducing the concept of not-yet-existing possibility and in insisting on the contingency of the future, Aristotle came very close to the idea of an "open future," which is the central theme of modern process philosophy.

It must also be noted that in spite of his insistence on the inseparability of time and motion, Aristotle was careful enough not to identify them. Since there are various motions of different speeds occurring simultaneously, "the time is absolutely the same for both" (*Physics*, IV, 14). There are thus absolutist elements in Aristotle's view of time which vaguely foreshadow Newton's view. This is also clear from his comment on his own definition of time. After defining time as the "numerical aspect of motion with respect to its successive parts," he raises the question whether time can exist without the counting activity of mind; and his answer is affirmative: time is *numerus numerabilis*, i.e., an objective reality susceptible of being counted but independent of the act of counting, consequently independent of the existence of the counting mind. The sphere of the fixed stars represents the absolutely uniform cosmic clock by which time is measured; its perfectly uniform rotation is, within the realm of change, the closest imitation of the immutability of the Prime Mover.

Aristotle apparently also accepted the idea of eternal return of all the events, at least if we accept his authorship of the following passage in *Problemata*: "Just as the course of the firmament and each of the stars is a circle, why should not also the coming into being and the decay of perishable things be of such a kind that the same things again come into being and decay?" (*The Works of Aristotle*, ed. W. D. Ross, Oxford [1923], VII, 916a). Aristotle realized that the cyclical character of becoming would imply a *relativization of succession:* if the Trojan War will inevitably recur, then in a sense we are living "prior" to it. The author of *Problemata*, however, refused to accept the ultimate consequence of the idea of eternal recurrence: "To demand that those who are coming into being should always be numerically identical, is foolish" (ibid). Like Plato, Aristotle associated the cosmic period ("the Great Year") not with a periodically recurring universal conflagration, but with a return of all celestial bodies to the same configuration. The idea of any cosmic cataclysm was incompatible with Aristotle's belief in the incorruptibility of the celestial clockwork.

The cyclicity of time was upheld also by the Stoics. According to them, at the end of each cosmic cycle the universe is dissolved into the original fire. This will coincide with the beginning of another cycle in which the events of the previous cycle will be reconstituted in all their details and in the same order. But Stoics followed Aristotle by believing that another Socrates who will marry another Xantippe and be accused by another Meletus will not be numerically identical with the previous Socrates since numerical identity implies an uninterrupted existence. Some younger Stoics, in conceding small differences between successive recurrences of Socrates, gave up the circularity of becoming

in all but name. Like Aristotle, the Stoics also speculated about the paradoxical nature of the present moment; according to Plutarch, Chrysippus denied the infinite divisibility of time, i.e., he accepted the existence of temporally extended moments, thus curiously anticipating the modern hypothesis of "chronons."

Although Plotinus' Ineffable One possesses all the attributes of the Eleatic Being, he retained change and time on the lower phenomenal level. He tried to make the relation between the temporal and timeless level more intelligible by his idea of *emanation*, i.e., by the process of degradation by which the lower degrees of reality proceed from the higher ones. This idea was implicitly present in Plato's view of the realm of change which "never truly is," forever oscillating between Being and Nothingness. According to Plotinus, change and time appear on the second level of emanation with the World Soul in which individual souls are contained. Unlike the Divine Intellect at the first level of emanation, souls are unable to grasp the timeless truth instantaneously, but only gradually, step by step, in a laborious process of reasoning. Succession and change are thus mere results of human inability to grasp everything at once. As in Plato, time is "the moving [and therefore imperfect] image of eternity"; but "motion" is understood by him in a psychological sense, as "movement of the soul"; without this movement time would disappear (*Enneads*, III, 7, 12). From this correlation of mind and time it follows that whenever there is time, there is mind at least in a rudimentary form, and vice versa. In this feature Plotinus' thought is near to modern temporalistic panpsychism (Bergson, Whitehead); but by his concept of timeless truth and by his adherence to the cyclical theory of time he stands at the opposite pole.

The Greek dualism of the timeless realm of perfection and the changing realm of decay, with the concomitant contrast between timeless divine insight and temporal (therefore incomplete) human knowledge dominated all medieval thought, Christian, Jewish, and Islamic. There were only a few theologians who did not accept predestination as an inevitable consequence of the time-transcending divine knowledge which embraces the totality of all successive events in one single act—*totum simul*. In the thought of Saint Augustine there were the same two trends as in Plotinus: on one side, time was characterized as "distension of soul" (*Confessions*, Book XI) and thus correlated with psychological reality. Augustine's description of our consciousness of time belongs to the finest and subtlest pieces of introspective analysis. On the other hand, again like Plotinus, he excluded time from the highest level of Being; time was created by God *with* the creation of the world: *Non in tempore, sed cum tempore finxit Deus mundum* (*De civitate Dei*, XI, 5).

Saint Thomas equally stressed the immutability of God (*Summa Theologica*, Qu. 9). It would seem then only consistent for Saint Thomas to accept complete predestination (Qu. 22, 23, 24). It was exceedingly difficult to reconcile this view with the freedom of will which he postulated on ethical grounds. More consistent on this point were the Protestant reformers of the sixteenth century who did not hesitate to negate freedom completely in the name of divive omniscience and predestination. The Greek influence can be seen also in the fact that some Christian thinkers, like Origen, accepted the eternity of the world and even metempsychosis (transmigration of souls); even Saint Thomas was aware that the Aristotelian proof of the Prime Mover did not imply the creation of the world in time, the truth of which must be accepted on faith, but cannot be proved (ibid., Qu. 46).

Even the idea of eternal return did not completely disappear during the Middle Ages as is shown by the decree of 1277 which threatened excommunication of those who accepted the Neo-Platonic idea of a Great Year lasting 36,000 years. It is true that because of the Judeo-Christian emphasis on the irreversibility of cosmic and human history this doctrine was foreign to that period: thus even Origen rejected the idea of eternal recurrence because of its incompatibility with human freedom, while Augustine rejected it on the ground that the incarnation of Christ could occur only once. Thomas Aquinas pointed out that the cyclical view of time implies the re-creation of numerically identical individuals—an operation which because of its intrinsically contradictory character is even beyond God's power. But neither Duns Scotus nor William of Ockham shared Thomas' view. Nicolas Bonnet and François de la Marche insisted on God's power to restore any past motion, and consequently, any past interval of time. Since the restoration of any past interval of time implies the concomitant elimination of that portion of the past which separates the re-created interval from the present moment, this claim was in direct opposition to Thomas' view of the intrinsic indestructibility of the past which even God's omnipotence is unable to change: *Praeterita autem non fuisse contradictionem implicat* (Qu. 25, art. 4).

***Time in Classical Science.*** While the time of the Aristotelian and medieval cosmology was relational, it was still uniform and in this sense universal since it was physically embodied in the uniform rotation of the sphere of the fixed stars which represented the absolute cosmic clock. But with the removal of this privileged cosmic clock by Giordano Bruno, the unity and uniformity of time was greatly compromised as

long as time was still regarded as inseparable from motion, in the sense of the relational theory. For what becomes of the unity and uniformity of time, if there is no uniform cosmic clock by which time can be measured? There are only two ways to avoid this difficulty: either to accept fully the consequence of the relational theory and to concede that without the privileged cosmic clock there should be as many times as there are motions—*tot tempora quot motus;* or to give up the relational theory altogether, that is, to make time completely independent of any concrete physical motion; only in this way would the unity and the uniformity of time not be affected by the diversity and variability of physical motions. It was the second solution which was gradually adopted by the incipient modern science. This separation of time from its physical content was made easier by the fact that doubts about the uniform cosmic clock began to arise even prior to the elimination of the last celestial sphere. The fact of the precessional motion, already known to the Greek astronomers, made it necessary to postulate an additional sphere beyond the eighth sphere; only to this ninth sphere—and not to the sphere of the "fixed stars"—did the truly uniform revolving motion belong.

Further observations raised the doubt whether any uniformly running celestial clock exists at all in nature. Doubts of this kind were expressed by Nicolas Bonnet and Grazadei d'Ascoli in the fourteenth century; they nevertheless insisted that the existence of true mathematical time does not depend on the existence of such a clock. Similarly, Bernardino Telesio in his *De rerum natura . . .* (1565), though he retained the Aristotelian cosmology, held that time is logically prior to motion and change; while motion cannot exist without time, time which, according to him, exists by itself (per se), can exist without motion. A similar foreshadowing of Newton's concept of absolute time can be seen in the thought of Francisco Suárez, even though he too retained the Aristotelian cosmic clockwork. He distinguishes two kinds of duration: "flowing imaginary extension" (*spatium imaginarium fluens*), which flows uniformly (*immutabile in suo fluxu*), and concrete change which coexists with it and, so to speak, fills it (*quasi replens*). Thus the distinction between time as a homogeneous container and its concrete changing content is clearly drawn; the former is intrinsically irreversible, the latter is not (*Disputationes metaphysicae*, C. L. sec. IX, 15).

But even after the definitive removal of the celestial clockwork, the concept of absolute time was formed only gradually and after some hesitation. This is clear in the thought of G. Bruno, in particular in articles 38–40 of his *Camoeracensis acrotismus seu rationes articulorum physicorum adversus Peripateticos* (Wittenberg, 1588). Certain of its passages show that Bruno was leaning toward the relational theory of time as, for instance, when he claims that there are as many times as there are stars (*tot tempora quot astra*). On the other hand, guided by the analogy of infinite space of which particular spaces are mere parts, he speaks of universal time (*tempus universale*) of which particular durations are finite portions. Time would exist even if all things were at rest and motionless; against Aristotle, Bruno holds that change is a necessary condition for the perception of time, but not for its existence.

Similar hesitancies may be traced in the thought of Pierre Gassendi. In his *Philosophiae Epicuri Syntagma* in 1649, only six years before his death, he speaks of time in the characteristically Epicurean way as an "accident of accidents," that is, *accidens accidentium*. Against this relational view of time, Gassendi equally unambiguously insists on its absolute and independent nature, e.g., when in his polemic with Descartes he says: "Whether things are or not, whether they move or rest, time always flows at an equal rate." This sentence occurs almost verbatim in the passage of Isaac Barrow, Newton's tutor (*Mathematical Works*, ed. W. Whewell [1860], II, 160f.), where it is stated that motion presupposes time, but not vice versa, and that time continues to flow even if all things stand still. Gassendi's influence on Barrow and Newton is also clear in his view linking the infinity of space and time with the divine omnipresence and everlasting duration, and his insistence that both time and space existed prior to the creation of the world (*Syntagma philosophicum, Opera omnia*, Lyons [1658], I, 183, 225). Newton's characterization of time, in the scholium of his *Philosophiae naturalis principia mathematica* (1687), was the culmination of the process by which the concept of time was separated from that of concrete physical change:

Absolute, true and mathematical time, of itself, and by its own nature, flows uniformly on, without regard to anything external. Relative, apparent and common time, is some sensible measure of absolute time (duration), estimated by the motions of bodies, whether accurate or inequable, and is commonly employed in place of true time; . . . (Andrew Motte's translation, revised by Florian Cajori).

For more than two centuries this concept of time remained practically unchallenged by physicists; James Clerk Maxwell's definition of time in his *Matter and Motion* (1877) is identical both in spirit as well as in letter with that of Newton.

**Time in Modern Philosophy.** Modern views of time (1500–1900) were shaped by the merging of two influences: of the previous philosophical tradition and of the nascent classical science. The Greek and medie-

val dualism of two realms, eternal and temporal, was retained in various systems of pantheistic monism and its echoes can be found in other systems too. The transcendent eternity of the medieval God was replaced by the impersonal immanent order of nature which was as much beyond time and change as the Eleatic Being, Plotinus' One, or Aristotle's and Aquinas' God. From Giordano Bruno to F. H. Bradley this basic pattern remained the same. "Thus also the divine mind contemplates everything in one altogether simple act at once and without succession, that is, without the difference between the past, present and future; to Him all things are present" (G. Bruno, *Opera latine conscripta*, Florence [1889], I, 4, pp. 32–33). "In eternity there is no 'before' and 'after'; for it follows exclusively from the divine perfection that God's decrees cannot be different and could not have been different" (B. Spinoza, *Ethica*, I, prop. 33).

The second quotation shows that the immutability of the eternal order of nature implies the strictest determinism. In this respect the ancient deterministic tradition was strengthened by the mechanistic physics of the seventeenth century. Galileo, like Bruno before him and Spinoza after him, upheld the dualism of timeless divine perfection and of imperfect, time-consuming human knowledge: "We proceed in step-by-step discussion from inference to inference, whereas He conceives through mere intuition. . . . The divine intellect . . . grasps the essence of the circle without any temporal discourse (*senza temporaneo discorso*) and thus apprehends the infinite array of its properties" (*Opere*, Florence [1855], VII, 129). Galileo still speaks of God; Spinoza speaks of *Deus sive natura*, while in Laplace the timeless order of nature is already thoroughly secularized and depersonalized: what was the omniscient divine insight in theology becomes in his thought the universal cosmic formula containing all the details of the cosmic history—past, present, as well as future (*Essai philosophique sur la probabilité*, Paris, 1814).

Neither Bruno nor Spinoza, nor certainly Laplace, ever denied temporal succession on the "lower" or phenomenal level; it was only on the "higher" level of the ultimate reality that time was abolished. This dualism of two realms, timeless and temporal, was retained by post-Kantian idealism. It was prepared by Kant's view that time is a mere form of sensibility, applicable legitimately only to the phenomenal, but not to the noumenal realm. This explains why the "Absolute Ego" of Fichte, in spite of his verbal emphasis on its becoming (*Werden*) and activity (*Urtätigkeit*), remains timeless (cf. *Grundlagen der Wissenschaftslehre*, Berlin [1845], p. 217: *Für die blosse reine Vernunft ist alles zugleich*). From such a point of view it was only consistent for Fichte to adhere to the most rigorous form of determinism (*Die Bestimmung des Menschen, Sämtliche Werke*, Berlin [1845], II, 182–83), while Kant used Laplacean language prior to Laplace when he claimed that a complete insight into the character of man would make his thoughts and actions as predictable as the solar and lunar eclipses (*Critique of Practical Reason*, trans. T. K. Abbot, 6th ed., London [1909], p. 193).

Schelling's view of time is similar, at least in that first phase of his thought which accounts for the close kinship of his *Identitätsphilosophie* with the thought of Bruno and Spinoza. The position of Hegel was far more ambiguous. On one side he stressed explicitly his agreement with Heraclitus; on the other side, he stressed the timelessness of his Absolute Idea. Hence two divergent interpretations of Hegel's dialectics: one interpreting it as the dynamic, historical process (Benedetto Croce, J. N. Findlay), the other, represented mainly by McTaggart, according to which the dialectical movement is merely in our mind, being nothing but a series of successive approximations by which we come closer to the timelessly realized "Infinite End," or Absolute Idea (J. M. E. McTaggart, *Studies in the Hegelian Dialectics*, 2nd ed., Cambridge [1922], p. 171).

On the other hand, Schopenhauer's view of time was quite unambiguous. Under the influence of Kant, he regarded time as only *phenomenally* real; the thing-in-itself which, according to him, is the Universal Will, is, despite the apparently dynamic connotation of this term, beyond both space and time, and he explicitly assimilated it to the Eleatic One and All (ἕν καὶ πᾶν). Only later, in the second edition of his main work (1844), did he realize that this view is incompatible with another of his basic claims, viz., that we directly intuit the cosmic Will in our own consciousness; how can we perceive the timeless reality directly through our essentially temporal introspection? He then corrected his view by saying that the will of which we are aware is not the thing-in-itself, but an appearance, even though somehow more basic (*Urphänomenon*) than other appearances. The same distinction between temporal appearances and the static substratum underlying them is found in F. H. Bradley, one of the most outspoken defenders of static monism in the twentieth century. In his main book, *Appearance and Reality* (1893), he tries to show the contradictory and therefore unreal character of change and of time as well as of diversity in general; the transcendent Absolute must be free of these contradictions.

The denial of time was frequently but not always associated with monistic tendencies as different kinds of static pluralism show. That the dynamic character of Leibniz's monad is more apparent than real is clear from its nature: the substance which contains in itself *all* its future states as its own predicates (*Discours de la métaphysique*, 8). His view that somebody with a sufficient insight "would see the future in the present as in a mirror" ("On Destiny or Mutual Dependence," *Leibniz Selections*, ed. P. P. Wiener, New York [1951], p. 571 followed from his theory of pre-established harmony and fully anticipated the passages of Kant, Fichte, and Laplace, quoted above. Far more explicit was the elimination of succession and change in J. F. Herbart and J. M. E. McTaggart. Herbart's immaterial units, *die Realen*, are qualitatively different, but absolutely immutable; the illusion of succession and change arises because to our shifting attention they appear in different aggregations. In McTaggart's monadism true reality belongs only to a timeless series of which the temporal series is merely apparent perspective representation. More recently, Bertrand Russell's "logical atomism" bears a clear similarity to the static pluralism of Herbart, as one historian of Anglo-American pluralism has noted (Jean Wahl, *Les philosophes pluralistes d'Angleterre et d'Amérique*, Paris [1920], p. 217). Wittgenstein's explicit denial of the passage of time (*Tractatus Logico-philosophicus* [1921], 6. 3611) is a consequence of his logical atomism.

These prevailing static tendencies explain why the concept of absolute time, upheld by Gassendi and Newton, has not been accepted by philosophers as unanimously as it has been by scientists. Closest to Newton's view was John Locke; but even Locke, in pointing out the impossibility of comparing two successive intervals of duration (which cannot be superposed because of their very succession), anticipated the later criticisms of Bergson and Poincaré in this regard. The most outstanding opponent of Newton was Leibniz, who was engaged in a long polemic with Newton's disciple, Samuel Clarke, about the status of space and time; Berkeley's objections were directed mainly against the concept of absolute space.

Both Berkeley and Leibniz upheld *the relational theory of space and time;* time is "the order of succession of perceptions," and as such it is inseparable from concrete events. From this standpoint the "flow of empty time" is without meaning. But while Berkeley claimed that the infinite divisibility of change and time (both being inseparable) is a mere fiction, since mathematical durationless instants are never perceptible and are therefore unreal, Leibniz—like Descartes—believed that both time and any concrete change is divisible ad infinitum, i.e., consists of ever-perishing instants. (It should be recalled that the alleged independence of perishing temporal instants was used by Descartes as the basis for his view that the world is maintained in existence by continuous divine creation.)

While David Hume accepted Berkeley's view of indivisible temporal moments (*minima sensibilia*), Kant sided with Leibniz in accepting the mathematical continuity (infinite divisibility) of all phenomenal changes. Thus for Berkeley and Hume, time shared the discreteness of perceptual changes, while for Leibniz and Kant concrete changes shared the infinite divisibility of mathematical time. Locke adopted an intermediate position in drawing the distinction between immediately experienced qualitative duration and the homogeneous duration of the physical world (*Essay Concerning Human Understanding*, Book II, Ch. 14). This distinction became the ground for another widely accepted distinction between the durational "specious present" in psychology and the mathematical present of physical and physiological time. On this point both Leibniz and Kant remained completely Newtonian and Cartesian.

The introspective approach to the problem of time, initiated by Locke, Berkeley, and Hume, led to two divergent developments: (1) to Kant's epistemological analysis of time in the *Critique of Pure Reason*, and its subsequent modifications in neo-Kantianism and phenomenology; (2) to the systematic investigation of temporal awareness in the empirical and experimental psychology of the nineteenth century. According to Kant, time is an *a priori* form of inner—and indirectly of outer—sense which is both "empirically real and transcendentally ideal"; it guarantees by its own nature the *a priori* and synthetic character of arithmetical operations, whose universal validity is independent of experience precisely because they take place in the ideal medium of time. But while time is a necessary condition of all experience—both introspective and sensory—it does not apply to transcendent "things-in-themselves," including our "intelligible character" which underlies our "empirical ego." In phenomenalizing both physical and psychological time, Kant greatly strengthened static modes of thought as the subsequent development of German philosophy showed.

Empirical psychologists in the nineteenth century were opposed to Kant's *a priori* view of time; they pointed out that the consciousness of time is subject to development and to individual and even pathological modifications. This view was strengthened by the theory of evolution and its applications to psychological phenomena; Herbert Spencer's *Principles of Psychology* (1855) contains long polemical passages showing the incompatibility of Kant's view with the observations of genetic psychology and psychopathology. But despite their opposition to Kant, empirical and genetic psychologists eventually reinforced the tendency to phenomenalize time and thus to weaken its ontological status. Arthur Schopenhauer's combination of the Kantian and of the empirical-psychological approach was only apparently paradoxical; he saw in the abnormal modifications of temporal awareness an additional corroboration of the phenomenal, and, ultimately, of the illusory character of time.

This is related to the fact that the theory of evolution, in spite of its emphasis on the historical aspects of reality, was not—in its initial impact at least—opposed to the static and substantialistic view of the world; on the contrary, since for some time it even strengthened it. Darwin's theory of the origin of species was strictly mechanistic and in this way fitted perfectly into the Laplacean framework of classical physics. Herbert Spencer, unquestionably the most influential philosophical interpreter of evolution in the last century, made an ambitious attempt at deriving "the law of evolution" from the law of conservation of energy. This law itself was regarded by him, as well as by Helmholtz, Häckel, Ostwald, and others, as the basis of the law of causality. Conversely, classical principles like *ex nihilo nil fit* and *causa aequat effectum* guided Robert Mayer (1814–78) in his experimental search for the law of the conservation of energy. Friedrich Nietzsche, in spite of his contempt for static concepts such as "substance," "Being," and others, did not find it incongruous to combine the evolutionary philosophy of Overman with the eternal return of all the events (*die ewige Wiederkunft der Gleichen*) in which becoming, in virtue of its own circularity, was subordinated to Being.

***Time in Contemporary Philosophy and Science.*** The radical reaffirmation—or as George Boas called it—the "acceptance of time," had to wait until the end of the last century. The main intellectual obstacle to it was the static determinism of the Spinoza-Laplacean type, which only a few "heretical" thinkers dared to question. Among them was Charles Renouvier who suggested the existence of absolute beginnings (*les commencements absolus*) in nature; Émile Boutroux who in his *De la contingence de la nature* (1874) suggested that physical determinism is valid only on the macrophysical scale and that there may be microphysical indeterminations too small to be detected by the methods available at that time (op. cit., Ch. IV). C. S. Peirce expressed a similar view about the merely approximative character of classical determinism ("The Doctrine of Necessity Examined," *The Monist*, **2** [April 1892], 321–37). Meanwhile William James also argued, as Peirce had, for the objectivity of the chance-element in nature ("Dilemma of Determinism," 1884); his rejection of determinism, though motivated mainly by ethical reasons, was also based on his rejection of the timeless "block-universe" which strict determinism implies, and which is incompatible with genuine plurality as well as with real succession.

A far more systematic formulation of James's pluralistic temporalism took place later, in his *A Pluralistic Universe* (1909) and his posthumous *Some Problems in Philosophy* (1911). In these books James's debt to Renouvier is still acknowledged, but far more decisive and explicitly acknowledged was the influence of Henri Bergson. In his first book *Essai sur les données immédiates de la conscience* (1889), Bergson reached a conclusion similar to a pivotal idea in James's *Principles of Psychology* (1890), namely, the continuity of introspective experience—"the stream of consciousness" or "true duration" (*durée réelle*)—which both thinkers stressed against artificial conceptualization and atomization. (It is fair to stress that some of the philosophically most important sections of *Principles of Psychology* had been published previously in *Mind* [1884] under the title "On Some Omissions of Introspective Psychology.") The dynamic continuity of psychological time is both unity and diversity; but it is neither the abstract homogeneous unity of mathematical time nor the dust-like multiplicity of the externally related durationless instants; it is the mnemic continuity in which no sharp separation can be drawn between the successive phases, despite their qualitative heterogeneity.

In his later books Bergson generalized his introspective analysis by applying its results to duration in general. Every duration, he held, is essentially incomplete in the sense that each of its moments introduces an element of novelty not contained in the past. In ignoring this irreducible element of novelty—previously stressed in Boutroux's contingentism and Peirce's tychism—radical determinism as well as radical finalism virtually and sometimes even explicitly eliminate time altogether in fusing the successive phases into a single instantaneous unity of the Laplacean formula or of the immutable Absolute. In such a "block universe"—whether of the naturalistic or idealistic kind—"everything is given" (*tout est donné*) which is contrary to the most obvious experience. Equally false is radical indeterminism, which, in positing *creatio ex nihilo* of each moment, ignores the dynamic continuity of duration and thus makes both memory and causation impossible. Mathematical continuity (infinite divisibility) belongs only to the spatial segment by which duration is inadequately symbolized, not to duration itself. In other words, the durationless present is a fiction not only in psychology, but in physics as well; even the physical processes have a fine pulsational structure, even though their temporal span is enormously shorter than that of mental events (*Matter and Memory*, Ch. IV). This view is also shared

by A. O. Lovejoy, although he insisted against Bergson that the temporal segments must have sharp boundaries if the genuine difference between the successive phases should be preserved. Although critical of some aspects of James's and Bergson's thought, Lovejoy shared with them their *temporalism*—the term which he himself coined for doctrines which took time as an essential category of all existence.

Another outstanding temporalist or "process philosopher" is Alfred North Whitehead; his metaphysics of events with its emphasis on "the creative advance of nature," "the immortality of the past" (from which the irreversibility of Becoming follows), and the denial of durationless instants was very close to the views of James and Bergson. Besides acknowledging his affinity with Bergson's views, Whitehead also stressed his debt to Samuel Alexander's work *Space, Time and Deity* (1920), and, to a lesser degree, to Lloyd Morgan and C. D. Broad. Like Alexander, and also under the influence of the relativity theory, Whitehead stressed the inseparability of space from time; but unlike Alexander, Morgan, and Broad, Whitehead regarded, in the later phase of his thought at least, his own concept of novelty as incompatible with classical determinism. Broad's original view about "the reality of the past and the unreality of the future" was given up later by his belief in precognition which requires the preexistence of the future in some form. John Dewey, who was one of the first to welcome Peirce's rejection of classical determinism ("The Superstition of Necessity," *Monist*, **3** [1893], 362–79), unlike other process philosophers, did not regard the reality of all-pervasive change as the source of cosmic optimism: "change is nothing to gloat over—" (*Experience and Nature*, Chicago [1925], p. 71). It is, however, fair to state that the term "meliorism," coined by William James, describes far more accurately than "optimism" the view of the process philosophers mentioned. An even more pessimistic view of time is that of Heidegger; his connotation of becoming is completely divorced from that of evolution and creativity; time is viewed only in its tragic and destructive aspects.

The interest in the problem of time was not confined to process philosophers only. Thus Josiah Royce used the durational present as a model for understanding the relation of time and eternity; the divine consciousness, "Eternal Now," is still temporal, although its temporal span is incomparably wider than that of the human specious present. Bertrand Russell, who favored the concept of mathematical instants in his *Principles of Mathematics* (1903), gave it up in his article "On the Experience of Time" in *Monist* (**25**, 1915). Husserl's phenomenological analysis of time in *Die Phänomenologie des inner Zeitbewusstsein* (1966) was in his own view in many respects similar to the introspective analysis of Bergson (cf. Roman Ingarden, "L'intuition bergsonienne et le problème phénoménologique de la constitution," in "Bergson et nous," *Bulletin de la Société Française de Philologie* [1959], 165–66).

The development of physics in the twentieth century profoundly modified the classical concepts, including that of time. The theory of relativity proposed the union of space with time; the significance of this union is still being discussed. According to the widespread, but very questionable view, it means an assimilation of time to the fourth dimension of the static, becoming-less continuum—"space-time." Serious objections have been raised against such interpretation not only by philosophers like Meyerson, Bergson, and Reichenbach, but also by scientists like Eddington, A. A. Robb, and Whitrow. Occasionally Einstein himself stressed that even within the relativistic "space-time" the time dimension is not equivalent to the spatial dimensions. It is far more correct to speak of the dynamization of space rather than of the spatialization of time; the relativization of simultaneity means that "instantaneous space," that is, the class of simultaneously existing events, cannot be unambiguously carved out of the four-dimensional world-process. It is also significant that while the succession of causally related events remains a topological invariant within relativity physics—i.e., the world-lines remain irreversible in any frame of reference—it is not so for the spatial distances; thus the relativity of simultaneity can equally appropriately be called the *relativity of justaposition*. It has been correctly pointed out that in the relativistic physics the past is separated from the future not by the durationless three-dimensional "Now" spreading instantaneously across the universe as in the physics of Newton, but, even more effectively, by the four-dimensional region of "Elsewhere." It can also be shown that an event which is in the causal future for a certain observer cannot be in the causal past of any conceivable observer. This follows from Minkowski's formula for the invariance of the world interval:

$$I = s^2 - c^2(t_2 - t_1)^2 = \text{const.}$$

$s$ is spatial distance separating two events, $(t_2 - t_1)$ being their separation in time.

The most common source of the antitemporalistic misinterpretations of the relativity theory is the confusion of the metrical invariance with the topological invariance of time; while the latter is preserved, the former is not. This can be shown when we analyze the popular relativistic paradoxes. Some of these "paradoxes" are due to sheer ignorance; for instance, under no circumstances can anybody or anything "travel backwards to the past" as it follows immedi-

ately from the relativistic space-time diagram. Even the famous "paradox of twins," first mentioned by Paul Langevin in 1911, implies the metrical, not the topological relativity of temporal intervals; the twins aging at different rates, both move in the direction of the future and it is a misunderstanding to claim that one can make an exploratory "round trip" to the future and back.

Dynamization of space is even more conspicuous in the general relativity theory which fuses the physical content with the variable spatiotemporal continuum, and thus challenges the classical container-like character of absolute space and time. Thus time is inseparable from concrete physical events in a sense much more radical than the classical relational theory of time suggested. Thus the gravitational and inertial field—both being according to the principle of equivalence two aspects of the same phenomenon—are not *in* space-time; they are nothing but certain local irregularities of space-time, and the changes in the local curvature of space-time appear to us as the displacements of bodies in the allegedly inert space. The recession of the galaxies which suggested the idea of the expanding space shows how far modern cosmologies are from the immutable space of Newton.

Significant changes of the concept of time are also suggested by the quantum theory and wave mechanics. The implications of these changes point in the same direction as those of the relativity theories. The quantum character of the microphysical processes makes probable the view that physical time—like psychological time—is not divisible ad infinitum: that is, that there are the minimum intervals of time which are not further divisible since they coincide with the elementary events of nature. This is the meaning of *"l'atome du temps"* of Poincaré, of "quantum of time" of Whitehead, and of "chronon" of some contemporary physicists. It is always possible to assume that underlying the temporally indivisible events of microphysics there is the mathematical, infinitely divisible duration of Newton and Locke; but this view implies the absolutist distinction between homogeneous container-like time and its concrete physical content, which the present trends in physics make improbable. It is true that for practical purposes, that is, on the macrophysical level where the magnitude of Planck's constant $h$ can be disregarded, and where the interval of chronon is practically equivalent to a mathematical instant, time remains very approximately continuous. The chronon theory would remove the distinction between physical, infinitely divisible duration and psychological time—or rather it would reduce this distinction to that of degree only, the physical "chronons" being of incomparably shorter temporal span than the temporal *minima sen-*

*sibilia* in psychology. But since these temporal minima cannot be conceived as sharply separated, a serious difficulty arises as to how to synthesize conceptually the individuality of events with the continuity of becoming. It is probable that without a radical modification of our conceptual tools this will be impossible. Such modification is suggested by some recent attempts at constructing "topology without points" or "fuzzy set theory."

Another even more important philosophical consequence of the existence of Planck's constant is the indeterminacy of the microphysical processes, formulated by Heisenberg (1927). The two different names of this principle—"uncertainty principle" or "indeterminacy principle"—suggest two radically different interpretations of it. The first interpretation, more conservative in its outlook and favored more by traditionally oriented philosophers than by physicists, regards microphysical indeterminacy as a result of the interference of the process of observation with the process observed. The second interpretation, more favored by physicists, regards it as a manifestation of objective indeterminacy in nature. The first interpretation leaves the Laplacean determinism intact; the second one suggests the objective status of chance in the sense of Boutroux and Peirce, that is, of the "open world" (H. Weyl's term), forever in growth and forever incomplete, in which the future remains genuinely ambiguous and, though influenced by the past, is not predetermined by it. While the first interpretation is more congruous with the philosophical tradition glorifying static and immutable Being, the second interpretation is viewed with sympathy by the process-oriented thinkers. Thus the discussion concerning the interpretation of this principle is merely the most recent phase of the ancient dialogue between Parmenides and Heraclitus.

### BIBLIOGRAPHY

For the history of the concept of time, Walter Gent, *Die Philosophie des Raumes und der Zeit,* 2nd ed. (Hildesheim, 1962) is a very useful sourcebook. For the concept of time in medieval cosmology see the relevant chapters in Pierre Duhem, *Le système du monde,* Vols. I–X (Paris, 1913–59). Z. Zawirski's *L'évolution de la notion du temps* (Krakow, 1934) includes the modifications of the concept of time in recent physics. A very extensive bibliography of recent English articles on time is in J. J. C. Smart, *Problems of Space and Time* (New York, 1964) while *The Voices of Time,* ed. J. T. Fraser (New York, 1965) is a cooperative volume dealing with the historical, psychological, biological, and physical aspects of time.

Modern restatement of the Eleatic denial of time are F. H. Bradley, *Appearance and Reality* (London, 1893), Chs. 4, 18 and J. M. E. McTaggart, "The Unreality of Time," in *Mind,* N.S., **17** (1908), while Josiah Royce, in Lecture 3, *The World and the Individual,* Vol. II (New York, 1901), tries to synthesize the temporalistic and eternalistic view. Reaffirmation of the reality of temporal succession are: Henri Bergson, *Oeuvres complètes* (Geneva, 1945); William James, *A Pluralistic Universe* (New York, 1910); idem, *Some Problems of Philosophy* (New York, 1911); Samuel Alexander, *Space, Time and Deity* (London, 1920); A. N. Whitehead, *Process and Reality* (Cambridge, 1929); Charles Hartshorne, "Contingency and the New Era in Metaphysics," *Journal of Philosophy,* **29** (1932); Mary F. Cleugh, *Time and Its Importance in Western Thought* (London, 1937); Paul Weiss, *Reality* (Princeton, 1938); A. O. Lovejoy, *Reason, the Understanding and Time* (Baltimore, 1964); Philip P. Wiener, "The Central Role of Time in Lovejoy's Philosophy," *Philosophy and Phenomenological Research,* **23** (1963).

On the physical status of time: H. Poincaré, "La mesure du temps," *Dernières pensées* (Paris, 1913); Einstein-Lorentz-Minkowski-Weyl, *The Principle of Relativity,* trans. W. Perret and G. B. Jeffrey (London, 1952); A. S. Eddington, *The Nature of the Physical World* (Cambridge, 1928), Chs. III–V; É. Meyerson, *Identité et réalité,* 5th ed. (Paris, 1951); idem, *La déduction relativiste* (Paris, 1925), Ch. 7; A. A. Robb, *The Absolute Relations of Time and Space* (Cambridge, 1921); H. Mehlberg, "Essai sur la théorie causale du temps," *Studia philosophica* (Leopolis [Lvov], 1935); H. Reichenbach, *The Philosophy of Space and Time* (New York, 1958); idem, *The Direction of Time* (Los Angeles, 1956); A. Grünbaum, *Philosophical Problems of Space and Time* (New York, 1964); M. Čapek, *The Philosophical Impact of Contemporary Physics* (Princeton, 1961); G. J. Whitrow, *The Natural Philosophy of Time* (London and Edinburgh, 1961); A. N. Prior, *Papers on Time and Sense* (London, 1968); idem, *Past, Present and Future* (London, 1967); idem, *Time and Modality* (London and New York, 1957).

On the perception of time, see William James, *Principles of Psychology,* Vol. I (New York, 1890), esp. Chs. 9, 15; Bertrand Russell, "On the Experience of Time," *Monist,* **25** (1915); Edmund Husserl, *Die Phänomenologie des innern Zeitbewusstsein,* ed. R. Boehm (The Hague, 1966); Paul Fraisse, *Psychologie du temps* (Paris, 1957) contains a very complete bibliography.

MILIČ ČAPEK

[See also Atomism; Cosmic Images; **Cycles;** Determinism; **Evolutionism;** God; **Pragmatism;** Pre-Platonic Conceptions; Pythagorean . . . ; **Relativity;** Skepticism; **Space;** Uniformitarianism.]

# TIME AND MEASUREMENT

### I

THE ORIGINS of the concept of time are lost in the mists of prehistory but from our knowledge of surviving primitive races it would seem highly probable that the lives of our remote ancestors were far less consciously dominated by time than are ours. For example, although the children of Australian aborigines are of similar mental capacity to white children, they have great difficulty in telling the time by the clock. They can read off the position of the hands on the face of a clock as a memory exercise but they are quite unable to relate it to the time of the day. There is a cultural gap between their conception of time and ours which they find difficult to cross. Nevertheless, all primitive peoples have some idea of time and some method of reckoning, usually based on astronomical observations. The Australian aborigine will fix the time for a proposed action by placing a stone in the fork of a tree, or some such place, so that the sun will strike it at the agreed time.

Primitive man's sense of rhythm was a vital factor in his intuition of time. Before he had any explicit idea of time, he seems to have been aware of temporal associations dividing time into intervals like bars in music. The principal transitions in nature were thought to occur suddenly, and similarly man's journey through life was visualized as a sequence of distinct stages—later epitomized in Shakespeare's "seven ages of man." Even in so culturally advanced a civilization as the ancient Chinese different intervals of time were regarded as separate discrete units, so that time was in effect discontinuous. Just as space was decomposed into regions, so time was split up into areas, seasons, and epochs. In other words, time was "boxed." Even in late medieval Europe the development of the mechanical clock did not spring from a desire to register the passage of time but rather from the monastic demand for accurate determination of the hours when the various religious offices and prayers should be said.

It was a long step from the inhomogeneity of magical time as generally imagined in antiquity and the Middle Ages with its specific holy days and lucky and unlucky secular days to the modern scientific conception of homogeneous linear time. Indeed, man was aware of different times long before he formulated the idea of time itself. This distinction is particularly well illustrated by the Maya priests of pre-Columbian central America, who, of all ancient peoples, were probably the most obsessed with the idea of time. Whereas in European antiquity the days of the week were regarded as being under the influence of the principal heavenly bodies, e.g., Saturn-day, Sun-day, Moon-day, etc., for the Mayas each day was itself divine. Every monument and every altar was erected to mark the passage of time. The Mayas pictured the divisions of time as burdens carried on the backs of a hierarchy of divine bearers who personified the respective numbers by which the different periods—days, months, years, dec-

ades, etc.—were distinguished. There were momentary pauses at the end of each prescribed period, for example, at the end of a day, when one god with his burden (in this case representing the next day) replaced another god with his. A remarkably precise astronomical calendar was developed embodying correction formulae that were even more accurate than our present leap year *correction* which was introduced about a thousand years later by Pope Gregory XIII in 1582. Our correction is too long by 0.03 days in a century, whereas the corresponding Maya correction was 0.02 days too short. Despite this astonishing achievement the Mayas never seem to have grasped the idea of time as the journey of one bearer and his load. Instead, each god's burden came to signify the particular omen of the division of time in question—one year the burden might be drought, another a good harvest and so on.

## II

Unlike the Mayas, the ancient Greeks were not obsessed by the temporal aspect of things. At the dawn of Greek literature two contrasting points of view are found in Homer and Hesiod. In the *Iliad* Olympian theology and morality are dominated by spatial concepts, the cardinal sin being hubris, that is going beyond one's assigned province. Homer was not interested in the origin of things and had no cosmogony. On the other hand, Hesiod in his *Works and Days* gave an account of the origin of the world, and his poem can be regarded as a moralistic study based on the time concept.

Two centuries or more later (sixth century B.C.) the Ionian pioneers of natural philosophy visualized the world as a geometrical organism or a live space-filling substance. Heraclitus, on the other hand, believed the world to be a soul involved in an endless cycle of death and rebirth, the very essence of the universe being transmutation. A similar emphasis on time and soul characterized the Orphic religion which appears to have provided the mythical background of Pythagoreanism. According to Plutarch, when asked what Time was, Pythagoras replied that it was the soul, or procreative element, of the universe. Pythagoras is a shadowy figure but to him was attributed the celebrated discovery, following experiments with a monochord, that the concordant intervals of the musical scale can be expressed by simple ratios of whole numbers. This was perhaps the most striking illustrative example of Pythagoras' doctrine that the nature, or ultimate principle, of things is not some kind of substance, as the Ionians thought, but is to be found in number.

For the early Pythagoreans the concept of number itself had both spatial and temporal significance. Num-

399

bers were represented by patterns of the type still found on dominoes and dice. This led to an elementary theory of numbers based on geometry. Number, however, was also regarded from a temporal point of view. This is evident in the Pythagorean use of the *gnomon*. Originally, this was a time-measuring instrument—a simple, upright sundial. The term then came to mean the figure that remains when a square is cut out of the corner of a larger square with its sides parallel to the sides of the latter. Eventually it denoted any number which when added to a figurate number, for example a square number, generates the next number of the same shape. The early Pythagoreans regarded the generation of numbers as an actual physical operation in space and time, beginning with the initial unit or monad. In general, they failed to make any clear distinction between the abstract and the concrete and between logical and chronological priority.

These distinctions were clearly drawn by Parmenides, the founding father of deductive argument and logical analysis. In his *Way of Truth* he criticized current cosmogonies for their common assumption that the universe began at some moment of time. "And what need," he asked, "could have stirred it up, starting from nothing, to be born later rather than sooner?" This question was answered by Plato who claimed that time is coexistent with the universe. But he was deeply impressed by Parmenides' acute criticism of the ideas of becoming and perishing and by his conclusion that time does not pertain to anything that is truly real.

The difficulties involved in producing a logically satisfactory theory of time and its measurement were emphasized by Parmenides' pupil Zeno of Elea in his famous paradoxes. For, although these paradoxes were primarily concerned with the problem of motion, they raised difficulties both for the idea of time as continuous or infinitely divisible and for the idea of temporal atomicity. Unlike the Pythagoreans, who tended to identify the chronological with the logical, Parmenides and Zeno argued that they are incompatible.

The influence of Parmenides and Zeno on Plato is evident in the different treatment of space and time in Plato's cosmological dialogue the *Timaeus*. Space exists in its own right as a given frame for the visible order of things, whereas time is merely a feature of that order based on an ideal timeless archetype or realm of static geometrical shapes (Eternity) of which it is the "moving image," being governed by a *regular* numerical sequence made manifest by the motions of the heavenly bodies. Plato's intimate association of time with the universe led him to regard time as being actually produced by the revolutions of the celestial sphere.

400    This conclusion was not accepted by Aristotle who

rejected the idea that time can be identified with any form of motion. For, he argued, motion can be uniform or nonuniform and these terms are themselves defined by time, whereas time cannot be defined by itself. Nevertheless, although time is not identical with motion, it seemed to him to be dependent on motion. Possibly influenced by the Pythagoreans, he argued that time is a kind of number, being the numerable aspect of motion. Time is therefore a numbering process founded on our perception of "before" and "after" in motion: "Time is the number of motion with respect to earlier and later" (*Physica*, ed. W. D. Ross, Vol II, Book IV, 219a). Aristotle regarded time and motion as reciprocal. "Not only do we measure the movement by the time, but also the time by the movement, because they define each other. The time marks the movement, since it is number; and the movement the time" (ibid.). Aristotle recognized that motion can cease whereas time cannot, but there is one motion that continues unceasingly, namely that of the heavens. Clearly, although he did not agree with Plato, he too was profoundly influenced by the cosmological view of time. Moreover, although he began by rejecting any association between time and a particular motion in favor of one between time and motion in general, he came to the conclusion that time is closely associated with the circular motion of the heavens, which he regarded as the perfect example of uniform motion.

For Aristotle the primary form of motion was uniform motion in a circle because it could continue indefinitely, whereas uniform rectilinear motion could not. Any straight line necessarily had finite end points, since he did not have the modern mathematical concept of the infinitely extended straight line. For Aristotle, therefore, time was intimately connected with uniform circular motion.

Belief in the cyclic nature of time was widespread in antiquity, since most ancient peoples tended to regard time as essentially periodic. Long before Aristotle, this idea led the Greeks to formulate the concept of the Great Year, and this is presumably what the Pythagorean Archytas of Tarentum had in mind when he said that time is the number of a certain movement and is the interval appropriate to the nature of the universe—a definition that may well have influenced Aristotle. There were, however, two distinct interpretations of the Great Year. On the one hand it was simply the period required for the Sun, Moon, and planets to attain the same positions in relation to each other as they had at a given time. This appears to have been the sense in which Plato used the idea in the *Timaeus*. On the other hand, for Heraclitus it signified the period of duration of the world from its formation to its destruction and rebirth. Whereas Plato seems to have refrained from giving any estimate of the length of the Great Year, Heraclitus, with no particular astronomical interpretation in mind, gave 10,800 years as its duration. He may have arrived at this figure by taking a generation of 30 years as a day and multiplying by 360, the (approximate) number of days in the year.

The two interpretations of the Great Year were combined by the Stoics who believed that, when the heavenly bodies return at fixed intervals of time to the same relative positions as they had at the beginning of the world, everything would be destroyed by fire. Then all would be restored anew just as it was before and the entire cycle would be renewed in every detail.

### III

The idea of time in antiquity differed from ours not only because it was thought to be cyclical but also because the lack of reliable mechanical clocks prevented its accurate measurement. This impeded the development of the modern metrical concept of time. Moreover, the scale of "hours" was not uniform. Indeed, our present system of dividing day and night together into twenty-four hours of equal length was not employed in civil life until the fourteenth century A.D., although it had already been used by astronomers. Previously, it was the general custom to divide the periods of light and darkness into an equal number of "temporal hours" (*horae temporales*, as they were called by the Romans). The number was usually twelve. Consequently, the length of an hour varied according to the time of year and also, except at the equinoxes, a daylight hour was not equal to a nocturnal hour. Strange as this mode of reckoning time may now seem, we must remember that most human activities took place in the hours of daylight and also that early civilizations were in latitudes where the period from sunrise to sunset varies far less than in more northerly parts. For their standard hours, the astronomers took "equinoctial hours" (*horae equinoctales*). These were the same as the temporal hours at the date of the spring equinox.

The only mechanical time-recorders in antiquity were water clocks, but until the fourteenth century A.D. the most reliable way to tell the time was by means of a sundial. Both types of clock were used by the Egyptians. Later they were introduced into Greece and eventually became widespread in the Roman Empire. Vitruvius, writing about 30 B.C., described more than a dozen different types of sundial. He also described a number of "clepsydrae" or water clocks. To obtain a uniform flow of water they were designed so as to keep the pressure head constant. In order to indicate "temporal" hours, either the rate of flow or the scale of hours had to be varied according to the time of year. The result was that many of the ancient water clocks were instruments of considerable complexity.

The earliest known attempt to produce mechanically a periodic standard of time is a device illustrated in a Chinese text written by Su Sung in A.D. 1092. It was powered by a waterwheel which advanced in a step-by-step motion, water being poured into a series of cups which emptied (or escaped) every quarter of an hour, when the weight of the water in the cup was sufficient to tilt a steelyard. The mechanism was then unlocked until the arrival of the next cup below the water stream when it was locked again. An astronomical check on timekeeping was made by a sighting tube pointed to a selected star. Since the timekeeping was governed mainly by the flow of water rather than by the escapement action itself, this device may be regarded as a link between the timekeeping properties of a steady flow of liquid and those of mechanically produced oscillations.

The fundamental distinction between water clocks and mechanical clocks, in the strict sense of the term, is that the former involve a continuous process (the flow of water through an orifice) whereas the latter are governed by a mechanical motion which continually repeats itself. The mechanical clock, in this sense, appears to have been a European invention of the late thirteenth or early fourteenth century. The first clocks of this type were public striking clocks, the earliest, as far as we know, being set up at Milan in 1309. The type of motion employed in these clocks, known as the "verge" escapement—probably from the Latin *virga*, a rod or twig—was an ingenious device in which a heavy bar pivoted near its center was pushed first one way and then the other by a toothed wheel driven by a weight suspended from a drum. The wheel advanced by the space of one tooth for each to and fro oscillation of the bar. Since the bar had no natural period of its own, the rate of the clock depended on the driving weight, but was also affected by variations of friction in the driving mechanism. Consequently, the accuracy of these clocks was low and they could not be relied on to keep time more closely than to about a quarter of an hour a day at best. An error of an hour was not unusual. Until the middle of the seventeenth century mechanical clocks had only one hand and the dial was divided only into hours and quarters.

The word "clock" is etymologically related to the French word *cloche*, meaning a bell. Bells played a prominent part in medieval life and mechanisms for ringing them, made of toothed wheels and oscillating levers, may have helped to prepare for the invention of mechanical clocks. Indeed, some early clocks were essentially mechanisms for striking the hours.

**401**

Music provides another instance of the growing importance of temporal concepts in the Middle Ages. Early medieval music was all plain chant in which notes had fluid time-values. Mensural music in which the duration of notes had an exact ratio among themselves appears to have been an Islamic invention. It was introduced into Europe about the twelfth century. About this time there appeared in Europe the system of notation in which the exact time-value of a note is indicated by a lozenge on a pole.

## IV

The cardinal factor, however, in causing time to become a concept of primary importance was the spread of Christianity. Its central doctrine of the Crucifixion was regarded as a *unique* event in time not subject to repetition and so implied that time must be linear rather than cyclic. Before the rise of Christianity only the Hebrews and Zoroastrian Iranians appear to have developed teleological conceptions of the universe implying that history is progressive. The historical view of time, with particular emphasis on the nonrepeatability of events was, however, the very essence of Christianity. The contrast with the Hebrew view is clearly brought out in the Epistle to the Hebrews (9:25–26): "Nor yet that he should offer himself often, as the high priest entereth into the holy place every year with the blood of others; For then must be often have suffered since the foundation of the world; but now once in the end of the world hath he appeared to put away sin by the sacrifice of himself."

Nevertheless, the idea of denominating the years serially in a single era count, such as the Olympic dating from 776 B.C. and the Seleucid from 311 B.C., did not originate in the Christian era until it was introduced by Dionysius Exiguus in A.D. 525, and the B.C. sequence extending backwards from the birth of Christ was only introduced in the latter part of the seventeenth century. In medieval Europe, as in medieval China, ancient Greece, and pre-Columbian America, time was not conceived as a continuous mathematical parameter but was split up into separate seasons, divisions of the Zodiac, and so on, each exerting its specific influence. In other words, magical time had not yet been superseded by scientific time. Moreover, throughout the whole medieval period, there was a conflict between the cyclic and linear concepts of time. The scientists and scholars, influenced by astronomy and astrology, tended to emphasize the cyclic concept. The linear concept was fostered by the mercantile class and the rise of a money economy. For, as long as power was concentrated in the ownership of land, time was felt to be plentiful and was associated with the unchanging cycle of the soil. With the circu-

lation of money, however, the emphasis was on mobility. In other words, men were beginning to believe that "time is money" and that one must try to use it economically and thus time came to be associated with the idea of linear progress.

In the course of the fourteenth century many public mechanical clocks that rang the hours were set up in European towns. They were very expensive and, despite their lack of accuracy, they were a source of pride to the citizens. Clocks were made with curious and complicated movements. It was easier to add wheels than to regulate the escapement. Moreover, in view of the general belief that a correct knowledge of the relative positions of the heavenly bodies was necessary for the success of most human activities, many early clocks involved elaborate astronomical representations. The most celebrated was the Strasbourg clock set up in 1350, but the most elaborate was the astronomical domestic clock made at about the same time by Giovanni de' Dondi. From about 1400 there are records of the purchase of domestic clocks by royalty, but until the latter part of the sixteenth century these clocks were very rare.

Although medieval scholars were not concerned with machines, they became more and more interested in clocks, particularly because of their connection with astronomy. Already in the fourteenth century Nicole Oresme (1323–82), Bishop of Lisieux, likened the universe to a vast mechanical clock created and set moving by God so that "all the wheels move as harmoniously as possible." The great leaders of the scientific revolution of the seventeenth century were much concerned with horological questions and metaphors. Early in the century Kepler specifically rejected the old quasi-animistic magical conception of the universe and asserted that it was similar to a clock, and later the same analogy was drawn by Robert Boyle and others. Thus the invention of the mechanical clock played a central role in the formulation of the mechanistic conception of nature that dominated natural philosophy from Descartes to Kelvin. An even more far-reaching influence has been claimed for the mechanical clock by Lewis Mumford who has argued that it "dissociated time from human events and helped create the belief in an independent world of mathematically measurable sequences: the special world of science" (*Technics and Civilization*, p. 15).

Nevertheless, this development was for a long time hampered by the lack of any accurate mechanical means for measuring small intervals of time. Thus, in his famous experiments on the rate of fall of bodies rolling down an inclined plane, Galileo measured time by weighing the quantity of water which emerged as a thin jet from a vessel with a small hole in it. It is not surprising that he refrained as far as possible from giving a concrete value for the acceleration due to gravity and that when he did state a value it was less than half the correct amount. The construction of precision timekeepers was stimulated by the needs of astronomy and navigators, and they contributed to the development of science itself.

### V

A new era opened in the history of chronometry when Galileo discovered a natural periodic process that could be conveniently adapted for the purposes of accurate timekeeping. As a result of much mathematical thinking on experiments with oscillating pendulums, he came to the conclusion that each simple pendulum has its own type of vibration depending on its length. In his old age he contemplated applying the pendulum to clockwork which could record mechanically the number of swings, but this step was first taken successfully by Huygens in 1656. Strictly speaking, the simple pendulum in which the bob describes circular arcs is not quite isochronous. Huygens discovered that theoretically perfect isochronism could be achieved by compelling the bob to describe a cycloidal arc. His first pendulum clock with cycloidal "cheeks" was constructed in 1656. Great as was Huygens' achievement, particularly from the point of view of theory, the ultimate practical solution of the problem came only after the invention of a new type of escapement. Huygens' clock incorporated the verge type, but about 1670 a much improved type, the anchor type, was invented that interfered less with the pendulum's free motion.

The invention of a satisfactory mechanical clock had a tremendous influence on the general concept of time. For, unlike the water clocks, etc. that preceded it, the mechanical clock if properly regulated can tick away continually for years on end, and so must have greatly influenced belief in the homogeneity and continuity of time. This belief was implicit in the idea of time put forward by Galileo in the dynamical part of *Two New Sciences* (1638). For, although he was not the first to represent time by a geometrical straight line, he became the most influential pioneer of this idea through his theory of motion.

Nevertheless, for the first explicit discussion of the concept of geometrical time it seems that we must go to the *Lectiones geometricae* (1669) of Isaac Barrow, written about thirty years after the publication of Galileo's book. Barrow, who occupied the chair of mathematics in Cambridge in which he was succeeded by Newton in 1669, was greatly impressed by the kinematic method in geometry that had been developed with great effect by Galileo's pupil Torricelli.

Barrow realized that to understand this method it was necessary to study time, and he was particularly concerned with the relation of time and motion. "Time does not imply motion, as far as its absolute and intrinsic nature is concerned; not any more than it implies rest; whether things move or are still, whether we sleep or wake, Time pursues the even tenour of its way." However, he argues, it is only by means of motion that time is measurable. "Time may be used as a measure of motion; just as we measure space from some magnitude, and then use this space to estimate other magnitudes commensurable with the first; i.e., we compare motions with one another by the use of time as an intermediary." Barrow regarded time as essentially a mathematical concept which has many analogies with a line "for time has length alone, is similar in all its parts and can be looked upon as constituted from a simple addition of successive instants or as from a continuous flow of one instant; either a straight or a circular line" (*Geometrical Lectures*, London [1735], Lecture 1, p. 35). The reference here to "a circular line" shows that Barrow was not completely emancipated from traditional ideas. Nevertheless, his statement goes further than any of Galileo's, for Galileo only used straight line *segments* to denote particular intervals of time. Barrow was very careful, however, not to push his analogy between time and a line too far. Time, in his view, was "the continuance of anything in its own being."

Barrow's views greatly influenced his illustrious successor in the Lucasian chair, Isaac Newton. In particular, Barrow's idea that irrespective of whether things move or are still time passes with a steady flow is echoed in the famous definition at the beginning of Newton's *Principia* (1687). "Absolute, true and mathematical time," wrote Newton, "of itself and from its own nature, flows equably without relation to anything external." Newton admitted that, in practice, there may be no such thing as a uniform motion by which time may be accurately measured, but he thought it necessary that, in principle, there should exist an ideal rate-measurer of time. Consequently, he regarded the moments of absolute time as forming a continuous sequence like the points on a geometrical line and he believed that the rate at which these moments succeed each other is a variable which is independent of all particular events and processes. His belief in absolute time was supported by the argument for absolute motion that he based on his celebrated experiment with a rotating bucket of water. He thought that it was not necessary to refer to any other body when attaching a physical meaning to saying that a particular body rotates, and from this he concluded that time as well as space must be absolute.

Newton's views made a great impression on the philosopher John Locke in whose *Essay concerning Human Understanding* (1690) we find the clearest statement of the "classical" scientific conception of time that was evolved in the seventeenth century:

. . . duration is but as it were the length of one straight line extended *in infinitum*, not capable of multiplicity, variation or figure, but is one common measure of all existence whatsoever, wherein all things, whilst they exist equally partake. For this present moment is common to all things that are now in being, and equally comprehends that part of their existence as much as if they were all but one single being; and we may truly say, they all exist in the same moment of time (Book II, Ch. 15, Para. 11).

Newton's conception of time has been frequently criticized. If time can be considered in isolation "without relation to anything external," what meaning could be attached to saying that its flow is not uniform and hence what point is there in saying that it "flows equally"? This objection does not apply to the idea of time formulated by Newton's contemporary Leibniz who rejected the idea that moments of absolute time exist in their own right. Instead, he thought of them as classes of events related by the concept of simultaneity and he defined time as the order of succession of phenomena. Today this is generally accepted, and we regard events as simultaneous not because they occupy the same moment of time but simply because they happen together. We derive time from events and not vice versa. Nevertheless, Leibniz' definition of time as "the order of succession of phenomena" is incomplete insofar as it concentrates on the ordinal aspect of time without *explicit* reference to its durational aspect and its continuity.

Newton recognized the practical difficulty of obtaining a satisfactory measure of time. He pointed out that, although commonly considered equal, the natural days are in fact unequal. We now know that in the long run we cannot base our definition of time on the observed motions of any of the heavenly bodies. For the Moon's revolutions are not strictly uniform but are subject to a small secular acceleration, minute irregularities have been discovered in the diurnal rotation of the Earth, and so on. Greater accuracy in the measurement of time can, however, be obtained by means of atomic and molecular clocks. Indeed, the greatest accuracy so far achieved is with a frequency standard in the radio range of the spectrum of the caesium atom and is of the order of one part in $10^{11}$, which corresponds to a clock error of only one second in 3000 years.

Implicit in these developments is the assumption that all atoms of a given element behave in exactly the same way, irrespective of place and epoch. The ultimate scale of time is therefore based on our concept of universal laws of nature. This was already recognized last century, long before the advent of modern ultraprecise time-keeping, in particular by Thomson and Tait in their treatise *Natural Philosophy* (1890). In discussing the law of inertia they argued that it could be stated in the form: the times during which any particular body not compelled by force to alter the speeds of its motions passes through equal spaces are equal; and in this form, they said, the law expresses our convention for measuring time. It is easily seen that this implies a unique time-scale except for the arbitrary choice of time unit and time zero.

In practical life the precise standardization of time measurement began with the foundation of the Royal Observatory in 1675, and was further developed when Greenwich time could be taken on each ship after John Harrison had perfected the chronometer, about 1760. The conventional nature of our choice of time zero in civil time was clearly revealed when, in 1885, to cope with the fact that solar time varies by four minutes in a degree of longitude, it was found necessary to divide the globe into a series of standard time-belts.

## VI

Until the beginning of the present century it was universally assumed that time is like a moving knife-edge covering all places in the universe simultaneously and that the only arbitrary elements in its determination were our choice of time unit and time zero. It therefore came as a great shock when, in 1905, Einstein discovered a previously unsuspected gap in the theory of time-measurement. For, in his analysis of the nature of the velocity of light it occurred to him that time-measurement depends on simultaneity, and that although this idea is perfectly clear when two events occur at the same place it was not equally clear for events in different places. Einstein realized that the concept of simultaneity for a distant event and one in close proximity to the observer is an inferred concept depending on the relative position of the distant event and the mode of connection between it and the observer's perception of it. If the distance of an external event is known and also the velocity of the signal that connects it and the resulting percept, the observer can calculate the epoch at which the event occurred and can correlate this with some previous instant in his own experience. This calculation will be a distinct operation for each observer, but until Einstein raised the question it had been tacitly assumed that, when we have found the rules according to which the time of perception is determined by the time of the event, all perceived events can be brought into a single objective time-sequence the same for all observers. Einstein not only realized that it was a hypothesis to assume that, if they calculate correctly, all observers must assign the same time to a given event, but he produced cogent reasons why, in general, this hypothesis should be rejected.

Einstein assumed that there are no instantaneous connections between external events and the observer. The classical theory of time, with its assumption of worldwide simultaneity for all observers, in effect presupposed that there were such connections. Instead, Einstein postulated that the most rapid form of communication is by means of electromagnetic signals (*in vacuo*), including light rays, and that their speed is the same for all observers at relative rest or in uniform relative motion. He regarded this assumption as a consequence of the principle of special relativity (as it is now called) which asserts that the laws of physics are the same for all such observers. He found that, although the invariance of the velocity of light is compatible with the idea of worldwide simultaneity for all observers at relative rest, those in uniform relative motion would, in general, be led to assign different times to the same event and that a moving clock would appear to run slow compared with an identical clock at rest with respect to the observer.

It is well known that Einstein's theory automatically explained the failure of the Michelson-Morley experiment for measuring the Earth's velocity through the luminiferous aether and has been successful in explaining many other results that could not be accounted for in the classical theory of time. The phenomenon of the apparent slowing down of a clock in motion relative to the observer is called "time dilatation." It is essentially a phenomenon of measurement applicable to all forms of matter and is a reciprocal effect: if *A* and *B* are two observers in uniform relative motion, *B*'s clock seems to *A* to run slow and equally *A*'s clock seems to run slow according to B. This reciprocity no longer holds, however, if forces are applied to change the motion of one of the observers. In particular, if *A* and *B* are together at some instant and at a later instant the motion of *B* is suddenly reversed so that he eventually comes back to *A* with the same speed, the time that elapses between the instant at which *B* left *A* and the instant when he returns to *A* will be shorter according to *B*'s clock than according to *A*'s. Consequently, although we accept Isaac Barrow's view that "Time is the continuance of anything in its own being," the special theory of relativity prevents our agreeing with him unconditionally when he went on to say "nor do I believe there is anyone but allows that those things existed equal times which rose and perished together."

Empirical evidence that can only be understood in terms of time dilatation has come from the study of cosmic-ray phenomena. Elementary particles known as mu-mesons, found in cosmic-ray showers, disintegrate spontaneously, their average "proper lifetime" (that is time from production to disintegration according to an observer travelling with a meson) being about two micro-seconds (two millionths of a second). These particles are mainly produced at heights of about ten kilometers above the Earth's surface. Consequently, those observed in the laboratory on photographic plates must have travelled that distance. But in two micro-seconds a particle that travelled with the velocity of light would cover less than a kilometer, and according to the theory of relativity all material particles travel with speeds less than that of light. However, the velocity of these particles has been found to be so close to that of light that the time-dilatation factor is about ten, which is the amount required to explain why it is that to the observer in the laboratory these particles appear to travel about ten times as far as they could in the absence of this effect.

Although the theory of relativity has undermined the classical concept of universal time, the same for all observers, it has led to time-measurement's becoming even more significant than before in physics, since time standards are now tending to be regarded as primary standards for spatial as well as for temporal measurement. This is because the theory leads us to reject the classical rigid body concept, since it implies the instantaneous transmission of a disturbance through the body from one end to the other, and this is incompatible with the basic assumption that no signal can travel faster than light. Instead of spatial measurement depending on the idea of the rigid body, it can be based on the radar principle. According to this, distance is measured in terms of the time taken by light (or other electromagnetic signals) to traverse it. This technique is now being used by radio astronomers to redetermine the scale of the solar system.

Although the laws of nature do not enable us to define a local standard of rest, in principle this can be determined by the bulk distribution of matter in the universe. According to most current cosmological theories, there is at each place in the universe a preferential time-scale for the description of the universe, being that associated with the local standard of rest, and these local time-scales all fit together to form one worldwide cosmic time. It is with reference to this that we can give objective meaning to such concepts as the age of the Earth, the age of the solar system, the age of our Galaxy, and the age of the universe. Thus, despite the theory of relativity, we can still retain the concept of a unique cosmic time-scale for our description of the physical universe and the dating of events.

## BIBLIOGRAPHY

The subject of time and measurement is discussed at length with many references in G. J. Whitrow, *The Natural Philosophy of Time* (London, 1961; New York, 1963). The history of practical time-measurement is outlined in F. A. B. Ward, *Time Measurement—Part I: Historical Review,* 4th ed. (London, 1958). A more popular account is given in F. le Lionnais, *Time,* trans. W. D. O'Gorman, Jr. (London, 1962). A classic work on ancient methods of time-measurement is M. P. Nilsson, *Primitive Time-Reckoning* (Lund, 1920). A good short account will be found in the chapter by E. R. Leach, "Primitive Time-Reckoning" in *A History of Technology,* ed. C. Singer et al., Vol. I (Oxford, 1954). Chinese views are discussed by J. Needham, *Time and Eastern Man* (London, 1965). See also J. Needham et al., *Heavenly Clockwork* (Cambridge, 1960). Maya achievements in time-measurement are described by J. E. S. Thompson, *The Rise and Fall of Maya Civilization* (Norman, Okla., 1956). Ancient ideas on time are discussed by S. G. F. Brandon, *History, Time and Deity* (New York, 1965); M. Eliade, *Cosmos and History: the Myth of the Eternal Return,* trans. W. R. Trask (New York, 1959); and J. F. Callahan, *Four Views of Time in Ancient Philosophy* (Cambridge, Mass., 1948). Greek ideas are briefly discussed by G. J. Whitrow, "The Concept of Time from Pythagoras to Aristotle," in *Proceedings VIII International Congress of the History of Science* (Ithaca, N.Y., 1962; Paris, 1964). The invention of the mechanical clock is discussed by C. M. Cipolla, *Clocks and Culture, 1300–1700* (London, 1967). Ideas on time in different civilizations are described in various chapters of *The Voices of Time,* ed. J. T. Fraser (New York, 1966).

The quotations of Aristotle are from Aristotle, *Physica,* trans. R. P. Hardie and R. K. Gaye, in *The Works of Aristotle,* ed. W. D. Ross, Vol. II (Oxford, 1930). The cultural influence of the mechanical clock in modern civilization is discussed by Lewis Mumford in *Technics and Civilization* (New York and London, 1934), Ch. I.

G. J. WHITROW

[See also Astrology; Continuity; **Cosmology;** Cycles; Music and Science; Newton on Method; Number; Pythagorean Doctrines; **Relativity;** Space; Time.]

# TOTALITARIANISM

### I. CONTROVERSIAL DEFINITIONS

IN THE strict sense of terminology, the concept of Totalitarianism originated with and was applied to Fascism in Italy, to National Socialism in Germany, and to the consolidation of Stalinism in Russia. Related to a specific form and state of modern dictatorship as developed during the 1920's and '30's the concept of totalitarianism became increasingly controversial after the transformations following Stalin's death (1953). Comparison of past Fascist regimes and evolving Communist systems posed many new problems of interpretation and methodology. This comparison was even more complicated by the fact that after World War II, when most of the standard works on totalitarianism were published, the discussion became closely related to the confrontations of the cold war. Hence, many mid-century critics denounced totalitarianism as a purely polemical term, an instrument of anti-ideology rather than a useful means of political analysis.

Though this growing criticism of the concept of totalitarianism refers to specific contemporary constellations as well as to deep differences between Fascism and Communism, the fact remains that modern dictatorship in its most elaborate forms is an important topic of comparative analysis. The search for common features and for a general theory explaining the structure and practice of such regimes has not only produced a wealth of pertinent material and interpretations, but at the same time has sharpened the eye for similarities and differences alike. This results in efforts to distinguish various types of totalitarianism rather than completely to abolish the idea itself. Communist theory has of course never adopted the term in its general sense but has always aimed at expanding the notion of Fascism by applying it very broadly to non-Communist states and "capitalistic" societies of various forms.

Aside from such ideological and propagandistic controversies, another question seems important whenever the concept of totalitarianism is discussed in a comparative analysis. The question is whether the structure and workings of "totalitarian" regimes can be seen as basically different from "classical" dictatorship, i.e., despotism or tyranny as described time and again since the days of Plato and Aristotle. Most definitions of totalitarianism concentrate on the fact that modern dictatorship tends to an extreme model of centralized, uniform control of all provinces of political, social, and intellectual life. This tendency leads far beyond older forms of absolutism and autocracy. A phenomenon of the twentieth century, totalitarianism is seen as primarily conditioned and facilitated by modern industrialism and technology in the "age of the masses." Modern organization, communication, and propaganda offer the means for all-embracing controls, for total mobilizing, and for terrorist regimentation (*Gleichschaltung*) of the life and thinking of every citizen as never before in history.

As a political system, totalitarianism appears to be a concrete product of the crises following World War

I. The emergence of Fascism and National Socialism as well as of Communism is clearly bound to the political and socioeconomic results and to the ideological confrontations associated with the war and its aftermath. At the same time, all the regimes tending to totalitarian forms of government are distinguished from older forms of absolutism and dictatorship by their ambiguous relation to modern democracy. While principally opposed to a pluralistic system of representative parliamentarism, such regimes claim a higher form of popular government and democratic legitimacy. This is demonstrated in the staged approval by plebiscite or acclamation of the acts of a Leader or of a monopoly party claiming to represent the *volonté générale* ("general will") in state and society. Different as the historical conditions, the social and national framework, the ideological positions and aims may be, the common denominator of totalitarianism is to be found in the methods and practice of ruling, in the techniques of domination.

First of all, totalitarian regimes deny the right of existence to competing political parties and groups as well as to individual freedom; tolerating autonomous sectors of life and culture would be a *contradictio in adjecto*. While the ideological superstructure may aim at a higher, definite form of freedom for all, the actual consequence is the abolition of personal liberties and the negation of all activities outside the state with respect to the regime. Individuals and groups are to be integrated into a closed, compulsory system defined in terms of a future order of state and society, and dynamized by an ideological sense of mission for a greater nation, a better race, a dominating class. This corresponds to the total monopoly of the government by a party, political clique, or a Leader. Decorated with the attributes of infallibility, these supreme rulers demand a pseudoreligious worship by the masses; the party—or the Leader—is always right, constitutes the new dogma of a total consensus, a complete identity between leadership and population.

The ideal-type definition of totalitarianism offers of course no more than a framework for a concrete analysis; but this is true for the concepts of social and political science in general. There are three main indices by which similarities and differences among totalitarian dictatorships may be measured: how they come to power, how they interpret themselves, and how they develop, when compared with other transitory or developmental dictatorships.

As to the first question, a distinction has been made between pseudolegal (Fascist) and revolutionary (Communist) seizure of power; yet in all cases a *Putschist, coup d'état* technique in completing the process of power seizure was at work, while the degree and form of veiling and legalizing differed. As to the second question, the situation seems reversed: Fascist and Nazi self-interpretation largely endorsed totalitarianism, while Communist ideology tended to avoid totalitarian terminology in justifying the claim for exclusive power; but this made little difference as soon as Stalin succeeded in supplanting party rule by one-man leadership. The third question evidently poses the main problems. Even Fascism and National Socialism show different stages of development, the Italian version lasting almost twice as long; yet both ended prematurely, by a military defeat from outside effecting the death of the Leaders. On the other hand, the Stalin regime was one important stage in a much longer process; after 1953, adherence to the Leader gave way again to one-party rule.

From such observations, the prime importance of Party-Leader relations for determining the type of dictatorship becomes evident. Moreover, any definition and application of the concept of totalitarianism depends on which historical frame of reference is used. In this respect three main groups of interpretation may be noticed. The one confines totalitarianism to the period from 1922 to 1953, reaching from Mussolini's advent to Stalin's death. Another school of thought emphasizes the Fascist character of totalitarianism, with the consequence of either limiting it to the "Fascist period" between the wars, or even extending it to all "fascistoid" tendencies and right-wing dictatorships before or after World War II. In a much broader sense, totalitarianism is defined as a tendency inherent in all modern states aiming at a perfectionist management of socioeconomic crisis, and development by means of political and ideological monopoly of power, be it in the name of capitalist or socialist one-way solutions. This last interpretation seems more appropriate to a comparative analysis asking for common traits in the exercise and sanction of power.

Totalitarian politics can indeed be reduced to a syndrome of traits based on four main arguments that characterize the sociopolitical structure and the ideological justification of a system: (1) an official ideology of exclusive and comprehensive claim based upon radical rejection of some aspects of the past and chiliastic claims for the future; (2) a centralized, unitary mass movement claiming classless equality but organized hierarchically as a single, monopolistic party under authoritarian leadership; (3) full control of the means of communication and coercion; and (4) the bureaucratic direction, via state control or socialization, of the economy and social relations. While a more differentiated view of totalitarian politics no longer keeps to the fiction of a monolithic, conflict-free rule, the distinction between modern and "classical" dictatorship remains clear: absolute, exclusive ideology, legalized terror justified by chiliastic promises, control of state and society by means of force, the forming of a "new man" to arise from such a perfect order, the negation of further conflicts and the suppression of opposition in favor of ideo-political unity and technological efficiency, and the irrational equation of oligarchical leadership with the interests of the "whole," the *Volksgemeinschaft* ("community of the people") or the workers and peasant class.

## II. HISTORICO-POLITICAL DEVELOPMENT

The origins and the main stages of the idea of totalitarianism reflect the problems of interpretation and the controversies surrounding the use of the term in social science, history, and philosophy. From the beginning, the concept of the total or totalitarian state and regime is basic to Fascism and remains so, while its transfer and application to Communist systems, i.e., the analogy of a rightist and leftist totalitarianism poses manifold problems. Earlier use of the term is rare and vague: the "total war" signifies, in the period from the French Revolution (Robespierre) to World War I (Ludendorff) and II (Goebbels), the *levée en masse* ("universal conscription") in its most radical form; *Totalität* ("organic wholeness or unity") is ascribed to the idea of the state by Hegel or Adam Müller; "total revolution" is occasionally to be found in the writings of Marx and Lassalle.

Yet Italian Fascism, for the first time, transformed such general notions into the systematic terms *totalitario* and *totalitarietà* that were to describe and prophesy a radically new political phenomenon: the unity of theory and action, of organization and consent in state and society alike. It was Mussolini who first (and then repeatedly) applied the idea in this sense to the Fascist state, in a speech of October 28, 1925: *Tutto nello Stato, niente al di fuori dello Stato, nulla contro lo Stato* ("Everything in the State, nothing outside the State, nothing against the State"). This formula was, however, more than simply extreme etatism; at the same time Mussolini and other leading Fascists proclaimed their *feroce volontà totalitaria* ("violent totalitarian will") and talked about the "totalitarian program of our Revolution."

What this early vocabulary of Fascism meant, is above all a political style of violence, determination, unconditional and absolute action, of radical demands and intolerance. The dual aspects of the idea of totalitarianism are clearly visible here, as later on, in other non-Italian contexts: not only full and absolute power, but also a political dynamism based on dictatorial decision and permanent action, as an emanation and confirmation of unlimited power. Both aspects, the

totalitarian-etatist (as presented dogmatically by Mussolini's Hegelian Philosopher-Minister G. Gentile) and the totalitarian activist (leading into imperialist and finally even racist radicalism) are present in the concept of totalitarian policy. German National Socialism, though under different national conditions, demonstrates a similar combination of state-absolutist and radical-absolutist revolutionary elements. But while the Hitler regime realized a dictatorship of utmost radical consequence, the rhetorical use and the philosophical exposition of the idea of totalitarianism remained a domain of the Italian fascists, whether it was concentrating on the etatist-institutional or (after 1933 and influenced by the triumph of National Socialism in Germany) on the dynamic radical-revolutionary meaning of the concept. The leading role of the party as a "movement," the continuation of a revolution never completed but in fact permanent was stressed, as against the traditional party and state structure.

On the other hand, since the term "totalitarianism" was applied by critical observers very early (1928) to both Fascism and Communism, its comparative use was not merely a product of the cold war after 1945, as critics of the term have suggested. Distinction should be made between the use of the term (negatively) by liberal analysts (like G. H. Sabine, 1937) or (positively) by political movements and systems posing as totalitarian: most emphatically Italian Fascism, National Socialism chiefly during the first years of the Third Reich (Hitler himself preferred the word *autoritär*). Communists reduced the phenomenon of totalitarianism to the confrontation of revolutionary and counter-revolutionary systems. The Fascist theory of totalitarianism in turn has never recognized the Soviet Union as a totalitarian state, but instead as a class dictatorship radically opposed to the Fascist idea of a unified and classless society.

In Germany, different from Italy, the idea of a "total state" was developed before the Nazi seizure of power (and even outside the Nazi Party) by political lawyers and theorists like Carl Schmitt; it was the antiliberal, antipluralistic consequence of a parliamentary democracy in crisis, the Weimar Republic. In the crucial period of 1932–33 this concept of a strong, monocratic state was applied to the new reality of the Hitler regime. Yet for this very reason, after an initial inflation of writings on the total state, it never became official doctrine (as in Fascism). Some protagonists of state absolutism were even suspected of contradicting the revolutionary and racist dynamism of National Socialism.

On the other hand, the structure and politics of the Third Reich corresponded, as no other dictatorial system, to the idea of totalitarian organization, power, and ideology. In fact, since the rise of the SS-state over the traditional state and legal system, the wartime regime of National Socialism with its policy of mobilization and expansion, of persecution, terror, and extermination, of a declared "total war" was meant to be as totalitarian as possible, even though the result was a guided chaos. Totalitarian order and efficiency turned out to consist of a system of arbitrary decisions and a state-party dualism, under the sole will of the Leader. But if the idea of the monolithic order of the totalitarian Leader system did not correspond to reality, it still was real as the principle dominating the reorganization of state and society. Much as we know today about the chaotic, improvised state of the Third Reich, its basic drive toward totalitarian organization and mobilization still presents the most appropriate point of departure for an analysis of National Socialism.

Does this Leader principle also hold true after a critical analysis of the Stalinist system? Communist theory never adopted the terminology of totalitarianism to explain or legitimize the rule of the dictator or the alleged dictatorship of the proletariat. But the idea to represent a more perfect, true form of democracy, at times even claimed by Hitler, does not in itself contradict the totalitarian character of a political movement or system. Indeed totalitarianism differs from former types of dictatorship by its capacity to handle democratic formulas and fictions, while using all the possibilities of modern communication and technology to manipulate the consent or submission of the masses. This pseudodemocratic base of totalitarian systems should however not be mistaken for reality, as is done by both conservative critics who explain totalitarianism simply as the consequence of democracy, and by apologists of Communist or Fascist systems who praise the "democratic" quality of plebiscites and acclamations. The very fact that the ruling clique or leader seek to legitimize their dictatorship by appeals to mass support does not prove the democratic quality of a regime but signifies the specific form of mass dictatorship in a democratic age. Thus the range of the idea of totalitarianism is not only a matter of definition but depends on the question, whether it is restricted to systems that proclaim to be (or become) totalitarian, or extended as a tool of critical analysis and comparison, to dictatorial systems with a different vocabulary and dogma. In the first case, the idea of totalitarianism would be no more than a rather curious piece of exaggerated power philosophy, typical of the self-styled superman attitude of Mussolini's Fascism, with little explanatory value as to the working of the Fascist system, and even less of the Hitler regime. In the second case, however, the idea of totalitarianism must be further developed to signify and explain the basic structural elements of modern, post-democratic dictatorship, independent of its self-interpretation as radical or progressive, democratic or revolutionary, left or right.

### III. POSSIBILITIES OF APPLICATION

As a critical concept to compare and analyze modern dictatorships, the idea of totalitarianism cannot be defined by a philological compilation of the uses and connotations of the term. Yet most attempts at a typology comprising the main elements of totalitarian systems have foundered on the contradiction between historical and systematic analysis. This criticism has been directed against the well-known theory of Carl J. Friedrich and Z. K. Brzezinski: its rigid form is easily attacked on the ground that more differentiated empirical evidence does not fit into the axiomatic scheme. Evidently modern dictatorship cannot be reduced to a few variables. A synopsis of various typologies ranging from Sigmund Neumann, Franz L. Neumann, and Hannah Arendt to Robert Tucker and Leonard Schapiro would offer a wider range of features and variables for comparisons capable of dealing with systems of very different historical and intellectual, economic and social conditions. Such a typology, while operating on various levels of comparison, presents a more complicated, less perspicuous picture than the gross equation of Fascist and Communist systems. But it remains the only way to reconcile social theory and historical evidence, and to save the concept of totalitarianism as a useful tool from its uncritical friends and its adversaries alike.

This means first of all that there can be no short definition of totalitarianism that will cover the pioneer example of the idea, Fascist Italy, together with Hitlerism and Stalinism. Instead certain features can be discerned as "typical," which then or now may also be discerned in other dictatorships (in Latin America, the Balkans, Spain, and notably China). The most important characteristic remains, in all cases, the extraordinary position of the Leader. His rise is of course bound to the general conditions allowing for dictatorial rule, but the character of a totalitarian system is unthinkable apart from Mussolini, Stalin, Hitler, or Franco and Mao. They rank as historical forces above any other factor, including ideology or doctrine which they use at will; this applies also to the use of Marxism by Stalin, quite contrary to attempts to distinguish principally between Fascist and Communist systems on the ground of their profound ideological differences. Hitler's neglect or violation of basic ideas of National Socialism or the contradictory insertion of a Leader cult into Marxism is ample proof of the dominating, all-important role of the Leader; it is typical also of his relationship to the (allegedly omnipotent) party as well as to all other agencies of power and influence. Either by purges or through the tactics of *divide et impera,* the Leader maintains a monopoly position—least successfully defended by Mussolini—that makes all authority derive from and depend on his arbitrary will, and not even on the will of the seemingly omnipotent one party.

It is the "Leader" state, indispensable as the one-party system may be for any totalitarian regime, that determines the real power structure of such dictatorship, whatever qualities may be ascribed to its aims, or doctrines. Here more than anywhere else the common totalitarian rationale is superior to any distinctions made between left or right, progressive or reactionary regimes. One may indeed conclude that the totalitarian character which allows for close comparison of different regimes is dependent on a cluster of forces in which the Leader supersedes party and ideology; consequently, Leninist or post-Stalinist dictatorship has to be defined in more specific terms.

The same applies to the unlimited power of the Leader versus state and law. This explains the typical coexistence of extremely arbitrary acts with administrative and legal continuity, in the sense of a "dual state" (E. Fraenkel) in which order and chaos, stability and revolution form a pair. In reality, such a dualism was only tolerated to provide pseudolegal cover for arbitrary actions, with no legal security or predictability available outside the will of the Leader. This was clearly the case in both the Hitler and the Stalin regimes, with only superficial differences of more pseudolegal (the German tradition) or more revolutionary camouflage; again Mussolini, while following the same line, was least successful in view of the powerful remnants of monarchy and church in Italy, despite his regime.

Another important feature also distinguishing totalitarian systems from older forms of dictatorship, is the degree to which individual and private life is controlled and subjugated to a "new morality" of collective behavior. The regime demands quite openly the complete politicizing of all realms of life, and its success in performing this part of totalitarian control reveals the degree to which the regime is able to realize its claim to fuse state and society, party and people, individual and collective into the ideal of total unity. It is here that ideology aims to perform its central function: to justify or even glorify the violation and abolition of existing laws and morals in favor of higher goals of national and racist, or social and class-oriented ideals of community, again in the sense of a totality of means and ends superseding individual sacrifices and sublimating terror and crime when they are used in the

service of the "whole" to which totalitarian ideology is geared.

It has become clear how important in this connection the pseudodemocratic appearance must be for a regime claiming total consent. To uphold the fiction of a *volonté générale* embodied in the regime of one leader and one party, as opposed to the empirical truth that different individuals and groups naturally ask for representation in different parties and power agencies, a totalitarian regime could not be satisfied with older techniques of autocratic rule by military repression or religious sanction. It is only by ruling in the name of the people that modern dictatorship can expect the more or less voluntary support of the masses which is necessary for large-scale mobilization and effective functioning. This is helped by the extensive use of modern propaganda, concentrating mainly on the glorification of the Leader and on the manipulation of his charismatic and pseudoreligious qualities. Among the basic preconditions of totalitarian dictatorship ranges the pseudodemocratic fiction that by mass meetings and other emotional processes of communication the individual is directly linked to, and represented by, the Leader—without the need of intermediate agencies like free parliaments or interest groups: it is the fiction of direct mass democracy.

In conclusion, the justification and usefulness of the concept of totalitarianism seems quite independent of the occasional misuse of the term in the service of cold war and other propaganda. If there is no doubt about some basic differences between Fascism and Communism in the realm of ideological goals and social policy, the distinction between right and left totalitarianism is much harder to establish in the actual working of systems like the Hitlerian or Stalinist; at the same time, the similarities of basic features of rule are striking. While those systems seem to be a matter of the past and history may not repeat itself, basic components of the idea of totalitarianism remain present in our age of democracy, of mass movements and profound social change. This is a potential to be mobilized by future Leaders whenever social crisis, emotional need for security, and ideological conviction, and the hunger for power coincide in the belief that only by concentrating all forces in one power agency and by completely subduing individual freedom to the chiliastic promises of a political movement and its deified leaders, can the problems of modern society be solved. In this way, the idea of totalitarianism is not a phenomenon of the past bound to the unique constellation of the interwar period, but is part of the modernizing process of nations and societies in the age of mass democracy, bureaucracy, and pseudoreligious ideologies.

*BIBLIOGRAPHY*

A. Aquarone, *L'organizzazione dello Stato totalitario* (Turin, 1965). H. Arendt, *The Origins of Totalitarianism*, 2nd ed. (New York, 1957). J. A. Armstrong, *The Politics of Totalitarianism* (New York, 1961). R. Aron, *Démocratie et totalitarisme* (Paris, 1964). K. D. Bracher, *The German Dictatorship* (New York, 1970); idem, with W. Sauer and G. Schulz, *Die nationalsozialistische Machtergreifung* (Köln, 1962). Z. K. Brzezinski, *The Permanent Purge* (Cambridge, Mass., 1956); idem, *Ideology and Power in Soviet Politics* (New York, 1962). H. Buchheim, *Totalitäre Herrschaft* (Munich, 1962). N. Cohn, *The Pursuit of the Millenium* (London, 1957). W. Ebenstein, *Totalitarianism* (New York, 1962). M. Fainsod, *How Russia is Ruled*, 2nd ed. (Cambridge, Mass., 1963). E. Fraenkel, *The Dual State* (New York, 1941). C. J. Friedrich, ed., *Totalitarianism* (Cambridge, Mass., 1954); idem, with Z. K. Brzezinski, *Totalitarian Dictatorship and Autocracy*, 2nd ed. (Cambridge, Mass., 1965); idem, "The Changing Theory and Practice of Totalitarianism," *Il Politico*, **33** (1968), 53ff. D. L. Germino, *The Italian Fascist Party in Power* (Minneapolis, 1959). J. A. Gregor, *The Ideology of Fascism* (New York, 1969). W. Kornhauser, *The Politics of Mass Society* (London, 1960). W. Laqueur and G. Mosse, eds. *International Fascism 1920–1945* (New York, 1966). A. G. Meyer, *The Soviet Political System* (New York, 1965). B. Moore, *Social Origins of Dictatorship and Democracy* (New York, 1966). F. L. Neumann, *Behemoth*, 2nd ed. (New York, 1944). S. Neumann, *Permanent Revolution* (New York, 1942). G. H. Sabine, *A History of Political Theory* (New York, 1937). L. Schapiro, "The Concept of Totalitarianism," *Survey*, No. 73 (1969), 93ff.; idem, with J. W. Lewis, "The Roles of the Monolithic Party under the Totalitarian Leader," *China Quarterly*, **40** (1969), 39ff.; idem, *The Origin of the Communist Autocracy* (London, 1955). B. Seidel and S. Jenker, eds., *Wege der Totalitarismus-Forschung* (Darmstadt, 1968). J. L. Talmon, *The Origins of Totalitarian Democracy* (Boston, 1952); idem, *Political Messianism* (New York, 1960). R. C. Tucker, *The Soviet Political Mind* (New York, 1963); idem, "The Dictator and Totalitarianism," *World Politics*, **17** (1965), 555ff.

KARL DIETRICH BRACHER

[See also **Authority**; Crisis in History; Democracy; Despotism; Nation; **State**.]

# SENSE OF THE TRAGIC

THE TERM "tragic" has always referred to some aspect of man's concrete involvement with evil and with his effort to comprehend it and to deal with it. As theory is to data, so the theory of evil might be thought to be related to tragedy. But a caution must be sounded, for evil is not an objective datum, as it were, presented for our inspection and understanding. It is also subjective; man himself is involved in it in a manner different from the theorist's impersonal study of the datum. This complexity may be expressed by observing that the struggle against evil may become ironic. For the evil is often in one's self; or it may be identified with the world to which one owes one's being, or with an unnamed and mysterious power in the world. Tragic action in its generic sense is an ironic struggle with evil.

Irony is understood here to be ambiguity in speech or human action used for purposes of communication. An evil event becomes ironic when its ambiguous character is perceived and used. The peculiar tragic character of the protagonist's struggle turns upon his perception of evil and upon his possible creative use of it. Therefrom follows the characteristic salvation of the tragic hero, his victory in defeat. This use of the evil in the struggle against it was recognized by Aristotle in his account of the function of tragedy as the catharsis of pity and terror by means of pity and terror (*Poetics*, 1449b 25–30). Hegel suggests the same recognition when he remarks that the tragic hero plucks for himself the fruit of his own deeds.

The most notable Western interpretations of the evil involved in dramatic encounter are the Tragic, the Orphic, and the Christian. The first of these, as the title suggests, has become standard or typical. The diversified forms of the tragic can be regarded as envisaging human action, according to a characteristic pattern or form, in the several contexts which are determined by these three ways of understanding evil.

## THE PATTERN OF TRAGEDY

Aristotle understood a tragedy to be an artificial thing, an imitation (*mimesis*) of the nature of man coming to mature self-realization. This dramatic doctrine should be interpreted within Aristotle's metaphysics and is skillfully replaced in this context by K. Telford (1965, pp. 89f.). An actual and complete human action must, Aristotle held, have a certain magnitude or significance. It is a whole having concrete parts. These parts, beginning, middle, and end (*Poetics*, 1450b 26f.), occur in temporal succession and can be understood as a unity by reference to a principle.

The principles of necessity ($\dot{\alpha}\nu\dot{\alpha}\gamma\kappa\eta$) and likelihood ($\tau\dot{o}$ $\epsilon\dot{\iota}\kappa\dot{o}s$, 1451b 1f.) are exhibited in the definitions of the three parts of an action. The beginning of an action is not altogether necessitated by preceding events but is reasonably (probably) followed by other events. The end is necessitated by all that precedes and is followed by no further part of that action. The middle is both necessitated by what precedes and points with probability to subsequent events. A man's action, consisting in his free decision and its consequences up to a termi-

411

nal effect, would satisfy these conditions. The consequence of a decision can be foreseen only with probability, but once enacted the decision takes its place in the necessary order and exercises compelling power upon the present. This necessity in its action upon the protagonist acquires the terrifying force of fate.

Aristotle may be interpreted to hold that the appropriate pleasure of tragedy follows upon a catharsis of the audience's emotions of pity and fear (and like emotions) effected by means of the dramatic presentation of incidents involving pity and fear. Pity is a human reaction to events which awaken our sympathy, or an inclination to identify one's self with the personages caught up in these events. Terror is the concurrent reaction to that which repels or overawes. By awakening the audience's pity the poet induces the audience to participate in the terror which the protagonist also senses. This is terror in the face of fate. Hence the audience comes to share to some degree in the heroic manner in which the protagonist confronts this fearful fate. The peculiar quality of the hero's suffering both attracts and repels the audience and readjusts its inclinations to approach the humanly attractive and to flee from evil.

It is essential now to determine how to recognize the completeness of an action involving the piteous and the terrible. This action must have a beginning, a middle, and an end, and be unified by the principles of necessity and likelihood. In Aristotle's favorite drama, the *Oedipus Rex* of Sophocles, these three parts are easy to recognize. Briefly, the beginning is Oedipus' identification of himself as the father of his family, the just king of Thebes, able and obligated to rid Thebes of the plague, sign of the gods' displeasure. The middle is the struggle to retain this character and also to effect the desired riddance. The end comes with his self-recognition as an offense to the gods and the cause of the plague through his foretold and foreordained incest and patricide. Thus, the drama moves through a decision concerning identity and role, a struggle to retain this identity and role, and an end or insight into the erroneously and arrogantly assumed identity and role. The completeness of the action may be interpreted as the return of the end to the beginning, a return in which the past is seen to bear unexpectedly upon the present yet in a manner which is in accord with fate. A complete action of this kind must be distinguished from a series of events which is merely calamitous, pathetic, or piteous but which is not accompanied by an insight, for the insight which reevaluates the series of events or sets it into a new perspective is essential.

Variations upon this pattern of decision, struggle, and insight-laden return to the decision are demonstrably descriptive of a great many, if not all, tragedies. To take one instance: in Sophocles' *Antigone*, both Creon and Antigone move through the pattern; but the insight of the play as a totality lies in the evident point that although each may be justified in his own course of action, no reconciliation between the two is possible; there is no just universe which includes both.

There are other accounts of the pattern of tragic action. Gilbert Murray develops an elaborate one in "An Excursus on the Ritual Forms Preserved in Greek Tragedy" contributed to *Themis* by Jane Harrison (Cambridge, 1917). Kenneth Burke describes his understanding of the tragic rhythm in terms of "purpose, passion, perception" in *A Grammar of Motives* (New York [1945], pp. 38f.); cf. also Francis Fergusson, *The Idea of a Theater* (Princeton [1949], Ch. I). These accounts are not inconsistent with the one presented here. The "three unities," however, which express what the neo-classic authors learned from Aristotle by way of J. C. Scaliger (*Poetics*, 1561) and L. Castelvetro (*Poetics*, 1570), communicate only a superficial grasp of this pattern.

The tragic view of life may, up to this point, be said to be the faith, or at least the hope, that the struggle will indeed be followed by an insight which will illuminate the decision or reaffirm the value of the struggle, even though the value may be affirmed only in an ironic sense. However, this faith or this hope, expressed in so abstract a manner, scarcely does justice to the hero's motivation to embark upon the tragic action. Moreover, this pattern may be discovered in other kinds of action; thus, it is not sufficient to define the tragic sense.

### TRAGIC ACTION

For a fuller understanding of the nature of the tragic struggle we must turn to the evil which precipitated it or which emerges from it. The situation is as if the tragedian had asked himself: Why is man involved with the evils of the world? Why does man seem to suffer unjustly? Then the poet seeks an answer to these questions by placing heroic men in extreme situations, those demanding the utmost of human exertion and wisdom, in order to see what emerges of value and what human wisdom can make of the evil. The tragic artist, of course, must work within a context which is already structured by a number of beliefs. The most pertinent of these beliefs concern the human being and his fate, his relation to the world, and his involvement with others. Such contexts, bearing upon the tragic sense, can most easily be specified by reference to the myths about the nature of evil which are characteristic of each belief. We shall, therefore, examine the tragic sense in its relation to three different myths concerning the nature of evil: the Ancient Greek (or Tragic), Orphic, and Christian.

*1. Ancient Greek Tragedy: The Dionysian Vision.* The Greek understanding of the nature of evil and man's relation to it cluster around the notion of fate or necessity. This compelling element in human life flows mainly from the past. Fate in the Homeric writings is an altogether obscure power, perhaps dominating the gods (in its older form) or perhaps obedient to the gods. It is most important to recognize that this fate is related to the sense of "noumenous" or divine power *before* that power had gone through the ethical phase of evolution which divided its good from its evil component. Both fate and the Homeric gods are indifferent to man's ideas of good or of justice. Precisely the nonhuman character of this power, a character which shades off into malevolence, is that which is terrible in itself and strikes terror to man's heart.

In addition, the gods are jealous and send evil fortune to the man of hybris who dares to rival or to challenge them. Hybris, although often translated as "pride," is not felt as a sin. Yet it is a dangerous possession, for it dares much and is regarded by Aristotle as a flaw of the heroic character. Hybris is the quality of self-confident greatness which makes for heroic virtue. It is the mask of divinity which certain men tend to assume and which is destined to be torn from them to expose the suffering humanity beneath. The presence of hybris in the persons of Hector, Achilles, or Agamemnon is their moving element. Such men are often blinded by a jealous god and brought low according to the standards of their world. The tragic spirit appears in their struggle to remain themselves and to retain their human dignity despite their checkmate by fate or by the gods. Though they acknowledge their defeat by the gods or their domination by fate, they transform this defeat and this domination into a kind of bitter victory. The hybris which was their undoing is also the occasion of their heroism. Thus, within this context two elements are essential to tragic action: a fateful power, which is indifferent or hostile to man, and a hero, one moved by hybris, who fears this fateful power but yet is undaunted by it.

Aristotle and many recent writers regard tragedy as a prolongation of the chthonic religion centered around the birth, life, and death of the god. Indeed the priest-king, leader of the Dionysiac chorus and ritual scapegoat, is said to have evolved into the hero of tragedy. Such a leader is caught up in the inexorable movements by which time is fulfilled. He is in an admirable position for exhibiting the hybris and suffering the fate of man in conflict with the indifference of time and seasonal change. Even if this genealogy of the tragic hero were historically incorrect, it would retain an aesthetic appropriateness, for it accords with the movement of the whole history of tragedy, to involve others in the hero's struggle and epiphany. Aeschylus and Sophocles illustrate especially well the quasi-religious character of the hero's trial, purifying insight, and its often revivifying public effect.

Aeschylus made frequent references to the indifference of the gods and the nonjustice or injustice of the events which they let occur. But he also makes explicit the law that the human good is wisdom and that wisdom is linked with suffering (e.g., *Agamemnon*, 160ff.). The Prometheus who can suffer without yielding to the injustice of Zeus is the true purveyor of wisdom to man. And Orestes, cursed before his birth by the curse upon the house of Atreus, was condemned by the gods no matter what choice he would make, yet he did not remain quiescent nor take refuge in suicide but pressed active obedience to the limit and accepted the consequent madness with the sacrificial fortitude which led finally to a change in the order of human justice. Sophocles dwelt upon the inscrutability of the gods and of fate, yet he saw heroic virtue in learning of the human status and in retaining it in spite of misfortune.

Euripides seemed to judge the gods to be irrational, and hence he turned with the practicality of the Sophists to study man's struggle with other persons or with himself in his effort to dominate his own destructive passions. His last play, the *Bacchae*, tells of Agave's discovery of the destructive character of a Dionysian fertility cult to which she was fondly attached. Pentheus, her son, slain by her and the chorus, also acquired a new evaluation of those passions which he had mistakenly thought easy to civilize. Perhaps fate becomes somewhat more humanized in this context, but it seems to become Apollonian or perspicuous in principle only with the philosophers.

The tragic vision of these writers, especially of Homer, Aeschylus, and Sophocles, has always been regarded as archetypal. The rationale of this evaluation most likely lies in their intuition of the trans-human and altogether mysterious character of the evil to which some men are subject. The remark of Heraclitus is descriptive of this trans-human quality: "To god all things are beautiful and good and just, both those which men call just and those which they call unjust" (frag. 61). The point is the inappropriateness to the divine of metaphors and explanations drawn from human life and its conventional values. The source of the evil of fate is external to man's being; it is visited upon men by impersonal force or by the nonhuman gods. Such an evil cannot be said to be deserved, nor to be excusable in terms of some obscure cosmic justice, nor to be explained away by a theodicy. But the significant

413

point is that certain of the men caught in this net are not passively resigned; they do not turn away in neurotic flight; they do not attempt to disguise their suffering in pious platitudes. On the contrary, these men around whom the tragic net is drawn become heroes. To a dark fate and to a superhuman malignancy, they oppose heroic virtue, the straightforward affirmation of human dignity and freedom.

The tragic sense is traditionally best understood against the background of this cosmic evil. What good, what rationality, what order or justice there is does not exist apart from man. And yet this impersonal and irrational evil which brings unmerited suffering upon a man is that which elicits his heroic character and brings him to those efforts which do build value, order, rationality, and justice in the world. The inhuman evil of the cosmos is, thus, ironic in that it is the source and provocation of human good. It is in the end only ambiguously evil.

We shall return presently to elements of this classic view of tragedy which are present in other contexts. We should first take note of some recent opinions to the effect that tragedy of an even approximately Greek kind can no longer be written at all, since the present climate of belief no longer nourishes the tragic sense.

Confidence in the power of technology to bring nature and fate itself under our control, to prolong life indefinitely, to cure suffering, even mental anguish, and to relieve all human wants by means of applied science have radically altered beliefs about the universe. They have also changed human character. The consequence is that only pathos, not tragedy, is the burden of much of recent literature. Nietzsche stands solidly with the view that the powerful Dionysiac conception of man and his relation to fate cannot be recaptured without radical and universal changes in human character (cf. his *Birth of Tragedy from The Spirit of Music*). Still attempts to communicate a sense of the tragic do exist in modern times. To take an example, Thomas Hardy attempted tragedy, but he is said to have offered only relatively quiescent actors caught in a fate made up of unforeseen accidents and mechanical determination. Again, Arthur Miller's Willy Loman, in *Death of a Salesman*, or the actors in Albee's *Who's Afraid of Virginia Woolf* have their illusions painfully stripped from them. But their illusions are said to be rather silly to begin with, and no one of them achieves a notable insight into human destiny and freedom.

On the other hand, one may speculate that contemporary literature of the absurd represents a return to something like the nonhuman cosmos of the Greek tragedy. However, emphasis in modern times is certainly placed upon the indifference rather than upon the malignancy of fate; one remembers here the final

attitude of Mersault in Camus' *L'Étranger* or of Bertrand Russell in "A Free Man's Worship." But again in modern times this fate or natural law is understood to be penetrable by the scientific intellect and even to be determinable by technology. At the same time, man is seen as just another sort of object within this universe. Thus, he tends in some recent writing to lose his unique status and his human value. He tends to fade into the cosmic background of objects. Samuel Beckett's characters in *Endgame* or in *Krapp's Last Tape* appear to be losing their human identity, and in Robbe-Grillet's novels objects may be more important than people just because they are not people. This meaningless modern cosmos has lost its ironic character; likewise, modern man has lost his tragic resolution and his hybris. He has become as meaningless as the cosmos itself. Thus, if the literature of the absurd preserves some awareness of the nonhuman character of the cosmos, its writers do not communicate the conviction that man retains the power of reaching tragic proportions within it.

*2. Orphic Evil and the Apollonian Vision.* After the great tragedians' contemplation of a nonhuman power of fate, power of this sort appears to become somewhat more perspicuous to the philosophers and their Apollonian minds. But although Plato asserted that philosophers produced the truest tragedies (*Laws*, VII, 817B), his meaning may perhaps be understood with reference to the Orphic religion by which, according to some scholars, he was influenced. The Orphic religion was a relatively late arrival upon the Greek scene and represents the evolution of religious feeling and concepts at a stage where the divine goodness had become distinct from evil. According to the Orphic dualistic myth, the gods are perfect and divine. And in this respect the human psyche is homogeneous with the gods; human evil is the consequence of the soul's falling or straying away from its natural domain and becoming imprisoned in the body. Thus the world of becoming, the body in particular, is the source of all evil and of all tragic action which responds to that evil. Philosophy offers that wisdom or gnosis which can free the soul from its prison and return it to its heaven. Hence philosophy is the art of separating the soul from its body; it is the practice of death.

Socrates, who held that we err only through ignorance, and who believed heaven to be blameless, quite reasonably turned his efforts, in *Republic*, II, toward purging the ancient myths of elements which might lead the youth astray. Suggestions of the gods' injustice, of their unconcern for human standards of virtue, of their double dealing, and of their jealousy—in short, of all those traits which belonged to a Titanic and uncivilized nature—were uncompromisingly censored by Socrates. Plato's fanciful mathematics of the marriage number (*Republic*, VIII, 546) suggests a conviction of the basic Apollonian character of fate. But undoubtedly Socrates' career best represents Plato's feeling for the tragic. In the *Apology, Crito,* and *Phaedo* Socrates is presented as reaffirming his life's decision to struggle against sophistry both within himself and in others and as achieving again his insight that his decision was a just one, that virtue is knowledge, and that the death which frees the soul from its prison is a good. Moreover, Socrates is presented as the artist of life; he has the art of manipulating circumstances and of utilizing whatever misfortune occurs, even death itself, as a means for affirming the nobility and integrity of the virtuous human soul.

Even so, Apollo does not triumph completely within the Platonic dialogues. God still withdraws his hand from the tiller of the universe for one-half of the cycle of the Great Year (*Politicus*, 270A, 273). Also there remains a scandalous and irrational factor in the temporal world. With a dash of imagination one may see an intellectualized version of Dionysian madness in the a-rational receptacle of the *Timaeus* (48D f.), which is the matrix of all becoming and the vessel of the Demiurge's making. Tragedy for Plato, then, may not be merely the simple drama of separating body from soul, for the human soul too is made by the Demiurge. It is at best an imperfect imitation of ideal perfection and retains some tincture of the a-rational character of the receptacle. In short, tragedy for Plato is the failure to achieve human virtue, but this failure involves a complex understanding and use of the a-rational element within the psyche itself.

The Gnostic dualism of soul and body passed into the Christian West through Saint Paul and Neo-Platonism and became allied with Stoic doctrine, especially the doctrine of virtue. This dualism of moral tragedy remains evident in persistently recurring Puritan traits, fear of the body, rejection of physical beauty, and reprobation of sensuousness and emotionality. Puritanism, however, as Nietzsche insisted, did not give birth to much of the kind of writing which can easily be recognized as tragic. Bunyan's *Pilgrim's Progress* is not a work of tragic art. However, Racine, schooled in Jansenism, may fairly be assigned a place in this part of the tradition. In his theater, for instance, in *Andromaque* or in *Bérénice*, the rule of reason and morality triumphs over emotions, mainly the emotions aroused by Venus. Racine's theater is a school of greatness of soul where the magnanimous soul succeeds in neutralizing passion, and in vindicating the aristocratic conception of virtue.

We should also take notice of a curious sort of reverse effect in consequence of which the rejection of the body came to appear as an inhuman evil that called for an intransigeant affirmation of the human. The beginnings of such an assertion might be discerned in the medieval poem, "Aucassin and Nicolette." Also it is possible to read Milton's epic, *Paradise Lost*, so that Satan is its real protagonist. This Satan manifests heroic dignity and virtue in his unequal combat with a frigidly perfect deity. Finally one may perceive a demythologized version of this Puritanism in reverse in some of Bernard Shaw's writings. Evil in his plays, even in *Saint Joan*, has been leveled down to ignorance, egoism, and middle-class hypocrisy. The virtues which he would inculcate are honesty and objectivity, and their precondition is rejection of the "manufactured logic about duty."

**3. The Universe of Christianity.** The Christian tradition inherited the Hebraic ethical monotheism. The Christian, devoted to the one and holy God, creator of heaven and earth, experienced difficulty from the very beginning in reconciling this devotion with the fact of evil in creation. Happily, though, the myth of Adam was at hand to indicate the human origin of evil and to provide a basis for interpreting the beginning of history as the fall of the first Adam and the culmination of history as the advent of the second Adam, the perfect man.

God's creation was, therefore, good; evil entered it later with Adam's desire to be "as a god, knowing good from evil." Evil, then, became man's doing, the result of his grandiose self-misidentification, of the consequent perversion of his love, and of his losing struggle to save himself. The tragic spirit might then be supposed to be exhausted in the assertion of man's hope for a return to Grace and to his original being. And so it might appear in the writings of Saint Augustine, or of Dante, or in the medieval ecclesiastical drama. The tragic form at the least remains in the sequence of man's acceptance of his own opinion as truth and of his own desire as determinative of value, his failing struggle to maintain this self-centered and autarchic conviction, and final insight, aided necessarily by the gift of faith, into his creaturely dependence upon the Creator. In these terms each individual man as well as mankind are potential tragic actors.

This basically good Christian universe, however, seems to fail in eliciting the range and possibility of human heroism with the fullness achieved in the context of Greek tragic thought. Christianity, in brief, seems to define all but human evil out of existence. And man's tragic plight seems almost too easily remedied by observance and discipline. Moreover, many facts do not seem to square with the Adamic account of evil. The suffering of animals and children are instances in point, so also is the disproportionate

415

misery of a "just" war. It must be recalled, though, that the Christian tradition is very rich, and there are in it elements which hark back to something like the Greek tragic sense. These elements ought not to be ignored.

Jaspers and others have argued that tragedy is no longer possible in a Christian universe, because evil is transcended. Yet Adam's original sin remains to place this transcendence into question. According to this doctrine Adam's guilt infected the essence of human nature. It is the presupposition of all human acts and cannot be considered to be the just desert of any man in the sense of being the appropriate consequence of his willed acts. In this respect, original sin bears some analogy to the blindness visited by a god upon the Greek hero.

Still another possibly older apprehension of the nature of evil present in Christianity can be discovered within the Adamic myth. There, it will be recalled, an account of Adam's fall was offered which carried his decision back to other beings. Thus, Adam was not alone in guilt, for he was tempted by Eve, who had been tempted by the serpent, who in turn had been inspired by Satan. Now it is quite possible to suppose that Satan and the serpent embody something of the nonhuman or prehuman evil fate which must in some inexplicable way have been present with or before creation. This prehuman evil emerges in the book of Job. Job clearly presents the contrast of the just and good aspect of God with a possibly more ancient and inscrutable concept of God whose ways may seem evil to the man who is suffering unjustly. Job does not attempt to justify this injustice; rather he acknowledges the mystery. Perhaps again, one catches a glimpse of this more ancient deity in the anguished cry of Christ on the Cross, "My God, my God, why hast thou forsaken me?" (Matthew 27:46). And it is also present between the lines of Saint Paul's remark to the effect that man's wisdom is foolishness to God.

It should occasion no surprise, therefore, that later writers, although imbued with Christian beliefs and attitudes, should sometimes seem to hark back to the spirit of Greek tragedy, whereas at other times they deal with merely human evil, remediable by religious or ethical discipline or even by personal or institutional rearrangements.

Evil, then, for the Christian tradition is both prehuman, an externally determined fate, and Adamic or human and ethical. Exemplifying the latter is Marlowe's *The Tragedy of Dr. Faustus*. Faustus has chosen to seek omnipotence by mastering nature through knowledge and magic. In the end the wheel turns, death and the Devil claim him, and he admits that the faith, which he can no longer recover, would have

saved him. His evil plight he sees as internally determined; his guilt is altogether his own.

Shakespeare, on the other hand, is not without a generous share of the ancient tragic spirit. This sense is manifested, for example, in *Hamlet* and emphasized by the failure of generations of critics to pluck out the heart of his mystery. The rottenness of Denmark, the inconstancy of the Queen, and Hamlet's own inability to determine the character of the evil and to restore health to himself and to the realm suggest the mysterious and prehuman origin of this evil. As in Greek tragedy, the action acquires magnitude by its involvement in the political order and even in the cosmic order. The kingdom participates in Hamlet's struggle with fate and might be reinvigorated by his dauntless though failing efforts. However, to see in Fortinbras, who would tempt fortune "even for an eggshell," the hope for victory in defeat may be a thin hope. No doubt there will always be something rotten in Denmark. King Lear also suffers disproportionately for his errors of judgment. His time of trial in the storm on the heath suggests the mysterious and cosmic character of the fate which has caught him up. To his anguished question, "Is man no more than this?" the powers of nature, human nature included, seem to answer affirmatively. Man is a reed to their careless power. Still, the tragic hero in his extremity reiterates with Pascal that he remains a thinking reed. And Lear accepts an old man's death with gentleness and dignity.

Among modern writers Dostoevsky manifests an especially profound sense of the Christian and the tragic. The Karamazov family exhibits the symptoms of inherited evil. This again is the prehuman evil of which Melville has given us the most impressive symbol in the great white whale, only with the Karamazov family this evil belongs to the soul and to the age. The brothers Demitri and Ivan thresh about in a meaningless universe. Nevertheless, Demitri and Ivan bear their extreme suffering with a determination to press their self-declared freedom to its utmost. In particular, Ivan is troubled to see how a universe such as theirs, ruled by impersonal forces, where the suffering of persons is intense and unjust, can be accepted by Alyosha in Christian faith. Like Job's, Ivan's dilemma is unresolved; nevertheless, his suffering is illuminated by intervals of insight, and these suggest something of the possibility of human transcendence. All in such a world is not lost, although much is.

Ibsen, deeply influenced by Kierkegaard and his enigmatic struggle for and against Christianity, composed dramas in which contemporary mores and middle-class conventions come into unexpected conflict with the past and its necessities. In *Ghosts* this past visits Oswald Alving in the guise of inherited disease which destroys his sanity. In order to involve the audience more intimately in the dramatic action, Ibsen left the insight or reconciliation of *Ghosts* inexplicitly expressed, with the expectation that the audience would complete it. Some critics, consequently, have found the play to be trivial or brutal, effecting no catharsis. Others regard the tragedy as belonging to Oswald's mother, for although her hopes are blasted by her son's insanity, she wins her way through to an understanding of the ghosts—the moral hypocrisy—which haunt them all in the twilight of their middle-class existence.

T. S. Eliot's *Murder in the Cathedral,* like his "The Waste Land," embodies a share of the complex Christian sense of the tragic. The author leads the Archbishop back to Canterbury, where everyone knows he will be unjustly killed by some agency of the King. The play, like *Antigone,* portrays the complete irreconcilability of the powers of the spirit and those of the world, an opposition which is the source of disorder, even within the mind of Becket himself.

In brief, then, the tragic sense is constituted by an awareness of the ironic character of man's struggle with evil. It is often embodied in a complete action which brings the protagonist's world into question. This questioning has proceeded within contexts defined by three mythological views. The consequences of this confrontation with evil, especially the confrontation with an evil deriving from a nonhuman source, have, when carried to the limit, resulted in the affirmation of human dignity and freedom. This affirmation constitutes a sort of victory despite the overpowering force of evil.

*BIBLIOGRAPHY*

A bibliography is included in T. R. Henn, *The Harvest of Tragedy* (London, 1956), pp. 295–98, and in W. Kerr, *Tragedy and Comedy* (New York, 1967), pp. 343–50. R. B. Sewall, *The Vision of Tragedy* (New Haven, 1959), pp. 148f. includes other listings. In addition see the following: W. Arrowsmith, "The Criticism of Greek Tragedy," *Tulane Drama Review*, **3** (1957), 31–57. E. G. Ballard, *Art and Analysis* (The Hague, 1957), pp. 154–84. J. L. Duchemin, L'AΓΩN *dans la tragédie grecque* (Paris, 1945). M. Esslin, *The Theater of the Absurd* (New York, 1961). W. C. Greene, *Moira: Fate, Good and Evil in Greek Thought* (Cambridge, Mass., 1944). K. Jaspers, *Tragedy is not Enough,* trans. H. A. Reiche, T. Moore, and W. H. Deutsch (Boston, 1952). J. W. Krutch, *The Modern Temper* (New York and London, 1930). A. C. Mahr, *Origin of the Greek Tragic Form* (New York, 1938). O. Mandel, *A Definition of Tragedy* (New York, 1961). G. Nebel, *Weltangst und Götterzorn, eine Deutung der Griechischen Tragödie* (Stuttgart, 1957). Friedrich Nietzsche, *Die Geburt der Tragödie aus dem Geiste der Musik* (1872), trans. from 1886 ed. as *The Birth of Tragedy* (1910), several versions. Anne and H. Paolucci, eds., *Hegel on Tragedy* (New York, 1962). M. Peckham, *Beyond the Tragic Vision* (New York, 1962). D. D. Raphael, *The Paradox of Tragedy* (Bloomington, Ind., 1960). P. Ricoeur, *The Symbolism of Evil,* trans. E. Buchanan (New York, 1967), pp. 218–31. M. Scheler, "Zum Phaenomen des Tragischen," *Vom Umsturz des Werte; Abhandlungen und Aufsätze,* 4th ed. (Bern, 1955). K. A. Telford, *Aristotle's Poetics* (Chicago, 1965), trans. and analysis. R. Wellek, *A History of Modern Criticism*, Vols. I and II (New Haven and London, 1955), Vols. III and IV (1965).

EDWARD G. BALLARD

[See also **Catharsis;** Dualism; **Empathy;** Evil; **Irony; Mimesis; Necessity;** Sin.]

# UNIFORMITARIANISM AND CATASTROPHISM

UNIFORMITARIANISM assumes the principle that the past history of the earth is uniform with the present in terms of the physical laws governing the natural order, the physical processes occurring both within the earth and on its surface, and the general scale and intensity of these processes. It asserts further that our only means of interpreting the history of the earth is to do so by analogy with events and processes in the present.

Catastrophism assumes the principle that conditions on the earth during the past were so different from those existing in the present that no comparison is possible, that earthquakes, volcanic eruptions, and the elevation of mountains and floods occurred during the past on a scale many times greater than that of any similar events observable in the modern world, and that geological events in the past were often so violent and catastrophic, that they sometimes destroyed all the species living in particular districts.

The questions raised by the conflicting assumptions of uniformitarianism and catastrophism apply most directly to the interpretation of geological history, but are not restricted to it. These questions arise in science whenever there is need to interpret natural events occurring at a distance in space or time. In these circumstances the separation of the events or processes from the observing scientist requires him either to interpret them by analogy with events and processes closer at hand and more directly observable, or, to assume that the distant events are the result of processes unknown to him and are, therefore, impossible to interpret. If a scientist attempts to interpret distant events by analogy, he is assuming the uniformity of the natural order through space and time.

417

The terms "catastrophism" and "uniformitarianism" were introduced in 1837 by William Whewell in his *History of the Inductive Sciences* to describe the two leading schools of theoretical geology at that time. Catastrophism, which was the older theoretical viewpoint, was in England widely accepted and defended by the older generation of geologists, but its leading exponents were then on the Continent. Leopold von Buch, the German geologist, had presented a theory of craters of elevation to account for the form of volcanic mountains. He supposed that such volcanoes as Teneriffe in the Canary Islands had not been built up gradually by many repeated volcanic eruptions carried on over an immense period of time, but by an upheaval of the surrounding rock strata, and that this upheaval had been essentially a single event, catastrophic in nature, and without parallel in the modern world. Von Buch presented this theory in 1824 after a visit to the Canary Islands, and in 1829 Léonce Élie de Beaumont published his theory of the sudden and simultaneous elevation of mountain chains. He had been struck by the fact that a number of ranges of mountains tended to be composed of rocks of similar geological age and showed similarities of structure. For instance, de Beaumont suggested that the Pyrenees had been uplifted in a single sudden upthrow (*en un seul jet*) and that this elevation had occurred at the same time as that of the Alps. Von Buch and de Beaumont suggested that in the geological past there had occurred events on such an enormous scale as to be catastrophic in nature and without counterpart in the modern experience of man. Their view of the history of the world was that while conditions on the earth's surface in modern times, that is, since the appearance of man on earth, had been relatively orderly and calm, undisturbed by any great changes which might destroy a significant portion of life on earth, this stable and reliable condition of the earth's surface was of relatively recent appearance. During the geological past, they assumed that, while there may have been long periods of calm conditions, the earth had also been subjected repeatedly to enormous changes, great shakings of the surface of the whole earth, which had resulted in the throwing up of mountain ranges, vast floods, subsidences, and other catastrophes.

In assuming the extraordinary and catastrophic nature of the earth's history, von Buch and de Beaumont were part of a tradition of geological thinking which extended back to the seventeenth century and was deeply influenced by the account of the Creation in Genesis. Genesis takes for granted that the condition of the world at the time of its creation was different from its present state, and this assumption was accepted unquestioningly by late seventeenth- and early eighteenth-century writers on the origin of the world. Even if one leaves aside extravagant and uncritical writers like Thomas Burnet whose *Sacred Theory of the Earth* (1681–89) was an imaginative but completely uncritical account of the origin and history of the earth, the ideas of a cautious and disciplined scientist like John Ray nonetheless take for granted that the account in Genesis did reflect the actual events which occurred at the origin of the world and, furthermore, that the present world was temporary and would disappear in a great conflagration at the day of judgment. In the early eighteenth century, it became generally recognized that the fossils found in rocks were the actual remains of once living animals. For geologists in Italy fossils demonstrated that the Italian rock strata had been laid down beneath the sea, because the well preserved fossil shells in the Italian strata were recognizably similar to the shells species living in the Mediterranean. For geologists in England and in northern Europe, however, the recognition of fossils as the remains of once living animals posed the difficulty that they belonged to species without counterparts in the north Atlantic, or in other parts of the world, for that matter. Thus the fossils of the English strata suggested the existence of multitudes of species in the past which had since died out. The disappearance of such multitudes of species also suggested that they must have been destroyed by some great catastrophic event on the earth's surface.

Of the geological theories put forward during the eighteenth century, perhaps the most influential was that of Abraham Gottlob Werner. As a professor at the School of Mines at Frêyburg, Werner became expert in the recognition of rocks and minerals.

In 1793 Peter Simon Pallas, as a result of his study of the two principal mountain ranges of Siberia, decided that the characteristic structure of mountain ranges was a central core of granite with schistose rocks containing no fossils along the flanks of the granite, and with fossil-bearing limestone rocks lying outside and above the schistose. Pallas' observations on the structure of mountain ranges, and those of Horace Bénédict de Saussure on the Alps, appear to have been used by Werner in the development of his theory of the earth. Werner assumed that the granite represented the original surface of the earth formed when the earth had cooled from a molten mass. He thought that the schistose rocks had been deposited from the universal ocean, which, in the first stages of the earth's history, had covered the whole surface of the earth and had been as deep as the mountains are high. The schistose rocks had been chemical precipitates from the primordial ocean, but at a later stage mechanical sediments had been deposited from this ocean, giving rise to the strata of limestone, shale, and sandstone.

Werner's assumption that granite represented the original surface of the earth and was consequently the oldest rock, was challenged in 1795 by James Hutton in his *Theory of the Earth with Proofs and Illustrations*. Hutton had been impressed by the fact that the stratified rocks were sediments which, to his mind, must have been laid down beneath the sea. These sediments, laid down originally as soft sand, mud, or marl, had somehow been consolidated into solid rock and had then been raised from the sea bottom to form dry land and even hills and mountains. The force which produced both the consolidation of sediments into rock and their elevation into hills and mountains was heat. Hutton was evidently impressed by the discovery of specific and latent heats by his friend Joseph Black, the physicist. Hutton considered heat as a force inherent in matter, moreover, as a repulsive force, derived ultimately from the sun. It might assume the form of specific heat; in which case it influenced the volume of matter, or, latent heat, which determined the fluidity of matter, or light, or electricity. Heat which was so diverse in its form and its effects, existed abundantly within the earth and acted both to consolidate sediments into rock and to elevate them. In 1788 Hutton discovered in Glen Tilt in the highlands of Scotland, a dyke of granite, which had clearly intruded into the surrounding schistose strata. Not only had the granite intruded into the stratified rock, but it had intruded in a molten condition because the strata in the vicinity of the dyke were much altered, as if by heat. Hutton was greatly excited by this discovery because it meant that the granite was not the oldest rock and did not represent the primordial surface of the earth. Instead, it represented a later intrusion, and the oldest rocks discoverable were stratified rocks which had themselves originated as sediments. However, these sediments represented the detritus of some preexisting land. Hutton was aware that the whole surface of the land was subject to relentless forces of erosion and was being worn down steadily by rain and running water. The wearing down of the land was necessary to create the sediments which were deposited on the sea bottom. These sediments accumulated over immense periods of time, were then in turn hardened into rock by heat, and elevated from the sea to form hills and mountains. Hutton saw this process of the wearing down of land, the deposition of sediments and their re-elevation extending indefinitely into the past and continuing indefinitely into the future. He saw the present surface of the earth, not as fixed and unchanging, but as intermediate stage in a continuous process.

Hutton's theory reflects the calm inquiring rational spirit of the eighteenth-century Enlightenment; Hutton possessed the same temper of mind as David Hume, the philosopher, or Adam Smith, the economist. His theory was attacked immediately as being dangerous to religion, and the force of this criticism was sharpened by the political consequences of the French Revolution. In Great Britain the French Revolution was felt to endanger the whole fabric of social order, of which the Christian religion was the essential foundation. Hutton's theory left no place for the Mosaic account of Creation and of the Flood. It assumed that the earth and the physical order of nature were eternal and unchanging. At the same time that Hutton's theory was being attacked on religious and scientific grounds, liberal political ideas had become unpopular in Britain, and a repressively reactionary tone dominated politics. At Edinburgh where Hutton's friends continued to support his theory after his death in 1797, Robert Jameson, professor of natural history at the University of Edinburgh, was one of the most vigorous exponents of the Wernerian theory. Consequently, the controversy between the Wernerians and Huttonians raged with a special vigor at Edinburgh between 1800 and 1810. Hutton's friends, several of whom were associated with the *Edinburgh Review*, tended to be liberal in their outlook, whereas the Wernerians were Tories, and these political associations tended to deepen and embitter the scientific controversy.

The Wernerian-Huttonian controversy at Edinburgh did have the effect of convincing geologists of the dangers of theoretical controversy. Thus, when the Geological Society of London was founded in 1807, its members decided to avoid theoretical discussion in favor of a broad program of geological field studies. Geological evidence, which could not be interpreted in terms of the Huttonian theory, was also accumulating. In 1811 Alexandre Brongniart and Georges Cuvier published their description of the Tertiary strata of the Paris basin. Among these strata Cuvier and Brongniart found a repeated alternation of fresh water and marine sediments. Such an alternation required either repeated incursion of the sea over the land, or repeated subsidences and re-elevations of the land. Hutton's theory provided for neither contingency. At the same time, Cuvier and Brongniart had described a whole series of sediments unknown to Werner. In 1812 Cuvier also published the first edition of his *Recherches sur les ossemens fossiles* (1812–26) based upon his reconstruction of fossil animals during the preceding fifteen years. This work presented to the scientific world a succession of populations of animals, all extinct, and

419

sometimes both larger in size and more numerous in species than the animals of modern times. Cuvier asserted that each successive assemblage of fossil species of animals had been destroyed by a geological catastrophe, such as might occur when the sea rose to cover the land. He did not hesitate to extend the consequences of his observations made in the Paris basin to the whole world. Cuvier was as skillful a politician as an anatomist, and his theory of successive catastrophes, the most recent of which was the flood described in the Bible, appealed strongly to the religions because it allowed the numerous and striking recent discoveries in paleontology to be reconciled, however uncritically, to the biblical account of creation. After 1815 Cuvier's catastrophism was perhaps keyed to the intellectual tone of the Bourbon restoration, but it was also popular in the English-speaking world. An English translation by Robert Kerr was published at Edinburgh in 1815 and again in many subsequent editions.

Perhaps paleontology tended to strengthen the plausibility of catastrophism by the fact that the discovery of so many large and remarkable fossil animals suggested that catastrophic events on earth must have been needed to bring about their disappearance. In 1812 the skeleton of a remarkable fossil reptile, seventeen feet long, was found in the blue Lias formation at Lyme Regis on the coast of Dorsetshire. This reptile, which had paddle-like appendages to equip it for swimming, and which in some respects resembled a fish, in 1816 was named Ichthyosaurus. In 1820 another large swimming reptile, also from the blue Lias, and with a remarkably long neck was described by William Daniel Conybeare and was named Plesiosaurus. This was followed by the discovery of the enormous Megalosaurus by the Reverend William Buckland in the Stonesfield slate, and of the Iguanodon by Gideon Mantell in Sussex. In 1825, in the third edition of his *Recherches*. . . , Cuvier described the Pterodactyls, a group of fossil flying reptiles. These discoveries all exerted a profound effect on both the scientific and popular imagination and presented a vivid picture of the abundance, diversity, and enormous size and strangeness of past forms of life.

One of the points which had been at issue between the Huttonians and Wernerians had been the question of the origin of basalt. Werner had considered that basalt had been formed by crystallization from water, whereas Hutton and such French geologists as Jean Étienne Guettard and Nicholas Desmarest considered it a volcanic rock. The volcanic origin of basalt was generally accepted in Britain after 1813 when the Reverend William Buckland and the Reverend William Daniel Conybeare visited the Giant's Causeway in

Ireland, where they found clear evidence that that particularly famous basalt formation had resulted from a volcanic outflow.

In general, British geologists tended to abandon Werner's idea that rock strata had been formed by crystallization or deposition from a universal ocean, and had accepted the Huttonian idea that the strata had been laid down beneath the sea and had subsequently been elevated. However, in accepting the concept of movements of the land they necessarily accepted the occurrence of catastrophes during the history of the earth, because they could not conceive how elevations sufficient to create the existing hills and mountains could occur without catastrophes. In 1814 the English geologist Thomas Webster published a description of the geology of the Isle of Wight in which he showed that the chalk strata forming the central range of hills in the island were vertical or very steeply inclined and that they formed one side of an anticlinal fold, the opposite side of which, he discovered on the south shore of the Isle of Wight. Webster showed that the strata must once have been continuous in a great arch extending across the whole Isle of Wight and that most of this arch had since been removed. The chalk strata which had formed this arch had been formed as horizontal beds of sediment in the sea, so that their upraising to form the arch had required their uplift, bending, and disturbance on a great scale. This kind of disturbance was explicable to Webster only by some enormous convulsion of a kind entirely different from anything experienced in modern times. The basic assumptions of geologists in the 1820's, whether Huttonian or Wernerian, was stated by William Whewell in 1831:

In the dislocation of provinces, in the elevation of hills from the bottom of the sea, in the comminution and dispersion of vast tracts of the hardest rock, in the obliteration and renewal of a whole creation they seemed to themselves to see . . . the manifestation of powers more energetic and extensive than those which belonged to the common course of every day nature. . . . They spoke of a break in the continuity of nature's operations; of the present state of things as permanent and tranquil, the past having been progressive and violent (William Whewell, review of Lyell's *Principles of Geology, British Critic,* 9 [1831], 190).

During the 1820's the evidence for convulsive and catastrophic changes in the history of the earth seemed so compelling and universal that the revival of James Hutton's concept of a continuous process shaping the earth's surface indefinitely through time is a development requiring some explanation. Two factors seemed to have played a role. The first may have been an increasing interest in the study of volcanic activity in different parts of the world.

Beginning in 1797 Leopold von Buch (1774–1852) made extensive studies in the Alps where he determined that their structure showed that they had been uplifted. From his further observations on the Alban Hills and Vesuvius in Italy and on Etna in Sicily he became convinced of the vast extent and power of volcanic activity, and of its capacity to uplift whole areas of country. In 1802 he visited the Auvergne district of France where he found a series of volcanoes of different ages, all of which were connected with an underlying platform of granite. He decided that the mass of trachyte forming the Puy-de-Dôme was simply granite which had been softened and pushed up as a protuberance. The other *Puys,* which possessed the conical forms and craters characteristic of volcanoes, had been formed by the ordinary process of volcanic eruption. After a visit to Norway, where he observed granite veins extending into an overlying fossil-bearing limestone which was highly altered along the lines of contact, von Buch travelled to Madeira and the Canary Islands. There he saw the results of volcanic activity on a still larger scale and studied the way in which the islands had been formed as a result of volcanic action. He concluded that most oceanic islands were the products of volcanic activity.

When von Buch studied the form of volcanoes he noted that they were both conical in form and stratified, with the strata sloping away on all sides from the crater's summit. He decided that this structure was not the result of accumulated lava flows, because the lava emerged in small streams which did not form continuous sheets over the whole surface of the mountain. When he compared his observations in the Canary Islands with those he had made in central France, von Buch decided that each volcano had resulted originally from a dome-shaped extrusion of molten rock from the interior of the earth. If this extrusion broke through to the surface, it solidified while retaining its form and gave rise to a dome-shaped mountain such as the Puy-de-Dôme in Auvergne. More often, however, the extrusion might burst like a bubble at the summit and collapse inward, thereby forming a cone-shaped volcano of typical form with a crater marking the site of explosion. In this theory each volcanic mountain was the product of a single violent eruption instead of the accumulated product of a long series of eruptions extended over a great period of time. Von Buch called the interior molten mass, whose extrusion from the interior of the earth had given rise to the volcano, a "Crater of Elevation." He thought that their extrusion uplifted the rock strata of the surrounding country in a catastrophic manner.

On his return to Europe, von Buch again studied the Alps for a number of years and decided that they had been formed by a process of upheaval from below, the upheaving force being volcanic rocks which could not find their way to the surface because of the thickness of the overlying rock strata.

In 1822 William Daniel Conybeare suggested that volcanic activity sustained over a long period might be able to produce a large scale elevation of the land. Volcanoes were studied by Charles Daubeny, and by George Poulett Scrope and both studied the area of extinct volcanoes in the Auvergne district of France as well as those in Italy and Sicily.

The other factor which may have played a role in extending the time scale of earth history was the development of paleontology, which had also seemed to support catastrophism by requiring the extinction of so many successive assemblages of animals and plants. However, the succession of floras and faunas revealed by paleontology also required greatly lengthened periods of time. In addition, the detailed study of the fossil animals and plants found together in a single bed frequently suggested the existence of conditions analogous to those of the present. For instance, in the Tilgate Forest bed, studied by Gideon Mantell in 1822 and subsequent years, there was a collection of the bones of turtles, one or more species of crocodiles, freshwater shells, and the remains of various plants including tree ferns and large weeds. There were successive layers of clay and sand, such as might have been laid down in a modern river delta, and the animals and plants were comparable to those which might live in a river delta in a modern tropical country. These fossils, therefore, suggested that conditions on the earth's surface at a very remote period of time had been comparable with those of modern times, although the climate and latitude of Great Britain had then been much warmer. In 1824 Charles Lyell gave a reverse kind of analogy when he compared the plants and animals living in modern freshwater lakes in Scotland with the fossil animals and plants found in freshwater marls of the Paris basin, and found the assemblage of species very similar in both instances.

From 1820 to 1828 Charles Lyell was first a law student and later a practicing barrister, but through the whole time, he was an enthusiastic amateur geologist and naturalist. He travelled frequently and extensively. In 1818 he had toured Switzerland and northern Italy. In 1820 he returned to Switzerland and this time went as far south in Italy as Rome. He made frequent excursions on horseback through southern England, and in 1823 spent many weeks in Paris where he became acquainted with the Parisian geologists and studied the geology of the Paris basin. In 1824 he spent an extended period in Scotland. These travels gave him a broader experience of landscape, geography, and geology than many of his contemporaries had. In 1828 Lyell travelled with Roderick Murchison through the Auvergne district of France, then southward to Nice and along the coast into Italy. At Padua, Murchison turned back, but Lyell went on south through Italy to Naples and made a tour of Sicily. One of his chief geological discoveries during this journey was that the Tertiary beds of the Paris basin formed only the earliest part of the succession of Tertiary formations, and that in Italy and Sicily there were three series of Tertiary strata, each successively younger than those of the Paris basin. Ultimately he named them the Eocene, Miocene, and older and newer Pliocene formations, of which the Eocene represented the beds of the Paris basin. Taken together, the whole series of Tertiary strata were at least equal in total depth to the succession of secondary strata in England. In southern Italy and Sicily Lyell found that the newer Pliocene strata contained fossil shells, almost entirely belonging to species still living in the Mediterranean. He also found that these strata which were close to the active volcanoes of Vesuvius and Etna appeared to have been uplifted by volcanic activity. He became convinced that volcanic activity and earthquakes were both the causes of and manifestations of uplift.

In a letter to Roderick Murchison written as he was returning northward, Lyell expressed the geological conviction to which his tour had led him:

That no causes whatever have from the earliest time to which we can look back, to the present, ever acted but those now acting and that they never acted with different degrees of energy from that which they now exert (*Life, Letters and Journals of Sir Charles Lyell Bart*, ed. K. M. Lyell, 2 vols., London [1881], I, 234).

He was stating the central principle of what was to be known as uniformitarianism. As a principle, it was the outgrowth of Lyell's geological experience, but it must be emphasized that it was not, and is not, a demonstrable scientific conclusion. Instead, it is a statement of faith and a working hypothesis which is, nonetheless, a hypothesis indispensable to the progress of geology as a science. Lyell assumed that gradual causes acting through long periods of time might exert large-scale effects. His further assumption, that all geological effects are the result of gradual causes acting over large periods, required him to study relentlessly the existing processes going on both in the earth and over its surface, to pursue their consequences, and to estimate their rates. His principle of uniformity required Lyell always to attempt to *explain* geological phenomena and never to abandon this attempt to seek explanation by dismissing phenomena as the result of

catastrophic events of unknown origin and magnitude. Lyell assumed that the order of nature and the physical laws of nature remained constant through time. He saw, too, that our only possibility of attaining knowledge of the geological past was by analogy with modern conditions. The geologist had to assume that conditions in the past were comparable to those of the present and that processes going on in the past were comparable to processes going on at the present time, or else he would have to abandon all hope of acquiring any knowledge of the past.

Furthermore, Lyell's principle of uniformity opened up to the geologist a multitude of questions for investigation because the whole present order of nature, existing both over the earth's surface and within its interior, became relevant to his purpose. Hence, the geologist must seek to learn what is going on at the present in order to understand what has gone on in the past. Catastrophism, on the other hand, removes the necessity for investigating modern processes because events in the past are considered to have no counterparts in the present. The explosion which occurred at the time of emergence of a "Crater of Elevation" occurred only once and is not to be understood from the study of modern volcanic activity. The effect of catastrophic explanations in each instance in which they were used and in which they are used today, is to close off further investigation. Lyell stressed that an enlarged view of the existing order of nature was the primary requisite for a geologist, and the chief means of attaining this enlarged view was travel. He wrote:

To travel is of first, second, and third importance to those who desire to originate just and comprehensive views concerning the structure of our globe (Lyell, *Principles of Geology*, 11th ed., 2 vols., London [1872], 1, 69).

During his lifetime Lyell upheld the principle of uniformity in eleven successive editions of his *Principles of Geology*, published between 1830 and 1872, and in other books and memoirs. With unequalled insight, he interpreted a vast range of geological data in terms of processes observable in the modern world. Of even more far-reaching significance was his influence on Charles Darwin. During the voyage of the H. M. S. Beagle, 1831–36, Darwin came to appreciate the great value of the approach to geology embodied in Lyell's *Principles*. He then applied the same principles to the interpretation of the geological history of species and considered what would be the effect of a modern process, namely, natural selection, if it had continued to act through an indefinite period of past time. Darwin's theory of the origin of species by natural selection may be considered an application of Lyell's principles of uniformity to the living world.

Towards the end of Lyell's life uniformitarianism was attacked by the physicist, Lord Kelvin, who in 1865 argued that if the earth had been formed originally as a hot molten body which had later cooled but which also continued to lose heat by radiation, its age could be calculated by extrapolating backward from its present rate of heat loss. Kelvin assumed that there was no source of heat within the earth, other than that which was present there when the earth was formed. On his assumptions he showed that the age of the earth could not be greater than 100,000,000 years and was probably much less. This short and restricted time span for the age of the earth would not allow sufficient time for the extremely slow gradual geological processes, as viewed by Lyell, to bring about the actual geological changes which had occurred. The history of the earth if thus compressed in time would necessarily become violent and catastrophic. This concept of the earth's severely limited age would not allow time, either, for the slow process of evolution of living species by natural selection, as viewed by Charles Darwin.

In the face of Kelvin's calculations, geologists tended to retreat from their advocacy of uniformitarianism after Lyell's death in 1875. In 1897 Sir Archibald Geikie wrote that uniformitarianism "in its extreme form is probably held by few geologists in any country." By "its extreme form" Geikie meant chiefly a uniformitarianism which would rule out events on a catastrophic level in volcanic activity and mountain building during the geological past. However, with the discovery of radioactivity, it was pointed out by Ernest Rutherford in 1904 that the radioactive elements did provide a steady source of heat within the earth. The assumptions on which Kelvin had based his estimates of the age of the earth were, therefore, invalid and his calculations meaningless. Geologists did not, however, recover immediately their confidence in uniformitarianism, and in many instances they continued to believe that volcanic activity and mountain building had gone on during particular periods of the geological past on a scale, and with an intensity, unparalleled in the present. In recent years, however, radioactive methods of dating rocks have shown that instances of supposed catastrophic volcanic activity and mountain building have, in fact, occurred over long periods of geological time. There is, therefore, little reason to believe that they ever involved systematic volcanic eruptions or earthquakes of magnitude greater than those which occur on earth today. The principle of uniformitarianism may be considered vindicated by modern science.

*BIBLIOGRAPHY*

Frank Dawson Adams, *The Birth and Development of the Geological Sciences* (Montreal, 1938). Loren Eiseley, *Darwin's Century* (New York, 1958). Archibald Geikie, *The Founders of Geology* (London, 1897). Patsy A. Gerstner, "James Hutton's Theory of the Earth and His Theory of Matter," *Isis*, **59** (1968), 26–31. Charles C. Gillispie, *Genesis and Geology* (Cambridge, Mass., 1951). Leonard G. Wilson, "The Origins of Charles Lyell's Uniformitarianism," *Uniformity and Simplicity*, ed. Claude Albritton, Geological Society of America, Special Paper 89 (New York, 1967), 35–62.

LEONARD G. WILSON

[See also **Continuity and Discontinuity; Evolutionism;** Religion and Science; **Uniformitarianism in Linguistics.**]

# UNIFORMITARIANISM IN LINGUISTICS

*1. Uniformitarianism in Geology.* The term "uniformitarianism" was introduced by William Whewell in 1840 to label a certain scientific theory, contrasted with catastrophism. The issue as discussed by Whewell and his contemporaries primarily presented itself in geology. Charles (later Sir Charles) Lyell (1830) was the most prominent advocate of uniformitarianism.

In geology, the issue arose for two main reasons. (1) It appeared from the geological record that there were changes, in both the inorganic and the organic realms, too great or too sudden to be accounted for by causes now known to be in operation. (2) Even more important, anything like a literal interpretation of the Bible seemed to call for a catastrophic view. It was not generally supposed that the Creation, or Work of the Six Days, took six twenty-four hour periods to complete, but it was generally supposed that, instead of setting the universe up by a "single decree" (as Leibniz called it, *Causa Dei*, §42, and Fifth Letter to Clarke, §66), after which only "secondary causes" were at work, the Creator divided his total act of creation into several separate acts, of which all but the first supervened upon and altered a world already in operation. In addition to the Creation, another episode from Genesis—the Flood—had obvious bearing on geology. And one who applies the uniformitarian idea not, as Lyell did, only in geology, but in all natural science would exclude all miracles, whether alleged in the Old Testament or the New: the burning bush, Aaron's rod turning into a serpent, the rolling back of the waters of the Red Sea, Christ walking on water, etc. And it happened that in Genesis there is a linguistic episode that poses scientific problems rather like those of the Creation and the Flood.

Lyell's uniformitarianism is commonly treated only as a precursor of Darwin's evolutionism. It is clear—see especially Eiseley (1958), who in effect (pp. 108, 113, 115) defends the way in which Huxley (1869) distinguishes evolutionism from uniformitarianism—that Darwin went beyond Lyell not merely in dealing with the biological realm, including man, but also in his positive theory of natural selection. Uniformitarianism (extended to organic evolution) said there was a law; Darwin said what the law was. And we may distinguish between uniformitarianism and evolutionism as follows. Uniformitarianism as such says nothing about the limits of change over time, but says only that the "laws" or "causes" of change are uniform over time, i.e., are the same at all times. We may call "qualified uniformitarianism" the doctrine that admits one exception to this, or at most two exceptions, namely a first moment of the universe and perhaps also a last moment, in which, respectively, creation was started and annihilation was completed. It was thought to be a corollary of uniformitarianism that only those laws, or those causes, which are at work now—adapting a phrase of Newton's, these were called *verae causae*— were ever at work.

Uniformitarianism so defined says nothing as to whether life evolved from inorganic matter, or man from brute, or some other species of living thing from another species. How it differs from evolutionism may be brought out by an example: the causal relation of life to inorganic matter. According to uniformitarianism, either (1) there was never a time when there were not living things on the earth, or (2) there was such a time, and a later time when there were living things, but the transition from the earlier to the later state could be exhaustively explained in terms of laws that held good at both states and indeed at all states. Of the two possibilities compatible with uniformitarianism, only the second is evolutionary. What uniformitarianism rules out is the supposed possibility that the transition from an earlier stage with no life to a later stage with life was accomplished not by the prevailing laws of nature but by a miracle or other extraordinary direct intervention of the Creator.

What was the argument for uniformitarianism? In retrospect we are inclined to see the issue as at bottom one of scientific autonomy. Was natural science to be guided—constrained, as those who deplored the guidance would say—by premises allegedly furnished by Revelation, or was natural reason to be its own sole lawgiver? Lyell and his contemporaries did not, however, see the issue in this way. Both sides, whether partisans or critics, put the issue in terms of "probability," this being determined by what was most conformable to the Creator's intention (Lyell [1830–33], 1, 164, quoted by Gillispie [1951], p. 121; Huxley, in Darwin [1888], 1, 541). Lyell's formulation was muddied by the self-imposed limitation, justified no doubt but trouble-making, that he only undertook to defend uniformitarianism in application to strictly geological phenomena, not carrying it back "beyond the veil of stratified rock" (Huxley [1869], p. 313) to the earliest stages of our terrestrial globe, nor forward to living organisms. In other words, he virtually situated geology in between physics (and chemistry and astronomy) and biology, and for the most part refrained from treating its border-sciences, either uniformitarianly or in any other manner. There is only a terminological difference between saying, with Huxley (ibid., pp. 315, 319) that this limitation of scope imposed by Lyell is inherent in uniformitarianism, and saying that Lyell himself was not an out-and-out uniformitarian. Lyell's views on organic evolution are very complicated (Eiseley, Ch. 4).

**2. Uniformitarianism and Linguistics.** Uniformitarianism did not have any detectable direct influence upon linguistics until more than thirty years after Lyell set it forth in geology. We first describe the circumstances of this detectable impact, and then go back to look at the situation in linguistics before then.

The impact was due, in part, to Lyell himself. Chapter 23 of his work, *Geologic Evidences of the Antiquity of Man* (1863), is entitled "Origin and development of languages and species compared." The leading thoughts are that (1) there are various analogies between languages and biological species as regards mutation, splitting of one species (or language) into two, arrested development, competition among different species (or languages), and so forth, and (2) sometimes we can see more clearly what happens to species, sometimes to languages. Lyell was looking for light on what happened to species, and he thought that some light might come from what happened to languages.

Lyell's concern with language was distinct from, and independent of, a concern with language as a power of man. The latter concern—seen for instance in Darwin's *Descent of Man* (1871) and *Expression of the Emotions in Man and Animals* (1872), includes such questions as how far language resembles and how far it differs from such other things as gestures, brute cries, etc., and whether it can be regarded as having evolved from any of them.

Lyell's Chapter 23 began with a quotation from F. Max Müller, and the next year Müller returned the compliment by quoting Lyell (Müller [1864], Ch. 5, pp. 232, 239ff.). Müller might have done so from mere courtesy or timeliness. But beyond this obvious acknowledgment, Müller in the same work took account of Lyell's ideas in a much profounder way. For in an earlier chapter (Ch. 2) he virtually incorporated uniformitarianism into linguistics, by formulating two "principles on which the science of language rests, namely, that what is real in modern formations must be admitted as possible in more ancient formations, and that what has been found to be true on a small scale may be true on a large scale." The eminent American linguist W. D. Whitney, in his review of this book (1865, p. 567), commented disdainfully, "We should have called these, not fundamental principles, but obvious considerations, which hardly required any illustrations." But this disparagement was unfair if, as seems to be the case, Müller was the first in linguistics to formulate them. It should be noted, moreover, that Whitney did not question the truth of Müller's principles. Again, in 1885, Whitney admitted their truth and questioned the importance of stating them. That he was himself uniformitarian was stressed, shortly after his death, by the great Indo-Europeanist Karl Brugmann ([1897]; cf. W. P. Lehmann, *Language*, 34 [1958], 179–80, n. 2).

Through the German linguist Friedrich Techmer we gain further information on the channel of influence. He cites (1880, 1, 119) a passing allusion by Geiger (1869, p. 65) which suggests that the uniformitarian-catastrophist issue was familiar; in Techmer himself, familiarity with the issue is simply one instance of a general familiarity and sympathy with British logic and scientific method. The same familiarity and sympathy are manifest in Kruszewski (1884–90, 1, 295; 3, 167) a few years later.

Besides the major influence of uniformitarianism, linguistics shows influence from geology in two minor ways, namely, in its metaphors "substratum" and "linguistic paleontology." On substratum, see Y. Malkiel, *Language*, 43 (1967), 231ff. On linguistic paleontology, see Pictet (1859–63); Techmer (1880), 1, 60–61; Saussure (1922), §5.4.3; Nehring (1931). The history of the latter metaphor deserves further investigation. It doubtless involves some connection between A. Pictet (1799–1875) and F.-J. Pictet (1809–72). Both Pictets were professors at the University of Geneva. F.-J. Pictet was an eminent paleontologist; both Darwin and Huxley speak respectfully of his review of *The Origin of Species*.

*3. Geology, Biology, and Linguistics.* The metaphor "linguistic paleontology" exploits a certain obvious analogy between "dead" languages and fossils. (It should be borne in mind that paleontology, the study of fossils, belongs both to geology and to biology; this fact leads us, when considering influences of geology

upon linguistics, to consider at the same time certain influences of biology upon linguistics.) For one thing, linguistics was concerned with normative questions to a far higher degree than was biology. There was, for example, a counterpart in linguistics but not in biology to the literary "quarrel of the ancients and the moderns." This dispute—ably described in Chapter 14 of Highet (1949) and in Wimsatt and Brooks (1966), pp. 214, 262, 437n., 523–24—concerned the relative value of ancient languages and literatures as compared with modern languages and literatures. Whereas there was never a time in biology when the study of fossils was more highly esteemed than the study of living plants and animals, it was only after centuries of debate that the study of living languages and literatures (written or oral) came to be considered not inferior to the study of Latin and Greek. And the debate was, in effect, ended sooner for literature than for language: the "progressive" view prevailed, very broadly speaking, for literature already in the Enlightenment, but for language not until romanticism. The chronicle is well told in the various writings of the ardently progressivist, and yet remarkably objective linguist Otto Jespersen (e.g., 1922).

The maxim, therefore, that we ought to interpret dead languages in the light of the living ones was more controversial in linguistics than its counterpart was in biology. It was countervailed by the argument that, as the living languages have degenerated from the dead classical languages, to use the former as a guide is to interpret the perfected and optimal form in the "light" of the corrupted and obscured form. In biology a like argument was heard only in a very few special cases, for instance, in the opinion about ancient man that "There were giants in those days." The superior importance of the classical languages was bolstered by a judgment about the superior importance of written language over spoken language. According to this judgment, if we have only written records of ancient languages, this is, to be sure, a loss, but not an essential loss. In biology, per contra, it was generally recognized that if, e.g., one classified fossil molluscs exclusively according to properties of their shells, this basis of classification, used for lack of anything better, was forced upon us by the circumstance that only their hard shells, and not their soft inner vital parts, got preserved. The view attained in the nineteenth century, that we lacked information about such "vital parts" of the classical languages as their system of intonation, the details of their pronunciation, and the full extent of differences of dialect, social class, and style within them, and that in drawing inferences about them we should take as our models the living languages that we could more fully observe—this view was in effect uniformitarian, though there was no demonstrable influence from geology.

Having seen that uniformitarianism involved taking a position on the interpretation of those episodes of the Bible that concerned geology, we may inquire what positions linguistics took on the corresponding linguistically relevant episode. Linguistics had no Lyell, and the problem arises, Why not?

Several ingredients of an explanation present themselves. One of them—the normative aspect of linguistics—has already been discussed. In the second place, the hypothesis of uniform change had a very different aspect in linguistics than in geology, and this for several reasons. (1) Rate of linguistic change was less easily quantified than, for example, rate of sedimentation, glacial advance, or lava flow. The point is not that it was less easily measured, but that the very definition of what to measure was less easy. (2) If one estimated the rate of language change impressionistically, one might well have had the impression that it was highly variable. In particular, it was plausible to suppose an acceleration in times of social upheaval, or of decline in level of education, etc. (3) The mathematics of probability and statistics, which could be put to good use in quantifying rate of linguistic change, had not been sufficiently developed until the early nineteenth century, and, when it was developed, it was not regarded by linguists as one of their available tools.

In the third place, there are significant differences between the linguistic aspects of the Confusion of Tongues at Babel and the geological aspects of the Creation and the Flood. The Babel story, taken literally, says that by extraordinary, supernatural intervention God replaced a linguistic unity by a linguistic diversity that was sufficient to frustrate universal communication, but this left room for great latitude of opinion about the nature of the replacement. One extreme possibility was that God maximized the diversity; the consequence of this for scientific linguistics would be that we could not by any set of regularities account for the relation between the *lingua adamica* (whether this was Hebrew or some other language) and all the now existing languages. The other extreme possibility was that God minimized the diversity; the post-Babelian languages, each of them describable as gotten by a set of regularities from the *lingua adamica,* differed from one another just barely enough to frustrate universal communication, yet not so much as to frustrate scientific understanding of their relationships. This seems to have been Leibniz' view, in keeping with his principles that God works everywhere by rules and that he achieves maximal results with the minimum means. Thus both the so-called

"polygenist" view and the "monogenist" view can claim compatibility with the Babel story. But neither in Leibniz' time nor in Müller's nor in ours has any great success been achieved in working out the monogenist view in any detail.

As for the hypothesis that the pre-Babelian language was Hebrew, linguistic science was not in a position to refute this hypothesis definitely until about the 1860's, i.e., until the Comparative Method reached the stage to which Schleicher brought it.

In the fourth place, linguistics was subject to more constraints than geology. Even if relieved of heteronomy from Revelation, linguistics was still subject to constraints external to it, from physics, from geology, and from biology. Archbishop Ussher's chronology, fixing the Babel episode at 2347 B.C., gave the linguist only several thousand years to work within, as noted by Sapir in his discussion of Herder ([1907], p. 117; cf. Jespersen [1922], p. 28), but the natural sciences did not allow him much more. Given the obvious fact that man is of relatively recent origin, and given the opinions prevailing in the nineteenth century about the age of the earth and the durations of the several geological periods, there were still only a few thousand years available to the linguist for the origin and diversification of language. Geology and evolutionary biology were themselves oppressively constrained in their available time span by current physics (Eiseley [1958], Ch. 9); for instance, in 1893 Lord Kelvin accepted an estimate of the earth's total age as 24 million years. Contrast this with the fact that by 1907 B. B. Boltwood, using the half-life principle of radioactive decay, had arrived at an estimate 100 times that of the earlier one (personal communication from Matt Walton, 1963; not in Eiseley). Present-day estimates agree more or less with Boltwood's value rather than Lord Kelvin's, and the antiquity of *Homo sapiens* has likewise greatly expanded.

In the fifth place, linguistics was preoccupied with another task. Whitney (1867, p. 3), sketching the history of linguistics, spoke for the prevailing view when he called the recognition of an Indo-European family "the turning point in this history, the true beginning of linguistic science." The challenge of following up this recognition led to devising the Comparative Method (Bloomfield [1933], Ch. 18), and to refinements of methods in historical linguistics. The grand project of working out, by the historical and the comparative methods, the detailed history of the Indo-European family and also of various other families (Semitic, Dravidian, etc.) occupied nearly all the energy put into linguistics in the nineteenth century. But the historical and comparative methods did not—except perhaps for their indications that Hebrew was not the same as

Proto-Semitic—yield any result that challenged received interpretations of the Bible. Besides the reason already given—great uncertainty about the rate of linguistic change—there was another, that needs to be set forth rather fully. This other reason was that the comparative method cannot settle the question whether all human languages are descended, by uniformitarianly acceptable processes, from a single ancestor. The diversity of known languages is such, and the imperfections of the method are such, that the method breaks down before it reaches the end of our quest, which is the beginning in time of language. This limitation became clear to linguists in the second half of the nineteenth century.

The reason for the incapacity is that the comparative method does not admit of unlimitedly recursive application. Taking historical, documented languages as our input, we get as output Proto-Indo-European. And taking other sets of documented languages as inputs, we get Proto-Semitic, Proto-Finno-Ugric, Proto-Algonquian, and so on. The idea occurs to us that we could treat these reconstructed proto-languages as inputs in their turn, and thus get further back in time to the beginning of language. But no one has succeeded in doing this in a generally accepted way, nor is there any prospect of it.

The incapacity may be stated in terms of time. The several outputs of the comparative method take us back perhaps 6,000 years. (This is the rough time-depth that Pedersen [1931, p. 319] proposes for Proto-Indo-European; the estimates reported in Cardona, Hoenigswald, and Senn [1970] do not go back so far.) According to any dating that places the origin of language appreciably earlier than that, there is an appreciable temporal gap between the origin(s) and the earliest states that we can reconstruct by the comparative method. According to Ussher's chronology, there would be a gap of about 1,700 years (since he gave 2347 B.C. as the date of the Babel episode); according to timetables furnished by the physics and the geology of the late nineteenth century, there could be at most a gap of a few thousand years; according to present-day timetables, the gap might be as great as some hundreds of thousands of years. (Haas, 1966, discusses repeated applications of the comparative method; she finds it possible to repeat the method as much as three times, but the time depth thereby reached is still only about five thousand years, i.e., to about 3,000 B.C. See p. 140, Table 12 and n. 66.)

The fifth point of difference between linguistics and geology may be summarized as follows. Uniformitarian geology began with a proposed straightforward method and a proposed limitation upon its scope. Comparative linguistics began (at about the same time as Lyell's

geology) with a roughly defined task, and required about thirty years to work its way through to a more precise conception of its task and to the formulation of a method—the comparative method—for achieving it. The culminating figure was August Schleicher (especially his work of 1861–62), to whom we next turn. The founders were Rasmus Rask, Jakob Grimm, Franz Bopp, and August Pott, whose manner of discovery has been aptly compared by Antoine Meillet (see Jespersen [1922], p. 55) with that of Columbus. By the 1860's, as the inherent limitation of the comparative method became clear, linguists became aware of a veil like the "veil of stratified rock" which Lyell (according to Huxley) acknowledged from the outset.

So much for the differences between geology and paleontology on the one hand, and linguistics on the other. Let us close this section by noting an important resemblance. Whitney, quoted above, called the recognition of the Indo-European family a turning point in linguistics. The reason why it was a turning point is revealed by a phrase in the famous remarks (1786) of Sir William Jones which are generally given credit for starting the new turn. Greek, Latin, and the newly discovered Sanskrit, Jones says, show an "affinity . . . so strong that no philologer could examine all the three without believing them to have sprung from some common source which, perhaps, no longer exists . . ." (Jones [1788], pp. 421–22). This prospect was exciting for two reasons. First, for the thought—not new, as Hoenigswald (1963, p. 3) notes, but newly interesting— that a major language should have entirely disappeared. The comparable interest in extinct plants and animals is well described by J. C. Greene (1959). In each case, apart from the supposed bearing upon the revelations of the Bible, there was food for uniformitarian thought: the proposition that the *laws* of nature do not change over time did not mean that the *states* of nature do not change; the uniformitarian did not have to maintain that at all times the species of plants and animals, and the languages, were just what they are now. The second reason for excitement was the hope, and the prospect, that the lost source language could be recovered. The analogy between the hoped-for method of recovering the lost language and the method of recovering extinct plants and animals— between the comparative method of linguistics and paleontology—is a rather remote one, but we know from remarks by Hegel, W. von Humboldt, and others, that Cuvier's comparative anatomy inspired the founders of comparative linguistics.

*4. August Schleicher (1821-68).* Schleicher's unusually complex views cannot be accurately described in brief compass. Here we are concerned only with his relation to uniformitarianism (cf. Hoenigswald

[1963]; [1966], pp. 1–2 and n. 13; Jespersen [1922], pp. 71–83; Maher [1966]; Oertel [1902], pp. 39–42, 53–54, 58–59; Pedersen [1931], Ch. 10 and pp. 311–13; Robins [1967], pp. 178–82; Schmidt [1890]).

Schleicher's work (1863) on Darwinism and linguistics is interestingly like Lyell's work of the same year in its comparison of languages with biological species. Schleicher says that whether or not Darwin's natural-selection hypothesis is true of species, it is certainly true of languages. This is far from entitling us to call Schleicher a Darwinian, but at least there is a measure of agreement.

On the other hand, Schleicher was no uniformitarian. Employing a certain interpretation of Hegel's contrast between Spirit (which expresses itself in History) and Nature, he eclectically combined it with the pre-Hegelian, eighteenth-century opinion that the historically attested language changes are deteriorations, or forms of decay; he posited an earlier stage of language in which languages were perfected, and a later stage during which they deteriorated; because only the earlier stage involves Spirit, he assigned it to History (in the Hegelian sense), with the result—confusing to us today—that his stage of History is prehistoric and his stage of Nature includes all the historically documented changes. Now obviously any such contrast between a stage of History and a stage of Nature in language is intensely un-uniformitarian. It is one thing to simply say nothing about prehistoric languages, i.e., to limit the scope of one's consideration to the historically documented languages, and another thing to make a positive claim, as Schleicher did, about prehistorical "History." We shall now see the reaction in the 1860's and '70's to this claim. In leaving Schleicher, let us remark as a last point that one of his major contributions—the family-tree model of relationships within a language-family—had an un-uniformitarian tinge, insofar as it committed itself to treating the split of one language into two as a sudden, cleancut separation, contrary to what we observe today as the ordinary, hardly observable process of language-change (Bloomfield [1933], pp. 347, 364, 394, 481). A few years after Schleicher, a more realistic model was proposed by his pupil Johannes Schmidt (Pedersen [1931], pp. 314–15; Bloomfield [1933], pp. 317–18, 340).

**5. The Neogrammarians.** Since the uniformitarian attempts to get at the origin of language by the comparative method showed no prospect of success, we are not surprised to encounter, in the decades following Schleicher, explicit recommendations to abandon "glottogonic" inquiries (Jespersen [1922], pp. 96 and 412 quotes the Société de Linguistique de Paris in 1868 and Whitney in 1871).

428 About fifteen years after Schleicher's *floruit*, the German movement called "Neogrammarianism" appeared on the linguistic scene. Neogrammarians' platform had many components, two of which are relevant here: (1) their conception of sound-laws, and (2) their view of sound-change as gradual and largely unconscious.

The thesis that "Sound-laws have no exceptions" is the best known Neogrammarian thesis. Cassirer incisively noted (1953, §1.7, esp. p. 169) the resemblance between this thesis and the doctrine of the physiologist Emil Du Bois-Reymond in his celebrated lecture of 1872 (only a few years before the launching of their program), proclaiming laws of nature that were exceptionless, over all time and all space. Apparently Cassirer meant to suggest the hypothesis that the Neogrammarians were deliberately intending to apply or adapt Du Bois-Reymond's doctrine to linguistics, and this hypothesis may well be true. But if that was their intention, their application was faulty in two notable ways. (1) The sound-laws did not hold for all time and all space; each law was expressly limited to a certain language over a certain limited period, and was only claimed to be a "law" in the respects that it (a) applied to all instances, within the stated language during the stated period, that fell within its scope, and (b) was not subject to voluntary control. (2) It is one thing to claim that sound-change is subject to exceptionless laws, and another to claim that those laws are the extremely simple ones that linguists are able to pick out, such as Grimm's Law. The first point is less of a fault than the second, because in spite of Du Bois-Reymond's thesis it was not established usage to make timelessness (invariance over all time) essential to the concept of "law of nature."

Effectively, Neogrammarianism separated language-changes into those that fell under (exceptionless) laws and those that did not; changes of the former sort were held to be unconscious, those of the latter sort conscious and moreover voluntary ( purposeful, deliberate). It was hypothesized that sound-changes were of the former sort. It was furthermore supposed that for the most part sound-change is not merely unconscious but gradual. The supposition was expressed by using the slogan that was always on Darwin's lips, *Natura non facit saltus* ("Nature does not make leaps"). Linguists' use of this slogan may look like an influence from Darwin, and thus eventually from uniformitarianism, but in fact this influence is superficial and the real source of the doctrine is to be found elsewhere, in psychology, as the following paragraphs will show.

First let us consider the slogan as used by Darwin himself. Darwin emphasized the *Non saltus* maxim even to the point where Huxley thought he overworked it. But Darwin's reason was that he saw that uniformitarianism admits of degrees, and in his effort to show that an impeccably uniformitarian explanation of organic evolution could be given, he chose as a matter of policy to be excessively rather than insufficiently uniformitarian whenever threatened with the prospect of erring either on the one side or the other. But when the slogan gained currency beyond the circle of geologists and biologists, it was construed not as a maxim of method but as an alleged fact about nature.

Taken as a maxim of method, *Non saltus* is perhaps compatible with uniformitarianism but surely not essential to it. One might even claim that a certain amount of discontinuity is an obvious fact of experience, and so a *vera causa*, just as the Hindu philosopher Shankara (also Śaṃkara) argued that "A person maintaining that the people of ancient times were no more able to converse with the gods than people are at present would thereby deny the (incontestable) variety of the world" (Sacred Books of the East, 34, 222–23; cited by Deussen [1912], p. 38), and as Charles Peirce, arguing against causal determinism, urged that chance presents itself as a *vera causa*.

Those who imported *Non saltus* into the description of language-change disregarded such considerations, it seems, and had only a rather loose analogy in mind. We can see easily enough what the analogy was. We know that languages change, but we know this by inference, not by direct observation, somewhat as we know that waterways wear away stone (the Colorado River system has excavated the Grand Canyon), or that the hour hand of a watch moves one twelfth as fast as the minute hand, and the minute hand one sixtieth as fast as the second hand. The *Non saltus* maxim is a rather clumsy attempt to harmonize the *Vera causa* maxim with uniformitarianism, simply brushing aside the necessary truth that unless a change is truly continuous in a strictly mathematical sense, it is a succession of discrete steps, and whether this succession is perceived as discrete or as continuous depends upon the discriminatory power of the perceiving agent. To put the point more bluntly, Darwin naively took man as the measure in deciding whether a change was big enough to count as a leap (*saltus*) or not.

It so happened that those who took the slogan over into linguistics, though naive as regards the deeper methodological issues involved, were not naive in taking man as the measure. It is true that they took man as the measure, but not true that they did it naively. For they were concerned not with change in general, but with man's perception of change; and in dealing with man's perception of change it was not naive, but rather was inherent in the nature of the project, to take man as the measure. In other words, for their project it was entirely suitable, relative to

a perceiving individual A, to divide language-changes into changes of which A is aware and changes of which he is unaware. (It was a feature of the psychology of their day to contrast consciousness or awareness, called apperception, with perception.) And in dealing with the perception, and the awareness, of language-changes, the Neogrammarians made use of the fairly recent psychological discovery called "the phenomenon of the just noticeable difference." This phenomenon was of interest to psychologists because of (1) Fechner's attempt to quantify it and (2) the prospect that such a quantitative treatment would make a scientific treatment of the mind-body relation possible. But it was of interest to linguists not for either of these reasons but for a third reason, a "qualitative" rather than a quantitative aspect, which we might call "the nontransitivity of indistinguishability." There is an important difference between identity and indistinguishability. Identity is a transitive relation, i.e., if A is identical with B and B is identical with C, then A is identical with C. But if A is indistinguishable from B and B is indistinguishable from C, then no conclusion can be drawn; it neither follows that A is indistinguishable from C nor that A is distinguishable from C. To use the technical labels, indistinguishability is neither a transitive nor an intransitive relation, but something in between, which is called "nontransitive."

That language-change may be so gradual as to escape notice—that it may be "insensible," to use the eighteenth-century term—was observed already in ancient times; but the hypothesis (1) that the presently observed language diversity could result from an original unity by changes that were in large part gradual, and (2) that the principal locus of language change lay in the imperfect imitation by children of the speech of their elders, had to wait until the nineteenth century to receive serious consideration. Neither hypothesis would be accepted without qualification at the present time; but what is relevant is that the hypotheses themselves are uniformitarian in character, and the question is whether the linguists who put them forward were actually influenced by Lyell. It appears probable that there was little direct influence, that there was a fair amount of indirect influence via Darwin (insofar as Darwinian ideas had become common property of the "average educated man"), but that in large part the influence came from psychology, and in particular from its recent heightened appreciation of the just-noticeable difference and the "threshold," and its accompanying recognition that indistinguishability (of sounds, etc.) is nontransitive.

**6. Uniformitarianism in Recent Linguistics.** In 1950 Morris Swadesh launched a method, glottochronology, that deserves mention here because it proposed a uniformitarian refinement of the comparative method. It had two main postulates: (1) The vocabulary of any language can be divided into two parts, the basic vocabulary and the rest; languages may differ in their nonbasic vocabularies, but all languages agree in the meanings expressed in their basic vocabularies. (2) Change in a language's basic vocabulary (which consists in the replacement of one item by another item with the same meaning) proceeds at a more or less constant rate for all languages at all times.

It is postulate (2), uniform rate of change for replacements in basic vocabularies, that makes the method uniformitarian. To determine this constant rate, it was assumed that replacement, which is discrete, could be represented without serious distortion as a continuous process amenable to the differential and integral calculus. Under that assumption, there resulted as a corollary to postulate (2) a half-life principle just as in the mathematical model for radioactive decay. And actually it was the application to radioactive decay, and especially its recent application in archeology to radiocarbon dating, that inspired Swadesh's method and aroused hopes for it (Swadesh, 1952).

After about a decade of discussion both postulates came to be judged unrealistic (Hymes [1964], pp. 567–663, including pp. 622–23, a bibliography). However, the basic ideas of the method have not been shown to be wrong in principle.

## BIBLIOGRAPHY

Leonard Bloomfield, *Language* (New York, 1933). Arno Borst, *Der Turmbau von Babel*, 4 vols. (Stuttgart, 1957–63). Karl Brugmann, *The Nature and Origin of the Noun Genders in the Indo-European Languages* (New York, 1897). George Cardona, Henry M. Hoenigswald, and Alfred Senn, eds., *Indo-European and Indo-Europeans . . .* (Philadelphia, 1970). Ernst Cassirer, *The Philosophy of Symbolic Forms*, Vol. I (New York, 1953). Francis Darwin, *Life and Letters of Charles Darwin*, 3 vols. (London, 1888); cited from the two-volume edition (New York, 1898). Paul Deussen, *The System of the Vedanta* (Chicago, 1912). Loren Eiseley, *Darwin's Century* (New York, 1958); cited from the 1961 reprint. Lazarus Geiger, *Die Ursprung der Sprache* (Stuttgart, 1869). Charles C. Gillispie, *Genesis and Geology* (Cambridge, Mass., 1951); cited from the reprint (New York, 1959). John C. Greene, *The Death of Adam* (Ames, Iowa, 1959); cited from the reprint (New York, 1961). Mary R. Haas, "Historical Linguistics and the Genetic Relationship of Languages," in *Current Trends in Linguistics*, eds. Thomas A. Sebeok and Charles A. Ferguson (The Hague, 1966), III, 113–53. Gilbert Highet, *The Classical Tradition* (New York, 1949); cited from the reprint (New York, 1957). Henry M. Hoenigswald, "On the History of the Comparative Method," *Anthropological Linguistics*, **5**, No. 1 (1963), 1–11; idem, "Criteria for the Subgrouping of Languages," in *Ancient Indo-European Dialects*, ed. Henrik Birnbaum and Jaan Puhvel (Los Angeles, 1966), pp. 1–12. Leonard Huxley, *Life and Letters of Thomas Henry Huxley*, 2 vols. (London, 1900); cited from the two-volume edition (New York, 1901). Thomas Henry Huxley, "Geological Reform," Presidential Address to the Geological Society of London (1869); reprinted in his *Collected Essays*, 8, 305–39; and cf. pp. viii–xi; idem, *Collected Essays*, 9 vols. (London, 1893–94); cited from (New York, 1897). Dell Hymes, ed., *Language in Culture and Society* (New York, 1964). Roman Jakobson, "Franz Boas's Approach to Language," *International Journal of American Linguistics*, **10** (1944), 188–95; reprinted in Sebeok, 2, 127–39. Otto Jespersen, *Language* (London, 1922); idem, *Linguistica* (London, 1933). Sir William Jones, "The Third Anniversary Discourse. On the Hindus," Feb. 2, 1786, in *Asiatick Researches*, Vol. I (Calcutta, 1788), reprinted, idem, *Works* (London, 1799), I, 19–34. Mikolaj Kruszewski, "Prinzipien der Sprachentwicklung," *Internationale Zeitschrift für Sprachwissenschaft*, **1** (1884), 295–307; **2** (1885), 258–68; **3** (1887), 145–87; **5** (1890), 133–44, 339–60. Charles Lyell, *Principles of Geology*, 3 vols. (London, 1830, 1832, 1833); idem, *The Geological Evidences of the Antiquity of Man* (London, 1863). John P. Maher, "More on the History of the Comparative Method," *Anthropological Linguistics*, **8**, No. 3, Part 2 (1966), 1–12. Friedrich Max Müller, *Lectures on the Science of Language, Second Series* (London, 1864); cited from (New York, 1865). Alfons Nehring, "Sprachwissenschaftliche Paläontologie," in *Actes du Deuxième Congrès International de Linguistes* (Geneva, 1931; published 1933), pp. 191–94. Hanns Oertel, *Lectures on the Study of Language* (New York, 1902). Holger Pedersen, *Linguistic Science in the Nineteenth Century* (Cambridge, Mass., 1931). Adolphe Pictet, *Les origines indo-européennes, ou les Aryas primitifs, Essai de paléontologie linguistique*, 2 vols. (Paris and Geneva, 1859, 1863). R. H. Robins, *A Short History of Linguistics* (Bloomington, 1968). Edward Sapir, "Herder's *Ursprung der Sprache*," *Modern Philology*, **5** (1907), 109–42. Ferdinand de Saussure, *Cours de linguistique générale*, 2nd ed. (Paris, 1922). August Schleicher, *Compendium der vergleichenden Grammatik der indogermanischen Sprachen*, 2 vols. (Weimar, 1861, 1862); idem, *Die darwinische Theorie und die Sprachwissenschaft* (1863); an English abstract arranged by Huxley appeared in *The Reader* (London, 27 February 1864); see L. Huxley, *Life and Letters . . .* , 1, 227 and T. H. Huxley, *Collected Essays*, 2, 80. Johannes Schmidt, "Schleicher" (1890), reprinted in Sebeok 1, 374–95. Thomas A. Sebeok, *Portraits of Linguists*, 2 vols. (Bloomington, 1966). Shankara (Śaṃkara), *Commentary on the Vedanta-Sutra*, in Sacred Books of the East, Vol. 34 (London, 1890); Vol. 38 (London, 1896). Morris Swadesh, "Salish Internal Relationships," *International Journal of American Linguistics*, **16** (1950), 157–67; idem, "Lexico-statistic Dating of Prehistoric Ethnic Contacts," *Proceedings of the American Philosophical Society*, **96** (1952), 452–63. Friedrich Techmer, *Phonetik*, 2 vols. (Leipzig, 1880). William Whewell, *Philosophy of the Inductive Sciences* (London, 1840). Andrew D. White, *A History of the Warfare of Science with Theology in Christendom*, 2 vols. (New York, 1896); see Ch. 17, "From Babel to Comparative Philology," 2, 168–208. William D. Whitney, review of Müller, *Lectures on the Science of Language*, Second Series, *North American Review*, **100** (1865), 565–81; reprinted in Whitney's *Oriental and Linguistic Studies* (New York, 1873), pp. 239–62; idem, *Language and the Study of Language* (New York, 1867); idem, "Remarks on F. A. March's Paper on The Neo-grammarians," *Proceedings of the American Philological Association* (1885), xxi. William K. Wimsatt and Cleanth Brooks, *Literary Criticism: A Short History* (New York, 1966).

RULON WELLS

[See also Classification of the Sciences; **Language; Linguistics;** Structuralism; **Uniformitarianism and Catastrophism.**]

# UNITY OF SCIENCE FROM PLATO TO KANT

"THE PROFESSORS of wisdom in Greece did pretend," says Francis Bacon, "to teach a universal *Sapience.* . . . And it is a matter of common discourse of the chain of the sciences how they are linked together, insomuch that the Grecians, who had terms at will, have fitted it of a name of *Circle Learning*" (*Valerius Terminus*, Ch. I, *Works*, VI, 43). The ideal of such a universal knowledge has played a dominant role in the course of European culture, both scientific and humanistic, whether expressed in the educational requirements for merely the Roman orator and architect or at its apogee in the eighteenth-century *Encyclopédie* for the enlightenment of a whole age. It is partly in relation to this ideal that the more limited concept of the unity of the exact sciences arises; partly, however, it arises from the nature of science itself. In a science the search for unity and for intelligibility are inseparable. It is natural for this search to extend itself beyond the confines of the individual science to all the sciences taken together.

The main conception of the unity of the sciences until the time of Kant can, for convenience of classification, be considered in relation to the ways in which the sciences were in general, following Aristotle, distinguished from one another: (1) by their principles or logical foundations, (2) by their subject matters, and (3) by their methods. Consequently there are conceptions of unity underlying the principles of the different sciences, of unity with respect to their subject matters, and of unity with respect to their methods. To these we can add a fourth conception of unity with respect to the end or ends of science.

## UNITY OF PRINCIPLES OF SCIENCE

In the case of principles two powerful traditions were established by Plato and Aristotle. Plato distin-

guished the five mathematical arts (arithmetic, plane and solid geometry, astronomy, and harmonics), from all the other arts, for though, like the others, they are undertaken for their practical utility, they contain some apprehension of true being. Those who study them, however, accept their principles uncritically as self-evident or absolute and no attempt is made to account for them. Plato envisaged a science, "dialectic," which is superior to the mathematical sciences, because it takes their assumptions not as principles, but as hypotheses, using them as stepping stones for ascending to a single principle, not itself hypothetical, the first principle of everything, or the Form of the good. In doing so dialectic destroys their hypothetical character, that is, renders them intelligible or known, for "that which imparts truth to the things that are known and the power of knowing to the knower you affirm to be the Form of the good. It is the cause of knowledge and truth" (*Republic* 508). Moreover, dialectic shows the interconnections of the sciences with one another and their relation to the nature of being. Plato asserts it to be the distinguishing mark of the dialectician that he has the ability to see the sciences as comprising one whole (ibid. 537).

In opposition to the Platonic conception of the unity of the sciences with respect to their principles, there is the Aristotelian view which denies the possibility of a supreme science from which the basic truths of the particular sciences can be deduced (*Analytica posteriora* 76a 16–25). These basic truths are indemonstrable. Nevertheless there is a science which embraces the others. "We suppose," says Aristotle, "that the wise man knows of all things, as far as possible, although he has not knowledge of them in detail" (*Metaphysica* 982a 10). "In knowing the most universal things he knows in a sense all the instances which fall under the universal" (ibid. 23). While each of the special sciences investigates some kind of being with a view to demonstrating its essential properties, the highest degree of universal knowledge, or first philosophy, investigates the properties of no genus, but only the properties of being as being. Included also in first philosophy are the common principles or axioms which hold for everything that is insofar as it is and not insofar as it belongs to some genus. The most certain of these is the principle that "the same attribute cannot at the same time belong and not belong to the same subject and in the same respect" (ibid., 1005b 19). Aristotle also mentions the law of excluded middle. Among the indemonstrable basic truths of a science some are peculiar to that science and some are common to all the sciences, "but common only in the sense of analogous, being of use only in so far as they fall within the genus constituting the province of the science in question"

431

(*Analytica posteriora* 76a 37). Taking "common" in this sense, Aristotle says, "In virtue of the common elements of demonstration—I mean the common axioms which are used as the premisses of demonstration, not the subjects or the attributes demonstrated as belonging to them—all the sciences have communion with one another" (ibid. 77a 26).

With the rediscovery of Aristotle in the West in the thirteenth century, the conception of a universal science of being as being emerges again. In his Commentary on Aristotle's *Metaphysics* Saint Thomas Aquinas defines metaphysics as the science which investigates the most intelligible things, that is to say, the most universal principles. These are being and the consequent attributes of being, such as one and many, potency and act. Without knowledge of these universal principles it is not possible to have a complete knowledge of any genus or species of things. Moreover, it should not be left to any one of the particular sciences to investigate these principles, for, as necessary to the knowledge of any genus whatever, they would equally have to be investigated in all the particular sciences. Aquinas concludes that there must be one universal science whose concern is these principles (*Expositio*, Prooemium).

It is not possible here to trace the meanings attached to "being" from Aristotle through the periods of scholasticism and into the eighteenth century when it became, as the highest abstraction, the vacuous subject of Wolff's ontology, a science given pride of place in the classification of the sciences in the *Discours préliminaire de l'Encyclopédie*. However, in the seventeenth century Francis Bacon, for the specific purpose of giving unity to the sciences, took over the Aristotelian notion of first philosophy, and adapted it to his own thoroughgoing philosophical materialism, substituting nature for being. For Bacon first philosophy is a universal science, "the mother of the rest," and prior to all divisions by subject matter (*De augmentis scientiarum*, Book III, Ch. I, *Works*, VIII, 471). It has two parts. First, it is a repository of all axioms not peculiar to any of the particular sciences. Unlike the axioms of Aristotle's first philosophy, however, they are not common to all the sciences, but are such as are shared by two or more. Moreover, where for Aristotle it is impossible in demonstration to pass from one genus to another, the principle function of the axioms for Bacon is precisely that of making these transitions possible, "in order that solution of continuity in sciences may always be avoided. For the contrary thereof has made particular sciences to become barren, shallow, and erroneous" (ibid., Book IV, Ch. I, *Works*, IX, 14). Secondly, first philosophy is a doctrine of transcendentals (Being, One, etc.), but again with im-

portant modifications of tradition. Where for the scholastics being was the first of the transcendentals, and the others were coextensive or convertible with it, either singly, as in the case of unity, truth and goodness, or in disjunction as in the case of substance-accident, necessary-contingent, actual-potential, etc., Bacon presents a list only of disjunctive transcendentals and assigns being to membership in one of the disjunctive pairs—"Much, Little; Like, Unlike; Possible, Impossible; likewise Being and Not Being, and the like" (ibid., Book III, Ch. I, *Works*, VIII, 473). He does not appear to regard these pairs of disjunctives as coextensive with anything. What he considers important, however, is that first philosophy be concerned with "the operation of these Common Adjuncts" insofar as "they have efficacy in nature," and without regard to divisions of the sciences.

Plato's notion that there is a single science which gives certainty to the principles of the other sciences emerges again in the seventeenth and eighteenth centuries, most notably with Descartes, Leibniz, Hume, and Kant. Descartes' metaphysics gives certainty to the other sciences in two ways; one, by the removal of the hyperbolical doubt to which even mathematics is subject—the atheist mathematician cannot know that his science is true—and the other by showing that the Cartesian physics is not merely a new hypothesis but is true, and that the physics of Aristotle is false. Prior to producing his *Principles of Philosophy* Descartes presented all his treatises in the physical sciences as resting on hypothetical principles, which, though confirmable by experience, he considered himself able to deduce from the primary truths of his metaphysics (*Discourse on Method*, Part VI). Later he was to claim for his *Meditations* that they "contain the entire foundations of my physics" or "contain all its principles" (*Oeuvres*, III, 297f., 233). It is more specifically *Meditation V*, determining the essence of material things to be extension, and *Meditation VI*, establishing the real distinction between the mind and the body, which banish substantial forms from nature and demonstrate that all physical phenomena, including living phenomena, whether plant, animal, or human, are governed by purely mechanical principles. These principles are extended even to the scientific treatment of the passions: "my aim has been to explain the passions . . . only as a physicist" (ibid., XI, 326). Thus Descartes aptly compared philosophy as a whole to "a tree, whose roots are metaphysics, whose trunk is physics, and whose branches, which issue from this trunk, are all the other sciences," in particular, medicine, mechanics, and morals (*Principia philosophiae*, Preface).

Leibniz attributes a similar role to metaphysics in relation to the natural sciences, but for different reasons. Because physical nature is the phenomenal expression to a perceiver of immaterial or metaphysical substances, the principles governing phenomena are ultimately grounded in metaphysical principles. "We acknowledge that all phenomena are indeed to be explained by mechanical efficient causes but that these mechanical laws are themselves to be derived in general from higher reasons and that we thus use a higher efficient cause only to establish the general and remote principles" (*Specimen Dynamicum*, Loemker, p. 722). Physicists must not, like the scholastics with their substantial forms, introduce metaphysics into physics. The two spheres are separate. The sole function of metaphysics in relation to the physical science is to provide the foundations of their principles (*Discourse on Metaphysics*, Sec. X).

What Descartes and Leibniz in their different ways claimed for metaphysics, Hume claimed for his new "science of man," an empirical psychology conceived by analogy with Newton's natural philosophy. Because all sciences "return back by one passage or another to the science of human nature," Hume proposed ". . . to march up directly to the capital or centre of these sciences, to human nature itself. . . . From this station we may extend our conquest over all these sciences. There is no question of importance, whose decision is not comprised in the science: and there is none which can be decided with any certainty, before we become acquainted with that science. In pretending therefore to explain the principles of human nature we in effect propose a compleat system of the sciences, built on foundations almost entirely new, and the only one on which they can stand with any security" (*Treatise of Human Nature*, Introduction). Hume mentions seven sciences: mathematics, natural philosophy, natural religion, logic, morals, criticism, and politics. Of the first three he says only that it is, "impossible to tell what changes and improvements we might make in these sciences" by bringing the science of man to bear on them. In the case of the last four sciences Hume carried out his project thoroughly and psychologized them all.

Kant, too, was to introduce a new science to lay the foundations of the other sciences. He raised three questions. How is pure mathematics possible? How is the pure science of nature possible? How is metaphysics as science possible? These can all be summed up in one question, how are *a priori* synthetic judgments possible, or what are the grounds for taking such judgments as true? This is the object of a "transcendental" inquiry. The first two of these sciences Kant considered secure and certain. They actually exist as sciences and therefore are possible. The only reason for undertaking an inquiry into their grounds was for the sake of metaphysics, whose possibility had not yet been established. Metaphysics for Kant is the same as for Aristotle, that is, it "considers everything in so far as it is" (*Critique of Pure Reason*, B 873). The outcome of the transcendental investigation was that of showing, however, that metaphysics is restricted to everything insofar as it is in nature, that is, insofar as it is an object of possible experience. Thus the only metaphysics which is possible is that which he had called the pure science of nature. Nature includes the objects of both psychology and physics. Physics becomes a subalternate of this pure science of nature when concepts of empirical origin such as motion, impenetrability, and inertia are introduced. Nevertheless physics must use principles of absolute universality for the whole realm of nature, both psychological and physical, such as "every substance is permanent" and "every event is determined by a cause according to constant laws." When Kant speaks of "the pure science of nature," he treats it as an existing science in no need of a transcendental deduction for its own sake. When, however, he speaks of the same thing under the name "metaphysics of nature," then he considers that his transcendental investigation will put that metaphysics on "the secure path of a science. For this new point of view will enable us . . . to furnish satisfactory proof of the laws which form the *a priori* basis of nature" (ibid., B xix). Moreover it will make possible an exhaustive knowledge of the principles which constitute this pure science. Kant also provided the same kind of foundation for the metaphysics of morals as for the metaphysics of nature, for the supreme principle of morality is an *a priori* synthetic practical proposition, and its possibility like that of the *a priori* synthetic propositions of the other sciences requires a demonstration in order "to prove that morality is no mere phantom of the brain."

(An *a priori* proposition, in contrast to *a posteriori* particular facts, is universal and necessary, e.g., truths of mathematics, laws of nature, rules of logic; a synthetic proposition, in contrast to an analytic truth by definition, goes beyond the definition of the subject, e.g., the planets all move in elliptical orbits around the sun; an *a priori* synthetic proposition is a universal, necessary judgment going beyond definition and sense-particulars.)

### UNITY OF SUBJECT MATTER

"Let no man," says Bacon, "look for much progress in the sciences . . . unless natural philosophy be carried on and applied to particular sciences and particular sciences be carried back again to natural philosophy." This holds not only for "astronomy, optics, music, a number of mechanical arts, medicine itself," but also for "what one might more wonder at, moral and political philosophy, and the logical sciences" (*Novum organum*, Book II, Aph. lxxx, *Works*, VIII, 112). Bacon does not regard these other sciences as parts of natural philosophy, but as having their "roots" in it. Natural philosophy itself, however, contains within it certain constituent sciences which form a pyramid. These are distinguished from one another not by their subjects, but by their levels of generality in knowledge of the one subject, nature. At the base of the pyramid is natural history. On that is built physics, which has two parts, one less general and one more general. On physics is built metaphysics (a science distinct from first philosophy) which brings the axioms of physics under still more general axioms. At the vertical point of the pyramid is "the summary law of nature"—i.e., "the force implanted by God in the first particles of matter from the multiplication whereof all the variety of things proceeds and is made up" (*De principiis, Works*, X, 345), though knowledge of it is probably beyond the reach of the human mind. The three inductively ordered levels, natural history, physics, and metaphysics, are "the true stages of knowledge." Given the one subject, nature, it is Bacon's logic of induction which alone determines both the divisions and the unity of the sciences which comprise natural philosophy. Bacon also divided all human learning on the basis of Memory (History), Imagination (Poetry), and Reason (Philosophy).

Hobbes's materialism taken in conjunction with *his* logic or method has similar reductive consequences for the division and unity of the sciences, though the method is now deductive, not inductive. As knowledge of causes, science is in every case knowledge of the motions of bodies by which effects are generated. These motions are the single subject of all sciences, one science being distinguished from another only by the complexity of the motions which it investigates. Thus after first philosophy—which consists of definitions of the most general names—comes geometry, the science of the simple motions of a body by which lines, surfaces, and figures are produced. Then follows the science concerned with the effects of the impact of moving bodies; then the science of the effects of the internal motions of bodies, that is, physics or the study of sensible phenomena such as light, colors, sounds, tastes, odors, heat, etc., and of the senses themselves; then moral philosophy or the science of the motions of the mind such as appetite, aversion, love, benevolence, etc., for these are motions consequent upon the motions of sense; and finally, because the motions of the mind are the causes of the commonwealth, there comes civil or political philosophy (*Concerning Body*, Ch. VI, Secs. 6, 7).

434 For Spinoza and Leibniz also the sciences are not diversified by the kinds of beings which they investigate. There is for Spinoza only one substance, God or nature, and for Leibniz only one kind of substance, monads. In Spinoza's world the essence of any individual finite thing is the power or effort by which it endeavors to persevere in its being. This *conatus* follows from, or is a mode of, the infinite power of God, a power which can be expressed to the perceiving intellect either as infinite extension or as infinite thought (*Ethics*, Part I, definitions 4, 6). Correspondingly, the *conatus* constituting the essence of the individual thing can be expressed either as body or as mind. Thus physics on the one hand and the science of the thoughts and emotions of the mind on the other are knowledge merely of the same *conatus*, but as differently expressed, and the order of causes in the one science will be identical with the order of causes in the other (ibid., Part II, prop. 7). Spinoza's proposed aim of acquiring "the knowledge of the union which the mind has with the whole of nature" required the study of Moral Philosophy, the Theory of the Education of Children, the science of Medicine and the art of Mechanics (*De emendatione*, II, 13–15). Leibniz too adopts a double aspect conception, but in his case it is used for correlating metaphysics, the science of beings as they are in themselves, that is, as indivisible spiritual substances, with physics, the science of these same beings as they appear, that is, as material phenomena or extended masses. "These two realms are distinct, each one being governed by its own laws. . . . But the two very different series are in mutual correspondence in the same corporeal substance and harmonize so perfectly that it is just as if one were ruled by the influence of the other" (Loemker, p. 675).

### UNITY OF METHOD

According to Aristotle there is not a single method applicable to all subject matters, but each has its own appropriate method (*Metaphysica* 995b; *De anima* 402a; *Ethica* 1094b). While this was being reiterated by Saint Thomas in the thirteenth century, two of his contemporaries formulated conceptions of a universal method of discovery applicable in all the sciences; Roger Bacon in his *scientia experimentalis*, and Raymond Lully in his *ars magna*, the one empirical, the other *a priori*. Bacon calls his experimental science, "this great mistress of the speculative sciences," attributing to it "the same relation to the other sciences as the science of navigation to the carpenter's art and the military art to that of the engineer. . . . It directs other sciences as its handmaids, and therefore the whole power of speculative science is attributed especially to this science" (*Opus maius*, Part VI, p. 633). Knowledge is acquired in two ways, either by reasoning or by experience. Experience includes what is learned not only through the external senses but also through internal illumination or divine inspiration, the latter being important for both religion and for the principles of the speculative sciences. Bacon worked out no rules of operation for his new experimental science and it is not a precursor of his namesake's logic of induction. However, he assigned to it three prerogatives. The first is that of verifying conclusions deduced from principles. This is not so much a method of testing hypotheses as of giving certainty to conclusions and removing doubt, and is not therefore properly a method of discovery. But in its second and third prerogatives it is one of discovery. In the second it discovers new truths *within* a science which are incapable of being deduced from the principles of that science, and in the third it operates without reference to the limits of any of the particular sciences, but by its own power investigates the secrets of nature.

Like Bacon, and those in the tradition of Aristotle, Lully believed that each branch of inquiry rested on a limited number of principles and basic concepts. To this he added the notion that if letters of the alphabet were substituted for these elements, and combined in every possible way in a purely mechanical fashion, everything which it is possible to know in that subject could be discovered. Thus the great art was capable of yielding universality of knowledge. Lully enjoyed as great a following among his contemporaries as Thomas Aquinas and the basic idea underlying the great art continued to exercise a fascination until the seventeenth century, when it became incorporated in the *ars combinatoria* of Leibniz. But where Lully assumed that each branch of knowledge had its own simple elements, Leibniz believed it to be possible to find a single set of irreducible concepts common to all the sciences. Once all these concepts were given their characteristic numbers or signs, their combinations could generate a complete "demonstrative encyclopaedia":

Now since all human knowledge can be expressed by letters of the Alphabet, and since we may say that whoever understands the use of the alphabet knows everything, it follows that we can calculate the number of truths which men are able to express, and that we can determine the size of a work which would contain all possible human knowledge, in which there would be everything which could ever be known, written, or discovered; and even more than that, for it would contain not only the true but also the false propositions which we can assert, and even expressions which signify nothing (ed. Wiener, p. 75).

Leibniz claimed to have derived the basic idea of the art of combinations from the study of Aristotle's formal logic, but it was, he says, arithmetic and algebra which revealed to him the role of signs or characters in making demonstration in the sciences possible. "It is as if God, when he bestowed these two sciences on mankind, wanted us to realize that our understanding conceals a far deeper secret, foreshadowed by these two sciences" (trans. Loemker, p. 340).

Descartes too had drawn his inspiration for a universal method for the sciences from the study of mathematics, but what he saw as significant was not, as with Leibniz, the use of symbols in algebra, but the logical interconnections of all the parts of geometry. These "had caused me to imagine that all those things which fall under the cognizance of man might very likely be mutually related in the same fashion" (*Discourse on Method*, Part II). This conviction is expressed in an early opuscule: "All the sciences are interconnected as by a chain; no one of them can be completely grasped without the others following of themselves and so without taking in the whole of the encyclopaedia at one and the same time" (*Oeuvres*, X, 255). Descartes began his first work on method, the *Regulae*, with an explicit attack on the Aristotelian specialization of methods according to subject matter. He did so on two grounds, first, that the mind in its cognitive exercise is no more differentiated by its subjects than is the sun by what it illuminates, and, second, that everything knowable is logically linked. The logical order, or "order of reasons" which proceeds from the simpler to the more difficult, runs directly counter to the "order of subject-matters," the latter being "good only for those for whom all reasons are detached" (ibid., III, 266f.). To isolate a branch of knowledge by subject is to deprive it of its scientific character and render it a mere collection. There can therefore be no plurality of sciences but only one universal science, whose parts are undifferentiated by subjects. Leibniz took the same view of his demonstrative encyclopaedia, pointing out that as in geometry the demonstrative order does not permit everything belonging to the same subject to be dealt with in the same place. Because the encyclopaedia would result in the dissolution of the divisions of the sciences by subject, an index would be an essential part of the project in order to make it possible to bring together all propositions bearing on any one subject (*New Essays*, Book IV, Ch. XXI).

In the eighteenth century the most insistent voice on the identity of method in all the sciences was Condillac's. Like Leibniz, he saw the perfect existing example of this method in algebra, with its use of signs. Algebra provided "a striking proof that the progress of the sciences depends uniquely on the progress of language, and that well constructed languages alone can give analysis the degree of simplicity and precision of which it is susceptible" (*Oeuvres*, II, 409 b). He did not, like Leibniz, conceive the possibility of a single language for all the sciences; each would have its own, while using exactly the same method of analysis. The more radical part of Leibniz' ideal, that of a universal language, emerges again, however, with Condorcet. This language would, he says, be like algebra, "the only really exact and analytical language yet in existence," containing within it "the principles of a universal instrument applicable to all combinations of ideas," and as easily available to all as the language of algebra itself (*Sketch*, pp. 197f.).

### TELEOLOGICAL UNITY

Says Socrates in the *Republic:*

If we do not know the Form of the good, though we should have the fullest knowledge possible of all else, you know that that would be of no use to us, anymore than is the possession of anything without the good. Or do you think there is any advantage in universal possession if it is not good, or in understanding the whole world except the good? (*Republic* 505).

In its relation to all other knowledge Aristotle's first philosophy exercises the same function as Plato's dialectic. It is "the most authoritative of the sciences and more authoritative than any ancillary science," for it knows the supreme good in the whole of nature, and therefore the end to which the other sciences are directed (*Metaphysica* 982b 5). Saint Thomas and the medieval philosophers follow Aristotle in assigning to metaphysics the status of ruler of all the other sciences as directed to one end, and for Kant this legislation as a regulative guide constitutes the very essence of philosophy. The pursuit of sciences with a view to attaining their greatest logical perfection he calls "the scholastic concept" of philosophy.

But there is likewise another concept of philosophy, a *conceptus cosmicus*, which has always formed the real basis of the term 'philosophy,' especially when it has been as it were personified and its archtype represented in the ideal philosopher. On this view philosophy is the science of the relation of all knowledge to the essential ends of human reason (*teleologia rationis humanae*), and the philosopher is not an artificer in the field of reason, but himself the lawgiver of human reason (*Critique of Pure Reason*, B 867).

Reason, in exercising its purely logical function, is concerned with bringing the manifold knowledge provided by the understanding to the highest degree of systematic unity. It is this unity which distinguishes science from a mere aggregate of things known. In pursuit of this end reason is compelled to operate with the idea of the form of the whole of the science in question, an idea which determines *a priori* the scope

of the content of the science and the relation of its parts to one another. This regulating idea gives the science the same kind of unity as that possessed by an animal organism, and just as the parts of each science form an organic whole, so also do all the sciences taken together. "Not only is each system articulated in accordance with an idea, but they are one and all organically united in a system of human knowledge, as members of one whole, and so as admitting an architectonic of all human knowledge" (ibid., B 863). This whole of human knowledge will be directed by an idea, in the same way as is each of its constituent sciences, in order that the essential ends of reason served by each will be viewed under one ultimate end, namely, "the whole vocation of man." The highest degree of formal unity in the natural sciences—psychology, physics, and a third science which is a systematic union of the first two—is pursued under the regulative idea of the whole of nature as the work of a supreme intelligence. Practical reason, or morality also operates under a regulating idea, that of a Kingdom of Ends. This idea provides a means of formulating the moral law: "every rational being must so act as if he were by his maxims in every case a legislating member in a universal kingdom of ends." Such a kingdom could be realized only if nature harmonized with human ends, that is, only if the kingdom of nature and the kingdom of ends were united under one supreme ruler. Hence the moral idea of God is that supreme regulating idea which brings all the sciences into systematic unity in the science of moral theology. It is moral theology which "enables us to fulfill our vocation," or attain our highest end.

### BIBLIOGRAPHY

*The Works of Aristotle Translated into English,* ed. J. A. Smith and W. D. Ross (Oxford, 1908–52). *The Works of Francis Bacon,* ed. Ellis, Spedding, and Heath (Boston, 1864). *The Opus Maius of Roger Bacon,* trans. R. B. Burke (Philadelphia, 1928). *Oeuvres philosophiques de Condillac,* ed. Georges Le Roy (Paris, 1947–51). A. N. de Condorcet, *Sketch for a Historical Picture of the Progress of the Human Mind* (1795), trans. J. Barraclough (New York, 1955). *Oeuvres de Descartes,* ed. C. Adam and P. Tannery (Paris, 1897–1913). *The English Works of Thomas Hobbes,* ed. W. Molesworth (London 1839–45). D. Hume, *A Treatise of Human Nature* (1739–40), ed. L. A. Selby-Bigge (Oxford, 1888). I. Kant, *Critique of Pure Reason,* trans. N. K. Smith (London, 1933). G. W. Leibniz, *Selections,* ed. P. P. Wiener (New York, 1951). *New Essays Concerning Human Understanding* (1704) trans. A. G. Langley (LaSalle, Ill., 1949). *Gottfried Wilhelm Leibniz, Philosophical Papers and Letters,* trans. and ed. L. E. Loemker (Chicago, 1956). *Raymundi Lullii Opera ea quae ad adinventam ab ipso artem universalem . . . pertinent* (Strassburg, 1617). Plato, *Republic,* trans. A. D. Lindsay

(London, 1920). *The Chief Works of Benedict de Spinoza*, trans. R. H. M. Elwes (London, 1883–84). Thomas Aquinas, *Expositio in libros Metaphysicorum*, ed. M. R. Cathala and R. M. Spiazzi (Turin, 1950); *The Division and Methods of the Sciences, Questions V and VI of his Commentary on the De Trinitate of Boethius*, trans. with an introduction by Armand Maurer (Toronto, 1953).

ROBERT McRAE

[See also **Baconianism;** Causation, Final Causes; Certainty; **Classification of the Sciences;** Enlightenment; God; Platonism.]

# UNIVERSAL MAN

THE TERM "universal man" was coined by Jacob Burckhardt, the Swiss historian and exponent of cultural history, in his classic study, *Die Kultur der Renaissance in Italien* (1860). He used it to characterize the fully developed personalities of fifteenth-century Italy, meaning by the *uomo universale* a distinctive social type: one who combines comprehensive learning with the practice of one or more of the arts or professions.

Although the idea has its source and most significant development in the context of Renaissance history, it also plays a role in pedagogical thought (discussed below) and social criticism. In these domains, it represents a cultural ideal—as it did for the Renaissance. Contemporary discussions of the complete man as an educational and social goal are marked, however, by nostalgia rather than by genuine aspiration. Renaissance universality is most often used as a foil, setting off by sharp contrast the specialization of knowledge, the one-sided personal development, and the philistinism fostered by modern technocratic society and its scientific culture. In the abundant literature on Leonardo da Vinci, for example, Morris Philipson has found a reflection of our own cultural discontent. If Leonardo has become a sort of archetype, it is ". . . as an ideal of fulfillment in an age of frequent frustration, as an idea of completeness in an era of fragmentation, as a joyous expression of how optimistic-dreamer and practical-planner might be combined in this world of narrow specialties giving lip-service to the gods of 'creativity'" (*Leonardo da Vinci, Aspects of the Renaissance Genius* [1966], p. vii).

This sense of wholeness, the versatility and unity of personality which Leonardo represents, seems to be denied us. Yet it is precisely because these characteristics are rarely realized today that the idea of universal man attracts (and deserves) attention. When a human type of great social worth threatens to pass out of existence, it is well to reflect upon its nature, to determine which of its features are peculiar to the age that brought it forth and which can be thought of as being of general cultural value. This can best be done by turning to the historical literature from which contemporary social and educational thought derives its conceptions of the universal man. His thought and mode of life, the intellectual and social conditions that once sustained him: these are subjects developed in several studies of Renaissance culture and of its representative personalities.

## I

Burckhardt maintained that citizens and subjects, condottieri and princes, artists and intellectuals, all contributed to the formation of a new and distinctive human type in Renaissance Italy. Powerful, highly individualistic natures were to be found in each of these groups: complete persons, as developed intellectually as they were emotionally, as capable in theoretical matters as they were in practical affairs. The merchants, statesmen, and rulers who patronized the arts and studied the classics, and the productive artists who added to their mastery of several arts and crafts a mastery of intellectual culture, found their counterpart in the humanists, the intellectuals who combined a scholarly passion for antiquity with concern for the practical needs of their own society: "While studying Pliny, [the humanist] made collections of natural history; the geography of the ancients was his guide in treating of modern geography, their history was his pattern in writing contemporary chronicles . . . ; and besides all this, he often acted as magistrate, secretary, and diplomatist . . ." (1950, p. 85). These were the "many-sided men," a type which markedly increased in number in the course of the fifteenth century; and among them arose the "all-sided," giants who "mastered all the elements of the culture of the age." This is the universal man, exemplified for Burckhardt by Leon Battista Alberti and Leonardo.

Since Burckhardt, Alberti and Leonardo, and many other Renaissance figures besides, have been seen and understood in the light of his idea of universality. Yet Burckhardt barely sketched the features of the comprehensive nature of the Renaissance man. He based his incisive portrayal of Alberti upon some of Alberti's literary works and upon an incomplete fifteenth-century biography which gives a naive but enthusiastic account of Alberti's gymnastic feats, of his study of music and law, physics and mathematics, of his work in the arts, his literary writings in Latin and the vernacular, and of the personality traits that sustained this vigorous, productive life: his iron will, his generosity, his sympathetic delight in all creation of form,

437

natural and human. Burckhardt did not venture to define the unifying principles or logical character of Alberti's world of thought. And in Leonardo's case, although he regarded him "as the finisher to the beginner, as the master to the dilettante," he refrained even from describing the range of his achievements. He left to future historians the task of analyzing the intellectual culture of the universal man. But if he did not investigate the theoretical grounds of Renaissance universality, he did show how the political institutions and conditions of life in the Italian city-states provided a social context from which this type of person could emerge.

The wealth and leisure, the municipal freedom and social equality obtaining in the urban centers of Renaissance Italy played a significant role in promoting man's recognition of himself as "a spiritual individual," much as these conditions had in ancient Greece. To them, Burckhardt added his distinctive conception of the "rational" or "artificial" character of the Renaissance state as particularly conducive to the full development of the individual's personality. Whether republics or despotisms, the political order of the Renaissance city-states was the "outcome of reflection and calculation." Public life, emancipated from the traditional constraints of feudal society, came to be deliberately shaped by the individuals and families who seized and held power. The precariousness of a social order that could invoke few customary sanctions to support it, and the fact that power and status within it could be won by intelligence and forcefulness, stimulated to the fullest possible degree the self-realization of the individual. Liberated from traditional conceptions of fixed class and corporate bounds, the individual was seized by the impulse to realize all his natural powers, to mold the self as well as the state as a work of art.

At this point, Burckhardt introduced his seminal idea of the development of the individual, and of the universal man. Although it gave rise to controversy as to whether "individualism" and "universality" were not also to be found in the Middle Ages (of course they are, but they assume a different form in medieval culture), this dispute has not been able to dislodge so apt and useful an idea. It has been thoroughly incorporated in Renaissance historical writing from John Addington Symonds' *Renaissance in Italy* (1875–86) down to the present, and its elaboration by subsequent historians has shed considerable light, not only upon several Renaissance personalities, but upon the course of Renaissance cultural and social developments as well. The treatment which the concept has received in Renaissance histories and biographies will be sketched below by considering the relations between

the universal man and the intellectual culture and social institutions of his time.

## II

***1. Humanism and the Universal Man.*** Most (but not all) of the complete personalities Burckhardt referred to had been educated in the classical, humanistic learning of their time. Burckhardt noted that the learning of the universal man was no longer identified with the encyclopaedic knowledge of the medieval thinker, but he did not establish a connection between humanism and the rise of the many-sided or all-sided man. He did not credit humanism with fashioning an ideal of the complete man nor with providing a curriculum appropriate to it. If anything, he tended to believe that no such objective was entertained by those who would seem to have striven to fulfill it.

It was an English historian of Renaissance classical education who showed that the full development of the personality which Burckhardt described corresponded to the avowed objectives of humanist educators. William Harrison Woodward's *Vittorino da Feltre and Other Humanist Educators* (1897) is based upon a close study of the famous teacher and upon humanistic treatises on education (many of which he translated and published in this work). He found in these writings, as in Vittorino's teaching, a conscious revival of both the ancient rhetorical tradition of general education (*encyklios paideia*) and its underlying ideal of the whole man. Vittorino called his method of education "encyclopaedic," by which he meant a balanced combination of intellectual, moral, and physical training. Another humanist educator, Battista Guarino, explicitly identified humanistic learning with Greek *paideia* and Roman *humanitas;* and Maffeo Vegio, in a treatise *De educatione liberorum* (ca. 1460), hailed the humanistic restoration of the "universal" education of the ancients (*qui orbis doctrinarum appellatus est*).

In point of fact, humanistic education was far from universal or encyclopaedic in the sense of all-encompassing. If anything, it represents a narrowing of the Seven Liberal Arts of medieval secondary education. It dropped the mathematical Quadrivium (arithmetic, geometry, music, astronomy) and deleted logic from the literary Trivium (grammar, rhetoric, dialectics). But it greatly expanded the study of "letters" by adding poetry, history, and moral philosophy (which was understood as a form of eloquence) to grammar and rhetoric, as well as by adding Greek to Latin letters (Kristeller, 1961, 1965). The Renaissance *studia humanitatis* was thus strictly literary and classical; but founded as it was upon the tradition of classical eloquence, it revived and adopted the ancient rhetorical ideas of general education. Its guiding principle was the ideal of classical *humanitas:* cultivation of "the whole man, body and soul, sense and reason, character and mind" (Marrou, 1948).

This "general" education (general because it was neither technical nor professional in nature) was regarded by the humanists as the finest preparation for public and private life. Bearing out Burckhardt's description of the union of theory and practice in the humanists, Woodward noted the humanistic conviction that the practical ends of the individual and society would be furthered by a general, i.e., liberal education. On the one hand, humanistic learning (particularly in the secondary schools) was directed toward formation of the person. The desire for distinction was encouraged by the humanists as a stimulus to learning, and distinction required not only intellectual culture but virtue, the cultivation of character, and the acquisition of certain personal and social graces as well: eloquence, dignity of bearing, accomplishment in various forms of recreation and diversion. Moreover, the *studia humanitatis* was to lead to the perfection of man as a political being (as citizen, courtier, or ruler, as the case may be). In this regard, the union of scholarly and practical interests was built into the very system of humanistic studies which is directed simultaneously toward thought and action: literature and society, poetry and history, rhetoric and moral philosophy—all were necessary for the complete man. Finally, classical studies provided authorities for a wide range of matters of social and public concern, from statecraft (Aristotle's *Politics*) to management of a household (Plutarch and Cicero), from agriculture (Vergil) to the art of war (Caesar).

The humanists thus appear to be directly responsible for popularizing the ideal of the well-rounded man. And formal education was not their only instrument for propagating and diffusing this ideal. They promoted it in their writings as well; universalizing the general, literary culture of the ancient orator, the humanists recommended it (as P. O. Kristeller has pointed out) in treatises addressed to diverse groups in Renaissance society, to princes and citizens, to women, courtiers, and artists—to all who professed "humanity." Several of Alberti's works exemplify this tendency, as does Baldassare Castiglione's *Il cortigiano* (1528). Castiglione required the courtier to join to his customary martial virtues and to his loyalty to his prince the humanistic virtues of eloquence, a literary education, and a certain accomplishment in painting, music, and dancing. In the same spirit, although written a century earlier and with a bourgeois audience in mind, Alberti's *De familia* (ca. 1434) sets forth, in the idealized figures of his own prominent merchant-banking family, a har-

monious marriage of classical culture with the political, economic, and social concerns of the urban patriciate. One of his late works gives the reverse of this picture. The subject of *De iciarchia* (1469) is the public responsibilities (chiefly educational) of the humanist scholar. Alberti also extended to the artist this conception of the whole man. In *De pictura* (1435) he urged the painter to become literate and acquire a general education. This first treatise on painting was also the first work to encourage development of that wide range of interests and general competence which in fact came to characterize the Renaissance artist.

The learning embraced by the artistic exponents of the humanistic ideal was not always, and not even typically, classical and literary, however. Alberti and Leonardo, the two whom Burckhardt singled out as most fully representative of his all-sided man, achieved their universality outside the confines of humanistic learning, as did Michelangelo who seemed to his age the truly universal artist of all time. Alberti was a humanist, to be sure. He was in fact the epitome of the Renaissance humanist, animated as he was by the desire to achieve that personal excellence which triumphs over human frailty, death, and time, and bending all his liberal learning at the same time to practical and social needs in characteristically humanistic fashion. Alberti the Latinist wrote vernacular dialogues on moral philosophy for the *non literatissimi cittadini* of the lay society of his time; and it was for the sake of justifying this use of the Tuscan tongue as an instrument of learning and prose literature that he worked out its first grammar. For the crafts of painting and sculpture he provided a theoretical basis and, by grounding them in the "sciences" of perspective and anthropometry, drew them into the circle of the liberal arts. Complementing this work, he applied the mathematical learning of the schools, and his humanistic knowledge of Ptolemy and Vitruvius, to problems of surveying, map-making, and the construction of measuring devices and simple machines. For a friend who was a Papal Secretary, he devised the method of coding by means of a cipher-wheel and of decoding by frequency analysis. And for architects and builders, he set forth in his famous *De re aedificatoria* (1452) the engineering knowledge of antiquity and his own day, the rules of classical architecture, and a theory of universal Harmony which formed the aesthetic outlook of his age and fostered its quest for proportionality.

This quest for proportionality, however, which was at once an aesthetic, a scientific, a moral, and a metaphysical objective, as Alberti's writings attest, bespeaks a mathematical rather than a humanistic treatment of problems. It belongs to a current of thought which is

439

just as fundamental to Renaissance culture as humanism but is logically distinct from it. Alberti embodies both currents, as did the classical culture of antiquity. His Platonic conviction that the intellectual should serve as guide and teacher of his age gave an ethical, a humanistic consistency to the diversity of his works. But methodologically, once he moved outside the sphere of literature, philology, and moral philosophy to accomplish this task, mathematics became the organon of all his undertakings. It was by holding to a mathematical intuition of reality (which he recovered from classical sources), by working it out in a variety of technical problems (often in accordance with classical exemplars) that Alberti's thought developed in several fields of learning—fields which were hitherto quite disparate, but in which he, and Leonardo after him, brought about a new methodological unity and achieved a new, nonliterary kind of universality.

**2. Mathesis Universalis.** Recent studies of Leonardo's thought have tended to find the basis of Leonardo's universality in his distinctive fusion of mathematics and sensory experience. Ernst Cassirer (1927), Ludwig H. Heydenreich (1944), Erwin Panofsky (1953), V. P. Zubov (1962), and Eugenio Garin (1965) all stress the significance of Leonardo's geometric formulation of technical and physical problems in accounting for the scope and unity of his thought. This also holds true for Alberti's artistic and scientific work. Burckhardt was right in maintaining that Leonardo brought to fulfillment what Alberti had begun, for Alberti and Leonardo are very much akin. They were both practicing artists, practicing surveyors and mapmakers, practicing engineers. Both figure in the history of astronomy, geography, mechanics, anatomy, optics, and perspective. Leonardo's chief art was painting, of course, whereas Alberti's was architecture; and Leonardo brought his mathematical vision to bear on a greater variety of problems than Alberti did and he penetrated them more deeply; but both had the same intention of discovering in the world of experience its lawful, proportional structure. This was the methodological objective that made it possible for them to unite art and science, and theory and practice, as they did. The diversity of their interests sprang in both cases from a commitment to practice and experience, "the common mother of all the sciences and arts" (Leonardo, ed. Richter, I, #18). And both used mathematics in the several arts and sciences they pursued as the instrument by which to grasp the rational principles of experience. If the *studia humanitatis* may be regarded as a revised and expanded Trivium, the disciplines comprehended by Alberti and Leonardo represent a Quadrivium systematically expanded to include all the sciences of measurement.

Alike as they are in their artistic and scientific pursuits, however, Alberti and Leonardo did not share the same "universe" of learning. It is not simply that Leonardo's thought includes sciences such as botany, zoology, geology, and hydraulics which are either not found at all, or found only in very rudimentary form, in Alberti. What is more remarkable is Leonardo's utter disregard of humanistic values and the classical, literary method of humanistic study. Leonardo was, as he confessed, an *omo sanza lettere*. But his disinterest in the *studia humanitatis* and his strictures against book-learning cannot be accounted for solely by the fact that he was trained as an apprentice in a workshop rather than educated, as Alberti was, in a humanistic *gymnasium*. Self-taught in almost everything he did, Leonardo would have mastered the humanistic learning of the time had he been vitally interested in it. He did teach himself Latin, in fact, when he was forty-two, but he used it to gain access to the physical knowledge, not the literary culture of antiquity and the Middle Ages. The humanistic mode of learning was alien to him because, as his work and statements prove, the kind of knowledge he sought was to be found in nature, not books. He restricted himself quite deliberately to *sperienza* (by which he meant chiefly visual experience), having won from its mathematical analysis, so he thought, the rare prize of certain knowledge.

This divergence between humanism and what was to become in the scientific academies of the seventeenth century an independent, empirical-mathematical mode of inquiry, is not yet felt in Alberti. In many respects, technical and empirical thought was still more primitive in the early fifteenth century than it had been in antiquity, so that Alberti found many of his most fruitful technical ideas in the classical authors. Moreover, his humanistic ideas mingle with his artistic and mathematical ones at the deeper level of his fundamental intuition of the world and man. The idea of proportion which figures in his thought as an ideal of morality and mores—an idea that echoes Cicero's notion of decorum and Plato's idea of justice—complements his vision of the "outer" world of nature. Balance, measure, or proportion in man reflects the definition Alberti gave of cosmic beauty, that natural "Harmony of all the parts, in whatsoever subject it appears, fitted together with such proportion and connection that nothing can be added, diminished, or altered but for the worse" (*De re aedificatoria* IX, 5). Alberti's successor knew nothing of this vital bond between the moral and the physical world, between man and nature. The proportion or measure that constitutes the form of both the inner and outer world in Alberti's thought is metaphysically conceived, of course, and Leonardo, who developed and sharpened the empirical-mathematical method he shared with Alberti, evidently could not admit this conception into his thought. With Leonardo's greater awareness of his distinctively "scientific" methods and objectives, the two currents of thought that Alberti held together in one view of man and the world parted ways.

The humanistic movement also encouraged this separation. In contrast to early humanistic treatises on education which included mathematics, dialectics, and astronomy in their ideal curricula, the humanistic curriculum of the late fifteenth and sixteenth centuries came to be strictly defined as a program of literary, historical, and ethical studies. The artistic-technical interests of an Alberti could not be an integral part of this *studia humanitatis* any more than the investigation of nature could be pursued by means of literature. Humanism and the natural-scientific mode of thought were found to follow different methodological principles, and this intellectual fact shaped the specific "universality," i.e., the particular completeness and comprehensive content of thought, of the two main examples of the Renaissance universal man.

*3. The Universal Man in Renaissance Society.* Different as they may be in method and objectives, humanism and empirical-mathematical thought are alike in their departure from the Scholastic form of medieval universality. For sheer comprehensiveness, neither the *studia humanitatis* nor the sciences of measurement embraced by an Alberti or a Leonardo can compete with Roger Bacon's proposed encyclopaedia of knowledge or the *Summa Theologiae* of Thomas Aquinas. The two forms of Renaissance learning are limited, first to the world of experience, then to the domain of either physical or cultural and social experience. But with this narrowing of scope came a rational grounding of knowledge. The principles of thought in the humanities and natural sciences are positive; those of the Scholastic organization of knowledge are metaphysical and theological. Roger Bacon intended to unify the sciences of his encyclopaedia by placing them in the service of theology; and the *Summa Theologiae*, as its name declares, is a work of metaphysics or philosophical theology which purports to ground the knowledge of all things in "truths" provided by Sacred Doctrine.

The representatives of Renaissance universality entertained no such systematic, metaphysical aim, nor was their learning encyclopaedic. The defining characteristic of their thought is not its generality, but rather (as Burckhardt saw and Cassirer demonstrated) its union of experience and reason, of practice and theory. This basic feature is manifest in the many-sided nature of the Renaissance man, as it is in the practical and positive cast of his knowledge. The Schoolman's life

was purely contemplative and academic; the mode of life of the Renaissance man includes practice of the arts or crafts or some form of public involvement. The Schoolman belonged to a religious order; the Renaissance man belongs to the lay world (even when, as in the case of Alberti, he has taken Holy Orders). The urban society of the time, not the cloister or the university, fostered his development and supported him.

This social fact is basic to the revival and ready acceptance of the humanistic ideal of *encyklios paideia*. What made the educational ideas of antiquity vital once more was their responsiveness to the needs of Italian society, particularly those of its dominant class, the urban patriciate. One such feature of classical *paideia* was its public-spirited ethos stemming from the Greco-Roman conviction that man, the complete man, is a political animal. In fifteenth-century Florence, this principle served both to elevate bourgeois life, and to reconcile intellectuals to public and political concerns. Moreover, the humanists found in the literary or rhetorical learning of antiquity an educational ideal that met the cultural aspirations of their society while satisfying its practical needs. Humanistic learning enhanced the dignity of despots, of the urban patriciate, and of the humanists themselves by making classical culture a sign of *nobilitas*, a nobility more rational (and hence a matter of *virtù*) than that of the old landed aristocracy which was an accident of birth, of *fortuna*. It provided a general preparation for the variety of practical and public positions that had to be filled. And because the state of social and technological development reached by the Italian states in the fifteenth century was comparable to that of classical civilization, Renaissance society could indeed profit from knowledge of its political and practical arts.

The esteem won by the manual and practical arts (such as painting and surveying) is also an index of their usefulness to the ruling class of the Italian states. They, too, enhanced the dignity of princes and patriciate and they furthered their very real interests of wealth and power. The methodical and practical spirit of Renaissance urban life is stamped upon the scientific achievements of the artistic-technical current of thought, products of applied mathematics in almost every case: cryptography, survey maps and scaled nautical charts, machines and mechanical principles. In this cultural domain, as in that of humanism, the kind of problems considered and the way those problems were handled depended in many ways upon the practical needs of Italian society and the level of institutional and technical development it had achieved.

Both types of the Renaissance universal man, the humanist and artist-scientist, grew out of the orderly, practical, and confident urban world of fourteenth- and fifteenth-century Italy, and when the bourgeois basis of that civilization collapsed, both they and the culture they bore were overcome by hostile social forces. Three major stages of social change were distinguished by Alfred von Martin in the first sociological study of Renaissance culture as a whole, *Soziologie der Renaissance* (1932). It is useful to consider these stages here, especially since the art historian, Arnold Hauser, has already shown how the three periods of Renaissance art to which Alberti, Leonardo, and Michelangelo belong correspond to and reflect certain social features of the "heroic age of capitalism," the classical "age of the rentier" which succeeded it (at least in Florence) toward the end of the fifteenth century, and the courtly society of sixteenth-century Italy dominated by Spain and the Counter-Reformation Church. Many of the features that characterize them as universal men have their source in this changing social context, too.

Alberti belongs to the expansive and public-spirited life of the first period whereas Leonardo belongs to the second, when Florence yielded to the princely rule of Lorenzo de' Medici and its culture came to be shaped by Neo-Platonic ideas, and he lived well into the time of the invasions that followed on the heels of Lorenzo's death. Leonardo sank no roots in Medici Florence (or in Medici Rome), nor did the republican tradition and civic outlook of Florentine humanism touch a vital chord in him. His patrons were great princes and condottieri, and finally the King of France; and as he passed from the service of one to the other, he remained peculiarly detached from political events and factions, peculiarly neutral. He served equally well both the brutal and ruthless Cesare Borgia and the Florentine Republic under Piero Soderini. When Ludovico Sforza met his sorry fate after having been Leonardo's patron at Milan from 1481 until 1499, Leonardo redirected many of the ideas he had developed for a Sforza equestrian monument toward a monument for the very condottiere who defeated Ludovico at the behest of the King of France.

This detachment from political and moral issues in matters of patronage also marks Leonardo's view of knowledge. Alberti, who never engaged in military engineering, could still bind his technical-scientific endeavors to his humanistic ethic, seeing that they served in fact some constructive social purpose. No such optimistic outlook was possible for Leonardo who advertised himself to Ludovico Sforza as a master of artillery, fortifications, and the advanced weaponry of the day. Yet for all the violent and destructive ends to which his science was immediately put, Leonardo adopted toward it a Faustian attitude of limitless expansion. The pursuit of physical knowledge which was checked and directed by ethical considerations in

Alberti became for Leonardo an autonomous intellectual endeavor: "The acquisition of any knowledge whatsoever is always useful to the intellect, because it will be able to banish the useless things and retain those which are good. For nothing can be either loved or hated unless it is first known" (*Notebooks* . . . , ed. MacCurdy, p. 95). Like Machiavelli, who was very much his counterpart, Leonardo sounds the keynote of the modern European ethos of ethically-indifferent scientific inquiry.

In Leonardo we see most clearly the separation of humanism and the artistic-technical current of thought as their distinctive methods were clarified and as the civic ethic, which bound the two for Alberti, dissolved. By the time Castiglione's *Courtier* (*Il cortigiano*) was published in 1528, the humanistic ideal of the complete man had shaken off its republican, bourgeois origins to attach itself to the courtly principles which were to dominate Italy and Europe in the succeeding age, and science and technology, severed from social considerations, began their autonomous career. The rational spirit of Renaissance civilization survived in the literary-historical and empirical-mathematical sciences it founded, but its once integral conception of man and the world had begun to pull apart. Then, in the following decades of the sixteenth century, as the combined forces of Spanish-Imperial arms and the Counter-Reformation Church dealt the death blow to the social institutions of Renaissance Italy, the classical culture which those institutions supported was utterly transformed. Michelangelo confronts us with a totally different outlook. Hailed by his contemporary Vasari as "the perfect exemplar in life, work, and behavior," the "divine" Michelangelo renounced the rational principles fundamental to Renaissance universality.

Painter, sculptor, architect, and poet, Michelangelo drew little from and contributed less to the two positive currents of Renaissance thought. His literary interests were centered in Dante and the Bible, not classical antiquity; and his moral, aesthetic, and cosmological conceptions were nourished by Savonarola and Florentine Neo-Platonism, not by humanism and the empirical-mathematical mode of thought. Michelangelo's genius, which felt constrained by man and matter, produced its gigantic works in isolation and out of an inner wrestling of the soul with its personal angels and demons. The public life of the Renaissance had been destroyed: "I keep to myself," he wrote to his nephew in 1548, in response to his warning not to associate in Rome with Florentines who had been banished from their (and his) native city. "I go about little, and I speak to nobody—least of all to Florentines. If a man salute me in the street I cannot do otherwise than answer him with fair words: then

I pass on. If I could know which of them were exiles I would pass by with no reply whatever . . ." (*Michelangelo*, ed. Carden, p. 232). To this witness of the cataclysmic changes of the sixteenth century—an age in which Rome was sacked by Imperial armies (1527), Florence besieged and her republic subverted for all time by the Medici and by Imperial forces (1529–30), and Italy subject to direct or indirect Spanish rule—the order of the world had again become incomprehensible and providential. Neither humanism nor science entered the circle of Michelangelo's interests. Art was his society and his world, and the Maker himself had become his patron: ". . . there are many who believe—myself among them—that it was God who laid this charge [the construction of St. Peter's] upon me" (ibid., p. 308).

It was Michelangelo who first detached art from the scientific preoccupations of the classical period. In Michelangelo the moral life came to be conceived in theological terms once again. Impelled by a religious longing for release and regeneration, this late embodiment of the Renaissance universal man unloosed the human spirit from its rational bonds to physical and social experience, and in so doing brought about the final dissolution of the Renaissance view of man and the world.

Art, science, and literary humanism henceforth pursued their own independent careers. The cohesion of Renaissance universality was gone, and it was not to be restored any more than were the peculiar social conditions which had once favored its rise. But the ideal of a rational unification of knowledge persisted; it passed from humanism and empirical-mathematical thought, which did not of themselves issue in a systematic ordering of knowledge, to philosophy which did. Renaissance universality holds a logical, as well as a chronological, place between the theological syntheses of medieval learning and the modern philosophical syntheses of rational knowledge. Neither the *studia humanitatis* nor the sciences of measurement could embrace the entire *globus intellectualis*, since neither is a system of philosophy; but they both prepared the way for the modern unifications of learning which, from the time of Francis Bacon and René Descartes, have regarded as "knowledge" only that which is grounded in experience and reason. The achievement of Renaissance thought is positive knowledge, the dual tradition of the cultural and the empirical-mathematical sciences. And it is this scientific tradition which has provided the cumulatively changing contents for the modern syntheses of knowledge from Francis Bacon to the *Encyclopédie* of Diderot and d'Alembert, from Leibniz to the twentieth-century philosophy of culture of Ernst Cassirer.

*BIBLIOGRAPHY*

The major works on Renaissance culture dealing with the idea of universal man are Jacob Burckhardt, *Die Kultur der Renaissance in Italien: Ein Versuch* (Basel, 1860) trans. S. G. C. Middlemore as *The Civilization of the Renaissance in Italy* (London, 1950, and other editions); John Addington Symonds, *Renaissance in Italy*, 7 vols. (London, 1875–86); Ernst Cassirer, *Individuum und Kosmos in der Philosophie der Renaissance* (Leipzig and Berlin, 1927), trans. Mario Domandi as *The Individual and the Cosmos in Renaissance Philosophy* (New York and Evanston, Ill., 1964); Erwin Panofsky, "Artist, Scientist, Genius: Notes on the 'Renaissance-Dämmerung,'" in *The Renaissance, A Symposium* (New York, 1953), pp. 77–93; Paul Oskar Kristeller, *Renaissance Thought I: The Classic, Scholastic, and Humanist Strains* (New York, Evanston, Ill., London, 1961), and idem, *Renaissance Thought II: Papers on Humanism and the Arts* (New York, Evanston, Ill., London, 1965); Eugenio Garin, *Scienza e vita civile nel Rinascimento italiano* (Bari, 1965), trans. Peter Munz as *Science and Civic Life in the Italian Renaissance* (New York, 1969). See also Joan Gadol, *Leon Battista Alberti, Universal Man of the Early Renaissance* (Chicago and London, 1969); Ludwig H. Heydenreich, *Leonardo da Vinci* (Berlin, 1944), English trans., 2 vols. (New York, 1955); V. P. Zubov, *Leonardo da Vinchi, 1452–1519* (Moscow and Leningrad, 1962), trans. David H. Kraus as *Leonardo da Vinci* (Cambridge, Mass., 1968); Morris Philipson, ed., *Leonardo da Vinci, Aspects of the Renaissance Genius* (New York, 1966). The Leonardo quotations are from *The Literary Works of Leonardo da Vinci*, ed. Jean Paul Richter, 2 vols. (London, 1883), and *The Notebooks of Leonardo da Vinci*, ed. Edward MacCurdy (London, 1908; New York, 1938); the Michelangelo quotations, *Michelangelo; A Record of His Life*, ed. R. W. Carden (London, 1913). For classical and humanistic education, Werner Jaeger, *Paideia* (Leipzig, 1933–34), English trans. Gilbert Highet, 3 vols. (New York, 1939–44); Henri Irénée Marrou, *Histoire de l'éducation dans l'antiquité* (Paris, 1948), trans. as *A History of Education in Antiquity* (London and New York, 1956); William Harrison Woodward, *Vittorino da Feltre and other Humanist Educators* (Cambridge, 1897); idem, *Studies in Education during the Age of the Renaissance* (Cambridge, 1924); Eugenio Garin, *Il pensiero pedagogico dell'umanesimo* (Florence, 1958). For Renaissance social history in relation to its culture, see the interpretive essays by Wallace K. Ferguson in *Renaissance Studies* (New York, Evanston, Ill., London, 1970); A. von Martin, *Soziologie der Renaissance* (Stuttgart, 1932), trans. as *Sociology of the Renaissance* (New York and Evanston, Ill., 1963); Arnold Hauser, *The Social History of Art* (New York, 1952); Hans Baron, *The Crisis of the Early Italian Renaissance* (Princeton, 1966); Lauro Martines, *The Social World of the Florentine Humanists, 1390–1460* (Princeton, 1963); Marvin Becker, *Florence in Transition* (Baltimore, 1967–68).

JOAN KELLY GADOL

[See also Education; Individualism; **Renaissance Humanism**.]

## UTILITARIANISM

THE CENTRAL thesis of utilitarianism, in its most general form, is that actions are to be judged solely by their consequences and are not right or wrong in themselves. The term is most commonly used, however, to refer to the more specific view put forward in the eighteenth century by Helvétius in France and Jeremy Bentham and his followers, the Philosophical Radicals, in England, that the rightness of any action is determined by a single criterion, its contribution to the greatest happiness of the greatest number. Utilitarians have often been moral reformers; but some have claimed to be merely stating what is implicit in the generally accepted moral rules. Most have combined these positions. They have said that the utilitarian principle underlies ordinary moral reasoning, but that, because this has not been realized, individuals and communities have often held moral beliefs which are inconsistent with utilitarianism and which a more careful analysis of their own views would lead them to renounce.

Utilitarianism needs to be distinguished from natural law theory, which in some ways it resembles. Many of the Greeks, including Aristotle, had said that the ultimate good is *eudaimonia*, but they seem to have meant, not happiness in Bentham's sense, but something like a happy (or blessed) condition of the soul. The crucial distinction is between the gratification of the desires a man actually has and the gratification of the desires a fully rational, or perfect, man would have. Most of Bentham's precursors are at least partly influenced by natural law theory. Thus Richard Cumberland, Bishop of Peterborough, sometimes considered the first English utilitarian, includes moral perfection as well as happiness in his common good.

Many members of the "moral sense" school came close to utilitarianism but in them, too, the theory is modified, though in varying degrees. Bishop Butler in a note to one of his sermons makes the tentative suggestion (which he may not mean to endorse) that God is probably a utilitarian, but that men had better not be. It is reasonable, he concedes, to suppose that God approves of those actions which lead to general happiness in the long run. Men, however, are likely to make mistakes in trying to decide which actions will in fact have this result. Consequently it is safer for them to trust to the immediate judgments of conscience, by which they may know immediately what actions are right, as distinct from what ultimately makes them right. Francis Hutcheson went much further than Butler by insisting that the rightness of an action simply consisted in its rousing feelings of approval in all normal men. Those actions which did rouse such approval, however, had another characteristic in common: they all showed evidence of benevolent intention. And benevolence was, for Hutcheson, a natural propensity to seek "the greatest happiness for the greatest numbers" (a phrase which he may have been the first in England to use). In saying this Hutcheson gave the moral sense theory a more definite utilitarian twist than either Butler or Shaftesbury. Shaftesbury thought that what those actions approved by the moral sense had in common was a tendency to promote the harmony of the universe. Consequently he is probably closer to natural law theory than to utilitarianism. Hume, whose moral theory follows Hutcheson quite closely, was more interested in Hutcheson's subjectivism than in his utilitarianism. His account of benevolence is closer to Butler's than to Hutcheson's: man's natural generosity is limited, and does not, as a rule, extend beyond his immediate acquaintances to mankind in general. On the other hand, the combination of self-interest, limited generosity, and the requirements of social living result in a moral sense which approves of those qualities that are useful to the possessor or to other people affected by them.

John Stuart Mill, in his essay on Bentham, says that he was anticipated by John Brown and Soames Jenyns; but, at least in part, their view was that, since the pains and pleasures of eternity far outweighed those of this life, and since God happened to reward those who considered others as well as themselves, the far-seeing egoist would adopt a utilitarian policy. This view attained great popularity, especially through the writings of William Paley; but it is a form of the self-interest theory rather than of utilitarianism proper.

Perhaps the most wholehearted English endorsement of utilitarianism apart from Bentham's was William Godwin's. Godwin summarizes his moral theory in just two sentences: "The end of virtue is to add to the sum of pleasurable sensations. The beacon and regulator of virtue is impartiality, that we shall not give that exertion to procure the pleasure of an individual, which might have been employed in procuring the pleasure of many individuals" (*Political Justice*, 3rd ed., II, 493). He did not hesitate to accept those consequences of utilitarianism that had made Butler shy away from it. He repudiated the virtue of promise-keeping, for example: if the promised act promoted the general happiness, one ought to do it, whether one had promised to or not; if it detracted from the general happiness, one ought not to do it, even if one had promised to. Promises, then, were either irrelevant to morality or hostile to it. He did not hesitate to say that, if one could save only one person from a burning building, and had to choose between one's own mother and some great man more likely to contribute to human happiness, one should save the latter.

It is hardly surprising that Godwin was the target of a pamphlet published in 1798 attacking "the leading principle of the new system of morals." The "leading principle" is utilitarianism, from which, according to the anonymous author (actually Thomas Green of Ipswich) Godwin's scandalous conclusion follows logically: that we are entitled, in the interests of the general happiness, to ignore all general rules, and hence law and convention, and also all emotions, such as friendship or filial affection.

The early utilitarians were fighting on two fronts: against the self-interest school and against the belief that moral rules are binding quite apart from their consequences. Inevitably both controversies became entangled in a different one, between naturalism on the one hand and, on the other, nonnaturalism and its concomitant, intuitionism. The "principle of utility" merely states that an action is right only if it contributes more to the general happiness than any alternative action open to the agent. That principle itself might result from the psychological fact that men (either instinctively or as a result of social conditioning) tend to subordinate all other considerations to the general happiness. But equally it might just be an irreducible fact that men ought to do this, whether they actually do or not. That they ought to do this, it might be said, is known by intuition. There is no reason, then, why utilitarianism should not be combined with intuitionism and nonnaturalism; and Henry Sidgwick did so combine it.

Bentham and his followers, however, derided intuitionism ("ipse-dixitism," Bentham called it) because, they said, it amounted to exalting one's own prejudices into eternal and immutable principles. Utilitarianism, they claimed, provided an objective criterion which its rivals lacked. In one way, this claim was justified. If happiness is simply the fulfillment of individual desires, whatever they may be, then utilitarianism can be said to aim at the gratification of everyone's desires (or as many as possible) instead of foisting on the individual what others happen to desire for him. Bentham, who was primarily a legal reformer, was anxious that criminals should be judged by the harm they actually did, not by the feelings of revulsion individual judges might have for their actions. But the desire that everyone's desires should be gratified is itself the desire, not of everyone, but of the utilitarian—who may therefore be accused, at least at this higher level, of foisting his own prejudice on others. To escape this charge by saying that the greatest happiness principle itself is an objective moral principle known by intuition is to weaken the force of Bentham's diatribe against intuition as another name for prejudice.

Consequently Bentham and Mill tried to base utilitarianism upon psychological hedonism. On this view, the desire to escape pain and obtain pleasure is simply a psychological (ultimately a biological) fact about men, and, since morality can be derived from it, there is no need for intuitions about special moral facts. But psychological hedonism leads to egoistic hedonism, not to utilitarianism. It is our own pleasure that nature bids us seek, not that of others. There is indeed one obvious way in which utilitarianism can be based on egoism. The relation between them can be said to be that of means to end. Though not a utilitarian, Hobbes had argued that men could satisfy their individual desires only by cooperating with other men, and that cooperation was only possible if men agreed to aim at a compromise between their various desires rather than insisting on those desires as such. The half-loaf offered by society was better than the no-bread of the state of nature. Brown, Jenyns, and Paley also regarded utilitarianism as a means to attaining happiness for oneself, through the mediation of God. Neither of these views was acceptable to Bentham and Mill. If the greatest happiness is good only as a means to one's own happiness, it will follow that self-interest should take precedence whenever the two conflict. Hobbes and Paley, for different reasons, maintained that they never could conflict in the long run, but this seems doubtful.

The usual view is that Bentham and Mill failed dismally in their attempts to base utilitarianism on egoism. Bentham seems simply to make the transition without arguing for it. Mill, in the notorious fourth chapter of *Utilitarianism* (1863), is said to have been betrayed into gross logical howlers by attempting to argue for it. Mill's argument may, however, be more subtle than is generally realized. The happiness of the individual consists simply in the realization of whatever desires he may happen to have. Some of these, of course, are biological in origin; but others (and even the biological ones to a limited extent) will depend on social conditioning, on what David Hartley called "associations." Now, if Hobbes is right, men in society will be conditioned to associate their own happiness with that of others. The ultimate justification of society is self-interest; but society will not work smoothly if men think of "the laws of nature" (the rules of behavior necessary to keep society together) as mere means to an end, to be broken whenever there is no chance of detection. Society will see to it that the individual will come to think of himself, in Mill's words, as "a being who *of course* pays regard to others" (*Utilitarianism*, Everyman ed., p. 30).

The happiness of others, that is to say, is not thought of as a means, but as an end in itself. We have been conditioned to desire it. Conditioning is not possible unless there is some inherent desire with which the conditioned desire can be associated; but the conditioned desire is quite as genuine a desire as (and may even, on occasion, be stronger than) the original desire which engendered it. Man's two masters, pain and pleasure, drive him into society, in the way outlined by Hobbes; but Hobbes failed to notice that, as a result, society will see to it that he forms the associations between his own pleasures and the pleasures of others which make him aim at the greatest happiness rather than simply at his own happiness. But this is an inaccurate way of putting it; for, since his happiness is whatever he desires, and he has been conditioned to desire the happiness of others as well as his own, the sharp distinction between his own happiness and that of others breaks down. We should distinguish rather between what he desires for himself and what he desires for others. Both are desires that he has; and, since his happiness consists in the gratification of his desires, we may say, paradoxically, that the happiness of others is part of his happiness. This is no contradiction. All that is meant is that one of the things the individual desires is that the desires of others shall be gratified so far as is possible. Whether or not this view is a sound one, to interpret Mill as putting it forward at least leaves him guiltless of the grosser confusions attributed to him. Moreover, this interpretation takes account of the influence on Mill of his father, James Mill, and of Hartley, who was of course one of the major influences on James Mill.

Utilitarianism, as formulated by Bentham, gives rise to some obvious objections. According to Bentham, the way to determine the rightness or wrongness of a given action is to ask oneself the question: Will this action cause more pleasure, on balance, to all those affected by it, than any alternative action open to the agent? But how can this be answered unless one can measure pleasures? Bentham seemed to think that it made sense to talk about the units of pleasure (or of pain) caused to a given person by a given action. In fact, however, there are no such units. Pleasures, the critics of utilitarianism insisted, are incommensurable. It is important, however, to distinguish between two different things that may be meant by this. If you say that you get more pleasure from music, say, than from reading detective stories, you do not mean that it is a matter of indifference whether you read two detective novels or attend one symphony concert. This is a valid criticism of the hedonic calculus if it is meant to be very precise. There is, however, a sense in which we can and do weigh one pleasure or pain against another. A judge, for example, may offer a convicted person a choice between a term of imprisonment or a fine

of a given amount. The job of finding equivalent sentences can be well or badly done. "One day in prison or a fine of $10,000" would be an absurd sentence. The two kinds of pain, then, are not wholly incommensurable. In ordinary life, we do constantly have to choose between alternative courses of action. Often the questions we ask ourselves are: Which will I enjoy more? Is it worth giving up this for the sake of that? These questions admit of no precise answer, but they can be answered. It is not absurd then, to suggest that the question: Ought I to do this or that? amounts to: Will this or that cause more pleasure in the long run to all concerned?

There is, however, something quite different that is often meant when it is said that pleasures are incommensurable. Most of us do not believe that, to use G. E. Moore's example, "the state of mind of a drunkard, when he is intensely pleased with breaking crockery, is just as valuable in itself—just as well worth having, as that of a man who is fully realizing all that is exquisite in the tragedy of King Lear, provided only the mere quantity of pleasure in both cases is the same" (*Ethics*, p. 238). Some kinds of pleasure, we think, are more valuable than other kinds; and this is not the same as saying that they yield greater pleasure.

In answering this objection Bentham and Mill part company. Bentham argues that, when the dimensions of pleasure are taken into account, the difference between higher and lower pleasures is, after all, a quantitative one. Mill does not, however, take this line. "It is quite compatible with the principle of utility," he says, "to recognize the fact, that some *kinds* of pleasure are more desirable and more valuable than others" (op. cit., p. 7). His critics have not thought so: in conceding that the distinction between higher and lower pleasures is qualitative and not quantitative Mill has, it is said, tacitly admitted that there is something else, apart from pleasure, that is intrinsically good.

This criticism has given rise to a modified version of utilitarianism, called Ideal Utilitarianism by Hastings Rashdall, and put forward by him and by G. E. Moore in the first years of this century. They differed from the older, or hedonistic, utilitarians in maintaining that other things (notably truth, beauty, and love) were good in themselves as well as pleasure or happiness. Consequently they altered the utilitarian formula to "the greatest *good* of the greatest number." They agreed with the hedonistic utilitarians, however, in judging actions solely by their consequences, their efficacy in producing good states of affairs. (Some philosophers, indeed, added moral perfection to the list of goods; but to say this is to abandon what is distinctive about utilitarianism.)

In one respect Sidgwick had already made a step

in the direction of ideal utilitarianism. It would seem to follow from the hedonic calculus that there is no moral difference between a situation in which A benefits (obtains 50 units of pleasure, say) at the expense of B (say 40 units of pain) and one in which A and B both obtain moderate benefits (say 5 units each). The total increase in human happiness (10 units) is the same whichever we choose. To meet this objection Sidgwick modified the greatest happiness formula by making the equal distribution of happiness a requirement as well as its maximization. It would seem to follow that equality, as well as happiness, is good in itself. Ideal utilitarianism does not escape this objection, since we need to amend the "greatest good" formula in the same way. It is, however, easier for the ideal utilitarian to accommodate the change: since he has already admitted a multiplicity of goods, he need not shrink from regarding the equalization of good as itself a good.

Most of the criticisms leveled at utilitarianism, however, apply with equal force to both kinds. This is true even of the objection that utilitarians put the promotion of happiness on a level with the relief of misery, which has seemed to many a more stringent obligation. The ideal utilitarian will be faced with the same problem, both because happiness is one of his goods, and because similar questions arise about truth and beauty, as contrasted with the removal of ugliness or error. Utilitarians have sometimes tried to meet both these objections and the one about equal distribution by invoking the economist's principle of marginal utility. This would not, however, explain why the obligation to relieve misery is felt to be of a different kind from the obligation to increase happiness; nor would it prevent equality of distribution from ever conflicting with maximization.

A more important objection is that we often judge an action right or wrong because of the motive or intention and not because of the actual consequences. (For this reason Hutcheson's utilitarianism went no further than making evidence of benevolent intention the feature which all actions approved by the moral sense have in common.) The utilitarian replies that this is merely because, in ordinary speech, we fail to distinguish between a right action and a praiseworthy one. If a man asks himself which of two alternative actions is right, he is not, as a rule, questioning his own motives. His only motive may be to do whatever is best in the circumstances; but he will not be satisfied if we say to him: "In that case, anything you do will be right, so you can stop worrying about which to do." "If you do what you sincerely think to be right, you will do what is right" does not mean that you can never make mistakes about what is right. What is meant is: "If you

do what you sincerely think to be right, you deserve praise, even if what you do is not actually right." Once the confusion between "right" and "praiseworthy" is cleared up, there is no further difficulty about motives for the utilitarian. He can, quite consistently, praise the man who acts from a benevolent motive even if the results are unfortunate in a particular case, since actions done from good motives generally have good results. It is indeed a corollary of utilitarianism that an action is to be praised if the consequences of praising it are good, not if the consequences of doing it are good.

The other objections are essentially those which Green brought against Godwin, and which made Butler decide that utilitarianism was better left to God. Utilitarianism, it is said, cannot account for contractual obligations: as Godwin realized, it makes the act of promising irrelevant to morality. Nor can it account for private and domestic obligations: to one's friends, one's wife or husband or children, or to the mother whom Godwin would leave to perish in the flames. The utilitarian, it is argued, denies all obligations except the single one of indiscriminate benevolence. To this most utilitarians have replied that promoting happiness (or good) requires a certain amount of organization. Division of labor may be necessary here as elsewhere: we are more likely to get results if everyone has a special responsibility for the welfare of a few individuals. This is the rationale of family obligations. A somewhat similar account may be given of promises. It would be impossible to cope with the world unless inanimate objects behaved predictably—according to fixed laws which can be discovered. In the same way society functions much more smoothly if human behavior is predictable. Even predictably hostile behavior may be easier to cope with than random behavior. The making and keeping of explicit undertakings is then a useful social device which, in spite of Godwin, may easily be justified on utilitarian grounds.

This may explain why we believe that private or contractual obligations have a special force. It would follow, however, that, if ever these obligations conflicted with the general obligation to promote happiness (or good) they should be subordinated to it. And it is just this that the opponents of utilitarianism deny. No one disputes that we are justified in breaking a promise in order to save a life, or gain some other end which far outweighs anything achieved by keeping the promise. But when there is only a slight advantage to be gained by breaking the promise, it would generally be said that the obligation to keep it comes first. Bentham accounted for this by distinguishing between first and second order evil. First order evil is the pain caused to particular individuals; second order evil is the harm done to the community in general by the shattering of public confidence in, for example, the institution of promise-making.

Second order evil, however, would seem to require publicity; and it is objected that we do not think it right to break a promise, for the sake of a slight increase in good, even if no one would know of the breach. A promise made to a dying man, for example, is usually held to be binding even after the man has died, whether others know about it or not.

Exactly the same sort of point can be made about justice. The utilitarian, it is said, is committed to the view that the end justifies the means, with all its totalitarian implications. One can imagine circumstances in which good consequences might result from punishing an innocent man (if he is generally believed to be guilty, say, and riots would result from acquitting him). Of course, if it were known that he were innocent, there might be general insecurity and loss of confidence in the law—the very great second order evil we associate with a police state. But most of us think it wrong to punish the innocent, even if the second order evil can be avoided.

Like the objection about higher and lower pleasures, this one has given rise to an amended utilitarian theory, sometimes called Rule Utilitarianism (in which case the more traditional theory is called Act Utilitarianism) and sometimes Restricted Utilitarianism (in which case the traditional theory is called Extreme Utilitarianism). According to this amended theory, the test of rightness is not whether an individual action will have better consequences than any alternative but whether it would have such consequences if it formed part of a general practice. Some statements of rule utilitarianism give it a slight flavor of conformism by suggesting that the test is whether the proposed action is or is not in conformity with an existing social norm: the test of such norms is whether their general adoption makes for the general good.

At least at first sight this revision of utilitarianism seems to meet the objections just discussed. Whatever may be said about individual acts of promise-breaking or injustice, a general practice of disregarding undertakings or punishing the innocent whenever it seemed expedient could hardly have good consequences.

It does not seem to have been noticed that rule utilitarianism was propounded by Bishop Berkeley in *Passive Obedience*. "In framing the general laws of nature," Berkeley says, "it is granted we must be entirely guided by the public good of mankind, but not in the ordinary moral actions of our lives. Such a rule, if universally observed hath, from the nature of things, a necessary fitness to promote the general well-being of mankind: therefore it is a law of nature. This is good reasoning. But if we should say, such an action doth in this instance produce much good and no harm to mankind; therefore it is lawful: this were wrong. The rule is framed with respect to the good of mankind, but our practice must be always shaped immediately by the rule" (*Works*, ed. Luce and Jessup, 6, 34).

This quite explicit statement of rule utilitarianism does not seem to have attracted much attention, and modern interest in the theory apparently stems from an article by R. F. Harrod in *Mind* for 1936. Even then, it was not till the nineteen-fifties that general interest was roused. Some of the modern exponents of rule utilitarianism have, however, suggested that the traditional utilitarians have been misinterpreted, and that they were, at least implicitly, rule rather than act utilitarians. This claim has been made by mid-twentieth-century philosophers: for Mill by J. O. Urmson, for Hume and Austin by J. Rawls, and for Hutcheson by J. D. Mabbott.

If rule utilitarianism is to be genuinely distinct from act utilitarianism, it will presumably assert that conforming to a rule is good in itself, and not merely good as a means. For if it is good as a means, and the end is the general welfare, what is in dispute is simply the factual question whether one ever can increase the general good by contravening a rule which could not advantageously be broken by everyone. The rule utilitarian says that even if the general good could be increased by such an action, it would still not be right. Why not, unless something else, namely the following of general rules, is good in itself as well as happiness (and, for the ideal utilitarian, truth, beauty, etc.)? It has seemed to some critics that this assertion is patently absurd, and they have called it derisively "rule-worship."

One way of defending the assertion is to invoke the universalization principle. This is often held to be a principle of reason, quite independent of utilitarianism. If so, it seems reasonable to suppose that a sound moral theory will comply with it as well as with the utilitarian formula. But a utilitarian who reaches the conclusion that he ought to break a promise made in secret to a dying man, or that he ought to punish an innocent man whom everyone else believes to be guilty, is not departing from the principle of universalization. Not only does he think it right to act as he is acting, in the peculiar circumstances in which he finds himself: he also thinks it right that everyone else in those circumstances should act in that way. One relevant circumstance is that no one else knows the truth about what he is doing. This can hardly be ignored: for it is only because of it that second order evil may be presumed not to occur, and the absence of second order evil is clearly a relevant circumstance. It would seem, then, that merely appealing to the universalization principle will not enable us to avoid the objections made to act utilitarianism.

What makes the difference is not the presence of universalizability, but the absence of secrecy. What the rule utilitarian needs to say is that one should always act according to principles one is prepared to acknowledge publicly. Is it clear, however, that this is an independent principle, and not one that can be derived from utilitarianism itself? Predictability would seem to demand that men should not profess one set of principles and act on another. Consider the consequences if a utilitarian does decide that the general welfare demands that on occasion he depart from certain "secondary principles" in secret. If he is asked whether utilitarianism ever does lead to this departure, he has to say that it never does. He cannot say that it follows from utilitarianism that it is permissible to break promises made to dying men; for then it would become impossible for a known utilitarian to comfort dying men by making promises to them. To avoid this second order evil he must practice deception, not only about his own actions, but about the true nature of utilitarianism itself. But it is presumably in the general interest that utilitarianism should be practiced with understanding. This deception, then, will in itself lead to second order evil.

It is at least arguable that, when Mill and other traditional utilitarians lay the stress they do on "secondary principles" and say things like "it would be unworthy of an intelligent agent not to be consciously aware that the action is of a class which, if practiced generally, would be generally injurious and that this is the ground of the obligation to abstain from it" (op. cit., p. 18), they are merely spelling out Bentham's contention about second order evil and are not departing from act utilitarianism. The case may have been different with Berkeley, since he did think that something else was good in itself besides attaining the general good, namely, loyal obedience to the commands of God. Even Berkeley, however, gives utilitarian reasons for God's willing us to conform to general rules. The reasons are that predictability is important, and that men are fallible in judging the consequences of their actions.

We would seem, then, to have this position: If the rule utilitarian is merely saying that it is not possible to promote the general interest by breaking general rules in secret, he does not differ from the act utilitarian, who has always maintained that, when second order evil is taken account of, his theory does not commit him to this kind of deception. To differ significantly from the act utilitarian, the rule utilitarian must maintain that it is sometimes possible to attain the general good in this way, and that, even then, the action is not right. This amounts to saying that something else is right, besides the maximization and equal distribution of welfare. But what? It is hardly plausible to say that conforming to rules is right in itself, apart from its consequences. Universalizability, as we have seen, will not do; and modern rule utilitarians are unlikely to follow Berkeley and invoke the will of God. One suspects that they have in mind something which is often confused with universalization: fairness or justice. Whether utilitarianism can account for justice is one of the crucial questions. If the principles of justice cannot be derived, as Mill thought, from the maximization of happiness principle, there remain two possibilities. It may be that justice is concerned with the equal distribution, rather than the maximization of happiness (or good), in which case we are faced with a conflict between two utilitarian principles, and obviously need to find some way of reconciling them. Or it may be that justice is right quite apart from its consequences, which is what the critics of utilitarianism have always said. In either case, the problem does not seem to be solved by making conformity to rules an independent good.

*BIBLIOGRAPHY*

N. Rescher, *Distributive Justice* (Indianapolis, 1966), has a comprehensive bibliography. The classical texts of hedonistic utilitarianism are: J. Bentham, *Introduction to the Principles of Morals and Legislation* (London, 1780); J. S. Mill, *Utilitarianism* (London, 1863); and H. Sidgwick, *The Methods of Ethics* (London, 1874; 7th ed., 1907). The chief works of the eighteenth-century forerunners of utilitarianism are: F. Hutcheson, *Inquiry into the Original of our Ideas of Beauty and Virtue* (London, 1725); idem, *Essay on the Nature and Conduct of the Passions, and Illustrations upon the Moral Sense* (London, 1728); idem, *System of Moral Philosophy* (London, 1755); J. Brown, *Essays on the Characteristics* (London, 1751); C.-A. Helvétius, *De l'esprit* (Paris, 1758); A. Tucker, *The Light of Nature Pursued* (London, 1768–77); W. Paley, *Principles of Moral and Political Philosophy* (London, 1785); W. Godwin, *Enquiry concerning Political Justice* (London, 1793). For ideal utilitarianism the main sources are G. E. Moore, *Principia ethica* (London, 1903); idem, *Ethics* (London, 1912); and H. Rashdall, *Theory of Good and Evil* (London, 1907). Apart from G. Berkeley, *Passive Obedience* (London, 1712), rule utilitarianism is developed mainly in articles by R. F. Harrod, J. Harrison, J. Rawls, R. B. Brandt, and others. There is a bibliography and a critique in D. Lyons, *Forms and Limits of Utilitarianism* (Oxford, 1967). General historical accounts of utilitarianism are: L. Stephen, *The English Utilitarians* (London, 1900); E. Albee, *A History of English Utilitarianism* (London, 1901); É. Halévy, *Growth of Philosophical Radicalism* (London, 1928); J. Plamenatz, *The English Utilitarians* (Oxford, 1949).

D. H. MONRO

[See also Equality; God; **Happiness and Pleasure;** Justice; Law, Natural; **Pragmatism;** Right and Good.]

## UTILITY AND VALUE
## IN ECONOMIC THOUGHT

### I

**1.** The common word "utility" was introduced into the special vocabulary of the social scientist only in the last half of the eighteenth century. By it the initiators understood that inherent property of a thing which in English is best rendered by "usefulness." Thus, Abbot Ferdinando Galiani (*Della moneta*, 1750) defined *utilità* as "the power of a thing to procure us felicity." Similarly, Jeremy Bentham at first spoke of utility as "that property in any object, whereby it tends to produce benefit, advantage, pleasure, good or happiness" (*An Introduction to the Principles of Morals and Legislation*, 1780). But the meaning of the term has shifted continuously and even today "utility" circulates with various, albeit cognate, connotations. By referring to the principle of utility as the principle of the greatest happiness of the greatest number, Bentham himself paved the way for this terminological license. The ensuing confusion prompted W. Stanley Jevons to insist that "*Utility is not an Intrinsic Quality*," but "the sum of the pleasure created and the pain prevented" (*The Theory of Political Economy*, 1871).

In the end, Bentham was disturbed by his license, but blamed the unfortunate choice of the term for his confusion, and the French for insisting on that choice. The choice was indeed unfortunate, especially in the case of those Romance languages which do not distinguish between "utility" and "usefulness." But even an English-speaking person needs some mental effort to relate "utility" to pleasure. Moreover, "utility" can hardly evoke a relationship between an individual and the things and services available to him, which is the core of every modern definition of the concept. Several other economists have also expressed their dissatisfaction with the term and made various suggestions, not always well inspired, for a new label. Unfortunately, even "ophelimity," the term coined by Vilfredo Pareto to cleanse the terminology of any vernacular overtones, did not prevail. The prestige of Jevons added to that of Bentham sufficed to enthrone "utility" in economics.

A passage from an Oxford lecture delivered in 1833 by W. F. Lloyd admirably illustrates how clear the whole picture becomes if one is not entrapped by the ambiguity of Bentham's license:

> The utility [usefulness] of corn is the same after an abundant harvest as in time of famine. . . . The term value [utility] therefore does not express a quality inherent in a commodity, [but] a feeling of the mind, and is variable with the variations of the external circumstances which can influence that feeling, without any variation of the intrinsic qualities of the commodity which is the object of it (pp. 174, 181).

Carl Menger, one of the founders of the modern theory of utility ("Principles of Economics," 1950; German original, 1871), also used "value" for what others called "utility" and even decried the use of this last term otherwise than as a synonym of "usefulness." Jevons himself began by emphasizing that "*value depends entirely on utility.*" And nowadays most economists would agree with his position. All this shows that the modern concept of utility is so intimately connected with that of economic value that it is well-nigh impossible to separate them in thought or analysis.

**2.** The notion of utility, in fact, goes back under other names twenty-five centuries to the philosophers of ancient Greece, who first raised the problem of what endows certain things with an economic value. The march of ideas has been unusually slow and exasperatingly tortuous, not only because there were numerous genuine obstacles to circumvent, but also because at times spurious ones were created. Nevertheless, one can distinguish four salient landmarks.

The earliest landmark is represented by a thought of a very modern facture. There are two elements involved in economic value: an intrinsic property of the commodity and the user's ability to enjoy it. As Xenophon observed in his *Oeconomicus*, even though a flute has no value for one who cannot play it, it has a market value because others can. However, the familiar conviction that science requires a monistic explanation led a long line of students to move away from this thought in order to look for a single cause of value.

Clearly, such a cause must be either in us or in things, but not in both. And since in early times hardly anyone could think of pleasure as a measurable entity, the tenet that "the value of a thing lies in the thing itself"—as J. B. Say was to formulate it not very long ago—won by default. Other factors, however, account for the long survival of this commodity fetishism, a second landmark. There was, first, the authority of Aristotle, from whom the idea originated (*Nicomachean Ethics* 1133a 25–26). Secondly, any thought that there may after all be a subjective element in economic value was stifled by the so-called paradox of value, which, according to Plato (*Euthydemus* 304), was known even to the poet Pindar. This paradox points out that some vitally important things (such as water) have a very low exchange value or none at all, while others (such as diamonds) have very little importance and a very high exchange value. Ergo, value cannot be in man.

Like many other traditional dogmas, commodity fetishism suffered a setback during the Age of the Enlightenment. And, as always, the reaction embraced the diametrically opposite view. This view, the third landmark, is that "a thing does not have value because, as is assumed, it has a cost; but it has a cost because it has value [in use]," as Étienne de Condillac summarized it about 1745 (*Oeuvres philosophiques . . . ,* 2 vols. [1948], 2, 246).

The fourth landmark is the modern theory which views utility as being neither in things nor in us, but in a relation between us and things, and which explains value as the balance determined by the members of an economy between utility and disutility.

## II

**1.** In retrospect it may seem curious that the rich intellectual legacy of ancient Greece included no systematic economic study apart from a few uninteresting works on *oikonomia*, on rules for good housekeeping. But the attention of an inquisitive mind will never be arrested by a stationary process. The ancient Greeks were a nation of busy traders and navigators over many seas, but their economy was nevertheless stationary, in the sense that, apart from random fluctuations caused by natural phenomena, economic life went from day to day without any perceptible change. What should surprise us, therefore, is that in spite of this fact many of their writings are studded with ideas on value and utility which even nowadays, after the theory of consumer behavior has become a highly developed branch of the economic science, retain their full significance.

No modern utilitarian has been able to add anything substantial to Plato's clear formulation of the doctrine. He tells us repeatedly that life is a "juxtaposition" of pleasure and pain, and that "each one of us has in his bosom two counsellors, both foolish and also antagonistic; of which we call the one pleasure, and the other pain" (*Protagoras* 357; *Laws* I. 644, V. 733). After more than two thousand years, Bentham, the modern architect of utilitarianism, echoed this very thought in the opening sentence of *An Introduction to Principles of Morals and Legislation:* "Nature has placed mankind under the governance of two sovereign masters, *pain* and *pleasure*." Hermann H. Gossen, the first author of a mathematical theory of utility, in 1854 also began his *Entwicklung der Gesetze des menschliches Verkehrs und der daraus fliessenden Regeln für menschliches Handeln* (1854; "Exposition of the Laws of Human Relations and the Resulting Principles for Human Actions") with it: "Man wants to enjoy life, and on this he sets his life goal," because this is the Creator's law. In a quite modern vein, Plato (*Philebus* 21, trans. B. Jowett), further argues that ". . . and if you had no power of calculation you would not be able to calculate on future pleasure, and your life would be the life, not of a man, but of an oyster or 'pulmo marinus.'"

This time, however, Bentham's echo—that "all men [even madmen] calculate" pleasure and pain—falls much short of the convincing power of Plato's original argument.

Even though Plato's analysis of pleasure and pain, spread throughout the *Dialogues*, is not as systematic as Bentham's, recent trends in utility theory show that Plato's is superior. Whilst Bentham maintains that pleasures and pains are "addible" so that in any situation the net result is a quantum of either pleasure or pain, Plato argues that although they "both admit of more and less" neither can be subtracted from the other because "the negation of pain will not be the same with pleasure" (*Philebus* 41, 43). This idea is further strengthened by several observations in *The Republic* on the nature of wants and, especially, on their hierarchy. Plato even notes that new wants emerge with the increase in income and also touches the important idea that basic wants are irreducible to one another. Elsewhere (*Euthydemus* 299), he adumbrates another vital principle for the theory of utility, namely, the principle that every want is satiable.

**2.** We owe to Aristotle the fundamental distinction between value in use and value in exchange (*Politics* 1257a). Less known is the fact that both his *Politics* and *Topics* contain many other first thoughts on utility. We find, for example, the idea that "the more conspicuous good" is the more desirable and also the concept of complementarity among commodities, which F. Y. Edgeworth was to introduce in economics more than two thousand years later. Also, the observation that wants satisfied by material consumption alone are subject to satiety was made again in 1855 by Richard Jennings. On the other hand, Aristotle's analysis becomes cumbersome as he forces upon it his strongly ethical views. While recognizing that the number of human wants is normally unlimited, he contends that a good household should aim at setting a limit to the satisfaction of these wants (*Politics* I. 9–10). He also denounces the craving for money on the part of money-making people as abnormal and the practice of "money-breeding" (money-lending) as the most obnoxious of all. So set was Aristotle on this point that he invoked the legend of King Midas in its support without realizing that the legend illustrates only the principle of want irreducibility. Even if everything Midas touched had turned into bread, he still would have died—of thirst.

Unfortunately, the most fateful of Aristotle's thoughts on value are crowded in a few pages of *Nicomachean Ethics* (1132a–1133b) and more often than not are off the mark. His argument that commodities could not be exchanged with one another if every commodity did not possess one measurable quality common to all, is the origin of commodity fetishism. In a somewhat cryptic sentence Aristotle asserted that what renders all commodities comparable is χρεία, which means "need" and may mean also "demand." Most likely, all he wanted to say was that exchange is possible because people, generally, have the same wants. Aristotle was very clear on the point which anticipates the teaching of classical economists: the quality that endows commodities with value is labor, and the value of a commodity is proportional to the amount of labor embodied in it. But, like many after him, he simply begged the question of whether every kind of labor is reducible to the same unit of measurement.

A logician of Aristotle's stature could not possibly overlook the logical implication that, if value is in things (in whatever form), then exchange cannot increase it—an idea that Karl Marx, in particular, was to defend in modern times. The point that after a *just* exchange or a *just* remuneration everyone must come out without gain or loss harmonized splendidly with Aristotle's ethical views. But the fallacy, shielded by such a high authority, constituted the sturdiest obstacle for more than two millennia to a clarification of the problem of utility.

3. With the fate that awaited knowledge after the Athenian *Akademeia* came to an end, the rekindled intellectual activity of the Middle Ages found no other authoritative guide than Aristotle's integrated philosophical system. So, as the Scholastic doctors turned their attention during the thirteenth century to man's secular problems, they found Aristotle's ethical views of economic life perfectly congenial to the Christian teachings. Aristotle's thought that the basis of value is χρεία offered to Saint Thomas Aquinas a splendid ground for arguing that value represents the need of the whole society, not the whimsical need of the individual. Moreover, this need must reflect social justice, without which any society is doomed. However, in the end the Scholastics began to ask what value is, instead of what it should be. It was Saint Antoninus who, about the middle of the fifteenth century, reached the highest point on a trail broken by Duns Scotus. In his explicit formulation, the value of an object involves (1) its quality in comparison with other similar objects, (2) its scarcity, and (3) its *complacibilitas*—a notion equivalent to that of utility as defined later by Galiani and Bentham.

4. During the next three hundred years or so—until the Enlightenment—the problem of value even suffered a regress. If some histories of economic thought leave a different impression it is only because the historian, either through ignorance of the older writings or through faulty logic, gratuitously credited

some authors with original thoughts. The truth is that this period contributed an erroneous idea which had grown out of the fact that throughout Western Europe the structure of production remained practically constant over the years. The idea, which constituted an analytical obstacle for a long time, is that demand is an invariant coordinate for each community. We find it first stated in an essay, *Della moneta: trattato mercantile* (1686), by an Italian scholar, Geminiano Montanari. But its clearest formulation came some twenty years later from the financier John Law: "If the Quantity of Wine brought from *France* be a 100 Tunn, and the Demand be for 500 Tunn, the Demand is greater than the Vent" (*Money and Trade . . .*, p. 4). Even Galiani spoke of the demand for wheat in the Kingdom of Naples as a fixed quantity. And, along with Montanari, he insisted that only fashion, "an affection of the mind," may change the demand.

The mercantilist mood induced later writers to represent demand by an invariant expenditure, instead of an invariant quantity. According to this view, the price of a commodity is the quotient between the money allocated for that purchase and the quantity of the commodity brought to the market, as Richard Cantillon neatly explained in a celebrated essay of 1755 (*Essai sur la nature du commerce en général*). This fallacy is stated in equally plain words by Adam Smith (*The Wealth of Nations* [1776], Ch. vii) and appears several times in Karl Marx's circuitous discussion of demand (*Capital*, III, Ch. x). J. B. Say derived from it the theorem that the rise of price is in direct ratio to the demand, and in inverse ratio to the supply.

One exception strengthens the view that this erroneous conception of demand was fostered by the constancy of economic patterns. The great variations in grain prices caused by climatic fluctuations led Gregory King to observe as early as 1686 that the smaller the crop, the greater its cash value. King, however, remained totally ignored for almost two centuries. Only much later—with A. A. Cournot (1838) in France and Fleeming Jenkin (1870) in England, and independently of King's work—did the notion of *demand at a price* emerge to clear the way for the modern theory of utility.

5. The publication of Galiani's *Della moneta* (1750) was an important event, not because the treatise abounded in remarks which redistilled systematically some thoughts of Plato's and Aristotle's or because it substituted *utilità* for Saint Antoninus' *complacibilitas*, but because it marked a change of temper. The treatise contains the first sparks of subjectivist ideas, of the recognition of man as the center of everything social, which was in line with the reformist ideas of the Age of Enlightenment. Galiani thus argues that the only

invariable standard of value is man himself, for while the value of all things changes, "man has been, is, and will be everywhere the same self." And in his analysis of man's behavior we find the thesis that the desire for "rank, titles, honor, nobility, authority" is stronger than that for luxuries, and the desire for luxuries stronger than the desire of the hungry for food—a thesis germane to a recent idea that man works harder for that additional income which elevates him on the social scale (Milton Friedmann and L. J. Savage, 1948).

Most important of all is the fact that Galiani anticipates the highest thought advanced on utility, namely, the modern theory of choice. Value, he says, is "an idea of the balance between the possession of one thing and that of another in the mind of an individual." No wonder then, that Galiani himself did not grasp the full relevance of this thought. Otherwise he would not have continued to cling to the Aristotelian fallacy that in a just exchange there can be neither loss nor gain. The idea of subjective choice is even more sharply outlined in a little known essay, "Valeurs et monnaies" by Turgot (1768):

If the same individual has a choice among several objects useful to him, he may prefer one to another. . . . He will judge that one object *values more* than another; he will compare them in his mind, . . . choose those he prefers and leave the others (*Oeuvres* . . . [1844], I, 80).

Turgot goes on to explain that choice reflects the hierarchy that exists among the individual wants. He also is the first writer to admit that in barter each party values what it gets more than what it gives. But, symptomatically, Turgot still could not free himself from the Aristotelian tradition completely, for he goes on to argue that in free barter the gains of both parties must be equal.

5. Thoughts such as Turgot's betrayed the increasing economic awareness brought about by the increased commercialization of economic life and, especially, by the ebullient transformation of the Industrial Revolution. Students of economic affairs not only became more visibly interested in the problem of value but also, on the disappearing trails of mercantilism, began searching for the *source* of value. An economy, such as that of France ruined by the wars of Louis XIV and crippled by a nobility who deserted the countryside for Versailles, led François Quesnay to see the source of value in natural resources, particularly in the agricultural ones. "Rich peasants, rich kingdom," is the way he epitomized his doctrine. Equally natural is the fact that an economy—such as England's during the same period—which could not find enough hands to keep pace with a revolutionary increase in the demand for manufactured wares, should have inspired Adam Smith to see in labor alone the source of value.

Unfortunately, the rise to glory of the classical school also meant a total return to the Aristotelian ideas and hence a setback for the correct approach to the problem of utility initiated by Galiani and Turgot. While classical economists freely admitted that a thing must have some use value in order to have a market value, they scorned—as David Ricardo did most clearly in the essay "Absolute Value and Exchangeable Value" written shortly before his death in 1823—any thought that the individual may have something to say about the value of a commodity. And with his excellent logic Ricardo could but acknowledge and defend the startling conclusion that the value of the income of a society does not increase at all if, after any technological innovations, the society produces more goods without employing more labor.

There certainly was an anachronism in the re-enthronement of the notion of an invariant demand, just as the forces of the Industrial Revolution began swaying markets and values. The problem of why people do not spend their income entirely on bread or entirely on pearls did not exist for the followers of Adam Smith even after Lord Lauderdale lectured them on its importance. Small wonder then that a consummate economist and philosopher such as J. S. Mill could proclaim in 1848 that "happily, there is nothing in the laws of value which remains for the present or for any future writer to clear up; the theory of the subject is complete" (*Principles of Political Economy* . . . 7th ed. [1961], p. 436).

The British as a whole spoke the language of utility, as the historian Élie Halévy judged. Only the British economists, who lived under the great shadow cast by Adam Smith and Ricardo, remained immune to Bentham's influence. Even in the awakening from their slumber Bentham's utilitarianism played a very small role. The event came as economists everywhere were compelled to pay attention to the increasing importance of the consumer in an expanding market capable of satisfying a growing spectrum of wants. It was not a mere coincidence that, almost at the same time and independently of each other, four authors came up with an almost identical theory of utility: H. H. Gossen in Germany (1854), W. Stanley Jevons in England (1871), Carl Menger in Austria (1871), and Léon Walras (1874) in France. Gossen alone poses a problem to the historian because at the time the historical school of thought ruled supreme in Germany. But this condition accounts for the injustice done to the author who not only anticipated the others by many years, but also excelled them in many respects. Even today his name is overshadowed by those of the others.

453

## III

*1.* The notion of utility, under whatever form, could never have acquired its importance in economics if it had not been for the law that came to be attached to it. This law, which is known as the Principle of Decreasing Marginal Utility, simply states that *for any given individual, each additional unit of a commodity increases utility by a decreasing magnitude.* Curiously, it was a mathematician, Daniel Bernoulli, who first formulated the principle (1738). As he tried to solve the St. Petersburg paradox (a gambling paradox), Bernoulli was led to argue that the *emolumentum* (Latin for "advantage") of the ducat a gambler gains is smaller than the *emolumentum* of the ducat he loses. Owing to the lack of mathematical interest of the traditional economists, Bernoulli's esoteric memoir remained unknown to them for almost two centuries. So, as far as social scientists are concerned, Bentham was the first to formulate the Principle of Decreasing Marginal Utility for the case of money (*Principles of the Civil Code*, 1802), and Lloyd (op. cit., 1833) the first to formulate it for a commodity.

Behind the apparently simple enunciation of the principle, there lie some strong assumptions and some intricate issues. The least vulnerable of these assumptions is that every commodity is *cardinally* measurable, which in common terms means that every instance of a commodity is a sum of perfectly identical parts (or units). Obviously, this is not true for a vacation or a stamp collection, for instance.

The truly vulnerable assumption, that utility, too, is cardinally measurable (in some fictitious units that have come to be called "utils"), goes back to Bernoulli and to Bentham. But Bentham went further and maintained that the utilities of all individuals have a common measure and hence can be added together to yield the total pleasure of a community, just as the addition of all individual farm areas yields the total farm area of a country. Once, he did admit that "you might as well pretend to add twenty apples to twenty pears" and even denounced the measurability of the individual's utility; but he set a lasting pattern for social scientists in arguing that without the addibility of different utilities "all political reasoning is at a standstill." Certainly, without this addibility Bentham's principle of the greatest happiness of the greatest number becomes vacuous. He therefore had a reason for dreaming about a "political thermometer." Vain though such a hope is, economists have kept looking for a "welfare function" by which to measure the welfare level of any economy. Even Alfred Marshall (1879), in a controversial argument which was first advanced by a French engineer, J. Dupuit (1844), claimed that the total utility of any community is measured by the amount of money its members would pay for each commodity rather than go without it.

*2.* Benthamism was so much in the air, both in England and on the Continent, that (with the notable exception of Carl Menger) the early writers on utility followed Bentham's hedonism and equated utility with the pleasure experienced by an individual during the act of consumption. This is especially true of Gossen and Edgeworth and, to some extent, of Jevons. It is from this position that Edgeworth, with whom hedonism reached its apogee in economics, was able to defend the cardinal measurability of utility by invoking the law of sensations enunciated by G. T. Fechner and E. H. Weber in 1860. Utility is measurable, he contended, because an actual pleasure may be measured in terms of its "atoms," i.e., in terms of "just perceptible increments" (*Mathematical Psychics*, 1881). And, even though not quite in the same vein as Bentham, Edgeworth expressed his belief in the eventual construction of a *hedonimeter* for measuring actual pleasures.

But economics could not go on indefinitely with a notion of utility which implies that the consumer decides whether or not to buy more coffee while drinking coffee. The modern notion of utility embodies an idea laboriously outlined by Richard Jennings in an essay that received hardly any attention at the time (1855). Utility (Jennings used "value") is the expression of the *expected pleasure* at which the individual arrives on the basis of his past *actual pleasures.* However, it is the unique, yet totally ignored, merit of Gossen to have perceived that one can go deeper than that. Indeed, Gossen alone saw that actual pleasure is governed by a second diminishing principle: *Any pleasure diminishes in intensity and duration with its repetition, and the sooner the repetition, the greater the diminution.*

When all is said and done and utility is taken in Jennings' sense, the fact that milk tastes better if consumed less frequently has more to do with the Principle of Decreasing Marginal Utility than the fact that the intensity of the pleasure of drinking milk decreases as one is drinking milk.

*3.* Still another idea of how man values things is that of Carl Menger (1871), who never accepted the view that value (by which he meant utility) is measurable. Menger's position was that man's wants are hierarchized and that the first unit of an individual's resources has a higher importance than the second because it satisfies a more urgent need. This simple idea is, in essence, a nonquantitative form of the Principle of Decreasing Marginal Utility for any commodity that may satisfy several wants. Perhaps this is why the first formulations of this principle, by Daniel Bernoulli and Bentham, pertained to money, not to a commodity.

Menger's nonmathematical approach soon died away under the mathematical landslide caused in economics by Jevons and Walras. Yet, every time a justification of the Principle of Decreasing Marginal Utility is offered in the current literature, it invokes only Menger's hierarchy of wants.

### IV

*1.* All founders of the utility theory had some doubts about the cardinal measurability of utility, but they took for granted that the utility of each commodity is independent of other commodities, that the utility of bacon, for instance, does not depend on how many eggs one has. This means that, if $x_1, x_2, \ldots, x_n$ denote the amounts of the various commodities possessed by an individual, his total utility is the sum of the single utilities, $U_1(x_1) + U_2(x_2) + \cdots + U_n(x_n)$. It goes without saying that the assumption greatly simplifies the analysis of value. Let John have six bushels of potatoes which he can trade at the price of four eggs for a bushel. In Figure 1, let the number of bushels be measured from $O_1$ to $X_1$ and the number of eggs from $O_2$ to $X_2$. Let $A_1C_1$ represent John's *direct* marginal utility of potatoes when consumed as such and let $A_2C_2$ represent his *indirect* marginal utility of potatoes derived from the eggs obtained by trading. If John wants to maximize his total utility—a basic assumption of every utility theory—he should, obviously, trade the sixth and fifth bushels: their indirect utility is greater than their direct utility. And he should stop trading at the point M, where the two curves intersect, because the direct utility of the fourth bushel is greater for him than its indirect utility. And if John possessed initially twenty-four eggs instead of six bushels of potatoes, he should end up with the same distribution of commodities, four bushels of potatoes and eight eggs. The same

result obtains in the equivalent case in which John has twelve dollars and the prices are two dollars for a bushel and fifty cents for an egg. But if, as it may well happen, the marginal utilities are such that $A_1C_1$ and $A_2C_2$ do not meet, then John must choose to have either only potatoes or only eggs, according to which commodity has everywhere a greater marginal utility. In any case, the optimal distribution of the budget is unique, which is a direct consequence of the Principle of Decreasing Marginal Utility.

The fact that a glance at Figure 1 suffices to clarify many issues of value is the reason why economists still use this highly unrealistic framework. For example, the diagram (with $A_1C_1$ and $A_2C_2$ being drawn as they are) shows that John's dollar buys more utility when spent on potatoes than on eggs. This simple point explains away the paradox of value. The same diagram shows that as a potato seller John gains the amount of utility represented by the area $MA_2C_1$, and as an egg seller he gains the greater amount $MA_1C_2$ (which may be infinite if the first potato is indispensable to life). There can be then no just exchange in Aristotle's sense. And to know whether there are just exchanges in Turgot's sense we need the interpersonal comparison of utilities in which Bentham believed.

*2.* The independence axiom was discarded as Edgeworth (*Mathematical Psychics*, 1881) proposed to represent total utility by a general function $U(x_1, x_2, \ldots, x_n)$. The diagram supplied by Edgeworth for the representation of exchange under these general conditions has become the most popular in economic analysis. Let potatoes and eggs be measured on $OX_1$ and $OX_2$, respectively (Figure 2). Let $C_1, C_2, C_3, \ldots$

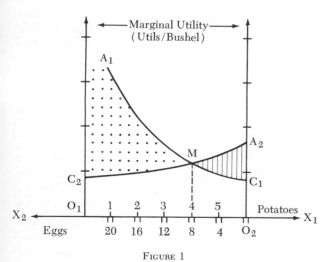

FIGURE 1

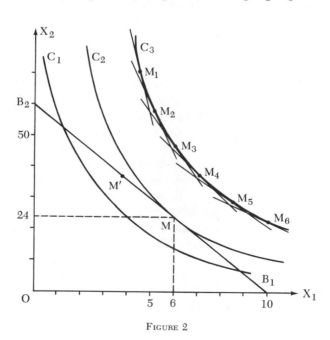

FIGURE 2

455

be John's utility isolines, a utility isoline being the loci of all combinations of potatoes and eggs that have the same utility. Naturally, utility increases as we move from an isoline to a "higher" one, from $C_2$ to $C_3$, for example. The alternatives open to John, whom we may now assume to have ten bushels and be able to trade one bushel for six eggs, are represented by the points of the *budget* line $B_1B_2$. The budget distribution that maximizes John's total utility is the point M at which one isoline is tangent to this budget line. Clearly, with isolines having the shape shown in Figure 2, all other possible distributions of John's budget lie on *lower* isolines. Therefore, John will trade four bushels of potatoes for twenty-four eggs and retain six bushels for his own consumption. The same solution is valid if John has, say, six dollars and the prices are sixty cents for one bushel and ten cents for an egg.

*3.* Obviously, for the optimal budget distribution to be unique the utility isolines must be convex toward O (as they have been drawn in Figure 2). A new difficulty arises now because the Principle of Decreasing Marginal Utility does not suffice to guarantee this convexity. The shape of the utility isolines depends, in addition, on the relation between the commodities. As Edgeworth noted, commodities may be rival—like margarine and butter—if an increase in one diminishes the marginal utility of the other. They may be complementary—like bread and butter—if an increase in one increases the marginal utility of the other. However, there is no way to reduce the convexity property to a property related to this classification. The convexity of the isolines had to be added as a new axiom for which no transparent explanation has yet been offered. The axiom says that *along any isoline* the marginal rate of substitution increases in favor of the commodity that is decreased.

V

*1.* Before the emergence of the modern school of utility, thoughts on value, demand, and exchange ordinarily reflected the economic conditions prevailing during each period. A turning point in this respect took place following the process of mathematization fostered by that school. Utility theory has ever since been its own source of new ideas, suggested primarily (and, at times, exclusively) by its mathematical framework. An excellent illustration is the observation made by Irving Fisher in his doctoral dissertation (1892). The pure geometry of Edgeworth's diagram led Fisher to note that in order to determine the optimal budget distribution we do not need to know how many utils each isoline represents: the knowledge of the isolines as such suffices. This simple geometrical truth caused the first serious dent in the idea that a cardinally

measurable utility is indispensable for explaining value.

It was, however, Vilfredo Pareto (*Manuale di economia politica*, 1905) who first constructed a consumer theory which does not require the notion of utility at all. His point of departure is that an individual confronted with two baskets of commodities will always either prefer one basket or be indifferent as to which one he gets. Given this faculty of *binary* choice, Pareto reasoned that, by asking the individual to choose between M and every other possible basket, we can determine an *indifference* curve, i.e., a curve that represents the loci of all baskets "indifferent" in relation to M. The procedure does not refer in any way to utility. And once the indifference curves are determined, they help determine the optimal distribution of any budget in exactly the same manner as the utility isolines. Furthermore, we can construct a function $V(x_1, x_2, \ldots, x_n)$ such that its value is constant on each indifference curve, just as the utility function $U(x_1, x_2, \ldots, x_n)$ is constant on each isoline. The only difference is that $V$ is not uniquely determined—any increasing function of $V$, say $V^2$, would do.

It is for the function $V$ that Pareto coined the term "ophelimity." But, as was argued in subsequent developments, we may still speak of utility and of $V$ as its *ordinal*, instead of cardinal, measure. This means that the value of $V$ simply *orders* all baskets according to the individual's preferences. Today the notion of an ordinal utility dominates consumer theory, the central problem of which is how to derive an ophelimity function from directly observable budget data.

*2.* In fact, this problem is relatively old. It was first formulated in a neglected memoir of an Italian engineer, G. Antonelli (1886). And, as happens quite often, the glory went to the more famous rediscoverer of the idea, in this case to Pareto (1905). In simple terms, Pareto's idea was this: if the optimal distribution of every possible budget has been determined by observation, every indifference curve can be determined by the tangential artifice shown in Figure 2 for $C_3$. But he ignored the fact that this artifice (which in mathematics is called "integration") is not always available for more than two commodities. An obvious paradox—known as the integrability problem—thus arose to intrigue many a mathematical economist. Some light was cast on Pareto's theory of choice and the integrability problem when it was shown (Georgescu-Roegen, 1936) that Pareto's argument failed to include two axioms (1) that any commodity may be substituted for another so that the first and the second basket be *completely* indifferent, and (2) that the binary choice is transitive. (Choice is transitive if A being chosen over B and B over C, A is chosen over C.)

*3.* In a signal contribution, Paul A. Samuelson (1938)

presented a theory of choice based, not on the comparison between two baskets, but on observable budget data. His point of departure is that John, by choosing the budget distribution M, reveals that he prefers M to any other distribution (such as M′) compatible with his budget. To this transparent definition, Samuelson added only an equally transparent axiom: *If a budget reveals that the basket A is preferred to B, no budget can reveal that B is preferred to A.* Samuelson claimed that this axiom alone suffices for deriving by integration the indifference varieties and hence for constructing an ophelimity function. In fact, the axiom expresses only a condition equivalent to the Principle of Decreasing Marginal Rate of Substitution. And as shown first by Jean Ville (1946) and later, but independently, by H. S. Houthakker (1950), Samuelson's idea calls for a stronger axiom (analogous to the transitivity of binary choice). But soon thereafter it was proved that even this stronger axiom does not entail the existence of an ophelimity function. It still leaves large domains for which there is no comparability among the commodity baskets (Georgescu-Roegen, 1954b). The problem of what set of economically meaningful postulates would make the Antonelli-Pareto idea work still awaits its solution. If it is ever solved, it will very probably cause a greater stir in mathematics than in economics.

## VI

*1.* Developments on an entirely different track suggest that economists have never abandoned the hope of proving that utility is after all cardinally measurable. A remarkably elegant scheme for determining a cardinal scale for utility was developed by Frank P. Ramsey (1926) and, independently, by O. Morgenstern and John von Neumann (1944). The scheme follows Bernoulli's idea in reverse. Bernoulli determined the stake of the gambler from the knowledge of the gambler's utility function. The authors just mentioned proposed to determine the utility function of an individual with the aid of the odds which that individual would be just willing to accept. They reasoned that if an individual is just willing to pay five dollars for a lottery ticket that gives him one chance in two of winning twelve dollars, we can infer that for that individual the utility of the additional seven dollars is equal to the utility of the five dollars that he may lose. By experimenting with various gambling propositions, we may thus determine step by step how great is the utility of the individual's $n$-th dollar in comparison with all his other dollars. This is tantamount to constructing a utility scale which, like that of temperature, is completely determined once the origin and the unit of measurement are chosen arbitrarily.

The idea was received with enthusiasm as well as with strong reservations. Some authorities on the subject of utility openly doubted their ability to construct a cardinal scale even for their own utility. Various suggestions have been made as to what piece of the theoretical apparatus may be at fault. Most probably, the culprit is the assumption that an individual may be *perfectly* indifferent between a dollar in hand and the probable prospect of winning ten dollars. Indeed, this assumption overlooks the fact that risk adds a new and irreducible dimension to man's choice (Georgescu-Roegen, 1954a).

Whatever the fault, the operational feasibility of the project has never moved beyond the paper-and-pencil stage and Ramsey's new vision of a psychogalvanometer had no better fate than Edgeworth's hedonimeter.

*2.* The conclusion of a recent approach to the process of choice is that utility is not even ordinally measurable (Georgescu-Roegen, 1954a). The point of departure is Menger's framework: man chooses in response to his varied wants and in accord with the hierarchy of these wants. But the new approach notes that at the bottom of the hierarchy are the most urgent wants, which are grounded in the biological nature of man and consequently are ordered alike for all human beings. These are followed by the social wants, which have the same order for all persons belonging to the same culture. Lastly, there are the personal wants; these vary irregularly from one individual to another. Moreover, only some of the personal wants may possibly compensate for each other. That is, a person might be *just* as happy with more records and fewer movies. But biological and social wants are irreducible. He who does not have enough to eat cannot satisfy his hunger by wearing more shirts.

In this framework, choice is determined by the least important want that can be satisfied in the given situation. For example, a person who does not have enough food will prefer the grocery basket with the greatest food value. But between two baskets with the same food value, the same person will choose the one with tastier foods, taste thus becoming the least important want. Should the baskets differ only with respect to, say, packaging, the next want will come into play. Choice, in this case, completely orders all possible baskets, but there are no completely indifferent baskets. The result is that choice no longer yields indifference lines and hence cannot be represented by an ophelimity index.

Several criticisms may be levelled against this approach. There is, first, the fact that wants are not sharply defined notions and hence fit poorly into a quantitative framework. Blurred as the hierarchy of wants may be, it offers a legitimate, *objective* basis for the interpersonal comparison of welfare—without which taxation must remain a completely arbitrary operation. It also justifies, for example, such useful analytical tools as the distinction between wage goods and luxury goods.

The preceding picture is foreign to the utility theory launched by Gossen, Jevons, and Walras. This theory has instead accumulated an impressive mathematical arsenal around the idea of the complete reducibility of wants, which is tantamount to the assumption of complete substitutability among commodities. The ultimate product needs unparsimonious stressing: the modern utility theory reduces all wants to one general abstract want called "utility." In line with this reduction, one need not say "these people need more shoes"; instead, "these people need more utility" should suffice. The reduction is responsible for the fact that the same theory teaches that there is no objective basis for interpersonal comparison of utility. All this may again be due to a particular feature of the economies in which the builders of the modern theory of utility lived. Those were not economies in which a low income kept basic wants in front of everybody's eyes; they were economies where most people were able to satisfy even many personal wants. Modern utility theory is a theory of a consumer who has a relatively ample income and whose economic choice is guided only by the quantities of commodities.

*BIBLIOGRAPHY*

In addition to the classic authors (ancient and modern), the following special works cited in the text may be consulted for details: Giovanni B. Antonelli, *Sulla teoria matematica della economia politica* (1866; Milan, 1952); M. Friedman and L. J. Savage, "The Utility Analysis of Choices Involving Risk," *Journal of Political Economy*, **56** (1948), 279–304; Ferdinando Galiani, *Della moneta* (1750; Bari, 1915); Nicholas Georgescu-Roegen (1936), "The Pure Theory of Consumer's Behavior," reprinted in Nicholas Georgescu-Roegen, *Analytical Economics: Issues and Problems* (Cambridge, Mass., 1966), pp. 133–70; idem, "Choice, Expectations, and Measurability" (1954a), reprinted ibid., pp. 184–215, from the *Quarterly Journal of Economics*, **68** (1954), 503–34; idem, "Choice and Revealed Preference" (1954b), reprinted ibid., pp. 216–27, from *Southern Economic Journal*, **21** (1954), 119–30; Hendrik S. Houthakker, "Revealed Preference and the Utility Function," *Economica*, N.S., **17** (1950), 159–74; John Law, *Money and Trade Considered with a Proposal for Supplying the Nation with Money* (1705), reprinted in *Oeuvres complètes*, 3 vols. (Paris, 1934) I, 4; William F. Lloyd, "A Lecture on the Notion of Value as Distinguishable Not Only From Utility But Also From Value in Exchange" (1833), *Economic History*, **1** (1927), 170–83; Alfred Marshall, *The Pure Theory of Domestic Value* (1879), Reprints of Scarce Tracts in Economics and Political Science, No. 1 (London, 1930); Oskar Morgenstern and John von Neumann, *Theory of Games and Economic Behavior* (New York, 1944); Vilfredo Pareto, *Manuel d'économie politique* (Paris, 1909), an expanded version of his *Manuale di economia politica* (Milan), published in 1905 but dated 1906; Frank P. Ramsey, *The Foundations of Mathematics and Other Logical Essays* (1926; New York, 1950); Paul A. Samuelson, "A Note on Pure Theory of Consumer's Behavior," *Economica*, N.S., **5** (1938), 61–71 and 353–54; Jean Ville, "The Existence-conditions of a Total Utility Function" (1946), *Review of Economic Studies*, **19** (1951–52), 123–28.

General surveys of the technical aspects of the problem of utility are: Kenneth J. Arrow, "Utilities, Attitudes, Choices: A Review Article," *Econometrica*, **26** (1958), 1–23; John S. Chipman, "The Foundations of Utility," *Econometrica*, **28** (1960), 193–224; Nicholas Georgescu-Roegen, "Utility," *International Encyclopedia of the Social Sciences*, 17 vols. (New York, 1968), 16, 236–67 (it includes a substantial bibliography); George J. Stigler, "The Development of Utility Theory" (1950), reprinted in J. J. Spengler and W. R. Allen, eds., *Essays in Economic Thought: Aristotle to Marshall* (Chicago, 1960), 606–55, from *Journal of Political Economy*, **18** (1950), 307–27, 373–96.

NICHOLAS GEORGESCU-ROEGEN

[See also **Economic History**; Economic Theory of Natural Liberty; Happiness and Pleasure; **Social Welfare**; **Utilitarianism**.]

# UTOPIA

THE WORD "utopia" derives from two Greek words, εὐτόπος and οὐτόπος, meaning respectively "good place" and "no place." Utopian writings have reflected this ambiguity, being sometimes visions of good and possibly attainable social systems and at other times fantasies of a desirable but unattainable perfection. The imaginary societies denoted by the term "utopia" are all presented as better than any existing society because of the rationality, harmony, utility, and order prevailing within them. Furthermore the imagined social systems they embody are better in the sense that men living in these regimes are either morally better people, happier, more self-fulfilled, or freer because conflicts have been eliminated from their environment and personality. Utopian writings have been one expression of the belief that given reasonable, natural, and truly just institutions man's lot can really be immeasurably improved. Since the seventeenth century utopian writings have been a constant expression of social idealism, hope, and optimism even though some utopists have stressed the illusory nature of their visions and have found in their impossibility a despairing statement of human finitude and man's radical imperfection. Most utopias have been produced within Western civilization. Though other cultures had myths of a golden age and other proto-utopian forms, only the Chinese seem to have produced indigenous utopian writings prior to the influence of Western culture. Even in China the genre did not flourish until Western civilization impinged upon Chinese consciousness influencing a few writers like K'ang Yieu Wei (1858–1927), whose *The United States of the World* appeared in 1935, fifty years after it was begun. In the West, utopias owed much to ancient classical images of ideal social existence.

Perhaps the earliest expression of utopianism in Greek culture is the portrayal of the Golden Age in the works of Hesiod (ca. 750 B.C.). Hesiod describes a time when ". . . the fruitful earth spontaneously bore [men] abundant fruit without stint. And they lived in ease and peace upon their land with many good things rich in flocks and beloved of the blessed gods" (Hesiod, *Works and Days*, 109–21). Here the perfect social condition is in the pre-urban past in which neither men nor classes struggled for power or property. Idleness, luxury, war, religious strife and other forms of conflict, ennui and malaise find no place in a rustic setting where men live simply, morally, and happily at peace with themselves and nature which abundantly supplies their needs. Many cultures preserve the image of such a golden age in the past and thus know of a utopia gone and not to be regained as long as life is complicated, urbanized, and filled with contention, and economic scarcities are man's inheritance. Lewis Mumford has argued (*Daedalus* [Spring 1965], 273) that "Such a society had indeed come into existence at the end of the last Ice Age, if not before, when the long process of domestication had come to a head in the establishment of small, stable communities, with an abundant and varied food supply. . . ." The first utopias would seem to be the pleasant but nostalgic folk memories of this state, standing in idealized contrast to the urban regulated world of war and social strife which succeeded as Iron-Age populations grew and rational and religious control systems were elaborated with the founding of the ancient cities. In Greek thought this second urban stage of civilization produced a series of visions of an ideal order which also harked back to a once real social condition. The ancient cities were rigidly structured institutions which Mumford has called (ibid., p. 283) "not only 'utopia' but the most impressive and most enduring of all utopias. . . . For to an extraordinary extent the archetypal [ancient] city [everywhere] placed the stamp of divine order and human purpose on all its institutions. . . ." The *Repub-*

*lic* of Plato owes something to this real, but in his time already archaic and passing, social organization.

The *Republic* (ca. 370–360 B.C.) is the first great extant utopian work detailing the institutions of an ideal social order. It is not, however, the first of such speculations in Greek culture, for Aristotle mentions in his *Politics* (Book II, Chs. 7 and 8, 1266a–1268b) Phaleas of Chalcedon who, he says, "was the first to affirm that the citizens of a state ought to have equal possessions," and Hippodamus of Miletus "who was the first person not a statesman who made inquiries about the best form of government." The *Republic* appeared at a time when the polis or city-state was proving to be an inadequate institution. Too small to organize large areas or to rule over subject peoples, it was large enough to contain unruly factions and demagogic leaders. Population growth and the militancy of the Greeks whose internecine quarrels tended to embroil city-states in each other's affairs had resulted in a period of warfare which would end only when the *Pax Romana* was imposed upon the ancient world. Plato's *Republic* attempted to provide guidance to Athens and its competitors in this time of troubles and to assure good men that the pursuit of justice and virtue would be rewarded in this life and the next (*Republic* X, 621).

The ideal republic as he sketched it was not only a reasoned contrivance enabling men to live the good life but the timeless, eternal, and good form of social organization. It was, like Plutarch's Sparta, the ultimate rationalization of the ancient city controlling every aspect of social existence in the name of justice, order, freedom, peace, strength, stability, and goodness. Ruled by wise men, protected by valiant warriors, and served by men of lesser abilities, Plato's republic, like most utopias conceived before the eighteenth century, was anything but democratic. The division of labor was elaborate and controlled by the governing intellectual elite who did not toil but organized production and distribution and kept the population limited to an optimal level. These philosopher-rulers regulated the beliefs of the people, teaching each class what it ought to know and training each for its social role. They decided all questions of government and maintained an ideal status quo in this most static and unhistorical of realms. Often described as a form of communism, the Platonic republic is perhaps more accurately described as a rationalized version of the communitarian ideal embodied in the polis. While the work is utopian in the sense of being an unrealizable ideal, many of the institutions with which it is provided were or were thought to have been in existence somewhere in the ancient world. As a guide to action, action which would realize only in imperfect and changeable form the idea of a perfect polis, the *Republic* was not wholly utopian and in this respect as in many others it served as model and source for later utopists.

Sparta, so well disciplined, pure and successful, inspired the admiration not only of Plato but of many other writers, one of whom left an account of its legislator which became a source for later utopists. Plutarch's *Life of Lycurgus* (ca. A.D. 100), the Spartan lawgiver, describes the social institutions which Lycurgus is supposed to have created for the Spartans and which made them austere, morally upright, simple, self-sacrificing, brave, hardy, and in a way happy in their freedom. Lycurgus stands in utopian and much nonutopian political writing as the archetypal legislator, the charismatic leader who, given the power and opportunity, shaped the destinies of a real people as decisively as have his descendants, who have in numerous utopias transformed the characters of ordinary men into perfect and ideal citizens. Lycurgus equalized property in Sparta, all but abolished money, regulated and ordered the lives of its citizens for their own and the state's good. The social order he created and the training and education which he designed to sustain it were directed to making the Spartans an efficient military power capable of defending their liberty and way of life which they saw almost as divine and unchangeable. Plutarch reports that the Spartans honored Lycurgus as a god, consecrating a temple to his memory. The image of Sparta and the possible changes which an enlightened legislator could make offered utopists a fascinating vision of rational social control and a means of realizing it if only the proper leader could be found.

Later descriptions of ideal societies owe much to other classical works. Idyllic depictions of the Golden Age among Arcadians, Hyperboreans, Panchaeans, and Atlanteans appeared in the works of Euhemerus, Ovid, Lucian of Samosata, and others. Plato's *Laws* (ca. 340), Aristotle's *Politics*, and Xenophon's *Cyropaedia*, while not utopias, provided materials from which later writers borrowed institutions, notions of enlightened rule and conceptions of human goodness and happiness to be found in civic, particularly urban, life. The founder of Stoicism, Zeno of Citium, and later Stoics as well as eclectic thinkers like Cicero, enlarged the image of an ideal social order to include all mankind and not merely those within a walled city.

The ancient world produced another profoundly different source of Western utopianism. The Hebraic tradition, as it came to the West in the Bible, has a number of utopian elements. The view of Eden in Genesis (Chapter 2) was sketchy enough to make men wish to describe it more fully. The conception of a theocratic state in which all is ordered for the glory of the god of a particular people endowed with a unique cult has attracted later writers. The vision of peace and harmony which possessed the Deutero-Isaiah also has its utopian aspects as do other eschatological and apocalyptic portions of the Bible. The pseudo-epigraphic works of the Jews and early Christians make much of epochs and eons to come which will be totally different and better than this decayed and sorrowful world. The vision of paradise held by early Christian writers added another not dissimilar utopian element. Nevertheless the biblical tradition has consistently worked against utopianism while furthering chiliastic and millenarian beliefs; it has done so because the transformations of man's life which are revealed are really the works of God and not of men, reordering their life in a rational and natural way. The apocalypse of Peter contains a typical and short account of such supernatural paradise which God, not men, will produce. (Cf. Eurich, p. 18.)

Speculations about such an ideal existence had perforce to be speculations about God's providence and not men's plans and efforts. The stress in the Christian tradition upon the sinfulness and imperfection of fallen man also worked against utopianism. There could be but one perfect man, Christ Jesus, and only the City of God, not of this world, manifested through grace the perfections for which utopians longed and hoped. The world as a place of sin, disorder, and suffering could be purged, judged, and redeemed, but it could not be radically reformed and perfected by fallen men. Paradise lost or regained was the only utopia possible and God alone held its keys. From the beginning of the Christian era to the sixteenth century Christian utopian longings usually took the form of millenarianism and utopia the appearance of a redeemed world.

Christianity did, however, provide one notable source and sanction for utopian thought and practice. The account of the first Christians contained in The Acts of the Apostles presents the apostle Peter as a preacher of a social as well as a religious gospel.

And they continued stedfastly in the apostles' doctrine and fellowship, and in breaking of bread, and in prayers. . . . And all that believed were together, and had all things common; And sold their possessions and goods, and parted them to all men, as every man had need. And they, continuing daily with one accord in the temple, and breaking bread from house to house, did eat their meat with gladness and singleness of heart, Praising God, and having favour with all the people. And the Lord added to the church daily such as should be saved (Acts 2:42, 44–47).

This passage so manifestly descriptive of a sectarian communist society gathered as a saved and saving remnant has been the favorite text of utopians claiming to be Christian since the Reformation. Used as a proof text it was the authorization appealed to by the leaders of most nineteenth-century American religious utopian communities such as the Rappites, the Inspirationists, and the Oneida Community. On the whole, Christianity has not been utopian in outlook and has branded as heretics those who took the apostle's message literally. There were consequently few utopian works written during the Christian Middle Ages. At best the land of Cockane, the realm of Prester John, and perhaps Dante's scheme for a universal monarchy show that a glimmer of utopianism persisted.

The Renaissance, which gave expression to so many new currents of optimism and secularism, saw a rebirth of utopian writing. Nicholas of Cusa in the fifteenth century postulated a semi-utopian order embracing all mankind in a world in which politics and religion had ceased to be disruptive forces. The burgeoning life of Italian city-states led men such as Leonardo da Vinci to think about remaking their world. The utopianism of such artists and architects, if it can be called that, was a reflection of urban growth. Its character has been nicely summed up by Eugenio Garin (in *Les utopies à la renaissance*, "La cité idéale de la renaissance italienne," p. 35). What mattered to these men were earthly ends and values. Political reorganization was to be the strategy to achieve them. Their plans were instinct with urban life and reflected its problems, notably international, and class conflict.

Urban development and consciousness provided but one stimulus to the production of Renaissance utopias. Religious turmoil, the upheaval of societies occasioned by economic growth, and the emergence of larger and stronger states, the exciting voyages of discovery were potent stimuli to the production of social visions and precise plans. The pre-Reformation *Utopia* (1516) of Sir Thomas More has its roots in all of these elements. More's projection of the ideal society is qualified in one important respect: Utopia is the best regime which fallen sinful men unaided by revelation are capable of creating. Because it lacks Christianity, it is a radically imperfect society. It is a proclamation of the limits of reason and human finitude as well as a statement of social idealism. It is consequently a statement of Christian humanism exemplifying the new-found moral and religious earnestness in which the Reformation and the Counter-Reformation were rooted. More's utopian society is one designed to humble the pride of its citizens through rigid controls. Its social policies are ideal solutions to the problems of poverty, economic dislocation, and bad government which sixteenth-century societies knew all too well. The narrator of the account of the Utopia, Ralph Hythloday, is presented as having been a companion of the Florentine navigator, Amerigo Vespucci, and himself an even more remarkable explorer. More's *Utopia*, like Plato's *Republic,* set a pattern and a style for the genre which was by and large unchanged until the late eighteenth century. The timeless, static society in which history is discounted, the totalitarian patterns of control, the location of the society in the present but in a remote, unexplored area, the concern with communism, natural religion, and the overcoming of the problem of economic scarcity by means of a strict control of production, distribution or population—all these became hallmarks of the genre in the sixteenth century.

Seventeenth-century utopias are perhaps the most fascinating of any period because they reveal so fully the intellectual currents of the time. The first important one of the century was Tommaso Campanella's *Civitas solis* (*The City of the Sun,* 1602–27). Betraying an interest in astrology, hermeticism, and esoteric knowledge, his work also shows this defender of Galileo to have been an ardent proponent of the new science and a reviler of Aristotle. Campanella's vision possesses an almost chiliastic dimension, for the future includes great changes, even the establishment of a universal Christian monarchy. Campanella's world is one replete with inventions in which new scientific knowledge is applied for man's welfare, but more interesting is his changed attitude toward the future and the sense of destiny, almost progress, which hangs over the world at the end of his book:

Indeed, since these people, who know only the natural law, so closely approach Christianity, which adds to the laws of nature only the sacraments, which give aid in observing these laws, I deduce the valid argument in favor of the Christian religion that it is the truest of all and that when its abuses have been removed it will be mistress over the whole world, as the more outstanding theologians teach and hope. They say that this is the reason the Spaniards discovered the New World (although the first discoverer is our great Genoese hero Columbus): that the whole world may be gathered under one law. Therefore, these philosophers must be witnesses of the truth, chosen by God. From this I realize that we do not know what we are doing but are the instruments of God. Those men seek new regions, led on by their desire for gold and riches; but God has a higher end in view. The sun attempts to burn up the earth, not to produce plants, men, etc., but God uses the struggle between it and them for the production of the latter things. Praise and glory to Him! (see Negley and Patrick, p. 345, trans. W. T. Gilstrap).

This is a far more positive attitude toward history and the possibilities of human life than More could have imagined.

The early German utopist, Johann Andreae, whose *Christianopolis* (1619) appeared before the final version of Campanella's work, resembled the Italian monk in many ways. Andreae had been a Rosicrucian and his    **461** esoteric interests mingle with an interest in the new science. His utopia, while less scientifically sophisticated than Campanella's or Bacon's *New Atlantis*, possesses laboratories staffed with scientists (or perhaps one should say natural magicians). This friend and correspondent of Kepler also tried to wed the new science to Christian beliefs and to design a system "to lessen the burden of our mortality."

Bacon's *New Atlantis* is not essentially different in aim though its reputation and effectiveness have been much greater because of the celebrity of Bacon's philosophical and methodological writings. Like the others, he wrote to show how a Christian society could be improved by increased knowledge and a better technology. There is, however, a fideistic streak in Bacon's thought which tended to separate the natural and supernatural realms that blend so easily in *The City of the Sun* or later in Samuel Hartlib's *Description of the Famous Kingdom of Macaria* (1641), a work written "to propagate religion and to endeavour the reformation of the whole world" through sound learning, well taught and made fruitful in practice. Bacon's description of Salomon's House, the first research institute dedicated to the advancement of learning by cooperative scientific endeavor in the interest of beneficial technological application, provided images of purpose and organization which inspired men as diverse as the Christian *virtuosi* who founded the Royal Society of London (1662) and the rather less pious authors of the great French encyclopedia edited by Denis Diderot and Jean le Rond d'Alembert.

This interest in science and utopian writing was not confined to the sober and successful only. Gerrard Winstanley, the Digger, in *The Law of Freedom* (1651) and other tracts, designed plans for the millennium which included a place for science and secular learning. He and other millenarians who surfaced in the turmoil of mid-seventeenth-century England, were forerunners of those nineteenth-century sectarians who thought, like the Shakers, that they were living in a postmillennial age. Christian sensibilities got utopian dress of a more conventional sort in Robert Burton's short sketch, "Democritis Junior to the Reader," included in his *Anatomy of Melancholy* (1620). This utopian work of erudition and realism is interesting in its attempts to make reforms plausible by citing authorities and historical precedents for many of his suggested innovations.

James Harrington's *Oceana* (1656), another work of great analytic realism, adopts a similar stance in its polemics against divine-right monarchists, Thomas Hobbes, and theocratic sectaries. *Oceana*, like other utopian works by Harrington, is most concerned with the problems of political stability, constitutional forms, and the economic foundations of both. Harrington's republicanism, his concern with agriculture, public order, toleration and a religious establishment which could not be fractious, and above all his earnest realism combine to make him an attractive thinker despite the dullness of his books.

Seventeenth-century utopias include two other types requiring notice. The *Histoire comique ou voyage dans la lune* (1650) of Cyrano de Bergerac and Gabriel de Foigny's *Terra Australis incognita* (1676) both describe utopias in which a wide range of questions is pursued in a rationalistic fashion. Such works look forward to the philosophic tale of the Enlightenment. By the end of the century a critique of Christianity in the form of deism had found expression in numerous works of which Simon Tysot de Patot's *Voyages et aventures de Jacques Massé* (1710) is perhaps the best known.

The succeeding age, the Enlightenment, saw the development of most of its cherished beliefs in numerous utopias. Deism continued to appear as the religion of the truly wise. Utopias, which had always been moral, even strenuously so, became happy places, and it was clear that this happiness would be the product of sensual gratification as it was for Diderot's Tahitians in *Supplément au voyage de Bougainville* (*The Supplement to Bougainville's Voyage*, 1772). Another change which is noticeable in eighteenth-century utopias is the greater equality of their inhabitants; some were communist societies with complete equality as a corollary. As a consequence the attitude toward labor tends to change as well. Earlier works had required labor as a discipline or moral good; many had relegated manual labor to a specific class. Eighteenth-century writers tended to see it as creative and not degrading. In real life the power of states over their subjects was increasing; a similar trend prevails in the utopias of the time as well. Morelly's *Code de la nature* (1755) offers a view of a static society which is highly regimented in the interest of a communist egalitarianism.

The greatest and most ingenious of the utopians were those who placed their utopias in the future and saw them as the inevitable culmination of human progress. The first to write a utopia set in the future was Louis Sébastien Mercier, the author of *An 2440 ou Rêve s'il en fut jamais* (1770). The conceptual novelty belongs to his contemporaries, Baron Anne Robert Jacques Turgot, Marie Jean Antoine Nicolas de Caritat, Marquis de Condorcet, Paul Henri Dietrich, Baron d'Holbach, and Claude Adrien Helvétius, all of whom elaborated theories of progress in which secular, dynamic social and psychological forces acted inevitably to bring about progress in the arts, sciences, and morals.

Condorcet's *L'esquisse d'un tableau historique des progrès de l'esprit humain* (1794) contains as its last section a sketch of the future state of mankind at last living freely in a rational and natural social order which continues to perfect itself. The static mold in which earlier utopias had been cast was broken. So also was the isolation of the utopian world for Condorcet's utopia was to be worldwide although not realizable at the same rate by all peoples. In England Richard Price had reached a rather similar conclusion although he still connected progress with the realization of a divine providential plan—a plan in which the founding of the United States and the French Revolution were, as they were for Condorcet, significant steps into a bright future.

The eighteenth century also produced a rather different kind of utopist in the person of Robert Wallace, a Scottish clergyman and the author of *Various Prospects of Mankind, Nature, and Providence* (1761). Wallace believed that utopias could function as analytic models helpful to the social theorist.

Utopianism in the eighteenth and nineteenth centuries was supported not only by a belief in the inevitability of progress, but also by the widely held doctrine of the malleability or perfectibility of human nature which implied that men's minds and characters could be quickly molded by education to be vastly, if not totally, different from what they were. Utopia could be quickly built. Nineteenth-century utopists, Saint-Simonians, Owenites, and other utopian socialists tended to concentrate more than their predecessors on the means of getting to utopia rather than on the precise form the new society would have. For most, education was the favored means. Robert Owen spoke for many when he wrote in the Second Essay of *The New View of Society* (1813):

Children are without exception passive and wonderfully contrived compounds; which, by an accurate previous and subsequent attention, *founded on a correct knowledge of the subject,* may be formed collectively to have any human character. And although these compounds, like all the other works of nature possess endless varieties, yet they partake of that plastic quality, which by perseverance under judicious management, may be ultimately moulded into the very image of rational wishes and desires.

Education was, however, but one means to this goal. Some socialists who looked back to the French Revolution found inspiration in the revolutionary ideals and practices of the Jacobins or of Gracchus Babeuf. For them political action, even revolution through force, was the road to utopia. For others, especially Charles Fourier, the functioning example of a successful utopian community or phalanstery would convince mankind to adopt schemes so obviously good.

Nineteenth-century utopias display another charac-

teristic generally lacking in earlier works: they are much more optimistic about the possibilities of human betterment. Utopists of the seventeenth and eighteenth centuries dreamt of making men good and happy; their nineteenth- and twentieth-century successors dreamt of overcoming disease and death to say nothing of poverty, disorder, ignorance, and crime. Science, technology, and new social institutions to promote both could lead to abundance while machines, relieving men of toil, would allow all to develop mentally and spiritually. A somewhat greater interest in the control of economic and political relationships tended to make utopian and socialist identical for many in the nineteenth century. Because of this identity utopian ideas became for the first time politically effective. By 1900 utopian thought had in this way affected the views of many in Europe and North and South America. Indeed, socialism in America in 1890 meant not Marxism but the views of Edward Bellamy, whose utopia, *Looking Backward* (1888), became a best seller, provoked much controversy, and was translated into many languages. Throughout the last years of the nineteenth century, *Looking Backward* and Theodor Hertzka's *Freeland* (1891)—a more or less free-enterprise utopia located in Africa as befitted a work coming during the imperialist scramble for African territory—found not only readers but enthusiastic supporters gathered in clubs to promote the competing ideologies.

The twentieth century has produced more utopias than had been written by 1900. Indeed, F. T. Russell estimated in 1932 that "the eighteenth century produced as many as the sixteenth and seventeenth together, that the nineteenth almost tripled that number, and that the twentieth [had then seen] . . . almost as many as the nineteenth" (F. T. Russell, p. 307). Divided about equally between the political "right" and "left" these works have come mainly from the pens of Frenchmen, Englishmen, and Americans outside the South. One might surmise that maritime activity, religious belief, the freedom of the press, and a lively political environment which allowed widespread involvement in political action as well as economic dynamism had something to do with both the geographic distribution of utopists and the rate of utopian publications. Perhaps increasing alienation and political frustration have been factors, since many recent utopias have been thinly disguised political tracts. While utopian writings have been concomitants of social and ideological change, it is not clear that the increase has been greater than the increase in the reading public or the number of authors. It may be that the urge to write utopias is a constant product of social idealism, revulsion at inefficiency, waste, and disorder, and a desire to do something about these evils

463

even though the required or envisioned remedies are of a magnitude which engenders as much pessimism and frustration as reforming zeal. Whatever the reason for the increased number of utopias, it has not resulted in literary greatness or substantial novelty.

H. G. Wells and Burrhus Frederic Skinner have been the most interesting and creative of the utopists of this century. Wells blended science fiction, prophecy, and realistic social analysis to produce works more predictive than utopian. He has had many imitators. Scientific achievement has already outrun his fantasies and verified Oscar Wilde's quip, "Progress is the realization of utopia." B. F. Skinner's *Walden II* (1947) is interesting because of its stress on the techniques of behavioristic social engineering which for this pioneering behaviorist psychologist open the way to utopia.

If twentieth-century utopists have not provided much of interest, the same cannot be said of the anti-utopians whose parodies of the genre have subjected it to searching and destructive criticism in many dystopias or anti-utopias. There have always been anti-utopians—realists, cautious reformers, doubters of man's ability to achieve rationality, questioners of the possibility of an harmonious natural social order, and most importantly scoffers who have maintained that the achievement of utopists' dreams would be living nightmares. They have been a small but respectable company, including Aristophanes, Jonathan Swift, perhaps Voltaire, Samuel Butler, and in the twentieth century E. M. Forster, Evelyn Waugh, Evgeni Zamyatin, George Orwell, and Aldous Huxley. The grim visions of a likely future, all too rational and orderly, which these men have conjured up have made dystopias rather than utopias of more interest since 1930.

Utopian writings have played many roles in Western thought. Some belong to the literature of whimsy and escape, others to science fiction, a considerable number to satire, and many to that ill-defined genre, the philosophic tale. Utopias have appeared in almost every literary form—travels, letters, visions, dialogues, novels, treatises, and in both prose and verse. They have been the vehicles of seriously argued religious, political, and philosophic views set out didactically in a succinct and interesting manner and of propaganda. Many have sought to move men to action, while others have been visions for contemplation, dreams to think on. They virtually defy orderly classification, though some writers have tried to divide them into restrictive, rigidly controlled societies, totalitarian in their social policies, or expansive realms of freedom knowing only a minimum of control. This division coincides roughly with a division between those in which harmony, statically conceived, is maintained by the repression of spontaneity, and those in which perfection is seen as a relative condition dependent upon progress and individual freedom of choice and action. The static, dynamic, repressive, and expansive characteristics may owe something to the kind of men who have written utopias and the role which these works played in their own lives and perhaps also in those of their readers.

There have been few literary masterpieces among the utopias, perhaps because it is difficult to write interestingly of perfection, of states without the usual conflicts which form the stuff of romance and tragedy. Moreover, the characters in utopian works must be types, exemplifying classes, so they often lack individuality. Nevertheless, at their best, utopists have shared in most of the great intellectual debates and their works have often been not only stimulants to change but prophetic of the future.

## BIBLIOGRAPHY

Bibliographical works. G. Negley, *The Utopia Collection of Duke University Library* (Durham, N.C., 1965), contains over 500 titles. United States Library of Congress, Public Affairs Information Service, Division of Bibliography, *Utopias* (Washington, 1922, 1924, 1926, 1928).

Anthologies of utopian writings containing bibliographical information. H. C. Baldry, *Ancient Utopias* (Southampton, 1956). G. Boas and A. O. Lovejoy, *Primitivism and Related Ideas in Antiquity* (Baltimore, 1935), the standard source for selections and references dealing with "the Golden Age." F. E. and F. P. Manuel, *French Utopias: An Anthology of Ideal Societies* (New York, 1966), mainly eighteenth- and nineteenth-century selections. G. Negley and J. M. Patrick, *The Quest for Utopia: An Anthology of Imaginary Societies* (New York, 1952), contains all or parts of thirty-three utopias and lists the titles of over 100 other utopias and dystopias as well as major secondary sources to 1950.

General works bearing on utopian writing containing bibliographical information. G. Atkinson, *The Extraordinary Voyage in French Literature before 1700* (New York, 1920); idem, *The Extraordinary Voyage in French Literature from 1700 to 1720* (Paris, 1922). W. Bentley, *The Communication of Utopian Thought: Its History, Forms, and Use* (San Francisco, 1955). M. Buber, *Paths in Utopia* (London, 1949). N. Cohn, *The Pursuit of the Millennium*, 2nd ed. (New York, 1961). G. D. H. Cole, *A History of Socialist Thought: The Forerunners 1779–1850* (London, 1955). R. C. Elliot, *The Shape of Utopia: Studies in a Literary Genre* (Chicago, 1970). N. Eurich, *Science in Utopia: A Mighty Design* (Cambridge, 1967), is necessary reading for those interested in seventeenth-century utopias. Fédération International des Instituts et Sociétés pour l'Étude de la Renaissance, *Les utopies à la renaissance: colloque international* (Liège, 1963); twelve essays dealing with Nicholas of Cusa, Robert Burton,

Jerome Cardan, Thomas More, Kaspar Stiblin, Johann Andreae, Rabelais, and others. S. R. Graubard, ed., *Daedalus*, **94**, 2, *The Proceedings of the American Academy of Arts and Sciences: Utopia* (Richmond, 1965), thirteen papers on various topics concerning utopia. J. O. Hertzler, *The History of Utopian Thought* (New York, 1923), dated but still useful. G. Kateb, *Utopia and Its Enemies* (Glencoe, 1963). H. Kern, *Staatsutopie und allgemeine Staatslehre: ein Beitrag zur allgemeine Staatslehre unter besonderer Berucksichtigung von Thomas Morus und H. G. Wells* (Mainz? 1951?). H. Levin, *The Myth of the Golden Age in the Renaissance* (Bloomington, 1969). K. Mannheim, *Ideologie und Utopie* (Bonn, 1929), trans. as *Ideology and Utopia* (London, 1936). A. E. Morgan, *Nowhere and Somewhere: How History Makes Utopias and How Utopias Make History* (Chapel Hill, 1946), argues that More's *Utopia* betrays European knowledge of Peru prior to its conquest. M. H. Nicolson, *Voyages to the Moon* (New York, 1948). F. T. Russell, *Touring Utopia* (New York, 1932). J. Servier, *Histoire de l'utopie* (St. Amand, 1967). J. Shklar, *After Utopia* (Princeton, 1957). J. L. Talmon, *The Origins of Totalitarian Democracy* (London, 1951), has an excellent section on how the eighteenth-century utopians conceived of a natural, rational political order. S. L. Thrupp, *Millennial Dreams in Action* (The Hague, 1962). E. L. Tuveson, *Millennium and Utopia: A Study in the Background of the Idea of Progress*, 2nd ed. (New York, 1964). C. Walsh, *From Utopia to Nightmare* (New York, 1962).

Studies of utopists and utopias. W. H. G. Armytage, *Heavens Below: Utopian Experiments in England 1560–1960* (London and Toronto, 1961). A. E. Bestor, *Backwoods Utopias: The Sectarian and Owenite Phases of Communitarian Socialism in America 1663–1829* (Philadephia, 1950), is particularly good on early American communities. C. Blitzer, *An Immortal Commonwealth: The Political Thought of James Harrington* (New Haven, 1960). E. R. Curtis, *A Season in Utopia: The Story of Brook Farm* (New York, 1961). J. H. Hexter, *More's Utopia: The Biography of an Idea* (Princeton, 1952). R. V. Hine, *California's Utopian Communities* (San Marino, 1953). H. J. N. Horsburgh, "The Relevance of the Utopian," *Ethics* (1967), 127–38. R. Owen, *Utopianism and Education: Robert Owen and the Owenites*, ed. J. F. C. Harrison (New York, 1968). F. E. Manuel, *The Prophets of Paris* (Cambridge, 1962). Morelly, *Code de la Nature . . . avec une introduction et des notes par Gilbert Chinard* (Paris, 1950). C. Nordhoff, *The Communist Societies of the United States* (New York, 1875; 1961; 1965), a famous eyewitness account of the American communities in 1874. J. H. Noyes, *History of American Socialisms* (New York, 1870; 1961), by the leader of the Oneida Community. C. Rihs, "Les Utopistes contre les lumières," *Studies on Voltaire and the Eighteenth Century*, **57** (1967), 1321–55. J. Shklar, *Men and Citizens: A Study of Rousseau's Social Theory* (Cambridge, 1969), a study of utopian elements in Rousseau's works. E. L. Surtz, S. J., *The Praise of Wisdom: A Commentary on the Religious and Moral Problems and Backgrounds of St. Thomas More's Utopia* (Chicago, 1957). L. G. Thompson, *Ta t'ung shu: The One World Philosophy of K'ang Yu Wei* (London, 1958). D. Winston, *Iambulus, A Literary Study in Greek Utopianism* (Ann Arbor, 1956). P. Yershov, *Science Fiction and Utopian Fantasy in Soviet Literature* (New York, 1954).

ROGER L. EMERSON

[See also City; **Millenarianism;** Perfectibility; Progress; Renaissance; Sin and Salvation; **Socialism.**]

## UT PICTURA POESIS

*Ut pictura poesis:* "as is painting so is poetry," is often either implicitly or explicitly reversed to "as is poetry so is painting," to indicate an extended analogy, if not an identification, between the two media. This classical theory of parallels between the arts was widely held and developed, especially from the Middle Ages through the Enlightenment, and served as the testing ground for theories of imitation and as the incubator for systematic aesthetics. The discussions often revolved around "natural" (painting) and "arbitrary" (language) signs and symbols, and the questions, usually unstated until the eighteenth century, were "How does painting or poetry communicate?" and "What are the limits of each medium in time and space?"

Particular emphasis was always placed on the ability of the poet (or orator) to make his listener see the object, and of the painter to make his viewer understand meaning as well as imagine action. The usual major developments of the parallel include the principles that both arts are imitative and that their subjects must be significant and unified human actions, usually drawn from history, epics, romances, and the Bible. They must, therefore, express moral or psychological truths, hold to consistency or "decorum," and offer to instruct, to delight, and to move, although these ends and their relative importance were much disputed. There were fairly regular demands that the painter as well as the poet possess "learning," along with innate capacity and technical training. Theorists were usually interested in justifying the arts in general, especially in the face of criticism from historians and philosophers who challenged their utility and morality.

The theory of *ut pictura poesis* is applied in many ways. It may mean that the poet, without any real attempt to compete with the painter, should give enough concrete detail for the reader to form an accurate and vivid picture. This position was particularly common in the early eighteenth century, especially when critics examined the nature of metaphor. An equally important meaning may involve the poet's control over the reception of detail. The poet may "frame" or "light" a scene, or he may carry a reader from "foreground" to "middle ground" to "background," often using the painter's terminology. A kind of stasis is often effected, even when, as in the novels of Henry James and Thomas Hardy, a visual composition evolves as characters enter a space and take places, almost as in a tableau. With *ekphrasis* (or *ecphrasis*), an essentially rhetorical device in which an object formed in one art becomes the matter for another, the theory only apparently changes or takes on another dimension. The poet may indeed compete with the painter or the painter with the poet to render some art object, may attempt, in effect, to translate it either literally or spiritually. The poet may, however, be responding to a painting, simply revealing his reactions rather than attempting in any way a reproduction. The converse is also true: the painter need not be trying to reproduce the poem, or even to illustrate a facet of it, but may be revealing his intellectual and emotional reaction to the verbal art work.

Many Renaissance theorists, while admitting, even urging, the parallels, tended to make a case for one medium as superior to, or at least competing with, the other. The most usual distinction was that poetry appealed to man's essential faculty, reason, while painting was simply and dangerously sensory; or, conversely, that poetry appealed merely to slow reason while painting rightly and immediately overwhelmed the viewer through sight, the greatest of the senses, by being clearly imitative of nature, by, to note a favorite metaphor, "holding up a mirror to life." Gregory the Great in the sixth century, and during the Renaissance Savonarola and Giulio Romano asserted that paintings are "the scriptures of the ignorant"—Christ gave not only the gospels but his picture on Veronica's veil—and so painting was seen as a simple and powerful alternative for language, "books of lay-men" (Thomas Fuller, *Worthies of England*, 1662). But there is an equally strong if not "popular" Neo-Platonic view, well voiced by Pico della Mirandola in *Heptaplus* (1489), that the picture is a form of revelation, an incarnation of the Word. The value of the image then is not to present truths to the illiterate nor is it to interact with language for a more intense impact on the viewer-reader. Rather, its emblematic mystery or complexity, by serving as a kind of vision, lures or thrusts the viewer to meditation on truths. Furthermore, since the picture can be taken in quickly (instantaneously?) the process of viewing immediately transcends the gross sensory act and is not far removed, at least conceptually, from Neo-Platonic intuitive perception. The knot was cut by G. P. Bellori,

*Vite de pittori, scultori ed architetti moderni* (1672), who claimed that both art forms appeal equally and concurrently to the senses and the understanding, and by Joseph Trapp, *Praelectiones poeticae* (1711–15; trans. 1742), who suggested that both art forms be combined to appeal to the whole man.

Some of the complexity surrounding the entire problem of *ut pictura poesis* may derive from or be reinforced by the intricacy of the word *sentio*, which in its various forms in Latin, English, and the Romance languages indicates "knowing" or "understanding" as well as "experiencing through the senses." Language symbolizes while painting can imitate by natural signs, and the interior confusion revealed through the ambivalent, perhaps ambiguous, use of *sentio* to record the experience both of language and of the plastic arts of painting and sculpture appears to be another aspect of the general confusion of art forms. It is worth noting that in Greek *graphein* means "to write" or "to paint" (as does *hsieh* in literary Chinese), while until the late eighteenth century Western knowledge of hieroglyphs was limited to seeing them as either literal or mystical representations of things, rather than as language.

Furthermore, the easy exchange in the arts of terms such as "harmony," "proportion," "highlight," and "decorum" encouraged difficulties as critical vocabularies were sought. Such terms may well have been the metaphors of a man who knew one art form well but wanted to talk of another less known. But once the engaging analogies were started, they were there to be extended. In addition, terms of plastic arts such as "chiaroscuro," "Claudian," and "sculpturesque," when applied to literature, are often limited to similar content rather than to similar form (Giovannini, 1950).

One major problem in considering *ut pictura poesis* is the difficulty of determining whether the many comments on the sister arts reflected a concern for aesthetics or for social and financial position. Until the eighteenth century there was little pursuit of what we would call the "aesthetics" of the parallel, as is evidenced by the general lack of systematic discrimination among all fields of learning or the arts. Even the "arts" and the "sciences" were not clearly distinguished until the resolution of the "quarrel between the ancients and the moderns" in the late seventeenth and early eighteenth century, so from the classical period through the seventeenth century, thinkers bundled together what to the twentieth-century man appear to be very strange bedfellows: musicians and astronomers, cooks and architects. Francis Bacon, in *De augmentis scientiarum* (1623), IV, 2, categorizes music and painting as arts of simply sensory pleasure with the cautionary note that they may overstimulate already wayward emotions; he indicates their low rank by not including them with the liberal arts of poetry and history, both of which demand reason and imagination. Well past the Renaissance, painters were seen as mere craftsmen who made things that appealed to the senses; they were hardly worthy of the status traditionally given the rational or inspired poet (Kristeller, 1951; 1952).

Within this context, from the fourteenth through the seventeenth centuries, art theorists in Italy, France, and England almost invariably claimed that painting, like poetry, was a liberal, not a mechanical art. The essentially sociological aim of raising the position of the painter through the parallel with the poet is nicely demonstrated by the arguments for the superiority of painting over poetry as found in Leonardo da Vinci's *Paragone* in the early sixteenth century and is carried on by the Comte de Caylus, *Tableaux tirés de l'Iliade, de l'Odyssée d'Homère, et de l'Énéide de Virgile* (1757), Joshua Reynolds, *Discourses* (1769–90), and J. M. W. Turner, *Lectures* (1811–23). In the latter half of the eighteenth century, however, social respect rose sharply for the painter who produced a unique work in a universally "read" form (R. Cohen [1964], Ch. IV).

Modern scholars concerned with the interrelations of the arts often fail to recognize the differences between the use of one art by another and the transference of styles from one art to another. Many studies in *Geistesgeschichte, Weltanschauung,* and *milieu* have been superficially attractive, but too often they are presumptuous or "hobbyhorsical" in the pursuit of parallels (R. Wellek [1942], and R. Cohen [1964], Ch. IV). The great danger in any specific application of the theory of the relations between poetry and painting is that the literary critic starts to see "pictures" in even the slightest touch of detail or suggestion of stasis. A critic's interest in *ekphrasis* may tempt him toward a full analogy between a particular poem and a particular painting on the basis of a few similar but minor details. A different type of danger is that many early theorists must be read with particular care since they often use the term "poetry" to mean, or to include, "drama."

Although the emphasis in this study is on the art object, whether verbal or plastic, as art object, the obvious must not be overlooked: a demonstrable intention and effect of crossing art forms has an historical, cultural, or contextual significance that transcends the formally aesthetic. The medieval ordered portrait of the blond heroine is not only painterly and further is not only "ideal beauty," but it is goodness as well, or even primarily. The landscapes of Pope, Balzac, the Brontës, Zola, and Hardy are far more than simply places in which characters move, just as are the paintings of Bosch, the Breughels, Watteau, Constable,

Turner, Henri Rousseau, and Cézanne. They may be worlds of the senses, but they are also the landscapes of meaning.

## HISTORICAL DEVELOPMENT OF THE CONCEPT

Although both Plato and Aristotle referred in passing to the parallels between poetry and painting, it was Horace in his *Ars poetica* (19–10 B.C.) who provided the basis for the comparison and supplied the tag, *ut pictura poesis* (line 361). The line itself is limited enough in its immediate context: Horace is quite simply saying that poetry is like painting in that a particular poem has its own virtues and so, like a particular painting, needs to be considered under different physical conditions and with different expectations (cf. Quintilian, *De institutione oratoria* [ca. A.D. 95], XII.10.3–9). Throughout the entire poetic essay, however, he is so very ready with analogies among the arts—poetry, painting, drama, music, and dance—that a reader's expansion of the meaning of *ut pictura poesis* from a minor comparison to a rich analogy, or even identification, is readily understandable. Since there was no *ars pictura* from antiquity, Horace's work was seized on by critics of painting as an easy and appropriate substitute, and during the Renaissance the theorists of poetry and painting were so close in their thinking about the two arts that in many treatises the terms "poet" and "painter" could be readily interchanged": B. Daniello's *Poetica* (1536) was the direct source in both form and context of the *Dialogo della pittura* (1557) by L. Dolce, who had earlier translated Horace's *Ars poetica* (1535).

Just as Bacon's expression of a *philosophia prima* (*Advancement of Learning,* I) is a notable attempt at persuading scientists to search for the first and simple cause, so the man of the Renaissance hardly needed to leap to find correspondences among the particular arts, since all art reflected—perhaps refined—nature, just as nature reflected God, in "harmony," "symmetry," and "proportion." Every major theorist of poetics in the sixteenth century assumed and repeatedly affirmed some unity of the arts by at least noting the relations between poetry and painting. Vida, Daniello, Alberti, Robortello, Fracastoro, Minturno, Scaliger, Castelvetro, Sidney, Tasso, F. Junius, and Vossius all represent a common belief or search often summarized by Horace's tempting line.

If Horace supplied the term for the parallel, Plutarch preserved a vivid expression that was used by almost every critic of poetry or painting from the Renaissance through the eighteenth century. In his *De gloria Atheniensium* he cites Simonides of Ceos (ca. 556–467 B.C.) as saying, "Painting is mute poetry and poetry a speaking picture" (346f.) and noted that the phrase was already commonplace (17f–18a).

The neatest and most widely disseminated verbal association of Horace and Plutarch is found in C. A. Dufresnoy's *De arte graphica* (Paris, 1667), of which the opening sentence is *Ut pictura poesis erit*. John Dryden's translation (London, 1695) reflects attitudes widely accepted: "Painting and Poesy are two sisters; which are so like in all things, that they mutually lend to each other both their Name and Office. One is called a dumb Poesy, and the other a speaking Picture." The popularity of the Renaissance critics, as well as of Dufresnoy and Dryden, helped assure, with remarkably little challenge, the continued awareness that the arts were "sisters" (Ovid, *Metamorphoses* II, 13–14) until G. E. Lessing's *Laokoön* (1766).

Attempts to over-refine the analogy of form extended Aristotle's argument for the primacy of plot in drama and of line in painting (*Poetics* 1450b 1–3). This simply illustrative point was fruitlessly developed in Dryden's rather lackluster preface to his translation of Dufresnoy's *De arte graphica*, "A Parallel of Poetry and Painting" (1695). He wrote, "Expression, and all that belongs to words, is that in a poem which colouring is in a picture" and compares "lights and shadows with tropes and figures," observing that "Strong and glowing colours are the just Resemblances of bold Metaphors." He ends with the dangerous commonplace that "words are . . . the clothing of thought, in the same sense as colours are the clothing of design" (cf. Richard Flecknoe, *A Short Discourse of the English Stage*, 1664). Much the same appears in the Abbé Batteux, *Les beaux arts réduits à un même principe* (Paris [1746], pp. 138, 140, and 247), and from the painter, Sir Joshua Reynolds, comes a confirming note: "Well-turned periods in eloquence, or harmony of numbers in poetry . . . are in those arts what colouring is in painting" (*Discourse* [1776], VII).

The development of *ut pictura poesis* may well be pursued through the complexity of rhetorical theory from the classical period through the Renaissance. Major canons of rhetoric—*inventio, dispositio,* and *elocutio*—were adapted from Cicero and Quintilian and applied to the art of the poet and painter. As early as L. B. Alberti in his *Della pittura* (1436), *inventio* was used to indicate the painter's general material, his ideas and forms; *dispositio,* the large aspects of arrangement or composition; and *elocutio,* the actual portrayal. L. Daniello in *La poetica* (1536) and B. Dolce in *Dialogo della pittura* (1557) apply more explicitly these traditional terms.

Within this large framework, most rhetoricians had traditionally agreed that the speaker must make an audience see as well as hear (Quintilian, *De institutione*

*oratoria,* VIII. 3; Richard Sherry, *A Treatise of Schemes and Tropes,* 1550; F. Patrizi, *Della Poetica,* 1586). The second-century A.D. handbooks of Aelius Theon, Hermogenes, and Aphtonius were popular throughout the Middle Ages and the Renaissance, and they dictated, as an essential part of the *progymnasmata* or preliminary rhetorical exercises, much work in description of persons, places, and things, treating "vivid description" under the general headings of *enargeia, ekphrasis,* or *hypotyposis.* Dozens of refinements on standard descriptions hold meaning for *ut pictura poesis* but the matter is complicated since many medieval and Renaissance rhetoricians are in conflict over both definitions and examples for *descriptio, characterismus, effictio, mimesis, notatio, informatio, diatyposis, prosopographia, prosopopoeia,* and many other categories that demand varying amounts of formed concrete detail. From classical rhetorical theory also came the *descriptio locorum,* which could include not only fields or general topography but cities and, more specifically, monuments or temples. For more generalized landscapes, the *descriptio temporum,* with its description of spring or winter with all their mythological or symbolic impact, could serve as a picture. Vergil and Ovid, Sannazaro, Ariosto, and Tasso, and Spenser and Milton, all give many examples of detailed landscape description for a variety of purposes.

Descriptive elements such as metaphor or personification could be accepted as "figures of thought" and therefore as parts of amplification, or they could be seen as elements of decoration included to trap the senses. The rhetorical principle of amplification through description was presented in Cicero, *De inventione* (I, xxiv) and the *Rhetorica ad Herennium* (IV, 49 and 50) and was supported in the rhetorical handbooks. Description, especially epideictic, was extensively developed in the poetics of Matthieu de Vendôme, *Ars versificatoria* (ca. 1175) and Geoffroi de Vinsauf, *Poetria nova* (ca. 1210). These theorists codified the portrait, demanding very complete physical details and an exact order of those details from the head to the feet. In general, the twelfth-century Latin *comoedia,* the Old French *fabliaux,* and the medieval romance reveal this rhetorical formula in highly finished pictures of ideal beauty or extreme ugliness with very little suggestion of personal observation or shaded attitude.

Of particular relevance to *ut pictura poesis,* however, is the rhetorical device of *ekphrasis* and "icon," since both were used to designate a description of a work of art following the εἰκόνες ("icon") of Philostratus (A.D. 3) and the ἐκφράσεις (*ekphrasis*) of Callistratus (A.D. 3 or 4). These elaborate descriptions of the second Sophistic rhetorical tradition, one of a gallery of paintings, the other of a group of statues, seem produced in competition with the plastic arts. The work before the writer is presented and then analyzed for its historical and moral value—its humanistic illustrative power?—but not dealt with aesthetically.

The writer and orator used the plastic arts or even competed with the plastic artist, and the detailed description of an art work—*ekphrasis*—is common to both art critics and creative writers.

Art critics have always needed to—or wanted to—offer the work before them through language and, it is fair to say, often saw themselves as painters with words. Philostratus and Callistratus strained to reproduce paintings and statues as well as to instruct the reader both in art appreciation and in the entire story of which the artifact offers but a part. These critics were widely praised and their descriptions imitated, especially in the Italian Renaissance (Philostratus was later translated by Goethe with enthusiasm). To complete the circle, Titian's *Bacchanal, Bacchus and Ariadne,* and *The Feast of Venus* were based on the descriptions by Philostratus. L. B. Alberti in *Della pittura* and, above all, G. Vasari in his *Lives* (1550; rev. ed. 1568) develop many careful descriptions while emphasizing the narrative and the allegorical or expressive material in the painting. Vasari, rather than interpreting the evidence before him, often described an unseen or expressionless face in a painting and assigned meaning based only on his previous knowledge of the scene's literary source (Alpers, 1960). Even with the increasingly refined techniques for visual reproduction, modern critics generally point out verbally—or even presumptuously restructure and so challenge the painter—both details and their arrangement to illuminate an *attached* print.

The list of poets, novelists, and playwrights who were active art critics is long and in each instance a case can be made for the interaction of forms. Bellori, Michelangelo, Lessing, Diderot, Stendhal, Baudelaire, Ruskin, Pater, Morris, Henry James, Klee, and Malraux all produced a significant mass of art criticism in which *ekphrasis* plays an important role.

But the most interesting use of *ekphrasis* is in the enormous number of actual or imaginary works of art portrayed by creative writers. The Greek romances and the writings of Vergil, Ovid, Statius, Martial, Lucian, Apuleius, Claudian, the authors of the *chansons de geste,* Chaucer, Ariosto, Spenser, and Balzac are particularly fruitful sources, as are those of many English poets in the eighteenth and nineteenth centuries (Hagstrum, 1958; Larrabee, 1943; Manwaring, 1925; Hussey, 1927; and Jack, 1967). Poe, Hawthorne, Browning, and Henry James constantly reveal their deep involvement with the plastic arts, while English and American poets of the 1950's and 1960's offer many examples of *ekphrasis,* the most famous being those of Brueghel's works by W. H. Auden and W. C. Williams. Of particular interest is the tradition of "gallery poems" in which the writer places himself in a real or imaginary gallery and describes the works for a usually philosophical end by examining his created microcosm. Common and attractive as these instances of *ekphrasis* are—and useful when considering *ut pictura poesis*—they nevertheless are simply verbal descriptions, and one question raised by Lessing must be asked: Can the reader, moving through time and adding detail after detail, in fact ever form a picture? Or is he finally left with but a general "impression" that might be better and more economically gained by a very few selected details or a telling metaphor?

The poets, then, used the painters, but the painters made still greater use of the poets. Just as Aristotle and Horace at least implicitly assumed that the writer would use known myth, fable, and history as *inventio,* so essentially did the Renaissance art theorist, from Alberti, *Della pittura* (1436) on, see the painter as telling a "story" in space. The generally accepted dictum was that the painter should draw his subject matter from poems, especially epics and romances, as well as from history. The painter, in turning to this "nature" to imitate, was competing directly for the audience's approval, tempting the comparison between the verbal and plastic rendering of a usually well-known event. It could be argued that the painter, rather than being limited by his medium, actually could rhetorically transcend the single, rigidly confined moment since his audience could immediately supply the larger action of the incident from the common knowledge of the entire poem or historical period. Furthermore, by the middle of the eighteenth century, critics began to emphasize the imagination's power in reaction to the plastic stimulus, so that the viewer in drawing on his memory as well as on his own creative powers joined with the painter in creating "moving pictures."

The primacy of "history" painting based on one source or another was essentially unchallenged (until J. J. Winckelmann and Lessing) as the painter caught a significant impassioned moment out of time. (Hogarth in his sequences had to leap the bounds of the single canvas, and he emphasized a "moral" rather than an actual history.) Scenes from Tasso formed the subject of many paintings in the seventeenth century, the greatest by Poussin and Lorrain (Lee [1940], pp. 242–50), and collections of extracts from the great poets, classical and contemporary, were gathered to provide a painter with suitable models of human actions and emotions (G. P. Lomazzo, *Trattato dell'arte della pittura, scultura ed architettura* [1595], VI, 65, and Comte de Caylus, *Tableaux tirés de l'Iliade . . .*). André Félibien set the hierarchy in painting as ranging from the low of still life to the high of meaningful events (preface, *Conférences de l'Académie Royale de Peinture et de Sculpture*, 1669), and Reynolds in his *Discourses* (1769–90) suggested much the same. In the late eighteenth century Diderot's critical scaling strongly supported the French Academy's emphasis on historical painting.

In the sixteenth and seventeenth centuries both the emblem book and the figure poem stand as vivid examples of *ut pictura poesis*, as well as of theories that presented the various arts either as mutually reinforcing agents or as a combination forming a hybrid art such as the masque, ballet, or opera.

The hugely popular emblem books—over 3,000 editions were issued from 1531 to 1700—can be considered a genre that demonstrates the view of poetry and painting as "sister arts." Stimulated by interest in medieval illuminated manuscripts and dream interpretation, as well as Egyptian hieroglyphics (Boas, 1950), the practitioner-theorists developed lengthy, subtle distinctions among "emblemata," *"imprese,"* "devices," "enseigns," "hieroglyphs," "blazons," and other terms (Praz, *Studies*, 1964). Most agreed in stressing the interrelation of a picture, motto, and poem, arguing that none of the elements could stand alone and be meaningful. In contrast to the *titulus*, a metrical description offered with a work of art and meaningless without that work, in the emblem books the poem could stand alone since the scene was often at least suggested in the language, the picture alone since it was in a tradition of iconographic interpretation. Their subjects might be natural phenomena, historical, mythical, or political events, moral doctrine or exhortation. Personifications or virtues, vices, and ideal or stock types as well as allegories were common; the title page of Cesare Ripa's *Iconologia* (1593) reads *non meno utile che necessaria a poete, pittori, scultori, per rappresentare le vitii, virtù, affetti, and passioni humane* ("not less useful than necessary to poets, painters, and sculptors for representing the vices, virtues, emotions, and human passions"). The attractions of the emblem books were not only visual and didactic but intellectual in that the picture and text often were something of a puzzle to be worked out for the pleasure of analogy. Some had a sophistic quality in that the puzzle could indeed be an ingenious display of wit; the poet, in particular, creates rather than derives a world of meaning from the picture.

The emblem, then, may represent an actuality, but it also means an abstract quality or relationship, means it so richly that the image-symbol may be, as it is in Marsilio Ficino's *De vita coelitus comparanda*, confused or merged with the reality it represents.

It has been persuasively argued that the emblem books generated a seventeenth-century poetics based on *ut pictura poesis*: the poet word-paints his emblem and then either reacts mystically or explores rationally, and discovers intricate, recondite, and surprising relations and meanings. The whole theory of correspondence, however, stands behind both the emblem books and "emblematic poetry" and so forms a general "real" basis for illuminating metaphor.

Later developments of the important interactions of language and picture are found in the works of Hogarth, Blake, J. M. W. Turner, and D. G. Rossetti as well as in the eighteenth-century political cartoon and the twentieth-century comic strip. Much of the theoretical discussion of the film centers on the relationship between the "moving image" and dialogue, critics often severely limiting the film's perimeters as a medium by arguing that language should be much reduced or even refined away, an argument that reflects an older one: the title of a plastic work is a statement *about* the work that may over-direct, needlessly reinforce, or seriously interfere with the statement *of* the work of art.

A figure or pattern poem (*carmen figuratum*) in which the line length presents a typographical image of the poem's subject may be considered a tour-de-force variation on the emblem books and their tradition. This form, which can be found in the *Greek Anthology* and Simias of Rhodes (ca. 300 B.C.) as well as in Persian and Chinese literature, was popular and respected throughout Europe in the seventeenth century although it is indeed a forced joining of poetry and painting. Few poems in this tradition, other than George Herbert's "Easter Wings" and "The Altar" (1633), now warrant a reading, and the form, often used for occasional pieces, survived in a sub-literary world of greeting cards and advertisements. One should consider, however, Apollinaire's *Calligrammes* (1918) in which the impact of the cubists' sense of "simultaneity" is apparent. But isolated examples, such as Mallarmé's complicated "Un coup de dés" (1897), Dylan Thomas' ambiguous "Vision and Prayer" (1946) and John Hollander's careful *Types of Shape* (1969), simply testify to the form's rarity. (Note the mouse's long sad tale/tail in Lewis Carroll's *Alice in Wonderland* [1865], Ch. III.) Far more worthy of serious consideration are the innovative "concrete poets" of post-World War II who extended radically the traditional typographical relation of form and content (Geoffroy Tory, *Champ Fleury*, 1529). Drawing on the traditional figure poem as well as on the works of Pound, Joyce, and Cummings, many international experimenters developed, especially in Brazil and Germany, the simply clever "word game" in which "hollow" is printed with very large "O's," "fear" with wavy lines, until a genuine unity of the linear and spatial is gained (Solt, 1968).

In the late seventeenth century many political poems were developed within a convention traced to the Anacreontea (200 B.C.–A.D. 500) as well as to Homer's *Iliad*, the making of Achilles' shield. A poet gives direct instructions to a painter on both the content and form for an historical, biographical, or allegorical painting that grows in the telling. (Robert Browning's "The Bishop Orders His Tomb" [1844] is a late variation on this lively use of point of view.) In *The Last Instructions to a Painter* (ca. 1667), probably by Andrew Marvell, the poet is quite conscious of his aesthetic as well as his more obvious political act since near the end he writes, "Painter, adieu! How well our arts agree,/ Poetic picture, painted poetry. . . ." In the course of the poem "portraits" have been "painted," as well as landscapes for the temporal action. But the poet is clearly aware of a commonly held distinction between the arts and suggests the limitation of expressiveness in paintings: "Where pencil cannot, there my pen shall do't/ That may his body, this his mind explain." He has explicated his own pictures in the course of his poem to gain his ends with double force (cf. Spenser, *The Fairie Queene*, III, Poem 2; Shakespeare, *Timon of Athens*, I; Jonson, *Timber*, pub. 1640, dated 1641; Hobbes, "The Virtues of an Heroic Poem," 1675).

Obviously the easy distinction which allots time to poetry and space to painting is challenged in both the paintings and poetry of this period. From classical times painters and sculptors do in fact present not a simple action or solitary incident but a narrative. The many separate sequences on Trajan's Column (A.D. 113) tell a long story which must be read as must Hogarth's sequences or the before-and-after paintings of the nineteenth-century Hudson River School. Many medieval paintings and sculptures depict within a single frame a variety of scenes from a saint's life. Lessing rejected these—he makes reference to Titian's *Life of the Prodigal Son*—as literary rather than painterly. But such paintings are "in time," and stylistic critics such as Leo Spitzer (1962) and Murray Krieger (1967) argue specifically, and Coleridge and Croce generally, that literature is an object or artifact, that poetry can ultimately be spatial or "still," that the reader combines the sequential details into a spatial moment, that Keats in his "Ode on a Grecian Urn" both uses and transcends time in both content and form.

Following the theories of the imagination of both Hobbes and Locke, early eighteenth-century literary critics, most notably Joseph Addison, along with Joseph

and Thomas Warton (Chapin, 1955; Cohen, 1964), considered description as the basis for poetry since the language appealed most vividly to the image-making faculty. Addison argued that the test of the "true metaphor" was whether or not there was sufficient detail for it to be painted and, in "The Pleasures of the Imagination," *Spectator*, Nos. 411–21 (1712), that a word brought forward the image of an object and that the imagination could paint more vividly than nature. Concurrently there was a developing scientific attitude that demanded careful observation and detailed recording of external actuality in order to approach reality. This provided a tradition for the realism and naturalism of the late eighteenth and nineteenth centuries, this in spite of constant "romantic" challenges that the artist's reactions were the genuine subject of art and that art itself must always reflect moral or psychological tension or conflict.

In the eighteenth century, then, "description" or "pictorialism" developed from being an occasional rhetorical device into almost the dominating matter of a poem. A major example is James Thomson's extraordinarily popular *The Seasons* (1730–46) in which the divine analogy of "God" offered by the book of "nature" reflected deistic as well as traditional Christian concerns and the natural world was a universal book in a universal language (Cohen). The old Renaissance argument of art versus nature was revived, and some of the competition shifted from between art forms to between any medium and nature. Can any language reflect the object? Can any art equal the variety or plenitude and the "vivacity" of nature?

Before the mid-eighteenth century the term "philosophical criticism" stood for what we now call "aesthetics." It is not remarkable at all, given the general preoccupations of the century with its concern for "taste" and tendency toward synaesthesia, that "aesthetics" as a branch of philosophy was finally "established" and named by A. G. Baumgarten in his *Aesthetica* (1750–58). Two French authors, widely popular and often translated, had continued the search for a common basis for the arts. The Abbé Dubos in *Réflexions critiques sur la poésie et sur la peinture* (1719) found the principle to be the imitation of the "beautiful" in nature, while the Abbé Batteux argued for "harmony" in *Les beaux arts réduits à un même principe*. Examples of such works could be multiplied throughout the century since the hundreds of critics who wrote on "taste" inevitably considered both *ut pictura poesis* and synaesthesia. In both David Hume, "On Taste" (1757), and Edmund Burke, *A Philosophical Enquiry into the Origin of our Ideas of the Sublime and Beautiful* (1757), there is a readiness to use not the metaphor but the analogy of the physical taste for

471

the mental. Obviously there was widespread confusion about the nature and function of the senses and faculties as well as of the properties of natural and art objects. Both senses and faculties were readily multiplied as answers to thorny psychological and aesthetic problems while there was a concurrent attempt to synthesize their functions.

The shift from imitative to affective poetry in the late eighteenth century must be considered as a function of the ever-growing concern with the interior of man, his emotional responses. It would be a falsification to underestimate the concurrent growth and change in the theory of language as it concerns *ut pictura poesis*. The enormous popularity of Burke's work on the sublime promulgated widely the theory of the associative value of language and to a significant degree overwhelmed the Lockean concept of language as image-maker. Such a change was the specific cause of the demise of descriptive writing, which was, of course, to be reborn in the early nineteenth-century local color and historical novel as a beginning of scientific realism. In 1761, both Daniel Webb (*An Inquiry into the Beauties of Painting*), and Lord Kames (*Elements of Criticism*) emphasized the importance of successive appeals to the reader in order to effect the true sublime; it cannot be done satisfactorily through the simple instance of the painting but can be gained in poetry (cf. Joseph Spence, *Polymetis* [1747], p. 67). Such theories placed greater emphasis on structure or *dispositio* in poetry and, in conjunction with Burke's argument that words do not cause mental images of things but produce emotion-laden associations, reduced faith in the primacy of set descriptive pieces. There was, furthermore, an increased concern for revealing discovered value in an object rather than for reproducing the object itself. Goethe commented that Ewald von Kleist would have rewritten his heavily descriptive *Der Frühling* (1749) with far less concrete detail and far more on reactions to the objects. This was part of a concern for interpretation characteristic of both science and deism and demonstrated by the sharp interest in physiognomy as well as in elocution with their great emphasis on facial configuration and limb movement.

The parallels between poetry and painting were not enough to satisfy thinkers on aesthetics or psychology, and more arts, particularly music, were widely considered. The rise of critical interest in poetry and music was supported by a developing or resurrected theory that since all arts rose from "nature" and all satisfied man's "taste," they should all work together in expressing and appealing to human emotions. The whole theory of "the association of ideas" encouraged the union or blending of contiguous objects in the memory if not in fact. Although such a union was always implicit in the drama and especially in the Renaissance masque, the popularity of the Italian opera in the eighteenth century was the most immediate demonstration of the concept which was expressed by the Abbé Batteux and by Francesco Algarotti in his *Saggio sopra l'opera in musica* (1755). Batteux was particularly influential since his ideas were given wide distribution by Diderot and d'Alembert in the *Encyclopédie*. The culmination of such theories was, of course, Richard Wagner's *Gesamtkunstwerk* thesis in the nineteenth century.

Parallels between poetry and music had long been made since both functioned in time, seeking "harmony," and, more precisely, both used accent, rhythm, and pause. Charles Avison, in *An Essay on Musical Expression* (London, 1752), developed the points that painting and music both have harmony and proportion and, above all, composition. Poetry with its direct appeal to the reason was seen as superior to music as well as to painting, both of which were essentially sensory, although J. J. Rousseau, Herder, and J. B. Monboddo—all cultural evolutionists—saw music as preceding language historically since it was expressive of man's pre-rational, perhaps spiritual, nature. Following the tradition of the lyric or song, poetry and music were united to gain intensity, just as poetry and painting combined their powers in the emblem books. In prefaces, however, both Dryden (*Albion and Albanius*, 1685) and Gluck (*Alceste*, 1767) warn of music overwhelming the language.

As long as the concept of "imitation" prevailed and the imagination was seen as an "image-making" faculty and language as the prompter of images, the natural analogy was between painting and language; and language with its powers of description dominated poetry. But in the latter half of the eighteenth century, with the rising interest in internal senses or psychological reactions over the reproduction of external objects and with language seen as material for associative emotions, music with its suggestive powers became the appropriate parallel for poetry. Through the general theories of the imagination and the particular one of "sensibility" or "sympathy" the analogy with music answered questions about the mysterious nature of creativity, the organization or "harmony" of subject matter, and the reader's or viewer's relation to the poem or painting. Poems such as Poe's "Bells" (1849) and Verlaine's "Chanson d'automne" (1866) were more than just experiments in sound. (One must recall, however, Dryden's "A Song for St. Cecilia's Day, 1687" and "Alexander's Feast," 1697). The ascendancy of music was such that in the nineteenth century Walter Pater could write that "All art constantly aspires toward the

472

condition of music" ("Giorgione," *The Renaissance*, 1873) and Verlaine, that music is all ("La poétique," 1884). The "symphonic poems" and "tone poems" of Franz Liszt, Hector Berlioz, and Richard Strauss are approaches to this problem of identity but from a different starting point.

The eighteenth-century interest in *ut pictura poesis* was further supported by an attempt to elucidate parallels between music and color. There was a tradition of comparing scales and colors of the spectrum that goes back to Aristotle in *De sensu et sensibili*, and can be found in Indian, Chinese, Persian, and Arabic studies (Albert Wellek, 1951; and see Praz, *Mnemosyne*, 1970, for mathematics and architecture, pp. 60ff.). Athanasius Kircher in his *Musurgia universalis* (1650) confusedly argued at length for the identity of colors and tones, so it remained for Newton in his *Opticks* (1704), Book I, Part II, to give the first generally acceptable account of the relationship. As the poet of Erasmus Darwin's *The Botanic Garden* (1791), Part II, Interlude III, says, "Sir Isaac Newton has observed, that the breadths of the seven primary colours in the Sun's image refracted by a prism, are proportional to the seven musical notes of the gamut, or to the intervals of the eight sounds contained in an octave. . . ." Loud colors, *schreiende Farben, couleurs criardes*, are more than imaginative and vivid expressions since, as Darwin continues, painters and musicians claim "a right to borrow metaphors from each other; musicians to speak of the brilliancy of sounds and the light and shade of a concerto; and painters of the harmony of colours, and the tone of a picture."

The most dramatic result of the scientific account was Louis Bertrand Castel's "ocular clavecin," an elaborate instrument for projecting colors by a keyboard, and this enthusiastic French Jesuit spent years attempting to perfect his color symphonies after the initial announcement of the project in 1725. This theory of "light shows" failed, as did that of Alexander Scriabin in *Prometheus, the Poem of Fire* (1909–10), in part because of technical problems (problems overcome in Walt Disney's film, *Fantasia* in 1940, and with the sophisticated projectors of the 1960's) and in part from the derision of such contemporaries as Diderot, Goethe, and J. J. Rousseau, the last calling him the "Don Quixote of Mathematics" (Mason, 1958). Castel anticipated instruments that would "play on" the senses of smell, taste, and touch, and it is fair to say that he helped prepare the way for the devotion to synaesthesia so prominent in romantic poetry (von Erhardt-Siebold, 1932) and in such works as Baudelaire's "Correspondances" (1857).

In spite of the late eighteenth-century interest in affective rather than imitative art, the vogue of the "picturesque" sustained the interest in *ut pictura poesis*. The term usually meant at this time a landscape "suitable for a painting" or a description of either the landscape or the painting. But it was a deceptively complicated sociological and aesthetic movement reviving with new vigor disputes on the primacy of nature and art, as well as the unity of various arts and crafts. The titles of major works indicate the variety of areas involved in the "picturesque" vision: William Gilpin, *Three Essays: On Picturesque Beauty; On Picturesque Travel; and On Sketching Landscape* (1792); Uvedale Price, *An Essay on the Picturesque, As Compared with the Sublime and the Beautiful; and, on the Use of Studying Pictures, for the Purpose of Improving Real Landscape* (1794); and Richard Payne Knight, *The Landscape* (1794); and *An Analytical Inquiry into the Principles of Taste* (1805). In discussions of "taste," the "picturesque" was seen as something of a middle ground between the relaxing smoothness of the "beautiful" or the exciting infinity of the "sublime," the middle ground achieved through a kind of irregularity or indefiniteness in a landscape. The theory supported the development of genre painting and local color writing as well as attitudes toward travel, local history, gardening, and architecture, with these areas unified not only through similar content but through a characteristic form of roughness, of tactility often suffused by pale light. The impact on the sentimental novel was enormous. It is fair to say that the picturesque is still very much alive with Sunday painters but that its most significant influence can be traced from Constable through J. M. W. Turner to the French impressionists.

Although landscape description looms so large in eighteenth-century literature, the human figure was not neglected. The period's concern with the rational rather than the mythic reading of epics, with ethics and psychology, and with Locke's view of the imagination and language, encouraged a wide use of the Renaissance tradition of "personification" by poets, painters, and sculptors, as well as by critics. Because of the often necessarily generalized visualization of the passions, the virtues and vices, and natural forces—the most usual subjects of personification and allegory—the temptation to see very close parallels among art forms is particularly strong (Hagstrum, 1958; Chapin, 1955) either because distinguishing details are absent or because theories of metaphor to which poets responded often demanded that "vividness" could be best attained by the detailed metaphor—or personification—that could be painted.

It is evident from these many concerns found in the eighteenth century that the search for a clarification of the use and limits of art forms was constant. In 473 general treatises on taste, language, and the association of ideas and in both the theory and practice of description, sublimity, personification, and the picturesque, thinkers and creators were keenly aware of the concept of *ut pictura poesis* or, increasingly, with analogies of music, poetry, and painting.

The major attempt at ordering or at least checking the chaos appeared in Lessing's *Laokoön* (1766). Through an adept use of example he affirmed the basic distinction between the spatial mode of painting and the temporal mode of poetry, a distinction derived from Moses Mendelssohn and J. J. Winckelmann and widely developed and promulgated in much of German aesthetic theory until the twentieth century (cf. Friedrich Schiller, *Über naive und sentimentalische Dichtung*, 1795). A major justification for this position is that a poet can establish and develop presented character so that a reader's sympathy and understanding will be with that character at any moment, even a moment that might make us reject an unknown figure. The painter does not have this opportunity to develop character but is limited to presenting the person or god in a single characteristic expressive pose, for otherwise a viewer simply cannot recognize and therefore understand the figure portrayed: an angry Venus is possible for the poet but not for the painter unless he gives us something in addition to the figure—a symbolic artifact or a name—to indicate that the figure does indeed represent Venus.

The entire problem is a very rich one not yet resolved. Any repeated motif, whether it be abstract design or realistically repeated identical figures, tends toward motion. Just as with a colonnade, the very repetition moves not only through space itself but, for the viewer, exists in time. Simply determining the interrelations of parts in a painting is often a complex exercise with time introduced into spatial objects by the use of intricate detail, an obscure theme, multiple points of views, or varied reactions to an event pictured within a single space. A viewer must explore and analyze these various components if he is to comprehend or realize the painting, sculpture, or building. For that matter any three-dimensional object suggests that movement must take place by either the object or the viewer if its totality is to be comprehended.

A significantly more complex aspect of time may be seen by considering the fact that any painting is in time, is within a culture and within a specific tradition. Time, then, is part of a painting. For the viewer of that painting there is the effect of memory in that culture and tradition, again a fact of time that complicates even further a viewer's exploration of the given art object. Both time and space then are aspects of individual memory and of history as well as simply objects of sensory perception, and the early and common argument, codified by Lessing, that a painting is seen and absorbed instantaneously is clearly untenable.

Lessing's position in general was weakened since he was so committed to a concern for beauty of bodily form, especially in sculpture, that he tended to confine the expression of the passions, long a key aspect of history painting, to poetry alone. At the same time, one must insist that he was not as rigid as some critics have suggested. He was clearly aware of the imagination's capacity to add time to a painting, to complete an action depicted, or for that matter, to understand, through the pictured act, that earlier acts had taken place and were still affecting the present impassioned moment.

One mark of the impact of Lessing is Irving Babbitt's *The New Laokoön: An Essay on the Confusion of the Arts* (1910). He saw the *ut pictura poesis* of the eighteenth century as a dehumanizing rejection of action for stasis. The emphasis on "things" to be imitated was compounded by the other imitation, that of diction, which led to a deadening of all poetry. Like his predecessor, Babbitt sought too neat a compartmentalization not only of art forms but of genre. The description of a landscape is "nonhumanistic," however, only if "humanistic" is defined as having man as its overt object. This position is a misrepresentation of the very humanistic position in the late eighteenth-century conception of landscape as meaningfully human since it was viewed as the book of God and was, in addition, a reflection of human perception or the human mind. Still further, and perhaps of greater importance ultimately, was the fact that a viewer was concerned with that landscape and that for him it had very human symbolic or emotive value.

In the nineteenth century, concrete detail was used to individuate character and place, to set, intellectually as well as visually, a particular entity apart from all others of its class. The formation of a picture with language was no longer seen as a significant goal, although many writers and painters revealed a warm preoccupation with each other's medium. The use of concrete detail took two basic directions, both easy to anticipate. The first was the continuation of scientific observation and reporting, close, precise, and extensive, which is best exemplified in the local color or historical novel popularized by Walter Scott. His long descriptions of both places and people are in defiance of Lessing's argument that no reader can "compose" a clear picture from a mass of detail; he can only admit to the existence of the facts. Balzac, of course, very consciously saw himself as an historian of his own time, and throughout the enormous bulk of his work he details clothing and architecture, making that record an essential part of his contemporary history. In keeping with both his scientific and his mystical bent, his facial descriptions always reflect the popular pseudo-sciences of physiognomy and phrenology in his attempts to use all observable means to reveal the truth.

The other direction of the use of concrete detail is in the suggestive; the selected dominant detail or very few details will give the reader a direction to pursue concerning a person or place. This more compressed approach may be easily seen in the works of Jane Austen and Stendhal, both of whom but very rarely describe the physical appearance of a person or place. The literature of the nineteenth century can well be examined by asking such simple questions as why the writer uses concrete detail and why just this much if there is to be anything approximating the painting of a picture. The nineteenth-century painter continued to develop the interest in the audience's imaginative involvement and so, through the use of vague suggestion rather than through the completeness of the medieval *effictio*. The cooperative creative art was, then, necessarily sequential: painting was moved from the simply spatial, poetry from the passively temporal. French criticism, since A. C. Quatremère de Quincy, *Essai sur la nature, le but et les moyens de l'imitation dans les beaux arts* (1823), is based on the audience's awareness that the art object is in fact an art object and that the audience will both cooperate with and submerge itself in the illusion (Gombrich, 1948).

Throughout the nineteenth and twentieth centuries both accidental and deliberate mixing of the arts is constantly evident. Rimbaud arbitrarily assigned color values to vowel sounds, and D. G. Rossetti both wrote and painted *The Blessed Damozel*. With the nineteenth-century Pre-Raphaelites and *parnassiens*, as well as the twentieth-century members of the *Bauhaus* and *De Stilj*, workers in a wide variety of art forms saw their arts as sisters (Fosca, 1960; Hatzfeld, 1952; Praz, *Studies*, 1964; and Ringe, 1960). Both opera and ballet grew enormously in popularity, bringing many art forms together to effect one whole. Many novelists clearly saw their world through the painter's eye. The film, especially the "animated cartoon," has enriched the complexities of the drama and opera since it is indeed an art of "moving images" with, usually but by no means necessarily, interaction of language and music. The old problems of space and time seem to merge in a film such as *Last Year at Marienbad* (1962).

In language development through "show and tell," in industrial and military training films, and in advertising on television, both language and visual image are deliberately combined to reinforce each other, both to clarify and to intensify meaning. In his prophetic *Brave New World* (1932) Aldous Huxley invented "feelies," films for which the audience was wired to receive tactile impressions analogous to, and thereby reinforcing, its visual ones. Post-World War II film makers have, admittedly only sporadically, attempted an olfactory reinforcement by having various scents carried through the ventilating systems to make more real their depictions of forest or sea movies.

In the older art forms the twentieth century has the concrete poetry discussed earlier, and Cézanne broke the space-time problem in painting. In Cubism, the eye moves through different planes on the flat surface and, in effect, moves around the object rather than viewing it from a fixed point. One can consider all art following Cézanne as little but a footnote, although Picasso was even more radical in that he not only moved around an object but through it. A variation on space-time in twentieth-century painting was the attempt in Futurism to give a single view of successive movements, which can be found in Balla's *Girl Running on the Balcony* (1912) and Duchamp's *Nude Descending a Staircase, No. 2* (1913). Extremely effective multiple-exposure photographs by such artists as Gjon Mili (*Life*, October, 3, 1969) give this sense of a full sequence of movement within a single frame, within a single figure. But perhaps the ultimate in the history of *ut pictura poesis* is found in the mobile of Alexander Calder. It is painting and sculpture and narrative as it continuously describes in time its own ever-varying space. If sound and language is included, as it often is in developments by such "New Tendency" artists as Jean Tinguely and Len Lye, the traditional questions about the discrimination of the arts seem fruitless.

### ORIENTAL CONCEPTIONS

In China, there is little doubt but that the nature of the ideograph as well as the use of the same brush for writing and for the usually monochromatic painting encouraged the identification of the sister arts. The Chinese poet, Su Shih (Su Tung-po, 1036–1101) wrote,

Tu Fu's poems are figureless paintings, Han Kan's paintings are wordless poems.

Developments in the relationship of poetry and painting are remarkably parallel to Western views. Although we know painting was seen as a respectable avocation by the second century, it was not until the Sung dynasty (960–1280) that it became clearly established as a fine art. In the twelfth century the state examinations for official posts included one in painting: the "problem" was set by asking the candidate to paint a scene suggested by a few lines of poetry. (This method reflects the re-creation of poetry by means of painting practiced at least as early as the fourth century.) During the later part of this period the premiss that the painter should be a learned man became generally accepted. From the fifteenth century "figure poems" were well-known.

Western culture since the eighteenth century has been rich in landscape poetry. Chinese literature, however, reveals an older and more constant interest since the end of the Han dynasty (A.D. 220), although a full development did not occur until about the fourth century when landscape, and especially mountains, symbolized cosmic forces. From the fourth century on, with the introduction of Buddhism and Taoism, nature became reality itself and, as a part of religion, an object of contemplation. Poetry reflected this pervading concern through regular pictorialization of landscape (Frankel, 1957, and Frodsham, 1967).

*BIBLIOGRAPHY*

Items of major importance are Ralph Cohen, *The Art of Discrimination* (Berkeley, 1964); Jean H. Hagstrum, *The Sister Arts* (Chicago, 1958); Renssalaer W. Lee, "*Ut Pictura Poesis:* The Humanistic Theory of Painting," *Art Bulletin,* **22** (1940), 197–269; and Mario Praz, *Mnemosyne: The Parallel between Literature and the Visual Arts* (Princeton, 1970). A full bibliography appears in *The Bulletin of Bibliography* (Oct.–Dec. 1971).

Important corrective warnings against easily imagined parallelisms among the arts are René Wellek and Austin Warren, "Literature and the Other Arts," *Theory of Literature* (New York, 1949); René Wellek, "The Parallelism Between Literature and the Arts," *English Institute Annual, 1941* (New York, 1942); and G. Giovannini, "Method in the Study of Literature in Its Relation to the other Fine Arts," *Journal of Aesthetics and Art Criticism,* **8** (1950), 185–95.

Of particular value for general context are George Boas, trans., *The Hieroglyphics of Horapollo (1505)* (New York, 1950) and Paul O. Kristeller, "The Modern System of the Arts: A Study of the History of Aesthetics," *Journal of the History of Ideas,* **12** (1951), 496–527, **13** (1952), 7–46.

The significance of the emblem books is handled in Robert J. Clements, *Picta Poesis: Literary and Humanistic Theory in Renaissance Emblem Books* (Rome, 1960). The rich area of *ekphrasis* calls for more study but the following item is particularly useful: S. L. Alpers, "Ekphrasis and Aesthetic Attitudes in Vasari's *Lives,*" *Journal of the Warburg and Courtauld Institutes,* **23** (1960), 190–215.

Various other aspects may be pursued in Chester F. Chapin, *Personification in Eighteenth Century English Poetry* (New York, 1955); H. H. Frankel, "Poetry and Painting: Chinese and Western Views of Their Convertibility," *Comparative Literature,* **9** (1957), 289–307; J. D. Frodsham, "Landscape Poetry in China and Europe," *Comparative Literature,* **19** (1967), 193–215; Walter John Hipple, Jr., *The Beautiful, The Sublime, and The Picturesque* (Carbondale, 1957); Wilton Mason, "Father Castel and His Color Clavecin," *Journal of Aesthetics and Art Criticism,* **17** (1958), 103–16; Mary Ellen Solt, ed., *Concrete Poetry: A World View* (Bloomington, Indiana, 1968); Erika von Erhardt-Siebold, "Harmony of the Senses in English, German, and French Romanticism," *Publications of the Modern Language Association,* **47** (1932), 577–92; and Albert Wellek, "Farbenmusik," *Musik im Geschichte und Gegenwart* (Kassel, 1951).

JOHN GRAHAM

[See also China: **Classification of the Arts;** Criticism, Literary; Iconography; **Mimesis; Poetry and Poetics;** Taste.]

# VIRTÙ IN AND SINCE THE RENAISSANCE

*1. Introduction.* The word "virtue" (and its counterparts in most other languages) is used to attribute some kind of value to conduct or action. Its meanings are therefore potentially as various as the bases on which men value their acts. The predominant meaning in English has become moral virtue; a virtuous man is one who lives in accord with certain moral standards. Even in our language, however, other senses of the word survive. When we speak of the virtue of a particular course of action, we mean its power to achieve certain results. We also speak (slightly archaically, perhaps) of the virtue of a drug, meaning its inherent potency or efficacy. These latter senses have in common their attribution of value to action (or to the potential for it) on the basis of power or efficacy, whereas the concept of moral virtue derives value from intent or result. This is the fundamental division among meanings of virtue: on the one hand, a "moral" sense which focuses on the conformity of actions to approved standards or ends, on the other a "non-moral" sense concerned with the power of an action (or an actor) to be effective or to achieve a desired end.

The history of the idea of virtue is the history of both these senses of the word, and of the relations between them. Often the two senses have existed side by side, and men have not been troubled by the differences between them. In times of moral crisis, however, the contradictions potentially present in "virtue" have come to the surface and have been employed by thinkers to criticize old values and aid in the development of new ones. The ambivalence of "virtue" provides a means to challenge dominant moral values through an emphasis on other values also inherent— while perhaps submerged—in existing language. This is what occurred during the Italian Renaissance. After a period in which the idea of virtue came increasingly into men's minds, Machiavelli set out a critique of traditional moral virtue through a reemphasis on virtue in the purely active sense.

**2. Early Renaissance Virtue.** It is not surprising that the age of the Renaissance in Italy saw a lively interest in the idea of virtue. A concern for understanding and evaluating human action was fostered by the many and often novel activities of Renaissance men. The citizens of the various towns witnessed more political activity than most other Europeans; each independent town was a political nucleus, organizing its own internal life and its relations with other towns. Economic activity was also more varied than in nonurban areas. Banking, trading, and manufacturing raised many questions about the effectiveness and the morality of human action. Yet the great traditional source of moral standards, the Church, was in the throes of a long and deep crisis, involving the "Babylonian captivity" of the papacy in Avignon and the scandal of the Great Schism which followed. Men were turning elsewhere for moral counsel, above all to the great traditions of Greece and Rome. It is significant too that many of the humanists who led the revival of antiquity were not professional philosophers or theologians in the tradition of the medieval schools, but poets, politicians, and rhetoricians with little commitment to systematic philosophical thought. They were therefore freer to develop the implications of living in the urban and secular society of the day.

In the period from Dante to Machiavelli, both the "moral" and the "non-moral" senses of virtue (*virtú* or *virtù* in Italian) were in general use. All the traditional virtues were denominated as such, but the same writers who regarded faith or justice or courage as prime virtues also used the term in the other sense. Dante, echoing Aristotle, wrote (*Convivio*, I, v) that "Everything is virtuous in its nature when it does that for which it is ordained." Following this definition, he regarded human speech as virtuous when it "makes clear human thought," since this was its purpose in the divine scheme. For Boccaccio too, a virtuous speech was an effective one; neither of these writers thought a speech had to be edifying to be virtuous. Using a similar definition, Dante attributed *virtù* to the devil as well as the saints: "He moved mist and wind by the *virtù* his nature gave" (*Purgatorio*, V, 114). Such connotations survived into the fifteenth century. When Savonarola said that Florence had become the instrument of the *"virtù divina,"* he meant God's power and purpose manifested in activity, not the realization of particular virtues. Savonarola regarded tyrants as the most vicious of men, but he attributed *virtù*—in the sense of ability or capacity—to them also. Observing that the tyrant will try to excel other men in every

activity, Savonarola added that "when he cannot do it by his *virtù*, he will try to be superior by fraud and deception" (*Prediche e scritti*, 171, 183).

In these citations—especially the last—glimmerings of Machiavelli's usage of *virtù* are visible. Yet there is a definite gap between these writers and Machiavelli. It is the space between accident and purposeful awareness. Both the moral and the non-moral senses existed in Renaissance Italian, and the two came to the minds of the period's writers with nearly equal facility. But one sense did not interfere with the other, a reference to the devil's or the tyrant's *virtù* neither reflected nor created any crisis of moral action or theory. This would come later.

Several currents of Renaissance thought demonstrate that the understanding of virtue was a matter of concern during the fourteenth and fifteenth centuries, and that the word's meaning was changing. First, some men began to evolve a conception of virtue as a generally admirable quality in human action, rather than the sum of particular qualities ("virtues") which conformed to religious or philosophical prescriptions. Artists sought to represent not only the traditional individual virtues, but "virtue in general" (*virtus generaliter sumpta*), and some complained that the existing iconographical tradition offered no models for them to follow. It is not entirely clear what these artists—Giovanni Pisano, Francesco da Barberino, Filarete, whose chosen name meant "lover of virtue"—meant by "virtue in general," but their use of Hercules to represent the quality they had in mind gives an indication. Herculean virtue is first of all manliness, courage, strength; what Petrarch thought about when he wrote (in lines that would be quoted by Machiavelli) "*Virtù* will take arms against violence,/And let the fight be short!" (*Italia Mia*, lines 93–96). Yet this may not have been all that was meant by *virtus generaliter sumpta* under the aspect of Hercules. In the early Renaissance, the story of "Hercules at the crossroads" returned to popularity after being practically forgotten during the Middle Ages. Hercules' choice, which Cicero had described as being between *virtus* and *voluptas* was recalled first by Petrarch, who compared it to the fundamental moral choice he thought all men faced. Moreover, following Cicero, Petrarch remarked on the closeness of "virtue" to the Latin word for man, *vir*, and thought that one probably derived from the other (*Fam.*, XXIII, 2, 28). Thus the "virtue in general" symbolized by Hercules could represent a wide range of admirable human qualities. From this point of view the lines between such usually distinct conceptions as "virtue," "humanity," and "virility" might become obscured.

The difficulty of keeping these notions separate appears clearly in one very common theme of Renaissance literature: the opposition of virtue and fortune. The theme had its source in antiquity, when fortune, either as an abstraction or as a goddess, was thought to have considerable control over human life. Livy tells that *Fortuna* ("fortune") was the favorite goddess of the Romans. Yet some classical writers—especially those in the tradition of the Stoics—preserved one realm of life free of the dominion of fortune: the realm of virtue. Seneca wrote that "Fortune can only take away what she has given; but she does not give virtue" (*De constantia sapientiae*, V, 2). The virtue he had in mind was moral worth, *honestas*. The man who recognized *honestas* as the only good worth seeking was free of fortune. "He who reckons other things as goods comes under fortune's power" (*Epistles*, 1, xiv, 1). The virtue which thereby triumphed over fortune had a highly moralistic coloration, but at the same time it connoted personal strength: the power to find fulfillment within one's self and remain indifferent to external rewards. Cicero often referred to the Stoics as the most manly or most virile of philosophers.

Both the element of moralism and the element of personal strength are present in Renaissance discussions of the power of virtue over fortune. Petrarch noted that fortune is "the ruler of all human things except for virtue" (*Fam.*, I, 2, 24). He wrote a whole work (*De remediis utriusque fortunae*) with the intention of providing men with material for strengthening their inner defenses against fortune. He also distinguished between "*fortunatos*" and the "outstanding men" whose lives he described in *De viris illustribus:* "Outstanding men overcome all things by the power of virtue." Leon Battista Alberti also wrote of virtue's dominion over fortune in terms derived from the Stoics. Virtue alone brings men happiness, he said; it is more than content with itself, worth far more than all the things subject to fortune (*Della famiglia*, 24, 80, 149).

At the same time that the traditional notion of virtue as moral worth was being merged with the separate sense of virtue as inner, personal strength, the humanists were also engaged in raising broad questions about the nature of moral virtue, and whether particular qualities should be accepted as virtues. These Renaissance debates about moral virtue also had an important classical background. Several of Cicero's writings report the disagreements between followers of the various ancient philosophic schools represented at Rome, and particularly between the Stoics and the Peripatetics. The Stoics regarded *honestas*, moral worth, as the only genuine good, and instructed the wise man in indifference to everything else. The Peripatetics agreed that moral worth or virtue was the chief good, but they thought that human nature required other supports if a man were to live well: health for one thing, and favorable circumstances for another. The Peripatetics thus recommended a different line of conduct than the Stoics, and as Cicero several times observed, it was a life much more in accord with the notions of ordinary men than the Stoic ideal. Cicero supported the Stoics in some of his writings and the Peripatetics in others, but for the public orator or statesman, addressing ordinary men in the language of everyday life, Peripatetic ethics was the most appropriate.

Petrarch recalled these themes in Cicero's writings. He often sought to approach the Stoic ideal of conduct (to which he gave a Christian coloration), and he addressed Stoic counsels both to himself in his *Secret*, and to friends and readers in his letters and other works. Yet he regarded the level of virtue to which the Stoics aspired as unattainable in this life. Stoicism made a fine philosophic ideal, but who could actually live according to it? "You will act differently as a philosopher and as a man," he wrote in one of his letters. "No one is so given to wisdom that he does not, when he returns to the common human state, condescend also to public ways of acting" (*Fam.*, XXI, 13, 1). The "public ways of acting" Petrarch sanctioned here were anything but libertine; they were the mores of the best public figures, not the worst. Yet in some other places (notably the *Secret*) Petrarch seemed to regard any lapse from philosophical morality as a descent to the level of the despised "crowd." Certainly he was aware that the morality of philosophers contrasted sharply with the way most men—even the best intentioned ones—actually lived their lives.

The separation between a strict philosophical morality and some Renaissance ideals of conduct was widened by later writers. Matteo Palmieri argued that anger (*ira*) could be an aid to the virtue of courage rather than a vice, "provided that the choice of the danger to be faced is made with virtue." To assert this was to remove some restraints on sheer human activity which had been proposed in the name of moral virtue. Comparing the active life and the virtues appropriate to it with the contemplative, the speaker in Palmieri's *Della vita civile* concluded that "The solitary life is placed after the active" and flatly declared that the "higher" forms of virtue, "being heavenly things, are not proper to men" (1529 ed., p. 34r). Palmieri went further. One of the features of Stoic morality as Cicero had presented it was the affirmation that there was no distinction between what was morally good, *honestum*, and what was useful for man. Man pursued his utility by pursuing morality. Matteo Palmieri agreed that according to "subtle philosophy" this was true enough, but pointed out that it did not fit the common opinion of ordinary men, who saw quite clearly the distinction between what was morally good and what was good for themselves. Since he was writing about ordinary life, Palmieri accepted the reality of the distinction between what was good and what was useful (ed. cit., p. 91r). A later humanist writer, Giovanni Pontano, also thought it necessary to separate the two, at least in the political sphere. Other humanists used the notions of common sense and the observation of ordinary life to push the criticism of traditional ideals of virtue further. Poggio Bracciolini was aware that "vice" might sometimes play a positive role in the world. He recognized that simple force was responsible for much of human accomplishment. A speaker in one of his dialogues asserted that empires had been established by force rather than by law; it followed that everything achieved within them depended on force too. "Everything excellent and worthy of remembrance has been achieved by wrong-doing, injustice and contempt for law," was the admittedly highly rhetorical conclusion (*Utra artium, medicinae an iuris civilis, praestet*, ed. Garin, p. 29). In such declarations as these, the gap between the early Renaissance concern for *virtù* and Machiavelli's development of the idea—the gap between accidental confusion of the two basic senses of the word and the purposeful confrontation of them—narrowed. Yet only Machiavelli would close it completely.

*3. Machiavelli.* Machiavelli was heir to the humanist discussions of virtue. In his intellectual formation and in his chief occupation—as a secretary in the Florentine chancery—he had many ties with the humanists. But the situation of Italy in his time was much more troubled than before. Machiavelli's lifetime (1469–1527) saw a new stage in the crisis of the Church and the invasion of Italy by foreign armies, bringing the rapid rise and fall of individual and group political fortunes there, and the increasingly apparent subjection of the peninsula to foreign powers. In this situation the problems of *virtù*, of morality and power, grew more intense. Much ink has been spilled on Machiavelli's use of the word *virtù*, and a great deal of confusion about it remains. Some of the difficulties can be cleared up if the linguistic and intellectual background discussed above is remembered, and if two different facets of Machiavelli's approach to *virtù* are kept separate. These are, in the order we shall discuss them: (1) the confrontation between traditional moral virtue and the non-moral sense of virtue as capacity for action; (2) the development of a theory of human action through the analysis of virtue in the second sense. The discussion of these two topics and of the relationship between them should show that, while Machiavelli had no "doctrine of *virtù*" (that is, he did not always use the word to the same effect), he did

have a sustained concern for its meaning which raised the consideration of it to an entirely new level.

Machiavelli used the word *virtù* in many of the senses current in his day. When he said that "A prince should show himself to be a lover of the virtues, and honor men excellent in every art" (*Prince*, XXI), the virtues he had in mind included the standard moral and intellectual ones. When he said that "The *virtù* of infantry is more powerful than that of cavalry," he meant military capacity or capacity for effective action in general (*Disc.*, II, xviii). His declaration that the fortune of a city depends on the *virtù* of its founder (*Disc.*, I, i) may seem less traditional, but it is not; here "virtue" means what it meant to Dante in *Convivio*: "Everything is virtuous in its nature when it does that which it is ordained to do." Machiavelli attributed virtue to the admittedly wicked Roman Emperor Severus (*Disc.*, I, x), but even Savonarola had admitted the *virtù* (talent or capacity) of a tyrant. The most common sense of *virtù* in all Machiavelli's writing is military. Most of the men described as *virtuosi* by Machiavelli are military leaders; very often, the *virtù* of an individual or a city is simply his or its military prowess. Sometimes the connotation is military even when on the surface it does not seem to be. For instance, the virtue despised in a corrupt city (*Disc.*, I, xviii) is revealed as military when Machiavelli explains that it was the city's security against its enemies which led to the diminishing regard for virtue.

Of all the specific meanings of "virtue," military virtue is the one which best embodies the general notion of capacity for effective action. In Machiavelli as in no other Renaissance writer, we see the other meanings of "virtue" measured against this fundamental one, and often discarded when they do not meet the standard. Machiavelli's rejection of traditional morality has sometimes been questioned, but he himself quite frankly admitted—indeed insisted on—it.

My intention being to write something of use to those who understand, it appears to me more proper to go to the real truth of the matter than to its imagination; . . . for how we live is so far removed from how we ought to live, that he who abandons what is done for what ought to be done will rather learn to bring about his own ruin than his preservation. A man who wishes to make a profession of goodness in everything must necessarily come to grief among so many who are not good (*Prince*, XV; trans. L. Ricci).

There is an echo here of Petrarch's comment about those who live in "the common human state" accepting "public ways of acting," but Machiavelli's moral stance was far more radical. His reason for rejecting a strict philosophical morality was not, as in Petrarch, the acceptance of ordinary human life, but the requirements of effective action in a world fraught with evil and danger. Consider Machiavelli's most general axiom about moral virtue: "He who ponders well the whole question will find one thing that looks like virtue, which to follow would be his ruin, and another that looks like vice, which when followed brings his security and well-being" (XV). Following this principle, Machiavelli argued that, in Hannibal, cruelty was a virtue. It was his "inhuman cruelty [condemned by Livy] which, together with his infinite virtues, made him always to be revered and fearful in the eyes of his soldiers; and without cruelty, his other virtues would not have sufficed for that effect. Imperceptive writers admire his action while condemning its principal cause. And that it is true that his other virtues would not have sufficed can be observed from [the comparison with] Scipio . . ." (*Prince*, XVII). The repetition of "his other virtues" makes the point quite clearly. The sense of virtue as what is morally right has been forced out by Machiavelli's overriding concern for effective action.

Machiavelli was not able to hold to his own conclusion with perfect consistency. Some princes had to be regarded as wicked despite their success. Machiavelli was puzzled by such men, as his account of Agathocles the Sicilian, tyrant of Syracuse, makes clear.

He who considers the actions and virtues of this man will see little or nothing that can be attributed to fortune. . . . Yet it cannot be called virtue to kill one's fellow citizens, betray one's friends, be without faith. . . . For all that, considering the virtue of Agathocles in getting in and out of dangers, and his greatness of soul in bearing with and overcoming adversities, there seems to be no reason for judging him inferior to the most excellent leaders. Nonetheless, his ferocious cruelty and inhumanity, together with infinite acts of wickedness, do not allow him to be enshrined with the most excellent men. Therefore, what was accomplished without either fortune or virtue cannot be attributed to either one (*Prince*, VIII).

"Yet . . . For all that . . . Nonetheless . . .": this is the grammar of uncertainty. Remembering the general statement about virtue and vice and the praise of Hannibal's cruelty already noted, it is hard to see what made Machiavelli hesitate about Agathocles. Cesare Borgia, whose place in Machiavelli's pantheon is so famous, was also guilty of cruelty, betrayal and lack of faith; besides, Machiavelli specifically justified each of these qualities in general terms elsewhere. It would seem that Machiavelli was himself somewhat awed by his own conclusions about the true nature of virtue. At least this passage shows that Machiavelli had a reluctance to give up some traditional moral standards; to understand what overcame this reluctance we must examine the second facet of his analysis of virtue.

Several writers on Machiavelli have compared his use of the word *virtù* to the sense defined by the physician Galen: *potestas quaedam efficiendi* (the power to do or accomplish something). Machiavelli's criticism of traditional moral virtue stemmed from its lack of this ability. Yet how could Machiavelli be confident that the virtue he envisioned would be effective in the world? To answer this question, we must examine the connection between Machiavellian virtue and five closely related topics: fortune, necessity, animality, audacity, and order.

The limit of Machiavellian *virtù* can be described in a word: *fortuna*. Like other Renaissance writers, Machiavelli sometimes described fortune's power as irresistible. "All the histories show that men can act in accord with fortune but not oppose themselves to her; they can weave her webs but not break them" (*Disc.*, II, xxix). This gave no justification for despair; fortune's plans were never known, and men could always hope that their own purposes would fit them. Still, in this passage at least, Machiavelli spoke of fortune and "the heavens" with the respect due the gods.

Yet many other statements in his writings show that Machiavelli did not think men's lives were wholly under fortune's sway. In a famous place in *The Prince* he limited her control to "half our actions, or thereabouts." What is most significant about Machiavelli's view of fortune's boundaries, however, is not their limits but their nature. Unlike other Renaissance writers, Machiavelli refused to accept fortune's strange power as a mystery beyond man's ken and separate from his nature. On the contrary, Machiavelli made fortune derive from human nature almost to the same extent as *virtù*. In Chapter XXV of *The Prince,* and in a nearly contemporaneous letter to Piero Soderini, Machiavelli attacked the perplexing question why the same actions at different times yielded opposite results, and why the same results followed at separate times from contrasting acts. The answer lay in the harmony or discord between men's ways of acting and the conditions of their time. "A family, a city, each man has his fortune founded on his style of action" (*modo del procedere*).

I believe that just as nature has given men differing faces, so has she given them differing minds and imaginations. From this it arises that everyone directs himself according to his mind and imagination. And because on the other side times and situations differ, those accomplish their desires and are happy who fit their style of action to the time, and those on the contrary are unlucky who argue with their time and situation by their actions (*Lettere*, ed. F. Gaeta, p. 230).

A man's fortune thus depended first of all on himself, on his personal style. This perspective sometimes led

Machiavelli to a strong affirmation of the power of *virtù*. The Romans were successful because of *virtù*, not *fortuna;* it was their reputation for valor that earned them the good fortune of having others fear to attack them (*Disc.*, I, ii). The men discussed in Chapter VI of *The Prince* had founded states by their own virtue, without the help of fortune. "Examining their lives and actions, one sees that they had nothing more from fortune than the occasion, which gave them material to shape in whatever way they liked." Without an appropriate occasion their virtue would have been wasted, but without their virtue the occasion would have passed unrecognized. "Their virtue made the occasion known."

Yet, the idea that those men succeed whose style of action fits the times defined the limitations of human action as well as its potential strength. In fact, Machiavelli's most consistent deduction from the idea that those men are happy whose character fits the time was not that men should change to fit the times, but that they are unable to do so. The fundamental notion in Machiavelli's theory of human action is not the flexibility of human nature but its rigidity. The man prudent enough to change his actions to suit the time will never be found, Machiavelli declared in *The Prince*, "both because one cannot deviate from the path to which nature inclines him, and because having always prospered by going in a certain way, one cannot persuade himself to depart from it" (XXV; see also *Lettere*, p. 231). Piero Soderini always acted with "humanity and patience," and succeeded as long as those qualities corresponded to the needs of action in his time. Julius II did everything with "force and fury"; luckily for him the situation required just his temper while he lived. Knowing how to act well in a certain way allowed men to succeed in their purposes when the times were right. But since this ability came from nature, not choice, it contained the seeds of failure as well as success.

Fabius Maximus proceeded with his army carefully and cautiously, removed from any fury and from Roman audacity; and good fortune made his style fit well with the times.... And that Fabius acted in this way from his nature and not by choice is apparent, since when Scipio wanted to take the armies into Africa to finish up the war, Fabius spoke much against it, like one who could not cut himself off from his own style and custom (*Disc.*, III, ix).

Speaking in this way, Machiavelli made fortune weigh more heavily in the balance than virtue.

There is only a rough consistency at best in Machiavelli's view of the relationship between virtue and fortune: he tempered his shifting emphasis from one to the other with the reflection that each had control about half the time. Yet he did not really mean (as the above quotation might imply) that *virtù* was only a fit between natural necessity and fortune. Everyone by nature had a personal character, but not everyone was a *virtuoso*. One thing that distinguished the man of virtue from others was precisely his ability to overcome the defects that the rigidity of nature entailed. Hannibal was a great general through making himself feared by his men, Scipio by making himself loved by them (*Disc.*, III, xxi; Machiavelli's choice for fear over love is not so clear here as in *The Prince*). Yet both these courses of action had inescapable dangers; the man who made himself feared would also be hated, the man who was loved would be despised. "Thus it matters little for a military leader which of these paths he takes, as long as he is virtuous and his virtue makes him respected among the men. For when the virtue is great, as it was in Hannibal and Scipio, it cancels out all the errors that are committed through making one's self loved or feared too much." This is not to say that these men were free of the necessary rigidity of human character: they were subject to the general rule that "No one can take the middle path, precisely because our nature does not allow it." But they were able to "make up for their excesses by an extraordinary virtue."

The other side of virtue's relationship with fortune, then, was her relationship with necessity. But whereas fortune was a limitation on the effectiveness even of the *virtuoso*, necessity was not a limitation on virtue; it was rather a precondition for it. Machiavelli was intensely preoccupied with necessity; by one count, the word (*necessità*) appears seventy-six times in *The Prince* alone. His acceptance of its place in man's life is strong and clear: soldiers who go to foreign countries "have more necessity to fight, and that necessity makes virtue, as I have said more than once" (*Disc.*, II, xii). Other writers had thought necessity strengthened virtue; to Machiavelli necessity created virtue. "Men never do anything well except through necessity. Where there is an abundance of choice, and where license can enter in, everything is immediately filled with confusion and disorder" (*Disc.*, I, iii). Because "virtue is greater where choice has less sway," wise founders of cities establish laws that prevent citizens from softening under the influence of prosperity (*Disc.*, I, i).

We can better understand the dimensions of Machiavelli's emphasis on necessity if we see that it is closely tied to another of his favorite themes: the animal or bestial element in human nature. In contrast to some other Renaissance writers (such as the Neo-Platonists), Machiavelli thought that man must not attempt to escape his animality. Not only did he use the well-known metaphors of the lion and the fox, and declare that "a prince must know how to use bestial conduct as well as human" (*Prince*, XVIII); he also

481

wrote an allegorical poem which made clear his acceptance of human bestiality and its connection with necessity. The poem, *The Golden Ass,* derives from a classical legend Apuleius popularized, but its themes included those of Machiavelli's major works: the rise and fall of political units and the general affirmation that "evil follows good and good evil, and the one is always the cause of the other" (lines 103ff.). The real moral of the work was that man cannot escape his nature (lines 88–90); it was for this reason that the hero had to assume the guise of an ass in order to find a way out of his difficulties. In the poem a pig explains why animals are happier than men: "We are more friends of nature than you; thus she bestows her virtue more on us, making you beggars for all her goods." Whatever the allegory of the golden ass meant to other Renaissance writers, to Machiavelli it meant that man must accept his own natural necessity, of which bestiality is both a metaphor and a part.

The animal element in human necessity brings this theme close to another of Machiavelli's favorite topics, audacity. In a famous passage in *The Prince,* Machiavelli said that, since fortune is a woman, the audacious and impetuous have a better chance to master her than the cautious or hesitating. A chapter title in the *Discourses* reads: "Many times one achieves with impetuousness and audacity things that could never be achieved by ordinary means" (III, xliv). Machiavelli's stress on audacity was sometimes tempered by his general principle that action must fit the times: after all, Fabius Maximus had success with his waiting game. Yet this should not be seen as a contradiction. Holding back one's forces might be good military strategy, but it was not the same thing as the hesitation that followed from indecisiveness. It was indecisiveness to which audacity was most strongly opposed, and this links it most clearly to the necessity which creates virtue in Machiavelli's mind: both are opposites of choice (*elezione*), and *virtù* dissolves in the realm of choice. "Let everyone do whatever his spirit tells him, and with audacity" (*Lettere,* p. 229). The *virtuoso* acts in accord with necessity, and with animal naturalness. "To Machiavelli, animals possess the pristine genuineness which, in man, is weakened by reason. Man's control over his world depends on his attaining a level of instinctiveness where he becomes part of the forces surrounding him" (Felix Gilbert, *Machiavelli and Guicciardini,* p. 197).

Machiavelli would not make man so purely animal as to destroy the reason which distinguishes him from the beasts. On the contrary, *ragione* and *prudenzia* are often close to *virtù*. But whereas in most traditional ethics reason's task is to oppose or temper the passions, in Machiavelli man's distinguishing and most useful quality is his ability to order his passions so as to use their power more effectively. The difference between the Roman army and its barbarian enemies lay not in superior forcefulness but in superior order; this allowed the Romans to fight longer and more effectively than their opponents. "Where an ordered virtue (*virtù ordinata*) uses passion with method and plan, no difficulty weakens the army or makes it lose heart. . . . The opposite occurs in those armies where there is passion but no order" (*Disc.,* III, xxxvi). "Order"—this word is close to the heart of Machiavellian virtue. It had many more senses in Machiavelli's language than in ours. An *ordine* was a method, an institution, a procedure; it was the *ordini* of the exemplars of *virtù* which Machiavelli told his readers to follow (*Prince,* XXVI). Fortune held sway where there was no *virtù ordinata* to resist her (*Prince,* XXV). What distinguished the Roman Republic (and the Roman army) from others was its *ordine* (*Discourses,* passim). Where there is good order there is virtue.

But order is also related to necessity. In a well-ordered army, soldiers have no choice but to fight; in a well-ordered state, the laws force citizens to virtuous conduct. Order is the main principle of political life for Machiavelli, because it is the bridge between the human world and the world of natural necessity; through political organization man creates his own world of necessity—the only environment in which his *virtù* can flourish.

In the theory of human action which emerges from Machiavelli's reflection on *virtù,* the idea of necessity is central. Only when we have surveyed the dimensions of Machiavelli's belief in the power of necessity are we prepared to appreciate the full extent of his rejection of traditional moral virtue.

We noted earlier that Machiavelli hesitated to give the title "virtuous" to Agathocles the Sicilian—despite his talent, spirit, and success—because of Agathocles' wickedness. But the category of necessity makes Machiavelli's hesitation irrelevant. The men described in *The Prince* are given as examples of conduct, and the question of whether the wicked ones are also *virtuosi* had no bearing on whether they were to be imitated. It was enough to give the examples of wickedness "without entering into the merits of their kind, because in my judgment it is sufficient that one driven by necessity imitate them." In the light of Machiavelli's enthusiasm for necessity, his hesitant declaration that the deeds of Agathocles "cannot be called virtue" seems to arise simply from an unwillingness to proclaim the most revolutionary implications of his new point of view.

This conclusion is strengthened by one element in Machiavelli's attitude toward virtue as he conceived it: his awareness that virtue could be dangerous. In quiet and peaceful times, virtue was valued less than in perilous and difficult ones; wealth and influence were valued more than personal merit. To give outstanding men less honor than was due them was a "disorder," Machiavelli said, "which has caused the ruin of many republics. For those citizens who see themselves despised, and who know that the cause of it is the times being easy and not dangerous, think up ways to disturb things, promoting new wars to the damage of the republic." There were only two ways to deal with this problem: either keep everyone poor so that wealth could not have unmerited influence, or else keep the state always at war or ready for it, in order to provide continuous opportunities for "the virtue of man" (*Disc.*, I, xvi). Thus virtue as Machiavelli understood it had a threatening aspect: if not given satisfaction, it became a harmful force.

All this underlines one of Machiavelli's most pervasive traits: his fundamental pessimism about human nature. Yet the discussion of his meditation on virtue would not be complete if we failed to recall that, side by side with this pessimism about man Machiavelli nurtured a spark of optimism about nature at large. His belief that good could come out of evil had a definite optimistic edge in times as bad as his own. Several times he affirmed his belief that virtue can shine most brightly when the night is darkest; one of these was the famous last chapter of *The Prince*, exhorting the Medici to unite Italy and drive out the foreign invaders. Despite his general pessimism, he did not believe that the total quantity of virtue in the world was less in his own day than it had been in Roman times; it was only so scattered about that its effects were felt less, and not at all in Italy. In affirming this belief, Machiavelli personified "the world" in a revealing way. In ancient times, he said, "the world" had moved its virtue successively from the Syrians to the Persians to the Romans, but after their time "the world no longer kept its virtue all together" in one place (*Disc.*, II, preface). The personification of "the world" in this passage recalls the medieval idea (still present in a quotation from Savonarola given above) that virtue came from God. Here, however, the notion has been secularized, so that virtue in a political body derives from "the world" instead of from God. The implications of this are optimistic, since Machiavelli entrusted man's destiny to "nature" with the same willingness that medieval men had entrusted it to the divinity.

Perhaps it is from the point of view of this optimism that we should consider one of the most characteristic elements of virtue in Machiavelli's thought: independence. To preserve ones independence is the first rule of politics. "A wise prince should build on foundations that are his, not on other people's." "Only those defenses are good, certain, and lasting, which depend on you yourself and on your virtue" (*Prince*, XVII, XXIV). Cesare Borgia's most significant accomplishment was establishing his independent power despite the fact that he had received his state by the power of the king of France. Certainly the celebration of independence has obvious immediate and practical import. But for Machiavelli it had a more philosophical meaning as well. In Machiavelli's day the political crisis of Italy and the moral crisis of the Church led men to lose confidence in themselves and in their power to live well in the world. Machiavelli's stress on independence was a response to this condition. He saw trust in outside powers instead of in one's own as the sickness of Italian politics; his basic objection to Christianity was that it turned men's efforts to a world beyond their own. In opposition to both, Machiavelli recalled men to a fundamental trust in themselves and in the natural world of which they were a part. The most enduring aspect of Machiavelli's message was his defiance of despair, his insistence that even in the worst of times men must trust in themselves: only to do so was virtue.

**4. Modern Virtue.** The history of the idea of virtue in the centuries since Machiavelli's time belongs in part to the vast history of ethical theory (a subject dealt with elsewhere in this work), and in part to the topic Machiavellism. Yet some indications about how later perspectives on virtue relate to Machiavelli may help to place Machiavelli's thought in a broader context, and suggest its wider importance.

Men's attitudes toward virtue have continued to be shaped by changing circumstances, and especially by the pressures on conduct and action which derive from the political situation in the widest sense. In post-Renaissance Europe the disorder Machiavelli had lamented gave way to something like the order he had desired. The agency of this change was a creation of which Machiavelli has often been called the prophet: the modern state. The governments of Europe gained more effective control of their territories, expanding and improving their administrative bureaucracies, and gaining a monopoly of violence through a centrally organized and controlled army. In this new situation the maintenance of political order seldom required the kind of unrestricted and audacious action for which Machiavelli called. By the eighteenth century, as Friedrich Meinecke has observed, there reigned in the European monarchies "deep peace, order and discipline. To continue making use of . . . Machiavellian methods within the state was now entirely superfluous, and therefore seemed hateful" (*Machiavellism . . .*, p. 284). Of course, rulers and governments still dealt with each other in ways that recalled Machiavelli's precepts, 483 but this was true only of relations between states, not of political life within them. While Machiavelli's thinking might be applauded with regard to foreign policy, his ideas were not likely to be seen as relevant to other spheres of conduct; because of this, the notion of virtue as effective action was restricted to one realm of human affairs—war and diplomacy—and was not apt to challenge the idea of virtue as morality. In the absence of this challenge, the discussion of virtue did not lead to a general consideration of human action as it had in Machiavelli's thought.

Most post-Renaissance writers simply affirmed the traditional notion of moral virtue in opposition to Machiavelli. What was happening to the idea of virtue, however, is best understood not with reference to one of these thinkers, but in connection with a man who has sometimes been compared to Machiavelli, Thomas Hobbes. Hobbes's political theory was based on a very stern recognition of the realities of early modern politics, but he did not generally consider virtue from a Machiavellian perspective. In Hobbes's view,

The sum of virtue is to be sociable with them that will be sociable, and formidable to them that will not. And the same is the sum of the law of nature; for in being sociable, the law of nature taketh place by the way of peace and society; and to be formidable, is the law of nature in war, where to be feared is a protection a man hath from his own power (*Elements of Law*, Part I, Ch. 17, para. 15).

For Hobbes, "force and fraud are the two cardinal virtues" in time of war, but the same is by no means true in time of peace or within a peaceful state (see John Laird, *Hobbes*, pp. 180–81). Hobbes saw a clear separation between a peaceful realm of moral virtue and warlike realm of virtue in the non-moral sense; the second presented no Machiavellian challenge to the first. The same observation applies to the views of Frederick the Great of Prussia (1712–86). In his *Réfutation du Prince de Machiavel* (1739; Voltaire altered the title to *Antimachiavell*), Frederick rejected Machiavellian virtue as meaning only the skill of a rogue. True virtue, he implied, is eternal and unchanging, and needs no favorable circumstances to make itself known. Frederick later questioned some of the harsh criticisms he had made of Machiavelli in his youthful *Réfutation*, but his change of heart regarded only foreign policy, not conduct in general, or the consideration of virtue.

Thus by the eighteenth century the moral sense of virtue reigned unchallenged by the alternative of "the power to act effectively." The article on "Vertu" in the famous *Encyclopédie* of Diderot and d'Alembert reflected this purely moral sense. There virtue was

described as "one, simple and unalterable in its essence, the same in all times, climes and governments" (p. 517). It was "the constant observation of the laws that are imposed on us." Virtue was an inner light, a sentiment given to all men by God, the foundation on which all human societies and all laws were built. The author of the article noted that the original sense of *vertu* had been strength or courage, and suggested that accordingly the word virtue retained a connection with effort and will which distinguished it from goodness: "We say that God is good, and not virtuous, because goodness is essential to his nature, and because he is fully perfect by necessity and without effort" (ibid.). But this statement was a mere gesture; in the rest of the article there is nothing to prevent our reading virtue as a synonym for goodness.

The Enlightenment's conviction that virtue was equivalent to morality and that its eternal essence was not threatened by the vicissitudes of fortune was a tribute to the high level of civilization and order achieved by the *ancien régime*, but the *vertu* of the *Encyclopédie* had lost the compelling drive to comprehend man's power to act in the world, the drive that shaped Machiavelli's meditation on *virtù*. It should be no surprise that when something like the Machiavellian approach to virtue reappeared, its spokesman was a man in revolt against the social and political order which had grown up in Europe since the Renaissance: Friedrich Nietzsche (1844–1900). Nietzsche's conception of virtue arose from his search for man's true self under the many layers of convention and coercion that hid it; his new man or "overman" (*Übermensch*) was the man who has "become what he is," as the subtitle of Nietzsche's book *Ecce Homo* put it. True virtue contributed to this human growth, but it had to be sharply distinguished from conventional morality.

Virtues are as dangerous as vices, in so far as they are allowed to rule over one as authorities and laws coming from outside, and not as qualities one develops one's self. The latter is the only right way; they should be the most personal means of defence and most individual needs—the determining factors of precisely our existence and growth, which we recognize and acknowledge independently of the question whether others grow with us with the help of the same or of different principles. . . . The extent to which one can dispense with virtue is the measure of one's strength; and a height may be imagined where the notion "virtue" is understood in such a way as to be reminiscent of *virtù*—the virtue of the Renaissance—free from moralic [sic] acid (*The Will to Power*, Secs., 326, 327).

Nietzsche's notion of virtue revived some of the essential elements of Machiavelli's; virtue was power over one's self and one's environment; it depended on the harmony of the self with the natural, biological world, and one of its major components was the individual's freedom or independence. Yet Nietzsche went beyond Machiavelli. Nietzsche admired the outstanding individuals of the Renaissance (he knew Jacob Burckhardt, in whose work the concept of the Renaissance became inseparably linked to the notion of individualism), but Nietzsche's own individualism was much more radical than Machiavelli's had been. In part this was due to the nineteenth century's developmental or historical conception of human personality, which stemmed from Hegel and the romantics, and which permitted a much greater attention to the uniqueness of the individual than Machiavelli's more static and typological psychology allowed. Yet Nietzsche's individualism and his conception of virtue also drew strength from his rejection of the very institution whose discipline Machiavelli required for most virtue: the political community or the state. Whereas Machiavelli's sense of human requirements always took him into the realm of politics, Nietzsche was convinced that only the individual, the "single one" could find human self-realization. The state blocked the way:

Now almost everything on earth is determined by the crudest and most evil forces, by the egotism of the purchasers and the military despots. The State, in the hands of the latter . . . wishes that people would lavish on it the same idolatrous cult that they used to lavish on the Church (*Schopenhauer as Educator*, Sec. 4; Kaufmann, *Nietzsche*, p. 166).

Earlier the development of the State had put an end to Machiavelli's political kind of speculation about virtue; now Nietzsche saw in the dominance of the state a force which stunted the development of real *virtù*. In this there was both great insight and great irony, for however brilliantly Nietzsche illuminated the condition of modern European man, he seems to have been unaware that his idealization of *virtù* was a celebration of one of the sources of that very condition. In Machiavelli's hero, Cesare Borgia, Nietzsche saw only a man of power and will whose self-control separated his *virtù* from vice (*The Will to Power*, Sec. 871); that the action of men like Cesare contributed to the oppressive growth of state power escaped him. The apolitical Nietzsche fixed his gaze on a virtue whose worst enemy was tyranny and whose political implications were anarchistic; he did not see that the Machiavellian *virtù* he invoked was an antidote to anarchy and that it contained a willingness to countenance tyranny in anarchy's place. Nietzsche's revival of Machiavellian *virtù* was not the result of an identical aim, but of the dialectical union of opposites; both

anarchy and tyranny render ordinary moral virtue invalid and demand that men seek within themselves a new foundation for their action. This is the moral of the history of "virtue."

### BIBLIOGRAPHY

Before Machiavelli, texts: L. B. Alberti, *I Libri della famiglia*, ed. Cecil Grayson, in *Opere volgari*, Vol. I (Bari, 1960). Matteo Palmieri, *Libro della vita civile* (Florence, 1529). Petrarch, *Le Familiari* (*Familiarum rerum libri*), here cited as *Fam.*, ed. in 4 vols. by Vittorio Rossi, the last vol. by Umberto Bosco (Florence, 1933–42). Girolamo Savonarola, *Prediche e scritti*, ed. Mario Ferrara (Milan, 1930).

Before Machiavelli, commentary: Werner Jaeger, *Paideia: the Ideals of Greek Culture*, trans. Gilbert Highet, 3 vols. (New York, 1939), on the Greek idea of virtue (*aretē*). Theodor E. Mommsen, "Petrarch and the Story of the Choice of Hercules," *Medieval and Renaissance Studies*, ed. Eugene F. Rice, Jr. (Ithaca, N.Y., 1959). Erwin Panofsky, "Artist, Scientist, Genius: Notes on the Renaissance—Dämmerung," *The Renaissance: Six Essays* (New York and Evanston, Ill., 1968), esp. p. 169 and n. (and the other works of Panofsky cited there).

Machiavelli, texts: The most recent edition in Italian is the Feltrinelli Edition, Vol. I, *Il Principe e Discorsi*, ed. Sergio Bertelli (Milan, 1960), here cited as *Prince* and *Disc.* respectively; Vol. II, *Arte della Guerra e scritti politici minori*, ed. Sergio Bertelli (Milan, 1961); Vol. VI, *Lettere*, ed. Franco Gaeta (Milan, 1961); Vol. VIII, *Il teatro e scritti letterari*, ed. Franco Gaeta (Milan, 1965); all vols. contain bibliographical essays. Translations, unless otherwise identified, are by Jerrold E. Seigel. The best English edition of the *Discorsi* is *The Discourses*, trans. with intro. and notes by Leslie J. Walker, S.J. (New Haven, 1950). The most recent translation is *Machiavelli, The Chief Works and Others*, trans. Allan Gilbert, 3 vols. (Durham, N.C., 1965).

Machiavelli, commentary: Eric W. Cochrane, "Machiavelli 1940–1960," *Journal of Modern History*, 33 (1961), 113–36, is a bibliographical article. Felix Gilbert, *Machiavelli and Guicciardini* (Princeton, 1965); idem, "On Machiavelli's Idea of *Virtù*," *Renaissance News*, 4 (1951), 53–55, and the discussion by L. C. MacKinney and Felix Gilbert, ibid., 5 (1952), 21–23 and 70–71. R. de Mattei, *Dal premachiavellismo all'antimachiavellismo europeo del cinquecento*, course of lectures at Rome University, 1955–56 (Rome, 1956). Eduard Mayer, *Machiavelli's Geschichtsauffassung und sein Begriff virtù* (Munich and Berlin, 1912). Friedrich Meinecke, *Machiavellism: The Doctrine of Raison D'Etat and Its Place in Modern History*, trans. Douglas Scott (London, 1957). Gennaro Sasso, *Niccolò Machiavelli: Storia del suo pensiero politico* (Naples, 1958). Neal Wood, "Machiavelli's Concept of Virtú Reconsidered," *Political Studies*, 15 (1967), 159–72.

After Machiavelli, texts: *Encyclopédie ou Dictionnaire raisonné des sciences* (Berne and Lausanne, 1781), Vol. 35,

485

art. "Vertu." Frederick the Great, *Réfutation du Prince de Machiavel (Antimachiavell)*, *Oeuvres* (Berlin, 1846–57), Vol. 8. Thomas Hobbes, *Elements of Law, Natural and Politic* (Cambridge, 1928); idem, *Leviathan* (London, 1651, and subsequent editions). Friedrich Nietzsche, *The Will to Power*, trans. Anthony M. Ludovici, 2 vols. in *The Complete Works of Friedrich Nietzsche*, ed. Oscar Levy (New York, 1964), Vols. 14 and 15.

After Machiavelli, commentary: the works of de Mattei and Meinecke cited above. John Laird, *Hobbes* (New York, 1934; 1968). Leo Strauss, *The Political Philosophy of Hobbes* (Chicago, 1952). Walter Kaufmann, *Nietzsche* (Princeton, 1960; 1968).

JERROLD E. SEIGEL

[See also Fortune; Happiness; **Machiavellism;** Necessity; Relativism in Ethics; **Renaissance Humanism;** Right and Good; State; Stoicism.]

# VIRTUOSO

THE TERM "virtuoso" originated in Italy and was used earlier there than in England. The first English use listed in the *Oxford English Dictionary* was in John Evelyn's *Diary* on March 1, 1644, when Evelyn had been travelling on the continent for some time. Writing from Paris, he mentioned "one of the greatest Virtuosas in France, for his Collection of Pictures, Achates, Medaills, & Flowers, especially Tulips & Anemonys." Walter E. Houghton, Jr., the first to write extensively on the subject, cites an earlier use by Henry Peacham whose *Complete Gentleman* (1634) became a sort of handbook to the virtuosi. Discussing classical antiquities such as statues, inscriptions, coins, he said that the possession of rarities, because of their cost, "doth properly belong to Princes, or rather to princely minds," then added, "such as are skilled in them, are by the Italians termed *Virtuosi.*"

But the movement in England had begun much earlier than the use of the word. As the term came to be used before the Restoration, it implied a collector or connoisseur of objets d'art, i.e., a gentleman—Mr. Houghton points out that the movement was extremely class-conscious—a man of wealth and leisure, a student but not a scholar. His studies were not devoted to such utilitarian ends as professional success or commercial gain. There seems to have been a fusion of the long traditions of scholar and courtier, the result being neither the one nor the other. The idea behind the term emerged in England particularly during the reign of James I in a period of wealth and comparative leisure. Sons did not feel the devotion to public service

with which many of their Elizabethan fathers had been occupied. Gentlemen lived less at court than on country estates, occupied with "learned Pleasure and delight." James's son, Prince Henry, who died in 1612 at the age of eighteen, had been well on the way to becoming the leader of the virtuosi. His Highness, wrote one of his subjects, perceiving the nobility and the gentry "too much given to ease," attempted to attract them to the study of antiquities and painting in which he himself took great pleasure. The heir presumptive had already made a good beginning on the fine gallery of paintings which his brother further developed. John Evelyn, writing to Samuel Pepys much later in the century, remembered that the prince had collected books and statues, and "a Cabinet of ten thousand Medals, not inferior to most Abroad, and far superior to any at Home."

In a lengthy passage in *The Anatomy of Melancholy* (Part II, sec. 2, member 4; first ed. 1621) Robert Burton seems almost to give a recipe for virtuosi, although his purpose was to recommend study as a cure for melancholy. He urged the melancholic to put himself to school to "Maps, Pictures, Statues, Jewels, Marbles." He advised him "to view those neat Architectures, Devices, Scutcheons, Coats of Arms," and added that he should "peruse old Coins, of several sorts in a fair Gallery, Artificial Works, Perspective Glasses, Old Reliques, Roman Antiquities." In his usual lavish fashion, he added other lists of objects, interest in which would distract the mind from melancholia and presumably produce a collector and a connoisseur. It is interesting to notice that at the conclusion of his lengthy account Burton turns to collection on the part of melancholy women, almost seeming to introduce a type that we shall find called the "virtuosa."

A contrasting attitude is shown in one of the most familiar passages in *The Advancement of Learning* (1605), in which Francis Bacon implied that what was to be called the "virtuoso" was really a dilettante. A majority of men who "entered into a desire for knowledge" did so for the wrong reasons from Bacon's point of view: "sometimes upon a natural curiosity and inquisitive appetite; sometimes to entertain their minds with variety and delight; sometimes for ornament and reputation; and sometimes to enable them to victory of wit and contradiction; and most times for lucre and profession." The true end of learning, to Bacon, should be "the benefit and use of man . . . the relief of man's estate." Bacon did not use the word "virtuoso" but the distinctions implied in his passage were to become overt when the term took on new meaning in the period of the Restoration.

John Evelyn is the best single example of the English virtuoso both before and after the Restoration.

Wherever he went on his extensive travels he collected curios, pictures, books, varieties of objets d'art. He visited museums and the estates of nobility and gentry, reporting their collections in dozens of letters and passages in the *Diary*. One entry for September 29, 1645 may give an idea of the range of his curiosity:

I went . . . to see the Collection of a Noble Venetian Signor Rugini; he has a stately Palace, richly furnish'd, with statues, heads of the Roman Empp, which are all plac'd in an ample room: In the next was a Cabinet of Medals both Latine & Greeke, with divers curious shells, & two faire Pearles in 2 of them: but above all, he abounded in things petrified, Walnuts, Eggs, in which the Yealk rattl'd, a Peare, a piece of beefe, with the bones in it; an whole hedg-hog, a plaice on a Wooden Trencher turnd into Stone, & very perfect: Charcoale, a morsel of Cork yet retaining its levitie, Sponges, Gutts, & a piece of Taffity: Part rolld up, with innumerable more; In another Cabinet, sustained by 12 pillars of oriental Achat, & raild about with Chrystal, he shew'd us several noble Intaglias, of Achat, especially a Tiberius's head, & a Woman in a Bath with her dog: Some rare Cornelians, Onixes, Chrystals &c in one of which was a drop of Water not Congeal'd but plainly moving up & down as it was (shaken); but above all was a Diamond which had growing in it a very faire Rubie; Then he shew'd us divers pieces of Amber wherein were several Insects intomb'd, in particular one cut like an heart that contain'd in it a Salamander (*Diary*, ed. de Beer, 1955).

In the years following the Restoration Evelyn combined with his other varied interests a knowledge of contemporary science.

In 1662 was established the Royal Society of London for Improving Natural Knowledge which brought together a group of what we today call "scientists," who added to their number intelligent laymen—divines, aristocrats, philosophers, men of letters. Scientists, in any technical sense, were in the minority. An excellent example of the inclusion of amateurs may be seen in the election of Samuel Pepys, then a naval official. Pepys, to be sure, was a "collector" of sorts—of ballads, pictures, music, books. Amateur of science though he was, Pepys became President of the Royal Society in 1684. It is interesting to notice that Pepys seldom referred to the organization as "the Royal Society." In many of his notations it was, as at his first meeting on February 15, 1667, "the college of vertuosoes."

With the establishment of the Royal Society, the term "virtuosi" came to take on new meaning, applied as it was to "collectors" in science. The term was used seriously by the scientists themselves. Robert Boyle, for example, frequently called himself and his fellow-workers "virtuosi," and one of his works was named *The Christian Virtuoso*. But the prevailing use of the term outside of the Society was satirical. Science—not

yet so-called—was still in its infancy, and a man who devoted himself to collecting in such a field seemed to outsiders, particularly satirists, an Autolycus, a snapper-up of unconsidered trifles. Laughter was led behind the scenes by no less a person than King Charles, officially the patron of the Royal Society. His Majesty prided himself on being a scientist, and had his own laboratory in which he experimented, particularly in chemistry. But Pepys reported in his *Diary* on February 1, 1664 that the King spent part of an evening laughing at the Royal Society. "Gresham College [the Royal Society] he mightily laughed at, for spending time only in weighing of ayre, and doing nothing else since they sat."

Satire after satire poured from the press, but we shall here concern ourselves only with the most popular one, *The Virtuoso* of Thomas Shadwell, first performed at the Dorset Theatre in May, 1676. This included the many themes satirized in most of the others. The experiments which Shadwell reduced to laughter were all real ones that had been performed before the Royal Society, several by Robert Boyle and Robert Hooke, whose places in the history of science have grown more and more important as time has gone on. Sir Nicholas Gimcrack, the "Virtuoso," is discovered lying upon a laboratory table where he is learning to swim by imitating the motions of a frog in a bowl of water. When asked whether he had practiced swimming in water, he replies that he hates the water and would never go near it. "I content myself," he said, "with the speculative part of swimming; I care not for the practical. I seldom bring anything to use. . . . Knowledge is my ultimate end." Robert Boyle's many studies on luminescence are parodied in the Virtuoso's reading the Geneva Bible by the light of a leg of pork. Robert Hooke's important microscopical observations, which laid the basis for modern microscopy, are reflected in Gimcrack's reiterated enthusiasm for his own expensive microscopes. Gimcrack's nieces, resenting his misuse of their money, say that he has spent two thousand pounds on microscopes to find out the nature of eels in vinegar, mites in a cheese, and the blue of plums, which he finds to be living creatures. He has made a profound study of spiders but is not concerned to understand mankind. Gimcrack offers his visitors a lecture on ants, whose eggs he has dissected under a microscope. One visitor says in an aside "What does it concern a man to know the nature of an ant," to which the other replies, "O it concerns a virtuoso mightily; so it be knowledge, 'tis no matter of what."

In common with many of his countrymen, Gimcrack's creator made him greatly interested in experiments by the Royal Society, a decade before *The Virtuoso*, on blood transfusions. These had begun with transfusions between dogs, continued with cross-transfusions between various animals, and came to a climax with human transfusions, performed in France a little earlier than in England. Sir Nicholas Gimcrack, too, had performed his first transfusions on dogs, but in human transfusion he went beyond the Royal Society, when he transfused the blood of a sheep into an insane man:

The patient from being maniacal or raging mad became wholly ovine or sheepish; he bleated perpetually and chew'd the cud; he had wool growing on him in great quantities; and a Northamptonshire sheep's tail did soon emerge or arise from his anus or human fundament.

Gimcrack's uncle, well-named Snarl, may have the last word, so far as *The Virtuoso* is concerned: "If the blood of an ass were transfus'd into a virtuoso, you would not know the emittent ass from the recipient philosopher."

Satire upon the virtuoso continued throughout the century and was still lively in the time of Addison and Steele. In *Tatler* 216 for August 26, 1710 appeared "The Will of a Virtuoso." At his death, all that Sir Nicholas Gimcrack left to his family were rarities such as "a dried cockatrice . . . three crocodile's eggs . . . my last year's collection of grasshoppers . . . my rat's testicles . . . all my flowers, plants, minerals, mosses, shells, pebbles, fossils, beetles, butterflies, caterpillars, grasshoppers and vermin." The third Earl of Shaftesbury in his *Characteristics* (1711) attempted to restore to their original position the "virtuosi or refin'd wits of the Age," and make them what he felt they should be, "the real fine Gentlemen, the Lovers of Art and Ingenuity," but throughout the eighteenth century the word largely denoted the pseudoscientist rather than the collector of objets d'art.

Since the New Science interested women almost as much as men, it is not surprising to find the development of a feminine counterpart to the virtuoso, the virtuosa or "Philosophical Girl," as she was frequently called. Her prototype may well be considered Margaret Cavendish, Duchess of Newcastle, whom Charles Lamb called "a dear favorite of mine in the last century but one," but who has frequently been considered "mad Madge." A voluminous writer, an encyclopedic reader, she was much interested in science. One of the more embarrassing occasions faced by the Royal Society was that upon which this spectacular noble lady practically ordered it to give a command performance for her. The most familiar account of the visit on May 23, 1667 is given by Pepys:

Anon came the Duchesse with her women attending her. . . . The Duchesse hath been a good comely woman; but her dress is so antic, and her deportment so ordinary, that I do not like her at all, nor did I hear her say anything that was worth hearing, but that she was full of admiration, all admiration. Several fine experiments were shown her of colours, loadstones, microscopes, and of liquors; among others, of one that did, while she was there, turn a piece of roasted mutton into pure blood, which was very rare. . . . After they had shown her many experiments, and she cried still she was full of admiration, she departed, being led out by several Lords that were there.

The minute-book of the Royal Society contains a list of the various experiments performed for the benefit of the Duchess. They were largely in the hands of Robert Boyle and Robert Hooke, except for the one that Pepys considered "very rare." This, the interested reader may be glad to know, was "the dissolving of meat in the oil of vitriol."

Under the influence of her husband, Mistress Pepys became to some extent a virtuosa. After Samuel Pepys had engaged a tutor to teach him arithmetic which, like a majority of his contemporaries, he had never learned, he noted on October 21, 1665, when a pair of globes had been delivered to him: "This evening . . . I begun to enter my wife in arithmetic, in order to her studying the globes, and, I hope, I shall bring her to understanding many fine things." He noted on February 15, 1663: "After prayers to bed, talking long with my wife and teaching her things in astronomy." On August 13, 1664 Pepys bought a microscope, through which he and Mistress Pepys attempted to observe, encountering characteristic beginners' problems: "my wife and I with great pleasure, but with great difficulty before we could come to find the manner of seeing anything."

The learned lady had already become a type, as Molière's comedies show, but Molière's were not virtuosae. The "Philosophical Girl," like the *femme savante*, came into her own in France. In 1686 Bernard le Bovier de Fontenelle published his *Entretiens sur la pluralité des mondes*. It is doubtful that any treatment of a woman character has ever been so successful. Seven editions had appeared by 1724, four more were published during the eighteenth century, and at least nine in the nineteenth century. The work became a world-classic with a total of almost one hundred editions in at least six languages. Within two years of its French publication it was translated into English three times, one of the translations, fittingly enough, by a woman, Aphra Behn's *A Discovery of New Worlds. From the French* (1688). Far from being satiric, the *Entretiens* is a charmingly sympathetic treatment of a beautiful Marchioness who for six evenings strolled with a Philosopher between clipped hedges of roses, while he taught her the elements of Cartesian astronomy, together with some principles of microscopy. The lady was an interested and highly intelligent auditor, who learned her lessons well. Here we find disquisitions on planets, the stars, the moon, Cartesian vortexes, the possibility of life in other planets, all that had been observed in the new universe of space discovered by Galileo's telescope, on the one hand, Giordano Bruno's philosophy on the other, with occasional excursions into the other new universe of microscopic life.

English women were not behind the French in reading Fontenelle. Joseph Addison left an amusing picture in *The Guardian* for September 8, 1713:

It is always the custom for one of the young ladies to read, while the others are at work. . . . I was mightily pleased, the other day, to find them all busy in preserving several fruits of the season . . . reading over *the plurality of worlds.* It was very entertaining to me to see them dividing their speculations between jellies and stars, and making a sudden transition from the sun to an apricot, or upon the Copernican system to the figure of a cheese-cake.

In more sober mood, Addison devoted part of *The Spectator* paper for October 25, 1712 to Fontenelle's discussion of a universe of life containing in large and small all possible varieties of life. Fontenelle's work set a pattern, both on the continent and in England for the writing of works on popular astronomy intended for the layman. Various of these imitations have been discussed by Gerald Dennis Meyer in *The Scientific Lady in England,* listed in the Bibliography of this article. The closest approach to the *Entretiens* was by Francesco Algarotti in *Il Newtonianismo per le dame* in 1737, in which the author clarified for ladies the theories of light and color in Newton's *Opticks.* Like Fontenelle Algarotti used the device of dialogue between a noble lady and a philosopher. Fittingly enough, this was translated into English by a virtuosa, Elizabeth Carter, one of the most learned ladies in England, who published in 1739 *Sir Isaac Newton's Philosophy Explain'd. For the Use of Ladies.*

Partly under the influence of Fontenelle, but largely because the English virtuosa was coming into her own, editors found a new buying public for journals. John Dunton's *Athenian Mercury* (1690–97) was intended equally for men and women readers. John Tipper's *Ladies Diary* (1704–1804) and Ambrose Philips' *Free Thinker* (1718–21) were issued specifically for women readers, who contributed letters to both. Some numbers of the various periodicals edited or written by Addison and Steele were expressly addressed to women. In addition, Steele published in 1714 *The Ladies' Library* in three volumes, each dedicated to a woman, and pretending to have been written by a woman. Steele himself posed only as a "Gentleman Usher," leading "the Fair into their Closets, to the perusal of this useful as well as delightful Entertainment." Some of the ex-

cerpts of which the volumes were composed were on religious, others on literary matters; a number were devoted to teaching ladies philosophical and scientific ideas. Again we find women instructed in astronomy and microbiology. The latter proved particularly interesting to women, many of whom by this time possessed microscopes. Like publishers, glass-grinders had found a new public (as advertisements show), preparing for women exquisite glasses in special cases which ladies could carry with them as gentlemen carried snuff-boxes. Something of this sort Jonathan Swift described in the *Journal to Stella* on November 15, 1710 when he offered to buy a microscope for Stella: "'Tis not the great bulky ones nor the common little ones, to impale a louse (saving your presence) upon a needle's point; but of a more exact sort, and clearer to the sight, with all its equipage in a little trunk that you may carry in your pocket. Tell me, sirra, shall I buy it or not for you?"

Popular science was growing apace in London in the earlier seventeenth century, certainly as early as 1713 when Alexander Pope was enthralled by an astronomical lecture given by William Whiston at Button's coffeehouse. Ladies did not go to coffeehouses, but when Whiston's lectures were removed to a larger hall, they were free to attend them. Richard Steele developed a lecture-hall, the Censorium, in which lectures were given on science as on many other subjects. In the advertising, the presence of women was particularly stressed: "Which Room is conveniently fitted for Ladies as well as Gentlemen."

In the second quarter of the century appeared various textbooks on science, particularly designed for women, such as Charles Leadbetter's *Astronomy: Or the True System of the Planets Demonstrated* (1727); Joshua Charlton's *The Ladies Astronomy and Chronology* (1735). A few years later Charlton added *A Compleat System of Astronomy* (1742) "for the Benefit of Young Students." Astronomy, as one forgotten writer phrased it, was coming to be "made clear to the meanest capacity, even that of women and children." John Newbery, a writer and publisher, particularly of children's books, published in the 1750's *The Newtonian System of Philosophy Adapted to the Capacities of Young Gentlemen and Ladies,* which went through many editions. The little volume consisted of six lectures supposed to have been delivered before the Lilliputian Society by Tom Telescope, who seems to some modern readers as obnoxious a prig as Elsie Dinsmore.

Since eighteenth-century women had become an important source of income to publishers of periodicals, it is not surprising to find that later in the century two women edited three of the most readable, all designed primarily for women readers: Eliza Haywood edited *The Female Spectator* (1744–46) and *Epistles for the Ladies* (1749–50), and Charlotte Lennox brought out *The Lady's Museum* a little later (1760–61). All three included many scientific essays. The best of them, *The Female Spectator*, was widely read both in England and in the colonies. This, says Gerald Meyer, was written "by a scientific lady, about scientific ladies, and for scientific ladies." The Female Spectator, fortunate in "an education more liberal than is ordinarily allowed to persons of our sex," was assisted in her editorial labors by Mira, a "philosophress," Euphrosine, whose intellectual attainments surpassed even her admitted beauty, and a nameless Widow of quality. With their microscopes the ladies went out to the country, where they made observations on caterpillars and snails which they reported as "not ugly and insignificant as they may seem to other people" but "peculiarly graceful and majestic." That did not surprise the Female Spectator, since "nothing made by God is in itself contemptible. Wonderful are all his works." Their observations led them to ponder on microscopic anatomy and to raise the question whether dissection had proved any fundamental distinction between the sexes, which in turn led them to reflect upon the possibility of great improvements in women's education. During their visit to the country they spent their evenings, when weather permitted, on visits to the roof of a friend who was the proud possessor of a telescope. So popular was *The Female Spectator* that it was imitated and the characters borrowed by Eliza Haywood in the two-volume *Epistles for the Ladies.*

We may conclude with an earlier portrait of a virtuosa written by a woman, a play *The Bassett-Table* by Mrs. Susannah Centlivre (1705), a most attractive and amusing picture of what its author called "a Philosophical Girl" and "the little She Philosopher." Instead of elegant trifles, her lover sends her specimens for microscopical dissection. We first see Valeria running across the stage in pursuit of "the finest Insect for Dissection, a huge Flesh Fly, which Mr. Lovely sent me just now, and opening the Box to try the Experiment, away it flew." Lady Reveller shrieks with horror to learn that Valeria had dissected her dove "to see whether it is true that doves lack gall." Lady Reveller sarcastically suggests that Valeria might found "a College for the Study of Philosophy, where none but Women should be admitted," which Valeria would gladly do if her fortune was under her control. The "bedroom scene," familiar in Restoration comedy, has undergone a change. Valeria has transformed her chamber into a laboratory, the center of which would seem to be a laboratory table fitted with microscopes, where fish are laid out for dissection. When her lover enters, she bids him look through the glass "and see

how the Blood circulates in the Tail of this Fish." Paying no attention to his finding the circulation of the blood much more attractive in Valeria's "fair Neck," she shows him, among other of her curiosities, the "Lumbricus, Laetus, or Fossile, as Hippocrates calls it, or vulgarly in English, the Tape-Worm." There is a nice variation, too, upon the "concealment," popular in Restoration comedy. When Valeria hears her father approaching, she hides her lover in a tub, in which she usually keeps fish, then warns her father not to touch it because it contains "a Bear's young cub that I have bought for Dissection." There are few more amusing rejoinders of a virtuosa than Valeria's when her lover proposes that she elope with him: "What! and leave my Microscopes?"

The term "virtuoso" has become much rarer in the English language since the eighteenth century, although it is occasionally used, particularly in the field of music; as women's education has caught up with men's, "virtuosa" has disappeared.

*BIBLIOGRAPHY*

Mary Benson, *Women in Eighteenth Century America: A Study of Opinion and Social Usage* (New York, 1935). Mrs. Susannah Centlivre, "The Bassett-Table" (1706), in *The Works of the Celebrated Mrs. Centlivre*, Vol. I (London, 1761). Sir Lionel Henry Cust, *History of the Society of Dilettanti*, comp. by Lionel Cust, ed. Sidney Colvin (London and New York, 1914). John Evelyn, *The Diary of John Evelyn*, ed. E. S. de Beer (Oxford, 1955). Walter E. Houghton, Jr., "The English Virtuoso in the Seventeenth Century," *Journal of the History of Ideas*, **3** (1942), 51–75, 190–219. Gerald Dennis Meyer, *The Scientific Lady in England, 1650–1760* (Berkeley and Los Angeles, 1955). Majorie Nicolson, *Science and Imagination* (Ithaca, 1956); idem, *Thomas Shadwell: The Virtuoso* (Lincoln, 1966), with David Rodes. Myra Reynolds, *The Learned Lady in England, 1650–1760* (Boston and New York, 1920). Louis Booker Wright, *Middle-Class Culture in Elizabethan England* (Chapel Hill, N.C., 1935). Thomas Wright, *The Female Virtuoso's. A Comedy: as it is acted at the Queen's theatre* (London, 1693).

MARJORIE HOPE NICOLSON

[See also Atomism in the Seventeenth Century; **Baconianism;** Biological Conceptions; Experimental Science; **Newton on Method;** Optics; Satire; Women.]

# *VOLKSGEIST*

*Volksgeist* (also *Volksseele, Nationalgeist* or *Geist der Nation, Volkscharakter,* and in English "national character") is a term connoting the productive principle of a spiritual or psychic character operating in different national entities and manifesting itself in various creations like language, folklore, mores, and legal order.

Connotatively, the German word *Geist* is related in meaning to the Hebrew *ruah*, to the Greek *pneuma*, and to the Latin *spiritus*. *Volksgeist* is the spirit (*Geist*) of a people expressing itself in certain articulated creations. The shift to spirit as against expression, follows the shift from the letter of the law to the spirit of the law as in Saint Paul (II Corinthians 3:6). To the extent that the term is related to genius or to *génie* (as a derivation from *genius*), it is associated with the Roman idea of *genius loci*, the attendant spirit of a place, household or city, e.g., *genius urbis Romae*. Along with other parallel terms, the term *Geist* and *Volksgeist*, however, connote a spirit not outside but inside a certain entity.

***1. Emergence of the Concept.*** The distinction introduced by Leibniz between dead power and living power (*vis viva*)—the latter being understood also as a directive power—became the philosophical basis for the idea of a directive principle within historical entities guiding their existence in time and expressing itself in their creations. As a guiding principle the living power is not a logical or rational principle and could thus be connected with various concepts expressing the irrational directive principle of human creations and evaluations as the French *goût*, the Italian *gusto*, the German *Geschmack*, or the English taste. *Gusto* has sometimes been associated with *ingenio*.

*Volksgeist* as a guiding principle of peoples and nations appears in the context of investigations into the historical existence of peoples. The formulation of the concept goes along with the stress laid on history. The emphasis of Vico on the genetic aspect of a people's life is thus one of the sources of the concept: "since each family had its own religion, language, lands, nuptials, name, arms, government, etc." Again, the importance attached by Vico to "common sense . . . judgment without reflection, shared by an entire class, an entire people, an entire nation, the entire human race" can also be interpreted in terms of this concept (I. Berlin, E. Auerbach).

Edmund Burke rejected the *a priori* character of the science concerned with the construction of a commonwealth, and put forward the experimental and historical aspect of this science and of political life in general. Burke's view served as one of the sources of the attempt to disclose the historical character of peoples and the factors shaping their historical course.

Montesquieu in his *L'Esprit des lois* explicitly uses the term "general spirit of nations": "Mankind is influenced by various causes: by the climate, by the religion, by the laws, by the maxims of government, by precedents, morals and customs; whence is formed a general spirit of nations." Here the "general spirit of nations" is actually a result of different causes, some of them of a natural character like climate. Climatic conditions are discussed extensively by Montesquieu and by many other writers who subsequently used the term *Volksgeist*. Elsewhere it appears as a result of factors like religion, laws, morals, and customs which were considered by many thinkers as expressions of the *Volksgeist* proper. Yet Montesquieu says: "The Government most conformable to nature is that which best agrees with the humor and disposition of the people in whose favor it is established." He thus combines the principle of nature as a norm with that of a people's genius as a standard of government. Montesquieu's analysis of the spirit of laws influenced a series of German thinkers concerned with the spirit of the laws of the *Teutschen* and inspired the concepts of a *teutscher Nationalgeist*, *teutsche Freiheit*, etc. Friedrich Carl von Moser in *Von dem Deutschen national-Geist* (1765), uses Montesquieu's concept and gives it a nationalistic and polemic turn.

In Hume we find the concept "national character," a concept which recurs often in the nineteenth century. In his description of this concept Hume stresses a peculiar set of manners; the factors determining national character are partly "moral" (psychological) and partly physical, the "moral" disposition being able to alter even the natural one. In the context of this discussion Hume considers also the difference between Negroes and whites, the former being, in his opinion, naturally inferior to the latter; nature itself made an original hierarchical distinction between these two breeds of men. Here Hume's concept of national character goes beyond the domain of description and enters the domain of evaluation.

Voltaire employs the term "genius of a people" in his *Philosophical Dictionary* with a more general description of the term *esprit*. Speaking about different cultural creations, he refers to the subtle spirit of the "genius" of a nation. The study of manners (*moeurs*) was one of the topics of Voltaire's reflections on history. Climate, government, and religion are for him the three factors influencing the human spirit.

The term *"Nationalgeist"* appears, possibly for the first time, in the title of Carl Friedrich Moser's above-mentioned book, *Vom deutschen national-Geist* (1765). The concept has no specific meaning here; it connotes merely the general patriotic ambiance. Moser is concerned with certain political and social factors which cause an artificial split among the Germans. He uses this term also in a polemic with the Catholic Church and its detrimental influence on Germany.

These ideas and their linguistic expressions found their synthesis in the German term *Volksgeist* and its derivations, *Geist* connoting—even in Kant's terminology—not the intellectual or rational but the vital directing factor in human life.

**2. Formulation of the Concept.** We can point to three major steps taken towards the formulation of the concept of *Volksgeist*, following which it became one of the key notions of historical and literary movements.

J. G. von Herder does not use the term *Volksgeist*, but only various expressions like *Geist des Volkes, Geist der Nation, Nationalgeist* (explicitly referring to Moser), *Genius des Volkes*, and *Nationalcharakter* (without mentioning Hume). In the line of the historical reflections mentioned above, Herder also stresses the importance of climatic conditions for the shaping of historical events and their direction. Yet in spite of the absence of the term, the trend towards the formulation of the characteristic features of the name of "*Volksgeist*" can be clearly discerned.

Herder refers also to "the spirit of the times" (*Geist der Zeiten*), which is close to the experience of past times and which is impressed on the soul. The spirit of the times can be best understood from its expression in folklore and from daily experience; it expresses itself in vernacular speech and in popular poetry. Hence Herder's interest in the study of language and literature as two branches of mankind's historical creativity. The reference to the expressions of spirit replaces the direct approach to the substance of spirit, since spirit as such can neither be described nor painted. Spirit expresses itself through words, movements, conflicts, forces, and effects. As to the stability or destructiveness of the national character, Herder oscillates between two views: on the one hand, he describes it as an "innate idea" (Descartes) and considers it as eternal and indestructible; on the other hand, he speaks of his own historical age as tending to blur the distinction between various national traits. He then calls for an urgent investigation of these expressions of national character before they disappear.

Hegel coined the term *Volksgeist* in 1801 in speaking about mores, laws, and constitutions as forming the inner life or spirit of a people. From Hegel the term apparently entered the vocabulary of different systems and intellectual movements, although the ground had been prepared gradually for this absorption through the scattered ideas analyzed before. Hegel took cognizance of Herder's work mainly in the area of folk-poetry. He referred explicitly to Montesquieu who, in Hegel's opinion, combined the true historical view with a genuine philosophical position. According to this view legislation—in general as well as in its particular provisions—is to be treated not as something isolated but rather as a subordinate component in a whole. For Hegel, legal systems express a general attitude of a people and therefore the Roman or German concepts of laws are for him comprehensive systems guided by certain principles which can be formulated. Hegel's indebtedness to his predecessors comes to the fore when, along with the characteristic features of a nation's spirit whose investigation belongs to the natural philosophy of world history, he points to the natural dispositions of the national spirit like the composition of the body and the ways of life, whose study belongs to the history of the nature of man. But Hegel's main contribution to the formulation of the concept of *Volksgeist* is the attribution of a historical character to the concept. The spirit of a nation is one of the manifestations of World Spirit (*Weltgeist*). That Spirit is essentially alive and active throughout mankind's history.

Now, the spirit of a nation is an intermediate stage of world history as the history of the World Spirit. The World Spirit gives impetus to the realization of the historical spirits of various nations (*Volksgeister*). The spirits of individual nations are both the articulations (*Gliederungen*) of an organization and its realization. The spirits of individual nations represent a segment of the World Spirit out of which emerges the unlimited universal spirit. A comparison is introduced here between the status of an individual and that of a nation's spirit. In the process of his formation the individual undergoes various changes without, however, losing his identity. As a part of world history, a nation—exhibiting a certain trend expressed in its *Volksgeist*—plays its part in the total process of world history. But once it contributes its share to world history it can no longer play a role in the process of world history. The submersion in the total process prevents a people's cultural rebirth, because it has exhausted its creativity in the historical growth of its guiding spirit. It is for this reason that one of Hegel's disciples, Michelet, considered the idea of a renaissance of the Jewish people as philosophically impossible. The relations of state to state are uncertain, and there is no imperial Praetor available to adjust them. The only higher judge is the universal absolute spirit, the World Spirit (*Weltgeist*). In keeping with his general philosophical view which stresses the actuality of spirit as a living expression of the World Spirit, Hegel identifies the spirit of a people with its historical and cultural accomplishments, namely its religions, its mores, its constitution, and its political laws. They are the work of a people, they are the people.

Yet in spite of this view which confers, as it were, an equal status on each accomplishment, Hegel tends to give priority to the political constitution and to the state. The actual state is inspired (*beseelt*) by the national spirit and this inspiration is expressed in the various occurrences related to the state. The national spirit has an intrinsic morality which expresses itself in the confidence prevailing among the individuals imbued with the same national spirit. In addition, all elements of the population participate in the decisions and actions of the government. Here again the national spirit, though not identical with government, is related to it. The principles of national spirits (*Volksgeister*) are wholly restricted on account of their particularity because, as existent individuals, they have their own objective actuality and self-consciousness. Out of the finitude of these minds arises the universal spirit, the spirit of the world, free from all restriction, producing itself as that which exercises its right, the highest right of all, over the finite spirits in the history of the world, which is the world's court of judgment. Hegel uses also the term "genius of a nation," following the terminology found in the preceding discussions, as well as the term "God of a people." The identification of the spirit of a people with God of the people is made explicit, possibly under the influence of Hegel's historical speculations, by Nachman Krochmal, who distinguishes between the partial spiritual elements characteristic of the people of the world, and "the absolute spirit" identical with the monotheistic God and characteristic of the Jewish people. Because of the absolute character of this spiritual element it does not exhaust itself in the limited span within the historical process, but emerges time and again as the guiding principle of the people in a cyclical process of rise and fall.

The third component which contributed to the formation of the concept of *Volksgeist* is the Historical School of Law where the issue of the relation between the national spirit and the legal system became the center of a lengthy controversy. F. K. von Savigny does not use the concept of *Volksgeist;* this, however, appears in the works of G. F. Puchta. In Savigny we find only terms like *Volksbewusstsein* or "the common conviction of the people"; the loose terminology which he uses conveys, however, the same meaning as the term *Volksgeist.* Civil law has a definite character which is the product of a people's specific character, just as language, customs or constitution. These expressions are linked into one whole by the people's common convictions, by the feeling of an inner necessity which excludes all notions of an accidental or arbitrary genesis of such expressions. Because of the historical character of the legal system, the law must be approached mainly as law based on a plurality of legal systems (*Gewohnheitsrecht*). Savigny, however, has some misgivings as to the accuracy of this definition. The idea of customary law emerging from inner and tacit forces must be juxtaposed to a legal system based on the arbitrary decision of a lawgiver. The stress on a law emerging from history enables Savigny to advocate the common German legal system. Just as there is no Prussian and Bavarian language, so there is no room and justification for a legal system based on the political split then prevailing in Germany. Hence the idea of *Volksgeist* ceased to be a mere descriptive concept and became a political slogan. In spite of the importance attached to the state, the interest of the Historical School shifts from the state to the historical people. This—as well as the absence of the idea of a World Spirit—distinguishes the conceptions of the Historical School from those of Hegel. The Historical School faced a specific problem as to the justification of a deliberate legislation. Savigny's view of this problem was moderate; for him the legislator must be the representative of a people's common convictions and feelings. Other thinkers of this School rejected the idea of deliberate legislation altogether.

Echoing the seventeenth-century criticism of natural science in the Middle Ages which was based on the principle of *hypotheses non fingo* ("I do not frame hypotheses"), some critics raised the objection that the term *Volksgeist* expresses that which we do not know or understand and reminds one of the primitive mind's furnishing the world with spirits—the spirit of life, of light, of fire. This criticism, however, does not diminish the impact of the concept of *Volksgeist* on various intellectual movements of the nineteenth and twentieth centuries.

***3. The Impact.*** Indeed, the idea of *Volksgeist* as a descriptive concept as well as a normative demand of faithfulness to a given national genius and spirit influenced various trends in political life, in historiography, in literature, in legal and philosophical discussions, etc.

The various nationalist ideologies in Germany, France, Italy, and Poland explicitly used the concept of *Volksgeist* and of *Volkstum;* the description of the latter pointed out a certain intellectual and spiritual trend within peoplehood. The nationalist ideologies based on the concept of *Volkstum* or *Le Peuple* are related to this concept. Whether these ideologies have been influenced directly by the masters of the notion of *Volksgeist* or by more popular thinkers who entertained the idea, like Justus Möser and Adam Müller in Germany, or Madame de Staël in France, is of secondary importance. Sometimes those who based their ideological demands on the notion of *Volksgeist* placed the political center of gravitation on the people as against dynasties, assuming that only the people is the authentic representative and transmitter of national tradition.

In the description of the subjects of the historical processes historical research took advantage of this concept. German historical literature, including the opus of Leopold von Ranke, displays this influence. But the same applies to a large extent to the contemporary historical writings in France which had been influenced by Herder and by the German romantic ideas. It is interesting to point out that Madame de Staël, who carried the German influence to France, took characterization of peoples as a basic principle for the high praise of the English people and its institutions.

In the literary sphere romanticism is closely related to the concept of *Volksgeist*. The shift toward the folk saga is due to the preference given to folkloric productions over individual creations. For Jakob Grimm the community was the creative force; law and poetry are closely related and have a common source. Wilhelm von Humboldt speaks about national spirit when dealing with Greek history; and in his philosophy of language, while stressing the inner activity expressed in language, he stresses along with the inner form of language also its relation to *Volksgeist*. Though the linguistic capacity is a characteristic feature of man as man, the individual languages are manifestations of the national spirits.

The Historical School of Law gave rise to a peculiar controversy as to the extent to which Germanic law may absorb elements of Roman law or whether it should be purified from the intrusion of elements which do not express the German mind. This controversy is known as the controversy between Germanists and Romanists; it centers to some extent around the problem known as the "reception" of Roman law into the texture of Germanic law. Savigny advocated this absorption, while those who took issue with him argued against him and his followers on the basis of his own ideas, pushed, as it were, to their decisive and ultimate conclusion. For Otto von Gierke the Germanic legal system is characterized by the preference given to organic ties between individuals and is thus close to the idea of the law of *Genossenschaften*. The Roman tradition and its manifestations in natural law, in economic liberalism, individualism and capitalism has a destructive effect on the Germanic tradition. Von Gierke took further the idea of *Volksgeist* as a slogan for nationalistic attitudes and stated, during World War I, that the *Volksgeist* amounts to a Common Ego (*Gesamt-Ich*). The mythological interpretations of the *Volksgeist*, the drawing of distinctions between *Volksgeist* and race, confused by the Nazi ideology, followed this line in their own way.

There is a close affinity between the application of the idea of *Volksgeist* in the legal sphere and the application of this idea or of some of its derivations in the sphere of economic theory. The counterpart of the rejection of the alleged individualism in the legal sphere is the rejection of the isolated *homo aeconomicus,* an idea allegedly characteristic of the English economic theory as it is stated in the polemic which accompany these discussions. The specific *Volksgeist* exhibits its uniqueness also in the economic domain. This idea was expressed by Friedrich List (1789–1846) when he said that every people has its own political economy, and every great nation has to strive to be a whole for itself. The mission of political economy is to furnish the economical education of the nation and to prepare it for its proper place in the universal association of the future.

*4. The Polemic Aspect.* In so far as the concept of *Volksgeist* implies a demand of faithfulness to a people's traditions and to its spiritual principles of creativity, it implies *pari passu* the awareness of a distinction between different peoples' characters and their traditions. In its turn this distinction may take a polemical shape in adopting a critical attitude towards certain traditions and in giving preference to others. This polemical aspect in the concept of a people's or a community spirit of peoples comes to the fore in the Slavic domain. A. I. Herzen speaks specifically about the Slav genius and about its incompatibility with centralized government. Adam Mickiewicz spoke about the Slav tribe as characterized by religiosity, straightforwardness, and force. In connection with religion as a characteristic feature of the Slavic peoples, Herzen said that Russia will never be Protestant nor will it be *juste-milieu*, and these two are interrelated, since for him Protestantism was a bourgeois religion. The Pan-Slavists followed the same line, stressing the interest in religion characteristic of the Russian people, an interest which is similar to that of the ancient Jews. In contradistinction to the Germans, the Poles, according to Mickiewicz, believe in the power of great personalities and not in the opinions of the masses; while Herzen points out that the *droit du seigneur* has never existed among Slav peoples. Hence there exists a natural affinity between the Slavic character and the inner disposition for communism. The slogan of *Volksgeist* here takes a messianic direction at times.

In a different context, John Dewey points to the abuse of the term in German philosophy which used it to assume constancy where constancy was absent.

*5. American Totality.* This expression, taken from Walt Whitman, can be understood as pointing in the direction of the absorption of the concept into the texture of the problematic ideology of the United States. The problem presented by such an ideology is clear in this context: the people of the United States are not a traditional people in the European sense of the term. Its institutions are based rather on the notion of natural or rational law than on the legal system which expresses an accepted historical tradition. Yet in spite of this diversified background rooted in principles and based on theoretical considerations, we do find traces of the concept of *Volksgeist*. Whitman refers explicitly to Herder's idea of a national spirit, though he places his reference in a reflection on the character of poetry. Really great poetry, like the Homeric or biblical canticles, he says, is the result of a national spirit and not of the privileges of a polished and select few. The idea seems to be that the national spirit is an expression of a whole people and against the whole people stand the privileged few. This identification of a national spirit with folk elements is close to Grimm's view of natural poetry as the poetry of the people and artificial poetry as the poetry of individual poets. Again this duality runs parallel to the duality between the law of the people and the imposed law of the jurists. The populist trend in Whitman finds its expression in his rejection of the poetry of the Old World. Here the polemic aspect of his national feeling emerges: as long as the United States remains unsupplied with autochthonous song the people lacks first-class nationality.

The influence of the German thinkers on the American version of the idea of *Volksgeist* is revealed in the fact that two American thinkers, Francis Lieber and Philip Schaff, who concerned themselves with this issue (though their terminology differs), were of German descent. Francis Lieber did not use the term *Volksgeist*; but he was aware of his relation to the German ideology and the use of the terms *Volkstum* and *Volksgeist*. Lieber placed the emphasis on the consciousness of unification of different peoples according to circumstances: either the consciousness of unity precedes the political unification as is the case of Germany and Italy, or the political unity precedes the ethnic and the cultural unity as is the case of the United States, Canada, and Australia. He spoke about races though he gave to the concept a cultural and historical meaning and not a biological one, and considered the Anglican race which achieved guarantees to human rights, civil liberties, and self-government superior to the Teutonic one.

Philip Schaff's sketch of the character of the American people and its components is another instance of German influence on American thinking. The concept used by Schaff is national character and not *Volksgeist*; but the two concepts are similar in their origin. When Schaff says that all depends ultimately upon the character of the nation, he echoes the idea of *Volksgeist*. His reference to history and his notion that every nation has its peculiar calling is based on the connection put forward in German thinking between the importance of history and the position of *Volksgeist* as a principle operating in history. Schaff is aware of the particular situation prevailing in America where,

in spite of the confused diversity, there resides, after all, a higher unity and where, in a babel of peoples, the traces of a specifically American national character may be discerned. The impulse towards freedom and the sense of law and order resting on moral basis are features of this character. Thus ultimately the ideas rooted in the conception of natural law and rational morality are presented as expressions of the national character. Here, too, a polemical note can be discerned: *gloire* is the motto of the Frenchman; "duty" that of the Englishman. A similar idea is voiced by Theodore Parker, and to some extent its echoes can be heard in the notion of "manifest destiny" which, though related to the physical expansion of the United States to the Pacific, absorbed also the view that it is God's design that each country should wear a peculiar physiognomy—as Thomas Starr King and John Fiske said. George Bancroft was in his own way influenced by similar ideas.

*6. Völkerpsychologie.* The psychology of the nineteenth century gave birth to a discipline known as *Völkerpsychologie*. The relation between this trend and the concept of *Volksgeist* comes to the fore in the use of this term by M. Lazarus (1824–1903), one of the founders of the school. The spirit of the people is inherent in the social constitution and in all that which makes a state. Not only is the term *Volksgeist* used here, but the relation between the formative *Volksgeist* and statehood is also put forward. The importance of language for expressing the spirit of a people also appears in the school, mainly in the works of H. Steinthal. The difference between the position of this school and the thinkers discussed above seems to lie in the fact that *Volksgeist* ceases to be an underlying principle expressing itself in the historical reality of peoples, but now becomes a product or a manifestation of the individuals themselves. *Volksgeist* subsists in the products of the minds of different peoples. From this point of view we may say that *Völkerpsychologie* was concerned with the subject matter created by individuals and not with one preceding them. Lazarus oscillates between a view which underlines the created and secondary character of a people's *psyche* (*Volksseele*) and a view which attributes to it an independent position of its own, in spite of its secondary status. There are thus elements and laws of the spiritual life of peoples and these have to be investigated by a special branch of science. Wilhelm Wundt took issue with the program of this school as presented by Lazarus and Steinthal, arguing that their program is based on a presupposition which defies the fundamentals of Herbart's psychology since it assumes a soul other than the individual one. Wundt tried to arrive at a conclusion which takes the soul of the people to be an outcome of individual elements

495

and experiences, to a greater extent than had been done by Lazarus in the implicit reflections of the traditional notion of *Volksgeist*. He stresses the genetic and causal investigation of the facts underlying human society. *Volksseele* is a result of individual souls which compose the collective *psyche*, but the individual souls are no less the results of the *Volksseele* in which they participate. Wundt distinguishes between the common consciousness (*Gesamtbewusstsein*) which finds its expression in language, myth, and customs, and the common will (*Gesamtwille*) which finds its expression in common decisions.

*7. Morphology of Cultures.* A scheme of types of cultures was presented by Huizinga; this, however, does not correspond to particular historical peoples and their mind. The orbit of a certain type comprises more than one people. The whole idea has, however, a considerable affinity with the concept of *Volksgeist*. Huizinga lists a Latin type of culture, an Anglo-Saxon one, and expresses doubts as to the existence of a Slavic type as well as of a Germanic type. In Huizinga's opinion, the Germanic type does not comprise a plurality of nations as the Latin or Anglo-Saxon type. In any case, the types which he lists are, in a certain sense, *Volksgeister* projected on groups of peoples and thus transcending any particular people in uniqueness.

*8. Wholes and Patterns.* The theory of *Volksgeist* was an attempt to understand cultures and civilizations as wholes and to point to empirical data as interrelated in these wholes. It was an attempt to identify the whole with a historical people. In this sense it guided empirical and anthropological research. The direction of recent anthropological research retains the idea of a whole but replaces it with an idea of a whole as a pattern or structure related to civilizations and not to peoples; wholes are not principles operating in civilizations but structures of interrelated elements present in them. This might be looked at as a turn away from the mythological understanding of a whole to the systematic understanding of it. Still, the rejection of "rationalism" in politics as advocated by Michael Oakeshott and the acceptance of the "tradition" as the guiding norm of politics, are echoes of the concept of *Volksgeist* in its normative if not in its descriptive sense.

## BIBLIOGRAPHY

M. Brasch, *Die Philosophie der Gegenwart* (Leipzig, 1888). This volume includes the relevant material on M. Lazarus, H. Steinthal, and W. Wundt. S. Brie, *Der Volksgeist bei Hegel und in der historischen Rechtsschule* (Berlin and Leipzig, 1909). E. Burke, *Reflections on the Revolution in France* (London, 1790; several reprints available). R. G. Collingwood, *An Essay on Metaphysics* (Oxford, 1940). O. Gierke, "Die historische Rechtsschule und die German-isten," *Universitätsreden* (Berlin, 1900–09). G. W. F. Hegel, *Phänomenologie des Geistes* (1807), trans. J. B. Baillie as *Phenomenology of Mind* (New York, 1964; also reprint); idem, *Encyklopädie der philosophischen Wissenschaften* (1817); idem, *Grundlinien der Philosophie des Rechts* (1818), trans. T. M. Knox as *Philosophy of Right* (Oxford, 1942); idem, *Vorlesungen über die Philosophie der Weltgeschichte* (1821), trans. J. Sibree as *Lectures on the Philosophy of History* (New York, reissue 1956). M. Heidegger, "Die Zeit des Weltbildes," *Holzwege* (Frankfurt a. M., 1950). J. G. von Herder, *Sämtliche Werke*, ed. B. Suphan (Berlin, 1877–1913), esp. Vols. V, IX, XII, XIII, XIV, XVII, XVIII, passim. A. Herzen, *From the Other Shore*, trans. Moura Budberg (London and New York, 1956). R. Hildebrand, *Geist* (Halle a. Saale, 1926). D. Hume, *Essays, Moral, Political, and Literary*, ed. T. H. Green, 2 vols. (London, 1875; London and New York, 1963). K. Jaspers, *Die geistige Situation der Zeit* (Berlin, 1932), trans. Eden and Cedar Paul as *Man in the Modern Age* (London, 1933); *Vom Ursprung und Ziel der Geschichte* (Zurich, 1949), trans. M. Bullock as *Origin and Goal of History* (New Haven, 1968). H. Kantorowicz, "Savigny and the Historical School of Law," *Law Quarterly Review*, **53** (1937), 326ff. F. List, *National System of Political Economy*, trans. G. A. Matile (Philadelphia, 1856). K. Löwith, *Von Hegel bis Nietzsche* (Zurich, 1941), trans. as *From Hegel to Nietzsche: The Revolution in Nineteenth Century Thought* (New York, 1964). M. de Montesquieu, *L'Esprit des lois* (Geneva, 1748). F. C. von Moser, *Von dem deutschen national-Geist* (location uncertain, 1765?). J.-P. Sartre, *Critique de la raison dialectique* (Paris, 1960). F. C. von Savigny, *Vom Beruf unserer Zeit für Gesetzgebung und Rechtswissenschaft* (Heidelberg, 1814). Philip Schaff, *America, A Sketch of Its Political, Social, and Religious Character*, ed. P. Miller (Cambridge, Mass., 1961). Friedrich Schiller, *Über die ästhetische Erziehung des Menschen* (1795), trans. R. Snell as *On the Aesthetic Education of Man* (New York, 1965). G. Vico, *Scienza nuova* (1725), trans. Max H. Fisch and Thoman S. Bergin as *The New Science of Giambattista Vico* (Ithaca, 1944; 1968). F. M. A. de Voltaire, *Essai sur les moeurs et l'esprit des nations* (1756); *Dictionnaire philosophique* (1764), esp. "Esprit"; trans. Peter Gay as *Philosophical Dictionary* (New York, 1967). A. N. Whitehead, *Science and the Modern World* (London and New York, 1925). Walt Whitman, *Complete Prose Works* (Boston, 1898); idem, *Leaves of Grass and Selected Prose*, ed. S. Bradley (New York, 1960).

NATHAN ROTENSTREICH

[See also Environment; Language; Law, Ancient Roman; **Nationalism;** Romanticism; State; *Zeitgeist.*]

## VOX POPULI

THE IDEA of "the People" contains both descriptive and normative elements. Descriptively it has referred to a racial, religious, political, and sometimes a social group of individuals. We still speak about the white and black people, the people of God, the electorate, and the working people, and in each case the reference is to a different group of men and women. Normatively it has been used in both a eulogistic and pejorative sense. Thus we find "popular" government, as democracy, contrasted with absolute monarchy, and we mean by the adjective a government of which we approve. But we also speak of popular taste as inferior to cultivated taste; few writers would think themselves complimented to be called popular writers if the epithet meant writers who appealed only to the masses. Few ideas have been so vague as the idea of the People.

Historically the idea that distinguishes the People from the other members of a community arose in Athens. A democracy was a government of the *Demos*, a term that originally meant the free inhabitants of a *deme* or locality. In time, however, it came to mean the free, native, male citizens of the city of Athens. It never included slaves, women, or resident aliens (*metoikoi*). The *Demos* had the right to vote for certain officers and on certain policies but was far from ever being omnicompetent. Its liberation was a gradual affair, starting with Solon (sixth century B.C.) and developing until the overthrow of Athenian independence under Philip of Macedon, after the Battle of Cheroneia (336 B.C.) There is a tradition that the Athenians were proud of their democracy. Some undoubtedly were. But neither Plato nor Aristotle thought highly of it.

The reason for their low opinion derived from a second usual meaning of "the People." To Plato the People were the artisan class, hand laborers, and in Plato's eyes such men existed simply to feed themselves and to procreate. In his view they corresponded to the appetites of an individual man in contrast to the military (the irascible or spirited class) and the philosophers (the rational). To his way of thinking in both his *Republic* and *The Laws*, a democracy would be government run by artisans, analogous to a man dominated by gluttony and lust.

In Aristotle a similar opinion obtained. No man, he believed, could live the life of virtue who was occupied solely in earning his living. He even excluded men engaged in retail trade from the class who should govern. But Aristotle also thought of each kind of government as constituted for the satisfaction of a set of interests. The problem of the political philosopher was to find that form of government that would satisfy the interests of all the citizens. And his fear of mob rule was based on the premiss that "the Many" would govern in the interests of the poor. Still both Plato and Aristotle were willing to admit that democracy, in the sense of a government by the working class, was the best of bad governments. States, they both felt, should be run by reason, and to cultivate the life of reason demanded leisure. The working class by definition has no leisure.

In Rome also, we find at least two meanings of "the People." The famous monogram, *SPQR*, standing for *The Senate and the Roman People*, implied a sharp cut between the lawmakers or the Senate, and those who were governed—though associating both in the results of legislation. But the Roman population had another distinction that was of social as well as of political importance, the distinction between the patricians and the plebeians.

The patrician was the social superior to the plebeian and his rank was determined by descent. The distinction became political when the plebeians seceded in 494 B.C. and there was instituted the Tribunate of the Plebs. Thus what began as a social distinction was preserved by law. No one is sure of the origin of either the patricians or plebeians, but we do know that the latter in historical times absorbed freedmen and resident aliens, whereas, at least during the Republic, the former were a closed caste.

Some Roman writers discussed the meaning of the word *populus*. Cicero, for instance, in his *Republic* (I, 25, 39) points out that the word does not refer to the whole population of a state but rather to a group associated in their agreement with the laws and who live in the community of service. To be a member of the *populus*, then, would seem to imply a conscious will to accept the laws and live for their observance. Livy too in speaking of the Tribunate of the Plebeians, says in his *History* (II, 25) that it is not an office of the people but only of the *plebs*, thus differentiating the *plebs* from the *populus*. Along with this political distinction ran a social distinction, as mentioned before.

The contempt that the upper-class Roman had for the plebeian is best illustrated in the characters who play ludicrous roles in Plautus: fishermen, pimps, slaves, parasites, freedmen. The people in the sense of the lower classes seemed to be inherently comic, a tradition that continued up to the nineteenth century. One has but to think of the plays of Shakespeare, *Julius Caesar, Coriolanus, A Midsummer Night's Dream*, to see this exemplified. It was not until such a novel as Mrs. Gaskell's *Mary Barton* (1848) was published that any writer took members of the working class seriously, though sympathy for their hard lot had often been expressed. It had been well established in the Italian Renaissance that only nobles could be tragic figures; comic figures came from the laboring classes. We retain this usage in adjectives such as "plebeian" and "vulgar" (Latin, *vulgus*), which are historically synonymous.

There was bound up in this confusion of ideas the notion that what is plentiful, and perhaps therefore cheap, is worse than that which is rare. The Greeks called the common people—and the word "common" is suggestive—"the Many" (*Hoi Polloi*) and the Romans similarly called them "the Multitude" (*multitudo*). We too have carried on this tradition in using "rare" for something precious, and "ordinary" or "common" for something cheap and *therefore* undesirable. Indeed this tradition may lie behind that contempt for the vulgar which has never died out and which only in the middle of the twentieth century began itself to be condemned.

Christianity, influenced perhaps by Stoicism, introduced the notion that all men, regardless of social position or nationality, are brothers. To the Stoic, the Emperor Marcus Aurelius and the slave Epictetus, were equals, at least before the law or "in the eyes of God." This notion was perpetuated in the Middle Ages in religious matters, though not in either political or social circles. In Pauline Christianity we are all members of one body, and in Saint Augustine all who belong to the City of God are equals. But neither man thought that this idea applied to all human beings. It applied only to true Christians. The City of God does not exist here on earth and "Thy people Israel" (*tua plebs Israel*) are far from being everyone. They are the elect. A *populus*, says Saint Augustine, following Cicero, are men bound together in harmonious communion (*concordi communione*) (*City of God*, XIX, 23–24). The existent city was founded by Cain and is inherently evil. Hence the people, as well as their princes, participate in hereditary guilt. This may seem like a rather discouraging outlook, but the fact remains that for Saint Augustine one's social position counted for nothing when it was a question of God's grace. This view was important and was kept alive throughout the Middle Ages when revolts of peasants and laborers, beginning with the Bagaudae in the fourth century and including the Lollards in the fourteenth, broke out frequently and were put down only by superior force. One sees the idea appearing in the slogan of John Ball (1381) when the couplet

> When Adam delved and Eve span
> Who was then the gentleman?

became popular. Though the Middle Ages, as appears in the feudal system of ranks (*dignitates*) and special privileges, was a period in which social position counted for everything in theory, there was also in the background the notion that God was not a respecter of persons.

In fact it was during the early Middle Ages (eighth century) that the proverb, *Vox populi vox Dei* was first recorded. It occurs in a letter of Alcuin to Charlemagne. In this letter Alcuin says that the proverb is a customary saying and that the Emperor ought to pay no attention to it, since the *populus* ought to be led,

not followed. Unfortunately no one has found the origin of the proverb, but the idea that there is something divine in general opinion goes back at least to Hesiod (eighth century B.C.). In I Samuel 8:7, where the people come to Samuel and ask for a king, God says to His high priest, "Listen to the voice of the people," or in the Vulgate, by which these words were transmitted to medieval Christians, *Audi vocem populi*. In this case the voice was not the voice of God at all, and God saw in the request something which His people would regret in time to come. But He did say to listen to them and grant their request. Thus biblical justification was given for the theory that in the beginning kings were elected by the *populus*. Similarly bishops, however nominated, had to be approved by the people and popular consent was expressed in all probability by acclamation. But there is no case of either a king or a bishop having been elected by popular vote in the sense of universal franchise. Kings were sometimes elected by the nobility and bishops chosen from a list submitted by a group of other bishops, but the phrase, "by the consent of the people," was always retained.

The People, in the sense of the working classes, took no part in such elections other than that of acclaiming the new bishop or king. In literature they retained their color of the comic or the brutal. The one exception to this rule occurred in the case of shepherds. In literary history two strains join here, that of the pastoral poetry of Theocritus and Vergil and that of the biblical account of the annunciation to the shepherds from Luke 2. This double strain gave shepherds as literary figures a special place of esteem, though the service of actual shepherds was far from delightful. This is not the place to expatiate on this curious bit of literary history, but it may be noted that it became traditional well into the eighteenth century when rural life began to take on romantic coloring. Its importance for us is that it contained in it the seeds of an element in the history of the People which has been neglected, if known. For sympathy with the shepherd led in the pastorals of the Renaissance and in the rococo period to a fantastic glorification of a kind of life and a class of men so far from reality that one wonders how it could ever have been treated seriously. At the same time it is possible that out of this glorification came a growing sympathy for rural life in general and a certain admiration for the peasant.

In the eighteenth century the songs of the peasants began to be collected, first as charming and delightful, and second as specimens of the voice of the people uncorrupted by sophistication. Bishop Thomas Percy published his famous *Reliques of Ancient English Poetry* in 1765 and stimulated a vogue for ballads and songs which has not seen its end today. Percy's ballads were so edited and revised that none could be taken as authentic in the form he gave it. But that fault was remedied by other editors as time went on. Percy himself believed that these poems were written and sung by "bards" at the courts of nobles, but his contemporary in Germany, Johann Gottfried von Herder, thought of them as literally the people's voice, *Volkslieder,* expressive of the collective soul of the folk. He collected and translated such verses from various countries, including some of the legendary Ossian, and was in all probability the source of the idea that the folk had a voice and that its voice expressed emotions that were more "authentic" than that of trained and sophisticated poets. It was in this vein that Wordsworth in the Preface to the *Lyrical Ballads* (1798) spoke of the speech of the rural folk as better than that of the urban dwellers. To him poetic diction was rural diction. Country people were supposed to be closer to nature in one of the many senses of that word, and to praise them was to elevate nature above art.

Meanwhile the social levels below that of the barons were gaining power in England and by 1832 the franchise was extended beyond the limits of the large property owners. The system of rotten boroughs was done away with or at least seriously threatened. This meant that the People, as opposed to the nobility and the gentry, were beginning to be represented in Parliament. In France the Revolution of 1789, though it gained the sympathy of some members of the nobility at the start—the Duc d'Orléans voting for the execution of his cousin, the king—gradually became the instrument of the urban mob; and the political gains made by the *menu peuple* were lost again under Napoleon and the Restoration. It has been said by Marxists that the French Revolution was a revolution of the bourgeoisie, and as far as permanent gains are concerned, that opinion is correct. The spread of the franchise to the total adult population, female as well as male, did not come about in France until after the second World War. In Western Europe and the United States, universal enfranchisement was gained only after the industrial workers and miners saw the advantage of organization, and then only very gradually. The Chartist movement in England, so eloquently described in Mrs. Gaskell's *Mary Barton,* was a failure, but nevertheless the strength of organized labor grew until in the twentieth century almost everyone had become a working man. Property qualifications for the franchise, which were universal in the early nineteenth century, were gradually abandoned and the slogan, attributed to John Jay, that he who owns the country should govern it, was dropped. This was perhaps because the public began to realize that the country was not only land but also stocks and bonds and muscles.

In spite of the progress of culture and political power, the People became too numerous to meet as a unit. Even some of the larger New England towns abandoned the old form of the town meeting and substituted representation. In a large industrial and hence urban country the actual political power is bound to be in the hands of an oligarchy, a very large one to be sure, and the People as a whole are in the position of voting for officers who have been nominated behind the scenes and of being represented, rather than present even in municipal affairs. From the county through the cities and states up to the federal congress, the People's voice has grown weaker and weaker, and though this may be deprecated, there seems to be no feasible alternative. On the social scene all forms of snobbery still obtain and an upper upper class, to use Professor Lloyd Warner's term, is still recognized. But as far as general culture is concerned, the United States has seen an uninterrupted spread of educational facilities, of concerts and exhibitions of fine arts open to the public and often crowded, of recreational possibilities that would have been undreamt of at the opening of the twentieth century. This movement has awakened the public to pleasures that it assumed belong to it by right, along with means of insuring public health and proper housing. The welfare state has raised the extension of the word "People" to include almost everyone. But the expression of its voice is bound to be more and more restricted except in extralegal ways. The distinction between patrician and plebeian has almost disappeared in the United States, though of course it still exists in social discrimination and in conversation. But the adjective "popular" would probably be replaced by "folk" as a term of praise, though no one seems to be sure of just who the folk are.

The history of the idea of the People is thus one in which the descriptive and normative connotations are closely intertwined. Whereas in the past the People were in general thought of either with pity or contempt, now the pity may be retained but the contempt is certainly abandoned. Moreover whereas the denotation of the People, even in the Preamble to the Constitution of the United States, applied to males and property owners only, represented by a small group of men from only twelve of the thirteen states, it is now applied to almost everyone. It is impossible to point to any one cause of this, but the predominant cause would appear to be economic. Though Mrs. Gaskell, Charles Kingsley, at times Dickens, always Zola and sometimes the Brothers Goncourt expressed warm sympathy with the lot of the working class, they had no power to change it. It was undoubtedly through the power of organized labor that increased wages, shorter hours, and all the fringe benefits that are now customary were obtained. This accomplishment has raised the working class in the United States out of the proletariat into the bourgeoisie.

In England class consciousness is still strong, if one may judge from novels and plays; in France the peasant class is clearly defined, as it is in Germany. Social democracy is still unrealized in the United States, but economic democracy is close to being realized. Political democracy is as close to being actualized as is possible in an urban society. One always finds in studying the history of an idea that old ideas hang on as residues of the past, and that is as true in the United States as in Spain, to take an example of an extremely conservative country. It is always the emotional coefficient of ideas that retains its potency after an idea has lost its descriptive meaning. It would be easy to make a selection of Americans who would believe in all the ideals of a medieval baron, both the noble ideas and the merely snobbish. But it is doubtful that such a selection would be a fair sample of the population as a whole.

*BIBLIOGRAPHY*

Alcuin, Letter 132, in *Epistolae Karolini Aevi. Monumenta Germaniae Historica*, Vol. 4 (Berlin, 1895). Aristophanes, *The Knights*, trans. Benjamin Bickley Rogers (London and Cambridge, Mass., 1924; 1960). Aristotle, *Politics*, trans. Benjamin Jowett (Oxford, 1885; 1923). Augustine, *The City of God, Corpus Scriptorum Ecclesiasticorum Latinorum*, Vol. 40. George Boas, *Vox Populi* (Baltimore, 1969). Paul Brandt, *Schaffende Arbeit und Bildende Kunst*, 2 vols. (Leipzig, 1927–28). R. W. and A. J. Carlyle, *A History of Medieval Political Theory in the West*, 6 vols. (London, 1903–36; New York, reprint n. d.), Vol. I. Francis James Child, *The English and Scottish Popular Ballads*, 5 vols. (Boston, 1883–98). G. William Domhoff, *Who Rules America?* (Englewood Cliffs, N.J., 1967). Max Farrand, ed., *The Records of the Federal Convention* (New Haven, 1911). Morris D. Forkosch, "Who are the 'People' in the Preamble to the Constitution?" *Case Western Reserve Law Review*, **19**, 3 (1968). S. A. Gallacher, "Vox Populi, Vox Dei," *Philological Quarterly*, **24**, 1 (1945). Otto Gierke, *Political Theories of the Middle Ages*, trans. F. W. Maitland (Cambridge, 1900). Arnold Hauser, *The Social History of Art* (New York, 1951). J. G. von Herder, *Auszug aus einem Briefwechsel über Ossian und die Lieder alter Völker*, in *Sämtliche Werke*, ed. B. Suphan, 33 vols. (Berlin, 1877–1913), Vol. 5. A. L. Lloyd, *Folk Song in England* (London, 1967). Jules Michelet, *Le Peuple*, ed. Lucien Refort (Paris, 1946). Kirk Harold Porter, *A History of Suffrage in the United States* (Chicago, 1918). Lily Ross Taylor, *Roman Voting Assemblies* (Ann Arbor, 1966). Gérard Walter, *Histoire des paysans de France* (Paris, 1963). W. L. Warner and P. S. Lunt, *The Social Life of a Modern Community* (New Haven, 1941). Michael Wilks, *The Problem of Sovereignty in the Later Middle Ages* (Cambridge, 1963).

Chilton Williamson, *American Suffrage, from Property to Democracy, 1760–1860* (Princeton, 1960).

GEORGE BOAS

[See also Class; **Democracy;** Equality; State; *Volksgeist.*]

# WAR AND MILITARISM

***General Images.*** The history of ideas about war and militarism is largely one of combinations of prevailing ideas in political, social, and moral philosophy. Modern war is an armed conflict among states. But war predates states and remains an expression of so pervasive and traumatic a feature of mankind's evolution that ideas about the origins of man's warlike tendencies are discussed in many philosophical systems. Classical and neo-classical military literature thus includes philosophical discourses which mention war along with military histories and practical soldiers' handbooks and manuals.

Ideas about war are peculiarly, though not uniquely, affected by historical events and social problems. The need to train large numbers of men to engage in potentially self-destructive acts, for example, grew greater after the French Revolution had shown the military value of more popular armies and after the Industrial and Agricultural Revolutions had increased the material resources and manpower which could be devoted to warfare. In what Herbert Spencer later saw as a resulting metamorphosis of institutions, the time required to train a soldier was cut from two years to two months, while compulsory education for a peaceful life in an industrialized society increased the citizen's preparation for and his personal resentment of military training.

A positivistic philosophy of war was developed during the nineteenth century. This combined Carl von Clausewitz' view of its nature, more explicit assumptions about its origins in human nature, society, or the state system, and a set of ideas for its management. These gave military "scientists" positive goals during a century of peace in which the major European military events were Prussia's scientifically managed victories over both Austria and France in 1886 and 1870–71. The result was a clarification of what Waltz (1959) sees as three images of the relations of man, the state, and war, and of war's origins in human nature, in social "containers," in which, like water in a boiler, men are "made to 'behave' in different ways." This latter view is inherent in Montesquieu's remark that "As soon as man enters into society he loses the sense of his weakness; equality ceases, and then commences the state of war" (*Esprit des lois*, Book I, Ch. III).

"Militarism" is a nineteenth-century liberal pejorative label for systems which overvalue the military virtues, glorify war, or give inordinate power or rewards to soldiers. These evils became clearer as more uniform states replaced the feudal orders and as national and democratic armies (in which noble officers were still favored) replaced bands of mercenary military artisans. But books on their art were still collections of maxims (from Sun Tsu's *Art of War*, 500 B.C., to Burnod's *Military Maxims of Napoleon*, 1827), handbooks (Vegetius' *Military Institutions of the Romans*, 390, or Frederick the Great's *Instructions for His Generals*, 1747), or formal treatises of advice to princes (Machiavelli's *Art of War* expands a paragraph in *The Prince*).

Clausewitz' work *On War* (published posthumously, 1832–36) became the writ of a positivistic philosophy of war after Prussia's victories in the mid-nineteenth century. Like the Marxist, Social Darwinist, and other social positivists of this era, Clausewitzians often used *On War* for incantational purposes, but all of their works reflected the events which had again freed "the primitive violence of war . . . from all conventional restrictions. . . . The cause was the participation of the people in this great affair of state, . . . [arising] partly from the effects of the French Revolution, . . . partly from the threatening attitude of the French toward all nations." The acceptance of his view that war is "not merely a political act but a political instrument" shifted debate to the right means of managing a "chameleon, . . . [which] in each concrete case . . . changes somewhat its character . . . of the original violence of its essence, . . . of the play of probabilities and chance, . . . and of the subordinate character of a political tool, through which it belongs to . . . pure intelligence" (Book VIII, Ch. iii; Book I, Chs. xxiv, xxviii; trans. Jollis).

Two world wars then shook this post-Napoleonic science of war. Failures in the Great War of 1914–18 came from unscientific evaluation of weapons. The more than Napoleonic victories in the Second World War confirmed a new faith in scientific mechanization. But "absolute" nuclear and biochemical weapons and "assured" delivery systems revived doubts about war as a political instrument, though analogies from ritualized intraspecific and primitive conflict revived the Garden of Eden for some observers.

*Classical Warfare.* Classical observers of primitive warriors had stressed not their play acting but their courage, treachery, and indiscipline. Greco-Roman political and social institutions were partly based on kinship groups, but "civilized" men saw few analogies between themselves and barbarians, perhaps because they had so largely overcome the restrictions which tribalism places on political and military efficiency, perhaps because the technological gap between civilized and barbarian peoples, even in metallurgy, remained relatively small. Barbarian incursions might also spark slave or social insurrections, and their few laws of war applied only to other civilized peoples.

War began with plunder. "Both Hellenes and Barbarians . . . were commanded by powerful chiefs, who took this means of increasing their wealth and providing for their poorer followers" (Thucydides, *Peloponnesian War*, trans. Benjamin Jowett, Book I. Chs. v–vi). This fitted the facts of legend and history. The Spartans "were virtually the first of the Greeks to feel . . . greed for the territory of their neighbors" (Polybius, *Histories*, trans. Mortimer Chambers, Book VI, Ch. xlix). To keep her gains Sparta made every citizen a professional soldier and mercenaries her main export. But Aristotle saw her constitution as a true union of aristocracy and democracy, though Polybius found Rome's less democratic one better for expansion. The Romans managed the most efficient city-smashing, land-grabbing, slave-catching machine of antiquity. As Montesquieu was to note of this "city without commerce, and almost without arts, pillage was the only means individuals had of enriching themselves" (*Grandeur et décadence des Romains*, Ch. I).

Aristotle related constitutions to military systems. Cavalry's replacement by infantry had been democratizing. But modern ideas of militarism came after the technology which ended the dangers of barbarian incursions had threatened to make civilized wars self-destructive. Disciplined and efficient soldiers were necessary for a state's survival in fighting barbarians with very similar hand weapons. The Romans benefited from "the abundance and convenient accessibility of their military supplies," but they also glorified war. "Their customs" provided "many incitements to develop . . . bodily strength and . . . personal bravery" (Polybius, Book VI, Chs. 1, lii).

Soldiers often fought each other for political power, but the social costs of ancient—and medieval—armaments and warfare are difficult to estimate. Fortifications which protected capital, surplus food, and occasionally a transportation network may have taken most of the social surpluses which went to armaments. Such public works usually used the seasonally unemployed labor of a "backward" agricultural system. Population pressures were relieved by more distant ventures which might add to a state's land and labor capital. And the disasters which overtook Rome were too insidious (soil erosion, malnutrition, endemic disease, anomie) or too traumatic (plagues, barbarian invasions, civil and foreign wars against equal enemies) to be regarded as other than acts of God.

Images of pacifism mirror a society's images of violence. Most of the ancients whom the moderns were to regard as rational saw internal and external political violence in terms which were not too incongruent with Clausewitz' view of "physical force (for no moral force exists apart from the state and law)" (Book I, Ch. i) as normal. Early Christians rejected as evil a society founded on coercion rather than on love. An established Church regarded those who felt that it should not defend itself as naive and sinful. Greco-Roman feelings of shock at Carthaginian child immolation—which modern Tunisian historians try to explain away—or at Christian pacifists are analogous to those later feelings of hatred which the Faithful directed at Peoples of the Book who were not True Believers. And as long as the military and technological balance between civilized and barbarian remained relatively even, both needed an enemy to be envied, feared, hated, enslaved, and plundered.

***Medieval and Early Modern Warfare.*** Medieval society's hieratic military, political, and other orders defy historical generalization. Armored horsemen and fortifications dominated war and an unarmed peasantry. But medieval societies were not easily seen as militaristic, and medieval Christians and Muslims had good reasons for "just" wars. Citizens of city-states saw their political and military problems as analogous to those of city-states in antiquity. The result was that there were few new generalizations about the relations of man, the state, and war before the eighteenth and early nineteenth centuries. By that time centralized sovereign states had taken away the right of declaring just wars from a broken Universal Church. And Fichte and Hegel had reconciled the individual moral imperatives which Kant had found in the natural right doctrines of Rousseau—"the Newton of the moral world"—with the historical imperatives of social ethics.

Long before Clausewitz, Machiavelli mixed ancient and modern examples with a philosophy, implicit in his case, which saw political violence and *raison d'état* as normal. "A wise prince . . . takes as his profession nothing else than war. . . . In peace he trains himself . . . to find the enemy, to choose encampments, to plan battles, and to besiege towns." His view of Ferdinand of Aragon's actions which grew "one from another" so that people had "no leisure for working against him" (*Prince*, trans. Allan Gilbert, Chs. XIV, XXI) was to be Bodin's idea that "the best way of preserving a state . . . against sedition . . . is to . . . find an enemy against

whom they [its subjects] can make common cause" (*Commonwealth*, Book V, Ch. v). The Romans, Machiavelli noted, had made "their wars, as the French say, short and big. . . . [They led] large armies . . . against the enemy and at once fought a battle." Cannon favor the offensive; infantry are more valuable than cavalry. "Fortresses generally are more harmful than useful." And "Roman generals were never excessively punished for any misdeeds; nor . . . ever punished . . . [for] incapacity or bad planning" (*Discourses*, trans. Allan Gilbert, Books I–II).

Machiavelli's maxims sound Napoleonic today but, except in the field of international law, the conservative, liberal, socialist, and internationalist sciences of the management of social violence did not appear until four centuries later. The events of those centuries were to simplify the problems of both politics and war. Gunpowder gradually made all men tall, the infantryman again dominated war. Better transportation and siege weapons forced soldiers to think of grand tactics involving whole countries. More food, forage, and metals were available to support masses of men and horses. The French Revolution had involved many middle-class citizens. For the first time, perhaps, since antiquity, enough literate and politically conscious citizens knew enough about war to "ask the right questions about . . . battle" (Polybius, Book XII, Ch. xxviii a). And Clausewitz was not to be the only veteran of the Napoleonic wars to write about an art which was no longer the sport of kings or the secret of cabinets and great captains.

***Modern and Contemporary Warfare.*** Every ancient soldier after him might try to be an Alexander. Every modern one may try to be a Napoleon. The failure of all the European armies' war plans in 1914 led B. H. Liddel Hart to exorcise *The Ghost of Napoleon* (London, 1934) by claiming that "the influence of thought upon thought is the most influential factor in history," and that Clausewitz had not been "the prophet . . . of Napoleon," but "the Mahdi of mass and mutual massacre" (pp. 11, 120). Liddell Hart admitted that Clausewitz was easy to misunderstand, but Clausewitz' contemporary, A. H. Jomini—who had reduced Frederick's and Napoleon's grand tactics to geometrical figures which are still used in military science—did not think that he was obscure, but that he was much too skeptical about military science. This was true, though many later mathematical military scientists failed to note in their Clausewitzian incantations his remark that while an enemy's "power of resistance" can be "expressed as a product of two inseparable factors: *the extent of the means at his disposal* and *the strength of his will*," only the first can be estimated in "figures," and that the second is "only approximately to be measured by the strength of the motive behind it" (*On War*, Book I, Ch. ii, 6).

The people had to be armed, although Clausewitz saw "a people's war in civilized Eurore . . . [as] a phenomenon of the nineteenth century" which might be "as dangerous to the social order at home as to the enemy." Prussia's conservative military reformers, especially after the Revolution of 1848, had to manage national and popular "passions," while carefully training and indoctrinating a mass conscript army which might again have to "advance against Paris, and engage the French army in a great battle." Prussia was still the weakest of the great powers. Hence Prussia and her allies should *act with as much concentration . . . [and] as swiftly as possible.*" Clausewitz could not have been expected to see that a new Napoleon would be more afraid of arming the people than Prussia's conservatives would be. But he did fear that since "bounds once thrown down, are not easily built up again, . . . at least whenever great interests are in question, mutual hostility will discharge itself in the same manner as it has done in our time" (ibid., Book VI, Ch. xxvii; Book VIII, Chs. ix, iii b).

Although "militarism" is a nineteenth-century term, its meaning received little attention from nineteenth-century philosophers. There is no index entry for it in the eleventh edition of the *Encyclopaedia Britannica* (1911). John H. Muirhead's article on Hegel ignores Hegel's idea that modern war fosters unselfishness and does not lead individuals to hate individuals, and stresses "the overpowering sense of the value of organization" which had led Hegel to feel that "a vital interconnexion between all parts of the body politic is the source of all good" (*Encycl. Brit.*, XIII, 203). Later, democratic propagandists saw Nietzsche's supermen and Treitschke's history as characteristically militaristic, conservative, German, Clausewitzian, and Hegelian. Tocqueville, on the other hand, feared that the inevitable growth of democracy would also lead to despotism and militarism. While "peace is peculiarly hurtful to democratic armies, war" and its popular passions give "them advantages which . . . cannot fail in the end to give them the victory." His "secret connection between the military character and . . . [that] of democracies" was the profit motive. "Men of democracies are . . . passionately eager to acquire what they covet and to enjoy it on easy conditions, . . . worship chance, and are much less afraid of death than of difficulty. . . . No kind of greatness is more pleasing to the imagination of a democratic people than military greatness—a greatness of vivid and sudden luster obtained without toil by nothing but the risk of life" (*Democracy in America*, trans. Henry Reeves, London [1840], IV, 239–40).

Tocqueville felt that "no protracted war can fail to endanger the freedom of a democratic country," if only because "it must increase the powers of civil government." Democracy's defenses against militarism and Bonapartism lay in "characteristics of officers, noncommissioned officers and men" which were not uniform "at all times and among all democratic nations. In every democratic army the noncommissioned officers will be the worst representatives of the pacific and orderly spirit, . . . and the private soldiers the best." If the "community is ignorant and weak," its soldiers may "be drawn by their leaders into disturbances; . . . if it is enlightened and energetic, the community will itself keep" its leaders "within the bounds of order" (ibid., IV, 231–32).

Tocqueville died in 1859, the year in which Prussia's conservatives began to strengthen her army against Napoleon III's designs on the Rhine. The next decade ended with their founding of a German Empire at minimal costs in "blood and iron." This left them in a good position to combat the industrial classes' growing egalitarianism by the deliberate promotion of a popular militarism which promised still more "vivid and sudden luster."

During the next long peace the English liberal Hegelian, T. H. Green, argued that more democratic states saw the general good less militaristically, were less prone to resort to war, and were more likely to "arrive at a passionless impartiality in dealing with each other" (*Principles of Political Obligation*, London [1890], para. 175). His Social Darwinist contemporary, Herbert Spencer, held that the individualism sparked by the profit motive was the main source of modern social progress and that the progress of democracy and industrialism had already resulted in "a growing personal independence, . . . a smaller faith in governments, and a more qualified patriotism." These would eventually lead democratic industrial societies to return to the norms of "certain uncultured peoples whose lives are passed in peaceful occupations, . . . honesty, truthfulness, forgivingness, kindness." The general "decrease of warfare" in the nineteenth century had already brought considerable relaxation of governmental controls and popular militancy, although Germany's upper classes had successfully combined feudal controls and popular nationalism to spark those "increases of armaments and of aggressive activities" which had forced a temporary regression "toward the militant social type; alike in the development of the civil organization with its accompanying sentiments and ideas, and in the spread of socialistic theories" (*Principles of Sociology*, New York [1897], Vol. II, Ch. XXIII) in Europe.

Hegel and Tocqueville were closer to the realities of people's wars and revolutions than Green and

503

Spencer were. But none of this was very new, and there were no major philosophical treatises on or major histories of militarism. Each philosopher put his examples of Spencerian "social metamorphosis" into his general social philosophy. *On War* remains the only major philosophical treatise on that subject. By 1914 Clausewitzian ideas on the scientific management of war dominated military thought, and Napoleonic military ideas were as uniformly widespread as Frederician ones had been in 1789. But, as in the other social sciences, the scientific method had been only partly applied to the resulting mixture of ancient and modern lore which bolstered the discipline and morale of the industrial nations in arms.

Clausewitz did not see how the nascent Industrial Revolution would change war. British arms and money had played only supporting roles in defeating Napoleon in Russia and Germany. Better planning, rather than better weapons, had built the German Empire, though everyone saw the importance of national industrial potential. War's "accelerating self-transformation" was to be partly due to the "institutionalization of . . . innovation in . . . research laboratories, universities, . . . [and] general staffs" (William H. McNeill, *The Rise of the West*, Chicago [1963], p. 567), but what Whitehead later called the "invention of the method of invention" had been only partly applied in the peacetime armies which took the field in 1914.

Ardant du Picq's *Battle Studies* (1880) and Colmar von der Goltz's *The Nation in Arms* (London, 1883) had argued that men could only be moved against modern firepower by the "internal power" of "national egotism." More important, France's outnumbered army thought that it could win a Napoleonic battle with Germany. General Ferdinand Foch cited Frederick the Great, de Maistre, Napoleon, G. J. D. von Scharnhorst, Marshal de Saxe, Xenophon, and Clausewitz to show that, "*A battle won, is a battle in which one does not confess oneself beaten,*" and that the "old theory" of "superior numbers, . . . guns, . . . positions" was as "radically wrong" (Foch, *Principles of War* [1903], London [1921], pp. 286, 3) as the Russian banker and economist Ivan S. Bloch's statistical projections of *The Future of War in Its Technical, Economic, and Political Relations* (1898). Bloch saw the future of war as one of technical military deadlock, economic collapse, and political and social revolution.

Fifty years after the deadlock began, just before a new test of military thinking, a United States Air Force *Basic Doctrine* (1964) declared that "technological and tactical improvements must be continuous." Many nineteenth-century officers came from a class which knew as little science as many of its classically educated critics. Weaponry was left to private contractors or branch specialists. Testing was hampered and general industrial progress aided by the longest general peace in modern times. And "physical force" was being used to uphold the "moral force" of international law. Despite the fact that Bloch's work on the future of war influenced Nicholas II's call for the International Peace Congress of 1899, international arbitration among the great powers was seen in the article on "Arbitration, International" in the *Encyclopaedia Britannica* (1911) as offering only faint hope amidst "the springs of warlike enterprise still found in commercial jealousies, in imperialistic ambitions and in the doctrine of the survival of the fittest which lends scientific support to both" (II, 331). The author, M. H. Crackanthorpe, was the President of the Eugenics Education Society.

Two generations of violence produced many new combinations of old ideas. Technology was the *deus ex machina* in most victory, peace, and prosperity of Western nations. Science, for example, is the basis for Kenneth E. Boulding's "great transition" out of the war, development, population, and entropy "traps" of *The Meaning of the Twentieth Century* (New York, 1964). But this prolonged military intellectual crisis produced no new ideas about the origins of war, and even the definition of militarism was greatly affected by national experience and by more general conservative, liberal, and socialist ideas of conflict resolution or management.

***Definitions of Militarism.*** Vagts's massive *History of Militarism: Romance and Realities of a Profession* (1937, p. 11) reflected a liberal exile's view of recent German history in its distinction between a scientific "military way" and an unscientific militarism. "The military way is marked by . . . concentration . . . on winning specific objectives of power . . . with the least expenditure of blood and treasure. It is limited in scope, confined to one function, and scientific. . . . Militarism is so constituted that it may hamper . . . the military way. . . . It may permeate all society and become dominant over all industry and arts. Rejecting the scientific character of the military way, militarism displays the qualities of caste and cult, authority and belief." But military authority rests partly on belief. The French army which had lost the Battle of the Frontiers defeated the Germans at the Marne, and faith kept both armies attacking until they were finally exhausted.

Middle-class Prussian liberals were the first to define militarism. With the economic fortunes of the landed aristocracy still in decline, the officer corps sheltered many refugees. The now traditional values of loyalty to a monarch as a personal feudal lord, of nobles whose ancestors had sold out to or been ennobled by him, were in even sharper contrast with the middle-class values of equal opportunity for hard work for private profit. The first Prussian debates had turned on the status of middle-class *Landwehr* officers whose units were to prove untrustworthy during the Revolution of 1848. While the same events made the middle class as afraid of socialism as were the conservatives, its growing wealth was not matched by more openings for its sons in the officer corps.

As the social effects of victory wore off, the German Empire's liberals returned to the attack. Prussia's conservatives did not invent "scientific management"—a late nineteenth-century term made popular by an American, Henry O. Taylor—but they had greatly extended the scope of military, educational, and political management in a system which won the loyalties of large segments of the middle and lower classes. Many of the most extreme Social Darwinist glorifications of war came from such late nineteenth-century military publicists as Friedrich von Bernhardi. Von der Goltz felt that *The Nation in Arms* demanded an *"increase* of our moral forces, . . . for . . . [in Scharnhorst's words] 'never are moral forces at rest; they fall as soon as they no longer increase'" (trans. Philip A. Ashworth, p. 290). These effusions did not halt the decline of the conservative parliamentary parties; they did warn Germany's neighbors of the dangers of German militarism. And Bismarck's constitution could not cope with a supreme warlord who sounded like the ghost of Napoleon, but could not act like the ghost of Frederick the Great.

The German Empire was militaristic in tone, but military men did not determine its policies. The German army could not check massive expenditures on a navy which helped to bring Great Britain into an anti-German coalition. No staffs for scientific weapons evaluation or research and development, for army-navy cooperation, or for coordinating foreign and military policy were set up to advise the Emperor. A popularly elected *Reichstag* could check spending, but not military or foreign policy action. Chancellor Bethmann-Hollweg later boasted that he had not interfered in a military policy which led to the invasion of neutral Belgium. Germany became a military dictatorship in 1916. Its war aims made the destruction of militarism and the democratization of Germany popular goals among her enemies. To link their weak attempts to secure those goals with their greater efforts to weaken Germany needed no Hitler.

Postwar fascism also influenced Vagts's views of militarism. Its rhetoric became still more flamboyant in imposing new orders on masses which had been deliberately led to hope for more revolutionary results from their sacrifices. Vagts was not sure of communist militarism. He did note that "Fascist and Communist armies alike appeal to honor in secular language," that "the old Christian international idea of honor" had survived "better in newer countries with less of a feudal heritage, as in the United States," and that much military history was "a phase of militarism" (pp. 484–85, 21). He could not have been expected to see that none of the totalitarian powers, except Japan, was militaristic in the sense that military scientists determined policy.

The totalitarian powers' evaluations of air power—the most important new weapon of the interwar era—were no more scientific than the evaluation of sea power by Wilhelmine Germany, and rather less so than those made by the "Anglo-Americans." Their politicians "interfered" in military operations more often than was the case with democracies which had improved their decision making institutions to cope with matters which the Great War had shown to be "too important to be left to the generals." The postwar Clausewitzians managed the populist version of conservative militarism as poorly as the nobles had managed France to support Tocqueville's view that "an aristocratic nation . . . [which] does not succeed in ruining" a democratic one "at the outset of the war . . . runs a great risk of being conquered by it" (*Democracy in America*, IV, 240).

Social Darwinism is not necessarily evidence of democratic militarism. Carolyn E. Playne's *The Neuroses of the Nations* (London, 1925), Edward Glover's *War, Sadism, and Pacifism* (London, 1947), and Alix Strachey's *The Unconscious Motives of War* (London, 1957) are typical popularizations of many efforts to apply social psychiatry to militarism. One can accept Playne's idea of a mass mind which "first in Germany, then in France, [showed] signs of nervous breakdown," but not that "parliamentary government in France abdicated to the War Office" and "military authority ruled the land, the Court and the Kaiser in Germany" (pp. 461, 464) before 1914. She saw "time" and "hope" as curatives, but German, Japanese, and Italian militarism were to be cured by outside powers, while militarism remains a plausible restorative for both conservative and radical nationalists in many countries.

The idea that militarism chiefly affects great powers which have accomplished something by war is supported by those who see contemporary American militarism as an outgrowth of her crusades against war, fascism, and communism. In 1890 there were less than 4000 American officers on active duty in a population of nearly 63,000,000. In spite of the demands of imperialism and navalism, there were fewer than 27,000 such officers—a quarter of the number of physicians—in a population of nearly 130,000,000 in 1938. By 1965 there were 350,000 officers for "normal"

505

armed forces of 2,500,000 in a population of 195,000,000. Until the second half of this century, the American soldiers' guild had to see war, S. P. Huntington noted in 1957, "as an independent science, . . . the practice . . . [of which] was the only purpose of military forces" (p. 255). The soundness of its professional advice was partly responsible for militarism's growth in a liberal society in which Huntington furthermore sees "the power of the military" as "the greatest threat to their professionalism" (p. 464). His "militarism" is Vagts's "military way." Its American strands are "technism, populism, and professionalism" (p. 193), its main "historical fact . . . the extent to which liberal ideology and conservative Constitution . . . dictate an inverse relation between political power and military professionalism" (p. 143).

This first major American treatise on civil-military relations found American and Soviet patterns historically "similar; . . . the dominance of a single anti-military ideology . . . put obstacles in the way of military professionalism." Better relations between the U.S. and Russia, he felt, would depend on both adopting a more "conservative outlook, divorced from universalistic pretensions." He defined the "military ethic" as one which combined a conservative view of "the permanence . . . [of] evil in human nature" with the Hegelian "supremacy of society over the individual," medieval ideas of "order, hierarchy, and division of function," and modern ones of "the nation state as the highest form of political organization, . . . the continuing likelihood of wars among nation states, . . . and the importance of power in international relations" (ibid., pp. 463, 79). If the United States and the Soviet Union have become militaristic by a "realistic and conservative" acceptance of the results of their victories, the process was rather like that by which defeat forced both democracy and militarism on France after 1870.

Realistic conservative nineteenth-century Marxists, such as Karl Liebknecht, saw the social evil of private ownership of the means of production as the source of all social conflict. Militarism "exhibits . . . the national, cultural, and class instinct of self-preservation, that most powerful of all instincts." Its history is that "of human development, . . . strained relations and jealousies between nations and states, arising from their desires for political and social power or economic advantage, . . . [and] class-struggles within nations and states for the same objects" (*Militarism* [1907], Eng. trans. New York [1917], p. 2). The Marxist contribution to military thought was practical rather than theoretical. Engels' ideas for training workers for the coming revolution did not allay conservative fears of mass armies' unreliability. The French socialist, Jean Jaurès,

agreed with Spencer that industrialized democracies were less likely to become militaristic; he wanted to begin military training at ten and to cut peacetime active service to six months (*L'Armée nouvelle*, Paris [1910]; trans. as *Democracy and Military Power*, London [1916]). But no democratic socialist general strikes erupted in 1914. That nations in arms have fought so well when "great interests" are involved underlines the populist and nationalist demands for military power which may result in what Janowitz (1964b, p. 16) calls "reactive militarism."

Contemporary research on militarism takes in developing societies in which militarism is mainly internal, as well as developed ones, and tries to fix the degrees of political and social power held by soldiers. Some advanced democracies now need only an internal or international "constabulary" for peacekeeping purposes (Janowitz [1964a], p. 12). The soldiers of some totalitarian popular democracies may well be quite realistic conservatives, but they are still subject to political interference in their professional affairs. In Huntington's view of professionalism in a liberal society, political involvement hampers professional soldiers, who seldom get the expertise to compete with its political, profit-making, and technological professionals. In its industrial-political-military complexes, soldiers may become the scapegoats of "reactive militarism." Liberals who are already suspicious of military men credit the guild's successes to its liberal indoctrination, and blame it for any political failures. Soldiers may then blame their failures on a "stab in the back" by the liberal politicians who ordered the war or the profit-makers who sold them a particular weapons system in the first place.

Finer (1962) sees the descent into covert or overt military rule beginning with threats of mass resignation or noncooperation. Then come vetoes of particular policies or politicians, manipulating or delaying elections in the interest of public order, or the preventive detention or murder of opposition politicians, and covert or overt rule by soldiers. While they can take advantage of the communications and intelligence networks needed by all modern armies, their heavy weapons may not produce for military politicians the force they were once supposed to have even against urban dissidents. And as Clausewitz once remarked about a romantic view of people's war: "Even if we do not consider it as an . . . unconquerable element, over which the mere force of an army has as little control as . . . over the wind, . . . we cannot drive armed peasants before us like a body of soldiers who keep together like a herd of cattle, and usually follow their noses" (*On War*, Book VI, Ch. xxvi).

The "reactive" theory of militarism best fits great

powers—such as Prussia—under constant foreign military pressure. The demand for weapons and professional military leadership was a popular national concern, though professional politicians with mass parties behind them can generally get military efficiency without sharing real political power. Existing democratic polities survived total wars in Great Britain and the United States, wars which led to more effective civilian governments in Russia and China. Postwar great power military aid programs increased soldiers' power in other states, but did so by increasing their managerial skills as much as by giving them better weapons. And realistic liberals, conservatives, nationalists, and socialists have tapped so many popular forces to strengthen their external and internal power positions that the resulting spectrum of attitudes toward the just uses of social violence can be made to fit almost any *a priori* definition of militarism.

Andreski's look at "war, its alleged evil or beneficial effects, its causes, and the possibilities of its abolition" (1954, p. 1) goes with his belief that only Weber and Mosca among sociology's founders had examined the role of "military factors in shaping societies." This reflects "the insidious utopianism which pervades sociological thinking" and soldiers' fears that a "critical examination of the exercise of violence . . . might besmirch . . . [their] idols." But his theoretical classification of societies by military population ratios and levels of subordination and cohesion is only another sign of the interests which turned Chicago scholars from the historical and legal studies of Wright (1942) to Janowitz' "elite analysis" of *The Professional Soldier* (1960) based on "empirical data on social background, career lines, professional ideology, and decision-making" (1964a, p. 15) without greatly illuminating war's fundamental causes.

*Origins of War.* Buchan's *War in Modern Society* shows that if "strategic studies, the analysis of the role of force in international relations, have yet to find their Keynes" (1966, p. xii), social psychologists are no better managers of what their predecessors called the instinct of aggression. McDougall's "instinct of pugnacity" was a secondary one, activated by inhibiting another. "Emulation" would replace it in advanced societies, to "end what has been . . . probably the most important factor of progressive evolution . . . [in] individuals and societies" (*Social Psychology*, London [1908], Ch. XI). William James felt that "our ancestors have bred pugnacity into our bone and marrow," and that "military instincts and ideals are as strong as ever." His argument for a "Moral Equivalent of War" (1910; Bramson [1964], pp. 21–31) was similar to those of Bloch or of Norman Angell's widely read *The Great Illusion: a Study of the Relation of Miltary Power in*

*Nations to their Economic and Social Advantage* (London, 1911). "Modern war," James held, "is so expensive that we feel trade to be a better avenue for plunder. . . . Competitive *preparation . . . is the real war,* . . . battles are only a sort of public verification of the mastery gained during the 'peace' interval. . . . When whole nations are the armies and the science of destruction vies in intellectual refinement with the sciences of production, . . . war becomes absurd and impossible."

Freud took years to admit an "aggressive instinct alongside of the familiar instincts of self-preservation and sex, and on an equal footing with them." But by 1930 he felt that "men are not gentle creatures who want to be loved, and who at the most can defend themselves if . . . attacked." Checks on aggression are one source of civilized man's discontents. It had "very probably" taken "the bees, the ants, the termites . . . thousands of years" to arrive "at the State institutions . . . for which we admire them." The "question for the human species . . . [is whether] their cultural development will . . . [master] the disturbance of their communal life by the human instinct of aggression . . . [now that] they have gained control over the forces of nature to such an extent that . . . they would have no difficulty in exterminating one another to the last man" (*Civilization and Its Discontents* [1930], New York [1961], pp. 8, 58, 92).

Some Freudians' views of militarism have been noted elsewhere. In "Personal Aggressiveness and War" (1938; Bramson [1964], pp. 81–103), E. F. M. Durbin and John Bowlby saw the projection of aggression to internal or external scapegoats as relieving social tensions. The work of John Dollard and others on *Human Frustration and Aggression* (New Haven, 1939) was followed by his practical *Fear in Battle* (New Haven, 1943) and official *Studies of Social Psychology in World War II* (4 vols., Princeton, 1949), but L. L. Bernard felt that *War and Its Causes* (New York [1944], p. 23) still eluded "all-purpose" definitions. And in the contemporary social explosion—from overpopulation, poverty, etc.—theory of war goes little beyond Machiavelli's or Bodin's maxims.

Konrad Lorenz' and other ethologists' works *On Aggression* (New York, 1966) enliven the 1960's. Lorenz sees aggression as a general instinct which is highly adaptive to ecological conditions. In territorial species it divides the habitat for their survival. In social ones it may create hierarchical structures in which authority and experience are predominant. Baboons' controlled group aggressiveness fits their feeding habits; related species act as if dominance were less important. But ethologists study species with highly stereotyped responses, and most of the argument is by analogy. Aggressive human responses to many situations are far from stereotyped even in individuals, and the social anthropologist Ashley Montagu (*On Being Human*, New York, 1966) sees all this as a new myth of original sin to project and displace the learned social evils of war and aggression to nature.

Our ideas of progress and states make it hard to take Polybius' view of history as "education . . . for political action" with "the memory of other people's calamities" as "the only source from which we can learn to bear the vicissitudes of Fortune with courage" (*Histories*, Book I, Ch. i). Wright (1964, p. 154) found so many historical causes of war that studying "the engineering of peace" was more profitable. After showing war as "the proximate cause of the breakdown of every civilization . . . known for certain to have broken down" and the failure of all universal empires, Toynbee (1951, pp. vii–xii) still hoped for "a voluntary association of peace-loving peoples" strong and wise enough "to avoid any serious wish to challenge its authority." And McNeill (*Rise* . . . , p. 806) hopes that power "which has dominated the whole history of mankind" will "coalesce under an overarching world sovereignty [until] the impetus now impelling men to develop new sources of power will largely cease."

The voluminous works of contemporary military intellectuals contain no new ideas on the origins of war. They deal with the scientific management of war in an atmosphere of popular fears of absolute weapons and revolutionary passions. While great powers are deterred from direct attacks on each other, this may produce nonevents which seem like victories, and old ideas of influence spark wars in which "irresponsible" small powers may manage their sponsors. Some resulting problems are familiar. Guerrillas may counter superior machines hiding among the people; Americans saved their men by using machines so indiscriminately that popular passions overturned their managers and imperiled the "great interests" allegedly in question.

In this situation a "satisfactory" scientific view of war is as remote as ever. The sociologist Raymond Aron (1959, pp. 114, 119) finds the "twentieth century an aggregate of past centuries, . . . [without] even the rudiments of an advance over them," or any hopes for the further neutralization of areas threatened by nuclear war, and notes that these "cannot be indefinitely extended." The economist Boulding (*Meaning* . . . , pp. 90–91) uses Bloch's argument. "In the age of civilization war was a stable social institution, and for mankind as a whole, a tolerable one. In the twentieth century the system of international relations . . . based on unilateral national defense has broken down because of the change in the fundamental parameters of the system, and war has therefore become intolerable." His

hope in the social sciences is James's hope that "the ordinary prides and shames of social man . . . are capable of organizing such a moral equivalent . . . [of war]. It is but a question of time, of skillful propagandism, and of opinion-making men seizing historic opportunities" ("Moral Equivalent of War," p. 29).

**Conclusion.** Social science has contributed to some understanding of the political, technological, and military causes of particular wars. It provides psychological props for the hope that it may help to kill that one of the four horsemen which did the most social damage in the first half of the twentieth century, or at least that one which is most clearly social in origin. But military science is so rooted in the particular actions of individuals and groups in so wide a variety of particular circumstances that the history of ideas about the causes of war and militarism remains one of new combinations of old philosophical insights and ideas.

*BIBLIOGRAPHY*

S. Andreski, *Military Organization and Society* (1954; 2d ed., Berkeley, 1968). R. Aron, *De la Guerre* (1957), trans. Terence Kilmartin as *On War* (Garden City, N.Y., 1959). L. Bramson, and G. W. Goethals, eds., *War: Studies from Psychology, Sociology, Anthropology* (New York, 1964) is a fine anthology. A. Buchan, *War in Modern Society: An Introduction* (London, 1966). C. von Clausewitz, *Vom Kriege* (1832–34), trans. O. M. J. Jollis as *On War* (New York, 1943). B. W. C. Cook et al., eds., *The Garland Library of War and Peace* (New York) is a reprint series. E. M. Earle, ed., *Makers of Modern Strategy: Military Thought from Machiavelli to Hitler* (1942; New York, 1966). S. E. Finer, *The Man on Horseback: The Role of the Military in Politics* (New York, 1962). S. P. Huntington, *The Soldier and the State: The Theory and Politics of Civil-Military Relations* (1957; New York, 1964). M. Janowitz, *The Professional Soldier: A Social and Political Portrait* (Glencoe, Ill., 1960); idem, ed., *The New Military: Changing Patterns of Organization* (New York, 1964a); idem, *The Military in the Political Development of New Nations: An Essay in Comparative Analysis* (Chicago, 1964b). T. R. Phillips, ed., *Roots of Strategy: A Collection of Military Classics* (Harrisburg, Pa., 1940). Polybius, *Histories*, trans. Mortimer Chambers, abridged, intro. by E. Badian (New York, 1966). D. B. Ralston, ed., *Soldiers and States: Civil-Military Relations in Modern Europe* (Boston, 1966) is a good anthology. L. F. Richardson, *Statistics of Deadly Quarrels*, ed. Q. Wright and C. C. Lienau (Pittsburgh, 1960), and *Arms and Insecurity: A Mathematical Study of the Causes and Origins of War*, ed. N. Rashevsky and E. Trucco (Pittsburgh, 1960) are attempts at mathematical analysis. G. Ritter, *Staatskunst und Kriegshandwerk: Das Problem des "Militarismus" in Deutschland* (1954–64), trans. Heinz Norden as *The Sword and the Scepter: The Problem of Militarism in Germany*, 3 vols. (Miami, Fla., 1969–). T. Ropp, *War in the Modern World*, 2d ed. (New York, 1962), history since the Hundred Years War. U.

Schwarz, *American Strategy: A New Perspective, the Growth of Politico-Military Thinking in the United States* (Garden City, N.Y., 1966) is a favorable Swiss view of contemporary American military intellectuals. A. Storr, *Human Aggression* (New York, 1968) covers the ethological debate. A. J. Toynbee, *War and Western Civilization* (New York, 1951). A. Vagts, *A History of Militarism: Civilian and Military* (1937; London, 1960) contains a mass of information. K. M. Waltz, *Man, the State and War: A Theoretical Analysis* (New York, 1959) is the most important single work. R. F. Weigley, ed., *The American Military: Readings in the History of the Military in American Society* (Reading, Mass., 1969). *The West Point Military Library* (Westport, Conn.) is a second important reprint series in this field. Q. Wright, *A Study of War,* 2 vols. (1942, abridged ed. Chicago, 1964).

Unless noted otherwise, translations are by the author of the article.

THEODORE ROPP

[See also **Nationalism; Peace;** State.]

# WELFARE STATE

THE TERM "welfare state" in English is of recent origin. First used during the Second World War, it passed into general currency only after 1945. There had been intermittent discussion, however, some of it sophisticated, about the contribution the state should make to the social welfare of all its citizens from the eighteenth century onwards. "It is the duty of a government to do whatever is conducive to the welfare of the governed," the political economist Nassau Senior, one of the main architects of the new English Poor Law of 1834, argued in his Oxford lectures of 1847–48. In the meantime, Richard Oastler, a tory-radical critic both of early factory industrialism and of political economy, had advocated in his journal, *The Fleet Papers,* in 1842 the creation of what he called the "social state." This state would seek "to secure the prosperity and happiness of every class of society": it would be particularly concerned, also, with "the protection of the poor and needy, because they require the shelter of the constitution and the laws more than any other classes."

Oastler was a traditionalist, and his conception of the "social state" was different from that of Senior, who believed in a market economy and in the substitution of contract for status in the pattern of social relations. Yet both men rejected the idea of the property-protecting "night-watchman state" caricatured by Ferdinand Lassalle in Germany (where the authority of the state was far greater than in Britain).

They both recognized that it was no longer possible to provide adequate welfare services to support individuals through the family, the Church, the guild or private "charity." They were both aware of the fact that the rise of factory industry had posed new problems which demanded urgent solutions. In particular, they identified, though in contrasting styles, social contingencies associated with industrialization, particularly unemployment.

Sickness, old age, and death entail hardships in any society: poverty was in no sense a postindustrial phenomenon. Yet the massing of large numbers of people in factories and in cities changed the language and content of social and political analysis. As the nineteenth century went by and, after struggles, new groups of the population had secured the right to vote, politics became more directly concerned with what to do with newly acquired political power. The demand for the provision by the state of particular social services—a piecemeal process explicable in terms of cumulative administrative processes and political pressures—was accompanied by the articulation of comprehensive theories of the state which rested on arguments for positive state intervention. Thus, John Ruskin, defying the fashionable economic orthodoxy of the day, urged that the state should ensure that all its citizens received a living wage and were guaranteed full employment in the name of social justice. Thus, T. H. Green, arguing that "citizenship makes the moral man," urged the case for "positive liberalism," and Arnold Toynbee (1852–83), historian of early industrialization, demanded in a popular lecture of 1882 that "where the people are unable to provide a thing for themselves, and that thing is *of primary social importance,* then . . . the state should interfere and provide it for them."

These were minority views, even then not always free from ambiguity. Throughout the nineteenth century there were four curbs on effective state action in Britain, for long the most industrialized society. First, political economists, even when they refused to talk in slogan terms of laissez-faire, were skeptical about the interference of the state with the operations of the market: at most, they pressed for an abandonment of social laissez-faire while accepting the need for economic laissez-faire and international free trade. Second, belief in the importance of individual self-help or mutual self-help through voluntary organizations (including the friendly society and the trade union) held back any effective talk of "reliance" on the state: people were expected to fend for themselves through savings and insurance. Action on the part of the state was deemed to be both expensive and debilitating. Third, the receipt of help from the state or from local

509

authorities carried with it a stigma. People who accepted "relief" were not thought of as full citizens. The Poor Law of 1834 was based on this assumption: it was never abandoned even when the operations of the 1834 Act were refined and mollified. Fourth, the apparatus of the state was viewed with suspicion not only by businessmen but by workingmen: they identified it with unpopular social institutions and coercive action, and judged it not in terms of purposes which it might fulfil but in terms of restraints which it imposed. Instead of looking to the state, they looked rather to the trade union and instead of seeking direct political action (or, except when deemed absolutely necessary, resort to the law), they preferred to work voluntarily through collective bargaining. There was, indeed, surprisingly little political talk of the state as such. As Matthew Arnold put it in 1861, "we have not the notion, so familiar on the Continent and to antiquity, of the state—the nation in its collective and corporate character, entrusted with stringent powers for the general advantage and controlling individual wills in the name of an interest wider than that of individuals."

In Germany the position was different. The word "state" was generally used, and was endowed with a sense of authority. Moreover, the extension of the administrative apparatus of the state long preceded the advent of industrialism. At the same time, belief in the autonomous market economy was far less strong, and an influential group of historically minded political economists argued fervently that national economy (*Volkswirtschaft*) had to be converted into state economy (*Staatswirtschaft*) with "welfare" as the objective. Bismarck did not go anywhere near as far as many of the "socialists of the Chair," academic protagonists of a state dedicated to welfare, but through laws passed in 1882, 1884, and 1889 he introduced compulsory national insurance against sickness, accidents, old age, and invalidity. "The state," it was laid down in his first unsuccessful bill of 1881, "is not merely a necessary but a beneficent institution." In the last years of his life Bismarck also contemplated insurance against unemployment and talked with assurance about "the right to work." His objectives were, of course, mixed. He wished to provide an alternative to laissez-faire liberalism, but he also wished to sap the strength of the rising socialist movement. The national state was to become an instrument of welfare within the limits set by the capitalist system and the traditional framework of the social order: in return the masses, he believed, would be attached through greater patriotism to the state. He conceived of social insurance, indeed, as a form of political insurance, and the kind of society in which he put his trust was as hierarchical as that extolled by Oastler.

Other continental countries introduced insurance schemes without necessarily accepting Bismarck's calculations, and in Australia and New Zealand there were politicians who believed in what the French called "socialism without doctrines" and went much further than any Europeans did in urging in the name of equal citizenship that "the more the state does for the citizen, the more it fulfills its purpose . . . the functions of the state shall be extended as much as possible. . . . True democracy consists in the extension of state activity" (from a speech by New Zealand politician, W. Pember Reeves, 1895). The New Zealand Old Age Pensions Act of 1898 was the first to be passed in a British dominion. Though it has been described as a "social palliative," it marked the all-important beginning of a noncontributory pensions system.

When in the early twentieth century the British Liberal party carried a series of social service measures which have been noted in retrospect as landmarks on the way to the welfare state, it had both German and "colonial" experience in mind. At the same time, the driving force behind three new welfare measures—the feeding of school children, the school medical service, and old age pensions—had indigenous motivation. By contrast, unemployment and health insurance, in particular, were strongly influenced by Germany, with Winston Churchill, then President of the Board of Trade, writing to H. Asquith in 1908 that "the Minister who will apply to this country the successful experiences of Germany in Social Organisation may or may not be supported at the polls, but he will at least have left a memorial which time will not deface of his administration." The self-helping activities of working-class movements were no longer thought to be adequate either by a growing number of socialists anxious to exert political influence to eliminate "poverty in the midst of plenty" or by trade-union groups like the miners and the agricultural laborers who, for various reasons, could not secure their union objectives (for example, a shortening of the length of the working day or a minimum wage) simply through the machinery of collective bargaining. The charitable efforts of philanthropists, it was increasingly recognized even by philanthropists themselves, could not alleviate all the social problems of an increasingly complex industrial society. In this recognition the publication of social statistics played a big part: well-documented poverty surveys by Charles Booth, Seebohm Rowntree, and others revealed the continuing extent of poverty in British cities after a century of economic growth and relative affluence. Once their statistics had been published, wrote the Fabian socialist Beatrice Webb, "the net effect was to give an entirely fresh impetus to the general adoption of the policy of securing to every individual, as the basis of his life and work, a prescribed national minimum of the requisites for efficient parenthood and citizenship" (*My Apprenticeship* [1926], p. 239).

Beatrice Webb was prominent in the campaign which accompanied and followed the meetings of the Royal Commission on the Poor Laws (1905–09) to substitute new welfare policies for the Poor Law of 1834, policies which would remove the stigma attaching to the receipt of public money. She claimed that the introduction of these policies would not only mark a new stage in the history of citizenship but would constitute a return to older theories of the relationship between the individual and the community. "The whole theory of the mutual obligation between the individual and the state, which I find myself working out in my poor law scheme, is taken straight out of the nobler aspect of the mediaeval manor. It will come as a new idea to the present generation—it is really a very old one that has been thrust out of sight in order to attain some measure of equality in political rights. There are some who wish to attain to a socialist state by the assertion of economic equality—they desire to force the property-owners to yield to the non-property owners. I prefer to have the forward movement based on the obligation of each individual to serve" (*Our Partnership*, London [1948], p. 385). Political affinities have often been traced between the Fabian socialists and the Benthamites who played such a big part in initiating and implementing the Poor Law of 1834: it is interesting to note that in this statement Beatrice Webb was echoing rather the kind of arguments used by Oastler, though in a very different kind of language.

Yet the socialists, Fabian or otherwise, were less important in the introduction of new welfare measures than the Liberals, some of whom called themselves "new liberals" and rejected all arguments in favor of laissez-faire. Their theories, well set out, for example, by J. A. Hobson, were reinforced by other sets of statistics besides those collected by Booth and Rowntree. Statistics released in the aftermath of the Boer War concerning ill health and malnutrition raised fundamental questions about "national efficiency." So, too, did later figures concerning rural distress. It was for reasons embedded in British history, therefore, that after 1906 a Liberal government with a large majority introduced legislation, much of it controversial, to extend welfare services. The Education (Provision of Meals) Act, 1906, permitting the provision of free meals at school for needy children, was the first of a number of measures which entailed direct intervention on the part of the state in an activity previously falling entirely within a sphere of family responsibility. Old Age Pensions followed in 1908, though the Act was hedged round with qualifications limiting the right to receive pensions. In 1900 trade boards were set up to deal with conditions and wages in sweated industries, where collective bargaining was ineffective, and in 1911, in face of Fabian as well as Conservative criticism, national insurance was introduced. The term "welfare state" was not used, but much of the language of parliamentary and public debate centered on the issue of state provision of welfare. "A new spirit was disclosing itself," wrote R. B. Haldane, a Liberal minister of the year 1906. "It is not about details that the people care or are stirred. What they seem to desire is that they should seem to have something approaching to equality of chance of life with those among whom they live.... There was earnestness about state intervention to be seen everywhere" (R. B. Haldane, *Autobiography* [1929], p. 213).

The measures initiated largely by Lloyd George and Churchill after 1908, culminating in the insurance acts, represented a major achievement. They were explicitly nonsocialist—they left the profit system intact—but they introduced a greater note of responsibility into social politics and a firmer basis of collective organization. They were pushed even further as a result of the First World War when Lloyd George, in a different capacity, talked of creating "a land fit for heroes," and a Ministry of Reconstruction turned to new proposals for change. "The public," a committee of 1918 reported, "not only has its conscience aroused and its heart stirred, but also has its mind open ... to an unprecedented degree." Immediate postwar reforms did not go far to meet the high hopes of the war years, but the Unemployment Insurance Act of 1920, passed with little criticism, greatly increased the numbers of people insured under national schemes, and the Housing Act of 1919 not only required local authorities to survey housing needs but offered government subsidies to help them to provide houses. Referring to this act, the National Housing and Town Planning Council commented that "it has needed the earthquake shock of war to bring the nation to the recognition of the truth ... that it is the duty of the community ... to take the necessary action, however drastic."

The process of extending the social services continued in Britain between 1919 and 1939 with public provision of housing constituting the major postwar innovation. Yet there was little doubt in Britain, as in other European countries and in the United States, that large-scale involuntary mass unemployment following the world depression of 1929 constituted a major watershed. Heavy unemployment strained poor law, social service, and above all insurance systems beyond the limit. Insurance benefits, limited to contributions, were stringently restricted, and while there were fierce arguments between socialists and nonsocialists about the imposition of a "means test" on those in receipt

511

of unemployment relief, an Unemployment Board, founded in 1934, was providing a second-line income maintenance service, centrally administered. Keynesian economic policies to eliminate unemployment were rejected by the government in power, but the social consequences of unemployment were studied carefully by advocates of a more active social service policy.

The main theorists of large-scale intervention were to be found not in Britain but in Sweden and in New Zealand, with spokesmen of the New Deal in the United States urging if not the creation of a "welfare state" the extension of "welfare capitalism." In Sweden, where a social democratic government came into power in the wake of the world depression (in Britain the Labour government went out of power) a series of welfare measures was introduced based on the assumption, as Gunnar Myrdal put it, that the state must achieve certain social goals: a high standard of nutrition, full employment, and social welfare for all its citizens. In New Zealand a Labour government, which took office in 1935, placed in the center of its program proposals which had been set out since 1919: sustenance payments instead of relief work (the right to work was proclaimed); a national health service as free as education; state housing and a statutory minimum wage. The 1938 Social Security Act marked "a radical and far-reaching effort to place the claims of welfare before those of wealth."

In the United States the position was more complex. There had always been Americans who had urged the need for state action in welfare matters. Thus, the institutional economist Richard T. Ely had argued in the late nineteenth century that the state was "an educational and ethical agency whose positive aim is an indispensable condition of human progress" and that "the doctrine of *laissez faire* is unsafe in politics and unsound in morals and . . . suggests an inadequate explanation of the relations between the state and the citizens." More than 1500 labor laws were passed by different American states in the decade after 1887. Yet American society had been shaped more by market forces than any other society in the world, and there were far more critics of state interference than there were supporters, both in periods of affluence and in periods of recession. There were over thirteen million unemployed when F. D. Roosevelt became President in 1933 and one of the objects of his New Deal was to widen the concept of social justice in the course of dealing with economic emergency. The policies of the New Deal were derived from many different sources, but they all entailed increasing state intervention. No comprehensive national structure of social security was introduced, but steps were taken to raise low incomes (through the Fair Labor Standards Act

of 1938), to offer aid to the disabled (through the important Social Security Act of 1935), and to reduce unemployment. Roosevelt's policies, eclectic in character, have been hailed as landmarks in the history of the welfare idea and in the evolution of empirical collectivism. They certainly generated enough bitter opposition to account for the fact that when the term "welfare state" began to be used after 1945 it was almost always used in the United States in a pejorative sense, even after a number of new welfare provisions had been introduced both in individual states and by the federal government. Yet it is certainly difficult to call the United States of the 1930's a "welfare state." At best it was a society where a series of improvisations reduced the extent to which the market dictated the living conditions of individuals and families and where social and political gospels were publicly expressed.

What was true of the United States was true, indeed, of most countries in 1939, with the possible exception of New Zealand and of the Soviet Union where there was no problem of relating a network of state social services to a market-based and privately owned industrial system. Russian social services were regulated rather in terms of the assessed exigencies of "socialist development," and there was no theory of welfare outside the framework of Marxist-Leninist analysis. In Britain, too, it was clear in 1939 that the network of social services which had been created during the nineteenth and twentieth centuries did not constitute a system. The services were financed separately, covered only limited sections of the population, and were restricted in duration and scope. They had certainly not proved adequate to deal with the brute facts of poverty and malnutrition, social insecurity and mass unemployment.

The great turning point came during the Second World War which was sufficiently protracted in length and extensive in its influence on the lives of the masses of the population everywhere to promote talk of a "better world" when the war ended. There was no shortage of such talk in the occupied countries and even in Nazi Germany itself, and in Britain, where the powers of the state were greatly extended after 1939, the belief was widely held that, in the words of an official paper on social security policy published in 1944, "in a matter so fundamental, it is right for all citizens to stand in together, without exclusion based on differences of status, function or wealth." The argument was not just that administrative processes affecting the operation of the social services would be simplified if structures were "comprehensive" or "universal," but that through universal services, "concrete expression would be given to the solidarity and unity of the nation." What had been achieved in war could be achieved in peace "in the fight against individual want and mischance."

In such statements, as in the writings of Sir William Beveridge who did much to propound and to publicize this philosophy, there was a significant shift from the idea of a social service state, improvising and extending welfare networks for people in misfortune, to that of a "welfare state" providing a basic minimum for everybody. There were other shifts too. As Richard Titmuss, the historian of British social policy during the war has remarked, "it was increasingly regarded as a proper function or even obligation of government to ward off distress and strain not only among the poor but among all classes of society. And because the area of responsibility had so perceptibly widened, it was no longer thought sufficient to provide through various branches of social assistance a standard of service hitherto considered appropriate for those in receipt of poor assistance" (*Problems of Social Policy* [1950], p. 506). In other words, the standards of provision on the part of the state were expected to rise. "The deep desire of men to free themselves from the fear of want," a desire identified in the deliberations of the International Labour Organisation Conference at Philadelphia in 1944, was a foundation of policy, but welfare policy would be expected to fulfill further aspirations also.

It was perhaps in relation to unemployment, however, the social scourge of the 1930's, that the war produced the greatest transformation of attitudes. The virtual disappearance of unemployment in war conditions suggested that it could be kept to a very low figure in peacetime. Sir William Beveridge, who had written his first study of unemployment as early as 1909, argued in his influential *Full Employment in a Free Society* (1945), which was strongly influenced by Keynes, that "it must be a function of the state . . . to protect its citizens against mass unemployment, as definitely as it is now the function of the state to defend the citizens against attack from abroad and against robbery and violence at home" (p. 25). The doctrine received less general assent in the United States, although it was strongly supported by a number of economists, including Alvin H. Hansen, and in 1946 an important Employment Act laid down that it was "the continuing policy and responsibility of the Federal Government to use all practicable means . . . to promote maximum employment, production and purchasing power [and] to co-ordinate and utilize all its plans, functions and resources for the purpose of creating and maintaining, in a manner calculated to foster and promote free competitive enterprise and the general welfare, conditions under which there will be afforded useful employment opportunities, including self-employment, for those able, willing and seeking to work."

Soon after the Employment Act was passed, the term "welfare state" began to be used on both sides of the Atlantic. It was the program of the British Labour government, brought into power at the general election of 1945, which, in particular, focussed international attention on welfare policies and stimulated both its critics and its supporters to sum up its objective as the creation of a "welfare state." In this connection, the National Health Act of 1947 was of central importance. "Homes, health, education and social security, these are your birthright," exclaimed Aneurin Bevan, its architect. The act provided a universal and comprehensive health service "without any insurance qualifications of any sort": "it is available," Bevan pointed out, "to the whole population, and not only is it available to the whole population freely, but it is intended, through the health service to generalise the best health advice and treatment." The Act was more strongly attacked in the United States, where there was no state-provided "medicare," than in Britain, and it did much to stimulate debate on the merits and pitfalls of a "welfare state."

Meanwhile, historians and sociologists as well as socialists and anti-socialists were connecting the policies of the British Labour government between 1945 and 1950 with earlier landmarks in the history of the social services and looking for "origins" and strands of continuity and "development." Different metaphors were employed. Hitherto, T. H. Marshall wrote in 1949—concerning himself less with the increased powers of the state than with the changing fabric of citizenship—social service policy had always been thought of as a remedial policy dealing with the basement of society and ignoring its upper floors. Now the purpose was being extended. "It has begun to re-model the whole building," and it might even end by "converting a skyscraper into a bungalow" or at least into a "bungalow surmounted by an architecturally insignificant turret." The "welfare state," to use a different metaphor, was seeking to provide a fence to ensure that people do not fall over a cliff, whereas the older social-service state provided an ambulance at the bottom of the cliff to carry away for treatment all those who fell.

Between 1947 and 1960 the term "welfare state" reached its peak currency. Two new developments took place. First, the term began to be used everywhere, even in relation to the policies of nonindustrialized societies like India. It was very fashionable in newly independent countries which were formerly part of the British Commonwealth, and where the British Colonial Office after 1945 had emphasized the need for framing comprehensive welfare programs. The International Labour Organisation spotlighted its universal implications. In an ILO report of 1950, for example, it was stated that "the transformation of social insurance is accompanied by the absorption of co-ordination of social assistance, and there begins to emerge a new organisation for social security, which we can only describe as a service for the citizenry at large. This new organisation now concerns society as a whole, though it is primarily directed to the welfare of the workers and their families. It tends, therefore, to become a part of national government, and social security policy accordingly becomes co-ordinated closely with national policy for raising the standard of welfare and, in particular, for promoting the vitality of the population."

Second, most "advanced" countries introduced substantial welfare legislation. Scandinavia led the way both in ideas and in scope of provision, but countries like France and Germany, which had inherited very different patterns of provision, developed new systems, particularly of social security, which by 1960 provided more generous benefits in real terms than those offered in Britain. The British "welfare state" survived the fall of the Labour government in 1951, but it was before that fall that the costs of providing certain services under the national health scheme forced the government—with Bevan resigning in protest—to impose new direct charges. Britain ceased to lead the way in welfare legislation after 1951, although nothing was done to dismantle existing structures, and in a period of increasing prosperity there was no danger of the problems of the 1930's repeating themselves in a new version of economic and social crisis. In all countries unemployment, the main catalyst of prewar discontent, was kept well below its prewar figures.

The term "welfare state" itself lost its initial force during the 1960's, when "welfare" issues were redefined, particularly in the United States. The Economic Opportunity Act of 1964 launched a "war on poverty," but the difficulties of dealing adequately (locally or federally) with poverty, in a society where the problem was inextricably entangled with ethnic questions, explicitly directed attention to the "values" underlying the approach to all welfare issues. They also led to a more searching examination of the basic economic and social structures which most, though not all, of the sociologists and historians of the "welfare state" had disposed of far too easily. New slogans emerged, and it became plain that the circumstances which had led to the coinage of a lively new term after the end of the Second World War had radically altered.

Given the difficulties of carrying over into historical analysis a term used in recent if not in current politics, it is possible nonetheless to identify descriptively what a "welfare state" seeks to do. It is a state in which organized power is deliberately used (through politics and administration) in an effort to modify the play of market forces in at least three directions: first, by guaranteeing individuals and families a minimum income irrespective of their work or their property; second, by narrowing the extent of insecurity by enabling individuals and families to meet certain "social contingencies" (for example, sickness, old age, and unemployment) which could lead otherwise to individual or family crises; and third, by ensuring that all individuals as citizens without distinction of status or class are offered the best services available in relation to a certain agreed, if never finally fixed, range of social services.

Such a definition points to some of the historical considerations which must always be emphasized. First, the concept of "market forces" sets the problems of the "welfare state" within the context of the age of modern political economy. In societies without market economics, the problem of "welfare" raises quite separate issues. Second, the concept of "social contingencies, is strongly influenced by the experience of industrialism. Third, the idea of using organized power (through politics and administration) to determine particular patterns of welfare services rather than relying on other agencies must be set within particular chronological frameworks. It was only with the advent of or the threat of democratic politics and with the introduction of administrations which included or employed experts that power could be deployed in this manner. Fourth, the range of agreed social services must be a shifting range, with both economic and political factors influencing the scope and scale of constituent items. Fifth, the idea of offering not "minima" but "optima," at least in relation to some specified services, represented the major historical shift, from "the social service state" to the "welfare state." Sixth, the definition leaves out motives and values. For some advocates of a "welfare state," like Archbishop William Temple, one of the first people to use the phrase in 1941, the "welfare state" rested on a moral ideal. For others it crystallized as a set of expedients. For others it emerged as the product of inexorable political pressures over a long period of time.

It follows from this historical account that the term "welfare state" even in its heyday has usually been used vaguely rather than precisely, and that it has been employed more frequently in political debate, often as a slogan, than in social and economic analysis. Most usually, it has been identified through contrast rather than through explicit definition—through contrast with a "laissez-faire" state or more recently with a "power state" or a "warfare state," and little attention has been devoted to the different social and political structures or institutions in the different societies to which the label has been attached. Socialist critics of the concept, like Richard M. Titmuss, have talked of going "beyond" the welfare state, drawing attention not only to its limits (in terms of redistribution of incomes and the implementation of economic planning) but also to the uneven efforts of its operations (for example, in satisfying the middle-class demand for health and education more completely than the working-class need for health and education). They have agreed, indeed, that the term hinders rather than assists an understanding of "what is actually being done in different societies." From a nonsocialist vantage point, Jacob Viner claimed in 1962 that "the welfare state is at best a hastily improvised system having characteristics stretching all the way through the range from near-statism to near-anarchy. It is an unplanned response to a host of historical forces and of political pressures which has not yet acquired and may never acquire, an internally coherent and logically formulated philosophy. It is undergoing constant change, and its movements forward, backwards and sideways, are not guided by any clear and widely accepted consensus as it knows where it is going or where it should go from here" (p. 226). Since 1962 the most interesting studies of the term have concentrated on persisting patterns of stratification, and on differences of values within the same society. The "consensus" of the wartime years helped to generate the dream, and the reality of the "welfare state" has itself passed into history.

*BIBLIOGRAPHY*

There is a useful collection of articles and papers in S. P. Aiyer, ed., *Perspectives on the Welfare State* (Bombay, 1966). There is no adequate history of the term or of the institutions associated with it, but M. Bruce, *The Coming of the Welfare State* (London, 1961) deals with British experience as a whole, and B. S. Gilbert, *The Evolution of National Insurance in Great Britain: the Origins of the Welfare State* (London, 1966) and idem, *British Social Policy, 1916–1939* (London, 1970) examine fully some of the critical chapters. T. H. Marshall, *Citizenship and Social Class* (Cambridge, 1949) is a basic analysis. See also B. Kirkman Gray, *Philanthropy and the State* (London, 1908); G. Myrdal, *Beyond the Welfare State* (New Haven, 1958); R. M. Titmuss, *Essays on "The Welfare State"* (London, 1958) and idem, *Income Distribution and Social Change* (London, 1962); W. G. Runciman, *Relative Deprivation and Social Justice* (Berkeley, 1966); J. B. Condliffe, *The Welfare State in New Zealand* (New York, 1959); S. B. Fry, "Bismarck's Welfare State," *Current History*, 18 (1950); C. W. Pitkin, *Social Politics and Modern Democracies*, 2 vols. (New York, 1931); H. L. Wilenski and C. N. Lebeaux, *Industrial Society and Social Welfare Services in the United States* (New York, 1958); J. Viner, "The United States as a Welfare State," in S. W. Higginbotham, ed., *Man, Science, Learning and Education* (Houston, 1962); M. L. Zald, ed., *Social Welfare Institutions* (New York, 1965).

ASA BRIGGS

[See also **Economic History**; Economic Theory of Natural Liberty; **Social Welfare**; **Socialism**; State; **Utilitarianism**.]

# WISDOM OF THE FOOL

THE PARADOXICAL idea that the fool may possess wisdom, though it was not to achieve its fullest articulation until the Renaissance, doubtless had its beginnings very early in the civilizing process. As soon as it was possible for man to feel nostalgia for a simpler way of life, he must also have wondered about the superiority of a simpler kind of wisdom, whether innate or inspired, over whatever knowledge of the world he had acquired through his own empirical deduction or from the instruction of others. Whenever reason has been able to question itself and acknowledge that the heart has its reasons that reason does not know, a kind of wisdom has been attributed to the fool. Men have often noticed that the untutored or simpleminded, in their purity of heart, could penetrate to profounder truths than those encumbered with learning and convention, in the same way that we sometimes sense a more resonant verity in homely sayings or popular proverbs than in rational exposition. It is, in fact, no accident that the fools of literature characteristically resort to proverbial expressions; for proverbs draw their strength, Antaeus-like, from the humble earth and the simple heart. Moreover, developing rationality, like developing civilization, has seemed to bring burdens along with benefits; and the more advanced the development of either, the more some men, longing for an earlier, simpler, more natural state, have experienced the beguilements of the uncivilized and the irrational. The concept of the wise fool, in opposing a wisdom that is natural or god-given to one that is self-acquired, is the most sophisticated and far-reaching of those primitivistic ideas with which man has questioned his own potentialities and achievements.

*I*

The implications inherent in the figure of the wise fool grow out of the attitudes most societies have held about real fools. The names he has been given suggest, in their etymological undertones, the various characteristics that have been attributed to the fool: that he is empty-headed (μάταιος, *inanis*, fool), dull-witted (μῶρος, *stultus*, dolt, clown), feebleminded (*imbécile*, dotard), and lacks understanding (ἄνοος, ἄφρων, *insipiens*); that he is different from normal men (idiot); that he is either inarticulate (*Tor*) or babbles incoherently (*fatuus*) and is given to boisterous merrymaking (*buffone*); that he does not recognize the codes of propriety (*ineptus*) and loves to mock others (*Narr*); that he acts like a child (νήπιος); and that he has a natural simplicity and innocence of heart (εὐήθης, natural, simpleton). Though violent madmen have, of necessity, usually had to be restrained or incarcerated by society, harmless fools have often enjoyed special privileges. Their helplessness has earned them the pitying protection of the more fortunate, just as their childishness has won them the license granted children for their irresponsible—and often irreverent—words or actions. Since they are guided by nothing but their natural instincts, the fool and the child are not held accountable to the rules of civilized society. For while mature adults are enjoined from breaking society's accepted codes of conduct and belief on the assumption that they ought to "know better," the fool, like the child, is not expected to "know" anything. Because of this, he has often been granted considerable freedom.

Perhaps more than anything else, it is this privilege of speaking with impunity that was to make the "all-licensed fool" so attractive to the literary imagination. Moreover, though the fact that fools stand apart from normal humanity sometimes caused them to be treated as objects of derision, it also sometimes caused them to be venerated. In the Middle Ages, as in certain primitive societies, they were thought to be under the special protection of God, and the possibility always existed that what sounded like inane chatter was, in actual fact, theopneustic glossolalia.

The modern psychologist has, retrospectively, taken special interest in the personality of the fool; for in Freudian terms he embodies the untrammeled expression of the id. Lacking any vestige of a superego, the fool surrenders shamelessly to his bodily appetites and natural desires, and he is regularly characterized by his hunger, thirst, lust, and obsession with obscenities. It has been pointed out that his very etymology has a genital suggestion (*follis*), and the familiar bauble of the professional fool is undeniably phallic. With no social personality to mask his emotions, he is childlike in the utter frankness of his responses: when happy, he laughs; when sad, he cries. Since he is equally short of memory and unable to follow anything to its logical conclusion, the past and the future are meaningless to him as he happily lives in and for the moment. Instructed only by his senses and his intuition and seeking only self-gratification, he is the pleasure-principle personified. His enemy, the superego, represents all the ordered conventions and civilizing rationality of society which he finds both incomprehensible and intolerably repressive. However we may choose to express the antithesis—id vs. superego, heart vs. head, chaos vs. order, anarchy vs. culture, nature vs. art, passion vs. reason, pleasure vs. virtue, Carnival vs. Lent—his allegiance is always unmistakably clear and one-sided.

By at least the end of the twelfth century (and probably earlier), the fool had achieved the eminence of having his own feast day. The famous, sometimes infamous, Fête des Fous gave the lower clergy, if only ephemerally, the traditional freedom accorded the fool. Related to the Roman Saturnalia and embodying the spirit of carnival misrule, the Feast of Fools found its Scriptural authority in a verse from the Magnificat: *Deposuit potentes de sede, et exaltavit humiles*. Almost three centuries later, when these blasphemous celebrations had been driven out of the church, they were taken over and expanded by the secular Sociétés Joyeuses in the towns and universities. Emulating the sub-deacons of the cathedrals, students and urban citizens took the opportunity to lord it over their betters and mock authority, both temporal and religious, with assumed amnesty. But the original Scriptural suggestion of The World Turned Upside-Down continued to be closely associated with the fool. For by his very nature, the fool is iconoclastic, not simply irreverent but potentially subversive in his inability to comprehend the assumptions on which authority is founded. He is too simpleminded to see the emperor's new clothes and too unsophisticated to refrain from pointing out the nakedness of the truth.

At the same time, the fools of the Fête des Fous and the Société Joyeuse were not, of course, genuinely simpleminded, and the distinction must be made between the authentic or natural fool and the artificial or professional fool. Though we do not know when it first appeared advantageous for a normal man to assume the guise of a simpleton, there are accounts in Xenophon, Athenaeus, Lucian, and Plautus of professionally amusing parasites who earned their bread and butter with idiocies, and wealthy Romans kept deformed buffoons in their households whose impudence was legendary. Their descendants are the Rigoletto-type fools of late-medieval and Renaissance Europe with their traditional costume of motley, cap and bells, and *marotte*. They had their heyday in the fifteenth and sixteenth centuries, and a few of them achieved such fame that their names are still known to us. At least one of them, the fool of François I, is supposed to have been truly witless, and the famous fool of Sir Thomas More had suffered brain damage as the result of a fall from a church-steeple; but most of them were men of normal intelligence who found it profitable to adopt motley for its ability to amuse and the impunity it gave them to speak freely. The professional jester, whose wry quips tended not only to amuse but often to correct his master, personifies the penchant all fools have for commenting on the morals of others and affairs of state. One of the most characteristic gestures of *le fou glossateur*, as one critic has called him, is to hold a mirror up for our scrutiny and to exclaim, *"tu quoque!"* It is this aspect of the fool which was to achieve its most moving realization in the nameless court fool who accompanies King Lear across the barren heath of the world.

## II

The idea of the wisdom (*sapientia*) of the fool always stands in contrast to the knowledge (*scientia*) of the learned or the "wisdom" of the worldly (*sapientia mundana*). In this respect, the oxymoron, "wise fool," is inherently reversible; for whenever it is acknowledged that the fool is wise, it is also suggested, expressly or tacitly, that the wise are foolish. Perhaps the earliest recorded expression of this paradox is Heraclitus' observation that much learning does not teach wisdom (frag. 40), but the theme was recurrent in ancient literature from Aeschylus to Horace. The classical archetype for the figure of the wise fool is Socrates, whom later theorists constantly invoked. Not only was his educational method based on exposing the folly of the supposedly wise, but he himself claimed that his own wisdom was derived from an awareness of his ignorance. In the *Apology* (20d–23b), he recounts how the oracle at Delphi had once said there was no man wiser than he. Knowing that he was not wise, however, he attempted to disprove the oracle by finding a wiser man among the Athenians; but he found that all those who professed wisdom were in fact ignorant, while he alone admitted his ignorance. Hence he concluded that what the Pythian god had meant was: "The wisest of you, O men, is he who, like Socrates, knows that as far as wisdom is concerned he is actually worthless."

Socrates' account of human ignorance, in attributing true wisdom only to the divine, anticipates Saint Paul's claim that God has made foolish the wisdom of this world (I Corinthians 1:20; 3:19). The Pauline concept of the Fool in Christ, which is given its fullest exposition in the Epistles to the Corinthians, affirms the worthlessness of wordly wisdom in contrast to the wisdom of the Christian, which to the world appears folly. Claiming that we are fools for Christ's sake but are wise in Christ (I Corinthians 4:10), he argues that "the foolishness of God is wiser than men" (I Corinthians 1:25), and he says of unbelievers that, "professing themselves to be wise, they became fools" (Romans 1:22). "Let no man deceive himself," he exhorts; "if any man among you seemeth to be wise in this world,

let him become a fool, that he may be wise" (I Corinthians 3:18). Christ Himself had exemplified this foolish wisdom, not only when as a child He answered the doctors in the temple, but also later when He confounded the scribes and pharisees in their wisdom. Moreover, His teaching was seen to be childlike in its simplicity, "foolish" in its homespun imagery; and, it was later argued, although we think of sheep as foolish creatures, He was the Lamb of God. This theological paradox of the Wise Fool in Christ, which was to provide the rationale for so many subsequent treatments of the wisdom of folly, was kept alive all during the Middle Ages by such writers as Gregory the Great, Scotus Erigena, Francis of Assisi, Jacopone da Todi, and Raimond Lull.

It is, however, in the late Middle Ages and out of that northern mysticism of the *devotio moderna* taught by the Brethren of the Common Life at Deventer that two of the most important Christian treatments of the wisdom of the fool appear. Almost simultaneously, near the middle of the fifteenth century, Thomas à Kempis, in his influential *Imitatio Christi*, urged a Christian life of "holy simplicity" in emulation of Christ the Fool, and Nicholas of Cusa (or Cusanus), in various writings, laid the philosophical groundwork for a new concept of learned ignorance. Cusanus' *docta ignorantia*, "the coincidence of knowledge and ignorance," in rejecting rational theology and attributing to God a wisdom unattainable by man, poses serious questions about the very possibility of human knowledge but finally derives a kind of wisdom from the antithesis between the irrational absolute and logical reason. For he argues, as Socrates had before him and as Montaigne would after him (though both in quite different contexts from Cusanus'), that knowledge of our ignorance is itself a kind of knowledge.

Throughout the Middle Ages, a less theological—and, admittedly, often less wise—figure of the fool capered through the *sotties*, carnival plays, proverbs, songs, and jestbooks that appeared all over Europe. Tyl Eulenspiegel, Marcolf, Scogin, Bertoldo, Robin Goodfellow, and a dozen others, though often nothing more than scurrilous buffoons and outrageous pranksters, sometimes give evidence in their jests that they are also vessels of wisdom. In their roguery, they are the direct forebears of the confidence men of later literature—the Elizabethan coney-catcher, Arlecchino, Lazarillo, Simplicius, Scapin, Melville's deaf-mute, Felix Krull; but in their wisdom, they display the characteristics of all fools. In particular, the legendary Marcolf, whose origins are distant and obscure, is one of the primordial manifestations of the wisdom of folly. Companion to the very personification of wisdom, King Solomon, he regularly bests the sage in their encounters by means of his earthy, natural, literal-minded acuity. At the same time, there were also literary fools who were only fools, and the medieval imagination took satiric delight in cataloguing them in such works as Wireker's *Speculum stultorum* or Lydgate's *The Ordre of Folys*. Their more ominous confrere, the Vice, who replaced the bauble with a dagger of lath, proffered temptations to Everyman on the medieval stage. Sebastian Brandt, gathering them all together at the end of the Middle Ages, was to confirm once more the old observation of the preacher of Ecclesiastes that *stultorum numerus infinitus est* (I:15). And, indeed, the passengers on the *Narrenschiff* (1494) are fools in the somberest sense; for, like all men, they are sinners.

By the end of the fifteenth century, a fairly complex set of ideas and associations had gathered around the figure of the fool. At worst, he was considered a sinful instrument of vice, who was blind to the truth and had no hope of salvation. It has been suggested that this attitude goes back to Saint Jerome, who translated the opening of Psalm 53/52 with *Dixit insipiens in corde suo*, rendering the Hebrew word "*nabal*" as "fool" rather than as "vile or morally deficient person." At best, the fool was a simple innocent, devoid of the pretensions of learning and the corruptions of worldly wisdom, into whom the spirit of God could most easily enter. The most universal characteristics of the fool, however, lay somewhere in between the two opposite poles represented by the fool of Saint Jerome and the fool of Saint Paul; for these are his social rather than his religious characteristics. On the one hand, he could be found in any rank of society; on the other, he was the shameless critic of all ranks. He saw through the hypocrisy of social status and noble sentiments; he exposed the vanity of beauty and learning. He did not believe in honor, order, measure, prudence, justice, chastity, or any of the stoical restraints society imposes upon itself. If Hercules at the crossroads between virtue and pleasure had traditionally opted for virtue, the fool resolutely took the other fork and sought gratification for the body rather than the spirit, arguing that there will still be cakes and ale though some are virtuous. It had long since been recognized, however, that he was a formidable adversary, not just because he refused to abide by the accepted rules, but because his jocose antics, like all play, could easily turn into high seriousness and his unbridled tongue was capable of truth as well as foolishness.

### III

It was out of these antecedents that the wisest, most important, most influential fool of all was created in the first decade of the sixteenth century. Erasmus'

*Moriae encomium*, written in 1509 and first published in 1511, is, for all its joking, the most profoundly serious and penetrating examination of the wise fool in Western literature. It is no exaggeration to say that all subsequent fools of note are, in one way or another, indebted to his figure of Stultitia, who delivers her own eulogy in *The Praise of Folly*. Not only does she sum up all earlier expressions of the paradox, but she also manages, through her deep sense of humanity and her polysemous irony, to give new dimensions to the concept. The foolish creation of the most learned man of his time, she is the literal embodiment of the word *oxymoron*, and in her idiotic wisdom she represents the finest flowering of that fusion of Italian humanistic thought and northern piety which has been called Christian Humanism.

Like all fools, Stultitia's basic impulse is satiric, and her widespread notoriety throughout sixteenth-century Europe was largely the result of those parts of her speech in which she irreverently boasts that all the chief secular, religious, and intellectual estates of the Renaissance world are under her dominion. No man, not even her own author, is exempted from her mordant ridicule as she anatomizes the follies of mankind. Yet in the last analysis, it is not her satiric catalogue but her ironic self-description which was to have the more lasting resonance. For in explaining who she is—in asking, that is, what it means to be a fool—she demonstrates that folly is not merely universal but necessary and even desirable to mankind, that to be a man is nothing other than to play the fool, and that the highest wisdom is to acknowledge this very fact.

Portraying herself as the personification of all natural instincts, she claims to be the life-force in the universe and argues that it is only she, Folly, who keeps men from committing suicide. Those impulses of man which attempt to curb or deny his own nature are objects of her deepest scorn. Behind this foolish naturalism lies Erasmus' deep belief, inherited from some of his humanistic predecessors, in the goodness of nature, especially human nature—a philosophical position which enabled Luther later to accuse him of Pelagianism. Stultitia, in reflecting this belief, emerges as the champion of φύσις (nature) over all forms of νόμος (law, custom, convention) which attempt to restrict nature. She is, accordingly, an enemy of the Stoics, as all fools inherently are. But this fool has philosophical and theological reasons to buttress her instinctive love of pleasure. In fact, she is one of the earliest spokesmen for the post-medieval revival of Epicurus and suggests, as Erasmus was to argue in detail elsewhere, that "if we take care to understand the words properly" the true Christian is an Epicurean (*Colloquia familiaria* [1516], "Epicureus"). Though she speaks in learned Latin decorated with Greek tags, Stultitia is equally scornful of the pretensions of learning, whether pedantic sophistry on the one hand or speculative metaphysics on the other. In opposition to both sets of "foolosophers," as she calls them (μωροσόφοι), she extolls the humility of ignorance and the simple knowledge drawn from experience and faith. Beyond this, she is, as always, acutely conscious of the cares of mankind and the pains of existence. She laments with Ecclesiastes that "He that increaseth knowledge increaseth sorrow" (I:18), and she sadly concedes with Sophocles that "to know nothing affords the happiest life" (*Ajax* 554).

The fool's traditional penchant for turning things upside-down is, in Stultitia, reinforced by the profound Erasmian ability to see both sides of a question. Not surprisingly, she invokes one of her author's most important adages, "The Sileni of Alcibiades" (*Adagiorum chiliades* III. iii. 1), in which it is argued that the inner essence of any matter is often the opposite of its outer appearance, to explain that the apparently foolish may actually be wise, the apparently wise, foolish. This is, to be sure, the basis of her irony; but it is also the burden of her message. For she proceeds to apply this technique of reversal to all aspects of worldly wisdom, reexamining those virtues and codes of conduct the world takes for granted to be wise, and demonstrating both their limitations and the wisdom of their foolish opposites. For example, she hails Self-love (Φιλαυτία) as her closest companion, only to ask if the Christian can really love his neighbor as himself if he does not, in fact, love himself. Similarly, she attacks Prudence, traditional enemy of Folly in medieval psychomachies, not simply because fools rush in where angels fear to tread, but in order to show that experience can be valuable and that judgments are always difficult. She acknowledges that his illusions and self-delusions are as important to man as his truths; she accepts the passions of the heart as well as the reasons of the mind; and she resolves the ancient antinomy between virtue and pleasure by arguing that pleasure is a virtue.

These radical reappraisals of common assumptions are derived throughout from a humane understanding of man's condition and a belief in the essential goodness of human nature if it is uncorrupted by man-made institutions, false learning, and perversions of the will. Once man has stripped himself of these false claims to wisdom, he becomes a proper receptacle to receive the wisdom of Christ, which is the only true wisdom. In the conclusion of her great speech, Stultitia invokes the figure of the Fool in Christ, derived from Saint Paul and Cusanus, and prescribes a pietistic simplicity of heart as the true way to divine wisdom. What is more, she effectively argues that, since to be a man is to be a fool, when the Son of God accepted the role of human frailty He became the greatest of all fools.

## IV

Erasmus' Stultitia ushers in that host of wise fools who were to play such a dominant role in European thought and literature for the next hundred years, from Murner's *Narrenbeschwörung* (1512) to Cervantes' *Don Quixote* (1605, 1615). It has often been observed that the great fools of the sixteenth century are essentially the creation of Renaissance humanism and their ironic wisdom the result of the assimilation of Lucian by such humanists as Alberti, More, and Erasmus himself. At the same time, it is equally important to recognize the evidence such fools supply that the hopeful ideals of humanist philosophy were already being subjected to increasing doubt. For the concept of folly, however "wise," is ultimately the antithesis of the concept of the dignity of man; and if the medieval Feast of Fools was religion on a holiday, the Renaissance triumph of the wise fool was humanism on a holiday—or, perhaps more accurately, humanism in mourning. The optimistic dream of man and the heaven-storming possibilities of human reason so proudly advanced by the humanists of the fifteenth century did not concede much if any wisdom to folly. Though the first humanist, Petrarch, had claimed the wisdom of his own ignorance, the ignorance he professed was not that of the fool but only that of the non-Averroist. It is, significantly, only in the sixteenth century, when the shadow of skepticism fell across humanist thought, that the wise fool emerges as the spokesman for his epoch. It is precisely when he can no longer determine whether man is the Godlike paragon of animals or the base quintessence of dust that Hamlet puts on the antic disposition of the fool and walks in the corridor reading Erasmus' *Praise of Folly*.

Down the length of the sixteenth century, the wisdom of folly is described in all its nuances by such diverse authors as Ariosto, Skelton, Rabelais, Folengo, Nashe, Hans Sachs, Cornelius Agrippa, Francisco Sanchez, Montaigne, and many others; the portrait of the wise fool is drawn again and again by Breughel and Bosch, Massys and Holbein, and countless minor illustrators. When Olivia, in *Twelfth Night*, says of the clown Feste, "This fellow is wise enough to play the fool" (III.i.60) and when Touchstone, in *As You Like It*, proverbially observes that "The fool doth think he is wise, but the wise man knows himself to be a fool" (V.i.31), they are uttering what had by then become 519 commonplaces. In the age of Elizabeth, foolery did indeed seem to walk about the orb like the sun and shine everywhere; and one of Ben Jonson's last characters, looking back over the drama of the preceding century, can nostalgically claim that "There was no play [that is, of any merit] without a fool" (*Staple of News*, 1st Intermean, 35). For in England especially, the wise fool found his true home in the drama of Heywood, Marston, Middleton, Dekker, Jonson, and, above all, Shakespeare. In both the comedies and the tragedies, the Shakespearean wise fool has his splendid role to play, from the bantering wit of Touchstone and Feste to Yorick's gibeless skull and Cleopatra's death-bearing clown. If Jaques, in the sun-dappled world of Arden, can learnedly quote *The Praise of Folly* to demonstrate that all the world's a stage, it remains for Lear, in the storm-tossed kingdom of tragedy, to acknowledge that the world is "this great stage of fools." Lear's own fool is only the greatest of many who, for all their motley, bring tears to our eyes because of the profundity of their wisdom. Nor are those who wear motley the only wise fools in Shakespeare: we better understand such otherwise dissimilar characters as Falstaff and Antony when we recognize that they too manifest many of the traditional traits of the wise fool.

Significantly, the last of the great Renaissance fools, Don Quixote, who rides forth as the age of humanism is drawing to a close, is known to the world not for his jesting motley but for his mournful countenance. To be sure, his companion, Sancho Panza, is something of a court jester without the office—or the court; but by the beginning of the seventeenth century the professional fool had almost had his day. Even his particolored costume only partially survives in the Commedia dell'Arte. The concept of folly, however, was far from dead. For fools, whether specifically identified as such or not, have continued down the centuries to call into question the claims of learning, religion, and civilization. Whenever human reason has most proudly vaunted its achievements, it has been inevitably challenged by the mocking laughter of the wise fool. Long after the Renaissance fool had made his exit from the scene, from Grimmelshausen and Molière and Swift to Dostoevsky's Prince Myshkin and Hauptmann's Emanuel Quint and Yeats's Crazy Jane, the idea of the wisdom of folly has persisted.

## BIBLIOGRAPHY

Important general studies of fools and folly include Carl F. Flögel, *Geschichte des Grotesk-Komischen*, ed. Max Bauer (Munich, 1914); Michel Foucault, *Folie et déraison: histoire de la folie à l'âge classique* (Paris, 1961); Joel Lefebvre, *Les Fols et la folie* (Paris, 1968); Barbara Swain, *Fools and Folly during the Middle Ages and the Renaissance* (New York, 1932); Erica Tietze-Conrat, *Dwarfs and Jesters in Art* (New York, 1957); and Enid Welsford, *The Fool: His Social and Literary History* (London, 1935).

Especially valuable studies on more specific aspects of late-medieval, Renaissance, and humanist fools, some of which contain important general and theoretical discussions, are: Walter Gaedik, *Der Weise Narr in der englischen Literatur von Erasmus bis Shakespeare* (Weimar and Leipzig, 1928); Hadumoth Hanckel, *Narrendarstellungen im Spätmittelalter* (Freiburg, 1952); Marieluise Held, *Das Narrenthema in der Satire am Vorabend und in der Frühzeit der Reformation* (Marburg, 1945); C. H. Herford, *Studies in the Literary Relations of England and Germany in the Sixteenth Century* (Cambridge, 1886); Walter Kaiser, *Praisers of Folly: Erasmus, Rabelais, Shakespeare* (Cambridge, Mass., 1963); Robert Klein, "Un aspect de l'herméneutique à l'âge de l'humanisme: le thème fou et l'ironie humaniste," *Umanesimo e Ermeneutica*, Archivio di Filosofia, 3 (1963), 11–25, reprinted in R. Klein, *La Forme et l'intelligible* (Paris, 1970), pp. 433–50; Barbara Könneker, *Wesen und Wandlung der Narrenidee im Zeitalter des Humanismus: Brant—Murner—Erasmus* (Wiesbaden, 1966); Irmgaard Meiners, *Schelm und Dümmling in Erzählungen des deutschen Mittelalters* (Munich, 1967); Rocco Montano, *Follia e saggezza nel Furioso e nell' Elogio di Erasmo* (Naples, 1942); and H. de Vocht, *De Invloed van Erasmus op de Engelsche Tooneelliteratuur der XVIe en XVIIe Eeuwen* (Ghent, 1908).

For court fools, see John Doran, *The History of Court Fools* (London, 1858) and Carl F. Flögel, *Geschichte der Hofnarren* (Leipzig, 1789). Johan Huizinga, *Homo Ludens: A Study of the Play-Element in Culture* (Boston, 1950) and William Willeford, *The Fool and His Scepter: A Study in Clowns and Their Audience* (Evanston, 1969) emphasize the sociological and psychological aspects of folly. The Fool in Christ is treated by Walter Nigg, *Der christliche Narr* (Zurich and Stuttgart, 1956); and E. Vansteenberghe has written a useful introduction to Cusanus' doctrine in *Autour de la docte ignorance. Une Controverse sur la théologie mystique au XVe siècle* (Münster, 1914). Three basic works for the fool in drama are E. K. Chambers, *The Mediaeval Stage*, 2 vols. (Oxford, 1903); Gustave Cohen, *Le Théâtre en France au Moyen Age* (Paris, 1928); and Allardyce Nicoll, *Masks, Mime, and Miracles* (New York, 1931; reprint 1964). Heinz Wyss has written an important monograph on *Der Narr im Schweizerischen Drama des 16. Jahrhunderts* (Bern, 1959). Among many studies on Elizabethan and Shakespearean dramatic fools, the following are particularly useful: C. L. Barber, *Shakespeare's Festive Comedy* (Princeton, 1959); Olive Busby, *The Development of the Fool in Elizabethan Drama* (Oxford, 1923); Robert Goldsmith, *Wise Fools in Shakespeare* (East Lansing, 1955); Leslie Hotson, *Shakespeare's Motley* (London, 1952); and Annemarie Schöne, "Die weisen Narren Shakespeares und ihre Vorfahren," *Jahrbuch für Aesthetik und allgemeine Kunstwissenschaft*, 5 (1960), 202ff.

WALTER KAISER

[See also **Comic**; **Irony**; Primitivism; **Rationality**.]

# WITCHCRAFT

THE UNIFYING element in the idea of witchcraft is the belief that an evil intent may be carried out by appeal to an evil incorporeal power. Some part of mankind has always believed in a cause and effect relation between an evil intent and a subsequent injury or death. While most societies (Egyptian, Greek, Roman, Germanic, African) have condemned witches and sorcerers for crimes associated with the belief, Hebrew and Christian societies have condemned the belief itself as well as the imputed crimes. In the polytheistic world of classical times, where the deities of the underworld and death were part of the pantheon and most deities had both good and evil aspects, the belief was generally included as one among many. Monotheistic Hebrew thought, however, associated the witch and sorcerer with the idolater, forbidding an error in religious attitude as well as any deeds that might result from it. It is this association that Christianity developed.

The history of the idea of witchcraft in the Christian period is mainly the history of the application by the Church of Judaic-Christian demonology to non-Christian—hence idolatrous—religious impulses among the baptized. Wherever a surviving or revived impulse came to the attention of Church writers they dealt with it in terms derived from biblical statements about witches, sorcerers, the Serpent, Satan, Leviathan, and evil spirits in the Old Testament and the Hebrew Apocrypha, and from references to Satan and evil demons in the New Testament (see Demonology). Despite the tendency throughout the Christian era to transmute "general supernatural power into the two schools of divine and anti-divine power," as Charles Williams suggests (*Witchcraft,* p. 60), the attitude in the early centuries was to treat magic and sorcery, frequently associated with the Triple Goddess Hecate or Diana, as a superstition to be overcome by persuasion. For a long time these arts were not treated by the Church as heresy but as infidelism. However, the common belief that they could result in injury or death was reflected in civil laws under Christian Roman Emperors as well as earlier pagan Emperors, especially when sorcery involved divination with its political threat to the ruler's life. The Church was long in developing the full implications of its position with regard to pagan worship and folk customs among the baptized despite the early Church Fathers' belief that *Omnes dei gentium sunt daemonia* (Psalm XCVI, 5 Vulgate) and Saint Augustine's view that sorcery involved a pact with demons.

The position of the Church just prior to Scholasticism is stated in the anonymous *Canon* (or *Capitulum*) *Episcopi* recorded by Regino of Prüm (ca. 900) and incorporated into Church law. Issues to be debated for eight centuries are raised in this ruling. The author distinguishes between those who follow the "pernicious art of sorcery and malefice invented by the devil"— which he condemns as heretical—and those "wicked women" who believe that they or other women can really "ride upon certain beasts with Diana . . . and . . . traverse great spaces of earth . . . to be summoned to her service on certain nights"—which he condemns as "in every way false" and as "phantasms . . . imposed on the minds of infidels and not by the divine but by the malignant spirit." He compares night-riding (a nearly universal folklore element) to "dreams and nocturnal visions" similar to those "in spirit" of Ezekiel, John, and Paul, and concludes that whoever believes that any creature can be changed into another species except by God is "beyond doubt an infidel" (trans. Lea, *Materials,* I, 178–80). Here, the heresy involved in a sorcerer's pact with demons is distinguished from the mental delusions of night-riding and of animal transformation. Yet, in the following period, influenced by Scholastic discussions of the powers of angels and demons, by the rise of dualistic heresies, and by the establishment of the Inquisition, the idea of the first sort of activity came to be applied to the second—to such an extent that by the time of the *Malleus maleficarum* (1487?) it was akin to heresy *not* to believe in the reality of night-riding. When what we must presume were the remnants of pagan observances—whether imaginary or acted out—came under the scrutiny of Inquisitors trained in the demonology of the Christian tradition and knowledgeable in the various dualistic heresies of the thirteenth century, they construed them as devil worship involving the pact with demons or the Devil and the implicit adherence to evil incorporeal power that had been regarded as heretical since the early period of the Church. In order to give a rational account within the Christian framework of ideas of the persistent belief in the night-flying witch, in such primitive ideas as that of the "evil eye," in the power of a curse, in the wise woman's control over wind and weather, and in the magical power of charms, the Church referred them to the agency of the Devil, the tempter of Adam and Christ. But each attempt to explain some local belief placed a new, comparatively intellectual construction upon it. The resulting interpretations sifted into sermons and books and thence into people's minds. Worse yet, it informed the Inquisitors' leading questions and the replies from prisoners under torture. The Inquisitors and the Protestant judges interpreted further the extracted testimony and codified it in Inquisitorial manuals of the fifteenth century such as Kramer and Sprenger, *Malleus maleficarum,* and in the judicial guides of the sixteenth century such as Martin Del Rio, *Disquisitiones magicae* (1599–1601), Nicholas Remy, *Daemonolatreia* (1595), Jean Bodin, *De magorum daemonomania* (1581) and Henri Boguet, *Discours des sorciers* (1590–1601). Almost unwittingly, the very attempt to eliminate one danger to the Church—latent infidelism and its peril to the soul—gave rise to a greater one—the elaboration within the Church of a dualistic system of ideas in which an evil incorporeal power assumed almost as much importance in men's lives as God.

Two circumstances, one legal and one theological, preceded the definition of witchcraft in both civil and canon law as a crime and the elaborate systematization of ideas about it. First, there occurred the theocratic union of Church and State in the Christian commonwealth, in regard to which any heresy could be called treason. By the thirteenth century Emperor Frederick II and Pope Innocent III had made this identification, for, as Frederick said, echoing an earlier letter of Innocent, "To offend the Divine majesty is a far greater crime than to offend the majesty of an Emperor" (Maycock, p. 88). Hence, when under the revived Roman law, death was applied as the penalty for treason, the way was clear for the legal extirpation of heretics through the Inquisition and the secular arm. The second circumstance, the theological identification of all witchcraft with heresy, was more complex. Throughout the latter half of the thirteenth century and during the fourteenth it was debated. Alexander IV's bull *Quod super nonnullis* (1258) suggested that those sorcerers who paid honor to demons savored of heresy, which was not new, and Nicholas Eymeric in his *Directorium* (1376) distinguished "simple" and "heretical" sorcerers in a similar manner and subjected the latter to the Inquisition. Lea notes the difficulty the Inquisition had in subjecting sorcery to itself, because it was supposed to deal only with beliefs not acts. The document that drew all beliefs and practices associated with witchcraft under the laws applicable to heresy was an article adopted by the theological faculty of the University of Paris in 1398 which declared that there was an implied contract with Satan in every superstitious observance of which the expected result was not reasonably to be anticipated from God and from nature. The biblical statement, "We have entered into a league with death; we have made a covenant with hell" (Isaiah 28:15), which had since the days of Saint Augustine implied the possibility of a pact with Satan, was taken to be the explanation for the witch's power over men's bodies and over natural forces—a power which was never doubted in popular belief. The witch as heretic and as evil-doer was the enemy of the state, the individual, and of her own salvation. Martin Luther much later summed up the common attitude with its emphasis upon the question of fealty: "Does not witchcraft, then, merit death, which is a revolt of the creature against the creator, a denial to God of the authority it accords to the demon?" (Luther, p. 252).

Long before the theoretical possibility of witchcraft was generally questioned, the Spanish Inquisitor Alonso de Salazar y Frias and the English Bishop Samuel Harsnett questioned the evidence for the crimes imputed to witches and checked the spread of accusations wherever their example penetrated. The abstract belief in the Devil and his power lingered, especially in the idea that he was the cause of the delusion concerning the Sabbat—a return essentially to the tenth-century position of the *Canon Episcopi*. It informs the work of the "hag-advocates," who called for common sense, justice, and reason—writers such as Reginald Scot, John Weyer, Friedrich von Spee, and even Balthasar Bekker, who, in *De Betoverde Weereld* (1690–93), argued from Scripture and reason that no evil spirit could be active in the world but did not deny the Devil's existence. The belief in the system lingered longest among Calvinists, it has been suggested, because of the doctrines of the depravity of man and of the double election, the literal interpretation of Scripture, Genevan theocracy, and Calvinism's origin in the regions of Switzerland and France where the dualistic heresies of the Middle Ages had flourished and lingered underground (Davies, pp. 4–12).

General belief in witchcraft declined with the eighteenth century, in part because of the rise of rationalism and the general skepticism of the marvelous, as outlined by Lecky, and in part because of the acceptance during the century of the idea of a fixed natural order under a benevolent deity. The triumph of the latter, essentially Christian, idea, combined with the growth of the scientific habit of observation of nature put an end to the belief except among the least educated.

With the romantic period literary interest in the idea of witchcraft took two directions which have continued into the twentieth century. There was a strong revival of interest in it as historical subject matter, as in Scott's popular *Letters on Demonology and Witchcraft* (1830), which led to many imitations and culminated in the great historical works of H. C. Lea and Joseph Hansen. As a theme of romantic literature all aspects were exploited, whether comic as in Burns' *Tam O'Shanter* (1791) or tragic as in Melville's *Moby Dick* (1851). Goya's *Caprichos* and *Pinturas negras* reflect the interest in art. It also began to receive scientific study both by proto-anthropologists as a survival of early European folk religion comparable to contemporary beliefs in primitive parts of the world, as in Joseph Ennemoser,

*History of Magic* (1854) and by psychologists as a mental disease, as in Samuel Hibbert, *Sketches of the Philosophy of Apparitions* (1825). In the twentieth century, studies of the nearly universal black African acceptance of the reality of witchcraft throw light upon the European experience, especially by suggesting that the problem for thinkers of the Middle Ages was to reconcile in a rational manner the prevalent popular belief with the Christian notion of a good and omnipotent God. Although they achieved this reconciliation by regarding the evil angel and his agents as operating under God, in so doing some thinkers yielded to the perennial hazards of dualistic theology.

### BIBLIOGRAPHY

R. Trevor Davies, *Four Centuries of Witch-Beliefs* (London, 1947). Joseph Hansen, *Zauberwahn, Inquisition und Hexenprozess im Mittelalter . . .* (Leipzig, 1900). Heinrich Kramer and Jacob Sprenger, *Malleus maleficarum*, trans. Montague Summers (London, 1926). Henry Charles Lea, *Materials Toward a History of Witchcraft*, ed. A. C. Howland (Philadelphia, 1939); idem, *A History of the Inquisition of the Middle Ages* (New York, 1921). W. E. H. Lecky, *History of the Rise and Influence of the Spirit of Rationalism in Europe* (London, 1946). Martin Luther, *Table-Talk*, ed. William Hazlitt (London, 1902). A. L. Maycock, *The Inquisition from its Establishment to the Great Schism* (New York and London, 1927). Geoffrey Parrinder, *Witchcraft: European and African* (London, 1963). Rossell H. Robbins, *Encyclopaedia of Witchcraft and Demonology* (New York, 1959). Ronald Seth, *Witches and Their Craft* (London, 1967). Charles Williams, *Witchcraft* (London, 1941).

HELEN P. TRIMPI

[See also **Demonology**; Dualism; **Heresy**; **Hermeticism**; Romanticism.]

# SOCIAL ATTITUDES TOWARDS WOMEN

THE SITUATION of women in Western society has always been fraught with ambiguity. The writings of innumerable authors in a variety of fields attest to the existence of the problem, although there is by no means agreement concerning the nature of the problem. Adherents of the "eternal feminine" mystique accept as normative the feminine stereotypes of our culture, according to which a "true woman" does not achieve self-actualization through intellectual creativity and participation in political, economic, and social life on a level equal to that of men. Rather, according to this view, her destiny lies in generic fulfillment through motherhood, physical or spiritual, and in being a helpmate to her husband. Opposition to this position is strong. Radically opposed to the idea that the feminine stereotype is "natural" are the findings of anthropology, which suggest that "many, if not all, of the personality traits that we have called masculine or feminine are as lightly linked to sex, as are the clothing, the manners, and the form of head-dress that a society at a given period assigns to sex" (Mead [1935], p. 279). Recent research in experimental psychology also tends to refute the idea that the cluster of qualities expressed by the "eternal feminine" stereotype are innate and peculiar to women (Maccoby, 1963 and 1966). A growing number of authors argue that the characteristics of the "eternal feminine" are opposed to those of a developing, authentic person, who must be unique, self-critical, active, and searching (De Beauvoir, 1949; Jeannière, 1964; Daly, 1968). Modern feminists argue that the biological burdens associated with maternity and the restrictions imposed by cultural conditioning have held women back from the attainment of full human stature. They note with irony that the compensation offered by society to women for acceptance of the restrictions which it has imposed upon them in the political, economic, social, educational, and moral spheres has been imprisonment upon a pedestal.

The oppressive situation of women in ancient times is reflected in the Bible. The authors of both the Old and the New Testaments were men of their times, and it would be naive to think that they were free of the prejudices of their epochs. Indeed, the Bible contains much to jolt the modern woman, who is accustomed to think of herself, at least to some extent, as an autonomous person. In the writings of the Old Testament, women emerge as subjugated and inferior beings. Although the wife of an Israelite was not on the level of a slave, and however much better off she was than wives in other Near-Eastern nations, it is indicative of her inferior condition that the wife addressed her husband as a slave addressed his master, or a subject his king. In the Decalogue a man's wife is listed among his possessions, along with such items as his ox and his ass (Exodus 20:17; Deuteronomy 5:21). While her husband could repudiate her, she could not claim a divorce. Misconduct on the part of the wife was severely punished among the ancient Hebrews, whereas infidelity on the part of the man was punished only if he violated the rights of another man by taking a married woman as his accomplice. A man could sell his daughter as well as his slaves. If a couple did not have children, it was assumed to be the fault of the wife. In summary, although Hebrew women were honored as parents and often treated with kindness,

523

their social and legal status was that of subordinate beings. Hebrew males prayed: "I thank thee, Lord, that thou has not created me a woman."

Throughout the centuries, Christian authors have placed great importance upon the account of the creation of Eve in the second chapter of Genesis. Combined with the story of the Fall, this seemed to present irrefutable evidence of woman's essentially inferior intellectual and moral stature. Indeed, through the ages the anti-feminine tradition in Christian culture has justified itself to a large extent on the story of the origin and activities of the "first mother," which until recently was not understood to be androcentric myth but rather was taken as straight historical fact. A psychoanalyst who is also a student of biblical literature has summarized the situation succinctly: "The biblical story of Eve's birth is the hoax of the millennia" (Reik [1960], p. 124).

Androcentric tendencies in Western culture, rooted also in the profound misogynism of the Greeks, are reflected in the New Testament as well, which in turn has served as a basis for their perpetuation throughout Christendom. The most strikingly anti-feminine passages are in the Pauline texts. Paul was greatly concerned with order in society and in Christian assemblies in particular. It seemed important to him that women should not have a predominant place in Christian assemblies, that they should not "speak" in public or unveil their heads. This could have caused scandal and ridicule of the new sect, which already had to face charges of immorality and effeminacy. Thus he repeatedly insisted upon "correct" sexual behavior, including the subjection of wives at meetings. Paul went further and looked for theological justification for the prevailing customs. Thus, for example: "For a man ought not to cover his head, since he is the image and glory of God; but woman is the glory of man. For man was not made from woman, but woman from man. Neither was man created for woman, but woman for man" (I Corinthians 11:7ff.). Paul was basing his theological assertion here upon the then commonly held interpretation of Genesis. The extent of the effect is inestimable. For nearly two thousand years sermons and pious literature have been based upon the "glory of man" theme, and this has been accepted as God's inspired word.

Another frequently quoted Pauline text (probably not written by Paul but traditionally attributed to him) based on the then current interpretation of Genesis and used ever since as authority for the subordination of women is the following:

Let a woman learn in silence with all submissiveness. I permit no woman to teach or to have authority over men; she is to keep silent. For Adam was formed first, then Eve; and Adam was not deceived, but the woman was deceived and became a transgressor. Yet woman will be saved through bearing children, if she continues in faith and love and holiness, with modesty (I Timothy 2:11–15).

As for women's place in domestic society, the Pauline teaching was most explicit: "As the Church is subject to Christ, so let wives be subject in everything to their husbands" (Ephesians 5:24).

Such texts, understood as divinely inspired and without reference to the cultural context in which they were written, have served as powerful instruments for the reinforcement of the subjection of women in Western society. They have been used by religious authorities down through the centuries as a guarantee of divine approval for the transformation of woman's subordinate status from a contingent fact into an immutable norm of the feminine condition. They have been instrumental in withholding from women equal education, legal and economic equality, and access to the professions.

The low esteem for women in Western society during the early centuries of Christianity is reflected in the writings of the Church Fathers. The characteristics they considered to be typically feminine include fickleness and shallowness, garrulousness and weakness, slowness of understanding, and instability of mind. There were some violent tirades, such as that of Tertullian: "Do you not know that you are Eve? . . . You are the devil's gateway. . . . How easily you destroyed man, the image of God. Because of the death which you brought upon us, even the Son of God had to die" (De cultu feminarum, libri duo I, 1). On the whole, the attitude was one of puzzlement over the seemingly incongruous fact of woman's existence. Augustine summed up the general idea in saying that he did not see in what way it could be said that woman was made to be a help for man, if the work of child-bearing be excluded.

The Fathers found in Genesis an "explanation" of woman's inferiority which served as a guarantee of divine approval for perpetuating the situation which made her inferior. There was uncritical acceptance of the androcentric myth of Eve's creation and refusal, in varying degrees of inflexibility, to grant that woman is the image of God—an attitude in large measure inspired by Paul's first epistle to the Corinthians. Thus Augustine wrote that only man is the image and glory of God. According to him, since the believing woman cannot lay aside her sex, she is restored to the image of God only where there is no sex, that is, in the spirit (De Trinitate, XII, 7).

Together with the biblical account and the teachings of Church Fathers, those living in the early centuries of the Christian era were confronted with an image of women produced by oppressive conditions which were universal. A girlhood of strict seclusion and of minimal education prepared them for the life of mindless subordinates. This was followed by an early marriage which effectively cut them off from the possibility of autonomous action for the rest of their lives. Their inferiority was a fact; it appeared to be "natural." Thus experience apparently supported the rib story just as the myth itself helped "explain" the common experience of women as incomplete and lesser humans. The vicious circle was complete.

In the Middle Ages the general opinion of women was hardly much higher, although some of the fierceness of tone was mitigated. In the twelfth century Peter the Lombard wrote that woman is sensuality itself, which is well signified by woman, since in woman this naturally prevails (*Collectanea in epist. D. Pauli in epist. ad Cor.*, cap. XI, 8–10).

The assimilation of Aristotelianism into theology provided new conceptual tools for fixing woman's place in the universe. The most influential medieval theologian, Thomas Aquinas, in the thirteenth century reasserted Aristotle's teaching that women are misbegotten males, whose existence is due to some defect in the active force (that of the father) or to some material indisposition, or to some external influence such as the south wind, which is moist (*Summa Theologica*, I, 92, 1, ad 1). For Thomas, following Aristotle, the role of the woman in reproduction is purely passive; she supplies the "matter" whereas the father disposes this for the "form." From this he drew some rather startling implications; for example, that one should love one's father more than one's mother. Yet, of course, woman is needed for generation. Indeed, this seemed to Aquinas to be the only reason for the existence of women as such, "since a man can be more efficiently helped by another man in other works" (*Summa Theologica*, I, 92, 1c). He taught that although there is proportional equality between man and wife, there is not strict equality; neither in regard to the conjugal act, in which that which is nobler is due to the man, nor in regard to the order of the home, in which the woman is ruled and the man rules (*Summa Theologica*, Suppl., 64, 3c). Women must be excluded from Holy Orders, since "in the female sex no eminence of degree can be signified" (*Summa Theologica*, Suppl., 39 1c). Thomas revealed the same puzzlement over woman's existence as did the Fathers. Since he was a more systematic thinker, he had to face the difficulty of assimilating the anomaly of woman into an otherwise orderly universe. At points the strain is evident. Thomas had to admit, for example, that woman is somehow the image of God, since this was the teaching

of Genesis. Yet Paul and the Fathers had seemed to deny this. Thomas resolved the puzzle with a distinction, affirming that "in a secondary sense the image of God is found in man and not in woman: for man is the beginning and end of woman; as God is the beginning and end of every creature" (*Summa Theologica*, I, 93, 4 ad 1). Since Thomas taught that the intellectual soul is natural and essential to both men and women and yet shared with the Fathers the feeling that women are not quite human, there is a basic disharmony in his thought on this subject. The deep roots of his philosophical anthropology—his conceptions concerning body-soul relationship and the person—would have supported a conception of genuine equality, but the combined influence of commonly accepted biblical exegesis, Aristotelian biology, and the prevailing image and status of women resulted in a discordant androcentrism.

It would be difficult to overestimate the influence of Thomism, in which Aristotelian theory was wedded to the standard biblical interpretations, so that the seeming weight of "science" was added to that of authority. Thomism came to have a place of unique pre-eminence in the church, a pre-eminence which, at least in Roman Catholicism, has lasted into modern times.

Despite medieval theories, there were some cases of powerful women in the Middle Ages. There were abbesses who exercised great power. The abbesses of Saint Cecilia in Cologne, for example, had the power of jurisdiction and of suspension over clerics. In some areas there were double monasteries in which both monks and nuns were ruled by an abbess. Although restrictive in some ways, nunneries did open for some women the road to learning and administrative posts.

There were of course some great individual women in the secular world. There were outstanding rulers such as Clotilde and Blanche of Castille, and learned women like Eleanor of Aquitaine and Blanche of Navarre. There were great saints: Catherine of Siena had enormous influence and the story of Joan of Arc has no parallel. However, it would be absurd to judge the general situation of women or the general attitude toward them by such examples. The prevailing low status of women was fixed by law and custom. By canon law a husband was entitled to beat his wife. Only the dowry system was allowed for matrimony, and under this system women were legally defenseless. In general they were considered as man's property. Since for feudal lords marriages were a means of accumulating property, women were pawns in the game of acquiring wealth. Complex marriage laws offered ample opportunity for trickery and abuse. Thus, although there were glorious feminine personalities in the Middle

Ages, there were multitudes of anonymous victims of hypocrisy and oppression.

The early modern period did not bring any startling changes in the general attitude toward women. It is significant that Theresa of Avila, one of the most remarkable women of all times, complained repeatedly of the ignorance and other obstacles imposed upon her sex: "The very thought that I am a woman is enough to make my wings droop" (*Life*, Ch. X). Yet in the Renaissance some upper-class women did study Greek and Roman classics. In the fifteenth century Christine de Pisan wrote in defense of her sex, thus acting as one of the first harbingers of the modern feminist movement. In the sixteenth century Erasmus of Rotterdam was sympathetic toward the education of women, as were some other Renaissance authors such as Sir Thomas Elyot and Sir Thomas More. However, general practice did not keep pace with theory. The vision of the early humanists was not fulfilled until centuries later.

Within the Church a number of courageous women struggled to break the old patterns. Among the most daring of the religious innovators was Mary Ward (1585–1645), who founded the "English Ladies." Her basic insight was that it was time for new possibilities for dedicated religious women beyond the confines of the cloister. She intended that her group would work "in the world," conducting schools for girls. They were to be like the Jesuits, but would not be subject to them. Rather, they were to be governed directly by women responsible solely to the pope, independently of bishops and of men's orders. A strong advocate of the emancipation of women, she planned to teach girls Latin and other secular subjects which heretofore had been reserved largely for men. For her pains, she was rewarded with persecution by clerical enemies and was arrested as a heretic and a schismatic. Mary Ward and other courageous contemporaries did not live to see the fulfillment of their aspirations, but they broke ground for the future.

Throughout the seventeenth, eighteenth, and nineteenth centuries consciousness of women's potential and of their plight continued to grow. In France, writers such as Molière, Poulain de la Barre, Voltaire, and Mercier wrote in favor of the emancipation of women. Diderot and Helvétius both recognized that woman's inferiority was created by society and by the absurdity of their education. Condorcet strongly advocated their political emancipation. Unfortunately for the feminist movement, however, the Napoleonic Code blocked the emancipation of Frenchwomen and kept them legally and politically powerless throughout the nineteenth century. In England, Mary Wollstonecraft's *A Vindication of the Rights of Woman* (1792) was

effective in sparking the struggle for equal rights. So also was John Stuart Mill's famous work, *On the Subjection of Women* (1869). In the United States the great leaders in the fight for women's rights—Lucy Stone, Susan B. Anthony, Elizabeth Cady Stanton, Carrie Chapman Catt, and others—carried on the struggle through every available means, writing, lecturing, organizing political support and public demonstrations.

Resistance to the liberation of women came from all sides. Philosophers as diverse as Comte and Hegel failed to get the message that a new age was dawning and that the movement could not be stopped. Queen Victoria expressed her fury over the "mad wicked folly of 'Women's Rights' with all its attendant horrors." Grover Cleveland, writing in *Ladies Home Journal* (October 1905), opposed the franchise on the grounds that "woman suffrage would give to the wives and daughters of the poor a new opportunity to gratify their envy and mistrust of the rich." In support of this he invoked a familiar stereotype: "We all know how much further women go than men in their social rivalries and jealousies."

Institutional religion was not generally disposed to welcome or encourage feminine emancipation. The official Catholic reaction in the nineteenth and twentieth centuries manifested the persistence of the conflict between the Christian concept of women as persons, made to the image of God, and the notion of them as inferior, derivative beings. Since this is the most dramatic and powerful example of institutionalized religion's resistence to feminism in Western culture, and since it reflects and reinforces idea patterns in other cultural institutions, it merits scrutiny.

The first pope to confront the emancipation movement was Leo XIII. Against the socialists, whom he saw as threatening the stability of marriage, he defended "paternal authority." As for the husband-wife relationship, he reaffirmed the subjection of the female, supporting this position by an interpretation of Genesis no longer acceptable to modern biblical scholarship (Encyclical *Arcanum Divinae*, 1880). Leo XIII viewed divorce as an unqualified evil, claiming that by divorce "the dignity of womanhood is lessened and brought low, and women run the risk of being deserted after having ministered to the pleasures of men" (Encyclical *Arcanum Divinae*, 1880). The other side of the picture, the fact that many wives desired to be freed from partners who exploited their wives' inability to obtain a divorce under existing laws was tacitly passed over.

In 1919 Benedict XV pronounced in favor of votes for women, but this did not represent any sweeping change in the official outlook. It would be naive to suppose that official attitudes were not affected by the consideration that women's votes would probably support conservative and religious parties.

Resistance to the striving for equal education for women was strongly put forth by Pius XI, who wrote:

False also and harmful to Christian education is the so-called method of "coeducation" . . . There is not in nature itself, which fashions the two quite different in organism, in temperament, in abilities, anything to suggest that there can be or ought to be promiscuity, and much less equality, in the training of the two sexes" (Encyclical *Divini Illius Magistri*, 1929).

It is noteworthy that Pius XI linked coeducation with equality and therefore opposed it. In the same encyclical he taught that the differences between the sexes should be "maintained and encouraged," thus unwittingly conceding that these differences may not be as natural in origin as he insists they are. It is striking that Pius XI's language more than once displays this characteristic of unwitting self-refutation. He attacked "false teachers" for proclaiming that the married woman should, to the neglect of her family, "be able to follow her own bent and devote herself to business and even public affairs" (Encyclical *Casti Connubii*, 1930). It is the admission of such an ambitious "bent" in women that reveals the shakiness of his views about "the natural disposition and temperament of the female sex." Closely allied to this phenomenon of self-contradictory expressions is the occurrence of ambivalent language. Thus, Piux XI could write: "True emancipation will not involve false liberty and unnatural equality with the husband" (*Casti Connubii*). Anyone interested in the analysis of language would be fascinated with the problem of what the adjectives in that sentence do to the nouns. Again, in the same letter, Pius XI refers to equality in dignity between husband and wife and then effectively negates this by affirming the necessity of "a certain inequality." It is obvious that he favored the traditional androcentric situation; yet the pressure of social evolution forced him to use expressions which have just enough ambiguity to leave the door open a crack for unavoidable social change. Thus: "This subjection of wife to husband in its degree and manner may vary according to the different conditions of persons, place, and time."

Pius XII in his copious utterances manifested the same resistance to change, the same ambivalence characteristic of an ideology in a state of transition. He saw the gainful employment of married women solely as an obligation taken on for the family, and not at all as a means of self-actualization or as a contribution to society. There is indecision between a supposedly ideal situation, that of a bygone agricultural society,

and the facts of modern life. A key concept in the whole adjustment to modern society was "spiritual motherhood," an easily manipulated concept which permitted some degree of expansion of the traditional role but with serious limitations. Thus he wrote that "a true woman cannot see and fully understand all the problems of human life otherwise than under the family aspect" (*Address to Women of Catholic Action*, October 21, 1945). The expression "true woman" is characteristic of this kind of ideology, implying that anyone who does not fit the stereotype is not what she should be. The ideology that shaped Pius XII's utterances on women was one in which they are seen as totally "other." It is not surprising, then, that there is little sign of sensitivity to their problems and personal aspirations. The following statement reveals this lack of compassion and imagination:

A cradle consecrates the mother of the family; and more cradles sanctify and glorify her before her husband and children, before church and homeland. The mother who complains because a new child presses against her bosom seeking nourishment at her breast is foolish, ignorant of herself, and unhappy. (*Address to Women of Catholic Action*, October 26, 1941).

Moreover, he affirmed that a mother "loves it [her child] the more, the more pain it has cost her" (*Address to Obstetricians*, October 29, 1951).

Pius XII was completely satisfied with his own views of women, insisting that "these peculiar characteristics which distinguish the two sexes reveal themselves so clearly to the eyes of all" that only obstinate blindness or doctrinairism could disregard them (*Address to Women of Catholic Action*, October 21, 1945). The idea that the stereotypes which he accepted as immutable nature might be the effect of social conditioning was not given serious consideration by this pope or his predecessors.

Catholic ideology on the official level took a promising swing upward with Pope John XXIII, who affirmed the equal rights and duties of man and woman in marriage, without the customary nullifying adjectives (Encyclical *Pacem in Terris*, 1963). Vatican II's *Pastoral Constitution on the Church in the Modern World* also reflected this upward swing, affirming that "with respect to the fundamental rights of the person, every type of discrimination, whether social or cultural, whether based on sex, race, color, social condition, language, or religion, is to be overcome and eradicated as contrary to God's law." Although the post-Vatican II years have witnessed a regression in official Catholic ideology, this official ideology has become less and less influential on thought and practice. Theology itself is

527

to a great extent becoming liberated from this official influence and turning with increasing interest to the data of experience analyzed by the methods of scientific disciplines. Although official Catholicism remains the most powerful bastion of conservatism, pressure continues to come both from outside its structures and from within its active membership, e.g., from a feminist organization of Catholic women, the Saint Joan's International Alliance (originally the Catholic Women's Suffrage Society, founded in England in 1911).

Although Protestantism on the whole has tended to be somewhat more advanced, the same basic patterns are observable both in ideology and in practice. Women are admitted to the ministry in a number of Protestant churches, but even in those churches discrimination persists. A significant proportion of major theologians, from Luther to Barth and Bonhoeffer, in a manner somewhat less blatant than that of their Catholic counterparts have perpetuated a fundamentally infrapersonal view of woman.

As already indicated, however, it would be a mistake to think that the infrapersonal conceptualizations of woman have been conserved and promulgated in the nineteenth and twentieth centuries only by institutional religion. The majority of philosophers seem to have suffered a suspension of their critical powers when it came to this question, although there have been outstanding exceptions such as Marx and John Stuart Mill. Freud, for all his genius, was not able to get beyond the conventional stereotype, and was convinced that a woman who wanted to be someone, who was ambitious and self-actualizing, must be sick with penis envy. Politicians who opposed woman suffrage and educators who opposed equal education have been legion.

Despite the opposition, the battle for women's suffrage was won in most countries in the West. In Great Britain and Germany it was granted in 1918, in the USSR in 1917, in the United States in 1920, in France in 1944. As far as education is concerned, there is hardly any field in which women today, after many years of denial, cannot obtain higher degrees.

Nevertheless, even basic legal equality does not yet exist for women in the United States. The Federal constitution was framed and adopted under the influence of the English Common Law valuation of women, which does not regard women as legal persons or entities. A historian of American feminism has pointed out:

Through the years, repeated Supreme Court decisions, as late as 1961, have held that women do not rate the "equal protection of the laws" because they were not regarded as legal "persons" when the Constitution and the Fourteenth Amendment were adopted. This means that women have no legal protection against discrimination (Lutz [1968], p. 298).

In effect, this absence of guarantee by the Fourteenth Amendment means that at any time a law can be passed by Congress or by any state which would discriminate against women or bar them from certain forms of work or education. Such a law would not be unconstitutional. In fact, laws in some states do today seriously limit the rights of married women. The Massachusetts Committee for the Equal Rights Amendment has pointed out that laws in some states limit a married woman's right to contract, to engage in business, to separate domicile, to the guardianship of children, to dispose of property by will, to serve on juries, to contract for her labor on the same terms as men. The Committee maintains that the Equal Rights for Women Amendment would wipe out the English Common Law valuation of women, giving them full protection under the constitution and making unconstitutional all laws discriminating against women as well as making it possible to enforce Title VII of the Civil Rights Act in cases of discrimination on the basis of sex. It also sees this amendment as the best hope for bringing the United States into compliance with the United Nations Charter, which upholds the "equal rights of men and women" and the United Nations Declaration on the elimination of discrimination against women, adopted by the General Assembly, November 7, 1967.

The Equal Rights for Women Amendment was first introduced in 1923 by the National Women's Party and has been reintroduced in every session of Congress. It was opposed through the years even by many who maintained that women need protective labor legislation. However, in very recent years a new wave of support for it has grown. Senator Eugene McCarthy sponsored the bill in the senate and a number of prominent national organizations have endorsed it.

It is increasingly recognized that women still do not participate on an equal basis with men in politics and the professions. In the 1960's a sense of desperation over the decline of women's participation in the United States since the end of World War II sparked a renewed concern over equal rights. It was noted with alarm that only 7% of doctors in the U.S. were women, less than 4% of lawyers, and less that 1% of federal judges, and that there was an increasing tendency for women to be concentrated at the bottom of the job ladder in the more menial and routine jobs. In 1966, in Washington D.C. a group of concerned persons formed the National Organization for Women (NOW), whose purpose is "to take action to bring women into full participation in the mainstream of American society *now*, exercising all the privileges and responsibilities thereof in truly equal partnership with men." Composed of men and women, NOW works to break through the "silken curtain" of discrimination against women in American life. NOW has been particularly industrious in pressuring the Equal Employment Opportunity Commission to carry out effectively the mandate against sex discrimination under Title VII of the Civil Rights Act of 1964. In 1968 it endorsed the Equal Rights Amendment. Its members seek nothing less than complete equality for women in government, industry, the professions, the churches, the political parties, the judiciary, the labor unions, and in all fields of importance in American life.

It is instructive to note that despite the struggles of modern-day feminists in the United States, there is little evidence that even those legal changes which already have taken place have in fact been translated into profound institutional change. The franchise and other legal victories, as many feminist authors (e.g., Betty Friedan) and social critics have observed, have to a large extent been hollow victories. They will remain such until they work their way into the very structures of society.

It has been pointed out that there is no sex equality until women actually participate on an equal basis with men in politics, occupations, and the family. That is, women must want to participate and be able to participate. This cannot happen "unless ways are devised to ease the combination of home and work responsibilities. This is precisely what has not occurred" (Rossi [1964], p. 610).

This observation invites serious reflection upon the history of the feminist movement. Historians and sociologists observe that it has never been a completely autonomous movement. It has been effective when joined with other reform movements. Alice Rossi notes this: "By linking the feminist cause to the antislavery or social welfare movement, women were able to work together with men of similar sympathies and in the process they enlisted the support of these men for the feminist cause" (Rossi [1964], p. 611). De Beauvoir reflects that feminism has been in part an epiphenomenon reflecting a deeper social drama. The problem has been that feminism's lack of autonomy has held it back from complete fulfillment. Thus women in the antislavery movement who petitioned Congress in the 1860's to enfranchise women either before or at the same time as Negroes were confronted with the slogan: This is the Negro's hour. "This slogan was repeated so constantly that people in general, and even some women, actually believed that it was more important to enfranchise thousands of illiterate Negroes than to confer the inherent right of citizenship upon educated,

intelligent women, granddaughters of the founders of the Republic" (Lutz [1968], pp. 294–95). Thus there has been an ambivalence in feminism's history; it obtains the necessary thrust toward action through union with other revolutionary movements and at the same time it tends to fall short of its goals by reason of its lack of autonomy. This has been witnessed again one hundred years later, when discrimination on the basis of sex became banned in Title VII of the Civil Rights Act as a sort of rider, when the basic concern was racial discrimination. Not too surprisingly, those charged with the implementing of Title VII have focused their attention chiefly on cases of racial discrimination, tending to overlook sex discrimination.

This lesson of history has not been lost on young women activists of the New Left. In many cases, the ability to comprehend the lesson arose from the experience of participation in meetings at which young women across the United States have shared the experience of gaining political sophistication and awareness of revolutionary tactics. They have also shared the discouraging experience of being cast into the traditional feminine role precisely within a movement which presents itself as engaged in struggle for the liberation of the oppressed classes. As a result of this complex experience of social awakening shared by many women university students in the late 1960's a significant and extraordinary movement has developed. Commonly known as the Women's Liberation Movement, it surfaced to public attention in 1968 and has been gaining momentum since then. Its most obvious qualities are the youthfulness and the political and social radicalness of its membership. Although they express solidarity with the members of NOW, the adherents of the Women's Liberation Movement profess a more revolutionary ideology. Their goal is not equal participation in the American political and economic system as it now is—a goal which they consider self-contradictory and self-defeating. Rather they see hope only in a radical transformation of that system. Basically in agreement with Engels' thesis that "the first class oppression coincides with that of the female sex by the male" they conclude that female liberation is basic to all other struggles, since it strikes at the foundation of all other forms of oppression.

It is interesting to note that whereas in 1964 sociologist Rossi had written that the decline of political radicalism and the general state of affluence and social conservatism in American society since World War II have contributed in subtle ways to the decline of feminism, by the end of the same decade a profound political polarization among the younger generation gave rise to a new feminist movement, the effectiveness of which cannot yet be judged.

BIBLIOGRAPHY

Jane Addams, *Twenty Years of Hull House* (New York, 1960). D. S. Bailey, *The Man-Woman Relation in Christian Thought* (London, 1959). M. Daly, *The Church and the Second Sex* (New York, 1968). S. De Beauvoir, *Le deuxième sexe* (Paris, 1949); trans. as *The Second Sex* (New York, 1953); many reprints). E. Flexner, *Century of Struggle* (Cambridge, 1959). B. Friedan, *The Feminine Mystique* (New York, 1963). J. Hole and E. Levine, *Rebirth of Feminism* (New York, 1972). A. Jeannière, *Anthropologie sexuelle* (Paris, 1964); see the Foreward by D. Sullivan to the American edition, trans. J. Kiernan (New York, 1967). A. S. Kraditor, ed., *Up from the Pedestal. Selected Writings in the History of American Feminism* (Chicago, 1968), and idem, *The Ideas of the Woman Suffrage Movement, 1890–1920* (New York, 1965). A. Lutz, *Crusade for Freedom: Women of the Antislavery Movement* (Boston, 1968) and idem, *Susan B. Anthony: Rebel, Crusader, Humanitarian* (Boston, 1959). E. Maccoby, ed., *The Development of Sex Differences* (Stanford, 1966) and "Woman's Intellect," *The Potential of Woman*, eds. S. M. Farber and R. H. L. Wilson (New York, 1963), pp. 24–39. H. Marcuse, *Eros and Civilization* (Boston, 1955). Marx, Engels, Lenin, and Stalin, *The Woman Question* (New York, 1951). M. Mead, *From the South Seas* (New York, 1939) and idem, *Sex and Temperament in Three Primitive Societies* (New York, 1935). Kate Millett, *Sexual Politics* (New York, 1970). R. Morgan, ed., *Sisterhood Is Powerful* (New York, 1970). William L. O'Neill, *Everyone Was Brave* (Chicago, 1969). T. Reik, *The Creation of Woman* (New York, 1960). Robert Riegel, *American Feminists* (Lawrence, Kan., 1963); idem, *American Women: A Story of Social Change* (Rutherford, N.J., 1970). A. Rossi, "Equality between the Sexes; An Immodest Proposal," *Daedalus* (Spring, 1964), 607–52. Page Smith, *Daughters of the Promised Land* (Boston, 1970). M. Thompson, ed., *Voices of the New Feminism* (Boston, 1970).

MARY DALY

[See also Church as Institution; Conservation; **Equality; Law, Equal Protection; Protest Movements.**]

# WORK

THE GREEK word *banausia* (βαναυσία) means mechanical skill, more generally manual work, and has a pejorative connotation. The opposing thought was that man's destiny should be linked to thinking, more specifically to contemplation. The Gods of Olympus watch the world from on high in the light of ideas, and bask in eternity.

Among many examples that may be given of this attitude, the following two will suffice. Xenophon says that the mechanical arts bear the mark of social decay and bring dishonor to Greek cities (*Economica*, IV, 203). His statement is not a haphazard one, but reflects actually the more general world view shared by two major thinkers of antiquity, Plato and Aristotle.

In the *Gorgias* (512b), Plato, through the words of Callicles, asserts that no matter how useful the maker of war machines may be, "you denigrate him and his art," so that "you would not wish to give your daughter in marriage to his son." Nor should it be thought that Aristotle is judging casually when he puts forth his theory that making and knowing how to make things is the servile activity of slaves under the dominion of their masters, the virtues peculiar to master and slave being clearly distinct (*Politics*, 1277ff.).

It is consequently natural for Aristotle to regard work as a secondary activity, in the sense that though work seems to emancipate us from things, it really imprisons us. It is better for man, and more in accord with his essence, to retire within his true self by thinking, and thus to participate in the work of God. It follows, for Aristotle, that living is essentially learning and understanding, for knowledge contains the supreme virtue which actualizes and consummates in man the work of divinity. Man's destiny is to keep himself immune from the sensory world and to advance steadily to the world of pure thought, not merely in work (ἐνέργεια) but in theorizing (θεωρία). In the activity of thinking man attains his highest felicity or blessedness; the happiness which man can attain through practical virtue is secondary and is associated with the life he is compelled to lead in dealing with the world's external things (*Nicomachean Ethics* 1169–70, 1177–78; *Metaphysics* 982a).

Ancient thought, however, does not lack various expressions of a certain appreciation of human labor, apart from any prejudice that others may have had. In general such assertions are found among authors belonging to the school of Sophists and other minor schools. For example, Antiphon proclaims the harsh necessity of work insofar as life is accepted for what it is. This life is certainly not easy or sweet, but it nevertheless acquires meaning when it is crowned with success (Stobaeus, IV, 22.2.66; a fragment translated in *I sofisti*, ed. M. T. Cardini, Bari [1923], p. 126; also in *Minor Attic Orators*, Loeb Library, Vol. I). But Prodicus of Chios, in the circle of the Sophists, states the definitive thesis about work in his apology, *Hercules at the Crossroad*. Referring to Xenophon's *Memorabilia* (II, 1, 21–34), Prodicus insists on the virtue of labor which gives dignity to the life of man.

An interpreter like R. Mondolfo bases his views on a dualism of ethnic groups by blaming the warlike aristocracy of the Dorians for imposing on the conquered Achaeans the yoke of laboring on the lands which had become their booty, even though such labor was contrary to the social rank of the conquered.

Conquering groups prefer a contemplative life to one burdened by work; the conquered consider that keeping their pledge of labor is a duty though far from achieving perfect liberty. Work is the ransom paid for the sake of keeping alive.

Reference to an eternal life in religious intuition comes out of the Greek world, but becomes determinant and definite in Judaism and finally in Christianity. The book of Genesis (3:17–19) says that hard work is a result of Adam's sin. Man is condemned to labor because he must expiate the original sin. Nevertheless it should not be thought that labor suffices to restore man's lost status or dignity before God. Holy Scripture says that "All the labor of man is for his mouth, and yet the appetite is not filled" (Ecclesiastes 6:7), which clearly means that the soul needs much more than work to redeem itself; it needs prayer and the contemplation of God. Merely economic activities or goods are not sufficient for salvation if the recognition of God is absent. On this recognition is based the alliance or covenant which links God to his people.

It is important to note that the Jews continue to cherish a world without drudgery or with little drudgery, a world independent of labor. God's gift is precisely a collection of temporal goods, the reward of faith in the one and only God. The intervention of God in the economy assures his people of the reestablishment of the more perfect conditions of existence, the reign on earth of the plenitude of his gifts. The regenerated earth will no longer require hard work; opulent and fruitful, it will satisfy the needs of the chosen people.

Such motives are taken up again by Christianity, but in the end, after a complex elaboration, there emerge, in the supernatural kingdom, values which are ever more distinctively spiritual and accessible to all people without discrimination.

At first the rejection of work seems radical and final, and echoes the most radical denial by the Prophets: "Therefore take no thought, saying, What shall we eat? or, What shall we drink? or, Wherewithal shall we be clothed? (For after all these things do the Gentiles seek:) for your heavenly Father knoweth that ye have need of all these things. But seek ye first the kingdom of God, and his righteousness; and all these things shall be added unto you" (Matthew 6:31–33).

However, little by little in place of such ideas, emerge other ideas which begin to dignify the idea of work, and work, though not considered exactly a blessing, ceases on the other hand to be conceived negatively. Jesus is a worker, born in a family of workers. "Is not this the carpenter, the son of Mary . . . ?" (Mark 6:3). And that is exactly why Paul can say that "he became poor, that ye through his poverty might be rich" (II Corinthians 8:9).

There are many reasons behind this revaluation of work; only some will be sketched here. Above all, work, while it assures one of being independent of political power (Philippians 4:11), furnishes one with the means for giving charitably "to him that needeth" (Ephesians 4:28). It thus comes about that this work is purified as a means and instrument of love among men. These are the reasons that pass from the apostle into the oldest Christian literature (Didache, Book IV; I John 3:17).

The antitheses sketched above lasted during the entire medieval period, which valued work to the extent that it might further the ends of asceticism, but the Middle Ages also subordinated work to the contemplative life, and to the spiritual adoration of God. It suffices to recall the Rule of Saint Benedict, its formula of "pray and work" (ora et labora), in order to understand the idea of enjoying the liberating spirit of work, obviously on the plane of a discipline of the mind, exactly what the discipline of genuine asceticism is said to be. Ecce labora et noli contristari ("There he works and refuses to be gloomy").

However, there is a larger picture that must include the view outlined; it makes reference to a doctrine that again refutes any definitely pragmatic attitude and orders man to concern himself with the spirit in a radical dedication to God.

It is a matter of defining the sphere of human knowledge, the arts (the "arts" signifying the same as the "sciences") which constitute it, being the very articulations of knowing. These arts proceeded in a particular way, starting with Martianus Capella and Boethius, going on to Isidore of Seville and Alcuin, and finally to Bede and Rabanus Maurus. What emerged was the classification called the "trivium" and the "quadrivium," the first embracing grammar, dialectic, and rhetoric, the second geometry, arithmetic, astronomy, and music. It was hence possible to conceive a comprehensive doctrinal learning such that, by its means, man reasons and discusses in the three arts called discursive (sermocinales), but at the same time endeavors to learn about things through the other four arts called real (reales). The totality of the resulting arts, whether discursive or real, is finally taken over and made subordinate and instrumental to philosophy, "the knowledge of human and divine things" (rerum humanarum divinarumque cognitio). Philosophy in turn is linked to religion and becomes its handmaid in a true and peculiar relation of dependence.

It is appropriate to declare the arts mentioned to be liberal arts, in the sense that they fulfil the educational aims which shape the mind of the free man, in

531

contrast to the lowly arts (*artes sordidae*) of the slave, thus crystallizing the traditional antithesis, just as it appears in Cassiodorus. It was in fact he who came to make a less drastic but more precise distinction. In his work on the liberal arts and disciplines, *De artibus et disciplinis liberalibus* (Migne, *Patrologiae latinae*, Vol. LXX, col. 1151), he contrasts the liberal arts, which are learned from books through the exercise of the mind, with the mechanical arts. If the two motifs, the mechanical (or more specifically the manual) and the lowly, are brought together, we have a context which can be compared to the modern idea of the antithesis of praxis and theory. The latter is praised, the other remains inferior.

In order to find the way in which thought did break through this dualism, which stubbornly and continually arises, and how it was superseded by the praise of the free man, it is necessary to look to the Renaissance, when that dualism was slowly and laboriously attacked. In investigating the concept of the humanities (*humanitas*), thinkers define not only what is usually called "humanism," which reflects precisely the first phase of the Renaissance, but on the contrary judge the Renaissance wholly humanistic in its very essence. Man is evaluated in every aspect, his reason as well as his will. The mind is investigated not merely through literary documents or literature called "humane," but much more through man's involvement in the world, through his mastery of things, and through his definite and exact intervention in nature. To the idea of a created nature (*natura naturata*) the Renaissance adds the idea of a creative nature (*natura naturans*), a second nature, as it were, made by man.

There follows the exaltation of man by minds like Giannozzo Manetti, Pico della Mirandola, Marsilio Ficino, Matteo Palmieri, Leon Battista Alberti, Leonardo da Vinci, Giordano Bruno, and Tommaso Campanella, to mention only the greatest and most important ones. Their emphasis is on the dignity and excellence of man, with praise for his open-eyed views of the world, and for his efficient and effective diligence as a worker, one who not only commands things and events but also enjoys working incessantly. Of course, work is often hard, painful, and exhausting, but how can one stop the wheels of progress? Leonardo goes so far as to say that in work "nature is surpassed: the raw materials of nature are finite, but the works that the eye orders the hands to make are infinite" (*Treatise on Painting*, sec. 28). Man is therefore exalted in his creative activity. It is not merely a matter of labor, even when accompanied by extreme fatigue, but it requires the whole complex of human conditions, social and historical, for a new and original work to emerge. The end product is created spontaneously by man

who comes close to being like God. Is man himself not a God? Everything would lead one to think so insofar as work and the process of working makes man divine. However, an immediate reservation is necessary: man may be like God without being a deity. Man makes himself similar to God in his capability and work, but he is not God. "Therefore, man who generally takes care of living and inanimate things is a kind of God" (Marsilio Ficino, *Theologia platonica*, XIII, 3). A recurrent theme in the Renaissance is ascertaining the boundaries of man's nature. Man can come close to God, can act like a little God in his image, but he is not God.

What must be added to mark the limits of human nature is the fatigue which accompanies human work; hence rest and leisure are necessary to restore man's energy. The thinker who devoted all of his thought to the relationship of man to God is surely Giordano Bruno. He insists, in fact, on the importance of the will, and for Bruno the will implies activity, as well as the laborious mastery of things. On the other hand, to the extent that work brings on fatigue, leisure is required, for through leisure man's energies are restored, and he is prepared to cope with subsequent fatigue from new work.

We have noted how work is praised for its infinite potentialities, but we also indicate the limitations of work, and have called on Bruno as a witness. Something has to be said of the way in which the depressing aspect of work is regarded. Whence the question: Can manual activity be eliminated, and above all to what extent? Campanella, in his *City of the Sun* (*Civitas solis*, 1623), not only advocates the communal sharing of goods and women, but sketches a whole social plan and educational system based on learning and work. He is cognizant, moreover, of the new role of science in both its creative and moral aspects, even while he invokes a thorough and effective discipline of work to maintain the aims of civilization and progress. With everyone working, whether in the intellectual field or in manual activity, for Campanella, the result attained in the work is complete human equality and a wholesale solution of the great problems of social life without the privileged states that intellectuals might claim at the expense of those condemned to be tied down to merely manual labor.

The Protestant Reformation contributed new elements to the theory of work. Without giving up the medieval idea of work as a remedy for sin (*remedium peccati*), Luther sketched the new concept of work as a service to God. God accomplishes everything through us; using us as a means, he attends to the most humble tasks, such as milking the cow and the kid, and all such labors are without exception pleasing to the Lord. The lowliest housemaid's servile work has its religious value generally enhanced through the inspiration with which it is imbued. "For God is present in such matters and his Spirit is in the work" (*Opera exegetica latina,* ed. Elsperger, Erlangen [1831], VII, 208f., 213f.). Finally, there is no occupation in the home or in the field which is so humble that it fails to reveal our divine calling, and which thus binds us to the Lord. The occupation becomes a religious profession, and the German word *Beruf* thus acquired the distinctive meaning of both "a calling" and "service to God."

However, it is with Calvin that the definitive religious implications of Protestantism stand out in high relief. In his *Institutio christiana* (1534–36), we find the Augustinian idea of predestination affirmed and developed. Predestined as man is, he must confront God alone, and then ask himself to verify whether he is one of the elect or damned, as Max Weber puts it. The answer to such a question no other man can give him, nor can society provide an answer; only his conscience can. Assuming that he is cognizant of being one of the elect rather than one of the condemned, the individual will feel and act like one of the elect, and show his gratitude by increasing the production of goods. Conduct for the greater glory of God will be rewarded by success, since success is the consequence of election and grace. Goods will be multiplied by the hands of the elect; these goods are not to be accumulated or to be hoarded but on the contrary they are to be channeled into the cycle of production, capital aimed at infinite production in praise of God. Capitalism is stimulated by arousing a psychological motivation, which in its turn finds a basis in religious dogma.

We now come to the modern era, and in particular to the contributions to the theme of work made by the philosophers concerned with modern civilization. There are two lines which will be pursued here: the first concerns the relationship between work and science due to technology; the second regards the discussion of whether a society based on work as an expression of the creative spirit of man truly suffices to satisfy man's deeper needs, or whether, on the contrary, it reveals itself to be spiritually deficient. Obviously in such arguments we are confronting a problematic situation constituting the most challenging question of contemporary speculative thought; in short, it comes to seeking the very reasons for living.

As to the first line of inquiry, there is no doubt that its source is in the Renaissance investigations of man's powers. Not only do his powers as they have been historically manifested form the subject of Renaissance thought, but there is much more persistent concern with the issues and limits of the new sciences and "arts" other than those previously known as the *trivium* and *quadrivium.* Renaissance philosophy is completely at harmony with science, and becomes the epistemology and methodology of the arts which occupy a prominent place in men's minds and demand their attention. It is not conceptually abstract knowledge but the quite different concrete kind of knowledge which is applied to nature and transforms it for the human ends of utility and enjoyment. The task of philosophy continues in the sense that it secures a methodological framework for the progress of science guaranteeing more flexible principles than were traditional, as well as adequate verification in experience. In any case, philosophy still depends on value judgments in aesthetics, ethics, and religion, that go beyond the scope of the sciences. Work emerges in science and technology as the means for the advancement of man committed to a toil that is ever renewed and yet never sufficient.

Francis Bacon is certainly the thinker to whom we owe much of the new perspective, for he is precisely the theorist of science with respect to its pragmatic ends. He attempted the construction of the kingdom of man (*regnum hominis*) by man's dominion over nature, through precise means and instruments which the individual arts, opportunely cultivated, could provide. Men ought to know that in the theater of life only God and the angels can properly be spectators (*De dignitate et augmentis scientiarum,* VIII, 1). A true son of the Renaissance, Bacon insists on considering the much proclaimed dignity of man to reside in the functional role of science. Intelligence and will converge in pragmatic knowledge.

On this point it is fitting to refer again to Leonardo to testify that for him also philosophy ends in science understood as technology. The result is the confirmed role of the machine to which the relief of man's weary labor is entrusted.

Instrumental or mechanical science is the most noble and most useful above all the others; it is a conscious thing by means of which living bodies in motion perform their operations (Fumagalli, pp. 57–58).

On this score Galileo says exactly the same thing, and even insists on such ideas in the wide context of experimental thought. Experiments not only repeat the operations of nature but, by duly interrogating her, can reveal her secrets.

Moreover, to mark the characteristic feature of the new conception of science there is the manual activity that accompanies the role of science as a "hunter," its "venatorial" function, to use a term dear to the language of Bacon's day. Things unveil their secrets through some means or instrument, that is to say, technologically. But we are reminded that it is the hand which controls the instrument, the hand which in its turn is guided by man looking to the mind and will to direct him. The "mechanical arts" acquire a new meaning and vigor, a new prestige from the positive results of the sciences, even directly from the discovery of a new world through machines or the mechanical approach to the world. Seen through the work entrusted to science and technology, the world looks like an enormous machine (*machina mundi*) with God the chief engineer and man the artisan who makes the machine and replaces its parts.

Contemplation plays a very small part in such views of natural science, and is not a vocational substitute for productive knowledge. With the Baconian and Leonardian innovations the legacy of the Renaissance flows into the Enlightenment and later thought.

We now understand the importance which the idea of work has acquired in political thinking with regard to the very concept of the State as well as to the purposes of life geared to the idea of progress. "Everyone," says J. G. Fichte, "should make his own living by work" (*Grundlage des Naturrechts*, sec. 16). It follows that anyone who will not work for his own livelihood in an orderly civil society will not be bound to respect the property of others so that in the end civil society will not even be a stepmother to him.

Hegel descends from his general idea of spiritual activity to that of work, and regards work as coming especially under the system of necessity. It is in order to meet this necessity that man works and creates wealth. Were it not for work no need would ever be satisfied; work is the absolute law of life, and accompanies life from its primitive forms to its complex structure. Hegel describes this process in great detail (*Enzyklop. der philos. Wissenschaften* [1817], para. 524–28).

From Hegel, Karl Marx derives his view of change as historical becoming, but treats all history as proceeding on an economic basis dependent on the productivity of labor. Moreover, Marx does not treat history merely as interpretation, or hermeneutics, but philosophically insists on viewing history as in need of being redirected through human effort along economic lines. The Hegelian "Idea" is inadequate to perform the tasks of shaping man's life in society, which has to be understood in economic terms by class-struggle, according to a law internal to history, a law which gives the struggle direction and its necessary development.

To the young Marx this view appeared to be decisive, but the later system which he worked out is no less important; it reflected all human values and goods themselves in the economic mode of production. In Marx's *Das Kapital* (III) labor determines value, and gives all goods their value. The individual who works

acquires a dignity which is reflected in the esteem supported by professional and class spirit and in the morality belonging to the profession or class. Consequently, though one may talk about the physiology of labor, it must not be forgotten that there is also a wholly pathological condition which Marx stressed and from which he derived the class struggle, the necessity of an ultimate social revolution and to provide a socialistic order, a classless society immune from the assumptions of private property and the weight of authority.

We have indicated a whole line of speculative thought devoted to the prestige of labor as a human value in civilized society and life itself. Many other thinkers could be named from Voltaire to David Hume, from Benjamin Franklin to Adam Smith, from Auguste Comte to Giuseppe Mazzini. However, we cannot hide the fact that there is a very different tendency to deny value to work as pictured above, or at least a tendency exists to pick on certain internal difficulties. We refer chiefly to J. J. Rousseau's *Discours sur les sciences et les arts* (1749), according to which the technological development of civilization in the arts is an absolute evil because it removes man from the simplicity of life in the state of nature. However, it is in the very theories that attribute a human and social value to work that the most discouraging antinomies occur. To give a prime example, Hegel maintains that in the process of work the very division of labor removes the worker from the complex vision of the organic whole, in short, from the entire global process, and thus produces alienation. This conception explains the reason for so many points of view, the theme of alienation being taken up and developed insistently by the Hegelian left, from Marx to L. A. Feuerbach, D. F. Strauss, B. Bauer, and A. Ruge. Alienated labor, viewed as the oppression of the worker in the immense mechanism of industry completely owned and controlled by capital, revives the theme of social reform, of the vindication of the worker, of subversion, and of revolution as the direct remedy.

However, it is from the very center of contemporary speculative thought that we find arising a limited view if not the denial of work as a life value. Max Scheler illustrates this negative view. He deems man in the modern world to be preoccupied with a frenzied fanaticism for work and earning money. Utility rather than the holy has become the supreme value, as Scheler likes to put it in his criticisms. And every philosophical system that exalts the sacred in a hierarchy of values is obviously in accord with Scheler and esteems his essay on "Work and Ethics" ("Arbeit und Ethik," *Schriften zur Soziologie und Weltanschauungslehre*, Leipzig [1924], III, 2).

We must also not forget in this vein some of the doctrines that come from chairs of sociology and adopt a critical attitude towards a whole society which forgets man and gives itself up entirely to the production and consumption of goods. One-dimensional man is an alienated man, H. Marcuse affirms. Man continues to be just as alienated as he is when he is subjected to the hard law of work.

But it is in Martin Heidegger's system that we find the most radical delineation of the denial that work is the law of life. By questioning himself inwardly man will find structures of thought that will refer to the historical world, to the order of time, that is to say, to man's temporal finitude. So we read in *Sein und Zeit* (*Being and Time*, 1927), in the author's best pages, as he pursues the deepest recesses of the nature of Being. In his *Brief über den Humanismus* (*Letter on Humanism*, 1949), it is Being which dominates, and man can only be on the watch against relinquishing to Being his home and his country.

Thus the rapidly changing diagnosis of work in our times is measured through the polar views of work as the law of life and work scanned against Being. The problem remains whether there is a third way aside from the two lines traced above, a way that would save values in our world and in history, apart from rubbish and beyond the labor that exhausts life.

*BIBLIOGRAPHY*

For the ancient world, see: R. Mondolfo, *La comprensione del soggetto humano nell'antichità classica* (Florence, 1958), pp. 574ff. For Leonardo da Vinci, see: G. Fumagalli, ed., *Leonardo* (Florence, 1952). For the Renaissance contributions of Bacon and their later history: B. Farrington, *Francis Bacon: Philosopher of Industrial Science* (New York, 1949). With respect to the spirit of the Reformation and capitalism, see: E. Troeltsch, *Die sozialen Lehren der christlichen Kirchen und Gruppen* (Tübingen, 1912); trans. O. Wyon as *The Social Teaching of the Christian Churches*, 2 vols. (London and New York, 1931). M. Weber, *The Protestant Ethic and the Spirit of Capitalism*, trans. Talcott Parsons (New York, 1930).

General works: H. Arvon, *La philosophie du travail* (Paris, 1961). Henri Bartoli, *Science économique et travail* (Paris, 1957). F. Battaglia, *Filosofia del lavoro* (Bologna, 1951). M. D. Chenu, *Pour une théologie du travail* (Paris, 1955); trans. as *Theology of Work* (Chicago, 1966). Georges Friedmann, *Où va le travail humain?* (Paris, 1951). R. Kwant, *Philosophy of Labor* (Pittsburgh, 1960). Jean Lacroix, *Personne et amour* (Paris, 1955). Emmanuel Mounier, *La petite peur du XXe siècle* (Paris, 1948). Lewis Mumford, *Technics and Civilization* (New York, 1934). P.-M. Schuhl, *Machinisme et philosophie* (Paris, 1969). J. Todoli, *Filosofia del trabajo* (Madrid 1954). H. Weinstock, *Arbeit und Bildung* (Heidelberg, 1954). S. Wyszinski, *Lo spirito del lavoro humano* (Brescia, 1964).

Various authors, article "Arbeit," *Sowietssystem und demokratische Gesellschaft* (Friburg, Basel, Vienna, 1964), cols. 246–367.

FELICE BATTAGLIA

[See also **Alienation; Baconianism;** Culture; Pragmatism; **Renaissance; Socialism; Technology.**]

## *ZEITGEIST*

ALONG WITH the concept of *Volkgeist* we can trace in literature the development of the cognate notion of *Zeitgeist* (*Geist der Zeit, Geist der Zeiten*). Just as the term *Volkgeist* was conceived as a definition of the spirit of a nation taken in its totality across generations, so *Zeitgeist* came to define the characteristic spirit of a historical era taken in its totality and bearing the mark of a preponderant feature which dominated its intellectual, political, and social trends. *Zeit* is taken in the sense of "era," of the French *siècle*. Philosophically, the concept is based on the presupposition that the time has a material meaning and is imbued with content. It is in this sense that the Latin *tempus* appears in such phrases as *tempora mutantur*. The expression "it is in the air" is latently related to the idea of *Zeitgeist*.

*Geist der Zeiten* meant originally the sum total of the spirit of generations through the ages. Gradually the meaning of this expression was contracted so as to describe the principle of a certain historical period as it conceives of itself (Karl Löwith). As such this shift is representative of the modern idea of historical self-consciousness and to some extent of severing the ties of continuity between generations.

In Voltaire and Herder the concept appears in their attempt to answer the question, "What is the spirit of the times?" Herder defined it as a powerful genius, a mighty demon to whom we are all subordinated, actively or passively.

For Hegel, philosophy is related to the preponderant spirit of the ages or of a particular age. Philosophy is its own time apprehended in thoughts, time connoting in this context the intellectual trend of the epoch. Hence Hegel considered the trend of his own philosophy towards an identification of subject and object as germane to the tendencies of his time. The conformity with the spirit of time was meant not only as a descriptive statement of a factual situation, but also as a justification, at least a partial one, for the systematic validity of Hegel's own philosophy and of every philosophy as related to an era. Hegel took the

*Zeitgeist* as a spiritual and intellectual reality which is not totally alien to the intellectual exposition present in a philosophical system. A philosophical system is but a conceptual, and as such a self-conscious formulation of the substance present in the *Zeitgeist*. This view brings philosophy close to reality and by the same token makes reality the guiding substance and standard for philosophy. The assumption that philosophy can transcend its contemporary world was for Hegel a mere fancy just as it is a fancy (to Hegel) to suggest that an individual can overleap his own age. Philosophy has to be related to a particular reality; it is to this relatedness that he refers in quoting the famous phrase, *Hic Rhodus, hic salta*. The concept of the spirit of the time has thus both a guiding and a limiting connotation. The latter connotation implies the historicist understanding of the spirit of the time.

Related to this historicist view is the conception that the thought and culture of peoples are correlated with certain historical periods, that is to say, to certain trends of the spirit of the time. Transcending a spirit of the time makes a trend not only impossible but sometimes obsolete, as in the case when an individual or a group of individuals cling to a trend which has already been overcome. It might be thus congenial for one period of history to be imbued with a religious world outlook, yet this world outlook is superseded by another spirit of the time which is scientific or philosophic and thus overcomes the limitations and the validity of the religious world outlook. Along this scheme, though without employing the term *Zeitgeist*, Marx presents the view that a social and economic system like feudalism or capitalism might be appropriate historically at a certain period of time but ceases to be so and even becomes reactionary at a later period of history. Continuing this line, Sartre (in his later stage, in *Critique de la raison dialectique*) speaks about Marxism as "the philosophy of our time." This philosophy cannot be transcended since the circumstances which caused its emergence have not been surpassed.

Kant considered the temper or import of his critical philosophy as reflecting the characteristic feature of his time which was essentially one of critique. One of Kant's critiques (*Bescheid*) speaks about "genius (spirit) of the age" (*genius saeculi*). Schiller used the term *Geist der Zeit* as pointing to the perversion and brutishness of nature, of superstition, and the absence of moral belief in his time. Fichte analyzed the major trends of the age on the assumption that an age can be characterized by a well-defined principle. In his own age he noticed a trend towards the undermining of the power of external authority; and in a polemic vein Goethe says, through his mouthpiece Faust, that the spirit of the times is at bottom the spirit of those (*die Herren*) in whom the times are mirrored. Thus this verse questions the reality of a "spirit of an age."

Heidegger put forward the notion that metaphysics established an epoch in time (*Zeitalter*), suggesting a certain interpretation of truth. "Modern times" in this sense is a period characterized by science, by technology, by positing the work of art as an object of experience; its feature is the disappearance of God or Gods (*Entgötterung*). The general principle of the modern era is to look at the world as a *Bild*, not to picture the world but to take it as a picture. The whole is there only when human beings refer to it by way of representing it and establishing it. This description implied a criticism of the modern era as replacing the concern for the totality of Being with specialized research of scientific data.

The term or the general meaning of *Zeitgeist* has entered various dictionary attempts at historical periodization and has also entered our everyday vocabulary. The very notion that a certain span of time can be conceived in terms of a defined content, e.g., the period of constitutional monarchy or of romanticism as a period and not only as a trend—these descriptions echo the concept of *Zeitgeist*. In this sense we speak of the technological era or the post-industrial period. In the usage of these features we eventually refer to a *Zeitgeist* as connoting a dominating idea or a dominating social force or a combination of both. In a different context it refers to the prevailing spirit of a literary period dominated by an outstanding author, e.g., to *Geist der Goethezeit*.

In various systems of twentieth-century philosophical literature we find a direct or indirect reference to the concept. Karl Jaspers goes out to analyze specifically the spiritual situation of the time, i.e., the present, and then in his historical-philosophical attempts to refer to the fifth century B.C. as to an "axis time." Whitehead speaks about a "climate of opinion" as the all-embracing intellectual atmosphere of a certain period within the development of modern science and its principal ideas. "Climate of opinion" connotes in this context a state of mind, conviction in the existence of an order of things or on an instinctive faith in an Order of Nature. The term "climate of opinion" is an investigation of a shift from the view which takes time as a totality of circumstances to a view which equates circumstances with "climate." Mill used the term "mental climate"—and in this sense we speak about an *atmosphere* of freedom, *atmosphere* of permissiveness, etc. We connect the concept of surroundings with mental or moral activity. This metaphor appears in German as *Zeitklima*. For Collingwood, metaphysics is a formulation of the presuppositions of science in a certain period of time, and is thus determined by the *Zeitgeist* (though the term is not used by him).

*BIBLIOGRAPHY*

R. G. Collingwood, *An Essay on Metaphysics* (Oxford, 1940). M. Heidegger, *Holzwege* (Frankfurt a. M., 1950). K. Jaspers, *Die geistige Situation der Zeit* (Berlin, 1932), trans. Eden and Cedar Paul as *Man in the Modern Age* (London, 1933); idem, *Vom Ursprung und Ziel der Geschichte* (Zurich, 1949), trans. M. Bullock as *Origin and Goal of History* (New Haven, 1968). K. Löwith, *Von Hegel bis Nietzsche* (Zurich, 1941), trans. as *From Hegel to Nietzsche: The Revolution in Nineteenth Century Thought* (New York, 1964). J.-P. Sartre, *Critique de la raison dialectique* (Paris, 1960). F. Schiller, *Über die ästhetische Erziehung des Menschen* (1795), trans. R. Snell as *The Aesthetic Education of Man* (New York, 1965). A. N. Whitehead, *Science and the Modern World* (London and New York, 1925).

NATHAN ROTENSTREICH

[See also Historicism; Marxism; **Periodization in History;** Time; *Volksgeist.*]

·DICTIONARY OF·

·THE HISTORY OF IDEAS·

## For Reference

Not to be taken from this room